MW01153493

# MODERN CHEMISTRY

SOUTH ... ED

Raymond E. Davis
Regina Frey
Mickey Sarquis
Jerry L. Sarquis

**HOLT, RINEHART AND WINSTON**
A Harcourt Education Company
Orlando • **Austin** • New York • San Diego • London

# Unpacking Chemistry Standards •••>

# South Carolina

As you read the following pages and work through the unpacking of the South Carolina Chemistry Standards, you will discover the big ideas and key concepts that your teacher expects you to learn and understand.

**You will see three things:**

1. **>**
   what the standard actually says
2. **What's it mean?**
   an explanation to help you understand the big ideas within the standard
3. **Review Question**
   a typical standards Review Question

# South Carolina
## The Palmetto State

State capitol, Columbia

Table Rock State Park

### Scientific Inquiry

**>C-1 The student will demonstrate an understanding of how scientific inquiry and technological design, including mathematical analysis, can be used appropriately to pose questions, seek answers, and develop solutions.**

**What's it mean?** The student will show an understanding of how creating scientific experiments, designing tools, and using math to analyze problems can all be used to ask questions, look for answers, and find solutions to problems. Go to Chapter 1, Introduction to Science, for help.

**>C-1.1 Apply established rules for significant digits, both in reading a scientific instrument and in calculating a derived quantity from measurement. Go to Chapter 1, Introduction to Science, for help.**

**What's it mean?** Use the rules for figuring out which digits in a number matter, when either reading a machine or using math to understand numbers gathered from measuring material.

**Review Question** When numbers are multiplied or divided, the answer can have no more

A. significant figures than are in the measurement that has the smallest number of significant figures.
B. significant figures than are in the measurement that has the largest number of significant figures.
C. digits to the right of the decimal point than are in the measurement that has the smallest number of digits to the right of the decimal point.
D. digits to the right of the decimal point than are in the measurement that has the largest number of digits to the right of the decimal point.

### >C-1.2 Use appropriate laboratory apparatuses, technology, and techniques safely and accurately when conducting a scientific investigation.

**What's it mean?** Use proper science tools, equipment, and procedures to carry out experiments safely and correctly. Go to Chapter 1, Introduction to Science, for help.

**Review Question** When working with radioactive elements, which of the following is most important?

A. protecting the data
B. protecting the equipment
C. protecting people
D. protecting the radioactive material

### >C-1.3 Use scientific instruments to record measurement data in appropriate metric units that reflect the precision and accuracy of each particular instrument.

**What's it mean?** Use scientific equipment to make measurements in units that show the correct value written to the correct number of decimal places. Go to Chapter 1, Introduction to Science, for help.

**Review Question** Which of the following measurements contains three significant figures?

A. 200 mL
B. 0.02 mL
C. 20.2 mL
D. 200.0 mL

### >C-1.4 Design a scientific investigation with appropriate methods of control to test a hypothesis (including independent and dependent variables), and evaluate the designs of sample investigations.

**What's it mean?** Design an experiment with a procedure that tests a prediction by comparing test groups that are the same except for one difference, and consider how well the effects of that difference test the prediction. Go to Chapter 1, Introduction to Science, for help.

**Review Question** A scientist wants to learn about the effect that different amounts of sunlight have on plants. Which of the following is the only variable that she should change?

A. the type of plant
B. the amount of light
C. the volume of water
D. the amount of nutrients

Answers: C-1.1) A, C-1.2) C, C-1.3) C, C-1.4) B

**>C-1.5 Organize and interpret the data from a controlled scientific investigation by using mathematics (including formulas, scientific notation, and dimensional analysis), graphs, models, and/or technology.**

**What's it mean?** Sort and analyze information collected in an experiment by using mathematical calculations, visual displays, or computers. Go to Chapter 1, Introduction to Science, for help.

**Densities of Common Substances***

| Substance | Density (q/cm3) | Substance | Density (q/cm3) |
|---|---|---|---|
| Helium (gas) | 0.0001663 | Copper (solid) | 8.96 |
| Oxygen (gas) | 0.001331 | Silver (solid) | 10.50 |
| Water (liquid) | 1.00 | Lead (solid) | 11.35 |
| Iron Pyrite (solid) | 5.02 | Mercury (liquid) | 13.55 |
| Zinc (solid) | 7.13 | Gold (solid) | 19.32 |

* at 20°C and normal atmospheric pressure

**Review Question** A chemistry student created the chart above, which compares the densities of common substances. Using the chart, what could the student conclude about mercury?

A. It is the densest substance listed.
B. Its density is less than the density of water.
C. It is solid at 20°C and normal atmospheric pressure.
D. It is the densest liquid listed in the chart.

**>C-1.6 Evaluate the results of a scientific investigation in terms of whether they verify or refute the hypothesis and what the possible sources of error are.**

**What's it mean?** Decide whether the information gathered during an experiment agrees with the predicted outcome. Go to Chapter 1, Introduction to Science, for help.

**Review Question** A consumer hypothesizes that more-expensive portable stereos sound better than less-expensive stereos. He consults a consumer magazine that published the following results from their tests of portable stereos.

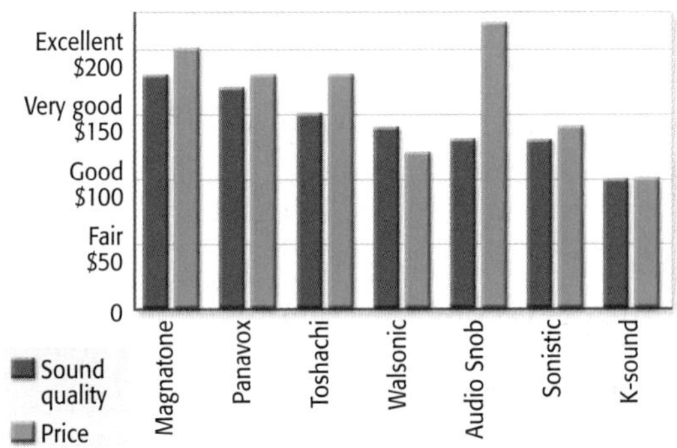


Which statement accurately reflects the relationship between price and sound quality?

A. More-expensive equipment always sounds better.
B. Less-expensive equipment always sounds better.
C. Less-expensive equipment sometimes performs better than more-expensive equipment.
D. More-expensive equipment has more features than less-expensive equipment.

## >C-1.7 Evaluate a technological design or product on the basis of designated criteria.

**What's it mean?** Decide whether an invention or tool is useful, based on what you are told about what the tool needs to do. Go to Chapter 1, Introduction to Science, for help.

**Review Question** A company is designing a new kind of electrical transformer for use on poles in rural areas. Which of the following design feature must the transformers have?

A. They must be lightweight.
B. They must be entirely made of metal.
C. They must be impervious to precipitation.
D. They must be more efficient than the transformers they replace.

## >C-1.8 Use appropriate safety procedures when conducting investigations.

**What's it mean?** Follow the correct rules for safely performing activities in the science classroom. Go to Chapter 1, Introduction to Science, for help.

**Review Question** What piece of safety equipment must you always wear in the lab?

A. safety goggles
B. heat resistant gloves
C. chemical-resistant gloves
D. a chemical-resistant apron.

## >C-2 Students will demonstrate an understanding of atomic structure and nuclear processes.

**What's it mean?** Students will show that they know the parts of an atom, and what happens in the nucleus of an atom. Go to Chapter 3, Atoms: The Building Blocks of Matter, for help.

## >C-2.1 Illustrate electron configurations by using orbital notation for representative elements.

**What's it mean?** Draw the arrangement of electrons in an atom using the correct format for specific elements. Go to Chapter 4, Arrangement of Electrons in Atoms, for help.

**Review Question** What is the maximum number of unpaired electrons that can be placed in a 3p sublevel?

A. 1 C. 3
B. 2 D. 4

## >C-2.2 Summarize atomic properties (including electron configuration, ionization energy, electron affinity, atomic size, and ionic size).

**What's it mean?** State briefly the properties of atoms. Go to Chapter 3, Atoms: the Building Blocks of Matter, for help.

**Review Question** An important result of Rutherford's experiments with gold foil was to establish that

A. atoms have mass.
B. electrons have a negative charge.
C. neutrons are uncharged particles.
D. the atom is mostly empty space.

Answers: C-1.5) D, C-1.6) C, C-1.7) C, C-1.8) A, C-2.1) C, C-2.2) D

**>C-2.3 Summarize the periodic table's property trends (including electron configuration, ionization energy, electron affinity, atomic size, ionic size, and reactivity).**

**What's it mean?** Briefly state how elements in the periodic table are similar to others in their area or column. Go to Chapter 5, Periodic Law for help.

**Review Question** As you move left to right across Period 3 from Mg to Cl, the energy needed to remove an electron from an atom

A. generally increases.
B. generally decreases.
C. does not change.
D. varies unpredictably.

**>C-2.4 Compare the nuclear reactions of fission and fusion to chemical reactions (including the parts of the atom involved and the relative amounts of energy released).**

**What's it mean?** Compare two kinds of reactions: reactions in which nuclear matter is converted to energy, and reactions in which atoms interact with other atoms. Go to Chapter 21, Nuclear Chemistry, for help.

**Review Question** Which of the following is true of nuclear reactions but not chemical reactions?

A. new chemicals are made
B. matter is converted to energy
C. reagents change
D. results can be measured quantitatively

**>C-2.5 Compare alpha, beta, and gamma radiation in terms of mass, charge, penetrating power, and the release of these particles from the nucleus.**

**What's it mean?** Compare three kinds of radiation in terms of the properties of the particles or rays released from the nucleus. Go to Chapter 21, Nuclear Chemistry, for help.

**Review Question** Which type of radiation has the most penetrating ability?

A. an alpha particle
B. a beta particle
C. a gamma ray
D. a neutron

**>C-2.6 Explain the concept of half-life, its use in determining the age of materials, and its significance to nuclear waste disposal.**

**What's it mean?** Explain the predictable rate of radioactive decay and how that property can be used to help determine how old something is, and its role in safely disposing nuclear wastes. Go to Go to Chapter 21, Nuclear Chemistry, for help.

**Review Question** It takes 5.2 min for a 4.0 g sample of francium-210 to decay until only 1.0 g is left. What is the half-life of francium-210?

A. 1.3 min
B. 2.6 min
C. 5.2 min
D. 7.8 min

**>C-2.7 Apply the predictable rate of nuclear decay (half-life) to determine the age of materials.**

**What's it mean?** Use an element's half-life to find out how old a material is. Go to Chapter 21, Nuclear Chemistry for help.

**Review Question** Carbon Dating can be used to measure the age of each of the following except

A. a 7000-year-old human body
B. a 1200-year-old wooden statue
C. a 2600-year-old iron sward
D. a 3500-year-old piece of fabric

## >C-2.8 Analyze a decay series chart to determine the products of successive nuclear reactions and write nuclear equations for disintegration of specified nuclides.

**What's it mean?** Examine a chart that shows the radioactive decay of an element to find out what is made during the decay. Also, write equations that explain how radioactive atoms predictably change to form other atoms. Go to Chapter 21, Nuclear Chemistry, for help.

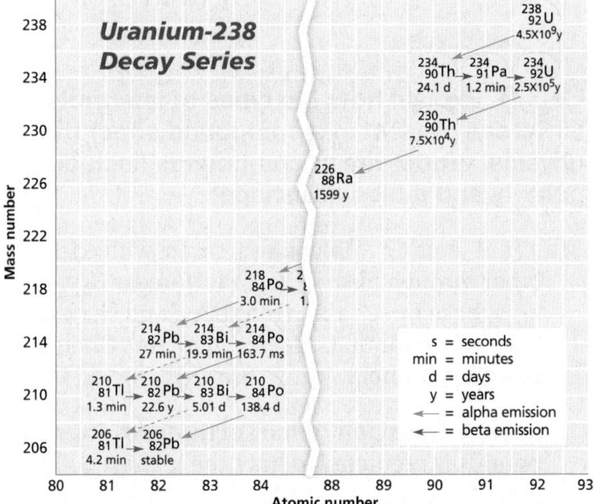


**Review Question** According to the chart, what is the daughter nuclide of U-238?

A. an isotope of thorium
B. an isotope of radon
C. an isotope of lead
D. an isotope of uranium

## >C-2.9 Use the equation $E = mc^2$ to determine the amount of energy released during nuclear reactions.

**What's it mean?** Use Einstein's equation of nuclear binding energy to find out how much energy is given off when protons and neutrons combine to form nuclei. Go to Chapter 21, Nuclear Chemistry, for help.

**Review Question** Calculate the binding energy for one mole of deuterium atoms. The measured mass of deuterium is 2.0140 amu.

A. $1.24 \times 10^{11}$ J/mole
B. $2.24 \times 10^{12}$ J/mole
C. $2.24 \times 10^{-11}$ J/mole
D. $2.24 \times 10^{11}$ J/mole

# >C-3 The student will demonstrate an understanding of the structures and classifications of chemical compounds.

**What's it mean?** The student will show an understanding of the makeup of chemical compounds and types of chemical compounds. Go to Chapter 7 Chemical Formulas and Chemical Compounds, for help.

## >C-3.1 Predict the type of bonding (ionic or covalent) and the shape of simple compounds by using Lewis dot structures and oxidation numbers.

**What's it mean?** Predict the kinds of chemical bonds in molecule, and the shape of the molecule, based on the way the structure of the molecule is described in conventional notation. Go to Chapter 6, Chemical Bonding, for help.

**Review Question** The Lewis structure of HCN contains

A. one double bond and one single bond.
B. one triple bond and one single bond.
C. two single bonds.
D. two double bonds.

Answers: C-2.3) A, C-2.4) B, C-2.5) C, C-2.6) B, C-2.7) C,
C-2.8) A, C-2.9) D, C-3.1) B

Park in Charleston

**>C-3.2 Interpret the names and formulas for ionic and covalent compounds.**

**What's it mean?** Explain the meaning of the names and formulas of compounds made with different kinds of bonds. Go to Chapter 7, Chemical Formulas and Compounds, for help.

**Review Question** The correct formula for ammonium phosphate is

A. $(NH_4)_3PO_4$.
B. $(NH_4)_2PO_4$.
C. $NH_4PO_4$.
D. $NH_4(PO_4)_2$.

**>C-3.3 Explain how the types of intermolecular forces present in a compound affect the physical properties of compounds (including polarity and molecular shape).**

**What's it mean?** Molecules interact with each other through electromagnetic forces. Explain how these forces affect the shape and characteristics of compounds. Go to Chapter 6, Chemical Bonding, for help.

**Review Question** Which of the following compounds is predicted to have the highest boiling point?

A. HCl
B. $CH_3COOH$ (Note the two oxygen atoms bond to the carbon.)
C. $Cl_2$
D. $SO_2$

**>C-3.4 Explain the unique bonding characteristics of carbon that have resulted in the formation of a large variety of organic structures.**

**What's it mean?** Explain why the kinds of bonds that carbon atoms can make have resulted in many different kinds and shapes of molecules made of carbon. Go to Chapter 22, Organic Chemistry, for help.

**Review Question** Why are carbon compounds so varied in kind and shape?

A. carbon atoms are larger than other atoms
B. carbon atoms are smaller than other atoms
C. carbon atoms have unique bonding characteristics
D. carbon atoms are polar

## >C-3.5 Illustrate the structural formulas and names of simple hydrocarbons (including alkanes and their isomers and benzene rings).

**What's it mean?** Draw the shape of some simple molecules made of carbon and hydrogen, and figure out the names of these compounds. Go to Chapter 22, Organic Chemistry, for help.

**Review Question** Examine the following structural formula:

```
          H
          |
        H-C-H
  H       |      H H
  |       |      | |
H-C-------C------C-C-H
  |       |      | |
  H       |      H H
        H-C-H
          |
          H
```

The correct name for this compound is

A. 2,2-dimethylbutane.
B. 1,1,1-trimethylpropane.
C. 2-ethyl-2-methylpropane.
D. 3,3-dimethylbutane.

## >C-3.6 Identify the basic structure of common polymers (including proteins, nucleic acids, plastics, and starches).

**What's it mean?** Identify the basic organization and shape of some common molecules that form chains. Go to Chapter 22, Organic Chemistry, for help.

**Review Question** What characterizes a polymer?

A. a small molecule
B. a large molecule made of at least 5 monomers
C. a radioactive molecule
D. a molecule soluble in water

## >C-3.7 Classify organic compounds in terms of their functional group.

**What's it mean?** Examine different kinds molecules made of carbon and organize them into groups based on the similarities among the chemically active parts of each molecule. Go to Chapter 22, Organic Chemistry, for help.

**Review Question** The organic molecule $CH_3OH$ is a(n)

A. alcohol.
B. alkyl halide.
C. alkane.
D. ketone.

## >C-3.8 Explain the effect of electronegativity and ionization energy on the type of bonding in a molecule.

**What's it mean?** Explain how a molecule's ability to form bonds is affected by its ability to attract and release electrons. Go to Chapter 5, Periodic Law, for help.

**Review Question** The noble gases are nonreactive because they have

A. high ionization energies.
B. high electron affinities.
C. large atomic radii.
D. a tendency to form both cations and anions.

Answers: C-3.2) A, C-3.3) B, C-3.4) C, C-3.5) A, C-3.6) B, C-3.7) A, C-3.8) A

**>C-3.9 Classify polymerization reactions as addition or condensation.**

**What's it mean?** Identify how different kinds of molecules react together to form long chains. Go to Chapter 22, Organic Chemistry, for help.

**Review Question** During a condensation polymerization reaction,

A. single bonds replace all double bonds that are present in the monomer.
B. water is often produced.
C. alcohol groups are formed.
D. an aldehyde group is changed to a ketone group.

**>C-3.10 Classify organic reactions as addition, elimination, or condensation.**

**What's it mean?** Identify the kind of reaction a carbon-based molecule undergoes. Chapter 22, Organic Chemistry, for help.

**Review Question** What type of chemical reaction would you expect to occur between 2-octene and bromide, HBr?

A. addition
B. elimination
C. condensation
D. condensation polymerization

**>C-4 The student will demonstrate an understanding of the types, the causes, and the effects of chemical reactions.**

**What's it mean?** The student will show an understanding about the kinds, causes, and effects of chemical reactions. Go to Chapter 8, Chemical Equations and Reactions, for help.

**>C-4.1 Analyze and balance equations for simple synthesis, decomposition, single replacement, double replacement, and combustion reactions.**

**What's it mean?** Analyze and balance chemical equations for the following kinds of reactions: 1) when two or more substances combine to form a single compound, 2) when a single compound changes to become two or more simpler materials, 3) when one element replaces a similar element in a compound, 4) when the charged particles of two compounds, dissolved in water, swap places with each other making two new compounds, 5) when a substance combines with oxygen. Go to Chapter 8, Chemical Equations and Reactions, for help.

**Review Question** Select the missing reactant for the following combustion reaction:

$$2\_\_\_\_ + 15O_2 \rightarrow 14CO_2 + 6H_2O.$$

A. $C_{14}H_{12}$
B. $C_{14}H_{12}O_4$
C. $C_7H_6$
D. $C_7H_6O_2$

**>C-4.2 Predict the products of acid-base neutralization and combustion reactions.**

**What's it mean?** Predict what will be made when an acid and a base combine, and when a substance combines with oxygen. Go to Chapter 15, Acid-Base Titration and pH, for help.

**Review Question** Identify the salt that forms when a solution of $H_2SO_4$ is titrated with a solution of $Ca(OH)_2$.

A. calcium sulfate
B. calcium hydroxide
C. calcium oxide
D. calcium phosphate

**>C-4.3 Analyze the energy changes (endothermic or exothermic) associated with chemical reactions.**

**What's it mean?** Examine carefully whether heat energy is gained or lost during a chemical reaction. Go to Chapter 16, Reaction Energy, for help.

**Review Question** Which of the following is true for the equation below?

$$C(s) + O_2(g) \rightarrow CO_2(g) + 393.51 \text{ kJ}$$

A. $\Delta H = -393.51$ kJ, exothermic
B. $\Delta H = 393.51$ kJ, exothermic
C. $\Delta H = -393.51$ kJ, endothermic
D. $\Delta H = 393.51$ kJ, endothermic

**>C-4.4 Apply the concept of moles to determine the number of particles of a substance in a chemical reaction, the percent composition of a representative compound, the mass proportions, and the mole-mass relationships.**

**What's it mean?** A mole is a unit used to measure an amount of particles. Use this unit to find the number of particles in chemical reaction and to determine the makeup of a compound, expressed several ways. Go to Chapter 9, Stoichiometry, for help.

**Review Question** What mass of NaCl can be produced by the reaction of 0.75 mol $Cl_2$?

$$2Na + Cl_2 \rightarrow 2NaCl$$

A. 0.75 g
B. 1.5 g
C. 44 g
D. 88 g

Answers: C-3.9) B, C-3.10) A, C-4.1) D, C-4.2) A, C-4.3) A, C-4.4) D

*Shrimp boats, McClellanville*

**>C-4.5 Predict the percent yield, the mass of excess, and the limiting reagent in chemical reactions.**

**What's it mean?** Predict how closely a reaction will make to its maximum amount of product. Also predict which material in a reaction will limit the amount of product that gets made, and how much unreacted material will be left over. Go to Chapter 9, Stoichiometry, for help.

**Review Question** If a chemist calculates the maximum amount of product that could be obtained in a chemical reaction, he or she is calculating the

A. percentage yield.
B. mole ratio.
C. theoretical yield.
D. actual yield.

**>C-4.6 Explain the role of activation energy and the effects of temperature, particle size, stirring, concentration, and catalysts in reaction rates.**

**What's it mean?** Explain the role of the energy needed to start a chemical reaction. Also explain how the reaction is affected by temperature, the size of the particles in the reactions, and other materials that can speed up the reaction. Go to Chapter 16, Reaction Energy, for help.

**Review Question** What does the height of the hill of the graph represent?

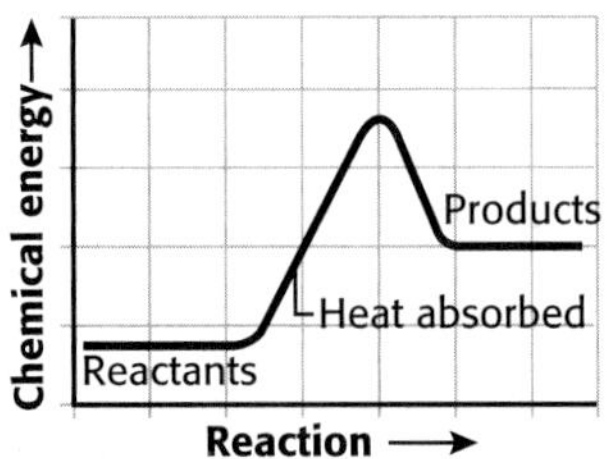


A. energy that must be added to the start of the reaction
B. energy released as the reactant molecules approach one another
C. the potential energy of the chemical bonds in the molecules of the reactants
D. the change in total chemical energy between the reactants and products.

Aerial view, Myrtle Beach

*The following indicators should be selected as appropriate to a particular course for additional content and depth:*

## >C-4.7 Summarize the oxidation and reduction processes (including oxidizing and reducing agents).

**What's it mean?** Explain briefly chemical reactions that involve the gain or loss of elections. Go to Chapter 19, Oxidation-Reduction Reactions for help.

**Review Question** Which answer contains the correct information about the following reaction:

$$2Pb(NO_3)_2 \longrightarrow 2PbO + 4NO_2 + O_2$$

A. This reaction is a decomposition reaction and not a redox reaction.
B. This reaction is a redox reaction in which the lead is reduced and the oxygen is oxidized.
C. This reaction is a disproportionation reaction.
D. This reaction is a redox reaction in which the nitrogen is reduced and the oxygen is oxidized.

## >C-4.8 Illustrate the uses of electrochemistry (including electrolytic cells, voltaic cells, and the production of metals from ore by electrolysis).

**What's it mean?** Describe how chemical reactions that use or make electricity are useful in everyday life. Go to Chapter 20, Electrochemistry, for help.

**Review Question** When silver is electroplated onto another metal, $Ag^+$ is

A. oxidized at the anode.
B. reduced at the anode.
C. oxidized at the cathode.
D. reduced at the cathode.

Answers: C-4.5) C, C-4.6) A, C-4.7) D, C-4.8) D

**>C-4.9 Summarize the concept of chemical equilibrium and Le Châtelier's principle.**

**What's it mean?** Explain briefly what is happening when chemicals are in a state of balance. Also explain how, when this balance is put under stress, the balance shifts to relieve the stress. Go to Chapter 18, Chemical Equilibrium, for help.

**Review Question** Le Châtelier's principle states that

A. at equilibrium, the forward and reverse reaction rates are equal.
B. stresses include changes in concentrations, pressure, and temperature.
C. to relieve stress, solids and solvents are omitted from equilibrium constant expressions.
D. chemical equilibria respond to reduce applied stress.

**>C-4.10 Explain the role of collision frequency, the energy of collisions, and the orientation of molecules in reaction rates.**

**What's it mean?** Explain how the speed and likelihood of a reaction is influenced by the number of times particles collide, how vigorously they collide, and how they are situated when they collide. Go to Chapter 17, Reaction Kinetics, for help.

**Review Question** To be effective, a collision requires

A. enough energy only.
B. favorable orientation only.
C. enough energy and a favorable orientation.
D. a reaction mechanism.

**>C-5 The student will demonstrate an understanding of the structure and behavior of the different phases of matter.**

**What's it mean?** The student will show an understanding of the differences of matter when it is a solid, liquid, gas, and plasma. Go to Chapter 10, States of Matter, for help.

**>C-5.1 Explain the effects of the intermolecular forces on the different phases of matter.**

**What's it mean?** Explain the forces that molecules exert on each other when matter is a solid, liquid, gas, and plasma. Go to Chapter 10, States of Matter, for help.

**Review Question** Which of the following is not a property of typical solids?

A. definite melting point
B. high density
C. easily compressible
D. low rate of diffusion

Oconee Station Falls

**>C-5.2 Explain the behaviors of gas; the relationship among pressure, volume, and temperature; and the significance of the Kelvin (absolute temperature) scale, using the kinetic-molecular theory as a model.**

**What's it mean?** Explain how gases behave. Explain how pressure, volume, and temperature affect gases. Explain the importance of the way temperature is measured and expressed, in terms of how the combined actions of molecules in a system affect the system as a whole. Go to Chapter 11 Gases, for help.

**Review Question** The graph below shows a plot of volume versus pressure for a particular gas sample at constant temperature. Answer the following questions by referring to the graph. No calculation is necessary.

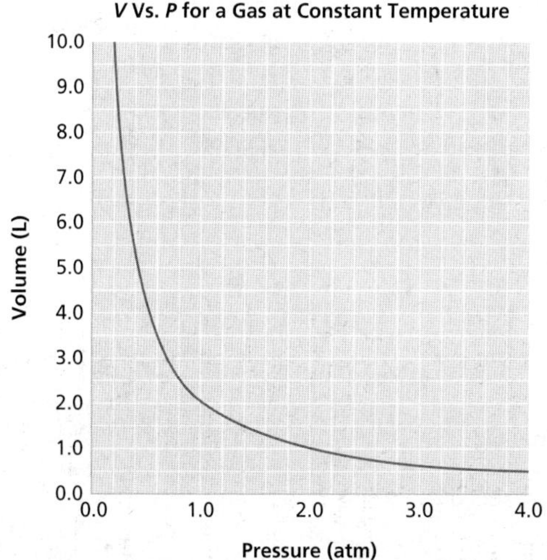


What is the volume of this gas sample at 4.0 atm pressure?

A. 0.25 L
B. 0.5 L
C. 1.0 L
D. 1.5 L

Answers: C-4.9) D, C-4.10) C, C-5.1) C, C-5.2) B

**>C-5.3 Apply the gas laws to problems concerning changes in pressure, volume, or temperature (including Charles's law, Boyle's law, and the combined gas law).**

**What's it mean?** Apply the known, predictable ways that gases behave to solve problems in gas systems. The problems will involve changes in pressure, volume, and temperature. Go to Chapter 10 States of Matter, for help.

**Review Question** A sample of gas in a closed container at a temperature of 100°C and 3.0 atm is heated to 300.0°C. What is the pressure of the gas at the higher temperature?

A. 35 atm
B. 4.6 atm
C. 59 atm
D. 9.0 atm

**>C-5.4 Illustrate and interpret heating and cooling curves (including how boiling and melting points can be identified and how boiling points vary with changes in pressure).**

**What's it mean?** Draw and show you understand graphs that show how materials change as they are heated and cooled. Go to Chapter 10 States of Matter, for help.

**Review Question** Using the graph below of vapor pressures of substances at various temperatures, estimate the boiling point of ethanol at an applied (external) pressure of 300 torr.

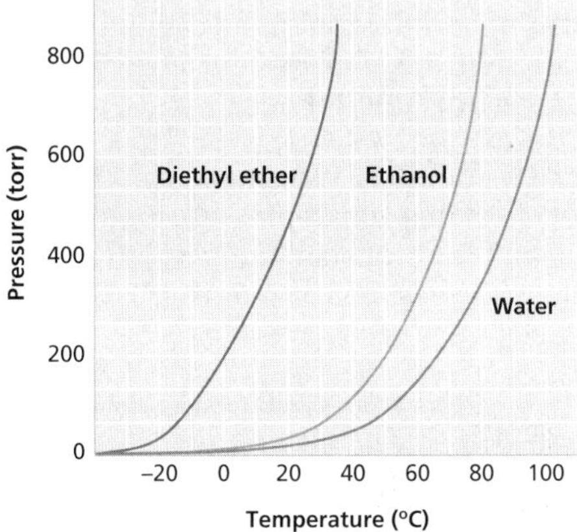



A. 40°C
B. 50°C
C. 60°C
D. 70°C

Boone Hall
Plantation

*The following indicators should be selected as appropriate to a particular course for additional content and depth:*

### >C-5.5 Analyze the energy changes involved in calorimetry by using the law of conservation of energy as it applies to temperature, heat, and phase changes (including the use of the formulas $q = mc\Delta T$ [temperature change] and $q = mLv$ and $q = mLf$ [phase change] to solve calorimetry problems).

**What's it mean?** Examine carefully the changes that take place when heat is absorbed or released in a chemical reaction or change of state. Go to Chapter 16, Reaction Energy, for help.

**Review Question** The gasification of coal is a method of producing methane by the following reaction.

$$C(s) + {}_2H_2(g) \rightarrow CH_4(g)\ \Delta H=?$$

Find ΔH by using the enthalpy changes in the following combustion reactions:

$C(s) + O_2(g) \rightarrow CO_2(g)\ \Delta H = -394\text{ kJ}$ $H_2(g) + O_2(g) \rightarrow H_2O(l)\ \Delta H = -286\text{ kJ}$ $CH_4(g) + 2O_2(g) \rightarrow CO_2(g) + 2H_2O(l)\ \Delta H = -891\text{ kJ}$

A. 75 kJ
B. −75 kJ
C. 1856 kJ
D. −1856 kJ

### >C-5.6 Use density to determine the mass, volume, or number of particles of a gas in a chemical reaction.

**What's it mean?** Use the density of a sample to find the mass, volume, or number of particles in a gas. Go to Chapter 11, Gases, for help.

**Review Question** What is the mass, in grams, of 11.2 L $H_2$ at STP?

A. 0.01 g
B. 1.00 g
C. 1.01 g
D. 10 g

### >C-5.7 Apply the ideal gas law ($pV = nRT$) to solve problems.

**What's it mean?** Solve problems, using a formula that expresses the known relationships between volume, temperature, pressure, and moles of gases. Go to Chapter 10, States of Matter, for help.

**Review Question** What is the pressure exerted by a 0.500 mol sample of nitrogen in a 10.0 L container at 20°C?

A. 1.2 kPa
B. 10 kPa
C. 0.10 kPa
D. 120 kPa

### >C-5.8 Analyze a product for purity by following the appropriate assay procedures.

**What's it mean?** Run tests on a sample of a product to determine if the product is pure. Go to Chapter 8, Chemical Equations and Reactions, for help.

**Review Question** Aspirin, $C_9H_8O_4$, is produced through the following reaction of salicylic acid, $C_7H_6O_3$, and acetic anhydride

$$C_4H_6O_3: C_7H_6O_3(s) + C_4H_6O_3(l) \rightarrow C_9H_8O_4(s) + HzC_2H_3O_2(l).$$

What other product is made when aspirin is made?

A. acetic acid
B. ethanol
C. methanol
D. acetone

Answers: C-5.3) B, C-5.4) C, C-5.5) B, C-5.6) C, C-5.7) D, C-5.8) A

# South Carolina
## The Palmetto State

**>C-5.9 Analyze a chemical process to account for the weight of all reagents and solvents by following the appropriate material balance procedures.**

**What's it mean?** Examine carefully a chemical process and keep track of the weight of all the chemicals and solvents in a reaction. Go to Chapter 8, Chemical Equations and Reactions, for help.

**Review Question** According to the law of conservation of mass, the total mass of the reacting substances is

A. always more than the total mass of the products.
B. always less than the total mass of the products.
C. sometimes more and sometimes less than the total mass of the products.
D. always equal to the total mass of the products.

## >C-6 The student will demonstrate an understanding of the nature and properties of various types of chemical solutions.

**What's it mean?** The student will show an understanding of how chemicals dissolved in liquids behave. Go to Chapter 12, Solutions, for help.

**>C-6.1 Summarize the process by which solutes dissolve in solvents, the dynamic equilibrium that occurs in saturated solutions, and the effects of varying pressure and temperature on solubility.**

**What's it mean?** Explain briefly how chemicals dissolve in liquids. Explain also the balance that occurs when a liquid is saturated with a dissolved chemical. Finally, explain how pressure and temperature affect the ability of a chemical to dissolve in a liquid. Go to Chapter 12, Solutions, for help.

**Review Question** Which one of the following statements is false?

A. Gases are generally more soluble in water under high pressures than under low pressures.
B. As temperature increases, the solubilities of some solids in water increase and the solubilities of other solids in water decrease.
C. Water dissolves many ionic solutes because of its ability to hydrate ions in solution.
D. Many solids dissolve more quickly in a cold solvent than in a warm solvent.

Old Cooper River Bridge

## >C-6.2 Compare solubility of various substances in different solvents (including polar and nonpolar solvents and organic and inorganic substances).

**What's it mean?** Compare the ability of different chemicals to dissolve in different liquids. Go to Chapter 12, Solutions, for help.

**Review Question** The graph below shows the solubilities of two different substances, cadmium selenate, $CdSeO_4$, and cobalt(II) chloride, $CoCl_2$, over a range of temperatures. According to the graph, at what temperature do both substances have the same solubility?

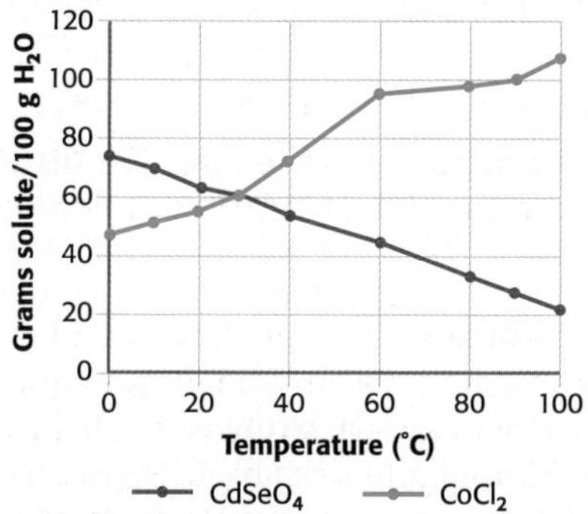


A. about 20 degrees
B. about 30 degrees
C. about 40 degrees
D. about 50 degrees

## >C-6.3 Illustrate the colligative properties of solutions (including freezing point depression and boiling point elevation and their practical uses).

**What's it mean?** Show some of the properties of particles in water that depend on the concentration of the particles, not on the nature of the particles. Go to Chapter 13 Ions in Aqueous Solutions and Colligative Properties, for help.

**Review Question:** The table below shows the freezing points of solutions of three nonvolatile solutes, X, Y, and Z, in water. The Kf for water is −1.86°C/m. According to the table below, which of the following statements is not true?

| Solute | Solute (mol) | Water (g) | Freezing Point (°C) |
|---|---|---|---|
| X | 1.00 | 1000 | −5.58% |
| Y | 1.00 | 1000 | −1.86% |
| Z | 1.00 | 1000 | −3.72% |

A. All three solutes are nonelectrolytes.
B. Solute X could be $Ca(NO_3)_2$.
C. Solute Y could be sucrose.
D. Solute Z could be KCl.

## C-6.4 Carry out calculations to find the concentration of solutions in terms of molarity and percent weight (mass).

**What's it mean?** Use mathematical procedures to find how much material has dissolved in a set amount of liquid, using conventional notation. Go to Chapter 13 Ions in Aqueous Solutions and Colligitive Properties, for help.

**Review Question** What mass of NaOH is contained in 2.5 L of a 0.010 M solution?
A. 0.010 g
B. 1.0 g
C. 2.5 g
D. 0.40 g

Answers: C-5.9) D, C-6.1) D, C-6.2) A, C-6.3) A, C-6.4) B

## >C-6.5 Summarize the properties of salts, acids, and bases.

**What's it mean?** Explain briefly the characteristics of salts, acids, and bases. Go to Chapter 14, Acids and Bases, for help.

**Review Question** Which of the following is not a characteristic of an acid?

A. An acid changes the color of an indicator.
B. An acid has a bitter taste.
C. An acid ionizes in water.
D. An acid produces hydronium ions in water.

## >C-6.6 Distinguish between strong and weak common acids and bases.

**What's it mean?** Tell the difference between strong and weak acids and bases. Go to Chapter 14, Acids and Bases, for help.

**Review Question** How can you distinguish between a strong acid and a weak acid?

A. A strong acid is highly concentrated.
B. A strong acid is 100% ionized.
C. A strong acid can be neutralized with a base.
D. A strong acid can react with metal.

## >C-6.7 Represent common acids and bases by their names and formulas.

**What's it mean?** Use common formulas and names to identify common acids and bases. Go to Chapter 14, Acids and Bases, for help.

**Review Question** What is the formula for acetic acid?

A. $CH_3COOH$ C. $HClO_4$
B. $HNO_3$ D. HCN

## >C-6.8 Use the hydronium or hydroxide ion concentration to determine the pH and pOH of aqueous solutions.

**What's it mean?** Determine how acidic or basic a liquid is based on the number of hydrogen ions or hydroxide ions in a set about of liquid. Go to Chapter 15, Acid-Base Titration and pH, for help.

**Review Question** The hydroxide ion concentration in a solution is $1.6 \times 10^{-11}$ M. What are the pH and the pOH of the solution, respectively?

A. 10.80 and 3.20 C. 3.80 and 1030
B. 10.30 and 3.80 D. 3.20 and 10.80

## >C-6.9 Explain how the use of a titration can determine the concentration of acid and base solutions

**What's it mean?** Explain how carefully adding a known amount of an acid of known strength to a base of unknown strength can help you figure out the strength of the base. Go to Chapter 15, Acid-Base Titration and pH, for help.

**Review Question** How many moles of NaOH would be the chemically equivalent amount of 1.0 mol HCl?

A. 0.1 M C. 1.0 M
B. 0.5 M D. 10.0 M

## >C-6.10 Interpret solubility curves to determine saturation at different temperatures.

**What's it mean?** Read and explain a graph that shows the changes in the amount of a chemical that will dissolve in a liquid at different temperatures. Go to Chapter 18, Chemical Equilibrium, for help.

**Review Question** According to the graph below, which of the following values is the amount of sodium nitrate that can be dissolved in 100 mL of water at 40°C?

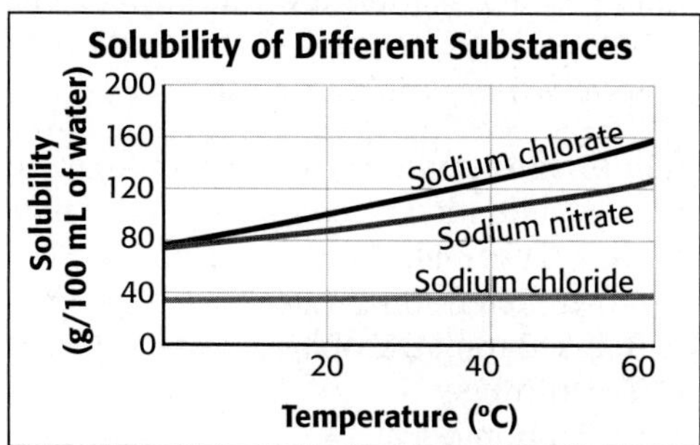


A. 0 g
B. 40 g
C. 100 g
D. 130 g

## >C-6.11 Use a variety of procedures for separating mixtures (including distillation, crystallization filtration, paper chromatography, and centrifuge).

**What's it mean?** Use several methods for separating mixtures. Go to Chapter 1, Matter and Change, for help.

**Review Question** Which method would you use to most efficiently separate ethanol and water?

A. crystal filtration
B. distillation
C. paper chromatography
D. centrifugation

## >C-6.12 Use solubility rules to write net ionic equations for precipitation reactions in aqueous solution.

**What's it mean?** Use known behaviors of chemicals that have dissolved in water to describe how those dissolved chemicals can interact and form chemicals that do not dissolve in water, and do come out of solution. Go to Chapter 13, Ions in Aqueous Solutions and Colligative Properties, for help.

**Review Question** Which of the following is the best representation of the precipitation reaction that occurs when aqueous solutions of sodium carbonate and calcium chloride are mixed?

A. $Na^+(aq) + Cl^-(aq) \rightarrow 2NaCl(s)$
B. $2Na^+(aq) + CO_3^{2-}(aq) + Ca^{2+}(aq) + 2Cl^-(aq) \rightarrow CaCO_3(s) + 2NaCl(s)$
C. $Ca^{2+}(aq) + CO_3^{2-}(aq) \rightarrow CaCO_3(s)$
D. No precipitation reaction occurs.

## >C-6.13 Use the calculated molality of a solution to calculate the freezing point depression and the boiling point elevation of a solution.

**What's it mean?** Find the change in boiling point and freezing point of a liquid based on the amount of known material dissolved in the liquid. Go to Chapter 13, Ions in Aqueous Solutions and Colligative Properties, for help.

**Review Question** Solution A contains 0.1 mol of sucrose, $C_{12}H_{22}O_{11}$, dissolved in 500 g of water. Solution B contains 0.1 mol of sodium chloride, NaCl, in 500 g of water. Which of the following statements about these solutions is true?

A. Both solutions have the same vapor pressure.
B. Solution A would boil at a higher temperature than solution B would.
C. Solution A would freeze at a higher temperature than solution B would.
D. Both solutions would boil at the same temperature.

Answers: C-6.5) B, C-6.6) B, C-6.7) A, C-6.8) D, C-6.9) C, C-6.10) C, C-6.11) B, C-6.12) C, C-6.13) C

# South Carolina
## The Palmetto State

**>C-6.14 Represent neutralization reactions and reactions between common acids and metals by using chemical equations.**

**What's it mean?** Use chemical equations to show how acids and bases neutralize each other, and how acids react with metals. Go to Chapter 13, Ions in Aqueous Solutions and Colligative Properties, for help.

**Review Question** Which of the following statements is true for the reaction below?

$$HF(aq) + HPO_4^{2-}(aq) \leftrightarrows F^-(aq) + H_2PO_4^-(aq)$$

A. HF is the base.
B. $HPO_4^{2-}$ is the acid.
C. $F^-$ is the conjugate base.
D. $H_2PO^{-4}$ is the conjugate base.

**>C-6.15 Analyze the composition of a chemical sample by using gas chromatography.**

**What's it mean?** Use a machine called a *gas chromatograph* to identify the make up of a chemical sample. Go to Chapter 1, Matter and Change, for help.

**Review Question** Which machine can best help you identify the composition of a tiny chemical sample?

A. pH meter
B. gas chromatograph
C. centrifuge
D. electronic scale

Answers: C-6.14) C, C-6.15) B

Night in Charleston

# MODERN CHEMISTRY®

Raymond E. Davis
Regina Frey
Mickey Sarquis
Jerry L. Sarquis

HOLT, RINEHART AND WINSTON
A Harcourt Education Company
Orlando • Austin • New York • San Diego • London

# Authors

**RAYMOND E. DAVIS, PH.D.**
**Professor Emeritus**
Department of Chemistry and Biochemistry
The University of Texas at Austin
Austin, TX

**MICKEY SARQUIS**
**Professor and Director, Center for Chemistry Education**
Department of Chemistry and Biochemistry
Miami University
Middletown, OH

**REGINA FREY, PH.D.**
**Senior Lecturer and Director of the Teaching Center**
Department of Chemistry
Washington University in St. Louis
St. Louis, MO

**JERRY L. SARQUIS, PH.D.**
**Professor**
Department of Chemistry and Biochemistry
Miami University
Oxford, OH

**On the cover:** A snow crystal image produced by using a low temperature scanning electron microscope.



Printed in the United States of America



ISBN-13: 978-0-03-036786-1

ISBN-10: 0-03-036786-7

2 3 4 5 6 7 048 11 10 09 08

# Acknowledgments

## Contributing Writers

**Lisa Saunders Baugh, Ph.D.**
*Senior Chemist*
Chemical Sciences Laboratory
ExxonMobil Research & Engineering Company
Corporate Strategic Research
Annandale, New Jersey

**Robert Davisson**
*Science Writer*
Albuquerque, New Mexico

**Seth Madej**
*Writer/Producer*
Pittsburgh, Pennsylvania

**Jim Metzner**
*Executive Producer*
*Pulse of the Planet* Radio Series
Jim Metzner Productions, Inc.
Accord, New York

**Jay A. Young, Ph.D.**
*Chemical Safety Consultant*
Silver Spring, Maryland

## Inclusion Specialists

**Joan Altobelli**
*Special Education Director*
Austin Independent School District
Austin, Texas

**John A. Solorio**
*Multiple Technologies Lab Facilitator*
Austin Independent School District
Austin, Texas

## Reviewers

**Eric V. Anslyn, Ph.D.**
*Professor*
Department of Chemistry and Biochemistry
University of Texas at Austin
Austin, Texas

**George F. Atkinson, Ph.D.**
*Professor of Chemistry*
Department of Chemistry
University of Waterloo
Waterloo, Ontario, Canada

**Sonal S.D. Blumenthal, Ph.D.**
*Life Science Consultant*
Austin, Texas

**G. Lynn Carlson, Ph.D.**
*Senior Lecturer Emeritus*
Department of Chemistry
University of Wisconsin—Parkside
Kenosha, Wisconsin

**Scott A. Darveau, Ph.D.**
*Associate Professor*
Department of Chemistry
University of Nebraska at Kearney
Kearney, Nebraska

**Cassandra T. Eagle, Ph.D.**
*Professor of Chemistry*
Department of Chemistry
Appalachian State University
Boone, North Carolina

**Linda Gaul, Ph.D., M.P.H.**
*Epidemiologist*
Infectious Disease Epidemiology and Surveillance
Department of State Health Services
Austin, Texas

**Pamela Gollhofer**
*Science Teacher*
Princeton High School
Cincinnati, Ohio

**Hima Joshi, Ph.D.**
Department of Chemistry
University of San Diego
San Diego, California

**Doris Ingram Lewis, Ph.D.**
*Professor of Chemistry*
Suffolk University
Boston, Massachusetts

**Gary E. Mueller, Ph.D.**
*Associate Professor*
Department of Nuclear Engineering
University of Missouri—Rolla
Rolla, Missouri

**Daniel B. Murphy, Ph.D.**
*Professor Emeritus of Chemistry*
Department of Chemistry
Herbert H. Lehman College
City University of New York
Bronx, New York

**R. Thomas Myers, Ph.D.**
*Professor Emeritus of Chemistry*
Kent State University
Kent, Ohio

**Keith B. Oldham, Ph.D.**
*Professor of Chemistry*
Trent University
Peterborough, Ontario, Canada

**Brian L. Pagenkopf, Ph.D.**
*Assistant Professor*
Department of Chemistry and Biochemistry
University of Texas at Austin
Austin, Texas

**Stanford Peppenhorst, Ed.D.**
*Chemistry Teacher*
Germantown High School
Germantown, Tennessee

**Charles Scaife, Ph.D.**
*Professor of Chemistry, Emeritus*
Union College
Schenectady, New York

**Peter Sheridan, Ph.D.**
*Professor*
Department of Chemistry and Biochemistry
Colgate University
Hamilton, New York

**Larry Stookey, P.E.**
*Physics and Chemistry Teacher*
Antigo High School
Antigo, Wisconsin

## Acknowledgments, continued

**David C. Taylor, Ph.D.**
*Professor of Chemistry*
Department of Chemistry
Slippery Rock University
Slippery Rock, Pennsylvania

**Richard S. Treptow, Ph.D.**
*Professor of Chemistry*
Department of Chemistry and Physics
Chicago State University
Chicago, Illinois

**Barry Tucker**
*Chemistry Teacher*
Colerain High School
Cincinnati, Ohio

**Martin Van Dyke, Ph.D.**
*Chemistry Professor, Emeritus*
Front Range Community College
Westminster, Colorado

**Joseph E. Vitt, Ph.D.**
*Associate Professor*
Chemistry Department
University of South Dakota
Vermillion, South Dakota

**Verne Weidler, Ph.D.**
*Professor of Chemistry, Retired*
Science and Engineering
Black Hawk College
Kewanee, Illinois

**Dale Wheeler, Ph.D.**
*Associate Professor of Chemistry*
A. R. Smith Department of Chemistry
Appalachian State University
Boone, North Carolina

**David Wilson, Ph.D.**
*Professor Emeritus*
Chemistry Department
Vanderbilt University
Nashville, Tennessee

**Candace Woodside**
*Science Teacher*
Winton Woods High School
Forest Park, Ohio

**Charles M. Wynn, Sr., Ph.D.**
*Professor of Chemistry*
Department of Physical Sciences
Eastern Connecticut State University
Willimantic, Connecticut

*continued on page 948*

# Contents in Brief

CHAPTER

# Contents

## Matter and Change 2



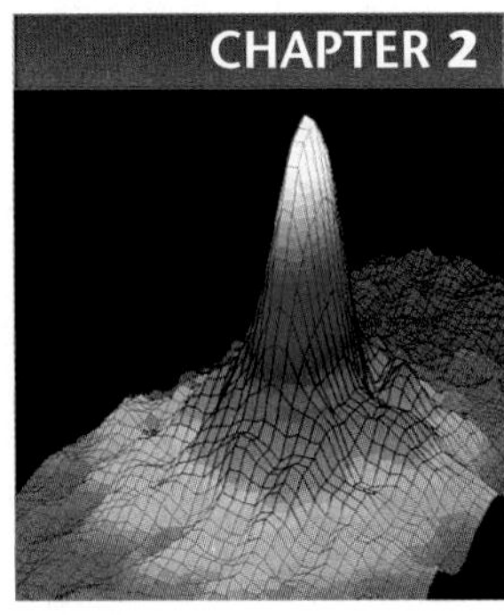


## Measurements and Calculations 28

## Atoms: The Building Blocks of Matter 66

## *Arrangement of Electrons in Atoms* 96



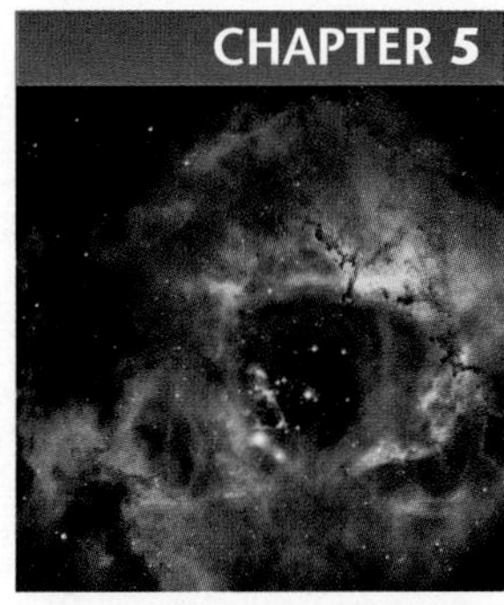


## *The Periodic Law* 132



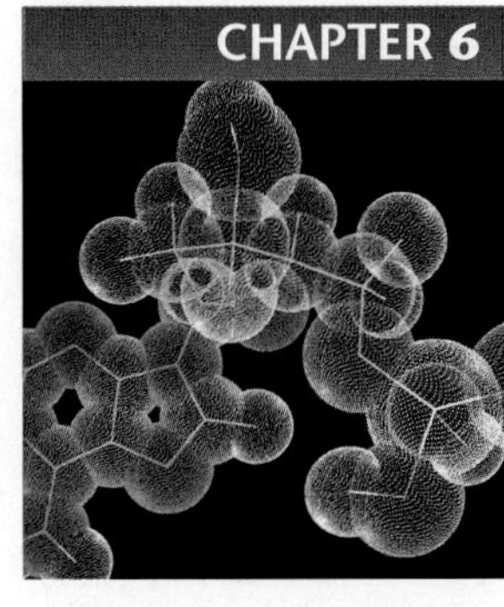


## *Chemical Bonding* 174

## Chemical Formulas and Chemical Compounds 218

## Chemical Equations and Reactions 260

## Stoichiometry 298

CHAPTER 10

## *States of Matter* 328

CHAPTER 11

## *Gases* 360

CHAPTER 12

## *Solutions* 400

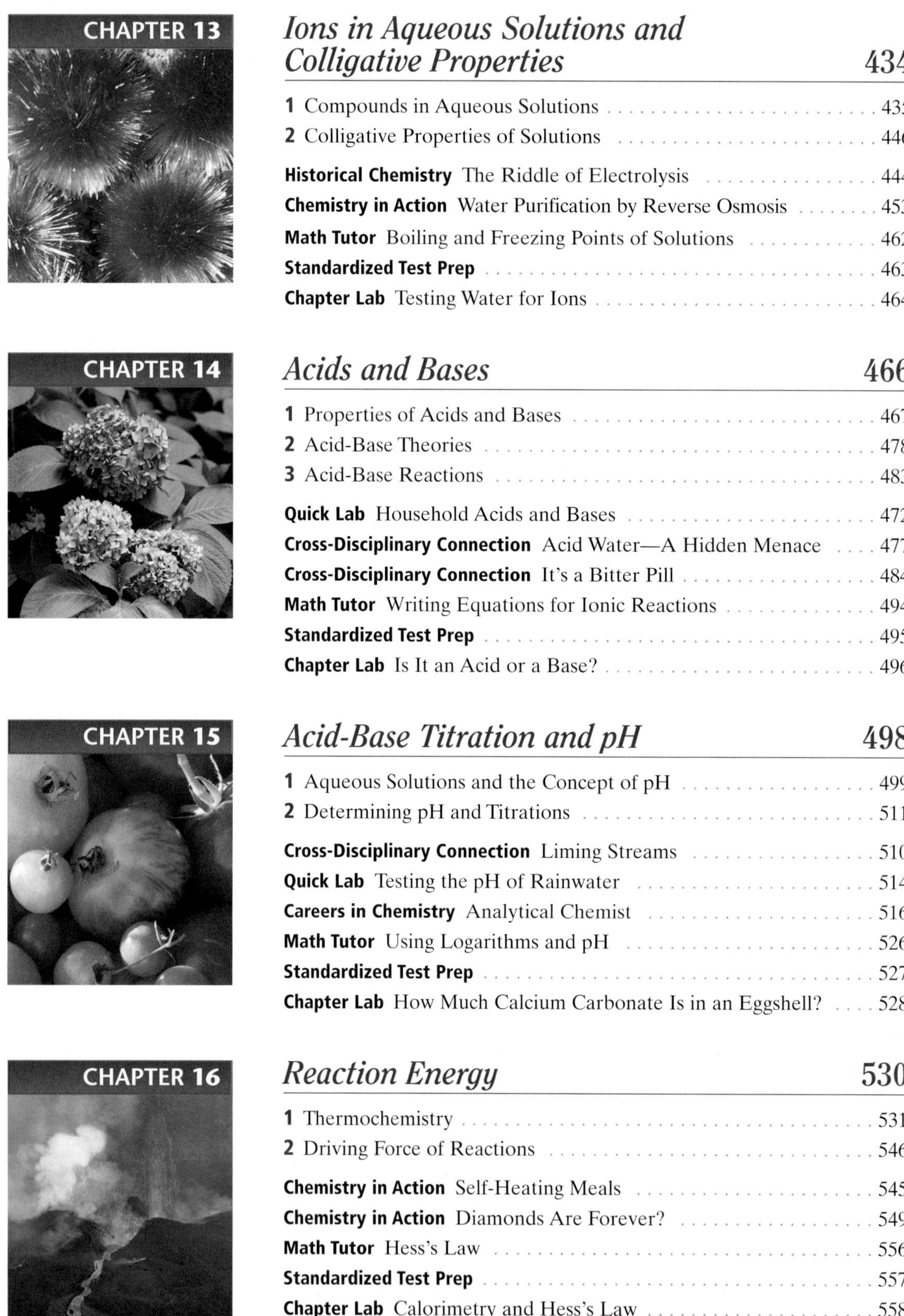

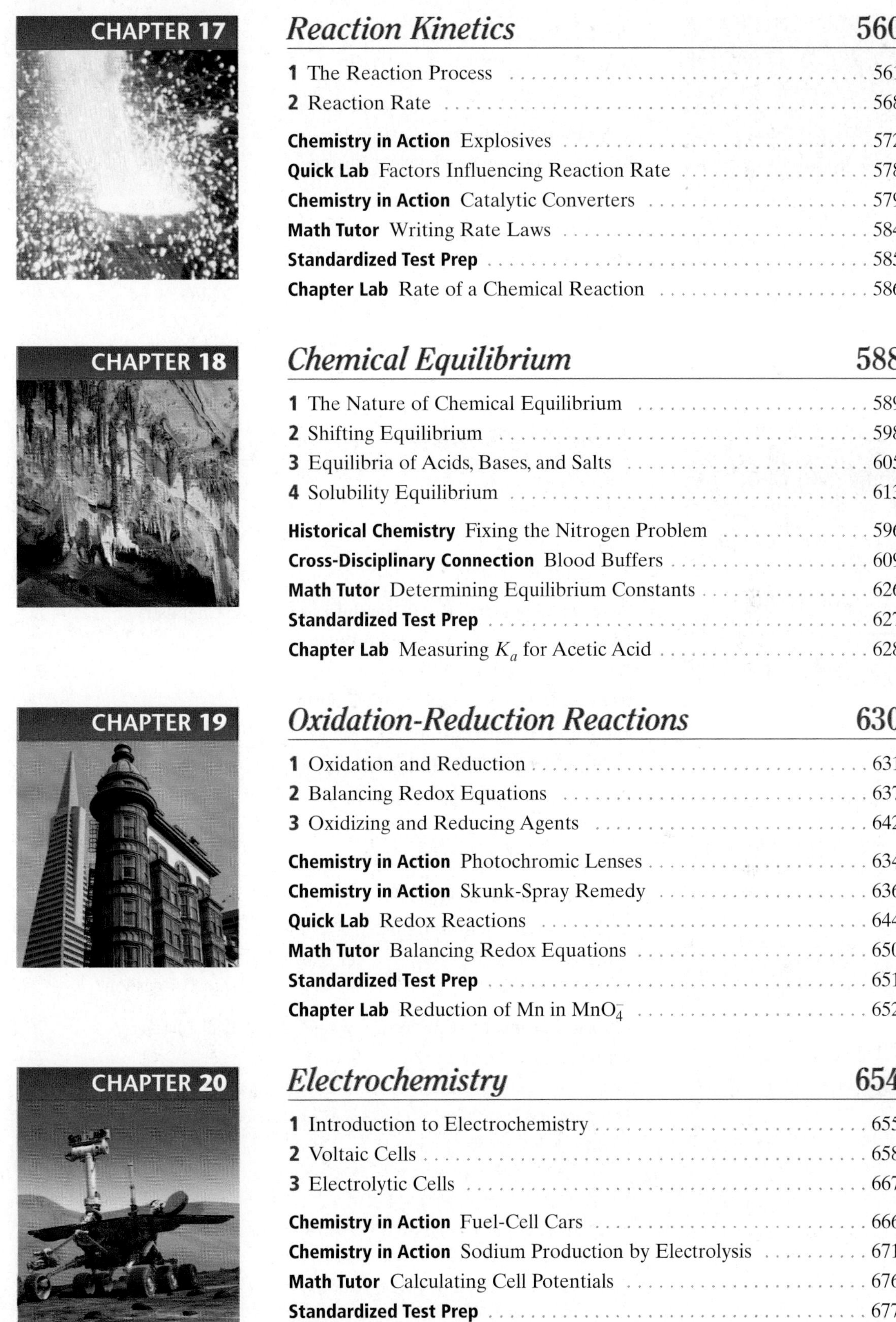

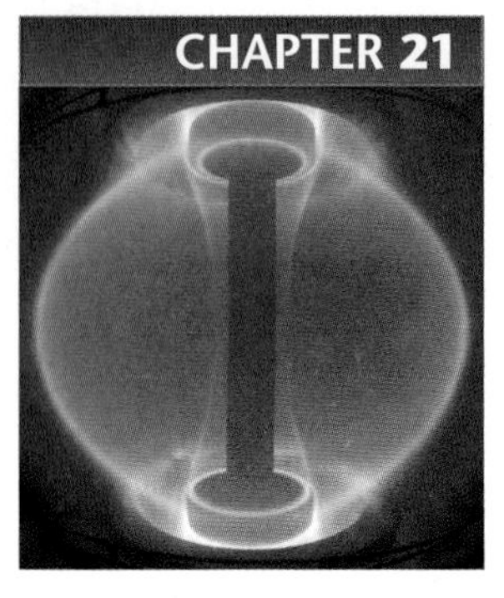


## *Nuclear Chemistry* 680



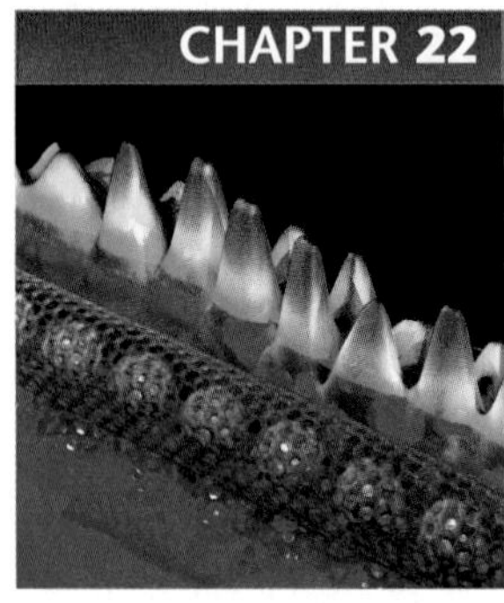


## *Organic Chemistry* 710

## *Biological Chemistry* 750

## Elements Handbook 784



## Reference

# Sample Problems and Math Tutors

# Safety in the Chemistry Laboratory

Any chemical can be dangerous if it is misused. Always follow the instructions for the experiment. Pay close attention to the safety notes. Do not do anything differently unless told to do so by your teacher.

Chemicals, even water, can cause harm. The challenge is to know how to use chemicals correctly. To make sure you are using chemicals correctly, follow the rules stated below, pay attention to your teacher's directions, and follow cautions on chemical labels and in the experiments.

Specific experiments will use a system of Safety Symbols to highlight specific types of precautions. No matter what Safety Symbols an experiment may contain, the following safety rules apply any time you are in the lab.

## Before You Begin

1. **Read the entire activity before entering the lab.** Be familiar with the instructions before beginning an activity. Do not start an activity until you have asked your teacher to explain any parts of the activity that you do not understand.
2. **Student-designed procedures or inquiry activities must be approved by your teacher before you attempt the procedures or activities.**
3. **Wear the right clothing for lab work.** Before beginning work, tie back long hair, roll up loose sleeves, and put on any required personal protective equipment as directed by your teacher. Remove your wristwatch and any necklaces or jewelry that could get caught in moving parts. Avoid or confine loose clothing that could knock things over, catch on fire, get caught in moving parts, contact electrical connections, or absorb chemical solutions. Wear pants rather than shorts or skirts. Nylon and polyester fabrics burn and melt more readily than cotton does. Protect your feet from chemical spills and falling objects. Do not wear open-toed shoes, sandals, or canvas shoes in the lab. In addition, chemical fumes may react with and ruin some jewelry, such as pearl jewelry. Do not apply cosmetics in the lab. Some hair care products and nail polish are highly flammable.
4. **Do not wear contact lenses in the lab.** Even though you will be wearing safety goggles, chemicals could get between contact lenses and your eyes and could cause irreparable eye damage. If your doctor requires that you wear contact lenses instead of glasses, then you should wear eye-cup safety goggles—similar to goggles worn for underwater swimming—in the lab. Ask your doctor or your teacher how to use eye-cup safety goggles to protect your eyes.
5. **Know the location of <u>all safety and emergency equipment</u> used in the lab.** Know proper fire-drill procedures and the location of all fire exits. Ask your teacher where the nearest eyewash stations, safety blankets, safety shower, fire extinguisher, first-aid kit, and chemical spill kit are located. Be sure that you know how to operate the equipment safely.

## While You Are Working

6. **Always wear a lab apron and safety goggles.** Wear these items even if you are not working on an activity. Labs contain chemicals that can damage your clothing, skin, and eyes. Keep the strings of your lab apron tied. If your safety goggles cloud up or are uncomfortable, ask your teacher for help. Lengthening the strap slightly, washing the goggles with soap and warm water, or using an anti-fog spray may help the problem.

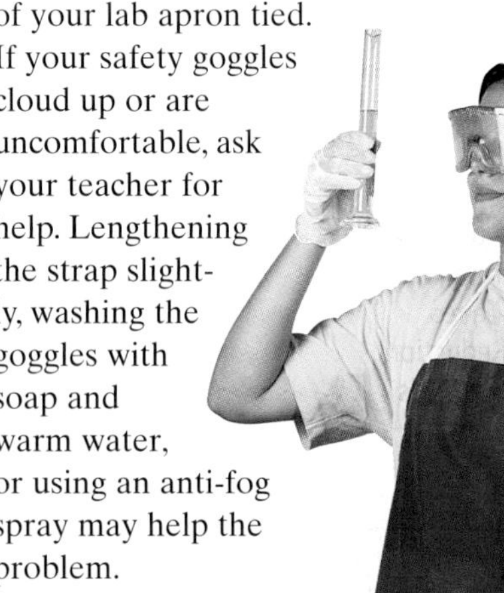

# Labs

## PRE-LABS



## CHAPTER LABS



## QUICK LABS

# Feature Articles

## Historical Chemistry

## Cross-Disciplinary Connection



extension

Go to **go.hrw.com** for full-length articles.

## Careers in Chemistry

## Chemistry in Action

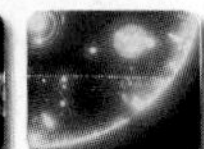

# Safety in the Chemistry Laboratory

Any chemical can be dangerous if it is misused. Always follow the instructions for the experiment. Pay close attention to the safety notes. Do not do anything differently unless told to do so by your teacher.

Chemicals, even water, can cause harm. The challenge is to know how to use chemicals correctly. To make sure you are using chemicals correctly, follow the rules stated below, pay attention to your teacher's directions, and follow cautions on chemical labels and in the experiments.

Specific experiments will use a system of Safety Symbols to highlight specific types of precautions. No matter what Safety Symbols an experiment may contain, the following safety rules apply any time you are in the lab.

## Before You Begin

1. **Read the entire activity before entering the lab.** Be familiar with the instructions before beginning an activity. Do not start an activity until you have asked your teacher to explain any parts of the activity that you do not understand.

2. **Student-designed procedures or inquiry activities must be approved by your teacher before you attempt the procedures or activities.**

3. **Wear the right clothing for lab work.** Before beginning work, tie back long hair, roll up loose sleeves, and put on any required personal protective equipment as directed by your teacher. Remove your wristwatch and any necklaces or jewelry that could get caught in moving parts. Avoid or confine loose clothing that could knock things over, catch on fire, get caught in moving parts, contact electrical connections, or absorb chemical solutions. Wear pants rather than shorts or skirts. Nylon and polyester fabrics burn and melt more readily than cotton does. Protect your feet from chemical spills and falling objects. Do not wear open-toed shoes, sandals, or canvas shoes in the lab. In addition, chemical fumes may react with and ruin some jewelry, such as pearl jewelry. Do not apply cosmetics in the lab. Some hair care products and nail polish are highly flammable.

4. **Do not wear contact lenses in the lab.** Even though you will be wearing safety goggles, chemicals could get between contact lenses and your eyes and could cause irreparable eye damage. If your doctor requires that you wear contact lenses instead of glasses, then you should wear eye-cup safety goggles—similar to goggles worn for underwater swimming—in the lab. Ask your doctor or your teacher how to use eye-cup safety goggles to protect your eyes.

5. **Know the location of <u>all safety and emergency equipment</u> used in the lab.** Know proper fire-drill procedures and the location of all fire exits. Ask your teacher where the nearest eyewash stations, safety blankets, safety shower, fire extinguisher, first-aid kit, and chemical spill kit are located. Be sure that you know how to operate the equipment safely.

## While You Are Working

6. **Always wear a lab apron and safety goggles.** Wear these items even if you are not working on an activity. Labs contain chemicals that can damage your clothing, skin, and eyes. Keep the strings of your lab apron tied. If your safety goggles cloud up or are uncomfortable, ask your teacher for help. Lengthening the strap slightly, washing the goggles with soap and warm water, or using an anti-fog spray may help the problem.

7. **NEVER work alone in the lab.** Work in the lab only when supervised by your teacher. Do not leave equipment unattended while it is in operation.

8. **Perform only activities specifically assigned by your teacher.** Do not attempt any procedure without your teacher's direction. Use only materials and equipment listed in the activity or authorized by your teacher. Steps in a procedure should be performed only as described in the activity or as approved by your teacher.

9. **Keep your work area neat and uncluttered.** Have only books and other materials that are needed to conduct the activity in the lab. Keep backpacks, purses, and other items in your desk, locker, or other designated storage areas.

10. **Always heed safety symbols and cautions listed in activities, listed on handouts, posted in the room, provided on chemical labels, and given verbally by your teacher.** Be aware of the potential hazards of the required materials and procedures, and follow all precautions indicated.

11. **Be alert, and walk with care in the lab.** Be aware of others near you and your equipment.

12. **Do not take food, drinks, chewing gum, or tobacco products into the lab.** Do not store or eat food in the lab.

13. **Use extreme caution when working with hot plates and other heating devices.** Keep your head, hands, hair, and clothing away from the flame or heating area. Remember that metal surfaces connected to the heated area will become hot by conduction. Use tongs when heating containers and never hold or touch them. Gas burners should be lit only with a spark lighter, not with matches. Make sure that all heating devices and gas valves are turned off before you leave the lab. Never leave a heating device unattended when it is in use. Metal, ceramic, and glass items do not necessarily look hot when they are hot. Allow all items to cool before storing them.

14. **Remember how easily glass can break and cause a serious cut.** Check the condition of any glassware before and after using it. Inform your teacher of any broken, chipped, or cracked glassware, because it should not be used. Never force glass tubing into rubber tubing, stoppers or wooden corks. To protect your hands, wear heavy cloth gloves or wrap toweling around the glass and the tubing, stopper, or cork, and gently push in the glass. Do not pick up broken glass with your bare hands. Dispose of broken glass in a specially designated disposal container.

15. **Exercise caution when working with electrical equipment.** Do not use electrical equipment with frayed or twisted wires. Be sure that your hands are dry before using electrical equipment. Do not let electrical cords dangle from work stations. Dangling cords can cause you to trip and can cause an electrical shock. The area under and around electrical equipment should be dry; cords should not lie in puddles of spilled liquid.

16. **Do not fool around in the lab.** Take your lab work seriously, and behave appropriately in the lab. Lab equipment and apparatus are not toys; never use lab time or equipment for anything other than the intended purpose. Be aware of the safety of your classmates as well as your safety at all times.

## Working With Chemicals

17. **NEVER taste chemicals or allow them to contact your skin.** Keep your hands away from your face and mouth, even if you are wearing gloves.

18. **Do not inhale fumes directly.** When instructed to smell a substance, use your hand to wave the fumes toward your nose, and inhale gently.

19. **Read chemical labels.** Follow the instructions and safety precautions stated on the labels.

20. **If you are working with flammable liquids, use only small amounts**. Be sure no one else is using a lit Bunsen burner or is planning to use one when you are working with flammable liquids, because the fumes can ignite.

21. **For all chemicals, take only what you need.** However, if you do happen to take too much and have some left over, DO NOT put it back in the bottle. If somebody accidentally puts a chemical into the wrong bottle, the next person to use it will have a contaminated sample. Ask your teacher what to do with any leftover chemicals.

22. **NEVER take any chemicals out of the lab.** (This is another one that you should already know. You probably know the remaining rules also, but read them anyway.)

## Emergency Procedures

23. **Follow standard fire-safety procedures.** If your clothing catches on fire, do not run; WALK to the safety shower, stand under it, and turn it on. While doing so, call to your teacher. In case of fire, alert your teacher and leave the lab.

24. **Report any accident, incident, or hazard—no matter how trivial—to your teacher immediately.** Any incident involving bleeding, burns, fainting, nausea, dizziness, chemical exposure, or ingestion should also be reported immediately to the school nurse or to a physician. If you have a close call, tell your teacher so that you and your teacher can find a way to prevent it from happening again.

25. **Report all spills to your teacher immediately.** Call your teacher rather than trying to clean a spill yourself. Your teacher will tell you whether it is safe for you to clean up the spill; if it is not safe, your teacher will know how to clean up the spill.

26. **If you spill a chemical on your skin, wash the chemical off in the sink and call your teacher.** If you spill a solid chemical onto your clothing, brush it off carefully without scattering it onto somebody else and call your teacher. If you get liquid on your clothing, wash it off right away by using the faucet at the sink and call your teacher. If the spill is on your pants or something else that will not fit under the sink faucet, use the safety shower. Remove the pants or other affected clothing while you are under the shower, and call your teacher. (It may be temporarily embarrassing to remove pants or other clothing in front of your classmates, but failure to flush the chemical off your skin could cause permanent damage.)

27. **If you get a chemical in your eyes, walk immediately to the eyewash station, turn it on, and lower your head so your eyes are in the running water.** Hold your eyelids open with your thumbs and fingers, and roll your eyeballs around. You have to flush your eyes continuously for at least 15 minutes. Call your teacher while you are doing this.

## When You Are Finished

28. **Clean your work area at the conclusion of each lab period as directed by your teacher.** Broken glass, chemicals, and other waste products should be disposed of in separate, special containers. Dispose of waste materials as directed by your teacher. Put away all material and equipment according to your teacher's instructions. Report any damaged or missing equipment or materials to your teacher.

29. **Wash your hands with soap and hot water after each lab period.** To avoid contamination, wash your hands at the conclusion of each lab period, and before you leave the lab.

## A Final Reminder

30. **Whether or not the lab instructions remind you, all of these rules apply all of the time.**

# Safety Symbols

To highlight specific types of precautions, the following symbols are used throughout the lab program. Remember that no matter what safety symbols you see in the textbook, all 30 of the lab safety rules previously described should be followed at all times.

## EYE PROTECTION

- Wear safety goggles in the lab at all times.
- Know how to use the eyewash station. If chemicals get into your eyes, flush your eyes (including under the eyelids) with running water at the eyewash station for at least 15 minutes. Use your thumb and fingers to hold your eyelids open and roll your eyeball around. While doing so, ask another student to notify your teacher.

## CLOTHING PROTECTION

- Wear an apron or lab coat at all times in the lab.
- Tie back long hair, secure loose clothing, and remove loose jewelry so that they do not knock over equipment or come into contact with hazardous materials.

## HAND SAFETY

- Wear protective gloves when working with chemicals.
- Use a hot mitt or tongs to handle equipment that may be hot.

## GLASSWARE SAFETY

- Inspect glassware before use; do not use chipped or cracked glassware.
- Never place glassware, containers of chemicals, or anything else near the edges of a lab bench or table.

## CHEMICAL SAFETY

- Never return unused chemicals to the original container. Take only what you need.
- Label the beakers and test tubes you use with the chemicals they contain.
- Never transfer substances by sucking on a pipet or straw; use a suction bulb.
- Do not mix any chemicals unless specifically instructed to do so by your teacher.
- If a chemical spills on the floor or lab bench, tell your teacher, and wait for instructions before cleaning it up yourself.

## CAUSTIC SUBSTANCE SAFETY

- Do not pour water into a strong acid or base. The mixture can produce heat and can splatter.

## HEATING SAFETY

- Avoid using open flames. If possible, work only with hot plates having an on/off switch and an indicator light.
- When heating a chemical in a test tube, point the open end of the test tube away from yourself and others.

## HYGIENE CARE

- Keep your hands away from your face and mouth while you work in the lab.
- Do not eat or drink any food from laboratory containers.
- Wash your hands thoroughly before you leave the lab.

## WASTE DISPOSAL

- Help protect our environment by following the instructions for proper disposal.

# How to Use Your Textbook

## Your Roadmap for Success with *Modern Chemistry*

### Get Organized

Keep a science notebook so that you are ready to take notes when your teacher reviews material in class. Keep your assignments in this notebook so that you can review them when studying for the chapter test.

**STUDY TIP Appendix B,** located in the back of the book, describes a number of Study Skills that can help you succeed in chemistry, including several approaches to note taking.

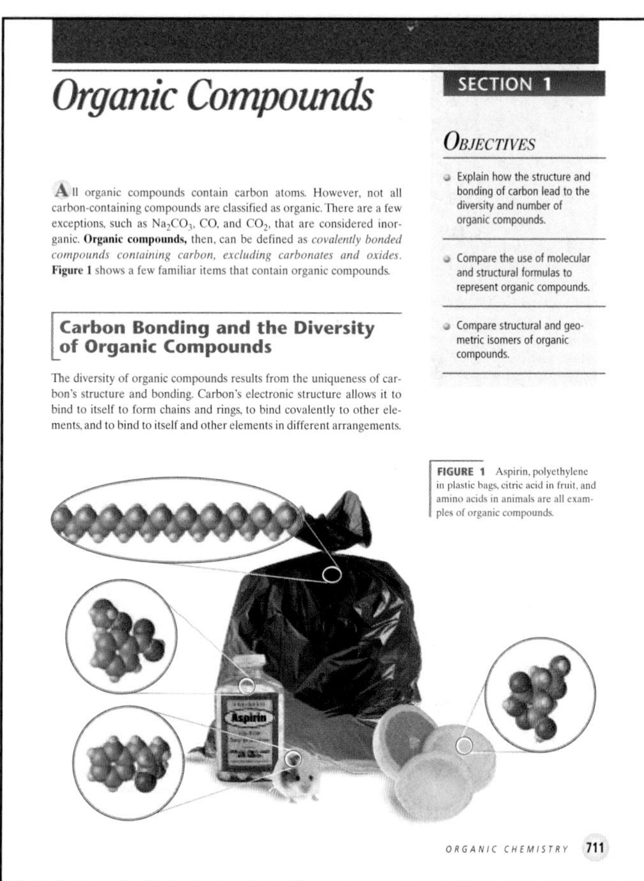

*Organic Compounds*

SECTION 1

*OBJECTIVES*

- Explain how the structure and bonding of carbon lead to the diversity and number of organic compounds.
- Compare the use of molecular and structural formulas to represent organic compounds.
- Compare structural and geometric isomers of organic compounds.

All organic compounds contain carbon atoms. However, not all carbon-containing compounds are classified as organic. There are a few exceptions, such as $Na_2CO_3$, CO, and $CO_2$, that are considered inorganic. **Organic compounds,** then, can be defined as *covalently bonded compounds containing carbon, excluding carbonates and oxides.* **Figure 1** shows a few familiar items that contain organic compounds.

**Carbon Bonding and the Diversity of Organic Compounds**

The diversity of organic compounds results from the uniqueness of carbon's structure and bonding. Carbon's electronic structure allows it to bind to itself to form chains and rings, to bind covalently to other elements, and to bind to itself and other elements in different arrangements.



**FIGURE 1** Aspirin, polyethylene in plastic bags, citric acid in fruit, and amino acids in animals are all examples of organic compounds.

ORGANIC CHEMISTRY 711

### Read for Meaning

Read the **Objectives** at the beginning of each section because they will tell you what you'll need to learn. **Key Terms** are boldfaced in each chapter. Use the glossary to locate definitions quickly. After reading each chapter, turn to the **Chapter Highlights** page. Then, review the list of key terms and read the brief summaries of the chapter's main ideas. You may want to do this even before you read the chapter.

**STUDY TIP** If you don't understand a definition, reread the page on which the term is introduced. The surrounding text should help make the definition easier to understand.

### Be Resourceful, Use the Web

**SciLinks** boxes in your textbook take you to resources that you can use for science projects, reports, and research papers. Go to **www.scilinks.org,** and type in the SciLinks code to get information on a topic.

**Visit go.hrw.com** Find resources and reference materials that go with your textbook. Visit **go.hrw.com,** and type in the keywords found in your textbook to access the available resources.

**SAMPLE PROBLEM B**

**Oxygen gas from the decomposition of potassium chlorate, $KClO_3$, was collected by water displacement. The barometric pressure and the temperature during the experiment were 731.0 torr and 20.0°C, respectively. What was the partial pressure of the oxygen collected?**

**SOLUTION**

1 *ANALYZE* Given: $PT = P_{atm} = 731.0$ torr

$P_{H_2O} = 17.5$ torr (vapor pressure of water at 20.0°C, from Table A-8)

$P_{atm} = P_{O_2} + P_{H_2O}$

Unknown: $P_{O_2}$ in torr

2 *PLAN* The partial pressure of the collected oxygen is found by subtracting the partial pressure of water vapor from the atmospheric pressure, according to Dalton's law of partial pressures.

$$P_{O_2} = P_{atm} - P_{H_2O}$$

3 *COMPUTE* Substituting values for $P_{atm}$ and $P_{H_2O}$ gives $P_{O_2}$.

$$P_{O_2} = 731.0 \text{ torr} - 17.5 \text{ torr} = 713.5 \text{ torr}$$

4 *EVALUATE* As expected, the oxygen partial pressure is less than atmospheric pressure. It is reasonably close to an estimated value of 713, calculated as 730 − 17.

**PRACTICE** *Answers in Appendix E*

1. Some hydrogen gas is collected over water at 20.0°C. The levels of water inside and outside the gas-collection bottle are the same. The partial pressure of hydrogen is 742.5 torr. What is the barometric pressure at the time the gas is collected?

**extension** Go to **go.hrw.com** for more practice problems that ask you to calculate partial pressure.

**CHAPTER REVIEW**

***The Development of a New Atomic Model***

**SECTION 1 REVIEW**

1. a. List five examples of electromagnetic radiation.
   b. What is the speed of all forms of electromagnetic radiation in a vacuum?
2. Prepare a two-column table. List the properties of light that can best be explained by the wave theory in one column. List those best explained by the particle theory in the second column. You may want to consult a physics textbook for reference.
3. What are the frequency and wavelength ranges of visible light?
4. List the colors of light in the visible spectrum in order of increasing frequency.
5. In the early twentieth century, what two experiments involving light and matter could not be explained by the wave theory of light?
6. a. How are the wavelength and frequency of electromagnetic radiation related?
   b. How are the energy and frequency of electromagnetic radiation related?
   c. How are the energy and wavelength of electromagnetic radiation related?
7. Which theory of light—the wave or particle theory—best explains the following phenomena?
   a. the interference of light
   b. the photoelectric effect
   c. the emission of electromagnetic radiation by an excited atom
8. Distinguish between the ground state and an excited state of an atom.
9. According to Bohr's model of the hydrogen atom, how is hydrogen's emission spectrum produced?

**PRACTICE PROBLEMS**

10. Determine the frequency of light whose wavelength is $4.257 \times 10^{-7}$ cm.
11. Determine the energy in joules of a photon whose frequency is $3.55 \times 10^{17}$ Hz.
12. Using the two equations $E = h\nu$ and $c = \lambda\nu$, derive an equation expressing $E$ in terms of $h$, $c$, and $\lambda$.
13. How long would it take a radio wave whose frequency is $7.25 \times 10^5$ Hz to travel from Mars to Earth if the distance between the two planets is approximately $8.00 \times 10^7$ km?
14. Cobalt-60 is an artificial radioisotope that is produced in a nuclear reactor and is used as a gamma-ray source in the treatment of certain types of cancer. If the wavelength of the gamma radiation from a cobalt-60 source is $1.00 \times 10^{-3}$ nm, calculate the energy of a photon of this radiation.

***The Quantum Model of the Atom***

**SECTION 2 REVIEW**

15. Describe two major shortcomings of Bohr's model of the atom.
16. a. What is the principal quantum number?
    b. How is it symbolized?
    c. What are shells?
    d. How does $n$ relate to the number of electrons allowed per main energy level?
17. a. What information is given by the angular momentum quantum number?
    b. What are sublevels, or subshells?
18. For each of the following values of $n$, indicate the numbers and types of sublevels possible for that main energy level. (Hint: See **Table 2.**)
    a. $n = 1$
    b. $n = 2$
    c. $n = 3$
    d. $n = 4$
    e. $n = 7$ (number only)
19. a. What information is given by the magnetic quantum number?
    b. How many orbital orientations are possible in each of the $s$, $p$, $d$, and $f$ sublevels?
    c. Explain and illustrate the notation for distinguishing between the different $p$ orbitals in a sublevel.

124 CHAPTER 4

## Work the Problems

**Sample Problems, Math Tutors,** and **Practice Problems** build your reasoning and problem-solving skills by guiding you through example problems.

## Prepare for Tests

**Section Reviews** and **Chapter Reviews** test your knowledge of the main points of the chapter. Critical Thinking items challenge you to think about the material in different ways and in greater depth. The **Standardized Test Prep** that is located after each Chapter Review helps you sharpen your test-taking abilities.

**STUDY TIP** Reread the Objectives and Chapter Highlights when studying for a test to be sure you know the material.

## Use the Appendix

Your **Appendix** contains a variety of resources designed to enhance your learning experience. The **Elements Handbook** provides additional information about the elements. **Appendix A** has tables which include essential problem-solving information. **Appendix D** provides more practice problems.

### Visit Holt Online Learning

If your teacher gives you a special password to log onto the **Holt Online Learning** site, you'll find your complete textbook on the Web. In addition, you'll find some great learning tools and online activities. You'll be able to see how well you know the material from your textbook.

CHAPTER 1

# Matter and Change

*Chemistry is central to all of the sciences.*

Tartaric Acid Crystals

SECTION 1

# Chemistry Is a Physical Science

## Objectives

- Define *chemistry.*
- List examples of the branches of chemistry.
- Compare and contrast basic research, applied research, and technological development.

The natural sciences were once divided into two broad categories: the biological sciences and the physical sciences. Living things are the main focus of the biological sciences. The physical sciences focus mainly on nonliving things. However, because we now know that both living and nonliving matter consist of chemical structures, chemistry is central to all the sciences, and there are no longer distinct divisions between the biological and physical sciences.

**Chemistry** *is the study of the composition, structure, and properties of matter, the processes that matter undergoes, and the energy changes that accompany these processes.* Chemistry deals with questions such as, What is a material's makeup? How does a material change when heated, cooled, or mixed with other materials and why does this behavior occur? Chemists answer these kinds of questions during their work.

Instruments are routinely used in chemistry to extend our ability to observe and make measurements. Instruments make it possible, for example, to look at microstructures—things too tiny to be seen with the unaided eye. The scanning electron microscope reveals tiny structures by beaming particles called electrons at materials. When the electrons hit a material, they scatter and produce a pattern that shows the material's microstructure. Invisible rays called X rays can also be used to

(a)

(b)

**FIGURE 1** A balance (a) is an instrument used to measure the mass of materials. A sample of DNA placed in a scanning tunneling microscope produces an image (b) showing the contours of the DNA's surface.

determine microstructures. The patterns that appear, called X-ray diffraction patterns, can be analyzed to reveal the arrangement of atoms, molecules, or other particles that make up the material. By learning about microstructures, chemists can explain the behavior of macrostructures—the visible things all around you.

## Branches of Chemistry

Chemistry includes many different branches of study and research. The following are six main areas, or branches, of study. But like the biological and physical sciences, these branches often overlap.

1. *Organic chemistry*—the study of most carbon-containing compounds
2. *Inorganic chemistry*—the study of non-organic substances, many of which have organic fragments bonded to metals (organometallics)
3. *Physical chemistry*—the study of the properties and changes of matter and their relation to energy
4. *Analytical chemistry*—the identification of the components and composition of materials
5. *Biochemistry*—the study of substances and processes occurring in living things
6. *Theoretical chemistry*—the use of mathematics and computers to understand the principles behind observed chemical behavior and to design and predict the properties of new compounds

In all areas of chemistry, scientists work with chemicals. *A* **chemical** *is any substance that has a definite composition.* For example, consider the material called sucrose, or cane sugar. It has a definite composition in terms of the atoms that compose it. It is produced by certain plants in the chemical process of photosynthesis. Sucrose is a chemical. Carbon dioxide, water, and countless other substances are chemicals as well.

Knowing the properties of chemicals allows chemists to find suitable uses for them. For example, researchers have synthesized new substances, such as artificial sweeteners and synthetic fibers. The reactions used to make these chemicals can often be carried out on a large scale to make new consumer products such as flavor enhancers and fabrics.

### Basic Research

Basic research is carried out for the sake of increasing knowledge, such as how and why a specific reaction occurs and what the properties of a substance are. Chance discoveries can be the result of basic research. The properties of Teflon™, for example, were first discovered by accident. A researcher named Roy Plunkett was puzzled by the fact that a gas cylinder used for an experiment appeared to be empty even though the measured mass of the cylinder clearly indicated there was something inside. Plunkett cut the cylinder open and found a white solid. Through basic research, Plunkett's research team determined the nonstick properties, molecular structure, and chemical composition of the new material.

## Applied Research

Applied research is generally carried out to solve a problem. For example, when certain refrigerants escape into the upper atmosphere, they damage the ozone layer, which helps block harmful ultraviolet rays from reaching the surface of Earth. In response to concerns that this atmospheric damage could pose health problems, chemists have developed new refrigerants. In applied research, researchers are driven not by curiosity or a desire to know but by a desire to solve a specific problem.

**FIGURE 2** The chemical structure of the material in an optical fiber gives it the property of total internal reflection. This property, which allows these fibers to carry light, was discovered through basic and applied research. The use of this property to build networks by sending data on light pulses is the technological development of fiber optics.

## Technological Development

Technological development typically involves the production and use of products that improve our quality of life. Examples include computers, catalytic converters for cars, and biodegradable materials.

Technological applications often lag far behind the discoveries that are eventually used in technologies. For example, nonstick cookware, a technological application, was developed well after the accidental discovery of Teflon. When it was later discovered that the Teflon coating on cookware often peeled off, a new challenge arose. Using applied research, scientists were then able to improve the bond between the Teflon and the metal surface of the cookware so that it did not peel.

Basic research, applied research, and technological development often overlap. Discoveries made in basic research may lead to applications that can result in new technologies. For example, knowledge of crystals and light that was gained from basic research was used to develop lasers. It was then discovered that pulses of light from lasers can be sent through optical fibers. Today, telephone messages and cable television signals are carried quickly over long distances using fiber optics.

## SECTION REVIEW

1. Define *chemistry*.
2. Name six branches of study in chemistry.
3. Compare and contrast basic research, applied research, and technological development.

**Critical Thinking**

4. **INFERRING RELATIONSHIPS** Scientific and technological advances are constantly changing how people live and work. Discuss a change that you have observed in your lifetime and that has made life easier or more enjoyable for you.

SECTION 2

# Matter and Its Properties

## OBJECTIVES

- Distinguish between the physical properties and chemical properties of matter.
- Classify changes of matter as physical or chemical.
- Explain the gas, liquid, and solid states in terms of particles.
- Explain how the law of conservation of energy applies to changes of matter.
- Distinguish between a mixture and a pure substance.

**C.5.2** Explain the behaviors of gas; the relationship among pressure, volume, and temperature; and the significance of the Kelvin (absolute temperature) scale, using the kinetic-molecular theory as a model

Look around you. You can see a variety of objects—books, desks, chairs, and perhaps trees or buildings outside. All those things are made up of matter, but exactly what is matter? What characteristics, or properties, make matter what it is? In this section, you will learn the answers to these questions.

Explaining what matter is involves finding properties that all matter has in common. That may seem difficult, given that matter takes so many different forms. For the moment, just consider one example of matter—a rock. The first thing you might notice is that the rock takes up space. In other words, it has *volume*. Volume is the amount of three-dimensional space an object occupies. All matter has volume. All matter also has a property called mass. **Mass** *is a measure of the amount of matter*. Mass is the measurement you make using a balance. **Matter** can thus be defined as *anything that has mass and takes up space*. These two properties are the general properties of all matter.

## Basic Building Blocks of Matter

Matter comes in many forms. The fundamental building blocks of matter are atoms and molecules. These particles make up elements and compounds. *An* **atom** *is the smallest unit of an element that maintains the chemical identity of that element. An* **element** *is a pure substance that cannot be broken down into simpler, stable substances and is made of one type of atom.* Carbon is an element and contains one kind of atom.

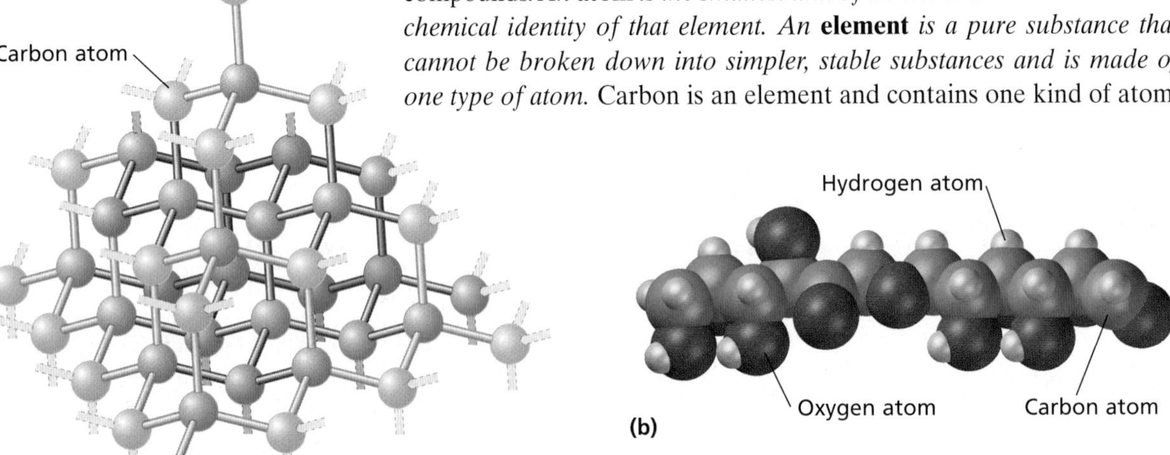


**FIGURE 3** Both elements and compounds are made of atoms, as shown in these models of (a) diamond and (b) sucrose (table sugar).

*A* **compound** *is a substance that can be broken down into simple stable substances. Each compound is made from the atoms of two or more elements that are chemically bonded.* Water is an example of a compound. It is made of two elements, hydrogen and oxygen. The atoms of hydrogen and oxygen are chemically bonded to form a water molecule. You will learn more about the particles that make up compounds when you study chemical bonding in Chapter 6. For now, you can think of a *molecule* as the smallest unit of an element or compound that retains all of the properties of that element or compound.

## Properties and Changes in Matter

Every substance, whether it is an element or a compound, has characteristic properties. Chemists use properties to distinguish between substances and to separate them. Most chemical investigations are related to or depend on the properties of substances.

A property may be a characteristic that defines an entire set of substances. That property can be used to classify an unknown substance as a member of that group. For example, many elements are classified as metals. The distinguishing property of metals is that they conduct electricity well. Therefore, if an unknown element is tested and found to conduct electricity well, it is a metal.

Properties can help reveal the identity of an unknown substance. However, conclusive identification usually cannot be made based on only one property. Comparisons of several properties can be used together to establish the identity of an unknown. Properties are either intensive or extensive. **Extensive properties** *depend on the amount of matter that is present.* Such properties include volume, mass, and the amount of energy in a substance. In contrast, **intensive properties** *do not depend on the amount of matter present.* Such properties include the melting point, boiling point, density, and ability to conduct electricity and to transfer energy as heat. Intensive properties are the same for a given substance regardless of how much of the substance is present. Properties can also be grouped into two general types: physical properties and chemical properties.

### Physical Properties and Physical Changes

*A* **physical property** *is a characteristic that can be observed or measured without changing the identity of the substance.* Physical properties describe the substance itself, rather than describing how it can change into other substances. Examples of physical properties are melting point and boiling point. Those points are, respectively, the temperature at which a substance melts from solid to liquid and the temperature at which it boils from liquid to gas. For example, water melts from ice to liquid at 0°C (273 K or 32°F). Liquid water boils to vapor at 100°C (373 K or 212°F).

*A change in a substance that does not involve a change in the identity of the substance is called a* **physical change.** Examples of physical

**FIGURE 4** Water boils at 100°C no matter how much water is in the container. Boiling point is an intensive property.

changes include grinding, cutting, melting, and boiling a material. These types of changes do not change the identity of the substance present.

Melting and boiling are part of an important class of physical changes called changes of state. As the name suggests, *a* **change of state** *is a physical change of a substance from one state to another.* The three common states of matter are solid, liquid, and gas.

*Matter in the* **solid** *state has definite volume and definite shape.* For example, a piece of quartz or coal keeps its size and its shape, regardless of the container it is in. Solids have this characteristic because the particles in them are packed together in relatively fixed positions. The particles are held close together by the strong attractive forces between them, and only vibrate about fixed points.

*Matter in the* **liquid** *state has a definite volume but an indefinite shape;* a liquid assumes the shape of its container. For example, a given quantity of liquid water takes up a definite amount of space, but the water takes the shape of its container. Liquids have this characteristic because the particles in them are close together but can move past one another. The particles in a liquid move more rapidly than those in a solid. This causes them to overcome temporarily the strong attractive forces between them, allowing the liquid to flow.

*Matter in the* **gas** *state has neither definite volume nor definite shape.* For example, a given quantity of helium expands to fill any size container and takes the shape of the container. All gases have this characteristic because they are composed of particles that move very rapidly and are at great distances from one another compared with the particles of liquids and solids. At these great distances, the attractive forces between gas particles have less of an effect than they do at the small distances between particles of liquids and solids.

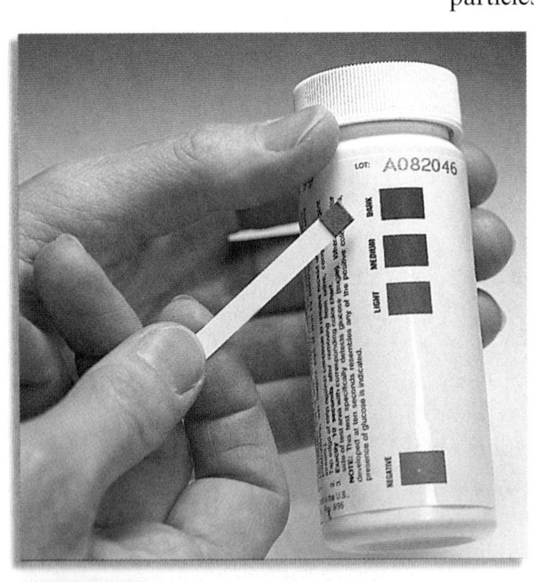


**FIGURE 5** Because it possesses certain chemical properties, a test strip containing Benedict's solution is used to test for the presence of sugar in urine. The test strip is dipped into the sample. The test strip is then matched to a color scale to determine the sugar level in the urine.

An important fourth state of matter is **plasma.** Plasma is a *high-temperature physical state of matter in which atoms lose most of their electrons, particles that make up atoms.* Plasma is found in fluorescent bulbs.

Melting, the change from solid to liquid, is an example of a change of state. Boiling is a change of state from liquid to gas. Freezing, the opposite of melting, is the change from a liquid to a solid. A change of state does not affect the identity of the substance. For example, when ice melts to liquid water or when liquid water boils to form water vapor, the same substance, water, is still present, as shown in **Figure 6.** The water has simply changed state, but it has not turned into a different compound. Only the distances and interactions between the particles that make up water have changed.

## Chemical Properties and Chemical Changes

Physical properties can be observed without changing the identity of the substance, but properties of the second type—chemical properties—cannot. *A* **chemical property** *relates to a substance's ability to undergo changes that transform it into different substances.* Chemical properties are easiest to see when

**FIGURE 6** Models for water in three states. The molecules are close together in the solid and liquid states but far apart in the gas state. The molecules in the solid state are relatively fixed in position, but those in the liquid and gas states can flow around each other.

substances react to form new substances. For example, the ability of charcoal (carbon) to burn in air is a chemical property. When charcoal burns, it combines with oxygen in air to become a new substance, carbon dioxide gas. After the chemical change, the amounts of the original substances, carbon and oxygen, are less than before. A different substance with different properties has been formed. Other examples of chemical properties include the ability of iron to rust by combining with oxygen in air and the ability of silver to tarnish by combining with sulfur.

*A change in which one or more substances are converted into different substances is called a* **chemical change** *or* **chemical reaction.** *The substances that react in a chemical change are called the* **reactants.** *The substances that are formed by the chemical change are called the* **products.** In the case of burning charcoal, carbon and oxygen are the reactants in a combustion, or burning, reaction. Carbon dioxide is the product. The chemical change can be described as follows:

Carbon plus oxygen yields (or forms) carbon dioxide.

Arrows and plus signs can be substituted for the words *yields* and *plus,* respectively:

$$\text{carbon} + \text{oxygen} \longrightarrow \text{carbon dioxide}$$

extension

**Historical Chemistry**

Go to **go.hrw.com** for a full-length article on the chemical reactions of noble gases.

**Keyword: HC6MTXX**

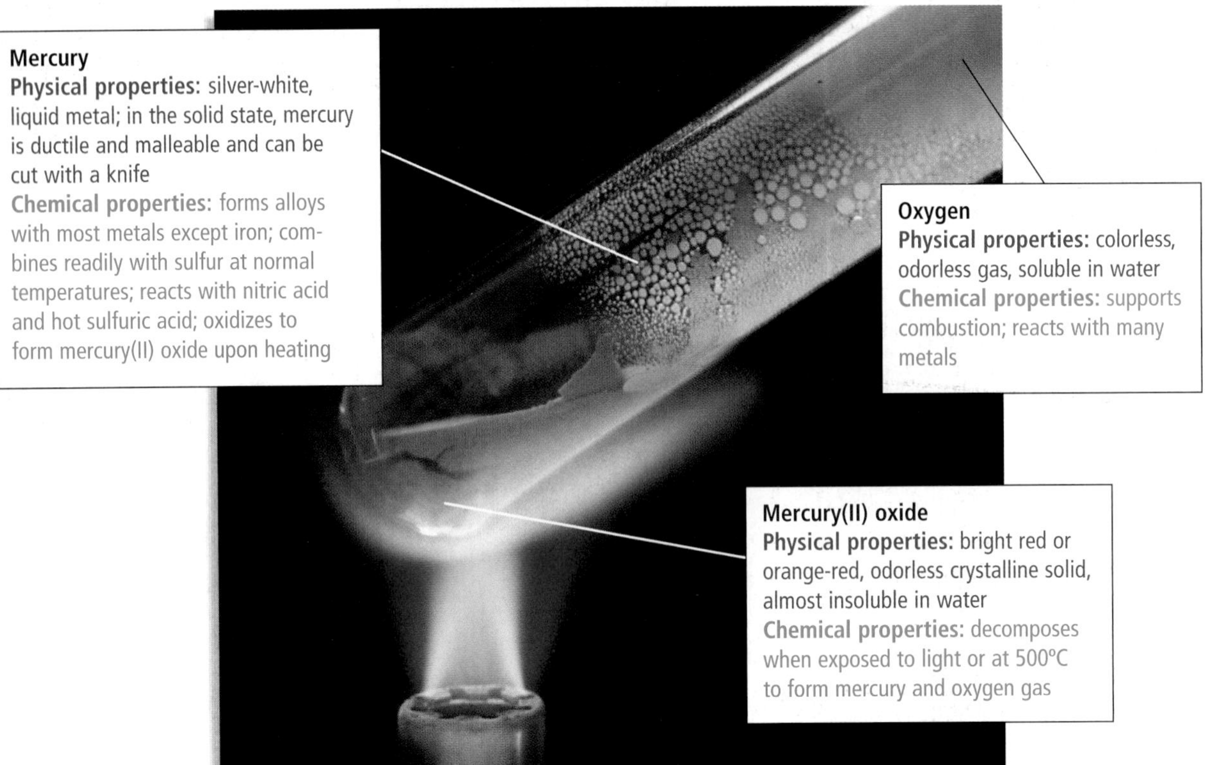


**FIGURE 7** When mercury(II) oxide is heated, it decomposes to form oxygen gas and mercury (which can be seen on the side of the test tube). Decomposition is a chemical change that can be observed by comparing the properties of mercury(II) oxide, mercury, and oxygen.

The decomposition of the mercury compound shown in **Figure 7** can be expressed as follows:

$$\text{mercury(II) oxide} \longrightarrow \text{mercury} + \text{oxygen}$$

Chemical changes and reactions, such as combustion and decomposition, form products whose properties differ greatly from those of the reactants. However, chemical changes do not affect the total amount of matter present before and after a reaction. The amount of matter, and therefore the total mass, remains the same.

## Energy and Changes in Matter

When physical or chemical changes occur, energy is always involved. The energy can take several different forms, such as heat or light. Sometimes heat provides enough energy to cause a physical change, as in the melting of ice, and sometimes heat provides enough energy to cause a chemical change, as in the decomposition of water vapor to form oxygen gas and hydrogen gas. But the boundary between physical and chemical changes isn't always so clear. For example, while most chemists would consider the dissolving of sucrose in water to be a physical change, many chemists would consider the dissolving of table salt in water to be a chemical change. As you learn more about the structure of matter, you will better understand why the boundaries between chemical and physical changes can be confusing.

Accounting for all the energy present before and after a change is not a simple process. But scientists who have done such experimentation are confident that the total amount of energy remains the same. Although energy can be absorbed or released in a change, it is not destroyed or created. It simply assumes a different form. This is the law of conservation of energy.

## Classification of Matter

Matter exists in an enormous variety of forms. Any sample of matter, however, can be classified either as a pure substance or as a mixture. The composition of a pure substance is the same throughout and does not vary from sample to sample. A pure substance can be an element or a compound. Mixtures, in contrast, contain more than one substance. They can vary in composition and properties from sample to sample and sometimes from one part of a sample to another part of the same sample. All matter, whether it is a pure substance or a mixture, can be classified in terms of uniformity of composition and properties of a given sample. **Figure 8** illustrates the overall classification of matter into elements, compounds, and mixtures.

### Mixtures

You deal with mixtures every day. Nearly every object around you, including most things you eat and drink and even the air you breathe, is a mixture. *A* **mixture** *is a blend of two or more kinds of matter, each*

**FIGURE 8** This classification scheme for matter shows the relationships among mixtures, compounds, and elements.

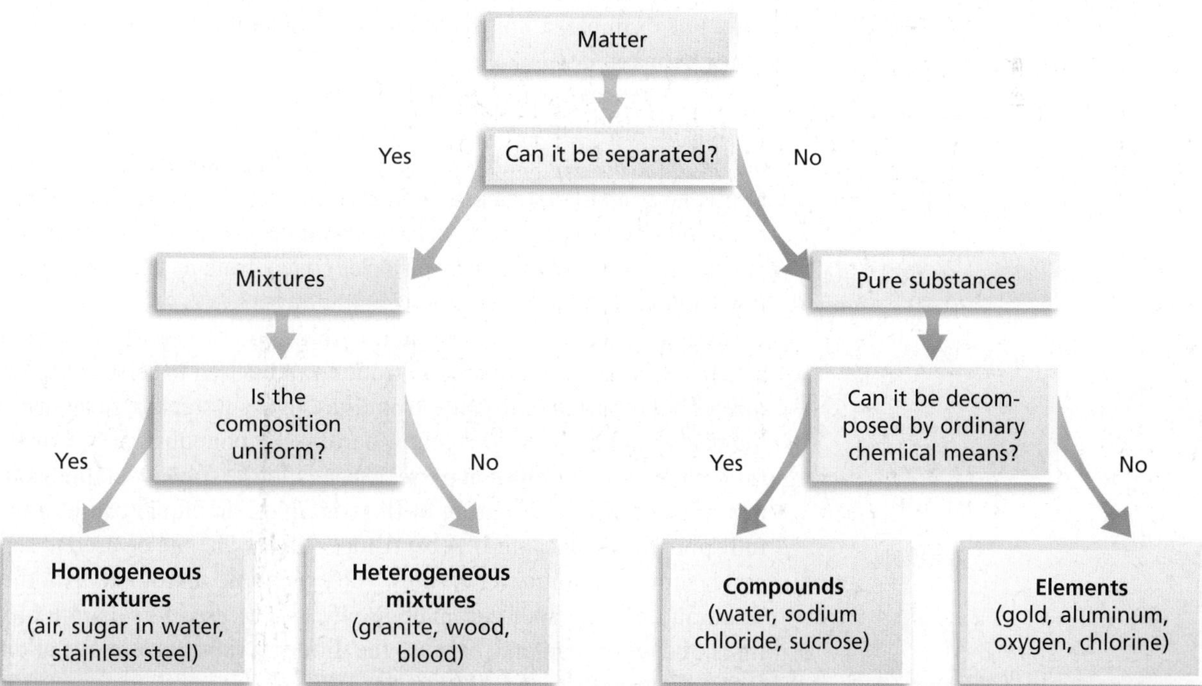

(a)

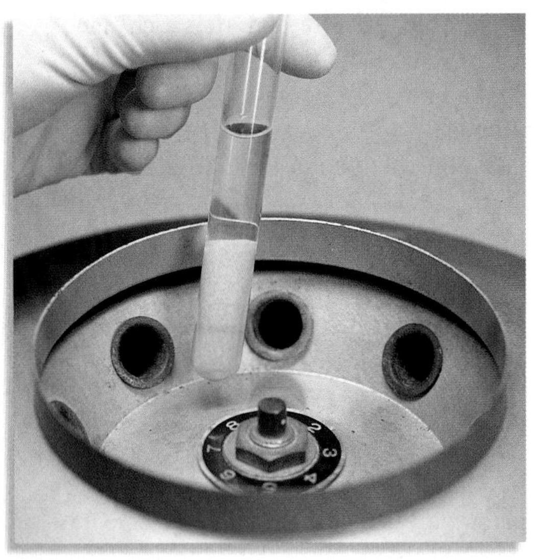
(b)

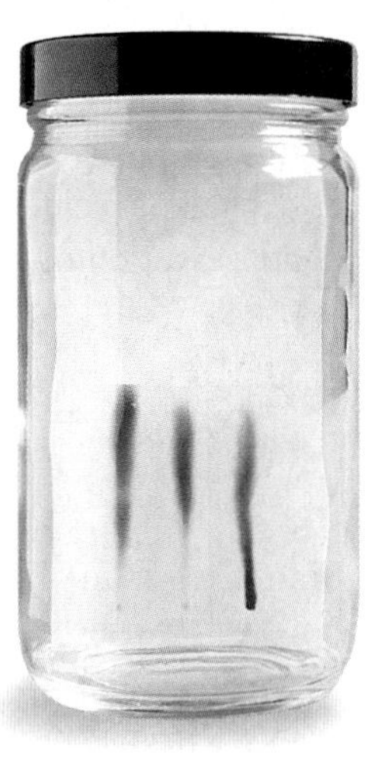
(c)

**FIGURE 9** (a) Barium chromate can be separated from the solution in the beaker using filtration. (b) A centrifuge can be used to separate certain solid components. The centrifuge spins rapidly, which causes the solids to settle to the bottom of the test tube. (c) The components of an ink can be separated using paper chromatography.

*of which retains its own identity and properties.* The parts, or components, of a mixture are simply mixed together physically and can usually be separated. As a result, the properties of a mixture are a combination of the properties of its components. Because mixtures can contain various amounts of different substances, a mixture's composition must be specified. This is often done in terms of percentage by mass or by volume. For example, a mixture might be 5% sodium chloride and 95% water by mass.

Some mixtures are *uniform in composition;* that is, they are said to be **homogeneous.** They have the same proportion of components throughout. *Homogeneous mixtures are also called* **solutions.** A salt-water solution is an example of such a mixture. Other mixtures are *not uniform throughout;* that is, they are **heterogeneous.** For example, in a mixture of clay and water, heavier clay particles concentrate near the bottom of the container.

Some mixtures can be separated by filtration or vaporized to separate the different components. Filtration can be used to separate a mixture of solid barium chromate from the other substances, as shown in the beaker in **Figure 9a.** The yellow barium compound is trapped by the filter paper, but the solution passes through. If the solid in a liquid-solid mixture settles to the bottom of the container, the liquid can be carefully poured off (decanted). A centrifuge **(Figure 9b)** can be used to separate some solid-liquid mixtures, such as those in blood. Another technique, called paper chromatography, can be used to separate mixtures of dyes or pigments because the different substances move at different rates on the paper **(Figure 9c).**

## Pure Substances

Any sample of a pure substance is homogeneous. *A* **pure substance** *has a fixed composition and differs from a mixture in the following ways:*

1. *Every sample of a given pure substance has exactly the same characteristic properties.* All samples of a pure substance have the same characteristic physical and chemical properties. These properties are so specific that they can be used to identify the substance. In contrast, the properties of a mixture depend on the relative amounts of the mixture's components.
2. *Every sample of a given pure substance has exactly the same composition.* Unlike mixtures, all samples of a pure substance have the same makeup. For example, pure water is always 11.2% hydrogen and 88.8% oxygen by mass.

Pure substances are either compounds or elements. A compound can be decomposed, or broken down, into two or more simpler compounds or elements by a chemical change. Water is a compound made of hydrogen and oxygen chemically bonded to form a single substance. Water can be broken down into hydrogen and oxygen through a chemical reaction called electrolysis, as shown in **Figure 10a.**

Sucrose is made of carbon, hydrogen, and oxygen. Sucrose breaks down to form the other substances shown in **Figure 10b.** Under intense heating, sucrose breaks down to produce carbon and water.

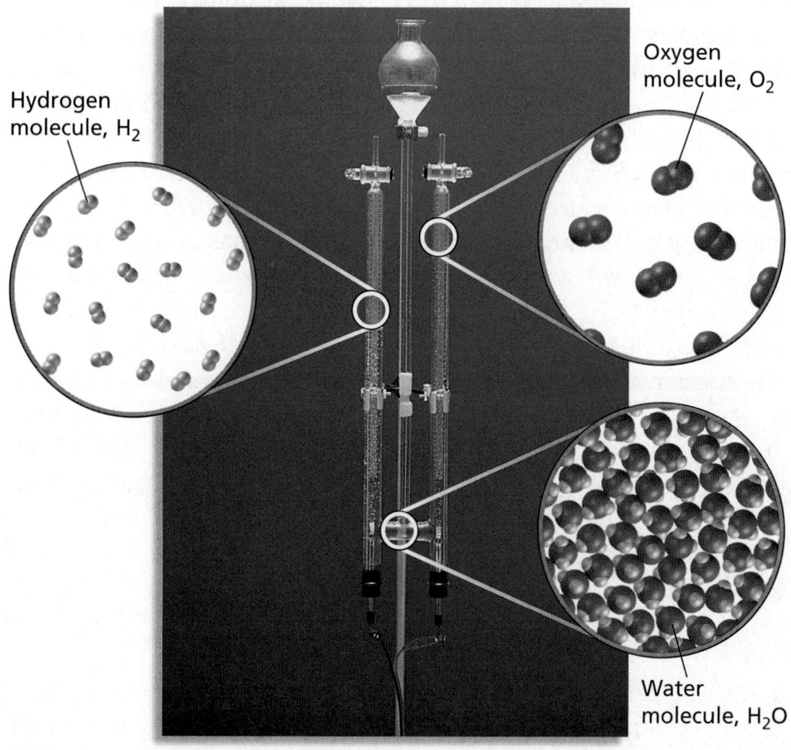


(a)

(b)

**FIGURE 10** (a) Passing an electric current through water causes the compound to break down into the elements hydrogen and oxygen, which differ in composition from water. (b) When sucrose is heated, it caramelizes. When it is heated to a high enough temperature, it breaks down completely into carbon and water.

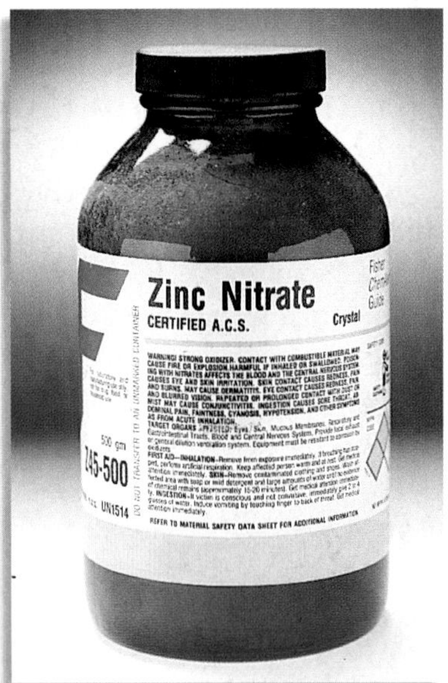


$Zn(NO_3)_2 \bullet 6H_2O$ F.W. 297.47

| Certificate of Actual Lot Analysis | |
|---|---|
| Acidity (as $HNO_3$) | 0.008% |
| Alkalies and Earths | 0.02% |
| Chloride (Cl) | 0.005% |
| Insoluble Matter | 0.001% |
| Iron (Fe) | 0.0002% |
| Lead (Pb) | 0.001% |
| Phosphate ($PO_4$) | 0.0002% |
| Sulfate ($SO_4$) | 0.002% |

**Store separately from and avoid contact with combustible materials. Keep container closed and in a cool, dry place. Avoid contact with skin, eyes and clothing.**

LOT NO. 917356

FL-02-0588 CAS 10196-18-6

**FIGURE 11** The labeling on a reagent bottle lists the grade of the reagent and the percentages of impurities for that grade. What grade is this chemical?

**TABLE 1** ***Some Grades of Chemical Purity***

| Increasing purity (↑) |
|---|
| Primary standard reagents |
| ACS (American Chemical Society–specified reagents) |
| USP (United States Pharmacopoeia standards) |
| CP (chemically pure; purer than technical grade) |
| NF (National Formulary specifications) |
| FCC (Food Chemical Code specifications) |
| Technical (industrial chemicals) |

## Laboratory Chemicals and Purity

The chemicals in laboratories are generally treated as if they are pure. However, all chemicals have some impurities. Chemical grades of purity are listed in **Table 1.** The purity ranking of the grades can vary when agencies differ in their standards. For some chemicals, the USP grade may specify higher purity than the CP grade. For other chemicals, the opposite may be true. However, the primary standard reagent grade is always purer than the technical grade for the same chemical. Chemists need to be aware of the kinds of impurities in a reagent because these impurities could affect the results of a reaction. For example, the chemical label shown in **Figure 11** shows the impurities for that grade. The chemical manufacturer must ensure that the standards set for that reagent by the American Chemical Society are met.

## SECTION REVIEW

1. **a.** What is the main difference between physical properties and chemical properties?
   **b.** Give an example of each.
2. Classify each of the following as either a physical change or a chemical change.
   **a.** tearing a sheet of paper
   **b.** melting a piece of wax
   **c.** burning a log
3. How do you decide whether a sample of matter is a solid, liquid, or gas?
4. Contrast mixtures with pure substances.

### Critical Thinking

5. **ANALYZING INFORMATION** Compare the composition of sucrose purified from sugar cane with the composition of sucrose purified from sugar beets. Explain your answer.

## CROSS-DISCIPLINARY CONNECTION

# Secrets of the Cremona Violins

What are the most beautiful sounding of all violins? Most professionals will pick the instruments created in Cremona, Italy, following the Renaissance. At that time, Antonio Stradivari, the Guarneri family, and other designers created instruments of extraordinary sound that have yet to be matched. The craftsmen were notoriously secretive about their techniques, but, based on 20 years of research, Dr. Joseph Nagyvary, a professor of biochemistry at Texas A&M University, thinks he has discovered the key to the violins' sound hidden in the chemistry of their materials.

According to Dr. Nagyvary, Stradivarius instruments are nearly free of the shrill, high-pitched noises produced by modern violins. Generally, violin makers attribute this to the design of the instrument, but Dr. Nagyvary traces it to a different source. In Stradivari's day, wood for the violins was transported by floating it down a river from the mountains to Venice, where it was stored in sea water. Dr. Nagyvary first theorized that the soaking process could have removed ingredients from the wood that made it inherently noisy. His experiments revealed that microbes and minerals also permeated the wood, making their own contribution to the mellow musical sound. Attempting to reproduce the effects of sea water, Dr. Nagyvary soaks all his wood in a "secret" solution. One of his favorite ingredients is a cherry-and-plum puree, which contains an enzyme called pectinase. The pectinase softens the wood, making it resonate more freely.

▲*Dr. Nagyvary and his violin*

"The other key factor in a violin's sound," says Dr. Nagyvary, "is the finish, which is the filler and the varnish covering the instrument. Most modern finishes are made from rubbery materials, which limit the vibrations of the wood." Modern analysis has revealed that the Cremona finish was different: it was a brittle mineral microcomposite of a very sophisticated nature. According to historical accounts, all violin makers, including Stradivari, procured their varnishes from the local drugstore chemist, and they didn't even know what they were using! Dr. Nagyvary and his co-workers have identified most of the key ingredients of the Cremona finish.

Many new violins made from the treated wood and replicated finish have been made, and their sound has been analyzed by modern signal analyzers. These violins have been favorably compared with authentic Stradivari violins.

A number of expert violinists have praised the sound of Dr. Nagyvary's instruments, but some violin makers remain skeptical of the chemist's claims. They insist that it takes many years to reveal just how good a violin is. In the meantime, almost everyone agrees that the art and science of violin making are still epitomized by the instruments of Cremona.

### Questions

1. According to Dr. Nagyvary, what are two factors that are believed to have created the unique sound of the Stradivari violins?
2. Use the library or Internet resources to find additional information about the Cremona violin makers. Who were some of the other instrument makers during the time period in which Stradivari was alive? Were other stringed instruments made by these artisans? What are the estimated present-day values of instruments made during this period in Cremona?

SECTION 3

# Elements

## OBJECTIVES

- Use a periodic table to name elements, given their symbols.
- Use a periodic table to write the symbols of elements, given their names.
- Describe the arrangement of the periodic table.
- List the characteristics that distinguish metals, nonmetals, and metalloids.

SC **C.2.3** Summarize the periodic table's property trends (including electron configuration, ionization energy, electron affinity, atomic size, ionic size, and reactivity)

As you have read, elements are pure substances that cannot be decomposed by chemical changes. The elements serve as the building blocks of matter. Each element has characteristic properties. The elements are organized into groups based on similar chemical properties. This organization of elements is the *periodic table,* which is shown in **Figure 12** on the next page.

## Introduction to the Periodic Table

Each small square of the periodic table shows the symbol for the element and the atomic number. For example, the first square, at the upper left, represents element 1, hydrogen, which has the symbol H. As you look through the table, you will see many familiar elements, including iron, sodium, neon, silver, copper, aluminum, sulfur, and lead. You can often relate the symbols to the English names of the elements. Some symbols are derived from the element's older name, which was often in Latin. Still others come from German. For example, wolfram comes from the German name for tungsten. **Table 2** lists some elements and their older names.

SCILINKS.
www.scilinks.org
**Topic:** Periodic Table
**Code:** HC61125

**TABLE 2 *Elements with Symbols Based on Older Names***

| Modern name | Symbol | Older name |
|---|---|---|
| Antimony | Sb | stibium |
| Copper | Cu | cuprum |
| Gold | Au | aurum |
| Iron | Fe | ferrum |
| Lead | Pb | plumbum |
| Mercury | Hg | hydrargyrum |
| Potassium | K | kalium |
| Silver | Ag | argentum |
| Sodium | Na | natrium |
| Tin | Sn | stannum |
| Tungsten | W | wolfram |

## Periodic Table

Metals
Metalloids
Nonmetals

| Group 1 | Group 2 | Group 3 | Group 4 | Group 5 | Group 6 | Group 7 | Group 8 | Group 9 | Group 10 | Group 11 | Group 12 | Group 13 | Group 14 | Group 15 | Group 16 | Group 17 | Group 18 |
|---|---|---|---|---|---|---|---|---|---|---|---|---|---|---|---|---|---|
| 1 H | | | | | | | | | | | | | | | | | 2 He |
| 3 Li | 4 Be | | | | | | | | | | | 5 B | 6 C | 7 N | 8 O | 9 F | 10 Ne |
| 11 Na | 12 Mg | | | | | | | | | | | 13 Al | 14 Si | 15 P | 16 S | 17 Cl | 18 Ar |
| 19 K | 20 Ca | 21 Sc | 22 Ti | 23 V | 24 Cr | 25 Mn | 26 Fe | 27 Co | 28 Ni | 29 Cu | 30 Zn | 31 Ga | 32 Ge | 33 As | 34 Se | 35 Br | 36 Kr |
| 37 Rb | 38 Sr | 39 Y | 40 Zr | 41 Nb | 42 Mo | 43 Tc | 44 Ru | 45 Rh | 46 Pd | 47 Ag | 48 Cd | 49 In | 50 Sn | 51 Sb | 52 Te | 53 I | 54 Xe |
| 55 Cs | 56 Ba | 57 La | 72 Hf | 73 Ta | 74 W | 75 Re | 76 Os | 77 Ir | 78 Pt | 79 Au | 80 Hg | 81 Tl | 82 Pb | 83 Bi | 84 Po | 85 At | 86 Rn |
| 87 Fr | 88 Ra | 89 Ac | 104 Rf | 105 Db | 106 Sg | 107 Bh | 108 Hs | 109 Mt | 110 Ds | 111 Rg | | | | | | | |

| | | | | | | | | | | | | | |
|---|---|---|---|---|---|---|---|---|---|---|---|---|---|
| 58 Ce | 59 Pr | 60 Nd | 61 Pm | 62 Sm | 63 Eu | 64 Gd | 65 Tb | 66 Dy | 67 Ho | 68 Er | 69 Tm | 70 Yb | 71 Lu |
| 90 Th | 91 Pa | 92 U | 93 Np | 94 Pu | 95 Am | 96 Cm | 97 Bk | 98 Cf | 99 Es | 100 Fm | 101 Md | 102 No | 103 Lr |

**FIGURE 12** The periodic table of elements. The names of the elements can be found on Table A-6 in the appendix.

*The vertical columns of the periodic table are called* **groups,** or **families.** Notice that they are numbered from 1 to 18 from left to right. Each group contains elements with similar chemical properties. For example, the elements in Group 2 are beryllium, magnesium, calcium, strontium, barium, and radium. All of these elements are reactive metals with similar abilities to bond to other kinds of atoms. The two major categories of elements are metals and nonmetals. Metalloids have properties intermediate between those of metals and nonmetals.

*The horizontal rows of elements in the periodic table are called* **periods.** Physical and chemical properties change somewhat regularly across a period. Elements that are close to each other in the same period tend to be more similar than elements that are farther apart. For example, in Period 2, the elements lithium and beryllium, in Groups 1 and 2, respectively, are somewhat similar in properties. However, their properties are very different from the properties of fluorine, the Period-2 element in Group 17.

The two sets of elements placed below the periodic table make up what are called the lanthanide series and the actinide series. These metallic elements fit into the table just after elements 57 and 89. They are placed below the table to keep the table from being too wide.

There is a section in the back of this book called the *Elements Handbook* which covers some elements in greater detail. You will use information from the handbook to complete the questions in the Using the Handbook sections in the chapter reviews.

## Chemistry in Action
### Superconductors

Any metal becomes a better conductor of electrical energy as its temperature decreases. In 1911, scientists discovered that when mercury is cooled to about −269°C, it loses all resistance and becomes a superconductor. Scientists have long tried to find a material that would superconduct at temperatures above −196°C, the boiling point of liquid nitrogen. In 1987, scientists discovered ceramic materials that became superconductors when cooled only to −183°C. These "high-temperature" superconductors are used to build very powerful electromagnets. Ceramic electromagnets are used in medical magnetic resonance imaging (MRI) machines and in high-efficiency electric motors and generators.

# Types of Elements

The periodic table is broadly divided into two main sections: metals and nonmetals. As you can see in **Figure 12,** the metals are at the left and in the center of the table. The nonmetals are toward the right. Some elements, such as boron and silicon, show characteristics of both metals and nonmetals.

## Metals

Some of the properties of metals may be familiar to you. For example, you can recognize metals by their shininess, or metallic luster. Perhaps the most important characteristic property of metals is the ease with which they conduct electricity and transfer energy. Thus, *a* **metal** *is an element that is a good electrical conductor and a good heat conductor.*

At room temperature, most metals are solids. Most metals also have the property of *malleability,* that is, they can be hammered or rolled into thin sheets. Metals also tend to be *ductile,* which means that they can be drawn into a fine wire. Metals behave this way because they have high *tensile strength,* the ability to resist breaking when pulled.

Although all metals conduct electricity well, metals also have very diverse properties. Mercury is a liquid at room temperature, whereas tungsten has the highest melting point of any element. The metals in Group 1 are so soft that they can be cut with a knife, yet others, such as chromium, are very hard. Some metals, such as manganese and bismuth, are very brittle, yet others, such as iron and copper, are very malleable and ductile. Most metals have a silvery or grayish white *luster.* Two exceptions are gold and copper, which are yellow and reddish brown, respectively. **Figure 13** shows examples of metals.

**FIGURE 13** (a) Gold has a low reactivity, which is why it may be found in nature in relatively pure form. (b) Copper is used in wiring because it is ductile and conducts electrical energy (c) Aluminum is malleable. It can be rolled into foil that is used for wrapping food.

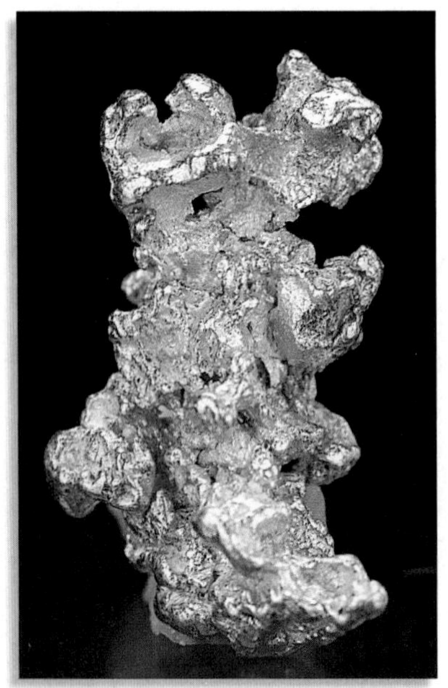

(a)

(b)

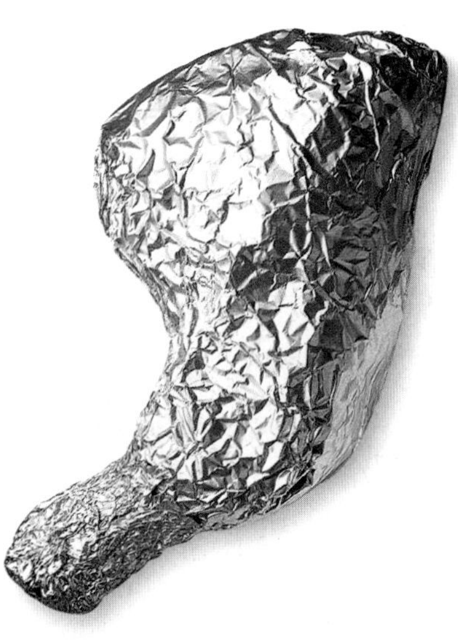

(c)

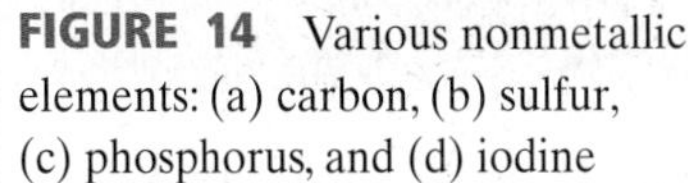
**FIGURE 14** Various nonmetallic elements: (a) carbon, (b) sulfur, (c) phosphorus, and (d) iodine

## Copper: A Typical Metal

Copper has a characteristic reddish color and a metallic luster. It is found naturally in minerals such as chalcopyrite and malachite. Pure copper melts at 1083°C and boils at 2567°C. It can be readily drawn into fine wire, pressed into thin sheets, and formed into tubing. Copper conducts electricity with little loss of energy.

Copper remains unchanged in pure, dry air at room temperature. When heated, it reacts with oxygen in air. It also reacts with sulfur and the elements in Group 17 of the periodic table. The green coating on a piece of weathered copper comes from the reaction of copper with oxygen, carbon dioxide, and sulfur compounds. Copper is an essential mineral in the human diet.

## Nonmetals

Many nonmetals are gases at room temperature. These include nitrogen, oxygen, fluorine, and chlorine. One nonmetal, bromine, is a liquid. The solid nonmetals include carbon, phosphorus, selenium, sulfur, and iodine. These solids tend to be brittle rather than malleable and ductile. Some nonmetals are illustrated in **Figure 14.**

Low conductivity can be used to define nonmetals. *A* **nonmetal** *is an element that is a poor conductor of heat and electricity.* If you look at **Figure 12,** you will see that there are fewer nonmetals than metals.

## Phosphorus: A Typical Nonmetal

Phosphorus is one of five solid nonmetals. Pure phosphorus is known in two common forms. Red phosphorus is a dark red powder that melts at 597°C. White phosphorus is a waxy solid that melts at 44°C. Because it ignites in air at room temperature, white phosphorus is stored under water.

Phosphorus is too reactive to exist in pure form in nature. It is present in huge quantities in phosphate rock, where it is combined with oxygen and calcium. All living things contain phosphorus.

**FIGURE 15** Selenium is a nonmetal, though it looks metallic.

## Metalloids

As you look from left to right on the periodic table, you can see that the metalloids are found between the metals and the nonmetals. *A* **metalloid**

**FIGURE 16** Some noble gases are used to make lighted signs of various colors.

*is an element that has some characteristics of metals and some characteristics of nonmetals.* All metalloids are solids at room temperature. They tend to be less malleable than metals but not as brittle as nonmetals. Some metalloids, such as antimony, have a somewhat metallic luster.

Metalloids tend to be semiconductors of electricity. That is, their ability to conduct electricity is intermediate between that of metals and that of nonmetals. Metalloids are used in the solid state circuitry found in desktop computers, digital watches, televisions, and radios.

## Noble Gases

The elements in Group 18 of the periodic table are the noble gases. These elements are generally unreactive. In fact, it was not until 1962 that the first noble gas compound, xenon hexafluoroplatinate, was prepared. Low reactivity makes the noble gases very different from the other families of elements. Group 18 elements are gases at room temperature. Neon, argon, krypton, and xenon are all used in lighting. Helium is used in party balloons and weather balloons because it is less dense than air.

## SECTION REVIEW

1. Use the periodic table to write the names for the following elements: O, S, Cu, Ag.
2. Use the periodic table to write the symbols for the following elements: iron, nitrogen, calcium, mercury.
3. Which elements are most likely to undergo the same kinds of reactions, those in a group or those in a period?
4. Describe the main differences between metals, nonmetals, and metalloids.

### Critical Thinking

5. **INFERRING CONCLUSIONS** If you find an element in nature in its pure elemental state, what can you infer about the element's chemical reactivity? How can you tell whether that element is a metal or a nonmetal?

# CHAPTER HIGHLIGHTS

## Chemistry Is a Physical Science

**Vocabulary**

chemistry
chemical

- Chemistry is the study of the composition, structure, and properties of matter and the changes that matter undergoes.
- A chemical is any substance that has a definite composition or is used or produced in a chemical process.
- Basic research is carried out for the sake of increasing knowledge. Applied research is carried out to solve practical problems. Technological development involves the use of existing knowledge to make life easier or more convenient.

## Matter and Its Properties

**Vocabulary**

mass
matter
atom
element
compound
extensive property
intensive property
physical property
physical change
change of state
solid
liquid
gas
plasma
chemical property
chemical change
chemical reaction
reactant

- All matter has mass and takes up space. Mass is one measure of the amount of matter.
- Chemical properties refer to a substance's ability to undergo changes that alter its composition and identity.
- An element is composed of one kind of atom. Compounds are made from two or more elements in fixed proportions.
- All substances have characteristic properties that enable chemists to tell the substances apart and to separate the substances.
- Physical changes do not involve changes in identity of a substance.
- The three major states of matter are solid, liquid, and gas. Changes of state, such as melting and boiling, are physical changes.
- In a chemical change—or a chemical reaction—the identity of the substance changes.
- Energy changes accompany physical and chemical changes. Energy may be released or absorbed, but it is neither created nor destroyed.
- Matter can be classified into mixtures and pure substances.

## Elements

**Vocabulary**

group
family
period
metal
nonmetal
metalloid

- Each element has a unique symbol. The periodic table shows the elements organized by their chemical properties. Columns on the table represent groups or families of elements that have similar chemical properties. Properties vary across the rows, or periods.
- The elements can be classified as metals, nonmetals, metalloids, and noble gases. These classes occupy different areas of the periodic table. Metals tend to be shiny, malleable, and ductile and tend to be good conductors. Nonmetals tend to be brittle and tend to be poor conductors.
- Metalloids are intermediate in properties between metals and nonmetals, and they tend to be semiconductors of electricity. The noble gases are generally unreactive elements.

# CHAPTER REVIEW

## Chemistry Is a Physical Science

### SECTION 1 REVIEW

1. What is chemistry?
2. What branch of chemistry is most concerned with the study of carbon compounds?
3. What is meant by the word *chemical*, as used by scientists?
4. In which of the six branches of chemistry would a scientist be working if he or she were doing the following:
   a. investigating energy relationships for various reactions
   b. comparing properties of alcohols with those of sugars
   c. studying reactions that occur during the digestion of food
5. Identify each of the following as an example of either basic research, applied research, or technological development:
   a. A new type of refrigerant that is less damaging to the environment is developed.
   b. A new element is synthesized in a particle accelerator.
   c. A computer chip is redesigned to increase the speed of the computer.

## Matter and Its Properties

### SECTION 2 REVIEW

6. a. What is mass?
   b. What is volume?
7. How does the composition of a pure compound differ from that of a mixture?
8. a. Define property.
   b. How are properties useful in classifying materials?
9. What is the difference between extensive properties and intensive properties?
10. a. Define chemical property.
    b. List two examples of chemical properties.
11. Distinguish between a physical change and a chemical change.
12. a. How does a solid differ from a liquid?
    b. How does a liquid differ from a gas?
    c. How is a liquid similar to a gas?
    d. What is a plasma?
13. What is meant by a change in state?
14. Identify the reactants and products in the following reaction:
    potassium + water ⟶
    potassium hydroxide + hydrogen
15. Suppose different parts of a sample material have different compositions. What can you conclude about the material?

## Elements

### SECTION 3 REVIEW

16. What is the significance of the vertical columns of the periodic table? What is the significance of the horizontal rows?
17. Compare the physical properties of metals, nonmetals, metalloids, and noble gases, and describe where in the periodic table each of these kinds of elements is located.
18. Suppose element X is a poor conductor of electricity and breaks when hit with a hammer. Element Z is a good conductor of electricity and heat. In what area of the periodic table does each element most likely belong?
19. Use the periodic table to write the names of the elements that have the following symbols, and identify each as a metal, nonmetal, metalloid, or noble gas.
    a. K c. Si e. Hg
    b. Ag d. Na f. He
20. An unknown element is shiny and is found to be a good conductor of electricity. What other properties would you predict for it?
21. Use the periodic table to identify the group numbers and period numbers of the following elements:
    a. carbon, C c. chromium, Cr
    b. argon, Ar d. barium, Ba

## MIXED REVIEW

**22.** a. Define physical property.
b. List two examples of physical properties.

**23.** How can you tell the difference between an element and a compound?

**24.** Identify each of the following as either a physical change or a chemical change. Explain your answers.
a. A piece of wood is sawed in half.
b. Milk turns sour.
c. Melted butter solidifies in the refrigerator.

**25.** Write a brief paragraph that shows that you understand the following terms and the relationships between them: *atom, molecule, compound,* and *element.*

**26.** Pick an object you can see right now. List three of the object's physical properties that you can observe. Can you also observe a chemical property of the object? Explain your answer.

## CRITICAL THINKING

**27. Interpreting Concepts** One way to make lemonade is to start by combining lemon juice and water. To make the lemonade taste better you could add some sugar. Is your lemonade-sugar combination classified as a compound or a mixture? Explain your answer.

**28. Analyzing Results** A pure white, solid material that looks like table salt releases gas when heated under certain conditions. There is no change in the appearance of the solid, but the reactivity of the material changes.
a. Did a chemical or physical change occur? How do you know?
b. Was the original material an element or a compound?

**29. Interpreting Concepts**
a. Is breaking an egg an example of a physical or chemical change? Explain your answer.
b. Is cooking an egg an example of a physical or chemical change? Explain your answer.

## USING THE HANDBOOK

**30.** Review the information on trace elements in the *Elements Handbook* in the back of this text.
a. What are the functions of trace elements in the body?
b. What transition metal plays an important role in oxygen transport throughout the body?
c. What two Group 1 elements are part of the electrolyte balance in the body?

## RESEARCH & WRITING

**31.** Research any current technological product of your choosing. Find out about its manufacture and uses. Also find out about the basic research and applied research that made its development possible.

**32.** Investigate current and proposed technological applications of superconductors. Find out which of these applications have been successfully tested or are already in use.

## ALTERNATIVE ASSESSMENT

**33.** During a 1 h period, make a list of all the changes that you see around you and that involve matter. Note whether each change seems to be a physical change or a chemical change. Give reasons for your answers.

**34.** Make a concept map using at least 15 terms from the vocabulary lists. An introduction to concept mapping is found in **Appendix B** of this book.

extension

Graphing Calculator
**Graphing Tabular Data**

Go to **go.hrw.com** for a graphing calculator exercise that asks you to graph temperature vs. time for a chemical reaction.

**Keyword : HC6MTXX**

# *Math Tutor* SIGNIFICANT FIGURES

The certainty of a measurement is expressed by significant figures. Significant figures in a measurement consist of all the digits known with certainty plus one final digit. Look at the reading below, which was obtained when measuring the mass of a paper clip.

mass of paperclip

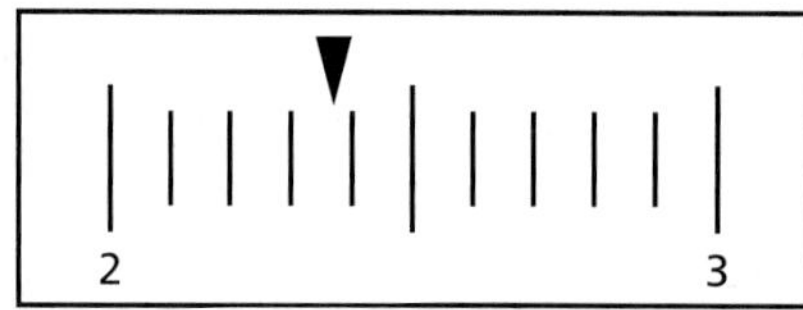


Balance reading = 2.37 g

You know with certainty that the paper clip has a mass of 2.3 g. You can also estimate an additional mass of 0.07 g for a total of 2.37 g. Each of the three digits in 2.37 g is significant because it is either certain or estimated.

## Problem-Solving *TIPS*

- Every nonzero digit is significant. Zeros between nonzero digits are significant.
- Zeros appearing in front of the first nonzero digit are not significant.
- If there is no decimal point, zeros that follow the last nonzero digit are not significant.
- If there is a decimal point, zeros that follow the last nonzero digit are significant.
- When measurements are added or subtracted, the result must be rounded to the same number of decimal places that the quantity with the fewest decimal places has.
- When measurements are multiplied or divided, the result must be rounded to the same number of significant figures that the quantity with the smallest number of significant figures has.

### SAMPLE 1

**How many significant figures does 0.007 09 kg have?**

All nonzero digits are significant. The zero between the 7 and 9 is significant. The zeros to the left of the decimal point are not significant. The quantity 0.007 09 kg has 3 significant figures.

### SAMPLE 2

**Divide 79.7 g by 0.89 $cm^3$.**

The quantity 79.7 g has 3 significant figures, but 0.89 $cm^3$ has only 2 significant figures. So, the product 8.955 056 18 $g/cm^3$ must be rounded to 2 significant figures. The rounded quantity is 9.0 $g/cm^3$.

### PRACTICE PROBLEMS

**1.** Determine the number of significant figures.

a. 42.200 L
b. 0.055 00 mol

**2.** Perform the following calculations and apply the rules for significant figures.

a. 56.05 g ÷ 13.3 $cm^3$ b. 1.057 g + 3.02 g + 12.4 g

# Standardized Test Prep

**Answer the following items on a separate piece of paper.**

**MULTIPLE CHOICE**

**1.** Magnesium reacts with hydrochloric acid to produce magnesium chloride and hydrogen gas. The reactants in this reaction are
**A.** magnesium and magnesium chloride.
**B.** hydrochloric acid and hydrogen gas.
**C.** magnesium and hydrochloric acid.
**D.** magnesium chloride and hydrogen gas.

**2.** Matter that has a definite shape and a definite volume is
**A.** a liquid. **C.** a solid.
**B.** an element. **D.** a gas.

**3.** We know that air is a mixture and not a compound because
**A.** it can be heated to a higher temperature.
**B.** it can be compressed to a smaller volume.
**C.** it is colorless.
**D.** its composition can vary.

**4.** Matter can be defined as anything that
**A.** has weight.
**B.** has mass and volume.
**C.** is uniform throughout.
**D.** exhibits both chemical and physical properties.

**5.** Which of the following is best classified as a homogeneous mixture?
**A.** pizza **C.** hot tea
**B.** blood **D.** copper wire

**6.** A compound differs from a mixture in that a compound
**A.** contains only one element.
**B.** varies in chemical composition depending on the sample size.
**C.** has a definite composition by mass of the elements that the compound contains.
**D.** can be classified as either heterogeneous or homogeneous.

**7.** Which of the following is *not* a physical state of matter?
**A.** solid **C.** element
**B.** gas **D.** liquid

**8.** Three of the following must contain two or more kinds of atoms. Which one does *not* contain two or more kinds of atoms?
**A.** element
**B.** compound
**C.** homogeneous mixture
**D.** heterogeneous mixture

**9.** Which of the following symbols does *not* match the element name given?
**A.** Al, aluminum
**B.** Co, copper
**C.** K, potassium
**D.** P, phosphorus

**SHORT ANSWER**

**10.** Give three examples of mixtures, and tell whether each one is homogeneous or heterogeneous. Give three examples of compounds.

**11.** In trying to identify a sample of a pure substance, we observe the following properties. Tell whether each one is a chemical property or a physical property.
**A.** Its mass is 124.3 g.
**B.** It is a shiny solid at room temperature.
**C.** It is easily etched by nitric acid.
**D.** It melts when heated to 670°C.
**E.** It is 31.7 centimeters long.
**F.** It is a good heat conductor.
**G.** It burns in air.
**H.** It is a good conductor of electrical energy.

**EXTENDED RESPONSE**

**12.** Describe the difference between a chemical change and a physical change. Give one example of each kind of change.

**13.** Describe general properties of metals, nonmetals, and metalloids.

**Test TIP** Remember that if you can eliminate two of the four answer choices, your chances of choosing the correct answer choice will double.

SEE PRE-LAB
EXTRACTION AND FILTRATION

INQUIRY LAB

# Mixture Separation

## OBJECTIVES

- ***Observe*** **the chemical and physical properties of a mixture.**
- ***Relate*** **knowledge of chemical and physical properties to the task of purifying the mixture.**
- ***Analyze*** **the success of methods of purifying the mixture.**

## MATERIALS

- **aluminum foil**
- **cotton balls**
- **distilled water**
- **filter funnels**
- **filter paper**
- **forceps**
- **magnet**
- **paper clips**
- **paper towels**
- **Petri dish**
- **pipets**
- **plastic forks**
- **plastic spoons**
- **plastic straws**
- **rubber stoppers**
- **sample of mixture and components (sand, iron filings, salt, poppy seeds)**
- **test tubes and rack**
- **tissue paper**
- **transparent tape**
- **wooden splints**

## BACKGROUND

The ability to separate and recover pure substances from mixtures is extremely important in scientific research and industry. Chemists need to work with pure substances, but naturally occurring materials are seldom pure. Often, differences in the physical properties of the components in a mixture provide the means for separating them. In this experiment, you will have an opportunity to design, develop, and implement your own procedure for separating a mixture. The mixture you will work with contains salt, sand, iron filings, and poppy seeds. All four substances are in dry, granular form.

## SAFETY

For review of safety, please see **Safety in the Chemistry Laboratory** in the front of your book.

## PREPARATION

1. Your task will be to plan and carry out the separation of a mixture. Before you can plan your experiment, you will need to investigate the properties of each component in the mixture. The properties will be used to design your mixture separation. Copy the data table on the following page in your lab notebook, and use it to record your observations.

## PROCEDURE

1. Obtain separate samples of each of the four mixture components from your teacher. Use the equipment you have available to make observations of the components and determine their properties. You will need to run several tests with each substance, so don't use all of your sample

| DATA TABLE | | | | |
|---|---|---|---|---|
| **Properties** | **Sand** | **Iron filings** | **Salt** | **Poppy seeds** |
| Dissolves | | | | |
| Floats | | | | |
| Magnetic | | | | |
| Other | | | | |

on the first test. Look for things like whether the substance is magnetic, whether it dissolves, or whether it floats. Record your observations in your data table.

2. Make a plan for what you will do to separate a mixture that includes the four components from step 1. Review your plan with your teacher.

3. Obtain a sample of the mixture from your teacher. Using the equipment you have available, run the procedure you have developed.

## CLEANUP AND DISPOSAL

4. Clean your lab station. Clean all equipment, and return it to its proper place. Dispose of chemicals and solutions in the containers designated by your teacher. Do not pour any chemicals down the drain or throw anything in the trash unless your teacher directs you to do so. Wash your hands thoroughly after all work is finished and before you leave the lab.

## ANALYSIS AND INTERPRETATION

1. **Evaluating Methods:** On a scale of 1 to 10, how successful were you in separating and recovering each of the four components: sand, salt, iron filings, and poppy seeds? Consider 1 to be the best and 10 to be the worst. Justify your ratings based on your observations.

## CONCLUSIONS

1. **Evaluating Methods:** How did you decide on the order of your procedural steps? Would any order have worked?

2. **Designing Experiments:** If you could do the lab over again, what would you do differently? Be specific.

3. **Designing Experiments:** Name two materials or tools that weren't available that might have made your separation easier.

4. **Applying Ideas:** For each of the four components, describe a specific physical property that enabled you to separate the component from the rest of the mixture.

## EXTENSIONS

1. **Evaluating Methods:** What methods could be used to determine the purity of each of your recovered components?

2. **Designing Experiments:** How could you separate each of the following two-part mixtures?
   a. aluminum filings and iron filings
   b. sand and gravel
   c. sand and finely ground polystyrene foam
   d. salt and sugar
   e. alcohol and water
   f. nitrogen and oxygen

3. **Designing Experiments:** One of the components of the mixture in this experiment is in a different physical state at the completion of this experiment that it was at the start. Which one? How would you convert that component back to its original state?

CHAPTER 2

# Measurements and Calculations

*Quantitative measurements are fundamental to chemistry.*

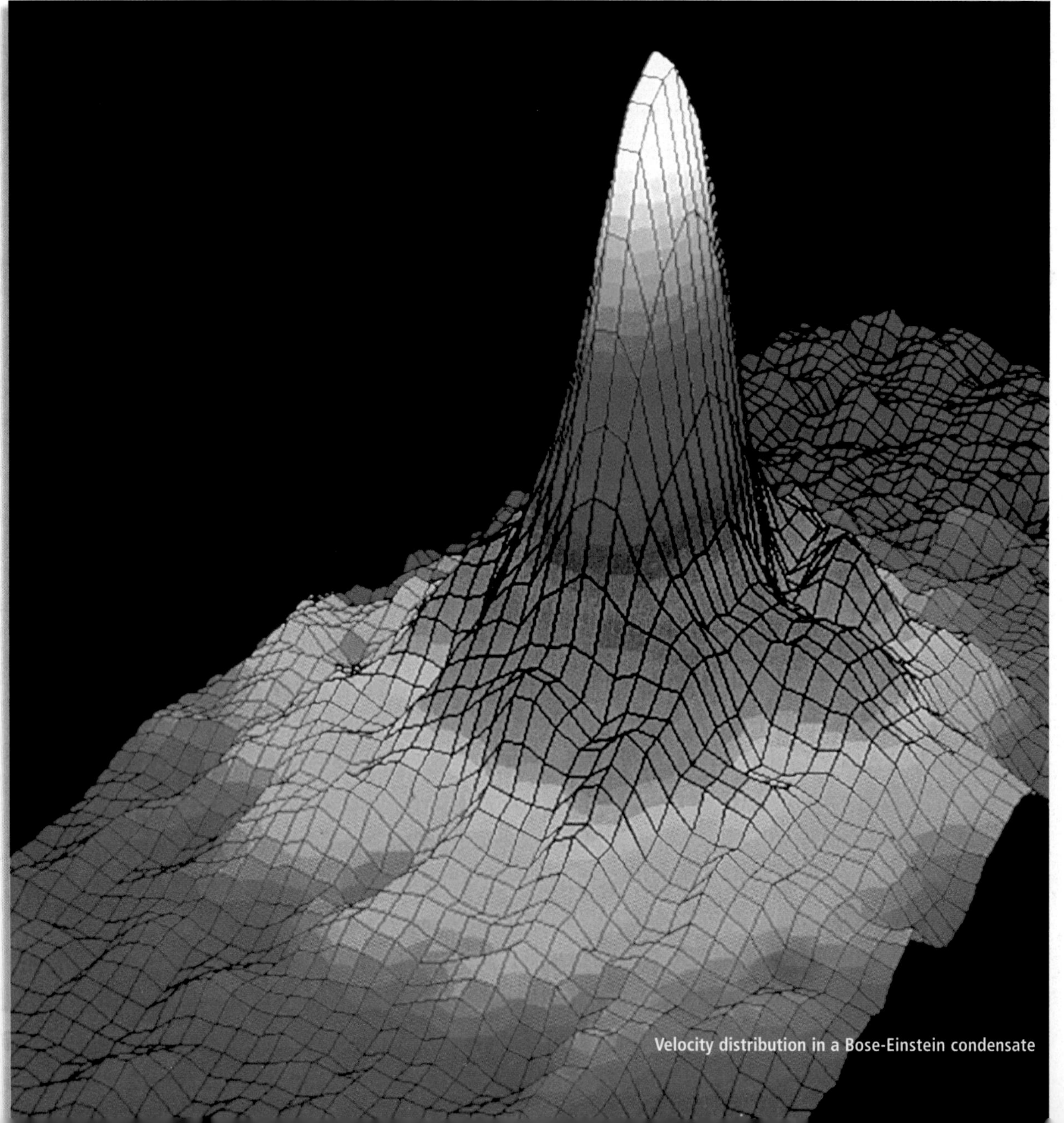

Velocity distribution in a Bose-Einstein condensate

# Scientific Method

SECTION 1

**C.1.4** Design a scientific investigation with appropriate methods of control to test a hypothesis (including independent and dependent variables), and evaluate the designs of sample investigations

## Objectives

- Describe the purpose of the scientific method.
- Distinguish between qualitative and quantitative observations.
- Describe the differences between hypotheses, theories, and models.

Sometimes progress in science comes about through accidental discoveries. Most scientific advances, however, result from carefully planned investigations. The process researchers use to carry out their investigations is often called the scientific method. *The* **scientific method** *is a logical approach to solving problems by observing and collecting data, formulating hypotheses, testing hypotheses, and formulating theories that are supported by data.*

## Observing and Collecting Data

*Observing* is the use of the senses to obtain information. Observation often involves making measurements and collecting data. The data may be descriptive (qualitative) or numerical (quantitative) in nature. Numerical information, such as the fact that a sample of copper ore has a mass of 25.7 grams, is *quantitative*. Non-numerical information, such as the fact that the sky is blue, is *qualitative*.

Experimenting involves carrying out a procedure under controlled conditions to make observations and collect data. To learn more about matter, chemists study systems. *A* **system** *is a specific portion of matter in a given region of space that has been selected for study during an experiment or observation.* When you observe a reaction in a test tube, the test tube and its contents form a system.

SCILINKS.
www.scilinks.org
**Topic:** Scientific Methods
**Code:** HC61359

**FIGURE 1** These students have designed an experiment to determine how to get the largest volume of popped corn from a fixed number of kernels. They think that the volume is likely to increase as the moisture in the kernels increases. Their experiment will involve soaking some kernels in water and observing whether the volume of the popped corn is greater than that of corn popped from kernels that have not been soaked.

**FIGURE 2** A graph of data can show relationships between two variables. In this case the graph shows data collected during an experiment to determine the effect of phosphorus fertilizer compounds on plant growth. The following is one possible hypothesis: *If* phosphorus stimulates corn-plant growth, *then* corn plants treated with a soluble phosphorus compound should grow faster, under the same conditions, than corn plants that are not treated.

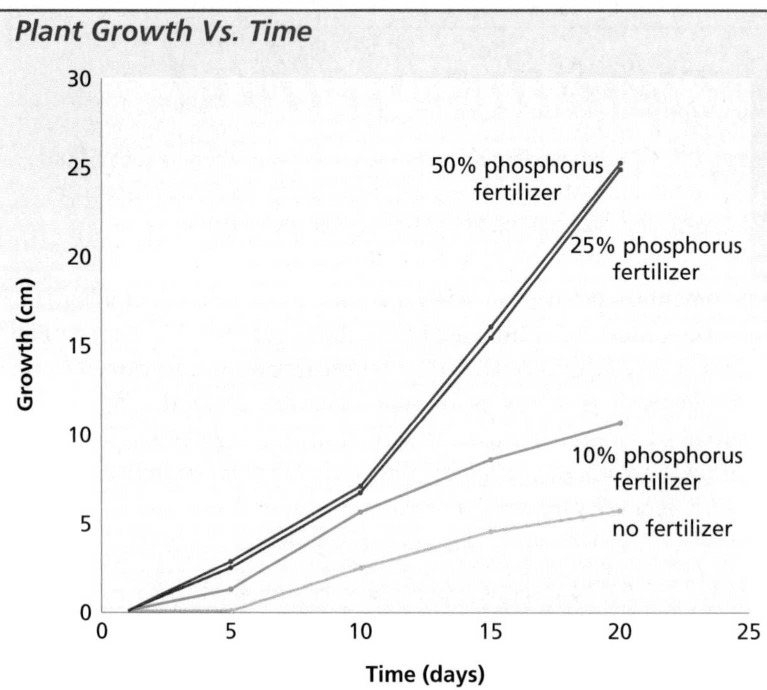


## Formulating Hypotheses

As scientists examine and compare the data from their own experiments, they attempt to find relationships and patterns—in other words, they make generalizations based on the data. Generalizations are statements that apply to a range of information. To make generalizations, data are sometimes organized in tables and analyzed using statistics or other mathematical techniques, often with the aid of graphs and a computer.

Scientists use generalizations about the data to formulate a **hypothesis,** *or testable statement.* The hypothesis serves as a basis for making predictions and for carrying out further experiments. Hypotheses are often drafted as "if-then" statements. The "then" part of the hypothesis is a prediction that is the basis for testing by experiment. **Figure 2** shows data collected to test a hypothesis.

## Testing Hypotheses

Testing a hypothesis requires experimentation that provides data to support or refute a hypothesis or theory. During testing, the experimental conditions that remain constant are called *controls,* and any condition that changes is called a *variable.* Any change observed is usually due to the effects of the variable. If testing reveals that the predictions were not correct, the hypothesis on which the predictions were based must be discarded or modified.

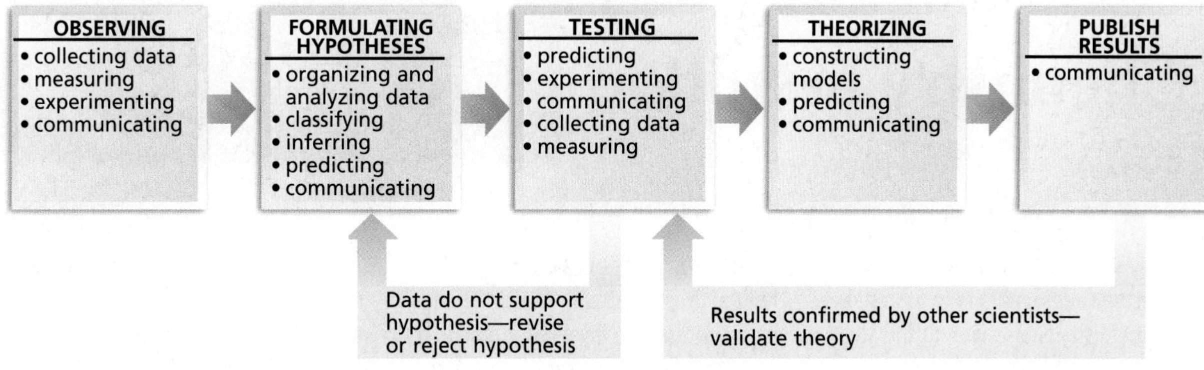


**FIGURE 3** The scientific method is not a single, fixed process. Scientists may repeat steps many times before there is sufficient evidence to formulate a theory. You can see that each stage represents a number of different activities.

## Theorizing

When the data from experiments show that the predictions of the hypothesis are successful, scientists typically try to explain the phenomena they are studying by constructing a model. *A* **model** *in science is more than a physical object; it is often an explanation of how phenomena occur and how data or events are related.* Models may be visual, verbal, or mathematical. One important model in chemistry is the atomic model of matter, which states that matter is composed of tiny particles called atoms.

If a model successfully explains many phenomena, it may become part of a theory. The atomic model is a part of the atomic theory, which you will study in Chapter 3. *A* **theory** *is a broad generalization that explains a body of facts or phenomena.* Theories are considered successful if they can predict the results of many new experiments. Examples of the important theories you will study in chemistry are kinetic-molecular theory and collision theory. **Figure 3** shows where theory fits in the scheme of the scientific method.

### SECTION REVIEW

1. What is the scientific method?
2. Which of the following are quantitative?
   **a.** the liquid floats on water
   **b.** the metal is malleable
   **c.** the liquid has a temperature of 55.6°C
3. How do hypotheses and theories differ?
4. How are models related to theories and hypotheses?

**Critical Thinking**

5. **INTERPRETING CONCEPTS** Suppose you had to test how well two types of soap work. Describe your experiment by using the terms *control* and *variable.*

# Chemistry in Action

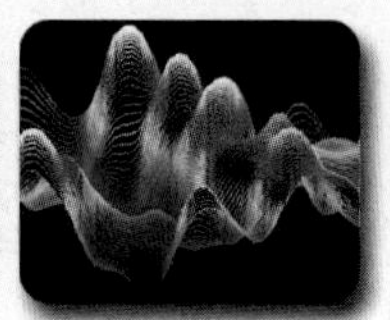
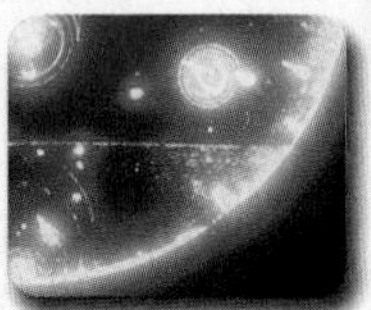

## Breaking Up Is Easy To Do

It may seem obvious that chemistry is important in the making of materials, but chemistry is also vital to the study of how materials break. Everyday items have to be made to withstand various types of force and pressure or they cannot be used. For example, scientists and engineers work to ensure that highway bridges do not collapse.

When excessive force is applied to an object, the material that the object is made of will break. The object breaks because the force creates stress on the bonds between the atoms of the material and causes the bonds to break. This creates microscopic cracks in the material. When a material breaks, it is said to have undergone *failure.* Materials typically break in one of two ways: *ductile failure* and *brittle failure.* Both types of failure start with microscopic cracks in the material. However, the way a material eventually breaks depends how its atoms are organized.

Shattering glass undergoes brittle failure. Glass shatters when the bonds between the two layers of atoms that are along the initial crack break. This breakage causes the layers to pull apart, which separates the material into pieces. This type of failure is common in materials that do not have a very orderly arrangement of atoms.

When a car bumper crumples, ductile failure happens. This type of failure tends to happen in materials such as metals, that have a regular, ordered arrangement of atoms. This arrangement of atoms is known as a *crystal structure.* Ductile failure happens when the bonds in the material break across many layers of atoms that are not in the same plane as the original crack. Rather than splitting apart, the layers slip past each other into new positions. The atoms form new chemical bonds, between them and the material stays in one piece; only the shape has changed.

microscopic defect

ductile failure

brittle failure

◀*A microscopic crack in a material can develop into brittle or ductile failure.*

In addition to the type of material influencing breakage, the quality of the material also influences breakage. All objects contain microscopic defects, such as bubbles in plastic pieces. A material will tend to undergo failure at its defect sites first. Careful fabrication procedures can minimize, but not completely eliminate, defects in materials.

Even though materials are designed to withstand a certain amount of force, the normal wear and tear that materials experience over their lifetimes creates defects in the material. This process is referred to as *fatigue.* If fatigue were to go undetected, the microscopic cracks that form could then undergo brittle or ductile failure. It would be catastrophic if the materials in certain products, such as airplane parts, failed. To avoid such a failure, people monitor materials that are exposed to constant stress for signs of fatigue. The defects in the metal parts of airplanes can be detected with nondestructive techniques, such as electromagnetic analysis.

### Questions

1. Can you name some ways in which metal or plastic parts might obtain defects caused by chemical reactions?
2. Does a ceramic dinner plate undergo brittle or ductile failure when it is dropped and breaks?

# Units of Measurement

SECTION 2

**C.1.1** Apply established rules for significant digits, both in reading a scientific instrument and in calculating a derived quantity from measurement

## Objectives

- Distinguish between a quantity, a unit, and a measurement standard.
- Name and use SI units for length, mass, time, volume, and density.
- Distinguish between mass and weight.
- Perform density calculations.
- Transform a statement of equality into a conversion factor.

Measurements are quantitative information. A measurement is more than just a number, even in everyday life. Suppose a chef were to write a recipe listing quantities such as 1 salt, 3 sugar, and 2 flour. The cooks could not use the recipe without more information. They would need to know whether the number 3 represented teaspoons, tablespoons, cups, ounces, grams, or some other unit for sugar.

Measurements *represent* quantities. *A* **quantity** *is something that has magnitude, size, or amount.* A quantity is not the same as a measurement. For example, the quantity represented by a teaspoon is volume. The teaspoon is a unit of measurement, while volume is a quantity. A teaspoon is a measurement standard in this country. Units of measurement compare what is to be measured with a previously defined size. Nearly every measurement is a number plus a unit. The choice of unit depends on the quantity being measured.

Many centuries ago, people sometimes marked off distances in the number of foot lengths it took to cover the distance. But this system was unsatisfactory because the number of foot lengths used to express a distance varied with the size of the measurer's foot. Once there was agreement on a standard for foot length, confusion as to the real length was eliminated. It no longer mattered who made the measurement, as long as the standard measuring unit was correctly applied.

## SI Measurement

Scientists all over the world have agreed on a single measurement system called *Le Système International d'Unités*, abbreviated **SI.** This system was adopted in 1960 by the General Conference on Weights and Measures. SI now has seven base units, and most other units are derived from these seven. Some non-SI units are still commonly used by chemists and are also used in this book.

SI units are defined in terms of standards of measurement. The standards are objects or natural phenomena that are of constant value, easy to preserve and reproduce, and practical in size. International organizations monitor the defining process. In the United States, the National Institute of Standards and Technology (NIST) plays the main role in maintaining standards and setting style conventions. For example, numbers are written in a form that is agreed upon internationally. The number seventy-five thousand is written 75 000, not 75,000, because the comma is used in other countries to represent a decimal point.

**TABLE 1 *SI Base Units***

| Quantity | Quantity symbol | Unit name | Unit abbreviation | Defined standard |
|---|---|---|---|---|
| Length | $l$ | meter | m | the length of the path traveled by light in a vacuum during a time interval of 1/299 792 458 of a second |
| Mass | $m$ | kilogram | kg | the unit of mass equal to the mass of the international prototype of the kilogram |
| Time | $t$ | second | s | the duration of 9 192 631 770 periods of the radiation corresponding to the transition between the two hyperfine levels of the ground state of the cesium-133 atom |
| Temperature | $T$ | kelvin | K | the fraction 1/273.16 of the thermodynamic temperature of the triple point of water |
| Amount of substance | $n$ | mole | mol | the amount of substance of a system which contains as many elementary entities as there are atoms in 0.012 kilogram of carbon-12 |
| Electric current | $I$ | ampere | A | the constant current which, if maintained in two straight parallel conductors of infinite length, of negligible circular cross section, and placed 1 meter apart in vacuum, would produce between these conductors a force equal to $2 \times 10^{-7}$ newton per meter of length |
| Luminous intensity | $I_v$ | candela | cd | the luminous intensity, in a given direction, of a source that emits monochromatic radiation of frequency $540 \times 10^{12}$ hertz and that has a radiant intensity in that direction of 1/683 watt per steradian |

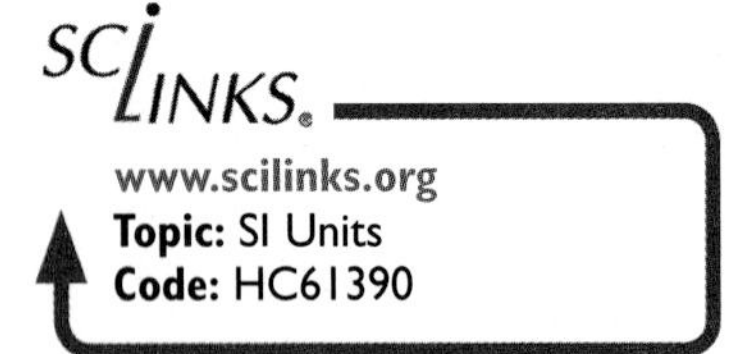


## SI Base Units

The seven SI base units and their standard abbreviated symbols are listed in **Table 1.** All the other SI units can be derived from the fundamental units.

Prefixes added to the names of SI base units are used to represent quantities that are larger or smaller than the base units. **Table 2** lists SI prefixes using units of length as examples. For example, the prefix *centi-*, abbreviated c, represents an exponential factor of $10^{-2}$, which equals 1/100. Thus, 1 centimeter, 1 cm, equals 0.01 m, or 1/100 of a meter.

### Mass

As you learned in Chapter 1, mass is a measure of the quantity of matter. The SI standard unit for mass is the kilogram. The standard for mass defined in **Table 1** is used to calibrate balances all over the world.

**TABLE 2 *SI Prefixes***

| Prefix | Unit abbreviation | Exponential factor | Meaning | Example |
|---|---|---|---|---|
| tera | T | $10^{12}$ | 1 000 000 000 000 | 1 terameter (Tm) = $1 \times 10^{12}$ m |
| giga | G | $10^{9}$ | 1 000 000 000 | 1 gigameter (Gm) = $1 \times 10^{9}$ m |
| mega | M | $10^{6}$ | 1 000 000 | 1 megameter (Mm) = $1 \times 10^{6}$ m |
| kilo | k | $10^{3}$ | 1000 | 1 kilometer (km) = 1000 m |
| hecto | h | $10^{2}$ | 100 | 1 hectometer (hm) = 100 m |
| deka | da | $10^{1}$ | 10 | 1 dekameter (dam) = 10 m |
| | | **$10^{0}$** | **1** | **1 meter (m)** |
| deci | d | $10^{-1}$ | 1/10 | 1 decimeter (dm) = 0.1 m |
| centi | c | $10^{-2}$ | 1/100 | 1 centimeter (cm) = 0.01 m |
| milli | m | $10^{-3}$ | 1/1000 | 1 millimeter (mm) = 0.001 m |
| micro | μ | $10^{-6}$ | 1/1 000 000 | 1 micrometer (μm) = $1 \times 10^{-6}$ m |
| nano | n | $10^{-9}$ | 1/1 000 000 000 | 1 nanometer (nm) = $1 \times 10^{-9}$ m |
| pico | p | $10^{-12}$ | 1/1 000 000 000 000 | 1 picometer (pm) = $1 \times 10^{-12}$ m |
| femto | f | $10^{-15}$ | 1/1 000 000 000 000 000 | 1 femtometer (fm) = $1 \times 10^{-15}$ m |
| atto | a | $10^{-18}$ | 1/1 000 000 000 000 000 000 | 1 attometer (am) = $1 \times 10^{-18}$ m |

The mass of a typical textbook is about 1 kg. The gram, g, which is 1/1000 of a kilogram, is more useful for measuring masses of small objects, such as flasks and beakers. For even smaller objects, such as tiny quantities of chemicals, the milligram, mg, is often used. One milligram is 1/1000 of a gram, or 1/1 000 000 of a kilogram.

Mass is often confused with weight because people often express the weight of an object in grams. Mass is determined by comparing the mass of an object with a set of standard masses that are part of the balance. **Weight** *is a measure of the gravitational pull on matter.* Unlike weight, mass does not depend on gravity. Mass is measured on instruments such as a balance, and weight is typically measured on a spring scale. Taking weight measurements involves reading the amount that an object pulls down on a spring. As the force of Earth's gravity on an object increases, the object's weight increases. The weight of an object on the moon is about one-sixth of its weight on Earth.

### Length

The SI standard unit for length is the meter. A distance of 1 m is about the width of an average doorway. To express longer distances, the kilometer, km, is used. One kilometer equals 1000 m. Road signs in the United States sometimes show distances in kilometers as well as miles. The kilometer is the unit used to express highway distances in most other countries of the world. To express shorter distances, the centimeter

**CROSS-DISCIPLINARY**

**Some Handy Comparisons of Units**

To become comfortable with units in the SI system, try relating some common measurements to your experience.

A meter stick is a little longer than a yardstick. A millimeter is about the diameter of a paper clip wire, and a centimeter is a little more than the width of a paper clip.

One gram is about the mass of a paper clip. A kilogram is about 2.2 pounds (think of two pounds plus one stick of butter). And there are about five milliliters in a teaspoon.

FIGURE 4 The meter is the SI unit of length, but the centimeter is often used to measure smaller distances. What is the length in cm of the rectangular piece of aluminum foil shown?

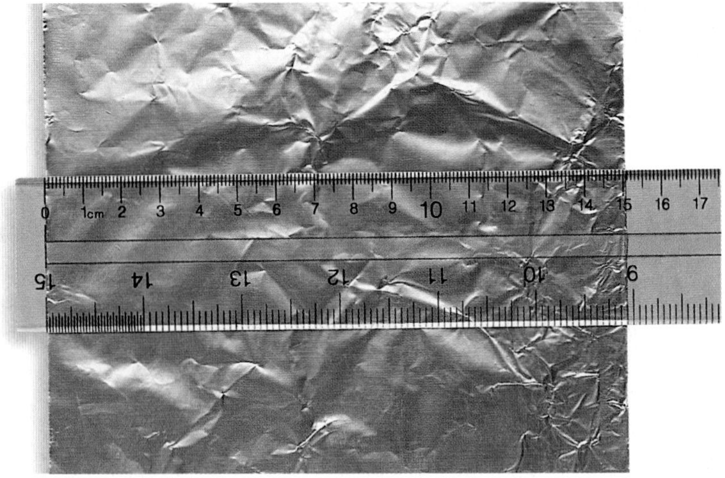

is often used. From **Table 2,** you can see that one centimeter equals 1/100 of a meter. The width of this book is just over 20 cm.

## Derived SI Units

Many SI units are combinations of the quantities shown in **Table 1.** *Combinations of SI base units form* **derived units.** Some derived units are shown in **Table 3.**

Derived units are produced by multiplying or dividing standard units. For example, area, a derived unit, is length times width. If both length and width are expressed in meters, the area unit equals meters times meters, or square meters, abbreviated $m^2$. The last column of

**TABLE 3 *Derived SI Units***

| Quantity | Quantity symbol | Unit | Unit abbreviation | Derivation |
|---|---|---|---|---|
| Area | $A$ | square meter | $m^2$ | length × width |
| Volume | $V$ | cubic meter | $m^3$ | length × width × height |
| Density | $D$ | kilograms per cubic meter | $\frac{kg}{m^3}$ | $\frac{\text{mass}}{\text{volume}}$ |
| Molar mass | $M$ | kilograms per mole | $\frac{kg}{mol}$ | $\frac{\text{mass}}{\text{amount of substance}}$ |
| Molar volume | $V_m$ | cubic meters per mole | $\frac{m^3}{mol}$ | $\frac{\text{volume}}{\text{amount of substance}}$ |
| Energy | $E$ | joule | J | force × length |

**Table 3** shows the combination of fundamental units used to obtain derived units.

Some combination units are given their own names. For example, pressure expressed in base units is the following.

$$kg/m{\bullet}s^2$$

The name *pascal,* Pa, is given to this combination. You will learn more about pressure in Chapter 11. Prefixes can also be added to express derived units. Area can be expressed in $cm^2$, square centimeters, or $mm^2$, square millimeters.

**FIGURE 5** The speed that registers on a speedometer represents distance traveled per hour and is expressed in the derived units kilometers per hour or miles per hour.

## Volume

**Volume** *is the amount of space occupied by an object.* The derived SI unit of volume is cubic meters, $m^3$. One cubic meter is equal to the volume of a cube whose edges are 1 m long. Such a large unit is inconvenient for expressing the volume of materials in a chemistry laboratory. Instead, a smaller unit, the cubic centimeter, $cm^3$, is often used. There are 100 centimeters in a meter, so a cubic meter contains 1 000 000 $cm^3$.

$$1\ m^3 \times \frac{100\ cm}{1\ m} \times \frac{100\ cm}{1\ m} \times \frac{100\ cm}{1\ m} = 1\ 000\ 000\ cm^3$$

When chemists measure the volumes of liquids and gases, they often use a non-SI unit called the liter. The liter is equivalent to one cubic decimeter. Thus, a liter, L, is also equivalent to 1000 $cm^3$. Another non-SI unit, the milliliter, mL, is used for smaller volumes. There are 1000 mL in 1 L. Because there are also 1000 $cm^3$ in a liter, the two units—milliliter and cubic centimeter—are interchangeable.

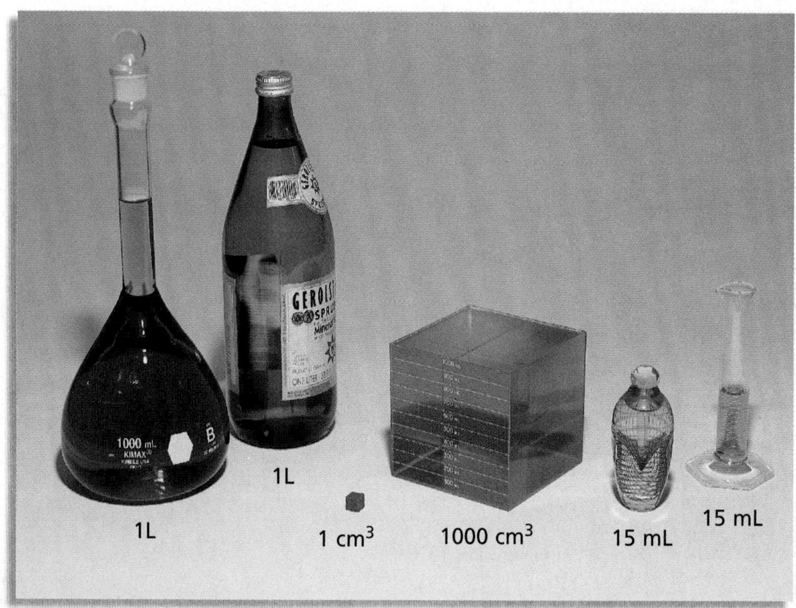


**FIGURE 6** The relationships between various volumes are shown here. One liter contains 1000 mL of liquid, and 1 mL is equivalent to 1 $cm^3$. A small perfume bottle contains about 15 mL of liquid. The volumetric flask (far left) and graduated cylinder (far right) are used for measuring liquid volumes in the lab.

**FIGURE 7** Density is the ratio of mass to volume. Both water and copper shot float on mercury because mercury is more dense.

## Density

An object made of cork feels lighter than a lead object of the same size. What you are actually comparing in such cases is how massive objects are compared with their size. This property is called density. **Density** *is the ratio of mass to volume, or mass divided by volume.* Mathematically, the relationship for density can be written in the following way.

$$density = \frac{mass}{volume} \text{ or } D = \frac{m}{V}$$

The quantity $m$ is mass, $V$ is volume, and $D$ is density.

The SI unit for density is derived from the base units for mass and volume—the kilogram and the cubic meter, respectively—and can be expressed as kilograms per cubic meter, $kg/m^3$. This unit is inconveniently large for the density measurements you will make in the laboratory. You will often see density expressed in grams per cubic centimeter, $g/cm^3$, or grams per milliliter, g/mL. The densities of gases are generally reported either in kilograms per cubic meter, $kg/m^3$, or in grams per liter, g/L.

Density is a characteristic physical property of a substance. It does not depend on the size of the sample because as the sample's mass increases, its volume increases proportionately, and the ratio of mass to volume is constant. Therefore, density can be used as one property to help identify a substance. **Table 4** shows the densities of some common materials. As you can see, cork has a density of only 0.24 $g/cm^3$, which is less than the density of liquid water. Because cork is less dense than water, it floats on water. Lead, on the other hand, has a density of 11.35 $g/cm^3$. The density of lead is greater than that of water, so lead sinks in water.

Note that **Table 4** specifies the temperatures at which the densities were measured. That is because density varies with temperature. Most objects expand as temperature increases, thereby increasing in volume. Because density is mass divided by volume, density usually decreases with increasing temperature.

**TABLE 4 Densities of Some Familiar Materials**

| Solids | Density at 20°C ($g/cm^3$) | Liquids | Density at 20°C (g/mL) |
|---|---|---|---|
| cork | 0.24* | gasoline | 0.67* |
| butter | 0.86 | ethyl alcohol | 0.791 |
| ice | 0.92† | kerosene | 0.82 |
| sucrose | 1.59 | turpentine | 0.87 |
| bone | 1.85* | water | 0.998 |
| diamond | 3.26* | sea water | 1.025** |
| copper | 8.92 | milk | 1.031* |
| lead | 11.35 | mercury | 13.6 |

† measured at 0°C
* typical density

** measured at 15°C

# QuickLAB  Wear safety goggles and an apron.

## Density of Pennies

### Materials

- balance
- 100 mL graduated cylinder
- 40 pennies dated before 1982
- 40 pennies dated after 1982
- water

### Procedure

1. Using the balance, determine the mass of the 40 pennies minted prior to 1982. Repeat this measurement two more times. Average the results of the three trials to determine the average mass of the pennies.
2. Repeat step 1 with the 40 pennies minted after 1982.
3. Pour about 50 mL of water into the 100 mL graduated cylinder. Record the exact volume of the water. Add the 40 pennies minted before 1982. CAUTION: Add the pennies carefully so that no water is splashed out of the cylinder. Record the exact volume of the water and pennies. Repeat this process two more times. Determine the volume of the pennies for each trial. Average the results of those trials to determine the average volume of the pennies.
4. Repeat step 3 with the 40 pennies minted after 1982.
5. Review your data for any large differences between trials that could increase the error of your results. Repeat those measurements.
6. Use the average volume and average mass to calculate the average density for each group of pennies.
7. Compare the calculated average densities with the density of the copper listed in Table 4.

### Discussion

1. Why is it best to use the results of three trials rather than a single trial for determining the density?
2. How did the densities of the two groups of pennies compare? How do you account for any difference?
3. Use the results of this investigation to formulate a hypothesis about the composition of the two groups of pennies. How could you test your hypothesis?

## SAMPLE PROBLEM A

**A sample of aluminum metal has a mass of 8.4 g. The volume of the sample is 3.1 cm$^3$. Calculate the density of aluminum.**

**SOLUTION** **Given:** mass ($m$) = 8.4 g

volume ($V$) = 3.1 cm$^3$

**Unknown:** density ($D$)

$$density = \frac{mass}{volume} = \frac{8.4 \text{ g}}{3.1 \text{ cm}^3} = 2.7 \text{ g/cm}^3$$

**PRACTICE** *Answers in Appendix E*

1. What is the density of a block of marble that occupies 310. $cm^3$ and has a mass of 853 g?
2. Diamond has a density of 3.26 $g/cm^3$. What is the mass of a diamond that has a volume of 0.351 $cm^3$?
3. What is the volume of a sample of liquid mercury that has a mass of 76.2 g, given that the density of mercury is 13.6 g/mL?

Go to **go.hrw.com** for more practice problems that ask you to calculate density.

Keyword: HC6MEAX

## Conversion Factors

*A* **conversion factor** *is a ratio derived from the equality between two different units that can be used to convert from one unit to the other.* For example, suppose you want to know how many quarters there are in a certain number of dollars. To figure out the answer, you need to know how quarters and dollars are related. There are four quarters per dollar and one dollar for every four quarters. Those facts can be expressed as ratios in four conversion factors.

$$\frac{4 \text{ quarters}}{1 \text{ dollar}} = 1 \qquad \frac{1 \text{ dollar}}{4 \text{ quarters}} = 1 \qquad \frac{0.25 \text{ dollar}}{1 \text{ quarter}} = 1 \qquad \frac{1 \text{ quarter}}{0.25 \text{ dollar}} = 1$$

Notice that each conversion factor equals 1. That is because the two quantities divided in any conversion factor are equivalent to each other—as in this case, where 4 quarters equal 1 dollar. Because conversion factors are equal to 1, they can be multiplied by other factors in equations without changing the validity of the equations. You can use conversion factors to solve problems through dimensional analysis. **Dimensional analysis** *is a mathematical technique that allows you to use units to solve problems involving measurements.* When you want to use a conversion factor to change a unit in a problem, you can set up the problem in the following way.

$$\text{quantity sought} = \text{quantity given} \times \text{conversion factor}$$

For example, to determine the number of quarters in 12 dollars, you would carry out the unit conversion that allows you to change from dollars to quarters.

$$\text{number of quarters} = 12 \text{ dollars} \times \text{conversion factor}$$

Next you would have to decide which conversion factor gives you an answer in the desired unit. In this case, you have dollars and you want quarters. To eliminate dollars, you must divide the quantity by dollars. Therefore, the conversion factor in this case must have dollars in the denominator and quarters in the numerator. That factor is 4 quarters/1 dollar. Thus, you would set up the calculation as follows.

$$? \text{ quarters} = 12 \text{ dollars} \times \text{conversion factor}$$

$$= 12 \text{ dollars} \times \frac{4 \text{ quarters}}{1 \text{ dollar}} = 48 \text{ quarters}$$

Notice that the dollars have divided out, leaving an answer in the desired unit—quarters.

Suppose you had guessed wrong and used 1 dollar/4 quarters when choosing which of the two conversion factors to use. You would have an answer with entirely inappropriate units.

$$? \text{ quarters} = 12 \text{ dollars} \times \frac{1 \text{ dollar}}{4 \text{ quarters}} = \frac{3 \text{ dollars}^2}{\text{quarter}}$$

It is always best to begin with an idea of the units you will need in your final answer. When working through the Sample Problems, keep track of the units needed for the unknown quantity. Check your final answer against what you've written as the unknown quantity.

## Deriving Conversion Factors

You can derive conversion factors if you know the relationship between the unit you have and the unit you want. For example, from the fact that *deci-* means "1/10," you know that there is 1/10 of a meter per decimeter and that each meter must have 10 decimeters. Thus, from the equality (1 m = 10 dm), you can write the following conversion factors relating meters and decimeters. In this book, when there is no digit shown in the denominator, you can assume the value is 1.

$$\frac{1 \text{ m}}{10 \text{ dm}} \text{ and } \frac{0.1 \text{ m}}{\text{dm}} \text{ and } \frac{10 \text{ dm}}{\text{m}}$$

The following sample problem illustrates an example of deriving conversion factors to make a unit conversion.

### SAMPLE PROBLEM B

**Express a mass of 5.712 grams in milligrams and in kilograms.**

**SOLUTION** **Given:** 5.712 g
**Unknown:** mass in mg and kg

The expression that relates grams to milligrams is

$$1 \text{ g} = 1000 \text{ mg}$$

The possible conversion factors that can be written from this expression are

$$\frac{1000 \text{ mg}}{\text{g}} \text{ and } \frac{1 \text{ g}}{1000 \text{ mg}}$$

To derive an answer in mg, you'll need to multiply 5.712 g by 1000 mg/g.

$$5.712\ \cancel{g} \times \frac{1000\ mg}{\cancel{g}} = 5712\ mg$$

This answer makes sense because milligrams is a smaller unit than grams and, therefore, there should be more of them.

The kilogram problem is solved similarly.

$$1\ kg = 1000\ g$$

Conversion factors representing this expression are

$$\frac{1\ kg}{1000\ g} \text{ and } \frac{1000\ g}{kg}$$

To derive an answer in kg, you'll need to multiply 5.712 g by 1 kg/1000 g.

$$5.712\ \cancel{g} \times \frac{1\ kg}{1000\ \cancel{g}} = 0.005712\ kg$$

The answer makes sense because kilograms is a larger unit than grams and, therefore, there should be fewer of them.

**PRACTICE**

*Answers in Appendix E*

1. Express a length of 16.45 m in centimeters and in kilometers.
2. Express a mass of 0.014 mg in grams.

**extension**

Go to **go.hrw.com** for more practice problems that ask you to perform unit conversions.

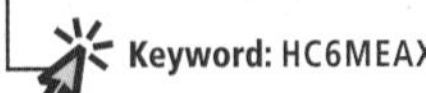


## SECTION REVIEW

1. Why are standards needed for measured quantities?
2. Label each of the following measurements by the quantity each represents. For instance, a measurement of 10.6 kg/m$^3$ represents density.
   - **a.** 5.0 g/mL
   - **b.** 37 s
   - **c.** 47 J
   - **d.** 39.56 g
   - **e.** 25.3 cm$^3$
   - **f.** 325 ms
   - **g.** 500 m$^2$
   - **h.** 30.23 mL
   - **i.** 2.7 mg
   - **j.** 0.005 L
3. Complete the following conversions.
   - **a.** 10.5 g = ____ kg
   - **b.** 1.57 km = ____ m
   - **c.** 3.54 µg = ____ g
   - **d.** 3.5 mol = ____ µmol
   - **e.** 1.2 L = ____ mL
   - **f.** 358 cm$^3$ = ____ m$^3$
   - **g.** 548.6 mL = ____ cm$^3$
4. Write conversion factors for each equality.
   - **a.** 1 m$^3$ = 1 000 000 cm$^3$
   - **b.** 1 in. = 2.54 cm
   - **c.** 1 µg = 0.000 001 g
   - **d.** 1 Mm = 1 000 000 m
5. **a.** What is the density of an 84.7 g sample of an unknown substance if the sample occupies 49.6 cm$^3$?
   **b.** What volume would be occupied by 7.75 g of this same substance?

**Critical Thinking**

6. **INFERRING CONCLUSIONS** A student converts grams to milligrams by multiplying by the conversion factor $\frac{1\ g}{1000\ mg}$. Is the student performing this calculation correctly?

# HISTORICAL CHEMISTRY

## Classical Ideas About Matter

The Greeks were among the many ancient cultures that sought to understand the nature of matter. One group of Greek philosophers, called the *atomists,* believed that matter could be broken down into pieces of a minute size. These pieces, called *atoms* or *atomos* which means "indivisible," possessed intrinsic, unchanging qualities. Another group of Greeks believed that matter could be divided an infinite number of times and could be changed from one type of matter into another.

Between 500 and 300 BCE, the Greek philosophers Leucippus and Democritus formulated the ideas that the atomists held. Leucippus and Democritus believed that all atoms were essentially the same but that the properties of all substances arose from the unique characteristics of their atoms. For example, solids, such as most metals, were thought to have uneven, jagged atoms. Because the atoms were rough, they could stick together and form solids. Similarly, water was thought to have atoms with smooth surfaces, which would allow the atoms to flow past one another. Though atomists did not have the same ideas about matter that we have today, they did believe that atoms were constantly in motion, even in objects that appeared to be solid.

Some Greek philosophers who studied matter between 700 and 300 BCE described matter in a way that differed from the way atomists described it. They attempted to identify and describe a fundamental substance from which all other matter was formed. Thales of Miletus (640–546 BCE) was among the first to suggest the existence of a basic element. He chose water, which exists as liquid, ice, and steam. He interpreted water's changeability to mean that water could transform into any other substance. Other philosophers suggested that the basic element was air or fire. Empedokles (ca. 490–ca. 430 BCE) focused on four elements: earth, air, fire, and water. He thought that these elements combined in various proportions to make all known matter.

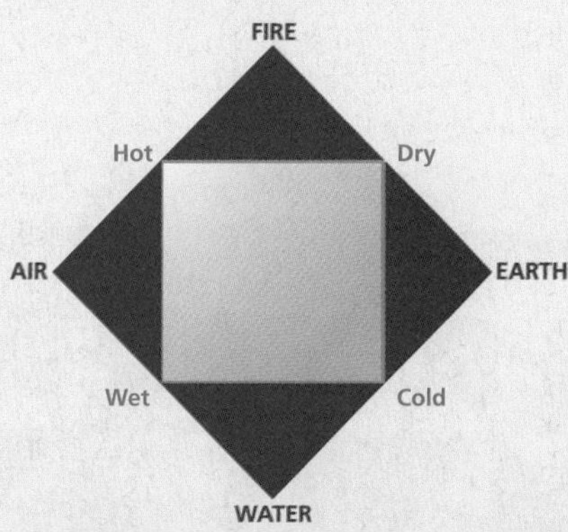


▲ *This diagram shows Aristotle's belief about the relationship between the basic elements and properties.*

Aristotle (384–322 BCE), a student of Plato, elaborated on the earlier ideas about elements. He argued that in addition to the four elements that make up all matter, there were four basic properties: hot, cold, wet, and dry. In Aristotle's view, the four elements could each have two of the basic properties. For example, water was wet and cold, while air was wet and hot. He thought that one element could change into another element if its properties were changed.

For more than 2,000 years, Aristotle's classical ideas dominated scientific thought. His ideas were based on philosophical arguments, not on the the scientific process. It was not until the 1700s that the existence of atoms was shown experimentally and that the incredible intuition of the atomists was realized.

### Questions

1. In Aristotle's system of elements, fire opposes water. Why do you think that he chose this relationship?
2. Use the ideas of the atomists to describe the atoms of the physical phases of matter—solid, liquid, and gas.

SECTION 3

# Using Scientific Measurements

## OBJECTIVES

- Distinguish between accuracy and precision.
- Determine the number of significant figures in measurements.
- Perform mathematical operations involving significant figures.
- Convert measurements into scientific notation.
- Distinguish between inversely and directly proportional relationships.

**C.1.3** Use scientific instruments to record measurement data in appropriate metric units that reflect the precision and accuracy of each particular instrument

If you have ever measured something several times, you know that the results can vary. In science, for a reported measurement to be useful, there must be some indication of its reliability or uncertainty.

## Accuracy and Precision

The terms *accuracy* and *precision* mean the same thing to most people. However, in science their meanings are quite distinct. **Accuracy** *refers to the closeness of measurements to the correct or accepted value of the quantity measured.* **Precision** *refers to the closeness of a set of measurements of the same quantity made in the same way.* Thus, measured values that are accurate are close to the accepted value. Measured values that are precise are close to one another but not necessarily close to the accepted value.

**Figure 8** can help you visualize the difference between precision and accuracy. A set of darts thrown separately at a dartboard may land in various positions, relative to the bull's-eye and to one another. The

**FIGURE 8** The sizes and locations of the areas covered by thrown darts illustrate the difference between precision and accuracy.

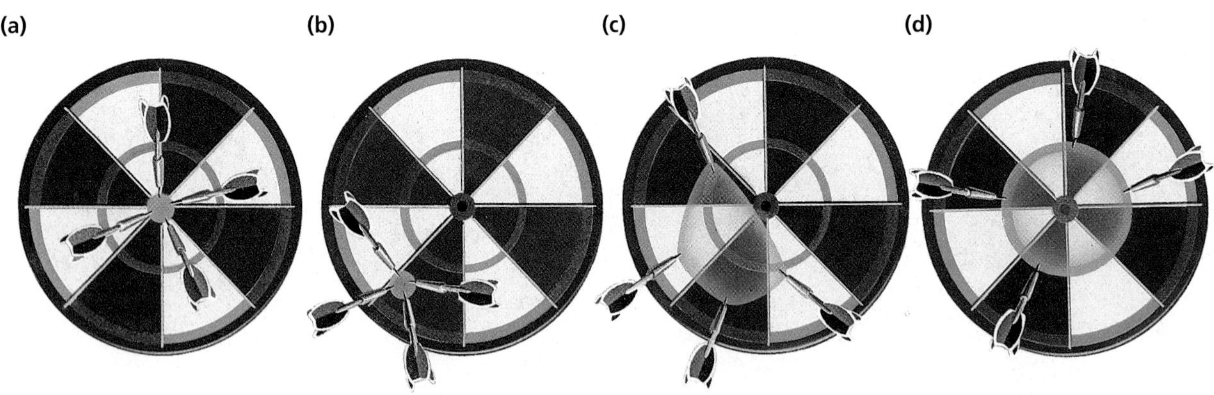


(a) Darts within small area = High precision

Area centered on bull's-eye = High accuracy

(b) Darts within small area = High precision

Area far from bull's-eye = Low accuracy

(c) Darts within large area = Low precision

Area far from bull's-eye = Low accuracy

(d) Darts within large area = Low precision

Area centered around bull's-eye = High accuracy (on average)

closer the darts land to the bull's-eye, the more accurately they were thrown. The closer they land to one another, the more precisely they were thrown. Thus, the set of results shown in **Figure 8a** is both accurate and precise because the darts are close to the bull's-eye and close to each other. In **Figure 8b,** the set of results is inaccurate but precise because the darts are far from the bull's-eye but close to each other. In **Figure 8c,** the set of results is both inaccurate and imprecise because the darts are far from the bull's-eye and far from each other. Notice also that the darts are not evenly distributed around the bull's-eye, so the set, even considered on average, is inaccurate. In **Figure 8d,** the set on average is accurate compared with the third case, but it is imprecise. That is because the darts are distributed evenly around the bull's-eye but are far from each other.

**extension**

**Chemistry in Action**

Go to **go.hrw.com** for a full-length article on using measurements to determine a car's pollution rating.

**Keyword: HC6MEAX**

## Percentage Error

The accuracy of an individual value or of an average experimental value can be compared quantitatively with the correct or accepted value by calculating the percentage error. **Percentage error** *is calculated by subtracting the accepted value from the experimental value, dividing the difference by the accepted value, and then multiplying by 100.*

$$Percentage\ error = \frac{Value_{experimental} - Value_{accepted}}{Value_{accepted}} \times 100$$

Percentage error has a negative value if the accepted value is greater than the experimental value. It has a positive value if the accepted value is less than the experimental value. The following sample problem illustrates the concept of percentage error.

### SAMPLE PROBLEM C

**A student measures the mass and volume of a substance and calculates its density as 1.40 g/mL. The correct, or accepted, value of the density is 1.30 g/mL. What is the percentage error of the student's measurement?**

**SOLUTION**

$$Percentage\ error = \frac{Value_{experimental} - Value_{accepted}}{Value_{accepted}} \times 100$$

$$= \frac{1.40\ g/\cancel{mL} - 1.30\ g/\cancel{mL}}{1.30\ g/\cancel{mL}} \times 100 = 7.7\%$$

**PRACTICE** *Answers in Appendix E*

1. What is the percentage error for a mass measurement of 17.7 g, given that the correct value is 21.2 g?
2. A volume is measured experimentally as 4.26 mL. What is the percentage error, given that the correct value is 4.15 mL?

**extension**

Go to **go.hrw.com** for more practice problems that ask you to calculate percentage error.

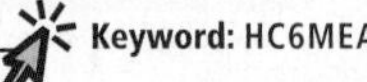

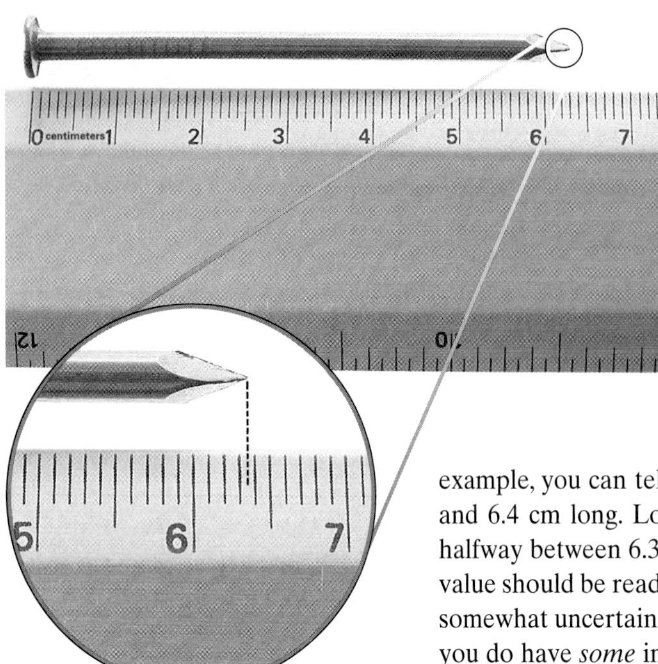


FIGURE 9 What value should be recorded for the length of this nail?

### Error in Measurement

Some error or uncertainty always exists in any measurement. The skill of the measurer places limits on the reliability of results. The conditions of measurement also affect the outcome. The measuring instruments themselves place limitations on precision. Some balances can be read more precisely than others. The same is true of rulers, graduated cylinders, and other measuring devices.

When you use a properly calibrated measuring device, you can be almost certain of a particular number of digits in a reading. For example, you can tell that the nail in **Figure 9** is definitely between 6.3 and 6.4 cm long. Looking more closely, you can see that the value is halfway between 6.3 and 6.4 cm. However, it is hard to tell whether the value should be read as 6.35 cm or 6.36 cm. The hundredths place is thus somewhat uncertain. Simply leaving it out would be misleading because you do have *some* indication of the value's likely range. Therefore, you would estimate the value to the final questionable digit, perhaps reporting the length of the nail as 6.36 cm. You might include a plus-or-minus value to express the range, for example, 6.36 cm ± 0.01 cm.

## Significant Figures

In science, measured values are reported in terms of significant figures. **Significant figures** *in a measurement consist of all the digits known with certainty plus one final digit, which is somewhat uncertain or is estimated.* For example, in the reported nail length of 6.36 cm discussed above, the last digit, 6, is uncertain. All the digits, including the uncertain one, are significant, however. All contain information and are included in the reported value. Thus, the term *significant* does not mean *certain*. In any correctly reported measured value, the final digit is significant but not certain. Insignificant digits are never reported. As a chemistry student, you will need to use and recognize significant figures when you work with measured quantities and report your results, and when you evaluate measurements reported by others.

### Determining the Number of Significant Figures

When you look at a measured quantity, you need to determine which digits are significant. That process is very easy if the number has no zeros because all the digits shown are significant. For example, in a number reported as 3.95, all three digits are significant. The significance of zeros in a number depends on their location, however. You need to learn and follow several rules involving zeros. After you have studied the rules in **Table 5,** use them to express the answers in the sample problem that follows.

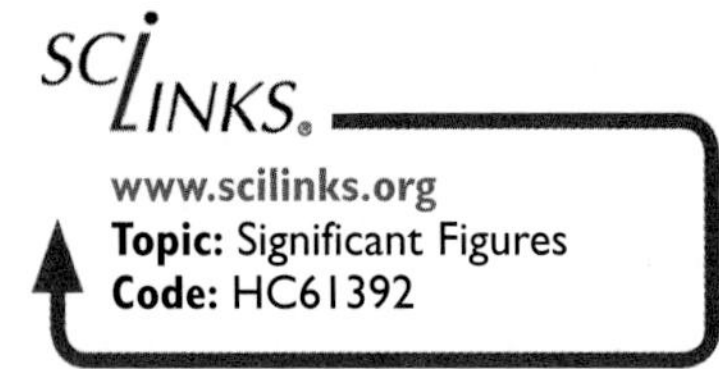

**TABLE 5 Rules for Determining Significant Zeros**

| Rule | Examples |
|---|---|
| 1. Zeros appearing between nonzero digits are significant. | a. 40.7 L has three significant figures.<br>b. 87 009 km has five significant figures. |
| 2. Zeros appearing in front of all nonzero digits are not significant. | a. 0.095 897 m has five significant figures.<br>b. 0.0009 kg has one significant figure. |
| 3. Zeros at the end of a number and to the right of a decimal point are significant. | a. 85.00 g has four significant figures.<br>b. 9.000 000 000 mm has 10 significant figures. |
| 4. Zeros at the end of a number but to the left of a decimal point may or may not be significant. If a zero has not been measured or estimated but is just a placeholder, it is not significant. A decimal point placed after zeros indicates that they are significant. | a. 2000 m may contain from one to four significant figures, depending on how many zeros are placeholders. **For measurements given in this text, assume that 2000 m has one significant figure.**<br>b. 2000. m contains four significant figures, indicated by the presence of the decimal point. |

## SAMPLE PROBLEM D

*For more help, go to the* ***Math Tutor*** *at the end of Chapter 1.*

**How many significant figures are in each of the following measurements?**

**a. 28.6 g**
**b. 3440. cm**
**c. 910 m**
**d. 0.046 04 L**
**e. 0.006 700 0 kg**

**SOLUTION** Determine the number of significant figures in each measurement using the rules listed in **Table 5.**

**a.** 28.6 g
There are no zeros, so all three digits are significant.

**b.** 3440. cm
By rule 4, the zero is significant because it is immediately followed by a decimal point; there are 4 significant figures.

**c.** 910 m
By rule 4, the zero is not significant; there are 2 significant figures.

**d.** 0.046 04 L
By rule 2, the first two zeros are not significant; by rule 1, the third zero is significant; there are 4 significant figures.

**e.** 0.006 700 0 kg
By rule 2, the first three zeros are not significant; by rule 3, the last three zeros are significant; there are 5 significant figures.

**PRACTICE** *Answers in Appendix E*

1. Determine the number of significant figures in each of the following.
   a. 804.05 g
   b. 0.014 403 0 km
   c. 1002 m
   d. 400 mL
   e. 30 000. cm
   f. 0.000 625 000 kg

2. Suppose the value "seven thousand centimeters" is reported to you. How should the number be expressed if it is intended to contain the following?
   a. 1 significant figure
   b. 4 significant figures
   c. 6 significant figures

Go to **go.hrw.com** for more practice problems that ask you to determine significant figures.

**Keyword: HC6MEAX**

## Rounding

When you perform calculations involving measurements, you need to know how to handle significant figures. This is especially true when you are using a calculator to carry out mathematical operations. The answers given on a calculator can be derived results with more digits than are justified by the measurements.

Suppose you used a calculator to divide a measured value of 154 g by a measured value of 327 mL. Each of these values has three significant figures. The calculator would show a numerical answer of 0.470948012. The answer contains digits not justified by the measurements used to calculate it. Such an answer has to be rounded off to make its degree of certainty match that in the original measurements. The answer should be 0.471 g/mL.

The rules for rounding are shown in **Table 6.** The extent of rounding required in a given case depends on whether the numbers are being added, subtracted, multiplied, or divided.

**TABLE 6** ***Rules for Rounding Numbers***

| If the digit following the last digit to be retained is: | then the last digit should: | Example (rounded to three significant figures) |
|---|---|---|
| greater than 5 | be increased by 1 | 42.68 g ⟶ 42.7 g |
| less than 5 | stay the same | 17.32 m ⟶ 17.3 m |
| 5, followed by nonzero digit(s) | be increased by 1 | 2.7851 cm ⟶ 2.79 cm |
| 5, not followed by nonzero digit(s), and preceded by an odd digit | be increased by 1 | 4.635 kg ⟶ 4.64 kg (because 3 is odd) |
| 5, not followed by nonzero digit(s), and the preceding significant digit is even | stay the same | 78.65 mL ⟶ 78.6 mL (because 6 is even) |

## Addition or Subtraction with Significant Figures

Consider two mass measurements, 25.1 g and 2.03 g. The first measurement, 25.1 g, has one digit to the right of the decimal point, in the tenths place. There is no information on possible values for the hundredths place. That place is simply blank and cannot be assumed to be zero. The other measurement, 2.03 g, has two digits to the right of the decimal point. It provides information up to and including the hundredths place.

Suppose you were asked to add the two measurements. Simply carrying out the addition would result in an answer of 25.1 g + 2.03 g = 27.13 g. That answer suggests there is certainty all the way to the hundredths place. However, that result is not justified because the hundredths place in 25.1 g is completely unknown. The answer must be adjusted to reflect the uncertainty in the numbers added.

*When adding or subtracting decimals, the answer must have the same number of digits to the right of the decimal point as there are in the measurement having the fewest digits to the right of the decimal point.* Comparing the two values 25.1 g and 2.03 g, the measurement with the fewest digits to the right of the decimal point is 25.1 g. It has only one such digit. Following the rule, the answer must be rounded so that it has no more than one digit to the right of the decimal point. The answer should therefore be rounded to 27.1 g. When working with whole numbers, the answer should be rounded so that the final significant digit is in the same place as the leftmost uncertain digit. (For example, 5400 + 365 = 5800.)

## Multiplication and Division with Significant Figures

Suppose you calculated the density of an object that has a mass of 3.05 g and a volume of 8.47 mL. The following division on a calculator will give a value of 0.360094451.

$$density = \frac{mass}{volume} = \frac{3.05 \text{ g}}{8.47 \text{ mL}} = 0.360094451 \text{ g/mL}$$

The answer must be rounded to the correct number of significant figures. The values of mass and volume used to obtain the answer have only three significant figures each. The degree of certainty in the calculated result is not justified. *For multiplication or division, the answer can have no more significant figures than are in the measurement with the fewest number of significant figures.* In the calculation just described, the answer, 0.360094451 g/mL, would be rounded to three significant figures to match the significant figures in 8.47 mL and 3.05 g. The answer would thus be 0.360 g/mL.

**SAMPLE PROBLEM E** *For more help, go to the **Math Tutor** at the end of Chapter 1.*

**Carry out the following calculations. Express each answer to the correct number of significant figures.**

**a. 5.44 m − 2.6103 m**

**b. 2.4 g/mL × 15.82 mL**

**SOLUTION** Carry out each mathematical operation. Follow the rules in **Table 5** and **Table 6** for determining significant figures and for rounding.

**a.** The answer is rounded to 2.83 m, because for subtraction there should be two digits to the right of the decimal point, to match 5.44 m.

**b.** The answer is rounded to 38 g, because for multiplication there should be two significant figures in the answer, to match 2.4 g/mL.

**PRACTICE** *Answers in Appendix E*

1. What is the sum of 2.099 g and 0.05681 g?
2. Calculate the quantity 87.3 cm – 1.655 cm.
3. Calculate the area of a rectangular crystal surface that measures 1.34 μm by 0.7488 μm. (Hint: Recall that *area* = *length* × *width* and is measured in square units.)
4. Polycarbonate plastic has a density of 1.2 g/cm$^3$. A photo frame is constructed from two 3.0 mm sheets of polycarbonate. Each sheet measures 28 cm by 22 cm. What is the mass of the photo frame?

Go to **go.hrw.com** for more practice problems that ask you to calculate using significant figures.

**Keyword: HC6MEAX**

### Conversion Factors and Significant Figures

Earlier in this chapter, you learned how conversion factors are used to change one unit to another. Such conversion factors are typically exact. That is, there is no uncertainty in them. For example, there are exactly 100 cm in a meter. If you were to use the conversion factor 100 cm/m to change meters to centimeters, the 100 would not limit the degree of certainty in the answer. Thus, 4.608 m could be converted to centimeters as follows.

$$4.608 \text{ m} \times \frac{100 \text{ cm}}{\text{m}} = 460.8 \text{ cm}$$

The answer still has four significant figures. Because the conversion factor is considered exact, the answer would not be rounded. Most exact conversion factors are defined, rather than measured, quantities. Counted numbers also produce conversion factors of unlimited precision. For example, if you counted that there are 10 test tubes for every student, that would produce an exact conversion factor of 10 test tubes/student. There is no uncertainty in that factor.

## Scientific Notation

*In* **scientific notation,** *numbers are written in the form* M × $10^n$, *where the factor* M *is a number greater than or equal to 1 but less than 10 and* n *is a whole number.* For example, to write the quantity 65 000 km in scientific notation and show the first two digits as significant, you would write the following.

$$6.5 \times 10^4 \text{ km}$$

Writing the *M* factor as 6.5 shows that there are exactly two significant figures. If, instead, you intended the first three digits in 65 000 to be significant, you would write $6.50 \times 10^4$ km. When numbers are written in scientific notation, only the significant figures are shown.

Suppose you are expressing a very small quantity, such as the length of a flu virus. In ordinary notation this length could be 0.000 12 mm. That length can be expressed in scientific notation as follows.

$$0.000\ 12 \text{ mm} = 1.2 \times 10^{-4} \text{ mm}$$

Move the decimal point four places to the right, and multiply the number by $10^{-4}$.

1. Determine *M* by moving the decimal point in the original number to the left or the right so that only one nonzero digit remains to the left of the decimal point.
2. Determine *n* by counting the number of places that you moved the decimal point. If you moved it to the left, *n* is positive. If you moved it to the right, *n* is negative.

## Mathematical Operations Using Scientific Notation

1. *Addition and subtraction* These operations can be performed only if the values have the same exponent (*n* factor). If they do not, adjustments must be made to the values so that the exponents are equal. Once the exponents are equal, the *M* factors can be added or subtracted. The exponent of the answer can remain the same, or it may then require adjustment if the *M* factor of the answer has more than one digit to the left of the decimal point. Consider the example of the addition of $4.2 \times 10^4$ kg and $7.9 \times 10^3$ kg.

   We can make both exponents either 3 or 4. The following solutions are possible.

$$\begin{array}{r} 4.2\ \times 10^4 \text{ kg} \\ +0.79 \times 10^4 \text{ kg} \\ \hline 4.99 \times 10^4 \text{ kg} \end{array} \text{ rounded to } 5.0 \times 10^4 \text{ kg}$$

or

$$\begin{array}{r} 7.9\ \times 10^3 \text{ kg} \\ +42\ \ \ \times 10^3 \text{ kg} \\ \hline 49.9\ \times 10^3 \text{ kg} \end{array} = 4.99 \times 10^4 \text{ kg rounded to } 5.0 \times 10^4 \text{ kg}$$

   Note that the units remain kg throughout.

**FIGURE 10** When you use a scientific calculator to work problems in scientific notation, don't forget to express the value on the display to the correct number of significant figures and show the units when you write the final answer.

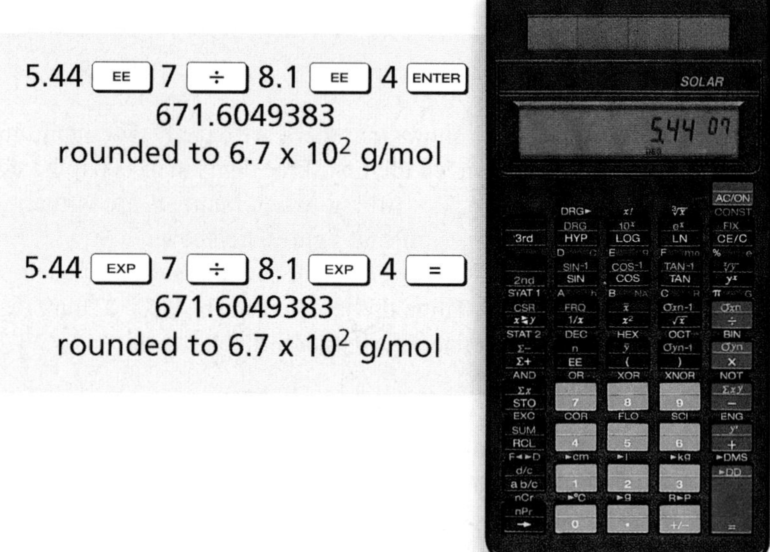


2. *Multiplication* The *M* factors are multiplied, and the exponents are added algebraically.

Consider the multiplication of $5.23 \times 10^6$ μm by $7.1 \times 10^{-2}$ μm.

$$(5.23 \times 10^6\ \mu\text{m})(7.1 \times 10^{-2}\ \mu\text{m}) = (5.23 \times 7.1)(10^6 \times 10^{-2})$$
$$= 37.133 \times 10^4\ \mu\text{m}^2 \text{ (adjust to two significant digits)}$$
$$= 3.7 \times 10^5\ \mu\text{m}^2$$

Note that when length measurements are multiplied, the result is area. The unit is now $\mu m^2$.

3. *Division* The *M* factors are divided, and the exponent of the denominator is subtracted from that of the numerator. The calculator keystrokes for this problem are shown in **Figure 10.**

$$\frac{5.44 \times 10^7\ \text{g}}{8.1 \times 10^4\ \text{mol}} = \frac{5.44}{8.1} \times 10^{7-4}\ \text{g/mol}$$
$$= 0.6716049383 \times 10^3 \text{ (adjust to two significant figures)}$$
$$= 6.7 \times 10^2\ \text{g/mol}$$

Note that the unit for the answer is the ratio of grams to moles.

## Using Sample Problems

Learning to analyze and solve such problems requires practice and a logical approach. In this section, you will review a process that can help you analyze problems effectively. Most Sample Problems in this book are organized by four basic steps to guide your thinking in how to work out the solution to a problem.

## Analyze

*The first step in solving a quantitative word problem is to read the problem carefully at least twice and to analyze the information in it.* Note any important descriptive terms that clarify or add meaning to the problem. Identify and list the data given in the problem. Also identify the unknown—the quantity you are asked to find.

## Plan

*The second step is to develop a plan for solving the problem.* The plan should show how the information given is to be used to find the unknown. In the process, reread the problem to make sure you have gathered all the necessary information. It is often helpful to draw a picture that represents the problem. For example, if you were asked to determine the volume of a crystal given its dimensions, you could draw a representation of the crystal and label the dimensions. This drawing would help you visualize the problem.

Decide which conversion factors, mathematical formulas, or chemical principles you will need to solve the problem. Your plan might suggest a single calculation or a series of them involving different conversion factors. Once you understand how you need to proceed, you may wish to sketch out the route you will take, using arrows to point the way from one stage of the solution to the next. Sometimes you will need data that are not actually part of the problem statement. For instance, you'll often use data from the periodic table.

## Compute

*The third step involves substituting the data and necessary conversion factors into the plan you have developed.* At this stage you calculate the answer, cancel units, and round the result to the correct number of significant figures. It is very important to have a plan worked out in step 2 before you start using the calculator. All too often, students start multiplying or dividing values given in the problem before they really understand what they need to do to get an answer.

## Evaluate

*Examine your answer to determine whether it is reasonable.* Use the following methods, when appropriate, to carry out the evaluation.

1. Check to see that the units are correct. If they are not, look over the setup. Are the conversion factors correct?
2. Make an estimate of the expected answer. Use simpler, rounded numbers to do so. Compare the estimate with your actual result. The two should be similar.
3. Check the order of magnitude in your answer. Does it seem reasonable compared with the values given in the problem? If you calculated the density of vegetable oil and got a value of 54.9 g/mL, you should know that something is wrong. Oil floats on water; therefore, its density is less than water, so the value obtained should be less than 1.0 g/mL.
4. Be sure that the answer given for any problem is expressed using the correct number of significant figures.

Look over the following quantitative Sample Problem. Notice how the four-step approach is used, and then apply the approach yourself in solving the practice problems that follow.

## SAMPLE PROBLEM F

**Calculate the volume of a sample of aluminum that has a mass of 3.057 kg. The density of aluminum is 2.70 g/cm$^3$.**

### SOLUTION

**1 *ANALYZE*** **Given:** mass = 3.057 kg, density = 2.70 g/cm$^3$
**Unknown:** volume of aluminum

**2 *PLAN*** The density unit in the problem is g/cm$^3$, and the mass given in the problem is expressed in kg. Therefore, in addition to using the density equation, you will need a conversion factor representing the relationship between grams and kilograms.

$$1000 \text{ g} = 1 \text{ kg}$$

Also, rearrange the density equation to solve for volume.

$$density = \frac{mass}{volume} \quad \text{or} \quad D = \frac{m}{V}$$

$$V = \frac{m}{D}$$

**3 *COMPUTE***

$$V = \frac{3.057 \text{ kg}}{2.70 \text{ g/cm}^3} \times \frac{1000 \text{ g}}{\text{kg}} = 1132.222 \ldots \text{cm}^3 \text{ (calculator answer)}$$

The answer should be rounded to three significant figures.

$$V = 1.13 \times 10^3 \text{ cm}^3$$

**4 *EVALUATE*** The unit of volume, cm$^3$, is correct. An order-of-magnitude estimate would put the answer at over 1000 cm$^3$.

$$\frac{3}{2} \times 1000$$

The correct number of significant figures is three, which matches that in 2.70 g/cm$^3$.

### PRACTICE

*Answers in Appendix E*

1. What is the volume, in milliliters, of a sample of helium that has a mass of $1.73 \times 10^{-3}$ g, given that the density is 0.178 47 g/L?
2. What is the density of a piece of metal that has a mass of $6.25 \times 10^5$ g and is 92.5 cm × 47.3 cm × 85.4 cm?
3. How many millimeters are there in $5.12 \times 10^5$ kilometers?
4. A clock gains 0.020 second per minute. How many seconds will the clock gain in exactly six months, assuming exactly 30 days per month?

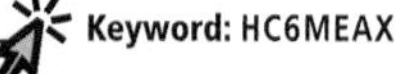


Go to **go.hrw.com** for more practice problems that ask you to calculate using scientific notation.

**Keyword: HC6MEAX**

## Direct Proportions

*Two quantities are* **directly proportional** *to each other if dividing one by the other gives a constant value*. For example, if the masses and volumes of different samples of aluminum are measured, the masses and volumes will be directly proportional to each other. As the masses of the samples increase, their volumes increase by the same factor, as you can see from the data in **Table 7.** Doubling the mass doubles the volume. Halving the mass halves the volume.

When two variables, $x$ and $y$, are directly proportional to each other, the relationship can be expressed as $y \propto x$, which is read as "$y$ is *proportional* to $x$." The general equation for a directly proportional relationship between the two variables can also be written as follows.

$$\frac{y}{x} = k$$

The value of $k$ is a constant called the proportionality constant. Written in this form, the equation expresses an important fact about direct proportion: the ratio between the variables remains constant. Note that using the mass and volume values in **Table 7** gives a mass-volume ratio that is constant (neglecting measurement error). The equation can be rearranged into the following form.

$$y = kx$$

The equation $y = kx$ may look familiar to you. It is the equation for a special case of a straight line. If two variables related in this way are graphed versus one another, a straight line, or linear plot that passes through the origin (0,0), results. The data for aluminum from **Table 7** are graphed in **Figure 11.** The mass and volume of a pure substance are directly proportional to each other. Consider mass to be $y$ and volume to be $x$. The constant ratio, $k$, for the two variables is density. The slope of the line reflects the constant density, or mass-volume ratio, of aluminum,

**TABLE 7** ***Mass-Volume Data for Aluminum at 20°C***

| Mass (g) | Volume (cm$^3$) | $\frac{m}{V}$ (g/cm$^3$) |
|---|---|---|
| 54.7 | 20.1 | 2.72 |
| 65.7 | 24.4 | 2.69 |
| 83.5 | 30.9 | 2.70 |
| 96.3 | 35.8 | 2.69 |
| 105.7 | 39.1 | 2.70 |

**FIGURE 11** The graph of mass versus volume shows a relationship of direct proportion. Notice that the line is extrapolated to pass through the origin.

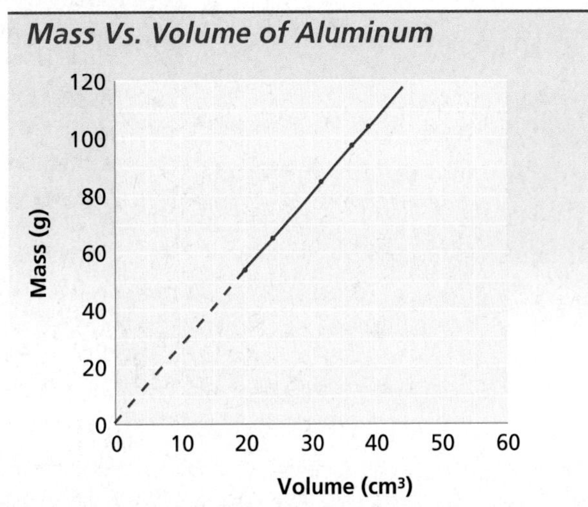

which is 2.70 g/cm$^3$ at 20°C. Notice also that the plotted line passes through the origin. All directly proportional relationships produce linear graphs that pass through the origin.

## Inverse Proportions

*Two quantities are* **inversely proportional** *to each other if their product is constant.* An example of an inversely proportional relationship is that between speed of travel and the time required to cover a fixed distance. The greater the speed, the less time that is needed to go a certain fixed distance. Doubling the speed cuts the required time in half. Halving the speed doubles the required time.

When two variables, $x$ and $y$, are inversely proportional to each other, the relationship can be expressed as follows.

$$y \propto \frac{1}{x}$$

This is read "$y$ is *proportional* to 1 divided by $x$." The general equation for an inversely proportional relationship between the two variables can be written in the following form.

$$xy = k$$

In the equation, $k$ is the proportionality constant. If $x$ increases, $y$ must decrease by the same factor to keep the product constant.

A graph of variables that are inversely proportional produces a curve called a hyperbola. Such a graph is illustrated in **Figure 12.** When the temperature of the gas is kept constant, the volume ($V$) of the gas sample decreases as the pressure ($P$) increases. Look at the data shown in **Table 8.** Note that $P \times V$ gives a reasonably constant value. The graph of this data is shown in **Figure 12.**

**TABLE 8** ***Pressure-Volume Data for Nitrogen at Constant Temperature***

| Pressure (kPa) | Volume (cm$^3$) | $P \times V$ |
|---|---|---|
| 100 | 500 | 50 000 |
| 150 | 333 | 50 000 |
| 200 | 250 | 50 000 |
| 250 | 200 | 50 000 |
| 300 | 166 | 49 800 |
| 350 | 143 | 50 100 |
| 400 | 125 | 50 000 |
| 450 | 110 | 49 500 |

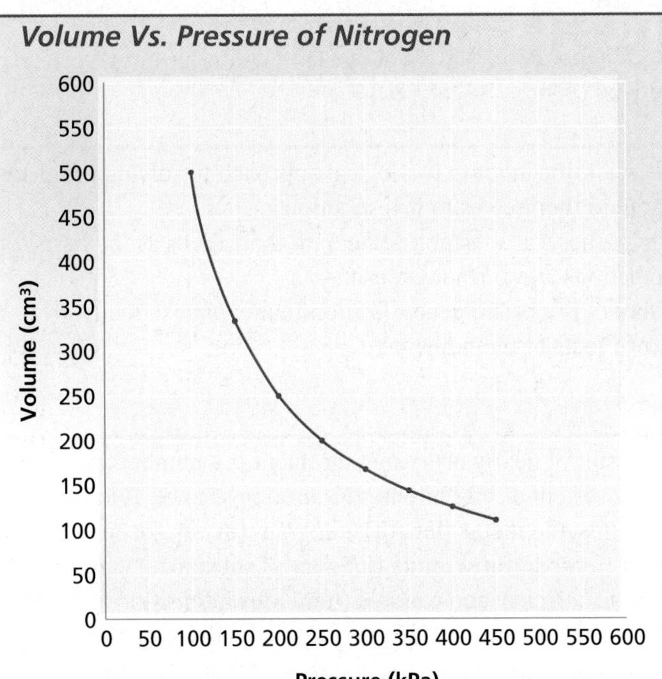


**FIGURE 12** The graph of volume versus pressure shows an inversely proportional relationship. Note the difference between the shape of this graph and that of the graph in Figure 11.

## SECTION REVIEW

1. The density of copper is listed as 8.94 g/cm$^3$. Two students each make three density determinations of samples of the substance. Student A's results are 7.3 g/mL, 9.4 g/mL, and 8.3 g/mL. Student B's results are 8.4 g/cm$^3$, 8.8 g/cm$^3$, and 8.0 g/cm$^3$. Compare the two sets of results in terms of precision and accuracy.
2. Determine the number of significant figures.
   **a.** 6.002 cm
   **b.** 0.0020 m
   **c.** 10.0500 g
   **d.** 7000 kg
   **e.** 7000. kg
3. Round 2.6765 to two significant figures.
4. Carry out the following calculations.
   **a.** 52.13 g + 1.7502 g
   **b.** 12 m × 6.41 m
   **c.** $\frac{16.25 \text{ g}}{5.1442 \text{ mL}}$
5. Perform the following operations. Express each answer in scientific notation.
   **a.** $(1.54 \times 10^{-2} \text{ g}) + (2.86 \times 10^{-1} \text{ g})$
   **b.** $(7.023 \times 10^{9} \text{ g}) - (6.62 \times 10^{7} \text{ g})$
   **c.** $(8.99 \times 10^{-4} \text{ m}) \times (3.57 \times 10^{4} \text{ m})$
   **d.** $\frac{2.17 \times 10^{-3} \text{ g}}{5.022 \times 10^{4} \text{ mL}}$
6. Write the following numbers in scientific notation.
   **a.** 560 000
   **b.** 33 400
   **c.** 0.000 4120
7. A student measures the mass of a beaker filled with corn oil. The mass reading averages 215.6 g. The mass of the beaker is 110.4 g.
   **a.** What is the mass of the corn oil?
   **b.** What is the density of the corn oil if its volume is 114 cm$^3$?
8. Calculate the mass of gold that occupies $5.0 \times 10^{-3}$ cm$^3$. The density of gold is 19.3 g/cm$^3$.
9. What is the difference between a graph representing data that are directly proportional and a graph of data that are inversely proportional?

### Critical Thinking

10. **APPLYING CONCEPTS** The mass of a liquid is 11.50 g and its volume is 9.03 mL. How many significant figures should its density value have? Explain the reason for your answer.

# CHAPTER HIGHLIGHTS

## Scientific Method

**Vocabulary**
scientific method
system
hypothesis
model
theory

- The scientific method is a logical approach to solving problems that lend themselves to investigation.
- A hypothesis is a testable statement that serves as the basis for predictions and further experiments.
- A theory is a broad generalization that explains a body of known facts or phenomena.

## Units of Measurement

**Vocabulary**
quantity
SI
weight
derived unit
volume
density
conversion factor
dimensional analysis

- The result of nearly every measurement is a number and a unit.
- The SI system of measurement is used in science. It has seven base units: the meter (length), kilogram (mass), second (time), kelvin (temperature), mole (amount of substance), ampere (electric current), and candela (luminous intensity).
- Weight is a measure of the gravitational pull on matter.
- Derived SI units include the square meter (area) and the cubic meter (volume).
- Density is the ratio of mass to volume.
- Conversion factors are used to convert from one unit to another.

## Using Scientific Measurements

**Vocabulary**
accuracy
precision
percentage error
significant figures
scientific notation
directly proportional
inversely proportional

- Accuracy refers to the closeness of a measurement to the correct or accepted value. Precision refers to the closeness of values for a set of measurements.
- Percentage error is the difference between the experimental and the accepted value that is divided by the accepted value and then multiplied by 100.
- The significant figures in a number consist of all digits known with certainty plus one final digit, which is uncertain.
- After addition or subtraction, the answer should be rounded so that it has no more digits to the right of the decimal point than there are in the measurement that has the smallest number of digits to the right of the decimal point. After multiplication or division, the answer should be rounded so that it has no more significant figures than there are in the measurement that has the fewest number of significant figures.
- Exact conversion factors are completely certain and do not limit the number of digits in a calculation.
- A number written in scientific notation is of the form $M \times 10^n$, in which $M$ is greater than or equal to 1 but less than 10 and $n$ is an integer.
- Two quantities are directly proportional to each other if dividing one by the other yields a constant value. Two quantities are inversely proportional to each other if their product has a constant value.

# CHAPTER REVIEW

For more practice, go to the Problem Bank in Appendix D.

## Scientific Method

### SECTION 1 REVIEW

1. How does quantitative information differ from qualitative information?
2. What is a hypothesis?
3. a. What is a model in the scientific sense?
   b. How does a model differ from a theory?

## Units of Measurement

### SECTION 2 REVIEW

4. Why is it important for a measurement system to have an international standard?
5. How does a quantity differ from a unit? Use two examples to explain the difference.
6. List the seven SI base units and the quantities they represent.
7. What is the numerical equivalent of each of the following SI prefixes?
   a. kilo-
   b. centi-
   c. mega-
   d. micro-
   e. milli-
8. Identify the SI unit that would be most appropriate for expressing the length of the following.
   a. width of a gymnasium
   b. length of a finger
   c. distance between your town and the closest border of the next state
   d. length of a bacterial cell
9. Identify the SI unit that would be most appropriate for measuring the mass of each of the following objects.
   a. table
   b. coin
   c. a 250 mL beaker
10. Explain why the second is not defined by the length of the day.
11. a. What is a derived unit?
    b. What is the SI-derived unit for area?
12. a. List two SI-derived units for volume.
    b. List two non-SI units for volume, and explain how they relate to the cubic centimeter.
13. a. Why are the units used that are to express the densities of gases different from those used to express the densities of solids or liquids?
    b. Name two units for density.
    c. Why is the temperature at which density is measured usually specified?
14. a. Which of the solids listed in **Table 4** will float on water?
    b. Which of the liquids will sink in milk?
15. a. Define *conversion factor.*
    b. Explain how conversion factors are used.

### PRACTICE PROBLEMS

16. What is the volume, in cubic meters, of a rectangular solid that is 0.25 m long, 6.1 m wide, and 4.9 m high?
17. Find the density of a material, given that a 5.03 g sample occupies 3.24 mL. (Hint: See Sample Problem A.)
18. What is the mass of a sample of material that has a volume of 55.1 $cm^3$ and a density of 6.72 $g/cm^3$?
19. A sample of a substance that has a density of 0.824 g/mL has a mass of 0.451 g. Calculate the volume of the sample.
20. How many grams are in 882 μg? (Hint: See Sample Problem B.)
21. Calculate the number of milliliters in 0.603 L.
22. The density of gold is 19.3 $g/cm^3$.
    a. What is the volume, in cubic centimeters, of a sample of gold that has a mass of 0.715 kg?
    b. If this sample of gold is a cube, what is the length of each edge in centimeters?
23. a. Find the number of kilometers in 92.25 m.
    b. Convert the answer in kilometers to centimeters.

## Using Scientific Measurements

### SECTION 3 REVIEW

24. Compare accuracy and precision.
25. a. Write the equation that is used to calculate percentage error.

b. Under what condition will percentage error be negative?

26. How is the average for a set of values calculated?

27. What is meant by a mass measurement expressed in this form: 4.6 g ± 0.2 g?

28. Suppose a graduated cylinder were not correctly calibrated. How would this affect the results of a measurement? How would it affect the results of a calculation using this measurement?

29. Round each of the following measurements to the number of significant figures indicated.
   a. 67.029 g to three significant figures
   b. 0.15 L to one significant figure
   c. 52.8005 mg to five significant figures
   d. 3.174 97 mol to three significant figures

30. State the rules governing the number of significant figures that result from each of the following operations.
   a. addition and subtraction
   b. multiplication and division

31. What is the general form for writing numbers in scientific notation?

32. a. By using *x* and *y*, state the general equation for quantities that are directly proportional.
   b. For two directly proportional quantities, what happens to one variable when the other variable increases?

33. a. State the general equation for quantities, *x* and *y*, that are inversely proportional.
   b. For two inversely proportional quantities, what happens to one variable when the other increases?

34. Arrange in the correct order the following four basic steps for finding the solution to a problem: compute, plan, evaluate, and analyze.

## PRACTICE PROBLEMS

35. A student measures the mass of a sample as 9.67 g. Calculate the percentage error, given that the correct mass is 9.82 g. (Hint: See Sample Problem C.)

36. A handbook gives the density of calcium as 1.54 g/cm$^3$. Based on lab measurements, what is the percentage error of a density calculation of 1.25 g/cm$^3$?

37. What is the percentage error of a length measurement of 0.229 cm if the correct value is 0.225 cm?

38. How many significant figures are in each of the following measurements? (Hint: See Sample Problem D.)
   a. 0.4004 mL
   b. 6000 g
   c. 1.000 30 km
   d. 400. mm

39. Calculate the sum of 6.078 g and 0.3329 g.

40. Subtract 7.11 cm from 8.2 cm. (Hint: See Sample Problem E.)

41. What is the product of 0.8102 m and 3.44 m?

42. Divide 94.20 g by 3.167 22 mL.

43. Write the following numbers in scientific notation.
   a. 0.000 673 0
   b. 50 000.0
   c. 0.000 003 010

44. The following numbers are in scientific notation. Write them in ordinary notation.
   a. $7.050 \times 10^3$ g
   b. $4.000\,05 \times 10^7$ mg
   c. $2.350\,0 \times 10^4$ mL

45. Perform the following operation. Express the answer in scientific notation and with the correct number of significant figures.
   0.002115m × 0.0000405m

46. A sample of a certain material has a mass of $2.03 \times 10^{-3}$ g. Calculate the volume of the sample, given that the density is $9.133 \times 10^{-1}$ g/cm$^3$. Use the four-step method to solve the problem. (Hint: See Sample Problem F.)

## MIXED REVIEW

47. A man finds that he has a mass of 100.6 kg. He goes on a diet, and several months later he finds that he has a mass of 96.4 kg. Express each number in scientific notation, and calculate the number of kilograms the man has lost by dieting.

48. A large office building is $1.07 \times 10^2$ m long, 31 m wide, and $4.25 \times 10^2$ m high. What is its volume?

**49.** An object has a mass of 57.6 g. Find the object's density, given that its volume is 40.25 $cm^3$.

**50.** A lab worker measures the mass of some sucrose as 0.947 mg. Convert that quantity to grams and to kilograms.

**51.** A student calculates the density of iron as 6.80 $g/cm^3$ by using lab data for mass and volume. A handbook reveals that the correct value is 7.86 $g/cm^3$. What is the percentage error?

## USING THE HANDBOOK

**52.** Find the table of properties for Group 1 elements in the *Elements Handbook*. Calculate the volume of a single atom of each element listed in the table by using the equation for the volume of a sphere.

$$\frac{4}{3}\pi \bullet r^3$$

**53.** Use the radius of a sodium atom from the *Elements Handbook* to calculate the number of sodium atoms in a row 5.00 cm long. Assume that each sodium atom touches the ones next to it.

**54.** a. A block of sodium that has the measurements 3.00 cm × 5.00 cm × 5.00 cm has a mass of 75.5 g. Calculate the density of sodium.

b. Compare your calculated density with the value in the properties table for Group 1 elements. Calculate the percentage error for your density determination.

## RESEARCH & WRITING

**55.** How does the metric system, which was once a standard for measurement, differ from SI? Why was it necessary for the United States to change to SI?

**56.** What are ISO 9000 standards? How do they affect industry on an international level?

## ALTERNATIVE ASSESSMENT

**57. Performance** Obtain three metal samples from your teacher. Determine the mass and volume of each sample. Calculate the density of each metal from your measurement data. (Hint: Consider using the water displacement technique to measure the volume of your samples.)

**58.** Use the data from the Nutrition Facts label below to answer the following questions:

a. Use the data given on the label for grams of fat and Calories from fat to construct a conversion factor that has the units Calories per gram.

b. Calculate the mass in kilograms for 20 servings of the food.

c. Calculate the mass of protein in micrograms for one serving of the food.

d. What is the correct number of significant figures for the answer in item a? Why?

**Nutrition Facts**

Serving Size ¾ cup (30g)
Servings Per Container About 14

| Amount Per Serving | Corn Crunch | with ½ cup skim milk |
|---|---|---|
| **Calories** | 120 | 160 |
| Calories from Fat | 15 | 20 |
| | **% Daily Value**** | |
| **Total Fat** 2g* | **3%** | **3%** |
| Saturated Fat 0g | **0%** | **0%** |
| **Cholesterol** 0mg | **0%** | **1%** |
| **Sodium** 160mg | **7%** | **9%** |
| **Potassium** 65mg | **2%** | **8%** |
| **Total Carbohydrate** 25g | **8%** | **10%** |
| Dietary Fiber 3g | | |
| Sugars 3g | | |
| Other Carbohydrate 11g | | |
| **Protein** 2g | | |

*Amount in Cereal. A serving of cereal plus skim milk provides 2g fat, less 5mg cholesterol, 220mg sodium, 270mg potassium, 31g carbohydrate (19g sugars) and 6g protein.

**Percent Daily Values are based on a 2,000 calorie diet. Your daily values may be higher or lower depending on your calorie needs:

| | Calories | 2,000 | 2,500 |
|---|---|---|---|
| Total Fat | Less than | 65g | 80g |
| Sat Fat | Less than | 20g | 25g |
| Cholesterol | Less than | 300mg | 300mg |
| Sodium | Less than | 2,400mg | 2,400mg |
| Potassium | | 3,500mg | 3,500mg |
| Total Carbohydrate | | 300g | 375g |
| Dietary Fiber | | 25g | 30g |

## CHAPTER 3

# Atoms: The Building Blocks of Matter

*An atom is the smallest particle of an element that retains the chemical properties of that element.*

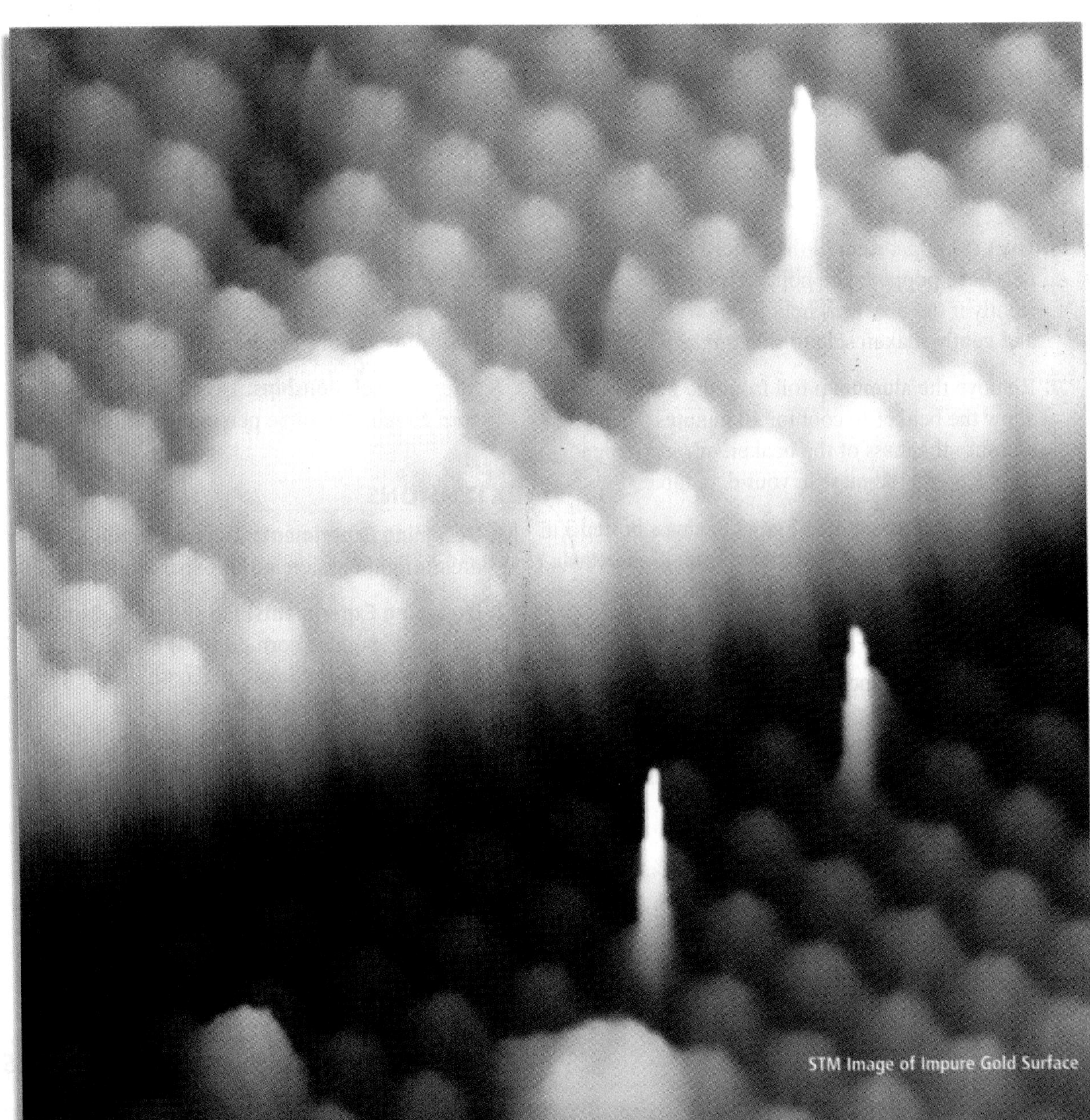

STM Image of Impure Gold Surface

# The Atom: From Philosophical Idea to Scientific Theory

SECTION 1

## *Objectives*

- Explain the law of conservation of mass, the law of definite proportions, and the law of multiple proportions.
- Summarize the five essential points of Dalton's atomic theory.
- Explain the relationship between Dalton's atomic theory and the law of conservation of mass, the law of definite proportions, and the law of multiple proportions.

SC **C.5.9** Analyze a chemical process to account for the weight of all reagents and solvents by following the appropriate material balance procedures

When you crush a lump of sugar, you can see that it is made up of many smaller particles of sugar. You may grind these particles into a very fine powder, but each tiny piece is still sugar. Now suppose you dissolve the sugar in water. The tiny particles seem to disappear completely. Even if you look at the sugar-water solution through a powerful microscope, you cannot see any sugar particles. Yet if you were to taste the solution, you'd know that the sugar is still there. Observations like these led early philosophers to ponder the fundamental nature of matter. Is it continuous and infinitely divisible, or is it divisible only until a basic, invisible particle that cannot be divided further is reached?

The particle theory of matter was supported as early as 400 B.C. by certain Greek thinkers, such as Democritus. He called nature's basic particle an *atom,* based on the Greek word meaning "indivisible." Aristotle was part of the generation that succeeded Democritus. His ideas had a lasting impact on Western civilization, and he did not believe in atoms. He thought that all matter was continuous, and his opinion was accepted for nearly 2000 years. Neither the view of Aristotle nor that of Democritus was supported by experimental evidence, so each remained speculation until the eighteenth century. Then scientists began to gather evidence favoring the atomic theory of matter.

extension

**Historical Chemistry**

Go to **go.hrw.com** for a full-length article on the history of atomic theory and transmutation.

**Keyword: HC6ATMX**

## Foundations of Atomic Theory

Virtually all chemists in the late 1700s accepted the modern definition of an element as a substance that cannot be further broken down by ordinary chemical means. It was also clear that elements combine to form compounds that have different physical and chemical properties than those of the elements that form them. There was great controversy, however, as to whether elements always combine in the same ratio when forming a particular compound.

The transformation of a substance or substances into one or more new substances is known as a *chemical reaction*. In the 1790s, the study of matter was revolutionized by a new emphasis on the quantitative

**FIGURE 1** Each of the salt crystals shown here contains exactly 39.34% sodium and 60.66% chlorine by mass.

analysis of chemical reactions. Aided by improved balances, investigators began to accurately measure the masses of the elements and compounds they were studying. This led to the discovery of several basic laws. One of these laws was the **law of conservation of mass,** *which states that mass is neither created nor destroyed during ordinary chemical reactions or physical changes.* This discovery was soon followed by the assertion that, regardless of where or how a pure chemical compound is prepared, it is composed of a fixed proportion of elements. For example, sodium chloride, also known as ordinary table salt, *always* consists of 39.34% by mass of the element sodium, Na, and 60.66% by mass of the element chlorine, Cl. *The fact that a chemical compound contains the same elements in exactly the same proportions by mass regardless of the size of the sample or source of the compound is known as the* **law of definite proportions.**

It was also known that two elements sometimes combine to form more than one compound. For example, the elements carbon and oxygen form two compounds, carbon dioxide and carbon monoxide. Consider samples of each of these compounds, each containing 1.00 g of carbon. In carbon dioxide, 2.66 g of oxygen combine with 1.00 g of carbon. In carbon monoxide, 1.33 g of oxygen combine with 1.00 g of carbon. The ratio of the masses of oxygen in these two compounds is 2.66 to 1.33, or 2 to 1. This illustrates the **law of multiple proportions:** *If two or more different compounds are composed of the same two elements, then the ratio of the masses of the second element combined with a certain mass of the first element is always a ratio of small whole numbers.*

## Dalton's Atomic Theory

In 1808, an English schoolteacher named John Dalton proposed an explanation for the law of conservation of mass, the law of definite proportions, and the law of multiple proportions. He reasoned that elements were composed of atoms and that only whole numbers of atoms can combine to form compounds. His theory can be summed up by the following statements.

1. All matter is composed of extremely small particles called atoms.
2. Atoms of a given element are identical in size, mass, and other properties; atoms of different elements differ in size, mass, and other properties.
3. Atoms cannot be subdivided, created, or destroyed.
4. Atoms of different elements combine in simple whole-number ratios to form chemical compounds.
5. In chemical reactions, atoms are combined, separated, or rearranged.

According to Dalton's atomic theory, the law of conservation of mass is explained by the fact that chemical reactions involve merely the combination, separation, or rearrangement of atoms and that during these processes atoms are not subdivided, created, or destroyed. This

(a)

Carbon, C
Mass x

Oxygen, O
Mass y

Carbon monoxide, CO
Mass x + Mass y

(b)

Carbon monoxide, CO
Mass x + Mass y

Carbon, C
Mass x

Oxygen, O
Mass y

**FIGURE 2** (a) An atom of carbon, C, and an atom of oxygen, O, can combine chemically to form a molecule of carbon monoxide, CO. The mass of the CO molecule is equal to the mass of the C atom plus the mass of the O atom. (b) The reverse holds true in a reaction in which a CO molecule is broken down into its elements.

idea is illustrated in **Figure 2** for the formation of carbon monoxide from carbon and oxygen.

The law of definite proportions, on the other hand, results from the fact that a given chemical compound is always composed of the same combination of atoms (see **Figure 3**). As for the law of multiple proportions, in the case of the carbon oxides, the 2-to-1 ratio of oxygen masses results because carbon dioxide always contains twice as many atoms of oxygen (per atom of carbon) as does carbon monoxide. This can also be seen in **Figure 3.**

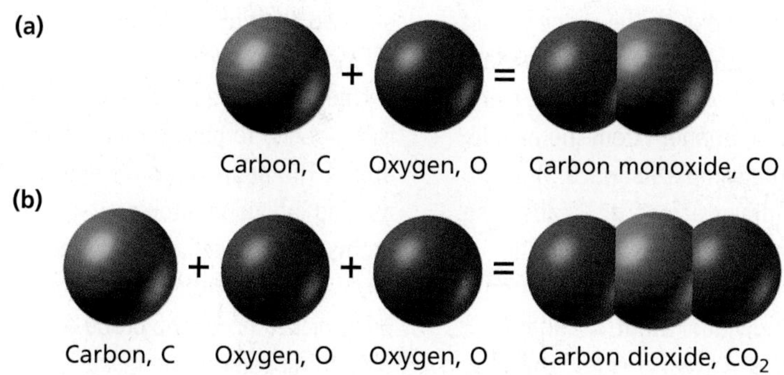


**FIGURE 3** (a) CO molecules are always composed of one C atom and one O atom. (b) $CO_2$ molecules are always composed of one C atom and two O atoms. Note that a molecule of carbon dioxide contains twice as many oxygen atoms as does a molecule of carbon monoxide.

## Modern Atomic Theory

By relating atoms to the measurable property of mass, Dalton turned Democritus's *idea* into a *scientific theory* that could be tested by experiment. But not all aspects of Dalton's atomic theory have proven to be correct. For example, today we know that atoms are divisible into even smaller particles (although the law of conservation of mass still holds true for chemical reactions). And, as you will see in Section 3, we know that a given element can have atoms with different masses. Atomic theory has not been discarded, however. Instead, it has been modified to explain the new observations. The important concepts that (1) all matter is composed of atoms and that (2) atoms of any one element differ in properties from atoms of another element remain unchanged.

# CAREERS in Chemistry

## Physical Chemist

Physical chemists focus on understanding the physical properties of atoms and molecules. They are driven by a curiosity of what makes things work at the level of atoms, and they enjoy being challenged. In addition to chemistry, they study mathematics and physics extensively. Laboratory courses involving experience with electronics and optics are typically part of their training. Often, they enjoy working with instruments and computers. Physical chemists can be experimentalists or theoreticians. They use sophisticated instruments to make measurements, or high-powered computers to perform intensive calculations. The instruments used include lasers, electron microscopes, nuclear magnetic resonance spectrometers, mass spectrometers, and particle accelerators. Physical chemists work in industry, government laboratories, research institutes, and academic institutions. Because physical chemists work on a wide range of problems, taking courses in other science disciplines is important.

### Scanning Tunneling Microscopy

For years, scientists have yearned for the ability to "see" individual atoms. Because atoms are so small, this had been nothing more than a dream. Now, the scanning tunneling microscope, STM, gives scientists the ability to look at individual atoms. It was invented in 1981 by Gerd Binnig and Heinrich Rohrer, scientists working for IBM in Zurich, Switzerland. They shared the 1986 Nobel Prize in physics for their discovery.

▲ *This STM image shows a "corral" of iron atoms on a copper surface.*

The basic principle of STM is based on the current that exists between a metallic needle that is sharpened to a single atom, the probe, and a conducting sample. As the probe passes above the surface of the sample at a distance of one or two atoms, electrons can "tunnel" from the needle tip to the sample's surface. The probe moves across, or "scans," the surface of the sample. When the probe comes close to the electrons of an individual atom, a signal is produced. A weaker signal is produced between atoms. These signals build a topographical (hill and valley) "map" of conducting and nonconducting regions. The resulting map shows the position and spacing of atoms.

Surface chemistry is a developing subdiscipline in physical chemistry, and STM is an important tool in the field. Scientists use STM to study surface reactions, such as those that take place in catalytic converters. Other areas of research in which STM is useful include semiconductors and microelectronics. Usually, STM is used with materials that conduct, but it has also been used to study biological molecules, such as DNA.

One innovative application of STM is the ability to position individual atoms. The figure shows the result of moving individual atoms. First, iron atoms were placed on a copper surface. Then, individual iron atoms were picked up by the probe and placed in position. The result is a "quantum corral" of 48 iron atoms on the surface of copper. The diameter of the corral is about 14 nm.

### Questions

1. In addition to chemistry, what kinds of courses are important for a student interested in a physical chemistry career?
2. What part of an atom is detected by STM?

# QuickLAB  Wear safety goggles and an apron.

## Constructing a Model

### Question

**How can you construct a model of an unknown object by (1) making inferences about an object that is in a closed container and (2) touching the object without seeing it?**

### Procedure

Record all of your results in a data table.

1. Your teacher will provide you with a can that is covered by a sock sealed with tape. Without unsealing the container, try to determine the number of objects inside the can as well as the mass, shape, size, composition, and texture of each. To do this, you may carefully tilt or shake the can. Record your observations in a data table.
2. Remove the tape from the top of the sock. Do *not* look inside the can. Put one hand through the opening, and make the same observations as in step 1 by handling the objects. To make more-accurate estimations, practice estimating the sizes and masses of some known objects outside the can. Then compare your estimates of these objects with actual measurements using a metric ruler and a balance.

### Discussion

1. Scientists often use more than one method to gather data. How was this illustrated in the investigation?
2. Of the observations you made, which were qualitative and which were quantitative?
3. Using the data you gathered, draw a model of the unknown object(s) and write a brief summary of your conclusions.

### Materials

- can covered by a sock sealed with tape
- one or more objects that fit in the container
- metric ruler
- balance

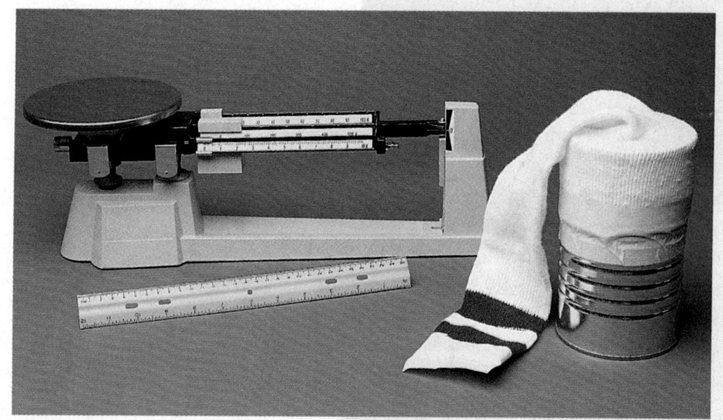

## SECTION REVIEW

1. List the five main points of Dalton's atomic theory.
2. What chemical laws can be explained by Dalton's theory?

### Critical Thinking

3. **ANALYZING INFORMATION** Three compounds containing potassium and oxygen are compared. Analysis shows that for each 1.00 g of O, the compounds have 1.22 g, 2.44 g, and 4.89 g of K, respectively. Show how these data support the law of multiple proportions.

SECTION 2

# The Structure of the Atom

## OBJECTIVES

- Summarize the observed properties of cathode rays that led to the discovery of the electron.
- Summarize the experiment carried out by Rutherford and his co-workers that led to the discovery of the nucleus.
- List the properties of protons, neutrons, and electrons.
- Define *atom.*

 **C.2.2** Summarize atomic properties (including electron configuration, ionization energy, electron affinity, atomic size, and ionic size)

Although John Dalton thought atoms were indivisible, investigators in the late 1800s proved otherwise. As scientific advances allowed a deeper exploration of matter, it became clear that atoms are actually composed of several basic types of smaller particles and that the number and arrangement of these particles within an atom determine that atom's chemical properties. Today we define an **atom** *as the smallest particle of an element that retains the chemical properties of that element.*

All atoms consist of two regions. The *nucleus* is a very small region located at the center of an atom. In every atom, the nucleus is made up of at least one positively charged particle called a *proton* and usually one or more neutral particles called *neutrons.* Surrounding the nucleus is a region occupied by negatively charged particles called *electrons.* This region is very large compared with the size of the nucleus. Protons, neutrons, and electrons are often referred to as *subatomic particles.*

## Discovery of the Electron

The first discovery of a subatomic particle resulted from investigations into the relationship between electricity and matter. In the late 1800s, many experiments were performed in which electric current was passed through various gases at low pressures. (Gases at atmospheric pressure don't conduct electricity well.) These experiments were carried out in glass tubes like the one shown in **Figure 4.** Such tubes are known as *cathode-ray tubes.*

**FIGURE 4** A simple cathode-ray tube. Particles pass through the tube from the *cathode,* the metal disk connected to the negative terminal of the voltage source, to the *anode,* the metal disk connected to the positive terminal.

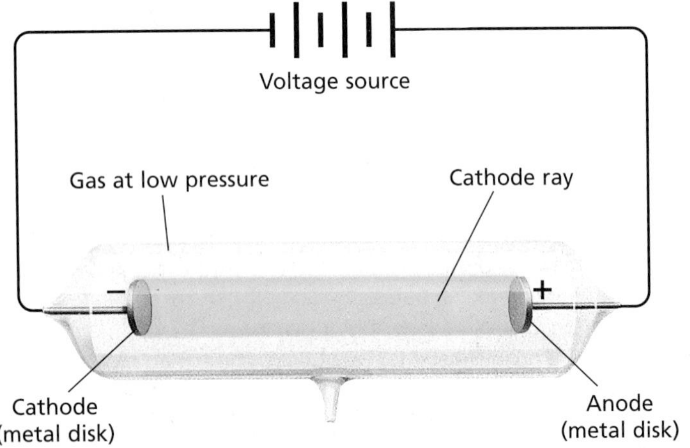


### Cathode Rays and Electrons

Investigators noticed that when current was passed through a cathode-ray tube, the surface of the tube directly opposite the cathode glowed. They hypothesized that the glow was caused by a stream of particles, which they called a cathode ray. The ray traveled from the cathode to the anode when current was passed through the tube. Experiments devised to test this hypothesis revealed the following observations.

1. Cathode rays were deflected by a magnetic field in the same manner as a wire carrying electric current, which was known to have a negative charge (see **Figure 5**).
2. The rays were deflected away from a negatively charged object.

These observations led to the hypothesis that the particles that compose cathode rays are negatively charged. This hypothesis was strongly supported by a series of experiments carried out in 1897 by the English physicist Joseph John Thomson. In one investigation, he was able to measure the ratio of the charge of cathode-ray particles to their mass. He found that this ratio was always the same, regardless of the metal used to make the cathode or the nature of the gas inside the cathode-ray tube. Thomson concluded that all cathode rays are composed of identical negatively charged particles, which were named electrons.

**FIGURE 5** A magnet near the cathode-ray tube causes the beam to be deflected. The deflection indicates that the particles in the beam have a negative charge.

## Charge and Mass of the Electron

Cathode rays have identical properties regardless of the element used to produce them. Therefore it was concluded that electrons are present in atoms of all elements. Thus, cathode-ray experiments provided evidence that atoms are divisible and that one of the atom's basic constituents is the negatively charged electron. Thomson's experiment also revealed that the electron has a very large charge-to-mass ratio. In 1909, experiments conducted by the American physicist Robert A. Millikan measured the charge of the electron. Scientists used this information and the charge-to-mass ratio of the electron to determine that the mass of the electron is about one two-thousandth the mass of the simplest type of hydrogen atom, which is the smallest atom known. More-accurate experiments conducted since then indicate that the electron has a mass of $9.109 \times 10^{-31}$ kg, or 1/1837 the mass of the simplest type of hydrogen atom.

Based on what was learned about electrons, two other inferences were made about atomic structure.

1. Because atoms are electrically neutral, they must contain a positive charge to balance the negative electrons.
2. Because electrons have so much less mass than atoms, atoms must contain other particles that account for most of their mass.

Thomson proposed a model for the atom that is called the *plum pudding model* (after the English dessert). He believed that the negative electrons were spread evenly throughout the positive charge of the rest of the atom. This arrangement is similar to that of seeds in a watermelon: the seeds are spread throughout the fruit but do not contribute much to the overall mass. However, shortly thereafter, new experiments disproved this model.

## Discovery of the Atomic Nucleus

More detail of the atom's structure was provided in 1911 by New Zealander Ernest Rutherford and his associates Hans Geiger and Ernest Marsden. The scientists bombarded a thin piece of gold foil with fast-moving *alpha particles,* which are positively charged particles with about four times the mass of a hydrogen atom. Geiger and Marsden assumed that mass and charge were uniformly distributed throughout the atoms of the gold foil. They expected the alpha particles to pass through with only a slight deflection, and for the vast majority of the particles, this was the case. However, when the scientists checked for the possibility of wide-angle deflections, they were shocked to find that roughly 1 in 8000 of the alpha particles had actually been deflected back toward the source (see **Figure 6**). As Rutherford later exclaimed, it was "as if you had fired a 15-inch [artillery] shell at a piece of tissue paper and it came back and hit you."

After thinking about the startling result for a few months, Rutherford finally came up with an explanation. He reasoned that the deflected alpha particles must have experienced some powerful force within the atom. And he figured that the source of this force must occupy a very small amount of space because so few of the total number of alpha particles had been affected by it. He concluded that the force must be caused by a very densely packed bundle of matter with a positive electric charge. Rutherford called this positive bundle of matter the nucleus (see **Figure 7**).

Rutherford had discovered that the volume of a nucleus was very small compared with the total volume of an atom. In fact, if the nucleus were the size of a marble, then the size of the atom would be about the size of a football field. But where were the electrons? This question was not answered until Rutherford's student, Niels Bohr, proposed a model in which electrons surrounded the positively charged nucleus as the planets surround the sun. Bohr's model will be discussed in Chapter 4.

**FIGURE 6** (a) Geiger and Marsden bombarded a thin piece of gold foil with a narrow beam of alpha particles. (b) Some of the particles were deflected by the gold foil back toward their source.

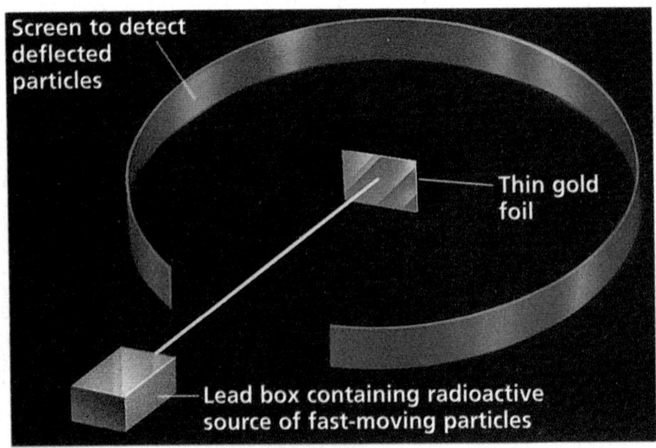


(a)

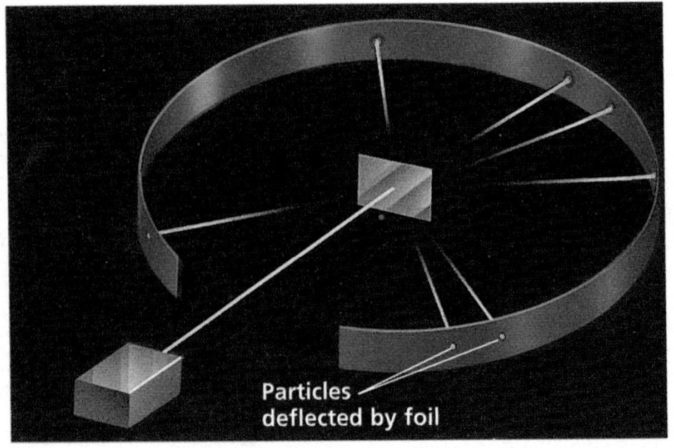


(b)

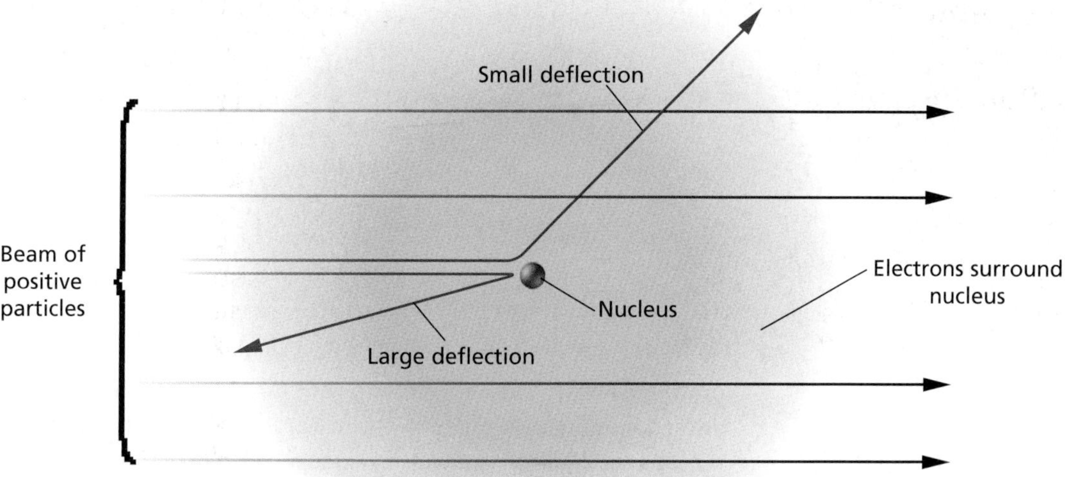


**FIGURE 7** Rutherford reasoned that each atom in the gold foil contained a small, dense, positively charged nucleus surrounded by electrons. A small number of the alpha particles directed toward the foil were deflected by the tiny nucleus (red arrows). Most of the particles passed through undisturbed (black arrows).

## Composition of the Atomic Nucleus

Except for the nucleus of the simplest type of hydrogen atom (discussed in the next section), all atomic nuclei are made of two kinds of particles, protons and neutrons. A proton has a positive charge equal in magnitude to the negative charge of an electron. Atoms are electrically neutral because they contain equal numbers of protons and electrons. A neutron is electrically neutral.

The simplest hydrogen atom consists of a single-proton nucleus with a single electron moving about it. A proton has a mass of $1.673 \times 10^{-27}$ kg, which is 1836 times greater than the mass of an electron and 1836/1837, or virtually all, of the mass of the simplest hydrogen atom. All atoms besides the simplest hydrogen atom also have neutrons. The mass of a neutron is $1.675 \times 10^{-27}$ kg—slightly larger than that of a proton.

The nuclei of atoms of different elements differ in their number of protons and therefore in the amount of positive charge they possess. Thus, the number of protons determines that atom's identity. Physicists have identified other subatomic particles, but particles other than electrons, protons, and neutrons have little effect on the chemical properties of matter. **Table 1** on the next page summarizes the properties of electrons, protons, and neutrons.

### Forces in the Nucleus

Generally, particles that have the same electric charge repel one another. Therefore, we would expect a nucleus with more than one proton to be unstable. However, when two protons are extremely close to each other, there is a strong attraction between them. In fact, as many as 83

**TABLE 1 *Properties of Subatomic Particles***

| Particle | Symbols | Relative electric charge | Mass number | Relative mass (amu*) | Actual mass (kg) |
|---|---|---|---|---|---|
| Electron | $e^-, {}^{0}_{-1}e$ | −1 | 0 | 0.000 5486 | $9.109 \times 10^{-31}$ |
| Proton | $p^+, {}^{1}_{1}\mathrm{H}$ | +1 | 1 | 1.007 276 | $1.673 \times 10^{-27}$ |
| Neutron | $n^\circ, {}^{1}_{0}n$ | 0 | 1 | 1.008 665 | $1.675 \times 10^{-27}$ |

*1 amu (atomic mass unit) = $1.660\,540 \times 10^{-27}$ kg

protons can exist close together to help form a stable nucleus. A similar attraction exists when neutrons are very close to each other or when protons and neutrons are very close together. *These short-range proton-neutron, proton-proton, and neutron-neutron forces hold the nuclear particles together and are referred to as* **nuclear forces.**

## The Sizes of Atoms

It is convenient to think of the region occupied by the electrons as an electron cloud—a cloud of negative charge. The radius of an atom is the distance from the center of the nucleus to the outer portion of this electron cloud. Because atomic radii are so small, they are expressed using a unit that is more convenient for the sizes of atoms. This unit is the picometer. The abbreviation for the picometer is pm (1 pm = $10^{-12}$ m = $10^{-10}$ cm). To get an idea of how small a picometer is, consider that 1 cm is the same fractional part of $10^3$ km (about 600 mi) as 100 pm is of 1 cm. Atomic radii range from about 40 to 270 pm. By contrast, the nuclei of atoms have much smaller radii, about 0.001 pm. Nuclei also have incredibly high densities, about $2 \times 10^8$ metric tons/cm$^3$.

## SECTION REVIEW

1. Define each of the following:

   **a.** atom **b.** electron **c.** nucleus **d.** proton **e.** neutron

2. Describe one conclusion made by each of the following scientists that led to the development of the current atomic theory:

   **a.** Thomson **b.** Millikan **c.** Rutherford

3. Compare the three subatomic particles in terms of location in the atom, mass, and relative charge.

4. Why is the cathode-ray tube in **Figure 4** connected to a vacuum pump?

**Critical Thinking**

5. **EVALUATING IDEAS** Nuclear forces are said to hold protons and neutrons together. What is it about the composition of the nucleus that requires the concept of nuclear forces?

SECTION 3

# Counting Atoms

**C.4.4** Apply the concept of moles to determine the number of particles of a substance in a chemical reaction, the percent composition of a representative compound, the mass proportions, and the mole-mass relationships

Consider neon, Ne, the gas used in many illuminated signs. Neon is a minor component of the atmosphere. In fact, dry air contains only about 0.002% neon. And yet there are about $5 \times 10^{17}$ atoms of neon present in each breath you inhale. In most experiments, atoms are much too small to be measured individually. Chemists can analyze atoms quantitatively, however, by knowing fundamental properties of the atoms of each element. In this section, you will be introduced to some of the basic properties of atoms. You will then discover how to use this information to count the number of atoms of an element in a sample with a known mass. You will also become familiar with the *mole,* a special unit used by chemists to express amounts of particles, such as atoms and molecules.

### OBJECTIVES

- Explain what isotopes are.
- Define *atomic number* and *mass number,* and describe how they apply to isotopes.
- Given the identity of a nuclide, determine its number of protons, neutrons, and electrons.
- Define *mole, Avogadro's number,* and *molar mass,* and state how all three are related.
- Solve problems involving mass in grams, amount in moles, and number of atoms of an element.

## Atomic Number

All atoms are composed of the same basic particles. Yet all atoms are not the same. Atoms of different elements have different numbers of protons. Atoms of the same element all have the same number of protons. *The* **atomic number** *(Z) of an element is the number of protons of each atom of that element.*

Turn to the inside back cover of this textbook. In the periodic table shown, an element's atomic number is indicated above its symbol. Notice that the elements are placed in order of increasing atomic number. At the top left of the table is hydrogen, H, which has atomic number 1. All atoms of the element hydrogen have one proton. Next in order is helium, He, which has two protons. Lithium, Li, has three protons (see **Figure 8**); beryllium, Be, has four protons; and so on.

The atomic number identifies an element. If you want to know which element has atomic number 47, for example, look at the periodic table. You can see that the element is silver, Ag. All silver atoms have 47 protons. Because atoms are neutral, we know from the atomic number that all silver atoms must also have 47 electrons.

3
Li
Lithium
6.941
[He]$2s^1$

**FIGURE 8** The atomic number in this periodic table entry reveals that an atom of lithium has three protons in its nucleus.

## Isotopes

The simplest atoms are those of hydrogen. All hydrogen atoms have only one proton. However, like many naturally occurring elements, hydrogen atoms can have different numbers of neutrons.

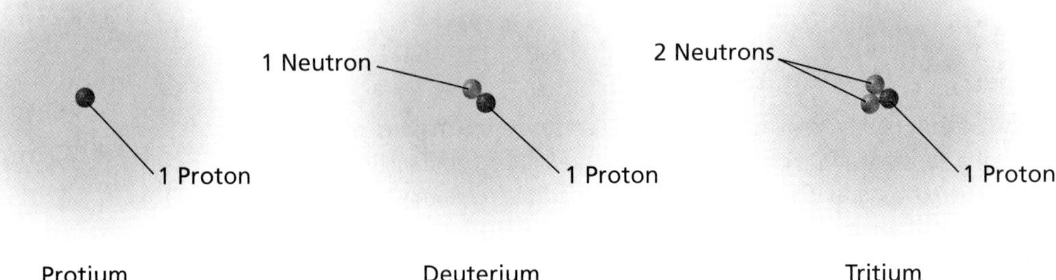


**FIGURE 9** The nuclei of different isotopes of the same element have the same number of protons but different numbers of neutrons. This is illustrated above by the three isotopes of hydrogen.

Three types of hydrogen atoms are known. The most common type of hydrogen is sometimes called *protium.* It accounts for 99.9885% of the hydrogen atoms found on Earth. The nucleus of a protium atom consists of one proton only, and it has one electron moving about it. There are two other known forms of hydrogen. One is called *deuterium,* which accounts for 0.0115% of Earth's hydrogen atoms. Each deuterium atom has a nucleus with one proton and one neutron. The third form of hydrogen is known as *tritium,* which is radioactive. It exists in very small amounts in nature, but it can be prepared artificially. Each tritium atom has one proton, two neutrons, and one electron.

Protium, deuterium, and tritium are isotopes of hydrogen. **Isotopes** *are atoms of the same element that have different masses.* The isotopes of a particular element all have the same number of protons and electrons but different numbers of neutrons. In all three isotopes of hydrogen, the positive charge of the single proton is balanced by the negative charge of the electron. Most of the elements consist of mixtures of isotopes. Tin has 10 stable isotopes, for example, the most of any element.

## Mass Number

Identifying an isotope requires knowing both the name or atomic number of the element and the mass of the isotope. *The* **mass number** *is the total number of protons and neutrons that make up the nucleus of an isotope.* The three isotopes of hydrogen described earlier have mass numbers 1, 2, and 3, as shown in **Table 2.**

**TABLE 2** ***Mass Numbers of Hydrogen Isotopes***

| | Atomic number (number of protons) | Number of neutrons | Mass number (protons + neutrons) |
|---|---|---|---|
| Protium | 1 | 0 | 1 + 0 = 1 |
| Deuterium | 1 | 1 | 1 + 1 = 2 |
| Tritium | 1 | 2 | 1 + 2 = 3 |

## Designating Isotopes

SCILINKS.
www.scilinks.org
Topic: Isotopes
Code: HC60820

The isotopes of hydrogen are unusual in that they have distinct names. Isotopes are usually identified by specifying their mass number. There are two methods for specifying isotopes. In the first method, the mass number is written with a hyphen after the name of the element. Tritium, for example, is written as hydrogen-3. We will refer to this method as *hyphen notation.* The uranium isotope used as fuel for nuclear power plants has a mass number of 235 and is therefore known as uranium-235. The second method shows the composition of a nucleus using the isotope's *nuclear symbol.* For example, uranium-235 is written as $^{235}_{92}U$. The superscript indicates the mass number (protons + neutrons) and the subscript indicates the atomic number (number of protons). The number of neutrons is found by subtracting the atomic number from the mass number.

mass number − atomic number = number of neutrons
235 (protons + neutrons) − 92 protons = 143 neutrons

Thus, a uranium-235 nucleus is made up of 92 protons and 143 neutrons.

**Table 3** gives the names, symbols, and compositions of the isotopes of hydrogen and helium. **Nuclide** *is a general term for a specific isotope of an element.* We could say that **Table 3** lists the compositions of five different nuclides, three hydrogen nuclides and two helium nuclides.

**TABLE 3 Isotopes of Hydrogen and Helium**

| Isotope | Nuclear symbol | Number of protons | Number of electrons | Number of neutrons |
|---|---|---|---|---|
| Hydrogen-1 (protium) | $^{1}_{1}H$ | 1 | 1 | 0 |
| Hydrogen-2 (deuterium) | $^{2}_{1}H$ | 1 | 1 | 1 |
| Hydrogen-3 (tritium) | $^{3}_{1}H$ | 1 | 1 | 2 |
| Helium-3 | $^{3}_{2}He$ | 2 | 2 | 1 |
| Helium-4 | $^{4}_{2}He$ | 2 | 2 | 2 |

### SAMPLE PROBLEM A

**How many protons, electrons, and neutrons are there in an atom of chlorine-37?**

**SOLUTION**

**1** *ANALYZE* **Given:** name and mass number of chlorine-37
**Unknown:** numbers of protons, electrons, and neutrons

**2** *PLAN* atomic number = number of protons = number of electrons
mass number = number of neutrons + number of protons

**3 COMPUTE** The mass number of chlorine-37 is 37. Consulting the periodic table reveals that chlorine's atomic number is 17. The number of neutrons can be found by subtracting the atomic number from the mass number.

mass number of chlorine-37 – atomic number of chlorine =
number of neutrons in chlorine-37

mass number – atomic number = 37 (protons plus neutrons) – 17 protons
= 20 neutrons

An atom of chlorine-37 is made up of 17 electrons, 17 protons, and 20 neutrons.

**4 EVALUATE** The number of protons in a neutral atom equals the number of electrons. And the sum of the protons and neutrons equals the given mass number.

**PRACTICE** *Answers in Appendix E*

1. How many protons, electrons, and neutrons make up an atom of bromine-80?
2. Write the nuclear symbol for carbon-13.
3. Write the hyphen notation for the isotope with 15 electrons and 15 neutrons.

Go to **go.hrw.com** for more practice problems that ask you to work with numbers of subatomic particles.

**Keyword: HC6ATMX**

## Relative Atomic Masses

Masses of atoms expressed in grams are very small. As we shall see, an atom of oxygen-16, for example, has a mass of $2.656 \times 10^{-23}$ g. For most chemical calculations it is more convenient to use *relative* atomic masses. As you read in Chapter 2, scientists use standards of measurement that are constant and are the same everywhere. In order to set up a relative scale of atomic mass, one atom has been arbitrarily chosen as the standard and assigned a mass value. The masses of all other atoms are expressed in relation to this defined standard.

The standard used by scientists to compare units of atomic mass is the carbon-12 atom. It has been arbitrarily assigned a mass of exactly 12 atomic mass units, or 12 amu. *One* **atomic mass unit,** *or 1 amu, is exactly 1/12 the mass of a carbon-12 atom.* The atomic mass of any other atom is determined by comparing it with the mass of the carbon-12 atom. The hydrogen-1 atom has an atomic mass of *about* 1/12 that of the carbon-12 atom, or about 1 amu. The precise value of the atomic mass of a hydrogen-1 atom is 1.007 825 amu. An oxygen-16 atom has about 16/12 (or 4/3) the mass of a carbon-12 atom. Careful measurements show the atomic mass of oxygen-16 to be 15.994 915 amu. The mass of a magnesium-24 atom is found to be slightly less than twice that of a carbon-12 atom. Its atomic mass is 23.985 042 amu.

Some additional examples of the atomic masses of the naturally occurring isotopes of several elements are given in **Table 4** on the next page. Isotopes of an element may occur naturally, or they may be made in the laboratory (*artificial isotopes*). *Although isotopes have different masses, they do not differ significantly in their chemical behavior.*

The masses of subatomic particles can also be expressed on the atomic mass scale (see **Table 1**). The mass of the electron is 0.000 5486 amu, that of the proton is 1.007 276 amu, and that of the neutron is 1.008 665 amu. Note that the proton and neutron masses are close to but not equal to 1 amu. You have learned that the mass number is the total number of protons and neutrons that make up the nucleus of an atom. You can now see that the mass number and relative atomic mass of a given nuclide are quite close to each other. They are not identical because the proton and neutron masses deviate slightly from 1 amu and the atomic masses include electrons. Also, as you will read in Chapter 21, a small amount of mass is changed to energy in the creation of a nucleus from its protons and neutrons.

## HISTORICAL CHEMISTRY

### Discovery of Element 43

The discovery of element 43, technetium, is credited to Carlo Perrier and Emilio Segrè, who artificially produced it in 1937. However, in 1925, a German chemist named Ida Tacke reported the discovery of element 43, which she called masurium, in niobium ores. At the time, her discovery was not accepted because it was thought technetium could not occur naturally. Recent studies confirm that Tacke and coworkers probably did discover element 43.

## Average Atomic Masses of Elements

Most elements occur naturally as mixtures of isotopes, as indicated in **Table 4.** The percentage of each isotope in the naturally occurring element on Earth is nearly always the same, no matter where the element is found. The percentage at which each of an element's isotopes occurs in nature is taken into account when calculating the element's average atomic mass. **Average atomic mass** *is the weighted average of the atomic masses of the naturally occurring isotopes of an element.*

The following is a simple example of how to calculate a *weighted average.* Suppose you have a box containing two sizes of marbles. If 25% of the marbles have masses of 2.00 g each and 75% have masses of 3.00 g each, how is the weighted average calculated? You could count the number of each type of marble, calculate the total mass of the mixture, and divide by the total number of marbles. If you had 100 marbles, the calculations would be as follows.

$$25 \text{ marbles} \times 2.00 \text{ g} = 50 \text{ g}$$
$$75 \text{ marbles} \times 3.00 \text{ g} = 225 \text{ g}$$

Adding these masses gives the total mass of the marbles.

$$50 \text{ g} + 225 \text{ g} = 275 \text{ g}$$

Dividing the total mass by 100 gives an average marble mass of 2.75 g.

A simpler method is to multiply the mass of each marble by the decimal fraction representing its percentage in the mixture. Then add the products.

$$25\% = 0.25 \qquad 75\% = 0.75$$
$$(2.00 \text{ g} \times 0.25) + (3.00 \text{ g} \times 0.75) = 2.75 \text{ g}$$

**TABLE 4 Atomic Masses and Abundances of Several Naturally Occurring Isotopes**

| Isotope | Mass number | Percentage natural abundance | Atomic mass (amu) | Average atomic mass of element (amu) |
|---|---|---|---|---|
| Hydrogen-1 | 1 | 99.9885 | 1.007 825 | 1.007 94 |
| Hydrogen-2 | 2 | 0.0115 | 2.014 102 | |
| Carbon-12 | 12 | 98.93 | 12 (by definition) | 12.0107 |
| Carbon-13 | 13 | 1.07 | 13.003 355 | |
| Oxygen-16 | 16 | 99.757 | 15.994 915 | 15.9994 |
| Oxygen-17 | 17 | 0.038 | 16.999 132 | |
| Oxygen-18 | 18 | 0.205 | 17.999 160 | |
| Copper-63 | 63 | 69.15 | 62.929 601 | 63.546 |
| Copper-65 | 65 | 30.85 | 64.927 794 | |
| Cesium-133 | 133 | 100 | 132.905 447 | 132.905 |
| Uranium-234 | 234 | 0.0054 | 234.040 945 | 238.029 |
| Uranium-235 | 235 | 0.7204 | 235.043 922 | |
| Uranium-238 | 238 | 99.2742 | 238.050 784 | |

### Calculating Average Atomic Mass

The average atomic mass of an element depends on both the mass and the relative abundance of each of the element's isotopes. For example, naturally occurring copper consists of 69.15% copper-63, which has an atomic mass of 62.929 601 amu, and 30.85% copper-65, which has an atomic mass of 64.927 794 amu. The average atomic mass of copper can be calculated by multiplying the atomic mass of each isotope by its relative abundance (expressed in decimal form) and adding the results.

$$0.6915 \times 62.929\ 601 \text{ amu} + 0.3085 \times 64.927\ 794 \text{ amu} = 63.55 \text{ amu}$$

The calculated average atomic mass of naturally occurring copper is 63.55 amu.

The average atomic mass is included for the elements listed in **Table 4.** As illustrated in the table, most atomic masses are known to four or more significant figures. *In this book, an element's atomic mass is usually rounded to two decimal places before it is used in a calculation.*

## Relating Mass to Numbers of Atoms

The relative atomic mass scale makes it possible to know how many atoms of an element are present in a sample of the element with a measurable mass. Three very important concepts—the mole, Avogadro's number, and molar mass—provide the basis for relating masses in grams to numbers of atoms.

## The Mole

The mole is the SI unit for amount of substance. *A* **mole** *(abbreviated* mol*) is the amount of a substance that contains as many particles as there are atoms in exactly 12 g of carbon-12.* The mole is a counting unit, just like a dozen is. We don't usually order 12 or 24 ears of corn; we order one dozen or two dozen. Similarly, a chemist may want 1 mol of carbon, or 2 mol of iron, or 2.567 mol of calcium. In the sections that follow, you will see how the mole relates to masses of atoms and compounds.

## Avogadro's Number

The number of particles in a mole has been experimentally determined in a number of ways. The best modern value is $6.022\ 141\ 79 \times 10^{23}$. This means that exactly 12 g of carbon-12 contains $6.022\ 141\ 79 \times 10^{23}$ carbon-12 atoms. The number of particles in a mole is known as Avogadro's number, named for the nineteenth-century Italian scientist Amedeo Avogadro, whose ideas were crucial in explaining the relationship between mass and numbers of atoms. **Avogadro's number**—*$6.022\ 141\ 79 \times 10^{23}$—is the number of particles in exactly one mole of a pure substance.* For most purposes, Avogadro's number is rounded to $6.022 \times 10^{23}$.

To get a sense of how large Avogadro's number is, consider the following: If every person living on Earth (6 billion people) worked to count the atoms in one mole of an element, and if each person counted continuously at a rate of one atom per second, it would take about 3 million years for all the atoms to be counted.

## Molar Mass

An alternative definition of *mole* is the amount of a substance that contains Avogadro's number of particles. Can you figure out the approximate mass of one mole of helium atoms? You know that a mole of carbon-12 atoms has a mass of exactly 12 g and that a carbon-12 atom has an atomic mass of 12 amu. The atomic mass of a helium atom is 4.00 amu, which is about one-third the mass of a carbon-12 atom. It follows that a mole of helium atoms will have about one-third the mass of a mole of carbon-12 atoms. Thus, one mole of helium has a mass of about 4.00 g.

*The mass of one mole of a pure substance is called the* **molar mass** *of that substance.* Molar mass is usually written in units of g/mol. The molar mass of an element is numerically equal to the atomic mass of the element in atomic mass units (which can be found in the periodic table). For example, the molar mass of lithium, Li, is 6.94 g/mol, while the molar mass of mercury, Hg, is 200.59 g/mol (rounding each value to two decimal places).

The molar mass of an element contains one mole of atoms. For example, 4.00 g of helium, 6.94 g of lithium, and 200.59 g of mercury all contain a mole of atoms. **Figure 10** shows molar masses of three common elements.

(a)

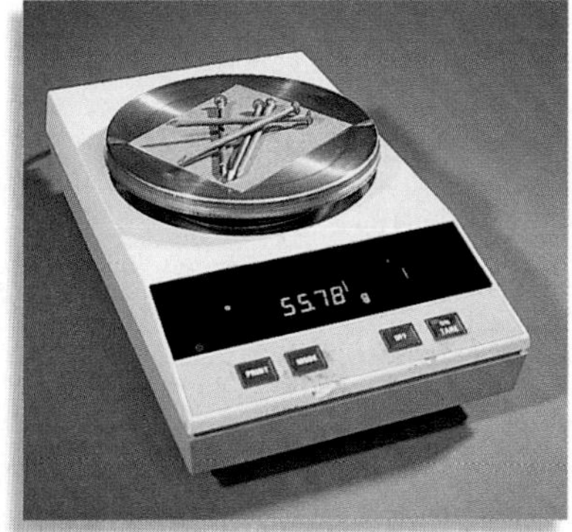

(b)

(c)

**FIGURE 10** Shown is approximately one molar mass of each of three elements: (a) carbon (graphite), (b) iron (nails), and (c) copper (wire).

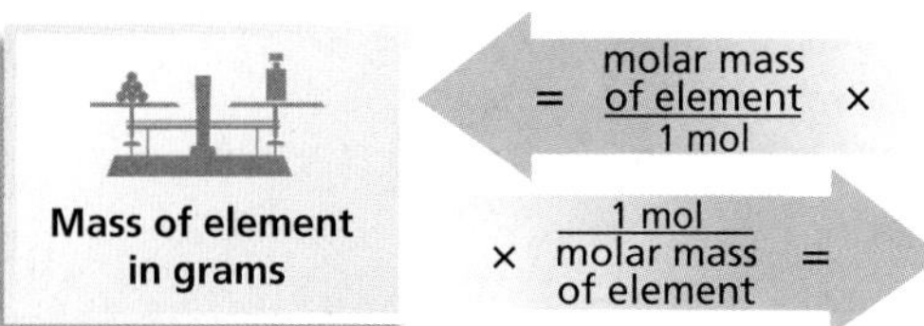

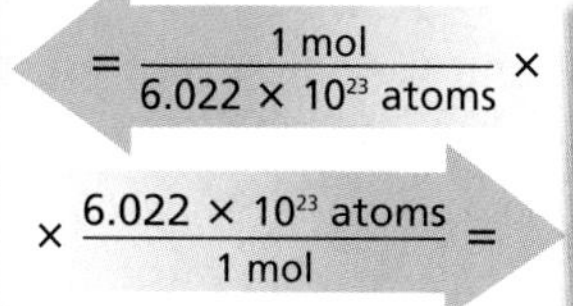

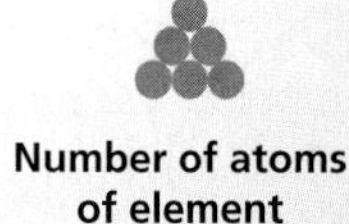


**FIGURE 11** The diagram shows the relationship between mass in grams, amount in moles, and number of atoms of an element in a sample.

## Gram/Mole Conversions

Chemists use molar mass as a conversion factor in chemical calculations. For example, the molar mass of helium is 4.00 g He/mol He. To find how many grams of helium there are in two moles of helium, multiply by the molar mass.

$$2.00 \cancel{\text{mol He}} \times \frac{4.00 \text{ g He}}{1 \cancel{\text{mol He}}} = 8.00 \text{ g He}$$

**Figure 11** shows how to use molar mass, moles, and Avogadro's number to relate mass in grams, amount in moles, and number of atoms of an element.

### SAMPLE PROBLEM B

*For more help, go to the* ***Math Tutor*** *at the end of this chapter.*

**What is the mass in grams of 3.50 mol of the element copper, Cu?**

**SOLUTION**

**1** *ANALYZE* **Given:** 3.50 mol Cu
**Unknown:** mass of Cu in grams

**2** *PLAN*

amount of Cu in moles ⟶ mass of Cu in grams

According to **Figure 11,** the mass of an element in grams can be calculated by multiplying the amount of the element in moles by the element's molar mass.

$$\text{moles Cu} \times \frac{\text{grams Cu}}{\text{moles Cu}} = \text{grams Cu}$$

**3** *COMPUTE* The molar mass of copper from the periodic table is rounded to 63.55 g/mol.

$$3.50 \cancel{\text{mol Cu}} \times \frac{63.55 \text{ g Cu}}{1 \cancel{\text{mol Cu}}} = 222 \text{ g Cu}$$

**4** *EVALUATE* Because the amount of copper in moles was given to three significant figures, the answer was rounded to three significant figures. The size of the answer is reasonable because it is somewhat more than 3.5 times 60.

**PRACTICE** *Answers in Appendix E*

1. What is the mass in grams of 2.25 mol of the element iron, Fe?
2. What is the mass in grams of 0.375 mol of the element potassium, K?
3. What is the mass in grams of 0.0135 mol of the element sodium, Na?
4. What is the mass in grams of 16.3 mol of the element nickel, Ni?

**extension**

Go to **go.hrw.com** for more practice problems that ask you to convert from amount in moles to mass.

**Keyword: HC6ATMX**

**SAMPLE PROBLEM C** *For more help, go to the* ***Math Tutor*** *at the end of this chapter.*

**A chemist produced 11.9 g of aluminum, Al. How many moles of aluminum were produced?**

**SOLUTION**

**1** ***ANALYZE*** **Given:** 11.9 g Al
**Unknown:** amount of Al in moles

**2** ***PLAN***

$$\text{mass of Al in grams} \longrightarrow \text{amount of Al in moles}$$

As shown in **Figure 11,** amount in moles can be obtained by *dividing* mass in grams by molar mass, which is mathematically the same as *multiplying* mass in grams by the *reciprocal* of molar mass.

$$\text{grams Al} \times \frac{\text{moles Al}}{\text{grams Al}} = \text{moles Al}$$

**3** ***COMPUTE*** The molar mass of aluminum from the periodic table is rounded to 26.98 g/mol.

$$11.9 \cancel{\text{ g Al}} \times \frac{1 \text{ mol Al}}{26.98 \cancel{\text{ g Al}}} = 0.441 \text{ mol Al}$$

**4** ***EVALUATE*** The answer is correctly given to three significant figures. The answer is reasonable because 11.9 g is somewhat less than half of 26.98 g.

**PRACTICE** *Answers in Appendix E*

1. How many moles of calcium, Ca, are in 5.00 g of calcium?
2. How many moles of gold, Au, are in $3.60 \times 10^{-5}$ g of gold?
3. How many moles of zinc, Zn, are in 0.535 g of zinc?

**extension**

Go to **go.hrw.com** for more practice problems that ask you to convert from mass to amount in moles.

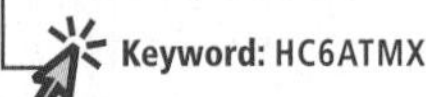

## Conversions with Avogadro's Number

**Figure 11** shows that Avogadro's number can be used to find the number of atoms of an element from the amount in moles or to find the amount of an element in moles from the number of atoms. While these types of problems are less common in chemistry than converting between amount in moles and mass in grams, they are useful in demonstrating the meaning of Avogadro's number. Note that in these calculations, Avogadro's number is expressed in units of atoms per mole.

### SAMPLE PROBLEM D

*For more help, go to the **Math Tutor** at the end of this chapter.*

**How many moles of silver, Ag, are in $3.01 \times 10^{23}$ atoms of silver?**

**SOLUTION**

**1** *ANALYZE* **Given:** $3.01 \times 10^{23}$ atoms of Ag
**Unknown:** amount of Ag in moles

**2** *PLAN*

$$\text{number of atoms of Ag} \longrightarrow \text{amount of Ag in moles}$$

From **Figure 11,** we know that number of atoms is converted to amount in moles by dividing by Avogadro's number. This is equivalent to multiplying numbers of atoms by the reciprocal of Avogadro's number.

$$\text{Ag atoms} \times \frac{\text{moles Ag}}{\text{Avogadro's number of Ag atoms}} = \text{moles Ag}$$

**3** *COMPUTE*

$$3.01 \times 10^{23}\ \text{Ag atoms} \times \frac{1\ \text{mol Ag}}{6.022 \times 10^{23}\ \text{Ag atoms}} = 0.500\ \text{mol Ag}$$

**4** *EVALUATE* The answer is correct—units cancel correctly and the number of atoms is one-half of Avogadro's number.

**PRACTICE** *Answers in Appendix E*

1. How many moles of lead, Pb, are in $1.50 \times 10^{12}$ atoms of lead?
2. How many moles of tin, Sn, are in 2500 atoms of tin?
3. How many atoms of aluminum, Al, are in 2.75 mol of aluminum?

Go to **go.hrw.com** for more practice problems that ask you to convert between atoms and moles.

**Keyword: HC6ATMX**

### SAMPLE PROBLEM E

*For more help, go to the **Math Tutor** at the end of this chapter.*

**What is the mass in grams of $1.20 \times 10^8$ atoms of copper, Cu?**

**SOLUTION**

**1** *ANALYZE* **Given:** $1.20 \times 10^8$ atoms of Cu
**Unknown:** mass of Cu in grams

**2 PLAN** number of atoms of Cu $\longrightarrow$ amount of Cu in moles $\longrightarrow$ mass of Cu in grams

As indicated in **Figure 11,** the given number of atoms must first be converted to amount in moles by dividing by Avogadro's number. Amount in moles is then multiplied by molar mass to yield mass in grams.

$$\text{Cu atoms} \times \frac{\text{moles Cu}}{\text{Avogadro's number of Cu atoms}} \times \frac{\text{grams Cu}}{\text{moles Cu}} = \text{grams Cu}$$

**3 COMPUTE** The molar mass of copper from the periodic table is rounded to 63.55 g/mol.

$$1.20 \times 10^{8}\ \cancel{\text{Cu atoms}} \times \frac{1\ \cancel{\text{mol Cu}}}{6.022 \times 10^{23}\ \cancel{\text{Cu atoms}}} \times \frac{63.55\ \text{g Cu}}{1\ \cancel{\text{mol Cu}}} = 1.27 \times 10^{-14}\ \text{g Cu}$$

**4 EVALUATE** Units cancel correctly to give the answer in grams. The size of the answer is reasonable—$10^8$ has been divided by about $10^{24}$ and multiplied by about $10^2$.

**PRACTICE** *Answers in Appendix E*

1. What is the mass in grams of $7.5 \times 10^{15}$ atoms of nickel, Ni?
2. How many atoms of sulfur, S, are in 4.00 g of sulfur?
3. What mass of gold, Au, contains the same number of atoms as 9.0 g of aluminum, Al?

**extension**

Go to **go.hrw.com** for more practice problems that ask you to convert among atoms, grams, and moles.

**Keyword:** HC6ATMX

## SECTION REVIEW

1. Define each of the following:
   - **a.** atomic number
   - **b.** mass number
   - **c.** relative atomic mass
   - **d.** average atomic mass
   - **e.** mole
   - **f.** Avogadro's number
   - **g.** molar mass
   - **h.** isotope
2. Determine the number of protons, electrons, and neutrons in each of the following isotopes:
   - **a.** sodium-23
   - **b.** calcium-40
   - **c.** $^{64}_{29}Cu$
   - **d.** $^{108}_{47}Ag$
3. Write the nuclear symbol and hyphen notation for each of the following isotopes:
   - **a.** mass number of 28 and atomic number of 14
   - **b.** 26 protons and 30 neutrons
4. To two decimal places, what is the relative atomic mass and the molar mass of the element potassium, K?
5. Determine the mass in grams of the following:
   - **a.** 2.00 mol N
   - **b.** $3.01 \times 10^{23}$ atoms Cl
6. Determine the amount in moles of the following:
   - **a.** 12.15 g Mg
   - **b.** $1.50 \times 10^{23}$ atoms F

### Critical Thinking

7. **ANALYZING DATA** Beaker A contains 2.06 mol of copper, and Beaker B contains 222 grams of silver. Which beaker contains the larger mass? Which beaker has the larger number of atoms?

# CHAPTER HIGHLIGHTS

## The Atom: From Philosophical Idea to Scientific Theory

**Vocabulary**
law of conservation of mass
law of definite proportions
law of multiple proportions

- The idea of atoms has been around since the time of the ancient Greeks. In the nineteenth century, John Dalton proposed a scientific theory of atoms that can still be used to explain properties of most chemicals today.
- Matter and its mass cannot be created or destroyed in chemical reactions.
- The mass ratios of the elements that make up a given compound are always the same, regardless of how much of the compound there is or how it was formed.
- If two or more different compounds are composed of the same two elements, then the ratio of the masses of the second element combined with a certain mass of the first element can be expressed as a ratio of small whole numbers.

## The Structure of the Atom

**Vocabulary**
atom
nuclear forces

- Cathode-ray tubes supplied evidence of the existence of electrons, which are negatively charged subatomic particles that have relatively little mass.
- Rutherford found evidence for the existence of the atomic nucleus by bombarding gold foil with a beam of positively charged particles.
- Atomic nuclei are composed of protons, which have an electric charge of +1, and (in all but one case) neutrons, which have no electric charge.
- Atomic nuclei have radii of about 0.001 pm (pm = picometers; 1 pm $\times$ $10^{-12}$ m), and atoms have radii of about 40–270 pm.

## Counting Atoms

**Vocabulary**
atomic number
isotope
mass number
nuclide
atomic mass unit
average atomic mass
mole
Avogadro's number
molar mass

- The atomic number of an element is equal to the number of protons of an atom of that element.
- The mass number is equal to the total number of protons and neutrons that make up the nucleus of an atom of that element.
- The relative atomic mass unit (amu) is based on the carbon-12 atom and is a convenient unit for measuring the mass of atoms. It equals $1.660\ 540 \times 10^{-24}$ g.
- The average atomic mass of an element is found by calculating the weighted average of the atomic masses of the naturally occurring isotopes of the element.
- Avogadro's number is equal to approximately $6.022 \times 10^{23}$. A sample that contains a number of particles equal to Avogadro's number contains a mole of those particles.

anode glows. In addition, a paddle wheel placed in the tube rolls from the anode toward the cathode when the current is on.

a. In which direction do particles pass through the gas?

b. What charge do the particles possess?

**34. Analyzing Data** Osmium is the element with the greatest density, 22.58 g/cm$^3$. How does the density of osmium compare to the density of a typical nucleus of $2 \times 10^8$ metric tons/cm$^3$? (1 metric ton = 1000 kg)

## USING THE HANDBOOK

**35.** Group 14 of the *Elements Handbook* describes the reactions that produce CO and $CO_2$. Review this section to answer the following:

a. When a fuel burns, what determines whether CO or $CO_2$ will be produced?

b. What happens in the body if hemoglobin picks up CO?

c. Why is CO poisoning most likely to occur in homes that are well sealed during cold winter months?

## RESEARCH & WRITING

**36.** Prepare a report on the series of experiments conducted by Sir James Chadwick that led to the discovery of the neutron.

**37.** Write a report on the contributions of Amedeo Avogadro that led to the determination of the value of Avogadro's number.

**38.** Trace the development of the electron microscope, and cite some of its many uses.

**39.** The study of atomic structure and the nucleus produced a new field of medicine called *nuclear medicine.* Describe the use of radioactive tracers to detect and treat diseases.

## ALTERNATIVE ASSESSMENT

**40.** Observe a cathode-ray tube in operation, and write a description of your observations.

**41. Performance Assessment** Using colored clay, build a model of the nucleus of each of carbon's three naturally occurring isotopes: carbon-12, carbon-13, and carbon-14. Specify the number of electrons that would surround each nucleus.

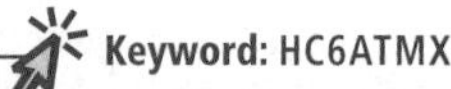

**extension**

Graphing Calculator **Calculating Numbers of Protons, Electrons, and Neutrons**

Go to **go.hrw.com** for a graphing calculator exercise that asks you to calculate numbers of protons, electrons, and neutrons.

Keyword: HC6ATMX

# Math Tutor CONVERSION FACTORS

Most calculations in chemistry require that all measurements of the same quantity (mass, length, volume, temperature, and so on) be expressed in the same unit. To change the units of a quantity, you can multiply the quantity by a conversion factor. With SI units, such conversions are easy because units of the same quantity are related by multiples of 10, 100, 1000, or 1 million. Suppose you want to convert a given amount in milliliters to liters. You can use the relationship 1 L = 1000 mL. From this relationship, you can derive the following conversion factors.

$$\frac{1000 \text{ mL}}{1 \text{ L}} \text{ and } \frac{1 \text{ L}}{1000 \text{ mL}}$$

The correct strategy is to multiply the given amount (in mL) by the conversion factor that allows milliliter units to cancel out and liter units to remain. Using the second conversion factor will give you the units you want.

These conversion factors are based on an exact definition (1000 mL = 1 L exactly), so significant figures do not apply to these factors. The number of significant figures in a converted measurement depends on the certainty of the measurement you start with.

## SAMPLE 1

**A sample of aluminum has a mass of 0.087 g. What is the sample's mass in milligrams?**

Based on SI prefixes, you know that 1 g = 1000 mg. Therefore, the possible conversion factors are

$$\frac{1000 \text{ mg}}{1 \text{ g}} \text{ and } \frac{1 \text{ g}}{1000 \text{ mg}}$$

The first conversion factor cancels grams, leaving milligrams.

$$0.087 \cancel{\text{g}} \times \frac{1000 \text{ mg}}{1 \cancel{\text{g}}} = 87 \text{ mg}$$

Notice that the values 0.087 g and 87 mg each have two significant figures.

## SAMPLE 2

**A sample of a mineral has $4.08 \times 10^{-5}$ mol of vanadium per kilogram of mass. How many micromoles of vanadium per kilogram does the mineral contain?**

The prefix *micro-* specifies $\frac{1}{1\,000\,000}$ or $1 \times 10^{-6}$ of the base unit.

So, 1 $\mu$mol = $1 \times 10^{-6}$ mol. The possible conversion factors are

$$\frac{1 \ \mu\text{mol}}{1 \times 10^{-6} \text{ mol}} \text{ and } \frac{1 \times 10^{-6} \text{ mol}}{1 \ \mu\text{mol}}$$

The first conversion factor will allow moles to cancel and micromoles to remain.

$$4.08 \times 10^{-5} \cancel{\text{mol}} \times \frac{1 \ \mu\text{mol}}{1 \times 10^{-6} \cancel{\text{mol}}} = 40.8 \ \mu\text{mol}$$

Notice that the values $4.08 \times 10^{-5}$ mol and 40.8 $\mu$mol each have three significant figures.

## PRACTICE PROBLEMS

**1.** Express each of the following measurements in the units indicated.

a. 2250 mg in grams
b. 59.3 kL in liters

**2.** Use scientific notation to express each of the following measurements in the units indicated.

a. 0.000 072 g in micrograms
b. $3.98 \times 10^{6}$ m in kilometers

# Standardized Test Prep

**Answer the following items on a separate piece of paper.**

**MULTIPLE CHOICE**

**1.** A chemical compound always has the same elements in the same proportions by mass regardless of the source of the compound. This is a statement of
**A.** the law of multiple proportions.
**B.** the law of isotopes.
**C.** the law of definite proportions.
**D.** the law of conservation of mass.

**2.** An important result of Rutherford's experiments with gold foil was to establish that
**A.** atoms have mass.
**B.** electrons have a negative charge.
**C.** neutrons are uncharged particles.
**D.** the atom is mostly empty space.

**3.** Which subatomic particle has a charge of +1?
**A.** electron
**B.** neutron
**C.** proton
**D.** meson

**4.** Which particle has the least mass?
**A.** electron
**B.** neutron
**C.** proton
**D.** All have the same mass.

**5.** Cathode rays are composed of
**A.** alpha particles.
**B.** electrons.
**C.** protons.
**D.** neutrons.

**6.** The atomic number of an element is the same as the number of
**A.** protons.
**B.** neutrons.
**C.** protons + electrons.
**D.** protons + neutrons.

**7.** How many neutrons are present in an atom of tin that has an atomic number of 50 and a mass number of 119?
**A.** 50
**B.** 69
**C.** 119
**D.** 169

**8.** What is the mass of 1.50 mol of sodium, Na?
**A.** 0.652 g
**B.** 0.478 g
**C.** 11.0 g
**D.** 34.5 g

**9.** How many moles of carbon are in a 28.0 g sample?
**A.** 336 mol
**B.** 72.0 mol
**C.** 2.33 mol
**D.** 0.500 mol

**SHORT ANSWER**

**10.** Which atom has more neutrons, potassium-40 or argon-40?

**11.** What is the mass of $1.20 \times 10^{23}$ atoms of phosphorus?

**EXTENDED RESPONSE**

**12.** Cathode rays emitted by a piece of silver and a piece of copper illustrate identical properties. What is the significance of this observation?

**13.** A student believed that she had discovered a new element and named it mythium. Analysis found it contained two isotopes. The composition of the isotopes was 19.9% of atomic mass 10.013 and 80.1% of atomic mass 11.009. What is the average atomic mass, and do you think mythium was a new element?

**Test TIP** Choose the best possible answer for each question, even if you think there is another possible answer that is not given.

# Conservation of Mass

## OBJECTIVES

- ***Observe*** **the signs of a chemical reaction.**
- ***Compare*** **masses of reactants and products.**
- ***Design*** **experiments.**
- ***Relate*** **observations to the law of conservation of mass.**

## MATERIALS

- **2 L plastic soda bottle**
- **5% acetic acid solution (vinegar)**
- **balance**
- **clear plastic cups, 2**
- **graduated cylinder**
- **hook-insert cap for bottle**
- **microplunger**
- **sodium hydrogen carbonate (baking soda)**

**FIGURE A** Slowly add the vinegar to prevent the reaction from getting out of control.

## BACKGROUND

The law of conservation of mass states that matter is neither created nor destroyed during a chemical reaction. Therefore, the mass of a system should remain constant during any chemical process. In this experiment, you will determine whether mass is conserved by examining a simple chemical reaction and comparing the mass of the system before the reaction with its mass after the reaction.

## SAFETY

For review of safety, please see **Safety in the Chemistry Laboratory** in the front of your book.

## PREPARATION

1. Make two data tables in your lab notebook, one for Part I and another for Part II. In each table, create three columns labeled "Initial mass (g)," "Final mass (g)," and "Change in mass (g)." Each table should also have space for observations of the reaction.

## PROCEDURE—PART I

1. Obtain a microplunger, and tap it down into a sample of baking soda until the bulb end is packed with a plug of the powder (4–5 mL of baking soda should be enough to pack the bulb).
2. Hold the microplunger over a plastic cup, and squeeze the sides of the microplunger to loosen the plug of baking soda so that it falls into the cup.
3. Use a graduated cylinder to measure 100 mL of vinegar, and pour it into a second plastic cup.
4. Place the two cups side by side on the balance pan, and measure the total mass of the system

(before reaction) to the nearest 0.01 g. Record the mass in your data table.

5. Add the vinegar to the baking soda a little at a time to prevent the reaction from getting out of control, as shown in **Figure A.** Allow the vinegar to slowly run down the inside of the cup. Observe and record your observations about the reaction.

6. When the reaction is complete, place both cups on the balance, and determine the total final mass of the system to the nearest 0.01 g. Calculate any change in mass. Record both the final mass and any change in mass in your data table.

7. Examine the plastic bottle and the hook-insert cap. Try to develop a modified procedure that will test the law of conservation of mass more accurately than the procedure in Part I.

8. In your notebook, write the answers to items 1 through 3 in Analysis and Interpretation—Part I.

## PROCEDURE—PART II

9. Your teacher should approve the procedure you designed in Procedure—Part I, step 7. Implement your procedure with the same chemicals and quantities you used in Part I, but use the bottle and hook-insert cap in place of the two cups. Record your data in your data table.

10. If you were successful in step 9 and your results reflect the conservation of mass, proceed to complete the experiment. If not, find a lab group that was successful, and discuss with them what they did and why they did it. Your group should then test the other group's procedure to determine whether their results are reproducible.

## CLEANUP AND DISPOSAL

11. Clean your lab station. Clean all equipment, and return it to its proper place. Dispose of chemicals and solutions in the containers designated by your teacher. Do not pour any chemicals down the drain or throw anything in the trash unless your teacher directs you to do so. Wash your hands thoroughly after all work is finished and before you leave the lab.

## ANALYSIS AND INTERPRETATION—PART I

1. **Drawing Conclusions:** What evidence was there that a chemical reaction occurred?

2. **Organizing Data:** How did the final mass of the system compare with the initial mass of the system?

3. **Resolving Discrepancies:** Does your answer to the previous question show that the law of conservation of mass was violated? (Hint: Another way to express the law of conservation of mass is to say that the mass of all of the products equals the mass of all of the reactants.) What do you think might cause the mass difference?

## ANALYSIS AND INTERPRETATION—PART II

1. **Drawing Conclusions:** Was there any new evidence in Part II indicating that a chemical reaction occurred?

2. **Organizing Ideas:** Identify the state of matter for each reactant in Part II. Identify the state of matter for each product.

## CONCLUSIONS

1. **Relating Ideas:** What is the difference between the system in Part I and the system in Part II? What change led to the improved results in Part II?

2. **Evaluating Methods:** Why did the procedure for Part II work better than the procedure for Part I?

## EXTENSIONS

1. **Applying Models:** When a log burns, the resulting ash obviously has less mass than the unburned log did. Explain whether this loss of mass violates the law of conservation of mass.

2. **Designing Experiments:** Design a procedure that would test the law of conservation of mass for the burning log described in Extension item 1.

CHAPTER 4

# Arrangement of Electrons in Atoms

*The emission of light is fundamentally related to the behavior of electrons.*

Neon Walkway

# The Development of a New Atomic Model

SECTION 1

## Objectives

- Explain the mathematical relationship among the speed, wavelength, and frequency of electromagnetic radiation.
- Discuss the dual wave-particle nature of light.
- Discuss the significance of the photoelectric effect and the line-emission spectrum of hydrogen to the development of the atomic model.
- Describe the Bohr model of the hydrogen atom.

SC **C.4.4** Apply the concept of moles to determine the number of particles of a substance in a chemical reaction, the percent composition of a representative compound, the mass proportions, and the mole-mass relationships

The Rutherford model of the atom was an improvement over previous models, but it was incomplete. It did not explain how the atom's negatively charged electrons are distributed in the space surrounding its positively charged nucleus. After all, it was well known that oppositely charged particles attract each other. So what prevented the negative electrons from being drawn into the positive nucleus?

In the early twentieth century, a new atomic model evolved as a result of investigations into the absorption and emission of light by matter. The studies revealed a relationship between light and an atom's electrons. This new understanding led directly to a revolutionary view of the nature of energy, matter, and atomic structure.

## Properties of Light

Before 1900, scientists thought light behaved solely as a wave. This belief changed when it was later discovered that light also has particle-like characteristics. Still, many of light's properties can be described in terms of waves. A quick review of these wavelike properties will help you understand the basic theory of light as it existed at the beginning of the twentieth century.

### The Wave Description of Light

Visible light is a kind of **electromagnetic radiation,** *which is a form of energy that exhibits wavelike behavior as it travels through space.* Other kinds of electromagnetic radiation include X rays, ultraviolet and infrared light, microwaves, and radio waves. *Together, all the forms of electromagnetic radiation form the* **electromagnetic spectrum.** The electromagnetic spectrum is represented in **Figure 1** on the next page. All forms of electromagnetic radiation move at a constant speed of $3.00 \times 10^8$ meters per second (m/s) through a vacuum and at slightly slower speeds through matter. Because air is mostly empty space, the value of $3.00 \times 10^8$ m/s is also light's approximate speed through air.

The significant feature of wave motion is its repetitive nature, which can be characterized by the measurable properties of wavelength and frequency. **Wavelength** ($\lambda$) *is the distance between corresponding points on adjacent waves.* The unit for wavelength is a distance unit. Depending on the type of electromagnetic radiation, it may be expressed in meters,

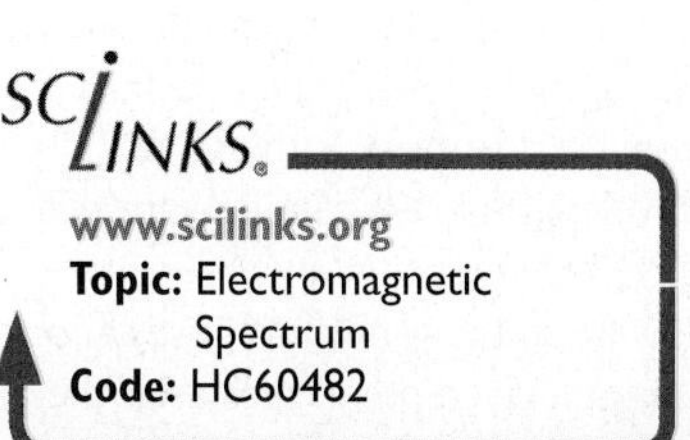

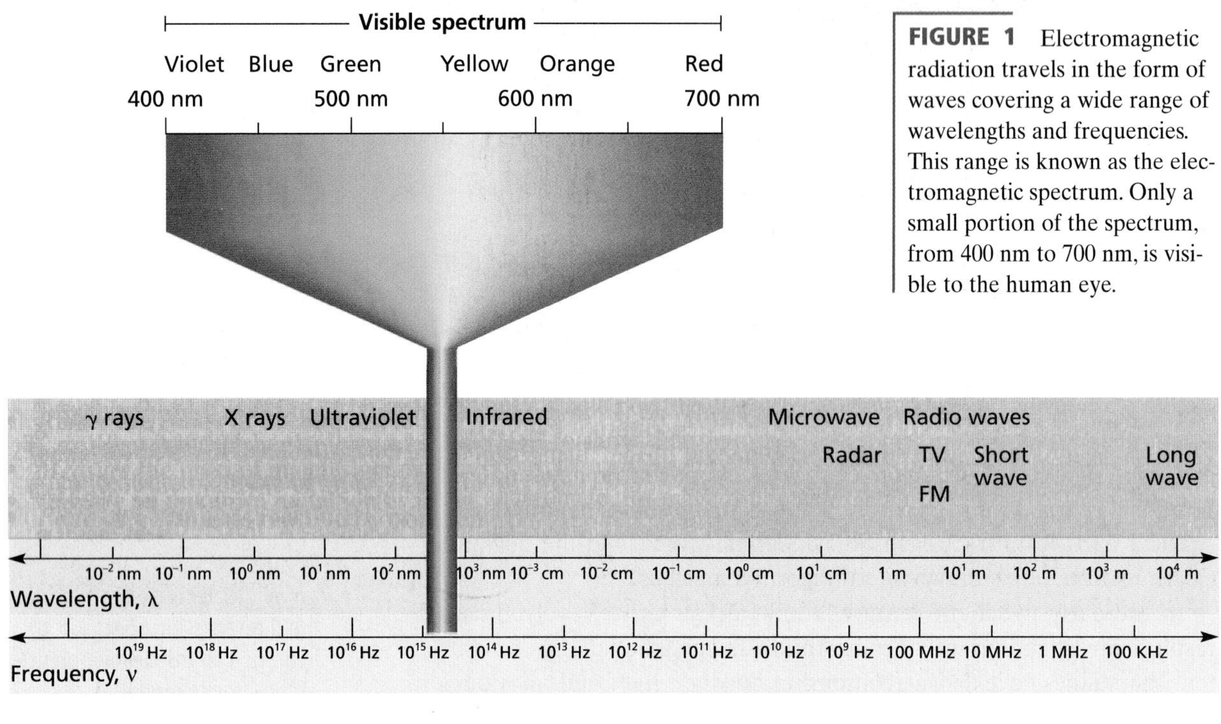


**FIGURE 1** Electromagnetic radiation travels in the form of waves covering a wide range of wavelengths and frequencies. This range is known as the electromagnetic spectrum. Only a small portion of the spectrum, from 400 nm to 700 nm, is visible to the human eye.

centimeters, or nanometers, as shown in **Figure 1. Frequency** (ν) *is defined as the number of waves that pass a given point in a specific time, usually one second.* Frequency is expressed in waves/second. One wave/second is called a hertz (Hz), named for Heinrich Hertz, who was a pioneer in the study of electromagnetic radiation. **Figure 2** illustrates the properties of wavelength and frequency for a familiar kind of wave, a wave on the surface of water. The wave in **Figure 2a** has a longer wavelength and a lower frequency than the wave in **Figure 2b.**

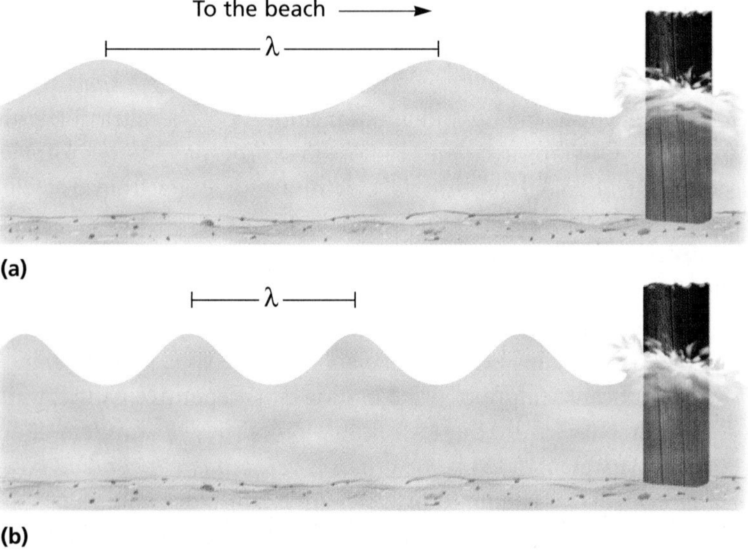


**FIGURE 2** The distance between any two corresponding points on one of these water waves, such as from crest to crest, is the wave's wavelength, λ. We can measure the wave's frequency, ν, by observing how often the water level rises and falls at a given point, such as at the post.

Frequency and wavelength are mathematically related to each other. For electromagnetic radiation, this relationship is written as follows.

$$c = \lambda\nu$$

In the equation, $c$ is the speed of light (in m/s), $\lambda$ is the wavelength of the electromagnetic wave (in m), and $\nu$ is the frequency of the electromagnetic wave (in $s^{-1}$). Because $c$ is the same for all electromagnetic radiation, the product $\lambda\nu$ is a constant. Consequently, we know that $\lambda$ is inversely proportional to $\nu$. In other words, as the wavelength of light decreases, its frequency increases, and vice versa.

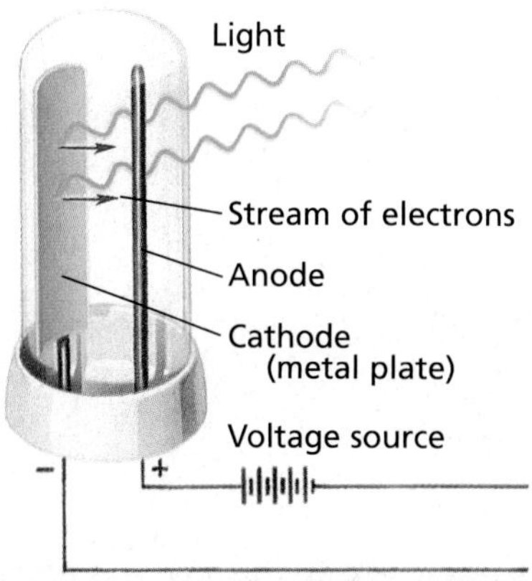


**FIGURE 3** The photoelectric effect: electromagnetic radiation strikes the surface of the metal, ejecting electrons from the metal and causing an electric current.

## The Photoelectric Effect

In the early 1900s, scientists conducted two experiments involving interactions of light and matter that could not be explained by the wave theory of light. One experiment involved a phenomenon known as the photoelectric effect. *The* **photoelectric effect** *refers to the emission of electrons from a metal when light shines on the metal,* as illustrated in **Figure 3.**

The mystery of the photoelectric effect involved the frequency of the light striking the metal. For a given metal, no electrons were emitted if the light's frequency was below a certain minimum—regardless of the light's intensity. Light was known to be a form of energy, capable of knocking loose an electron from a metal. But the wave theory of light predicted that light of any frequency could supply enough energy to eject an electron. Scientists couldn't explain why the light had to be of a minimum frequency in order for the photoelectric effect to occur.

### The Particle Description of Light

The explanation of the photoelectric effect dates back to 1900, when German physicist Max Planck was studying the emission of light by hot objects. He proposed that a hot object does not emit electromagnetic energy continuously, as would be expected if the energy emitted were in the form of waves. Instead, Planck suggested that the object emits energy in small, specific packets called quanta. *A* **quantum** *of energy is the minimum quantity of energy that can be lost or gained by an atom.* Planck proposed the following relationship between a quantum of energy and the frequency of radiation.

$$E = h\nu$$

In the equation, $E$ is the energy, in joules, of a quantum of radiation, $\nu$ is the frequency, in $s^{-1}$, of the radiation emitted, and $h$ is a fundamental physical constant now known as Planck's constant; $h = 6.626 \times 10^{-34}$ J•s.

In 1905, Albert Einstein expanded on Planck's theory by introducing the radical idea that electromagnetic radiation has a dual wave-particle nature. While light exhibits many wavelike properties, it can also be

thought of as a stream of particles. Each particle of light carries a quantum of energy. Einstein called these particles photons. *A* **photon** *is a particle of electromagnetic radiation having zero mass and carrying a quantum of energy.* The energy of a particular photon depends on the frequency of the radiation.

$$E_{photon} = h\nu$$

Einstein explained the photoelectric effect by proposing that electromagnetic radiation is absorbed by matter only in whole numbers of photons. In order for an electron to be ejected from a metal surface, the electron must be struck by a single photon possessing at least the minimum energy required to knock the electron loose. According to the equation $E_{photon} = h\nu$, this minimum energy corresponds to a minimum frequency. If a photon's frequency is below the minimum, then the electron remains bound to the metal surface. Electrons in different metals are bound more or less tightly, so different metals require different minimum frequencies to exhibit the photoelectric effect.

## The Hydrogen-Atom Emission-Line Spectrum

**FIGURE 4** Excited neon atoms emit light when electrons in higher energy levels fall back to the ground state or to a lower-energy excited state.

When current is passed through a gas at low pressure, the potential energy of the gas atoms increases. *The lowest energy state of an atom is its* **ground state.** *A state in which an atom has a higher potential energy than it has in its ground state is an* **excited state.** There are many possible excited states, each with a unique energy, but only one ground state energy for atoms of a given element. When an excited atom returns to its ground state or a lower energy excited state, it gives off the energy it gained in the form of electromagnetic radiation. The production of colored light in neon signs, as shown in **Figure 4,** is a familiar example of this process.

When investigators passed electric current through a vacuum tube containing hydrogen gas at low pressure, they observed the emission of a characteristic pinkish glow. *When a narrow beam of the emitted light was shined through a prism, it was separated into four specific colors of the visible spectrum.* The four bands of light were part of what is known as hydrogen's **emission-line spectrum.** The production of hydrogen's emission-line spectrum is illustrated in **Figure 5.** Additional series of lines were discovered in the ultraviolet and infrared regions of hydrogen's emission-line spectrum. The wavelengths of some of the spectral series are shown in **Figure 6.** They are known as the Lyman, Balmer, and Paschen series, after their discoverers.

Classical theory predicted that the hydrogen atoms would be excited by whatever amount of energy was added to them. Scientists had thus expected to observe *the emission of a continuous range of frequencies of electromagnetic radiation,* that is, a **continuous spectrum.** Why had the hydrogen atoms given off only specific frequencies of light? Attempts to explain this observation led to an entirely new atomic theory called *quantum theory.*

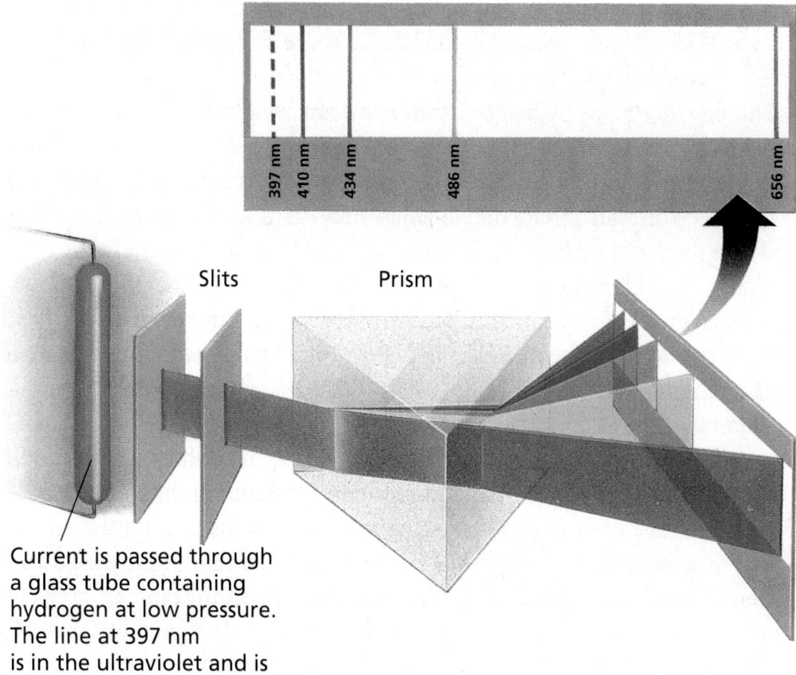


**FIGURE 5** Excited hydrogen atoms emit a pinkish glow, as is shown in this diagram. When the visible portion of the emitted light is passed through a prism, it is separated into specific wavelengths that are part of hydrogen's emission-line spectrum. The line at 397 nm is in the ultraviolet and is not visible to the human eye.

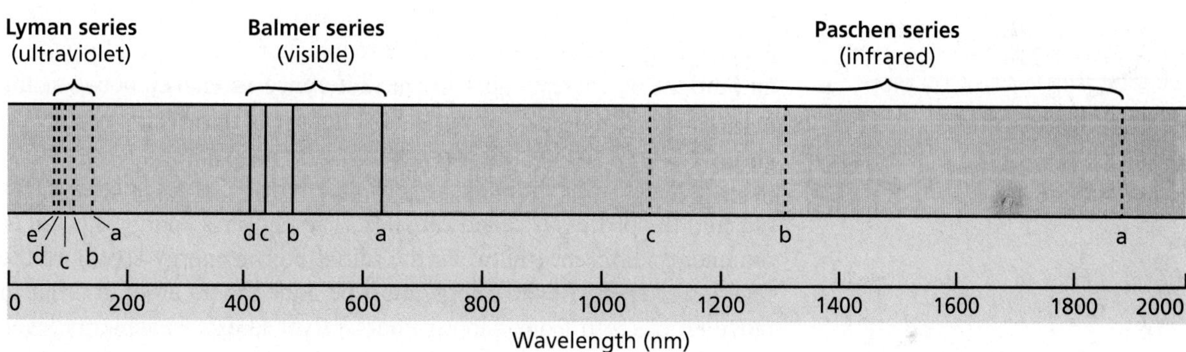


**FIGURE 6** A series of specific wavelengths of emitted light makes up hydrogen's emission-line spectrum. The letters below the lines label hydrogen's various energy-level transitions. Niels Bohr's model of the hydrogen atom provided an explanation for these transitions.

Whenever an excited hydrogen atom falls to its ground state or to a lower-energy excited state, it emits a photon of radiation. The energy of this photon ($E_{photon} = h\nu$) is equal to the difference in energy between the atom's initial state and its final state, as illustrated in **Figure 7.** The fact that hydrogen atoms emit only specific frequencies of light indicated that the energy differences between the atoms' energy states were fixed. This suggested that the electron of a hydrogen atom exists only in very specific energy states.

In the late nineteenth century, a mathematical formula that related the various wavelengths of hydrogen's emission-line spectrum was discovered. The challenge facing scientists was to provide a model of the hydrogen atom that accounted for this relationship.

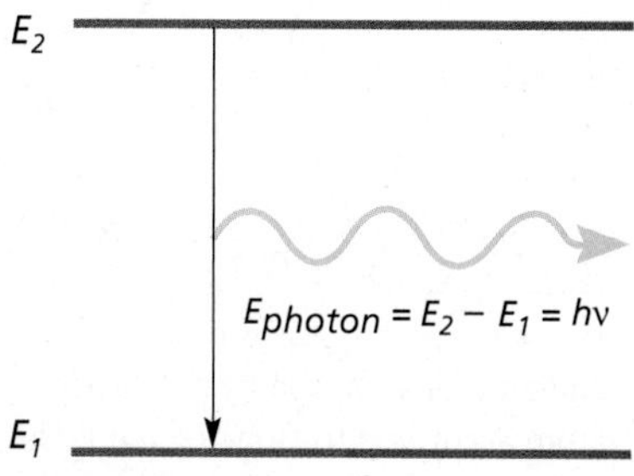


**FIGURE 7** When an excited atom with energy $E_2$ falls back to energy $E_1$, it releases a photon that has energy $E_2 - E_1 = E_{photon} = h\nu$.

## Bohr Model of the Hydrogen Atom

The puzzle of the hydrogen-atom spectrum was solved in 1913 by the Danish physicist Niels Bohr. He proposed a hydrogen-atom model that linked the atom's electron to photon emission. According to the model, the electron can circle the nucleus only in allowed paths, or *orbits*. When the electron is in one of these orbits, the atom has a definite, fixed energy. The electron—and therefore the hydrogen atom—is in its lowest energy state when it is in the orbit closest to the nucleus. This orbit is separated from the nucleus by a large empty space where the electron cannot exist. The energy of the electron is higher when the electron is in orbits that are successively farther from the nucleus.

The electron orbits, or atomic energy levels, in Bohr's model can be compared to the rungs of a ladder. When you are standing on a ladder, your feet are on one rung or another. The amount of potential energy that you possess corresponds to standing on the first rung, the second rung, and so forth. Your energy cannot correspond to standing between two rungs because you cannot stand in midair. In the same way, an electron can be in one orbit or another, but not in between.

**Chemistry in Action**

**Fireflies**

What kinds of reactions produce light? In this chapter, you are learning how excited atoms can produce light. In parts of the United States, summer is accompanied by the appearance of fireflies, or lightning bugs. What makes them glow? A bioluminescent chemical reaction that involves luciferin, luciferase (an enzyme), adenosine triphosphate (ATP), and oxygen takes place in the firefly and produces the characteristic yellow-green glow. Unlike most reactions that produce light, bioluminescent reactions do not generate energy in the form of heat.

How does Bohr's model of the hydrogen atom explain the observed spectral lines? While in a given orbit, the electron is neither gaining nor losing energy. It can, however, move to a higher-energy orbit by gaining an amount of energy equal to the difference in energy between the higher-energy orbit and the initial lower-energy orbit. When a hydrogen atom is in an excited state, its electron is in one of the higher-energy orbits. When the electron falls to a lower energy level, a photon is emitted, and the process is called *emission*. The photon's energy is equal to the energy difference between the initial higher energy level and the final lower energy level. Energy must be added to an atom in order to move an electron from a lower energy level to a higher energy level. This process is called *absorption*. Absorption and emission of radiation in Bohr's model of the hydrogen atom are illustrated in **Figure 8.** The energy of each absorbed or emitted photon corresponds to a particular frequency of emitted radiation, $E_{photon} = h\nu$.

Based on the different wavelengths of the hydrogen emission-line spectrum, Bohr calculated the allowed energy levels for the hydrogen

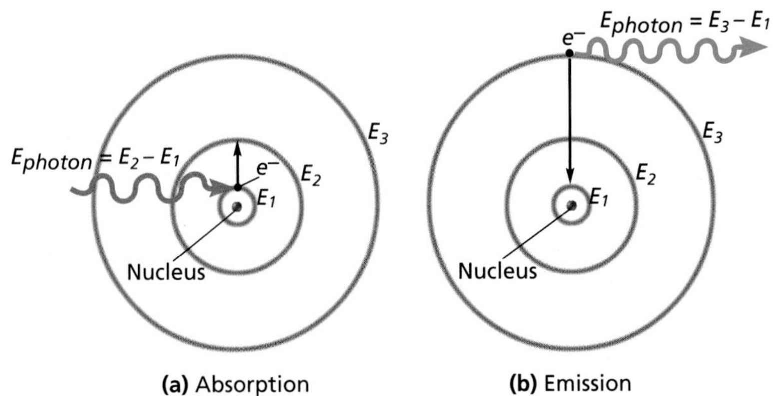


**FIGURE 8** (a) Absorption and (b) emission of a photon by a hydrogen atom according to Bohr's model. The frequencies of light that can be absorbed and emitted are restricted because the electron can only be in orbits corresponding to the energies $E_1$, $E_2$, $E_3$, and so forth.

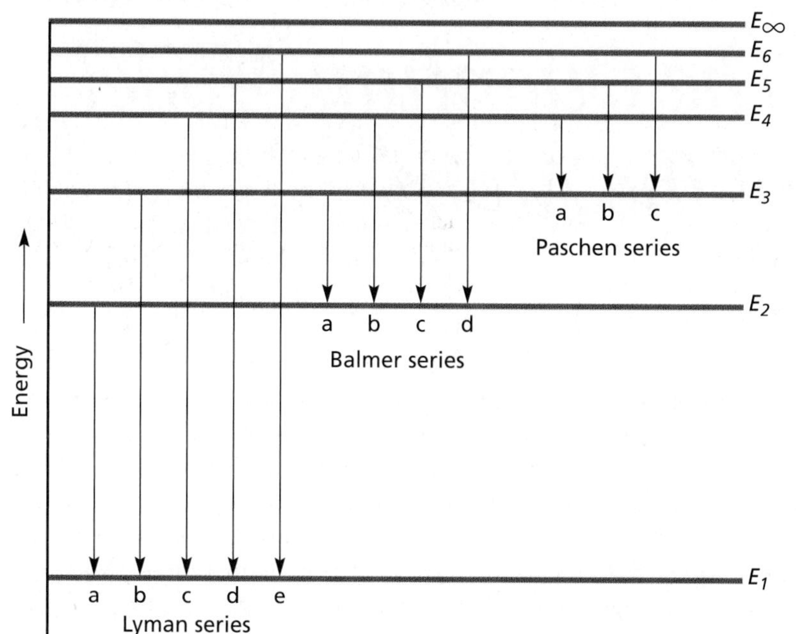


**FIGURE 9** This energy-state diagram for a hydrogen atom shows some of the energy transitions for the Lyman, Balmer, and Paschen spectral series. Bohr's model of the atom accounted mathematically for the energy of each of the transitions shown.

atom. He then related the possible energy-level changes to the lines in the hydrogen emission-line spectrum. The five lines in the Lyman series, for example, were shown to be the result of electrons dropping from energy levels $E_6$, $E_5$, $E_4$, $E_3$, and $E_2$ to the ground-state energy level $E_1$.

Bohr's calculated values agreed with the experimentally observed values for the lines in each series. The origins of three of the series of lines in hydrogen's emission-line spectrum are shown in **Figure 9.**

Bohr's model of the hydrogen atom explained observed spectral lines so well that many scientists concluded that the model could be applied to all atoms. It was soon recognized, however, that Bohr's approach did not explain the spectra of atoms with more than one electron. Nor did Bohr's theory explain the chemical behavior of atoms.

## SECTION REVIEW

1. What was the major shortcoming of Rutherford's model of the atom?
2. Write and label the equation that relates the speed, wavelength, and frequency of electromagnetic radiation.
3. Define the following:
   **a.** electromagnetic radiation **b.** wavelength
   **c.** frequency **d.** quantum **e.** photon
4. What is meant by the dual wave-particle nature of light?
5. Describe the Bohr model of the hydrogen atom.

**Critical Thinking**

6. **INTERPRETING GRAPHICS** Use the diagram in **Figure 9** to answer the following:
   **a.** Characterize each of the following as absorption or emission: an electron moves from $E_2$ to $E_1$; an electron moves from $E_1$ to $E_3$; and an electron moves from $E_6$ to $E_3$.
   **b.** Which energy-level change above emits or absorbs the highest energy? the lowest energy?

SECTION 2

# The Quantum Model of the Atom

## OBJECTIVES

- Discuss Louis de Broglie's role in the development of the quantum model of the atom.
- Compare and contrast the Bohr model and the quantum model of the atom.
- Explain how the Heisenberg uncertainty principle and the Schrödinger wave equation led to the idea of atomic orbitals.
- List the four quantum numbers and describe their significance.
- Relate the number of sublevels corresponding to each of an atom's main energy levels, the number of orbitals per sublevel, and the number of orbitals per main energy level.

SC **C.2.1** Illustrate electron configurations by using orbital notation for representative elements; **C.2.2** Summarize atomic properties (including electron configuration, ionization energy, electron affinity, atomic size, and ionic size)

To the scientists of the early twentieth century, Bohr's model of the hydrogen atom contradicted common sense. Why did hydrogen's electron exist around the nucleus only in certain allowed orbits with definite energies? Why couldn't the electron exist in a limitless number of orbits with slightly different energies? To explain why atomic energy states are quantized, scientists had to change the way they viewed the nature of the electron.

## Electrons as Waves

The investigations into the photoelectric effect and hydrogen's emission-line spectrum revealed that light could behave as both a wave and a particle. Could electrons have a dual wave-particle nature as well? In 1924, the French scientist Louis de Broglie asked himself this very question. And the answer that he proposed led to a revolution in our basic understanding of matter.

De Broglie pointed out that in many ways the behavior of electrons in Bohr's quantized orbits was similar to the known behavior of waves. For example, scientists at the time knew that any wave confined to a space can have only certain frequencies. De Broglie suggested that electrons be considered waves confined to the space around an atomic nucleus. It followed that the electron waves could exist only at specific frequencies. And according to the relationship $E = h\nu$, these frequencies corresponded to specific energies—the quantized energies of Bohr's orbits.

Other aspects of de Broglie's hypothesis that electrons have wave-like properties were soon confirmed by experiments. Investigators demonstrated that electrons, like light waves, can be bent, or diffracted. *Diffraction* refers to the bending of a wave as it passes by the edge of an object or through a small opening. Diffraction experiments and other investigations also showed that electron beams, like waves, can interfere with each other. *Interference* occurs when waves overlap (see the Quick Lab in this section). This overlapping results in a reduction of energy in some areas and an increase of energy in others. The effects of diffraction and interference can be seen in **Figure 10.**

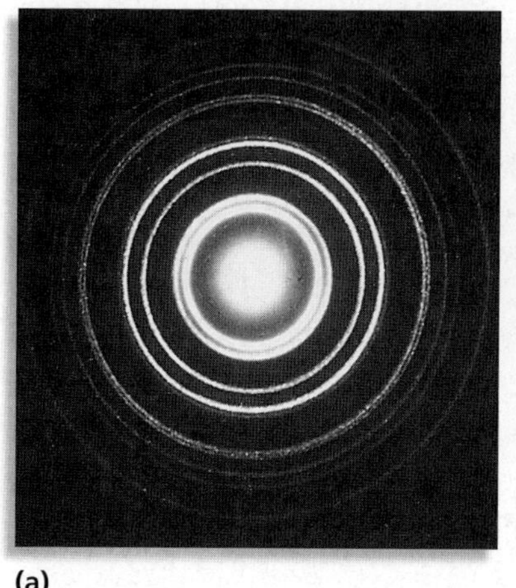
(a)

(b)

**FIGURE 10** Diffraction patterns produced by (a) a beam of electrons passed through a substance and (b) a beam of visible light passed through a tiny aperture. Each pattern shows the results of bent waves that have interfered with each other. The bright areas correspond to areas of increased energy, while the dark areas correspond to areas of decreased energy.

## The Heisenberg Uncertainty Principle

The idea of electrons having a dual wave-particle nature troubled scientists. If electrons are both particles and waves, then where are they in the atom? To answer this question, it is important to consider a proposal first made in 1927 by the German theoretical physicist Werner Heisenberg.

Heisenberg's idea involved the detection of electrons. Electrons are detected by their interaction with photons. Because photons have about the same energy as electrons, any attempt to locate a specific electron with a photon knocks the electron off its course. As a result, there is always a basic uncertainty in trying to locate an electron (or any other particle). *The* **Heisenberg uncertainty principle** *states that it is impossible to determine simultaneously both the position and velocity of an electron or any other particle.* Although it was difficult for scientists to accept this fact at the time, it has proven to be one of the fundamental principles of our present understanding of light and matter.

## The Schrödinger Wave Equation

In 1926, the Austrian physicist Erwin Schrödinger used the hypothesis that electrons have a dual wave-particle nature to develop an equation that treated electrons in atoms as waves. Unlike Bohr's theory, which assumed quantization as a fact, quantization of electron energies was a natural outcome of Schrödinger's equation. Only waves of specific energies, and therefore frequencies, provided solutions to the equation. Together with the Heisenberg uncertainty principle, the Schrödinger wave equation laid the foundation for modern quantum theory. **Quantum theory** *describes mathematically the wave properties of electrons and other very small particles.*

# QuickLAB

Wear safety goggles and an apron.

## The Wave Nature of Light: Interference

### Materials

- scissors
- manila folders
- thumbtack
- masking tape
- aluminum foil
- white poster board or cardboard
- flashlight

### Question

**Does light show the wave property of interference when a beam of light is projected through a pinhole onto a screen?**

### Procedure

Record all your observations.

1. To make the pinhole screen, cut a 20 cm × 20 cm square from a manila folder. In the center of the square, cut a 2 cm square hole. Cut a 7 cm × 7 cm square of aluminum foil. Using a thumbtack, make a pinhole in the center of the foil square. Tape the aluminum foil over the 2 cm square hole, making sure the pinhole is centered as shown in the diagram.
2. Use white poster board to make a projection screen 35 cm × 35 cm.
3. In a dark room, center the light beam from a flashlight on the pinhole. Hold the flashlight about 1 cm from the pinhole. The pinhole screen should be about 50 cm from the projection screen, as shown in the diagram. Adjust the distance to form a sharp image on the projection screen.

### Discussion

1. Did you observe interference patterns on the screen?
2. As a result of your observations, what do you conclude about the nature of light?

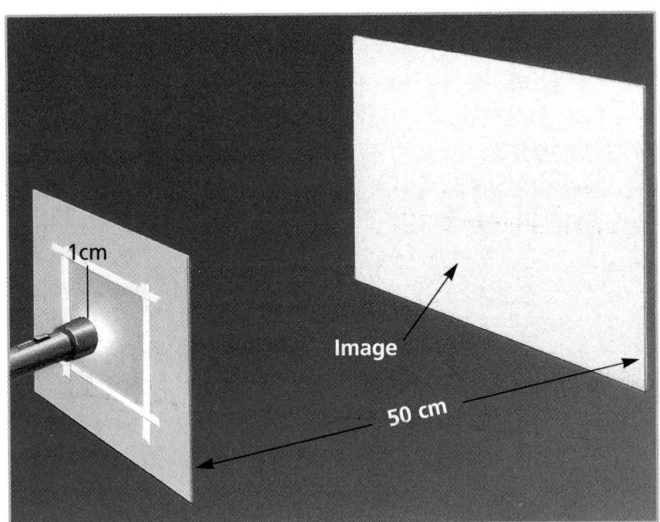


Solutions to the Schrödinger wave equation are known as wave functions. Based on the Heisenberg uncertainty principle, the early developers of quantum theory determined that wave functions give only the *probability* of finding an electron at a given place around the nucleus. Thus, electrons do not travel around the nucleus in neat orbits, as Bohr had postulated. Instead, they exist in certain regions called orbitals. *An* **orbital** *is a three-dimensional region around the nucleus that indicates the probable location of an electron.*

**Figure 11** illustrates two ways of picturing one type of atomic orbital. As you will see later in this section, atomic orbitals have different shapes and sizes.

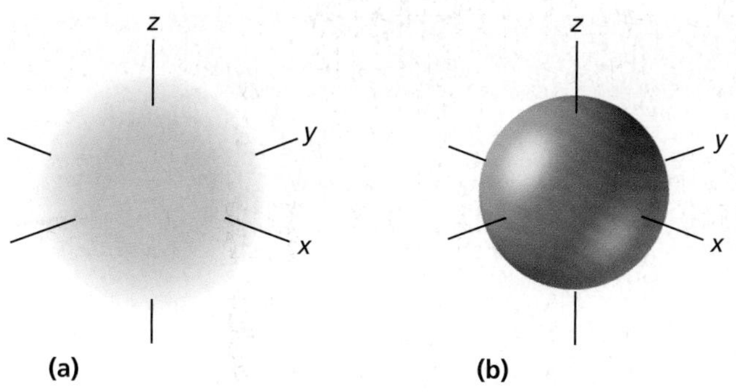


**FIGURE 11** Two ways of showing a simple atomic orbital are presented. In (a) the probability of finding the electron is proportional to the density of the cloud. Shown in (b) is a surface within which the electron can be found a certain percentage of the time, conventionally 90%.

## Atomic Orbitals and Quantum Numbers

In the Bohr atomic model, electrons of increasing energy occupy orbits farther and farther from the nucleus. According to the Schrödinger equation, electrons in atomic orbitals also have quantized energies. An electron's energy level is not the only characteristic of an orbital that is indicated by solving the Schrödinger equation.

In order to completely describe orbitals, scientists use quantum numbers. **Quantum numbers** *specify the properties of atomic orbitals and the properties of electrons in orbitals.* The first three quantum numbers result from solutions to the Schrödinger equation. They indicate the main energy level, the shape, and the orientation of an orbital. The fourth, the spin quantum number, describes a fundamental state of the electron that occupies the orbital. As you read the following descriptions of the quantum numbers, refer to the appropriate columns in **Table 2.**

### Principal Quantum Number

*The* **principal quantum number,** *symbolized by n, indicates the main energy level occupied by the electron.* Values of $n$ are positive integers only—1, 2, 3, and so on. As $n$ increases, the electron's energy and its average distance from the nucleus increase (see **Figure 12**). For example, an electron for which $n = 1$ occupies the first, or lowest, main energy level and is located closest to the nucleus. As you will see, more than one electron can have the same $n$ value. These electrons are sometimes said to be in the same electron *shell.* The total number of orbitals that exist in a given shell, or main energy level, is equal to $n^2$.

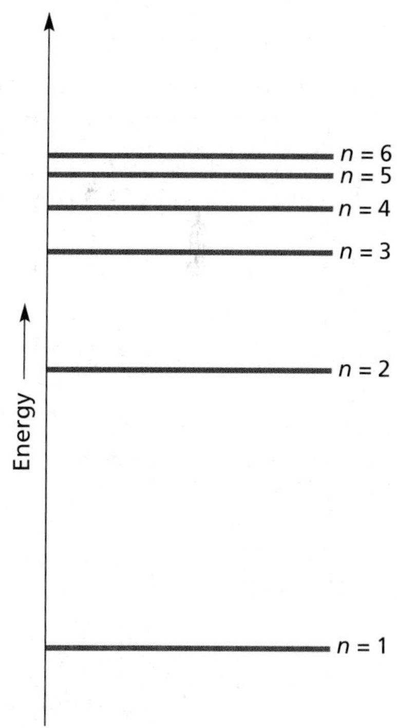


**FIGURE 12** The main energy levels of an atom are represented by the principal quantum number, $n$.

### Angular Momentum Quantum Number

Except at the first main energy level, orbitals of different shapes—known as *sublevels*—exist for a given value of $n$. *The* **angular momentum quantum number,** *symbolized by l, indicates the shape of the orbital.* For a specific main energy level, the number of orbital shapes possible is equal to $n$. The values of $l$ allowed are zero and all positive integers less

**TABLE 1 Orbital Letter Designations According to Values of *l***

| *l* | Letter |
|---|---|
| 0 | *s* |
| 1 | *p* |
| 2 | *d* |
| 3 | *f* |

than or equal to $n - 1$. For example, orbitals for which $n = 2$ can have one of two shapes corresponding to $l = 0$ and $l = 1$. Depending on its value of $l$, an orbital is assigned a letter, as shown in **Table 1.**

As shown in **Figure 13,** *s* orbitals are spherical, *p* orbitals have dumbbell shapes, and *d* orbitals are more complex. (The *f* orbital shapes are even more complex.) In the first energy level, $n = 1$, there is only one sublevel possible—an *s* orbital. As mentioned, the second energy level, $n = 2$, has two sublevels—the *s* and *p* orbitals. The third energy level, $n = 3$, has three sublevels—the *s*, *p*, and *d* orbitals. The fourth energy level, $n = 4$, has four sublevels—the *s*, *p*, *d*, and *f* orbitals. In an *n*th main energy level, there are *n* sublevels.

Each atomic orbital is designated by the principal quantum number followed by the letter of the sublevel. For example, the 1*s* sublevel is the *s* orbital in the first main energy level, while the 2*p* sublevel is the set of three *p* orbitals in the second main energy level. On the other hand, a 4*d* orbital is part of the *d* sublevel in the fourth main energy level. How would you designate the *p* sublevel in the third main energy level? How many other sublevels are in the third main energy level with this one?

## Magnetic Quantum Number

Atomic orbitals can have the same shape but different orientations around the nucleus. *The* **magnetic quantum number,** *symbolized by m, indicates the orientation of an orbital around the nucleus.* Values of *m* are whole numbers, including zero, from $-l$ to $+l$. Because an *s* orbital is spherical and is centered around the nucleus, it has only one possible orientation. This orientation corresponds to a magnetic quantum num-

**FIGURE 13** The orbitals *s*, *p*, and *d* have different shapes. Each of the orbitals shown occupies a different region of space around the nucleus.

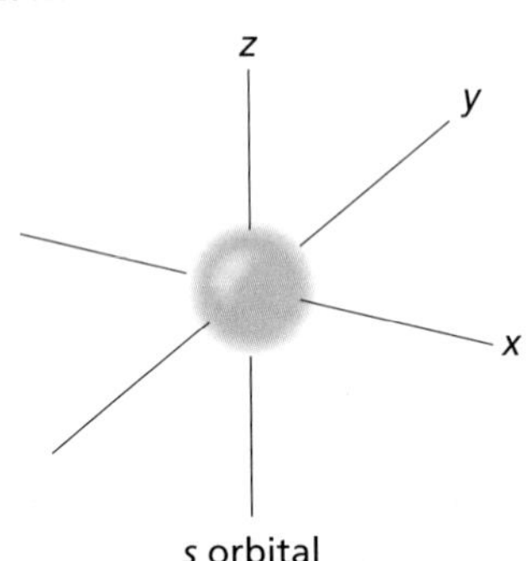

*s* orbital

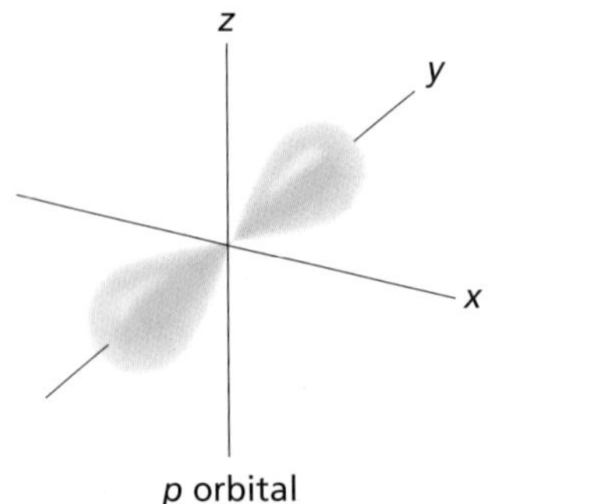

*p* orbital

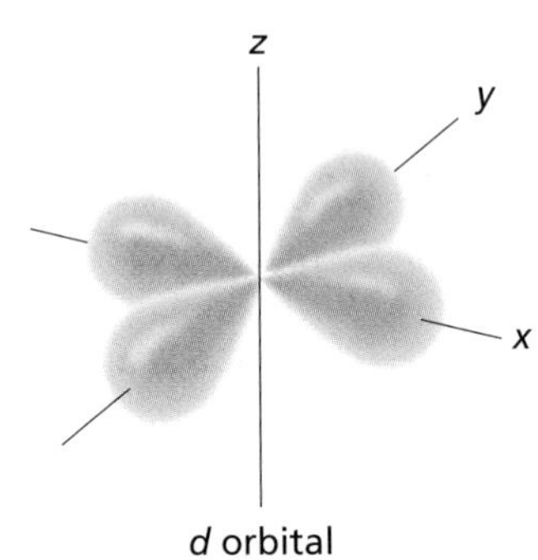

*d* orbital

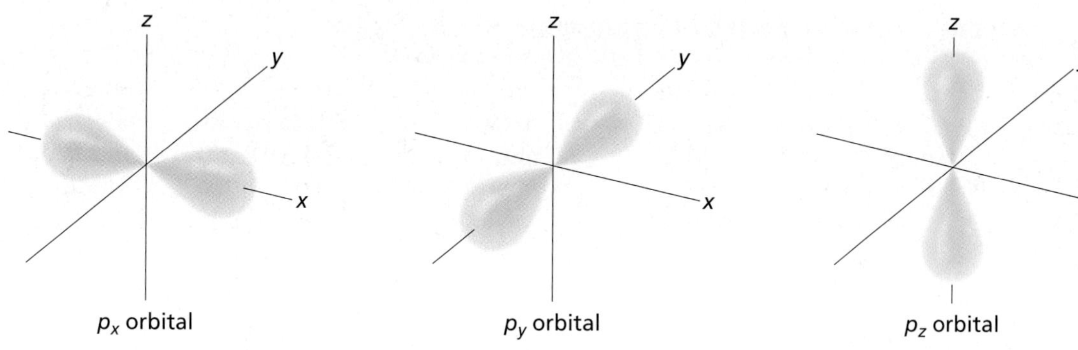


**FIGURE 14** The subscripts *x*, *y*, and *z* indicate the three different orientations of *p* orbitals. The intersection of the *x*, *y*, and *z* axes indicates the location of the center of the nucleus.

ber of $m = 0$. There is therefore only one *s* orbital in each *s* sublevel. As shown in **Figure 14,** the lobes of a *p* orbital extend along the *x, y,* or *z* axis of a three-dimensional coordinate system. There are therefore three *p* orbitals in each *p* sublevel, which are designated as $p_x$, $p_y$, and $p_z$ orbitals. The three *p* orbitals occupy different regions of space and those regions are related to values of $m = -1$, $m = 0$, and $m = +1$.

There are five different *d* orbitals in each *d* sublevel (see **Figure 15**). The five different orientations, including one with a different shape, correspond to values of $m = -2$, $m = -1$, $m = 0$, $m = +1$, and $m = +2$. There are seven different *f* orbitals in each *f* sublevel.

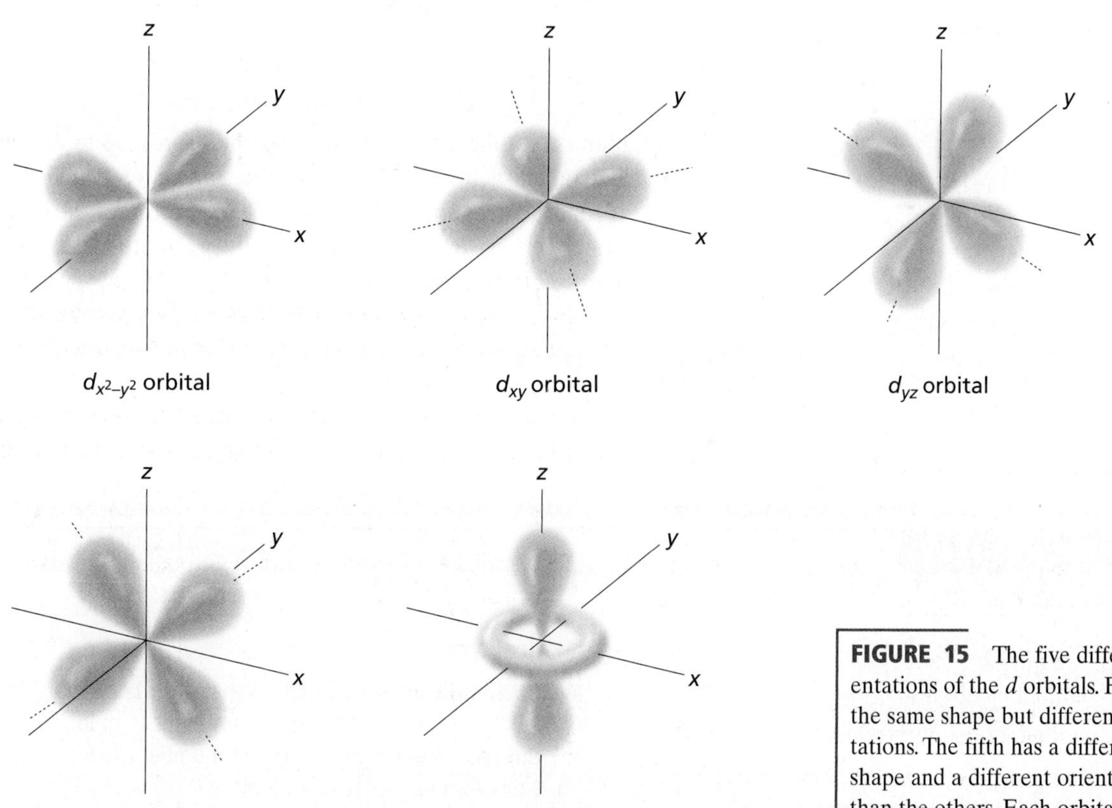


**FIGURE 15** The five different orientations of the *d* orbitals. Four have the same shape but different orientations. The fifth has a different shape and a different orientation than the others. Each orbital occupies a different region of space.

**TABLE 2 *Quantum Number Relationships in Atomic Structure***

| Principal quantum number: main energy level ($n$) | Sublevels in main energy level ($n$ sublevels) | Number of orbitals per sublevel | Number of orbitals per main energy level ($n^2$) | Number of electrons per sublevel | Number of electrons per main energy level ($2n^2$) |
|---|---|---|---|---|---|
| 1 | *s* | 1 | 1 | 2 | 2 |
| 2 | *s*<br>*p* | 1<br>3 | 4 | 2<br>6 | 8 |
| 3 | *s*<br>*p*<br>*d* | 1<br>3<br>5 | 9 | 2<br>6<br>10 | 18 |
| 4 | *s*<br>*p*<br>*d*<br>*f* | 1<br>3<br>5<br>7 | 16 | 2<br>6<br>10<br>14 | 32 |

**CROSS-DISCIPLINARY**

Go to **go.hrw.com** for for a full-length article on spintronics.

**Keyword: HC6ARRX**

As you can see in **Table 2,** the total number of orbitals in a main energy level increases with the value of $n$. In fact, the number of orbitals at each main energy level equals the square of the principal quantum number, $n^2$. What is the total number of orbitals in the third energy level? Specify each of the sublevels using the orbital designations you've learned so far.

## Spin Quantum Number

An electron in an orbital behaves in some ways like Earth spinning on an axis. The electron exists in one of two possible spin states, which creates a magnetic field. To account for the magnetic properties of the electron, theoreticians of the early twentieth century created the spin quantum number. *The* **spin quantum number** *has only two possible values—(+½, −½)—which indicate the two fundamental spin states of an electron in an orbital.* A single orbital can hold a maximum of two electrons, but the two electrons must have opposite spin states.

## SECTION REVIEW

1. Define the following:
   **a.** main energy levels
   **b.** quantum numbers
2. **a.** List the four quantum numbers.
   **b.** What general information about atomic orbitals is provided by the quantum numbers?
3. Describe briefly what specific information is given by each of the four quantum numbers.

**Critical Thinking**

4. **INFERRING RELATIONSHIPS** What are the possible values of the magnetic quantum number $m$ for $f$ orbitals? What is the maximum number of electrons that can exist in $4f$ orbitals?

# Electron Configurations

SECTION 3

## OBJECTIVES

- List the total number of electrons needed to fully occupy each main energy level.
- State the Aufbau principle, the Pauli exclusion principle, and Hund's rule.
- Describe the electron configurations for the atoms of any element using orbital notation, electron-configuration notation, and, when appropriate, noble-gas notation.

SC **C.2.1** Illustrate electron configurations by using orbital notation for representative elements

The quantum model of the atom improves on the Bohr model because it describes the arrangements of electrons in atoms other than hydrogen. *The arrangement of electrons in an atom is known as the atom's* **electron configuration.** Because atoms of different elements have different numbers of electrons, a unique electron configuration exists for the atoms of each element. Like all systems in nature, electrons in atoms tend to assume arrangements that have the lowest possible energies. The lowest-energy arrangement of the electrons for each element is called the element's *ground-state electron configuration.* A few simple rules, combined with the quantum number relationships discussed in Section 2, allow us to determine these ground-state electron configurations.

## Rules Governing Electron Configurations

To build up electron configurations for the ground state of any particular atom, first the energy levels of the orbitals are determined. Then electrons are added to the orbitals, one by one, according to three basic rules. (Remember that real atoms are not built up by adding protons and electrons one at a time.)

The first rule shows the order in which electrons occupy orbitals. According to the **Aufbau principle,** *an electron occupies the lowest-energy orbital that can receive it.* **Figure 16** shows the atomic orbitals in order of increasing energy. The orbital with the lowest energy is the 1*s* orbital. In a ground-state hydrogen atom, the electron is in this orbital. The 2*s* orbital is the next highest in energy, then the 2*p* orbitals. Beginning with the third main energy level, $n = 3$, the energies of the sublevels in different main energy levels begin to overlap.

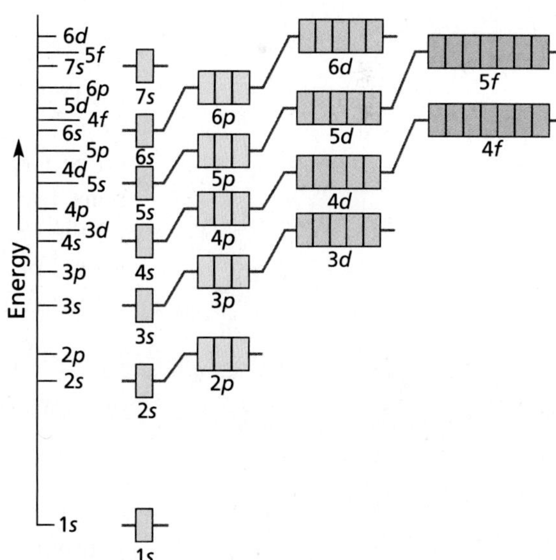


**FIGURE 16** The order of increasing energy for atomic sublevels is shown on the vertical axis. Each individual box represents an orbital.

Note in the figure, for example, that the 4*s* sublevel is lower in energy than the 3*d* sublevel. Therefore, the 4*s* orbital is filled before any electrons enter the 3*d* orbitals. (Less energy is required for two electrons to pair up in the 4*s* orbital than for those two electrons to

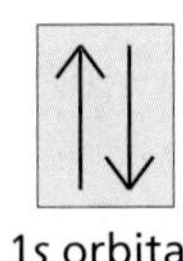

1s orbital

**FIGURE 17** According to the Pauli exclusion principle, an orbital can hold two electrons of opposite spin states. In this electron configuration of a helium atom, each arrow represents one of the atom's two electrons. The direction of the arrow indicates the electron's spin state.

occupy a 3*d* orbital.) Once the 3*d* orbitals are fully occupied, which sublevel will be occupied next?

The second rule reflects the importance of the spin quantum number. According to the **Pauli exclusion principle,** *no two electrons in the same atom can have the same set of four quantum numbers.* The principal, angular momentum, and magnetic quantum numbers specify the energy, shape, and orientation of an orbital. The two values of the spin quantum number reflect the fact that for two electrons to occupy the same orbital, they must have opposite spin states (see **Figure 17**).

The third rule requires placing as many unpaired electrons as possible in separate orbitals in the same sublevel. In this way, electron-electron repulsion is minimized so that the electron arrangements have the lowest energy possible. According to **Hund's rule,** *orbitals of equal energy are each occupied by one electron before any orbital is occupied by a second electron, and all electrons in singly occupied orbitals must have the same spin state.* Applying this rule shows, for example, that one electron will enter each of the three *p* orbitals in a main energy level before a second electron enters any of them. This is illustrated in **Figure 18.** What is the maximum number of unpaired electrons in a *d* sublevel?

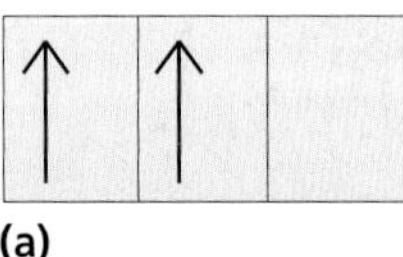

(a)

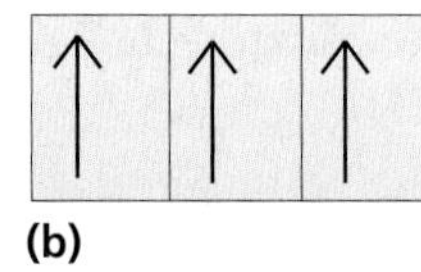

(b)

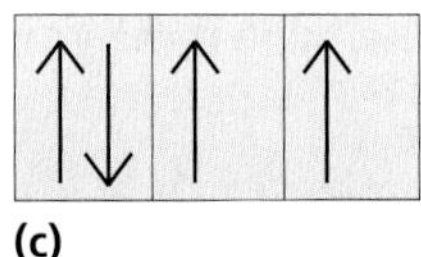

(c)

**FIGURE 18** The figure shows how (a) two, (b) three, and (c) four electrons fill the *p* sublevel of a given main energy level according to Hund's rule.

## Representing Electron Configurations

Three methods, or notations, are used to indicate electron configurations. Two of these notations will be discussed in the next two sections for the first-period elements, hydrogen and helium. The third notation is used mostly with elements of the third period and higher. It will be discussed in the section on third-period elements.

In a ground-state hydrogen atom, the single electron is in the lowest-energy orbital, the 1*s* orbital. The electron can be in either one of its two spin states. Helium has two electrons, which are paired in the 1*s* orbital.

### Orbital Notation

In orbital notation, an unoccupied orbital is represented by a line, ____, with the orbital's name written underneath the line. An orbital containing one electron is represented as $\underline{\ \uparrow\ }$. An orbital containing two electrons is represented as $\underline{\ \uparrow\downarrow\ }$, showing the electrons paired and with opposite spin states. The lines are labeled with the principal quantum number and sublevel letter. For example, the orbital notations for hydrogen and helium are written as follows.

$$\text{H}\ \underset{1s}{\underline{\uparrow}} \qquad \text{He}\ \underset{1s}{\underline{\uparrow\downarrow}}$$

## Electron-Configuration Notation

Electron-configuration notation eliminates the lines and arrows of orbital notation. Instead, the number of electrons in a sublevel is shown by adding a superscript to the sublevel designation. The hydrogen configuration is represented by $1s^1$. The superscript indicates that one electron is present in hydrogen's $1s$ orbital. The helium configuration is represented by $1s^2$. Here the superscript indicates that there are two electrons in helium's $1s$ orbital.

### SAMPLE PROBLEM A

*For more help, go to the* ***Math Tutor*** *at the end of Chapter 5.*

**The electron configuration of boron is $1s^22s^22p^1$. How many electrons are present in an atom of boron? What is the atomic number for boron? Write the orbital notation for boron.**

**SOLUTION** The number of electrons in a boron atom is equal to the sum of the superscripts in its electron-configuration notation: 2 + 2 + 1 = 5 electrons. The number of protons equals the number of electrons in a neutral atom. So we know that boron has 5 protons and thus has an atomic number of 5. To write the orbital notation, first draw the lines representing orbitals.

$$\underset{1s}{\underline{\quad}}\ \underset{2s}{\underline{\quad}}\ \underbrace{\underline{\quad}\,\underline{\quad}\,\underline{\quad}}_{2p}$$

Next, add arrows showing the electron locations. The first two electrons occupy $n = 1$ energy level and fill the $1s$ orbital.

$$\underset{1s}{\underline{\uparrow\downarrow}}\ \underset{2s}{\underline{\quad}}\ \underbrace{\underline{\quad}\,\underline{\quad}\,\underline{\quad}}_{2p}$$

The next three electrons occupy the $n = 2$ main energy level. Two of these occupy the lower-energy $2s$ orbital. The third occupies a higher-energy $p$ orbital.

$$\underset{1s}{\underline{\uparrow\downarrow}}\ \underset{2s}{\underline{\uparrow\downarrow}}\ \underbrace{\underline{\uparrow}\,\underline{\quad}\,\underline{\quad}}_{2p}$$

### PRACTICE

*Answers in Appendix E*

1. The electron configuration of nitrogen is $1s^22s^22p^3$. How many electrons are present in a nitrogen atom? What is the atomic number of nitrogen? Write the orbital notation for nitrogen.
2. The electron configuration of fluorine is $1s^22s^22p^5$. What is the atomic number of fluorine? How many of its $p$ orbitals are filled?

**extension**

Go to **go.hrw.com** for more practice problems that deal with electron configurations.

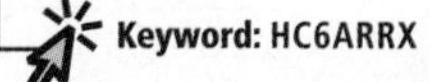

# HISTORICAL CHEMISTRY

## The Noble Decade

By the late nineteenth century, the science of chemistry had begun to be organized. In 1860, the First International Congress of Chemistry established the field's first standards. And Dmitri Mendeleev's periodic table of elements gave chemists across the globe a systematic understanding of matter's building blocks. But many important findings—including the discovery of a family of rare, unreactive gases that were unlike any substances known at the time—were yet to come.

### Cross-Disciplinary Correspondence

In 1888, the British physicist Lord Rayleigh encountered a small but significant discrepancy in the results of one of his experiments. In an effort to redetermine the atomic mass of nitrogen, he measured the densities of several samples of nitrogen gas. Each sample had been prepared by a different method. All samples that had been isolated from chemical reactions exhibited similar densities. But they were about one-tenth of a percent less dense than the nitrogen isolated from air, which at the time was believed to be a mixture of nitrogen, oxygen, water vapor, and carbon dioxide.

*This excerpt from Lord Rayleigh's letter was originally published in* Nature *magazine in 1892.*▼

SEPTEMBER 29, 1892 — *NATURE*

*LETTERS TO THE EDITOR.*

[*The Editor does not hold himself responsible for opinions expressed by his correspondents. Neither can he undertake to return, or to correspond with the writers of, rejected manuscripts intended for this or any other part of* NATURE. *No notice is taken of anonymous communications.*]

Density of Nitrogen.

I AM much puzzled by some recent results as to the density of *nitrogen*, and shall be obliged if any of your chemical readers can offer suggestions as to the cause. According to two methods of preparation I obtain quite distinct values. The relative difference, amounting to about $\frac{1}{1000}$ part, is small in itself; but it lies entirely outside the errors of experiment, and can only be attributed to a variation in the character of the gas...

Is it possible that the difference is independent of impurity, the nitrogen itself being to some extent in a different (dissociated) state?...

RAYLEIGH.

Terling Place, Witham, September 24.

Rayleigh was at a loss to explain his discovery. Finally, in 1892, he published a letter in *Nature* magazine to appeal to his colleagues for an explanation. A month later, he received a reply from a Scottish chemist named William Ramsay. Ramsay related that he too had been stumped by the density difference between chemical and atmospheric nitrogen. Rayleigh decided to report his findings to the Royal Society.

### A Chemist's Approach

With Rayleigh's permission, Ramsay attempted to remove all known components from a sample of air and to analyze what, if anything, remained. Having removed water vapor, carbon dioxide, and oxygen from the air, Ramsay repeatedly passed the sample over hot magnesium. The nitrogen reacted with the magnesium to form solid magnesium nitride. As a result, all of the then-known components of air were removed. What remained was a minuscule portion of a mysterious gas.

Ramsay tried to cause the gas to react with chemically active substances, such as hydrogen, sodium, and caustic soda, but the gas remained unaltered. He decided to name this new atmospheric component *argon* (Greek for "inert" or "idle").

### Periodic Problems

Rayleigh and Ramsay were sure that they had discovered a new element. But this created a problem. Their calculations indicated that argon had an atomic mass of about 40. However, as it appeared in 1894, the periodic table had no space for such an element. The elements with atomic masses closest to that of argon were chlorine and potassium. Unfortunately, the chemical properties of the families of each of these elements were completely dissimilar to those of the strange gas.

Ramsay contemplated argon's lack of reactivity. He knew that Mendeleev had created the periodic table on the basis of valence, or the number of atomic partners an element bonds with in forming a compound. Because Ramsay could not cause argon to form any compounds, he assigned it a valence of zero. And because the valence of the elements in

▲*In 1893, Scottish chemist William Ramsay isolated a previously unknown component of the atmosphere.*

| Periods \ Groups | III b | IV b | V b | VI b | VII b | VIII b | I b | II b | III a | IV a | V a | VI a | VII a | 0 | I a | II a |
|---|---|---|---|---|---|---|---|---|---|---|---|---|---|---|---|---|
| 1 | | | | | | | | | | | | | | | H | He |
| 2 | | | | | | | | | | | | | | | Li | Be |
| 3 | | | | | | | | | B | C | N | O | F | Ne | Na | Mg |
| 4 | | | | | | | | | Al | Si | P | S | Cl | Ar | K | Ca |
| 5 | Sc | Ti | V | Cr | Mn | Fe Co Ni | Cu | Zn | Ga | Ge | As | Se | Br | Kr | Rb | Sr |
| 6 | Y | Zr | Nb | Mo | Tc | Ru Rh Pd | Ag | Cd | In | Sn | Sb | Te | I | Xe | Cs | Ba |
| 7 | La | Hf | Ta | W | Re | Os Ir Pt | Au | Hg | Tl | Pb | Bi | Po | At | Rn | Fr | Ra |
| 8 | Ac | | | | | | | | | | | | | | | |
| | Transition elements | | | | | | | | Main-group elements | | | | | | | |

▲*This version of the periodic table shows how it looked after the discovery of the noble gases. The placement of the Group 1 and 2 elements at the far right of the table shows clearly how the noble gases fit in between the chlorine family and the potassium family of elements. The 0 above the noble-gas family indicates the zero valency of the gases.*

the families of both chlorine and potassium was one, perhaps argon fit in between them.

Ramsay's insight that argon merited a new spot between the halogen family and the alkali metal family on the periodic table was correct. And as Ramsay would soon confirm, his newly discovered gas was indeed one of a previously unknown family of elements.

### New Neighbors

In 1895, Ramsay isolated a light, inert gas from a mineral called *cleveite.* Physical analysis revealed that the gas was the same as one that had been identified in the sun in 1868—helium. Helium was the second zero-valent element found on Earth, and its discovery made chemists aware that the periodic table had been missing a whole column of elements.

Over the next three years, Ramsay and his assistant, Morris Travers, identified three more inert gases present in the atmosphere: neon (Greek for "new"), krypton ("hidden"), and xenon ("stranger"). Finally in 1900, German chemist Friedrich Ernst Dorn discovered radon, the last of the new family of elements known today as the *noble gases.* For his discovery, Ramsay received the Nobel Prize in 1904.

## Questions

1. What evidence led Ramsay to report that the mysterious gas was inert?
2. What property of argon caused Ramsay to propose a new column in the periodic table?

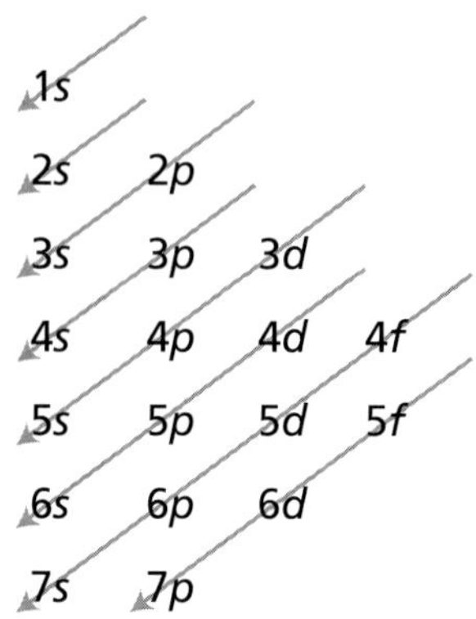


**FIGURE 19** Follow the diagonal arrows from the top to get the order in which atomic orbitals are filled according to the Aufbau principle.

## Elements of the Second Period

In the first-period elements, hydrogen and helium, electrons occupy the orbital of the first main energy level. The ground-state configurations in **Table 3** illustrate how the Aufbau principle, the Pauli exclusion principle, and Hund's rule are applied to atoms of elements in the second period. **Figure 19** provides a pattern to help you remember the order in which orbitals are filled according to the Aufbau principle.

According to the Aufbau principle, after the 1*s* orbital is filled, the next electron occupies the *s* sublevel in the second main energy level. Thus, lithium, Li, has a configuration of $1s^22s^1$. The electron occupying the 2*s* level of a lithium atom is in the atom's highest, or outermost, occupied level. The *highest-occupied energy level* is the electron-containing main energy level with the highest principal quantum number. The two electrons in the 1*s* sublevel of lithium are no longer in the outermost main energy level. They have become *inner-shell electrons,* which are electrons that are not in the highest-occupied energy level.

The fourth electron in an atom of beryllium, Be, must complete the pair in the 2*s* sublevel because this sublevel is of lower energy than the 2*p* sublevel. With the 2*s* sublevel filled, the 2*p* sublevel, which has three vacant orbitals of equal energy, can be occupied. One of the three *p* orbitals is occupied by a single electron in an atom of boron, B. Two of the three *p* orbitals are occupied by unpaired electrons in an atom of carbon, C. And all three *p* orbitals are occupied by unpaired electrons in an atom of nitrogen, N. Hund's rule applies here, as is shown in the orbital notations in **Table 3.**

According to the Aufbau principle, the next electron must pair with another electron in one of the 2*p* orbitals rather than enter the third main energy level. The Pauli exclusion principle allows the electron to pair with

**TABLE 3** ***Electron Configurations of Atoms of Second-Period Elements Showing Two Notations***

| | | Orbital notation | | | | | Electron-configuration notation |
|---|---|---|---|---|---|---|---|
| Name | Symbol | 1*s* | 2*s* | 2*p* | | | |
| Lithium | Li | ↑↓ | ↑ | ___ | ___ | ___ | $1s^22s^1$ |
| Beryllium | Be | ↑↓ | ↑↓ | ___ | ___ | ___ | $1s^22s^2$ |
| Boron | B | ↑↓ | ↑↓ | ↑ | ___ | ___ | $1s^22s^22p^1$ |
| Carbon | C | ↑↓ | ↑↓ | ↑ | ↑ | ___ | $1s^22s^22p^2$ |
| Nitrogen | N | ↑↓ | ↑↓ | ↑ | ↑ | ↑ | $1s^22s^22p^3$ |
| Oxygen | O | ↑↓ | ↑↓ | ↑↓ | ↑ | ↑ | $1s^22s^22p^4$ |
| Fluorine | F | ↑↓ | ↑↓ | ↑↓ | ↑↓ | ↑ | $1s^22s^22p^5$ |
| Neon | Ne | ↑↓ | ↑↓ | ↑↓ | ↑↓ | ↑↓ | $1s^22s^22p^6$ |

one of the electrons occupying the $2p$ orbitals as long as the spins of the paired electrons are opposite. Thus, atoms of oxygen, O, have the configuration $1s^22s^22p^4$. Oxygen's orbital notation is shown in **Table 3.**

Two $2p$ orbitals are filled in fluorine, F, and all three are filled in neon, Ne. Atoms such as those of neon, which have the $s$ and $p$ sublevels of their highest occupied level filled with eight electrons, are said to have an *octet* of electrons. Examine the periodic table inside the back cover of the text. Notice that neon is the last element in the second period.

## Elements of the Third Period

After the outer octet is filled in neon, the next electron enters the $s$ sublevel in the $n = 3$ main energy level. Thus, atoms of sodium, Na, have the configuration $1s^22s^22p^63s^1$. Compare the configuration of a sodium atom with that of an atom of neon in **Table 3.** Notice that the first 10 electrons in a sodium atom have the same configuration as a neon atom, $1s^22s^22p^6$. In fact, the first 10 electrons in an atom of each of the third-period elements have the same configuration as neon. This similarity allows us to use a shorthand notation for the electron configurations of the third-period elements.

### Noble-Gas Notation

Neon is a member of the Group 18 elements. *The Group 18 elements (helium, neon, argon, krypton, xenon, and radon) are called the* **noble gases.** To simplify sodium's notation, the symbol for neon, enclosed in square brackets, is used to represent the complete neon configuration: $[Ne] = 1s^22s^22p^6$. This allows us to write sodium's electron configuration as $[Ne]3s^1$, which is called sodium's *noble-gas notation.* **Table 4** shows the electron configuration of each of the third-period elements using noble-gas notation.

**TABLE 4 *Electron Configurations of Atoms of Third-Period Elements***

| Name | Symbol | Atomic number | Number of electrons in sublevels | | | | | Noble-gas notation |
|---|---|---|---|---|---|---|---|---|
| | | | 1*s* | 2*s* | 2*p* | 3*s* | 3*p* | |
| Sodium | Na | 11 | 2 | 2 | 6 | 1 | | *$[Ne]3s^1$ |
| Magnesium | Mg | 12 | 2 | 2 | 6 | 2 | | $[Ne]3s^2$ |
| Aluminum | Al | 13 | 2 | 2 | 6 | 2 | 1 | $[Ne]3s^23p^1$ |
| Silicon | Si | 14 | 2 | 2 | 6 | 2 | 2 | $[Ne]3s^23p^2$ |
| Phosphorus | P | 15 | 2 | 2 | 6 | 2 | 3 | $[Ne]3s^23p^3$ |
| Sulfur | S | 16 | 2 | 2 | 6 | 2 | 4 | $[Ne]3s^23p^4$ |
| Chlorine | Cl | 17 | 2 | 2 | 6 | 2 | 5 | $[Ne]3s^23p^5$ |
| Argon | Ar | 18 | 2 | 2 | 6 | 2 | 6 | $[Ne]3s^23p^6$ |

*$[Ne] = 1s^22s^22p^6$

The last element in the third period is argon, Ar, which is a noble gas. As in neon, the highest-occupied energy level of argon has an octet of electrons, [Ne]$3s^23p^6$. In fact, each noble gas other than He has an electron octet in its highest energy level. *A* **noble-gas configuration** *refers to an outer main energy level occupied, in most cases, by eight electrons.*

## Elements of the Fourth Period

The electron configurations of atoms in the fourth-period elements are shown in **Table 5.** The period begins by filling the 4*s* orbital, the empty orbital of lowest energy. Thus, the first element in the fourth period is potassium, K, which has the electron configuration [Ar]$4s^1$. The next element is calcium, Ca, which has the electron configuration [Ar]$4s^2$.

With the 4*s* sublevel filled, the 4*p* and 3*d* sublevels are the next available vacant orbitals. **Figure 16** shows that the 3*d* sublevel is lower in energy than the 4*p* sublevel. Therefore, the five 3*d* orbitals are next to

**TABLE 5** ***Electron Configuration of Atoms of Elements in the Fourth Period***

| Name | Symbol | Atomic number | Number of electrons in sublevels above 2*p* | | | | | Noble-gas notation |
|---|---|---|---|---|---|---|---|---|
| | | | 3*s* | 3*p* | 3*d* | 4*s* | 4*p* | |
| Potassium | K | 19 | 2 | 6 | | 1 | | *[Ar]$4s^1$ |
| Calcium | Ca | 20 | 2 | 6 | | 2 | | [Ar]$4s^2$ |
| Scandium | Sc | 21 | 2 | 6 | 1 | 2 | | [Ar]$3d^14s^2$ |
| Titanium | Ti | 22 | 2 | 6 | 2 | 2 | | [Ar]$3d^24s^2$ |
| Vanadium | V | 23 | 2 | 6 | 3 | 2 | | [Ar]$3d^34s^2$ |
| Chromium | Cr | 24 | 2 | 6 | 5 | 1 | | [Ar]$3d^54s^1$ |
| Manganese | Mn | 25 | 2 | 6 | 5 | 2 | | [Ar]$3d^54s^2$ |
| Iron | Fe | 26 | 2 | 6 | 6 | 2 | | [Ar]$3d^64s^2$ |
| Cobalt | Co | 27 | 2 | 6 | 7 | 2 | | [Ar]$3d^74s^2$ |
| Nickel | Ni | 28 | 2 | 6 | 8 | 2 | | [Ar]$3d^84s^2$ |
| Copper | Cu | 29 | 2 | 6 | 10 | 1 | | [Ar]$3d^{10}4s^1$ |
| Zinc | Zn | 30 | 2 | 6 | 10 | 2 | | [Ar]$3d^{10}4s^2$ |
| Gallium | Ga | 31 | 2 | 6 | 10 | 2 | 1 | [Ar]$3d^{10}4s^24p^1$ |
| Germanium | Ge | 32 | 2 | 6 | 10 | 2 | 2 | [Ar]$3d^{10}4s^24p^2$ |
| Arsenic | As | 33 | 2 | 6 | 10 | 2 | 3 | [Ar]$3d^{10}4s^24p^3$ |
| Selenium | Se | 34 | 2 | 6 | 10 | 2 | 4 | [Ar]$3d^{10}4s^24p^4$ |
| Bromine | Br | 35 | 2 | 6 | 10 | 2 | 5 | [Ar]$3d^{10}4s^24p^5$ |
| Krypton | Kr | 36 | 2 | 6 | 10 | 2 | 6 | [Ar]$3d^{10}4s^24p^6$ |

*[Ar] = $1s^22s^22p^63s^23p^6$

be filled. A total of 10 electrons can occupy the 3*d* orbitals. These are filled successively in the 10 elements from scandium (atomic number 21) to zinc (atomic number 30).

Scandium, Sc, has the electron configuration $[Ar]3d^14s^2$. Titanium, Ti, has the configuration $[Ar]3d^24s^2$. And vanadium, V, has the configuration $[Ar]3d^34s^2$. Up to this point, three electrons with the same spin have been added to three separate *d* orbitals, as required by Hund's rule.

Surprisingly, chromium, Cr, has the electron configuration $[Ar]3d^54s^1$. Not only did the added electron go into the fourth 3*d* orbital, but an electron also moved from the 4*s* orbital into the fifth 3*d* orbital, leaving the 4*s* orbital with a single electron. Chromium's electron configuration is contrary to what is expected according to the Aufbau principle. However, in reality the $[Ar]3d^54s^1$ configuration is of lower energy than a $[Ar]3d^44s^2$ configuration. For chromium, having six orbitals, all with unpaired electrons, is a more stable arrangement than having four unpaired electrons in the 3*d* orbitals and forcing two electrons to pair up in the 4*s* orbital. On the other hand, for tungsten, W, which is in the same group as chromium, having four electrons in the 5*d* orbitals and two electrons paired in the 6*s* orbital is the most stable arrrangement. Unfortunately, there is no simple explanation for such deviations from the expected order given in **Figure 19.**

Manganese, Mn, has the electron configuration $[Ar]3d^54s^2$. The added electron goes to the 4*s* orbital, completely filling this orbital while leaving the 3*d* orbitals still half-filled. Beginning with the next element, electrons continue to pair in the *d* orbitals. Thus, iron, Fe, has the configuration $[Ar]3d^64s^2$; cobalt, Co, has the configuration $[Ar]3d^74s^2$; and nickel, Ni, has the configuration $[Ar]3d^84s^2$. Next is copper, Cu, in which an electron moves from the 4*s* orbital to pair with the electron in the fifth 3*d* orbital. The result is an electron configuration of $[Ar]3d^{10}4s^1$—the lowest-energy configuration for Cu. As with Cr, there is no simple explanation for this deviation from the expected order.

In atoms of zinc, Zn, the 4*s* sublevel is filled to give the electron configuration $[Ar]3d^{10}4s^2$. In atoms of the next six elements, electrons add one by one to the three 4*p* orbitals. According to Hund's rule, one electron is added to each of the three 4*p* orbitals before electrons are paired in any 4*p* orbital.

## Elements of the Fifth Period

In the 18 elements of the fifth period, sublevels fill in a similar manner as in elements of the fourth period. However, they start at the 5*s* orbital instead of the 4*s*. Successive electrons are added first to the 5*s* orbital, then to the 4*d* orbitals, and finally to the 5*p* orbitals. This can be seen in **Table 6.** There are occasional deviations from the predicted configurations here also. The deviations differ from those for fourth-period elements, but in each case the preferred configuration has the lowest possible energy.

**TABLE 6 Electron Configurations of Atoms of Elements in the Fifth Period**

| Name | Symbol | Atomic number | Number of electrons in sublevels above 3d | | | | | Noble-gas notation |
|---|---|---|---|---|---|---|---|---|
| | | | 4s | 4p | 4d | 5s | 5p | |
| Rubidium | Rb | 37 | 2 | 6 | | 1 | | *[Kr]$5s^1$ |
| Strontium | Sr | 38 | 2 | 6 | | 2 | | [Kr]$5s^2$ |
| Yttrium | Y | 39 | 2 | 6 | 1 | 2 | | [Kr]$4d^15s^2$ |
| Zirconium | Zr | 40 | 2 | 6 | 2 | 2 | | [Kr]$4d^25s^2$ |
| Niobium | Nb | 41 | 2 | 6 | 4 | 1 | | [Kr]$4d^45s^1$ |
| Molybdenum | Mo | 42 | 2 | 6 | 5 | 1 | | [Kr]$4d^55s^1$ |
| Technetium | Tc | 43 | 2 | 6 | 6 | 1 | | [Kr]$4d^65s^1$ |
| Ruthenium | Ru | 44 | 2 | 6 | 7 | 1 | | [Kr]$4d^75s^1$ |
| Rhodium | Rh | 45 | 2 | 6 | 8 | 1 | | [Kr]$4d^85s^1$ |
| Palladium | Pd | 46 | 2 | 6 | 10 | | | [Kr]$4d^{10}$ |
| Silver | Ag | 47 | 2 | 6 | 10 | 1 | | [Kr]$4d^{10}5s^1$ |
| Cadmium | Cd | 48 | 2 | 6 | 10 | 2 | | [Kr]$4d^{10}5s^2$ |
| Indium | In | 49 | 2 | 6 | 10 | 2 | 1 | [Kr]$4d^{10}5s^25p^1$ |
| Tin | Sn | 50 | 2 | 6 | 10 | 2 | 2 | [Kr]$4d^{10}5s^25p^2$ |
| Antimony | Sb | 51 | 2 | 6 | 10 | 2 | 3 | [Kr]$4d^{10}5s^25p^3$ |
| Tellurium | Te | 52 | 2 | 6 | 10 | 2 | 4 | [Kr]$4d^{10}5s^25p^4$ |
| Iodine | I | 53 | 2 | 6 | 10 | 2 | 5 | [Kr]$4d^{10}5s^25p^5$ |
| Xenon | Xe | 54 | 2 | 6 | 10 | 2 | 6 | [Kr]$4d^{10}5s^25p^6$ |

*[Kr] = $1s^22s^22p^63s^23p^63d^{10}4s^24p^6$

## SAMPLE PROBLEM B

*For more help, go to the* ***Math Tutor*** *at the end of Chapter 5.*

**a. Write both the complete electron-configuration notation and the noble-gas notation for iron, Fe.**

**b. How many electron-containing orbitals are in an atom of iron? How many of these orbitals are completely filled? How many unpaired electrons are there in an atom of iron? In which sublevel are the unpaired electrons located?**

**SOLUTION**

a. The complete electron-configuration notation of iron is $1s^22s^22p^63s^23p^63d^64s^2$. The periodic table inside the back cover of the text reveals that $1s^22s^22p^63s^23p^6$ is the electron configuration of the noble gas argon, Ar. Therefore, as shown in **Table 5**, iron's noble-gas notation is [Ar]$3d^64s^2$.

b. An iron atom has 15 orbitals that contain electrons. They consist of one 1s orbital, one 2*s* orbital, three 2*p* orbitals, one 3*s* orbital, three 3*p* orbitals, five 3*d* orbitals, and one 4*s* orbital. Eleven of these orbitals are filled, and there are four unpaired electrons. They are located in the 3*d* sublevel. The notation $3d^6$ represents

$$3d\ \underline{\uparrow\downarrow}\ \underline{\uparrow}\ \underline{\uparrow}\ \underline{\uparrow}\ \underline{\uparrow}$$

**PRACTICE** *Answers in Appendix E*

1. a. Write both the complete electron-configuration notation and the noble-gas notation for iodine, I. How many inner-shell electrons does an iodine atom contain?

   b. How many electron-containing orbitals are in an atom of iodine? How many of these orbitals are filled? How many unpaired electrons are there in an atom of iodine?

2. a. Write the noble-gas notation for tin, Sn. How many unpaired electrons are there in an atom of tin?

   b. How many electron-containing *d* orbitals are there in an atom of tin? Name the element in the fourth period whose atoms have the same number of electrons in their highest energy levels that tin's atoms do.

3. a. Write the complete electron configuration for the element with atomic number 25. You may use the diagram shown in **Figure 19.**

   b. Identify the element described in item 3a.

4. a. How many orbitals are completely filled in an atom of the element with atomic number 18? Write the complete electron configuration for this element.

   b. Identify the element described in item 4a.

Go to **go.hrw.com** for more practice problems that deal with electron configurations.

**Keyword: HC6ARRX**

## Elements of the Sixth and Seventh Periods

The sixth period consists of 32 elements. It is much longer than the periods that precede it in the periodic table. To build up electron configurations for elements of this period, electrons are added first to the 6*s* orbital in cesium, Cs, and barium, Ba. Then, in lanthanum, La, an electron is added to the 5*d* orbital.

With the next element, cerium, Ce, the 4*f* orbitals begin to fill, giving cerium atoms a configuration of $[Xe]4f^1 5d^1 6s^2$. In the next 13 elements, the 4*f* orbitals are filled. Next the 5*d* orbitals are filled and the period is completed by filling the 6*p* orbitals. Because the 4*f* and the 5*d* orbitals are very close in energy, numerous deviations from the simple rules occur as these orbitals are filled. The electron configurations of the sixth-period elements can be found in the periodic table inside the back cover of the text.

The seventh period is incomplete and consists largely of synthetic elements, which will be discussed in Chapter 21.

## SAMPLE PROBLEM C

For more help, go to the *Math Tutor* at the end of Chapter 5.

**a. Write both the complete electron-configuration notation and the noble-gas notation for a rubidium atom.**

**b. Identify the elements in the second, third, and fourth periods that have the same number of highest-energy-level electrons as rubidium.**

**SOLUTION** a. $1s^22s^22p^63s^23p^63d^{10}4s^24p^65s^1$, $[Kr]5s^1$

b. Rubidium has one electron in its highest energy level (the fifth). The elements with the same outermost configuration are, in the second period, lithium, Li; in the third period, sodium, Na; and in the fourth period, potassium, K.

**PRACTICE** *Answers in Appendix E*

1. a. Write both the complete electron-configuration notation and the noble-gas notation for a barium atom.

   b. Identify the elements in the second, third, fourth, and fifth periods that have the same number of highest-energy-level electrons as barium.

2. a. Write the noble-gas notation for a gold atom.

   b. Identify the elements in the sixth period that have one unpaired electron in their 6*s* sublevel.

Go to **go.hrw.com** for more practice problems that deal with electron configurations.

**Keyword: HC6ARRX**

## SECTION REVIEW

1. **a.** What is an atom's electron configuration?
   **b.** What three principles guide the electron configuration of an atom?
2. What three methods are used to represent the arrangement of electrons in atoms?
3. What is an octet of electrons? Which elements contain an octet of electrons?
4. Write the complete electron-configuration notation, the noble-gas notation, and the orbital notation for the following elements:
   **a.** carbon **b.** neon **c.** sulfur
5. Identify the elements having the following electron configurations:
   **a.** $1s^22s^22p^63s^23p^3$
   **b.** $[Ar]4s^1$
   **c.** contains four electrons in its third and outer main energy level
   **d.** contains one set of paired and three unpaired electrons in its fourth and outer main energy level

**Critical Thinking**

6. **RELATING IDEAS** Write the electron configuration for the third-period elements Al, Si, P, S, and Cl. Is there a relationship between the group number of each element and the number of electrons in the outermost energy level?

# CHAPTER HIGHLIGHTS

## The Development of a New Atomic Model

**Vocabulary**
electromagnetic radiation
electromagnetic spectrum
wavelength
frequency
photoelectric effect
quantum
photon
ground state
excited state
line-emission spectrum
continuous spectrum

- In the early twentieth century, light was determined to have a dual wave-particle nature.
- Quantum theory was developed to explain observations such as the photoelectric effect and the line-emission spectrum of hydrogen.
- Quantum theory states that electrons can exist only at specific atomic energy levels.
- When an electron moves from one main energy level to a main energy level of lower energy, a photon is emitted. The photon's energy equals the energy difference between the two levels.
- An electron in an atom can move from one main energy level to a higher main energy level only by absorbing an amount of energy exactly equal to the difference between the two levels.

## The Quantum Model of the Atom

**Vocabulary**
Heisenberg uncertainty principle
quantum theory
orbital
quantum number
principal quantum number
angular momentum quantum number
magnetic quantum number
spin quantum number

- In the early twentieth century, electrons were determined to have a dual wave-particle nature.
- The Heisenberg uncertainty principle states that it is impossible to determine simultaneously the position and velocity of an electron or any other particle.
- Quantization of electron energies is a natural outcome of the Schrödinger wave equation, which describes the properties of an atom's electrons.
- An orbital, a three-dimensional region around the nucleus, shows the region in space where an electron is most likely to be found.
- The four quantum numbers that describe the properties of electrons in atomic orbitals are the principal quantum number, the angular momentum quantum number, the magnetic quantum number, and the spin quantum number.

## Electron Configurations

**Vocabulary**
electron configuration
Aufbau principle
Pauli exclusion principle
Hund's rule
noble gas
noble-gas configuration

- The ground-state electron configuration of an atom can be written by using the Aufbau principle, Hund's rule, and the Pauli exclusion principle.
- Electron configurations can be depicted by using different types of notation. In this book, three types of notation are used: orbital notation, electron-configuration notation, and noble-gas notation.
- Electron configurations of some atoms, such as chromium, deviate from the predictions of the Aufbau principle, but the ground-state configuration that results is the configuration with the minimum possible energy.

# CHAPTER REVIEW

## The Development of a New Atomic Model

### SECTION 1 REVIEW

1. a. List five examples of electromagnetic radiation.
   b. What is the speed of all forms of electromagnetic radiation in a vacuum?
2. Prepare a two-column table. List the properties of light that can best be explained by the wave theory in one column. List those best explained by the particle theory in the second column. You may want to consult a physics textbook for reference.
3. What are the frequency and wavelength ranges of visible light?
4. List the colors of light in the visible spectrum in order of increasing frequency.
5. In the early twentieth century, what two experiments involving light and matter could not be explained by the wave theory of light?
6. a. How are the wavelength and frequency of electromagnetic radiation related?
   b. How are the energy and frequency of electromagnetic radiation related?
   c. How are the energy and wavelength of electromagnetic radiation related?
7. Which theory of light—the wave or particle theory—best explains the following phenomena?
   a. the interference of light
   b. the photoelectric effect
   c. the emission of electromagnetic radiation by an excited atom
8. Distinguish between the ground state and an excited state of an atom.
9. According to Bohr's model of the hydrogen atom, how is hydrogen's emission spectrum produced?

### PRACTICE PROBLEMS

10. Determine the frequency of light whose wavelength is $4.257 \times 10^{-7}$ cm.
11. Determine the energy in joules of a photon whose frequency is $3.55 \times 10^{17}$ Hz.
12. Using the two equations $E = hv$ and $c = \lambda v$, derive an equation expressing $E$ in terms of $h$, $c$, and $\lambda$.
13. How long would it take a radio wave whose frequency is $7.25 \times 10^5$ Hz to travel from Mars to Earth if the distance between the two planets is approximately $8.00 \times 10^7$ km?
14. Cobalt-60 is an artificial radioisotope that is produced in a nuclear reactor and is used as a gamma-ray source in the treatment of certain types of cancer. If the wavelength of the gamma radiation from a cobalt-60 source is $1.00 \times 10^{-3}$ nm, calculate the energy of a photon of this radiation.

## The Quantum Model of the Atom

### SECTION 2 REVIEW

15. Describe two major shortcomings of Bohr's model of the atom.
16. a. What is the principal quantum number?
    b. How is it symbolized?
    c. What are shells?
    d. How does $n$ relate to the number of electrons allowed per main energy level?
17. a. What information is given by the angular momentum quantum number?
    b. What are sublevels, or subshells?
18. For each of the following values of $n$, indicate the numbers and types of sublevels possible for that main energy level. (Hint: See **Table 2.**)
    a. $n = 1$
    b. $n = 2$
    c. $n = 3$
    d. $n = 4$
    e. $n = 7$ (number only)
19. a. What information is given by the magnetic quantum number?
    b. How many orbital orientations are possible in each of the *s*, *p*, *d*, and *f* sublevels?
    c. Explain and illustrate the notation for distinguishing between the different *p* orbitals in a sublevel.

**20.** a. What is the relationship between $n$ and the total number of orbitals in a main energy level?
b. How many total orbitals are contained in the third main energy level? in the fifth?

**21.** a. What information is given by the spin quantum number?
b. What are the possible values for this quantum number?

**22.** How many electrons could be contained in the following main energy levels with $n$ equal to the number provided?
a. 1
b. 3
c. 4
d. 6
e. 7

**PRACTICE PROBLEMS**

**23.** Sketch the shape of an $s$ orbital and a $p$ orbital.

**24.** How does a $2s$ orbital differ from a $1s$ orbital?

**25.** How do a $2p_x$ and a $2p_y$ orbital differ?

## *Electron Configurations*

**SECTION 3 REVIEW**

**26.** a. In your own words, state the Aufbau principle.
b. Explain the meaning of this principle in terms of an atom with many electrons.

**27.** a. In your own words, state Hund's rule.
b. What is the basis for this rule?

**28.** a. In your own words, state the Pauli exclusion principle.
b. What is the significance of the spin quantum number?

**29.** a. What is meant by the highest occupied energy level in an atom?
b. What are inner-shell electrons?

**30.** Determine the highest occupied energy level in the following elements:
a. He
b. Be
c. Al
d. Ca
e. Sn

**31.** Write the orbital notation for the following elements. (Hint: See Sample Problem A.)
a. P
b. B
c. Na
d. O

**32.** Write the electron-configuration notation for the element whose atoms contain the following number of electrons:
a. 3
b. 6
c. 8
d. 13

**33.** Given that the electron configuration for oxygen is $1s^22s^22p^4$, answer the following questions:
a. How many electrons are in each oxygen atom?
b. What is the atomic number of this element?
c. Write the orbital notation for oxygen's electron configuration.
d. How many unpaired electrons does oxygen have?
e. What is the highest occupied energy level?
f. How many inner-shell electrons does the atom contain?
g. In which orbital(s) are these inner-shell electrons located?

**34.** a. What are the noble gases?
b. What is a noble-gas configuration?
c. How does noble-gas notation simplify writing an atom's electron configuration?

**35.** Write the noble-gas notation for the electron configuration of each of the elements below. (Hint: See Sample Problem B.)
a. Cl
b. Ca
c. Se

**36.** a. What information is given by the noble-gas notation [Ne]$3s^2$?
b. What element does this represent?

**37.** Write both the complete electron-configuration notation and the noble-gas notation for each of the elements below. (Hint: See Sample Problem C.)
a. Na
b. Sr
c. P

**38.** Identify each of the following atoms on the basis of its electron configuration:
a. $1s^22s^22p^1$
b. $1s^22s^22p^5$
c. $[Ne]3s^2$
d. $[Ne]3s^23p^2$
e. $[Ne]3s^23p^5$
f. $[Ar]4s^1$
g. $[Ar]3d^64s^2$

## PRACTICE PROBLEMS

**39.** List the order in which orbitals generally fill, from the 1*s* to the 7*p* orbital.

**40.** Write the noble-gas notation for the electron configurations of each of the following elements:
a. As
b. Pb
c. Lr
d. Hg
e. Sn
f. Xe
g. La

**41.** How do the electron configurations of chromium and copper contradict the Aufbau principle?

## MIXED REVIEW

**42.** a. Which has a longer wavelength: green light or yellow light?
b. Which has a higher frequency: an X ray or a microwave?
c. Which travels at a greater speed: ultraviolet light or infrared light?

**43.** Write both the complete electron-configuration and noble-gas notation for each of the following:
a. Ar
b. Br
c. Al

**44.** Given the speed of light as $3.00 \times 10^8$ m/s, calculate the wavelength of the electromagnetic radiation whose frequency is $7.500 \times 10^{12}$ Hz.

**45.** a. What is the electromagnetic spectrum?
b. What units can be used to express wavelength?
c. What unit is used to express frequencies of electromagnetic waves?

**46.** Given that the electron configuration for phosphorus is $1s^22s^22p^63s^23p^3$, answer the following questions:
a. How many electrons are in each atom?
b. What is the atomic number of this element?
c. Write the orbital notation for this element.
d. How many unpaired electrons does an atom of phosphorus have?
e. What is its highest occupied energy level?
f. How many inner-shell electrons does the atom contain?
g. In which orbital(s) are these inner-shell electrons located?

**47.** What is the frequency of a radio wave whose energy is $1.55 \times 10^{-24}$ J per photon?

**48.** Write the noble-gas notation for the electron configurations of each of the following elements:
a. Hf
b. Sc
c. Fe
d. At
e. Ac
f. Zn

**49.** Describe the major similarities and differences between Schrödinger's model of the atom and the model proposed by Bohr.

**50.** When sodium is heated, a yellow spectral line whose energy is $3.37 \times 10^{-19}$ J per photon is produced.
a. What is the frequency of this light?
b. What is the wavelength of this light?

**51.** a. What is an orbital?
b. Describe an orbital in terms of an electron cloud.

## CRITICAL THINKING

**52. Inferring Relationships** In the emission spectrum of hydrogen shown in **Figure 5,** each colored line is produced by the emission of photons with specific energies. Substances also produce absorption spectra when electromagnetic radiation passes through them. Certain wavelengths are absorbed. Using the diagram below, predict what the wavelengths of the absorption lines will be when white light (all of the colors of the visible spectrum) is passed through hydrogen gas.

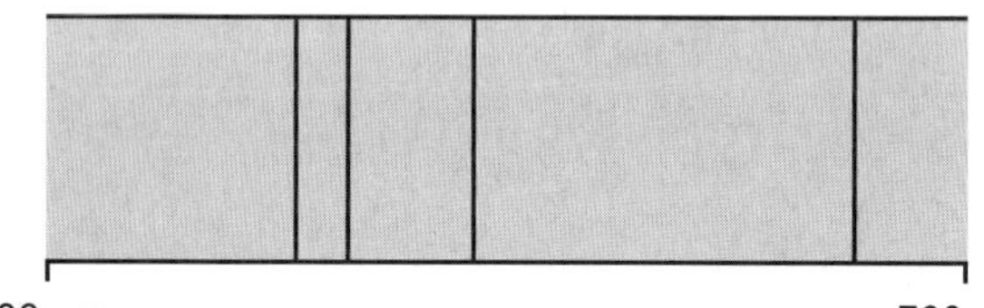


Hydrogen absorption spectrum

**53. Applying Models** In discussions of the photoelectric effect, the minimum energy needed to remove an electron from the metal is called the *threshold energy* and is a characteristic of the metal. For example, chromium, Cr, will emit electrons when the wavelength of the radiation is 284 nm or less. Calculate the threshold energy for chromium. (Hint: You will need to use the two equations that describe the relationships between wavelength, frequency, speed of light, and Planck's constant.)

**54. Analyzing Information** Four electrons in an atom have the four sets of quantum numbers given below. Which electrons are in the same orbital? Explain your answer.

a. 1, 0, 0, −__
b. 1, 0, 0, +__
c. 2, 1, 1, +__
d. 2, 1, 0, +__

**55. Relating Ideas** Which of the sets of quantum numbers below are possible? Which are impossible? Explain your choices.

a. 2, 2, 1, +__
b. 2, 0, 0, −__
c. 2, 0, 1, −__

## USING THE HANDBOOK

**56.** Sections 1 and 2 of the *Elements Handbook* contain information on an analytical test and a technological application for Group 1 and 2 elements. The test and application are based on the emission of light from atoms. Review these sections to answer the following:

a. What analytical technique utilizes the emission of light from excited atoms?
b. What elements in Groups 1 and 2 can be identified by this technique?
c. What types of compounds are used to provide color in fireworks?
d. What wavelengths within the visible spectrum would most likely contain emission lines for barium?

## RESEARCH & WRITING

**57.** Neon signs do not always contain neon gas. The various colored lights produced by the signs are due to the emission of a variety of low-pressure gases in different tubes. Research other kinds of gases used in neon signs, and list the colors that they emit.

**58.** Prepare a report about the photoelectric effect, and cite some of its practical uses. Explain the basic operation of each device or technique mentioned.

## ALTERNATIVE ASSESSMENT

**59. Performance** A spectroscope is a device used to produce and analyze spectra. Construct a simple spectroscope, and determine the absorption spectra of several elemental gases. (Your teacher will provide you with the gas discharge tubes containing samples of different gases.)

extension

Graphing Calculator **Calculating Quantum Number Relationships**

Go to **go.hrw.com** for a graphing calculator exercise that asks you to calculate quantum number relationships.

**Keyword:** HC6ARRX

# Math Tutor WEIGHTED AVERAGES AND ATOMIC MASS

You have learned that the mass of a proton is about 1 amu and that a neutron is only slightly heavier. Because atomic nuclei consist of whole numbers of protons and neutrons, you might expect that the atomic mass of an element would be very near a whole number. However, if you look at the periodic table, you will see that the atomic masses of many elements lie somewhere between whole numbers. In fact, the atomic masses listed on the table are *average* atomic masses. The atomic masses are averages because most elements occur in nature as a specific mixture of isotopes. For example, 75.76% of chlorine atoms have a mass of 34.969 amu, and 24.24% have a mass of 36.966 amu. If the isotopes were in a 1 : 1 ratio, you could simply add the masses of the two isotopes together and divide by 2. However, to account for the differing abundance of the isotopes, you must calculate a *weighted average*. For chlorine, the weighted average is 35.45 amu. The following two examples demonstrate how weighted averages are calculated.

## SAMPLE 1

**Naturally occurring silver consists of 51.839% Ag-107 (atomic mass 106.905 093) and 48.161% Ag-109 (atomic mass 108.904 756). What is the average atomic mass of silver?**

To find average atomic mass, convert each percentage to a decimal equivalent and multiply by the atomic mass of the isotope.

$$\begin{array}{r} 0.518\,39 \times 106.905\,093 \text{ amu} = 55.419 \text{ amu} \\ 0.481\,61 \times 108.904\,756 \text{ amu} = 52.450 \text{ amu} \\ \hline 107.869 \text{ amu} \end{array}$$

Adding the masses contributed by each isotope gives an average atomic mass of 107.869 amu. Note that this value for the average atomic mass of silver is very near the one given in the periodic table.

## SAMPLE 2

**Naturally occurring magnesium consists of 78.99% Mg-24 (atomic mass 23.985 042), 10.00% Mg-25 (atomic mass 24.985 837), and 11.01% Mg-26 (atomic mass 25.982 593). What is the average atomic mass of magnesium?**

Again, convert each percentage to a decimal and multiply by the atomic mass of the isotope to get the mass contributed by each isotope.

$$\begin{array}{r} 0.7899 \times 23.985\,042 \text{ amu} = 18.95 \text{ amu} \\ 0.1000 \times 24.985\,837 \text{ amu} = 2.499 \text{ amu} \\ 0.1101 \times 25.982\,593 \text{ amu} = 2.861 \text{ amu} \\ \hline 24.31 \text{ amu} \end{array}$$

Adding the masses contributed by each isotope gives an average atomic mass of 24.31 amu.

## PRACTICE PROBLEMS

**1.** Rubidium occurs naturally as a mixture of two isotopes, 72.17% Rb-85 (atomic mass 84.911 792 amu) and 27.83% Rb-87 (atomic mass 86.909 186 amu). What is the average atomic mass of rubidium?

**2.** The element silicon occurs as a mixture of three isotopes: 92.22% Si-28, 4.69% Si-29, and 3.09% Si-30. The atomic masses of these three isotopes are as follows: Si-28 = 27.976 926 amu, Si-29 = 28.976 495 amu, and Si-30 = 29.973 770 amu.

Find the average atomic mass of silicon.

# Standardized Test Prep

Answer the following items on a separate piece of paper.

**MULTIPLE CHOICE**

**1.** Which of the following relationships is true?
- **A.** Higher-energy light has a higher frequency than lower-energy light does.
- **B.** Higher-energy light has a longer wavelength than lower-energy light does.
- **C.** Higher-energy light travels at a faster speed than lower-energy light does.
- **D.** Higher-frequency light travels at a slower speed than lower-energy light does.

**2.** The energy of a photon is greatest for
- **A.** visible light.
- **B.** ultraviolet light.
- **C.** infrared light.
- **D.** X-ray radiation.

**3.** What is the wavelength of radio waves that have a frequency of 88.5 MHz?
- **A.** 3.4 m
- **B.** 8.9 nm
- **C.** 0.30 m
- **D.** 300 nm

**4.** Which transition in an excited hydrogen atom will emit the longest wavelength of light?
- **A.** $E_5$ to $E_1$
- **B.** $E_4$ to $E_1$
- **C.** $E_3$ to $E_1$
- **D.** $E_2$ to $E_1$

**5.** Which of the following quantum numbers is often designated by the letters *s, p, d,* and *f* instead of by numbers?
- **A.** *n*
- **B.** *l*
- **C.** *m*
- **D.** *s*

**6.** Which quantum number is related to the shape of an orbital?
- **A.** *n*
- **B.** *l*
- **C.** *m*
- **D.** *s*

**7.** What is the maximum number of unpaired electrons that can be placed in a 3*p* sublevel?
- **A.** 1
- **B.** 2
- **C.** 3
- **D.** 4

**8.** What is the maximum number of electrons that can occupy a 3*s* orbital?
- **A.** 1
- **B.** 2
- **C.** 6
- **D.** 10

**9.** Which element has the noble-gas notation $[Kr]5s^24d^2$?
- **A.** Se
- **B.** Sr
- **C.** Zr
- **D.** Mo

**SHORT ANSWER**

**10.** When a calcium salt is heated in a flame, a photon of light with an energy of $3.2 \times 10^{-19}$ J is emitted. On the basis of this fact and the table below, what color would be expected for the calcium flame?

| **Frequency, $s^{-1}$** | $7.1 \times 10^{14}$ | $6.4 \times 10^{14}$ | $5.7 \times 10^{14}$ |
|---|---|---|---|
| **Wavelength, nm** | 422 | 469 | 526 |
| **Color** | violet | blue | green |
| **Frequency, $s^{-1}$** | $5.2 \times 10^{14}$ | $4.8 \times 10^{14}$ | $4.3 \times 10^{14}$ |
| **Wavelength, nm** | 577 | 625 | 698 |
| **Color** | yellow | orange | red |

**11.** The electron configuration of sulfur is $1s^22s^22p^63s^23p^4$. Write the orbital notation for sulfur.

**EXTENDED RESPONSE**

**12.** Explain the reason for the hydrogen line-emission spectrum.

**13.** When blue light shines on potassium metal in a photocell, electrons are emitted. But when yellow light shines on the metal, no current is observed. Explain.

**Test TIP** If time permits, take short mental breaks during the test to improve your concentration.

# Flame Tests

## OBJECTIVES

- ***Identify*** **a set of flame-test color standards for selected metal ions.**
- ***Relate*** **the colors of a flame test to the behavior of excited electrons in a metal ion.**
- ***Identify*** **an unknown metal ion by using a flame test.**
- ***Demonstrate*** **proficiency in performing a flame test and in using a spectroscope.**

## MATERIALS

- **250 mL beaker**
- **Bunsen burner and related equipment**
- **cobalt glass plates**
- **crucible tongs**
- **distilled water**
- **flame-test wire**
- **glass test plate (or a microchemistry plate with wells)**
- **spectroscope**
- **1.0 M HCl solution**
- **$CaCl_2$ solution**
- **$K_2SO_4$ solution**
- **$Li_2SO_4$ solution**
- **$Na_2SO_4$ solution**
- **$SrCl_2$ solution**
- **unknown solution**

## OPTIONAL EQUIPMENT

- **wooden splints**

## BACKGROUND

The characteristic light emitted by an element is the basis for the chemical test known as a *flame test.*

To identify an unknown substance, you must first determine the characteristic colors produced by different elements. You will do this by performing a flame test on a variety of standard solutions of metal compounds. Then, you will perform a flame test with an unknown sample to see if it matches any of the standard solutions. The presence of even a speck of another substance can interfere with the identification of the true color of a particular type of atom, so be sure to keep your equipment very clean and perform multiple trials to check your work.

## SAFETY

For review of safety, please see **Safety in the Chemistry Laboratory** in the front of your book.

## PREPARATION

1. Prepare a data table in your lab notebook. Include rows for each of the solutions of metal compounds listed in the materials list and an unknown solution. The table should have three wide columns for the three trials you will perform with each substance. Each column should have room to record the colors and wavelengths of light. Be sure you have plenty of room to write your observations about each test.
2. Label a beaker *Waste*. Thoroughly clean and dry a well strip. Fill the first well one-fourth full with 1.0 M HCl on the plate. Clean the test wire by first dipping it in the HCl and then holding it in the colorless flame of the Bunsen burner. Repeat this procedure until the flame is not colored by the wire. When the wire is ready, rinse

the well with distilled water and collect the rinse water in the waste beaker.

3. Put 10 drops of each metal ion solution listed in the materials list in a row in each well of the well strip. Put a row of 1.0 M HCl drops on a glass plate across from the metal ion solutions. Record the positions of all of the chemicals placed in the wells. The wire will need to be cleaned thoroughly between each test solution with HCl to avoid contamination from the previous test.

## PROCEDURE

1. Dip the wire into the $CaCl_2$ solution, and then hold it in the Bunsen burner flame. Observe the color of the flame, and record it in the data table. Repeat the procedure again, but this time look through the spectroscope to view the results. Record the wavelengths you see from the flame. Repeat each test three times. Clean the wire with the HCl as you did in Preparation step 2.

2. Repeat step 1 with the $K_2SO_4$ and with each of the remaining solutions in the well strip.

3. Test another drop of $Na_2SO_4$, but this time view the flame through two pieces of cobalt glass. Clean the wire, and repeat the test. Record in your data table the colors and wavelengths of the flames as they appear when viewed through the cobalt glass. Clean the wire and the well strip, and rinse the well strip with distilled water. Pour the rinse water into the waste beaker.

4. Put a drop of $K_2SO_4$ in a clean well. Add a drop of $Na_2SO_4$. Perform a flame test for the mixture. Observe the flame without the cobalt glass. Repeat the test again, but this time observe the flame through the cobalt glass. Record in your data table the colors and wavelengths of the flames. Clean the wire, and rinse the well strip with distilled water. Pour the rinse water into the waste beaker.

5. Obtain a sample of the unknown solution. Perform flame tests for it with and without the cobalt glass. Record your observations. Clean the wire, and rinse the well strip with distilled water. Pour the rinse water into the waste beaker.

## CLEANUP AND DISPOSAL

6. Dispose of the contents of the waste beaker in the container designated by your teacher. Wash your hands thoroughly after cleaning up the area and equipment.

## ANALYSIS AND INTERPRETATION

1. **Organizing Data:** Examine your data table, and create a summary of the flame test for each metal ion.

2. **Analyzing Data:** Account for any differences in the individual trials for the flame tests for the metals ions.

3. **Organizing Ideas:** Explain how viewing the flame through cobalt glass can make it easier to analyze the ions being tested.

4. **Relating Ideas:** For three of the metal ions tested, explain how the flame color you saw relates to the lines of color you saw when you looked through the spectroscope.

## CONCLUSIONS

1. **Inferring Conclusions:** What metal ions are in the unknown solution?

2. **Evaluating Methods:** How would you characterize the flame test with respect to its sensitivity? What difficulties could there be when identifying ions by the flame test?

## EXTENSIONS

1. **Inferring Conclusions:** A student performed flame tests on several unknowns and observed that they all were shades of red. What should the student do to correctly identify these substances? Explain your answer.

2. **Applying Ideas:** During a flood, the labels from three bottles of chemicals were lost. The three unlabeled bottles of white solids were known to contain the following: strontium nitrate, ammonium carbonate, and potassium sulfate. Explain how you could easily test the substances and relabel the three bottles. (Hint: Ammonium ions do not provide a distinctive flame color.)

CHAPTER 5

# The Periodic Law

*Atoms of the heavier elements form when stars explode, such as when a supernova caused this nebula.*

Rosette Nebula

# History of the Periodic Table

SECTION 1

## Objectives

- Explain the roles of Mendeleev and Moseley in the development of the periodic table.
- Describe the modern periodic table.
- Explain how the periodic law can be used to predict the physical and chemical properties of elements.
- Describe how the elements belonging to a group of the periodic table are interrelated in terms of atomic number.

**C.2.3** Summarize the periodic table's property trends (including electron configuration, ionization energy, electron affinity, atomic size, ionic size, and reactivity)

Imagine the confusion among chemists during the middle of the nineteenth century. By 1860, more than 60 elements had been discovered. Chemists had to learn the properties of these elements as well as those of the many compounds that they formed—a difficult task. And to make matters worse, there was no method for accurately determining an element's atomic mass or the number of atoms of an element in a particular chemical compound. Different chemists used different atomic masses for the same elements, resulting in different compositions being proposed for the same compounds. This made it nearly impossible for one chemist to understand the results of another.

In September 1860, a group of chemists assembled at the First International Congress of Chemists in Karlsruhe, Germany, to settle the issue of atomic mass as well as some other matters that were making communication difficult. At the Congress, Italian chemist Stanislao Cannizzaro presented a convincing method for accurately measuring the relative masses of atoms. Cannizzaro's method enabled chemists to agree on standard values for atomic mass and initiated a search for relationships between atomic mass and other properties of the elements.

SCILINKS.
www.scilinks.org
**Topic:** Periodic Table
**Code:** HC61125

## Mendeleev and Chemical Periodicity

When the Russian chemist Dmitri Mendeleev heard about the new atomic masses discussed at Karlsruhe, he decided to include the new values in a chemistry textbook that he was writing. In the book, Mendeleev hoped to organize the elements according to their properties. He went about this much as you might organize information for a research paper. He placed the name of each known element on a card, together with the atomic mass of the element and a list of its observed physical and chemical properties. He then arranged the cards according to various properties and looked for trends or patterns.

Mendeleev noticed that when the elements were arranged in order of increasing atomic mass, certain similarities in their chemical properties appeared at regular intervals. Such a repeating pattern is referred to as *periodic*. The second hand of a watch, for example, passes over any given mark at periodic, 60-second intervals. The circular waves created by a drop of water hitting a water surface are also periodic.

**FIGURE 1** The regularly spaced water waves represent a simple periodic pattern.

**FIGURE 2** In his first published periodic table, Mendeleev arranged the elements in vertical periods according to relative atomic mass. The atomic mass for each element is indicated by the number following the element's symbol. The unknown elements indicated by question marks at estimated atomic masses 45, 68, and 70 were later identified as scandium, Sc, gallium, Ga, and germanium, Ge.

но въ ней, мнѣ кажется, уже ясно выражается примѣнимость выставляемаго мною начала ко всей совокупности элементовъ, пай которыхъ извѣстенъ съ достовѣрностію. На этотъ разъ я и желалъ преимущественно найдти общую систему элементовъ. Вотъ этотъ опытъ:

| | | | | | |
|---|---|---|---|---|---|
| | | | Ti=50 | Zr=90 | ?=180. |
| | | | V=51 | Nb=94 | Ta=182. |
| | | | Cr=52 | Mo=96 | W=186. |
| | | | Mn=55 | Rh=104,4 | Pt=197,4 |
| | | | Fe=56 | Ru=104,4 | Ir=198. |
| | | | Ni=Co=59 | Pl=106,6, | Os=199. |
| H=1 | | | Cu=63,4 | Ag=108 | Hg=200. |
| | Be=9,4 | Mg=24 | Zn=65,2 | Cd=112 | |
| | B=11 | Al=27,4 | ?=68 | Ur=116 | Au=197? |
| | C=12 | Si=28 | ?=70 | Su=118 | |
| | N=14 | P=31 | As=75 | Sb=122 | Bi=210 |
| | O=16 | S=32 | Se=79,4 | Te=128? | |
| | F=19 | Cl=35,5 | Br=80 | I=127 | |
| Li=7 | Na=23 | K=39 | Rb=85,4 | Cs=133 | Tl=204 |
| | | Ca=40 | Sr=87,6 | Ba=137 | Pb=207. |
| | | ?=45 | Ce=92 | | |
| | | ?Er=56 | La=94 | | |
| | | ?Yt=60 | Di=95 | | |
| | | ?In=75,6 | Th=118? | | |

а потому приходится въ разныхъ рядахъ имѣть различное измѣненіе разностей, чего нѣтъ въ главныхъ числахъ предлагаемой таблицы. Или же придется предполагать при составленіи системы очень много недостающихъ членовъ. То и другое мало выгодно. Мнѣ кажется притомъ, наиболѣе естественнымъ составить

Mendeleev created a table in which elements with similar properties were grouped together—a periodic table of the elements. His first periodic table, shown in **Figure 2,** was published in 1869. Note that Mendeleev placed iodine, I (atomic mass 127), after tellurium, Te (atomic mass 128). Although this contradicted the pattern of listing the elements in order of increasing atomic mass, it allowed Mendeleev to place tellurium in a group of elements with which it shares similar properties. Reading horizontally across Mendeleev's table, this group includes oxygen, O, sulfur, S, and selenium, Se. Iodine could also, then, be placed in the group it resembles chemically, which includes fluorine, F, chlorine, Cl, and bromine, Br.

Mendeleev's procedure left several empty spaces in his periodic table (see **Figure 2**). In 1871, the Russian chemist boldly predicted the existence and properties of the elements that would fill three of the spaces. By 1886, all three elements had been discovered. Today these elements are known as scandium, Sc, gallium, Ga, and germanium, Ge. Their properties are strikingly similar to those predicted by Mendeleev.

The success of Mendeleev's predictions persuaded most chemists to accept his periodic table and earned him credit as the discoverer of the periodic law. Two questions remained, however. (1) Why could most of the elements be arranged in the order of increasing atomic mass but a few could not? (2) What was the reason for chemical periodicity?

## Moseley and the Periodic Law

The first question was not answered until more than 40 years after Mendeleev's first periodic table was published. In 1911, the English scientist Henry Moseley, who was working with Ernest Rutherford, examined the spectra of 38 different metals. When analyzing his data, Moseley discovered a previously unrecognized pattern. The elements in the periodic table fit into patterns better when they were arranged in increasing order according to nuclear charge, or the number of protons in the nucleus. Moseley's work led to both the modern definition of atomic number and the recognition that atomic number, not atomic mass, is the basis for the organization of the periodic table.

Moseley's discovery was consistent with Mendeleev's ordering of the periodic table by properties rather than strictly by atomic mass. For example, according to Moseley, tellurium, with an atomic number of 52, belongs before iodine, which has an atomic number of 53. Today, Mendeleev's principle of chemical periodicity is correctly stated in what is known as the **periodic law:** *The physical and chemical properties of the elements are periodic functions of their atomic numbers.* In other words, when the elements are arranged in order of increasing atomic number, elements with similar properties appear at regular intervals.

## The Modern Periodic Table

The periodic table has undergone extensive change since Mendeleev's time (see **Figure 6** on pages 140–141). Chemists have discovered new elements and, in more recent years, synthesized new ones in the laboratory. Each of the more than 40 new elements, however, can be placed in a group of other elements with similar properties. *The* **periodic table** *is an arrangement of the elements in order of their atomic numbers so that elements with similar properties fall in the same column, or group.*

| | | | 2 He |
|---|---|---|---|
| 7 N | 8 O | 9 F | 10 Ne |
| 15 P | 16 S | 17 Cl | 18 Ar |
| 33 As | 34 Se | 35 Br | 36 Kr |
| 51 Sb | 52 Te | 53 I | 54 Xe |
| 83 Bi | 84 Po | 85 At | 86 Rn |

**FIGURE 3** The noble gases, also known as the Group 18 elements, are all rather unreactive. As you will read, the reason for this low reactivity also accounts for the special place occupied by the noble gases in the periodic table.

### The Noble Gases

Perhaps the most significant addition to the periodic table came with the discovery of the noble gases. In 1894, English physicist John William Strutt (Lord Rayleigh) and Scottish chemist Sir William Ramsay discovered argon, Ar, a gas in the atmosphere that had previously escaped notice because of its total lack of chemical reactivity. Back in 1868, another noble gas, helium, He, had been discovered as a component of the sun, based on the emission spectrum of sunlight. In 1895, Ramsay showed that helium also exists on Earth.

In order to fit argon and helium into the periodic table, Ramsay proposed a new group. He placed this group between the groups now known as Group 17 (the fluorine family) and Group 1 (the lithium family). In 1898, Ramsay discovered two more noble gases to place in his new group, krypton, Kr, and xenon, Xe. The final noble gas, radon, Rn, was discovered in 1900 by the German scientist Friedrich Ernst Dorn.

## The Lanthanides

The next step in the development of the periodic table was completed in the early 1900s. It was then that the puzzling chemistry of the lanthanides was finally understood. *The* **lanthanides** *are the 14 elements with atomic numbers from 58 (cerium, Ce) to 71 (lutetium, Lu).* Because these elements are so similar in chemical and physical properties, the process of separating and identifying them was a tedious task that required the effort of many chemists.

## The Actinides

Another major step in the development of the periodic table was the discovery of the actinides. *The* **actinides** *are the 14 elements with atomic numbers from 90 (thorium, Th) to 103 (lawrencium, Lr).* The lanthanides and actinides belong in Periods 6 and 7, respectively, of the periodic table, between the elements of Groups 3 and 4. To save space, the lanthanides and actinides are usually set off below the main portion of the periodic table, as shown in **Figure 6** on pages 140–141.

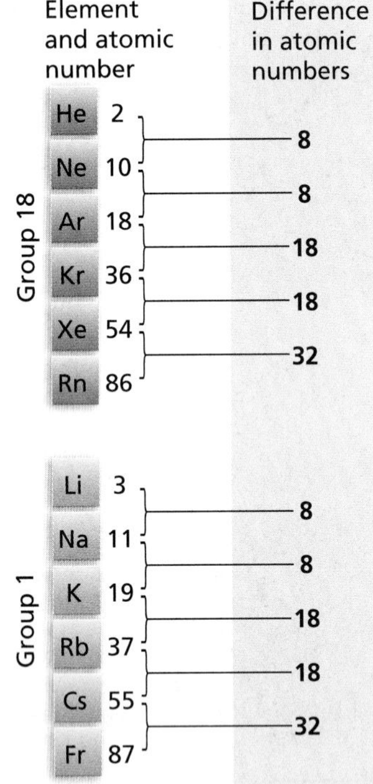


**FIGURE 4** In each of Groups 1 and 18, the differences between the atomic numbers of successive elements are 8, 8, 18, 18, and 32, respectively. Groups 2 and 13–17 follow a similar pattern.

## Periodicity

Periodicity with respect to atomic number can be observed in any group of elements in the periodic table. Consider the noble gases of Group 18. The first noble gas is helium, He. It has an atomic number of 2. The elements following helium in atomic number have completely different properties until the next noble gas, neon, Ne, which has an atomic number of 10, is reached. The remaining noble gases in order of increasing atomic number are argon (Ar, atomic number 18), krypton (Kr, atomic number 36), xenon (Xe, atomic number 54), and radon (Rn, atomic number 86). The differences in atomic number between successive noble gases are shown in **Figure 4.** Also shown in **Figure 4** are atomic-number differences between the elements of Group 1, which are all solid, silvery metals. As you can see, the differences in atomic number between the Group 1 metals follow the same pattern as the differences in atomic number between the noble gases.

Starting with the first member of Groups 13–17, a similar periodic pattern is repeated. The atomic number of each successive element is 8, 18, 18, and 32 higher than the atomic number of the element above it. In Section 2, you will see that the second mystery presented by Mendeleev's periodic table—the reason for periodicity—is explained by the arrangement of the electrons around the nucleus.

## QuickLAB

### *Designing Your Own Periodic Table*

**Materials**

- index cards

**Question**

**Can you design your own periodic table using information similar to that available to Mendeleev?**

**Procedure**

1. Write down the information available for each element on separate index cards. The following information is appropriate: a letter of the alphabet (A, B, C, etc.) to identify each element; atomic mass; state; density; melting point; boiling point; and any other readily observable physical properties. Do not write the name of the element on the index card, but keep a separate list indicating the letters you have assigned to each element.
2. Organize the cards for the elements in a logical pattern as you think Mendeleev might have done.

**Discussion**

1. Keeping in mind that the information you have is similar to that available to Mendeleev in 1869, answer the following questions.
   a. Why are atomic masses given instead of atomic numbers?
   b. Can you identify each element by name?
2. How many groups of elements, or families, are in your periodic table? How many periods, or series, are in the table?
3. Predict the characteristics of any missing elements. When you have finished, check your work using your separate list of elements and a periodic table.

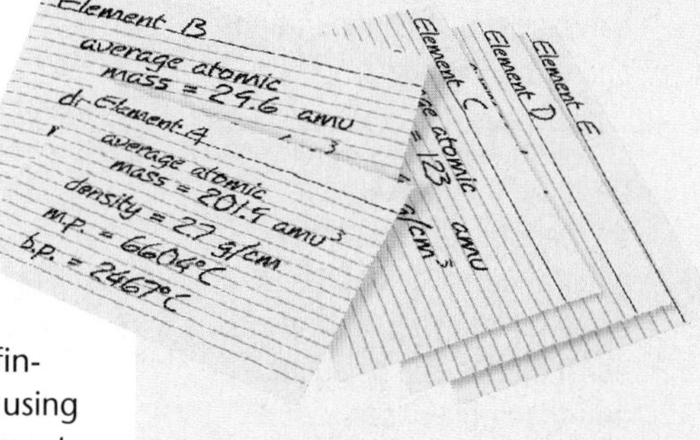


## SECTION REVIEW

1. a. Who is credited with developing a method that led to the determination of standard relative atomic masses?
   b. Who discovered the periodic law?
   c. Who established atomic numbers as the basis for organizing the periodic table?
2. State the periodic law.
3. Name three sets of elements that have been added to the periodic table after Mendeleev's time.
4. How do the atomic numbers of the elements within each of Groups 1, 2, and 13–18 of the periodic table vary? (Refer to **Figure 4** as a guide.)

**Critical Thinking**

5. **RELATING IDEAS** Why are elements' atomic masses not in strict increasing order in the periodic table, even though the properties of the elements are similar? For example, by atomic mass, tellurium, Te, should be in group 17 and iodine, I, should be in Group 16, but grouping by properties has Te in Group 16 and I in Group 17.

SECTION 2

## Objectives

- Describe the relationship between electrons in sub-levels and the length of each period of the periodic table.
- Locate and name the four blocks of the periodic table. Explain the reasons for these names.
- Discuss the relationship between group configurations and group numbers.
- Describe the locations in the periodic table and the general properties of the alkali metals, the alkaline-earth metals, the halogens, and the noble gases.

# Electron Configuration and the Periodic Table

SC **C.2.3** Summarize the periodic table's property trends (including electron configuration, ionization energy, electron affinity, atomic size, ionic size, and reactivity)

The Group 18 elements of the periodic table (the noble gases) undergo few chemical reactions. This stability results from the gases' special electron configurations. Helium's highest occupied level, the 1*s* orbital, is completely filled with electrons. And the highest occupied levels of the other noble gases contain stable octets. Generally the electron configuration of an atom's highest occupied energy level governs the atom's chemical properties.

## Periods and Blocks of the Periodic Table

While the elements are arranged vertically in the periodic table in groups that share similar chemical properties, they are also organized horizontally in rows, or *periods.* (As shown in **Figure 6,** there are a total of seven periods of elements in the modern periodic table.) As can be seen in **Table 1,** the length of each period is determined by the number of electrons that can occupy the sublevels being filled in that period.

**TABLE 1** ***Relationship Between Period Length and Sublevels Being Filled in the Periodic Table***

| Period number | Number of elements in period | Sublevels in order of filling |
|---|---|---|
| 1 | 2 | 1*s* |
| 2 | 8 | 2*s* 2*p* |
| 3 | 8 | 3*s* 3*p* |
| 4 | 18 | 4*s* 3*d* 4*p* |
| 5 | 18 | 5*s* 4*d* 5*p* |
| 6 | 32 | 6*s* 4*f* 5*d* 6*p* |
| 7 | 32 | 7*s* 5*f* 6*d* 7*p* |

In the first period, the 1*s* sublevel is being filled. The 1*s* sublevel can hold a total of two electrons. Therefore, the first period consists of two elements—hydrogen and helium. In the second period, the 2*s* sublevel, which can hold two electrons, and the 2*p* sublevel, which can hold six electrons, are being filled. Consequently, the second period totals eight elements. Similarly, filling of the 3*s* and 3*p* sublevels accounts for the eight elements of the third period. Filling 3*d* and 4*d* sublevels in addition to the *s* and *p* sublevels adds 10 elements to both the fourth and fifth periods. Therefore, each of these periods totals 18 elements. Filling 4*f* sublevels in addition to *s, p,* and *d* sublevels adds 14 elements to the sixth period, which totals 32 elements. And as new elements are created, the 25 named elements in Period 7 could, in theory, be extended to 32.

The period of an element can be determined from the element's electron configuration. For example, arsenic, As, has the electron configuration [Ar]$3d^{10}4s^24p^3$. The 4 in $4p^3$ indicates that arsenic's highest occupied energy level is the fourth energy level. Arsenic is therefore in the fourth period in the periodic table. The period and electron configuration for each element can be found in the periodic table on pages 140–141.

Based on the electron configurations of the elements, the periodic table can be divided into four blocks, the *s, p, d,* and *f* blocks. This division is illustrated in **Figure 5.** The name of each block is determined by whether an *s, p, d,* or *f* sublevel is being filled in successive elements of that block.

**FIGURE 5** Based on the electron configurations of the elements, the periodic table can be subdivided into four sublevel blocks.

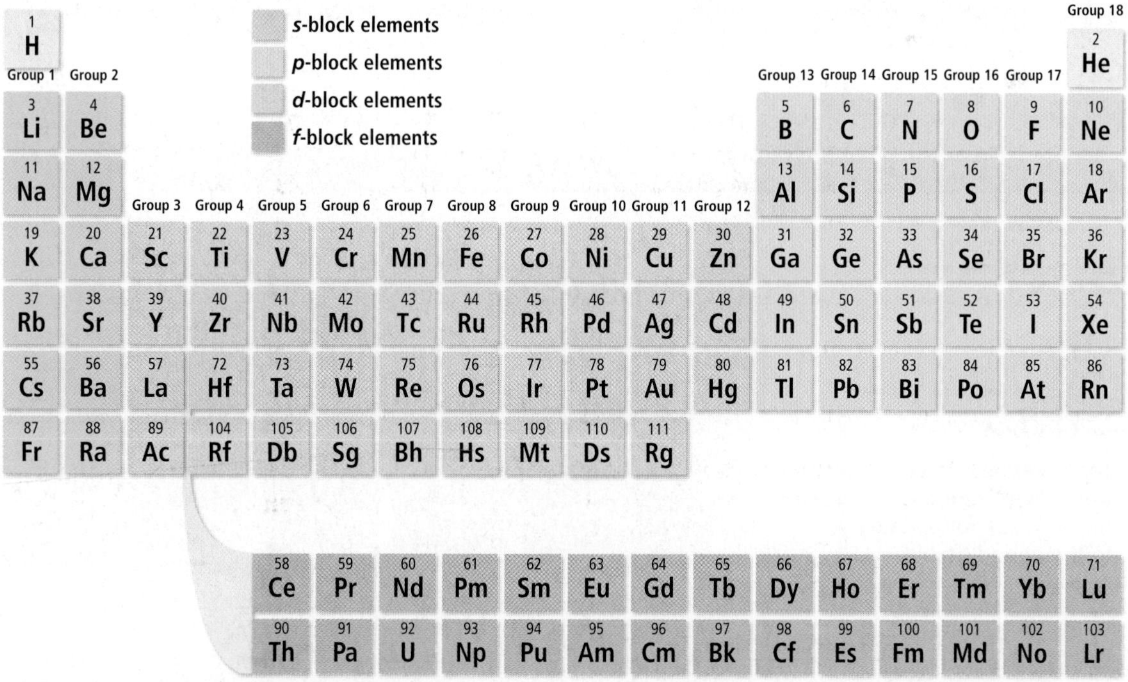

*s*-block elements
*p*-block elements
*d*-block elements
*f*-block elements

| Group 1 | Group 2 | Group 3 | Group 4 | Group 5 | Group 6 | Group 7 | Group 8 | Group 9 | Group 10 | Group 11 | Group 12 | Group 13 | Group 14 | Group 15 | Group 16 | Group 17 | Group 18 |
|---|---|---|---|---|---|---|---|---|---|---|---|---|---|---|---|---|---|
| 1 H | | | | | | | | | | | | | | | | | 2 He |
| 3 Li | 4 Be | | | | | | | | | | | 5 B | 6 C | 7 N | 8 O | 9 F | 10 Ne |
| 11 Na | 12 Mg | | | | | | | | | | | 13 Al | 14 Si | 15 P | 16 S | 17 Cl | 18 Ar |
| 19 K | 20 Ca | 21 Sc | 22 Ti | 23 V | 24 Cr | 25 Mn | 26 Fe | 27 Co | 28 Ni | 29 Cu | 30 Zn | 31 Ga | 32 Ge | 33 As | 34 Se | 35 Br | 36 Kr |
| 37 Rb | 38 Sr | 39 Y | 40 Zr | 41 Nb | 42 Mo | 43 Tc | 44 Ru | 45 Rh | 46 Pd | 47 Ag | 48 Cd | 49 In | 50 Sn | 51 Sb | 52 Te | 53 I | 54 Xe |
| 55 Cs | 56 Ba | 57 La | 72 Hf | 73 Ta | 74 W | 75 Re | 76 Os | 77 Ir | 78 Pt | 79 Au | 80 Hg | 81 Tl | 82 Pb | 83 Bi | 84 Po | 85 At | 86 Rn |
| 87 Fr | 88 Ra | 89 Ac | 104 Rf | 105 Db | 106 Sg | 107 Bh | 108 Hs | 109 Mt | 110 Ds | 111 Rg | | | | | | | |

| | | | | | | | | | | | | | |
|---|---|---|---|---|---|---|---|---|---|---|---|---|---|
| 58 Ce | 59 Pr | 60 Nd | 61 Pm | 62 Sm | 63 Eu | 64 Gd | 65 Tb | 66 Dy | 67 Ho | 68 Er | 69 Tm | 70 Yb | 71 Lu |
| 90 Th | 91 Pa | 92 U | 93 Np | 94 Pu | 95 Am | 96 Cm | 97 Bk | 98 Cf | 99 Es | 100 Fm | 101 Md | 102 No | 103 Lr |

# Periodic Table of the Elements

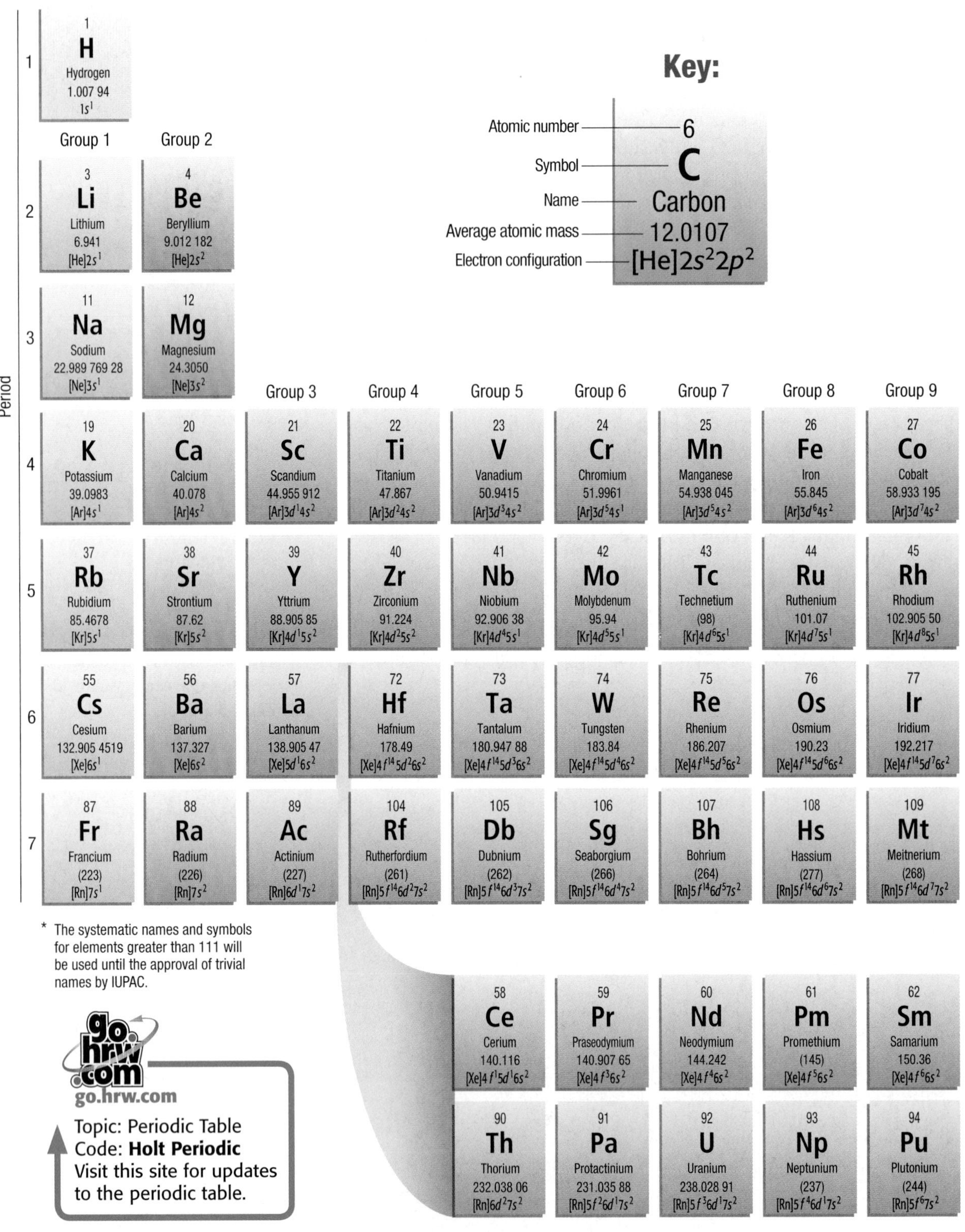

| Period | Group 1 | Group 2 | Group 3 | Group 4 | Group 5 | Group 6 | Group 7 | Group 8 | Group 9 |
|---|---|---|---|---|---|---|---|---|---|
| 1 | 1<br>**H**<br>Hydrogen<br>1.007 94<br>$1s^1$ | | | | | | | | |
| 2 | 3<br>**Li**<br>Lithium<br>6.941<br>$[He]2s^1$ | 4<br>**Be**<br>Beryllium<br>9.012 182<br>$[He]2s^2$ | | | | | | | |
| 3 | 11<br>**Na**<br>Sodium<br>22.989 769 28<br>$[Ne]3s^1$ | 12<br>**Mg**<br>Magnesium<br>24.3050<br>$[Ne]3s^2$ | | | | | | | |
| 4 | 19<br>**K**<br>Potassium<br>39.0983<br>$[Ar]4s^1$ | 20<br>**Ca**<br>Calcium<br>40.078<br>$[Ar]4s^2$ | 21<br>**Sc**<br>Scandium<br>44.955 912<br>$[Ar]3d^14s^2$ | 22<br>**Ti**<br>Titanium<br>47.867<br>$[Ar]3d^24s^2$ | 23<br>**V**<br>Vanadium<br>50.9415<br>$[Ar]3d^34s^2$ | 24<br>**Cr**<br>Chromium<br>51.9961<br>$[Ar]3d^54s^1$ | 25<br>**Mn**<br>Manganese<br>54.938 045<br>$[Ar]3d^54s^2$ | 26<br>**Fe**<br>Iron<br>55.845<br>$[Ar]3d^64s^2$ | 27<br>**Co**<br>Cobalt<br>58.933 195<br>$[Ar]3d^74s^2$ |
| 5 | 37<br>**Rb**<br>Rubidium<br>85.4678<br>$[Kr]5s^1$ | 38<br>**Sr**<br>Strontium<br>87.62<br>$[Kr]5s^2$ | 39<br>**Y**<br>Yttrium<br>88.905 85<br>$[Kr]4d^15s^2$ | 40<br>**Zr**<br>Zirconium<br>91.224<br>$[Kr]4d^25s^2$ | 41<br>**Nb**<br>Niobium<br>92.906 38<br>$[Kr]4d^45s^1$ | 42<br>**Mo**<br>Molybdenum<br>95.94<br>$[Kr]4d^55s^1$ | 43<br>**Tc**<br>Technetium<br>(98)<br>$[Kr]4d^65s^1$ | 44<br>**Ru**<br>Ruthenium<br>101.07<br>$[Kr]4d^75s^1$ | 45<br>**Rh**<br>Rhodium<br>102.905 50<br>$[Kr]4d^85s^1$ |
| 6 | 55<br>**Cs**<br>Cesium<br>132.905 4519<br>$[Xe]6s^1$ | 56<br>**Ba**<br>Barium<br>137.327<br>$[Xe]6s^2$ | 57<br>**La**<br>Lanthanum<br>138.905 47<br>$[Xe]5d^16s^2$ | 72<br>**Hf**<br>Hafnium<br>178.49<br>$[Xe]4f^{14}5d^26s^2$ | 73<br>**Ta**<br>Tantalum<br>180.947 88<br>$[Xe]4f^{14}5d^36s^2$ | 74<br>**W**<br>Tungsten<br>183.84<br>$[Xe]4f^{14}5d^46s^2$ | 75<br>**Re**<br>Rhenium<br>186.207<br>$[Xe]4f^{14}5d^56s^2$ | 76<br>**Os**<br>Osmium<br>190.23<br>$[Xe]4f^{14}5d^66s^2$ | 77<br>**Ir**<br>Iridium<br>192.217<br>$[Xe]4f^{14}5d^76s^2$ |
| 7 | 87<br>**Fr**<br>Francium<br>(223)<br>$[Rn]7s^1$ | 88<br>**Ra**<br>Radium<br>(226)<br>$[Rn]7s^2$ | 89<br>**Ac**<br>Actinium<br>(227)<br>$[Rn]6d^17s^2$ | 104<br>**Rf**<br>Rutherfordium<br>(261)<br>$[Rn]5f^{14}6d^27s^2$ | 105<br>**Db**<br>Dubnium<br>(262)<br>$[Rn]5f^{14}6d^37s^2$ | 106<br>**Sg**<br>Seaborgium<br>(266)<br>$[Rn]5f^{14}6d^47s^2$ | 107<br>**Bh**<br>Bohrium<br>(264)<br>$[Rn]5f^{14}6d^57s^2$ | 108<br>**Hs**<br>Hassium<br>(277)<br>$[Rn]5f^{14}6d^67s^2$ | 109<br>**Mt**<br>Meitnerium<br>(268)<br>$[Rn]5f^{14}6d^77s^2$ |

| | | | | |
|---|---|---|---|---|
| 58<br>**Ce**<br>Cerium<br>140.116<br>$[Xe]4f^15d^16s^2$ | 59<br>**Pr**<br>Praseodymium<br>140.907 65<br>$[Xe]4f^36s^2$ | 60<br>**Nd**<br>Neodymium<br>144.242<br>$[Xe]4f^46s^2$ | 61<br>**Pm**<br>Promethium<br>(145)<br>$[Xe]4f^56s^2$ | 62<br>**Sm**<br>Samarium<br>150.36<br>$[Xe]4f^66s^2$ |
| 90<br>**Th**<br>Thorium<br>232.038 06<br>$[Rn]6d^27s^2$ | 91<br>**Pa**<br>Protactinium<br>231.035 88<br>$[Rn]5f^26d^17s^2$ | 92<br>**U**<br>Uranium<br>238.028 91<br>$[Rn]5f^36d^17s^2$ | 93<br>**Np**<br>Neptunium<br>(237)<br>$[Rn]5f^46d^17s^2$ | 94<br>**Pu**<br>Plutonium<br>(244)<br>$[Rn]5f^67s^2$ |



**FIGURE 6** In the common periodic table, the elements are arranged in vertical groups and in horizontal periods.

Hydrogen
Semiconductors
(also known as metalloids)

**Metals**
- Alkali metals
- Alkaline-earth metals
- Transition metals
- Other metals

**Nonmetals**
- Halogens
- Noble gases
- Other nonmetals

| Group 10 | Group 11 | Group 12 | Group 13 | Group 14 | Group 15 | Group 16 | Group 17 | Group 18 |
|---|---|---|---|---|---|---|---|---|
| | | | | | | | | 2<br>**He**<br>Helium<br>4.002 602<br>$1s^2$ |
| | | | 5<br>**B**<br>Boron<br>10.811<br>$[He]2s^22p^1$ | 6<br>**C**<br>Carbon<br>12.0107<br>$[He]2s^22p^2$ | 7<br>**N**<br>Nitrogen<br>14.0067<br>$[He]2s^22p^3$ | 8<br>**O**<br>Oxygen<br>15.9994<br>$[He]2s^22p^4$ | 9<br>**F**<br>Fluorine<br>18.998 4032<br>$[He]2s^22p^5$ | 10<br>**Ne**<br>Neon<br>20.1797<br>$[He]2s^22p^6$ |
| | | | 13<br>**Al**<br>Aluminum<br>26.981 5386<br>$[Ne]3s^23p^1$ | 14<br>**Si**<br>Silicon<br>28.0855<br>$[Ne]3s^23p^2$ | 15<br>**P**<br>Phosphorus<br>30.973 762<br>$[Ne]3s^23p^3$ | 16<br>**S**<br>Sulfur<br>32.065<br>$[Ne]3s^23p^4$ | 17<br>**Cl**<br>Chlorine<br>35.453<br>$[Ne]3s^23p^5$ | 18<br>**Ar**<br>Argon<br>39.948<br>$[Ne]3s^23p^6$ |
| 28<br>**Ni**<br>Nickel<br>58.6934<br>$[Ar]3d^84s^2$ | 29<br>**Cu**<br>Copper<br>63.546<br>$[Ar]3d^{10}4s^1$ | 30<br>**Zn**<br>Zinc<br>65.409<br>$[Ar]3d^{10}4s^2$ | 31<br>**Ga**<br>Gallium<br>69.723<br>$[Ar]3d^{10}4s^24p^1$ | 32<br>**Ge**<br>Germanium<br>72.64<br>$[Ar]3d^{10}4s^24p^2$ | 33<br>**As**<br>Arsenic<br>74.921 60<br>$[Ar]3d^{10}4s^24p^3$ | 34<br>**Se**<br>Selenium<br>78.96<br>$[Ar]3d^{10}4s^24p^4$ | 35<br>**Br**<br>Bromine<br>79.904<br>$[Ar]3d^{10}4s^24p^5$ | 36<br>**Kr**<br>Krypton<br>83.798<br>$[Ar]3d^{10}4s^24p^6$ |
| 46<br>**Pd**<br>Palladium<br>106.42<br>$[Kr]4d^{10}5s^0$ | 47<br>**Ag**<br>Silver<br>107.8682<br>$[Kr]4d^{10}5s^1$ | 48<br>**Cd**<br>Cadmium<br>112.411<br>$[Kr]4d^{10}5s^2$ | 49<br>**In**<br>Indium<br>114.818<br>$[Kr]4d^{10}5s^25p^1$ | 50<br>**Sn**<br>Tin<br>118.710<br>$[Kr]4d^{10}5s^25p^2$ | 51<br>**Sb**<br>Antimony<br>121.760<br>$[Kr]4d^{10}5s^25p^3$ | 52<br>**Te**<br>Tellurium<br>127.60<br>$[Kr]4d^{10}5s^25p^4$ | 53<br>**I**<br>Iodine<br>126.904 47<br>$[Kr]4d^{10}5s^25p^5$ | 54<br>**Xe**<br>Xenon<br>131.293<br>$[Kr]4d^{10}5s^25p^6$ |
| 78<br>**Pt**<br>Platinum<br>195.084<br>$[Xe]4f^{14}5d^96s^1$ | 79<br>**Au**<br>Gold<br>196.966 569<br>$[Xe]4f^{14}5d^{10}6s^1$ | 80<br>**Hg**<br>Mercury<br>200.59<br>$[Xe]4f^{14}5d^{10}6s^2$ | 81<br>**Tl**<br>Thallium<br>204.3833<br>$[Xe]4f^{14}5d^{10}6s^26p^1$ | 82<br>**Pb**<br>Lead<br>207.2<br>$[Xe]4f^{14}5d^{10}6s^26p^2$ | 83<br>**Bi**<br>Bismuth<br>208.980 40<br>$[Xe]4f^{14}5d^{10}6s^26p^3$ | 84<br>**Po**<br>Polonium<br>(209)<br>$[Xe]4f^{14}5d^{10}6s^26p^4$ | 85<br>**At**<br>Astatine<br>(210)<br>$[Xe]4f^{14}5d^{10}6s^26p^5$ | 86<br>**Rn**<br>Radon<br>(222)<br>$[Xe]4f^{14}5d^{10}6s^26p^6$ |
| 110<br>**Ds**<br>Darmstadtium<br>(271)<br>$[Rn]5f^{14}6d^97s^1$ | 111<br>**Rg**<br>Roentgenium<br>(272)<br>$[Rn]5f^{14}6d^{10}7s^1$ | 112<br>**Uub***<br>Ununbium<br>(285)<br>$[Rn]5f^{14}6d^{10}7s^2$ | | 114<br>**Uuq***<br>Ununquadium<br>(289)<br>$[Rn]5f^{14}6d^{10}7s^27p^2$ | | 116<br>**Uuh***<br>Ununhexium<br>(292)<br>$[Rn]5f^{14}6d^{10}7s^27$ | | |

The discoveries of elements with atomic numbers 112, 114, and 116 have been reported but not fully confirmed.

| | | | | | | | | |
|---|---|---|---|---|---|---|---|---|
| 63<br>**Eu**<br>Europium<br>151.964<br>$[Xe]4f^76s^2$ | 64<br>**Gd**<br>Gadolinium<br>157.25<br>$[Xe]4f^75d^16s^2$ | 65<br>**Tb**<br>Terbium<br>158.925 35<br>$[Xe]4f^96s^2$ | 66<br>**Dy**<br>Dysprosium<br>162.500<br>$[Xe]4f^{10}6s^2$ | 67<br>**Ho**<br>Holmium<br>164.930 32<br>$[Xe]4f^{11}6s^2$ | 68<br>**Er**<br>Erbium<br>167.259<br>$[Xe]4f^{12}6s^2$ | 69<br>**Tm**<br>Thulium<br>168.934 21<br>$[Xe]4f^{13}6s^2$ | 70<br>**Yb**<br>Ytterbium<br>173.04<br>$[Xe]4f^{14}6s^2$ | 71<br>**Lu**<br>Lutetium<br>174.967<br>$[Xe]4f^{14}5d^16s^2$ |
| 95<br>**Am**<br>Americium<br>(243)<br>$[Rn]5f^77s^2$ | 96<br>**Cm**<br>Curium<br>(247)<br>$[Rn]5f^76d^17s^2$ | 97<br>**Bk**<br>Berkelium<br>(247)<br>$[Rn]5f^97s^2$ | 98<br>**Cf**<br>Californium<br>(251)<br>$[Rn]5f^{10}7s^2$ | 99<br>**Es**<br>Einsteinium<br>(252)<br>$[Rn]5f^{11}7s^2$ | 100<br>**Fm**<br>Fermium<br>(257)<br>$[Rn]5f^{12}7s^2$ | 101<br>**Md**<br>Mendelevium<br>(258)<br>$[Rn]5f^{13}7s^2$ | 102<br>**No**<br>Nobelium<br>(259)<br>$[Rn]5f^{14}7s^2$ | 103<br>**Lr**<br>Lawrencium<br>(262)<br>$[Rn]5f^{14}6d^17s^2$ |

The atomic masses listed in this table reflect the precision of current measurements. (Each value listed in parentheses is the mass number of that radioactive element's most stable or most common isotope.)

(a)

(b)

**FIGURE 7** (a) Like other alkali metals, potassium reacts so strongly with water that (b) it must be stored in kerosene or oil to prevent it from reacting with moisture in the air.

## The *s*-Block Elements: Groups 1 and 2

The elements of the *s* block are chemically reactive *metals.* The Group 1 metals are more reactive than those of Group 2. The outermost energy level in an atom of each Group 1 element contains a single *s* electron. For example, the configurations of lithium and sodium are [He]$2s^1$ and [Ne]$3s^1$, respectively. As you will learn in Section 3, the ease with which the single electron is lost helps to make the Group 1 metals extremely reactive. Using $n$ for the number of the highest occupied energy level, the outer, or group, configurations of the Group 1 and 2 elements are written $ns^1$ and $ns^2$, respectively. For example, the configuration of Na is [Ne]$3s^1$, so the group configuration is written $ns^1$, where $n = 3$.

*The elements of Group 1 of the periodic table (lithium, sodium, potassium, rubidium, cesium, and francium) are known as the* **alkali metals.** In their pure state, all of the alkali metals have a silvery appearance and are soft enough to cut with a knife. However, because they are so reactive, alkali metals are not found in nature as free elements. They combine vigorously with most nonmetals. And they react strongly with water to produce hydrogen gas and aqueous solutions of substances known as alkalis. Because of their extreme reactivity with air or moisture, alkali metals are usually stored in kerosene. Proceeding down the column, the elements of Group 1 melt at successively lower temperatures.

*The elements of Group 2 of the periodic table (beryllium, magnesium, calcium, strontium, barium, and radium) are called the* **alkaline-earth metals.** Atoms of alkaline-earth metals contain a pair of electrons in their outermost *s* sublevel. Consequently, the group configuration for Group 2 is $ns^2$. The Group 2 metals are harder, denser, and stronger than the alkali metals. They also have higher melting points. Although they are less reactive than the alkali metals, the alkaline-earth metals are also too reactive to be found in nature as free elements.

## Hydrogen and Helium

Before discussing the other blocks of the periodic table, let's consider two special cases in the classification of the elements—hydrogen and helium. Hydrogen has an electron configuration of $1s^1$, but despite the $ns^1$ configuration, it does not share the same properties as the elements

(a)

(b)

**FIGURE 8** Calcium, an alkaline-earth metal, is too reactive to be found in nature in its pure state (a). Instead, it exists in compounds, such as in the minerals that make up marble (b).

of Group 1. Although it is located above the Group 1 elements in many periodic tables, hydrogen is a unique element, with properties that do not closely resemble those of any group.

Like the Group 2 elements, helium has an $ns^2$ group configuration. Yet it is part of Group 18. Because its highest occupied energy level is filled by two electrons, helium possesses special chemical stability, exhibiting the unreactive nature of a Group 18 element. By contrast, the Group 2 metals have no special stability; their highest occupied energy levels are not filled because each metal has an empty available *p* sublevel.

SCI LINKS.
www.scilinks.org
**Topic:** Alkali Metals
**Code:** HC60043
**Topic:** Alkaline-Earth Metals
**Code:** HC60044

## SAMPLE PROBLEM A

*For more help, go to the* ***Math Tutor*** *at the end of this chapter.*

**a. Without looking at the periodic table, identify the group, period, and block in which the element that has the electron configuration [Xe]6*s*$^2$ is located.**

**b. Without looking at the periodic table, write the electron configuration for the Group 1 element in the third period. Is this element likely to be more reactive or less reactive than the element described in (a)?**

**SOLUTION**

a. The element is in Group 2, as indicated by the group configuration of $ns^2$. It is in the sixth period, as indicated by the highest principal quantum number in its configuration, 6. The element is in the *s* block.

b. In a third-period element, the highest occupied energy level is the third main energy level, $n = 3$. The 1*s*, 2*s*, and 2*p* sublevels are completely filled (see **Table 1**). A Group 1 element has a group configuration of $ns^1$, which indicates a single electron in its highest *s* sublevel. Therefore, this element has the following configuration:

$$1s^22s^22p^63s^1 \quad \text{or} \quad [\text{Ne}]3s^1$$

Because it is in Group 1 (the alkali metals), this element is likely to be more reactive than the element described in (a), which is in Group 2 (the alkaline-earth metals).

**PRACTICE**

*Answers in Appendix E*

1. Without looking at the periodic table, identify the group, period, and block in which the element that has the electron configuration [Kr]5$s^1$ is located.
2. a. Without looking at the periodic table, write the group configuration for the Group 2 elements.

   b. Without looking at the periodic table, write the complete electron configuration for the Group 2 element in the fourth period.

   c. Refer to **Figure 6** to identify the element described in (b). Then, write the element's noble-gas notation.

extension
Go to **go.hrw.com** for more practice problems that ask you to relate positions of elements in the periodic table with electron configurations.

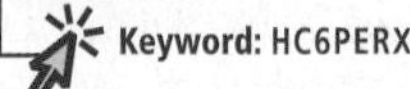

**FIGURE 9** The diagram shows the electron configuration of scandium, Sc, the Group 3 element of the fourth period. In general, the $(n - 1)d$ sublevel in Groups 3–12 is occupied by electrons after the $ns$ sublevel is filled.

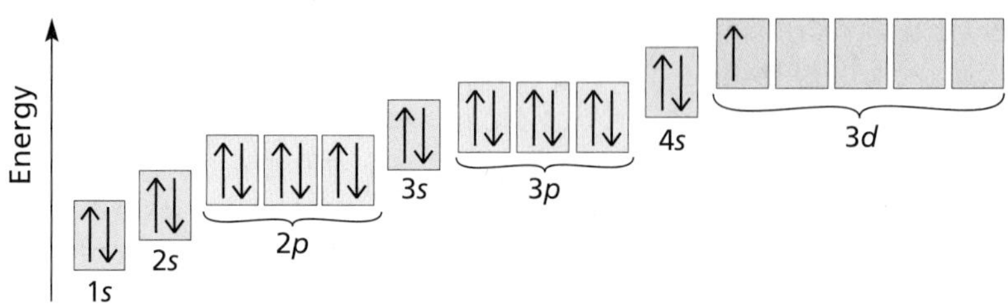


## The *d*-Block Elements: Groups 3–12

For energy level $n$, there are $n$ possible sublevels, so the $d$ sublevel first appears when $n = 3$. This $3d$ sublevel is slightly higher in energy than the $4s$ sublevel, so these are filled in the order $4s3d$ (see **Figure 9**). This order of filling is also seen for higher values of $n$. Each $d$ sublevel consists of five orbitals with a maximum of two electrons each, or up to 10 electrons possible in each $d$ sublevel. In addition to the two $ns$ electrons of Group 2, atoms of the Group 3 elements each have one electron in the $d$ sublevel of the $(n - 1)$ energy level. The group configuration for Group 3 is therefore $(n - 1)d^1ns^2$. Atoms of the Group 12 elements have 10 electrons in the $d$ sublevel plus two electrons in the $ns$ sublevel. The group configuration for Group 12 is $(n - 1)d^{10}ns^2$.

As you read in Chapter 4, some deviations from orderly $d$ sublevel filling occur in Groups 4–11. As a result, elements in these $d$-block groups, unlike those in $s$-block and $p$-block groups, do not necessarily have identical outer electron configurations. For example, in Group 10, nickel, Ni, has the electron configuration $[Ar]3d^84s^2$. Palladium, Pd, has the configuration $[Kr]4d^{10}5s^0$. And platinum, Pt, has the configuration $[Xe]4f^{14}5d^96s^1$. Notice, however, that in each case the sum of the outer $s$ and $d$ electrons is equal to the group number.

*The d-block elements are metals with typical metallic properties and are often referred to as* **transition elements.** They are good conductors of electricity and have a high luster. They are typically less reactive than the alkali metals and the alkaline-earth metals. Some are so unreactive that they do not easily form compounds, existing in nature as free elements. Palladium, platinum, and gold are among the least reactive of all the elements. Some $d$-block elements are shown in **Figure 10.**

**FIGURE 10** Mercury, tungsten, and vanadium are transition elements. Locate them in the $d$ block of the periodic table on pages 140–141.

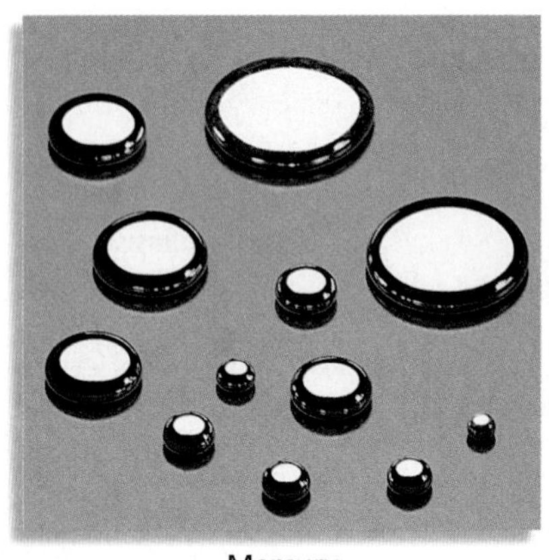
Mercury

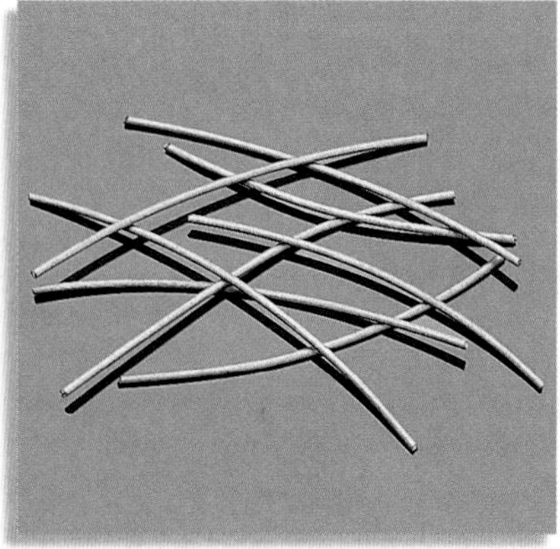
Tungsten

Vanadium

# CAREERS in Chemistry

## Materials Scientist

Almost everything we use or wear is composed of materials. Materials can include metals, ceramics, polymers, semiconductors, and composites. Metals have been used for thousands of years. Metals are good conductors of heat and electricity. They are strong but deformable. Ceramics are typically compounds made up of both metals and nonmetals. Usually, ceramics are insulators and are resistant to high temperatures. Examples of products that contain ceramics are dishes, building materials, bone and tooth replacements, and high-speed communications equipment. Polymers are generally organic compounds and have very large molecular structures. Polymer products include toys, storage containers, paints, and biomedical items; plastics (polymers) are everywhere. The electrical properties of semiconductors are between those of conductors and insulators. Computers, calculators, and cell phones are just a few examples of products that use semiconductors. Composites, such as ceramics and polymers, are found in flooring, tiles, bicycles, space shuttles, and insulation.

Materials science includes the study of the processing, structure, properties, and performance of materials. Processing involves manufacturing the material from its raw components. Structure refers to the arrangement of the material's components from an atomic to a macro scale. Understanding the structure helps materials scientists develop new materials that have the desired properties. Typical properties of interest are mechanical, such as tensile strength or hardness; electrical, such as conductivity or resistivity; magnetic, such as magnetic susceptibility; optical, such as refractive index; thermal, such as heat capacity or thermal conductivity; and environmental, such as corrosion behavior. Performance testing and analysis ensures that the product has the desired properties. Because a property or a structural characterization of a material closely depends on the processing used, evaluation often improves the process used to make the material.

### Careers in Materials Science

Materials scientists go by many different titles, such as process or production engineers, research scientists, metallurgists, polymer scientists, ceramic engineers, plant managers, and quality control engineers. Materials scientists are employed in industries such as transportation, electronics, aerospace, and biomedical engineering or work for research laboratories, the government, or universities. Materials scientists help determine what materials should be used in products based on desired properties, help synthesize new materials, and help produce these materials efficiently.

Because of the interdisciplinary nature of this field, many kinds of programs, disciplines, or majors can prepare a person for a career in materials science. An undergraduate degree in materials science and engineering, chemistry, physics, or engineering can lead to a career in this field. Many materials scientists obtain a more advanced degree, such as a master's degree in materials science and engineering or a doctorate (Ph.D.) in chemistry, physics, or engineering.

▲ *Materials scientists study the microstructure of materials, testing how they behave under various conditions.*

The materials field is exciting and expanding. The ability to create materials to meet specific needs is just starting to be realized. With the developing field of materials science, many say we are living in the Materials Age.

### Questions

1. Choose a product you might use in your daily life. Discuss the materials that compose the product and the properties that those materials give the product.
2. Using the Internet, find a profile of a materials scientist or engineer, and describe what that scientist or engineer does in her or his position.

**SAMPLE PROBLEM B** *For more help, go to the Math Tutor at the end of this chapter.*

**An element has the electron configuration [Kr]4$d^5$5$s^1$. Without looking at the periodic table, identify the period, block, and group in which this element is located. Then, consult the periodic table to identify this element and the others in its group.**

**SOLUTION** The number of the highest occupied energy level is 5, so the element is in the fifth period. There are five electrons in the *d* sublevel, which means that it is incompletely filled. The *d* sublevel can hold 10 electrons. Therefore, the element is in the *d* block. For *d*-block elements, the number of electrons in the *ns* sublevel (1) plus the number of electrons in the $(n - 1)d$ sublevel (5) equals the group number, 6. This Group 6 element is molybdenum. The others in Group 6 are chromium, tungsten, and seaborgium.

**PRACTICE** *Answers in Appendix E*

1. Without looking at the periodic table, identify the period, block, and group in which the element that has the electron configuration [Ar]3$d^8$4$s^2$ is located.
2. Without looking at the periodic table, write the outer electron configuration for the Group 12 element in the fifth period.

Go to **go.hrw.com** for more practice problems that ask you to use the electron configurations of elements to locate those elements in the periodic table.

**Keyword:** HC6PERX

## The *p*-Block Elements: Groups 13–18

The *p*-block elements consist of all the elements of Groups 13–18 except helium. Electrons add to a *p* sublevel only after the *s* sublevel in the same energy level is filled. Therefore, atoms of all *p*-block elements contain two electrons in the *ns* sublevel. *The p-block elements together with the s-block elements are called the* **main-group elements.** For Group 13 elements, the added electron enters the *np* sublevel, giving a group configuration of $ns^2np^1$. Atoms of Group 14 elements contain two electrons in the *p* sublevel, giving $ns^2np^2$ for the group configuration. This pattern continues in Groups 15–18. In Group 18, the stable noble-gas configuration of $ns^2np^6$ is reached. The relationships among group numbers and electron configurations for all the groups are summarized in **Table 2.**

For atoms of *p*-block elements, the total number of electrons in the highest occupied level is equal to the group number minus 10. For example, bromine is in Group 17. It has 17 – 10 = 7 electrons in its highest energy level. Because atoms of *p*-block elements contain two electrons in the *ns* sublevel, we know that bromine has five electrons in its outer *p* sublevel. The electron configuration of bromine is [Ar]3$d^{10}$4$s^2$4$p^5$.

The properties of elements of the *p* block vary greatly. At its right-hand end, the *p* block includes all of the *nonmetals* except hydrogen and helium. All six of the *metalloids* (boron, silicon, germanium, arsenic,

**TABLE 2 Relationships Among Group Numbers, Blocks, and Electron Configurations**

| Group number | Group configuration | Block | Comments |
|---|---|---|---|
| 1, 2 | $ns^{1,2}$ | *s* | One or two electrons in *ns* sublevel |
| 3–12 | $(n-1)d^{1-10}ns^{0-2}$ | *d* | Sum of electrons in *ns* and $(n-1)d$ levels equals group number |
| 13–18 | $ns^2np^{1-6}$ | *p* | Number of electrons in *np* sublevel equals group number minus 12 |

antimony, and tellurium) are also in the *p* block. At the left-hand side and bottom of the block, there are eight *p*-block metals. The locations of the nonmetals, metalloids, and metals in the *p* block are shown with distinctive colors in **Figure 6.**

*The elements of Group 17 (fluorine, chlorine, bromine, iodine, and astatine) are known as the* **halogens,** shown in **Figure 11.** The halogens are the most reactive nonmetals. They react vigorously with most metals to form examples of the type of compound known as salts. As you will see later, the reactivity of the halogens is based on the presence of seven electrons in their outer energy levels—one electron short of the stable noble-gas configuration. Fluorine and chlorine are gases at room temperature, bromine is a reddish liquid, and iodine is a dark purple solid. Astatine is a synthetic element prepared in only very small quantities. Most of its properties are estimated, although it is known to be a solid.

The metalloids, or semiconducting elements, are located between nonmetals and metals in the *p* block. They are mostly brittle solids with some properties of metals and some of nonmetals. The metalloid elements have electrical conductivity intermediate between that of metals, which are good conductors, and nonmetals, which are nonconductors.

The metals of the *p* block are generally harder and denser than the *s*-block alkaline-earth metals, but softer and less dense than the *d*-block metals. With the exception of bismuth, these metals are sufficiently reactive to be found in nature only in the form of compounds. Once obtained as free metals, however, they are stable in the presence of air.

**FIGURE 11** Fluorine, chlorine, bromine, and iodine are members of Group 17 of the periodic table, also known as the halogens. Locate the halogens in the *p* block of the periodic table on pages 140–141.

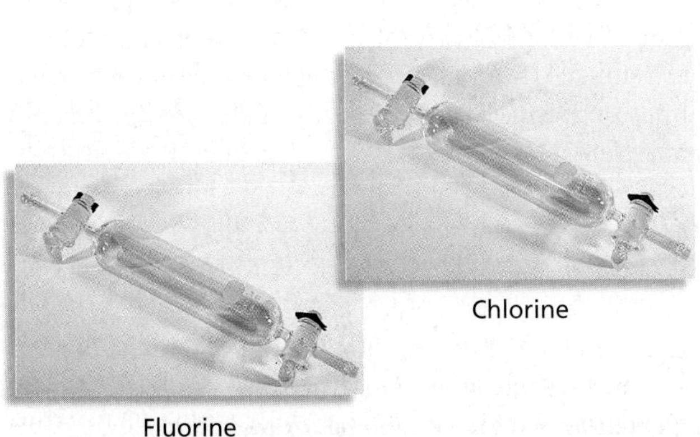

**SAMPLE PROBLEM C** *For more help, go to the Math Tutor at the end of this chapter.*

**Without looking at the periodic table, write the outer electron configuration for the Group 14 element in the second period. Then, name the element, and identify it as a metal, nonmetal, or metalloid.**

**SOLUTION** The group number is higher than 12, so the element is in the *p* block. The total number of electrons in the highest occupied *s* and *p* sublevels is therefore equal to the group number minus 10 (14 – 10 = 4). Two electrons are in the *s* sublevel, so two electrons must also be present in the 2*p* sublevel, which means that the outer electron configuration is $2s^22p^2$. The element is carbon, C, which is a nonmetal.

**PRACTICE** *Answers in Appendix E*

1. a. Without looking at the periodic table, write the outer electron configuration for the Group 17 element in the third period.

   b. Name the element described in (a), and identify it as a metal, nonmetal, or metalloid.

2. a. Without looking at the periodic table, identify the period, block, and group of an element that has the electron configuration $[Ar]3d^{10}4s^24p^3$.

   b. Name the element described in (a), and identify it as a metal, nonmetal, or metalloid.

Go to **go.hrw.com** for more practice problems that ask you to classify elements and write their electron configurations based on their period and group.

**Keyword: HC6PERX**

## The *f*-Block Elements: Lanthanides and Actinides

In the periodic table, the *f*-block elements are wedged between Groups 3 and 4 in the sixth and seventh periods. The position of these inner transition elements reflects the fact that they involve the filling of the 4*f* sublevel. With seven 4*f* orbitals to be filled with two electrons each, there are a total of 14 *f*-block elements between lanthanum, La, and hafnium, Hf, in the sixth period. The lanthanides are shiny metals similar in reactivity to the Group 2 alkaline-earth metals.

There are also 14 *f*-block elements, the actinides, between actinium, Ac, and element 104, Rf, in the seventh period. In these elements the 5*f* sublevel is being filled with 14 electrons. The actinides are all radioactive. The first four actinides (thorium, Th, through neptunium, Np) have been found naturally on Earth. The remaining actinides are known only as laboratory-made elements.

**SAMPLE PROBLEM D**

**The electron configurations of atoms of four elements are written at the top of page 149. Name the block and group in which each of these elements is located in the periodic table. Then, use the periodic table on pages 140–141 to name each element. Identify each element as a metal, nonmetal, or metalloid.**

**Finally, describe whether each element has high reactivity or low reactivity.**

a. $[Xe]4f^{14}5d^{9}6s^{1}$
b. $[Ne]3s^{2}3p^{5}$
c. $[Ne]3s^{2}3p^{6}$
d. $[Xe]4f^{6}6s^{2}$

**SOLUTION**

a. The 4*f* sublevel is filled with 14 electrons. The 5*d* sublevel is partially filled with nine electrons. Therefore, this element is in the *d* block. The element is the transition metal platinum, Pt, which is in Group 10 and has a low reactivity.

b. The incompletely filled *p* sublevel shows that this element is in the *p* block. A total of seven electrons are in the *ns* and *np* sublevels, so this element is in Group 17, the halogens. The element is chlorine, Cl, and is highly reactive.

c. This element has a noble-gas configuration and thus is in Group 18 in the *p* block. The element is argon, Ar, which is an unreactive nonmetal and a noble gas.

d. The incomplete 4*f* sublevel shows that the element is in the *f* block and is a lanthanide. Group numbers are not assigned to the *f* block. The element is samarium, Sm. All of the lanthanides are reactive metals.

**PRACTICE**

*Answers in Appendix E*

1. For each of the following, identify the block, period, group, group name (where appropriate), element name, element type (metal, nonmetal, or metalloid), and relative reactivity (high or low):

a. $[He]2s^{2}2p^{5}$
b. $[Ar]3d^{10}4s^{1}$

**extension**

Go to **go.hrw.com** for more practice problems that ask you to locate elements on the periodic table and predict their properties based on their electron configurations.

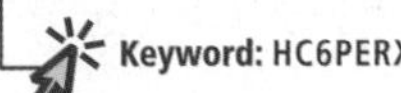


## SECTION REVIEW

1. Into what four blocks can the periodic table be divided to illustrate the relationship between the elements' electron configurations and their placement in the periodic table?
2. What name is given to each of the following groups of elements in the periodic table?
   **a.** Group 1 **b.** Group 2 **c.** Groups 3–12 **d.** Group 17 **e.** Group 18
3. What are the relationships between group configuration and group number for elements in the *s, p,* and *d* blocks?
4. Without looking at the periodic table, write the outer electron configuration for the Group 15 element in the fourth period.
5. Without looking at the periodic table, identify the period, block, and group of the element that has the electron configuration $[Ar]3d^{7}4s^{2}$.

**Critical Thinking**

6. **APPLYING MODELS** Period 7 contains elements in the *s, p, d,* and *f* blocks. Suppose that there were a Period 8 and it contained elements in the "g" block, where "g" had the angular momentum quantum number $\ell = 4$. If a hypothetical element in Period 8 had an atomic number of 120, into what group in the periodic table would the element fit, and what properties might it have (assuming it does not radioactively decay)?

SECTION 3

## *Objectives*

- Define *atomic* and *ionic radii, ionization energy, electron affinity,* and *electronegativity.*
- Compare the periodic trends of atomic radii, ionization energy, and electronegativity, and state the reasons for these variations.
- Define *valence electrons,* and state how many are present in atoms of each main-group element.
- Compare the atomic radii, ionization energies, and electronegativities of the *d*-block elements with those of the main-group elements.

# *Electron Configuration and Periodic Properties*

**C.2.3** Summarize the periodic table's property trends (including electron configuration, ionization energy, electron affinity, atomic size, ionic size, and reactivity)

So far, you have learned that the elements are arranged in the periodic table according to their atomic number and that there is a rough correlation between the arrangement of the elements and their electron configurations. In this section, the relationship between the periodic law and electron configurations will be further explored.

## Atomic Radii

Ideally, the size of an atom is defined by the edge of its orbital. However, this boundary is fuzzy and varies under different conditions. Therefore, to estimate the size of an atom, the conditions under which the atom exists must be specified. One way to express an atom's radius is to measure the distance between the nuclei of two identical atoms that are chemically bonded together, then divide this distance by two. As illustrated in **Figure 12, atomic radius** *may be defined as one-half the distance between the nuclei of identical atoms that are bonded together.*

### Period Trends

**Figure 13** gives the atomic radii of the elements and **Figure 14** presents this information graphically. Note that there is a gradual decrease in atomic radii across the second period from lithium, Li, to neon, Ne. *The*

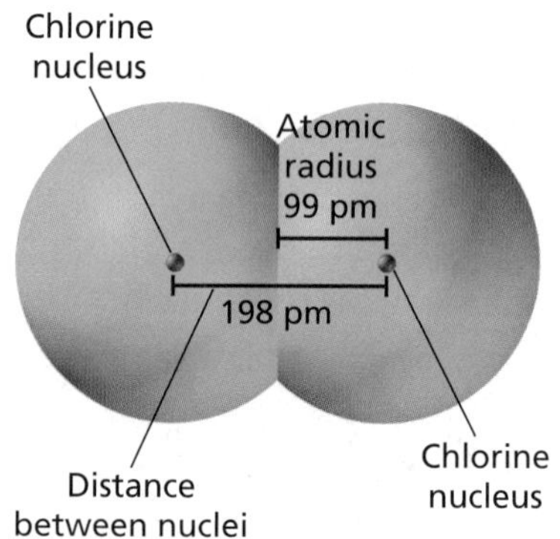


**FIGURE 12** One method of determining atomic radius is to measure the distance between the nuclei of two identical atoms that are bonded together in an element or compound, then divide this distance by two. The atomic radius of a chlorine atom, for example, is 100 picometers (pm).

## Periodic Table of Atomic Radii (pm)

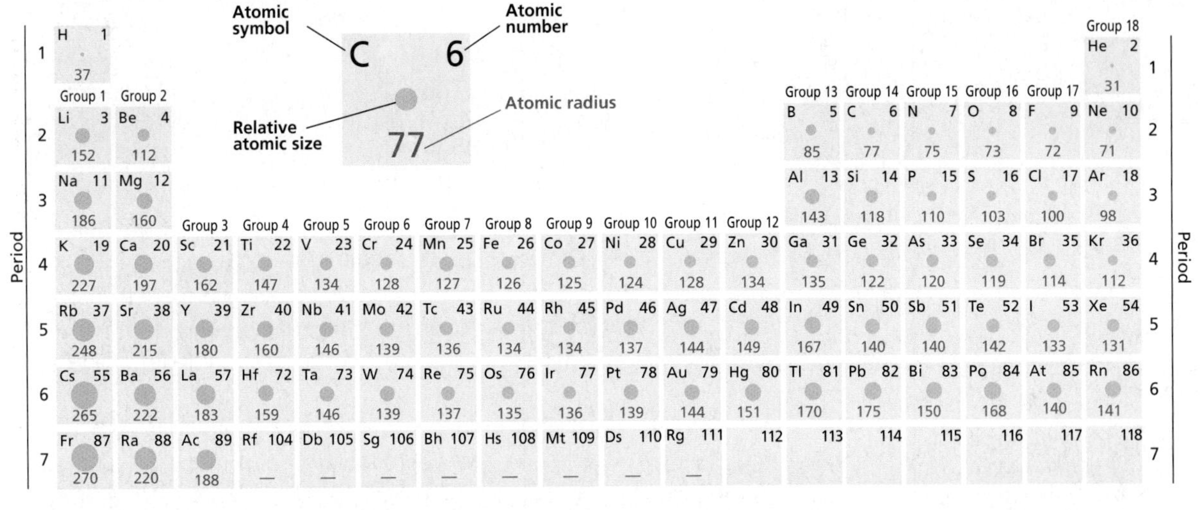


Lanthanide series

| Ce 58 | Pr 59 | Nd 60 | Pm 61 | Sm 62 | Eu 63 | Gd 64 | Tb 65 | Dy 66 | Ho 67 | Er 68 | Tm 69 | Yb 70 | Lu 71 |
|---|---|---|---|---|---|---|---|---|---|---|---|---|---|
| 182 | 182 | 181 | 183 | 180 | 208 | 180 | 177 | 178 | 176 | 176 | 176 | — | 174 |
| **Th 90** | **Pa 91** | **U 92** | **Np 93** | **Pu 94** | **Am 95** | **Cm 96** | **Bk 97** | **Cf 98** | **Es 99** | **Fm 100** | **Md 101** | **No 102** | **Lr 103** |
| 179 | 163 | 156 | 155 | 159 | 173 | 174 | — | 186 | 186 | — | — | — | — |

Actinide series

**FIGURE 13** Atomic radii decrease from left to right across a period and increase down a group.

*trend to smaller atoms across a period is caused by the increasing positive charge of the nucleus.* As electrons add to *s* and *p* sublevels in the same main energy level, they are gradually pulled closer to the more highly charged nucleus. This increased pull results in a decrease in atomic radii. The attraction of the nucleus is somewhat offset by repulsion among the increased number of electrons in the same outer energy level. As a result, the difference in radii between neighboring atoms in each period grows smaller, as shown in **Figure 13.**

## Group Trends

Examine the atomic radii of the Group 1 elements in **Figure 13.** Notice that the radii of the elements increase as you read down the group. As electrons occupy sublevels in successively higher main energy levels located farther from the nucleus, the sizes of the atoms increase. *In general, the atomic radii of the main-group elements increase down a group.*

Now examine the radii of the Group 13 elements. Although gallium, Ga, follows aluminum, Al, it has a slightly smaller atomic radius than does aluminum. This is because gallium, unlike aluminum, is preceded in its period by the 10 *d*-block elements. The expected increase in gallium's radius caused by the filling of the fourth main-energy level is outweighed by a shrinking of the electron cloud caused by a nuclear charge that is considerably higher than that of aluminum.

## *Atomic Radius vs. Atomic Number*

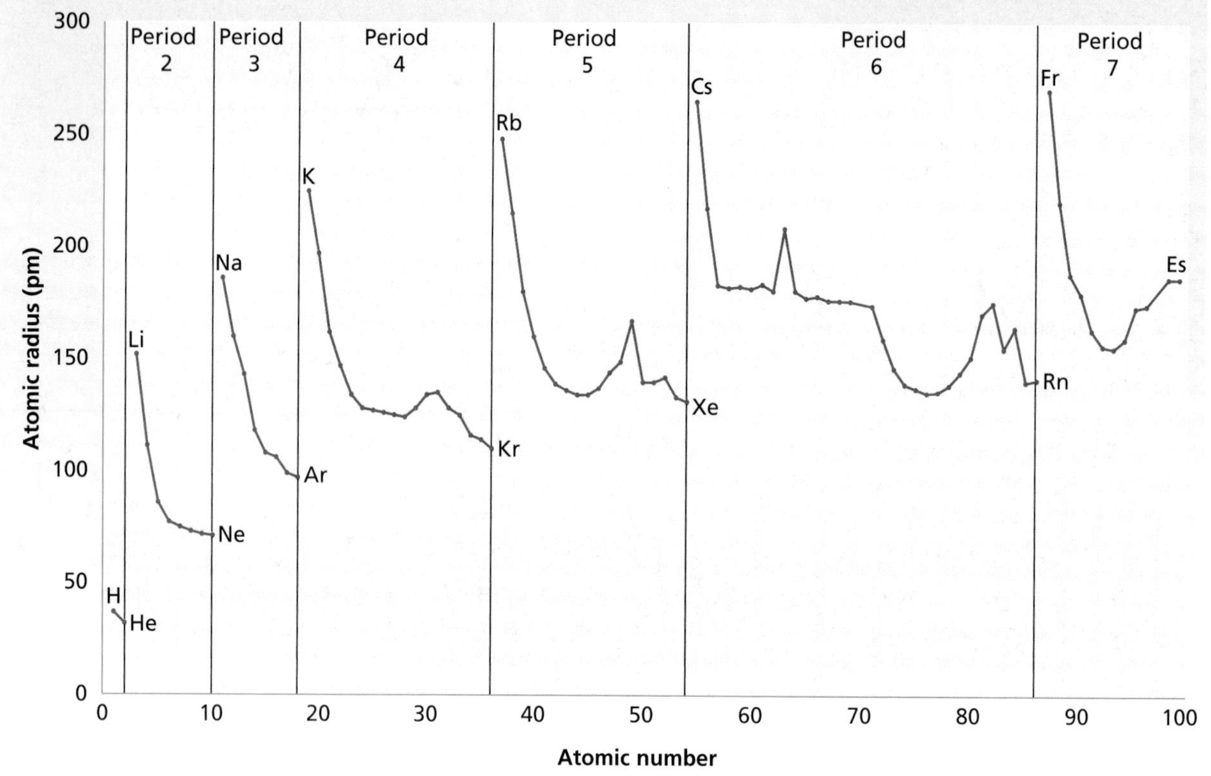

Period 2 | Period 3 | Period 4 | Period 5 | Period 6 | Period 7

H, He, Li, Ne, Na, Ar, K, Kr, Rb, Xe, Cs, Rn, Fr, Es

Atomic radius (pm): 0, 50, 100, 150, 200, 250, 300

Atomic number: 0, 10, 20, 30, 40, 50, 60, 70, 80, 90, 100

**FIGURE 14** The plot of atomic radius versus atomic number shows period and group trends.

## SAMPLE PROBLEM E

**Of the elements magnesium, Mg, chlorine, Cl, sodium, Na, and phosphorus, P, which has the largest atomic radius? Explain your answer in terms of trends in the periodic table.**

**SOLUTION** All of the elements are in the third period. Of the four, sodium has the lowest atomic number and is the first element in the period. Therefore, sodium has the largest atomic radius because atomic radii decrease across a period.

## PRACTICE

*Answers in Appendix E*

1. Which of the following elements has the largest atomic radius: Li, O, C, or F? Which has the smallest atomic radius?
2. Of the elements calcium, Ca, beryllium, Be, barium, Ba, and strontium, Sr, which has the largest atomic radius? Explain your answer in terms of trends in the periodic table.
3. Of the elements aluminum, Al, magnesium, Mg, silicon, Si, and sodium, Na, which has the smallest atomic radius? Explain your answer in terms of trends in the periodic table.

**extension**

Go to **go.hrw.com** for more practice problems that ask you to use periodic trends in atomic radius to predict relative sizes of atoms.

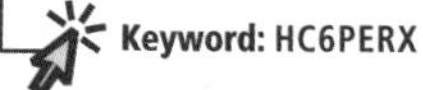

# Ionization Energy

An electron can be removed from an atom if enough energy is supplied. Using A as a symbol for an atom of any element, the process can be expressed as follows.

$$A + \text{energy} \rightarrow A^+ + e^-$$

The $A^+$ represents an ion of element A with a single positive charge, referred to as a 1+ ion. *An* **ion** *is an atom or group of bonded atoms that has a positive or negative charge.* Sodium, for example, forms an $Na^+$ ion. *Any process that results in the formation of an ion is referred to as* **ionization.**

To compare the ease with which atoms of different elements give up electrons, chemists compare ionization energies. *The energy required to remove one electron from a neutral atom of an element is the* **ionization energy, *IE*** *(or first ionization energy, $IE_1$).* To avoid the influence of nearby atoms, measurements of ionization energies are made on isolated atoms in the gas phase. **Figure 15** gives the first ionization energies for the elements in kilojoules per mole (kJ/mol). **Figure 16** presents this information graphically.

**FIGURE 15** In general, first ionization energies increase across a period and decrease down a group.

***Periodic Table of Ionization Energies (kJ/mol)***

Key: 6 (Atomic number) / C (Symbol) / 1086 (First ionization energy)

| Period | Group 1 | Group 2 | Group 3 | Group 4 | Group 5 | Group 6 | Group 7 | Group 8 | Group 9 | Group 10 | Group 11 | Group 12 | Group 13 | Group 14 | Group 15 | Group 16 | Group 17 | Group 18 |
|---|---|---|---|---|---|---|---|---|---|---|---|---|---|---|---|---|---|---|
| 1 | 1 H 1312 | | | | | | | | | | | | | | | | | 2 He 2372 |
| 2 | 3 Li 520 | 4 Be 900 | | | | | | | | | | | 5 B 801 | 6 C 1086 | 7 N 1402 | 8 O 1314 | 9 F 1681 | 10 Ne 2081 |
| 3 | 11 Na 496 | 12 Mg 738 | | | | | | | | | | | 13 Al 578 | 14 Si 787 | 15 P 1012 | 16 S 1000 | 17 Cl 1251 | 18 Ar 1521 |
| 4 | 19 K 419 | 20 Ca 590 | 21 Sc 633 | 22 Ti 659 | 23 V 651 | 24 Cr 653 | 25 Mn 717 | 26 Fe 762 | 27 Co 760 | 28 Ni 737 | 29 Cu 746 | 30 Zn 906 | 31 Ga 579 | 32 Ge 762 | 33 As 947 | 34 Se 941 | 35 Br 1140 | 36 Kr 1351 |
| 5 | 37 Rb 403 | 38 Sr 550 | 39 Y 600 | 40 Zr 640 | 41 Nb 652 | 42 Mo 684 | 43 Tc 702 | 44 Ru 710 | 45 Rh 720 | 46 Pd 804 | 47 Ag 731 | 48 Cd 868 | 49 In 558 | 50 Sn 709 | 51 Sb 834 | 52 Te 869 | 53 I 1008 | 54 Xe 1170 |
| 6 | 55 Cs 376 | 56 Ba 503 | 57 La 538 | 72 Hf 659 | 73 Ta 761 | 74 W 770 | 75 Re 760 | 76 Os 839 | 77 Ir 878 | 78 Pt 868 | 79 Au 890 | 80 Hg 1007 | 81 Tl 589 | 82 Pb 716 | 83 Bi 703 | 84 Po 812 | 85 At — | 86 Rn 1038 |
| 7 | 87 Fr — | 88 Ra 509 | 89 Ac 490 | 104 Rf — | 105 Db — | 106 Sg — | 107 Bh — | 108 Hs — | 109 Mt — | 110 Ds — | 111 Rg — | 112 | 113 | 114 | 115 | 116 | 117 | 118 |

Lanthanide series

| 58 Ce 534 | 59 Pr 527 | 60 Nd 533 | 61 Pm 536 | 62 Sm 545 | 63 Eu 547 | 64 Gd 592 | 65 Tb 566 | 66 Dy 573 | 67 Ho 581 | 68 Er 589 | 69 Tm 597 | 70 Yb 603 | 71 Lu 523 |
|---|---|---|---|---|---|---|---|---|---|---|---|---|---|

Actinide series

| 90 Th 587 | 91 Pa 570 | 92 U 598 | 93 Np 600 | 94 Pu 585 | 95 Am 578 | 96 Cm 581 | 97 Bk 601 | 98 Cf 608 | 99 Es 619 | 100 Fm 627 | 101 Md 635 | 102 No 642 | 103 Lr — |
|---|---|---|---|---|---|---|---|---|---|---|---|---|---|

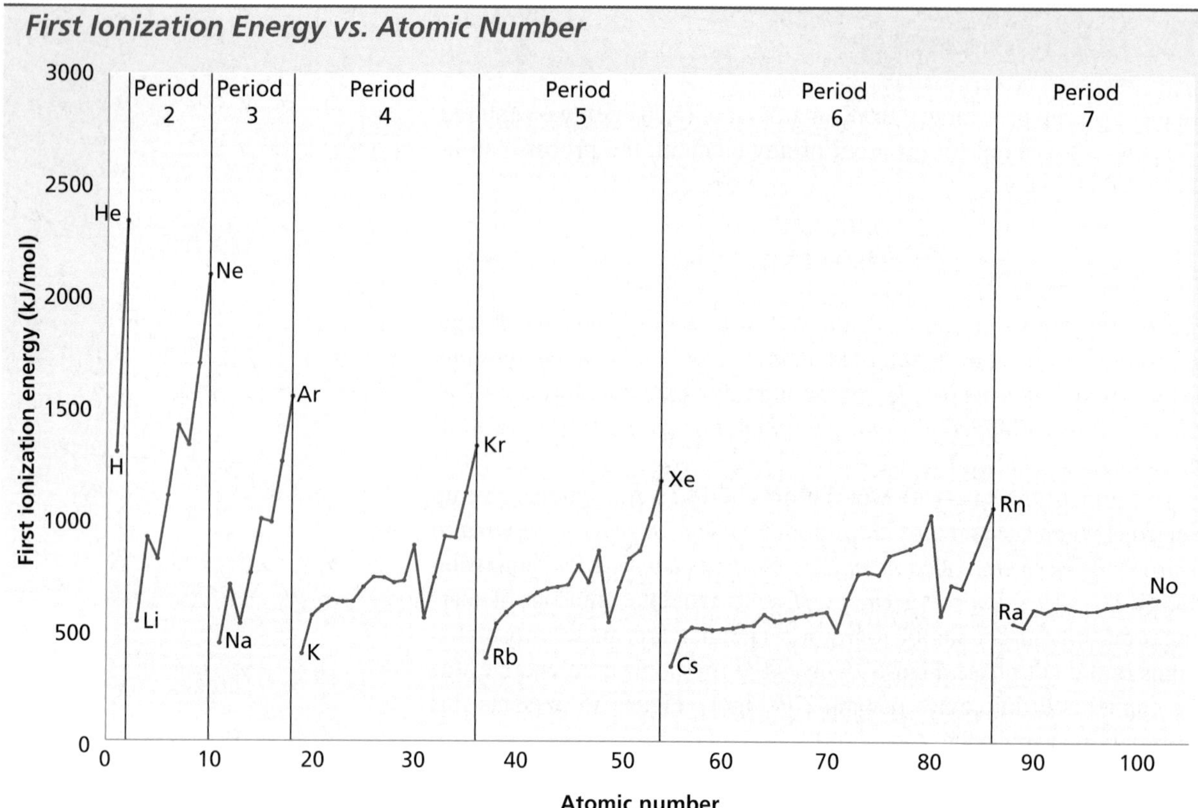


**FIGURE 16** Plot of first ionization energy, $IE_1$, versus atomic number. As atomic number increases, both the period and the group trends become less pronounced.

## Period Trends

In **Figures 15** and **16,** examine the ionization energies for the first and last elements in each period. You can see that the Group 1 metals have the lowest first ionization energies in their respective periods. Therefore, they lose electrons most easily. This ease of electron loss is a major reason for the high reactivity of the Group 1 (alkali) metals. The Group 18 elements, the noble gases, have the highest ionization energies. They do not lose electrons easily. The low reactivity of the noble gases is partly based on this difficulty of electron removal.

*In general, ionization energies of the main-group elements increase across each period.* This increase is caused by increasing nuclear charge. A higher charge more strongly attracts electrons in the same energy level. Increasing nuclear charge is responsible for both increasing ionization energy and decreasing radii across the periods. Note that, in general, nonmetals have higher ionization energies than metals do. In each period, the element of Group 1 has the lowest ionization energy and the element of Group 18 has the highest ionization energy.

## Group Trends

*Among the main-group elements, ionization energies generally decrease down the groups.* Electrons removed from atoms of each succeeding element in a group are in higher energy levels, farther from the nucleus. Therefore, they are removed more easily. Also, as atomic number increases going down a group, more electrons lie between the nucleus and the electrons in the highest occupied energy levels. This partially shields the outer electrons from the effect of the nuclear charge. Together, these influences overcome the attraction of the electrons to the increasing nuclear charge.

**extension**

**CROSS-DISCIPLINARY**

Go to **go.hrw.com** for a full-length article on elements and nutrition.

**Keyword: HC6PERX**

### Removing Electrons from Positive Ions

With sufficient energy, electrons can be removed from positive ions as well as from neutral atoms. The energies for removal of additional electrons from an atom are referred to as *the second ionization energy* ($IE_2$), *third ionization energy* ($IE_3$), and so on.

**Table 3** shows the first five ionization energies for the elements of the first, second, and third periods. You can see that the second ionization energy is always higher than the first, the third is always higher than the second, and so on. This is because as electrons are removed in successive ionizations, fewer electrons remain within the atom to shield the attractive force of the nucleus. *Thus, each successive electron removed from an ion feels an increasingly stronger effective nuclear charge (the nuclear charge minus the electron shielding).*

The first ionization energies in **Table 3** show that removing a single electron from an atom of a Group 18 element is more difficult than removing an electron from atoms of other elements in the same period. This special stability of the noble-gas configuration also applies to ions that have noble-gas configurations. Notice in **Table 3** the large increases between the first and second ionization energies of lithium, Li, and between the second and third ionization energies of beryllium, Be. Even larger increases in ionization energy exist between the third and fourth

**TABLE 3 *Ionization Energies (in kJ/mol) for Elements of Periods 1–3***

| | Period 1 | | Period 2 | | | | | | | |
|---|---|---|---|---|---|---|---|---|---|---|
| | H | He | Li | Be | B | C | N | O | F | Ne |
| $IE_1$ | 1312 | 2372 | 520 | 900 | 801 | 1086 | 1402 | 1314 | 1681 | 2081 |
| $IE_2$ | | 5250 | 7298 | 1757 | 2427 | 2353 | 2856 | 3388 | 3374 | 3952 |
| $IE_3$ | | | 11 815 | 14 849 | 3660 | 4621 | 4578 | 5300 | 6050 | 6122 |
| $IE_4$ | | | | 21 007 | 25 026 | 6223 | 7475 | 7469 | 8408 | 9370 |
| $IE_5$ | | | | | 32 827 | 37 830 | 9445 | 10 990 | 11 023 | 12 178 |
| | | | Period 3 | | | | | | | |
| | | | Na | Mg | Al | Si | P | S | Cl | Ar |
| $IE_1$ | | | 496 | 738 | 578 | 787 | 1012 | 1000 | 1251 | 1521 |
| $IE_2$ | | | 4562 | 1451 | 1817 | 1577 | 1903 | 2251 | 2297 | 2666 |
| $IE_3$ | | | 6912 | 7733 | 2745 | 3232 | 2912 | 3361 | 3822 | 3931 |
| $IE_4$ | | | 9544 | 10 540 | 11 578 | 4356 | 4957 | 4564 | 5158 | 5771 |
| $IE_5$ | | | 13 353 | 13 628 | 14 831 | 16 091 | 6274 | 7013 | 6540 | 7238 |

ionization energies of boron, B, and between the fourth and fifth ionization energies of carbon, C. In each case, the jump in ionization energy occurs when an ion assumes a noble-gas configuration. For example, the removal of one electron from a lithium atom ([He]$2s^1$) leaves the helium noble-gas configuration. The removal of four electrons from a carbon atom ([He]$2s^22p^2$) also leaves the helium configuration. A bigger table would show that this trend continues across the entire periodic system.

## SAMPLE PROBLEM F

**Consider two main-group elements, A and B. Element A has a first ionization energy of 419 kJ/mol. Element B has a first ionization energy of 1000 kJ/mol. Decide if each element is more likely to be in the *s* block or *p* block. Which element is more likely to form a positive ion?**

**SOLUTION** Element A has a very low ionization energy, which means that atoms of A lose electrons easily. Therefore, element A is most likely to be an *s*-block metal because ionization energies increase across the periods.

Element B has a very high ionization energy which means that atoms of B have difficulty losing electrons. Element B would most likely lie at the end of a period in the *p* block.

Element A is more likely to form a positive ion because it has a much lower ionization energy than element B does.

**PRACTICE** *Answers in Appendix E*

1. Consider four hypothetical main-group elements, Q, R, T, and X, that have the outer electron configurations indicated below. Then, answer the questions that follow.

   Q: $3s^23p^5$   R: $3s^1$   T: $4d^{10}5s^25p^5$   X: $4d^{10}5s^25p^1$

   a. Identify the block location of each hypothetical main-group element.

   b. Which of these elements are in the same period? Which are in the same group?

   c. Which element would you expect to have the highest first ionization energy? Which would have the lowest first ionization energy?

   d. Which element would you expect to have the highest second ionization energy?

   e. Which of the elements is most likely to form a 1+ ion?

**extension**
Go to **go.hrw.com** for more practice problems that ask you to use periodic trends in ionization energy.

**Keyword: HC6PERX**

## Electron Affinity

Neutral atoms can also acquire electrons. *The energy change that occurs when an electron is acquired by a neutral atom is called the atom's* **electron affinity.** Most atoms release energy when they acquire an electron.

$$A + e^- \longrightarrow A^- + \text{energy}$$

On the other hand, some atoms must be "forced" to gain an electron by the addition of energy.

$$A + e^- + \text{energy} \longrightarrow A^-$$

The quantity of energy absorbed would be represented by a positive number, but ions produced in this way are very unstable and hence the electron affinity for them is very difficult to determine. An ion produced in this way will be unstable and will lose the added electron spontaneously.

**Figure 17** shows the electron affinity in kilojoules per mole for the elements. Positive electron affinities, because they are so difficult to determine with any accuracy, are denoted in **Figure 17** by "(0)." **Figure 18,** on the next page, presents these data graphically.

### Period Trends

Among the elements of each period, the halogens (Group 17) gain electrons most readily. This is indicated in **Figure 17** by the large negative values of halogens' electron affinities. The ease with which halogen atoms gain electrons is a major reason for the high reactivities of the Group 17 elements. In general, as electrons add to the same *p* sublevel of atoms with increasing nuclear charge, electron affinities become more negative across each period within the *p* block. An exception to this trend occurs between Groups 14 and 15. Compare the electron affinities of carbon ([He]$2s^2 2p^2$) and nitrogen ([He]$2s^2 2p^3$). Adding an electron to a carbon atom gives a half-filled *p* sublevel. This occurs much more easily

**FIGURE 17** The values listed in parentheses in this periodic table of electron affinities are approximate. Electron affinity is estimated to be −50 kJ/mol for each of the lanthanides and 0 kJ/mol for each of the actinides.

*Periodic Table of Electron Affinities (kJ/mol)*

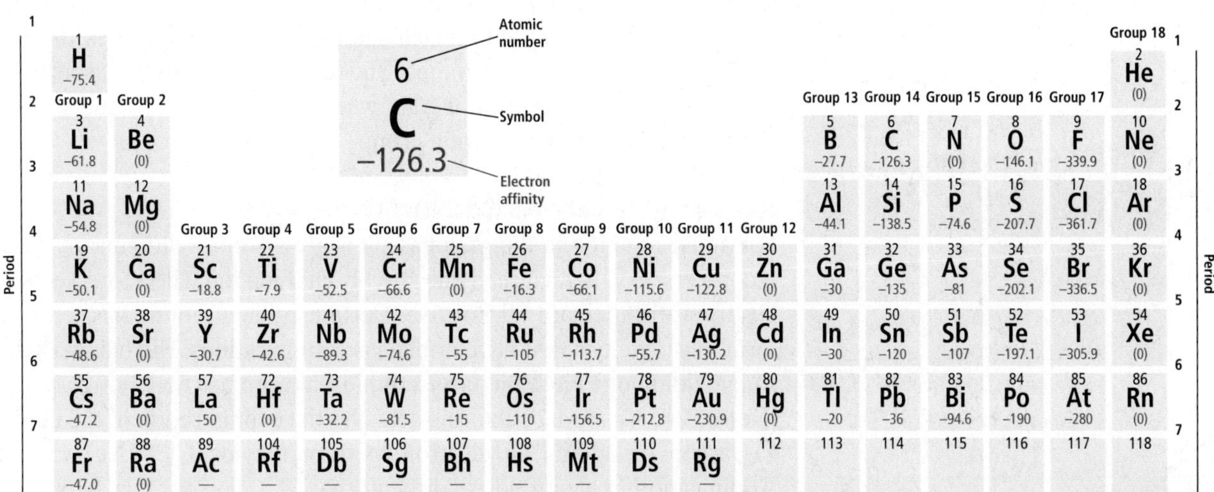


| Period | Group 1 | Group 2 | Group 3 | Group 4 | Group 5 | Group 6 | Group 7 | Group 8 | Group 9 | Group 10 | Group 11 | Group 12 | Group 13 | Group 14 | Group 15 | Group 16 | Group 17 | Group 18 |
|---|---|---|---|---|---|---|---|---|---|---|---|---|---|---|---|---|---|---|
| 1 | 1 H −75.4 | | | | | | | | | | | | | | | | | 2 He (0) |
| 2 | 3 Li −61.8 | 4 Be (0) | | | | | | | | | | | 5 B −27.7 | 6 C −126.3 | 7 N (0) | 8 O −146.1 | 9 F −339.9 | 10 Ne (0) |
| 3 | 11 Na −54.8 | 12 Mg (0) | | | | | | | | | | | 13 Al −44.1 | 14 Si −138.5 | 15 P −74.6 | 16 S −207.7 | 17 Cl −361.7 | 18 Ar (0) |
| 4 | 19 K −50.1 | 20 Ca (0) | 21 Sc −18.8 | 22 Ti −7.9 | 23 V −52.5 | 24 Cr −66.6 | 25 Mn (0) | 26 Fe −16.3 | 27 Co −66.1 | 28 Ni −115.6 | 29 Cu −122.8 | 30 Zn (0) | 31 Ga −30 | 32 Ge −135 | 33 As −81 | 34 Se −202.1 | 35 Br −336.5 | 36 Kr (0) |
| 5 | 37 Rb −48.6 | 38 Sr (0) | 39 Y −30.7 | 40 Zr −42.6 | 41 Nb −89.3 | 42 Mo −74.6 | 43 Tc −55 | 44 Ru −105 | 45 Rh −113.7 | 46 Pd −55.7 | 47 Ag −130.2 | 48 Cd (0) | 49 In −30 | 50 Sn −120 | 51 Sb −107 | 52 Te −197.1 | 53 I −305.9 | 54 Xe (0) |
| 6 | 55 Cs −47.2 | 56 Ba (0) | 57 La −50 | 72 Hf (0) | 73 Ta −32.2 | 74 W −81.5 | 75 Re −15 | 76 Os −110 | 77 Ir −156.5 | 78 Pt −212.8 | 79 Au −230.9 | 80 Hg (0) | 81 Tl −20 | 82 Pb −36 | 83 Bi −94.6 | 84 Po −190 | 85 At −280 | 86 Rn (0) |
| 7 | 87 Fr −47.0 | 88 Ra (0) | 89 Ac — | 104 Rf — | 105 Db — | 106 Sg — | 107 Bh — | 108 Hs — | 109 Mt — | 110 Ds — | 111 Rg — | 112 | 113 | 114 | 115 | 116 | 117 | 118 |

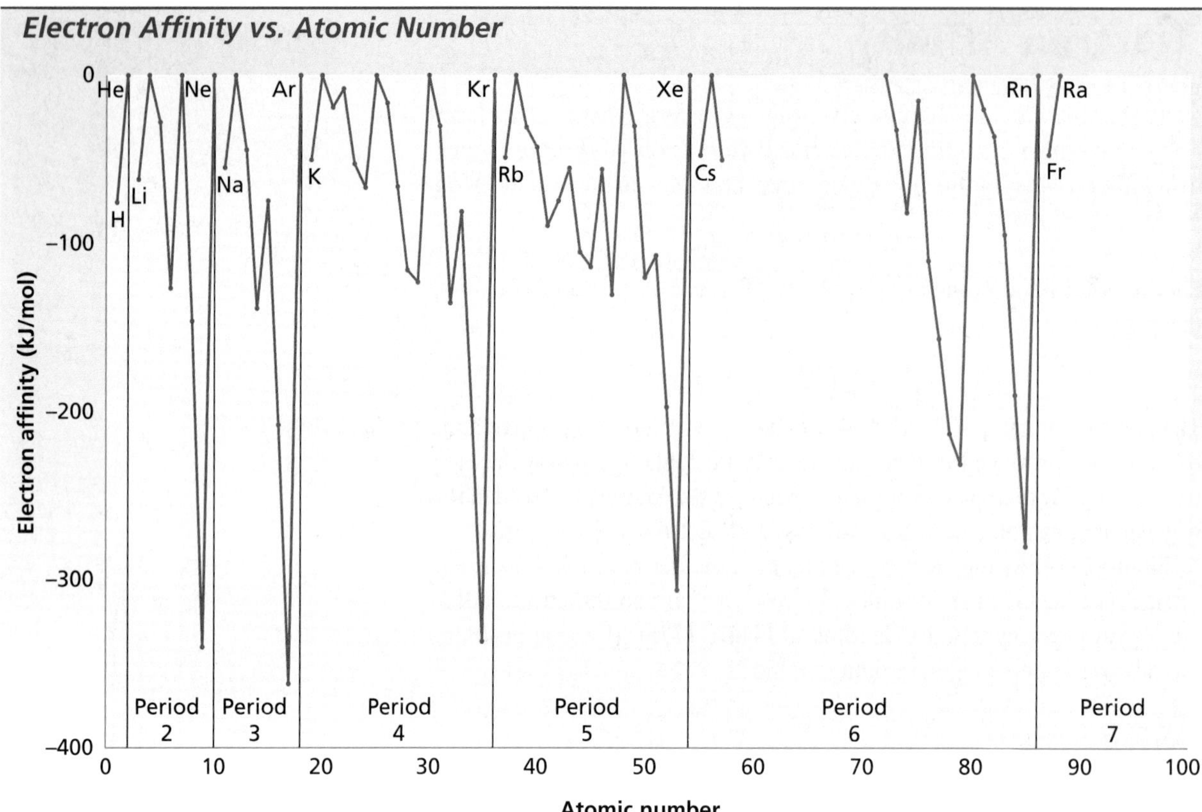


**FIGURE 18** The plot of electron affinity versus atomic number shows that most atoms release energy when they acquire an electron, as indicated by negative values.

than forcing an electron to pair with another electron in an orbital of the already half-filled *p* sublevel of a nitrogen atom.

## Group Trends

Trends for electron affinities within groups are not as regular as trends for ionization energies. As a general rule, electrons add with greater difficulty down a group. This pattern is a result of two competing factors. The first is a slight increase in effective nuclear charge down a group, which increases electron affinities. The second is an increase in atomic radius down a group, which decreases electron affinities. In general, the size effect predominates. But there are exceptions, especially among the heavy transition metals, which tend to be the same size or even decrease in radius down a group.

## Adding Electrons to Negative Ions

For an isolated ion in the gas phase, it is always more difficult to add a second electron to an already negatively charged ion. Therefore, second electron affinities are all positive. Certain *p*-block nonmetals tend to form negative ions that have noble gas configurations. The halogens do so by adding one electron. For example, chlorine has the configuration $[Ne]3s^23p^5$. An atom of chlorine achieves the configuration of the noble gas argon by adding an electron to form the ion $Cl^-$ ($[Ne]3s^23p^6$). Adding another electron is so difficult that $Cl^{2-}$ never occurs. Atoms of

Group 16 elements are present in many compounds as 2– ions. For example, oxygen ([He]$2s^22p^4$) achieves the configuration of the noble gas neon by adding two electrons to form the ion $O^{2-}$([He]$2s^22p^6$).

## Ionic Radii

**Figure 19** shows the radii of some of the most common ions of the elements. Positive and negative ions have specific names.

*A positive ion is known as a* **cation.** The formation of a cation by the loss of one or more electrons always leads to a decrease in atomic radius because the removal of the highest-energy-level electrons results in a smaller electron cloud. Also, the remaining electrons are drawn closer to the nucleus by its unbalanced positive charge.

*A negative ion is known as an* **anion.** The formation of an anion by the addition of one or more electrons always leads to an increase in atomic radius. This is because the total positive charge of the nucleus remains unchanged when an electron is added to an atom or an ion. So the electrons are not drawn to the nucleus as strongly as they were before the addition of the extra electron. The electron cloud also spreads out because of greater repulsion between the increased number of electrons.

### Period Trends

Within each period of the periodic table, the metals at the left tend to form cations and the nonmetals at the upper right tend to form anions. Cationic radii decrease across a period because the electron cloud shrinks due to the increasing nuclear charge acting on the electrons in the same main energy level. Starting with Group 15, in which atoms assume stable noble-gas configurations by gaining three electrons,

**FIGURE 19** The ionic radii of the ions most common in chemical compounds are shown. Cations are smaller and anions are larger than the atoms from which they are formed.

*Periodic Table of Ionic Radii (pm)*

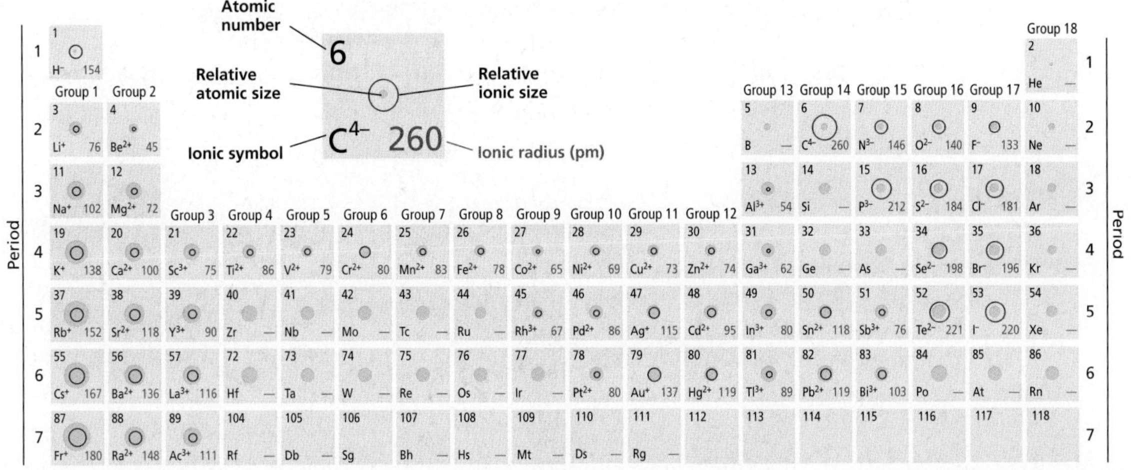

anions are more common than cations. Anionic radii decrease across each period for the elements in Groups 15–18. The reasons for this trend are the same as the reasons that cationic radii decrease from left to right across a period.

### Group Trends

As they are in atoms, the outer electrons in both cations and anions are in higher energy levels as one reads down a group. Therefore, just as there is a gradual increase of atomic radii down a group, there is also a gradual increase of ionic radii.

## Valence Electrons

Chemical compounds form because electrons are lost, gained, or shared between atoms. The electrons that interact in this manner are those in the highest energy levels. These are the electrons most subject to the influence of nearby atoms or ions. *The electrons available to be lost, gained, or shared in the formation of chemical compounds are referred to as* **valence electrons.** Valence electrons are often located in incompletely filled main-energy levels. For example, the electron lost from the 3*s* sublevel of Na to form $Na^+$ is a valence electron.

For main-group elements, the valence electrons are the electrons in the outermost *s* and *p* sublevels. The inner electrons are in filled energy levels and are held too tightly by the nucleus to be involved in compound formation. The Group 1 and Group 2 elements have one and two valence electrons, respectively, as shown in **Table 4.** The elements of Groups 13–18 have a number of valence electrons equal to the group number minus 10. In some cases, both the *s* and *p* sublevel valence electrons of the *p*-block elements are involved in compound formation. In other cases, only the electrons from the *p* sublevel are involved.

**TABLE 4** ***Valence Electrons in Main-Group Elements***

| Group number | Group configuration | Number of valence electrons |
|---|---|---|
| 1 | $ns^1$ | 1 |
| 2 | $ns^2$ | 2 |
| 13 | $ns^2p^1$ | 3 |
| 14 | $ns^2p^2$ | 4 |
| 15 | $ns^2p^3$ | 5 |
| 16 | $ns^2p^4$ | 6 |
| 17 | $ns^2p^5$ | 7 |
| 18 | $ns^2p^6$ | 8 |

# Electronegativity

Valence electrons hold atoms together in chemical compounds. In many compounds, the negative charge of the valence electrons is concentrated closer to one atom than to another. This uneven concentration of charge has a significant effect on the chemical properties of a compound. It is therefore useful to have a measure of how strongly one atom attracts the electrons of another atom within a compound.

Linus Pauling, one of America's most famous chemists, devised a scale of numerical values reflecting the tendency of an atom to attract electrons. **Electronegativity** *is a measure of the ability of an atom in a chemical compound to attract electrons from another atom in the compound.* The most electronegative element, fluorine, is arbitrarily assigned an electronegativity value of four. Values for the other elements are then calculated in relation to this value.

## Period Trends

*As shown in **Figure 20,** electronegativities tend to increase across each period, although there are exceptions.* The alkali and alkaline-earth metals are the least electronegative elements. In compounds, their atoms have a low attraction for electrons. Nitrogen, oxygen, and the halogens are the most electronegative elements. Their atoms attract electrons strongly in compounds. *Electronegativities tend to either decrease down a group or remain about the same.* The noble gases are unusual in that some of them

**FIGURE 20** Shown are the electronegativities of the elements according to the Pauling scale. The most-electronegative elements are located in the upper right of the *p* block. The least-electronegative elements are located in the lower left of the *s* block.

### *Periodic Table of Electronegativities*

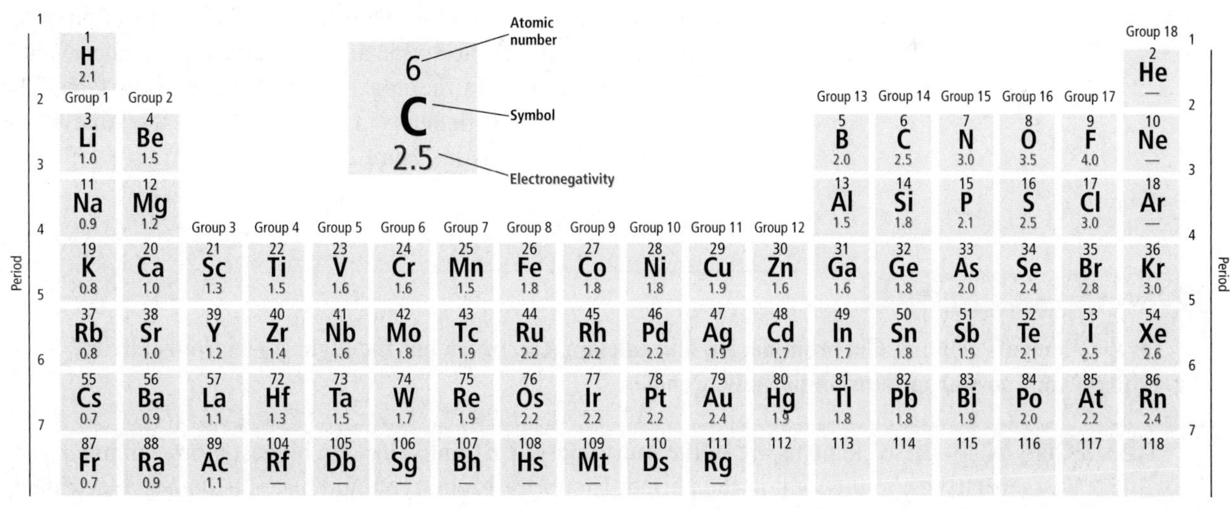


Lanthanide series

| 58 Ce 1.1 | 59 Pr 1.1 | 60 Nd 1.1 | 61 Pm 1.1 | 62 Sm 1.2 | 63 Eu 1.1 | 64 Gd 1.2 | 65 Tb 1.1 | 66 Dy 1.2 | 67 Ho 1.2 | 68 Er 1.2 | 69 Tm 1.3 | 70 Yb 1.1 | 71 Lu 1.3 |
|---|---|---|---|---|---|---|---|---|---|---|---|---|---|
| 90 Th 1.3 | 91 Pa 1.5 | 92 U 1.4 | 93 Np 1.4 | 94 Pu 1.3 | 95 Am 1.3 | 96 Cm 1.3 | 97 Bk 1.3 | 98 Cf 1.3 | 99 Es 1.3 | 100 Fm 1.3 | 101 Md 1.3 | 102 No 1.3 | 103 Lr — |

Actinide series

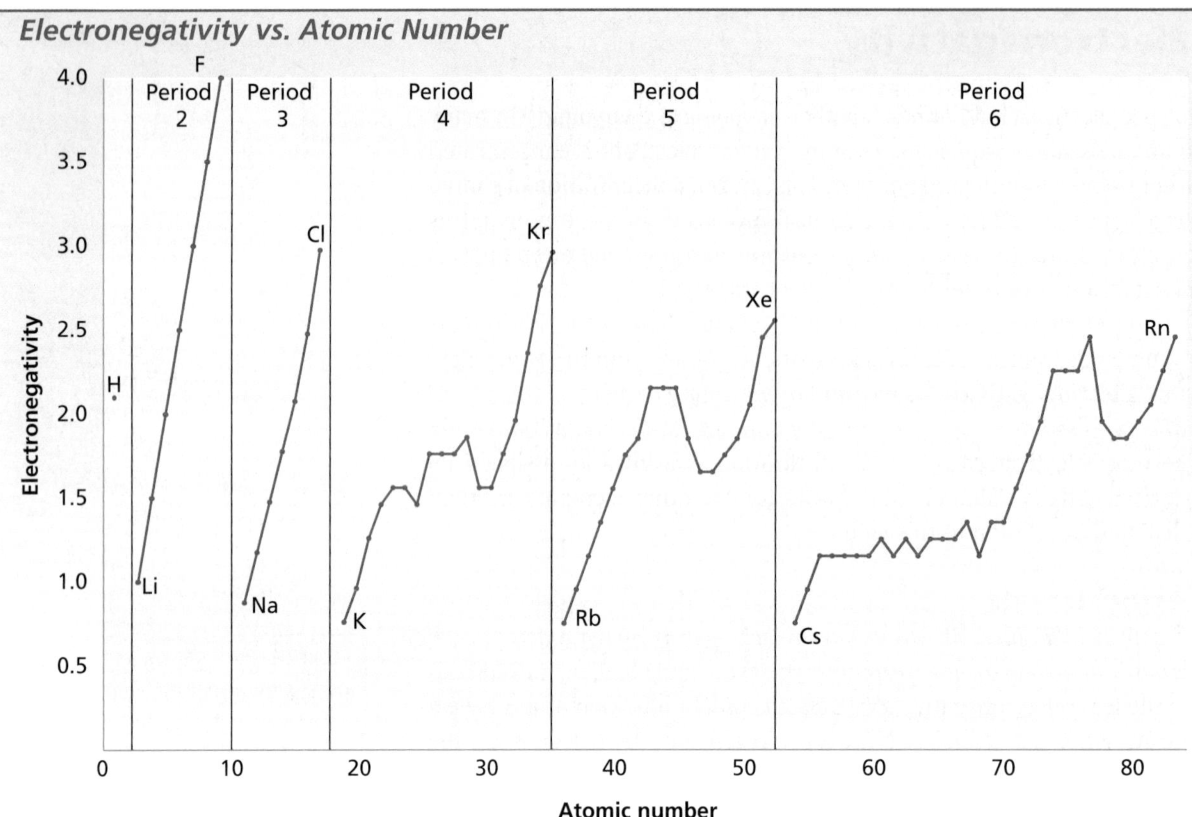


**FIGURE 21** The plot shows electronegativity versus atomic number for Periods 1–6.

do not form compounds and therefore cannot be assigned electronegativities. When a noble gas does form a compound, its electronegativity is rather high, similar to the values for the halogens. The combination of the period and group trends in electronegativity results in the highest values belonging to the elements in the upper right of the periodic table. The lowest values belong to the elements in the lower left of the table. These trends are shown graphically in **Figure 21.**

## SAMPLE PROBLEM G

**Of the elements gallium, Ga, bromine, Br, and calcium, Ca, which has the highest electronegativity? Explain your answer in terms of periodic trends.**

**SOLUTION** All of these elements are in the fourth period. Bromine has the highest atomic number and is farthest to the right in the period. Therefore, bromine should have the highest electronegativity because electronegativity increases across the periods.

**PRACTICE** *Answers in Appendix E*

1. Consider five hypothetical main-group elements, E, G, J, L, and M, that have the outer electron configurations shown at the top of the next page.

$$E = 2s^22p^5 \quad G = 4d^{10}5s^25p^5 \quad J = 2s^22p^2$$

$$L = 5d^{10}6s^26p^5 \quad M = 2s^22p^4$$

**a.** Identify the block location for each element. Then, determine which elements are in the same period and which are in the same group.

**b.** Which element would you expect to have the highest electron affinity? Which would you expect to form a 1– ion? Which should have the highest electronegativity?

**c.** Compare the ionic radius of the typical ion formed by the element G with the radius of the atom from which the ion was formed.

**d.** Which element(s) contain seven valence electrons?

Go to **go.hrw.com** for more practice problems that ask you to predict periodic properties.

**Keyword: HC6PERX**

## Periodic Properties of the *d*- and *f*-Block Elements

The properties of the *d*-block elements (which are all metals) vary less and with less regularity than those of the main-group elements. This trend is indicated by the curves in **Figures 14** and **16,** which flatten where the *d*-block elements fall in the middle of Periods 4–6.

Recall that atoms of the *d*-block elements contain from zero to two electrons in the *s* orbital of their highest occupied energy level and one to ten electrons in the *d* sublevel of the next-lower energy level. Therefore, electrons in both the *ns* sublevel and the $(n-1)d$ sublevel are available to interact with their surroundings. As a result, electrons in the incompletely filled *d* sublevels are responsible for many characteristic properties of the *d*-block elements.

### Atomic Radii

The atomic radii of the *d*-block elements generally decrease across the periods. However, this decrease is less than that for the main-group elements because the electrons added to the $(n-1)d$ sublevel shield the outer electrons from the nucleus. Also, note in **Figure 14** that the radii dip to a low and then increase slightly across each of the four periods that contain *d*-block elements. As the number of electrons in the *d* sublevel increases, the radii increase because of repulsion among the electrons.

In the sixth period, the *f*-block elements fall between lanthanum (Group 3) and hafnium (Group 4). Because of the increase in atomic number that occurs from lanthanum to hafnium, the atomic radius of hafnium is actually slightly less than that of zirconium, Zr, the element immediately above it. The radii of elements following hafnium in the sixth period vary with increasing atomic number in the usual manner.

## Ionization Energy

As they do for the main-group elements, ionization energies of the *d*-block and *f*-block elements generally increase across the periods. In contrast to the decrease down the main groups, however, the first ionization energies of the *d*-block elements generally increase down each group. This is because the electrons available for ionization in the outer *s* sublevels are less shielded from the increasing nuclear charge by electrons in the incomplete $(n - 1)d$ sublevels.

## Ion Formation and Ionic Radii

Among all atoms of the *d*-block and *f*-block elements, electrons in the highest occupied sublevel are always removed first. For the *d*-block elements, this means that although newly added electrons occupy the *d* sublevels, the first electrons to be removed are those in the outermost *s* sublevels. For example, iron, Fe, has the electron configuration $[Ar]3d^64s^2$. First, it loses two 4*s* electrons to form $Fe^{2+}$ ($[Ar]3d^6$). $Fe^{2+}$ can then lose a 3*d* electron to form $Fe^{3+}$ ($[Ar]3d^5$).

Most *d*-block elements commonly form 2+ ions in compounds. Some, such as iron and chromium, also commonly form 3+ ions. The Group 3 elements form only ions with a 3+ charge. Copper forms 1+ and 2+ ions, and silver usually forms only 1+ ions. As expected, the cations have smaller radii than the atoms do. Comparing 2+ ions across the periods shows a decrease in size that parallels the decrease in atomic radii.

## Electronegativity

The *d*-block elements all have electronegativities between 1.1 and 2.54. Only the active metals of Groups 1 and 2 have lower electronegativities. The *d*-block elements also follow the general trend for electronegativity values to increase as radii decrease, and vice versa. The *f*-block elements all have similar electronegativities, which range from 1.1 to 1.5.

## SECTION REVIEW

1. State the general period and group trends among main-group elements with respect to each of the following properties:
   - **a.** atomic radii
   - **b.** first ionization energy
   - **c.** electron affinity
   - **d.** ionic radii
   - **e.** electronegativity
2. **a.** In general, how do the periodic properties of the *d*-block elements compare with those of the main-group elements?
   **b.** Explain the comparisons made in (a).
3. For each main-group element, what is the relationship between its group number and the number of valence electrons that the group members have?

**Critical Thinking**

4. **RELATING IDEAS** Graph the general trends (left to right and top to bottom) in the second ionization energy ($IE_2$) of an element as a function of its atomic number, over the range Z = 1–20. Label the minima and maxima on the graph with the appropriate element symbol.

# CHAPTER HIGHLIGHTS

## History of the Periodic Table

**Vocabulary**
periodic law
periodic table
lanthanide
actinide

- The periodic law states that the physical and chemical properties of the elements are periodic functions of their atomic numbers.
- The periodic table is an arrangement of the elements in order of their atomic numbers so that elements with similar properties fall in the same column.
- The columns in the periodic table are referred to as groups.

## Electron Configuration and the Periodic Table

**Vocabulary**
alkali metals
alkaline-earth metals
transition elements
main-group elements
halogens

- The rows in the periodic table are called periods.
- Many chemical properties of the elements can be explained by the configurations of the elements' outermost electrons.
- The noble gases exhibit unique chemical stability because their highest occupied levels have an octet of electrons, $ns^2np^6$ (with the exception of helium, whose stability arises from its highest occupied level being completely filled with two electrons, $1s^2$).
- Based on the electron configurations of the elements, the periodic table can be divided into four blocks: the *s* block, the *p* block, the *d* block, and the *f* block.

## Electron Configuration and Periodic Properties

**Vocabulary**
atomic radius
ion
ionization
ionization energy
electron affinity
cation
anion
valence electrons
electronegativity

- The groups and periods of the periodic table display general trends in the following properties of the elements: electron affinity, electronegativity, ionization energy, atomic radius, and ionic radius.
- The electrons in an atom that are available to be lost, gained, or shared in the formation of chemical compounds are referred to as valence electrons.
- In determining the electron configuration of an ion, the order in which electrons are removed from the atom is the reverse of the order given by the atom's electron-configuration notation.

# CHAPTER REVIEW

## History of the Periodic Table

### SECTION 1 REVIEW

1. Describe the contributions made by the following scientists to the development of the periodic table:
   a. Stanislao Cannizzaro
   b. Dmitri Mendeleev
   c. Henry Moseley
2. State the periodic law.
3. How is the periodic law demonstrated within the groups of the periodic table?

## Electron Configuration and the Periodic Table

### SECTION 2 REVIEW

4. a. How do the electron configurations within the same group of elements compare?
   b. Why are the noble gases relatively unreactive?
5. What determines the length of each period in the periodic table?
6. What is the relationship between the electron configuration of an element and the period in which that element appears in the periodic table?
7. a. What information is provided by the specific block location of an element?
   b. Identify, by number, the groups located within each of the four block areas.
8. a. Which elements are designated as the alkali metals?
   b. List four of their characteristic properties.
9. a. Which elements are designated as the alkaline-earth metals?
   b. How do their characteristic properties compare with those of the alkali metals?
10. a. Write the group configuration notation for each *d*-block group.
    b. How do the group numbers of those groups relate to the number of outer *s* and *d* electrons?
11. What name is sometimes used to refer to the entire set of *d*-block elements?
12. a. What types of elements make up the *p* block?
    b. How do the properties of the *p*-block metals compare with those of the metals in the *s* and *d* blocks?
13. a. Which elements are designated as the halogens?
    b. List three of their characteristic properties.
14. a. Which elements are metalloids?
    b. Describe their characteristic properties.
15. Which elements make up the *f* block in the periodic table?
16. a. What are the main-group elements?
    b. What trends can be observed across the various periods within the main-group elements?

### PRACTICE PROBLEMS

17. Write the noble-gas notation for the electron configuration of each of the following elements, and indicate the period in which each belongs.
    a. Li  c. Cu  e. Sn
    b. O  d. Br
18. Without looking at the periodic table, identify the period, block, and group in which the elements with the following electron configurations are located. (Hint: See Sample Problem A.)
    a. $[Ne]3s^2 3p^4$
    b. $[Kr]4d^{10} 5s^2 5p^2$
    c. $[Xe]4f^{14} 5d^{10} 6s^2 6p^5$
19. Based on the information given below, give the group, period, block, and identity of each element described. (Hint: See Sample Problem B.)
    a. $[He]2s^2$
    b. $[Ne]3s^1$
    c. $[Kr]5s^2$
    d. $[Ar]4s^2$
    e. $[Ar]3d^5 4s^1$
20. Without looking at the periodic table, write the expected outer electron configuration for each of the following elements. (Hint: See Sample Problem C.)
    a. Group 7, fourth period
    b. Group 3, fifth period
    c. Group 12, sixth period

**21.** Identify the block, period, group, group name (where appropriate), element name, element type, and relative reactivity for the elements with the following electron configurations. (Hint: See Sample Problem D.)
a. $[Ne]3s^23p^1$
b. $[Ar]3d^{10}4s^24p^6$
c. $[Kr]4d^{10}5s^1$
d. $[Xe]4f^15d^16s^2$

## *Electron Configuration and Periodic Properties*

### SECTION 3 REVIEW

**22.** a. What is meant by atomic radius?
b. What trend is observed among the atomic radii of main-group elements across a period?
c. Explain this trend.

**23.** a. What trend is observed among the atomic radii of main-group elements down a group?
b. Explain this trend.

**24.** Define each of the following terms:
a. ion
b. ionization
c. first ionization energy
d. second ionization energy

**25.** a. How do the first ionization energies of main-group elements vary across a period and down a group?
b. Explain the basis for each trend.

**26.** a. What is electron affinity?
b. What signs are associated with electron affinity values, and what is the significance of each sign?

**27.** a. Distinguish between a cation and an anion.
b. How does the size of each compare with the size of the neutral atom from which it is formed?

**28.** a. What are valence electrons?
b. Where are such electrons located?

**29.** For each of the following groups, indicate whether electrons are more likely to be lost or gained in compound formation and give the number of such electrons typically involved.
a. Group 1
b. Group 2
c. Group 13
d. Group 16
e. Group 17
f. Group 18

**30.** a. What is electronegativity?
b. Why is fluorine special in terms of electronegativity?

**31.** Identify the most- and least-electronegative groups of elements in the periodic table.

### PRACTICE PROBLEMS

**32.** Of cesium, Cs, hafnium, Hf, and gold, Au, which element has the smallest atomic radius? Explain your answer in terms of trends in the periodic table. (Hint: see Sample Problem E.)

**33.** a. Distinguish between the first, second, and third ionization energies of an atom.
b. How do the values of successive ionization energies compare?
c. Why does this occur?

**34.** Without looking at the electron affinity table, arrange the following elements in order of *decreasing* electron affinities: C, O, Li, Na, Rb, and F.

**35.** a. Without looking at the ionization energy table, arrange the following elements in order of decreasing first ionization energies: Li, O, C, K, Ne, and F.
b. Which of the elements listed in (a) would you expect to have the highest second ionization energy? Why?

**36.** a. Which of the following cations is least likely to form: $Sr^{2+}$, $Al^{3+}$, $K^{2+}$?
b. Which of the following anions is least likely to form: $I^-$, $Cl^-$, $O^{2-}$?

**37.** Which element is the most electronegative among C, N, O, Br, and S? Which group does it belong to? (Hint: See Sample Problem G.)

**38.** The two ions $K^+$ and $Ca^{2+}$ each have 18 electrons surrounding the nucleus. Which would you expect to have the smaller radius? Why?

## MIXED REVIEW

**39.** Without looking at the periodic table, identify the period, block, and group in which each of the following elements is located.
a. $[Rn]7s^1$
b. $[Ar]3d^24s^2$
c. $[Kr]4d^{10}5s^1$
d. $[Xe]4f^{14}5d^96s^1$

**40.** a. Which elements are designated as the noble gases?
b. What is the most significant property of these elements?

**41.** Which of the following does not have a noble-gas configuration: $Na^+$, $Rb^+$, $O^{2-}$, $Br^-$ $Ca^+$, $Al^{3+}$, $S^{2-}$?

**42.** a. How many groups are in the periodic table?
b. How many periods are in the periodic table?
c. Which two blocks of the periodic table make up the main-group elements?

**43.** Write the noble-gas notation for the electron configuration of each of the following elements, and indicate the period and group in which each belongs.
a. Mg
b. P
c. Sc
d. Y

**44.** Use the periodic table to describe the chemical properties of the following elements:
a. fluorine, F
b. xenon, Xe
c. sodium, Na
d. gold, Au

**45.** For each element listed below, determine the charge of the ion that is most likely to be formed and the identity of the noble gas whose electron configuration is thus achieved.

| | | |
|---|---|---|
| a. Li | e. Mg | i. Br |
| b. Rb | f. Al | j. Ba |
| c. O | g. P | |
| d. F | h. S | |

**46.** Describe some differences between the *s*-block metals and the *d*-block metals.

**47.** Why do the halogens readily form 1– ions?

**48.** Identify which trends in the diagrams below describe atomic radius, ionization energy, electron affinity, and electronegativity.

a.

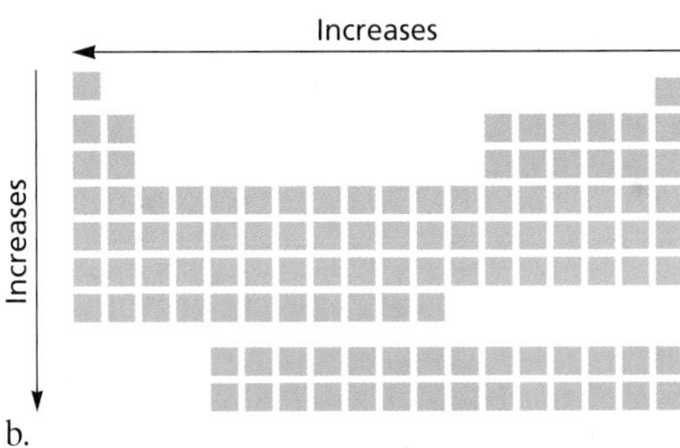

b.

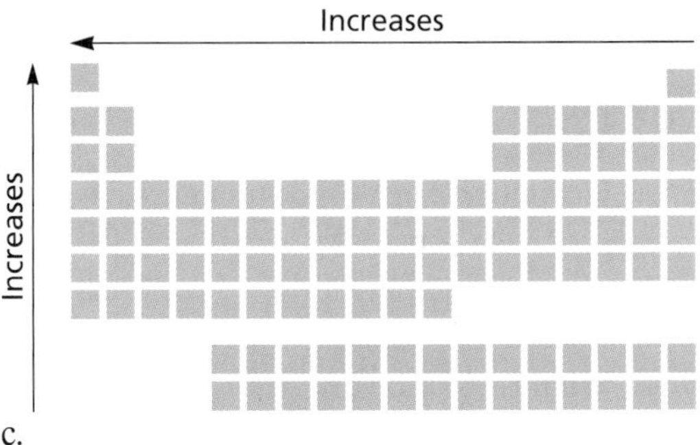

c.

**49.** The electron configuration of argon differs from those of chlorine and potassium by one electron each. Compare the reactivity of these three elements.

## CRITICAL THINKING

As a member on the newly-inhabited space station Alpha, you are given the task of organizing information on newly discovered elements as it comes in from the laboratory. To date, five elements have been discovered and have been assigned names and symbols from the Greek alphabet. An analysis of the new elements has yielded the following data:

| Element name | Atomic no. | Atomic mass | Properties |
|---|---|---|---|
| Epsilon ε | 23 | 47.33 | nonmetal, very reactive, produces a salt when combined with a metal, gaseous state |
| Beta β | 13 | 27.01 | metal, very reactive, soft solid, low melting point |
| Gamma γ | 12 | 25.35 | nonmetal, gaseous element, extremely unreactive |
| Delta Δ | 4 | 7.98 | nonmetal, very abundant, forms compounds with most other elements |
| Lambda Λ | 9 | 16.17 | metal, solid state, good conductor, high luster, hard and dense |

50. **Applying Models** Create a periodic table based on the properties of the five new elements.

51. **Predicting Outcomes** Using your newly created periodic table, predict the atomic number of an element with an atomic mass of 11.29 that has nonmetallic properties and is very reactive.

52. **Predicting Outcomes** Predict the atomic number of an element having an atomic mass of 15.02 that exhibits metallic properties but is softer than lambda and harder than beta.

53. **Analyzing Information** Analyze your periodic table for trends, and describe those trends.

## USING THE HANDBOOK

54. Review the boiling point and melting point data in the tables of the *Elements Handbook.* Make a list of the elements that exist as liquids or gases at the boiling point of water, 100°C.

55. Because transition metals have vacant *d* orbitals, they form a greater variety of colored compounds than do the metals of Groups 1 and 2. Review the section of the *Elements Handbook* on transition metals (pages 798–807) and answer the following:
    a. What colors are exhibited by chromium in its common oxidation states?
    b. What gems contain chromium impurities?
    c. What colors are often associated with the following metal ions: copper, cadmium, cobalt, zinc, and nickel?
    d. What transition elements are considered noble metals? What are the characteristics of a noble metal?

## RESEARCH & WRITING

56. Prepare a report tracing the evolution of the current periodic table since 1900. Cite the chemists involved and their major contributions.

57. Write a report describing the contributions of Glenn Seaborg toward the discovery of many of the actinide elements.

## ALTERNATIVE ASSESSMENT

58. Construct your own periodic table or obtain a poster that shows related objects, such as fruits or vegetables, in periodic arrangement. Describe the organization of the table and the trends it illustrates. Use this table to make predictions about your subject matter.

extension

**Graphing Calculator**
**Graphing Atomic Radii**

Go to **go.hrw.com** for a graphing calculator exercise that asks you to graph atomic radii versus atomic number for the Period 2 elements.

**Keyword:** HC6PERX

# Math Tutor WRITING ELECTRON CONFIGURATIONS

The arrangement of elements in the periodic table reflects the arrangement of electrons in an atom. Each period begins with an atom that has an electron in a new energy level and, with the exception of the first period, ends with an atom that has a filled set of *p* orbitals. To write the electron configuration of an element, you must fill the sublevels in order of increasing energy. If you follow the arrows in either of the two types of mnemonics shown below, you will get correct configurations for most elements.

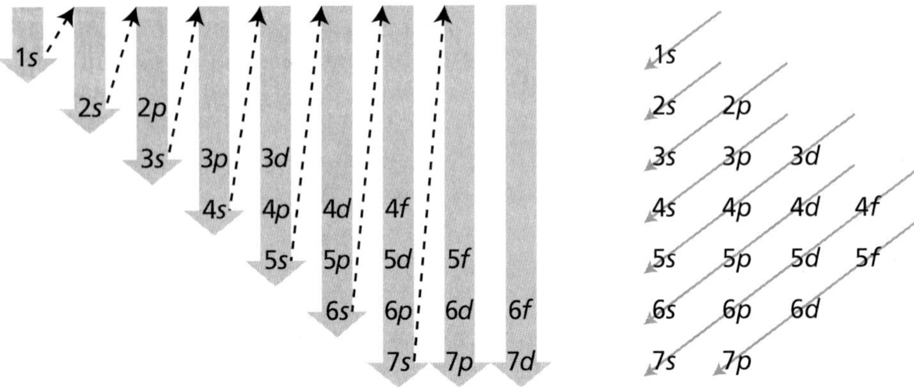


You also need to know how many orbitals are in each sublevel and that each orbital can contain two electrons of opposite spins. As shown in the following table, the sublevels *s, p, d,* and *f* have 1, 3, 5, and 7 available orbitals, respectively.

| Sublevel | *s* | *p* | *d* | *f* |
|---|---|---|---|---|
| No. of orbitals | 1 | 3 | 5 | 7 |
| No. of electrons | 2 | 6 | 10 | 14 |

## SAMPLE

**Write the full electron configuration for phosphorus.**

The atomic number of phosphorus is 15, so a phosphorus atom has 15 protons and electrons. Assign each of the 15 electrons to the appropriate sublevels. The final sublevel can be unfilled and will contain the number of valence electrons.

$$1s^2 \quad 2s^2 \quad 2p^6 \quad 3s^2 \quad 3p^3$$

$$2e^- + 2e^- + 6e^- + 2e^- + 3e^- = 15e^-$$

So, the full electron configuration of phosphorus is $1s^22s^22p^63s^23p^3$.

## PRACTICE PROBLEMS

1. Write full electron configurations for the following elements.

   a. aluminum
   b. neon
   c. tin
   d. potassium

2. Use noble gas symbols to write shorthand electron configurations for the following elements.

   a. silicon
   b. rubidium
   c. antimony
   d. arsenic

# Standardized Test Prep

**Answer the following items on a separate piece of paper.**

**MULTIPLE CHOICE**

**1.** In the modern periodic table, elements are arranged according to
**A.** decreasing atomic mass.
**B.** Mendeleev's original model.
**C.** increasing atomic number.
**D.** when they were discovered.

**2.** Group 17 elements, the halogens, are the most reactive of the nonmetal elements because they
**A.** require only one electron to fill their outer energy level.
**B.** have the highest ionization energies.
**C.** have the largest atomic radii.
**D.** are the farthest to the right in the periodic table.

**3.** The periodic law states that
**A.** the chemical properties of elements can be grouped according to periodicity.
**B.** the properties of the elements are functions of atomic mass.
**C.** all elements in the same group have the same number of valence electrons.
**D.** all elements with the same number of occupied energy levels must be in the same group.

**4.** As you move left to right across Period 3 from Mg to Cl, the energy needed to remove an electron from an atom
**A.** generally increases.
**B.** generally decreases.
**C.** does not change.
**D.** varies unpredictably.

**5.** Which of the following elements has the highest electronegativity?
**A.** oxygen
**B.** hydrogen
**C.** fluorine
**D.** carbon

**6.** The noble gases have
**A.** high ionization energies.
**B.** high electron affinities.
**C.** large atomic radii.
**D.** a tendency to form both cations and anions.

**7.** Which electron configuration is *not* correct?
**A.** $O^{2-}$ [He]$2s^22p^6$
**B.** $Mg^{2+}$ [He]$2s^22p^6$
**C.** $V^{3+}$ [Ar]$3d^2$
**D.** $Al^{3+}$ [Ar]$2s^22p^6$

**8.** Which two elements are more likely to have the same charge on their ions?
**A.** Se and As
**B.** Sn and Si
**C.** Ca and Rb
**D.** I and Xe

**9.** Using only the periodic table, choose the list that ranks the elements Sr, Te, Kr, Ru, and Cs in order of increasing ionization energy.
**A.** $Sr < Te < Ru < Cs < Kr$
**B.** $Te < Ru < Sr < Cs < Kr$
**C.** $Cs < Sr < Ru < Te < Kr$
**D.** $Kr < Cs < Sr < Ru < Te$

**SHORT ANSWER**

**10.** The second ionization energies for the elements S–Ti are listed in a scrambled order below. Assign the correct $IE_2$ value to each element. (Hint: S has $IE_2 = 2251$ kJ/mol, and Ti has $IE_2 = 1310$ kJ/mol.) Explain your reasoning.

$IE_2$ values (kJ/mol): 2666, 2297, 3051, 1235, 2251, 1310, and 1145

**11.** What group most commonly forms 2– ions? Explain your reasoning.

**EXTENDED RESPONSE**

**12.** An ordered list of atomic radii for 14 consecutive elements is shown below. Without using **Figure 13** on page 151, make a graph of these atomic radii versus the element's atomic number. Explain your reasoning.

Atomic radii (pm): 75, 73, 72, 71, 186, 160, 143, 118, 110, 103, 100, 98, 227, and 197

**Test TIP** If you are short on time, quickly scan the unanswered questions to see which might be easiest to answer.

# The Mendeleev Lab of 1869

## OBJECTIVES

- ***Observe*** **the physical properties of common elements.**
- ***Observe*** **the properties and trends in the elements on the periodic table.**
- ***Draw conclusions*** **and** ***identify*** **unknown elements based on observed trends in properties.**

## MATERIALS

- **blank periodic table**
- **elemental samples: Ar, C, Sn, and Pb**
- **note cards, 3 in. × 5 in.**
- **periodic table**

## BACKGROUND

Russian chemist Dmitri Mendeleev is generally credited with being the first chemist to observe that patterns emerge when the elements are arranged according to their properties. Mendeleev's arrangement of the elements was unique because he left blank spaces for elements that he claimed were undiscovered as of 1869. Mendeleev was so confident that he even predicted the properties of these undiscovered elements. His predictions were eventually proven to be quite accurate, and these new elements fill the spaces that originally were blank in his table. Use your knowledge of the periodic table to determine the identity of each of the nine unknown elements in this activity. These unknown elements are from the periodic table's groups that are listed below. Each of these groups contains at least one unknown element.

1 2 11 13 14 17 18

None of the known elements serves as one of the nine unknown elements. No radioactive elements are used during this experiment. The relevant radioactive elements include Fr, Ra, At, and Rn. You may not use your textbook or other reference materials. You have been provided with enough information to determine each of the unknown elements.

## SAFETY

For review of safety, please see **Safety in the Chemistry Laboratory** in the front of your book.

## PREPARATION

1. Make a data table to record the properties of each unknown that you test.
2. Use the note cards to copy the information listed on each of the sample cards. If the word *observe* is listed, you will need to visually inspect the sample and then write the observation in the appropriate space.

## PROCEDURE

1. Arrange the note cards of the known elements in a rough representation of the periodic table. In other words, all of the known elements from Group 1 should be arranged in the appropriate order. Arrange all of the other cards accordingly.
2. Inspect the properties of the unknowns to see where properties would best "fit" the trends of the elements of each group.
3. Assign the proper element name to each of the unknowns. Add the symbol for each one of the unknown elements to your data table.

## CLEANUP AND DISPOSAL

4. Clean up your lab station, and return the leftover note cards and samples of the elements to your teacher. Do not pour any of the samples down the drain or place them in the trash unless your teacher directs you to do so. Wash your hands thoroughly before you leave the lab and after all your work is finished.

## ANALYSIS AND INTERPRETATION

1. **Organizing Ideas:** In what order did your group arrange the properties to determine the unknowns? Explain your reasoning. Would a different order have been better? If so, what is the better order and why?
2. **Evaluating Methods:** What properties were the most useful in sorting the unknowns? What properties were the least useful? Explain your answer.

## CONCLUSIONS

1. **Interpreting Information:** Summarize your group's reasoning for the assignment of each unknown. Explain in a few sentences exactly how you predicted the identity of the nine unknown elements.

## EXTENSIONS

1. **Predicting Outcomes:** Use only the data from your group's experiment to predict the properties of the not yet discovered element, which has an atomic number of 120 (assuming it does not radioactively decay).

CHAPTER 6

# Chemical Bonding

*In nature, most atoms are joined to other atoms by chemical bonds.*

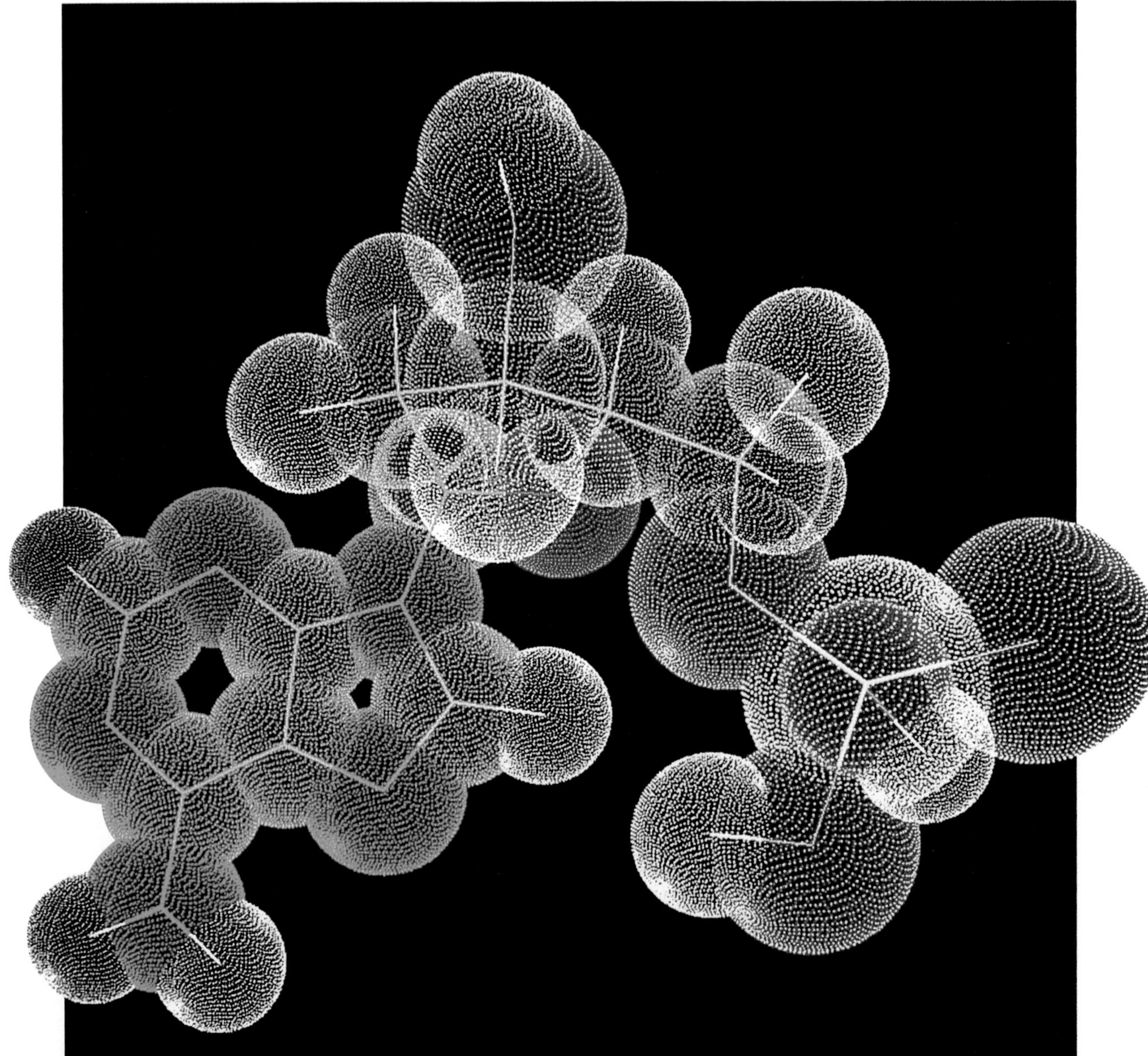

Computer Graphic Representation of a Molecule of Adenosine Monophosphate

# Introduction to Chemical Bonding

 **C.3.1** Predict the type of bonding (ionic or covalent) and the shape of simple compounds by using Lewis dot structures and oxidation numbers

SECTION 1

## OBJECTIVES

- Define *chemical bond.*
- Explain why most atoms form chemical bonds.
- Describe ionic and covalent bonding.
- Explain why most chemical bonding is neither purely ionic nor purely covalent.
- Classify bonding type according to electronegativity differences.

Atoms seldom exist as independent particles in nature. The oxygen you breathe, the water you drink, and nearly all other substances consists of combinations of atoms that are held together by chemical bonds. *A* **chemical bond** *is a mutual electrical attraction between the nuclei and valence electrons of different atoms that binds the atoms together.*

Why are most atoms chemically bonded to each other? As independent particles, most atoms are at relatively high potential energy. Nature, however, favors arrangements in which potential energy is minimized. This means that most atoms are less stable existing by themselves than when they are combined. By bonding with each other, atoms decrease in potential energy, thereby creating more stable arrangements of matter.

## Types of Chemical Bonding

When atoms bond, their valence electrons are redistributed in ways that make the atoms more stable. The way in which the electrons are redistributed determines the type of bonding. In Chapter 5, you read that main-group metals tend to lose electrons to form positive ions, or cations, and nonmetals tend to gain electrons to form negative ions, or anions. *Chemical bonding that results from the electrical attraction between cations and anions is called* **ionic bonding.** In purely ionic bonding, atoms completely give up electrons to other atoms, as illustrated in **Figure 1** on the next page. In contrast to atoms joined by ionic bonding, atoms joined by covalent bonding share electrons. **Covalent bonding** *results from the sharing of electron pairs between two atoms* (see **Figure 1**). In a purely covalent bond, the shared electrons are "owned" equally by the two bonded atoms.

### Ionic or Covalent?

Bonding between atoms of different elements is rarely purely ionic or purely covalent. It usually falls somewhere between these two extremes, depending on how strongly the atoms of each element attract electrons. Recall that electronegativity is a measure of an atom's ability to attract electrons. The degree to which bonding between atoms of two elements is ionic or covalent can be estimated by calculating the difference in

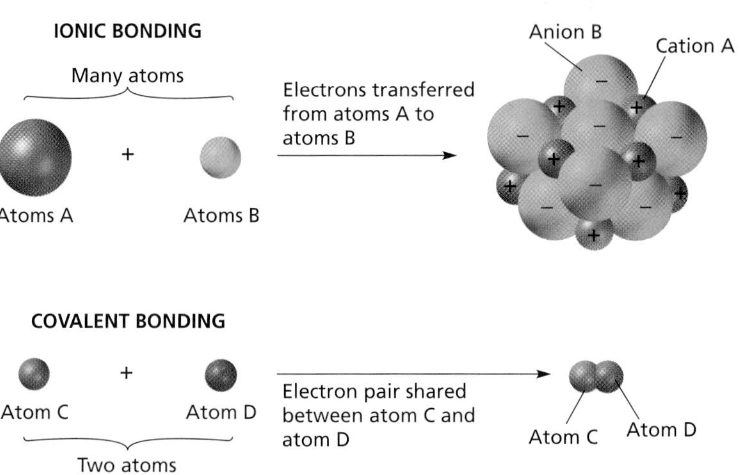


**FIGURE 1** In ionic bonding, many atoms transfer electrons. The resulting positive and negative ions combine due to mutual electrical attraction. In covalent bonding, atoms share electron pairs to form independent molecules.

the elements' electronegativities (see **Figure 2**). For example, the electronegativity difference between fluorine, F, and cesium, Cs, is 4.0 – 0.7 = 3.3. (See **Figure 20** on page 161 for a periodic table of electronegativity values.) So, according to **Figure 2,** cesium-fluorine bonding is ionic. Fluorine atoms, which are highly electronegative, gain valence electrons, causing the atoms to become anions. Cesium atoms, which are less electronegative, lose valence electrons, causing the atoms to become cations.

Bonding between atoms with an electronegativity difference of 1.7 or less has an ionic character of 50% or less. These compounds are typically classified as covalent. Bonding between two atoms of the same element is completely covalent. Hydrogen, for example, exists in nature not as isolated atoms, but as pairs of atoms held together by covalent bonds. The hydrogen-hydrogen bond is a **nonpolar-covalent bond,** *a covalent bond in which the bonding electrons are shared equally by the bonded atoms, resulting in a balanced distribution of electrical charge.* Bonds having 0% to 5% ionic character, corresponding to electronegativity differences of roughly 0 to 0.3, are generally considered nonpolar-covalent bonds. In bonds with significantly different electronegativities, the electrons are more strongly attracted by the more-electronegative atom. *Such bonds are* **polar,** *meaning that they have an uneven distribution of charge.* Covalent bonds having 5% to 50% ionic character, corresponding to electronegativity differences of 0.3 to 1.7, are classified as polar. *A* **polar-covalent bond** *is a covalent bond in which the bonded atoms have an unequal attraction for the shared electrons.*

Nonpolar- and polar-covalent bonds are compared in **Figure 3,** which illustrates the electron density distribution in hydrogen-hydrogen and hydrogen-chlorine bonds. The electronegativity difference between chlorine and hydrogen is 3.0 − 2.1 = 0.9, indicating a polar-covalent bond. The electrons in this bond are closer to the more-electronegative chlorine atom than to the hydrogen atom, as indicated in **Figure 3b.** Consequently, the chlorine end of the bond has a partial negative charge, indicated by the symbol δ–. The hydrogen end of the bond then has an equal partial positive charge, δ+.

Difference in electronegativities | Percentage ionic character
3.3 | 100%
Ionic
1.7 | 50%
Polar-covalent
0.3 | 5%
Nonpolar-covalent
0 | 0%

**FIGURE 2** Differences in electronegativities reflect the character of bonding between elements. The electronegativity of the less-electronegative element is subtracted from that of the more-electronegative element. The greater the electronegativity difference, the more ionic is the bonding.

(a) Nonpolar-covalent bond (b) Polar-covalent bond

**FIGURE 3** Comparison of the electron density in (a) a nonpolar, hydrogen-hydrogen bond and (b) a polar, hydrogen-chlorine bond. Because chlorine is more electronegative than hydrogen, the electron density in the hydrogen-chlorine bond is greater around the chlorine atom.

## SAMPLE PROBLEM A

**Use electronegativity differences and Figure 2 to classify bonding between sulfur, S, and the following elements: hydrogen, H; cesium, Cs; and chlorine, Cl. In each pair, which atom will be more negative?**

**SOLUTION** From **Figure 20** on page 161, we know that the electronegativity of sulfur is 2.5. The electronegativities of hydrogen, cesium, and chlorine are 2.1, 0.7, and 3.0, respectively. In each pair, the atom with the larger electronegativity will be the more-negative atom.

| Bonding between sulfur and | Electronegativity difference | Bond type | More-negative atom |
|---|---|---|---|
| hydrogen | 2.5 − 2.1 = 0.4 | polar-covalent | sulfur |
| cesium | 2.5 − 0.7 = 1.8 | ionic | sulfur |
| chlorine | 3.0 − 2.5 = 0.5 | polar-covalent | chlorine |

**PRACTICE** *Answers in Appendix E*

Use electronegativity differences and **Figure 2** to classify bonding between chlorine, Cl, and the following elements: calcium, Ca; oxygen, O; and bromine, Br. Indicate the more-negative atom in each pair.

Go to **go.hrw.com** for more practice problems that ask you to classify bonds.

**Keyword: HC6BNDX**

## SECTION REVIEW

1. What is the main distinction between ionic and covalent bonding?
2. How is electronegativity used in determining the ionic or covalent character of the bonding between two elements?
3. What type of bonding would be expected between the following atoms?
   **a.** Li and F
   **b.** Cu and S
   **c.** I and Br
4. List the three pairs of atoms referred to in the previous question in order of increasing ionic character of the bonding between them.

**Critical Thinking**

5. **INTERPRETING CONCEPTS** Compare the following two pairs of atoms: Cu and Cl; I and Cl.
   **a.** Which pair would have a bond with a greater percent ionic character?
   **b.** In which pair would Cl have the greater negative charge?
6. **INFERRING RELATIONSHIPS** The isolated K atom is larger than the isolated Br atom.
   **a.** What type of bond is expected between K and Br?
   **b.** Which ion in the compound KBr is larger?

SECTION 2

# Covalent Bonding and Molecular Compounds

## OBJECTIVES

- Define *molecule* and *molecular formula.*
- Explain the relationships among potential energy, distance between approaching atoms, bond length, and bond energy.
- State the octet rule.
- List the six basic steps used in writing Lewis structures.
- Explain how to determine Lewis structures for molecules containing single bonds, multiple bonds, or both.
- Explain why scientists use resonance structures to represent some molecules.

SC **C.3.3** Explain how the types of intermolecular forces present in a compound affect the physical properties of compounds (including polarity and molecular shape)

Many chemical compounds, including most of the chemicals that are in living things and are produced by living things, are composed of molecules. *A* **molecule** *is a neutral group of atoms that are held together by covalent bonds.* A single molecule of a chemical compound is an individual unit capable of existing on its own. It may consist of two or more atoms of the same element, as in oxygen, or of two or more different atoms, as in water or sugar (see **Figure 4** below). *A chemical compound whose simplest units are molecules is called a* **molecular compound.**

The composition of a compound is given by its chemical formula. *A* **chemical formula** *indicates the relative numbers of atoms of each kind in a chemical compound by using atomic symbols and numerical subscripts.* The chemical formula of a molecular compound is referred to as a molecular formula. *A* **molecular formula** *shows the types and numbers of atoms combined in a single molecule of a molecular compound.* The molecular formula for water, for example, is $H_2O$, which reflects the fact that a single water molecule consists of one oxygen atom joined by separate covalent bonds to two hydrogen atoms. A molecule of oxygen, $O_2$, is an example of a diatomic molecule. A *diatomic molecule* is a molecule containing only two atoms.

**(a)** Water molecule, $H_2O$

**(b)** Oxygen molecule, $O_2$

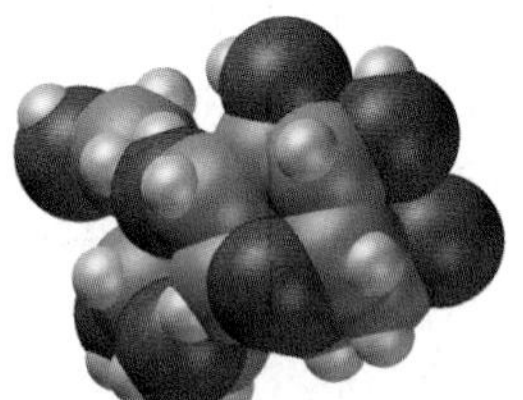

**(c)** Sucrose molecule, $C_{12}H_{22}O_{11}$

**FIGURE 4** The models for (a) water, (b) oxygen, and (c) sucrose, or table sugar, represent a few examples of the many molecular compounds in and around us. Atoms within molecules may form one or more covalent bonds.

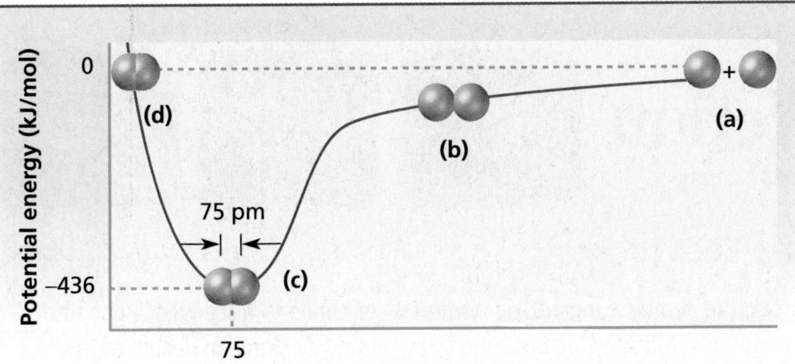


**FIGURE 5** Potential energy changes during the formation of a hydrogen-hydrogen bond. (a) The separated hydrogen atoms do not affect each other. (b) Potential energy decreases as the atoms are drawn together by attractive forces. (c) Potential energy is at a minimum when attractive forces are balanced by repulsive forces. (d) Potential energy increases when repulsion between like charges outweighs attraction between opposite charges.

## Formation of a Covalent Bond

As you read in Section 1, nature favors chemical bonding because most atoms have lower potential energy when they are bonded to other atoms than they have as they are independent particles. In the case of covalent bond formation, this idea is illustrated by a simple example, the formation of a hydrogen-hydrogen bond.

Picture two isolated hydrogen atoms separated by a distance large enough to prevent them from influencing each other. At this distance, the overall potential energy of the atoms is arbitrarily set at zero, as shown in part (a) of **Figure 5.**

Now consider what happens if the hydrogen atoms approach each other. Each atom has a nucleus containing a single positively charged proton. The nucleus of each atom is surrounded by a negatively charged electron in a spherical 1*s* orbital. As the atoms near each other, their charged particles begin to interact. As shown in **Figure 6,** the approaching nuclei and electrons are *attracted* to each other, which corresponds to a *decrease* in the total potential energy of the atoms. At the same time, the two nuclei *repel* each other and the two electrons *repel* each other, which results in an *increase* in potential energy.

The relative strength of attraction and repulsion between the charged particles depends on the distance separating the atoms. When the atoms first "sense" each other, the electron-proton attraction is stronger than the electron-electron and proton-proton repulsions. Thus, the atoms are drawn to each other and their potential energy is lowered, as shown in part (b) of **Figure 5.**

The attractive force continues to dominate and the total potential energy continues to decrease until, eventually, a distance is reached at which the repulsion between the like charges equals the attraction of the opposite charges. This is shown in part (c) of **Figure 5.** At this point, which is represented by the bottom of the valley in the curve, potential energy is at a minimum and a stable hydrogen molecule forms. A closer approach of the atoms, shown in part (d) of **Figure 5,** results in a sharp rise in potential energy as repulsion becomes increasingly greater than attraction.

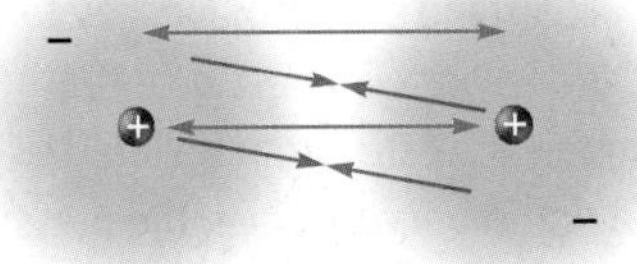


**FIGURE 6** The arrows indicate the attractive and repulsive forces between the electrons (shown as electron clouds) and nuclei of two hydrogen atoms. Attraction between particles corresponds to a decrease in potential energy of the atoms, while repulsion corresponds to an increase.

# Chemistry in Action

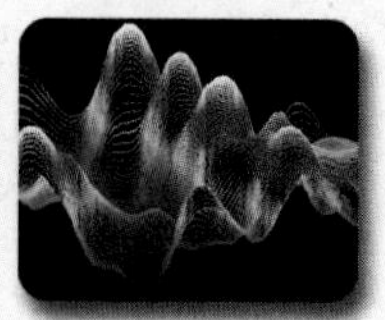
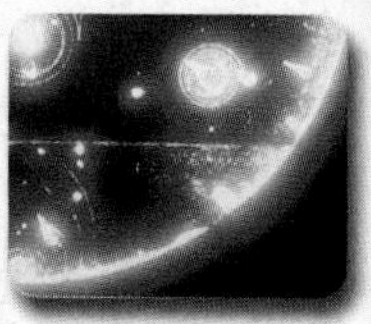

## Ultrasonic Toxic-Waste Destroyer

Paints, pesticides, solvents, and sulfides are just a few components of the 3 million tons of toxic waste that flow out of U.S. factories every year. Some of this waste ends up in groundwater and contaminates our streams and drinking water.

Eliminating hazardous waste is a constant challenge. Unfortunately, today's disposal methods often damage the environment as much as they help it. Incinerators burning certain waste, for example, produce dioxins, one of the most dangerous class of toxins known to man.

Finding new methods to destroy toxic waste is a puzzle. Michael Hoffmann, a professor of environmental chemistry at the California Institute of Technology, thinks that part of the solution lies in sound-wave technology.

According to Hoffmann, cavitation is the key to eliminating certain chemical wastes from polluted water. Cavitation occurs when the pressure in water is made to fluctuate from slightly above to slightly below normal, causing bubbles. The bubbles are unstable and collapse, creating tiny areas of extremely high pressure and heat. The pressure inside a collapsing bubble can be 1000 times greater than normal, and the temperature reaches about 5000°C—just a bit cooler than the surface of the sun. These conditions are harsh enough to combust most toxic-waste compounds in the water, breaking them down into harmless components.

Hoffmann has employed a device that uses ultrasound—sound waves at frequencies just above the range of human hearing—to create cavitation in polluted water. As water flows between two panels that generate ultrasound at different frequencies, the ultrasonic waves generated by one panel form cavitation bubbles. An instant later, the ultrasound produced by the other panel collapses the bubbles. The intense pressure and heat generated break down toxic compounds into innocuous substances, such as carbon dioxide, chloride ions, and hydrogen ions.

"With ultrasound," says Hoffmann, "we can harness frequencies . . . of about 16 kilohertz up to 1 megahertz, and different . . . compounds are destroyed more readily at one frequency versus another . . . applying a particular frequency range, we can destroy a very broad range of chemical compounds."

The device destroys simple toxins in a few minutes and other toxins in several hours. To be destroyed completely, some compounds must form intermediate chemicals first and then be treated again. To be sure the waste is totally removed, scientists use sophisticated tracking methods to trace what happens to every single molecule of the toxin.

The ultrasound toxic-waste destroyer treats about 10% of all types of waste, eliminating both organic and inorganic compounds, such as hydrogen cyanide, TNT, and many pesticides. While the device cannot destroy complex mixtures of compounds, such as those found in raw sewage, it does have many advantages over current technologies. Aside from having no harmful environmental side effects, ultrasonic waste destruction is cheaper and simpler than the process of combustion.

### Questions

1. How does Dr. Hoffmann's ultrasound device benefit society?
2. Briefly explain why the bulk temperature of the water remains low (at room temperature).

## Characteristics of the Covalent Bond

In **Figure 5,** the bottom of the valley in the curve represents the balance between attraction and repulsion in a stable covalent bond. At this point, the electrons of each hydrogen atom of the hydrogen molecule are shared between the nuclei. As shown below in **Figure 7,** the molecule's electrons can be pictured as occupying overlapping orbitals, moving about freely in either orbital.

The bonded atoms vibrate a bit, but as long as their potential energy remains close to the minimum, they are covalently bonded to each other. The distance between two bonded atoms at their minimum potential energy, that is, the average distance between two bonded atoms, is the *bond length.* The bond length of a hydrogen-hydrogen bond is 75 pm.

In forming a covalent bond, the hydrogen atoms release energy as they change from isolated individual atoms to parts of a molecule. The amount of energy released equals the difference between the potential energy at the zero level (separated atoms) and that at the bottom of the valley (bonded atoms) in **Figure 5.** The same amount of energy must be added to separate the bonded atoms. **Bond energy** *is the energy required to break a chemical bond and form neutral isolated atoms.* Scientists usually report bond energies in kilojoules per mole (kJ/mol), which indicates the energy required to break one mole of bonds in isolated molecules. For example, 436 kJ of energy is needed to break the hydrogen-hydrogen bonds in one mole of hydrogen molecules and form two moles of separated hydrogen atoms.

The energy relationships described here for the formation of a hydrogen-hydrogen bond apply generally to all covalent bonds. However, bond lengths and bond energies vary with the types of atoms that have combined. Even the energy of a bond between the same two types of atoms varies somewhat, depending on what other bonds the atoms have formed. These facts should be considered when examining the data in **Table 1** on the next page. The first three columns in the table list bonds, bond lengths, and bond energies of atoms in specific diatomic molecules. The last three columns give average values of specified bonds in many different compounds.

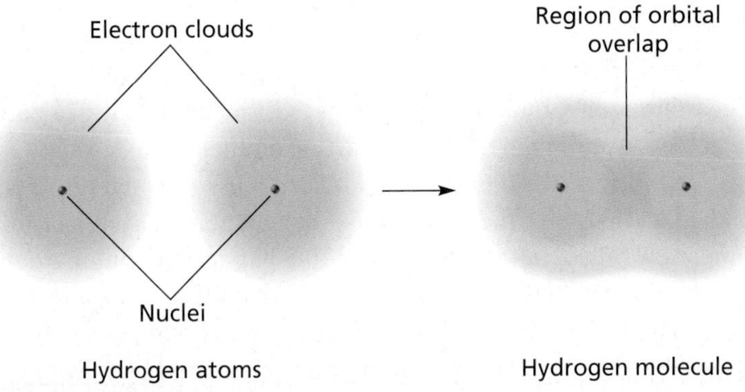


**FIGURE 7** The orbitals of the hydrogen atoms in a hydrogen molecule overlap, allowing each electron to feel the attraction of both nuclei. The result is an increase in electron density between the nuclei.

**TABLE 1 Bond Lengths and Bond Energies for Selected Covalent Bonds**

| Bond | Average bond length (pm) | Average bond energy (kJ/mol) | Bond | Average bond length (pm) | Average bond energy (kJ/mol) |
|---|---|---|---|---|---|
| H–H | 75 | 436 | C–C | 154 | 346 |
| F–F | 142 | 159 | C–N | 147 | 305 |
| Cl–Cl | 199 | 243 | C–O | 143 | 358 |
| Br–Br | 229 | 193 | C–H | 109 | 418 |
| I–I | 266 | 151 | C–Cl | 177 | 327 |
| H–F | 92 | 569 | C–Br | 194 | 285 |
| H–Cl | 127 | 432 | N–N | 145 | 163 |
| H–Br | 141 | 366 | N–H | 101 | 386 |
| H–I | 161 | 299 | O–H | 96 | 459 |

All individual hydrogen atoms contain a single, unpaired electron in a 1*s* atomic orbital. When two hydrogen atoms form a molecule, they share electrons in a covalent bond. As **Figure 8** shows, sharing electrons allows each atom to have the stable electron configuration of helium, $1s^2$. This tendency for atoms to achieve noble-gas configurations by bonding covalently extends beyond the simple case of a hydrogen molecule.

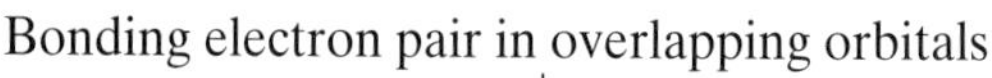


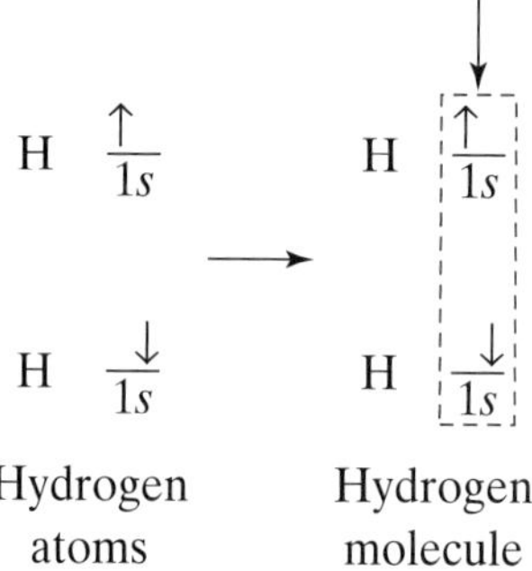


**FIGURE 8** By sharing electrons in overlapping orbitals, each hydrogen atom in a hydrogen molecule experiences the effect of a stable $1s^2$ configuration.

## The Octet Rule

Unlike other atoms, the noble-gas atoms exist independently in nature. They possess a minimum of energy existing on their own because of the special stability of their electron configurations. This stability results from the fact that, with the exception of helium and its two electrons in a completely filled outer shell, the noble-gas atoms' outer *s* and *p* orbitals are completely filled by a total of eight electrons. Other main-group atoms can effectively fill their outermost *s* and *p* orbitals with electrons by sharing electrons through covalent bonding. Such bond formation follows the *octet rule:* Chemical compounds tend to form so that each atom, by gaining, losing, or sharing electrons, has an octet of electrons in its highest occupied energy level.

Let's examine how the bonding in a fluorine molecule illustrates the octet rule. An independent fluorine atom has seven electrons in its highest energy level ([He]$2s^22p^5$). Like hydrogen atoms, fluorine atoms bond covalently with each other to form diatomic molecules, $F_2$. When two fluorine atoms bond, each atom shares one of its valence electrons with its partner. The shared electron pair effectively fills each atom's outermost energy level with an octet of electrons, as illustrated in **Figure 9a. Figure 9b** shows another example of the octet rule, in which the chlorine atom in a molecule of hydrogen chloride, HCl, achieves an outermost octet by sharing an electron pair with an atom of hydrogen.

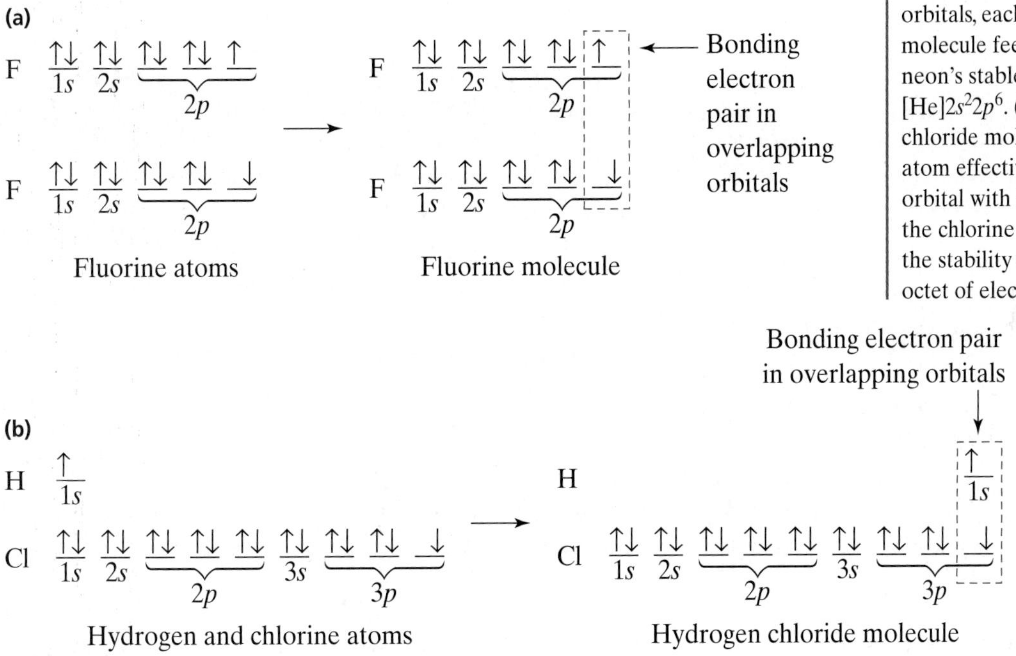

**FIGURE 9** (a) By sharing valence electrons in overlapping orbitals, each atom in a fluorine molecule feels the effect of neon's stable configuration, [He]$2s^22p^6$. (b) In a hydrogen chloride molecule, the hydrogen atom effectively fills its 1*s* orbital with two electrons, while the chlorine atom experiences the stability of an outermost octet of electrons.

## Exceptions to the Octet Rule

Most main-group elements tend to form covalent bonds according to the octet rule. However, there are exceptions. As you have seen, hydrogen forms bonds in which it is surrounded by only two electrons. Boron, B, has just three valence electrons ([He]$2s^22p^1$). Because electron pairs are shared in covalent bonds, boron tends to form bonds in which it is surrounded by six electrons. In boron trifluoride, $BF_3$, for example, the boron atom is surrounded by its own three valence electrons plus one from each of the three fluorine atoms bonded to it. Other elements can be surrounded by *more* than eight electrons when they combine with the highly electronegative elements fluorine, oxygen, and chlorine. In these cases of *expanded valence,* bonding involves electrons in *d* orbitals as well as in *s* and *p* orbitals. Examples of compounds that have an expanded valence include $PF_5$ and $SF_6$, as shown in **Table 5.**

| Number of valence electrons | Electron-dot notation | Example |
|---|---|---|
| 1 | X· | Na· |
| 2 | ·X· | ·Mg· |
| 3 | ·Ẋ· | ·Ḃ· |
| 4 | ·Ẋ· (with dot below) | ·Ċ· (with dot below) |
| 5 | ·Ẋ: (with dot below) | ·Ṅ: (with dot below) |
| 6 | :Ẋ: (with dot below) | :Ȯ: (with dot below) |
| 7 | :Ẍ: (with dot below) | :F̈: (with dot below) |
| 8 | :Ẍ: (with two dots below) | :N̈e: (with two dots below) |

**FIGURE 10** To write an element's electron-dot notation, determine the element's number of valence electrons. Then place a corresponding number of dots around the element's symbol, as shown.

## Electron-Dot Notation

Covalent bond formation usually involves only the electrons in an atom's outermost energy levels, or the atom's valence electrons. To keep track of these electrons, it is helpful to use electron-dot notation. **Electron-dot notation** *is an electron-configuration notation in which only the valence electrons of an atom of a particular element are shown, indicated by dots placed around the element's symbol.* The inner-shell electrons are not shown. For example, the electron-dot notation for a fluorine atom (electron configuration $[He]2s^22p^5$) may be written as follows.

:F̈: (with dot below)

In general, an element's number of valence electrons can be determined by adding the superscripts of the element's noble-gas notation. In this book, the electron-dot notations for elements with 1–8 valence electrons are written as shown in **Figure 10.**

**SAMPLE PROBLEM B** *For more help, go to the* ***Math Tutor*** *at the end of this chapter.*

**a. Write the electron-dot notation for hydrogen.**
**b. Write the electron-dot notation for nitrogen.**

**SOLUTION** a. A hydrogen atom has only one occupied energy level, the $n = 1$ level, which contains a single electron. Therefore, the electron-dot notation for hydrogen is written as follows.

H·

b. The group notation for nitrogen's family of elements is $ns^2np^3$, which indicates that nitrogen has five valence electrons. Therefore, the electron-dot notation for nitrogen is written as follows.

·Ṅ: (with dot below)

## Lewis Structures

Electron-dot notation can also be used to represent molecules. For example, a hydrogen molecule, $H_2$, is represented by combining the notations of two individual hydrogen atoms, as follows.

H:H

The pair of dots represents the shared electron pair of the hydrogen-hydrogen covalent bond. For a molecule of fluorine, $F_2$, the electron-dot notations of two fluorine atoms are combined.

$$:\underset{\cdot\cdot}{\overset{\cdot\cdot}{F}}:\underset{\cdot\cdot}{\overset{\cdot\cdot}{F}}:$$

Here also the pair of dots between the two symbols represents the shared pair of a covalent bond. In addition, each fluorine atom is surrounded by three pairs of electrons that are not shared in bonds. An *unshared pair,* also called a *lone pair,* is a pair of electrons that is not involved in bonding and that belongs exclusively to one atom.

The pair of dots representing a shared pair of electrons in a covalent bond is often replaced by a long dash. According to this convention, hydrogen and fluorine molecules are represented as follows.

$$H{-}H \quad :\underset{\cdot\cdot}{\overset{\cdot\cdot}{F}}{-}\underset{\cdot\cdot}{\overset{\cdot\cdot}{F}}:$$

These representations are all **Lewis structures,** *formulas in which atomic symbols represent nuclei and inner-shell electrons, dot-pairs or dashes between two atomic symbols represent electron pairs in covalent bonds, and dots adjacent to only one atomic symbol represent unshared electrons.* It is common to write Lewis structures that show only the electrons that are shared, using dashes to represent the bonds. *A* **structural formula** *indicates the kind, number, arrangement, and bonds but not the unshared pairs of the atoms in a molecule.* For example, F–F and H–Cl are structural formulas.

The Lewis structures (and therefore the structural formulas) for many molecules can be drawn if one knows the composition of the molecule and which atoms are bonded to each other. The following sample problem illustrates the basic steps for writing Lewis structures. The molecule described in this problem contains bonds with single shared electron pairs. A single covalent bond, or a **single bond,** *is a covalent bond in which one pair of electrons is shared between two atoms.*

## SAMPLE PROBLEM C

*For more help, go to the* ***Math Tutor*** *at the end of this chapter.*

**Draw the Lewis structure of iodomethane, $CH_3I$.**

**SOLUTION**

1. *Determine the type and number of atoms in the molecule.*
   The formula shows one carbon atom, one iodine atom, and three hydrogen atoms.

2. *Write the electron-dot notation for each type of atom in the molecule.*
   Carbon is from Group 14 and has four valence electrons. Iodine is from Group 17 and has seven valence electrons. Hydrogen has one valence electron.

$$\cdot\underset{\cdot}{\overset{\cdot}{C}}\cdot \quad :\underset{\cdot}{\overset{\cdot\cdot}{I}}: \quad H\cdot$$

3. *Determine the total number of valence electrons available in the atoms to be combined.*

| | | |
|---|---|---|
| **C** | $1 \times 4e^- =$ | $4e^-$ |
| **I** | $1 \times 7e^- =$ | $7e^-$ |
| **3H** | $3 \times 1e^- =$ | $3e^-$ |
| | | $14e^-$ |

4. *Arrange the atoms to form a skeleton structure for the molecule. If carbon is present, it is the central atom. Otherwise, the least-electronegative atom is central (except for hydrogen, which is never central). Then connect the atoms by electron-pair bonds.*

```
  H
  ..
H:C:I
  ..
  H
```

5. *Add unshared pairs of electrons to each nonmetal atom (except hydrogen) such that each is surrounded by eight electrons.*

```
  H               H
  .. ..           |  ..
H:C:I:    or    H–C–I:
  .. ..           |  ..
  H               H
```

6. *Count the electrons in the structure to be sure that the number of valence electrons used equals the number available. Be sure the central atom and other atoms besides hydrogen have an octet.*

There are eight electrons in the four covalent bonds and six electrons in the three unshared pairs, giving the correct total of 14 valence electrons.

**PRACTICE** *Answers in Appendix E*

1. Draw the Lewis structure of ammonia, $NH_3$.
2. Draw the Lewis structure for hydrogen sulfide, $H_2S$.
3. Draw the Lewis structure for silane, $SiH_4$.
4. Draw the Lewis structure for phosphorus trifluoride, $PF_3$.

Go to **go.hrw.com** for more practice problems that ask you to draw Lewis structures.

**Keyword: HC6BNDX**

## Multiple Covalent Bonds

Atoms of some elements, especially carbon, nitrogen, and oxygen, can share more than one electron pair. A double covalent bond, or simply a *double bond,* is a covalent bond in which two pairs of electrons are shared between two atoms. A double bond is shown either by two side-by-side pairs of dots or by two parallel dashes. All four electrons in a double bond "belong" to both atoms. In ethene, $C_2H_4$, for example, two electron pairs are simultaneously shared by two carbon atoms.

```
H       H        H       H
 \     /          \     /
  C::C     or      C=C
 /     \          /     \
H       H        H       H
```

A triple covalent bond, or simply a *triple bond,* is a covalent bond in which three pairs of electrons are shared between two atoms. For example, elemental nitrogen, $N_2$, like hydrogen and the halogens, normally exists as diatomic molecules. In this case, however, each nitrogen atom, which has five valence electrons, acquires three electrons to complete an octet by sharing three pairs of electrons with its partner. This is illustrated in the Lewis structure and the formula structure for $N_2$, as shown below.

:N:::N: or :N≡N:

**Figure 11** represents nitrogen's triple bond through orbital notation. Like the single bonds in hydrogen and halogen molecules, the triple bond in nitrogen molecules is nonpolar.

Carbon forms a number of compounds containing triple bonds. For example, the compound ethyne, $C_2H_2$, contains a carbon-carbon triple bond.

H:C:::C:H or H−C≡C−H

*Double and triple bonds are referred to as* **multiple bonds,** or multiple covalent bonds. Double bonds in general have greater bond energies and are shorter than single bonds. Triple bonds are even stronger and shorter. **Table 2** compares average bond lengths and bond energies for some single, double, and triple bonds.

In writing Lewis structures for molecules that contain carbon, nitrogen, or oxygen, one must remember that multiple bonds between pairs of these atoms are possible. (A hydrogen atom, on the other hand, has only one electron and therefore always forms a single covalent bond.) The need for a multiple bond becomes obvious if there are not enough valence electrons to complete octets by adding unshared pairs. Sample Problem D on the next page shows how to deal with this situation.

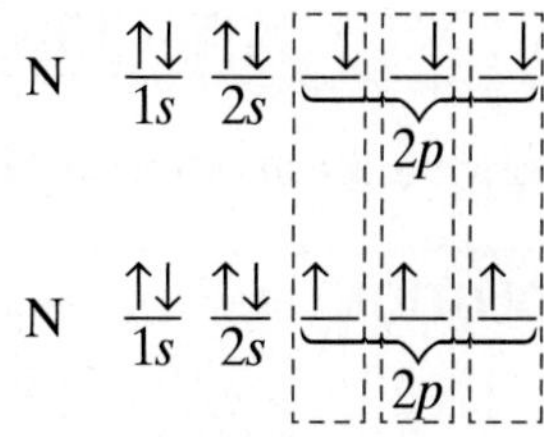

Nitrogen molecule

**FIGURE 11** In a molecule of nitrogen, $N_2$, each nitrogen atom is surrounded by six shared electrons plus one unshared pair of electrons. Thus, each nitrogen atom follows the octet rule in forming a triple covalent bond.

**TABLE 2 Bond Lengths and Bond Energies for Single and Multiple Covalent Bonds**

| Bond | Average bond length (pm) | Average bond energy (kJ/mol) | Bond | Average bond length (pm) | Average bond energy (kJ/mol) |
|---|---|---|---|---|---|
| C−C | 154 | 346 | C−O | 143 | 358 |
| C=C | 134 | 612 | C=O | 120 | 732 |
| C≡C | 120 | 835 | C≡O | 113 | 1072 |
| C−N | 147 | 305 | N−N | 145 | 163 |
| C=N | 132 | 615 | N=N | 125 | 418 |
| C≡N | 116 | 887 | N≡N | 110 | 945 |

## SAMPLE PROBLEM D

*For more help, go to the* ***Math Tutor*** *at the end of this chapter.*

**Draw the Lewis structure for methanal, $CH_2O$, which is also known as formaldehyde.**

**SOLUTION**

1. *Determine the number of atoms of each element present in the molecule.*
   The formula shows one carbon atom, two hydrogen atoms, and one oxygen atom.

2. *Write the electron-dot notation for each type of atom.*
   Carbon is from Group 14 and has four valence electrons. Oxygen, which is in Group 16, has six valence electrons. Hydrogen has only one electron.

   ·Ċ·  :Ö:  H·

3. *Determine the total number of valence electrons available in the atoms to be combined.*

| | | |
|---|---|---|
| **C** | **$1 \times 4e^-$ =** | **$4e^-$** |
| **O** | **$1 \times 6e^-$ =** | **$6e^-$** |
| **2H** | **$2 \times 1e^-$ =** | **$2e^-$** |
| | | **$12e^-$** |

4. *Arrange the atoms to form a skeleton structure for the molecule, and connect the atoms by electron-pair bonds.*

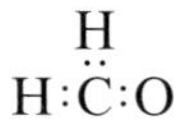

```
  H
  ··
H:C:O
```

5. *Add unshared pairs of electrons to each nonmetal atom (except hydrogen) such that each is surrounded by eight electrons.*

```
  H
  ·· ··
H:C:O:
  ·· ··
```

6a. *Count the electrons in the Lewis structure to be sure that the number of valence electrons used equals the number available.*
   The structure above has six electrons in covalent bonds and eight electrons in four lone pairs, for a total of 14 electrons. The structure has two valence electrons too many.

6b. *If too many electrons have been used, subtract one or more lone pairs until the total number of valence electrons is correct. Then move one or more lone electron pairs to existing bonds between non-hydrogen atoms until the outer shells of all atoms are completely filled.*
   Subtract the lone pair of electrons from the carbon atom. Then move one lone pair of electrons from the oxygen to the bond between carbon and oxygen to form a double bond.

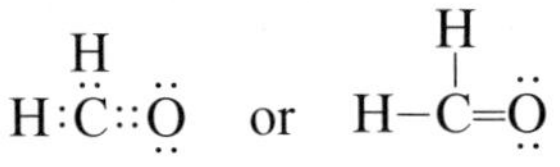

```
  H                 H
  ··   ··           |  ··
H:C::O     or    H—C=O
       ··              ··
```

   There are eight electrons in covalent bonds and four electrons in lone pairs, for a total of 12 valence electrons.

**PRACTICE**

*Answers in Appendix E*

1. Draw the Lewis structure for carbon dioxide, $CO_2$.
2. Draw the Lewis structure for hydrogen cyanide, which contains one hydrogen atom, one carbon atom, and one nitrogen atom.

**extension**

Go to **go.hrw.com** for more practice problems that ask you to draw Lewis structures.

## Resonance Structures

Some molecules and ions cannot be represented adequately by a single Lewis structure. One such molecule is ozone, $O_3$, which can be represented by either of the following Lewis structures.

$$\ddot{\underset{..}{O}}{=}\ddot{O}{-}\ddot{\underset{..}{O}}\colon \quad \text{or} \quad \colon\ddot{\underset{..}{O}}{-}\ddot{O}{=}\ddot{\underset{..}{O}}$$

Notice that each structure indicates that the ozone molecule has two types of O—O bonds, one single and one double. Chemists once speculated that ozone split its time existing as one of these two structures, constantly alternating, or "resonating," from one to the other. Experiments, however, revealed that the oxygen-oxygen bonds in ozone are identical. Therefore, scientists now say that ozone has a single structure that is the average of these two structures. Together the structures are referred to as *resonance structures* or *resonance hybrids*. **Resonance** *refers to bonding in molecules or ions that cannot be correctly represented by a single Lewis structure*. To indicate resonance, a double-headed arrow is placed between a molecule's resonance structures.

$$\ddot{\underset{..}{O}}{=}\ddot{O}{-}\ddot{\underset{..}{O}}\colon \longleftrightarrow \colon\ddot{\underset{..}{O}}{-}\ddot{O}{=}\ddot{\underset{..}{O}}$$

## Covalent-Network Bonding

All the covalent compounds that you have read about so far are molecular. They consist of many identical molecules held together by forces acting between the molecules. (You will read more about these intermolecular forces in Section 5.) There are many covalently bonded compounds that do not contain individual molecules, but instead can be pictured as continuous, three-dimensional networks of bonded atoms. You will read more about covalently bonded networks in Chapter 7.

### SECTION REVIEW

1. Define the following:
   **a.** bond length **b.** bond energy
2. State the octet rule.
3. How many pairs of electrons are shared in the following types of covalent bonds?
   **a.** a single bond
   **b.** a double bond
   **c.** a triple bond
4. Draw the Lewis structures for the following molecules:
   **a.** IBr
   **b.** $CH_3Br$
   **c.** $C_2HCl$
   **d.** $SiCl_4$
   **e.** $OF_2$

**Critical Thinking**

5. **APPLYING MODELS** Compare the molecules $H_2NNH_2$ and HNNH. Which molecule has the stronger N-N bond?

SECTION 3

# Ionic Bonding and Ionic Compounds

## OBJECTIVES

- Compare and contrast a chemical formula for a molecular compound with one for an ionic compound.
- Discuss the arrangements of ions in crystals.
- Define *lattice energy* and explain its significance.
- List and compare the distinctive properties of ionic and molecular compounds.
- Write the Lewis structure for a polyatomic ion given the identity of the atoms combined and other appropriate information.

C.3.8 Explain the effect of electronegativity and ionization energy on the type of bonding in a molecule

Most of the rocks and minerals that make up Earth's crust consist of positive and negative ions held together by ionic bonding. A familiar example of an ionically bonded compound is sodium chloride, or common table salt, which is found in nature as rock salt. A sodium ion, $Na^+$, has a charge of 1+. A chloride ion, $Cl^-$, has a charge of 1−. There is an electrical force of attraction between oppositely charged ions. In sodium chloride, these ions combine in a one-to-one ratio—$Na^+Cl^-$—so that each positive charge is balanced by a negative charge. The chemical formula for sodium chloride is usually written simply as NaCl.

*An* **ionic compound** *is composed of positive and negative ions that are combined so that the numbers of positive and negative charges are equal.* Most ionic compounds exist as crystalline solids (see **Figure 12**). A crystal of any ionic compound is a three-dimensional network of positive and negative ions mutually attracted to one another. As a result, in contrast to a molecular compound, an ionic compound is not composed of independent, neutral units that can be isolated and examined. The chemical formula of an ionic compound merely represents the simplest ratio of the compound's combined ions that gives electrical neutrality.

The chemical formula of an ionic compound shows the ratio of the ions present in a sample of any size. *A* **formula unit** *is the simplest collection of atoms from which an ionic compound's formula can be established.* For example, one formula unit of sodium chloride, NaCl, is one sodium cation plus one chloride anion. (In the naming of a monatomic anion, the ending of the element's name is replaced with *-ide*. See Chapter 7 for more details.)

The ratio of ions in a formula unit depends on the charges of the ions combined. For example, to achieve electrical neutrality in the ionic compound calcium fluoride, two fluoride anions, $F^-$, each with a charge of 1−, must balance the 2+ charge of each calcium cation, $Ca^{2+}$. Therefore, the formula of calcium fluoride is $CaF_2$.

**FIGURE 12** Like most ionic compounds, sodium chloride is a crystalline solid.

## Formation of Ionic Compounds

Electron-dot notation can be used to demonstrate the changes that take place in ionic bonding. Ionic compounds do not ordinarily form by the combination of isolated ions, but consider for a moment a sodium atom and a chlorine atom approaching each other. The two atoms are neutral and have one and seven valence electrons, respectively.

| Na· | :C̈l: |
|---|---|
| Sodium atom | Chlorine atom |

We have already seen that atoms of sodium and the other alkali metals readily lose one electron to form cations. And we have seen that atoms of chlorine and the other halogens readily gain one electron to form anions. The combination of sodium and chlorine atoms to produce one formula unit of sodium chloride can thus be represented as follows.

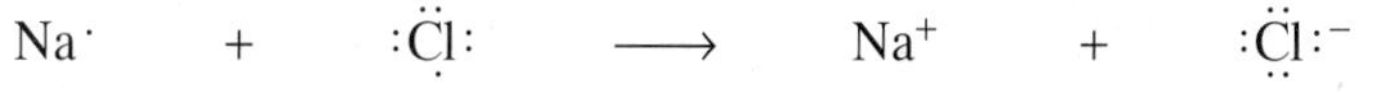

| Sodium atom | Chlorine atom | Sodium cation | Chloride anion |
|---|---|---|---|

The transfer of an electron from the sodium atom to the chlorine atom transforms each atom into an ion with a noble-gas configuration. In the combination of calcium with fluorine, two fluorine atoms are needed to accept the two valence electrons given up by one calcium atom.

$$\cdot Ca \cdot + :\ddot{F}: + :\ddot{F}: \longrightarrow Ca^{2+} + :\ddot{F}:^- + :\ddot{F}:^-$$

| Calcium atom | Fluorine atoms | Calcium cation | Fluoride anions |
|---|---|---|---|

**FIGURE 13** The ions in an ionic compound lower their potential energy by forming an orderly, three-dimensional array in which the positive and negative charges are balanced. The electrical forces of attraction between oppositely charged ions extend over long distances, causing a large decrease in potential energy.

## Characteristics of Ionic Bonding

Recall that nature favors arrangements in which potential energy is minimized. In an ionic crystal, ions minimize their potential energy by combining in an orderly arrangement known as a *crystal lattice* (see **Figure 13**). The attractive forces at work within an ionic crystal include those between oppositely charged ions and those between the nuclei and electrons of adjacent ions. The repulsive forces include those between like-charged ions and those between electrons of adjacent ions. The distances between ions and their arrangement in a crystal represent a balance among all these forces. Sodium chloride's crystal structure is shown in **Figure 14** below.

SCILINKS.
www.scilinks.org
**Topic:** Ionic Bonding
**Code:** HC60815

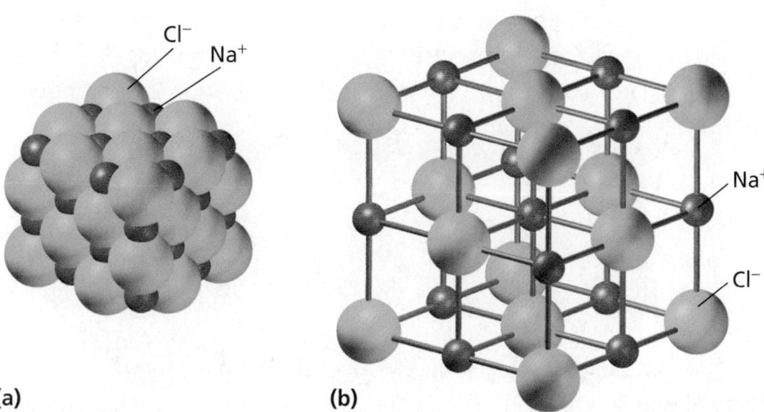


**FIGURE 14** Two models of the crystal structure of sodium chloride are shown. (a) To illustrate the ions' actual arrangement, the sodium and chloride ions are shown with their electron clouds just touching. (b) In an expanded view, the distances between ions have been exaggerated in order to clarify the positioning of the ions in the structure.

**FIGURE 15** The figure shows the ions that most closely surround a chloride anion and a sodium cation within the crystal structure of NaCl. The structure is composed such that (a) six $Na^+$ ions surround each $Cl^-$ ion. At the same time, (b) six $Cl^-$ ions surround each $Na^+$ ion (which cannot be seen but whose location is indicated by the dashed outline).

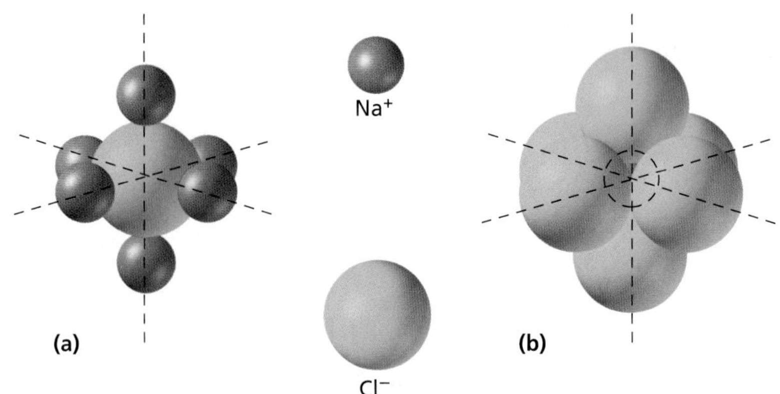


**Figure 15** shows the crystal structure of sodium chloride in greater detail. Within the arrangement, each sodium cation is surrounded by six chloride anions. At the same time, each chloride anion is surrounded by six sodium cations. Attraction between the adjacent oppositely charged ions is much stronger than repulsion by other ions of the same charge, which are farther away.

The three-dimensional arrangements of ions and the strengths of attraction between them vary with the sizes and charges of the ions and the numbers of ions of different charges. For example, in calcium fluoride, there are two anions for each cation. Each calcium cation is surrounded by eight fluoride anions. At the same time, each fluoride ion is surrounded by four calcium cations, as shown in **Figure 16.**

To compare bond strengths in ionic compounds, chemists compare the amounts of energy released when separated ions in a gas come together to form a crystalline solid. **Lattice energy** *is the energy released when one mole of an ionic crystalline compound is formed from gaseous ions.* Lattice energy values for a few common ionic compounds are shown in **Table 3.** The negative energy values indicate that energy is *released* when the crystals are formed.

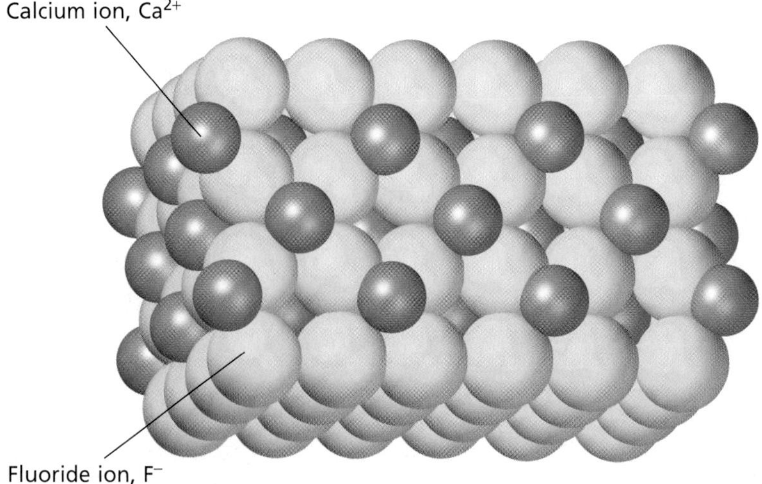


**FIGURE 16** In the crystal structure of calcium fluoride, $CaF_2$, each calcium cation is surrounded by eight fluoride anions and each fluoride ion is surrounded by four calcium cations. This is the closest possible packing of the ions in which the positive and negative charges are balanced.

## A Comparison of Ionic and Molecular Compounds

The force that holds ions together in ionic compounds is a very strong overall attraction between positive and negative charges. In a molecular compound, the covalent bonds of the atoms making up each molecule are also strong. But the forces of attraction *between* molecules are much weaker than the forces among formula units in ionic bonding. This difference in the strength of attraction between the basic units of molecular and ionic compounds gives rise to different properties in the two types of compounds.

The melting point, boiling point, and hardness of a compound depend on how strongly its basic units are attracted to each other. Because the forces of attraction between individual molecules are not very strong, many molecular compounds melt at low temperatures. In fact, many molecular compounds are already completely gaseous at room temperature. In contrast, the ions in ionic compounds are held together by strong attractive forces, so ionic compounds generally have higher melting and boiling points than do molecular compounds.

Ionic compounds are hard but brittle. Why? In an ionic crystal, even a slight shift of one row of ions relative to another causes a large buildup of repulsive forces, as shown in **Figure 17.** These forces make it difficult for one layer to move relative to another, causing ionic compounds to be hard. If one layer is moved, however, the repulsive forces make the layers part completely, causing ionic compounds to be brittle.

In the solid state, the ions cannot move, so the compounds are not electrical conductors. In the molten state, ionic compounds are electrical conductors because the ions can move freely to carry electrical current. Many ionic compounds can dissolve in water. When they dissolve, their ions separate from each other and become surrounded by water molecules. These ions are free to move through the solution, so such solutions are electrical conductors. Other ionic compounds do not dissolve in water, however, because the attractions between the water molecules and the ions cannot overcome the attractions between the ions.

**TABLE 3 *Lattice Energies of Some Common Ionic Compounds***

| Compound | Lattice energy (kJ/mol) |
|---|---|
| NaCl | −787.5 |
| NaBr | −751.4 |
| $CaF_2$ | −2634.7 |
| LiCl | −861.3 |
| LiF | −1032 |
| MgO | −3760 |
| KCl | −715 |

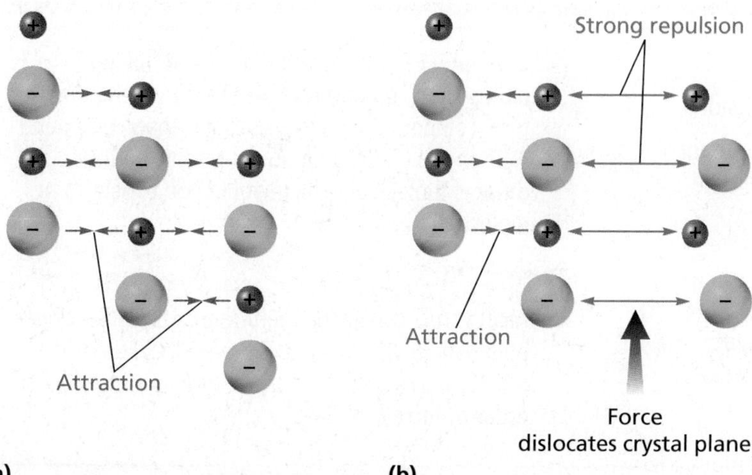


**FIGURE 17** (a) The attraction between positive and negative ions in a crystalline ionic compound causes layers of ions to resist motion. (b) When struck with sufficient force, the layers shift so that ions of the same charge approach each other, causing repulsion. As a result, the crystal shatters along the planes.

## Polyatomic Ions

Certain atoms bond covalently with each other to form a group of atoms that has both molecular and ionic characteristics. *A charged group of covalently bonded atoms is known as a* **polyatomic ion.** Polyatomic ions combine with ions of opposite charge to form ionic compounds. The charge of a polyatomic ion results from an excess of electrons (negative charge) or a shortage of electrons (positive charge). For example, an ammonium ion, a common positively charged polyatomic ion, contains one nitrogen atom and four hydrogen atoms and has a single positive charge. Its formula is $NH_4^+$, sometimes written as $[NH_4]^+$ to show that the group of atoms *as a whole* has a charge of 1+. The seven protons in the nitrogen atom plus the four protons in the four hydrogen atoms give the ammonium ion a total positive charge of 11+. An independent nitrogen atom has seven electrons, and four independent hydrogen atoms have a total of four electrons. When these atoms combine to form an ammonium ion, one of their electrons is lost, giving the polyatomic ion a total negative charge of 10–.

**extension**

**Chemistry in Action**

Go to **go.hrw.com** for a full-length article on nanoscale computers.

 **Keyword:** HC6BNDX

Lewis structures for the ammonium ion and some common negative polyatomic ions—the nitrate, sulfate, and phosphate ions—are shown below. To find the Lewis structure for a polyatomic ion, follow the steps of Sample Problem D, with the following exception. If the ion is negatively charged, add to the total number of valence electrons a number of electrons corresponding to the ion's negative charge. If the ion is positively charged, subtract from the total number of valence electrons a number of electrons corresponding to the ion's positive charge.

| $\left[\begin{matrix} & H & \\ H & :N: & H \\ & H & \end{matrix}\right]^+$ | $\left[\begin{matrix} :\ddot{O}: & \\ \ddot{N} & ::\ddot{O} \\ :\ddot{O}: & \end{matrix}\right]^-$ | $\left[\begin{matrix} & :\ddot{O}: & \\ :\ddot{O}: & \ddot{S} & :\ddot{O}: \\ & :\ddot{O}: & \end{matrix}\right]^{2-}$ | $\left[\begin{matrix} & :\ddot{O}: & \\ :\ddot{O}: & \ddot{P} & :\ddot{O}: \\ & :\ddot{O}: & \end{matrix}\right]^{3-}$ |
|---|---|---|---|
| Ammonium ion | Nitrate ion | Sulfate ion | Phosphate ion |

## SECTION REVIEW

1. Give two examples of an ionic compound.
2. Use electron-dot notation to demonstrate the formation of ionic compounds involving the following:
   **a.** Li and Cl
   **b.** Ca and I
3. Distinguish between ionic and molecular compounds in terms of the basic units that each is composed of.
4. Compound B has lower melting and boiling points than compound A. At the same temperature, compound B vaporizes faster than compound A. If one of these compounds is ionic and the other is molecular, which would you expect to be molecular? ionic? Explain your reasoning.

**Critical Thinking**

5. **ANALYZING DATA** The melting points for the compounds $Li_2S$, $Rb_2S$, and $K_2S$ are 900°C, 530°C, and 840°C, respectively. List these three compounds in order of increasing lattice energy.

# Metallic Bonding

SECTION 4

C.3.3 Explain how the types of intermolecular forces present in a compound affect the physical properties of compounds (including polarity and molecular shape)

## Objectives

- Describe the electron-sea model of metallic bonding, and explain why metals are good electrical conductors.
- Explain why metal surfaces are shiny.
- Explain why metals are malleable and ductile but ionic-crystalline compounds are not.

Chemical bonding is different in metals than it is in ionic, molecular, or covalent-network compounds. This difference is reflected in the unique properties of metals. They are excellent electrical conductors in the solid state—much better conductors than even molten ionic compounds. This property is due to the highly mobile valence electrons of the atoms that make up a metal. Such mobility is not possible in molecular compounds, in which valence electrons are localized in electron-pair bonds between neutral atoms. Nor is it possible in solid ionic compounds, in which electrons are bound to individual ions that are held in place in crystal structures.

## The Metallic-Bond Model

The highest energy levels of most metal atoms are occupied by very few electrons. In *s*-block metals, for example, one or two valence electrons occupy the outermost orbital, and all three outermost *p* orbitals, which can hold a total of six electrons, are vacant. In addition to completely vacant outer *p* orbitals, *d*-block metals also possess many vacant *d* orbitals in the energy level just below their highest energy level.

Within a metal, the vacant orbitals in the atoms' outer energy levels overlap. This overlapping of orbitals allows the outer electrons of the atoms to roam freely throughout the entire metal. The electrons are *delocalized,* which means that they do not belong to any one atom but move freely about the metal's network of empty atomic orbitals. These mobile electrons form a *sea of electrons* around the metal atoms, which are packed together in a crystal lattice (see **Figure 18**). *The chemical bonding that results from the attraction between metal atoms and the surrounding sea of electrons is called* **metallic bonding.**

SCILINKS.
www.scilinks.org
**Topic:** Metallic Bonding
**Code:** HC60944

**FIGURE 18** The model shows a portion of the crystal structure of solid sodium. The atoms are arranged so that each sodium atom is surrounded by eight other sodium atoms. The atoms are relatively fixed in position, while the electrons are free to move throughout the crystal, forming an electron sea.

### Metallic Properties

The freedom of electrons to move in a network of metal atoms accounts for the high electrical and thermal conductivity characteristic of all metals. In addition, metals are both strong absorbers and reflectors of light. Because they contain many orbitals separated by extremely small energy differences, metals can absorb a wide range of light frequencies. This absorption of light results in the excitation of the metal atoms' electrons to higher energy levels. However, in metals the electrons immediately fall back down to lower levels, emitting energy in the form of light at a frequency similar to the absorbed frequency. This re-radiated (or reflected) light is responsible for the metallic appearance or luster of metal surfaces.

**FIGURE 19** Unlike ionic crystalline compounds, most metals are malleable. This property allows iron, for example, to be shaped into useful tools.

Most metals are also easy to form into desired shapes. Two important properties related to this characteristic are malleability and ductility. **Malleability** *is the ability of a substance to be hammered or beaten into thin sheets.* **Ductility** *is the ability of a substance to be drawn, pulled, or extruded through a small opening to produce a wire.* The malleability and ductility of metals are possible because metallic bonding is the same in all directions throughout the solid. When struck, one plane of atoms in a metal can slide past another without encountering resistance or breaking bonds. By contrast, recall from Section 3 that shifting the layers of an ionic crystal causes the bonds to break and the crystal to shatter.

## Metallic Bond Strength

Metallic bond strength varies with the nuclear charge of the metal atoms and the number of electrons in the metal's electron sea. Both of these factors are reflected in a metal's *enthalpy of vaporization.* The amount of energy as heat required to vaporize the metal is a measure of the strength of the bonds that hold the metal together. The enthalpy of vaporization is defined as the amount of energy absorbed as heat when a specified amount of a substance vaporizes at constant pressure. Some enthalpies of vaporization for metals are given in **Table 4.**

**TABLE 4** ***Enthalpies of Vaporization of Some Metals (kJ/mol)***

| Period | Element | | |
|---|---|---|---|
| Second | Li<br>147 | Be<br>297 | |
| Third | Na<br>97 | Mg<br>128 | Al<br>294 |
| Fourth | K<br>77 | Ca<br>155 | Sc<br>333 |
| Fifth | Rb<br>76 | Sr<br>137 | Y<br>365 |
| Sixth | Cs<br>64 | Ba<br>140 | La<br>402 |

## SECTION REVIEW

1. Describe the electron-sea model of metallic bonding.
2. What is the relationship between metallic bond strength and enthalpy of vaporization?
3. Explain why most metals are malleable and ductile but ionic crystals are not.

**Critical Thinking**

4. **ORGANIZING IDEAS** Explain why metals are good electrical conductors.

# Molecular Geometry

SECTION 5

**C.3.3** Explain how the types of intermolecular forces present in a compound affect the physical properties of compounds (including polarity and molecular shape)

*OBJECTIVES*

- Explain VSEPR theory.
- Predict the shapes of molecules or polyatomic ions using VSEPR theory.
- Explain how the shapes of molecules are accounted for by hybridization theory.
- Describe dipole-dipole forces, hydrogen bonding, induced dipoles, and London dispersion forces and their effects on properties such as boiling and melting points.
- Explain what determines molecular polarity.

The properties of molecules depend not only on the bonding of atoms but also on molecular geometry—the three-dimensional arrangement of a molecule's atoms in space. The polarity of each bond, along with the geometry of the molecule, determines *molecular polarity,* or the uneven distribution of molecular charge. As you will read, molecular polarity strongly influences the forces that act *between* molecules in liquids and solids.

A chemical formula reveals little information about a molecule's geometry. After performing many tests designed to reveal the shapes of various molecules, chemists developed two different, equally successful theories to explain certain aspects of their findings. One theory accounts for molecular bond angles. The other is used to describe the orbitals that contain the valence electrons of a molecule's atoms.

## VSEPR Theory

As shown in **Figure 20,** diatomic molecules, like those of hydrogen, $H_2$, and hydrogen chloride, HCl, must be linear because they consist of only two atoms. To predict the geometries of more-complicated molecules, one must consider the locations of all electron pairs surrounding the bonded atoms. This is the basis of VSEPR theory.

The abbreviation VSEPR stands for "valence-shell, electron-pair repulsion," referring to the repulsion between pairs of valence electrons of the atoms in a molecule. **VSEPR theory** *states that repulsion between the sets of valence-level electrons surrounding an atom causes these sets to be oriented as far apart as possible.* How does the assumption that electrons in molecules repel each other account for molecular shapes? For now let us consider only molecules with no unshared valence electron pairs on the central atom.

Let's examine the simple molecule $BeF_2$. The beryllium atom forms a covalent bond with each fluorine atom and does not follow the octet rule. It is surrounded by only the two electron pairs that it shares with the fluorine atoms.

$$:\ddot{\underset{..}{F}}:Be:\ddot{\underset{..}{F}}:$$

According to VSEPR theory, the shared pairs will be as far away from each other as possible. As shown in **Figure 21a** on the next page, the distance between electron pairs is maximized if the bonds to fluorine are

**(a)** Hydrogen, $H_2$

**(b)** Hydrogen chloride, HCl

**FIGURE 20** Ball-and-stick models illustrate the linearity of diatomic molecules. (a) A hydrogen molecule is represented by two identical balls (the hydrogen atoms) joined by a solid bar (the covalent bond). (b) A hydrogen chloride molecule is composed of dissimilar atoms, but it is still linear.

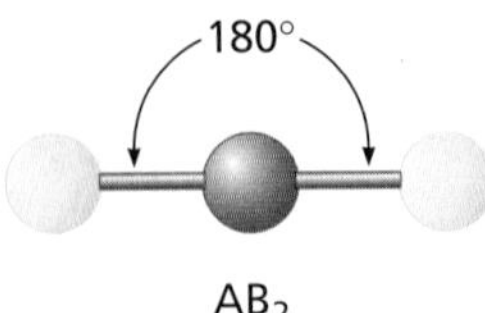


$AB_2$

**(a)** Beryllium fluoride, $BeF_2$

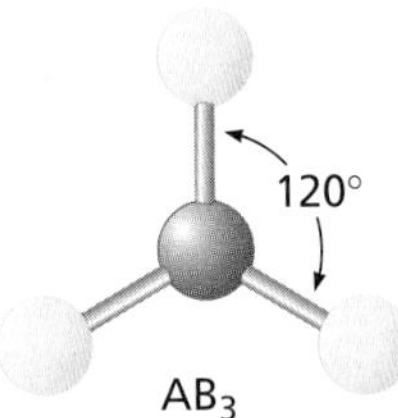


$AB_3$

**(b)** Boron trifluoride, $BF_3$

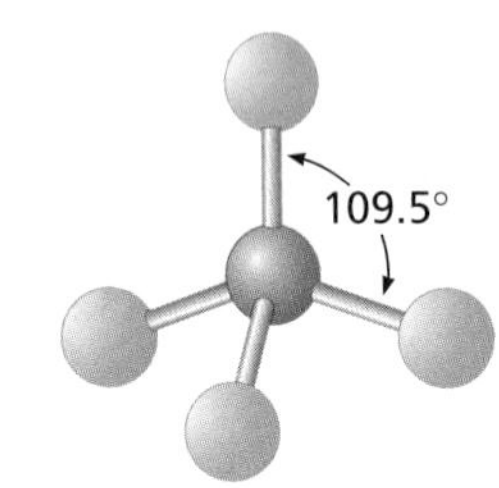


$AB_4$

**(c)** Methane, $CH_4$

**FIGURE 21** Ball-and-stick models show the shapes of (a) $AB_2$, (b) $AB_3$, and (c) $AB_4$ molecules according to VSEPR theory.

on opposite sides of the beryllium atom, 180° apart. Thus, all three atoms lie on a straight line. The molecule is linear.

If we represent the central atom in a molecule by the letter *A* and we represent the atoms bonded to the central atom by the letter *B*, then according to VSEPR theory, $BeF_2$ is an example of an $AB_2$ molecule, which is linear. Can you determine what an $AB_3$ molecule looks like? The three A—B bonds stay farthest apart by pointing to the corners of an equilateral triangle, giving 120° angles between the bonds. This trigonal-planar geometry is shown in **Figure 21b** for the $AB_3$ molecule boron trifluoride, $BF_3$.

The central atoms in $AB_4$ molecules follow the octet rule by sharing four electron pairs with B atoms. The distance between electron pairs is maximized if each A—B bond points to one of four corners of a tetrahedron. This geometry is shown in **Figure 21c** for the $AB_4$ molecule methane, $CH_4$. The same figure shows that in a tetrahedral molecule, each of the bond angles formed by the A atom and any two of the B atoms is equal to 109.5°.

The shapes of various molecules are summarized in **Table 5.** B can represent a single type of atom, a group of identical atoms, or a group of different atoms on the same molecule. The shape of the molecule will still be based on the forms given in the table. However, different sizes of B groups distort the bond angles, making some bond angles larger or smaller than those given in the table.

## SAMPLE PROBLEM E

**Use VSEPR theory to predict the molecular geometry of boron trichloride, $BCl_3$.**

**SOLUTION** First write the Lewis structure for $BCl_3$. Boron is in Group 13 and has three valence electrons.

$$\cdot\dot{\mathrm{B}}\cdot$$

Chlorine is in Group 17, so each chlorine atom has seven valence electrons.

$$:\ddot{\underset{\cdot}{\mathrm{Cl}}}:$$

The total number of available valence electrons is therefore $24e^-$ ($3e^-$ from boron and $21e^-$ from chlorine). The following Lewis structure uses all $24e^-$.

$$\begin{array}{c} :\ddot{\mathrm{Cl}}: \\ :\underset{\cdot\cdot}{\ddot{\mathrm{Cl}}}:\mathrm{B}:\underset{\cdot\cdot}{\ddot{\mathrm{Cl}}}: \end{array}$$

This molecule is an exception to the octet rule because in this case B forms only three bonds. Boron trichloride is an $AB_3$ type of molecule. Therefore, according to VSEPR theory, it should have trigonal-planar geometry.

**PRACTICE** *Answers in Appendix E*

1. Use VSEPR theory to predict the molecular geometry of the following molecules:

 a. HI  b. $CBr_4$  c. $CH_2Cl_2$

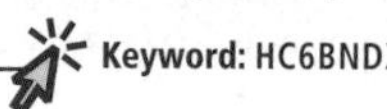

Go to **go.hrw.com** for more practice problems that ask you to predict molecular geometry.

Keyword: HC6BNDX

## VSEPR Theory and Unshared Electron Pairs

Ammonia, $NH_3$, and water, $H_2O$, are examples of molecules in which the central atom has both shared and unshared electron pairs (see **Table 5** on the next page for their Lewis structures). How does VSEPR theory account for the geometries of these molecules?

The Lewis structure of ammonia shows that in addition to the three electron pairs it shares with the three hydrogen atoms, the central nitrogen atom has one unshared pair of electrons.

$$\mathrm{H}:\ddot{\mathrm{N}}:\mathrm{H}$$
$$\quad\ddot{\mathrm{H}}$$

VSEPR theory postulates that the lone pair occupies space around the nitrogen atom just as the bonding pairs do. Thus, as in an $AB_4$ molecule, the electron pairs maximize their separation by assuming the four corners of a tetrahedron. Lone pairs do occupy space, but our description of the observed shape of a molecule refers to the *positions of atoms only*. Consequently, as shown in **Figure 22a,** the molecular geometry of an ammonia molecule is that of a pyramid with a triangular base. The general VSEPR formula for molecules such as ammonia is $AB_3E$, where E represents the unshared electron pair.

A water molecule has two unshared electron pairs. It is an $AB_2E_2$ molecule. Here, the oxygen atom is at the center of a tetrahedron, with two corners occupied by hydrogen atoms and two by the unshared pairs **(Figure 22b)**. Again, VSEPR theory states that the lone pairs occupy space around the central atom but that the actual shape of the molecule is determined by the positions of the atoms only. In the case of water, this results in a "bent," or angular, molecule.

SCILINKS.
www.scilinks.org
**Topic:** VSEPR Theory
**Code:** HC61621

**FIGURE 22** The locations of bonds and unshared electrons are shown for molecules of (a) ammonia and (b) water. Although unshared electrons occupy space around the central atoms, the shapes of the molecules depend only on the position of the molecules' atoms, as clearly shown by the ball-and-stick models.

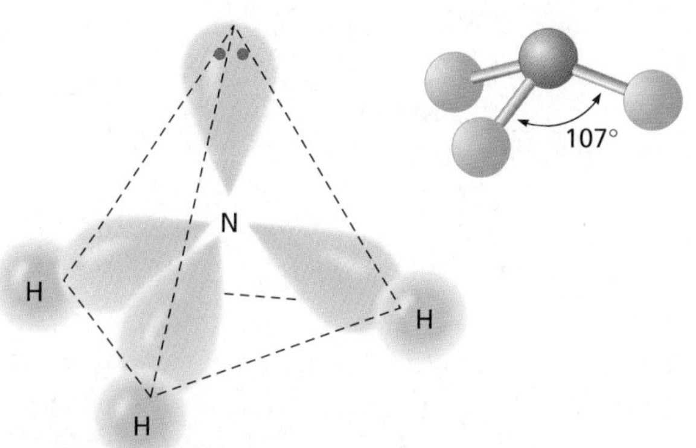


**(a)** Ammonia, $NH_3$

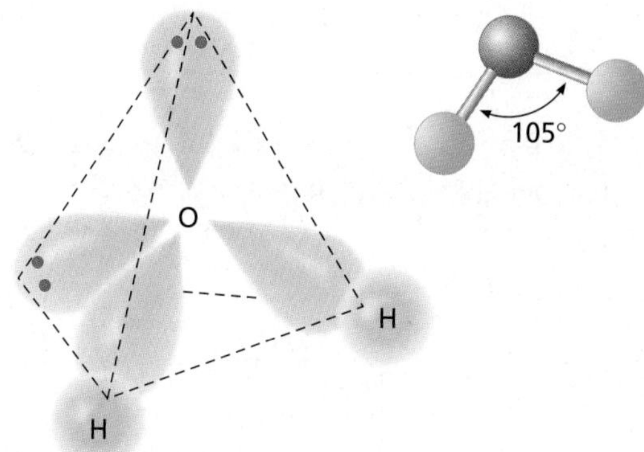


**(b)** Water, $H_2O$

In **Figure 22b,** note that the bond angles in ammonia and water are somewhat less than the 109.5° bond angles of a perfectly tetrahedral molecule. These angles are smaller because the unshared electron pairs repel electrons more strongly than do bonding electron pairs.

**Table 5** also includes an example of an $AB_2E$ type molecule. This type of molecule results when a central atom forms two bonds and retains one unshared electron pair.

Finally, in VSEPR theory, double and triple bonds are treated in the same way as single bonds. And polyatomic ions are treated similarly to molecules. (Remember to consider *all* of the electron pairs present in any ion or molecule.) Thus, Lewis structures and **Table 5** can be used together to predict the shapes of polyatomic ions as well as molecules with double or triple bonds.

**TABLE 5 *VSEPR Theory and Molecular Geometry***

| | Molecular shape | Atoms bonded to central atom | Lone pairs of electrons | Type of molecule | Formula example | Lewis structure |
|---|---|---|---|---|---|---|
| Linear | | 2 | 0 | $AB_2$ | $BeF_2$ | :F–Be–F: |
| Trigonal-planar | | 3 | 0 | $AB_3$ | $BF_3$ | :F–B(–F:)–F: |
| Bent or Angular | | 2 | 1 | $AB_2E$ | ONF | O=N–F: |
| Tetrahedral | | 4 | 0 | $AB_4$ | $CH_4$ | H–C(H)(H)–H |
| Trigonal-pyramidal | | 3 | 1 | $AB_3E$ | $NH_3$ | :N(H)(H)H |
| Bent or Angular | | 2 | 2 | $AB_2E_2$ | $H_2O$ | H–:O:–H |
| Trigonal-bipyramidal | 90°, 120° | 5 | 0 | $AB_5$ | $PCl_5$ | :Cl–P(Cl)(Cl)(Cl)Cl: |
| Octahedral | 90°, 90° | 6 | 0 | $AB_6$ | $SF_6$ | S(:F:)₆ |

SAMPLE PROBLEM F

**a. Use VSEPR theory to predict the shape of a molecule of carbon dioxide, $CO_2$.**
**b. Use VSEPR theory to predict the shape of a chlorate ion, $ClO_3^-$.**

**SOLUTION**

**a.** The Lewis structure of carbon dioxide shows two carbon-oxygen double bonds and no unshared electron pairs on the carbon atom. To simplify the molecule's Lewis structure, we represent the covalent bonds with lines instead of dots.

$$\ddot{O}=C=\ddot{O}$$

This is an $AB_2$ molecule, which is linear.

**b.** The Lewis structure of a chlorate ion shows three oxygen atoms and an unshared pair of electrons surrounding a central chlorine atom. Again, lines are used to represent the covalent bonds.

$$\left[ :\ddot{O} \; :\ddot{O}: \; \ddot{O}: \text{ bonded to } \ddot{Cl} \right]^-$$

The chlorate ion is an $AB_3E$ type. It has trigonal-pyramidal geometry, with the three oxygen atoms at the base of the pyramid and the chlorine atom at the top.

**PRACTICE**

*Answers in Appendix E*

1. Use VSEPR theory to predict the molecular geometries of the molecules whose Lewis structures are given below.

   **a.** $:\ddot{F}-\ddot{S}-\ddot{F}:$   **b.** $:\ddot{Cl}-\ddot{P}(-:\ddot{Cl}:)-\ddot{Cl}:$

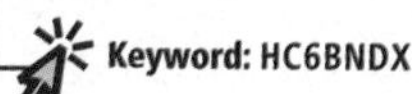

Go to **go.hrw.com** for more practice problems that ask you to use VSEPR theory.

**Keyword: HC6BNDX**

## Hybridization

VSEPR theory is useful for explaining the shapes of molecules. However, it does not reveal the relationship between a molecule's geometry and the orbitals occupied by its bonding electrons. To explain how the orbitals of an atom become rearranged when the atom forms covalent bonds, a different model is used. This model is called **hybridization,** *which is the mixing of two or more atomic orbitals of similar energies on the same atom to produce new hybrid atomic orbitals of equal energies.*

Methane, $CH_4$, provides a good example of how hybridization is used to explain the geometry of molecular orbitals. The orbital notation for a carbon atom shows that it has four valence electrons, two in the $2s$ orbital and two in $2p$ orbitals.

$$C \quad \underset{1s}{\uparrow\downarrow} \; \underset{2s}{\uparrow\downarrow} \; \underbrace{\underline{\uparrow} \; \underline{\uparrow} \; \underline{\;\;}}_{2p}$$

We know from experiments that a methane molecule has tetrahedral geometry. How does carbon form four equivalent, tetrahedrally arranged covalent bonds by orbital overlap with four other atoms?

Two of carbon's valence electrons occupy the 2*s* orbital, and two occupy the 2*p* orbitals. Recall that the 2*s* orbital and the 2*p* orbitals have different shapes. To achieve four equivalent bonds, carbon's 2*s* and three 2*p* orbitals *hybridize* to form four new, identical orbitals called $sp^3$ orbitals. The superscript 3 indicates that three *p* orbitals were included in the hybridization; the superscript 1 on the *s* is understood. The $sp^3$ orbitals all have the same energy, which is greater than that of the 2*s* orbital but less than that of the 2*p* orbitals, as shown in **Figure 23.**

**FIGURE 23** The $sp^3$ hybridization of carbon's outer orbitals combines one *s* and three *p* orbitals to form four $sp^3$ hybrid orbitals. Whenever hybridization occurs, the resulting hybrid orbitals are at an energy level between the levels of the orbitals that have combined.

Energy

↑ ↑ _ 2*p*

↑↓ 2*s*

↑↓ 1*s*

Hybridization

↑ ↑ ↑ ↑ $sp^3$

↑↓ 1*s*

Carbon's orbitals before hybridization

Carbon's orbitals after $sp^3$ hybridization

**Hybrid orbitals** *are orbitals of equal energy produced by the combination of two or more orbitals on the same atom.* The number of hybrid orbitals produced equals the number of orbitals that have combined. Bonding with carbon $sp^3$ orbitals is illustrated in **Figure 24a** for a molecule of methane.

Hybridization also explains the bonding and geometry of many molecules formed by Group 15 and 16 elements. The $sp^3$ hybridization of a nitrogen atom ([He]$2s^2 2p^3$) yields four hybrid orbitals—one orbital containing a pair of electrons and three orbitals that each contain an unpaired electron. Each unpaired electron is capable of forming a single bond, as shown for ammonia in **Figure 24b.** Similarly, two of the four $sp^3$ hybrid orbitals on an oxygen atom ([He]$2s^2 2p^4$) are occupied by two electron pairs and two are occupied by unpaired electrons. Each unpaired electron can form a single bond, as shown for water in **Figure 24c.**

**FIGURE 24** Bonds formed by the overlap of the 1*s* orbitals of hydrogen atoms and the $sp^3$ orbitals of (a) carbon, (b) nitrogen, and (c) oxygen. For the sake of clarity, only the hybrid orbitals of the central atoms are shown.

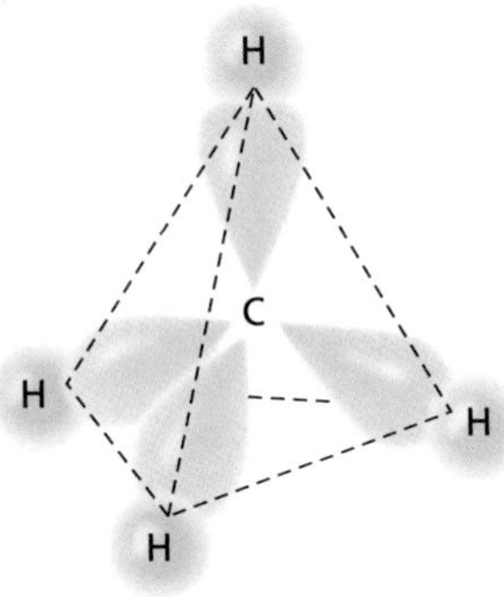


**(a)** Methane, $CH_4$

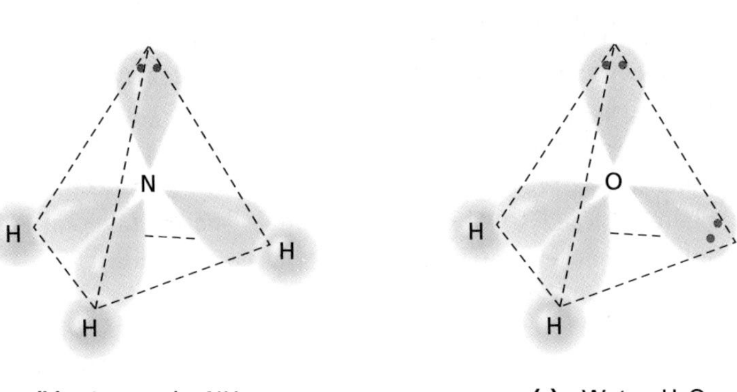


**(b)** Ammonia, $NH_3$

**(c)** Water, $H_2O$

**TABLE 6 Geometry of Hybrid Orbitals**

| Atomic orbitals | Type of hybridization | Number of hybrid orbitals | Geometry |
|---|---|---|---|
| *s*, *p* | *sp* | 2 | Linear (180°) |
| *s*, *p*, *p* | $sp^2$ | 3 | Trigonal-planar (120°) |
| *s*, *p*, *p*, *p* | $sp^3$ | 4 | Tetrahedral (109.5°) |

The linear geometry of molecules such as beryllium fluoride, $BeF_2$, (see **Table 5**) is made possible by hybridization involving the *s* orbital and one available empty *p* orbital to yield *sp* hybrid orbitals. The trigonal-planar geometry of molecules such as boron fluoride, $BF_3$, is made possible by hybridization involving the *s* orbital, one singly occupied *p* orbital, and one empty *p* orbital to yield $sp^2$ hybrid orbitals. The geometries of *sp*, $sp^2$, and $sp^3$ hybrid orbitals are summarized in **Table 6.**

## Intermolecular Forces

As a liquid is heated, the kinetic energy of its particles increases. At the boiling point, the energy is sufficient to overcome the force of attraction between the liquid's particles. The particles pull away from each other and enter the gas phase. Boiling point is therefore a good measure of the force of attraction between particles of a liquid. The higher the boiling point, the stronger the forces between particles.

The forces of attraction between molecules are known as *intermolecular forces.* Intermolecular forces vary in strength but are generally weaker than bonds that join atoms in molecules, ions in ionic compounds, or metal atoms in solid metals. Compare the boiling points of the metals and ionic compounds in **Table 7** on the next page with those of the molecular substances listed. Note that the values for ionic compounds and metals are much higher than those for molecular substances.

**TABLE 7 Boiling Points and Bonding Types**

| Bonding type | Substance | bp (1 atm, °C) |
|---|---|---|
| Nonpolar-covalent (molecular) | $H_2$ | −253 |
| | $O_2$ | −183 |
| | $Cl_2$ | −34 |
| | $Br_2$ | 59 |
| | $CH_4$ | −164 |
| | $CCl_4$ | 77 |
| | $C_6H_6$ | 80 |
| Polar-covalent (molecular) | $PH_3$ | −88 |
| | $NH_3$ | −33 |
| | $H_2S$ | −61 |
| | $H_2O$ | 100 |
| | HF | 20 |
| | HCl | −85 |
| | ICl | 97 |
| Ionic | NaCl | 1413 |
| | $MgF_2$ | 2239 |
| Metallic | Cu | 2567 |
| | Fe | 2750 |
| | W | 5660 |

## Molecular Polarity and Dipole-Dipole Forces

The strongest intermolecular forces exist between polar molecules. Polar molecules act as tiny dipoles because of their uneven charge distribution. *A* **dipole** *is created by equal but opposite charges that are separated by a short distance.* The direction of a dipole is from the dipole's positive pole to its negative pole. A dipole is represented by an arrow with a head pointing toward the negative pole and a crossed tail situated at the positive pole. The dipole created by a hydrogen chloride molecule, which has its negative end at the more electronegative chlorine atom, is indicated as follows.

$$\overset{+\!\!\longrightarrow}{\text{H—Cl}}$$

The negative region in one polar molecule attracts the positive region in adjacent molecules, and so on throughout a liquid or solid. The forces of attraction between polar molecules are known as *dipole-dipole forces.* These forces are short-range forces, acting only between nearby molecules. The effect of dipole-dipole forces is reflected, for example, by the significant difference between the boiling points of iodine chloride, I—Cl, and bromine, Br—Br. The boiling point of polar iodine chloride is 97°C, whereas that of nonpolar bromine is only 59°C. The dipole-dipole forces responsible for the relatively high boiling point of ICl are illustrated schematically in **Figure 25.**

### CAREERS in Chemistry

**Computational Chemist**

Computational chemistry is the study of molecules, their properties, and the interaction between molecules using mathematical equations that are based on the laws of quantum mechanics and which describe the motion of the electrons. Today, widely-available software packages exist that allow chemists to solve these equations for molecules under study.

Computational chemists combine their expertise in mathematics, their computer skills, and their love of chemistry. Computational chemistry has been used in industry to aid in the discovery of new pharmaceutical drugs and of new catalysts. Computational chemists are employed in all areas of chemistry and work closely with experimental chemists.

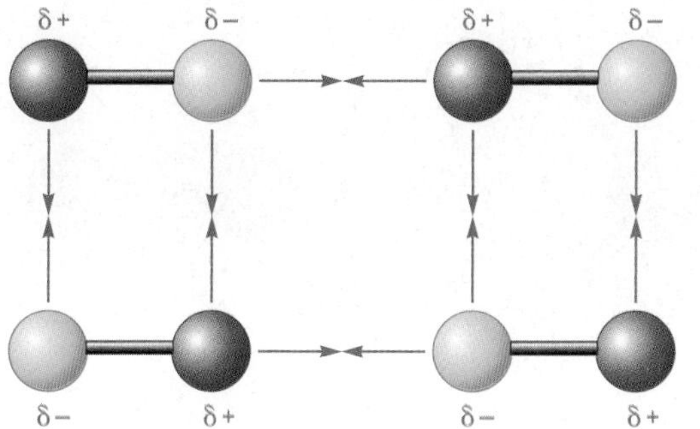


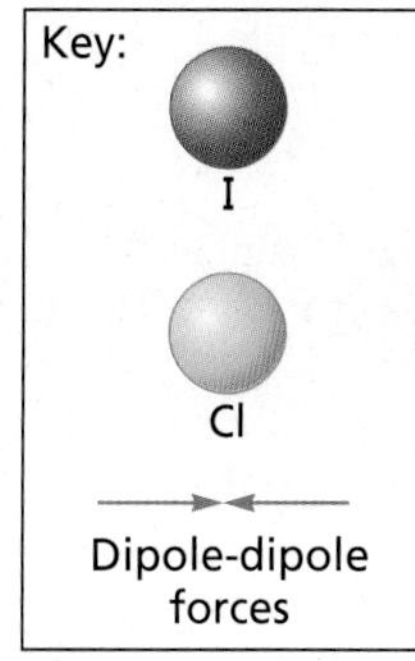


**FIGURE 25** Ball-and-stick models illustrate the dipole-dipole forces between molecules of iodine chloride, ICl. In each molecule, the highly electronegative chlorine atom has a partial negative charge, leaving each iodine atom with a partial positive charge. Consequently, the negative and positive ends of neighboring molecules attract each other.

The polarity of diatomic molecules such as ICl is determined by just one bond. For molecules containing more than two atoms, molecular polarity depends on both the polarity and the orientation of each bond. A molecule of water, for example, has two hydrogen-oxygen bonds in which the more-electronegative oxygen atom is the negative pole of each bond. Because the molecule is bent, the polarities of these two bonds combine to make the molecule highly polar, as shown in **Figure 26.** An ammonia molecule is also highly polar because the dipoles of the three nitrogen-hydrogen bonds are additive, combining to create a net molecular dipole. In some molecules, individual bond dipoles cancel one another, causing the resulting molecular polarity to be zero. Carbon dioxide and carbon tetrachloride are molecules of this type.

A polar molecule can *induce* a dipole in a nonpolar molecule by temporarily attracting its electrons. The result is a short-range intermolecular force that is somewhat weaker than the dipole-dipole force. The force of an induced dipole accounts for the solubility of nonpolar $O_2$ in water. The positive pole of a water molecule attracts the outer electrons

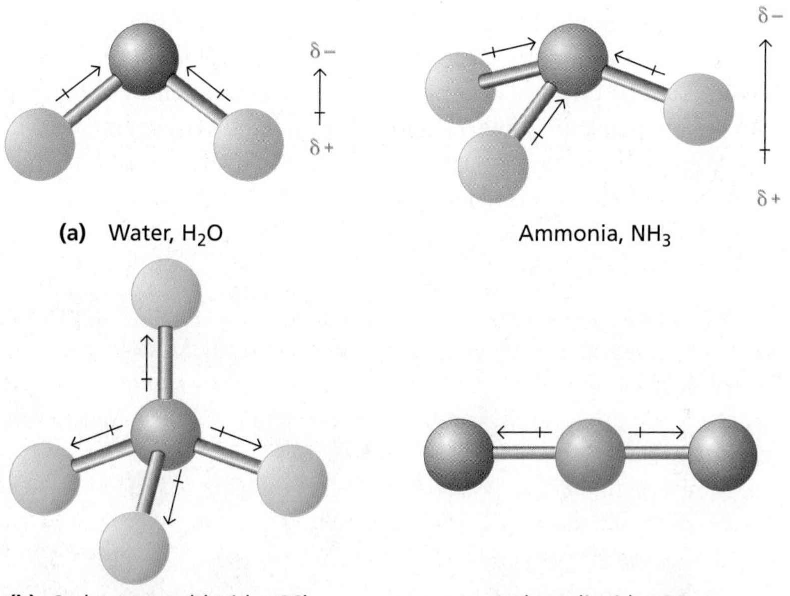


**FIGURE 26** (a) The bond polarities in a water or an ammonia molecule are additive, causing the molecule as a whole to be polar. (b) In molecules of carbon tetrachloride and carbon dioxide, the bond polarities extend equally and symmetrically in different directions, canceling each other's effect and causing each molecule as a whole to be nonpolar.

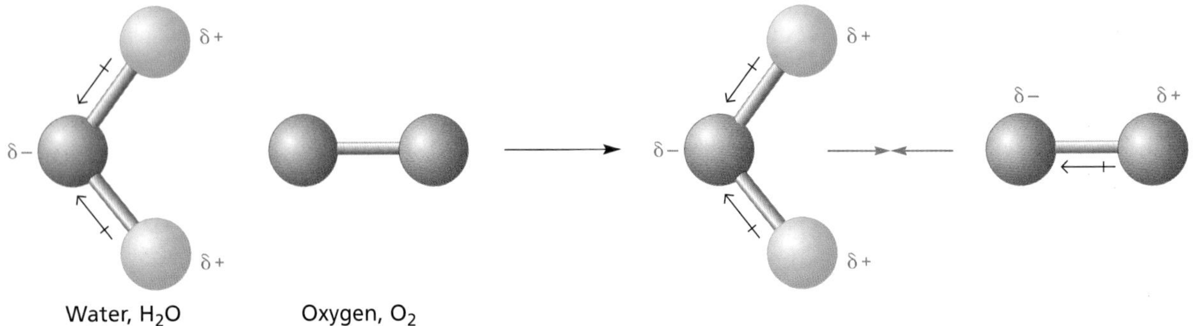


**FIGURE 27** Dipole-induced dipole interaction. The positive pole of a water molecule causes a temporary change in the electron distribution of an oxygen molecule. The negative pole induced in the oxygen molecule is then attracted to the positive pole of the water molecule.

of an adjacent oxygen molecule. The oxygen molecule, then, has an induced negative pole on the side toward the water molecule and an induced positive pole on the opposite side. The result is an attraction to the water molecule, as shown in **Figure 27.**

## Hydrogen Bonding

Some hydrogen-containing compounds, such as hydrogen fluoride (HF), water ($H_2O$), and ammonia ($NH_3$), have unusually high boiling points. This is explained by the presence of a particularly strong type of dipole-dipole force. In compounds containing H−F, H−O, or H−N bonds, the large electronegativity differences between hydrogen atoms and fluorine, oxygen, or nitrogen atoms make the bonds connecting them highly polar. This gives the hydrogen atom a positive charge that is almost half as large as that of a proton. Moreover, the small size of the hydrogen atom allows the atom to come very close to an unshared pair of electrons on an adjacent molecule. *The intermolecular force in which a hydrogen atom that is bonded to a highly electronegative atom is attracted to an unshared pair of electrons of an electronegative atom in a nearby molecule is known as* **hydrogen bonding.**

SCILINKS.
www.scilinks.org
**Topic:** Hydrogen Bonding
**Code:** HC60777

Hydrogen bonds are usually represented by dotted lines connecting the hydrogen-bonded hydrogen to the unshared electron pair of the electronegative atom to which it is attracted, as illustrated for water in **Figure 28.** The effect of hydrogen bonding can be seen by comparing the boiling points in **Table 7.** Look at phosphine, $PH_3$, compared with hydrogen-bonded ammonia, $NH_3$. How does hydrogen sulfide, $H_2S$, compare with hydrogen-bonded water, $H_2O$?

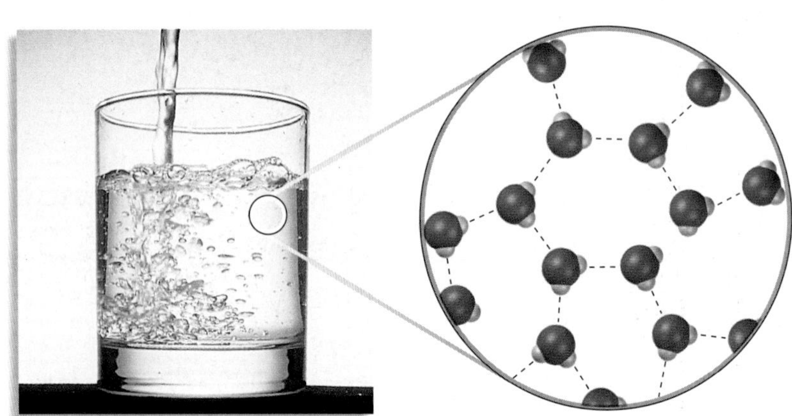

**FIGURE 28** Space-filling models illustrate hydrogen bonding between water molecules. The dotted lines indicate the attraction between electronegative oxygen atoms and electropositive hydrogen atoms of neighboring molecules.

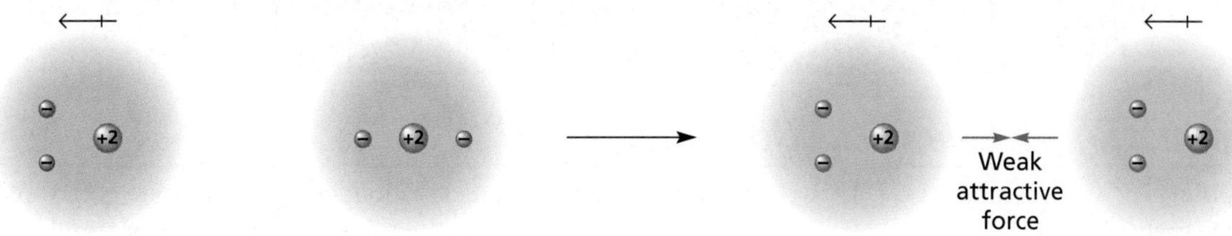


**FIGURE 29** When an instantaneous, temporary dipole develops in a helium atom, it induces a dipole in a neighboring atom.

## London Dispersion Forces

Even noble-gas atoms and molecules that are nonpolar experience a weak intermolecular attraction. In any atom or molecule—polar or nonpolar—the electrons are in continuous motion. As a result, at any instant the electron distribution may be slightly uneven. The momentary, uneven charge creates a positive pole in one part of the atom or molecule and a negative pole in another. This temporary dipole can then induce a dipole in an adjacent atom or molecule. The two are held together for an instant by the weak attraction between the temporary dipoles, as illustrated in **Figure 29.** *The intermolecular attractions resulting from the constant motion of electrons and the creation of instantaneous dipoles are called* **London dispersion forces,** after Fritz London, who first proposed their existence in 1930.

London forces act between all atoms and molecules. But they are the *only* intermolecular forces acting among noble-gas atoms and nonpolar molecules. This fact is reflected in the low boiling points of the noble gases and nonpolar molecular compounds listed in **Table 7.** Because London forces are dependent on the motion of electrons, their strength increases with the number of electrons in the interacting atoms or molecules. In other words, London forces increase with increasing atomic or molar mass. This trend can be seen by comparing the boiling points of the gases helium, He, and argon, Ar; hydrogen, $H_2$, and oxygen, $O_2$; and chlorine, $Cl_2$, and bromine, $Br_2$.

## SECTION REVIEW

1. What two theories can be used to predict molecular geometry?
2. Draw the Lewis structure and predict the molecular geometry of the following molecules:
   **a.** $SO_2$ **b.** $CI_4$ **c.** $BCl_3$
3. What factors affect the geometry of a molecule?
4. Explain what is meant by $sp^3$ hybridization.
5. What type of intermolecular force contributes to the high boiling point of water? Explain.

**Critical Thinking**

6. **INFERRING RELATIONSHIPS** What experimental property directly correlates with the strength of the intermolecular forces? Briefly explain your answer.

# CHAPTER HIGHLIGHTS

## Introduction to Chemical Bonding

**Vocabulary**

chemical bond
ionic bonding
covalent bonding
nonpolar-covalent bond
polar
polar-covalent bond

- Most atoms are chemically bonded to other atoms. The three major types of chemical bonding are ionic, covalent, and metallic.
- In general, atoms of metals bond ionically with atoms of nonmetals, atoms of metals bond metallically with each other, and atoms of nonmetals bond covalently with each other.

## Covalent Bonding and Molecular Compounds

**Vocabulary**

molecule
molecular compound
chemical formula
molecular formula
bond energy
electron-dot notation
Lewis structure
structural formula
single bond
multiple bond
resonance

- Atoms in molecules are joined by covalent bonds. In a covalent bond, two atoms share one or more pairs of electrons.
- The octet rule states that many chemical compounds tend to form bonds so that each atom shares or has eight electrons in its highest occupied energy level.
- Bonding within many molecules and ions can be indicated by a Lewis structure. Molecules or ions that cannot be correctly represented by a single Lewis structure are represented by resonance structures.

## Ionic Bonding and Ionic Compounds

**Vocabulary**

ionic compound
formula unit
lattice energy
polyatomic ion

- An ionic compound is a three-dimensional network of positive and negative ions mutually attracted to one another.
- Ionic compounds tend to be harder and more brittle and to have higher boiling points than materials containing only covalently bonded atoms.

## Metallic Bonding

**Vocabulary**

metallic bonding
malleability
ductility

- The "electron sea" formed in metallic bonding gives metals their properties of high electrical and thermal conductivity, malleability, ductility, and luster.

## Molecular Geometry

**Vocabulary**

VSEPR theory
hybridization
hybrid orbitals
dipole
hydrogen bonding
London dispersion forces

- VSEPR theory is used to predict the shapes of molecules based on the fact that electron pairs strongly repel each other.
- Hybridization theory is used to predict the shapes of molecules based on the fact that orbitals within an atom can mix to form orbitals of equal energy.
- Intermolecular forces include dipole-dipole forces and London dispersion forces. Hydrogen bonding is a special case of dipole-dipole forces.

# CHAPTER REVIEW

## *Introduction to Chemical Bonding*

### SECTION 1 REVIEW

1. What is a chemical bond?
2. Identify and define the three major types of chemical bonding.
3. What is the relationship between electronegativity and the ionic character of a chemical bond?
4. a. What is the meaning of the term polar, as applied to chemical bonding?
   b. Distinguish between polar-covalent and nonpolar-covalent bonds.
5. In general, what determines whether atoms will form chemical bonds?

### PRACTICE PROBLEMS

6. Determine the electronegativity difference, the probable bond type, and the more-electronegative atom with respect to bonds formed between the following pairs of atoms. (Hint: See Sample Problem A.)
   a. H and I
   b. S and O
   c. K and Br
   d. Si and Cl
   e. K and Cl
   f. Se and S
   g. C and H
7. List the bonding pairs described in item 6 in order of increasing covalent character.
8. Use orbital notation to illustrate the bonding in each of the following molecules:
   a. chlorine, $Cl_2$
   b. oxygen, $O_2$
   c. hydrogen fluoride, HF
9. The lattice energy of sodium chloride, NaCl, is –787.5 kJ/mol. The lattice energy of potassium chloride, KCl, is –715 kJ/mol. In which compound is the bonding between ions stronger? Why?

## *Covalent Bonding and Molecular Compounds*

### SECTION 2 REVIEW

10. What is a molecule?
11. a. What determines bond length?
    b. In general, how are bond energies and bond lengths related?
12. Describe the general location of the electrons in a covalent bond.
13. As applied to covalent bonding, what is meant by an unshared or lone pair of electrons?
14. Describe the octet rule in terms of noble-gas configurations and potential energy.
15. Determine the number of valence electrons in an atom of each of the following elements:
    a. H
    b. F
    c. Mg
    d. O
    e. Al
    f. N
    g. C
16. When drawing Lewis structures, which atom is usually the central atom?
17. Distinguish between single, double, and triple covalent bonds by defining each and providing an illustration of each type.
18. In writing Lewis structures, how is the need for multiple bonds generally determined?

### PRACTICE PROBLEMS

19. Use electron-dot notation to illustrate the number of valence electrons present in one atom of each of the following elements. (Hint: See Sample Problem B.)
    a. Li
    b. Ca
    c. Cl
    d. O
    e. C
    f. P
    g. Al
    h. S

**20.** Use electron-dot structures to demonstrate the formation of ionic compounds involving the following elements:
a. Na and S
b. Ca and O
c. Al and S

**21.** Draw Lewis structures for each of the following molecules. (Hint: See Sample Problem D.)
a. contains one C and four F atoms
b. contains two H and one Se atom
c. contains one N and three I atoms
d. contains one Si and four Br atoms
e. contains one C, one Cl, and three H atoms

**22.** Determine the type of hybrid orbitals formed by the boron atom in a molecule of boron fluoride, $BF_3$.

**23.** Draw Lewis structures for each of the following molecules. Show resonance structures, if they exist.
a. $O_2$
b. $N_2$
c. CO
d. $SO_2$

**24.** Draw Lewis structures for each of the following polyatomic ions. Show resonance structures, if they exist.
a. $OH^-$
b. $H_3C_2O_2^-$
c. $BrO_3^-$

## *Ionic Bonding and Ionic Compounds*

### SECTION 3 REVIEW

**25.** a. What is an ionic compound?
b. In what form do most ionic compounds occur?

**26.** a. What is a formula unit?
b. What are the components of one formula unit of $CaF_2$?

**27.** a. What is lattice energy?
b. In general, what is the relationship between lattice energy and the strength of ionic bonding?

**28.** a. In general, how do ionic and molecular compounds compare in terms of melting points, boiling points, and ease of vaporization?
b. What accounts for the observed differences in the properties of ionic and molecular compounds?
c. Cite three physical properties of ionic compounds.

**29.** a. What is a polyatomic ion?
b. Give two examples of polyatomic ions.
c. In what form do such ions often occur in nature?

## *Metallic Bonding*

### SECTION 4 REVIEW

**30.** a. How do the properties of metals differ from those of both ionic and molecular compounds?
b. What specific property of metals accounts for their unusual electrical conductivity?

**31.** What properties of metals contribute to their tendency to form metallic bonds?

**32.** a. What is metallic bonding?
b. How can the strength of metallic bonding be measured?

## *Molecular Geometry*

### SECTION 5 REVIEW

**33.** a. How is the VSEPR theory used to classify molecules?
b. What molecular geometry would be expected for $F_2$ and HF?

**34.** According to the VSEPR theory, what molecular geometries are associated with the following types of molecules?
a. $AB_2$
b. $AB_3$
c. $AB_4$
d. $AB_5$
e. $AB_6$

**35.** Describe the role of each of the following in predicting molecular geometries:
a. unshared electron pairs
b. double bonds

**36.** a. What are hybrid orbitals?
b. What determines the number of hybrid orbitals produced by the hybridization of an atom?

**37.** a. What are intermolecular forces?
b. In general, how do these forces compare in strength with those in ionic and metallic bonding?
c. What types of molecules have the strongest intermolecular forces?

**38.** What is the relationship between electronegativity and the polarity of a chemical bond?

**39.** a. What are dipole-dipole forces?
b. What determines the polarity of a molecule?

**40.** a. What is meant by an induced dipole?
b. What is the everyday importance of this type of intermolecular force?

**41.** a. What is hydrogen bonding?
b. What accounts for its extraordinary strength?

**42.** What are London dispersion forces?

## PRACTICE PROBLEMS

**43.** According to the VSEPR theory, what molecular geometries are associated with the following types of molecules?
a. $AB_3E$
b. $AB_2E_2$
c. $AB_2E$

**44.** Use hybridization to explain the bonding in methane, $CH_4$.

**45.** For each of the following polar molecules, indicate the direction of the resulting dipole:
a. H–F
b. H–Cl
c. H–Br
d. H–I

**46.** Determine whether each of the following bonds would be polar or nonpolar:
a. H–H
b. H–O
c. H–F
d. Br–Br
e. H–Cl
f. H–N

**47.** On the basis of individual bond polarity and orientation, determine whether each of the following molecules would be polar or nonpolar:
a. $H_2O$
b. $I_2$
c. $CF_4$
d. $NH_3$
e. $CO_2$

**48.** Draw a Lewis structure for each of the following molecules, and then use the VSEPR theory to predict the molecular geometry of each:
a. $SCl_2$
b. $PI_3$
c. $Cl_2O$
d. $NH_2Cl$
e. $SiCl_3Br$
f. ONCl

**49.** Draw a Lewis structure for each of the following polyatomic ions, and then use VSEPR theory to determine the geometry of each:
a. $NO_3^-$
b. $NH_4^+$
c. $SO_4^{2-}$
d. $ClO_2^-$

## MIXED REVIEW

**50.** Arrange the following pairs from strongest to weakest attraction:
a. polar molecule and polar molecule
b. nonpolar molecule and nonpolar molecule
c. polar molecule and ion
d. ion and ion

**51.** Determine the geometry of the following molecules:
a. $CCl_4$
b. $BeCl_2$
c. $PH_3$

**52.** What types of atoms tend to form the following types of bonding?
a. ionic
b. covalent
c. metallic

**53.** What happens to the energy level and stability of two bonded atoms when they are separated and become individual atoms?

**54.** Draw the three resonance structures for sulfur trioxide, $SO_3$.

**55.** a. How do ionic and covalent bonding differ?
b. How does an ionic compound differ from a molecular compound?
c. How does an ionic compound differ from a metal?

**56.** Write the electron-dot notation for each of the following elements:
a. He
b. Cl
c. O
d. P
e. B

**57.** Write the structural formula for methanol, $CH_3OH$.

**58.** How many $K^+$ and $S^{2-}$ ions would be in one formula unit of the ionic compound formed by these ions?

**59.** Explain metallic bonding in terms of the sparsely populated outermost orbitals of metal atoms.

**60.** Explain the role of molecular geometry in determining molecular polarity.

**61.** How does the energy level of a hybrid orbital compare with the energy levels of the orbitals it was formed from?

**62.** Aluminum's enthalpy of vaporization is 284 kJ/mol. Beryllium's enthalpy of vaporization is 224 kJ/mol. In which element is the bonding stronger between atoms?

**63.** Determine the electronegativity difference, the probable bonding type, and the more-electronegative atom for each of the following pairs of atoms:
a. Zn and O
b. Br and I
c. S and Cl

**64.** Draw the Lewis structure for each of the following molecules:
a. $PCl_3$
b. $CCl_2F_2$
c. $CH_3NH_2$

**65.** Write the Lewis structure for $BeCl_2$. (Hint: Beryllium atoms do not follow the octet rule.)

**66.** Draw a Lewis structure for each of the following polyatomic ions and determine their geometries:
a. $NO_2^-$
b. $NO_3^-$
c. $NH_4^+$

**67.** Why do most atoms tend to chemically bonded to other atoms?

## CRITICAL THINKING

**68. Inferring Relationships** The length of a bond varies depending on the type of bond formed. Predict and compare the lengths of the carbon-carbon bonds in the following molecules. Explain your answer. (Hint: See Table 2.)

```
 H H           H H
 | |           | |
H-C-C-H      H-C=C-H      H-C≡C-H
 | |
 H H
```

$C_2H_6$ $C_2H_4$ $C_2H_2$

**69.** Why does F generally form covalent bonds with great polarity?

**70.** Explain what is wrong with the following Lewis structures, and then correct each one.

a. H–H–$\ddot{\text{S}}$:

b. H–C(=:O:)=Ö–H

c. :Cl: double-bonded (‖) to N, with N bonded to :Cl and Cl: (a. H–H–S̤̈:, b. H–C(=O)=O–H, c. Cl=N(–Cl)–Cl as drawn)

**71.** Ionic compounds tend to have higher boiling points than covalent substances do. Both ammonia, $NH_3$, and methane, $CH_4$, are covalent compounds, yet the boiling point of ammonia is 130°C higher than that of methane. What might account for this large difference?

## USING THE HANDBOOK

**72.** Figure 18 shows a model for a body-centered cubic crystal. Review the Properties tables for all of the metals in the *Elements Handbook*. What metals exist in body-centered cubic structures?

**73.** Group 14 of the *Elements Handbook* contains a discussion of semiconductors and the band theory of metals. How does this model explain the electrical conductivity of metals?

## RESEARCH & WRITING

**74.** Prepare a report on the work of Linus Pauling.
  a. Discuss his work on the nature of the chemical bond.
  b. Linus Pauling was an advocate of the use of vitamin C as a preventative for colds. Evaluate Pauling's claims. Determine if there is any scientific evidence that indicates whether vitamin C helps prevent colds.

**75.** Covalently bonded solids, such as silicon, an element used in computer components, are harder than pure metals. Research theories that explain the hardness of covalently bonded solids and their usefulness in the computer industry. Present your findings to the class.

**76.** Natural rubber consists of long chains of carbon and hydrogen atoms covalently bonded together. When Goodyear accidentally dropped a mixture of sulfur and rubber on a hot stove, the energy from the stove joined these chains together to make vulcanized rubber. Vulcan was the Roman god of fire. The carbon-hydrogen chains in vulcanized rubber are held together by two sulfur atoms that form covalent bonds between the chains. These covalent bonds are commonly called disulfide bridges. Explore other molecules that have such disulfide bridges. Present your findings to the class.

**77.** Searching for the perfect artificial sweetener—great taste with no Calories—has been the focus of chemical research for some time. Molecules such as sucralose, aspartamine, and saccharine owe their sweetness to their size and shape. One theory holds that any sweetener must have three sites that fit into the proper taste buds on the tongue. This theory is appropriately known as the "triangle theory." Research artificial sweeteners to develop a model to show how the triangle theory operates.

## ALTERNATIVE ASSESSMENT

**78.** Devise a set of criteria that will allow you to classify the following substances as ionic or nonionic: $CaCO_3$, Cu, $H_2O$, NaBr, and C (graphite). Show your criteria to your instructor.

**79.** **Performance Assessment** Identify 10 common substances in and around your home, and indicate whether you would expect these substances to contain ionic, covalent, or metallic bonds.

**Graphing Calculator**
**Classifying Bond Type**
Go to **go.hrw.com** for a graphing calculator exercise that asks you to classify bonding type based on electronegativities of atoms.

**Keyword:** HC6BNDX

# Types of Bonding in Solids

## OBJECTIVES

- ***Observe*** **the physical properties of different solids.**
- ***Relate*** **knowledge of these properties to the type of bonding in each solid.**
- ***Identify*** **the type of bonding in an unknown solid.**

## MATERIALS

- **beakers, 50 mL (6)**
- **Bunsen burner**
- **copper wire**
- **deionized water**
- **evaporating dishes or crucibles (6)**
- **graduated cylinder, 10 mL**
- **aluminum shot**
- **LED conductivity tester**
- **silicon dioxide (sand)**
- **sodium chloride (NaCl)**
- **spatula**
- **sucrose**
- **test tubes, small, with solid rubber stoppers (6)**
- **test-tube rack**
- **tongs**
- **unknown substance**
- **wire gauze, support stand, iron ring, and clay triangle**

## BACKGROUND

The purpose of this experiment is to relate certain properties of solids to the type of bonding the solids have. These observable properties depend on the type of bonding that holds the molecules, atoms, or ions together in each solid. Depending on the type of bonding, solids may be described as ionic, molecular, metallic, or covalent network solids. The properties to be studied are relative melting point, solubility in aqueous solution, and electrical conductivity.

## SAFETY

For review of safety, please see the **Safety in the Chemistry Laboratory** in the front of your book.

## PREPARATION

1. Make a data table in which to record the results of melting, water solubility, solid conductivity, aqueous solution conductivity, and type of bonding of each substance tested.

## PROCEDURE

1. Place 1 g samples of each substance into separate evaporating dishes.
2. Touch the electrodes of the conductivity tester to each solid. After each test, rinse with distilled water and carefully dry the electrodes. Note which substances conducted electricity.
3. Place one evaporating dish on a triangle, and heat with a Bunsen burner. As soon as a solid melts, remove the flame.
4. Repeat this procedure for every substance. Do not heat any substance for more than 5 min. There may be some substances that will not melt.

5. Note which substances melted and how long the substances took to melt.
6. Place five test tubes in the test-tube rack. Place 0.5 g of each solid into its own individual test tube. Add 5 mL of deionized water to each test tube. Stopper and shake each test tube in an attempt to dissolve the solid.
7. Note which substances dissolved in the water.
8. Place the solutions or mixtures into separate 50 mL beakers, and immerse the electrodes of the conductivity tester. Rinse the electrodes with the solvent (deionized water) before and after each test. Note which substances conduct electricity.

## CLEANUP AND DISPOSAL

9. Dispose of solids and solutions in containers designated by your teacher.
10. Clean all equipment and return it to its proper place.
11. Wash your hands thoroughly after cleaning up your area and equipment.

## ANALYSIS AND INTERPRETATION

1. **Analyzing Methods:** Why did you rinse the electrodes before each conductivity test?
2. **Analyzing Methods:** Why did you use deionized water in making the solutions?
3. **Organizing Data:** List the results that each type of bonding should show.

## CONCLUSIONS

1. **Inferring Conclusions:** What type of bonding describes each substance? Explain your reasoning.
2. **Inferring Conclusions:** Comparing the properties of your unknown solid with the properties of the known solids, determine the type of bonding present in your unknown solid.

## EXTENSIONS

1. **Evaluating Methods:** Is it possible, for a specific type of bonding, for these properties to vary from what was observed in this experiment? If so, give an example of such a variance.
2. **Applying Conclusions:** Think about diamond. What would you predict to be the results of this experiment performed on diamond, and what would you predict the bond type to be?

CHAPTER 7

# Chemical Formulas and Chemical Compounds

*Chemists use chemical names and formulas to describe the atomic composition of compounds.*

Chemicals and Pigments

# Chemical Names and Formulas

SECTION 1

C.3.2 Interpret the names and formulas for ionic and covalent compounds

## Objectives

- Explain the significance of a chemical formula.
- Determine the formula of an ionic compound formed between two given ions.
- Name an ionic compound given its formula.
- Using prefixes, name a binary molecular compound from its formula.
- Write the formula of a binary molecular compound given its name.

The total number of natural and synthetic chemical compounds runs in the millions. For some of these substances, certain common names remain in everyday use. For example, calcium carbonate is better known as limestone, and sodium chloride is usually referred to simply as table salt. And everyone recognizes dihydrogen monoxide by its popular name, water.

Unfortunately, common names usually give no information about chemical composition. To describe the atomic makeup of compounds, chemists use systematic methods for naming compounds and for writing chemical formulas. In this chapter, you will be introduced to some of the rules used to identify simple chemical compounds.

## Significance of a Chemical Formula

Recall that a chemical formula indicates the relative number of atoms of each kind in a chemical compound. For a molecular compound, the chemical formula reveals the number of atoms of each element contained in a single molecule of the compound, as shown below for the hydrocarbon octane. (*Hydrocarbons* are molecular compounds composed solely of carbon and hydrogen.)

$$C_8H_{18}$$

Subscript indicates that there are 8 carbon atoms in a molecule of octane.

Subscript indicates that there are 18 hydrogen atoms in a molecule of octane.

Unlike a molecular compound, an ionic compound consists of a lattice of positive and negative ions held together by mutual attraction. The chemical formula for an ionic compound represents one formula unit—the simplest ratio of the compound's positive ions (cations) and its negative ions (anions). The chemical formula for aluminum sulfate, an ionic compound consisting of aluminum cations and polyatomic sulfate anions, is written as shown on the next page.

SciLinks.
www.scilinks.org
**Topic:** Chemical Formulas
**Code:** HC60271

$Al_2(SO_4)_3$



Note how the parentheses are used. They surround the polyatomic anion to identify it as a unit. The subscript 3 refers to the entire unit. Notice also that there is no subscript written next to the symbol for sulfur. When there is no subscript written next to an atom's symbol, the value of the subscript is understood to be 1.

## Monatomic Ions

By gaining or losing electrons, many main-group elements form ions with noble-gas configurations. For example, Group 1 metals lose one electron to give 1+ cations, such as $Na^+$. Group 2 metals lose two electrons to give 2+ cations, such as $Mg^{2+}$. *Ions formed from a single atom are known as* **monatomic ions.** The nonmetals of Groups 15, 16, and 17 gain electrons to form anions. For example, in ionic compounds nitrogen forms the 3– anion, $N^{3-}$. The three added electrons plus the five outermost electrons in nitrogen atoms give a completed outermost octet. Similarly, the Group 16 elements oxygen and sulfur form 2– anions, and the Group 17 halogens form 1– anions.

Not all main-group elements readily form ions, however. Rather than gain or lose electrons, atoms of carbon and silicon form covalent bonds in which they share electrons with other atoms. Other elements tend to form ions that do not have noble-gas configurations. For instance, it is difficult for the Group 14 metals tin and lead to lose four electrons to achieve a noble-gas configuration. Instead, they tend to lose the two electrons in their outer *p* orbitals but retain the two electrons in their outer *s* orbitals to form 2+ cations. (Tin and lead can also form molecular compounds in which all four valence electrons are involved in covalent bonding.)

Elements from the *d*-block form 2+, 3+, or, in a few cases, 1+ or 4+ cations. Many *d*-block elements form two ions of different charges. For example, copper forms 1+ and 2+ cations. Iron and chromium each form 2+ cations as well as 3+ cations. And vanadium forms 2+, 3+, and 4+ cations.

**Examples of Cations**

$K^+$
Potassium cation

$Mg^{2+}$
Magnesium cation

### Naming Monatomic Ions

Monatomic cations are identified simply by the element's name, as illustrated by the examples at left. Naming monatomic anions is slightly more complicated. First, the ending of the element's name is dropped. Then the ending *-ide* is added to the root name, as illustrated by the examples at right.

The names and symbols of the common monatomic cations and anions are organized according to their charges in **Table 1.** The names of many of the ions in the table include Roman numerals. These numerals are part of the *Stock system* of naming chemical ions and elements. You will read more about the Stock system and other systems of naming chemicals later in this chapter.

**Examples of Anions**

| Element | Anion |
|---|---|
| F | $F^-$ |
| Fluor*ine* | Fluor*ide* anion |
| N | $N^{3-}$ |
| Nitr*ogen* | Nitr*ide* anion |

**TABLE 1 Some Common Monatomic Ions**

**Main-group elements**

| 1+ | | 2+ | | 3+ | | | |
|---|---|---|---|---|---|---|---|
| lithium | $Li^+$ | beryllium | $Be^{2+}$ | aluminum | $Al^{3+}$ | | |
| sodium | $Na^+$ | magnesium | $Mg^{2+}$ | | | | |
| potassium | $K^+$ | calcium | $Ca^{2+}$ | | | | |
| rubidium | $Rb^+$ | strontium | $Sr^{2+}$ | | | | |
| cesium | $Cs^+$ | barium | $Ba^{2+}$ | | | | |
| **1–** | | **2–** | | **3–** | | | |
| fluoride | $F^-$ | oxide | $O^{2-}$ | nitride | $N^{3-}$ | | |
| chloride | $Cl^-$ | sulfide | $S^{2-}$ | phosphide | $P^{3-}$ | | |
| bromide | $Br^-$ | | | | | | |
| iodide | $I^-$ | | | | | | |

***d*-Block elements and others with multiple ions**

| 1+ | | 2+ | | 3+ | | 4+ | |
|---|---|---|---|---|---|---|---|
| copper(I) | $Cu^+$ | vanadium(II) | $V^{2+}$ | vanadium(III) | $V^{3+}$ | vanadium(IV) | $V^{4+}$ |
| silver | $Ag^+$ | chromium(II) | $Cr^{2+}$ | chromium(III) | $Cr^{3+}$ | tin(IV) | $Sn^{4+}$ |
| | | manganese(II) | $Mn^{2+}$ | iron(III) | $Fe^{3+}$ | lead(IV) | $Pb^{4+}$ |
| | | iron(II) | $Fe^{2+}$ | cobalt(III) | $Co^{3+}$ | | |
| | | cobalt(II) | $Co^{2+}$ | | | | |
| | | nickel(II) | $Ni^{2+}$ | | | | |
| | | copper(II) | $Cu^{2+}$ | | | | |
| | | zinc | $Zn^{2+}$ | | | | |
| | | cadmium | $Cd^{2+}$ | | | | |
| | | tin(II) | $Sn^{2+}$ | | | | |
| | | mercury(II) | $Hg^{2+}$ | | | | |
| | | lead(II) | $Pb^{2+}$ | | | | |

## CAREERS in Chemistry

### Pharmacist

Pharmacists work in many areas of healthcare. Traditionally, they have dispensed medications in pharmacies. Today, pharmacists work with other health professionals to develop and implement customized drug treatment plans. They advise medical professionals on the side effects of and interactions between medicines. Increasingly, pharmacists are working in nontraditional settings, such as in managed-care companies, pharmaceutical companies, and governmental agencies. In these settings, pharmacists establish drug guidelines, conduct drug reviews, and assist in the research and development of new drugs.

# Binary Ionic Compounds

*Compounds composed of two elements are known as* **binary compounds.** In a binary ionic compound, the total numbers of positive charges and negative charges must be equal. Therefore, the formula for such a compound can be written given the identities of the compound's ions. For example, magnesium and bromine combine to form the ionic compound magnesium bromide. Magnesium, a Group 2 metal, forms the $Mg^{2+}$ cation. Note that the $^{2+}$ in $Mg^{2+}$ is written as a superscript. Bromine, a halogen, forms the $Br^-$ anion when combined with a metal. In each formula unit of magnesium bromide, two $Br^-$ anions are required to balance the 2+ charge of the $Mg^{2+}$ cation. The compound's formula must therefore indicate one $Mg^{2+}$ cation and two $Br^-$ anions. The symbol for the cation is written first.

*Ions combined:* $Mg^{2+}$, $Br^-$, $Br^-$ *Chemical formula:* $MgBr_2$

Note that the $_2$ in $Br_2$ is written as a subscript. The charges of the ions are not included in the formula. This is usually the case when writing formulas for binary ionic compounds.

As an aid to determining subscripts in formulas for ionic compounds, the positive and negative charges can be "crossed over." Crossing over is a method of balancing the charges between ions in an ionic compound. For example, the formula for the compound formed by the aluminum ion, $Al^{3+}$, and the oxide ion, $O^{2-}$, is determined as follows.

1. *Write the symbols for the ions side by side. Write the cation first.*

$$Al^{3+}\ O^{2-}$$

2. *Cross over the charges by using the absolute value of each ion's charge as the subscript for the other ion.*

$$Al_2^{3+}\ O_3^{2-}$$

3. *Check the subscripts and divide them by their largest common factor to give the smallest possible whole-number ratio of ions. Then write the formula.*

   Multiplying the charge by the subscript shows that the charge on two $Al^{3+}$ cations ($2 \times 3+ = 6+$) equals the charge on three $O^{2-}$ anions ($3 \times 2- = 6-$). The largest common factor of the subscripts is 1. The correct formula is therefore written as follows.

$$Al_2O_3$$

# Naming Binary Ionic Compounds

The **nomenclature,** *or naming system,* of binary ionic compounds involves combining the names of the compound's positive and negative ions. The name of the cation is given first, followed by the name of the anion. For most simple ionic compounds, the ratio of the ions is not indicated in the compound's name because it is understood based on the relative charges of the compound's ions. The naming of a simple binary ionic compound is illustrated below.

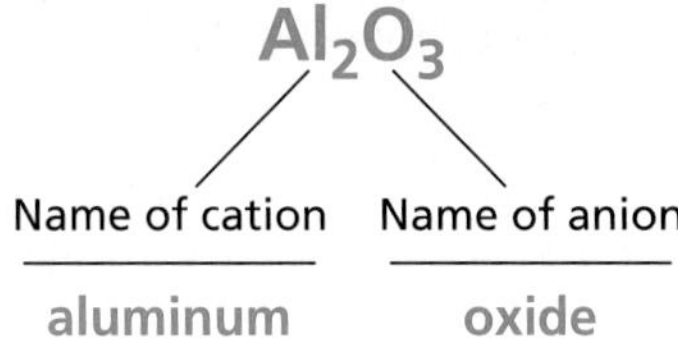


## SAMPLE PROBLEM A

**Write the formulas for the binary ionic compounds formed between the following elements:**
**a. zinc and iodine** **b. zinc and sulfur**

**SOLUTION** *Write the symbols for the ions side by side. Write the cation first.*

**a.** $Zn^{2+}$ $I^{-}$
**b.** $Zn^{2+}$ $S^{2-}$

*Cross over the charges to give subscripts.*

**a.** $Zn_1^{2+}$ $I_2^{-}$
**b.** $Zn_2^{2+}$ $S_2^{2-}$

*Check the subscripts and divide them by their largest common factor to give the smallest possible whole-number ratio of ions. Then write the formula.*

**a.** The subscripts are mathematically correct because they give equal total charges of $1 \times 2+ = 2+$ and $2 \times 1- = 2-$. The largest common factor of the subscripts is 1. The smallest possible whole-number ratio of ions in the compound is therefore 1:2. *The subscript 1 is not written,* so the formula is $ZnI_2$.

**b.** The subscripts are mathematically correct because they give equal total charges of $2 \times 2+ = 4+$ and $2 \times 2- = 4-$. The largest common factor of the subscripts is 2. The smallest whole-number ratio of ions in the compound is therefore 1:1. The correct formula is ZnS.

**PRACTICE** *Answers in Appendix E*

**1.** Write formulas for the binary ionic compounds formed between the following elements:
**a.** potassium and iodine
**b.** magnesium and chlorine
**c.** sodium and sulfur
**d.** aluminum and sulfur
**e.** aluminum and nitrogen

**2.** Name the binary ionic compounds indicated by the following formulas:
**a.** AgCl
**b.** ZnO
**c.** $CaBr_2$
**d.** $SrF_2$
**e.** BaO
**f.** $CaCl_2$

**extension**
Go to **go.hrw.com** for more practice problems that ask you to write formulas for binary ionic compounds.

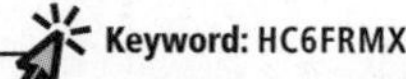
**Keyword: HC6FRMX**

## The Stock System of Nomenclature

Some elements, such as iron, form two or more cations with different charges. To distinguish the ions formed by such elements, scientists use the Stock system of nomenclature. This system uses a Roman numeral to indicate an ion's charge. The numeral is enclosed in parentheses and placed *immediately* after the metal name.

| $Fe^{2+}$ | $Fe^{3+}$ |
|---|---|
| iron(II) | iron(III) |

Names of metals that commonly form only one cation do *not* include a Roman numeral.

| $Na^{+}$ | $Ba^{2+}$ | $Al^{3+}$ |
|---|---|---|
| sodium | barium | aluminum |

There is no element that commonly forms more than one monatomic anion.

Naming a binary ionic compound according to the Stock system is illustrated below.

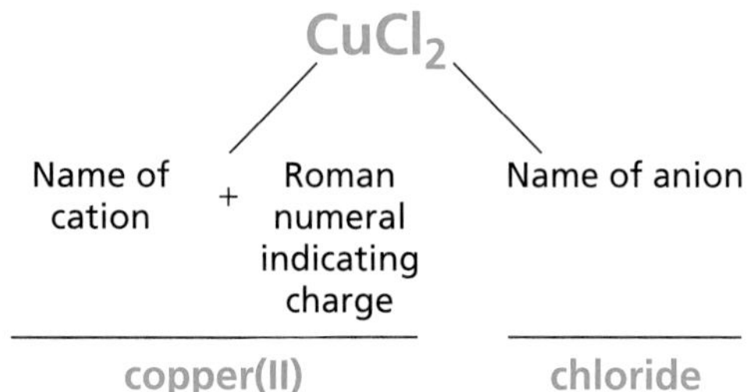

**FIGURE 1** Different cations of the same metal form different compounds even when they combine with the same anion. Compare (a) lead(IV) oxide, $PbO_2$, with (b) lead(II) oxide, PbO.

## SAMPLE PROBLEM B

**Write the formula and give the name for the compound formed by the ions $Cr^{3+}$ and $F^-$.**

**SOLUTION** *Write the symbols for the ions side by side. Write the cation first.*

$$Cr^{3+}\ F^-$$

*Cross over the charges to give subscripts.*

$$Cr_1^{3+}\ F_3^-$$

*Check the subscripts and write the formula.*
The subscripts are correct because they give charges of $1 \times 3+ = 3+$ and $3 \times 1- = 3-$. The largest common factor of the subscripts is 1, so the smallest whole-number ratio of the ions is 1:3. The formula is therefore $CrF_3$. As **Table 1** shows, chromium forms more than one ion. Therefore, the name of the 3+ chromium ion must be followed by a Roman numeral indicating its charge. The compound's name is chromium(III) fluoride.

**PRACTICE** *Answers in Appendix E*

1. Write the formula and give the name for the compounds formed between the following ions:
   a. $Cu^{2+}$ and $Br^-$
   b. $Fe^{2+}$ and $O^{2-}$
   c. $Pb^{2+}$ and $Cl^-$
   d. $Hg^{2+}$ and $S^{2-}$
   e. $Sn^{2+}$ and $F^-$
   f. $Fe^{3+}$ and $O^{2-}$
2. Give the names for the following compounds:
   a. CuO
   b. $CoF_3$
   c. $SnI_4$
   d. FeS

**extension**
Go to **go.hrw.com** for more practice problems that ask you to write formulas for ionic compounds.

Keyword: HC6FRMX

## Compounds Containing Polyatomic Ions

**Table 2** on the next page lists some common polyatomic ions. Most are negatively charged and most are **oxyanions**—*polyatomic ions that contain oxygen.* Some elements can combine with oxygen to form more than one type of oxyanion. For example, nitrogen can form $NO_3^-$ or $NO_2^-$. The name given a compound containing such an oxyanion depends on the number of oxygen atoms in the oxyanion. The name of the ion with the greater number of oxygen atoms ends in *-ate.* The name of the ion with the smaller number of oxygen atoms ends in *-ite.*

| $NO_2^-$ | $NO_3^-$ |
|---|---|
| nitrite | nitrate |

Sometimes, an element can form more than two types of oxyanions. In this case, an anion that has one fewer oxygen atom than the *-ite* anion

**TABLE 2 Some Polyatomic Ions**

| 1+ | | 2+ | | | |
|---|---|---|---|---|---|
| ammonium | $NH_4^+$ | dimercury* | $Hg_2^{2+}$ | | |
| | | | | | |
| | | | | | |
| | | | | | |
| | | | | | |
| **1−** | | **2−** | | **3−** | |
| acetate | $CH_3COO^-$ | carbonate | $CO_3^{2-}$ | arsenate | $AsO_4^{3-}$ |
| bromate | $BrO_3^-$ | chromate | $CrO_4^{2-}$ | phosphate | $PO_4^{3-}$ |
| chlorate | $ClO_3^-$ | dichromate | $Cr_2O_7^{2-}$ | | |
| chlorite | $ClO_2^-$ | hydrogen phosphate | $HPO_4^{2-}$ | | |
| cyanide | $CN^-$ | oxalate | $C_2O_4^{2-}$ | | |
| dihydrogen phosphate | $H_2PO_4^-$ | peroxide | $O_2^{2-}$ | | |
| hydrogen carbonate (bicarbonate) | $HCO_3^-$ | sulfate | $SO_4^{2-}$ | | |
| hydrogen sulfate | $HSO_4^-$ | sulfite | $SO_3^{2-}$ | | |
| hydroxide | $OH^-$ | | | | |
| hypochlorite | $ClO^-$ | | | | |
| nitrate | $NO_3^-$ | | | | |
| nitrite | $NO_2^-$ | | | | |
| perchlorate | $ClO_4^-$ | | | | |
| permanganate | $MnO_4^-$ | | | | |

*The mercury(I) cation exists as two $Hg^+$ ions joined together by a covalent bond and is written as $Hg_2^{2+}$.

has is given the prefix *hypo-*. An anion that has one more oxygen atom than the *-ate* anion has is given the prefix *per-*. This nomenclature is illustrated by the four oxyanions formed by chlorine.

| $ClO^-$ | $ClO_2^-$ | $ClO_3^-$ | $ClO_4^-$ |
|---|---|---|---|
| hypochlorite | chlorite | chlorate | perchlorate |

Compounds containing polyatomic ions are named in the same manner as binary ionic compounds. The name of the cation is given first, followed by the name of the anion. For example, the two compounds formed with silver by the nitrate and nitrite anions are named *silver nitrate,* $AgNO_3$, and *silver nitrite,* $AgNO_2$, respectively. When multiples of a polyatomic ion are present in a compound, the formula for the polyatomic ion is enclosed in parentheses, as shown on page 220 for aluminum sulfate, $Al_2(SO_4)_3$. The formula indicates that an aluminum sulfate formula unit has two aluminum cations and three sulfate anions.

**SAMPLE PROBLEM C**

**Write the formula for tin(IV) sulfate.**

**SOLUTION** *Write the symbols for the ions side by side. Write the cation first.*

$$Sn^{4+}\ SO_4^{2-}$$

*Cross over the charges to give subscripts. Add parentheses around the polyatomic ion if necessary.*

$$Sn_2^{4+}\ (SO_4)_4^{2-}$$

*Check the subscripts and write the formula.*
The total positive charge is $2 \times 4+ = 8+$. The total negative charge is $4 \times 2- = 8-$. The charges are equal. The largest common factor of the subscripts is 2, so the smallest whole-number ratio of ions in the compound is 1:2. The correct formula is therefore $Sn(SO_4)_2$.

**PRACTICE** *Answers in Appendix E*

1. Write formulas for the following ionic compounds:
   - **a.** sodium iodide
   - **b.** calcium chloride
   - **c.** potassium sulfide
   - **d.** lithium nitrate
   - **e.** copper(II) sulfate
   - **f.** sodium carbonate
   - **g.** calcium nitrite
   - **h.** potassium perchlorate

2. Give the names for the following compounds:
   - **a.** $Ag_2O$
   - **b.** $Ca(OH)_2$
   - **c.** $KClO_3$
   - **d.** $NH_4OH$
   - **e.** $Fe_2(CrO_4)_3$
   - **f.** $KClO$

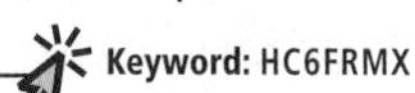


Go to **go.hrw.com** for more practice problems that ask you to name ionic compounds.

**Keyword: HC6FRMX**

## Naming Binary Molecular Compounds

Unlike ionic compounds, molecular compounds are composed of individual covalently bonded units, or molecules. Chemists use two nomenclature systems to name binary molecules. The newer system is the Stock system for naming molecular compounds, which requires an understanding of oxidation numbers. This system will be discussed in Section 2.

The old system of naming molecular compounds is based on the use of prefixes. For example, the molecular compound $CCl_4$ is named carbon *tetra*chloride. The prefix *tetra-* indicates that four chloride atoms are present in a single molecule of the compound. The two oxides of carbon, CO and $CO_2$, are named carbon *mon*oxide and carbon *di*oxide, respectively.

**TABLE 3 Numerical Prefixes**

| Number | Prefix |
|---|---|
| 1 | mono- |
| 2 | di- |
| 3 | tri- |
| 4 | tetra- |
| 5 | penta- |
| 6 | hexa- |
| 7 | hepta- |
| 8 | octa- |
| 9 | nona- |
| 10 | deca- |

In these names, the prefix *mon-* (from *mono-*) indicates one oxygen atom, and the prefix *di-* indicates two oxygen atoms. The prefixes used to specify the number of atoms in a molecule are listed in **Table 3.**

The rules for the prefix system of nomenclature of binary molecular compounds are as follows.

1. The element that has the smaller group number is usually given first. If both elements are in the same group, the element whose period number is greater is given first. The element is given a prefix only if it contributes more than one atom to a molecule of the compound.
2. The second element is named by combining (a) a prefix indicating the number of atoms contributed by the element, (b) the root of the name of the element, and (c) the ending *-ide*. With few exceptions, the ending *-ide* indicates that a compound contains only two elements.
3. The *o* or *a* at the end of a prefix is usually dropped when the word following the prefix begins with another vowel. For example, one would write *monoxide* and *pentoxide* instead of *mono-oxide* and *penta-oxide.*

The prefix system is illustrated below.

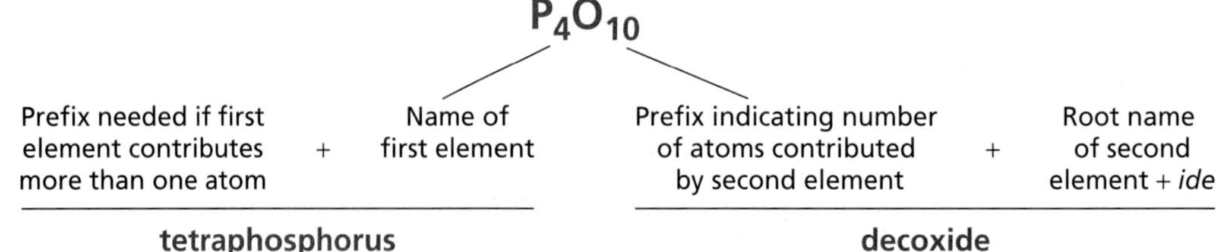


In general, the order of nonmetals in binary compound names and formulas is C, P, N, H, S, I, Br, Cl, O, and F.

**TABLE 4 Binary Compounds of Nitrogen and Oxygen**

| Formula | Prefix-system name |
|---|---|
| $N_2O$ | dinitrogen monoxide |
| NO | nitrogen monoxide |
| $NO_2$ | nitrogen dioxide |
| $N_2O_3$ | dinitrogen trioxide |
| $N_2O_4$ | dinitrogen tetroxide |
| $N_2O_5$ | dinitrogen pentoxide |

The prefix system is illustrated further in **Table 4,** which lists the names of the six oxides of nitrogen. Note the application of rule 1, for example, in the name *nitrogen dioxide* for $NO_2$. No prefix is needed with *nitrogen* because only one atom of nitrogen is present in a molecule of $NO_2$. On the other hand, according to rule 2, the prefix *di-* in *dioxide* is needed to indicate the presence of two atoms of oxygen. Take a moment to review the prefixes in the other names in **Table 4.**

## SAMPLE PROBLEM D

**a. Give the name for $As_2O_5$.**
**b. Write the formula for oxygen difluoride.**

**SOLUTION** a. A molecule of the compound contains two arsenic atoms, so the first word in the name is *diarsenic.* The five oxygen atoms are indicated by adding the prefix *pent-* to the word *oxide.* The complete name is *diarsenic pentoxide.*

b. The first symbol in the formula is that for oxygen. Oxygen is first in the name because it is less electronegative than fluorine. Since there is no prefix, there must be only one oxygen atom. The prefix *di-* in *difluoride* shows that there are two fluorine atoms in the molecule. The formula is $OF_2$.

**PRACTICE** *Answers in Appendix E*

1. Name the following binary molecular compounds:
   a. $SO_3$
   b. $ICl_3$
   c. $PBr_5$
2. Write formulas for the following compounds:
   a. carbon tetraiodide
   b. phosphorus trichloride
   c. dinitrogen trioxide

**extension**
Go to **go.hrw.com** for more practice problems that ask you to write names and formulas for binary molecular compounds.

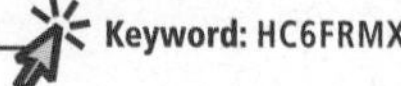

## Covalent-Network Compounds

As you read in Chapter 6, some covalent compounds do not consist of individual molecules. Instead, each atom is joined to all its neighbors in a covalently bonded, three-dimensional network. There are no distinct units in these compounds, just as there are no such units in ionic compounds. The subscripts in a formula for a covalent-network compound indicate the smallest whole-number ratio of the atoms in the compound. Naming such compounds is similar to naming molecular compounds. Some common examples are given below.

| $SiC$ | $SiO_2$ | $Si_3N_4$ |
|---|---|---|
| silicon carbide | silicon dioxide | trisilicon tetranitride |

## Acids and Salts

An *acid* is a distinct type of molecular compound about which you will read in detail in Chapter 14. Most acids used in the laboratory can be classified as either binary acids or oxyacids. *Binary acids* are acids that consist of two elements, usually hydrogen and one of the halogens—fluorine, chlorine, bromine, iodine. *Oxyacids* are acids that contain hydrogen, oxygen, and a third element (usually a nonmetal).

Acids were first recognized as a specific class of compounds based on their properties in solutions of water. Consequently, in chemical nomenclature, the term *acid* usually refers to a solution in water of one of these special compounds rather than to the compound itself. For example, *hydrochloric acid* refers to a water solution of the molecular compound hydrogen chloride, HCl. Some common binary and oxyacids are listed in **Table 5.**

Many polyatomic ions are produced by the loss of hydrogen ions from oxyacids. A few examples of the relationship between oxyacids and oxyanions are shown below.

| | | | |
|---|---|---|---|
| sulfuric acid | $H_2SO_4$ | sulfate | $SO_4^{2-}$ |
| nitric acid | $HNO_3$ | nitrate | $NO_3^-$ |
| phosphoric acid | $H_3PO_4$ | phosphate | $PO_4^{3-}$ |

**TABLE 5 Common Binary Acids and Oxyacids**

| | | | | | |
|---|---|---|---|---|---|
| HF | hydrofluoric acid | $HNO_2$ | nitrous acid | HClO | hypochlorous acid |
| HCl | hydrochloric acid | $HNO_3$ | nitric acid | $HClO_2$ | chlorous acid |
| HBr | hydrobromic acid | $H_2SO_3$ | sulfurous acid | $HClO_3$ | chloric acid |
| HI | hydriodic acid | $H_2SO_4$ | sulfuric acid | $HClO_4$ | perchloric acid |
| $H_3PO_4$ | phosphoric acid | $CH_3COOH$ | acetic acid | $H_2CO_3$ | carbonic acid |

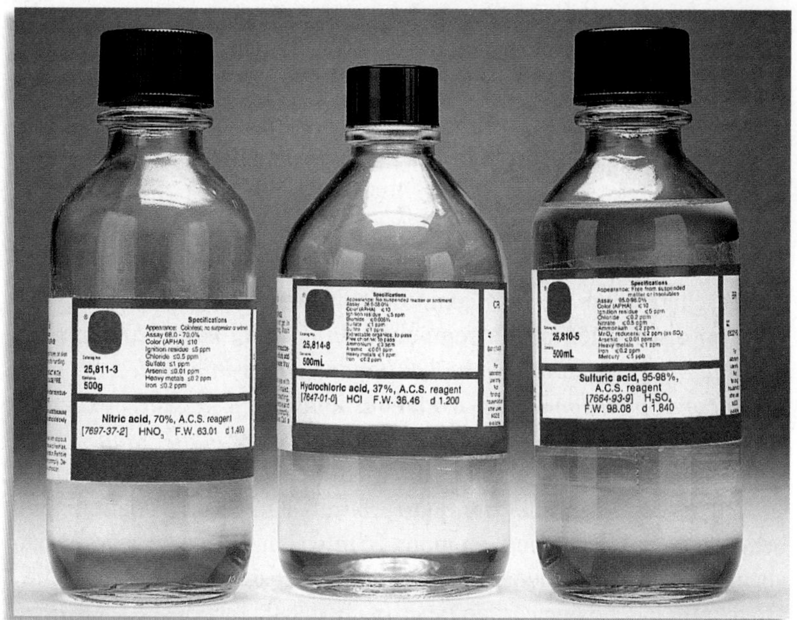


**FIGURE 2** Some common laboratory acids. Acids should always be handled with care and according to instructions. They can burn the skin, and they burn holes in clothing.

*An ionic compound composed of a cation and the anion from an acid is often referred to as a* **salt.** Table salt, NaCl, contains the anion from hydrochloric acid. Calcium sulfate, $CaSO_4$, is a salt containing an anion from sulfuric acid. Some salts contain anions in which one or more hydrogen atoms from the acid are retained. Such anions are named by adding the word *hydrogen* or the prefix *bi-* to the anion name. The best known such anion comes from carbonic acid, $H_2CO_3$.

$HCO_3^-$
hydrogen carbonate ion
bicarbonate ion

## SECTION REVIEW

1. What is the significance of a chemical formula?
2. Write formulas for the compounds formed between the following:
   - **a.** aluminum and bromine
   - **b.** sodium and oxygen
   - **c.** magnesium and iodine
   - **d.** $Pb^{2+}$ and $O^{2-}$
   - **e.** $Sn^{2+}$ and $I^-$
   - **f.** $Fe^{3+}$ and $S^{2-}$
   - **g.** $Cu^{2+}$ and $NO_3^-$
   - **h.** $NH_4^+$ and $SO_4^{2-}$
3. Name the following compounds by using the Stock system:
   - **a.** NaI
   - **b.** MgS
   - **c.** CaO
   - **d.** $K_2S$
   - **e.** CuBr
   - **f.** $FeCl_2$
4. Write formulas for each of the following compounds:
   - **a.** sodium hydroxide
   - **b.** lead(II) nitrate
   - **c.** iron(II) sulfate
   - **d.** diphosphorus trioxide
   - **e.** carbon diselenide
   - **f.** acetic acid
   - **g.** chloric acid
   - **h.** sulfurous acid

### Critical Thinking

5. **RELATING IDEAS** Draw the Lewis structure, give the name, and predict VSEPR geometry of $SCl_2$.

SECTION 2

# Oxidation Numbers

 C.3.2 Interpret the names and formulas for ionic and covalent compounds

## OBJECTIVES

- List the rules for assigning oxidation numbers.
- Give the oxidation number for each element in the formula of a chemical compound.
- Name binary molecular compounds using oxidation numbers and the Stock system.

The charges on the ions composing an ionic compound reflect the electron distribution of the compound. *In order to indicate the general distribution of electrons among the bonded atoms in a molecular compound or a polyatomic ion,* **oxidation numbers,** *also called* **oxidation states,** *are assigned to the atoms composing the compound or ion.* Unlike ionic charges, oxidation numbers do not have an exact physical meaning. In fact, in some cases they are quite arbitrary. However, oxidation numbers are useful in naming compounds, in writing formulas, and in balancing chemical equations. And, as will be discussed in Chapter 19, they are helpful in studying certain types of chemical reactions.

## Assigning Oxidation Numbers

As a general rule in assigning oxidation numbers, shared electrons are assumed to belong to the more electronegative atom in each bond. More specific rules for determining oxidation numbers are provided by the following guidelines.

1. The atoms in a pure element have an oxidation number of zero. For example, the atoms in pure sodium, Na, oxygen, $O_2$, phosphorus, $P_4$, and sulfur, $S_8$, all have oxidation numbers of zero.
2. The more-electronegative element in a binary molecular compound is assigned the number equal to the negative charge it would have as an anion. The less-electronegative atom is assigned the number equal to the positive charge it would have as a cation.
3. Fluorine has an oxidation number of –1 in all of its compounds because it is the most electronegative element.
4. Oxygen has an oxidation number of –2 in almost all compounds. Exceptions include when it is in peroxides, such as $H_2O_2$, in which its oxidation number is –1, and when it is in compounds with fluorine, such as $OF_2$, in which its oxidation number is +2.
5. Hydrogen has an oxidation number of +1 in all compounds containing elements that are more electronegative than it; it has an oxidation number of –1 in compounds with metals.
6. The algebraic sum of the oxidation numbers of all atoms in a neutral compound is equal to zero.
7. The algebraic sum of the oxidation numbers of all atoms in a polyatomic ion is equal to the charge of the ion.
8. Although rules 1 through 7 apply to covalently bonded atoms, oxidation numbers can also be assigned to atoms in ionic compounds.

**9.** A monatomic ion has an oxidation number equal to the charge of the ion. For example, the ions $Na^+$, $Ca^{2+}$, and $Cl^-$ have oxidation numbers of +1, +2, and −1, respectively.

Let's examine the assignment of oxidation numbers to the atoms in two molecular compounds, hydrogen fluoride, HF, and water, $H_2O$. Both compounds have polar-covalent bonds. In HF, the fluorine atom should have an oxidation number of −1 (see Rule 3 on the previous page). Rule 5 tells us that hydrogen should have an oxidation number of +1. This makes sense because fluorine is more electronegative than hydrogen, and in a polar-covalent bond, shared electrons are assumed to belong to the more-electronegative element. For water, Rules 4 and 5 tell us that the oxidation number of oxygen should be −2 and the oxidation number of each hydrogen atom should be +1. Again, oxygen is more electronegative than hydrogen, so the shared electrons are assumed to belong to oxygen.

Because the sum of the oxidation numbers of the atoms in a compound must satisfy Rule 6 or 7 of the guidelines on the previous page, it is often possible to assign oxidation numbers when they are not known. This is illustrated in Sample Problem E.

## SAMPLE PROBLEM E

**Assign oxidation numbers to each atom in the following compounds or ions:**

**a. $UF_6$**

**b. $H_2SO_4$**

**c. $ClO_3^-$**

**SOLUTION** a. Start by placing known oxidation numbers above the appropriate elements. From the guidelines, we know that fluorine always has an oxidation number of −1.

$$\overset{\quad -1}{UF_6}$$

Multiply known oxidation numbers by the appropriate number of atoms and place the totals underneath the corresponding elements. There are six fluorine atoms, 6 × −1 = −6.

$$\underset{\quad -6}{\overset{\quad -1}{UF_6}}$$

The compound $UF_6$ is molecular. According to the guidelines, the sum of the oxidation numbers must equal zero. The total of positive oxidation numbers is therefore +6.

$$\underset{+6\ -6}{\overset{\quad -1}{UF_6}}$$

Divide the total calculated oxidation number by the appropriate number of atoms. There is only one uranium atom in the molecule, so it must have an oxidation number of +6.

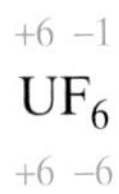


**b.** Oxygen and sulfur are each more electronegative than hydrogen, so hydrogen has an oxidation number of +1. Oxygen is not combined with a halogen, nor is $H_2SO_4$ a peroxide. Therefore, the oxidation number of oxygen is −2. Place these known oxidation numbers above the appropriate symbols. Place the total of the oxidation numbers underneath.

$$\overset{+1}{H_2}S\overset{-2}{O_4}$$
$$\underset{+2}{\phantom{H}}\quad\underset{-8}{\phantom{O}}$$

The sum of the oxidation numbers must equal zero, and there is only one sulfur atom in each molecule of $H_2SO_4$. Because (+2) + (−8) = −6, the oxidation number of each sulfur atom must be +6.

**c.** To assign oxidation numbers to the elements in $ClO_3^-$, proceed as in parts (a) and (b). Remember, however, that the total of the oxidation numbers should equal the overall charge of the anion, 1−. The oxidation number of a single oxygen atom in the ion is −2. The total oxidation number due to the three oxygen atoms is −6. For the chlorate ion to have a 1− charge, chlorine must be assigned an oxidation number of +5.

$$\overset{+5}{Cl}\overset{-2}{O_3^-}$$
$$\underset{+5}{\phantom{Cl}}\quad\underset{-6}{\phantom{O}}$$

**PRACTICE** *Answers in Appendix E*

1. Assign oxidation numbers to each atom in the following compounds or ions:

| | | |
|---|---|---|
| **a.** HCl | **e.** $HNO_3$ | **h.** $HClO_3$ |
| **b.** $CF_4$ | **f.** KH | **i.** $N_2O_5$ |
| **c.** $PCl_3$ | **g.** $P_4O_{10}$ | **j.** $GeCl_2$ |
| **d.** $SO_2$ | | |

Go to **go.hrw.com** for more practice problems that ask you to assign oxidation numbers.

**Keyword: HC6FRMX**

## Using Oxidation Numbers for Formulas and Names

As shown in **Table 6,** many nonmetals can have more than one oxidation number. (A more extensive list of oxidation numbers is given in Appendix Table A-15.) These numbers can sometimes be used in the same manner as ionic charges to determine formulas. Suppose, for example, you want to know the formula of a binary compound formed between sulfur and oxygen. From the common +4 and +6 oxidation states of sulfur, you could expect that sulfur might form $SO_2$ or $SO_3$. Both are known compounds. Of course, a formula must represent facts. Oxidation numbers alone cannot be used to prove the existence of a compound.

**TABLE 6 Common Oxidation Numbers of Some Nonmetals That Have Variable Oxidation States***

| | | |
|---|---|---|
| Group 14 | carbon | −4, +2, +4 |
| Group 15 | nitrogen | −3, +1, +2, +3, +4, +5 |
| | phosphorus | −3, +3, +5 |
| Group 16 | sulfur | −2, +4, +6 |
| Group 17 | chlorine | −1, +1, +3, +5, +7 |
| | bromine | −1, +1, +3, +5, +7 |
| | iodine | −1, +1, +3, +5, +7 |

*In addition to the values shown, atoms of each element in its pure state are assigned an oxidation number of zero.

In Section 1 we introduced the use of Roman numerals to denote ionic charges in the Stock system of naming ionic compounds. The Stock system is actually based on oxidation numbers, and it can be used as an alternative to the prefix system for naming binary molecular compounds. In the prefix system, for example, $SO_2$ and $SO_3$ are named sulfur dioxide and sulfur trioxide, respectively. Their names according to the Stock system are sulfur(IV) oxide and sulfur(VI) oxide. The international body that governs nomenclature has endorsed the Stock system, which is more practical for complicated compounds. Prefix-based names and Stock-system names are still used interchangeably for many simple compounds, however. A few additional examples of names in both systems are given below.

| | Prefix system | Stock system |
|---|---|---|
| $PCl_3$ | phosphorus trichloride | phosphorus(III) chloride |
| $PCl_5$ | phosphorus pentachloride | phosphorus(V) chloride |
| $N_2O$ | dinitrogen monoxide | nitrogen(I) oxide |
| NO | nitrogen monoxide | nitrogen(II) oxide |
| $PbO_2$ | lead dioxide | lead(IV) oxide |
| $Mo_2O_3$ | dimolybdenum trioxide | molybdenum(III) oxide |

## SECTION REVIEW

**1.** Assign oxidation numbers to each atom in the following compounds or ions:

**a.** HF
**b.** $CI_4$
**c.** $H_2O$
**d.** $PI_3$
**e.** $CS_2$
**f.** $Na_2O_2$
**g.** $H_2CO_3$
**h.** $NO_2^-$
**i.** $SO_4^{2-}$

**2.** Name each of the following binary molecular compounds according to the Stock system:

**a.** $CI_4$
**b.** $SO_3$
**c.** $As_2S_3$
**d.** $NCl_3$

### Critical Thinking

**3. DRAWING CONCLUSIONS** Determine the oxidation numbers for iron oxide, $Fe_3O_4$. (Recall that oxidation numbers are integers.)

# Chemistry in Action

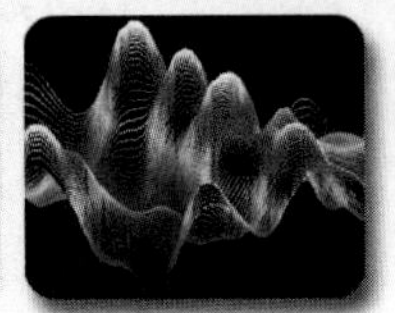

## Mass Spectrometry: Identifying Molecules

Tests for locating oil deposits in the ground and detecting dioxins in our food supply are commonly performed today. These tests can be performed by using a technique known as *mass spectrometry.* Mass spectrometry is now used in many fields, such as medicine, chemistry, forensic science, and astronomy.

What is mass spectrometry? It is the most accurate technique available to measure the mass of an individual molecule or atom. Knowing the molecular mass is an essential part of identifying an unknown compound and determining the structure of a molecule of the compound. As the diagram of a mass spectrometer shows, the molecules in a gaseous sample are converted into ions. The ions then are separated and sorted according to their mass-to-charge ratio by a combination of electric and magnetic fields. The fields cause the ions' trajectories to change based on the ions' masses and charges. Then, the sorted ions are detected, and a mass spectrum is obtained. The mass spectrum is a graph of relative intensity (related to the number of ions detected) versus mass-to-charge ratio. Mass spectrometry uses a very small sample size ($10^{-12}$ g) to obtain results.

The resulting spectrum is like a puzzle. It contains numerous peaks that correspond to fragments of the initial molecule. The largest peak (parent peak) corresponds to the molecular mass of the molecular ion. By analyzing the peaks, scientists can determine the identity and structure of a compound. Computers are used to help interpret the spectrum and identify the molecule by using online spectral database libraries.

Mass spectrometry has been an essential tool for scientists since its invention in the early 1900s. But its use was limited to small molecules from which ion creation was easy. Large biological molecules could not be studied because they would break down or decompose during conventional ion-formation techniques. In the late 1980s, two groups developed ion-formation methods that are used today in commercial mass spectrometers. John Fenn (Virginia Commonwealth University) developed electrospray ionization mass spectrometry, and Koichi Tanaka (Shimadzu Corporation, Japan) developed matrix-assisted laser desorption ionization (MALDI) mass spectrometry. In 2002, both scientists received the Nobel Prize in chemistry for their work. Their methods opened the field to the study of large molecules, allowing scientists to use mass spectrometry to study the structure of macromolecules such as nucleic acids and steroids and to identify the sequence of proteins.

### Questions

1. Why is it necessary to convert the sample into ions in the mass spectrometer?
2. How have recent developments in mass spectrometry contributed to the field of medicine?

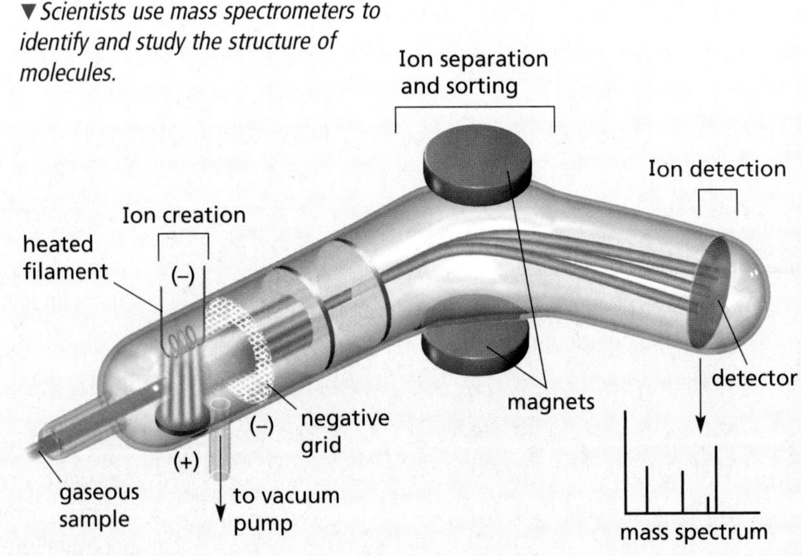


▼ *Scientists use mass spectrometers to identify and study the structure of molecules.*

# Using Chemical Formulas

SECTION 3

## Objectives

- Calculate the formula mass or molar mass of any given compound.
- Use molar mass to convert between mass in grams and amount in moles of a chemical compound.
- Calculate the number of molecules, formula units, or ions in a given molar amount of a chemical compound.
- Calculate the percentage composition of a given chemical compound.

**C.4.4** Apply the concept of moles to determine the number of particles of a substance in a chemical reaction, the percent composition of a representative compound, the mass proportions, and the mole-mass relationships

As you have seen, a chemical formula indicates the elements as well as the relative number of atoms or ions of each element present in a compound. Chemical formulas also allow chemists to calculate a number of characteristic values for a given compound. In this section, you will learn how to use chemical formulas to calculate the *formula mass,* the *molar mass,* and the *percentage composition* by mass of a compound.

## Formula Masses

In Chapter 3, we saw that hydrogen atoms have an average atomic mass of 1.007 94 amu and that oxygen atoms have an average atomic mass of 15.9994 amu. Like individual atoms, molecules, formula units, or ions have characteristic average masses. For example, we know from the chemical formula $H_2O$ that a single water molecule is composed of exactly two hydrogen atoms and one oxygen atom. The mass of a water molecule is found by adding the masses of the three atoms in the molecule. (In the calculation, the average atomic masses have been rounded to two decimal places.)

$$\text{average atomic mass of H: } 1.01 \text{ amu}$$
$$\text{average atomic mass of O: } 16.00 \text{ amu}$$

$$2 \cancel{\text{H atoms}} \times \frac{1.01 \text{ amu}}{\cancel{\text{H atom}}} = 2.02 \text{ amu}$$

$$1 \cancel{\text{O atom}} \times \frac{16.00 \text{ amu}}{\cancel{\text{O atom}}} = 16.00 \text{ amu}$$

$$\text{average mass of } H_2O \text{ molecule} = 18.02 \text{ amu}$$

The mass of a water molecule can be correctly referred to as a *molecular mass.* The mass of one NaCl formula unit, on the other hand, is not a molecular mass because NaCl is an ionic compound. The mass of *any* unit represented by a chemical formula, whether the unit is a molecule, a formula unit, or an ion, is known as the formula mass. *The* **formula mass** *of any molecule, formula unit, or ion is the sum of the average atomic masses of all atoms represented in its formula.*

The procedure illustrated for calculating the formula mass of a water molecule can be used to calculate the mass of any unit represented by a chemical formula. In each of the problems that follow, the atomic masses from the periodic table in the back of the book have been rounded to two decimal places.

## SAMPLE PROBLEM F

**Find the formula mass of potassium chlorate, $KClO_3$.**

**SOLUTION** The mass of a formula unit of $KClO_3$ is found by summing the masses of one K atom, one Cl atom, and three O atoms. The required atomic masses can be found in the periodic table in the back of the book. In the calculation, each atomic mass has been rounded to two decimal places.

$$1\ \cancel{\text{K atom}} \times \frac{39.10\ \text{amu}}{\cancel{\text{K atom}}} = 39.10\ \text{amu}$$

$$1\ \cancel{\text{Cl atom}} \times \frac{35.45\ \text{amu}}{\cancel{\text{Cl atom}}} = 35.45\ \text{amu}$$

$$3\ \cancel{\text{O atoms}} \times \frac{16.00\ \text{amu}}{\cancel{\text{O atom}}} = 48.00\ \text{amu}$$

$$\text{formula mass of } KClO_3 = 122.55\ \text{amu}$$

**PRACTICE** *Answers in Appendix E*

1. Find the formula mass of each of the following:
   a. $H_2SO_4$
   b. $Ca(NO_3)_2$
   c. $PO_4^{3-}$
   d. $MgCl_2$

**extension**
Go to **go.hrw.com** for more practice problems that ask you to calculate formula mass.

## Molar Masses

In Chapter 3 you learned that the molar mass of a substance is equal to the mass in grams of one mole, or approximately $6.022 \times 10^{23}$ particles, of the substance. For example, the molar mass of pure calcium, Ca, is 40.08 g/mol because one mole of calcium atoms has a mass of 40.08 g.

The molar mass of a compound is calculated by summing the masses of the elements present in a mole of the molecules or formula units that make up the compound. For example, one mole of water molecules contains exactly two moles of H atoms and one mole of O atoms. Rounded to two decimal places, a mole of hydrogen atoms has a mass of 1.01 g, and a mole of oxygen atoms has a mass of 16.00 g. The molar mass of water is calculated as follows.

$$2 \text{ mol H} \times \frac{1.01 \text{ g H}}{\text{mol H}} = 2.02 \text{ g H}$$

$$1 \text{ mol O} \times \frac{16.00 \text{ g O}}{\text{mol O}} = 16.00 \text{ g O}$$

$$\text{molar mass of } H_2O = 18.02 \text{ g/mol}$$

**Figure 3** shows a mole of water as well as a mole of several other substances.

You may have noticed that *a compound's molar mass is numerically equal to its formula mass*. For instance, in Sample Problem F the formula mass of $KClO_3$ was found to be 122.55 amu. Therefore, because molar mass is numerically equal to formula mass, we know that the molar mass of $KClO_3$ is 122.55 g/mol.

**FIGURE 3** Every compound has a characteristic molar mass. Shown here are one mole each of nitrogen (in balloon), water (in graduated cylinder), cadmium sulfide, CdS (yellow substance), and sodium chloride, NaCl (white substance).

## SAMPLE PROBLEM G

**What is the molar mass of barium nitrate, $Ba(NO_3)_2$?**

**SOLUTION** One mole of barium nitrate contains exactly one mole of $Ba^{2+}$ ions and two moles of $NO_3^-$ ions. The two moles of $NO_3^-$ ions contain two moles of N atoms and six moles of O atoms. Therefore, the molar mass of $Ba(NO_3)_2$ is calculated as follows.

$$1 \text{ mol Ba} \times \frac{137.33 \text{ g Ba}}{\text{mol Ba}} = 137.33 \text{ g Ba}$$

$$2 \text{ mol N} \times \frac{14.01 \text{ g N}}{\text{mol N}} = 28.02 \text{ g N}$$

$$6 \text{ mol O} \times \frac{16.00 \text{ g O}}{\text{mol O}} = 96.00 \text{ g O}$$

$$\text{molar mass of } Ba(NO_3)_2 = 261.35 \text{ g/mol}$$

**PRACTICE** *Answers in Appendix E*

1. How many moles of atoms of each element are there in one mole of the following compounds?
   a. $Al_2S_3$
   b. $NaNO_3$
   c. $Ba(OH)_2$
2. Find the molar mass of each of the compounds listed in item 1.

**extension**

Go to **go.hrw.com** for more practice problems that ask you to calculate molar mass.

Keyword: HC6FRMX

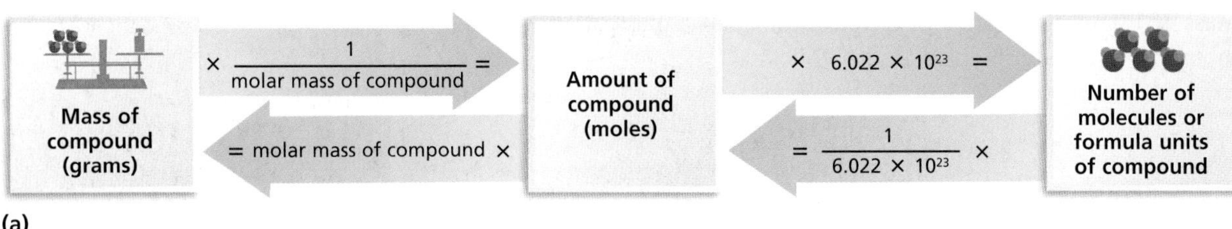

(a)

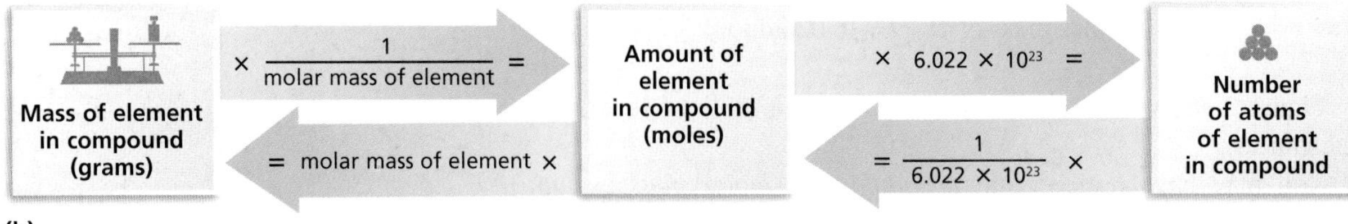


(b)

**FIGURE 4** (a) The diagram shows the relationships between mass in grams, amount in moles, and number of molecules or atoms for a given compound. (b) Similar relationships exist for an element within a compound.

## Molar Mass as a Conversion Factor

The molar mass of a compound can be used as a conversion factor to relate an amount in moles to a mass in grams for a given substance. Recall that molar mass usually has the units of grams per mole. To convert a known amount of a compound in moles to a mass in grams, multiply the amount in moles by the molar mass.

$$\text{amount in moles} \times \text{molar mass (g/mol)} = \text{mass in grams}$$

Conversions of this type for elements and compounds are summarized above in **Figure 4.**

### SAMPLE PROBLEM H

**What is the mass in grams of 2.50 mol of oxygen gas?**

**SOLUTION**

**1** *ANALYZE* **Given:** 2.50 mol $O_2$
**Unknown:** mass of $O_2$ in grams

**2** *PLAN* moles $O_2 \longrightarrow$ grams $O_2$
To convert amount of $O_2$ in moles to mass of $O_2$ in grams, multiply by the molar mass of $O_2$.

$$\text{amount of } O_2 \text{ (mol)} \times \text{molar mass of } O_2 \text{ (g/mol)} = \text{mass of } O_2 \text{ (g)}$$

**3 COMPUTE** First the molar mass of $O_2$ must be calculated.

$$2 \cancel{\text{mol O}} \times \frac{16.00 \text{ g O}}{\cancel{\text{mol O}}} = 32.00 \text{ g (mass of one mole of } O_2\text{)}$$

The molar mass of $O_2$ is therefore 32.00 g/mol. Now do the calculation shown in step 2.

$$2.50 \cancel{\text{mol } O_2} \times \frac{32.00 \text{ g } O_2}{\cancel{\text{mol } O_2}} = 80.0 \text{ g } O_2$$

**4 EVALUATE** The answer is correctly given to three significant figures and is close to an estimated value of 75 g (2.50 mol × 30 g/mol).

To convert a known mass of a compound in grams to an amount in moles, the mass must be divided by the molar mass. Or you can invert the molar mass and multiply so that units are easily canceled.

$$\text{mass in grams} \times \frac{1}{\text{molar mass (g/mol)}} = \text{amount in moles}$$

## SAMPLE PROBLEM I

**Ibuprofen, $C_{13}H_{18}O_2$, is the active ingredient in many nonprescription pain relievers. Its molar mass is 206.31 g/mol.**

**a. If the tablets in a bottle contain a total of 33 g of ibuprofen, how many moles of ibuprofen are in the bottle?**

**b. How many molecules of ibuprofen are in the bottle?**

**c. What is the total mass in grams of carbon in 33 g of ibuprofen?**

### SOLUTION

**1 ANALYZE** **Given:** 33 g of $C_{13}H_{18}O_2$, molar mass 206.31 g/mol

**Unknown:** a. moles $C_{13}H_{18}O_2$

b. molecules $C_{13}H_{18}O_2$

c. total mass of C

**2 PLAN** a. grams ⟶ moles

To convert mass of ibuprofen in grams to amount of ibuprofen in moles, multiply by the inverted molar mass of $C_{13}H_{18}O_2$.

$$\text{g } C_{13}H_{18}O_2 \times \frac{1 \text{ mol } C_{13}H_{18}O_2}{206.31 \text{ g } C_{13}H_{18}O_2} = \text{mol } C_{13}H_{18}O_2$$

b. moles ⟶ molecules

To find the number of molecules of ibuprofen, multiply amount of $C_{13}H_{18}O_2$ in moles by Avogadro's number.

$$\text{mol } C_{13}H_{18}O_2 \times \frac{6.022 \times 10^{23} \text{ molecules}}{\text{mol}} = \text{molecules } C_{13}H_{18}O_2$$

**c.** moles $C_{13}H_{18}O_2 \longrightarrow$ moles C $\longrightarrow$ grams C

To find the mass of carbon present in the ibuprofen, the two conversion factors needed are the amount of carbon in moles per mole of $C_{13}H_{18}O_2$ and the molar mass of carbon.

$$\text{mol } C_{13}H_{18}O_2 \times \frac{13 \text{ mol C}}{\text{mol } C_{13}H_{18}O_2} \times \frac{12.01 \text{ g C}}{\text{mol C}} = \text{g C}$$

**3 COMPUTE**

**a.** $33 \cancel{\text{g } C_{13}H_{18}O_2} \times \frac{1 \text{ mol } C_{13}H_{18}O_2}{206.31 \cancel{\text{g } C_{13}H_{18}O_2}} = 0.16 \text{ mol } C_{13}H_{18}O_2$

**b.** $0.16 \cancel{\text{mol}}\ C_{13}H_{18}O_2 \times \frac{6.022 \times 10^{23} \text{ molecules}}{\cancel{\text{mol}}} = 9.6 \times 10^{22} \text{ molecules } C_{13}H_{18}O_2$

**c.** $0.16 \cancel{\text{mol } C_{13}H_{18}O_2} \times \frac{13 \cancel{\text{mol C}}}{\cancel{\text{mol } C_{13}H_{18}O_2}} \times \frac{12.01 \text{ g C}}{\cancel{\text{mol C}}} = 25 \text{ g C}$

The bottle contains 0.16 mol of ibuprofen, which is $9.6 \times 10^{22}$ molecules of ibuprofen. The sample of ibuprofen contains 25 g of carbon.

**4 EVALUATE** Checking each step shows that the arithmetic is correct, significant figures have been used correctly, and units have canceled as desired.

**PRACTICE** *Answers in Appendix E*

1. How many moles of compound are there in the following?
   a. 6.60 g $(NH_4)_2SO_4$
   b. 4.5 kg $Ca(OH)_2$
2. How many molecules are there in the following?
   a. 25.0 g $H_2SO_4$
   b. 125 g of sugar, $C_{12}H_{22}O_{11}$
3. What is the mass in grams of 6.25 mol of copper(II) nitrate?

Go to **go.hrw.com** for more practice problems that ask you to use molar mass as a conversion factor.

**Keyword:** HC6FRMX

## Percentage Composition

It is often useful to know the percentage by mass of a particular element in a chemical compound. For example, suppose the compound potassium chlorate, $KClO_3$, were to be used as a source of oxygen. It would be helpful to know the percentage of oxygen in the compound. To find the mass percentage of an element in a compound, one can divide the mass of the element in a sample of the compound by the total mass of the sample, then multiply this value by 100.

$$\frac{\text{mass of element in sample of compound}}{\text{mass of sample of compound}} \times 100 = \begin{array}{c}\text{\% element in}\\ \text{compound}\end{array}$$

The mass percentage of an element in a compound is the same regardless of the sample's size. Therefore, a simpler way to calculate the percentage of an element in a compound is to determine how many grams of the element are present in one mole of the compound. Then divide this value by the molar mass of the compound and multiply by 100.

$$\frac{\text{mass of element in 1 mol of compound}}{\text{molar mass of compound}} \times 100 = \begin{array}{c}\text{\% element in} \\ \text{compound}\end{array}$$

*The percentage by mass of each element in a compound is known as the* **percentage composition** *of the compound.*

## SAMPLE PROBLEM J

For more help, go to the *Math Tutor* at the end of this chapter.

**Find the percentage composition of copper(I) sulfide, $Cu_2S$.**

### SOLUTION

1 *ANALYZE* **Given:** formula, $Cu_2S$
**Unknown:** percentage composition of $Cu_2S$

2 *PLAN* formula ⟶ molar mass ⟶ mass percentage of each element

The molar mass of the compound must be found. Then the mass of each element present in one mole of the compound is used to calculate the mass percentage of each element.

3 *COMPUTE*

$$2 \cancel{\text{mol Cu}} \times \frac{63.55 \text{ g Cu}}{\cancel{\text{mol Cu}}} = 127.1 \text{ g Cu}$$

$$1 \cancel{\text{mol S}} \times \frac{32.07 \text{ g S}}{\cancel{\text{mol S}}} = 32.07 \text{ g S}$$

$$\text{molar mass of } Cu_2S = 159.2 \text{ g}$$

$$\frac{127.1 \text{ g Cu}}{159.2 \text{ g } Cu_2S} \times 100 = 79.85\% \text{ Cu}$$

$$\frac{32.07 \text{ g S}}{159.2 \text{ g } Cu_2S} \times 100 = 20.15\% \text{ S}$$

4 *EVALUATE* A good check is to see if the results add up to about 100%. (Because of rounding, the total may not always be exactly 100%.)

## SAMPLE PROBLEM K

For more help, go to the *Math Tutor* at the end of this chapter.

**As some salts crystallize from a water solution, they bind water molecules in their crystal structure. Sodium carbonate forms such a *hydrate,* in which 10 water molecules are present for every formula unit of sodium carbonate. Find the mass percentage of water in sodium carbonate decahydrate, $Na_2CO_3•10H_2O$, which has a molar mass of 286.19 g/mol.**

**SOLUTION**

**1 ANALYZE** **Given:** chemical formula, $Na_2CO_3 \cdot 10H_2O$
molar mass of $Na_2CO_3 \cdot 10H_2O$
**Unknown:** mass percentage of $H_2O$

**2 PLAN** chemical formula $\longrightarrow$ mass $H_2O$ per mole of $Na_2CO_3 \cdot 10H_2O$ $\longrightarrow$ % water

The mass of water per mole of sodium carbonate decahydrate must first be found. This value is then divided by the mass of one mole of $Na_2CO_3 \cdot 10H_2O$.

**3 COMPUTE** One mole of $Na_2CO_3 \cdot 10H_2O$ contains 10 mol $H_2O$. Recall from page 239 that the molar mass of $H_2O$ is 18.02 g/mol. The mass of 10 mol $H_2O$ is calculated as follows.

$$10 \text{ mol } H_2O \times \frac{18.02 \text{ g } H_2O}{\text{mol } H_2O} = 180.2 \text{ g } H_2O$$

$$\text{mass of } H_2O \text{ per mole of } Na_2CO_3 \cdot 10H_2O = 180.2 \text{ g}$$

The molar mass of $Na_2CO_3 \cdot 10H_2O$ is 286.19 g/mol, so we know that 1 mol of the hydrate has a mass of 286.19g. The mass percentage of 10 mol $H_2O$ in 1 mol $Na_2CO_3 \cdot 10H_2O$ can now be calculated.

$$\text{mass percentage of } H_2O \text{ in } Na_2CO_3 \cdot 10H_2O = \frac{180.2 \text{ g } H_2O}{286.19 \text{ g } Na_2CO_3 \cdot 10H_2O} \times 100 = 62.97\% \text{ } H_2O$$

**4 EVALUATE** Checking shows that the arithmetic is correct and that units cancel as desired.

**PRACTICE** *Answers in Appendix E*

1. Find the percentage compositions of the following:
   a. $PbCl_2$ b. $Ba(NO_3)_2$
2. Find the mass percentage of water in $ZnSO_4 \cdot 7H_2O$.
3. Magnesium hydroxide is 54.87% oxygen by mass. How many grams of oxygen are in 175 g of the compound? How many moles of oxygen is this?

Go to **go.hrw.com** for more practice problems that ask you to calculate percentage composition.

**Keyword: HC6FRMX**

## SECTION REVIEW

1. Determine both the formula mass and molar mass of ammonium carbonate, $(NH_4)_2CO_3$.
2. How many moles of atoms of each element are there in one mole of $(NH_4)_2CO_3$?
3. What is the mass in grams of 3.25 mol $Fe_2(SO_4)_3$?
4. How many molecules of aspirin, $C_9H_8O_4$, are there in a 100.0 mg tablet of aspirin?
5. Calculate the percentage composition of $(NH_4)_2CO_3$.

**Critical Thinking**

6. **RELATING IDEAS** A sample of hydrated copper(II) sulfate ($CuSO_4 \cdot nH_2O$) is heated to 150°C and produces 103.74 g anhydrous copper(II) sulfate and 58.55 g water. How many moles of water molecules are present in 1.0 mol of hydrated copper(II) sulfate?

# Determining Chemical Formulas

SECTION 4

## OBJECTIVES

- Define *empirical formula,* and explain how the term applies to ionic and molecular compounds.
- Determine an empirical formula from either a percentage or a mass composition.
- Explain the relationship between the empirical formula and the molecular formula of a given compound.
- Determine a molecular formula from an empirical formula.

**C.4.4** Apply the concept of moles to determine the number of particles of a substance in a chemical reaction, the percent composition of a representative compound, the mass proportions, and the mole-mass relationships

When a new substance is synthesized or is discovered, it is analyzed quantitatively to reveal its percentage composition. From these data, the empirical formula is then determined. *An* **empirical formula** *consists of the symbols for the elements combined in a compound, with subscripts showing the smallest whole-number mole ratio of the different atoms in the compound.* For an ionic compound, the formula unit is usually the compound's empirical formula. For a molecular compound, however, the empirical formula does not necessarily indicate the actual numbers of atoms present in each molecule. For example, the empirical formula of the gas diborane is $BH_3$, but the molecular formula is $B_2H_6$. In this case, the number of atoms given by the molecular formula corresponds to the empirical ratio multiplied by two.

## Calculation of Empirical Formulas

To determine a compound's empirical formula from its percentage composition, begin by converting percentage composition to a mass composition. Assume that you have a 100.0 g sample of the compound. Then calculate the amount of each element in the sample. For example, the percentage composition of diborane is 78.1% B and 21.9% H. Therefore, 100.0 g of diborane contains 78.1 g of B and 21.9 g of H.

Next, the mass composition of each element is converted to a composition in moles by dividing by the appropriate molar mass.

$$78.1 \cancel{\text{g B}} \times \frac{1 \text{ mol B}}{10.81 \cancel{\text{g B}}} = 7.22 \text{ mol B}$$

$$21.9 \cancel{\text{g H}} \times \frac{1 \text{ mol H}}{1.01 \cancel{\text{g H}}} = 21.7 \text{ mol H}$$

These values give a mole ratio of 7.22 mol B to 21.7 mol H. However, this is not a ratio of smallest whole numbers. To find such a ratio, divide each number of moles by the smallest number in the existing ratio.

$$\frac{7.22 \text{ mol B}}{7.22} : \frac{21.7 \text{ mol H}}{7.22} = 1 \text{ mol B} : 3.01 \text{ mol H}$$

## Calculation of Molecular Formulas

CROSS-DISCIPLINARY

Go to **go.hrw.com** for a full-length article on the importance of molecular shape in odors.

**Keyword: HC6FRMX**

Remember that the *empirical formula* contains the smallest possible whole numbers that describe the atomic ratio. The *molecular formula* is the actual formula of a molecular compound. An empirical formula may or may not be a correct molecular formula. For example, diborane's empirical formula is $BH_3$. Any multiple of $BH_3$, such as $B_2H_6$, $B_3H_9$, $B_4H_{12}$, and so on, represents the same ratio of B atoms to H atoms. The molecular compounds ethene, $C_2H_4$, and cyclopropane, $C_3H_6$, also share an identical atomic ratio (2 H:1 C), yet they are very different substances. How is the correct formula of a molecular compound found from an empirical formula?

The relationship between a compound's empirical formula and its molecular formula can be written as follows.

$$x(\text{empirical formula}) = \text{molecular formula}$$

The number represented by $x$ is a whole-number multiple indicating the factor by which the subscripts in the empirical formula must be multiplied to obtain the molecular formula. (The value of $x$ is sometimes 1.) The formula masses have a similar relationship.

$$x(\text{empirical formula mass}) = \text{molecular formula mass}$$

To determine the molecular formula of a compound, you must know the compound's formula mass. For example, experimentation shows the formula mass of diborane to be 27.67 amu. The formula mass for the empirical formula, $BH_3$, is 13.84 amu. Dividing the experimental formula mass by the empirical formula mass gives the value of $x$ for diborane.

$$x = \frac{27.67 \text{ amu}}{13.84 \text{ amu}} = 2.000$$

The molecular formula of diborane is therefore $B_2H_6$.

$$2(BH_3) = B_2H_6$$

Recall that a compound's molecular formula mass is numerically equal to its molar mass, so a compound's molecular formula can also be found given the compound's empirical formula and its molar mass.

**SAMPLE PROBLEM N** *For more help, go to the Math Tutor at the end of Chapter 22.*

**In Sample Problem M, the empirical formula of a compound of phosphorus and oxygen was found to be $P_2O_5$. Experimentation shows that the molar mass of this compound is 283.89 g/mol. What is the compound's molecular formula?**

**SOLUTION**

1 *ANALYZE* **Given:** empirical formula
**Unknown:** molecular formula

**2 PLAN**

$$x(\text{empirical formula}) = \text{molecular formula}$$

$$x = \frac{\text{molecular formula mass}}{\text{empirical formula mass}}$$

**3 COMPUTE** Molecular formula mass is numerically equal to molar mass. Thus, changing the g/mol unit of the compound's molar mass to amu yields the compound's molecular formula mass.

$$\text{molecular molar mass} = 283.89 \text{ g/mol}$$
$$\text{molecular formula mass} = 283.89 \text{ amu}$$

The empirical formula mass is found by adding the masses of each of the atoms indicated in the empirical formula.

$$\text{mass of phosphorus atom} = 30.97 \text{ amu}$$
$$\text{mass of oxygen atom} = 16.00 \text{ amu}$$
$$\text{empirical formula mass of } P_2O_5 = 2 \times 30.97 \text{ amu} + 5 \times 16.00 \text{ amu} = 141.94 \text{ amu}$$

Dividing the experimental formula mass by the empirical formula mass gives the value of $x$. The formula mass is numerically equal to the molar mass.

$$x = \frac{283.89 \cancel{\text{ amu}}}{141.94 \cancel{\text{ amu}}} = 2.0001$$

The compound's molecular formula is therefore $P_4O_{10}$.

$$2 \times (P_2O_5) = P_4O_{10}$$

**4 EVALUATE** Checking the arithmetic shows that it is correct.

**PRACTICE** *Answers in Appendix E*

1. Determine the molecular formula of the compound with an empirical formula of CH and a formula mass of 78.110 amu.
2. A sample of a compound with a formula mass of 34.00 amu is found to consist of 0.44 g H and 6.92 g O. Find its molecular formula.

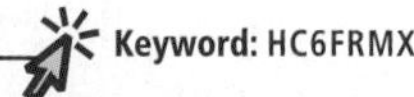


Go to **go.hrw.com** for more practice problems that ask you to determine molecular formulas.

**Keyword: HC6FRMX**

## SECTION REVIEW

1. A compound contains 36.48% Na, 25.41% S, and 38.11% O. Find its empirical formula.
2. Find the empirical formula of a compound that contains 53.70% iron and 46.30% sulfur.
3. Analysis of a compound indicates that it contains 1.04 g K, 0.70 g Cr, and 0.86 g O. Find its empirical formula.
4. If 4.04 g of N combine with 11.46 g O to produce a compound with a formula mass of 108.0 amu, what is the molecular formula of this compound?

**Critical Thinking**

5. **RELATING IDEAS** A compound containing sodium, chlorine, and oxygen is 25.42% sodium by mass. A 3.25 g sample gives $4.33 \times 10^{22}$ atoms of oxygen. What is the empirical formula?

# CHAPTER HIGHLIGHTS

## Chemical Names and Formulas

**Vocabulary**
monatomic ion
binary compound
nomenclature
oxyanion
salt

- A positive monatomic ion is identified simply by the name of the appropriate element. A negative monatomic ion is named by dropping parts of the ending of the element's name and adding *-ide* to the root.
- The charge of each ion in an ionic compound may be used to determine the simplest chemical formula for the compound.
- Binary compounds are composed of two elements.
- Binary ionic compounds are named by combining the names of the positive and negative ions.
- The old system of naming binary molecular compounds uses prefixes. The new system, known as the *Stock system,* uses oxidation numbers.

## Oxidation Numbers

**Vocabulary**
oxidation number
oxidation state

- Oxidation numbers are useful in naming compounds, in writing formulas, and in balancing chemical equations.
- Compounds containing elements that have more than one oxidation state are named by using the Stock system.
- Stock-system names and prefix-system names are used interchangeably for many molecular compounds.
- Oxidation numbers of each element in a compound may be used to determine the compound's simplest chemical formula.
- By knowing oxidation numbers, we can name compounds without knowing whether they are ionic or molecular.

## Using Chemical Formulas

**Vocabulary**
formula mass
percentage composition

- Formula mass, molar mass, and percentage composition can be calculated from the chemical formula for a compound.
- The percentage composition of a compound is the percentage by mass of each element in the compound.
- Molar mass is used as a conversion factor between amount in moles and mass in grams of a given compound or element.

## Determining Chemical Formulas

**Vocabulary**
empirical formula

- An empirical formula shows the simplest whole-number ratio of atoms in a given compound.
- Empirical formulas indicate how many atoms of each element are combined in the simplest unit of a chemical compound.
- A molecular formula can be found from the empirical formula if the molar mass is measured.

# CHAPTER REVIEW

For more practice, go to the Problem Bank in Appendix D.

## Chemical Names and Formulas

### SECTION 1 REVIEW

1. a. What are monatomic ions?
   b. Give three examples of monatomic ions.
2. How does the chemical formula for the nitrite ion differ from the chemical formula for the nitrate ion?
3. Using only the periodic table, write the symbol of the ion most typically formed by each of the following elements:
   a. K  d. Cl
   b. Ca  e. Ba
   c. S  f. Br
4. Write the formula for and indicate the charge on each of the following ions:
   a. sodium ion
   b. aluminum ion
   c. chloride ion
   d. nitride ion
   e. iron(II) ion
   f. iron(III) ion
5. Name each of the following monatomic ions:
   a. $K^+$  d. $Cl^-$
   b. $Mg^{2+}$  e. $O^{2-}$
   c. $Al^{3+}$  f. $Ca^{2+}$
6. Write formulas for the binary ionic compounds formed between the following elements. (Hint: See Sample Problem A.)
   a. sodium and iodine
   b. calcium and sulfur
   c. zinc and chlorine
   d. barium and fluorine
   e. lithium and oxygen
7. Give the name of each of the following binary ionic compounds. (Hint: See Sample Problem B.)
   a. KCl  c. $Li_2O$
   b. $CaBr_2$  d. $MgCl_2$
8. Write the formulas for and give the names of the compounds formed by the following ions:
   a. $Cr^{2+}$ and $F^-$
   b. $Ni^{2+}$ and $O^{2-}$
   c. $Fe^{3+}$ and $O^{2-}$
9. What determines the order in which the component elements of binary molecular compounds are written?
10. Name the following binary molecular compounds according to the prefix system. (Hint: See Sample Problem D.)
    a. $CO_2$  d. $SeF_6$
    b. $CCl_4$  e. $As_2O_5$
    c. $PCl_5$
11. Write formulas for each of the following binary molecular compounds. (Hint: See Sample Problem D.)
    a. carbon tetrabromide
    b. silicon dioxide
    c. tetraphosphorus decoxide
    d. diarsenic trisulfide
12. Distinguish between binary acids and oxyacids, and give two examples of each.
13. a. What is a salt?
    b. Give two examples of salts.
14. Name each of the following acids:
    a. HF  d. $H_2SO_4$
    b. HBr  e. $H_3PO_4$
    c. $HNO_3$
15. Give the molecular formula for each of the following acids:
    a. sulfurous acid
    b. chloric acid
    c. hydrochloric acid
    d. hypochlorous acid
    e. perchloric acid
    f. carbonic acid
    g. acetic acid

### PRACTICE PROBLEMS

16. Write formulas for each of the following compounds:
    a. sodium fluoride
    b. calcium oxide
    c. potassium sulfide
    d. magnesium chloride
    e. aluminum bromide
    f. lithium nitride
    g. iron(II) oxide

**17.** Name each of the following ions:
a. $NH_4^+$
b. $ClO_3^-$
c. $OH^-$
d. $SO_4^{2-}$
e. $NO_3^-$
f. $CO_3^{2-}$
g. $PO_4^{3-}$
h. $CH_3COO^-$
i. $HCO_3^-$
j. $CrO_4^{2-}$

**18.** Write the formula and charge for each of the following ions:
a. ammonium ion
b. acetate ion
c. hydroxide ion
d. carbonate ion
e. sulfate ion
f. phosphate ion
g. copper(II) ion
h. tin(II) ion
i. iron(III) ion
j. copper(I) ion
k. mercury(I) ion
l. mercury(II) ion

## Oxidation Numbers

### SECTION 2 REVIEW

**19.** Name each of the following ions according to the Stock system:
a. $Fe^{2+}$
b. $Fe^{3+}$
c. $Pb^{2+}$
d. $Pb^{4+}$
e. $Sn^{2+}$
f. $Sn^{4+}$

**20.** Name each of the binary molecular compounds in item 11 by using the Stock system.

**21.** Write formulas for each of the following compounds:
a. phosphorus(III) iodide
b. sulfur(II) chloride
c. carbon(IV) sulfide
d. nitrogen(V) oxide

**22.** a. What are oxidation numbers?
b. What useful functions do oxidation numbers serve?

### PRACTICE PROBLEMS

**23.** Name each of the following ionic compounds by using the Stock system:
a. NaCl
b. KF
c. CaS
d. $Co(NO_3)_2$
e. $FePO_4$
f. $Hg_2SO_4$
g. $Hg_3(PO_4)_2$

**24.** Assign oxidation numbers to each atom in the following compounds. (Hint: See Sample Problem E.)
a. HI
b. $PBr_3$
c. $GeS_2$
d. KH
e. $As_2O_5$
f. $H_3PO_4$

**25.** Assign oxidation numbers to each atom in the following ions. (Hint: See Sample Problem E.)
a. $NO_3^-$
b. $ClO_4^-$
c. $PO_4^{3-}$
d. $Cr_2O_7^{2-}$
e. $CO_3^{2-}$

## Using Chemical Formulas

### SECTION 3 REVIEW

**26.** a. Define *formula mass.*
b. In what unit is formula mass expressed?

**27.** What is meant by the molar mass of a compound?

### PRACTICE PROBLEMS

**28.** Determine the formula mass of each of the following compounds or ions. (Hint: See Sample Problem F.)
a. glucose, $C_6H_{12}O_6$
b. calcium acetate, $Ca(CH_3COO)_2$
c. the ammonium ion, $NH_4^+$
d. the chlorate ion, $ClO_3^-$

**29.** Determine the number of moles of each type of monatomic or polyatomic ion in one mole of the following compounds. For each polyatomic ion, determine the number of moles of each atom present in one mole of the ion.
a. $KNO_3$
b. $Na_2SO_4$
c. $Ca(OH)_2$
d. $(NH_4)_2SO_3$
e. $Ca_3(PO_4)_2$
f. $Al_2(CrO_4)_3$

**30.** Determine the molar mass of each compound listed in item 29. (Hint: See Sample Problem G.)

**31.** Determine the number of moles of compound in each of the following samples. (Hint: See Sample Problem I.)
a. 4.50 g $H_2O$
b. 471.6 g $Ba(OH)_2$
c. 129.68 g $Fe_3(PO_4)_2$

**32.** Determine the percentage composition of each of the following compounds. (Hint: See Sample Problem J.)
a. NaCl
b. $AgNO_3$
c. $Mg(OH)_2$

**33.** Determine the percentage by mass of water in the hydrate $CuSO_4 \cdot 5H_2O$. (Hint: See Sample Problem K.)

## *Determining Chemical Formulas*

### SECTION 4 REVIEW

**34.** What three types of information are used to find an empirical formula from percentage composition data?

**35.** What is the relationship between the empirical formula and the molecular formula of a compound?

### PRACTICE PROBLEMS

**36.** Determine the empirical formula of a compound containing 63.50% silver, 8.25% nitrogen, and 28.25% oxygen. (Hint: See Sample Problem L.)

**37.** Determine the empirical formula of a compound found to contain 52.11% carbon, 13.14% hydrogen, and 34.75% oxygen.

**38.** What is the molecular formula of the molecule that has an empirical formula of $CH_2O$ and a molar mass of 120.12 g/mol?

**39.** A compound with a formula mass of 42.08 amu is found to be 85.64% carbon and 14.36% hydrogen by mass. Find its molecular formula.

## MIXED REVIEW

**40.** Chemical analysis shows that citric acid contains 37.51% C, 4.20% H, and 58.29% O. What is the empirical formula for citric acid?

**41.** Name each of the following compounds by using the Stock system:
a. LiBr
b. $Sn(NO_3)_2$
c. $FeCl_2$
d. MgO
e. KOH
f. $Fe_2O_3$
g. $AgNO_3$
h. $Fe(OH)_2$
i. $CrF_2$

**42.** What is the mass in grams of each of the following samples?
a. 1.000 mol NaCl
b. 2.000 mol $H_2O$
c. 3.500 mol $Ca(OH)_2$
d. 0.625 mol $Ba(NO_3)_2$

**43.** Determine the formula mass and molar mass of each of the following compounds:
a. $XeF_4$
b. $C_{12}H_{24}O_6$
c. $Hg_2I_2$
d. CuCN

**44.** Write the chemical formulas for the following compounds:
a. aluminum fluoride
b. magnesium oxide
c. vanadium(V) oxide
d. cobalt(II) sulfide
e. strontium bromide
f. sulfur trioxide

**45.** How many atoms of each element are contained in a single formula unit of iron(III) formate, $Fe(CHO_2)_3 \cdot H_2O$? What percentage by mass of the compound is water?

**46.** Name each of the following acids, and assign oxidation numbers to the atoms in each:
a. $HNO_2$
b. $H_2SO_3$
c. $H_2CO_3$
d. HI

**47.** Determine the percentage composition of the following compounds:
a. NaClO
b. $H_2SO_3$
c. $C_2H_5COOH$
d. $BeCl_2$

**48.** Name each of the following binary compounds:

a. $MgI_2$
b. NaF
c. $CS_2$
d. $N_2O_4$
e. $SO_2$
f. $PBr_3$
g. $CaCl_2$
h. AgI

**49.** Assign oxidation numbers to each atom in the following molecules and ions:

a. $CO_2$
b. $NH_4^+$
c. $MnO_4^-$
d. $S_2O_3^{2-}$
e. $H_2O_2$
f. $P_4O_{10}$
g. $OF_2$

**50.** A 175.0 g sample of a compound contains 56.15 g C, 9.43 g H, 74.81 g O, 13.11 g N, and 21.49 g Na. What is the compound's empirical formula?

## CRITICAL THINKING

**51. Analyzing Information** Sulfur trioxide is produced in the atmosphere through a reaction of sulfur dioxide and oxygen. Sulfur dioxide is a primary air pollutant. Analyze the formula for sulfur trioxide. Then, list all of the chemical information from the analysis that you can.

**52. Analyzing Data** In the laboratory, a sample of pure nickel was placed in a clean, dry, weighed crucible. The crucible was heated so that the nickel would react with the oxygen in the air. After the reaction appeared complete, the crucible was allowed to cool and the mass was determined. The crucible was reheated and allowed to cool. Its mass was then determined again to be certain that the reaction was complete. The following data were collected:

| | |
|---|---|
| Mass of crucible | = 30.02 g |
| Mass of nickel and crucible | = 31.07 g |
| Mass of nickel oxide and crucible | = 31.36 g |

Determine the following information based on the data given above:

| | |
|---|---|
| Mass of nickel | = |
| Mass of nickel oxide | = |
| Mass of oxygen | = |

Based on your calculations, what is the empirical formula for the nickel oxide?

## USING THE HANDBOOK

**53.** Review the common reactions of Group 1 metals in the *Elements Handbook,* and answer the following questions:

a. Some of the Group 1 metals react with oxygen to form superoxides. Write the formulas for these compounds.
b. What is the charge on each cation for the formulas that you wrote in (a)?
c. How does the charge on the anion vary for oxides, peroxides, and superoxides?

**54.** Review the common reactions of Group 2 metals in the *Elements Handbook,* and answer the following questions:

a. Some of the Group 2 metals react with oxygen to form oxides. Write the formulas for these compounds.
b. Some of the Group 2 metals react with oxygen to form peroxides. Write the formulas for these compounds.
c. Some of the Group 2 metals react with nitrogen to form nitrides. Write the formulas for these compounds.
d. Most Group 2 elements form hydrides. What is hydrogen's oxidation state in these compounds?

**55.** Review the analytical tests for transition metals in the *Elements Handbook,* and answer the following questions:

a. Determine the oxidation state of each metal in the precipitates shown for cadmium, zinc, and lead.
b. Determine the oxidation state of each metal in the complex ions shown for iron, manganese, and cobalt.
c. The copper compound shown is called a *coordination compound.* The ammonia shown in the formula exists as molecules that do not have a charge. Determine copper's oxidation state in this compound.

56. Review the common reactions of Group 15 elements in the *Elements Handbook,* and answer the following questions:
  a. Write formulas for each of the oxides listed for the Group 15 elements.
  b. Determine nitrogen's oxidation state in the oxides listed in (a).

## RESEARCH & WRITING

57. **Nomenclature** Biologists who name newly discovered organisms use a system that is structured very much like the one used by chemists in naming compounds. The system used by biologists is called the *Linnaeus system,* after its creator, Carolus Linnaeus. Research this system in a biology textbook, and then note similarities and differences between the Linnaeus system and chemical nomenclature.

58. **Common Chemicals** Find out the systematic chemical name and write the chemical formula for each of the following common compounds:
  a. baking soda
  b. milk of magnesia
  c. Epsom salts
  d. limestone
  e. lye
  f. wood alcohol

## ALTERNATIVE ASSESSMENT

59. **Performance Assessment** Your teacher will supply you with a note card that has one of the following formulas on it: $NaCH_3COO \cdot 3H_2O$, $MgCl_2 \cdot 6H_2O$, $LiC_2H_3O_2 \cdot 2H_2O$, or $MgSO_4 \cdot 7H_2O$. Design an experiment to determine the percentage of water by mass in the hydrated salt assigned to you. Be sure to explain what steps you will take to ensure that the salt is completely dry. If your teacher approves your design, obtain the salt and perform the experiment. What percentage of water does the salt contain?

60. Both ammonia, $NH_3$, and ammonium nitrate, $NH_4NO_3$, are used in fertilizers as a source of nitrogen. Which compound has the higher percentage of nitrogen? Research the physical properties of both compounds, and find out how each compound is manufactured and used. Explain why each compound has its own particular application. (Consider factors such as the cost of raw ingredients, the ease of manufacture, and shipping costs.)

extension

**Graphing Calculator Calculating Molar Mass**

Go to **go.hrw.com** for a graphing calculator exercise that asks you to calculate the molar mass of a compound.

# Math Tutor CALCULATING PERCENTAGE COMPOSITION

Chemists can analyze an unknown substance by determining its percentage composition by mass. Percentage composition is determined by finding the mass of each element in a sample of the substance as a percentage of the mass of the whole sample. The results of this analysis can then be compared with the percentage composition of known compounds to determine the probable identity of the unknown substance. Once you know a compound's formula, you can determine its percentage composition by mass.

## SAMPLE 1

**Determine the percentage composition of potassium chlorate, $KClO_3$.**

First, calculate the molar mass of $KClO_3$. The formula shows you that one mole of $KClO_3$ consists of 1 mol K atoms, 1 mol Cl atoms, and 3 mol O atoms. Thus, the molar mass of $KClO_3$ is molar mass K + molar mass Cl + 3(molar mass O) = 39.10 g K + 35.45 g Cl + 3(16.00 g O).

$$\text{molar mass } KClO_3 = 122.55 \text{ g}$$

The percentage composition of $KClO_3$ is determined by calculating the percentage of the total molar mass contributed by each element.

$$\frac{\text{mass of element in 1 mol of compound}}{\text{molar mass of compound}} \times 100 = \text{\% element in compound}$$

$$\text{\% K in } KClO_3 = \frac{39.10 \text{ g K}}{122.55 \text{ g } KClO_3} \times 100 = 31.91\%$$

$$\text{\% Cl in } KClO_3 = \frac{35.45 \text{ g Cl}}{122.55 \text{ g } KClO_3} \times 100 = 28.93\%$$

$$\text{\% O in } KClO_3 = \frac{48.00 \text{ g O}}{122.55 \text{ g } KClO_3} \times 100 = 39.17\%$$

## SAMPLE 2

**Determine the percentage of nitrogen in ammonium sulfate, $(NH_4)_2SO_4$.**

Even though you want to find the percentage of only one element, you must calculate the molar mass of $(NH_4)_2SO_4$. To do that, examine the formula to find the number of moles of each element in the compound. The two ammonium groups, indicated by $(NH_4)_2$, contain 2 mol N and 8 mol H per mole of $(NH_4)_2SO_4$. The sulfate group, $SO_4$, contains 1 mol S and 4 mol O per mole of $(NH_4)_2SO_4$.

$$\begin{aligned}
2 \text{ mol N} = 2 \times 14.01 \text{ g} &= 28.02 \text{ g}\\
8 \text{ mol H} = 8 \times 1.01 \text{ g} &= 8.08 \text{ g}\\
1 \text{ mol S} = 1 \times 32.07 &= 32.07 \text{ g}\\
4 \text{ mol O} = 4 \times 16.00 &= 64.00 \text{ g}\\
\text{molar mass } (NH_4)_2SO_4 &= 132.17 \text{ g}
\end{aligned}$$

Now, you can determine the percentage of nitrogen in the compound as follows.

$$\text{\% N in } (NH_4)_2SO_4 = \frac{28.02 \text{ g N}}{132.17 \text{ g } (NH_4)_2SO_4} \times 100 = 21.20\%$$

## PRACTICE PROBLEMS

1. What is the percentage composition of sodium carbonate, $Na_2CO_3$?

2. What is the percentage of iodine in zinc iodate, $Zn(IO_3)_2$?

# Standardized Test Prep

**Answer the following items on a separate piece of paper.**

**MULTIPLE CHOICE**

**1.** Which of the following compounds does not contain a polyatomic ion?
**A.** sodium carbonate
**B.** sodium sulfate
**C.** sodium sulfite
**D.** sodium sulfide

**2.** The correct formula for ammonium phosphate is
**A.** $(NH_4)_3PO_4$.
**B.** $(NH_4)_2PO_4$.
**C.** $NH_4PO_4$.
**D.** $NH_4(PO_4)_2$.

**3.** When writing the formula for a compound that contains a polyatomic ion,
**A.** write the anion's formula first.
**B.** use superscripts to show the number of polyatomic ions present.
**C.** use parentheses if the number of polyatomic ions is greater than 1.
**D.** always place the polyatomic ion in parentheses.

**4.** The correct name for $NH_4CH_3COO$ is
**A.** ammonium carbonate.
**B.** ammonium hydroxide.
**C.** ammonium acetate.
**D.** ammonium nitrate.

**5.** Which of the following is the correct formula for iron(III) sulfate?
**A.** $Fe_3SO_4$
**B.** $Fe_3(SO_4)_2$
**C.** $Fe_2(SO_4)_3$
**D.** $3FeSO_4$

**6.** The molecular formula for acetylene is $C_2H_2$. The molecular formula for benzene is $C_6H_6$. The empirical formula for both is
**A.** CH.
**B.** $C_2H_2$.
**C.** $C_6H_6$.
**D.** $(CH)_2$.

**7.** Which of the following shows the percentage composition of $H_2SO_4$?
**A.** 2.5% H, 39.1% S, 58.5% O
**B.** 2.1% H, 32.7% S, 65.2% O
**C.** 28.6% H, 14.3% S, 57.1% O
**D.** 33.3% H, 16.7% S, 50% O

**8.** Which of the following compounds has the highest percentage of oxygen?
**A.** $CH_4O$
**B.** $CO_2$
**C.** $H_2O$
**D.** $Na_2CO_3$

**9.** The empirical formula for a compound that is 1.2% H, 42.0% Cl, and 56.8% O is
**A.** HClO.
**B.** $HClO_2$.
**C.** $HClO_3$.
**D.** $HClO_4$.

**SHORT ANSWER**

**10.** When a new substance is synthesized or is discovered experimentally, the substance is analyzed quantitatively. What information is obtained from this typical analysis, and how is this information used?

**11.** An oxide of selenium is 28.8% O. Find the empirical formula. Assuming that the empirical formula is also the molecular formula, name the oxide.

**EXTENDED RESPONSE**

**12.** What is an empirical formula, and how does it differ from a molecular formula?

**13.** What are Stock system names based on?

**Test TIP** Whenever possible, highlight or underline numbers or words critical to answering a question correctly.

SEE PRE-LAB
GRAVIMETRIC ANALYSIS

# Determining the Empirical Formula of Magnesium Oxide

## OBJECTIVES

- ***Measure*** **the mass of magnesium oxide.**
- ***Perform*** **a synthesis reaction by using gravimetric techniques.**
- ***Determine*** **the empirical formula of magnesium oxide.**
- ***Calculate*** **the class average and standard deviation for moles of oxygen used.**

## MATERIALS

- **15 cm magnesium ribbon, 2**
- **25 mL beaker**
- **Bunsen burner assembly**
- **clay triangle**
- **crucible and lid, metal or ceramic**
- **crucible tongs**
- **distilled water**
- **eyedropper or micropipet**
- **ring stand**

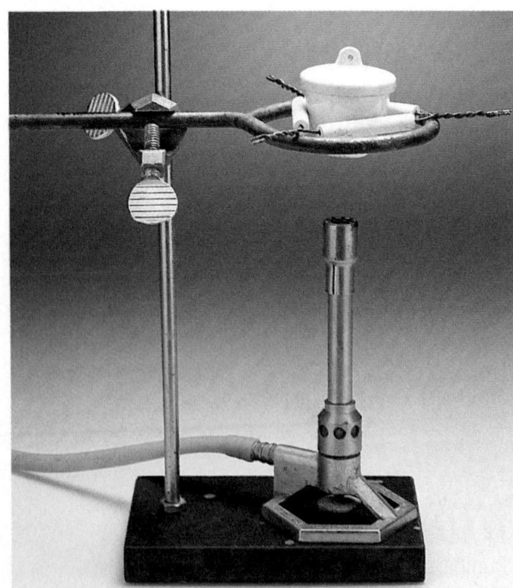

FIGURE A

## BACKGROUND

This gravimetric analysis involves the combustion of magnesium metal in air to synthesize magnesium oxide. The mass of the product is greater than the mass of magnesium used because oxygen reacts with the magnesium metal. As in all gravimetric analyses, success depends on attaining a product yield near 100%. Therefore, the product will be heated and cooled and have its mass measured until two of these mass measurements are within 0.02% of one another. When the masses of the reactant and product have been carefully measured, the amount of oxygen used in the reaction can be calculated. The ratio of oxygen to magnesium can then be established, and the empirical formula of magnesium oxide can be determined.

## SAFETY

For review of safety, please see **Safety in the Chemistry Laboratory** in the front of your book.

## PREPARATION

1. Copy the following data table in your lab notebook.

DATA TABLE

| | Trial 1 | Trial 2 |
|---|---|---|
| 1. Mass of crucible, lid, and metal (g) | | |
| 2. Mass of crucible, lid, and product (g) | | |
| 3. Mass of crucible and lid (g) | | |

## PROCEDURE

1. Construct a setup for heating a crucible as shown in Figure A and as demonstrated in the Pre-Laboratory Procedure "Gravimetric Analysis."

2. Heat the crucible and lid for 5 min to burn off any impurities.

3. Cool the crucible and lid to room temperature. Measure their combined mass, and record the measurement on line 3 of your data table.

   NOTE: Handle the crucible and lid with crucible tongs at all times during this experiment. Such handling prevents burns and the transfer of dirt and oil from your hands to the crucible and lid.

4. Polish a 15 cm strip of magnesium with steel wool. The magnesium should be shiny. Cut the strip into small pieces to make the reaction proceed faster, and place the pieces in the crucible.

5. Cover the crucible with the lid, and measure the mass of the crucible, lid, and metal. Record the measurement on line 1 of your data table.

6. Use tongs to replace the crucible on the clay triangle. Heat the covered crucible gently. Lift the lid occasionally to allow air in.

   CAUTION: Do not look directly at the burning magnesium metal. The brightness of the light can blind you.

7. When the magnesium appears to be fully reacted, partially remove the crucible lid and continue heating for 1 min.

8. Remove the burner from under the crucible. After the crucible has cooled, use an eyedropper to carefully add a few drops of water to decompose any nitrides that may have formed.

   CAUTION: Use care when adding water. Using too much water can cause the crucible to crack.

9. Cover the crucible completely. Replace the burner under the crucible, and continue heating for about 30 to 60 s.

10. Turn off the burner. Cool the crucible, lid, and contents to room temperature. Measure the mass of the crucible, lid, and product. Record the measurement in the margin of your data table.

11. Replace the crucible, lid, and contents on the clay triangle, and reheat for another 2 min. Cool to room temperature, and remeasure the mass of the crucible, lid, and contents. Compare this mass measurement with the measurement obtained in step 10. If the new mass is ±0.02% of the mass in step 10, record the new mass on line 2 of your data table and go on to step 12. If not, your reaction is still incomplete, and you should repeat step 11.

12. Clean the crucible, and repeat steps 2–11 with a second strip of magnesium ribbon. Record your measurements under Trial 2 in your data table.

## CLEANUP AND DISPOSAL

13. Put the solid magnesium oxide in the designated waste container. Return any unused magnesium ribbon to your teacher. Clean your equipment and lab station. Thoroughly wash your hands after completing the lab session and cleanup.

## ANALYSIS AND INTERPRETATION

1. **Applying Ideas:** Calculate the mass of the magnesium metal and the mass of the product.

2. **Evaluating Data:** Determine the mass of the oxygen consumed.

3. **Applying Ideas:** Calculate the number of moles of magnesium and the number of moles of oxygen in the product.

## CONCLUSIONS

1. **Inferring Relationships:** Determine the empirical formula for magnesium oxide, $Mg_xO_y$.

CHAPTER 8

# *Chemical Equations and Reactions*

*The evolution of energy as light and heat is an indication that a chemical reaction is taking place.*

Fireworks

# Describing Chemical Reactions

SECTION 1

C.4.1 Analyze and balance equations for simple synthesis, decomposition, single replacement, double replacement, and combustion reactions

## OBJECTIVES

- List three observations that suggest that a chemical reaction has taken place.
- List three requirements for a correctly written chemical equation.
- Write a word equation and a formula equation for a given chemical reaction.
- Balance a formula equation by inspection.

A *chemical reaction* is the process by which one or more substances are changed into one or more different substances. In any chemical reaction, the original substances are known as the *reactants* and the resulting substances are known as the *products*. According to the law of conservation of mass, the total mass of reactants must equal the total mass of products for any given chemical reaction.

Chemical reactions are described by chemical equations. *A* **chemical equation** *represents, with symbols and formulas, the identities and relative molecular or molar amounts of the reactants and products in a chemical reaction.* For example, the following chemical equation shows that the reactant ammonium dichromate yields the products nitrogen, chromium(III) oxide, and water.

$$(NH_4)_2Cr_2O_7(s) \longrightarrow N_2(g) + Cr_2O_3(s) + 4H_2O(g)$$

This strongly exothermic reaction is shown in **Figure 1.**

## Indications of a Chemical Reaction

To know for certain that a chemical reaction has taken place requires evidence that one or more substances have undergone a change in identity. Absolute proof of such a change can be provided only by chemical analysis of the products. However, certain easily observed changes usually indicate that a chemical reaction has occurred.

1. *Evolution of energy as heat and light.* A change in matter that releases energy as both heat and light is strong evidence that a chemical reaction has taken place. For example, you can see in **Figure 1** that the decomposition of ammonium dichromate is accompanied by the evolution of energy as heat and light. And you can see evidence that a chemical reaction occurs between natural gas and oxygen if you burn gas for cooking in your house. Some reactions involve only heat or only light. But heat or light by itself is not necessarily a sign of chemical change, because many physical changes also involve either heat or light.

**FIGURE 1** The decomposition of ammonium dichromate proceeds rapidly, releasing energy in the form of light and heat.

carbon dioxide and water," or simply, "methane and oxygen yield carbon dioxide and water."

The next step in writing a correct chemical equation is to replace the names of the reactants and products with appropriate symbols and formulas. Methane is a molecular compound composed of one carbon atom and four hydrogen atoms. Its chemical formula is $CH_4$. Recall that oxygen exists in nature as diatomic molecules; it is therefore represented as $O_2$. The correct formulas for carbon dioxide and water are $CO_2$ and $H_2O$, respectively.

*A* **formula equation** *represents the reactants and products of a chemical reaction by their symbols or formulas.* The formula equation for the reaction of methane and oxygen is written as follows.

$$CH_4(g) + O_2(g) \longrightarrow CO_2(g) + H_2O(g) \text{ (not balanced)}$$

The *g* in parentheses after each formula indicates that the corresponding substance is in the gaseous state. Like a word equation, a formula equation is a qualitative statement. It gives no information about the amounts of reactants or products.

A formula equation meets two of the three requirements for a correct chemical equation. It represents the facts and shows the correct symbols and formulas for the reactants and products. To complete the process of writing a correct equation, the law of conservation of mass must be taken into account. The relative amounts of reactants and products represented in the equation must be adjusted so that the numbers and types of atoms are the same on both sides of the equation. This process is called *balancing an equation* and is carried out by inserting coefficients. Once it is balanced, a formula equation is a correctly written chemical equation.

Look again at the formula equation for the reaction of methane and oxygen.

$$CH_4(g) + O_2(g) \longrightarrow CO_2(g) + H_2O(g) \text{ (not balanced)}$$

To balance the equation, begin by counting atoms of elements that are combined with atoms of other elements and that appear only once on each side of the equation. In this case, we could begin by counting either carbon or hydrogen atoms. Usually, the elements hydrogen and oxygen are balanced only after balancing all other elements in an equation. (You will read more about the rules of balancing equations later in the chapter.) Thus, we begin by counting carbon atoms.

Inspecting the formula equation reveals that there is one carbon atom on each side of the arrow. Therefore, carbon is already balanced in the equation. Counting hydrogen atoms reveals that there are four hydrogen atoms in the reactants but only two in the products. Two additional hydrogen atoms are needed on the right side of the equation. They can be added by placing the coefficient 2 in front of the chemical formula $H_2O$.

$$CH_4(g) + O_2(g) \longrightarrow CO_2(g) + 2H_2O(g) \text{ (partially balanced)}$$

A coefficient multiplies the number of atoms of each element indicated in a chemical formula. Thus, $2H_2O$ represents *four* H atoms and *two* O atoms. To add two more hydrogen atoms to the right side of the equation, one may be tempted to change the subscript in the formula of water so that $H_2O$ becomes $H_4O$. However, this would be a mistake because changing the subscripts of a chemical formula changes the *identity* of the compound. $H_4O$ is not a product in the combustion of methane. In fact, there is no such compound. One must use only coefficients to change the relative number of atoms in a chemical equation because coefficients change the numbers of atoms without changing the identities of the reactants or products.

Now consider the number of oxygen atoms. There are four oxygen atoms on the right side of the arrow in the partially balanced equation. Yet there are only two oxygen atoms on the left side of the arrow. One can increase the number of oxygen atoms on the left side to four by placing the coefficient 2 in front of the molecular formula for oxygen. This results in a correct chemical equation, or *balanced formula equation,* for the burning of methane in oxygen.

$$CH_4(g) + 2O_2(g) \longrightarrow CO_2(g) + 2H_2O(g)$$

This reaction is further illustrated in **Figure 3.**

## Additional Symbols Used in Chemical Equations

**Table 2** on the next page summarizes the symbols commonly used in chemical equations. Sometimes a gaseous product is indicated by an arrow pointing upward, ↑, instead of (*g*), as shown in the table. A downward arrow, ↓, is often used to show the formation of a precipitate during a reaction in solution.

The conditions under which a reaction takes place are often indicated by placing information above or below the reaction arrow. The word *heat,*

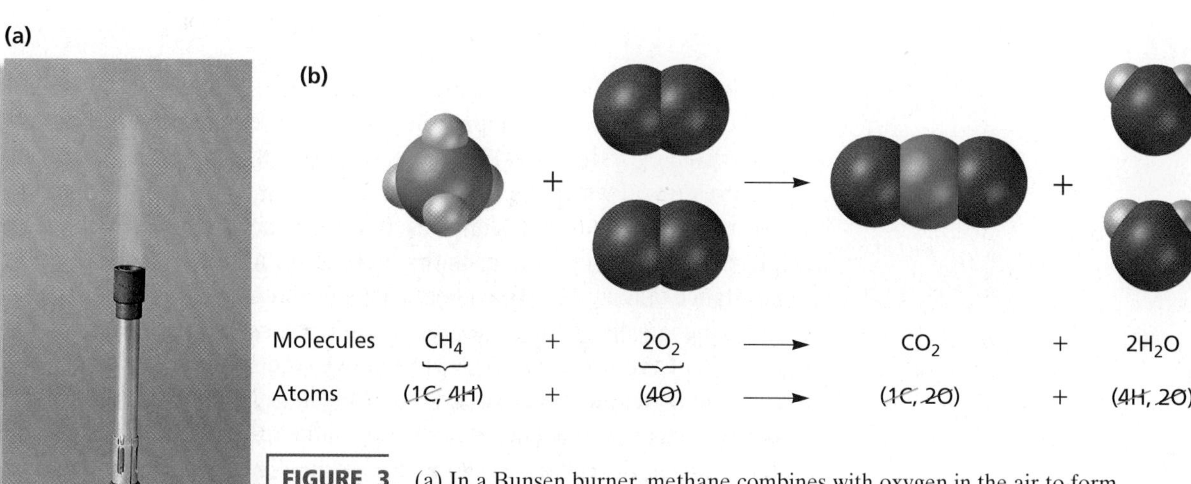


**FIGURE 3** (a) In a Bunsen burner, methane combines with oxygen in the air to form carbon dioxide and water vapor. (b) The reaction is represented by both a molecular model and a balanced equation. Each shows that the number of atoms of each element in the reactants equals the number of atoms of each element in the products.

| **TABLE 2** *Symbols Used in Chemical Equations* | |
|---|---|
| **Symbol** | **Explanation** |
| $\longrightarrow$ | "Yields"; indicates result of reaction |
| $\rightleftarrows$ | Used in place of a single arrow to indicate a reversible reaction |
| $(s)$ | A reactant or product in the solid state; also used to indicate a precipitate |
| $\downarrow$ | Alternative to $(s)$, but used only to indicate a precipitate |
| $(l)$ | A reactant or product in the liquid state |
| $(aq)$ | A reactant or product in an aqueous solution (dissolved in water) |
| $(g)$ | A reactant or product in the gaseous state |
| $\uparrow$ | Alternative to $(g)$, but used only to indicate a gaseous product |
| $\xrightarrow{\Delta}$ or $\xrightarrow{\text{heat}}$ | Reactants are heated |
| $\xrightarrow{\text{2 atm}}$ | Pressure at which reaction is carried out, in this case 2 atm |
| $\xrightarrow{\text{pressure}}$ | Pressure at which reaction is carried out exceeds normal atmospheric pressure |
| $\xrightarrow{0°\text{C}}$ | Temperature at which reaction is carried out, in this case 0°C |
| $\xrightarrow{MnO_2}$ | Formula of catalyst, in this case manganese dioxide, used to alter the rate of the reaction |

symbolized by a Greek capital delta, Δ, indicates that the reactants must be heated. The specific temperature at which a reaction occurs may also be written over the arrow. For some reactions, it is important to specify the pressure at which the reaction occurs or to specify that the pressure must be above normal. Many reactions are speeded up and can take place at lower temperatures in the presence of a *catalyst.* A catalyst is a substance that changes the rate of a chemical reaction but can be recovered unchanged. To show that a catalyst is present, the formula for the catalyst or the word *catalyst* is written over the reaction arrow.

In many reactions, as soon as the products begin to form, they immediately begin to react with each other and re-form the reactants. In other words, the reverse reaction also occurs. The reverse reaction may occur to a greater or lesser degree than the original reaction, depending on the specific reaction and the conditions. *A* **reversible reaction** *is a chemical reaction in which the products re-form the original* *reactants.* The reversibility of a reaction is indicated by writing two arrows pointing in opposite directions. For example, the reversible reaction between iron and water vapor is written as follows.

$$3Fe(s) + 4H_2O(g) \rightleftharpoons Fe_3O_4(s) + 4H_2(g)$$

With an understanding of all the symbols and formulas used, it is possible to translate a chemical equation into a sentence. Consider the following equation.

$$2HgO(s) \xrightarrow{\Delta} 2Hg(l) + O_2(g)$$

Translated into a sentence, this equation reads, "When heated, solid mercury(II) oxide yields liquid mercury and gaseous oxygen."

It is also possible to write a chemical equation from a sentence describing a reaction. Consider the sentence, "Under pressure and in the presence of a platinum catalyst, gaseous ethene and hydrogen form gaseous ethane." This sentence can be translated into the following equation.

$$C_2H_4(g) + H_2(g) \xrightarrow{\text{pressure, Pt}} C_2H_6(g)$$

Throughout this chapter we will often include the symbols for physical states (*s, l, g,* and *aq*) in balanced formula equations. You should be able to interpret these symbols when they are used and to supply them when the necessary information is available.

## SAMPLE PROBLEM A

*For more help, go to the **Math Tutor** at the end of this chapter.*

**Write word and formula equations for the chemical reaction that occurs when solid sodium oxide is added to water at room temperature and forms sodium hydroxide (dissolved in the water). Include symbols for physical states in the formula equation. Then balance the formula equation to give a balanced chemical equation.**

**SOLUTION** The word equation must show the reactants, sodium oxide and water, to the left of the arrow. The product, sodium hydroxide, must appear to the right of the arrow.

$$\text{sodium oxide} + \text{water} \longrightarrow \text{sodium hydroxide}$$

The word equation is converted to a formula equation by replacing the name of each compound with the appropriate chemical formula. To do this requires knowing that sodium has an oxidation state of +1, that oxygen usually has an oxidation state of −2, and that a hydroxide ion has a charge of 1−.

$$Na_2O + H_2O \longrightarrow NaOH \quad \text{(not balanced)}$$

Adding symbols for the physical states of the reactants and products and the coefficient 2 in front of NaOH produces a balanced chemical equation.

$$Na_2O(s) + H_2O(l) \longrightarrow 2NaOH(aq)$$

## SAMPLE PROBLEM B

**Translate the following chemical equation into a sentence:**

$$BaCl_2(aq) + Na_2CrO_4(aq) \longrightarrow BaCrO_4(s) + 2NaCl(aq)$$

**SOLUTION** Each reactant is an ionic compound and is named according to the rules for such compounds. Both reactants are in aqueous solution. One product is a precipitate and the other remains in solution. The equation is translated as follows: Aqueous solutions of barium chloride and sodium chromate react to produce a precipitate of barium chromate plus sodium chloride in aqueous solution.

**PRACTICE** *Answers in Appendix E*

1. Write word and balanced chemical equations for the following reactions. Include symbols for physical states when indicated.
   a. Solid calcium reacts with solid sulfur to produce solid calcium sulfide.
   b. Hydrogen gas reacts with fluorine gas to produce hydrogen fluoride gas. (Hint: See **Table 1.**)
   c. Solid aluminum metal reacts with aqueous zinc chloride to produce solid zinc metal and aqueous aluminum chloride.
2. Translate the following chemical equations into sentences:
   a. $CS_2(l) + 3O_2(g) \longrightarrow CO_2(g) + 2SO_2(g)$
   b. $NaCl(aq) + AgNO_3(aq) \longrightarrow NaNO_3(aq) + AgCl(s)$
3. Hydrazine, $N_2H_4$, is used as rocket fuel. Hydrazine reacts violently with oxygen to produce gaseous nitrogen and water. Write the balanced chemical equation.

Go to **go.hrw.com** for more practice problems that ask you to write balanced chemical equations.

**Keyword:** HC6RXNX

## Significance of a Chemical Equation

Chemical equations are very useful in doing quantitative chemical work. The arrow in a balanced chemical equation is like an equal sign. And the chemical equation as a whole is similar to an algebraic equation in that it expresses an equality. Let's examine some of the quantitative information revealed by a chemical equation.

1. *The coefficients of a chemical reaction indicate relative, not absolute, amounts of reactants and products.* A chemical equation usually shows the smallest numbers of atoms, molecules, or ions that will satisfy the law of conservation of mass in a given chemical reaction.

Consider the equation for the formation of hydrogen chloride from hydrogen and chlorine.

$$H_2(g) + Cl_2(g) \longrightarrow 2HCl(g)$$

The equation indicates that 1 molecule of hydrogen reacts with 1 molecule of chlorine to produce 2 molecules of hydrogen chloride, giving the following molecular ratio of reactants and products.

$$1 \text{ molecule } H_2 : 1 \text{ molecule } Cl_2 : 2 \text{ molecules } HCl$$

This ratio shows the smallest possible relative amounts of the reaction's reactants and products. To obtain larger relative amounts, we simply multiply each coefficient by the same number. Thus, 20 molecules of hydrogen would react with 20 molecules of chlorine to yield 40 molecules of hydrogen chloride. The reaction can also be considered in terms of amounts in moles: 1 mol of hydrogen molecules reacts with 1 mol of chlorine molecules to yield 2 mol of hydrogen chloride molecules.

2. *The relative masses of the reactants and products of a chemical reaction can be determined from the reaction's coefficients.* Recall from **Figure 4** in Chapter 7 that an amount of an element or compound in moles can be converted to a mass in grams by multiplying by the appropriate molar mass. We know that 1 mol of hydrogen reacts with 1 mol of chlorine to yield 2 mol of hydrogen chloride. The relative masses of the reactants and products are calculated as follows.

$$\cancel{1 \text{ mol } H_2} \times \frac{2.02 \text{ g } H_2}{\cancel{\text{mol } H_2}} = 2.02 \text{ g } H_2$$

$$\cancel{1 \text{ mol } Cl_2} \times \frac{70.90 \text{ g } Cl_2}{\cancel{\text{mol } Cl_2}} = 70.90 \text{ g } Cl_2$$

$$\cancel{2 \text{ mol } HCl} \times \frac{36.46 \text{ g } HCl}{\cancel{\text{mol } HCl}} = 72.92 \text{ g } HCl$$

The chemical equation shows that 2.02 g of hydrogen will react with 70.90 g of chlorine to yield 72.92 g of hydrogen chloride.

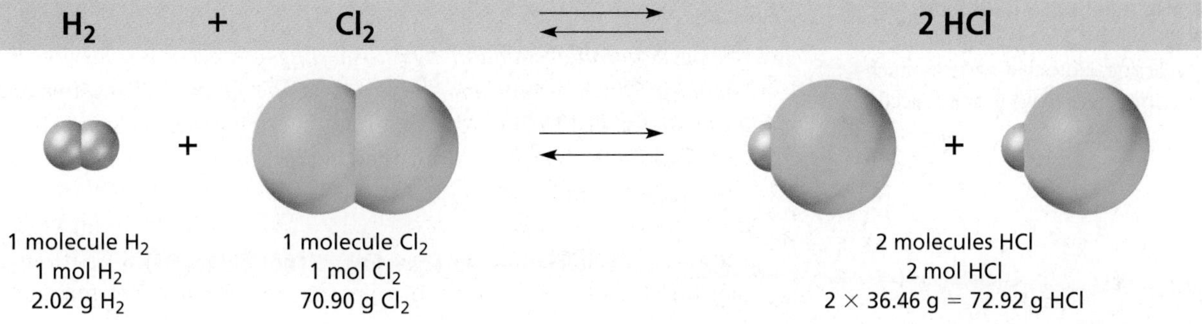


**FIGURE 4** This representation of the reaction of hydrogen and chlorine to yield hydrogen chloride shows several ways to interpret the quantitative information of a chemical reaction.

3. *The reverse reaction for a chemical equation has the same relative amounts of substances as the forward reaction.* Because a chemical equation is like an algebraic equation, the equality can be read in either direction. Reading the hydrogen chloride formation equation on the previous page from right to left, we can see that 2 molecules of hydrogen chloride break down to form 1 molecule of hydrogen plus 1 molecule of chlorine. Similarly, 2 mol (72.92 g) of hydrogen chloride yield 1 mol (2.02 g) of hydrogen and 1 mol (70.90 g) of chlorine.

We have seen that a chemical equation provides useful quantitative information about a chemical reaction. However, there is also important information that is *not* provided by a chemical equation. For instance, an equation gives no indication of whether a reaction will actually occur. A chemical equation can be written for a reaction that may not even take place. Some guidelines about the types of simple reactions that can be expected to occur are given in Sections 2 and 3. And later chapters provide additional guidelines for other types of reactions. In all these guidelines, it is important to remember that experimentation forms the basis for confirming that a particular chemical reaction will occur.

In addition, chemical equations give no information about the speed at which reactions occur or about how the bonding between atoms or ions changes during the reaction. These aspects of chemical reactions are discussed in Chapter 17.

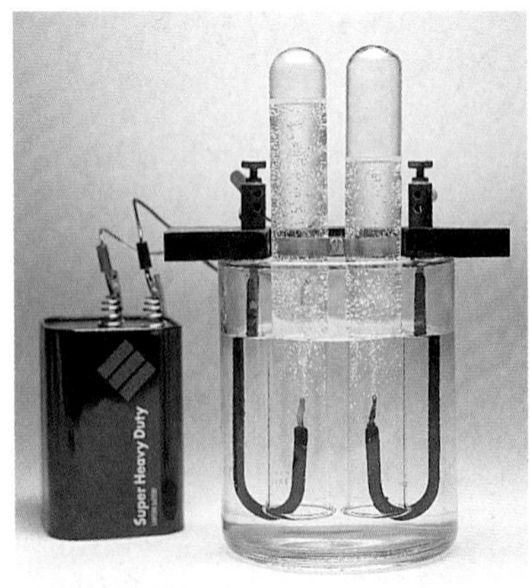

**FIGURE 5** When an electric current is passed through water that has been made slightly conductive, the water molecules break down to yield hydrogen (in tube at right) and oxygen (in tube at left). Bubbles of each gas are evidence of the reaction. Note that twice as much hydrogen as oxygen is produced.

## Balancing Chemical Equations

Most of the equations in the remainder of this chapter can be balanced by inspection. The following procedure demonstrates how to master balancing equations by inspection using a step-by-step approach. The equation for the decomposition of water (see **Figure 5**) will be used as an example.

1. *Identify the names of the reactants and the products, and write a word equation.* The word equation for the reaction shown in **Figure 5** is written as follows.

$$\text{water} \longrightarrow \text{hydrogen} + \text{oxygen}$$

2. *Write a formula equation by substituting correct formulas for the names of the reactants and the products.* We know that the formula for water is $H_2O$. And recall that both hydrogen and oxygen exist as diatomic molecules. Therefore, their correct formulas are $H_2$ and $O_2$, respectively.

$$H_2O(l) \longrightarrow H_2(g) + O_2(g) \quad \text{(not balanced)}$$

**3.** *Balance the formula equation according to the law of conservation of mass.* This last step is done by trial and error. Coefficients are changed and the numbers of atoms are counted on both sides of the equation. When the numbers of each type of atom are the same for both the products and the reactants, the equation is balanced. The trial-and-error method of balancing equations is made easier by the use of the following guidelines.

- Balance the different types of atoms one at a time.
- First balance the atoms of elements that are combined and that appear only once on each side of the equation.
- Balance polyatomic ions that appear on both sides of the equation as single units.
- Balance H atoms and O atoms after atoms of all other elements have been balanced.

The formula equation in our example shows that there are two oxygen atoms on the right and only one on the left. To balance oxygen atoms, the number of $H_2O$ molecules must be increased. Placing the coefficient 2 before $H_2O$ gives the necessary two oxygen atoms on the left.

$$2H_2O(l) \longrightarrow H_2(g) + O_2(g) \quad \text{(partially balanced)}$$

The coefficient 2 in front of $H_2O$ has upset the balance of hydrogen atoms. Placing the coefficient 2 in front of hydrogen, $H_2$, on the right, gives an equal number of hydrogen atoms (4) on both sides of the equation.

$$2H_2O(l) \longrightarrow 2H_2(g) + O_2(g)$$

**4.** *Count atoms to be sure that the equation is balanced.* Make sure that equal numbers of atoms of each element appear on both sides of the arrow.

$$\begin{array}{ccc} 2H_2O(l) & \longrightarrow & 2H_2(g) + O_2(g) \\ (4\not{H} + 2\not{O}) & = & (4\not{H}) \;+\; (2\not{O}) \end{array}$$

Occasionally at this point, the coefficients do not represent the smallest possible whole-number ratio of reactants and products. When this happens, the coefficients should be divided by their greatest common factor in order to obtain the smallest possible whole-number coefficients.

Balancing chemical equations by inspection becomes easier as you gain experience. Learn to avoid the most common mistakes: (1) writing incorrect chemical formulas for reactants or products and (2) trying to balance an equation by changing subscripts. Remember that subscripts cannot be added, deleted, or changed. Eventually, you will probably be able to skip writing the word equation and each separate step. However, *do not* leave out the final step of counting atoms to be sure the equation is balanced.

## SAMPLE PROBLEM C

For more help, go to the *Math Tutor* at the end of this chapter.

**The reaction of zinc with aqueous hydrochloric acid produces a solution of zinc chloride and hydrogen gas. This reaction is shown at right in Figure 6. Write a balanced chemical equation for the reaction.**

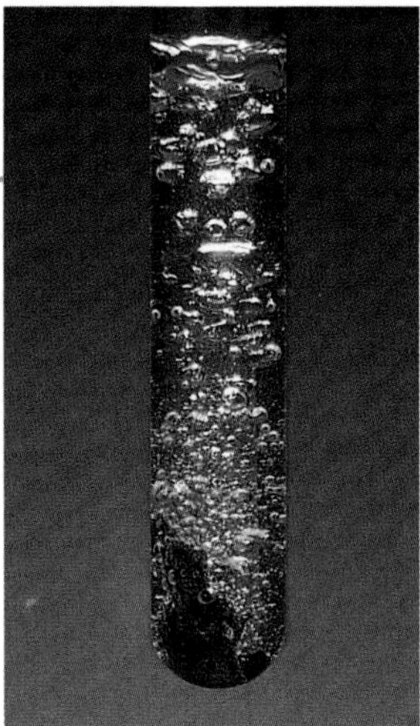

**FIGURE 6** Solid zinc reacts with hydrochloric acid to form aqueous zinc chloride and hydrogen gas.

### SOLUTION

**1 ANALYZE** *Write the word equation.*

zinc + hydrochloric acid ⟶ zinc chloride + hydrogen

**2 PLAN** *Write the formula equation.*

$$Zn(s) + HCl(aq) \longrightarrow ZnCl_2(aq) + H_2(g) \text{ (not balanced)}$$

**3 COMPUTE** *Adjust the coefficients.* Note that chlorine and hydrogen each appear only once on each side of the equation. We balance chlorine first because it is combined on both sides of the equation. Also, recall from the guidelines on the previous page that hydrogen and oxygen are balanced only after all other elements in the reaction are balanced. To balance chlorine, we place the coefficient 2 before HCl. Two molecules of hydrogen chloride also yield the required two hydrogen atoms on the right. Finally, note that there is one zinc atom on each side in the formula equation. Therefore, no further coefficients are needed.

$$Zn(s) + 2HCl(aq) \longrightarrow ZnCl_2(aq) + H_2(g)$$

**4 EVALUATE** *Count atoms to check balance.*

$$Zn(s) + 2HCl(aq) \longrightarrow ZnCl_2(aq) + H_2(g)$$
$$(1\cancel{Zn}) + (2\cancel{H} + 2\cancel{Cl}) = (1\cancel{Zn} + 2\cancel{Cl}) + (2\cancel{H})$$

The equation is balanced.

### PRACTICE

Answers in Appendix E

1. Write word, formula, and balanced chemical equations for each of the following reactions:
   a. Solid magnesium and aqueous hydrochloric acid react to produce aqueous magnesium chloride and hydrogen gas.
   b. Aqueous nitric acid reacts with solid magnesium hydroxide to produce aqueous magnesium nitrate and water.
2. Solid calcium metal reacts with water to form aqueous calcium hydroxide and hydrogen gas. Write a balanced chemical equation for this reaction.

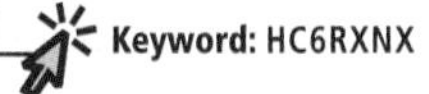

**extension**

Go to **go.hrw.com** for more practice problems that ask you to write balanced chemical equations.

**Keyword: HC6RXNX**

## SAMPLE PROBLEM D

*For more help, go to the* ***Math Tutor*** *at the end of this chapter.*

**Solid aluminum carbide, $Al_4C_3$, reacts with water to produce methane gas and solid aluminum hydroxide. Write a balanced chemical equation for this reaction.**

**SOLUTION** The reactants are aluminum carbide and water. The products are methane and aluminum hydroxide. The formula equation is written as follows.

$$Al_4C_3(s) + H_2O(l) \longrightarrow CH_4(g) + Al(OH)_3(s) \quad \text{(not balanced)}$$

Begin balancing the formula equation by counting either aluminum atoms or carbon atoms. (Remember that hydrogen and oxygen atoms are balanced last.) There are four Al atoms on the left. To balance Al atoms, place the coefficient 4 before $Al(OH)_3$ on the right.

$$Al_4C_3(s) + H_2O(l) \longrightarrow CH_4(g) + 4Al(OH)_3(s) \quad \text{(partially balanced)}$$

Now balance the carbon atoms. With three C atoms on the left, the coefficient 3 must be placed before $CH_4$ on the right.

$$Al_4C_3(s) + H_2O(l) \longrightarrow 3CH_4(g) + 4Al(OH)_3(s) \quad \text{(partially balanced)}$$

Balance oxygen atoms next because oxygen, unlike hydrogen, appears only once on each side of the equation. There is one O atom on the left and 12 O atoms in the four $Al(OH)_3$ formula units on the right. Placing the coefficient 12 before $H_2O$ balances the O atoms.

$$Al_4C_3(s) + 12H_2O(l) \longrightarrow 3CH_4(g) + 4Al(OH)_3(s)$$

This leaves the hydrogen atoms to be balanced. There are 24 H atoms on the left. On the right, there are 12 H atoms in the methane molecules and 12 in the aluminum hydroxide formula units, totaling 24 H atoms. The H atoms are balanced.

$$\begin{array}{ccccccc} Al_4C_3(s) & + & 12H_2O(l) & \longrightarrow & 3CH_4(g) & + & 4Al(OH)_3(s) \\ (\cancel{4Al} + \cancel{3C}) & + & (\cancel{24H} + \cancel{12O}) & = & (\cancel{3C} + \cancel{12H}) & + & (\cancel{4Al} + \cancel{12H} + \cancel{12O}) \end{array}$$

The equation is balanced.

## SAMPLE PROBLEM E

*For more help, go to the* ***Math Tutor*** *at the end of this chapter.*

**Aluminum sulfate and calcium hydroxide are used in a water-purification process. When added to water, they dissolve and react to produce two insoluble products, aluminum hydroxide and calcium sulfate. These products settle out, taking suspended solid impurities with them. Write a balanced chemical equation for the reaction.**

**SOLUTION** Each of the reactants and products is an ionic compound. Recall from Chapter 7 that the formulas of ionic compounds are determined by the charges of the ions composing each compound. The formula reaction is thus written as follows.

$$Al_2(SO_4)_3 + Ca(OH)_2 \longrightarrow Al(OH)_3 + CaSO_4 \quad \text{(not balanced)}$$

There is one Ca atom on each side of the equation, so the calcium atoms are already balanced. There are two Al atoms on the left and one Al atom on the right. Placing the coefficient 2 in front of $Al(OH)_3$ produces the same number of Al atoms on each side of the equation.

$$Al_2(SO_4)_3 + Ca(OH)_2 \longrightarrow 2Al(OH)_3 + CaSO_4 \text{ (partially balanced)}$$

Next, checking $SO_4^{2-}$ ions shows that there are three $SO_4^{2-}$ ions on the left side of the equation and only one on the right side. Placing the coefficient 3 before $CaSO_4$ gives an equal number of $SO_4^{2-}$ ions on each side.

$$Al_2(SO_4)_3 + Ca(OH)_2 \longrightarrow 2Al(OH)_3 + 3CaSO_4 \text{ (partially balanced)}$$

There are now three Ca atoms on the right, however. By placing the coefficient 3 in front of $Ca(OH)_2$, we once again have an equal number of Ca atoms on each side. This last step also gives six $OH^-$ ions on both sides of the equation.

$$Al_2(SO_4)_3(aq) + 3Ca(OH)_2(aq) \longrightarrow 2Al(OH)_3(s) + 3CaSO_4(s)$$
$$(2\cancel{Al} + \cancel{3SO_4^{2-}}) + (\cancel{3Ca} + \cancel{6OH^-}) = (2\cancel{Al} + \cancel{6OH^-}) + (\cancel{3Ca} + \cancel{3SO_4^{2-}})$$

The equation is balanced.

**PRACTICE**

*Answers in Appendix E*

1. Write balanced chemical equations for each of the following reactions:
   a. Solid sodium combines with chlorine gas to produce solid sodium chloride.
   b. When solid copper reacts with aqueous silver nitrate, the products are aqueous copper(II) nitrate and solid silver.
   c. In a blast furnace, the reaction between solid iron(III) oxide and carbon monoxide gas produces solid iron and carbon dioxide gas.

Go to **go.hrw.com** for more practice problems that ask you to write balanced chemical equations.

**Keyword: HC6RXNX**

## SECTION REVIEW

1. Describe the differences between word equations, formula equations, and chemical equations.
2. Write word and formula equations for the reaction in which aqueous solutions of sulfuric acid and sodium hydroxide react to form aqueous sodium sulfate and water.
3. Translate the following chemical equations into sentences:
   **a.** $2K(s) + 2H_2O(l) \longrightarrow 2KOH(aq) + H_2(g)$
   **b.** $2Fe(s) + 3Cl_2(g) \longrightarrow 2FeCl_3(s)$
4. Write the word, formula, and chemical equations for the reaction between hydrogen sulfide gas and oxygen gas that produces sulfur dioxide gas and water vapor.

**Critical Thinking**

5. **INTEGRATING CONCEPTS** The reaction of vanadium(II) oxide with iron(III) oxide results in the formation of vanadium(V) oxide and iron(II) oxide. Write the balanced chemical equation.

# Chemistry in Action

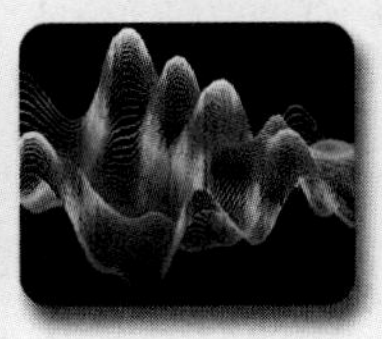

## Carbon Monoxide Catalyst

Colorless, odorless, and deadly—carbon monoxide, "the silent killer," causes the deaths of hundreds of Americans every year. When fuel does not burn completely in a combustion process, carbon monoxide is produced. Often this occurs in a malfunctioning heater, furnace, or fireplace. When the carbon monoxide is inhaled, it bonds to the hemoglobin in the blood, leaving the body oxygen starved. Before people realize a combustion device is malfunctioning, it's often too late.

$$O_2Hb + CO \rightarrow COHb + O_2$$

*Carbon monoxide, CO, has almost 200 times the affinity to bind with the hemoglobin, Hb, in the blood as oxygen. This means that hemoglobin will bind to carbon monoxide rather than oxygen in the body. If enough carbon monoxide is present in the blood, it can be fatal.*

Carbon monoxide poisoning can be prevented by installing filters that absorb the gas. After a time, however, filters become saturated, and then carbon monoxide can pass freely into the air. The best way to prevent carbon monoxide poisoning is not just to filter out the gas, but to eliminate it completely.

The solution came to research chemists at NASA who were working on a problem with a space-based laser. In order to operate properly, NASA's space-based carbon dioxide laser needed to be fed a continuous supply of $CO_2$. This was necessary because as a byproduct of its operation, the laser degraded some of the $CO_2$ into carbon monoxide and oxygen. To address this problem, NASA scientists developed a catalyst made of tin oxide and platinum that oxidized the waste carbon monoxide back into carbon dioxide. The NASA scientists then realized that this catalyst had the potential to be used in many applications here on Earth, including removing carbon monoxide from houses and other buildings.

Typically, a malfunctioning heater circulates the carbon monoxide it produces through its air intake system back into a dwelling space. Installing the catalyst in the air intake would oxidize any carbon monoxide to nontoxic carbon dioxide before it reentered the room.

"The form of our catalyst is a very thin coating on some sort of a support, or substrate as we call it," says NASA chemist David Schryer. "And that support, or substrate, can be any one of a number of things. The great thing about a catalyst is that the only thing that matters about it is its surface. So a catalyst can be incredibly thin and still be very effective."

The idea of using catalysts to oxidize gases is not a new one. Catalytic converters in cars oxidize carbon monoxide and unburned hydrocarbons to minimize pollution. Many substances are oxidized into new materials for manufacturing purposes. But both of these types of catalytic reactions occur at very high temperatures. NASA's catalyst is special, because it's able to eliminate carbon monoxide at room temperature.

According to David Schryer, low-temperature catalysts constitute a whole new class of catalysts with abundant applications for the future.

### Questions

1. How did NASA's research on the space-based carbon dioxide laser result in a benefit for consumers?
2. According to the chemical reaction, if there are 4.5 mol of oxygenated hemoglobin present in an excess of carbon monoxide, how many moles of hemoglobin would release oxygen and bind to carbon monoxide? Explain your answer.

SCILINKS.
www.scilinks.org
**Topic:** Carbon Monoxide
**Code:** HC60219

SECTION 2

# Types of Chemical Reactions

## Objectives

- Define and give general equations for *synthesis, decomposition, single-displacement,* and *double-displacement* reactions.
- Classify a reaction as a synthesis, decomposition, single-displacement, double-displacement, or combustion reaction.
- List three kinds of synthesis reactions and six kinds of decomposition reactions.
- List four kinds of single-displacement reactions and three kinds of double-displacement reactions.
- Predict the products of simple reactions given the reactants.

**C.4.1** Analyze and balance equations for simple synthesis, decomposition, single replacement, double replacement, and combustion reactions

Thousands of known chemical reactions occur in living systems, in industrial processes, and in chemical laboratories. Often it is necessary to predict the products formed in one of these reactions. Memorizing the equations for so many chemical reactions would be a difficult task. It is therefore more useful and realistic to classify reactions according to various similarities and regularities. This general information about reaction types can then be used to predict the products of specific reactions.

There are several ways to classify chemical reactions, and none are entirely satisfactory. The classification scheme described in this section provides an introduction to five basic types of reactions: synthesis, decomposition, single-displacement, double-displacement, and combustion reactions. In later chapters, you will be introduced to categories that are useful in classifying other types of chemical reactions.

## Synthesis Reactions

*In a* **synthesis reaction,** *also known as a composition reaction, two or more substances combine to form a new compound.* This type of reaction is represented by the following general equation.

$$A + X \longrightarrow AX$$

A and X can be elements or compounds. AX is a compound. The following examples illustrate several kinds of synthesis reactions.

### Reactions of Elements with Oxygen and Sulfur

One simple type of synthesis reaction is the combination of an element with oxygen to produce an *oxide* of the element. Almost all metals react with oxygen to form oxides. For example, when a thin strip of magnesium metal is placed in an open flame, it burns with bright white light. When the metal strip is completely burned, only a fine white powder of magnesium oxide is left. This chemical reaction, shown in **Figure 7** on the next page, is represented by the following equation.

$$2Mg(s) + O_2(g) \longrightarrow 2MgO(s)$$

The other Group 2 elements react in a similar manner, forming oxides with the formula MO, where M represents the metal. The Group 1 metals form oxides with the formula $M_2O$, for example, $Li_2O$. The Group 1 and Group 2 elements react similarly with sulfur, forming *sulfides* with the formulas $M_2S$ and MS, respectively. Examples of these types of synthesis reactions are shown below.

$$16Rb(s) + S_8(s) \longrightarrow 8Rb_2S(s)$$
$$8Ba(s) + S_8(s) \longrightarrow 8BaS(s)$$

Some metals, such as iron, combine with oxygen to produce two different oxides.

$$2Fe(s) + O_2(g) \longrightarrow 2FeO(s)$$
$$4Fe(s) + 3O_2(g) \longrightarrow 2Fe_2O_3(s)$$

In the product of the first reaction, iron is in an oxidation state of +2. In the product of the second reaction, iron is in an oxidation state of +3. The particular oxide formed depends on the conditions surrounding the reactants. Both oxides are shown below in **Figure 8.**

Nonmetals also undergo synthesis reactions with oxygen to form oxides. Sulfur, for example, reacts with oxygen to form sulfur dioxide. And when carbon is burned in air, carbon dioxide is produced.

$$S_8(s) + 8O_2(g) \longrightarrow 8SO_2(g)$$
$$C(s) + O_2(g) \longrightarrow CO_2(g)$$

In a limited supply of oxygen, carbon monoxide is formed.

$$2C(s) + O_2(g) \longrightarrow 2CO(g)$$

Hydrogen reacts with oxygen to form dihydrogen monoxide, better known as water.

$$2H_2(g) + O_2(g) \longrightarrow 2H_2O(g)$$

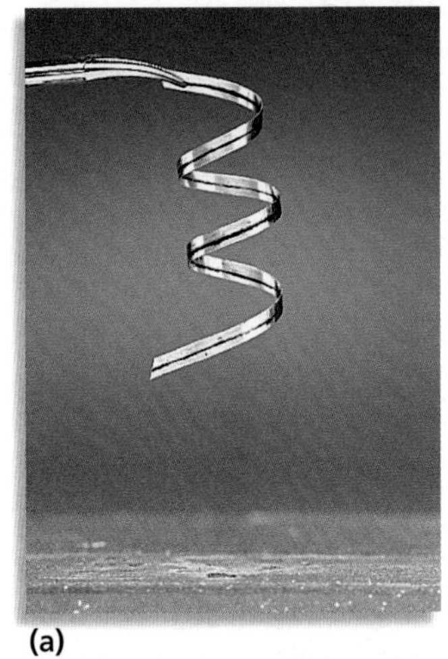

(a)

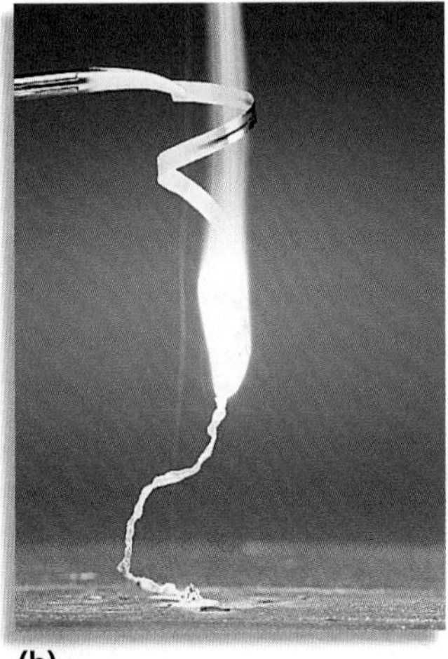

(b)

**FIGURE 7** Magnesium, Mg, pictured in (a), undergoes a synthesis reaction with oxygen, $O_2$, in the air to produce magnesium oxide, MgO, as shown in (b).

(a) (b)

**FIGURE 8** Iron, Fe, and oxygen, $O_2$, combine to form two different oxides: (a) iron(II) oxide, FeO, and (b) iron(III) oxide, $Fe_2O_3$.

## QuickLAB

Wear safety goggles and an apron.

# Balancing Equations Using Models

### Materials

- large and small gumdrops in at least four different colors
- toothpicks

### Question

**How can molecular models and formula-unit ionic models be used to balance chemical equations and classify chemical reactions?**

### Procedure

Examine the partial equations in Groups A–E. Using different-colored gumdrops to represent atoms of different elements, make models of the reactions by connecting the appropriate "atoms" with toothpicks. Use your models to (1) balance equations (a) and (b) in each group, (2) determine the products for reaction (c) in each group, and (3) complete and balance each equation (c). Finally, (4) classify each group of reactions by type.

**Group A**

**a.** $H_2 + Cl_2 \longrightarrow HCl$

**b.** $Mg + O_2 \longrightarrow MgO$

**c.** $BaO + H_2O \longrightarrow$ ______

**Group B**

**a.** $H_2CO_3 \longrightarrow CO_2 + H_2O$

**b.** $KClO_3 \longrightarrow KCl + O_2$

**c.** $H_2O \xrightarrow{\text{electricity}}$ ______

**Group C**

**a.** $Ca + H_2O \longrightarrow Ca(OH)_2 + H_2$

**b.** $KI + Br_2 \longrightarrow KBr + I_2$

**c.** $Zn + HCl \longrightarrow$ ______

**Group D**

**a.** $AgNO_3 + NaCl \longrightarrow AgCl + NaNO_3$

**b.** $FeS + HCl \longrightarrow FeCl_2 + H_2S$

**c.** $H_2SO_4 + KOH \longrightarrow$ ______

**Group E**

**a.** $CH_4 + O_2 \longrightarrow CO_2 + H_2O$

**b.** $CO + O_2 \longrightarrow CO_2$

**c.** $C_3H_8 + O_2 \longrightarrow$ ______

## SECTION REVIEW

1. List five types of chemical reactions.
2. Classify each of the following reactions as a synthesis, decomposition, single-displacement, double-displacement, or combustion reaction:
   - **a.** $N_2(g) + 3H_2(g) \longrightarrow 2NH_3(g)$
   - **b.** $2Li(s) + 2H_2O(l) \longrightarrow 2LiOH(aq) + H_2(g)$
   - **c.** $2NaNO_3(s) \longrightarrow 2NaNO_2(s) + O_2(g)$
   - **d.** $2C_6H_{14}(l) + 19O_2(g) \longrightarrow 12CO_2(g) + 14H_2O(l)$
3. For each of the following reactions, identify the missing reactant(s) or products(s) and then balance the resulting equation. Note that each empty slot may require one or more substances.
   - **a.** synthesis: ______ $\longrightarrow Li_2O$
   - **b.** decomposition: $Mg(ClO_3)_2 \longrightarrow$ ______
   - **c.** double displacement: $HNO_3 + Ca(OH)_2 \longrightarrow$ ______
   - **d.** combustion: $C_5H_{12} + O_2 \longrightarrow$ ______
4. For each of the following reactions, write the missing product(s) and then balance the resulting equation. Identify each reaction by type.
   - **a.** $Br_2 + KI \longrightarrow$ ______
   - **b.** $NaClO_3 \xrightarrow{\Delta}$ ______
   - **c.** $C_7H_{14} + O_2 \longrightarrow$ ______
   - **d.** $CuCl_2 + Na_2S \longrightarrow$ ______

### Critical Thinking

5. **INFERRING RELATIONSHIPS** In an experiment, an iron sample is oxidized to iron(III) oxide by oxygen, which is generated in the thermal decomposition of potassium chlorate. Write the two chemical reactions in the correct sequence.

SECTION 3

# Activity Series of the Elements

C.4.3 Analyze the energy changes (endothermic or exothermic) associated with chemical reactions

## OBJECTIVES

- Explain the significance of an activity series.
- Use an activity series to predict whether a given reaction will occur and what the products will be.

The ability of an element to react is referred to as the element's *activity*. The more readily an element reacts with other substances, the greater its activity is. *An* **activity series** *is a list of elements organized according to the ease with which the elements undergo certain chemical reactions.* For metals, greater activity means a greater ease of *loss* of electrons, to form positive ions. For nonmetals, greater activity means a greater ease of *gain* of electrons, to form negative ions.

The order in which the elements are listed is usually determined by single-displacement reactions. The most-active element, placed at the top in the series, can replace each of the elements below it from a compound in a single-displacement reaction. An element farther down can replace any element below it but not any above it. For example, in the discussion of single-displacement reactions in Section 2, it was noted that each halogen will react to replace any halogen listed below it in the periodic table. Therefore, an activity series for the Group 17 elements lists them in the same order, from top to bottom, as they appear in the periodic table. This is shown in **Table 3** on the next page.

As mentioned in Section 1, the fact that a chemical equation can be written does not necessarily mean that the reaction it represents will actually take place. Activity series are used to help predict whether certain chemical reactions will occur. For example, according to the activity series for metals in **Table 3,** aluminum replaces zinc. Therefore, we could predict that the following reaction does occur.

$$2Al(s) + 3ZnCl_2(aq) \longrightarrow 3Zn(s) + 2AlCl_3(aq)$$

Cobalt, however, cannot replace sodium. Therefore, we write the following.

$$Co(s) + 2NaCl(aq) \longrightarrow \text{no reaction}$$

It is important to remember that like many other aids used to predict the products of chemical reactions, activity series are based on experiment. The information that they contain is used as a general guide for predicting reaction outcomes. For example, the activity series reflects the fact that some metals (potassium, for example) react vigorously with water and acids, replacing hydrogen to form new compounds. Other metals, such as iron or zinc, replace hydrogen in acids such as hydrochloric acid but react with water only when the water is hot

SCILINKS.
www.scilinks.org
Topic: Activity Series
Code: HC60019

# Chemistry in Action

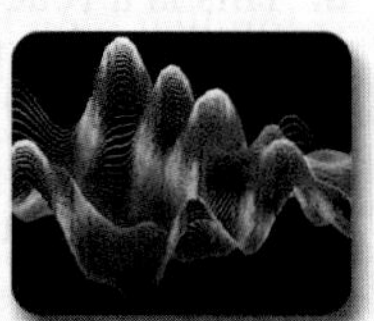

## Combustion Synthesis

What do aerospace materials, cutting tools, catalytic materials, ceramic engine parts, ball bearings, high-temperature superconductors, hydrogen storage, and fuel cells have in common? They are made of ceramics, composites, and other advanced materials.

Conventional techniques used to make these materials consist of a high-temperature furnace, with temperatures ranging from 500°C to 2000°C, to supply the energy needed for the reaction to take place. Because these furnaces may reach only 2000°C, it may take minutes to hours to convert reactants to solid-state products, and the mixtures are heated unevenly. As a result, flaws can be introduced into the structures, which can cause stress points in the materials.

A different high-temperature technique is *combustion synthesis,* which generates its own energy to keep the reaction continuing. Once the reactant mixture is ignited, a heat wave moves through the sample, producing the solid-state product. The mixture can reach temperatures up to 4000°C, twice what is possible with conventional high-temperature furnaces. Combustion synthesis also allows reactions to be completed in just seconds. Hence, this technique produces the desired material faster and requires less supplied energy than conventional techniques do. In addition, the intense and quick heating produces materials that are chemically homogeneous. More than 500 compounds, such as lightweight and heat-resistant aerospace materials, are created by combustion synthesis.

In a typical combustion synthesis procedure, the reactant powders are mixed and then pressed into a cylindrical pellet. The pellet is ignited by an intense heat source, such as an electrically heated coil or a laser. Because the combustion-synthesis reaction is very exothermic, the reaction is self-propagating, and the process does not need any further input of energy. This type of self-propagation is called a *reaction wave,* in which the reaction propagates through the starting material in a self-sustained manner. Therefore, compared with conventional high-temperature methods, this technique is an energy-saving process. In addition, the high temperatures and short reaction times can produce materials that would not be synthesized under conventional conditions. Currently, scientists are studying reaction waves, including how they move through the initial mixtures. As scientists better understand the characteristics of combustion synthesis, they can refine the technique to be more useful in advanced materials production.

### Questions

1. Why is this technique called *combustion synthesis?*
2. Why might this technique result in a more chemically homogeneous material?

▼ *Once the reactant mixture is ignited, the combustion wave moves through the sample, synthesizing the solid-state product.*

# CHAPTER HIGHLIGHTS

## Describing Chemical Reactions

**Vocabulary**
chemical equation
precipitate
coefficient
word equation
formula equation
reversible reaction

- Four observations that suggest a chemical reaction is taking place are the evolution of energy as heat and light, the production of gas, a change in color, and the formation of a precipitate.
- A balanced chemical equation represents, with symbols and formulas, the identities and relative amounts of reactants and products in a chemical reaction.

## Types of Chemical Reactions

**Vocabulary**
synthesis reaction
decomposition reaction
electrolysis
single-displacement reaction
double-displacement reaction
combustion reaction

- Synthesis reactions are represented by the general equation $A + X \longrightarrow AX$.
- Decomposition reactions are represented by the general equation $AX \longrightarrow A + X$.
- Single-displacement reactions are represented by the general equations $A + BX \longrightarrow AX + B$ and $Y + BX \longrightarrow BY + X$.
- Double-displacement reactions are represented by the general equation $AX + BY \longrightarrow AY + BX$.
- In a combustion reaction, a substance combines with oxygen, releasing energy in the form of heat and light.

## Activity Series of the Elements

**Vocabulary**
activity series

- Activity series list the elements in order of their chemical reactivity and are useful in predicting whether a chemical reaction will occur.
- Chemists determine activity series through experiments.

## Describing Chemical Reactions

### SECTION 1 REVIEW

1. List four observations that indicate that a chemical reaction may be taking place.
2. List the three requirements for a correctly written chemical equation.
3. a. What is meant by the term *coefficient* in relation to a chemical equation?
   b. How does the presence of a coefficient affect the number of atoms of each type in the formula that the coefficient precedes?
4. Give an example of a word equation, a formula equation, and a chemical equation.
5. What quantitative information is revealed by a chemical equation?
6. What limitations are associated with the use of both word and formula equations?
7. Define each of the following terms:
   a. aqueous solution
   b. catalyst
   c. reversible reaction
8. Write formulas for each of the following compounds:
   a. potassium hydroxide
   b. calcium nitrate
   c. sodium carbonate
   d. carbon tetrachloride
   e. magnesium bromide
9. What four guidelines are useful in balancing an equation?
10. How many atoms of each type are represented in each of the following?
    a. $3N_2$
    b. $2H_2O$
    c. $4HNO_3$
    d. $2Ca(OH)_2$
    e. $3Ba(ClO_3)_2$
    f. $5Fe(NO_3)_2$
    g. $4Mg_3(PO_4)_2$
    h. $2(NH_4)_2SO_4$
    i. $6Al_2(SeO_4)_3$
    j. $4C_3H_8$

### PRACTICE PROBLEMS

11. Write the chemical equation that relates to each of the following word equations. Include symbols for physical states in the equation.
    a. solid zinc sulfide + oxygen gas $\longrightarrow$ solid zinc oxide + sulfur dioxide gas
    b. aqueous hydrochloric acid + aqueous barium hydroxide $\longrightarrow$ aqueous barium chloride + water
    c. aqueous nitric acid + aqueous calcium hydroxide $\longrightarrow$ aqueous calcium nitrate + water
12. Translate each of the following chemical equations into a sentence.
    a. $2ZnS(s) + 3O_2(g) \longrightarrow 2ZnO(s) + 2SO_2(g)$
    b. $CaH_2(s) + 2H_2O(l) \longrightarrow Ca(OH)_2(aq) + 2H_2(g)$
    c. $AgNO_3(aq) + KI(aq) \longrightarrow AgI(s) + KNO_3(aq)$
13. Balance each of the following:
    a. $H_2 + Cl_2 \longrightarrow HCl$
    b. $Al + Fe_2O_3 \longrightarrow Al_2O_3 + Fe$
    c. $Pb(CH_3COO)_2 + H_2S \longrightarrow PbS + CH_3COOH$
14. Identify and correct each error in the following equations, and then balance each equation.
    a. $Li + O_2 \longrightarrow LiO_2$
    b. $H_2 + Cl_2 \longrightarrow H_2Cl_2$
    c. $MgCO_3 \longrightarrow MgO_2 + CO_2$
    d. $NaI + Cl_2 \longrightarrow NaCl + I$
15. Write chemical equations for each of the following sentences:
    a. Aluminum reacts with oxygen to produce aluminum oxide.
    b. Phosphoric acid, $H_3PO_4$, is produced through the reaction between tetraphosphorus decoxide and water.
    c. Iron(III) oxide reacts with carbon monoxide to produce iron and carbon dioxide.
16. Carbon tetrachloride is used as an intermediate chemical in the manufacture of other chemicals. It is prepared in liquid form by reacting chlorine gas with methane gas. Hydrogen chloride gas is also formed in this reaction. Write the balanced chemical equation for the production of carbon tetrachloride. (Hint: See Sample Problems C and D.)

**17.** For each of the following synthesis reactions, identify the missing reactant(s) or product(s), and then balance the resulting equation.
a. $Mg + \_\_\_\_ \longrightarrow MgO$
b. $\_\_\_\_ + O_2 \longrightarrow Fe_2O_3$
c. $Li + Cl_2 \longrightarrow \_\_\_\_$
d. $Ca + \_\_\_\_ \longrightarrow CaI_2$

## *Types of Chemical Reactions*

### SECTION 2 REVIEW

**18.** Define and give general equations for the five basic types of chemical reactions introduced in Chapter 8.
**19.** How are most decomposition reactions initiated?
**20.** A substance is decomposed by an electric current. What is the name of this type of reaction?
**21.** a. In what environment do many single-displacement reactions commonly occur?
b. In general, how do single-displacement reactions compare with synthesis and decomposition reactions in terms of the amount of energy involved?

### PRACTICE PROBLEMS

**22.** Complete each of the following synthesis reactions by writing both a word equation and a chemical equation.
a. sodium + oxygen $\longrightarrow$ ____
b. magnesium + fluorine $\longrightarrow$ ____
**23.** Complete and balance the equations for the following decomposition reactions:
a. $HgO \xrightarrow{\Delta}$
b. $H_2O(l) \xrightarrow{\text{electricity}}$
c. $Ag_2O \xrightarrow{\Delta}$
d. $CuCl_2 \xrightarrow{\text{electricity}}$
**24.** Complete and balance the equations for the following single-displacement reactions:
a. $Zn + Pb(NO_3)_2 \longrightarrow \_\_\_\_$
b. $Al + Hg(CH_3COO)_2 \longrightarrow \_\_\_\_$
c. $Al + NiSO_4 \longrightarrow \_\_\_\_$
d. $Na + H_2O \longrightarrow \_\_\_\_$
**25.** Complete and balance the equations for the following double-displacement reactions:
a. $AgNO_3(aq) + NaCl(aq) \longrightarrow \_\_\_\_$
b. $Mg(NO_3)_2(aq) + KOH(aq) \longrightarrow \_\_\_\_$
c. $LiOH(aq) + Fe(NO_3)_3(aq) \longrightarrow \_\_\_\_$
**26.** Complete and balance the equations for the following combustion reactions:
a. $CH_4 + O_2 \longrightarrow \_\_\_\_$
b. $C_3H_6 + O_2 \longrightarrow \_\_\_\_$
c. $C_5H_{12} + O_2 \longrightarrow \_\_\_\_$
**27.** Write and balance each of the following equations, and then identify each by type.
a. hydrogen + iodine $\longrightarrow$ hydrogen iodide
b. lithium + hydrochloric acid $\longrightarrow$ lithium chloride + hydrogen
c. sodium carbonate $\longrightarrow$ sodium oxide + carbon dioxide
d. mercury(II) oxide $\longrightarrow$ mercury + oxygen
e. magnesium hydroxide $\longrightarrow$ magnesium oxide + water
**28.** Identify the compound that could undergo decomposition to produce the following products, and then balance the final equation.
a. magnesium oxide and water
b. lead(II) oxide and water
c. lithium chloride and oxygen
d. barium chloride and oxygen
e. nickel chloride and oxygen
**29.** In each of the following combustion reactions, identify the missing reactant(s), product(s), or both, and then balance the resulting equation.
a. $C_3H_8 + \_\_\_\_ \longrightarrow \_\_\_\_ + H_2O$
b. $\_\_\_\_ + 8O_2 \longrightarrow 5CO_2 + 6H_2O$
c. $C_2H_5OH + \_\_\_\_ \longrightarrow \_\_\_\_ + \_\_\_\_$
**30.** Complete and balance the equations for the following reactions, and then identify each by type.
a. zinc + sulfur $\longrightarrow$ ____
b. silver nitrate + potassium iodide $\longrightarrow$ ____
c. toluene, $C_7H_8$ + oxygen $\longrightarrow$ ____
d. nonane, $C_9H_{20}$ + oxygen $\longrightarrow$ ____

## *Activity Series of the Elements*

### SECTION 3 REVIEW

**31.** a. What is meant by the *activity* of an element?
b. How does this description differ for metals and nonmetals?

**32.** a. What is an activity series of elements?
b. What is the basis for the ordering of the elements in the activity series?

**33.** a. What chemical principle is the basis for the activity series of metals?
b. What is the significance of the distance between two metals in the activity series?

## PRACTICE PROBLEMS

**34.** Based on the activity series of metals and halogens, which element within each pair is more likely to replace the other in a compound?

| | |
|---|---|
| a. K and Na | e. Au and Ag |
| b. Al and Ni | f. Cl and I |
| c. Bi and Cr | g. Fe and Sr |
| d. Cl and F | h. I and F |

**35.** Using the activity series in **Table 3** on page 286, predict whether each of the possible reactions listed below will occur. For the reactions that will occur, write the products and balance the equation.
a. $Ni(s) + CuCl_2(aq) \longrightarrow$ ______
b. $Zn(s) + Pb(NO_3)_2(aq) \longrightarrow$ ______
c. $Cl_2(g) + KI(aq) \longrightarrow$ ______
d. $Cu(s) + FeSO_4(aq) \longrightarrow$ ______
e. $Ba(s) + H_2O(l) \longrightarrow$ ______

**36.** Use the activity series to predict whether each of the following synthesis reactions will occur, and write the chemical equations for those predicted to occur.
a. $Ca(s) + O_2(g) \longrightarrow$ ______
b. $Ni(s) + O_2(g) \longrightarrow$ ______
c. $Au(s) + O_2(g) \longrightarrow$ ______

## MIXED REVIEW

**37.** Ammonia reacts with oxygen to yield nitrogen and water.
$$4NH_3(g) + 3O_2(g) \longrightarrow 2N_2(g) + 6H_2O(l)$$
Given this chemical equation, as well as the number of moles of the reactant or product indicated below, determine the number of moles of all remaining reactants and products.

| | |
|---|---|
| a. 3.0 mol $O_2$ | c. 1.0 mol $N_2$ |
| b. 8.0 mol $NH_3$ | d. 0.40 mol $H_2O$ |

**38.** Complete the following synthesis reactions by writing both the word and chemical equation for each:
a. potassium + chlorine $\longrightarrow$ ______
b. hydrogen + iodine $\longrightarrow$ ______
c. magnesium + oxygen $\longrightarrow$ ______

**39.** Use the activity series to predict which metal—Sn, Mn, or Pt—would be the best choice as a container for an acid.

**40.** Aqueous sodium hydroxide is produced commercially by the electrolysis of aqueous sodium chloride. Hydrogen and chlorine gases are also produced. Write the balanced chemical equation for the production of sodium hydroxide. Include the physical states of the reactants and products.

**41.** Balance each of the following:
a. $Ca(OH)_2 + (NH_4)_2SO_4 \longrightarrow CaSO_4 + NH_3 + H_2O$
b. $C_2H_6 + O_2 \longrightarrow CO_2 + H_2O$
c. $Cu_2S + O_2 \longrightarrow Cu_2O + SO_2$
d. $Al + H_2SO_4 \longrightarrow Al_2(SO_4)_3 + H_2$

**42.** Use the activity series to predict whether each of the following reactions will occur, and write the balanced chemical equations for those predicted to occur.
a. $Al(s) + O_2(g) \longrightarrow$ ______
b. $Pb(s) + ZnCl_2(s) \longrightarrow$ ______

**43.** Complete and balance the equations for the following reactions, and identify the type of reaction that each equation represents.
a. $(NH_4)_2S(aq) + ZnCl_2(aq) \longrightarrow$ ______ $+ ZnS(s)$
b. $Al(s) + Pb(NO_3)_2(aq) \longrightarrow$ ______
c. $Ba(s) + H_2O(l) \longrightarrow$ ______
d. $Cl_2(g) + KBr(aq) \longrightarrow$
e. $NH_3(g) + O_2(g) \xrightarrow{Pt} NO(g) + H_2O(l)$
f. $H_2O(l) \longrightarrow H_2(g) + O_2(g)$

**44.** Write and balance each of the following equations, and then identify each by type.
a. copper + chlorine $\longrightarrow$ copper(II) chloride
b. calcium chlorate $\longrightarrow$ calcium chloride + oxygen
c. lithium + water $\longrightarrow$ lithium hydroxide + hydrogen
d. lead(II) carbonate $\longrightarrow$ lead(II) oxide + carbon dioxide

45. How many moles of HCl can be made from 6.15 mol $H_2$ and an excess of $Cl_2$?

46. What product is missing in the following equation?

$$MgO + 2HCl \longrightarrow MgCl_2 + \_\_\_\_\_$$

47. Balance the following equations:
   a. $Pb(NO_3)_2(aq) + NaOH(aq) \longrightarrow Pb(OH)_2(s) + NaNO_3(aq)$
   b. $C_{12}H_{22}O_{11}(l) + O_2(g) \longrightarrow CO_2(g) + H_2O(l)$
   c. $Al(OH)_3(s) + H_2SO_4(aq) \longrightarrow Al_2(SO_4)_3(aq) + H_2O(l)$

## CRITICAL THINKING

48. **Inferring Relationships** Activity series are prepared by comparing single-displacement reactions between metals. Based on observations, the metals can be ranked by their ability to react. However, reactivity can be explained by the ease with which atoms of metals lose electrons. Using information from the activity series, identify the locations in the periodic table of the most reactive metals and the least reactive metals. Using your knowledge of electron configurations and periodic trends, infer possible explanations for the metals' reactivity and position in the periodic table.

49. **Analyzing Results** Formulate an activity series for the hypothetical elements A, J, Q, and Z by using the following reaction information:

$$A + ZX \longrightarrow AX + Z$$

$$J + ZX \longrightarrow \text{no reaction}$$

$$Q + AX \longrightarrow QX + A$$

## USING THE HANDBOOK

50. Find the common-reactions section for Group 1 metals in the *Elements Handbook*. Use this information to answer the following:
   a. Write a balanced chemical equation for the formation of rubidium hydroxide from rubidum oxide.
   b. Write a balanced chemical equation for the formation of cesium iodide.
   c. Classify the reactions you wrote in (a) and (b).
   d. Write word equations for the reactions you wrote in (a) and (b).

51. Find the common-reactions section for Group 13 in the *Elements Handbook*. Use this information to answer the following:
   a. Write a balanced chemical equation for the formation of gallium bromide prepared from hydrobromic acid.
   b. Write a balanced chemical equation for the formation of gallium oxide.
   c. Classify the reactions you wrote in (a) and (b).
   d. Write word equations for the reactions you wrote in (a) and (b).

## RESEARCH & WRITING

52. Trace the evolution of municipal water fluoridation. What advantages and disadvantages are associated with this practice?

53. Research how a soda-acid fire extinguisher works, and write the chemical equation for the reaction. Check your house and other structures for different types of fire extinguishers, and ask your local fire department to verify the effectiveness of each type of extinguisher.

## ALTERNATIVE ASSESSMENT

54. **Performance Assessment** For one day, record situations that show evidence of a chemical change. Identify the reactants and the products, and determine whether there is proof of a chemical reaction. Classify each of the chemical reactions according to the common reaction types discussed in the chapter.

# Math Tutor BALANCING CHEMICAL EQUATIONS

A chemical equation is a written expression of an actual chemical reaction in which certain atoms, ions, or molecules become rearranged in a specific way. Therefore, the equation must represent exactly what happens in the reaction. Recall that atoms are never created or destroyed in chemical reactions. A balanced chemical equation shows that all of the atoms present in reactants are still present in products.

## Problem-Solving TIPS

- First, identify reactants and products. (You may find it helpful to write a word equation first.)
- Using correct formulas and symbols, write an unbalanced equation for the reaction.
- Balance atoms one element at a time by inserting coefficients.
- Identify elements that appear in only one reactant and one product, and balance the atoms of those elements first.
- If a polyatomic ion appears on both sides of the equation, treat it as a single unit.
- Double-check to be sure that the number of atoms of each element is the same on both sides of the equation.

## SAMPLE

**When an aqueous solution of ammonium sulfate, $(NH_4)_2SO_4(aq)$, is combined with an aqueous solution of silver nitrate, $AgNO_3(aq)$, a precipitate of solid silver sulfate, $Ag_2SO_4(s)$, forms, leaving ammonium nitrate, $NH_4NO_3(aq)$, in solution. Balance the equation for this reaction.**

As before, first write an equation with correct formulas for all reactants and products.

$$(NH_4)_2SO_4(aq) + AgNO_3(aq) \longrightarrow NH_4NO_3(aq) + Ag_2SO_4(s)$$

If you compare the number of silver atoms on each side, you can see that the equation is not balanced. This equation may look very complex, but it is really fairly simple. In many reactions involving polyatomic ions such as sulfate, nitrate, and ammonium, the ions do not change. In the equation above, you can see that $NO_3$ is present on both sides, as are $SO_4$ and $NH_4$. You can balance the equation by treating the groups as if they were single atoms. To balance the $NH_4$ groups, place a 2 in front of $NH_4NO_3$. This gives you two ammonium groups on the left and two on the right. Now, because you have two nitrate groups on the right, place a 2 in front of $AgNO_3$ to give two nitrate groups on the left. Finally, check silver atoms and sulfate groups, and you find that they balance.

$$(NH_4)_2SO_4(aq) + 2AgNO_3(aq) \longrightarrow 2NH_4NO_3(aq) + Ag_2SO_4(s)$$

## PRACTICE PROBLEMS

1. When propane burns completely in air, the reaction forms carbon dioxide and water vapor. Balance the equation for this reaction.

$$C_3H_8 + O_2 \longrightarrow CO_2 + H_2O$$

2. Balance the following chemical equations:
   a. $KI(aq) + Cl_2(g) \longrightarrow KCl(aq) + I_2(s)$
   b. $Al(s) + H_2SO_4(aq) \longrightarrow Al_2(SO_4)_3(aq) + H_2(g)$

# Standardized Test Prep

**Answer the following items on a separate piece of paper.**

**MULTIPLE CHOICE**

**1.** According to the law of conservation of mass, the total mass of the reacting substances is
**A.** always more than the total mass of the products.
**B.** always less than the total mass of the products.
**C.** sometimes more and sometimes less than the total mass of the products.
**D.** always equal to the total mass of the products.

**2.** To balance a chemical equation, you may adjust the
**A.** coefficients.
**B.** subscripts.
**C.** formulas of the products.
**D.** either the coefficients or the subscripts.

**3.** Which is the correct chemical equation for the following formula equation: $(NH_4)_2S \longrightarrow NH_3 + H_2S$?
**A.** $2(NH_4)_2S \longrightarrow 2NH_3 + H_2S_2$
**B.** $2(NH_4)_2S \longrightarrow 2NH_3 + H_2S$
**C.** $(NH_4)_2S \longrightarrow 2NH_3 + H_2S$
**D.** None of the above

**4.** Select the missing reactant(s) for the double-displacement reaction that produces $PF_5$ and $AsCl_3$.
**A.** $PCl_5$ and $AsF_3$
**B.** $PCl_3$ and $AsF_5$
**C.** $PCl_3$ and $AsF_3$
**D.** None of the above

**5.** Select the missing reactant for the following combustion reaction: 2______ $+ 15O_2 \longrightarrow 14CO_2 + 6H_2O$.
**A.** $C_{14}H_{12}$
**B.** $C_{14}H_{12}O_4$
**C.** $C_7H_6$
**D.** $C_7H_6O_2$

**6.** A mixture consists of Ag, Pb, and Fe metals. Which of these metals will react with $ZnCl_2$?
**A.** Ag(s)
**B.** Pb(s)
**C.** Fe(s)
**D.** None of these metals

**7.** Which of the following statements is true about the reaction $2F_2 + 2H_2O \longrightarrow 4HF + O_2$?
**A.** Two grams of $O_2$ are produced when 2 g $F_2$ reacts with 2 g $H_2O$.
**B.** Two moles of HF are produced when 1 mol $F_2$ reacts with 1 mol $H_2O$.
**C.** For every 2 mol $O_2$ produced, 6 mol HF are produced.
**D.** For every 1 mol $H_2O$ that reacts, 2 mol $O_2$ are produced.

**SHORT ANSWER**

**8.** Determine the products and write a balanced equation for the reaction of solid magnesium and water.

**9.** A precipitation of iron(III) hydroxide is produced by reacting an aqueous solution of iron(III) chloride with an aqueous solution of sodium hydroxide. Write a balanced chemical equation.

**EXTENDED RESPONSE**

**10.** List the hypothetical metals A, E, M, and R in increasing order of reactivity by using the reaction data in the table below. The reaction of interest is of the form $C + ZX \longrightarrow CX + Z$. Explain your reasoning.

| | AX | EX | MX | RX |
|---|---|---|---|---|
| A | — | no reaction | reaction | no reaction |
| E | reaction | — | reaction | reaction |
| M | no reaction | no reaction | — | no reaction |
| R | reaction | no reaction | reaction | — |

**11.** Calcium hypochlorite, $Ca(OCl)_2$, is a bleaching agent produced from sodium hydroxide, calcium hydroxide, and chlorine. Sodium chloride and water are also produced in the reaction. Write the balanced chemical equation. If 2 mol NaOH react, how many moles of calcium hypochlorite can be produced?

**Test TIP** Focus on one question at a time unless you are asked to refer to previous answers.

CHAPTER LAB

# Blueprint Paper

## OBJECTIVES

- ***Prepare* blueprint paper and create a blueprint.**

## MATERIALS

- **10% iron(III) ammonium citrate solution**
- **10% potassium hexacyanoferrate(III) solution**
- **25 mL graduated cylinders, 2**
- **corrugated cardboard, 20 cm × 30 cm, 2 pieces**
- **glass stirring rod**
- **Petri dish**
- **thumbtacks, 4**
- **tongs**
- **white paper, 8 cm × 15 cm, 1 piece**

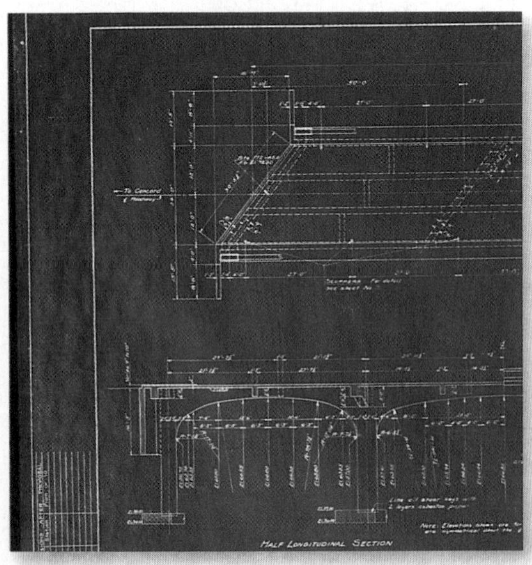

## BACKGROUND

Blueprint paper is prepared by coating paper with a solution of two soluble iron(III) salts—potassium hexacyanoferrate(III), commonly called *potassium ferricyanide,* and iron(III) ammonium citrate. These two salts do not react with each other in the dark. However, when exposed to UV light, the iron(III) ammonium citrate is converted to an iron(II) salt. Potassium hexacyanoferrate(III), $K_3Fe(CN)_6$, reacts with iron(II) ion, $Fe^{2+}$, to produce an insoluble blue compound, $KFeFe(CN)_6 \cdot H_2O$. In this compound, iron appears to exist in both the +2 and +3 oxidation states.

A blueprint is made by using black ink to make a sketch on a piece of tracing paper or clear, colorless plastic. This sketch is placed on top of a piece of blueprint paper and exposed to ultraviolet light. Wherever the light strikes the paper, the paper turns blue. The paper is then washed to remove the soluble unexposed chemical and is allowed to dry. The result is a blueprint—a blue sheet of paper with white lines.

## SAFETY

For review of safety, please see **Safety in the Chemistry Laboratory** in the front of your book.

## PROCEDURE

1. Pour 15 mL of a 10% solution of potassium hexacyanoferrate(III) solution into a Petri dish. With most of the classroom lights off or dimmed, add 15 mL of 10% iron(III) ammonium citrate solution. Stir the mixture.

2. Write your name on an 8 cm × 15 cm piece of white paper. Carefully coat one side of the piece of paper by using tongs to drag it over the top of the solution in the Petri dish.

3. With the coated side up, tack your wet paper to a piece of corrugated cardboard, and cover the paper with another piece of cardboard. **Wash your hands before proceeding to step 4.**

4. Take your paper and cardboard assembly outside into the direct sunlight. Remove the top piece of cardboard so that the paper is exposed. Quickly place an object such as a fern, a leaf, or a key on the paper. If it is windy, you may need to put small weights, such as coins, on the object to keep it in place, as shown in **Figure A.**

5. After about 20 min, remove the object and again cover the paper with the cardboard. Return to the lab, remove the tacks, and *thoroughly* rinse the blueprint paper under cold running water. Allow the paper to dry. In your notebook, record the amount of time that the paper was exposed to sunlight.

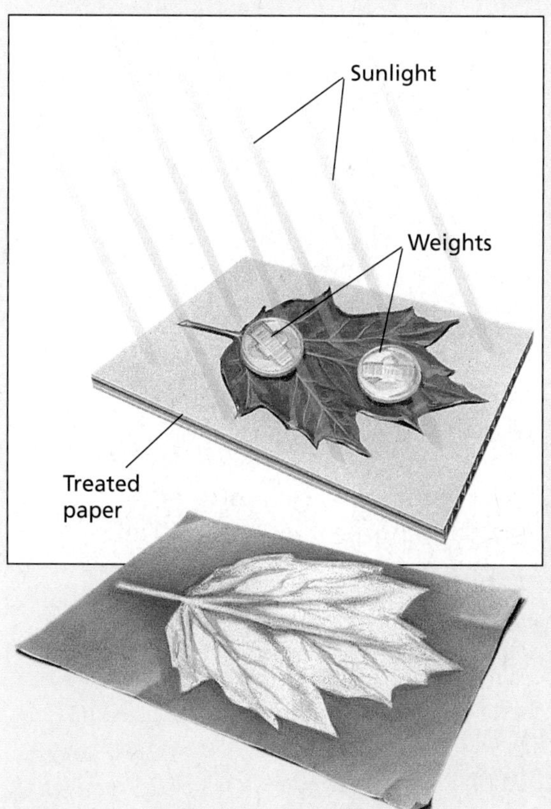


**FIGURE A** To produce a sharp image, the object must be flat, with its edges on the blueprint paper, and it must not move.

## CLEANUP AND DISPOSAL

6. Clean all equipment and your lab station. Return equipment to its proper place. Dispose of chemicals and solutions in the containers designated by your teacher. Do not pour any chemicals down the drain or in the trash unless your teacher directs you to do so. Wash your hands thoroughly before you leave the lab and after all work is finished.

## ANALYSIS AND INTERPRETATION

1. **Relating Ideas:** Why is the iron(III) ammonium citrate solution stored in a brown bottle?

2. **Organizing Ideas:** When iron(III) ammonium citrate is exposed to light, the oxidation state of the iron changes. What is the new oxidation state of the iron?

3. **Analyzing Methods:** What substances were washed away when you rinsed the blueprint in water after it had been exposed to sunlight? (Hint: Compare the solubilities of the two ammonium salts that you used to coat the paper and of the blue product that formed.)

## CONCLUSIONS

1. **Applying Ideas:** Insufficient washing of the exposed blueprints results in a slow deterioration of images. Suggest a reason for this deterioration.

2. **Relating Ideas:** Photographic paper can be safely exposed to red light in a darkroom. Do you think the same would be true of blueprint paper? Explain your answer.

## EXTENSIONS

1. **Applying Ideas:** How could you use this blueprint paper to test the effectiveness of a brand of sunscreen lotion?

2. **Designing Experiments:** Can you think of ways to improve this procedure? If so, ask your teacher to approve your plan, and create a new blueprint. Evaluate both the efficiency of the procedure and the quality of blueprint.

CHAPTER 9

# *Stoichiometry*

Stoichiometry *comes from the Greek words* stoicheion, *meaning "element," and* metron, *meaning "measure."*

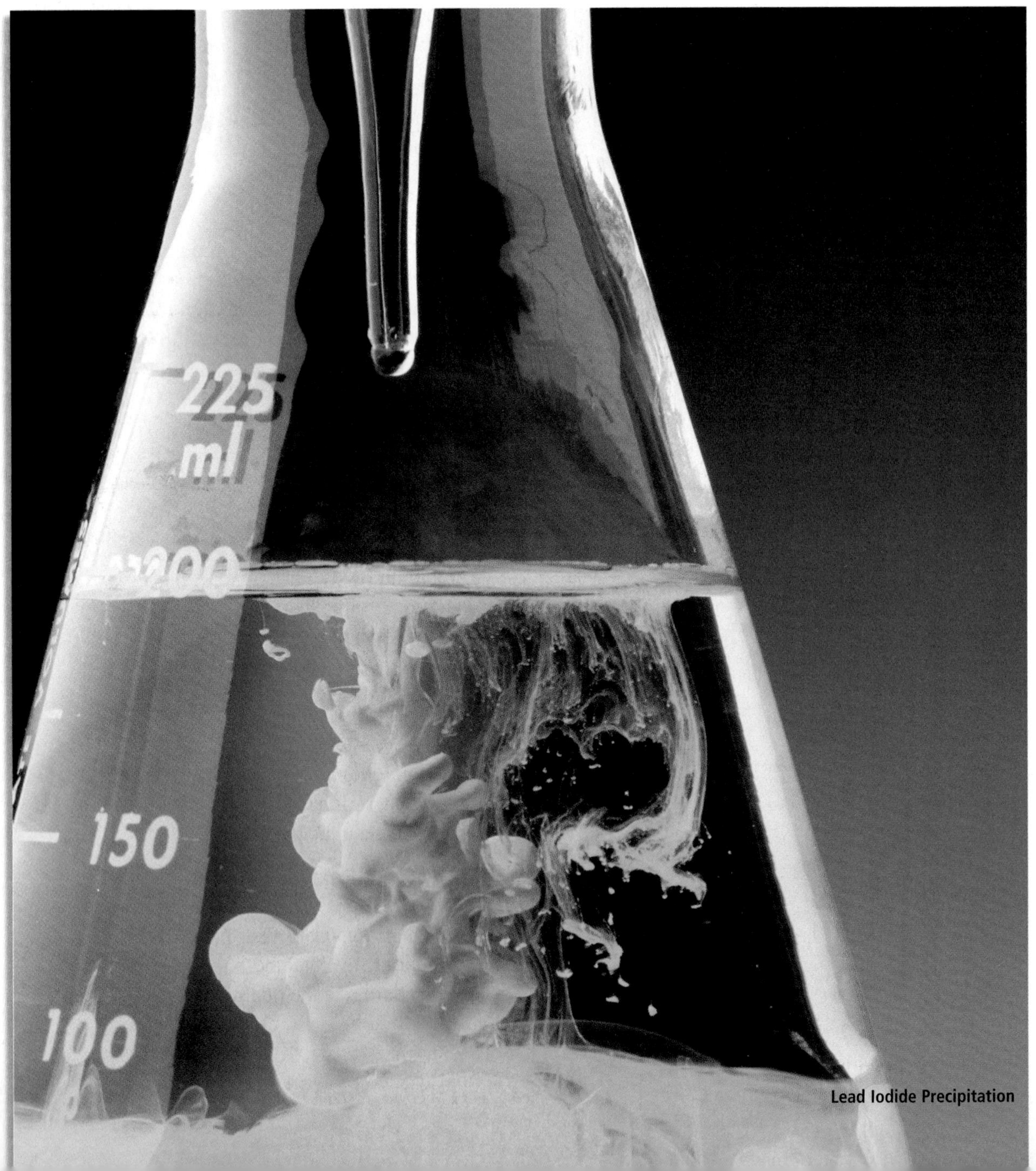

Lead Iodide Precipitation

# Introduction to Stoichiometry

SECTION 1

## OBJECTIVES

- Define *stoichiometry.*
- Describe the importance of the *mole ratio* in stoichiometric calculations.
- Write a mole ratio relating two substances in a chemical equation.

SC **C.4.4** Apply the concept of moles to determine the number of particles of a substance in a chemical reaction, the percent composition of a representative compound, the mass proportions, and the mole-mass relationships

Much of our knowledge of chemistry is based on the careful quantitative analysis of substances involved in chemical reactions. **Composition stoichiometry** (which you studied in Chapter 3) *deals with the mass relationships of elements in compounds.* **Reaction stoichiometry** *involves the mass relationships between reactants and products in a chemical reaction.* Reaction stoichiometry is the subject of this chapter and it is based on chemical equations and the law of conservation of mass. All reaction stoichiometry calculations start with a balanced chemical equation. This equation gives the relative numbers of moles of reactants and products.

## Reaction Stoichiometry Problems

The reaction stoichiometry problems in this chapter can be classified according to the information *given* in the problem and the information you are expected to find, the *unknown*. The *given* and the *unknown* may both be reactants, they may both be products, or one may be a reactant and the other a product. The masses are generally expressed in grams, but you will encounter both large-scale and microscale problems with other mass units, such as kg or mg. Stoichiometric problems are solved by using ratios from the balanced equation to convert the given quantity using the methods described here.

**Problem Type 1: *Given* and *unknown* quantities are amounts in moles.**
When you are given the amount of a substance in moles and asked to calculate the amount in moles of another substance in the chemical reaction, the general plan is

$$\begin{matrix}\text{amount of} \\ \textit{given}\text{ substance (mol)}\end{matrix} \longrightarrow \begin{matrix}\text{amount of} \\ \textit{unknown}\text{ substance (mol)}\end{matrix}$$

**Problem Type 2: *Given* is an amount in moles and *unknown* is a mass that is often expressed in grams.**
When you are given the amount in moles of one substance and asked to calculate the mass of another substance in the chemical reaction, the general plan is

$$\begin{matrix}\text{amount of} \\ \textit{given}\text{ substance} \\ \text{(mol)}\end{matrix} \longrightarrow \begin{matrix}\text{amount of} \\ \textit{unknown}\text{ substance} \\ \text{(mol)}\end{matrix} \longrightarrow \begin{matrix}\text{mass of} \\ \textit{unknown}\text{ substance} \\ \text{(g)}\end{matrix}$$

**Problem Type 3: *Given* is a mass in grams and *unknown* is an amount in moles.**

When you are given the mass of one substance and asked to calculate the amount in moles of another substance in the chemical reaction, the general plan is

$$\begin{matrix} \text{mass of} & & \text{amount of} & & \text{amount of} \\ \textit{given}\text{ substance} & \longrightarrow & \textit{given}\text{ substance} & \longrightarrow & \textit{unknown}\text{ substance} \\ \text{(g)} & & \text{(mol)} & & \text{(mol)} \end{matrix}$$

**Problem Type 4: *Given* is a mass in grams and *unknown* is a mass in grams.**

When you are given the mass of one substance and asked to calculate the mass of another substance in the chemical reaction, the general plan is

$$\begin{matrix} \text{mass of} & & \text{amount of} & & \text{amount of} & & \text{mass of} \\ \textit{given}\text{ substance} & \longrightarrow & \textit{given}\text{ substance} & \longrightarrow & \textit{unknown}\text{ substance} & \longrightarrow & \textit{unknown}\text{ substance} \\ \text{(g)} & & \text{(mol)} & & \text{(mol)} & & \text{(g)} \end{matrix}$$

## Mole Ratio

Solving any reaction stoichiometry problem requires the use of a mole ratio to convert from moles or grams of one substance in a reaction to moles or grams of another substance. *A* **mole ratio** *is a conversion factor that relates the amounts in moles of any two substances involved in a chemical reaction.* This information is obtained directly from the balanced chemical equation. Consider, for example, the chemical equation for the electrolysis of melted aluminum oxide to produce aluminum and oxygen.

$$2Al_2O_3(l) \longrightarrow 4Al(s) + 3O_2(g)$$

Recall from Chapter 8 that the coefficients in a chemical equation satisfy the law of conservation of matter and represent the relative amounts in moles of reactants and products. Therefore, 2 mol of aluminum oxide decompose to produce 4 mol of aluminum and 3 mol of oxygen gas. These relationships can be expressed in the following mole ratios.

$$\frac{2 \text{ mol } Al_2O_3}{4 \text{ mol Al}} \text{ or } \frac{4 \text{ mol Al}}{2 \text{ mol } Al_2O_3}$$

$$\frac{2 \text{ mol } Al_2O_3}{3 \text{ mol } O_2} \text{ or } \frac{3 \text{ mol } O_2}{2 \text{ mol } Al_2O_3}$$

$$\frac{4 \text{ mol Al}}{3 \text{ mol } O_2} \text{ or } \frac{3 \text{ mol } O_2}{4 \text{ mol Al}}$$

For the decomposition of aluminum oxide, the appropriate mole ratio would be used as a conversion factor to convert a given amount in moles of one substance to the corresponding amount in moles of another

### CAREERS in Chemistry

**Chemical Technician**

Chemical technicians are highly skilled scientific professionals who bring valuable skills to the development of new products, the processing of materials, the management of hazardous waste, regulatory compliance, and many other aspects of getting products and services to the consumer. Chemical technicians must have a solid background in applied chemistry and mathematics and be highly skilled in laboratory methods. Earning an associate's degree in applied science or chemical technology is one good way to prepare for this career. Many chemical technicians have a bachelor's degree in chemical technology, chemistry, or other sciences.

substance. To determine the amount in moles of aluminum that can be produced from 13.0 mol of aluminum oxide, the mole ratio needed is that of Al to $Al_2O_3$.

$$13.0 \text{ mol } Al_2O_3 \times \frac{4 \text{ mol Al}}{2 \text{ mol } Al_2O_3} = 26.0 \text{ mol Al}$$

Mole ratios are exact, so they do not limit the number of significant figures in a calculation. The number of significant figures in the answer is therefore determined only by the number of significant figures of any measured quantities in a particular problem.

**Chemistry in Action**

Go to **go.hrw.com** for a full-length article on stoichiometry and air bags.

**Keyword: HC6STCX**

## Molar Mass

Recall from Chapter 7 that the molar mass is the mass, in grams, of one mole of a substance. The molar mass is the conversion factor that relates the mass of a substance to the amount in moles of that substance. To solve reaction stoichiometry problems, you will need to determine molar masses using the periodic table.

Returning to the previous example, the decomposition of aluminum oxide, the rounded masses from the periodic table are the following.

$1 \text{ mol } Al_2O_3 = 101.96 \text{ g}$ $\quad$ $1 \text{ mol Al} = 26.98 \text{ g}$ $\quad$ $1 \text{ mol } O_2 = 32.00 \text{ g}$

These molar masses can be expressed by the following conversion factors.

$$\frac{101.96 \text{ g } Al_2O_3}{1 \text{ mol } Al_2O_3} \text{ or } \frac{1 \text{ mol } Al_2O_3}{101.96 \text{ g } Al_2O_3}$$

$$\frac{26.98 \text{ g Al}}{1 \text{ mol Al}} \text{ or } \frac{1 \text{ mol Al}}{26.98 \text{ g Al}}$$

$$\frac{32.00 \text{ g } O_2}{1 \text{ mol } O_2} \text{ or } \frac{1 \text{ mol } O_2}{32.00 \text{ g } O_2}$$

To find the number of grams of aluminum equivalent to 26.0 mol of aluminum, the calculation would be as follows.

$$26.0 \text{ mol Al} \times \frac{26.98 \text{ g Al}}{1 \text{ mol Al}} = 701 \text{ g Al}$$

## SECTION REVIEW

1. What is stoichiometry?

2. For each equation, write all possible mole ratios.

   **a.** $2HgO(s) \longrightarrow 2Hg(l) + O_2(g)$

   **b.** $4NH_3(g) + 6NO(g) \longrightarrow 5N_2(g) + 6H_2O(l)$

3. How is a mole ratio used in stoichiometry?

**Critical Thinking**

4. **RELATING IDEAS** What step must be performed before any stoichiometry problem is solved? Explain.

# HISTORICAL CHEMISTRY

## The Case of Combustion

***People throughout history have transformed substances by burning them in air. Yet at the dawn of the scientific revolution, very little was known about the process of combustion. In attempting to explain this common phenomenon, chemists of the 18th century developed one of the first universally accepted theories in their field. But as one man would show, scientific theories do not always stand the test of time.***

### Changing Attitudes

Shunning the ancient Greek approach of logical argument based on untested premises, investigators of the 17th century began to understand the laws of nature by observing, measuring, and performing experiments on the world around them. However, this scientific method was incorporated into chemistry slowly. Although early chemists experimented extensively, most considered measurement to be unimportant. This viewpoint hindered the progress of chemistry for nearly a century.

### A Flawed Theory

By 1700, combustion was assumed to be the decomposition of a material into simpler substances. People saw burning substances emitting smoke and energy as heat and light. To account for this emission, scientists proposed a theory that combustion depended on the emission of a substance called *phlogiston,* which appeared as a combination of energy as heat and light while the material was burning but which could not be detected beforehand.

The phlogiston theory was used to explain many chemical observations of the day. For example, a lit candle under a glass jar burned until the surrounding air became saturated with phlogiston, at which time the flame died because the air inside could not absorb more phlogiston.

### A New Phase of Study

By the 1770s, the phlogiston theory had gained universal acceptance. At that time, chemists also began to experiment with air, which was generally believed to be an element.

In 1772, when Daniel Rutherford found that a mouse kept in a closed container soon died, he explained the results based on the phlogiston theory. Like a burning candle, the mouse emitted phlogiston; when the air could hold no more phlogiston, the mouse died. Thus, Rutherford figured that the air in the container had become "phlogisticated air."

▲*Antoine Laurent Lavoisier helped establish chemistry as a science.*

A couple of years later, Joseph Priestley obtained a reddish powder when he heated mercury in the air. He assumed that the powder was mercury devoid of phlogiston. But when he heated the powder, an unexpected result occurred: Metallic mercury, along with a gas that allowed a candle to burn, formed. Following the phlogiston theory, he believed this gas that supports combustion to be "dephlogisticated air."

### Nice Try, But . . .

Antoine Laurent Lavoisier was a meticulous scientist. He realized that Rutherford and Priestley had carefully observed and described their experiments but had not measured the mass of anything. Unlike his colleagues, Lavoisier knew the importance of using a balance. He measured the masses of reactants and products and compared them. He observed that the total mass of the reactants equaled the total mass of the products. Based on these observations, which supported what would become known as the *law of conservation of mass,* Lavoisier endeavored to explain the results of Rutherford and Priestley.

Lavoisier put some tin in a closed vessel and weighed the entire system. He then burned the tin. When he opened the vessel, air rushed into it as if something had been *removed* from the air in the vessel during combustion. He then measured the mass of the burned metal and observed that this mass was greater than the mass of the original tin. Curiously, this increase in mass equaled the mass of the air that had rushed into the vessel. To Lavoisier, this change in mass did not support the idea of phlogiston escaping the burning material. Instead, it indicated that during combustion, part of the air reacted with the tin.

After obtaining similar results by using various substances, Lavoisier concluded that air was not an element but a mixture composed principally of two gases, Priestley's "dephlogisticated air" (which Lavoisier renamed *oxygen*) and Rutherford's "phlogisticated air" (which was mostly nitrogen but had traces of other nonflammable atmospheric gases). When a substance burned, it chemically combined with oxygen, resulting in a product Lavoisier named an *oxide.* Lavoisier's theory of combustion persists today. He used the name *oxygen* because he thought that all acids contained oxygen. *Oxygen* means "acid former."

### The Father of Chemistry

By emphasizing the importance of quantitative analysis, Lavoisier helped establish chemistry as a science. His work on combustion laid to rest the phlogiston theory and the theory that air is an element. He also explained why hydrogen burned in oxygen to form water, or hydrogen oxide. He later published one of the first chemistry textbooks, which established a common naming system of compounds and elements and helped unify chemistry worldwide. These accomplishments earned Lavoisier the reputation of being the father of chemistry.

## Questions

1. Why does the mass of tin increase when tin is heated in air?

2. What was the composition of Priestley's "dephlogisticated air" and Rutherford's "phlogisticated air"?

TABLE OF SIMPLE SUBSTANCES.

*Simple fubftances belonging to all the kingdoms of nature, which may be confidered as the elements of bodies.*

| New Names. | Correfpondent old Names. |
|---|---|
| Light | *Light.* |
| Caloric | *Heat.*<br>*Principle or element of heat.*<br>*Fire. Igneous fluid.*<br>*Matter of fire and of heat.* |
| Oxygen | *Dephlogifticated air.*<br>*Empyreal air.*<br>*Vital air, or*<br>*Bafe of vital air.* |
| Azote | *Phlogifticated air or gas.*<br>*Mephitis, or its bafe.* |
| Hydrogen | *Inflammable air or gas,*<br>*or the bafe of inflammable air.* |

▲ *Lavoisier's concept of simple substances was published in his book* Elements of Chemistry *in 1789.*

SECTION 2

# Ideal Stoichiometric Calculations

## Objectives

- Calculate the amount in moles of a reactant or product from the amount in moles of a different reactant or product.
- Calculate the mass of a reactant or product from the amount in moles of a different reactant or product.
- Calculate the amount in moles of a reactant or product from the mass of a different reactant or product.
- Calculate the mass of a reactant or product from the mass of a different reactant or product.

SC **C.4.4** Apply the concept of moles to determine the number of particles of a substance in a chemical reaction, the percent composition of a representative compound, the mass proportions, and the mole-mass relationships

The balanced chemical equation is the key step in all stoichiometric calculations because the mole ratio is obtained directly from it. Solving any reaction stoichiometry problem must begin with a balanced equation.

Chemical equations help us plan the amounts of reactants to use in a chemical reaction without having to run the reactions in the laboratory. The reaction stoichiometry calculations described in this chapter are theoretical. They tell us the amounts of reactants and products for a given chemical reaction under *ideal conditions,* in which all reactants are completely converted into products. However, many reactions do not proceed such that all reactants are completely converted into products. Theoretical stoichiometric calculations allow us to determine the maximum amount of product that could be obtained in a reaction when the reactants are not pure or byproducts are formed in addition to the expected products.

Solving stoichiometric problems requires practice. These problems are extensions of the composition stoichiometry problems that you solved in Chapters 3 and 7. Practice by working the sample problems in the rest of this chapter. Using a logical, systematic approach will help you successfully solve these problems.

## Conversions of Quantities in Moles

In these stoichiometric problems, you are asked to calculate the amount in moles of one substance that will react with or be produced from the given amount in moles of another substance. The plan for a simple mole conversion problem is

$$\begin{array}{c}\text{amount of} \\ \textit{given}\text{ substance (mol)}\end{array} \longrightarrow \begin{array}{c}\text{amount of} \\ \textit{unknown}\text{ substance (mol)}\end{array}$$

This plan requires one conversion factor—the stoichiometric mole ratio of the *unknown* substance to the *given* substance from the balanced equation. To solve this type of problem, simply multiply the *known* quantity by the appropriate conversion factor.

$$\textit{given}\text{ quantity} \times \text{conversion factor} = \textit{unknown}\text{ quantity}$$

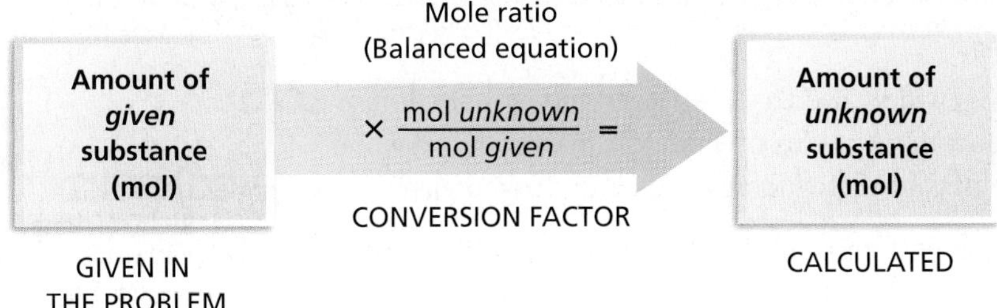


**FIGURE 1** This is a solution plan for problems in which the given and unknown quantities are expressed in moles.

## SAMPLE PROBLEM A

*For more help, go to the **Math Tutor** at the end of this chapter.*

**In a spacecraft, the carbon dioxide exhaled by astronauts can be removed by its reaction with lithium hydroxide, LiOH, according to the following chemical equation.**

$$CO_2(g) + 2LiOH(s) \longrightarrow Li_2CO_3(s) + H_2O(l)$$

**How many moles of lithium hydroxide are required to react with 20 mol $CO_2$, the average amount exhaled by a person each day?**

### SOLUTION

**1 *ANALYZE***

**Given:** amount of $CO_2$ = 20 mol
**Unknown:** amount of LiOH (mol)

**2 *PLAN***

amount of $CO_2$ (mol) $\longrightarrow$ amount of LiOH (mol)

This problem requires one conversion factor—the mole ratio of LiOH to $CO_2$. The mole ratio is obtained from the balanced chemical equation. Because you are given moles of $CO_2$, select a mole ratio that will cancel mol $CO_2$ and give you mol LiOH in your final answer. The correct ratio has the following units.

$$\frac{\text{mol LiOH}}{\text{mol } CO_2}$$

This ratio cancels mol $CO_2$ and gives the units mol LiOH in the answer.

$$\text{mol } CO_2 \times \overbrace{\frac{\text{mol LiOH}}{\text{mol } CO_2}}^{\text{mol ratio}} = \text{mol LiOH}$$

**3 *COMPUTE***

Substitute the values in the equation in step 2, and compute the answer.

$$20 \cancel{\text{mol } CO_2} \times \frac{2 \text{ mol LiOH}}{1 \cancel{\text{mol } CO_2}} = 40 \text{ mol LiOH}$$

**4 *EVALUATE***

The answer is written correctly with one significant figure to match the number of significant figures in the given 20 mol $CO_2$, and the units cancel to leave mol LiOH, which is the unknown. The balanced equation shows that twice the amount in moles of LiOH reacts with $CO_2$. Therefore, the answer should be $2 \times 20 = 40$.

**PRACTICE** *Answers in Appendix E*

1. Ammonia, $NH_3$, is widely used as a fertilizer and in many household cleaners. How many moles of ammonia are produced when 6 mol of hydrogen gas react with an excess of nitrogen gas?

2. The decomposition of potassium chlorate, $KClO_3$, into KCl and $O_2$ is used as a source of oxygen in the laboratory. How many moles of potassium chlorate are needed to produce 15 mol of oxygen gas?

Go to **go.hrw.com** for more practice problems that ask you to calculate unknown quantities by using mole ratios.

**Keyword: HC6STCX**

## Conversions of Amounts in Moles to Mass

In these stoichiometric calculations, you are asked to calculate the mass (usually in grams) of a substance that will react with or be produced from a given amount in moles of a second substance. The plan for these mole-to-gram conversions is

$$\begin{array}{ccccc} \text{amount of} & & \text{amount of} & & \text{mass of} \\ \textit{given} \text{ substance} & \longrightarrow & \textit{unknown} \text{ substance} & \longrightarrow & \textit{unknown} \text{ substance} \\ \text{(mol)} & & \text{(mol)} & & \text{(g)} \end{array}$$

This plan requires two conversion factors—the mole ratio of the *unknown* substance to the *given* substance and the molar mass of the *unknown* substance for the mass conversion. To solve this kind of problem, you simply multiply the known quantity, which is the amount in moles, by the appropriate conversion factors.

**FIGURE 2** This is a solution plan for problems in which the given quantity is expressed in moles and the unknown quantity is expressed in grams.

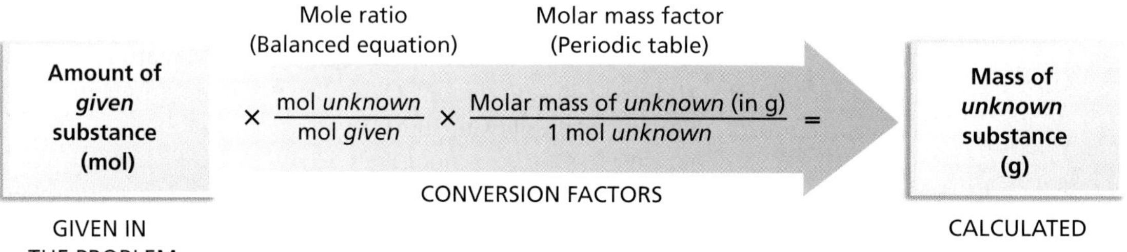


**SAMPLE PROBLEM B** *For more help, go to the Math Tutor at the end of this chapter.*

**In photosynthesis, plants use energy from the sun to produce glucose, $C_6H_{12}O_6$, and oxygen from the reaction of carbon dioxide and water. What mass, in grams, of glucose is produced when 3.00 mol of water react with carbon dioxide?**

**SOLUTION**

**1** *ANALYZE* **Given:** amount of $H_2O$ = 3.00 mol

**Unknown:** mass of $C_6H_{12}O_6$ produced (g)

**2 PLAN** You must start with a balanced equation.

$$6CO_2(g) + 6H_2O(l) \longrightarrow C_6H_{12}O_6(s) + 6O_2(g)$$

Given the amount in mol of $H_2O$, you need to get the mass of $C_6H_{12}O_6$ in grams. Two conversion factors are needed—the mole ratio of $C_6H_{12}O_6$ to $H_2O$ and the molar mass of $C_6H_{12}O_6$.

$$\text{mol } H_2O \times \overset{\text{mol ratio}}{\frac{\text{mol } C_6H_{12}O_6}{\text{mol } H_2O}} \times \overset{\text{molar mass factor}}{\frac{\text{g } C_6H_{12}O_6}{\text{mol } C_6H_{12}O_6}} = \text{g } C_6H_{12}O_6$$

**3 COMPUTE** Use the periodic table to compute the molar mass of $C_6H_{12}O_6$.

$$C_6H_{12}O_6 = 180.18 \text{ g/mol}$$

$$3.00 \text{ mol } H_2O \times \frac{1 \text{ mol } C_6H_{12}O_6}{6 \text{ mol } H_2O} \times \frac{180.18 \text{ g } C_6H_{12}O_6}{1 \text{ mol } C_6H_{12}O_6} = 90.1 \text{ g } C_6H_{12}O_6$$

**4 EVALUATE** The answer is correctly rounded to three significant figures, to match those in 3.00 mol $H_2O$. The units cancel in the problem, leaving g $C_6H_{12}O_6$ as the units for the answer, which matches the unknown. The answer is reasonable because it is one-half of 180.

## SAMPLE PROBLEM C

*For more help, go to the* ***Math Tutor*** *at the end of this chapter.*

**What mass of carbon dioxide, in grams, is needed to react with 3.00 mol $H_2O$ in the photosynthetic reaction described in Sample Problem B?**

### SOLUTION

**1 ANALYZE**

**Given:** amount of $H_2O$ = 3.00 mol
**Unknown:** mass of $CO_2$ (g)

**2 PLAN**

The chemical equation from Sample Problem B is

$$6CO_2(g) + 6H_2O(l) \longrightarrow C_6H_{12}O_6(s) + 6O_2(g).$$

Two conversion factors are needed—the mole ratio of $CO_2$ to $H_2O$ and the molar mass factor of $CO_2$.

$$\text{mol } H_2O \times \overset{\text{mol ratio}}{\frac{\text{mol } CO_2}{\text{mol } H_2O}} \times \overset{\text{molar mass factor}}{\frac{\text{g } CO_2}{\text{mol } CO_2}} = \text{g } CO_2$$

**3 COMPUTE**

Use the periodic table to compute the molar mass of $CO_2$.

$$CO_2 = 44.01 \text{ g/mol}$$

$$3.00 \text{ mol } H_2O \times \frac{6 \text{ mol } CO_2}{6 \text{ mol } H_2O} \times \frac{44.01 \text{ g } CO_2}{1 \text{ mol } CO_2} = 132 \text{ g } CO_2$$

**4 EVALUATE**

The answer is rounded correctly to three significant figures to match those in 3.00 mol $H_2O$. The units cancel to leave g $CO_2$, which is the unknown. The answer is close to an estimate of 120, which is $3 \times 40$.

**PRACTICE** *Answers in Appendix E*

1. When magnesium burns in air, it combines with oxygen to form magnesium oxide according to the following equation.

$$2Mg(s) + O_2(g) \longrightarrow 2MgO(s)$$

What mass in grams of magnesium oxide is produced from 2.00 mol of magnesium?

2. What mass of glucose can be produced from a photosynthesis reaction that occurs using 10 mol $CO_2$?

$$6CO_2(g) + 6H_2O(l) \longrightarrow C_6H_{12}O_6(aq) + 6O_2(g)$$

Go to **go.hrw.com** for more practice problems that ask you to calculate unknown quantities by using mole ratios.

**Keyword: HC6STCX**

## Conversions of Mass to Amounts in Moles

In these stoichiometric calculations, you are asked to calculate the amount in moles of one substance that will react with or be produced from a given mass of another substance. In this type of problem, you are starting with a mass (probably in grams) of some substance. The plan for this conversion is

$$\begin{matrix}\text{mass of} & & \text{amount of} & & \text{amount of} \\ \textit{given}\text{ substance} & \longrightarrow & \textit{given}\text{ substance} & \longrightarrow & \textit{unknown}\text{ substance} \\ \text{(g)} & & \text{(mol)} & & \text{(mol)}\end{matrix}$$

This route requires two additional pieces of data: the molar mass of the *given* substance and the mole ratio. The molar mass is determined by using masses from the periodic table. We will follow a procedure much like the one used previously by using the units of the molar mass conversion factor to guide our mathematical operations. Because the known quantity is a mass, the conversion factor will need to be 1 mol divided by molar mass. This conversion factor cancels units of grams and leaves units of moles.

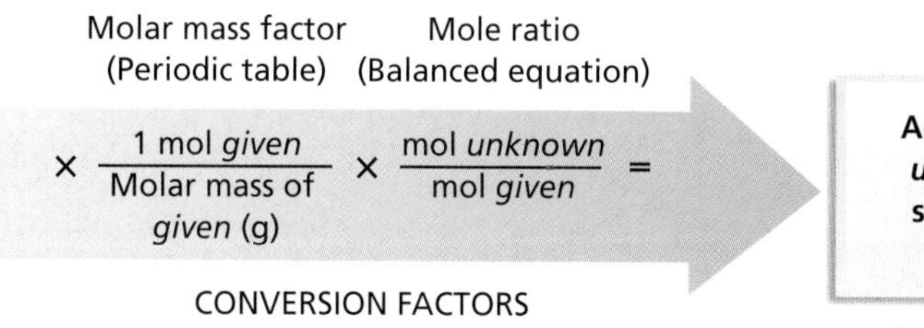


**FIGURE 3** This is a solution plan for problems in which the given quantity is expressed in grams and the unknown quantity is expressed in moles.

## SAMPLE PROBLEM D

For more help, go to the *Math Tutor* at the end of this chapter.

**The first step in the industrial manufacture of nitric acid is the catalytic oxidation of ammonia.**

$$NH_3(g) + O_2(g) \longrightarrow NO(g) + H_2O(g) \text{ (unbalanced)}$$

**The reaction is run using 824 g $NH_3$ and excess oxygen.**

**a. How many moles of NO are formed?**

**b. How many moles of $H_2O$ are formed?**

### SOLUTION

**1 ANALYZE** **Given:** mass of $NH_3$ = 824 g

**Unknown:** **a.** amount of NO produced (mol)

**b.** amount of $H_2O$ produced (mol)

**2 PLAN** First, write the balanced chemical equation.

$$4NH_3(g) + 5O_2(g) \longrightarrow 4NO(g) + 6H_2O(g)$$

Two conversion factors are needed to solve part (a)—the molar mass factor for $NH_3$ and the mole ratio of NO to $NH_3$. Part (b) starts with the same conversion factor as part (a), but then the mole ratio of $H_2O$ to $NH_3$ is used to convert to the amount in moles of $H_2O$. The first conversion factor in each part is the molar mass factor of $NH_3$.

$$\textbf{a. } \text{g } NH_3 \times \underbrace{\frac{1 \text{ mol } NH_3}{\text{g } NH_3}}_{\text{molar mass factor}} \times \underbrace{\frac{\text{mol NO}}{\text{mol } NH_3}}_{\text{mol ratio}} = \text{mol NO}$$

$$\textbf{b. } \text{g } NH_3 \times \underbrace{\frac{1 \text{ mol } NH_3}{\text{g } NH_3}}_{\text{molar mass factor}} \times \underbrace{\frac{\text{mol } H_2O}{\text{mol } NH_3}}_{\text{mol ratio}} = \text{mol } H_2O$$

**3 COMPUTE** Use the periodic table to compute the molar mass of $NH_3$.

$$1 \text{ mol } NH_3 = 17.04 \text{ g/mol}$$

$$\textbf{a. } 824 \text{ g } NH_3 \times \frac{1 \text{ mol } NH_3}{17.04 \text{ g } NH_3} \times \frac{4 \text{ mol NO}}{4 \text{ mol } NH_3} = 48.4 \text{ mol NO}$$

$$\textbf{b. } 824 \text{ g } NH_3 \times \frac{1 \text{ mol } NH_3}{17.04 \text{ g } NH_3} \times \frac{6 \text{ mol } H_2O}{4 \text{ mol } NH_3} = 72.5 \text{ mol } H_2O$$

**4 EVALUATE** The answers are correctly given to three significant figures. The units cancel in the two problems to leave mol NO and mol $H_2O$, respectively, which are the unknowns.

### PRACTICE

*Answers in Appendix E*

Oxygen was discovered by Joseph Priestley in 1774 when he heated mercury(II) oxide to decompose it to form its constituent elements.

1. How many moles of mercury(II) oxide, HgO, are needed to produce 125 g of oxygen, $O_2$?
2. How many moles of mercury are produced?

**extension**

Go to **go.hrw.com** for more practice problems that ask you to calculate unknown quantities by using mole ratios.

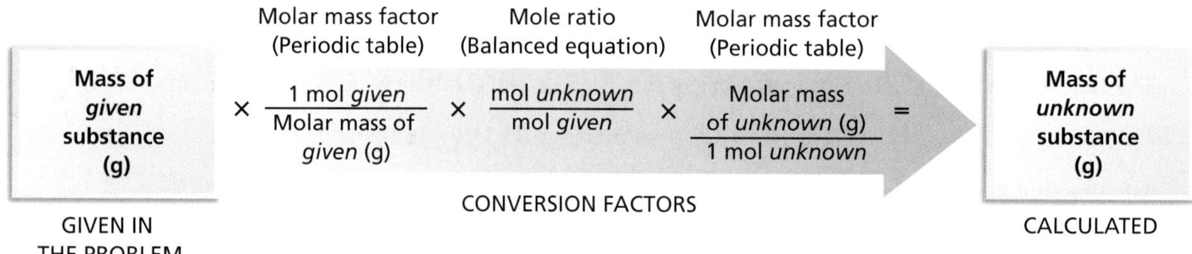


**FIGURE 4** This is a solution plan for problems in which the given quantity is expressed in grams and the unknown quantity is also expressed in grams.

## Mass-Mass Calculations

Mass-mass calculations are more practical than other mole calculations you have studied. You can never measure moles directly. You are generally required to calculate the amount in moles of a substance from its mass, which you can measure in the lab. Mass-mass problems can be viewed as the combination of the other types of problems. The plan for solving mass-mass problems is

$$\begin{matrix} \text{mass of} & & \text{amount of} & & \text{amount of} & & \text{mass of} \\ \textit{given}\text{ substance} & \longrightarrow & \textit{given}\text{ substance} & \longrightarrow & \textit{unknown}\text{ substance} & \longrightarrow & \textit{unknown}\text{ substance} \\ \text{(g)} & & \text{(mol)} & & \text{(mol)} & & \text{(g)} \end{matrix}$$

Three additional pieces of data are needed to solve mass-mass problems: the molar mass of the *given* substance, the mole ratio, and the molar mass of the *unknown* substance.

### SAMPLE PROBLEM E

*For more help, go to the* ***Math Tutor*** *at the end of this chapter.*

**Tin(II) fluoride, $SnF_2$, is used in some toothpastes. It is made by the reaction of tin with hydrogen fluoride according to the following equation.**

$$\mathbf{Sn(\mathit{s}) + 2HF(\mathit{g}) \longrightarrow SnF_2(\mathit{s}) + H_2(\mathit{g})}$$

**How many grams of $SnF_2$ are produced from the reaction of 30.00 g HF with Sn?**

**SOLUTION**

**1** *ANALYZE*

**Given:** amount of HF = 30.00 g

**Unknown:** mass of $SnF_2$ produced (g)

**2** *PLAN*

The conversion factors needed are the molar masses of HF and $SnF_2$ and the mole ratio of $SnF_2$ to HF.

$$\text{g HF} \times \underbrace{\frac{\text{mol HF}}{\text{g HF}}}_{\text{molar mass factor}} \times \underbrace{\frac{\text{mol SnF}_2}{\text{mol HF}}}_{\text{mol ratio}} \times \underbrace{\frac{\text{g SnF}_2}{\text{mol SnF}_2}}_{\text{molar mass factor}} = \text{g SnF}_2$$

**3 COMPUTE** Use the periodic table to compute the molar masses of HF and $SnF_2$.

$$1 \text{ mol HF} = 20.01 \text{ g}$$
$$1 \text{ mol } SnF_2 = 156.71 \text{ g}$$

$$30.00 \text{ g HF} \times \frac{1 \text{ mol HF}}{20.01 \text{ g HF}} \times \frac{1 \text{ mol } SnF_2}{2 \text{ mol HF}} \times \frac{156.71 \text{ g } SnF_2}{1 \text{ mol } SnF_2} = 117.5 \text{ g } SnF_2$$

**4 EVALUATE** The answer is correctly rounded to four significant figures. The units cancel to leave g $SnF_2$, which matches the unknown. The answer is close to an estimated value of 120.

**PRACTICE** *Answers in Appendix E*

1. Laughing gas (nitrous oxide, $N_2O$) is sometimes used as an anesthetic in dentistry. It is produced when ammonium nitrate is decomposed according to the following reaction.

$$NH_4NO_3(s) \longrightarrow N_2O(g) + 2H_2O(l)$$

   a. How many grams of $NH_4NO_3$ are required to produce 33.0 g $N_2O$?

   b. How many grams of water are produced in this reaction?

2. When copper metal is added to silver nitrate in solution, silver metal and copper(II) nitrate are produced. What mass of silver is produced from 100. g Cu?

3. What mass of aluminum is produced by the decomposition of 5.0 kg $Al_2O_3$?

Go to **go.hrw.com** for more practice problems that ask you to calculate unknown quantities by using mole ratios.

**Keyword: HC6STCX**

## SECTION REVIEW

1. Balance the following equation. Then, given the moles of reactant or product below, determine the corresponding amount in moles of each of the other reactants and products.

$$NH_3 + O_2 \longrightarrow N_2 + H_2O$$

   **a.** 4 mol $NH_3$ **b.** 4 mol $N_2$ **c.** 4.5 mol $O_2$

2. One reaction that produces hydrogen gas can be represented by the following unbalanced chemical equation:

$$Mg(s) + HCl(aq) \longrightarrow MgCl_2(aq) + H_2(g)$$

   **a.** What mass of HCl is consumed by the reaction of 2.50 moles of magnesium?

   **b.** What mass of each product is produced in part (a)?

3. Acetylene gas, $C_2H_2$, is produced as a result of the following reaction:

$$CaC_2(s) + 2H_2O(l) \longrightarrow C_2H_2(g) + Ca(OH)_2(aq)$$

   **a.** If 32.0 g $CaC_2$ are consumed in this reaction, how many moles of $H_2O$ are needed?

   **b.** How many moles of each product would form?

4. When sodium chloride reacts with silver nitrate, silver chloride precipitates. What mass of AgCl is produced from 75.0 g $AgNO_3$?

### Critical Thinking

5. **RELATING IDEAS** Carbon and oxygen react to form carbon monoxide: $2C + O_2 \longrightarrow 2CO$. What masses of carbon and oxygen are needed to make 56.0 g CO? Which law does this illustrate?

SECTION 3

# Limiting Reactants and Percentage Yield

## Objectives

- Describe a method for determining which of two reactants is a limiting reactant.
- Calculate the amount in moles or mass in grams of a product, given the amounts in moles or masses in grams of two reactants, one of which is in excess.
- Distinguish between theoretical yield, actual yield, and percentage yield.
- Calculate percentage yield, given the actual yield and quantity of a reactant.

 **C.4.5** Predict the percent yield, the mass of excess, and the limiting reagent in chemical reactions

In the laboratory, a reaction is rarely carried out with exactly the required amount of each of the reactants. In many cases, one or more reactants is present in excess; that is, there is more than the exact amount required to react.

Once one of the reactants is used up, no more product can be formed. The substance that is completely used up first in a reaction is called the limiting reactant. *The* **limiting reactant** *is the reactant that limits the amount of the other reactant that can combine and the amount of product that can form in a chemical reaction. The substance that is not used up completely in a reaction is called the* **excess reactant.** A limiting reactant may also be referred to as a *limiting reagent.*

The concept of the limiting reactant is analogous to the relationship between the number of bicycles that can be made from the number of frames and wheels available. How many bicycles can you make if you have 100 frames and 250 wheels? You have frames to make 100 bicycles and wheels to make 125. The maximum number is *limited* by the number of frames, 100. Because you put two wheels on each frame, you will use 200 wheels and have 50 wheels left over.

The same reasoning can be applied to chemical reactions. Consider the reaction between carbon and oxygen to form carbon dioxide.

$$C(s) + O_2(g) \longrightarrow CO_2(g)$$

According to the equation, one mole of carbon reacts with one mole of oxygen to form one mole of carbon dioxide. Suppose you could mix 5 mol C with 10 mol $O_2$ and allow the reaction to take place. **Figure 5** shows that there is more oxygen than is needed to react with the carbon. Carbon is the limiting reactant in this situation, and it limits the amount of $CO_2$ that is formed. Oxygen is the excess reactant, and 5 mol $O_2$ will be left over at the end of the reaction.

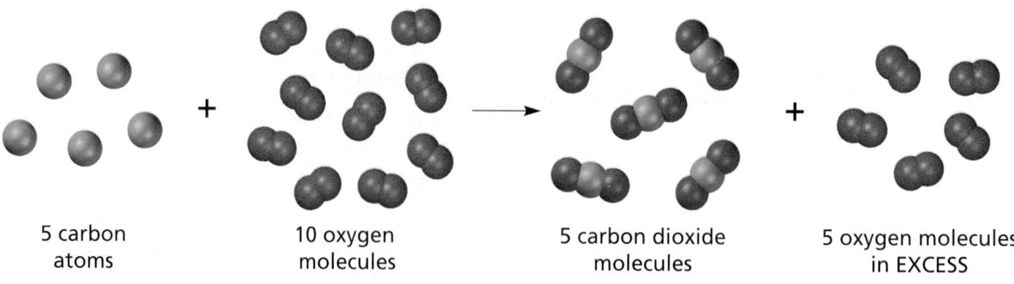


**FIGURE 5** If you think of a mole as a multiple of molecules and atoms, you can see why the amount of $O_2$ is in excess.

## SAMPLE PROBLEM F

**Silicon dioxide (quartz) is usually quite unreactive but reacts readily with hydrogen fluoride according to the following equation.**

$$SiO_2(s) + 4HF(g) \longrightarrow SiF_4(g) + 2H_2O(l)$$

**If 6.0 mol HF is added to 4.5 mol $SiO_2$, which is the limiting reactant?**

### SOLUTION

**1 ANALYZE**

**Given:** amount of HF = 6.0 mol
amount of $SiO_2$ = 4.5 mol

**Unknown:** limiting reactant

**2 PLAN**

Pick one of the products, in this case $SiF_4$. Use the given amounts of each reactant to calculate the amount of $SiF_4$ that could be produced from that reactant. Compare the amounts of $SiF_4$. The limiting reactant is the reactant that produces the smallest number of moles of $SiF_4$. The smallest amount of product is also the maximum amount that can be formed.

$$\text{mol HF} \times \frac{\text{mol } SiF_4}{\text{mol HF}} = \text{mol } SiF_4 \text{ produced} \qquad \text{mol } SiO_2 \times \frac{\text{mol } SiF_4}{\text{mol } SiO_2} = \text{mol } SiF_4 \text{ produced}$$

**3 COMPUTE**

$$6.0 \cancel{\text{mol HF}} \times \frac{1 \text{ mol } SiF_4}{4 \cancel{\text{mol HF}}} = 1.5 \text{ mol } SiF_4 \text{ produced}$$

$$4.5 \cancel{\text{mol } SiO_2} \times \frac{1 \text{ mol } SiF_4}{1 \cancel{\text{mol } SiO_2}} = 4.5 \text{ mol } SiF_4 \text{ produced}$$

Under ideal conditions, 6.0 mol HF can make 1.5 mol $SiF_4$, and 4.5 mol $SiO_2$ present can make 4.5 mol $SiF_4$. Because 1.5 mol $SiF_4$ is smaller than 4.5 mol $SiF_4$, the HF is the limiting reactant and $SiO_2$ is the excess reactant.

**4 EVALUATE**

From the balanced equation, we can see that the reaction requires four times the number of moles of HF as it does moles of $SiO_2$. Because the molar amount of HF that we have is less than four times the moles of $SiO_2$, our calculations clearly show that HF is the limiting reactant.

### PRACTICE

*Answers in Appendix E*

1. Some rocket engines use a mixture of hydrazine, $N_2H_4$, and hydrogen peroxide, $H_2O_2$, as the propellant. The reaction is given by the following equation.

$$N_2H_4(l) + 2H_2O_2(l) \longrightarrow N_2(g) + 4H_2O(g)$$

   a. Which is the limiting reactant in this reaction when 0.750 mol $N_2H_4$ is mixed with 0.500 mol $H_2O_2$?

   b. How much of the excess reactant, in moles, remains unchanged?

   c. How much of each product, in moles, is formed?

**extension**

Go to **go.hrw.com** for more practice problems that ask you to determine the limiting reactant.

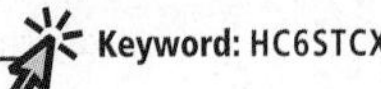

## SAMPLE PROBLEM G

**The black oxide of iron, $Fe_3O_4$, occurs in nature as the mineral magnetite. This substance can also be made in the laboratory by the reaction between red-hot iron and steam according to the following equation.**

$$3Fe(s) + 4H_2O(g) \longrightarrow Fe_3O_4(s) + 4H_2(g)$$

**a. When 36.0 g $H_2O$ is mixed with 67.0 g Fe, which is the limiting reactant?**
**b. What mass in grams of black iron oxide is produced?**
**c. What mass in grams of excess reactant remains when the reaction is completed?**

### SOLUTION

**1** *ANALYZE*

**Given:** mass of $H_2O$ = 36.0 g
mass of Fe = 67.0 g

**Unknown:** limiting reactant
mass of $Fe_3O_4$, in grams
mass of excess reactant remaining

**2** *PLAN*

**a.** First, convert both given masses in grams to amounts in moles. Then, calculate the number of moles of one of the products. Because the problem asks for the mass of $Fe_3O_4$ formed, we will calculate moles of $Fe_3O_4$. The reactant yielding the smaller number of moles of product is the limiting reactant.

$$\text{g Fe} \times \overset{\text{molar mass factor}}{\frac{\text{mol Fe}}{\text{g Fe}}} \times \overset{\text{mol ratio}}{\frac{\text{mol } Fe_3O_4}{\text{mol Fe}}} = \text{mol } Fe_3O_4$$

$$\text{g } H_2O \times \overset{\text{molar mass factor}}{\frac{\text{mol } H_2O}{\text{g } H_2O}} \times \overset{\text{mol ratio}}{\frac{\text{mol } Fe_3O_4}{\text{mol } H_2O}} = \text{mol } Fe_3O_4$$

**b.** To find the maximum mass of $Fe_3O_4$ that can be produced, we must use the amount of $Fe_3O_4$ in moles from the limiting reactant in a simple stoichiometric problem.

$$\text{mole } Fe_3O_4 \text{ from limiting reactant} \times \overset{\text{molar mass factor}}{\frac{\text{g } Fe_3O_4}{\text{mol } Fe_3O_4}} = \text{g } Fe_3O_4 \text{ produced}$$

**c.** To find the amount of excess reactant remaining, we must first determine the amount of the excess reactant that is consumed. The calculated moles of the product (from the limiting reactant) is used to determine the amount of excess reactant that is consumed.

$$\text{mol product} \times \frac{\text{mol excess reactant}}{\text{mol product}} \times \frac{\text{g excess reactant}}{\text{mol excess reactant}} = \text{g excess reactant consumed}$$

The amount of excess reactant remaining can then be found by subtracting the amount consumed from the amount originally present.

original g excess reactant − g excess reactant consumed = g excess reactant remaining

**3** *COMPUTE*

**a.** Use the periodic table to determine the molar masses of $H_2O$, Fe, and $Fe_3O_4$. Then, determine how many mol $Fe_3O_4$ can be produced from each reactant.

1 mol $H_2O$ = 18.02 g
1 mol Fe = 55.85 g
1 mol $Fe_3O_4$ = 231.55 g

$$67.0 \text{ g Fe} \times \frac{1 \text{ mol Fe}}{55.85 \text{ g Fe}} \times \frac{1 \text{ mol } Fe_3O_4}{3 \text{ mol Fe}} = 0.400 \text{ mol } Fe_3O_4$$

$$36.0 \text{ g } H_2O \times \frac{1 \text{ mol } H_2O}{18.02 \text{ g } H_2O} \times \frac{1 \text{ mol } Fe_3O_4}{4 \text{ mol } H_2O} = 0.499 \text{ mol } Fe_3O_4$$

Fe is the limiting reactant because the given amount of Fe can make only 0.400 mol $Fe_3O_4$, which is less than the 0.499 mol $Fe_3O_4$ that the given amount of $H_2O$ would produce.

**b.** $0.400 \text{ mol } Fe_3O_4 \times \frac{231.55 \text{ g } Fe_3O_4}{1 \text{ mol } Fe_3O_4} = 92.6 \text{ g } Fe_3O_4$

**c.** $0.400 \text{ mol } Fe_3O_4 \times \frac{4 \text{ mol } H_2O}{1 \text{ mol } Fe_3O_4} \times \frac{18.02 \text{ g } H_2O}{1 \text{ mol } H_2O} = 28.8 \text{ g } H_2O$ consumed

36.0 g $H_2O$ – 28.8 g $H_2O$ consumed = 7.2 g $H_2O$ remaining

**4** *EVALUATE*

The mass of original reactants is 67.0 + 36.0 = 103.0 g; the mass of $Fe_3O_4$ + unreacted water is 92.6 g + 7.2 g = 99.8 g. The difference of 3.2 g is the mass of hydrogen that is produced with the $Fe_3O_4$.

**PRACTICE** *Answers in Appendix E*

**1.** Zinc and sulfur react to form zinc sulfide according to the following equation.

$$8Zn(s) + S_8(s) \longrightarrow 8ZnS(s)$$

**a.** If 2.00 mol of Zn are heated with 1.00 mol of $S_8$, identify the limiting reactant.

**b.** How many moles of excess reactant remain?

**c.** How many moles of the product are formed?

**2.** Carbon reacts with steam, $H_2O$, at high temperatures to produce hydrogen and carbon monoxide.

**a.** If 2.40 mol of carbon are exposed to 3.10 mol of steam, identify the limiting reactant.

**b.** How many moles of each product are formed?

**c.** What mass of each product is formed?

**extension**

Go to **go.hrw.com** for more practice problems that ask you to calculate the amount of excess reactant and the amount of product formed.

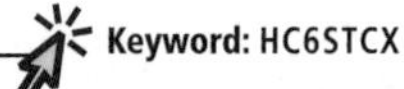

# QuickLAB  Wear oven mitts when handling heated items.

## *Limiting Reactants in a Recipe*

### Materials

- 1/2 cup sugar
- 1/2 cup brown sugar
- 1 1/3 stick margarine (at room temperature)
- 1 egg
- 1/2 tsp. salt
- 1 tsp. vanilla
- 1/2 tsp. baking soda
- 1 1/2 cup flour
- 1 1/3 cup chocolate chips
- mixing bowl
- mixing spoon
- measuring spoons and cups
- cookie sheet
- oven preheated to 350°F

### Procedure

1. In the mixing bowl, combine the sugars and margarine together until smooth. (An electric mixer will make this process go much faster.)
2. Add the egg, salt, and vanilla. Mix well.
3. Stir in the baking soda, flour, and chocolate chips. Chill the dough for an hour in the refrigerator for best results.
4. Divide the dough into 24 small balls about 3 cm in diameter. Place the balls on an ungreased cookie sheet.
5. Bake at 350°F for about 10 minutes, or until the cookies are light brown.

Yield: 24 cookies

### Discussion

1. Suppose you are given the following amounts of ingredients:
   1 dozen eggs
   24 tsp. of vanilla
   1 lb. (82 tsp.) of salt
   1 lb. (84 tsp.) of baking soda
   3 cups of chocolate chips
   5 lb. (11 cups) of sugar
   2 lb. (4 cups) of brown sugar
   1 lb. (4 sticks) of margarine

   **a.** For each ingredient, calculate how many cookies could be prepared if all of that ingredient were consumed. (For example, the recipe shows that using 1 egg—with the right amounts of the other ingredients—yields 24 cookies. How many cookies can you make if the recipe is increased proportionately for 12 eggs?)

   **b.** To determine the limiting reactant for the new ingredients list, identify which ingredient will result in the fewest number of cookies.

   **c.** What is the maximum number of cookies that can be produced from the new amounts of ingredients?

## Percentage Yield

The amounts of products calculated in the ideal stoichiometry problems in this chapter so far represent theoretical yields. *The* **theoretical yield** *is the maximum amount of product that can be produced from a given amount of reactant.* In most chemical reactions, the amount of product obtained is less than the theoretical yield. There are many reasons for this result. Reactants may contain impurities or may form byproducts in competing side reactions. Also, in many reactions, all reactants are not converted to products. As a result, less product is produced than ideal stoichiometric calculations predict. *The measured amount of a product obtained from a reaction is called the* **actual yield** *of that product.*

Chemists are usually interested in the efficiency of a reaction. The efficiency is expressed by comparing the actual and theoretical yields. *The* **percentage yield** *is the ratio of the actual yield to the theoretical yield, multiplied by 100.*

$$\text{percentage yield} = \frac{\text{actual yield}}{\text{theoretical yield}} \times 100$$

### SAMPLE PROBLEM H

**Chlorobenzene, $C_6H_5Cl$, is used in the production of many important chemicals, such as aspirin, dyes, and disinfectants. One industrial method of preparing chlorobenzene is to react benzene, $C_6H_6$, with chlorine, as represented by the following equation.**

$$C_6H_6(l) + Cl_2(g) \longrightarrow C_6H_5Cl(l) + HCl(g)$$

**When 36.8 g $C_6H_6$ react with an excess of $Cl_2$, the actual yield of $C_6H_5Cl$ is 38.8 g. What is the percentage yield of $C_6H_5Cl$?**

#### SOLUTION

**1** *ANALYZE*

**Given:** mass of $C_6H_6$ = 36.8 g
mass of $Cl_2$ = excess
actual yield of $C_6H_5Cl$ = 38.8 g
**Unknown:** percentage yield of $C_6H_5Cl$

**2** *PLAN*

First do a mass-mass calculation to find the theoretical yield of $C_6H_5Cl$.

$$\text{g } C_6H_6 \times \overset{\text{molar mass factor}}{\frac{\text{mol } C_6H_6}{\text{g } C_6H_6}} \times \overset{\text{mol ratio}}{\frac{\text{mol } C_6H_5Cl}{\text{mol } C_6H_6}} \times \overset{\text{molar mass}}{\frac{\text{g } C_6H_5Cl}{\text{mol } C_6H_5Cl}} = \text{g } C_6H_5Cl \text{ (theoretical yield)}$$

Then the percentage yield can be found.

$$\text{percentage yield } C_6H_5Cl = \frac{\text{actual yield}}{\text{theoretical yield}} \times 100$$

**3 COMPUTE** Use the periodic table to determine the molar masses of $C_6H_6$ and $C_6H_5Cl$.

$$1 \text{ mol } C_6H_6 = 78.12 \text{ g}$$
$$1 \text{ mol } C_6H_5Cl = 112.56 \text{ g}$$

$$36.8 \text{ g } C_6H_6 \times \frac{1 \text{ mol } C_6H_6}{78.12 \text{ g } C_6H_6} \times \frac{1 \text{ mol } C_6H_5Cl}{1 \text{ mol } C_6H_6} \times \frac{112.56 \text{ g } C_6H_5Cl}{1 \text{ mol } C_6H_5Cl} = 53.0 \text{ g } C_6H_5Cl \text{ (theoretical yield)}$$

$$\text{percentage yield} = \frac{38.8 \text{ g}}{53.0 \text{ g}} \times 100 = 73.2\%$$

**4 EVALUATE** The answer is correctly rounded to three significant figures to match those in 36.8 g $C_6H_6$. The units have canceled correctly. The theoretical yield is close to an estimated value of 50 g, (one-half of 100 g). The percentage yield is close to an estimated value of 80%, (40/50 × 100).

**PRACTICE** *Answers in Appendix E*

1. Methanol can be produced through the reaction of CO and $H_2$ in the presence of a catalyst.

$$CO(g) + 2H_2(g) \xrightarrow{\text{catalyst}} CH_3OH(l)$$

If 75.0 g of CO reacts to produce 68.4 g $CH_3OH$, what is the percentage yield of $CH_3OH$?

2. Aluminum reacts with excess copper(II) sulfate according to the reaction given below. If 1.85 g of Al react and the percentage yield of Cu is 56.6%, what mass of Cu is produced?

$$Al(s) + CuSO_4(aq) \longrightarrow Al_2(SO_4)_3(aq) + Cu(s) \text{ (unbalanced)}$$

**extension**

Go to **go.hrw.com** for more practice problems that ask you to calculate percentage yield.

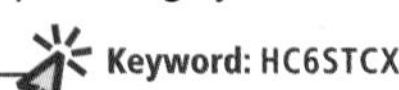
**Keyword: HC6STCX**

## SECTION REVIEW

1. Carbon disulfide burns in oxygen to yield carbon dioxide and sulfur dioxide according to the following chemical equation.

$$CS_2(l) + 3O_2(g) \longrightarrow CO_2(g) + 2SO_2(g)$$

   **a.** If 1.00 mol $CS_2$ reacts with 1.00 mol $O_2$, identify the limiting reactant.

   **b.** How many moles of excess reactant remain?

   **c.** How many moles of each product are formed?

2. Metallic magnesium reacts with steam to produce magnesium hydroxide and hydrogen gas.

   **a.** If 16.2 g Mg are heated with 12.0 g $H_2O$, what is the limiting reactant?

   **b.** How many moles of the excess reactant are left?

   **c.** How many grams of each product are formed?

3. Quicklime, CaO, can be prepared by roasting limestone, $CaCO_3$, according to the following reaction.
$CaCO_3(s) \xrightarrow{\Delta} CaO(s) + CO_2(g)$.
When $2.00 \times 10^3$ g $CaCO_3$ are heated, the actual yield of CaO is $1.05 \times 10^3$ g. What is the percentage yield?

**Critical Thinking**

4. **ANALYZING DATA** A chemical engineer calculated that 15.0 mol $H_2$ was needed to react with excess $N_2$ to prepare 10.0 mol $NH_3$. But the actual yield is 60.0%. Write a balanced chemical equation for the reaction. Is the amount of $H_2$ needed to make 10.0 mol $NH_3$ more, the same, or less than 15 mol? How many moles of $H_2$ are needed?

# CHAPTER HIGHLIGHTS

## Introduction to Stoichiometry

**Vocabulary**
composition stoichiometry
reaction stoichiometry
mole ratio

- Reaction stoichiometry involves the mass relationships between reactants and products in a chemical reaction.
- Relating one substance to another requires expressing the amount of each substance in moles.
- A mole ratio is the conversion factor that relates the amount in moles of any two substances in a chemical reaction. The mole ratio is derived from the balanced equation.
- Amount of a substance is expressed in moles, and mass of a substance is expressed by using mass units such as grams, kilograms, or milligrams.
- Mass and amount of substance are quantities, whereas moles and grams are units.
- A balanced chemical equation is necessary to solve any stoichiometric problem.

## Ideal Stoichiometric Calculations

- In an ideal stoichiometric calculation, the mass or the amount of any reactant or product can be calculated if the balanced chemical equation and the mass or amount of any other reactant or product is known.

## Limiting Reactants and Percentage Yield

**Vocabulary**
limiting reactant
excess reactant
theoretical yield
actual yield
percentage yield

- In actual reactions, the reactants may be present in proportions that differ from the stoichiometric proportions required for a complete reaction in which all of each reactant is converted to product.
- The limiting reactant controls the maximum possible amount of product formed.
- For many reactions, the quantity of a product is less than the theoretical maximum for that product. Percentage yield shows the relationship between the theoretical yield and actual yield for the product of a reaction.

# CHAPTER REVIEW

*For more practice, go to the Problem Bank in Appendix D.*

## Introduction to Stoichiometry

### SECTION 1 REVIEW

1. a. Explain the concept of mole ratio as used in reaction stoichiometry problems.
   b. What is the source of this ratio?
2. For each of the following balanced chemical equations, write all possible mole ratios:
   a. $2Ca + O_2 \longrightarrow 2CaO$
   b. $Mg + 2HF \longrightarrow MgF_2 + H_2$

### PRACTICE PROBLEMS

3. Given the chemical equation $Na_2CO_3(aq) + Ca(OH)_2 \longrightarrow 2NaOH(aq) + CaCO_3(s)$, determine to two decimal places the molar masses of all substances involved. Then, write the molar masses as conversion factors.

## Ideal Stoichiometric Calculations

### SECTION 2 REVIEW

4. a. What is molar mass?
   b. What is its role in reaction stoichiometry?

### PRACTICE PROBLEMS

5. Hydrogen and oxygen react under a specific set of conditions to produce water according to the following: $2H_2(g) + O_2(g) \longrightarrow 2H_2O(g)$.
   a. How many moles of hydrogen would be required to produce 5.0 mol of water?
   b. How many moles of oxygen would be required? (Hint: See Sample Problem A.)
6. a. If 4.50 mol of ethane, $C_2H_6$, undergo combustion according to the unbalanced equation $C_2H_6 + O_2 \longrightarrow CO_2 + H_2O$, how many moles of oxygen are required?
   b. How many moles of each product are formed?
7. Sodium chloride is produced from its elements through a synthesis reaction. What mass of each reactant would be required to produce 25.0 mol of sodium chloride?
8. In a blast furnace, iron(III) oxide is used to produce iron by the following (unbalanced) reaction: $Fe_2O_3(s) + CO(g) \longrightarrow Fe(s) + CO_2(g)$
   a. If 4.00 kg $Fe_2O_3$ are available to react, how many moles of CO are needed?
   b. How many moles of each product are formed?
9. Methanol, $CH_3OH$, is an important industrial compound that is produced from the following (unbalanced) reaction: $CO(g) + H_2(g) \longrightarrow CH_3OH(g)$. What mass of each reactant would be needed to produce 100.0 kg of methanol? (Hint: See Sample Problem E.)
10. Nitrogen combines with oxygen in the atmosphere during lightning flashes to form nitrogen monoxide, NO, which then reacts further with $O_2$ to produce nitrogen dioxide, $NO_2$.
    a. What mass of $NO_2$ is formed when NO reacts with 384 g $O_2$?
    b. How many grams of NO are required to react with this amount of $O_2$?
11. As early as 1938, the use of NaOH was suggested as a means of removing $CO_2$ from the cabin of a spacecraft according to the following (unbalanced) reaction: $NaOH + CO_2 \longrightarrow Na_2CO_3 + H_2O$.
    a. If the average human body discharges 925.0 g $CO_2$ per day, how many moles of NaOH are needed each day for each person in the spacecraft?
    b. How many moles of each product are formed?
12. The double-replacement reaction between silver nitrate and sodium bromide produces silver bromide, a component of photographic film.
    a. If 4.50 mol of silver nitrate react, what mass of sodium bromide is required?
    b. What mass of silver bromide is formed?
13. In a soda-acid fire extinguisher, concentrated sulfuric acid reacts with sodium hydrogen carbonate to produce carbon dioxide, sodium sulfate, and water.
    a. How many moles of sodium hydrogen carbonate would be needed to react with 150.0 g of sulfuric acid?
    b. How many moles of each product would be formed?

**14.** Sulfuric acid reacts with sodium hydroxide according to the following:
$H_2SO_4 + NaOH \longrightarrow Na_2SO_4 + H_2O$.
a. Balance the equation for this reaction.
b. What mass of $H_2SO_4$ would be required to react with 0.75 mol NaOH?
c. What mass of each product is formed by this reaction? (Hint: See Sample B.)

**15.** Copper reacts with silver nitrate through single replacement.
a. If 2.25 g of silver are produced from the reaction, how many moles of copper(II) nitrate are also produced?
b. How many moles of each reactant are required in this reaction? (Hint: See Sample Problem D.)

**16.** Aspirin, $C_9H_8O_4$, is produced through the following reaction of salicylic acid, $C_7H_6O_3$, and acetic anhydride, $C_4H_6O_3$: $C_7H_6O_3(s) + C_4H_6O_3(l) \longrightarrow C_9H_8O_4(s) + HC_2H_3O_2(l)$.
a. What mass of aspirin (kg) could be produced from 75.0 mol of salicylic acid?
b. What mass of acetic anhydride (kg) would be required?
c. At 20°C, how many liters of acetic acid, $HC_2H_3O_2$, would be formed? The density of $HC_2H_3O_2$ is 1.05 g/mL.

## *Limiting Reactants and Percentage Yield*

### SECTION 3 REVIEW

**17.** Distinguish between ideal and real stoichiometric calculations.

**18.** Distinguish between the limiting reactant and the excess reactant in a chemical reaction.

**19.** a. Distinguish between the theoretical yield and actual yield in stoichiometric calculations.
b. How does the value of the theoretical yield generally compare with the value of the actual yield?

**20.** What is the percentage yield of a reaction?

**21.** Why are actual yields usually less than calculated theoretical yields?

### PRACTICE PROBLEMS

**22.** Given the reactant amounts specified in each chemical equation, determine the limiting reactant in each case:
a. $\underset{2.0\text{ mol}}{HCl} + \underset{2.5\text{ mol}}{NaOH} \longrightarrow NaCl + H_2O$
b. $\underset{2.5\text{ mol}}{Zn} + \underset{6.0\text{ mol}}{2HCl} \longrightarrow ZnCl_2 + H_2$
c. $\underset{4.0\text{ mol}}{2Fe(OH)_3} + \underset{6.5\text{ mol}}{3H_2SO_4} \longrightarrow Fe_2(SO_4)_3 + 6H_2O$
(Hint: See Sample Problem F.)

**23.** For each reaction specified in Problem 22, determine the amount in moles of excess reactant that remains. (Hint: See Sample Problem G.)

**24.** For each reaction specified in Problem 22, calculate the amount in moles of each product formed.

**25.** a. If 2.50 mol of copper and 5.50 mol of silver nitrate are available to react by single replacement, identify the limiting reactant.
b. Determine the amount in moles of excess reactant remaining.
c. Determine the amount in moles of each product formed.
d. Determine the mass of each product formed.

**26.** Sulfuric acid reacts with aluminum hydroxide by double replacement.
a. If 30.0 g of sulfuric acid react with 25.0 g of aluminum hydroxide, identify the limiting reactant.
b. Determine the mass of excess reactant remaining.
c. Determine the mass of each product formed. Assume 100% yield.

**27.** The energy used to power one of the Apollo lunar missions was supplied by the following overall reaction: $2N_2H_4 + (CH_3)_2N_2H_2 + 3N_2O_4 \longrightarrow 6N_2 + 2CO_2 + 8H_2O$. For the phase of the mission when the lunar module ascended from the surface of the moon, a total of 1200. kg $N_2H_4$ was available to react with 1000. kg $(CH_3)_2N_2H_2$ and 4500. kg $N_2O_4$.
a. For this portion of the flight, which of the allocated components was used up first?
b. How much water, in kilograms, was put into the lunar atmosphere through this reaction?

**28.** Calculate the indicated quantity for each of the various chemical reactions given:
a. theoretical yield = 20.0 g, actual yield = 15.0 g, percentage yield = ?
b. theoretical yield = 1.0 g, percentage yield = 90.0%, actual yield = ?
c. theoretical yield = 5.00 g, actual yield = 4.75 g, percentage yield = ?
d. theoretical yield = 3.45 g, percentage yield = 48.0%, actual yield = ?

**29.** The percentage yield for the reaction

$$PCl_3 + Cl_2 \longrightarrow PCl_5$$

is 83.2%. What mass of $PCl_5$ is expected from the reaction of 73.7 g $PCl_3$ with excess chlorine?

**30.** The Ostwald process for producing nitric acid from ammonia consists of the following steps:

$4NH_3(g) + 5O_2(g) \longrightarrow 4NO(g) + 6H_2O(g)$
$2NO(g) + O_2(g) \longrightarrow 2NO_2(g)$
$3NO_2(g) + H_2O(g) \longrightarrow 2HNO_3(aq) + NO(g)$

If the yield in each step is 94.0%, how many grams of nitric acid can be produced from 5.00 kg of ammonia?

## MIXED REVIEW

**31.** Magnesium is obtained from sea water. $Ca(OH)_2$ is added to sea water to precipitate $Mg(OH)_2$. The precipitate is filtered and reacted with HCl to produce $MgCl_2$. The $MgCl_2$ is electrolyzed to produce Mg and $Cl_2$. If 185.0 g of magnesium are recovered from 1000. g $MgCl_2$, what is the percentage yield for this reaction?

**32.** Phosphate baking powder is a mixture of starch, sodium hydrogen carbonate, and calcium dihydrogen phosphate. When mixed with water, phosphate baking powder releases carbon dioxide gas, causing a dough or batter to bubble and rise.

$$2NaHCO_3(aq) + Ca(H_2PO_4)_2(aq) \longrightarrow Na_2HPO_4(aq) + CaHPO_4(aq) + 2CO_2(g) + 2H_2O(l)$$

If 0.750 L $CO_2$ is needed for a cake and each kilogram of baking powder contains 168 g of $NaHCO_3$, how many grams of baking powder must be used to generate this amount $CO_2$? The density of $CO_2$ at baking temperature is about 1.20 g/L.

**33.** Coal gasification is a process that converts coal into methane gas. If this reaction has a percentage yield of 85.0%, what mass of methane can be obtained from 1250 g of carbon?

$$2C(s) + 2H_2O(l) \longrightarrow CH_4(g) + CO_2(g)$$

**34.** If the percentage yield for the coal gasification process is increased to 95%, what mass of methane can be obtained from 2750 g of carbon?

**35.** Builders and dentists must store plaster of Paris, $CaSO_4{\cdot}\frac{1}{2}H_2O$, in airtight containers to prevent it from absorbing water vapor from the air and changing to gypsum, $CaSO_4{\cdot}2H_2O$. How many liters of water vapor evolve when 2.00 kg of gypsum are heated at 110°C to produce plaster of Paris? At 110°C, the density of water vapor is 0.574 g/L.

**36.** Gold can be recovered from sea water by reacting the water with zinc, which is refined from zinc oxide. The zinc displaces the gold in the water. What mass of gold can be recovered if 2.00 g of ZnO and an excess of sea water are available?

$2ZnO(s) + C(s) \longrightarrow 2Zn(s) + CO_2(g)$
$2Au^{3+}(aq) + 3Zn(s) \longrightarrow 3Zn^{2+}(aq) + 2Au(s)$

## CRITICAL THINKING

**37. Relating Ideas** The chemical equation is a good source of information concerning a reaction. Explain the relationship between the actual yield of a reaction product and the chemical equation of the product.

**38. Analyzing Results** Very seldom are chemists able to achieve a 100% yield of a product from a chemical reaction. However, the yield of a reaction is usually important because of the expense involved in producing less product. For example, when magnesium metal is heated in a crucible at high temperatures, the product magnesium oxide, MgO, is formed. Based on your analysis of the reaction, describe some of the actions that you would take to increase your percentage yield. The reaction is as follows:

$$2Mg(s) + O_2(g) \longrightarrow 2MgO(s)$$

39. **Analyzing Results** In the lab, you run an experiment that appears to have a percentage yield of 115%. Propose reasons for this result. Can an actual yield ever exceed a theoretical yield? Explain your answer.

40. **Relating Ideas** Explain the stoichiometry of blowing air on a smoldering campfire to keep the coals burning.

## USING THE HANDBOOK

41. The steel-making process described in the Transition Metal section of the *Elements Handbook* shows the equation for the formation of iron carbide. Use this equation to answer the following questions:
    a. If $3.65 \times 10^3$ kg of iron is used in a steel-making process, what is the minimum mass of carbon needed to react with all of the iron?
    b. What is the theoretical mass of iron carbide that is formed?

42. The reaction of aluminum with oxygen to produce a protective coating for the metal's surface is described in the discussion of aluminum in Group 13 of the *Elements Handbook*. Use this equation to answer the following questions:
    a. What mass of aluminum oxide would theoretically be formed if a 30.0 g piece of aluminum foil reacted with excess oxygen?
    b. Why would you expect the actual yield from this reaction to be far less than the mass you calculated in item (a)?

43. The reactions of oxide compounds to produce carbonates, phosphates, and sulfates are described in the section on oxides in Group 16 of the *Elements Handbook*. Use those equations to answer the following questions:
    a. What mass of $CO_2$ is needed to react with 154.6 g MgO?
    b. What mass of magnesium carbonate is produced?
    c. When 45.7 g $P_4O_{10}$ is reacted with an excess of calcium oxide, what mass of calcium phosphate is produced?

## RESEARCH & WRITING

44. Research the history of the Haber process for the production of ammonia. What was the significance of this process in history? How is this process related to the discussion of reaction yields in this chapter?

## ALTERNATIVE ASSESSMENT

45. **Performance** Just as reactants combine in certain proportions to form a product, colors can be combined to create other colors. Artists do this all the time to find just the right color for their paintings. Using poster paint, determine the proportions of primary pigments used to create the following colors. Your proportions should be such that anyone could mix the color perfectly.

46. **Performance** Write two of your own sample problems that are descriptions of how to solve a mass-mass problem. Assume that your sample problems will be used by other students to learn how to solve mass-mass problems.

**extension**

**Graphing Calculator Limiting Reactants and Percentage Yield**

Go to **go.hrw.com** for a graphing calculator exercise that asks you to use a theoretical yield graph to make predictions about limiting reactants and percentage yield.

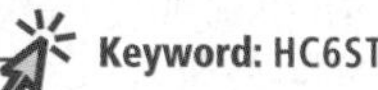

# Math Tutor USING MOLE RATIOS

An unbalanced chemical equation tells you what substances react and what products are produced. A balanced chemical equation gives you even more information. It tells you how many atoms, molecules, or ions react and how many atoms, molecules, or ions are produced. The coefficients in a balanced equation represent the relative amounts in moles of reactants and products. Using this information, you can set up a mole ratio. A mole ratio is a conversion factor that relates the amounts in moles of any two substances involved in a chemical reaction.

## Problem-Solving TIPS

- When solving stoichiometric problems, always start with a balanced chemical equation.
- Identify the amount known from the problem (in moles or mass).
- If you are given the mass of a substance, use the molar mass factor as a conversion factor to find the amount in moles. If you are given the amount in moles of a substance, use the molar mass factor as a conversion factor to find the mass.

## SAMPLE

**If 3.61 g of aluminum reacts completely with excess $CuCl_2$, what mass of copper metal is produced? Use the balanced equation below.**

$$2Al(s) + 3CuCl_2(aq) \longrightarrow 2AlCl_3(aq) + 3Cu(s)$$

You know the mass of aluminum that reacts. If you convert that mass to moles, you can apply the mole ratio of aluminum to copper in this reaction to find the moles of copper produced.

$$\text{mol Al} = 3.61\ \cancel{\text{g Al}} \times \frac{1\ \text{mol Al}}{26.98\ \cancel{\text{g Al}}} = 0.134\ \text{mol Al}$$

$$\cancel{\text{mol Al}} \times \frac{3\ \text{mol Cu}}{2\ \cancel{\text{mol Al}}} = \text{mol Cu}$$

$$0.134\ \cancel{\text{mol Al}} \times \frac{3\ \text{mol Cu}}{2\ \cancel{\text{mol Al}}} = 0.201\ \text{mol Cu}$$

Then, convert moles of Cu to mass of Cu by applying the following factor:

$$\text{mol Cu} \times \frac{\text{molar mass Cu}}{1\ \text{mol Cu}} = \text{mass Cu, or } 0.201\ \text{mol Cu} \times \frac{63.55\ \text{g Cu}}{1\ \text{mol Cu}} = 12.8\ \text{g Cu}$$

## PRACTICE PROBLEMS

1. If 12.24 moles of $O_2$ react with excess $SO_2$, how many moles of $SO_3$ are formed? Use the balanced equation below.

$$2SO_2(g) + O_2(g) \longrightarrow 2SO_3(g)$$

2. If 78.50 g $KClO_3$ decomposes, what mass of $O_2$ is produced? Use the balanced equation below.

$$2KClO_3(s) \longrightarrow 2KCl(s) + 3O_2(g)$$

# Standardized Test Prep

Answer the following items on a separate piece of paper.

**MULTIPLE CHOICE**

**1.** In stoichiometry, chemists are mainly concerned with

**A.** the types of bonds found in compounds.
**B.** mass relationships in chemical reactions.
**C.** energy changes occurring in chemical reactions.
**D.** the speed with which chemical reactions occur.

**2.** Assume ideal stoichiometry in the reaction $CH_4 + 2O_2 \longrightarrow CO_2 + 2H_2O$. If you know the mass of $CH_4$, you can calculate

**A.** only the mass of $CO_2$ produced.
**B.** only the mass of $O_2$ reacting.
**C.** only the mass of $CO_2 + H_2O$ produced.
**D.** the mass of $O_2$ reacting and $CO_2 + H_2O$ produced.

**3.** Which mole ratio for the equation $6Li + N_2 \longrightarrow 2Li_3N$ is incorrect?

**A.** $\frac{6 \text{ mol Li}}{2 \text{ mol } N_2}$ **C.** $\frac{2 \text{ mol } Li_3N}{1 \text{ mol } N_2}$

**B.** $\frac{1 \text{ mol } N_2}{6 \text{ mol Li}}$ **D.** $\frac{2 \text{ mol } Li_3N}{6 \text{ mol Li}}$

**4.** For the reaction below, how many moles of $N_2$ are required to produce 18 mol $NH_3$?

$$N_2 + 3H_2 \longrightarrow 2NH_3$$

**A.** 4.5 **C.** 18
**B.** 9.0 **D.** 36

**5.** What mass of NaCl can be produced by the reaction of 0.75 mol $Cl_2$?

$$2Na + Cl_2 \longrightarrow 2NaCl$$

**A.** 0.75 g **C.** 44 g
**B.** 1.5 g **D.** 88 g

**6.** What mass of $CO_2$ can be produced from 25.0 g $CaCO_3$ given the decomposition reaction

$$CaCO_3 \longrightarrow CaO + CO_2$$

**A.** 11.0 g **C.** 25.0 g
**B.** 22.0 g **D.** 56.0 g

**7.** If a chemical reaction involving substances A and B stops when B is completely used up, then B is referred to as the

**A.** excess reactant. **C.** limiting reactant.
**B.** primary reactant. **D.** primary product.

**8.** If a chemist calculates the maximum amount of product that could be obtained in a chemical reaction, he or she is calculating the

**A.** percentage yield.
**B.** mole ratio.
**C.** theoretical yield.
**D.** actual yield.

**9.** What is the maximum number of moles of $AlCl_3$ that can be produced from 5.0 mol Al and 6.0 mol $Cl_2$?

$$2Al + 3Cl_2 \longrightarrow 2AlCl_3$$

**A.** 2.0 mol $AlCl_3$ **C.** 5.0 mol $AlCl_3$
**B.** 4.0 mol $AlCl_3$ **D.** 6.0 mol $AlCl_3$

**SHORT ANSWER**

**10.** Why is a balanced equation necessary to solve a mass-mass stoichiometry problem?

**11.** What data are necessary to calculate the percentage yield of a reaction?

**EXTENDED RESPONSE**

**12.** A student makes a compound in the laboratory and reports an actual yield of 120%. Is this result possible? Assuming that all masses were measured correctly, give an explanation.

**13.** Benzene, $C_6H_6$, is reacted with bromine, $Br_2$, to produce bromobenzene, $C_6H_5Br$, and hydrogen bromide, HBr, as shown below. When 40.0 g of benzene are reacted with 95.0 g of bromine, 65.0 g of bromobenzene is produced.

$$C_6H_6 + Br_2 \longrightarrow C_6H_5Br + HBr$$

a. Which compound is the limiting reactant?
b. What is the theoretical yield of bromobenzene?
c. What is the reactant in excess, and how much remains after the reaction is completed?
d. What is the percentage yield?

**Test TIP** Choose an answer to a question based on both information that you already know and information that is presented in the question.

SEE PRE-LAB
EXTRACTION AND FILTRATION

# Stoichiometry and Gravimetric Analysis

## OBJECTIVES

- ***Observe*** **the double-displacement reaction between solutions of strontium chloride and sodium carbonate.**
- ***Demonstrate*** **proficiency with gravimetric methods.**
- ***Measure*** **the mass of the precipitate that forms.**
- ***Relate*** **the mass of the precipitate that forms to the mass of the reactants before the reaction.**
- ***Calculate*** **the mass of sodium carbonate in a solution of unknown concentration.**

## MATERIALS

- **15 mL $Na_2CO_3$ solution of unknown concentration**
- **50 mL 0.30 M $SrCl_2$ solution**
- **50 mL graduated cylinder**
- **250 mL beakers, 2**
- **balance**
- **beaker tongs**
- **distilled water**
- **drying oven**
- **filter paper**
- **glass funnel or Büchner funnel with related equipment**
- **glass stirring rod**
- **paper towels**
- **ring and ring stand**
- **spatula**
- **water bottle**

## BACKGROUND

This gravimetric analysis involves a double-displacement reaction between strontium chloride, $SrCl_2$, and sodium carbonate, $Na_2CO_3$. This type of reaction can be used to determine the amount of a carbonate compound in a solution. For accurate results, essentially all of the reactant of unknown amount must be converted into product. If the mass of the product is carefully measured, you can use stoichiometric calculations to determine how much of the reactant of unknown amount was involved in the reaction.

## SAFETY

For review of safety, please see **Safety in the Chemistry Laboratory** in the front of your book.

## PREPARATION

1. Make a data table that has 2 columns and 5 rows. In the first column write each of the following phrases in a separate row: "Volume of $Na_2CO_3$ solution added"; "Volume of $SrCl_2$ solution added"; "Mass of dry filter paper"; "Mass of beaker with paper towel"; "Mass of beaker with paper towel, filter paper, and precipitate."
2. Clean all of the necessary lab equipment with soap and water, and rinse with distilled water.
3. Measure the mass of a piece of filter paper to the nearest 0.01 g, and record it in your table.
4. Set up a filtering apparatus. Use the Pre-Laboratory Procedure "Extraction and Filtration."

5. Label a paper towel with your name and the date. Place the towel in a clean, dry 250 mL beaker, and measure and record the mass of the paper towel and beaker to the nearest 0.01 g.

## PROCEDURE

1. Measure about 15 mL of the $Na_2CO_3$ solution into the graduated cylinder. Record this volume to the nearest 0.5 mL. Pour the $Na_2CO_3$ solution into an empty 250 mL beaker. Carefully wash the graduated cylinder, and rinse it with distilled water.

2. Measure about 25 mL of the 0.30 M $SrCl_2$ solution into the graduated cylinder. Record this volume to the nearest 0.5 mL. Pour the $SrCl_2$ solution into the beaker with the $Na_2CO_3$ solution, as shown in **Figure A.** Gently stir with a glass stirring rod.

3. Measure another 10 mL of the $SrCl_2$ solution into the graduated cylinder. Record the volume to the nearest 0.5 mL. Slowly add the solution to the beaker, and stir gently. Repeat this step until no more precipitate forms.

4. Slowly pour the mixture into the funnel. Do not overfill the funnel—some of the precipitate could be lost between the filter paper and the funnel.

5. Rinse the beaker several more times with distilled water. Pour the rinse water into the funnel each time.

6. After all of the solution and rinses have drained through the funnel, use distilled water to slowly rinse the precipitate on the filter paper in the funnel to remove any soluble impurities.

7. Carefully remove the filter paper from the funnel, and place it on the paper towel that you labeled with your name. Unfold the filter paper, and place the paper towel, filter paper, and precipitate in the rinsed beaker. Then, place the beaker in the drying oven. For best results, allow the precipitate to dry overnight.

8. Using beaker tongs, remove your sample from the oven, and let it cool. Record the total mass of the beaker, paper towel, filter paper, and precipitate to the nearest 0.01 g.

FIGURE A The precipitate is a product of the reaction between $Na_2CO_3$ and $SrCl_2$. Add enough $SrCl_2$ to react with all of the $Na_2CO_3$ present.

## CLEANUP AND DISPOSAL

9. Dispose of the precipitate and the filtrate in designated waste containers. Clean up all equipment after use, and dispose of substances according to your teacher's instructions. Wash your hands thoroughly after all lab work is finished.

## ANALYSIS AND INTERPRETATION

1. **Organizing Ideas:** Write a balanced equation for the reaction. What is the precipitate?

2. **Applying Ideas:** Calculate the mass of the dry precipitate. Calculate the number of moles of precipitate produced in the reaction.

3. **Applying Ideas:** How many moles of $Na_2CO_3$ were present in the 15 mL sample? How many grams of $Na_2CO_3$ were present?

## CONCLUSIONS

1. **Applying Conclusions:** There are 0.30 mol $SrCl_2$ in every liter of solution. Calculate the number of moles of $SrCl_2$ that were added. What is the limiting reactant?

# CHAPTER 10

# *States of Matter*

*The total three-dimensional arrangement of particles of a crystal is its crystal structure.*

Icicle Sculpture

# The Kinetic-Molecular Theory of Matter

SECTION 1

## Objectives

- State the kinetic-molecular theory of matter, and describe how it explains certain properties of matter.
- List the five assumptions of the kinetic-molecular theory of gases. Define the terms ideal gas and real gas.
- Describe each of the following characteristic properties of gases: expansion, density, fluidity, compressibility, diffusion, and effusion.
- Describe the conditions under which a real gas deviates from "ideal" behavior.

SC **C.5.2** Explain the behaviors of gas; the relationship among pressure, volume, and temperature; and the significance of the Kelvin (absolute temperature) scale, using the kinetic-molecular theory as a model

In Chapter 1, you read that matter exists on Earth in the forms of solids, liquids, and gases. Although it is not usually possible to observe individual particles directly, scientists have studied large groups of these particles as they occur in solids, liquids, and gases.

In the late nineteenth century, scientists developed the kinetic-molecular theory of matter to account for the behavior of the atoms and molecules that make up matter. *The* **kinetic-molecular theory** *is based on the idea that particles of matter are always in motion.* The theory can be used to explain the properties of solids, liquids, and gases in terms of the energy of particles and the forces that act between them. In this section, you will study the theory as it applies to gas molecules.

## The Kinetic-Molecular Theory of Gases

The kinetic-molecular theory can help you understand the behavior of gas molecules and the physical properties of gases. The theory provides a model of what is called an ideal gas. *An* **ideal gas** *is a hypothetical gas that perfectly fits all the assumptions of the kinetic-molecular theory.*

The kinetic-molecular theory of gases is based on the following five assumptions:

1. *Gases consist of large numbers of tiny particles that are far apart relative to their size.* These particles, usually molecules or atoms, typically occupy a volume that is about 1000 times greater than the volume occupied by an equal number of particles in the liquid or solid state. Thus, molecules of gases are much farther apart than molecules of liquids or solids. Most of the volume occupied by a gas is empty space, which is the reason that gases have a lower density than liquids and solids do. This also explains the fact that gases are easily compressed.
2. *Collisions between gas particles and between particles and container walls are elastic collisions. An* **elastic collision** *is one in which there is no net loss of total kinetic energy.* Kinetic energy is transferred between two particles during collisions. However, the total kinetic energy of the two particles remains the same as long as temperature is constant.

www.scilinks.org
**Topic:** Gases
**Code:** HC60638

Diffusion is a process by which particles of a gas spread out spontaneously and mix with other gases. In contrast, **effusion** *is a process by which gas particles pass through a tiny opening*. The rates of effusion of different gases are directly proportional to the velocities of their particles. Because of this proportionality, molecules of low mass effuse faster than molecules of high mass.

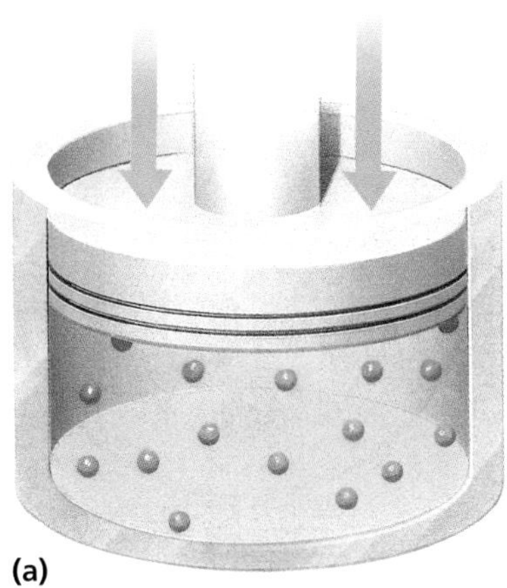

(a)

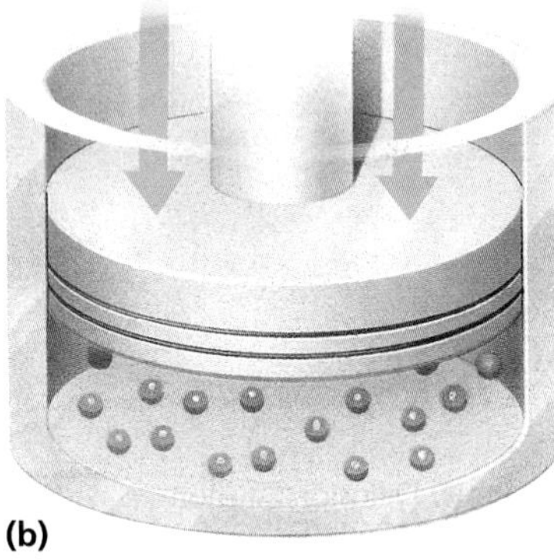

(b)

**FIGURE 3** (a) Gas molecules in a car engine cylinder expand to fill the cylinder. (b) As pressure is exerted on them, the gas molecules move closer together, reducing their volume.

## Deviations of Real Gases from Ideal Behavior

Because particles of gases occupy space and exert attractive forces on each other, all real gases deviate to some degree from ideal gas behavior. *A* **real gas** *is a gas that does not behave completely according to the assumptions of the kinetic-molecular theory*. At very high pressures and low temperatures, the gas particles will be closer together and their kinetic energy will be insufficient to overcome completely the attractive forces. At such conditions, the gas is most likely to behave like a nonideal gas. These conditions are illustrated in **Figure 3.**

The kinetic-molecular theory is more likely to hold true for gases whose particles have little attraction for each other. The noble gases, such as helium, He, and neon, Ne, show essentially ideal gas behavior over a wide range of temperatures and pressures. The particles of these gases are monatomic and thus nonpolar. The particles of gases, such as nitrogen, $N_2$, and hydrogen, $H_2$, are nonpolar diatomic molecules. The behavior of these gases most closely approximates that of the ideal gas under certain conditions. The more polar the molecules of a gas are, the greater the attractive forces between them and the more the gas will deviate from ideal gas behavior. For example, highly polar gases, such as ammonia, $NH_3$, and water vapor, deviate from ideal behavior to a larger degree than nonpolar gases.

## SECTION REVIEW

1. Use the kinetic-molecular theory to explain each of the following properties of gases: expansion, fluidity, low density, compressibility, and diffusion.
2. Describe the conditions under which a real gas is most likely to behave ideally.
3. Which of the following gases would you expect to deviate significantly from ideal behavior: He, $O_2$, $H_2$, $H_2O$, $N_2$, HCl, or $NH_3$?
4. How does the kinetic-molecular theory explain the pressure exerted by gases?
5. What happens to gas particles when a gas is compressed?
6. What happens to gas particles when a gas is heated?

**Critical Thinking**

7. **DRAWING CONCLUSIONS** Molecules of hydrogen escape from Earth, but molecules of oxygen and nitrogen are held to the surface and remain in the atmosphere. Explain.

# Liquids

C.5.1 Explain the effects of the intermolecular forces on the different phases of matter

SECTION 2

## OBJECTIVES

- Describe the motion of particles in liquids and the properties of liquids according to the kinetic-molecular theory.
- Discuss the process by which liquids can change into a gas. Define *vaporization*.
- Discuss the process by which liquids can change into a solid. Define *freezing*.

The water in the waves crashing on a beach and the molten lava rushing down the sides of a volcano are examples of matter in the liquid state. When you think of Earth's oceans, lakes, and rivers and the many liquids you use every day, it is hard to believe that liquids are the *least* common state of matter in the universe. Liquids are less common than solids and gases because a substance can exist in the liquid state only within a relatively narrow range of temperatures and pressures.

In this section, you will examine the properties of the liquid state. You will also compare them with those of the solid state and the gas state. These properties will be discussed in terms of the kinetic-molecular theory.

## Properties of Liquids and the Kinetic-Molecular Theory

A liquid can be described as a form of matter that has a definite volume and takes the shape of its container. The properties of liquids can be understood by applying the kinetic-molecular theory, considering the motion and arrangement of molecules and the attractive forces between them.

As in a gas, particles in a liquid are in constant motion. However, the particles in a liquid are closer together than the particles in a gas are. Therefore, the attractive forces between particles in a liquid are more effective than those between particles in a gas. This attraction between liquid particles is caused by the intermolecular forces discussed in Chapter 6: dipole-dipole forces, London dispersion forces, and hydrogen bonding. Some molecules at the surface of a liquid can have enough kinetic energy to overcome these forces, and enter the gas state.

Liquids are more ordered than gases because of the stronger intermolecular forces and the lower mobility of the liquid particles. According to the kinetic-molecular theory of liquids, the particles are not bound together in fixed positions. Instead, they move about constantly. This particle mobility explains why liquids and gases are referred to as fluids. *A* **fluid** *is a substance that can flow and therefore take the shape of its container.* Most liquids naturally flow downhill because of gravity. However, some liquids can flow in other directions as well. For example, liquid helium near absolute zero has the unusual property of being able to flow uphill.

SCILINKS.
www.scilinks.org
**Topic:** Properties of Liquids
**Code:** HC61228

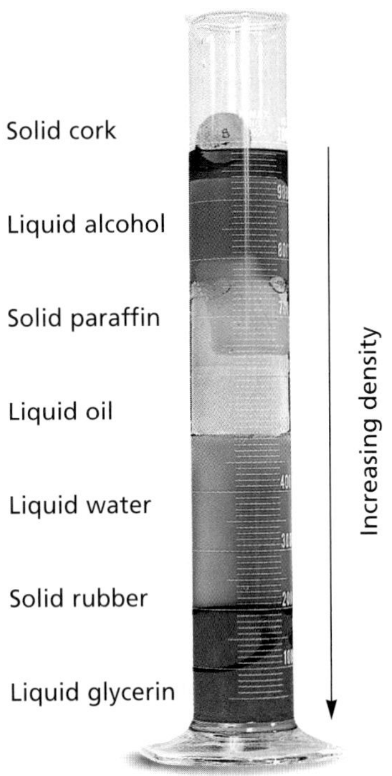


**FIGURE 4** Solids and liquids of different densities are shown. The densest materials are at the bottom. The least dense are at the top. (Dyes have been added to the liquids to make the layers more visible.)

## Relatively High Density

At normal atmospheric pressure, most substances are hundreds of times denser in a liquid state than in a gaseous state. This higher density is a result of the close arrangement of liquid particles. Most substances are only slightly less dense (about 10%) in a liquid state than in a solid state, however. Water is one of the few substances that becomes less dense when it solidifies, as will be discussed further in Section 5.

At the same temperature and pressure, different liquids can differ greatly in density. **Figure 4** shows some liquids and solids with different densities. The densities differ to such an extent that the liquids form layers.

## Relative Incompressibility

When liquid water at 20°C is compressed by a pressure of 1000 atm, its volume decreases by only 4%. Such behavior is typical of all liquids and is similar to the behavior of solids. In contrast, a gas under a pressure of 1000 atm would have only about 1/1000 of its volume at normal atmospheric pressure. Liquids are much less compressible than gases because liquid particles are more closely packed together. Like gases, liquids can transmit pressure equally in all directions.

## Ability to Diffuse

As described in Section 1, gases diffuse and mix with other gas particles. Liquids also diffuse and mix with other liquids, as shown in **Figure 5.** Any liquid gradually diffuses throughout any other liquid in which it can dissolve. The constant, random motion of particles causes diffusion in liquids, as it does in gases. Yet diffusion is much slower in liquids than in gases because liquid particles are closer together. Also, the attractive forces between the particles of a liquid slow their movement. As the temperature of a liquid is increased, diffusion occurs more rapidly. The reason is that the average kinetic energy, and therefore the average speed of the particles, is increased.

**FIGURE 5** Like gases, the two liquids in this beaker diffuse over time. The green liquid food coloring from the drop will eventually form a uniform solution with the water.

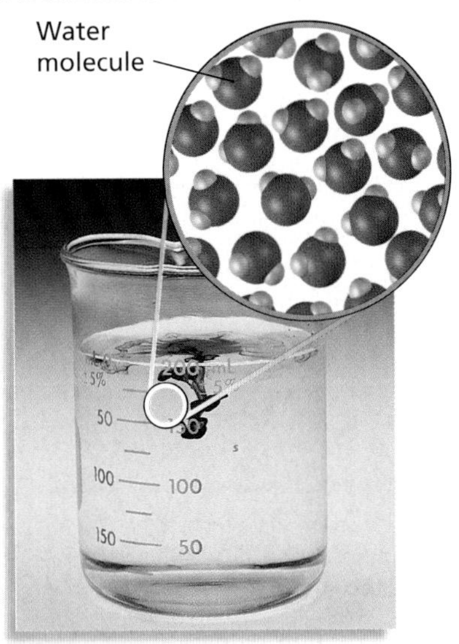


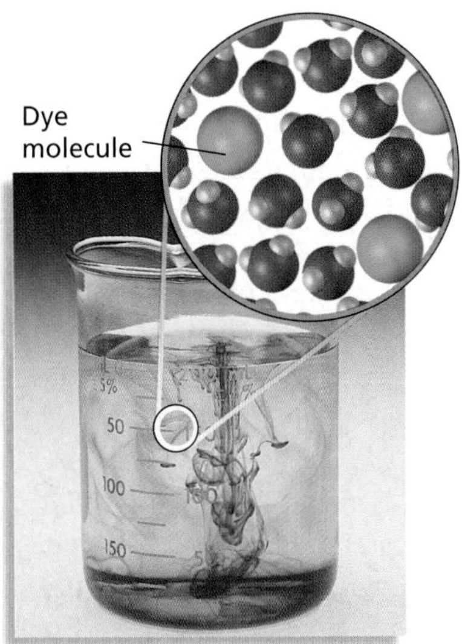

## Surface Tension

A property common to all liquids is **surface tension,** *a force that tends to pull adjacent parts of a liquid's surface together, thereby decreasing surface area to the smallest possible size.* Surface tension results from the attractive forces between particles of a liquid. The higher the force of attraction, the higher the surface tension. Water has a higher surface tension than most liquids. This is due in large part to the hydrogen bonds water molecules can form with each other. The molecules at the surface of the water are a special case. They can form hydrogen bonds with the other water molecules beneath them and beside them, but not with the molecules in the air above them. As a result, the surface water molecules are drawn together and toward the body of the liquid, creating a high surface tension. Surface tension causes liquid droplets to take on a spherical shape because a sphere has the smallest possible surface area for a given volume. An example of this phenomenon is shown in **Figure 6.**

**Capillary action,** *the attraction of the surface of a liquid to the surface of a solid,* is a property closely related to surface tension. A liquid will rise quite high in a very narrow tube and will wet the tube if a strong attraction exists between the liquid molecules and the molecules that make up the surface of the tube. This attraction tends to pull the liquid molecules upward along the surface and against the pull of gravity. This process continues until the attractive forces between the liquid molecules and the surface of the tube are balanced by the weight of the liquid. Capillary action can occur between water molecules and paper fibers, as shown in **Figure 7.** Capillary action is at least partly responsible for the transportation of water from the roots of a plant to its leaves. The same process is responsible for the concave liquid surface, called a *meniscus,* that forms in a test tube or graduated cylinder.

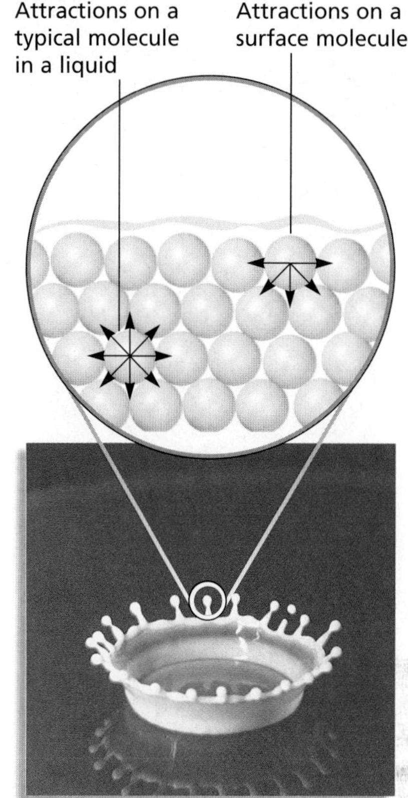


**FIGURE 6** As a result of surface tension, liquids form roughly spherical drops. The net attractive forces between the particles pull the molecules on the surface of the drop inward. The molecules are pulled very close together, which minimizes the surface area.

## Evaporation and Boiling

*The process by which a liquid or solid changes to a gas is* **vaporization.** Evaporation is a form of vaporization. **Evaporation** *is the process by which particles escape from the surface of a nonboiling liquid and enter the gas state.*

(a)

(b)

**FIGURE 7** The attraction between polar water molecules and polar cellulose molecules in paper fibers causes the water to move up in the paper. The water-soluble ink placed near the bottom of the paper in (a) rises up the paper along with the water, as seen in (b). As the ink moves up the paper, it is separated into its various components, producing the different bands of color. This separation occurs because the water and the paper attract the molecules of the ink components differently. These phenomena are used in the separation process of paper chromatography seen here.

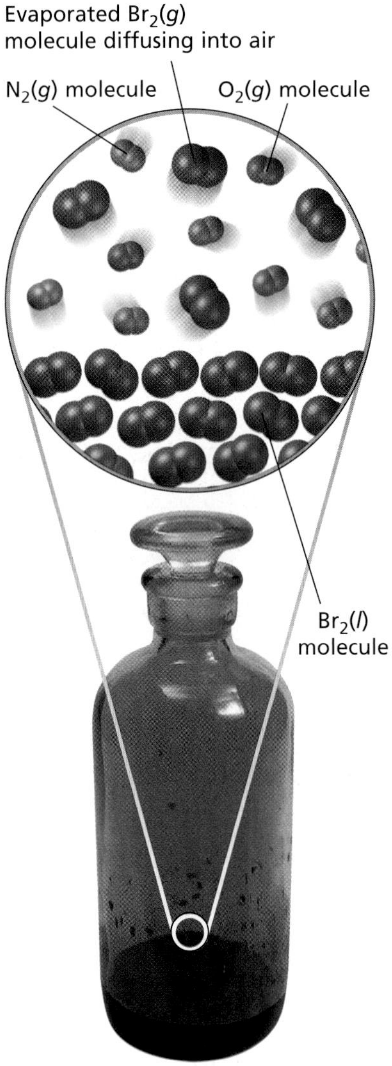

Evaporated $Br_2(g)$ molecule diffusing into air

$N_2(g)$ molecule

$O_2(g)$ molecule

$Br_2(l)$ molecule

**FIGURE 8** Liquid bromine, $Br_2$, evaporates near room temperature. The resulting brownish red gas diffuses into the air above the surface of the liquid.

A small amount of liquid bromine was added to the bottle shown in **Figure 8.** Within a few minutes, the air above the liquid bromine turned brownish-red because some bromine molecules escaped from the surface of the liquid. These molecules became gas molecules, or bromine vapor, which mixed with the air. A similar phenomenon occurs if you apply perfume to your wrist. Within seconds, you become aware of the perfume's fragrance. Scent molecules evaporate from your skin and diffuse through the air, where your nose detects them.

Evaporation occurs because the particles of a liquid have different kinetic energies. Particles with higher-than-average energies move faster. Some surface particles with higher-than-average energies can overcome the intermolecular forces that bind them to the liquid. They can then escape into the gas state.

Evaporation is a crucial process in nature. Evaporation removes fresh water from the surface of the ocean, leaving behind a higher concentration of salts. In tropical areas, evaporation occurs at a higher rate, causing the surface water to be saltier. All water that falls to Earth in the form of rain and snow previously evaporated from oceans, lakes, and rivers. Evaporation of perspiration plays an important role in keeping you cool. Perspiration, which is mostly water, cools you by absorbing body heat when it evaporates. Energy as heat is absorbed from the skin, causing the cooling effect.

*Boiling* is the change of a liquid to bubbles of vapor that appear throughout the liquid. Boiling differs from evaporation, as you will see in Section 4.

## Formation of Solids

When a liquid is cooled, the average energy of its particles decreases. If the energy is low enough, attractive forces pull the particles into an even more orderly arrangement. The substance then becomes a solid. *The physical change of a liquid to a solid by removal of energy as heat is called* **freezing** *or solidification.* Perhaps the best-known example of freezing is the change of liquid water to solid water, or ice, at 0°C. Another familiar example is the solidification of paraffin at room temperature. All liquids freeze, although not necessarily at temperatures you normally encounter. Ethanol, for example, freezes near –114°C.

## SECTION REVIEW

1. Describe the liquid state according to the kinetic-molecular theory.
2. List the properties of liquids.
3. How does the kinetic-molecular theory explain the following properties of liquids: (a) relatively high density, (b) ability to diffuse, and (c) ability to evaporate?
4. Explain why liquids in a test tube form a meniscus.
5. Compare vaporization and evaporation.

**Critical Thinking**

6. **INTERPRETING CONCEPTS** The evaporation of liquid water from the surface of Earth is an important step in the water cycle. How do water molecules obtain enough kinetic energy to escape into the gas state?

# Solids

SECTION 3

C.5.1 Explain the effects of the intermolecular forces on the different phases of matter

## Objectives

- Describe the motion of particles in solids and the properties of solids according to the kinetic-molecular theory.
- Distinguish between the two types of solids.
- Describe the different types of crystal symmetry. Define *crystal structure* and *unit cell.*

The common expression "solid as a rock" suggests that something is hard or unyielding and has a definite shape and volume. In this section you will examine the properties of solids and compare them with those of liquids and gases. The properties of solids are explained in terms of the kinetic-molecular theory, as the other states of matter are.

## Properties of Solids and the Kinetic-Molecular Theory

The particles of a solid are more closely packed than those of a liquid or gas. Intermolecular forces between particles are therefore much more effective in solids. All interparticle attractions such as dipole-dipole attractions, London dispersion forces, and hydrogen bonding exert stronger effects in solids than in the corresponding liquids or gases. Attractive forces tend to hold the particles of a solid in relatively fixed positions, with only vibrational movement around fixed points. Because the motions of the particles are restricted in this way, solids are more ordered than liquids and are much more ordered than gases. The importance of order and disorder in physical and chemical changes will be discussed in Chapter 16. Compare the physical appearance and molecular arrangement of the element in **Figure 9** in solid, liquid, and gas form.

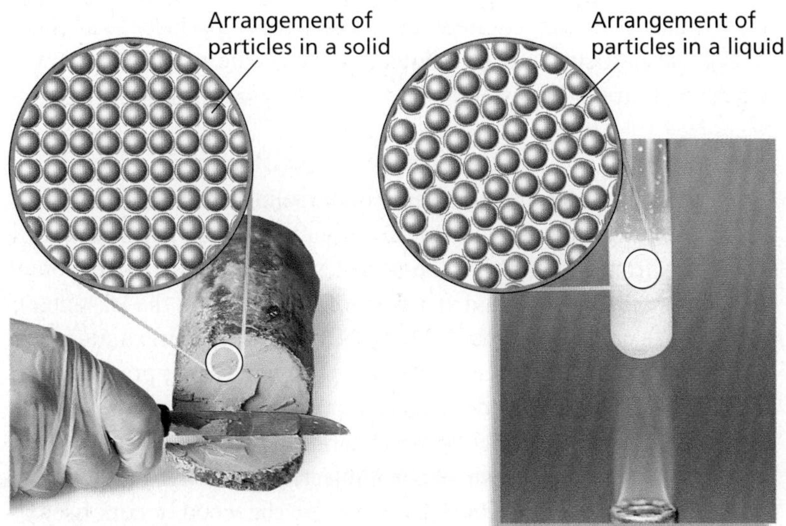


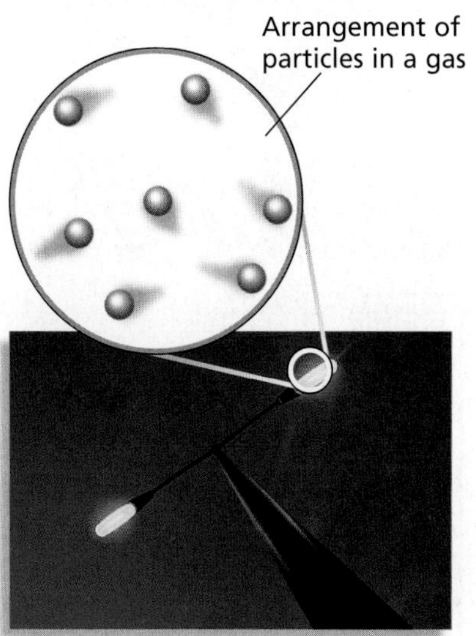


**FIGURE 9** Particles of sodium metal in three different states are shown. Sodium exists in a gaseous state in a sodium-vapor lamp.

There are two types of solids: crystalline solids and amorphous solids. Most solids are **crystalline solids**—*they consist of crystals. A* **crystal** *is a substance in which the particles are arranged in an orderly, geometric, repeating pattern.* Noncrystalline solids, including glass and plastics, are called amorphous solids. *An* **amorphous solid** *is one in which the particles are arranged randomly.* The two types of solids will be discussed in more detail later in this section.

## Definite Shape and Volume

Unlike liquids and gases, solids can maintain a definite shape without a container. In addition, crystalline solids are geometrically regular. Even the fragments of a shattered crystalline solid have distinct geometric shapes that reflect their internal structure. Amorphous solids maintain a definite shape, but they do not have the distinct geometric shapes of crystalline solids. For example, glass can be molded into any shape. If it is shattered, glass fragments can have a wide variety of irregular shapes.

The volume of a solid changes only slightly with a change in temperature or pressure. Solids have definite volume because their particles are packed closely together. There is very little empty space into which the particles can be compressed. Crystalline solids generally do not flow because their particles are held in relatively fixed positions.

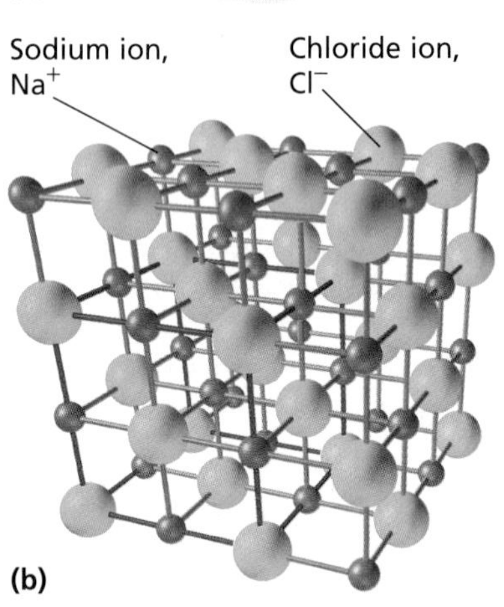


**FIGURE 10** (a) This is a scanning electron micrograph (SEM) of a sodium chloride crystal. A sodium chloride crystal can be represented by its crystal structure (b), which is made up of individual unit cells represented regularly in three dimensions. Here, one unit cell is outlined in red.

## Definite Melting Point

**Melting** *is the physical change of a solid to a liquid by the addition of energy as heat. The temperature at which a solid becomes a liquid is its* **melting point.** At this temperature, the kinetic energies of the particles within the solid overcome the attractive forces holding them together. The particles can then break out of their positions in crystalline solids, which have definite melting points. In contrast, amorphous solids, such as glass and plastics, have no definite melting point. They have the ability to flow over a range of temperatures. Therefore, amorphous solids are sometimes classified as **supercooled liquids,** *which are substances that retain certain liquid properties even at temperatures at which they appear to be solid.* These properties exist because the particles in amorphous solids are arranged randomly, much like the particles in a liquid. Unlike the particles in a true liquid, however, the particles in amorphous solids are not constantly changing their positions.

## High Density and Incompressibility

In general, substances are most dense in the solid state. Solids tend to be slightly denser than liquids and much denser than gases. The higher density results from the fact that the particles of a solid are more closely packed than those of a liquid or a gas. Solid hydrogen is the least dense solid; it has a density of about 1/320 of the densest element, osmium, Os.

Solids are generally less compressible than liquids. For practical purposes, solids can be considered incompressible. Some solids, such as wood and cork, may *seem* compressible, but they are not. They contain pores that are filled with air. When subjected to intense pressure, the pores are compressed, not the solid matter in the wood or cork itself.

**FIGURE 11** Shown are the seven basic crystalline systems and representative minerals of each.

### Low Rate of Diffusion

If a zinc plate and a copper plate are clamped together for a long time, a few atoms of each metal will diffuse into the other. This observation shows that diffusion does occur in solids. The rate of diffusion is millions of times slower in solids than in liquids, however.

## Crystalline Solids

Crystalline solids exist either as single crystals or as groups of crystals fused together. *The total three-dimensional arrangement of particles of a crystal is called a* **crystal structure.** The arrangement of particles in the crystal can be represented by a coordinate system called a *lattice. The smallest portion of a crystal lattice that shows the three-dimensional pattern of the entire lattice is called a* **unit cell.** Each crystal lattice contains many unit cells packed together. **Figure 10** shows the relationship between a crystal lattice and its unit cell. A crystal and its unit cells can have any one of seven types of symmetry. This fact enables scientists to classify crystals by their shape. Diagrams and examples of each type of crystal symmetry are shown in **Figure 11.**

### Binding Forces in Crystals

Crystal structures can also be described in terms of the types of particles in them and the types of chemical bonding between the particles.

**TABLE 1 Melting and Boiling Points of Representative Crystalline Solids**

| Type of substance | Formula | Melting point (°C) | Boiling point at 1 atm (°C) |
|---|---|---|---|
| Ionic | NaCl | 801 | 1413 |
| | $MgF_2$ | 1266 | 2239 |
| Covalent network | $(SiO_2)_x$ | 1610 | 2230 |
| | $C_x$ (diamond) | 3500 | 3930 |
| Metallic | Hg | −39 | 357 |
| | Cu | 1083 | 2567 |
| | Fe | 1535 | 2750 |
| | W | 3410 | 5660 |
| Covalent molecular (nonpolar) | $H_2$ | −259 | −253 |
| | $O_2$ | −218 | −183 |
| | $CH_4$ | −182 | −164 |
| | $CCl_4$ | −23 | 77 |
| | $C_6H_6$ | 6 | 80 |
| Covalent molecular (polar) | $NH_3$ | −78 | −33 |
| | $H_2O$ | 0 | 100 |

According to this method of classification, there are four types of crystals. These types are listed in **Table 1.** Refer to this table as you read the following discussion.

1. *Ionic crystals.* The ionic crystal structure consists of positive and negative ions arranged in a regular pattern. The ions can be monatomic or polyatomic. Generally, ionic crystals form when Group 1 or Group 2 metals combine with Group 16 or Group 17 nonmetals or nonmetallic polyatomic ions. The strong binding forces between the positive and negative ions in the crystal structure give the ionic crystals certain properties. For example, these crystals are hard and brittle, have high melting points, and are good insulators.
2. *Covalent network crystals.* In covalent network crystals, each atom is covalently bonded to its nearest neighboring atoms. The covalent bonding extends throughout a network that includes a very large number of atoms. Three-dimensional covalent network solids include diamond, $C_x$, quartz, $(SiO_2)_x$—shown in **Figure 12**—silicon carbide, $(SiC)_x$, and many oxides of transition metals. Such solids are essentially giant molecules. The subscript $x$ in these formulas indicates that the component within the parentheses extends indefinitely. The network solids are nearly always very hard and brittle. They have rather high melting points and are usually nonconductors or semiconductors.
3. *Metallic crystals.* The metallic crystal structure consists of metal cations surrounded by a sea of delocalized valence electrons. The electrons come from the metal atoms and belong to the crystal as a whole. The freedom of these delocalized electrons to move throughout the crystal explains the high electric conductivity of metals.

4. *Covalent molecular crystals.* The crystal structure of a covalent molecular substance consists of covalently bonded molecules held together by intermolecular forces. If the molecules are nonpolar—for example, hydrogen, $H_2$, methane, $CH_4$, and benzene, $C_6H_6$—then there are only weak London dispersion forces between molecules. In a polar covalent molecular crystal—for example, water, $H_2O$, and ammonia, $NH_3$—molecules are held together by dispersion forces, by somewhat stronger dipole-dipole forces, and sometimes by even stronger hydrogen bonding. The forces that hold polar or nonpolar molecules together in the structure are much weaker than the covalent chemical bonds between the atoms within each molecule. Covalent molecular crystals thus have low melting points. They are easily vaporized, are relatively soft, and are good insulators. Ice crystals, the most familiar molecular crystals, are discussed in Section 5.

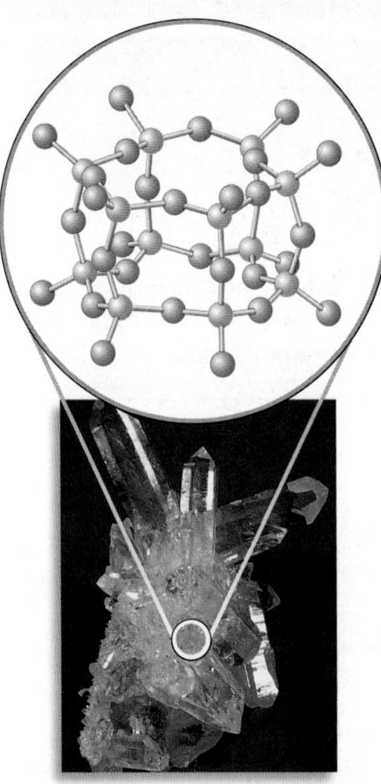

**FIGURE 12** Covalent network crystals include three-dimensional network solids, such as this quartz, $(SiO_2)_x$, shown here with its three-dimensional atomic structure.

## Amorphous Solids

The word *amorphous* comes from the Greek for "without shape." Unlike the atoms that form crystals, the atoms that make up amorphous solids, such as glasses and plastics, are not arranged in a regular pattern.

Glasses are made by cooling certain molten materials in a way that prevents them from crystallizing. The properties that result make glasses suitable for many uses, including windows, light bulbs, transformer cores, and optical fibers that carry telephone conversations.

Plastics, another type of amorphous solid, are easily molded at high temperatures and pressures. They are used in many structural materials.

Other, more recently created amorphous solids have been placed in many important applications. Amorphous semiconductors are used in electronic devices, including solar cells, copiers, laser printers, and flat-panel displays for computer monitors and television screens.

### SECTION REVIEW

1. Describe the solid state according to the kinetic-molecular theory.
2. What is the difference between an amorphous solid and a crystalline solid?
3. Account for each of the following properties of solids: (a) the definite volume, (b) the relatively high density of solids, (c) the extremely low rate of diffusion.
4. Compare and contrast the four types of crystals.
5. Why do crystalline solids shatter into regularly shaped fragments when broken?

**Critical Thinking**

6. **RELATING IDEAS** Explain why ionic crystals melt at much higher temperatures than typical covalent molecular crystals?

SECTION 4

## OBJECTIVES

- Explain the relationship between equilibrium and changes of state.
- Interpret phase diagrams.
- Explain what is meant by equilibrium vapor pressure.
- Describe the processes of boiling, freezing, melting, and sublimation.

# Changes of State

**C.5.4** Illustrate and interpret heating and cooling curves (including how boiling and melting points can be identified and how boiling points vary with changes in pressure)

Matter on Earth can exist in any of these states—gas, liquid, or solid—and can change from one state to another. **Table 2** lists the possible changes of state. In this section, you will examine these changes of state and the factors that determine them.

## Changes of State and Equilibrium

Some liquid chemical substances, such as rubbing alcohol, have an odor that is very easily detected. This is because some molecules at the upper surface of the liquid have enough energy to overcome the attraction of neighboring molecules. These molecules leave the liquid phase and evaporate. *A* **phase** *is any part of a system that has uniform composition and properties.* In a closed bottle of rubbing alcohol, the gas molecules are confined to the area under the cap. Some of the gas molecules strike the liquid surface and reenter the liquid phase through *condensation.* **Condensation** *is the process by which a gas changes to a liquid.* A gas in contact with its liquid or solid phase is often called a *vapor.*

If the temperature of the liquid remains constant and the cap remains closed, the rate at which molecules move from the liquid phase to the vapor phase remains constant. Near the beginning of the evaporation process, very few molecules are in the gas phase, so the rate of condensation is very low. But as more liquid evaporates, the increasing number of gas molecules causes the rate of condensation to increase. Eventually, the rate of condensation equals the rate of evaporation, and a state of equilibrium is established, as shown in **Figure 13. Equilibrium** *is a dynamic condition in which two opposing changes occur at equal rates in a closed system.* Even though molecules are constantly moving

**TABLE 2 Possible Changes of State**

| Change of state | Process | Example |
|---|---|---|
| Solid $\longrightarrow$ liquid | melting | ice $\longrightarrow$ water |
| Solid $\longrightarrow$ gas | sublimation | dry ice $\longrightarrow$ $CO_2$ gas |
| Liquid $\longrightarrow$ solid | freezing | water $\longrightarrow$ ice |
| Liquid $\longrightarrow$ gas | vaporization | liquid bromine $\longrightarrow$ bromine vapor |
| Gas $\longrightarrow$ liquid | condensation | water vapor $\longrightarrow$ water |
| Gas $\longrightarrow$ solid | deposition | water vapor $\longrightarrow$ ice |

SCILINKS.
www.scilinks.org
**Topic:** Factors Affecting Equilibrium
**Code:** HC60561

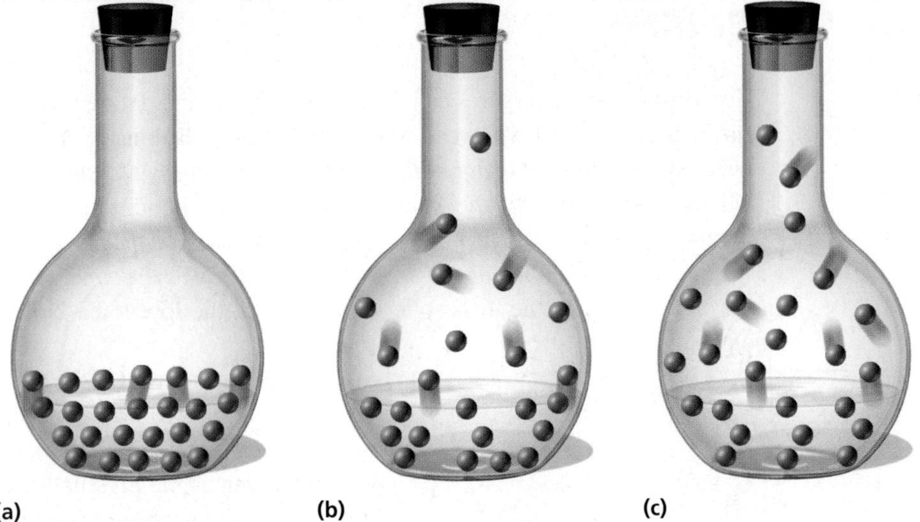


**FIGURE 13** A liquid-vapor equilibrium develops in a closed system. (a) At first there is only liquid present, but molecules are beginning to evaporate. (b) Evaporation continues at a constant rate. Some vapor molecules are beginning to condense to liquid. (c) Equilibrium has been reached between the rate of condensation and the rate of evaporation.

between liquid and gas phases, there is no net change in the amount of substance in either phase.

## Equilibrium Vapor Pressure of a Liquid

Vapor molecules in equilibrium with a liquid in a closed system exert a pressure proportional to the concentration of molecules in the vapor phase. *The pressure exerted by a vapor in equilibrium with its corresponding liquid at a given temperature is called the* **equilibrium vapor pressure** *of the liquid.*

The increase in equilibrium vapor pressure with increasing temperature can be explained in terms of the kinetic-molecular theory for the liquid and gaseous states. Increasing the temperature of a liquid increases the average kinetic energy of the liquid's molecules. This energy change increases the number of molecules that have enough energy to escape from the liquid phase into the vapor phase. The resulting increased evaporation rate increases the number of molecules in the vapor phase, which in turn increases the equilibrium vapor pressure.

Because all liquids have characteristic forces of attraction between their particles, every liquid has a specific equilibrium vapor pressure at a given temperature. The stronger these attractive forces are, the smaller the percentage of liquid particles that can evaporate at any given temperature is. A low percentage of evaporation results in a low equilibrium vapor pressure is. **Volatile liquids,** *which are liquids that evaporate readily,* have relatively weak forces of attraction between their particles. Ether is a typical volatile liquid. Nonvolatile liquids do not evaporate readily, and have relatively strong attractive forces between their particles. Molten ionic compounds are examples of nonvolatile liquids.

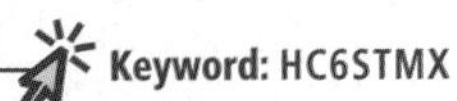


**Chemical Content**

Go to **go.hrw.com** for more information on equilibrium and changes of state.

**Keyword: HC6STMX**

## Boiling

Equilibrium vapor pressures can be used to explain and define the concept of boiling, which you read about in Section 3. **Boiling** *is the conversion of a liquid to a vapor within the liquid as well as at its surface.*

If the temperature of the liquid is increased, the equilibrium vapor pressure also increases. *The* **boiling point** *of a liquid is the temperature at which the equilibrium vapor pressure of the liquid equals the atmospheric pressure.* The lower the atmospheric pressure is, the lower the boiling point is.

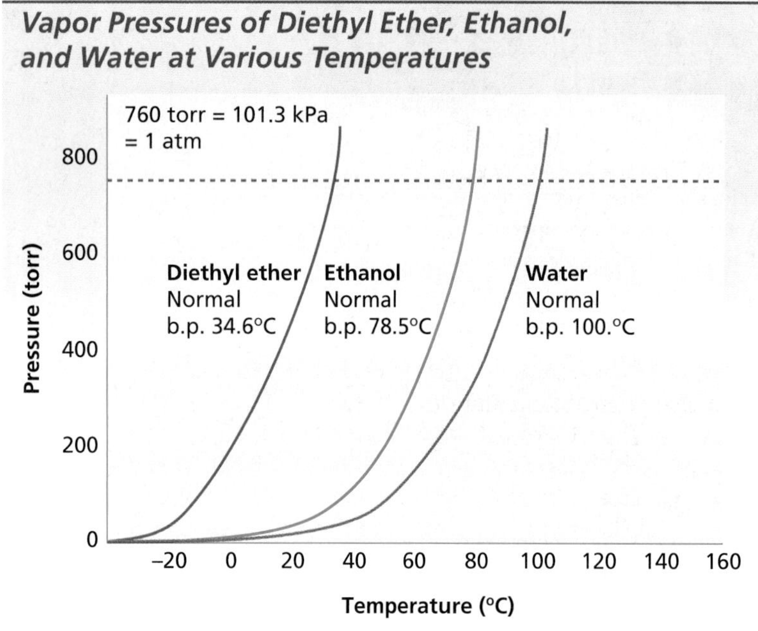


**FIGURE 14** The vapor pressure of any liquid increases as its temperature increases. A liquid boils when its vapor pressure equals the pressure of the atmosphere.

At the boiling point, all of the energy absorbed is used to evaporate the liquid, and the temperature remains constant as long as the pressure does not change. If the pressure above the liquid being heated is increased, the temperature of the liquid will rise until the vapor pressure equals the new pressure and the liquid boils once again. This is the principle behind the operation of a pressure cooker. The cooker is sealed so that steam pressure builds up over the surface of the boiling water inside. The pressure increases the boiling temperature of the water, resulting in shorter cooking times. Conversely, a device called a *vacuum evaporator* causes boiling at lower-than-normal temperatures. Vacuum evaporators are used to remove water from milk and sugar solutions. Under reduced pressure, the water boils away at a temperature low enough to avoid scorching the milk or sugar. This process is used to prepare evaporated milk and sweetened condensed milk.

At normal atmospheric pressure (1 atm, 760 torr, or 101.3 kPa), the boiling point of water is exactly 100°C. This temperature is known as the *normal* boiling point of water. **Figure 14** shows that the normal boiling point of each liquid is the temperature at which the liquid's equilibrium vapor pressure equals 760 torr.

### Energy and Boiling

Energy must be added continuously in order to keep a liquid boiling. A pot of boiling water stops boiling almost immediately after it is removed from the stove. If you were to carefully measure the temperature of a boiling liquid and its vapor you would find that they are at the same constant temperature. The temperature at the boiling point remains constant despite the continuous addition of energy. The added energy is used to overcome the attractive forces between molecules of the liquid during the liquid-to-gas change and is stored in the vapor as potential energy.

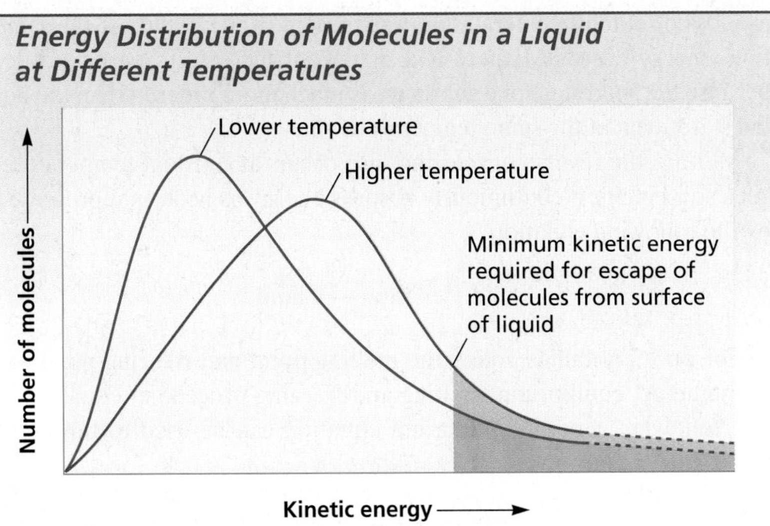


**FIGURE 15** The number of molecules in a liquid with various kinetic energies is represented at two different temperatures. Notice the shaded area, which shows the fraction of the molecules that have at least the minimum amount of kinetic energy required for evaporation to take place.

### Molar Enthalpy of Vaporization

*The amount of energy as heat that is needed to vaporize one mole of liquid at the liquid's boiling point at constant pressure is called the liquid's* **molar enthalpy of vaporization,** $\Delta H_v$. The magnitude of the molar enthalpy of vaporization is a measure of the attraction between particles of the liquid. The stronger this attraction is, the more energy that is required to overcome it, which results in a higher molar enthalpy of vaporization. Each liquid has a characteristic molar enthalpy of vaporization. Compared with other liquids, water has an unusually high molar enthalpy of vaporization due to the extensive hydrogen bonding in liquid water. This property makes water a very effective cooling agent. When water evaporates from your skin, the escaping molecules carry a great deal of energy as heat away with them. **Figure 15** shows the distribution of the kinetic energies of molecules in a liquid at two different temperatures. You can see that at the higher temperature, a greater portion of the molecules have the kinetic energy required to escape from the liquid surface and become vapor.

## Freezing and Melting

As you learned in Section 2, *the physical change of a liquid to a solid is called* **freezing.** Freezing involves a loss of energy in the form of heat by the liquid and can be represented by the following reaction.

$$\text{liquid} \longrightarrow \text{solid} + \text{energy}$$

In the case of a pure crystalline substance, this change occurs at constant temperature. *The normal* **freezing point** *is the temperature at which the solid and liquid are in equilibrium at 1 atm (760 torr, or 101.3 kPa) pressure.* At the freezing point, particles of the liquid and the solid have the same average kinetic energy. Therefore, the energy loss during freezing is a loss of potential energy that was present in the liquid. At the same time energy decreases, there is a significant increase in particle order because the solid state of a substance is much more ordered than the liquid state, even at the same temperature.

Melting, the reverse of freezing, also occurs at constant temperature. As a solid melts, it continuously absorbs energy as heat, as represented by the following equation.

$$\text{solid} + \text{energy} \longrightarrow \text{liquid}$$

For pure crystalline solids, the melting point and freezing point are the same. At equilibrium, melting and freezing proceed at equal rates. The following general equilibrium equation can be used to represent these states.

$$\text{solid} + \text{energy} \rightleftarrows \text{liquid}$$

At normal atmospheric pressure, the temperature of a system containing ice and liquid water will remain at 0.°C as long as both ice and water are present. That temperature will persist no matter what the surrounding temperature. Adding energy in the form of heat to such a system shifts the equilibrium to the right. That shift increases the proportion of liquid water and decreases that of ice. Only after all the ice has melted will the addition of energy increase the temperature of the system.

## Chemistry in Action

### Surface Melting

Freezing of water and melting of ice are phase changes that are familiar to all of us. Yet physicists and chemists have only recently begun to understand the basic aspects of these phase changes, with experimental and theoretical studies of a phenomenon known as surface melting. Experimental studies in the mid-1980s confirmed that the rigid surface arrangements of metals can become increasingly disordered several degrees below the melting point of the metal, forming a "quasi-liquid layer." Many different techniques have now shown that ice also has such a fluid surface layer just a few molecules thick. This surface melting of ice might explain observations as diverse as the origin of lightning, the unique shapes of snowflakes, and ice skating.

### Molar Enthalpy of Fusion

*The amount of energy as heat required to melt one mole of solid at the solid's melting point is the solid's* **molar enthalpy of fusion,** $\Delta H_f$. The energy absorbed increases the solid's potential energy as its particles are pulled apart, overcoming the attractive forces holding them together. At the same time, there is a significant decrease in particle order as the substance makes the transformation from solid to liquid. Similar to the molar enthalpy of vaporization, the magnitude of the molar enthalpy of fusion depends on the attraction between the solid particles.

### Sublimation and Deposition

At sufficiently low temperature and pressure conditions, a liquid cannot exist. Under such conditions, a solid substance exists in equilibrium with its vapor instead of its liquid, as represented by the following equation.

$$\text{solid} + \text{energy} \rightleftarrows \text{vapor}$$

*The change of state from a solid directly to a gas is known as* **sublimation.** The reverse process is called **deposition,** *the change of state from a gas directly to a solid.* Among the common substances that sublime at ordinary temperatures are dry ice (solid $CO_2$) and iodine. Ordinary ice sublimes slowly at temperatures lower than its melting point (0.°C). This explains how a thin layer of snow can eventually disappear, even if the temperature remains below 0.°C. Sublimation occurs in frost-free refrigerators when the temperature in the freezer compartment is periodically raised to cause any ice that has formed to sublime. A blower then removes the water vapor that has formed. The formation of frost on a cold surface is a familiar example of deposition.

## Phase Diagrams

*A* **phase diagram** *is a graph of pressure versus temperature that shows the conditions under which the phases of a substance exist.* A phase diagram also reveals how the states of a system change with changing temperature or pressure.

**Figure 16** shows the phase diagram for water over a range of temperatures and pressures. Note the three curves, AB, AC, and AD. Curve AB indicates the temperature and pressure conditions at which ice and water vapor can coexist at equilibrium. Curve AC indicates the temperature and pressure conditions at which liquid water and water vapor coexist at equilibrium. Similarly, curve AD indicates the temperature and pressure conditions at which ice and liquid water coexist at equilibrium. Because ice is less dense than liquid water, an increase in pressure lowers the melting point. (Most substances have a positive slope for this curve.) Point A is the triple point of water. *The* **triple point** *of a substance indicates the temperature and pressure conditions at which the solid, liquid, and vapor of the substance can coexist at equilibrium.* Point C is the critical point of water. *The* **critical point** *of a substance indicates the critical temperature and critical pressure. The* **critical temperature** *($t_c$) is the temperature above which the substance cannot exist in the liquid state.* The critical temperature of water is 373.99°C. Above this

**extension**

**CROSS-DISCIPLINARY**

Go to **go.hrw.com** for a full-length article on how cloud seeding is used to produce precipitation.

**Keyword: HC6STMX**

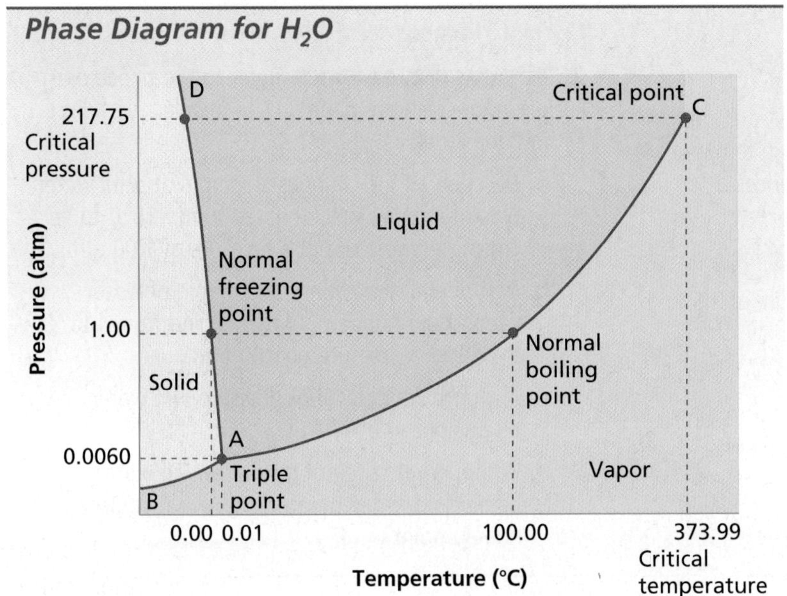


**FIGURE 16** This phase diagram shows the relationships between the physical states of water and its pressure and temperature.

**FIGURE 17** Solids, liquids, and gases can undergo various changes of state. The changes shown in green are exothermic, and those shown in blue are endothermic.

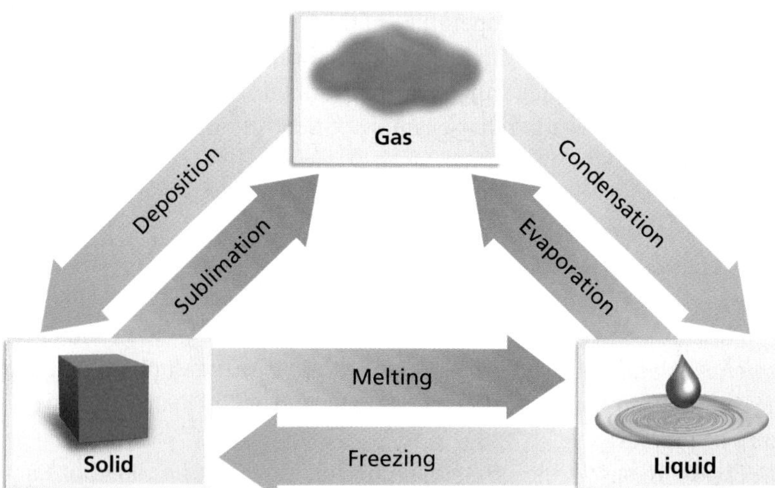


extension

**Chemistry in Action**

Go to **go.hrw.com** for a full-length article on phase-change materials.

**Keyword: HC6STMX**

temperature, water cannot be liquefied, no matter how much pressure is applied. *The* **critical pressure** *($P_c$) is the lowest pressure at which the substance can exist as a liquid at the critical temperature.* The critical pressure of water is 217.75 atm.

The phase diagram in **Figure 16** indicates the normal boiling point and the normal freezing point of water. It also shows how boiling point and freezing point change with pressure. As shown by the slope of line AD, ice melts at a higher temperature with decreasing pressure. Below the triple point, the temperature of sublimation decreases with decreasing pressure. Foods are freeze-dried by freezing the food and then lowering the pressure to cause the ice in the food to sublime rather than melt. **Figure 17** summarizes the changes of state of solids, liquids, and gases.

## SECTION REVIEW

1. What is equilibrium?
2. What happens when a liquid-vapor system at equilibrium experiences an increase in temperature? What happens when it experiences a decrease in temperature?
3. What would be an example of deposition?
4. What is the equilibrium vapor pressure of a liquid? How is it measured?
5. What is the boiling point of a liquid?
6. In the phase diagram for water, what is meant by the triple point and the critical point?

**Critical Thinking**

7. **INTERPRETING GRAPHICS** Refer to the phase diagram for water on page 347 to answer the following questions.
   - **a.** Describe all the changes a sample of solid water would undergo when heated from −10°C to its critical temperature at a pressure of 1.00 atm.
   - **b.** Describe all the changes a sample of water vapor would undergo when cooled from 110°C to 5°C at a pressure of 1.00 atm.
   - **c.** At approximately what pressure will water be a vapor at 0°C?
   - **d.** Within what range of pressures will water be a liquid at temperatures above its normal boiling point?

# Water

SECTION 5

C.6.1 Summarize the process by which solutes dissolve in solvents, the dynamic equilibrium that occurs in saturated solutions, and the effects of varying pressure and temperature on solubility

Water is a familiar substance in all three physical states: solid, liquid, and gas. On Earth, water is by far the most abundant liquid. Oceans, rivers, and lakes cover about 75% of Earth's surface. Significant quantities of water are also frozen in glaciers. Water is an essential component of all organisms; 70% to 90% of the mass of living things is water. The chemical reactions of most life processes take place in water, and water is frequently a reactant or product in such reactions. In order to better understand the importance of water, let us take a closer look at its structure and its properties.

## Objectives

- Describe the structure of a water molecule.
- Discuss the physical properties of water. Explain how they are determined by the structure of water.
- Calculate the amount of energy absorbed or released when a quantity of water changes state.

## Structure of Water

As discussed in Chapter 6, water molecules consist of two atoms of hydrogen and one atom of oxygen united by polar-covalent bonds. Research shows that a water molecule is bent. The structure can be represented as follows.

$$\underset{H\quad\ \ H}{\ddot{\dot{O}}}\quad 105^\circ$$

The angle between the two hydrogen-oxygen bonds is about 105°. This is close to the angle expected for $sp^3$ hybridization of the oxygen-atom orbitals.

The molecules in solid or liquid water are linked by hydrogen bonding. The number of linked molecules decreases with increasing temperature because increases in kinetic energy make hydrogen bond formation difficult. Nevertheless, there are usually from four to eight molecules per group in liquid water, as shown in **Figure 18.** If it were not for these molecular groups, water would be a gas at room temperature. Nonpolar molecules, such as methane, $CH_4$, that are similar in size and mass to water molecules do not undergo hydrogen bonding. Such substances are gases at room temperature.

Ice consists of water molecules in the hexagonal arrangement shown in **Figure 19.** The empty spaces between molecules in this pattern account for the relatively low density of ice. As ice is heated, the increased energy of the molecules causes them to move and vibrate more vigorously. When the melting point is reached, the energy of the

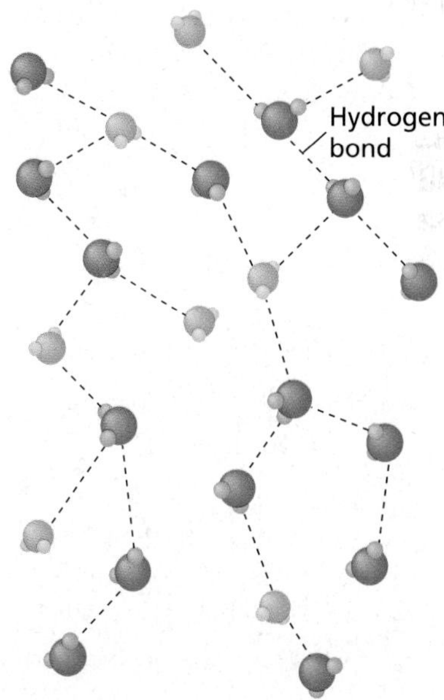


**FIGURE 18** The structure of liquid water shows that within the water molecule, oxygen and hydrogen are covalently bonded to each other, while the molecules are held together in groups by hydrogen bonds.

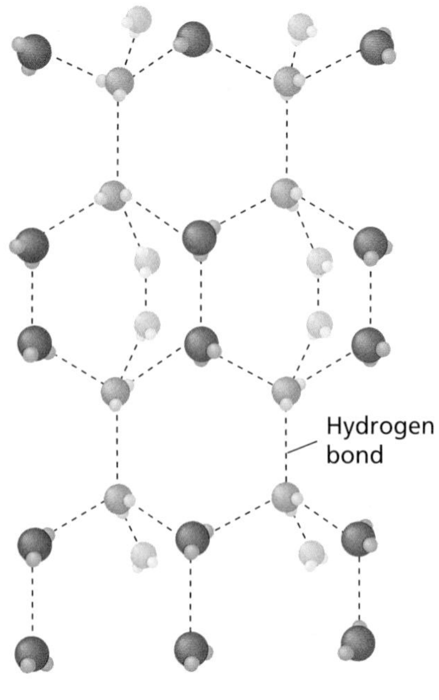


**FIGURE 19** Ice contains the same types of bonding as liquid water. However, the structure of the hydrogen bonding is much more rigid and open than it is in liquid water.

molecules is so great that the rigid open structure of the ice crystals breaks down, and ice turns into liquid water.

**Figures 18 and 19** also show that the hydrogen bonds between molecules of liquid water at 0.°C are fewer and more disordered than those between molecules of ice at the same temperature. Because the rigid open structure of ice has broken down, water molecules can crowd closer together. Thus, liquid water is denser than ice.

As the liquid water is warmed from 0.°C, the water molecules crowd still closer together. Water molecules are as tightly packed as possible at 3.98°C. At temperatures above 3.98°C, the increasing kinetic energy of the water molecules causes them to overcome molecular attractions. The molecules move farther apart as the temperature continues to rise. As the temperature approaches the boiling point, groups of liquid water molecules absorb enough energy to break up into separate molecules. Because of hydrogen bonding between water molecules, a high kinetic energy is needed, causing water's boiling point to be relatively high (100.°C) compared to other liquids that have similar molar masses.

## Physical Properties of Water

At room temperature, pure liquid water is transparent, odorless, tasteless, and almost colorless. Any observable odor or taste is caused by impurities, such as dissolved minerals, liquids, or gases.

As shown by its phase diagram in **Figure 16,** water freezes and ice melts at 0.°C at a pressure of 1 atm (101.3 kPa). The molar enthalpy of fusion of ice is 6.009 kJ/mol. That value is relatively large compared with the molar enthalpy of fusion of other solids. As you have read, water has the unusual property of expanding in volume as it freezes, because its molecules form an open rigid structure. As a result, ice at 0.°C has a density of only about 0.917 g/cm$^3$, but liquid water at 0.°C has a density of 0.999 84 g/cm$^3$.

This lower density explains why ice floats in liquid water. The insulating effect of floating ice is particularly important in the case of large bodies of water. If ice were more dense than liquid water, it would sink to the bottom of lakes and ponds, where it would be less likely to melt completely. The water of such bodies of water in temperate climates would eventually freeze solid, killing nearly all the living things in it.

Under a pressure of 1 atm (101.3 kPa), water boils at 100.°C. At this temperature, water's molar enthalpy of vaporization is 40.79 kJ/mol. Both the boiling point and the molar enthalpy of vaporization of water are quite high compared with those of nonpolar substances of comparable molecular mass, such as methane. The values are high because of the strong hydrogen bonding that must be overcome for boiling to occur. The high molar enthalpy of vaporization makes water useful for household steam-heating systems. The steam (vaporized water) stores a great deal of energy as heat. When the steam condenses in radiators, great quantities of energy are released.

## SAMPLE PROBLEM A

For more help, go to the ***Math Tutor*** at the end of this chapter.

**How much energy is absorbed when 47.0 g of ice melts at STP? How much energy is absorbed when this same mass of liquid water boils?**

### SOLUTION

**1 *ANALYZE*** **Given:** mass of $H_2O(s)$ = 47.0 g; mass of $H_2O(l)$ = 47.0 g; molar enthalpy of fusion of ice = 6.009 kJ/mol; molar enthalpy of vaporization = 40.79 kJ/mol

**Unknown:** energy absorbed when ice melts; energy absorbed when liquid water boils

**2 *PLAN*** First, convert the mass of water from grams to moles.

$$47.0 \text{ g } H_2O \times \frac{1 \text{ mol } H_2O}{18.02 \text{ g } H_2O} = 2.61 \text{ mol } H_2O$$

Then, use the molar enthalpy of fusion of a solid to calculate the amount of energy absorbed when the solid melts. Multiply the number of moles by the amount of energy needed to melt one mole of ice at its melting point (the molar enthalpy of fusion of ice). Using the same method, calculate the amount of energy absorbed when water boils by using the molar enthalpy of vaporization.

amount of substance (mol) × molar enthalpy of fusion or vaporization (kJ/mol) = energy (kJ)

**3 *COMPUTE***

$$2.61 \text{ mol} \times 6.009 \text{ kJ/mol} = 15.7 \text{ kJ (on melting)}$$

$$2.61 \text{ mol} \times 40.79 \text{ kJ/mol} = 106 \text{ kJ (on vaporizing or boiling)}$$

**4 *EVALUATE*** Units have canceled correctly. The answers have the proper number of significant digits and are reasonably close to estimated values of 18 (3 × 6) and 120 (3 × 40), respectively.

### PRACTICE

*Answers in Appendix E*

1. What quantity of energy is released when 506 g of liquid water freezes?
2. What mass of steam is required to release $4.97 \times 10^5$ kJ of energy on condensation?

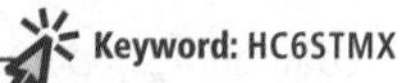


Go to **go.hrw.com** for more practice problems that ask you to use enthalpies to calculate energies absorbed or released.

**Keyword: HC6STMX**

## SECTION REVIEW

1. Why is a water molecule polar?
2. How is the structure of water responsible for some of water's unique characteristics?
3. Describe the arrangement of molecules in liquid water and in ice.
4. Why does ice float? Why is this phenomenon important?
5. Why is ice less dense than liquid water?
6. Is more energy required to melt one gram of ice at 0°C or to boil one gram of water at 100°C? How do you know?

**Critical Thinking**

7. **RELATING IDEAS** Why is exposure to steam dangerous?

# CHAPTER HIGHLIGHTS

## The Kinetic-Molecular Theory of Matter

**Vocabulary**

kinetic-molecular theory
ideal gas
elastic collision
diffusion
effusion
real gas

- The kinetic-molecular theory of matter can be used to explain the properties of gases, liquids, and solids.
- The kinetic-molecular theory of gases describes a model of an ideal gas.
- Gases consist of large numbers of tiny, fast-moving particles that are far apart relative to their size.

## Liquids

**Vocabulary**

fluid
surface tension
capillary action
vaporization
evaporation
freezing

- The particles of a liquid are closer together and more ordered than those of a gas and are less ordered than those of a solid.
- Liquids have a definite volume and a fairly high density, and they are relatively incompressible. Like gases, liquids can flow and thus are considered to be fluids.

## Solids

**Vocabulary**

crystalline solids
crystal
amorphous solids
melting
melting point
supercooled liquids
crystal structure
unit cell

- The particles of a solid are not nearly as free to move about as those of a liquid or a gas are.
- Solids have a definite shape and may be crystalline or amorphous. They have a definite volume and are generally nonfluid.
- A crystal structure is the total three-dimensional array of points that describes the arrangement of the particles of a crystal.
- Unlike crystalline solids, amorphous solids do not have a highly ordered structure or a regular shape.

## Changes of State

**Vocabulary**

phase
condensation
equilibrium
equilibrium vapor pressure
volatile liquids
boiling
boiling point
molar enthalpy of vaporization
freezing point
molar enthalpy of fusion
sublimation
deposition
phase diagram
triple point
critical point
critical temperature
critical pressure

- A liquid in a closed system will gradually reach a liquid-vapor equilibrium as the rate at which molecules condense equals the rate at which they evaporate.
- When two opposing changes occur at equal rates in the same closed system, the system is said to be in dynamic equilibrium.

## Water

- Water is a polar covalent compound.
- The structure and the hydrogen bonding in water are responsible for its relatively high melting point, molar enthalpy of fusion, boiling point, and molar enthalpy of vaporization.

# CHAPTER REVIEW

## The Kinetic-Molecular Theory of Matter

### SECTION 1 REVIEW

1. What idea is the kinetic-molecular theory based on?
2. What is an ideal gas?
3. State the five basic assumptions of the kinetic-molecular theory.
4. How do gases compare with liquids and solids in terms of the distance between their molecules?
5. What is the relationship between the temperature, speed, and kinetic energy of gas molecules?
6. a. What is diffusion?
   b. What factors affect the rate of diffusion of one gas through another?

## Liquids

### SECTION 2 REVIEW

7. What is a fluid?
8. What is surface tension?
9. Give two reasons why evaporation is a crucial process in nature.

## Solids

### SECTION 3 REVIEW

10. List six properties of solids, and explain each in terms of the kinetic-molecular theory of solids.
11. List four common examples of amorphous solids.
12. List and describe the four types of crystals in terms of the nature of their component particles and the type of bonding between them.

## Changes of State

### SECTION 4 REVIEW

13. Using **Figure 14,** estimate the approximate equilibrium vapor pressure of each of the following at the specified temperature.
    a. water at 80°C
    b. diethyl ether at 20°C
    c. ethanol at 60°C
14. a. What is sublimation?
    b. Give two examples of common substances that sublime at ordinary temperatures.
15. What is meant by the normal freezing point of a substance?
16. Explain how the attractive forces between the particles in a liquid are related to the equilibrium vapor pressure of that liquid.
17. Explain the relationship between atmospheric pressure and the actual boiling point of a liquid.
18. Explain the relationship between the molar enthalpy of fusion of a solid and the strength of attraction between that solid's particles.

### PRACTICE PROBLEMS

19. a. The molar enthalpy of vaporization for water is 40.79 kJ/mol. Express this enthalpy of vaporization in joules per gram.
    b. The molar enthalpy of fusion for water is 6.009 kJ/mol. Express this enthalpy of fusion in joules per gram.
20. Calculate the molar enthalpy of vaporization of a substance given that 0.433 mol of the substance absorbs 36.5 kJ of energy when it is vaporized.
21. Given that a substance has a molar mass of 259.0 g/mol and a 71.8 g sample of the substance absorbs 4.307 kJ when it melts,
    a. calculate the number of moles in the sample.
    b. calculate the molar enthalpy of fusion.
22. a. Calculate the number of moles in a liquid sample of a substance that has a molar enthalpy of fusion of 3.811 kJ/mol, given that the sample releases 83.2 kJ when it freezes.
    b. Calculate the molar mass of this substance if the mass of the sample is 5519 g.

## Water

### SECTION 5 REVIEW

**23.** Describe the structure of a water molecule.
**24.** List at least eight physical properties of water.

### PRACTICE PROBLEMS

**25.** Which contains more molecules of water: 5.00 $cm^3$ of ice at 0°C or 5.00 $cm^3$ of liquid water at 0.°C? How many more? What is the ratio of the numbers of molecules in these two samples?

**26.** a. What volume and mass of steam at 100.°C and 1.00 atm would release the same amount of energy during condensation as 100. $cm^3$ of liquid water would release during freezing?
b. What do you note, qualitatively, about the relative volumes and masses of steam and liquid water required to release the same amount of heat? (Hint: See Sample Problem A)

## MIXED REVIEW

**27.** Find the molar enthalpy of vaporization for a substance, given that 3.21 mol of the substance absorbs 28.4 kJ of energy as heat when the substance changes from a liquid to a gas.

**28.** Water's molar enthalpy of fusion is 6.009 kJ/mol. Calculate the amount of energy as heat required to melt $7.95 \times 10^5$ g of ice.

**29.** A certain substance has a molar enthalpy of vaporization of 31.6 kJ/mol. How much of the substance is in a sample that requires 57.0 kJ to vaporize?

**30.** Given that water has a molar enthalpy of vaporization of 40.79 kJ/mol, how many grams of water could be vaporized by 0.545 kJ?

**31.** Calculate the amount of energy released as heat by the freezing of 13.3 g of a liquid substance, given that the substance has a molar mass of 82.9 g/mol and a molar enthalpy of fusion of 4.60 kJ/mol.

**32.** What volume and mass of steam at 100.°C and 760. torr would release the same amount of energy as heat during condensation as 65.5 $cm^3$ of liquid water would release during freezing?

**33.** The following liquid-vapor system is at equilibrium at a given temperature in a closed system.

$$\text{liquid} + \text{energy} \rightleftarrows \text{vapor}$$

Suppose the temperature is increased and equilibrium is established at the higher temperature. How does the final value of each of the following compare with its initial value? (In each case, answer either higher, lower, or the same.)
a. the rate of evaporation
b. the rate of condensation
c. the final concentration of vapor molecules
d. the final number of liquid molecules

**34.** Given a sample of water at any point on curve AB in **Figure 16,** what effect would each of the following changes have on that sample?
a. adding energy at constant pressure
b. decreasing the volume at constant temperature
c. removing energy at constant pressure
d. increasing the volume at constant temperature

**35.** Using the phase diagram for $CO_2$, describe all the phase changes that would occur when $CO_2$ is heated from –100°C to –10°C at a constant pressure of 6 atm.

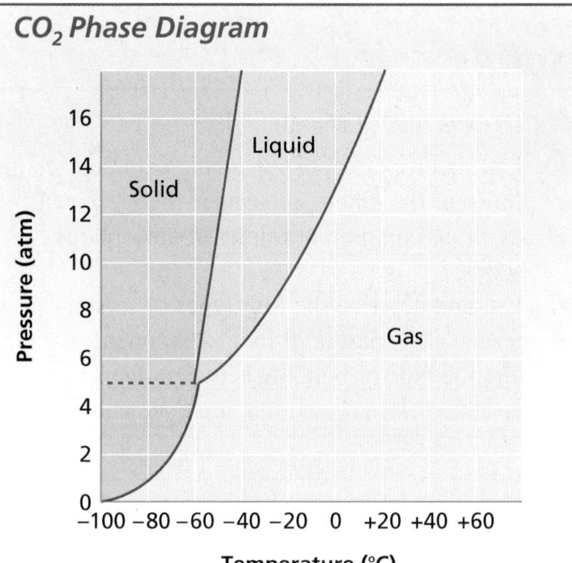

## CRITICAL THINKING

**36. Interpreting Concepts** During the freezing of a substance, energy is being removed from that substance. Yet the temperature of the liquid-solid system remains constant. Explain this phenomenon.

**37. Applying Models** At normal atmospheric pressure, the temperature of an ice-water system remains at 0°C as long as both ice and liquid water are present, regardless of the surrounding temperature. Explain why this occurs.

**38. Predicting Outcomes** Given a sample of water at any point on curve AD in **Figure 16,** how could more of the liquid water in that sample be converted into a solid without changing the temperature? Explain your reasoning.

**39. Interpreting Diagrams** Refer to the phase diagram in question 44.

a. Explain what happens when solid $CO_2$ ("dry ice") warms up to room temperature at normal atmospheric pressure.

b. Is there a pressure below which liquid $CO_2$ cannot exist? Estimate that pressure from the graph.

## USING THE HANDBOOK

**40.** The *Elements Handbook* contains a table of properties for each group that includes information on the crystal structures of the elements. Most metals crystallize in one of three lattice arrangements: body-centered cubic, face-centered cubic, or hexagonal close-packed. **Figure 10** shows a model of the face-centered cubic lattice for sodium chloride. Use this figure and the information in the *Elements Handbook* to answer the following.

a. What elements in Group 2 have the same lattice structure as sodium chloride?

b. How would the model of an element in a face-centered cubic lattice differ from the compound shown in **Figure 10**?

c. The body-centered cubic lattice is the least-efficient packing structure of the metals. What elements in Groups 1 and 2 show this arrangement?

## RESEARCH & WRITING

**41.** Ceramics are formed from silicates found in the soil. Artists use them to create pottery, but engineers and scientists have created ceramics with superconductive properties. Investigate the growing field of superconductive ceramics.

**42.** Liquid crystals are substances that possess the combined properties of both liquids and crystals. Write a report on these substances and the various uses we are finding for them.

## ALTERNATIVE ASSESSMENT

**43.** Compile separate lists of crystalline and amorphous solids found in your home. Compare your lists with those of your classmates.

**44.** Design an experiment to grow crystals of various safe, common household materials. Record the conditions under which each type of crystal is best grown.

extension

**Graphing Calculator**
**Vapor Pressure**

Go to **go.hrw.com** for a graphing calculator exercise that asks you to create a graph of the vapor pressure of water as a function of temperature.

# Math Tutor CALCULATIONS USING ENTHALPIES OF FUSION

When one mole of a liquid freezes to a solid, energy is released as attractive forces between particles pull the disordered particles of the liquid into a more orderly crystalline solid. When the solid melts to a liquid, the solid must absorb the same quantity of energy in order to separate the particles of the crystal and overcome the attractive forces opposing separation. This quantity of energy used to melt or freeze one mole of a substance at its melting point is called its molar enthalpy of fusion, $\Delta H_f$.

## Problem-Solving TIPS

- The enthalpy of fusion of a substance can be given as either joules per gram or kilojoules per mole.
- *Molar* enthalpy of fusion is most commonly used in calculations.
- The enthalpy of fusion is the energy absorbed or given off as heat when a substance melts or freezes at the melting point of the substance.
- No net change in temperature occurs as the state change occurs.

## SAMPLE 1

**7.30 kJ of energy is required to melt 0.650 mol of ethylene glycol ($C_2H_6O_2$) at its melting point. Calculate the molar enthalpy of fusion, $\Delta H_f$, of ethylene glycol and the energy absorbed.**

$$\text{molar enthalpy of fusion} = \Delta H_f = \frac{\text{energy absorbed}}{\text{moles of substance}}$$

$$\Delta H_{f,\text{ethylene glycol}} = \frac{7.30 \text{ kJ}}{0.065 \text{ mol}} = 11.2 \frac{\text{kJ}}{\text{mol}}$$

## SAMPLE 2

**Determine the quantity of energy that will be needed to melt $2.50 \times 10^5$ kg of iron at its melting point, 1536°C. The $\Delta H_f$ of iron is 13.807 kJ/mol.**

To calculate the number of moles of iron, use the equation below.

$$\text{moles of substance} = \frac{\text{mass of substance}}{\text{molar mass of substance}}$$

Next, use the following equation for energy as heat absorbed.

$$\text{energy absorbed} = \Delta H_f \times \text{moles of substance}$$

Now, substitute the calculation for moles of substance, and solve.

$$\text{energy absorbed} = \Delta H_f \times \frac{\text{grams of substance}}{\text{molar mass of substance}} =$$

$$13.807 \frac{\text{kJ}}{\text{mol}} \times \frac{2.50 \times 10^8 \text{ g Fe}}{55.847 \text{ g Fe/mol Fe}}$$

$$\text{energy absorbed} = 6.18 \times 10^7 \text{ kJ}$$

## PRACTICE PROBLEMS

1. Calculate the molar enthalpy of fusion of silver if 1.940 mol of silver requires 22.60 kJ of energy to change from a solid to a liquid at its melting point, 961°C.

2. What quantity of energy in kJ must be absorbed by 6.47 mol of solid acetic acid, $C_2H_4O_2$, to melt it at its melting point, 16.7°C? The $\Delta H_f$ for acetic acid is 11.54 kJ/mol.

# Standardized Test Prep

**Answer the following items on a separate piece of paper.**

**MULTIPLE CHOICE**

**1.** Surface tension is
**A.** skin on the surface of a liquid.
**B.** the tendency of the surface of liquids to decrease the area.
**C.** the spontaneous mixing of two substances.
**D.** the same as vapor pressure.

**2.** Pure liquids boil at higher temperatures under high pressures than they do under low pressures, because
**A.** the molecules of liquid are closer together under higher pressures.
**B.** it takes a higher temperature for the vapor pressure to equal the higher external pressure.
**C.** the molecules of vapor are farther apart under higher pressures.
**D.** the vapor diffuses more rapidly at higher pressures.

**3.** The formation of frost is an example of
**A.** condensation.
**B.** evaporation.
**C.** deposition.
**D.** melting point.

**4.** The graph that shows the pressure and temperature conditions under which the phases of a substance exist is called
**A.** a phase diagram.
**B.** a vapor pressure curve.
**C.** a unit cell.
**D.** the kinetic-molecular theory of matter.

**5.** Water boils at 100°C. Ethanol boils at 78.5°C. Which of the following statements is true?
**A.** Water has the higher vapor pressure at 78.5°C.
**B.** Ethanol has the higher vapor pressure at 78.5°C.
**C.** Both have the same vapor pressure at 78.5°C.
**D.** Vapor pressure is not related to boiling point.

**6.** Which of the following is not a property of typical solids?
**A.** definite melting point
**B.** high density
**C.** easily compressible
**D.** low rate of diffusion

**7.** The kinetic-molecular theory states that ideal gas molecules
**A.** are in constant, rapid, random motion.
**B.** have mass and take up space.
**C.** exert forces of attraction and repulsion on each other.
**D.** have high densities compared with liquids and solids.

**SHORT ANSWER**

**8.** Using this graph of vapor pressures of substances at various temperatures, estimate the boiling point of ethanol at an applied (external) pressure of 300 torr.

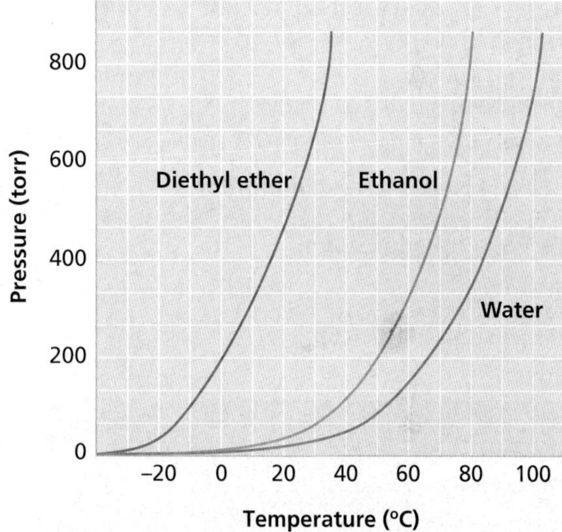


**9.** It is found that 60.0 J of energy are required to melt 15 g of a substance. The molar mass of the substance is 120 g/mol. Calculate the enthalpy of fusion of the substance in kilojoules per mole.

**EXTENDED RESPONSE**

**10.** Describe how a pressure cooker works.

**11.** What is meant by the statement that a liquid and its vapor in a closed container are in a state of dynamic equilibrium?

**Test TIP** Test questions are not necessarily arranged in order of increasing difficulty. If you are unable to answer a question, mark it and move on to other questions.

# "Wet" Dry Ice

## OBJECTIVES

- *Interpret* a phase diagram.
- *Observe* the melting of $CO_2$ while varying pressure.
- *Relate* observations of $CO_2$ to its phase diagram.

## MATERIALS

- 4–5 g $CO_2$ as dry ice, broken into rice-sized pieces
- forceps
- metric ruler
- plastic pipets, 5 mL, shatterproof
- pliers
- scissors
- transparent plastic cup

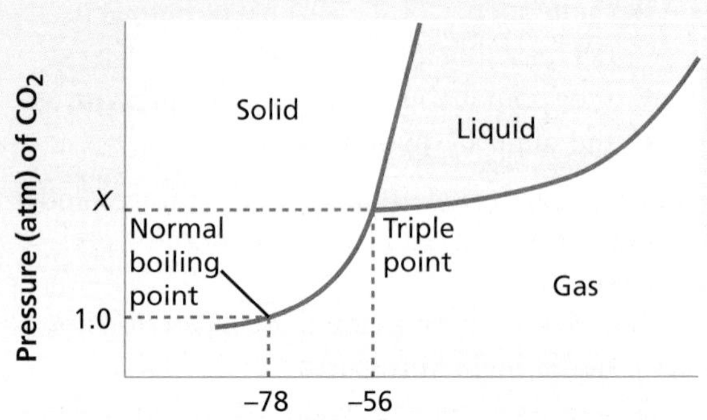


**FIGURE A** The phase diagram for $CO_2$ shows the temperatures and pressures at which $CO_2$ can undergo phase changes.

## BACKGROUND

The phase diagram for carbon dioxide in **Figure A** shows that $CO_2$ can exist only as a gas at ordinary room temperature and pressure. To observe the transition of solid $CO_2$ to liquid $CO_2$, you must increase the pressure until it is at or above the triple point pressure, which is labeled $X$ in the diagram.

## SAFETY

For review of safety, please see **Safety in the Chemistry Laboratory** in the front of your book.

## PREPARATION

1. Organize a place in your lab notebook for recording your observations.

## PROCEDURE

1. Use forceps to place 2–3 very small pieces of dry ice on the table, and observe them until they have completely sublimed. **Caution:** Dry ice will freeze skin very quickly. Do not attempt to pick up the dry ice with your fingers.

2. Fill a plastic cup with tap water to a depth of 4–5 cm.
3. Cut the tapered end (tip) off the graduated pipet.
4. Use forceps to carefully slide 8–10 pieces of dry ice down the stem and into the bulb of the pipet.
5. Use a pair of pliers to clamp the opening of the pipet stem securely shut so that no gas can escape. Use the pliers to hold the tube and to lower the pipet into the cup just until the bulb is submerged, as shown in **Figure B.** From the side of the cup, observe the behavior of the dry ice.
6. As soon as the dry ice has begun to melt, quickly loosen the pliers while still holding the bulb in the water. Observe the $CO_2$.
7. Tighten the pliers again, and observe.
8. Repeat Procedure steps 6 and 7 as many times as possible.

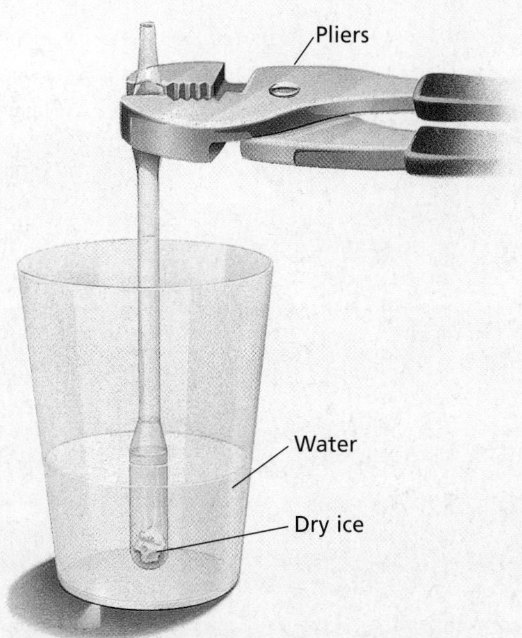


**FIGURE B** Clamp the end of the pipet shut with the pliers. Submerge the bulb in water in a transparent cup.

## CLEANUP AND DISPOSAL

9. Clean all apparatus and your lab station. Return equipment to its proper place. Dispose of chemicals and solutions in the containers designated by your teacher. Do not pour any chemicals down the drain or place them in the trash unless your teacher directs you to do so. Wash your hands thoroughly before you leave the lab and after all work is finished.

## ANALYSIS AND INTERPRETATION

1. **Analyzing Results:** What differences did you observe between the subliming and the melting of $CO_2$?
2. **Analyzing Methods:** As you melted the $CO_2$ sample over and over, why did it eventually disappear? What could you have done to make the sample last longer?
3. **Analyzing Methods:** What purpose(s) do you suppose the water in the cup served?

## EXTENSIONS

1. **Predicting Outcomes:** What would have happened if fewer pieces of dry ice (only 1 or 2) had been placed inside the pipet bulb? If time permits, test your prediction.
2. **Predicting Outcomes:** What might have happened if too much dry ice (20 or 30 pieces, for example) had been placed inside the pipet bulb? How quickly would the process have occurred? If time permits, test your prediction.
3. **Predicting Outcomes:** What would have happened if the pliers had not been released once the dry ice melted? If time permits, test your prediction.

CHAPTER 11

# Gases

*The density of a gas decreases as the temperature of the gas increases.*

# Gases and Pressure

SECTION 1

C.5.2 Explain the behaviors of gas; the relationship among pressure, volume, and temperature; and the significance of the Kelvin (absolute temperature) scale, using the kinetic-molecular theory as a model

In the chapter "States of Matter," you read about the kinetic-molecular theory, which is based on the idea that particles of matter are always in motion. In this section, you will study the implications of the kinetic-molecular theory of gases.

You have learned that the temperature of a gas is related to the kinetic energy of the gas molecules. In this chapter, you will learn about other properties of gases, including pressure, volume, and amount of gas present, and the relationship between these properties.

## OBJECTIVES

- Define *pressure*, give units of pressure, and describe how pressure is measured.
- State the standard conditions of temperature and pressure and convert units of pressure.
- Use Dalton's law of partial pressures to calculate partial pressures and total pressures.

## Pressure and Force

If you pump air into an automobile tire, the pressure in the tire will increase. The pressure increase is caused by the increase in the number of collisions of molecules of air with the inside walls of the tire. The collisions cause an outward push, or force, against the inside walls. Gas molecules exert pressure on any surface with which they collide. The pressure exerted by a gas depends on volume, temperature, and the number of molecules present. **Pressure** *(P) is defined as the force per unit area on a surface.* The equation defining pressure is shown in **Figure 1.**

**FIGURE 1** The pressure the ballet dancer exerts against the floor depends on the area of contact. The smaller the area of contact, the greater the pressure.

(a) Area of contact = 325 cm$^2$

$$\text{Pressure} = \frac{\text{force}}{\text{area}} = \frac{500\ \text{N}}{325\ \text{cm}^2} = 1.5\ \text{N/cm}^2$$

(b) Area of contact = 13 cm$^2$

$$\text{Pressure} = \frac{\text{force}}{\text{area}} = \frac{500\ \text{N}}{13\ \text{cm}^2} = 38\ \text{N/cm}^2$$

(c) Area of contact = 6.5 cm$^2$

$$\text{Pressure} = \frac{\text{force}}{\text{area}} = \frac{500\ \text{N}}{6.5\ \text{cm}^2} = 77\ \text{N/cm}^2$$

The SI unit for force is the **newton,** (N). *It is the force that will increase the speed of a one-kilogram mass by one meter per second each second that the force is applied.* At Earth's surface, gravity has an acceleration of 9.8 $m/s^2$. Consider a ballet dancer with a mass of 51 kg, as shown in **Figure 1.** A mass of 51 kg exerts a force of 500 N (51 kg × 9.8 $m/s^2$) on Earth's surface. No matter how the dancer stands, she exerts that much force against the floor. But the pressure exerted against the floor depends on the area of contact. When the dancer rests her weight on the soles of both feet, as shown in **Figure 1a,** the area of contact with the floor is about 325 $cm^2$. The pressure, or force per unit area, when she stands in this manner is 500 N/325 $cm^2$, or roughly 1.5 $N/cm^2$. When she stands on her toes, as in **Figure 1b,** the total area of contact with the floor is only 13 $cm^2$. The pressure exerted is then equal to 500 N/13 $cm^2$—roughly 38 $N/cm^2$. And when she stands on one toe, as in **Figure 1c,** the pressure exerted is twice that, or about 77 $N/cm^2$. Thus, the same force applied to a smaller area results in a greater pressure.

The atmosphere—the shell of air surrounding Earth—exerts pressure. **Figure 2** shows that atmospheric pressure at sea level is about equal to the weight of a 1.03 kg mass per square centimeter of surface, or 10.1 $N/cm^2$. The pressure of the atmosphere can be thought of as caused by the weight of the gases that compose the atmosphere. The atmosphere contains about 78% nitrogen, 21% oxygen, and 1% other gases, including argon and carbon dioxide. Atmospheric pressure is the sum of the individual pressures of the various gases in the atmosphere.

Your ears "pop" when you fly in an airplane because the density—and therefore the pressure—of the air is lower at higher altitudes. The popping happens when the air pressure inside your ears changes to reach the same pressure as the air inside the cabin.



**FIGURE 2** Air molecules—most of which are nitrogen or oxygen—collide with Earth's surface, creating a pressure of 10.1 $N/cm^2$.

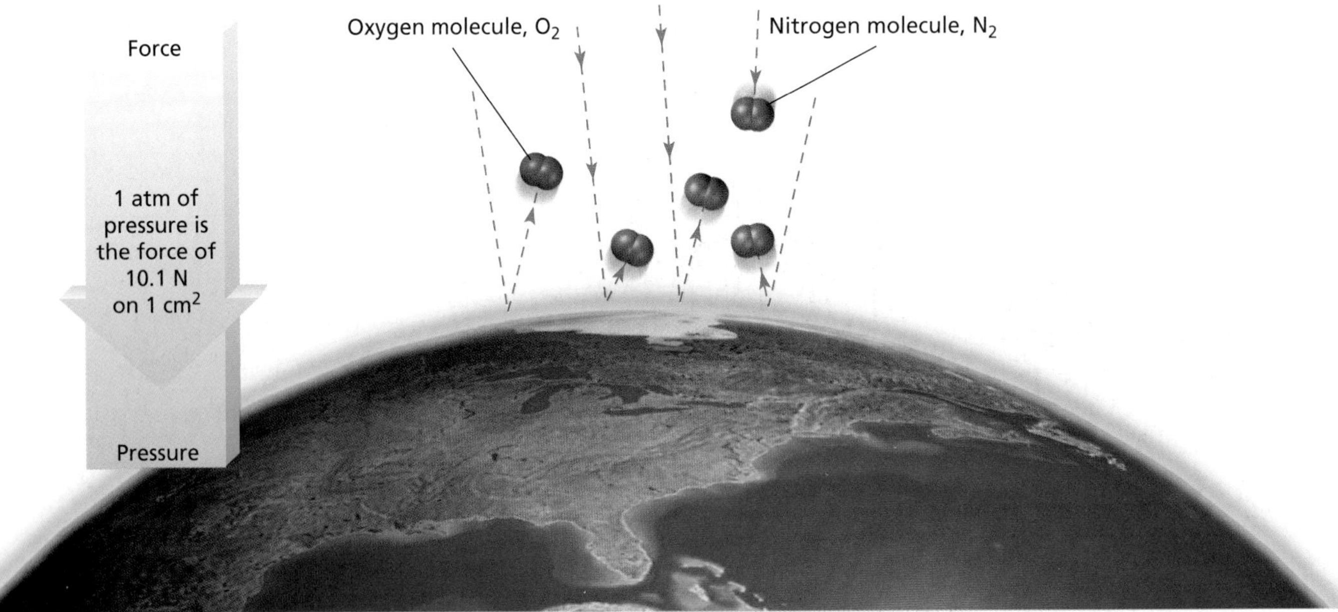

## Measuring Pressure

*A* **barometer** *is a device used to measure atmospheric pressure.* The first type of barometer, illustrated in **Figure 3,** was introduced by Evangelista Torricelli during the early 1600s. Torricelli wondered why water pumps could raise water to a maximum height of only about 34 feet. He thought that the height must depend somehow on the weight of water compared with the weight of air. He reasoned that liquid mercury, which is about 14 times as dense as water, could be raised only 1/14 as high as water. To test this idea, Torricelli sealed a long glass tube at one end and filled it with mercury. Holding the open end with his thumb, he inverted the tube into a dish of mercury without allowing any air to enter the tube. When he removed his thumb, the mercury column in the tube dropped to a height of about 30 in. (760 mm) above the surface of the mercury in the dish. He repeated the experiment with tubes of different diameters and lengths longer than 760 mm. In every case, the mercury dropped to a height of about 760 mm.

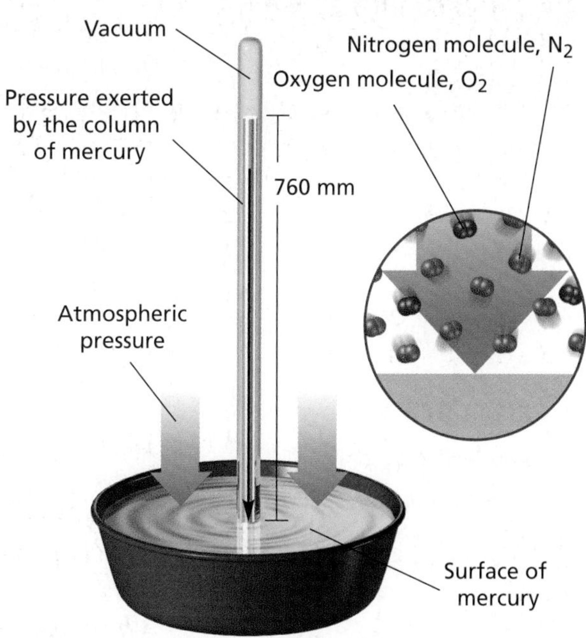


**FIGURE 3** Torricelli discovered that the pressure of the atmosphere supports a column of mercury about 760 mm above the surface of the mercury in the dish.

The space above the mercury in such a tube is nearly a vacuum. The mercury in the tube pushes downward because of gravitational force. The column of mercury in the tube is stopped from falling beyond a certain point because the atmosphere exerts a pressure on the surface of the mercury outside the tube. This pressure is transmitted through the fluid mercury and is exerted upward on the column of mercury. The mercury in the tube falls only until the pressure exerted by its weight is equal to the pressure exerted by the atmosphere.

The exact height of the mercury in the tube depends on the atmospheric pressure, or force per unit area. The pressure is measured in terms of the mercury column's height in the barometer tube.

From experiments like Torricelli's, it is known that at sea level and at 0°C, the average pressure of the atmosphere can support a 760 mm column of mercury. The atmospheric pressure at any given place depends on the elevation and the weather conditions. If the atmospheric pressure is greater than the average at sea level, the height of the mercury column in a barometer will be greater than 760 mm. If the atmospheric pressure is less, the height of the mercury column will be less than 760 mm.

All gases, not only those in the atmosphere, exert pressure. A device called a manometer can be used to measure the pressure of an enclosed gas sample, as shown in **Figure 4.** The difference in the height of mercury in the two arms of the U-tube is a measure of the oxygen gas pressure in the container.

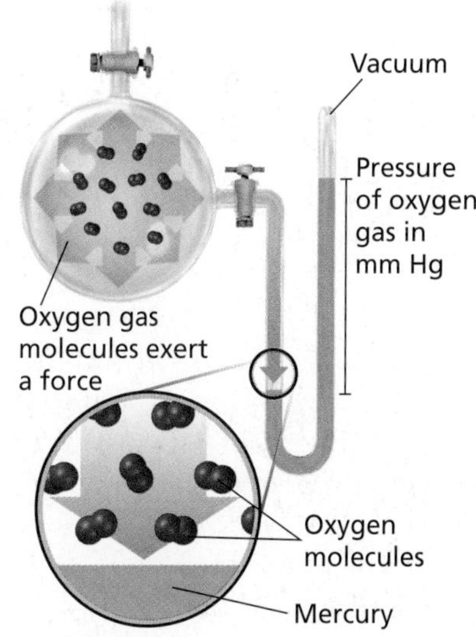


**FIGURE 4** In the manometer above, the pressure of the oxygen gas in the flask pushes on the mercury column. The difference in the height of the mercury in the two arms of the U-tube indicates the oxygen gas pressure.

To understand gas pressure, consider a can that is filled with air. The atmosphere exerts a pressure against the outside of the can. The air inside the can pushes outward and balances the atmosphere's inward-pushing force. If a vacuum pump is used to remove the air from the can, the balancing outward force is removed. As a result, the unbalanced force due to atmospheric pressure immediately crushes the can.

## Units of Pressure

A number of different units are used to measure pressure. Because atmospheric pressure is often measured by a mercury barometer, pressure can be expressed in terms of the height of a mercury column. *Thus, the common unit of pressure is* **millimeters of mercury,** *symbolized mm Hg.* A pressure of 1 mm Hg is also called 1 torr in honor of Torricelli for his invention of the barometer. The average atmospheric pressure at sea level at 0°C is 760 mm Hg.

Pressures are often measured in units of atmospheres. *One* **atmosphere of pressure** *(atm) is defined as being exactly equivalent to 760 mm Hg.*

In SI, pressure is expressed in derived units called pascals. The unit is named for Blaise Pascal, a French mathematician and philosopher who studied pressure during the seventeenth century. *One* **pascal** *(Pa) is defined as the pressure exerted by a force of one newton (1 N) acting on an area of one square meter.*

In many cases, it is more convenient to express pressure in kilopascals (kPa). The standard atmosphere (1 atm) is equal to $1.013\,25 \times 10^5$ Pa, or 101.325 kPa. The pressure units used in this book are summarized in **Table 1.**

### Chemical Content

Go to **go.hrw.com** for another version of this content. See the chapters "Physical Characteristics of Gases" and "Molecular Composition of Gases."

**Keyword: HC6GASX**

## Standard Temperature and Pressure

To compare volumes of gases, one must know the temperature and pressure at which the volumes are measured. *For purposes of comparison, scientists have agreed on standard conditions of exactly 1 atm pressure and 0°C.* These conditions are called *standard temperature and pressure* and are commonly abbreviated STP.

**TABLE 1** ***Units of Pressure***

| Unit | Symbol | Definition/relationship |
|---|---|---|
| pascal | Pa | SI pressure unit<br>$1\ \text{Pa} = \frac{1\ \text{N}}{\text{m}^2}$ |
| millimeter of mercury | mm Hg | pressure that supports a 1 mm mercury column in a barometer |
| torr | torr | 1 torr = 1 mm Hg |
| atmosphere | atm | average atmospheric pressure at sea level and 0°C<br>1 atm = 760 mm Hg<br>= 760 torr<br>= $1.013\,25 \times 10^5$ Pa<br>= 101.325 kPa |
| pounds per square inch | psi | 1 psi = $6.892\,86 \times 10^3$ Pa<br>1 atm = 14.700 psi |

## SAMPLE PROBLEM A

**The average atmospheric pressure in Denver, Colorado, is 0.830 atm. Express this pressure in (a) millimeters of mercury (mm Hg) and (b) kilopascals (kPa).**

### SOLUTION

**1 ANALYZE** **Given:** $P$ of atmosphere = 0.830 atm

760 mm Hg = 1 atm (definition); 101.325 kPa = 1 atm (definition)

**Unknown:** **a.** $P$ of atmosphere in mm Hg; **b.** $P$ of atmosphere in kPa

**2 PLAN**

**a.** atm ⟶ mm Hg; $\cancel{\text{atm}} \times \frac{760 \text{ mm Hg}}{\cancel{\text{atm}}} = \text{mm Hg}$

**b.** atm ⟶ kPa; $\cancel{\text{atm}} \times \frac{101.325 \text{ kPa}}{\cancel{\text{atm}}} = \text{kPa}$

**3 COMPUTE**

**a.** $0.830 \cancel{\text{atm}} \times \frac{760 \text{ mm Hg}}{\cancel{\text{atm}}} = 631 \text{ mm Hg}$

**b.** $0.830 \cancel{\text{atm}} \times \frac{101.325 \text{ kPa}}{\cancel{\text{atm}}} = 84.1 \text{ kPa}$

**4 EVALUATE** Units have canceled to give the desired units, and answers are expressed to the correct number of significant figures. The known pressure and the calculated pressures are about 80% of the atmospheric pressure, as expressed in the new units.

**PRACTICE** *Answers in Appendix E*

1. Convert a pressure of 1.75 atm to kPa and to mm Hg.
2. The critical pressure of carbon dioxide is 72.7 atm. What is this value in units of pascals?

**extension**

Go to **go.hrw.com** for more practice problems that ask you to convert between units of pressure.

## Dalton's Law of Partial Pressures

John Dalton, the English chemist who proposed the atomic theory, also studied gas mixtures. The pressure exerted by each gas in an unreactive mixture is independent of that exerted by other gases present. *The pressure of each gas in a mixture is called the* **partial pressure** *of that gas.* **Dalton's law of partial pressures** *states that the total pressure of a gas mixture is the sum of the partial pressures of the component gases.* The law is true regardless of the number of different gases that are present. Dalton's law may be expressed as follows.

$$P_T = P_1 + P_2 + P_3 + \ldots$$

$P_T$ is the total pressure of the mixture. $P_1$, $P_2$, $P_3$, and so on are the partial pressures of component gases 1, 2, 3, and so on.

# Chemistry in Action

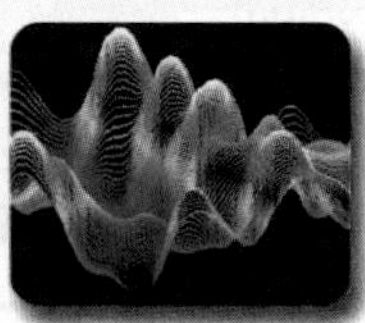
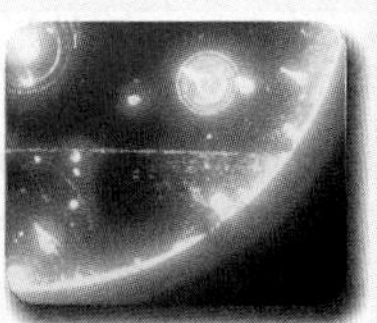

## The Gas Laws and Scuba Diving

An understanding of Dalton's law and Henry's law is essential to safe scuba diving. Dalton's law states that the total pressure of a gas mixture is equal to the sum of the partial pressures of the component gases. Henry's law predicts that the solubility of a gas in a liquid is a direct function of the partial pressure of that gas.

For every 33 ft of sea water that a diver descends, he or she feels one additional atmosphere of pressure because of the increasing weight of water overhead. Most divers use compressed air tanks to breathe underwater. The air in these tanks, which contains approximately 78% nitrogen and 21% oxygen, is the same as the air that we breathe. Once the compressed air enters the diver's lungs, it is subjected to the pressure caused by the water. The increase in the air pressure leads to an increase in the partial pressures of the nitrogen and oxygen in air, as predicted by Dalton's law. Henry's law predicts that this increase in partial pressures will increase the solubility of nitrogen and oxygen in the diver's bloodstream.

The increase in the partial pressure of oxygen is not problematic under typical diving conditions because a diver's body can metabolize the extra oxygen that is present in the bloodstream. The body does not metabolize nitrogen, however, so it can accumulate in a diver's body during a dive. The extra nitrogen can affect the nerve cells of the diver, causing *nitrogen narcosis.* Divers suffering from nitrogen narcosis become disoriented and experience symptoms similar to intoxication. This impairment of a diver's judgment can be very dangerous. To decrease the probability of contracting nitrogen narcosis, divers can use gas mixtures that contain less nitrogen than compressed air does.

Dissolved nitrogen can also be harmful if a diver ascends too quickly. As Henry's law predicts, nitrogen becomes less soluble in the blood as the pressure decreases. This decrease in solubility causes nitrogen to leave the diver's tissues and blood. Normally, the excess nitrogen is discharged through the lungs. However, if the diver comes up too rapidly, the nitrogen will form bubbles in the tissues and veins. This condition is known as *decompression sickness,* or "the bends." If the bubbles block blood flow, a wide range of effects, including severe joint pain, may occur. For this reason, divers are very careful to ascend slowly after diving.

At extreme depths, even the increased pressure of oxygen becomes a problem for scuba divers. Although oxygen is necessary for life, extended exposure to large concentrations of oxygen can result in *oxygen toxicity.* This condition can cause damage to the lungs and nervous system. Divers can avoid oxygen toxicity by breathing gas mixtures that contain more helium and less oxygen than compressed air does.

### Questions

1. Why is the concentration of helium increased in some gas mixtures that divers breathe in order to reduce the partial pressure of oxygen?
2. Although carbon monoxide, CO, is normally present in trace quantities in air, compressed air scuba tanks that are filled improperly can contain elevated levels of CO. Why is this particularly dangerous for divers?

◀ *In order to dive safely, scuba divers must be aware of some of the basic gas laws.*

# The Gas Laws

SECTION 2

C.5.3 Apply the gas laws to problems concerning changes in pressure, volume, or temperature (including Charles's law, Boyle's law, and the combined gas law)

Scientists have been studying physical properties of gases for hundreds of years. In 1662, Robert Boyle discovered that gas pressure and volume are related mathematically. The observations of Boyle and others led to the development of the gas laws. The *gas laws* are simple mathematical relationships between the volume, temperature, pressure, and amount of a gas.

### *Objectives*

- Use the kinetic-molecular theory to explain the relationships between gas volume, temperature, and pressure.
- Use Boyle's law to calculate volume-pressure changes at constant temperature.
- Use Charles's law to calculate volume-temperature changes at constant pressure.
- Use Gay-Lussac's law to calculate pressure-temperature changes at constant volume.
- Use the combined gas law to calculate volume-temperature-pressure changes.

## Boyle's Law: Pressure-Volume Relationship

Robert Boyle discovered that doubling the pressure on a sample of gas at constant temperature reduces its volume by one-half. Reducing the pressure on a gas by one-half allows the volume of the gas to double. As one variable increases, the other decreases. **Figure 6** shows that as the volume of gas in the syringe decreases, the pressure of the gas increases.

You can use the kinetic-molecular theory to understand why this pressure-volume relationship holds. The pressure of a gas is caused by moving molecules hitting the container walls. Suppose the volume of a container is decreased but the same number of gas molecules is present at the same temperature. There will be more molecules per unit volume. The number of collisions with a given unit of wall area per unit time will increase as a result. Therefore, pressure will also increase.

Lower pressure

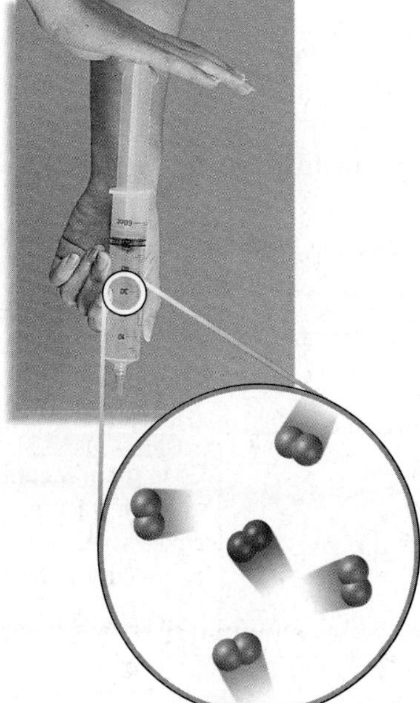

Higher pressure

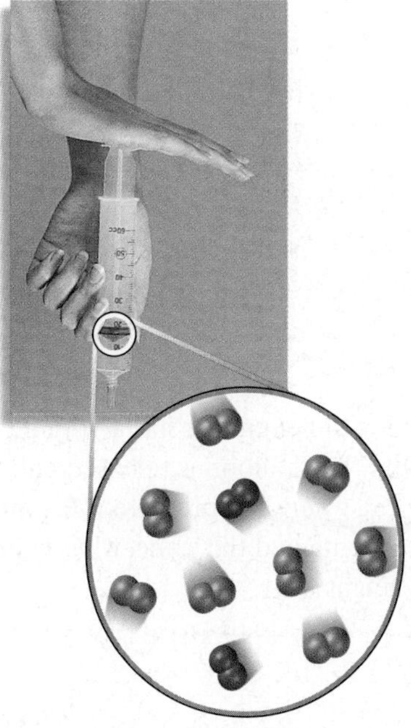

**FIGURE 6** The volume of gas in the syringe shown in the photo is reduced when the plunger is pushed down. The gas pressure increases as the volume is reduced because the molecules collide more frequently with the walls of the container in a smaller volume.

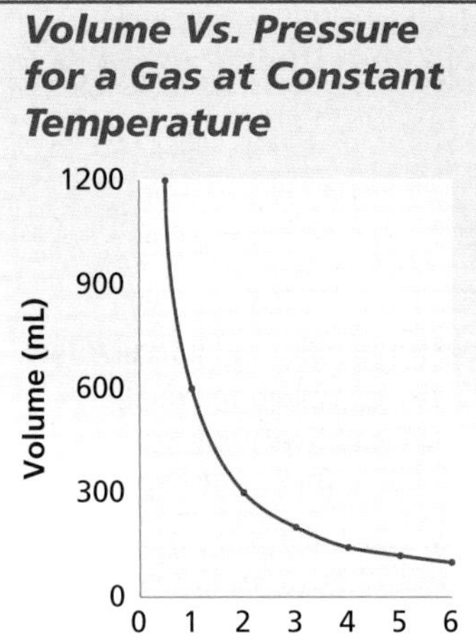


**FIGURE 7** This graph shows that there is an inverse relationship between volume and pressure.

Plotting the values of volume versus pressure for a gas at constant temperature gives a curve like that in **Figure 7.** The general volume-pressure relationship that is illustrated is called Boyle's law. **Boyle's law** *states that the volume of a fixed mass of gas varies inversely with the pressure at constant temperature.*

Mathematically, Boyle's law can be expressed as follows:

$$PV = k$$

In the equation above, $P$ is the pressure, $V$ is the volume, and $k$ is a constant. Since $P$ and $V$ vary inversely, their product remains the same. Because two quantities that are equal to the same thing are equal to each other, the relationship between changes of pressure and volume can be expressed as shown below.

$$P_1V_1 = P_2V_2$$

$P_1$ and $V_1$ represent initial conditions. $P_2$ and $V_2$ represent a different set of conditions. Given three of the four values $P_1$, $V_1$, $P_2$, and $V_2$, you can use this equation to calculate the fourth value for a system at constant temperature.

## SAMPLE PROBLEM C

*For more help, go to the **Math Tutor** at the end of this chapter.*

**A sample of oxygen gas has a volume of 150.0 mL when its pressure is 0.947 atm. What will the volume of the gas be at a pressure of 0.987 atm if the temperature remains constant?**

### SOLUTION

**1 ANALYZE** **Given:** $V_1$ of $O_2$ = 150.0 mL; $P_1$ of $O_2$ = 0.947 atm; $P_2$ of $O_2$ = 0.987 atm
**Unknown:** $V_2$ of $O_2$ in mL

**2 PLAN** Rearrange the equation for Boyle's law ($P_1V_1 = P_2V_2$) to obtain $V_2$.

$$V_2 = \frac{P_1V_1}{P_2}$$

**3 COMPUTE** Substitute values for $P_1$, $V_1$, and $P_2$ to obtain the new volume, $V_2$.

$$V_2 = \frac{P_1V_1}{P_2} = \frac{(0.947\ \cancel{atm})(150.0\ mL\ O_2)}{0.987\ \cancel{atm}} = 144\ mL\ O_2$$

**4 EVALUATE** When the pressure is increased slightly at constant temperature, the volume decreases slightly, as expected. Units cancel to give milliliters, a volume unit.

### PRACTICE

*Answers in Appendix E*

1. A balloon filled with helium gas has a volume of 500 mL at a pressure of 1 atm. The balloon is released and reaches an altitude of 6.5 km, where the pressure is 0.5 atm. If the temperature has remained the same, what volume does the gas occupy at this height?

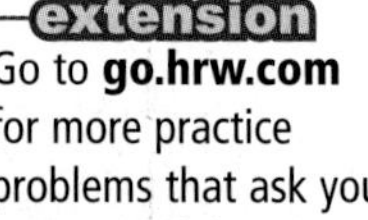


Go to **go.hrw.com** for more practice problems that ask you to use Boyle's Law.

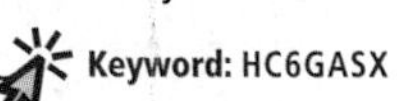

## Charles's Law: Volume-Temperature Relationship

Balloonists, such as those in the photo at the beginning of this chapter, are making use of a physical property of gases: if pressure is constant, gases expand when heated. When the temperature increases, the volume of a fixed number of gas molecules must increase if the pressure is to stay constant. At the higher temperature, the gas molecules move faster. They collide with the walls of the container more frequently and with more force. The volume of a flexible container must then increase in order for the pressure to remain the same.

The quantitative relationship between volume and temperature was discovered by the French scientist Jacques Charles in 1787. Charles's experiments showed that all gases expand to the same extent when heated through the same temperature interval. Charles found that the volume changes by 1/273 of the original volume for each Celsius degree, at constant pressure and an initial temperature of 0°C. For example, raising the temperature to 1°C causes the gas volume to increase by 1/273 of the volume it had at 0°C. If the temperature is increased by 273°C, the volume increases by 273/273 of the original, that is, the volume doubles. The same regularity of volume change occurs if a gas is cooled at constant pressure, as the balloons in **Figure 8** show.

The Kelvin temperature scale is a scale that starts at a temperature corresponding to –273.15°C. That temperature is the lowest one possible. *The temperature –273.15°C is referred to as* **absolute zero** *and is given a value of zero in the Kelvin scale.* This fact gives the following relationship between the two temperature scales.

$$K = 273.15 + {}^\circ C$$

For calculations in this book, 273.15 is rounded off to 273.

**FIGURE 8** As air-filled balloons are exposed to liquid nitrogen, they shrink greatly in volume because the air molecules in the balloon get closer together. When the balloons are removed from the liquid nitrogen and the air inside them is warmed to room temperature, they expand to their original volume.

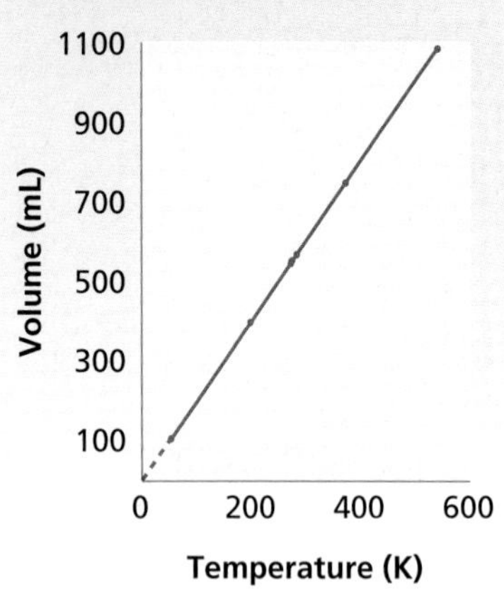


**FIGURE 9** This graph shows the plot of the volume versus the Kelvin temperature data of a sample of gas at constant pressure.

Gas volume and Kelvin temperature are directly proportional to each other at constant pressure as shown in **Figure 9.**

The relationship between Kelvin temperature and gas volume is known as Charles's law. **Charles's law** *states that the volume of a fixed mass of gas at constant pressure varies directly with the Kelvin temperature.* Charles's law may be expressed as follows:

$$V = kT \quad \text{or} \quad \frac{V}{T} = k$$

The value of $T$ is the Kelvin temperature, and $k$ is a constant. The ratio $V/T$ for any set of volume-temperature values always equals the same $k$. The form of Charles's law that can be applied directly to most volume-temperature problems involving gases is as follows:

$$\frac{V_1}{T_1} = \frac{V_2}{T_2}$$

$V_1$ and $T_1$ represent initial conditions. $V_2$ and $T_2$ represent a different set of conditions. When three of the four values $T_1$, $V_1$, $T_2$, and $V_2$ are known, you can use this equation to calculate the fourth value for a system at constant pressure.

## SAMPLE PROBLEM D

*For more help, go to the Math Tutor at the end of this chapter.*

**A sample of neon gas occupies a volume of 752 mL at 25°C. What volume will the gas occupy at 50°C if the pressure remains constant?**

### SOLUTION

**1 ANALYZE**

**Given:** $V_1$ of Ne = 752 mL; $T_1$ of Ne = 25°C + 273 = 298 K; $T_2$ of Ne = 50°C + 273 = 323 K
**Unknown:** $V_2$ of Ne in mL

**2 PLAN**

Because the gas remains at constant pressure, an increase in temperature will cause an increase in volume. To obtain $V_2$, rearrange the equation for Charles's law.

**3 COMPUTE**

Substitute values for $V_1$, $T_1$, and $T_2$ to obtain the new volume, $V_2$.

$$V_2 = \frac{V_1T_2}{T_1} = \frac{(752 \text{ mL Ne})(323 \text{ K})}{298 \text{ K}} = 815 \text{ mL Ne}$$

**4 EVALUATE**

As expected, the volume of the gas increases as the temperature increases. Units cancel to yield milliliters, as desired. The answer contains the appropriate number of significant figures.

### PRACTICE

*Answers in Appendix E*

1. A sample of neon gas has a volume of 752 mL at 25.0°C. What will the volume at 100.0°C be if pressure is constant?
2. A sample of nitrogen gas is contained in a piston with a freely moving cylinder. At 0.0°C, the volume of the gas is 375 mL. To what temperature must the gas be heated to occupy a volume of 500.0 mL?

**extension**

Go to **go.hrw.com** for more practice problems that ask you to use Charles's law.

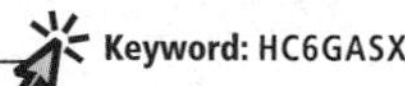

## Gay-Lussac's Law: Pressure-Temperature Relationship

You have just learned about the quantitative relationship between volume and temperature at constant pressure. What would you predict about the relationship between pressure and temperature at constant volume? You have seen that pressure is the result of collisions of molecules with container walls. The energy and frequency of collisions depend on the average kinetic energy of molecules. For a fixed quantity of gas at constant volume, the pressure should be directly proportional to the Kelvin temperature, which depends directly on average kinetic energy.

That prediction turns out to be correct. For every kelvin of temperature change, the pressure of a confined gas changes by 1/273 of the pressure at 0°C. Joseph Gay-Lussac is given credit for recognizing this in 1802. The data plotted in **Figure 10** illustrate **Gay-Lussac's law:** *The pressure of a fixed mass of gas at constant volume varies directly with the Kelvin temperature.* Mathematically, Gay-Lussac's law is expressed as follows.

$$P = kT \quad \text{or} \quad \frac{P}{T} = k$$

The value of $T$ is the temperature in kelvins, and $k$ is a constant that depends on the quantity of gas and the volume. For a given mass of gas at constant volume, the ratio $P/T$ is the same for any set of pressure-temperature values. Unknown values can be found using the following form of Gay-Lussac's law.

$$\frac{P_1}{T_1} = \frac{P_2}{T_2}$$

$P_1$ and $T_1$ represent initial conditions. $P_2$ and $T_2$ represent a different set of conditions. When values are known for three of the four quantities, the fourth value can be calculated for a system at constant volume.

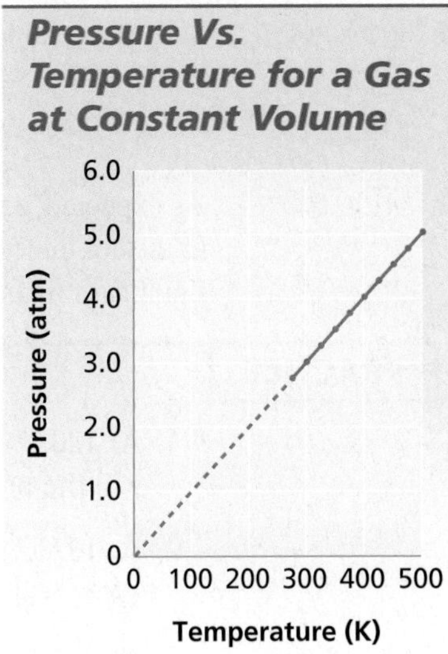


**FIGURE 10** A graph of pressure versus temperature of a sample of gas at constant volume is a straight line, indicating a direct relationship between pressure and temperature.

**SAMPLE PROBLEM E** *For more help, go to the* ***Math Tutor*** *at the end of this chapter.*

**The gas in a container is at a pressure of 3.00 atm at 25°C. Directions on the container warn the user not to keep it in a place where the temperature exceeds 52°C. What would the gas pressure in the container be at 52°C?**

**SOLUTION**

**1** *ANALYZE* **Given:** $P_1$ of gas = 3.00 atm

$T_1$ of gas = 25°C + 273 = 298 K; $T_2$ of gas = 52°C + 273 = 325 K

**Unknown:** $P_2$ of gas in atm

**2** *PLAN* Because the gaseous contents remain at the constant volume of the container, an increase in temperature will cause an increase in pressure. Rearrange Gay-Lussac's law to obtain $P_2$.

$$P_2 = \frac{P_1 T_2}{T_1}$$

**3 COMPUTE** Substitute values for $P_1$, $T_2$, and $T_1$ to obtain the new pressure, $P_2$.

$$P_2 = \frac{(3.00 \text{ atm})(325 \text{ K})}{298 \text{ K}} = 3.27 \text{ atm}$$

**4 EVALUATE** As expected, a temperature increase at constant volume causes the pressure of the contents in the container to increase. Units cancel correctly. The answer contains the proper number of significant figures. It is close to an estimated value of 3.25, calculated as (3 × 325)/300.

**PRACTICE** *Answers in Appendix E*

1. At 120.0°C, the pressure of a sample of nitrogen is 1.07 atm. What will the pressure be at 205°C, assuming constant volume?
2. At 122°C the pressure of a sample of nitrogen gas is 1.07 atm. What will the pressure be at 205°C, assuming constant volume?
3. A sample of helium gas has a pressure of 1.20 atm at 22°C. At what Celsius temperature will the helium reach a pressure of 2.00 atm, assuming constant volume?

**extension**

Go to **go.hrw.com** for more practice problems that ask you to use Gay-Lussac's law.

**Keyword:** HC6GASX

## The Combined Gas Law

A gas sample often undergoes changes in temperature, pressure, and volume all at the same time. When this happens, three variables must be dealt with at once. Boyle's law, Charles's law, and Gay-Lussac's law can be combined into a single expression that is useful in such situations. *The* **combined gas law** *expresses the relationship between pressure, volume, and temperature of a fixed amount of gas.* The combined gas law can be expressed as follows.

$$\frac{PV}{T} = k$$

In the equation, $k$ is constant and depends on the amount of gas. The combined gas law can also be written as follows.

$$\frac{P_1V_1}{T_1} = \frac{P_2V_2}{T_2}$$

The subscripts in the equation above indicate two different sets of conditions, and $T$ represents Kelvin temperature.

From this expression, any value can be calculated if the other five are known. Note that each of the gas laws can be obtained from the combined gas law when the proper variable is constant. For example, Boyle's law is obtained when the temperature is constant. Because $T_1 = T_2$, $T_1$ and $T_2$ will cancel out on both sides of the combined gas law equation, giving Boyle's law.

$$P_1V_1 = P_2V_2$$

www.scilinks.org
**Topic:** Gas Laws
**Code:** HC60637

### Chemical Content

Go to **go.hrw.com** for more information on how the combined gas law can be derived from Boyle's law, Charles's law, and Gay-Lussac's law.

**Keyword:** HC6GASX

## SAMPLE PROBLEM F

For more help, go to the *Math Tutor* at the end of this chapter.

**A helium-filled balloon has a volume of 50.0 L at 25°C and 1.08 atm. What volume will it have at 0.855 atm and 10.0°C?**

### SOLUTION

**1 ANALYZE**

**Given:** $V_1$ of He = 50.0 L; $T_1$ of He = 25°C + 273 = 298 K; $T_2$ of He = 10°C + 273 = 283 K
$P_1$ of He = 1.08 atm; $P_2$ of He = 0.855 atm

**Unknown:** $V_2$ of He in L

**2 PLAN**

Because the gas changes in both temperature and pressure, the combined gas law is needed. Rearrange the combined gas law to solve for the final volume, $V_2$.

$$\frac{P_1V_1}{T_1} = \frac{P_2V_2}{T_2} \longrightarrow V_2 = \frac{P_1V_1T_2}{P_2T_1}$$

**3 COMPUTE**

Substitute the known values into the equation to obtain a value for $V_2$.

$$V_2 = \frac{(1.08 \text{ atm})(50.0 \text{ L He})(283 \text{ K})}{(0.855 \text{ atm})(298 \text{ K})} = 60.0 \text{ L He}$$

**4 EVALUATE**

Here the pressure decreases much more than the temperature decreases. As expected, the net result of the two changes gives an increase in the volume, from 50.0 L to 60.0 L. Units cancel appropriately. The answer is correctly expressed to three significant figures. It is also reasonably close to an estimated value of 50, calculated as (50 × 300)/300.

### PRACTICE

Answers in Appendix E

1. The volume of a gas is 27.5 mL at 22.0°C and 0.974 atm. What will the volume be at 15.0°C and 0.993 atm?
2. A 700.0 mL gas sample at STP is compressed to a volume of 200.0 mL, and the temperature is increased to 30.0°C. What is the new pressure of the gas in Pa?

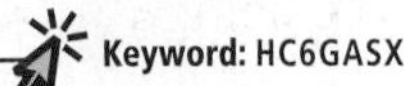

Go to **go.hrw.com** for more practice problems that ask you to use the combined gas law.

**Keyword: HC6GASX**

## SECTION REVIEW

1. Relate the effect of temperature and pressure on a gas to the model of a gas given by the kinetic-molecular theory.
2. A sample of helium gas has a volume of 200.0 mL at 0.960 atm. What pressure, in atmospheres, is needed to reduce the volume at constant temperature to 50.0 mL?
3. A sample of nitrogen gas occupies 1.55 L at 27.0°C and 1.00 atm. What will the volume be at −100.0°C and the same pressure?
4. A gas occupies 2.0 m$^3$ at 100.0 K and exerts a pressure of 100.0 kPa. What volume will the gas occupy if the temperature is increased to 400.0 K and the pressure is increased to 200.0 kPa?

**Critical Thinking**

5. **ANALYZING RESULTS** A student has the following data: $V_1$ = 822 mL, $T_1$ = 75°C, and $T_2$ = −25°C. He calculates $V_2$ and gets −274 mL. Is this value correct? Explain why or why not.
6. **APPLYING MODELS** Explain Charles's law in terms of the kinetic-molecular theory.

# HISTORICAL CHEMISTRY

## Chemistry's First Law

### Historical Perspective

The notion that "nature abhors a vacuum"—meaning that there is no such thing as "empty space"—was proposed by the Greek philosopher Aristotle, whose word was unchallenged for nearly 2000 years. Then, in the mid-1600s, a new breed of thinkers known as *natural philosophers*—what we now know as "scientists"—began testing the long-held assumption that all space must contain matter. These investigations were some of the earliest experiments with gases, and they led to the discovery of the first empirical principle of chemistry, Boyle's law.

### Overturning an Ancient Assumption

The first scientist to demonstrate the existence of a vacuum was Evangelista Torricelli. In 1643, he showed that when a glass tube that was 3 ft. long and about 1 in. in diameter was sealed at one end, filled with mercury, and inverted in a container full of mercury, the mercury in the tube fell to a height of about 30 in. above the level of mercury in the container. Some thinkers remained skeptical, but it was generally accepted that the space between the mercury and the sealed end of the tube was indeed a vacuum.

▲*Evangelista Torricelli invented the mercury barometer.*

Torricelli then turned his attention to how the mercury in the glass tube of his apparatus was supported. The fact that liquids exert a pressure on objects immersed in them inspired him to hypothesize that a "sea of air" surrounded Earth. He further hypothesized that the air exerted pressure on the mercury in the container and thus supported the mercury in the column.

### Support for the New Theory

Although the idea of an atmosphere that has weight and exerts a pressure on the objects within it seems obvious today, it was a radical theory at the time.

To test the effects of the atmosphere, Robert Boyle, one of the period's great scientists, had his talented assistant, Robert Hooke, create a piece of equipment that would revolutionize the study of air. The apparatus was an improved version of a pump designed by the German experimenter Otto von Guericke; the pump had a large receptacle in which a partial vacuum could be created.

Boyle placed Torricelli's setup, known today as a *barometer*, in the receptacle of the pump and observed the mercury column as he reduced the pressure around it. The height of the mercury decreased as the pressure surrounding the mercury in the container dropped, strongly supporting Torricelli's atmospheric theory.

Using Hooke's pump, Boyle performed additional studies that verified the idea that air exerted pressure and had weight. Boyle's experiments also led to the important conclusion that air was elastic: that is, it could expand and contract. Boyle discovered the fundamental law that bears his name during an investigation into air's elasticity.

### An Ingenious Experiment

In response to a criticism of his findings, Boyle performed an experiment to show that air could be compressed to a pressure greater than that of the atmosphere. First, he prepared a glass J-tube with the short end sealed off and the long end left open. Then, he poured mercury into the tube, making sure that the levels in the two ends were the same and letting air travel freely between the ends, to ensure that each column was at atmospheric pressure.

Then, by pouring more mercury into the long end of the tube until it was about 30 in. above the level of mercury in the short end, Boyle exposed the trapped air to about twice as much atmospheric pressure. He observed that the

◀ *We can measure the difference between the atmospheric pressure on a mountaintop and the atmospheric pressure at sea level thanks to the work of Torricelli and Boyle.*

volume of the trapped air was halved. He continued to add mercury until the total pressure on the trapped air was about 4 times that of the atmosphere. Noting that the air had been compressed to a volume about one-fourth of what it originally was, Boyle discovered the inverse relationship between air's pressure and volume.

### A Long-Standing Contribution

Boyle went on to show that the relationship between air pressure and volume, $P \propto 1/V$ (at constant temperature), held not only when the gas was compressed but also when it was allowed to expand. Future investigators would show that the law is a principle that applies to gases in general. Along with the findings of other researchers, such as Jacques Charles, Joseph Gay-Lussac, and Amadeo Avogadro, Boyle's discovery led chemists to the famous ideal gas law, $PV = nRT$, which serves as a starting point in the study of chemistry today.

### Questions

1. Why was it necessary for Boyle to seal one end of his J-tube?
2. What would have happened if Boyle had allowed the temperature of the trapped air sample to change as he added mercury to the tube?

SCI LINKS®
www.scilinks.org
**Topic:** Torricelli
**Code:** HC61539
**Topic:** Robert Boyle
**Code:** HC61317

SECTION 3

## OBJECTIVES

- State the law of combining volumes.
- State Avogadro's law and explain its significance.
- Define *standard molar volume of a gas* and use it to calculate gas masses and volumes.
- State the ideal gas law.
- Using the ideal gas law, calculate pressure, volume, temperature, or amount of gas when the other three quantities are known.

# Gas Volumes and the Ideal Gas Law

**C.5.7** Apply the ideal gas law (pV = nRT) to solve problems

In this section, you will study the relationships between the volumes of gases that react with each other. You will also learn about the relationship between molar amount of gas and volume, and a single gas law that unifies all the basic gas laws into a single equation.

## Measuring and Comparing the Volumes of Reacting Gases

In the early 1800s, French chemist Joseph Gay-Lussac studied gas volume relationships involving a chemical reaction between hydrogen and oxygen. He observed that 2 L of hydrogen can react with 1 L of oxygen to form 2 L of water vapor at constant temperature and pressure.

$$\begin{array}{ccccc} \text{hydrogen gas} & + & \text{oxygen gas} & \longrightarrow & \text{water vapor} \\ \text{2 L (2 volumes)} & & \text{1 L (1 volume)} & & \text{2 L (2 volumes)} \end{array}$$

In other words, this reaction shows a simple and definite 2:1:2 relationship between the volumes of the reactants and the product. Two volumes of hydrogen react with 1 volume of oxygen to produce 2 volumes of water vapor. The 2:1:2 relationship for this reaction applies to any proportions for volume—for example, 2 mL, 1 mL, and 2 mL; 600 L, 300 L, and 600 L; or 400 $cm^3$, 200 $cm^3$, and 400 $cm^3$.

Gay-Lussac also noticed simple and definite proportions by volume in other reactions of gases, such as in the reaction between hydrogen gas and chlorine gas.

$$\begin{array}{ccccc} \text{hydrogen gas} & + & \text{chlorine gas} & \longrightarrow & \text{hydrogen choloride gas} \\ \text{1 L (1 volume)} & & \text{1 L (1 volume)} & & \text{2 L (2 volumes)} \end{array}$$

In 1808, Gay-Lussac summarized the results of his experiments in a statement known today as **Gay-Lussac's law of combining volumes of gases.** The law states that *at constant temperature and pressure, the volumes of gaseous reactants and products can be expressed as ratios of small whole numbers.* This simple observation, combined with the insight of Avogadro, provided more understanding of how gases react and combine with each other.

## Avogadro's Law

Recall an important point of Dalton's atomic theory: atoms are indivisible. Dalton also thought that the particles of gaseous elements exist in the form of isolated single atoms. He believed that one atom of one element always combines with one atom of another element to form a single particle of the product. However, some of the volume relationships observed by Gay-Lussac could not be accounted for by Dalton's theory. For example, in reactions such as the formation of water vapor, mentioned on the preceding page, it would seem that the oxygen atoms involved would have to divide into two parts.

In 1811, Avogadro found a way to explain Gay-Lussac's simple ratios of combining volumes without violating Dalton's idea of indivisible atoms. He did this by rejecting Dalton's idea that reactant elements are always in monatomic form when they combine to form products. He reasoned that these molecules could contain more than one atom. Avogadro also put forth an idea known today as **Avogadro's law.** The law states that *equal volumes of gases at the same temperature and pressure contain equal numbers of molecules.* **Figure 11** illustrates Avogadro's law. It follows that at the same temperature and pressure, the volume of any given gas varies directly with the number of molecules. Avogadro's law also indicates that gas volume is directly proportional to the amount of gas, at a given temperature and pressure. Note the equation for this relationship.

$$V = kn$$

Here, $n$ is the amount of gas, in moles, and $k$ is a constant.

Avogadro's reasoning applies to the combining volumes for the reaction of hydrogen and oxygen to form water vapor. Dalton had guessed that the formula of water was HO, because this formula seemed to be the most likely formula for such a common compound. But Avogadro's reasoning established that water must contain twice as many H atoms as O atoms, consistent with the formula $H_2O$. As shown below, the coefficients in a chemical reaction involving gases indicate the relative numbers of molecules, the relative numbers of moles, and the relative volumes.

| $2H_2(g)$ | + $O_2(g)$ | $\longrightarrow 2H_2O(g)$ |
|---|---|---|
| 2 molecules | 1 molecule | 2 molecules |
| 2 mol | 1 mol | 2 mol |
| 2 volumes | 1 volume | 2 volumes |

The simplest hypothetical formula for oxygen indicated two oxygen atoms, which turns out to be correct. The simplest possible molecule of water indicated two hydrogen atoms and one oxygen atom per molecule, which is also correct. Experiments eventually showed that all elements that are gases near room temperature, except the noble gases, normally exist as diatomic molecules.

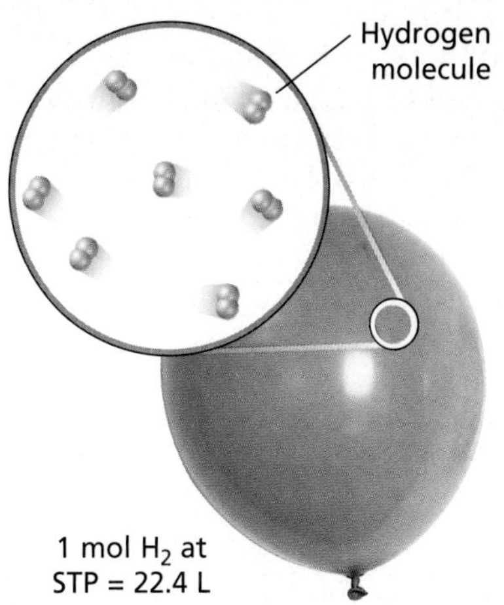


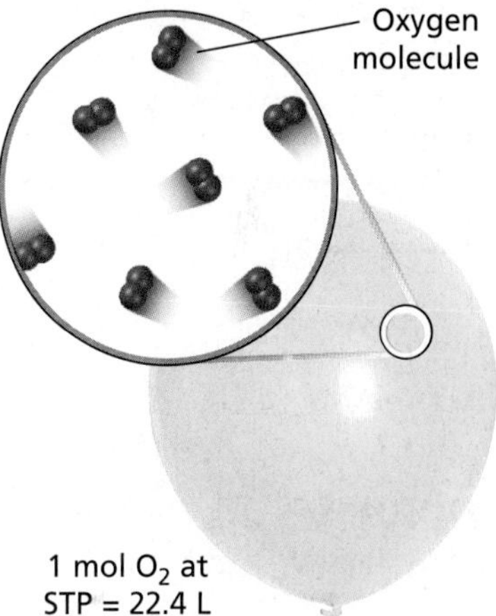


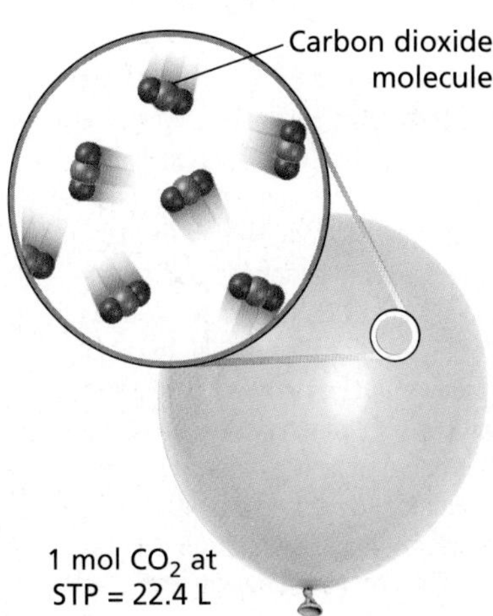


**FIGURE 11** At the same temperature and pressure, balloons of equal volume have equal numbers of molecules, regardless of which gas they contain.

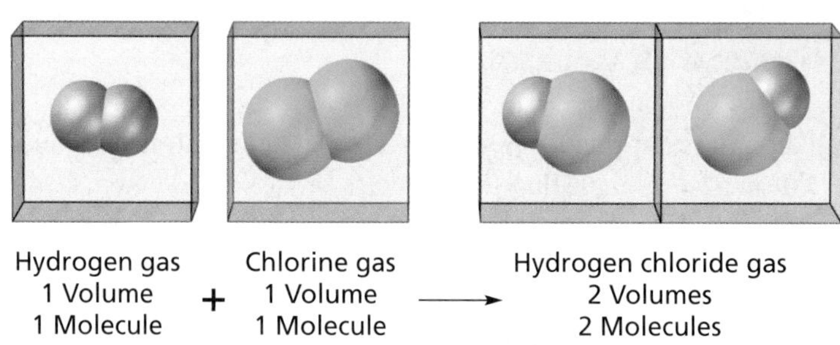


**FIGURE 12** Hydrogen molecules combine with chlorine molecules in a 1:1 volume ratio to produce 2 volumes of hydrogen chloride. Avogadro's law thus demonstrates that hydrogen and chlorine gases are diatomic.

Consider the reaction of hydrogen and chlorine to produce hydrogen chloride, illustrated in **Figure 12.** According to Avogadro's law, equal volumes of hydrogen and chlorine contain the same number of molecules. Avogadro's idea of diatomic gases applies to this reaction also. He concluded that the hydrogen and chlorine components must each consist of two or more atoms joined together. The simplest assumption was that hydrogen and chlorine molecules are composed of two atoms each. That assumption leads to the following balanced equation for the reaction of hydrogen with chlorine.

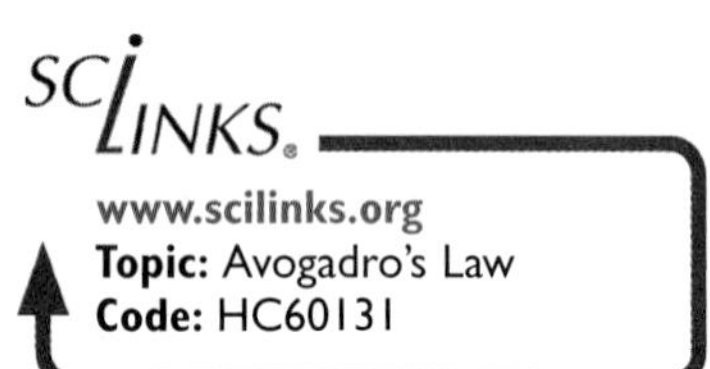


$$\begin{array}{lll} H_2(g) \quad + & Cl_2(g) \longrightarrow & 2HCl(g) \\ \text{1 volume} & \text{1 volume} & \text{2 volumes} \\ \text{1 molecule} & \text{1 molecule} & \text{2 molecules} \end{array}$$

The simplest hypothetical formula for hydrogen chloride, HCl, indicates that the molecule contains one hydrogen atom and one chlorine atom. Given the ratios of the combined volumes, the simplest formulas for hydrogen and chlorine must be $H_2$ and $Cl_2$, respectively.

## Chemistry in Action
### Automobile Air Bags

Since the late 1980s, air bags have been offered as a safety feature in cars to minimize injuries in the event of a high-speed collision. Modern automobile air bags use a series of very rapid chemical reactions to inflate the bag. When a collision is detected by sensors, an igniter triggers decomposition of solid sodium azide, $Na_3N$, to form $N_2$ gas. The hazardous sodium metal that also forms reacts with $KNO_3$ to form $Na_2O$, also producing additional $N_2$. Finally, the highly reactive $Na_2O$ is removed by reaction with $SiO_2$ to form harmless silicate glass. This entire sequence of reactions occurs to inflate the air bag with nitrogen gas in as few as 40 milliseconds (0.04 s) after a collision is detected by sensors.

## Molar Volume of a Gas

Recall that one mole of a molecular substance contains a number of molecules equal to Avogadro's constant ($6.022 \times 10^{23}$). One mole of oxygen, $O_2$, contains $6.022 \times 10^{23}$ diatomic oxygen molecules and has a mass of 31.9988 g. One mole of helium, a monatomic gas, contains the same number of helium atoms and has a mass of 4.002 602 g.

According to Avogadro's law, one mole of any gas will occupy the same volume as one mole of any other gas at the same temperature and pressure, despite mass differences. *The volume occupied by one mole of a gas at STP is known as the* **standard molar volume of a gas.** *It has been found to be 22.414 10 L.* For calculations in this book, we use 22.4 L as the standard molar volume.

Knowing the volume of a gas, you can use 1 mol/22.4 L as a conversion factor to find the number of moles, and therefore the mass, of a given volume of a given gas at STP. You can also use the molar volume of a gas to find the volume, at STP, of a known number of moles or a known mass of a gas.

## SAMPLE PROBLEM G

**a. What volume does 0.0685 mol of gas occupy at STP?**
**b. What quantity of gas, in moles, is contained in 2.21 L at STP?**

**SOLUTION**

**a.** Multiply the amount in moles by the conversion factor, $\frac{22.4 \text{ L}}{1 \text{ mol}}$.

$$0.0685 \text{ mol} \times \frac{22.4 \text{ L}}{1 \text{ mol}} = 1.53 \text{ L}$$

**b.** Multiply the volume in liters by the conversion factor, $\frac{1 \text{ mol}}{22.4 \text{ L}}$.

$$2.21 \text{ L} \times \frac{1 \text{ mol}}{22.4 \text{ L}} = 0.0987 \text{ mol}$$

**PRACTICE** *Answers in Appendix E*

1. At STP, what is the volume of 7.08 mol of nitrogen gas?
2. A sample of hydrogen gas occupies 14.1 L at STP. How many moles of the gas are present?

Go to **go.hrw.com** for more practice problems that ask you to calculate molar volume.

**Keyword: HC6GASX**

## Gas Stoichiometry

You can apply the discoveries of Gay-Lussac and Avogadro to calculate the stoichiometry of reactions involving gases. For gaseous reactants or products, the coefficients in chemical equations not only indicate molar amounts and mole ratios but also reveal volume ratios, assuming conditions remain the same. For example, consider the reaction of carbon monoxide with oxygen to give carbon dioxide.

| $2CO(g)$ | + $O_2(g)$ | $\longrightarrow$ $2CO_2(g)$ |
|---|---|---|
| 2 molecules | 1 molecule | 2 molecules |
| 2 mol | 1 mol | 2 mol |
| 2 volumes | 1 volume | 2 volumes |

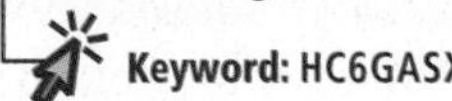


**Chemical Content**

Go to **go.hrw.com** for more information on gas stoichiometry.

**Keyword: HC6GASX**

The possible volume ratios can be expressed in the following ways.

**a.** $\frac{2 \text{ volumes CO}}{1 \text{ volume } O_2}$ or $\frac{1 \text{ volume } O_2}{2 \text{ volumes CO}}$

**b.** $\frac{2 \text{ volumes CO}}{2 \text{ volumes } CO_2}$ or $\frac{2 \text{ volumes } CO_2}{2 \text{ volumes CO}}$

**c.** $\frac{1 \text{ volume } O_2}{2 \text{ volumes } CO_2}$ or $\frac{2 \text{ volumes } CO_2}{1 \text{ volume } O_2}$

## SAMPLE PROBLEM H

**Propane, $C_3H_8$, is a gas that is sometimes used as a fuel for cooking and heating. The complete combustion of propane occurs according to the following balanced equation.**

$$C_3H_8(g) + 5O_2(g) \longrightarrow 3CO_2(g) + 4H_2O(g)$$

**(a) What will be the volume, in liters, of oxygen required for the complete combustion of 0.350 L of propane? (b) What will be the volume of carbon dioxide produced in the reaction? Assume that all volume measurements are made at the same temperature and pressure.**

### SOLUTION

**1** *ANALYZE* **Given:** balanced chemical equation

$V$ of propane = 0.350 L

**Unknown:** **a.** $V$ of $O_2$ in L

**b.** $V$ of $CO_2$ in L

**2** *PLAN*

**a.** $V$ of $C_3H_8 \longrightarrow V$ of $O_2$

**b.** $V$ of $C_3H_8 \longrightarrow V$ of $CO_2$

All volumes are to be compared at the same temperature and pressure. Therefore, volume ratios can be used like mole ratios to find the unknowns.

**3** *COMPUTE*

**a.** $0.350\ \cancel{L\ C_3H_8} \times \dfrac{5\ L\ O_2}{1\ \cancel{L\ C_3H_8}} = 1.75\ L\ O_2$

**b.** $0.350\ \cancel{L\ C_3H_8} \times \dfrac{3\ L\ CO_2}{1\ \cancel{L\ C_3H_8}} = 1.05\ L\ CO_2$

**4** *EVALUATE* Each result is correctly given to three significant figures. The answers are reasonably close to estimated values of 2, calculated as $0.4 \times 5$, and 1.2, calculated as $0.4 \times 3$, respectively.

### PRACTICE

*Answers in Appendix E*

1. Assuming all volume measurements are made at the same temperature and pressure, what volume of hydrogen gas is needed to react completely with 4.55 L of oxygen gas to produce water vapor?
2. What volume of oxygen gas is needed to react completely with 0.626 L of carbon monoxide gas, CO, to form gaseous carbon dioxide? Assume all volume measurements are made at the same temperature and pressure.
3. Nitric acid can be produced by the reaction of gaseous nitrogen dioxide with water, according to the following balanced chemical equation.

$$3NO_2(g) + H_2O(l) \longrightarrow 2HNO_3(l) + NO(g)$$

If 708 L of $NO_2$ gas react with water, what volume of NO gas will be produced? Assume the gases are measured under the same conditions before and after the reaction.

**extension**

Go to **go.hrw.com** for more practice problems that ask you to use mole ratios in stoichiometry.

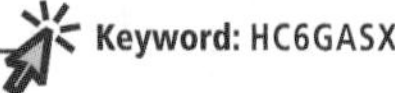

**Keyword: HC6GASX**

## The Ideal Gas Law

**Chemical Content**

Go to **go.hrw.com** for more information on how the ideal gas law can be derived from Boyle's law, Charles's law, and Avogadro's law.

**Keyword: HC6GASX**

You have learned about equations describing the relationships between two or three of the four variables—pressure, volume, temperature, and moles—needed to describe a gas sample. All the gas laws you have learned thus far can be combined into a single equation. *The* **ideal gas law** *is the mathematical relationship among pressure, volume, temperature, and the number of moles of a gas.* It is the equation of state for an ideal gas, because the state of a gas can be defined by its pressure, volume, temperature, and number of moles. It is stated as shown below, where $R$ is a constant.

$$PV = nRT$$

The ideal gas law reduces to Boyle's law, Charles's law, Gay-Lussac's law, or Avogadro's law when the appropriate variables are held constant.

The number of molecules or moles present will always affect at least one of the other three quantities. The collision rate of molecules per unit area of container wall depends on the number of molecules present. If the number of molecules is increased for a sample at constant volume and temperature, the collision rate increases. Therefore, the pressure increases, as shown by the model in **Figure 13a.** Consider what would happen if the pressure and temperature were kept constant while the number of molecules increased. According to Avogadro's law, the volume would increase. As **Figure 13b** shows, an increase in volume keeps the pressure constant at constant temperature. Increasing the volume keeps the collision rate per unit of wall area constant.

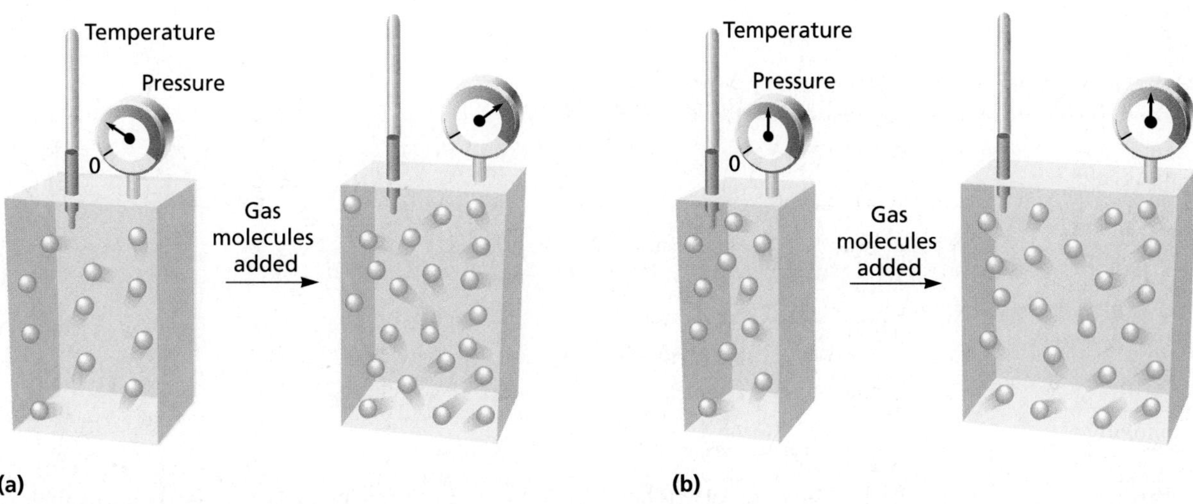


**FIGURE 13** (a) When volume and temperature are constant, gas pressure increases as the number of molecules increases. (b) When pressure and temperature are constant, gas volume increases as the number of molecules increases.

### Chemical Content

Go to **go.hrw.com** for information on how the ideal gas law can be formulated in terms of molar mass and density.

**Keyword: HC6GASX**

## The Ideal Gas Constant

In the equation representing the ideal gas law, *the constant R is known as the* **ideal gas constant.** Its value depends on the units chosen for pressure, volume, and temperature. Measured values of *P, V, T,* and *n* for a gas at near-ideal conditions can be used to calculate *R*. Recall that the volume of one mole of an ideal gas at STP (1 atm and 273.15 K) is 22.414 10 L. Substituting these values and solving the ideal gas law equation for *R* gives the following.

$$R = \frac{PV}{nT} = \frac{(1\ \text{atm})(22.414\ 10\ \text{L})}{(1\ \text{mol})(273.15\ \text{K})} = 0.082\ 058\ \frac{\text{L•atm}}{\text{mol•K}}$$

This calculated value of *R* is usually rounded to 0.0821 L • atm/(mol•K). Use this value in ideal gas law calculations when the volume is in liters, the pressure is in atmospheres, and the temperature is in kelvins. See **Table 2** for the value of *R* when other units for *n, P, V,* and *T* are used.

### Finding P, V, T, or n from the Ideal Gas Law

The ideal gas law can be applied to determine the existing conditions of a gas sample when three of the four variables, *P, V, T,* and *n,* are known. It can also be used to calculate the molar mass or density of a gas sample.

Be sure to match the units of the known quantities and the units of *R*. In this book, you will be using *R* = 0.0821 L•atm/(mol•K). Your first step in solving any ideal gas law problem should be to check the known values to be sure you are working with the correct units. If necessary, you must convert volumes to liters, pressures to atmospheres, temperatures to kelvins, and masses to numbers of moles before using the ideal gas law.

**TABLE 2 Numerical Values of Gas Constant, *R***

| Unit of *R* | Numerical value of *R* | Unit of *P* | Unit of *V* | Unit of *T* | Unit of *n* |
|---|---|---|---|---|---|
| $\frac{\text{L•mm Hg}}{\text{mol•K}}$ | 62.4 | mm Hg | L | K | mol |
| $\frac{\text{L•atm}}{\text{mol•K}}$ | 0.0821 | atm | L | K | mol |
| $\frac{\text{J}}{\text{mol•K}}$ * | 8.314 | Pa | $m^3$ | K | mol |
| $\frac{\text{L•kPa}}{\text{mol•K}}$ | 8.314 | kPa | L | K | mol |

*Note:* 1 L•atm = 101.325 J; 1 J = 1 Pa•$m^3$

* SI units

## SAMPLE PROBLEM I

**What is the pressure in atmospheres exerted by a 0.500 mol sample of nitrogen gas in a 10.0 L container at 298 K?**

### SOLUTION

**1 ANALYZE**

**Given:** $V$ of $N_2$ = 10.0 L
$n$ of $N_2$ = 0.500 mol
$T$ of $N_2$ = 298 K

**Unknown:** $P$ of $N_2$ in atm

**2 PLAN**

$$n, V, T \longrightarrow P$$

The gas sample undergoes no change in conditions. Therefore, the ideal gas law can be rearranged and used to find the pressure as follows.

$$P = \frac{nRT}{V}$$

**3 COMPUTE**

$$P = \frac{(0.500\ \cancel{\text{mol}})\left(\frac{0.0821\ \cancel{\text{L}} \cdot \text{atm}}{\cancel{\text{mol}} \cdot \cancel{\text{K}}}\right)(298\ \cancel{\text{K}})}{10.0\ \cancel{\text{L}}} = 1.22\ \text{atm}$$

**4 EVALUATE**

All units cancel correctly to give the result in atmospheres. The answer is properly limited to three significant figures. It is also close to an estimated value of 1.5, computed as $(0.5 \times 0.1 \times 300)/10$.

### PRACTICE

*Answers in Appendix E*

1. What pressure, in atmospheres, is exerted by 0.325 mol of hydrogen gas in a 4.08 L container at 35°C?
2. A gas sample occupies 8.77 L at 20°C. What is the pressure, in atmospheres, given that there are 1.45 mol of gas in the sample?

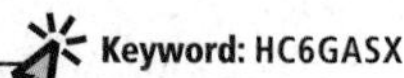

Go to **go.hrw.com** for more practice problems that ask you to use the ideal gas law.

**Keyword: HC6GASX**

## SECTION REVIEW

1. State Avogadro's law, and explain its significance.
2. What volume (in milliliters) at STP will be occupied by 0.0035 mol of methane, $CH_4$?
3. State the ideal gas law equation, and tell what each term means.
4. What would be the units for $R$ if $P$ is in pascals, $T$ is in kelvins, $V$ is in liters, and $n$ is in moles?
5. A 4.44 L container holds 15.4 g of oxygen at 22.55°C. What is the pressure?
6. A tank of hydrogen gas has a volume of 22.9 L and holds 14.0 mol of the gas at 12°C. What is the pressure of the gas in atmospheres?

**Critical Thinking**

7. **ANALYZING DATA** Nitrous oxide is sometimes used as a source of oxygen gas:

$$2N_2O(g) \longrightarrow 2N_2(g) + O_2(g)$$

What volume of each product will be formed from 2.22 L $N_2O$? At STP, what is the density of the product gases when they are mixed?

SECTION 4

# Diffusion and Effusion

## OBJECTIVES

- Describe the process of diffusion.
- State Graham's law of effusion.
- State the relationship between the average molecular velocities of two gases and their molar masses.

SC C.5.2 Explain the behaviors of gas; the relationship among pressure, volume, and temperature; and the significance of the Kelvin (absolute temperature) scale, using the kinetic-molecular theory as a model

The constant motion of gas molecules causes them to spread out to fill any container in which they are placed. The gradual mixing of two or more gases due to their spontaneous, random motion is known as *diffusion,* illustrated in **Figure 14.** *Effusion* is the process whereby the molecules of a gas confined in a container randomly pass through a tiny opening in the container. In this section, you will learn how effusion can be used to estimate the molar mass of a gas.

## Graham's Law of Effusion

The rates of effusion and diffusion depend on the relative velocities of gas molecules. The velocity of a gas varies inversely with the square root of its molar mass. Lighter molecules move faster than heavier molecules at the same temperature.

Recall that the average kinetic energy of the molecules in any gas depends only on the temperature and equals $\frac{1}{2}mv^2$. For two different gases, A and B, at the same temperature, the following relationship is true.

$$\frac{1}{2}M_Av_A{}^2 = \frac{1}{2}M_Bv_B{}^2$$

**Chemical Content**

Go to **go.hrw.com** for more information on how Graham's law can be derived from the equality of the kinetic energy of two gases.

**Keyword:** HC6GASX

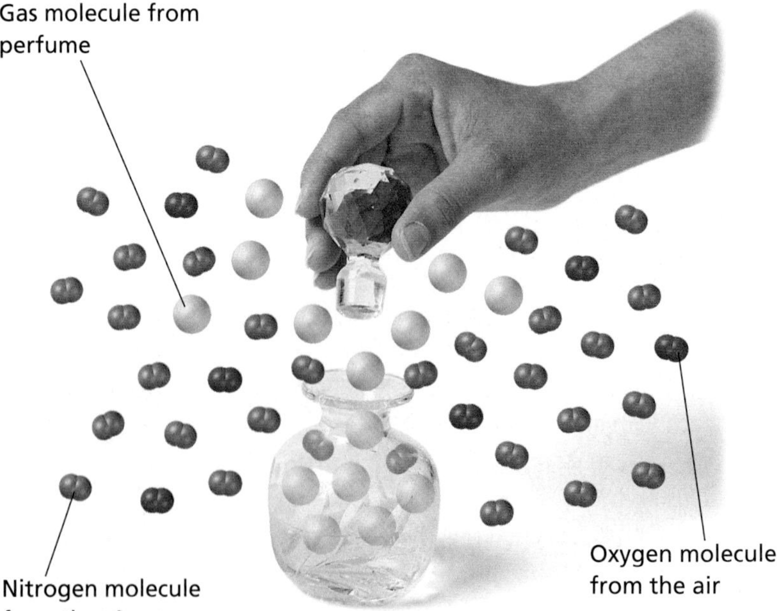


**FIGURE 14** When a bottle of perfume is opened, some of its molecules diffuse into the air and mix with the molecules in the air. At the same time, molecules from the air, such as nitrogen and oxygen, diffuse into the bottle and mix with the gaseous scent molecules.

From the equation relating the kinetic energy of two different gases at the same conditions, one can derive an equation relating the rates of effusion of two gases with their molecular mass. This equation is shown below.

$$\frac{\textit{rate of effusion of A}}{\textit{rate of effusion of B}} = \frac{\sqrt{M_B}}{\sqrt{M_A}}$$

In the mid-1800s, the Scottish chemist Thomas Graham studied the effusion and diffusion of gases. The above equation is a mathematical statement of some of Graham's discoveries. It describes the rates of effusion. It can also be used to find the molar mass of an unknown gas. **Graham's law of effusion** *states that the rates of effusion of gases at the same temperature and pressure are inversely proportional to the square roots of their molar masses.*

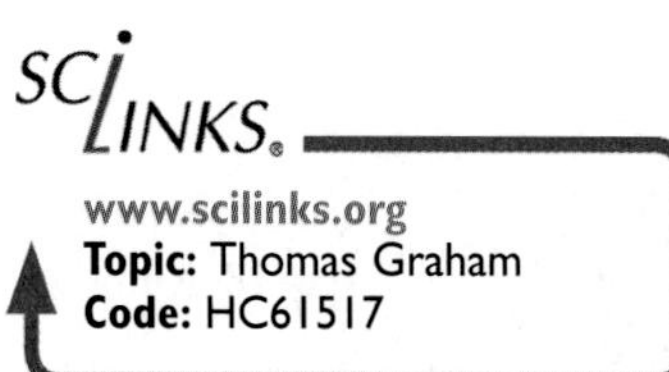


## QuickLAB  Wear safety goggles and an apron.

### *Diffusion*

#### Question

**Do different gases diffuse at different rates?**

#### Procedure

Record all of your results in a data table.

1. Outdoors or in a room separate from the one in which you will carry out the rest of the investigation, pour approximately 10 mL of the household ammonia into one of the 250 mL beakers, and cover it with a watch glass. Pour roughly the same amount of perfume or cologne into the second beaker. Cover it with a watch glass also.
2. Take the two samples you just prepared into a large, draft-free room. Place the samples about 12 to 15 ft apart and at the same height. Position someone as the observer midway between the two beakers. Remove both watch glass covers at the same time.
3. Note whether the observer smells the ammonia or the perfume first. Record how long this takes. Also, record how long it takes the vapor of the other substance to reach the observer. Air the room after you have finished.

#### Discussion

1. What do the times that the two vapors took to reach the observer show about the two gases?
2. What factors other than molecular mass (which determines diffusion rate) could affect how quickly the observer smells each vapor?

#### Materials

- household ammonia
- perfume or cologne
- two 250 mL beakers
- two watch glasses
- 10 mL graduated cylinder
- clock or watch with second hand

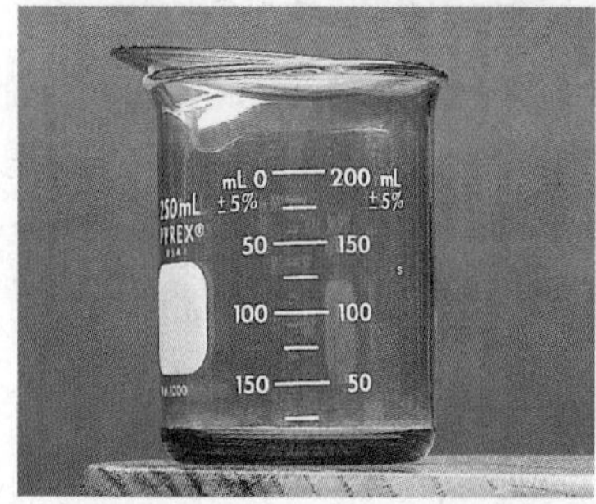

## SAMPLE PROBLEM J

**Compare the rates of effusion of hydrogen and oxygen at the same temperature and pressure.**

### SOLUTION

**1 *ANALYZE*** **Given:** identities of two gases, $H_2$ and $O_2$
**Unknown:** relative rates of effusion

**2 *PLAN*** molar mass ratio ⟶ ratio of rates of effusion

The ratio of the rates of effusion of two gases at the same temperature and pressure can be found from Graham's law.

$$\frac{\text{rate of effusion of A}}{\text{rate of effusion of B}} = \frac{\sqrt{M_B}}{\sqrt{M_A}}$$

**3 *COMPUTE***

$$\frac{\text{rate of effusion of } H_2}{\text{rate of effusion of } O_2} = \frac{\sqrt{M_{O_2}}}{\sqrt{M_{H_2}}} = \frac{\sqrt{32.00 \text{ g/mol}}}{\sqrt{2.02 \text{ g/mol}}} = \sqrt{\frac{32.00 \text{ g/mol}}{2.02 \text{ g/mol}}} = 3.98$$

Hydrogen effuses 3.98 times faster than oxygen.

**4 *EVALUATE*** The result is correctly reported to three significant figures. It is also approximately equivalent to an estimated value of 4, calculated as $\sqrt{32} / \sqrt{2}$.

**PRACTICE** *Answers in Appendix E*

1. Compare the rate of effusion of carbon dioxide with that of hydrogen chloride at the same temperature and pressure.
2. A sample of hydrogen effuses through a porous container about 9 times faster than an unknown gas. Estimate the molar mass of the unknown gas.
3. If a molecule of neon gas travels at an average of 400. m/s at a given temperature, estimate the average speed of a molecule of butane gas, $C_4H_{10}$, at the same temperature.

Go to **go.hrw.com** for additional problems that ask you to compare rates of effusion.

**Keyword: HC6GASX**

## SECTION REVIEW

1. Compare diffusion with effusion.
2. State Graham's law of effusion.
3. Estimate the molar mass of a gas that effuses at 1.6 times the effusion rate of carbon dioxide.
4. Determine the molecular mass ratio of two gases whose rates of effusion have a ratio of 16:1.
5. List the following gases in order of increasing average molecular velocity at 25°C: $H_2O$, He, HCl, BrF, and $NO_2$.

**Critical Thinking**

6. **ANALYZING INFORMATION** An unknown gas effuses at one-half the speed of oxygen. What is the molar mass of the unknown? The gas is known to be either HBr or HI. Which gas is it?

# CHAPTER HIGHLIGHTS

## Gases and Pressure

**Vocabulary**

pressure
newton
barometer
millimeters of mercury
atmosphere of pressure
pascal
partial pressure
Dalton's law of partial pressures

- The kinetic-molecular theory of gases describes an ideal gas. The behavior of most gases is nearly ideal except at very high pressures and low temperatures.
- A barometer measures atmospheric pressure.
- Dalton's law of partial pressure states that in a mixture of unreacting gases, the total pressure equals the sum of the partial pressures of each gas.

## The Gas Laws

**Vocabulary**

Boyle's law
absolute zero
Charles's law
Gay-Lussac's law
combined gas law

- Boyle's law states the inverse relationship between the volume and the pressure of a gas:
$$PV = k$$
- Charles's law illustrates the direct relationship between a gas's volume and its temperature in kelvins:
$$V = kT$$
- Gay-Lussac's law represents the direct relationship between a gas's pressure and its temperature in kelvins:
$$P = kT$$
- The combined gas law, as its name implies, combines the previous relationships into the following mathematical expression:
$$\frac{PV}{T} = k$$

## Gas Volumes and the Ideal Gas Law

**Vocabulary**

Gay-Lussac's law of combining volumes of gases
Avogadro's law
standard molar volume of a gas
ideal gas law
ideal gas constant

- Gay-Lussac's law of combining volumes states that the volumes of reacting gases and their products at the same temperature and pressure can be expressed as ratios of whole numbers.
- Avogadro's law states that equal volumes of gases at the same temperature and pressure contain equal numbers of molecules.
- The volume occupied by one mole of an ideal gas at STP is called the *standard molar volume,* which is 22.414 10 L.
- Charles's law, Boyle's law, and Avogadro's law can be combined to create the ideal gas law:
$$PV = nRT$$

## Diffusion and Effusion

**Vocabulary**

Graham's law of effusion

- Gases *diffuse,* or become more spread out, due to their constant random molecular motion.
- Graham's law of effusion states that the relative rates of effusion of gases at the same temperature and pressure are inversely proportional to the square roots of their molar masses.

# CHAPTER REVIEW

*For more practice, go to the Problem Bank in Appendix D.*

## Gases and Pressure

### SECTION 1 REVIEW

1. State the assumptions that the kinetic-molecular theory makes about the characteristics of gas particles.
2. What is an ideal gas?
3. a. Why does a gas in a closed container exert pressure?
   b. What is the relationship between the area a force is applied to and the resulting pressure?
4. a. Why does a column of mercury in a tube that is inverted in a dish of mercury have a height of about 760 mm at sea level?
   b. The density of water is approximately 1/13.5 the density of mercury. What height would be maintained by a column of water inverted in a dish of water at sea level?
   c. What accounts for the difference in the heights of the mercury and water columns?
5. a. Identify three units used to express pressure.
   b. Convert one atmosphere to millimeters of mercury.
   c. What is a pascal?
   d. What is the SI equivalent of one standard atmosphere of pressure?
6. a. Explain what is meant by the partial pressure of each gas within a mixture of gases.
   b. How do the partial pressures of gases in a mixture affect each other?

### PRACTICE PROBLEMS

7. If the atmosphere can support a column of mercury 760 mm high at sea level, what height of a hypothetical liquid whose density is 1.40 times the density of mercury could be supported?
8. Convert each of the following into a pressure reading expressed in torrs.
   a. 1.25 atm
   b. $2.48 \times 10^{-3}$ atm
   c. $4.75 \times 10^{4}$ atm
   d. $7.60 \times 10^{6}$ atm
9. Convert each of the following into the unit specified.
   a. 125 mm Hg into atmospheres
   b. 3.20 atm into pascals
   c. 5.38 kPa into millimeters of mercury
10. Three of the primary components of air are carbon dioxide, nitrogen, and oxygen. In a sample containing a mixture of only these gases at exactly 1 atm, the partial pressures of carbon dioxide and nitrogen are given as $P_{CO_2} = 0.285$ torr and $P_{N_2} = 593.525$ torr. What is the partial pressure of oxygen?
11. A sample of gas is collected over water at a temperature of 35.0°C when the barometric pressure reading is 742.0 torr. What is the partial pressure of the dry gas?

## The Gas Laws

### SECTION 2 REVIEW

12. How are the volume and pressure of a gas at constant temperature related?
13. Explain why pressure increases as a gas is compressed into a smaller volume.
14. How are the absolute temperature and volume of a gas at constant pressure related?
15. How are the pressure and absolute temperature of a gas at constant volume related?
16. Explain Gay-Lussac's law in terms of the kinetic-molecular theory.
17. State the combined gas law.

### PRACTICE PROBLEMS

18. Use Boyle's law to solve for the missing value in each of the following:
    a. $P_1 = 350.0$ torr, $V_1 = 200.0$ mL, $P_2 = 700.0$ torr, $V_2 = ?$
    b. $V_1 = 2.4 \times 10^5$ L, $P_2 = 180$ mm Hg, $V_2 = 1.8 \times 10^3$ L, $P_1 = ?$
19. Use Charles's law to solve for the missing value in each of the following:
    a. $V_1 = 80.0$ mL, $T_1 = 27°C$, $T_2 = 77°C$, $V_2 = ?$
    b. $V_1 = 125$ L, $V_2 = 85.0$ L, $T_2 = 127°C$, $T_1 = ?$
    c. $T_1 = -33°C$, $V_2 = 54.0$ mL, $T_2 = 160.0°C$, $V_1 = ?$

20. A sample of air has a volume of 140.0 mL at 67°C. At what temperature would its volume be 50.0 mL at constant pressure?
21. The pressure exerted on a 240.0 mL sample of hydrogen gas at constant temperature is increased from 0.428 atm to 0.724 atm. What will the final volume of the sample be?
22. A sample of hydrogen at 47°C exerts a pressure of 0.329 atm. The gas is heated to 77°C at constant volume. What will its new pressure be?
23. A sample of gas at 47°C and 1.03 atm occupies a volume of 2.20 L. What volume would this gas occupy at 107°C and 0.789 atm?
24. The pressure on a gas at –73°C is doubled, but its volume is held constant. What will the final temperature be in degrees Celsius?
25. A flask containing 155 $cm^3$ of hydrogen was collected under a pressure of 22.5 kPa. What pressure would have been required for the volume of the gas to have been 90.0 $cm^3$, assuming the same temperature?
26. A gas has a volume of 450.0 mL. If the temperature is held constant, what volume would the gas occupy if the pressure were
    a. doubled? (Hint: Express $P_2$ in terms of $P_1$.)
    b. reduced to one-fourth of its original value?
27. A sample of oxygen that occupies $1.00 \times 10^6$ mL at 575 mm Hg is subjected to a pressure of 1.25 atm. What will the final volume of the sample be if the temperature is held constant?
28. To what temperature must a sample of nitrogen at 27°C and 0.625 atm be taken so that its pressure becomes 1.125 atm at constant volume?
29. A gas has a volume of 1.75 L at –23°C and 150.0 kPa. At what temperature would the gas occupy 1.30 L at 210.0 kPa?
30. A gas at $7.75 \times 10^4$ Pa and 17°C occupies a volume of 850.0 $cm^3$. At what temperature, in degrees Celsius, would the gas occupy 720.0 $cm^3$ at $8.10 \times 10^4$ Pa?
31. A meteorological balloon contains 250.0 L He at 22°C and 740.0 mm Hg. If the volume of the balloon can vary according to external conditions, what volume would it occupy at an altitude at which the temperature is –52°C and the pressure is 0.750 atm?
32. The balloon in the previous problem will burst if its volume reaches 400.0 L. Given the initial conditions specified in that problem, determine at what temperature, in degrees Celsius, the balloon will burst if its pressure at that bursting point is 0.475 atm.
33. The normal respiratory rate for a human being is 15.0 breaths per minute. The average volume of air for each breath is 505 $cm^3$ at 20.0°C and $9.95 \times 10^4$ Pa. What is the volume of air at STP that an individual breathes in one day? Give your answer in cubic meters.

## *Gas Volumes and the Ideal Gas Law*

### SECTION 3 REVIEW

34. a. What are the restrictions on the use of Gay-Lussac's law of combining volumes?
    b. At the same temperature and pressure, what is the relationship between the volume of a gas and the number of molecules present?
35. a. In a balanced chemical equation, what is the relationship between the molar ratios and the volume ratios of gaseous reactants and products?
    b. What restriction applies to the use of the volume ratios in solving stoichiometry problems?
36. According to Avogadro,
    a. what is the relationship between gas volume and number of moles at constant temperature and pressure?
    b. what is the mathematical expression denoting this relationship?
37. What is the relationship between the number of molecules and the mass of 22.4 L of different gases at STP?
38. a. In what situations is the ideal gas law most suitable for calculations?
    b. When using this law, why do you have to pay particular attention to units?
39. a. Write the equation for the ideal gas law.
    b. What relationship is expressed in the ideal gas law?

**PRACTICE PROBLEMS**

**40.** Suppose a 5.00 L sample of $O_2$ at a given temperature and pressure contains $1.08 \times 10^{23}$ molecules. How many molecules would be contained in each of the following at the same temperature and pressure?
a. 5.0 L $H_2$
b. 5.0 L $CO_2$
c. 10.0 L $NH_3$

**41.** How many moles are contained in each of the following at STP?
a. 22.4 L $N_2$
b. 5.60 L $Cl_2$
c. 0.125 L Ne
d. 70.0 mL $NH_3$

**42.** Find the mass, in grams, of each of the following at STP.
a. 11.2 L $H_2$
b. 2.80 L $CO_2$
c. 15.0 mL $SO_2$
d. 3.40 $cm^3$ $F_2$

**43.** Find the volume, in liters, of each of the following at STP.
a. 8.00 g $O_2$
b. 3.50 g CO
c. 0.0170 g $H_2S$
d. $2.25 \times 10^5$ kg $NH_3$

**44.** Acetylene gas, $C_2H_2$, undergoes combustion to produce carbon dioxide and water vapor. If 75.0 L $CO_2$ is produced,
a. how many liters of $C_2H_2$ are required?
b. what volume of $H_2O$ vapor is produced?
c. what volume of $O_2$ is required?

**45.** Assume that 5.60 L $H_2$ at STP reacts with excess CuO according to the following equation:

$$CuO(s) + H_2(g) \longrightarrow Cu(s) + H_2O(g)$$

Make sure the equation is balanced before beginning your calculations.
a. How many moles of $H_2$ react?
b. How many moles of Cu are produced?
c. How many grams of Cu are produced?

**46.** If 29.0 L of methane, $CH_4$, undergoes complete combustion at 0.961 atm and 140°C, how many liters of each product would be present at the same temperature and pressure?

**47.** If air is 20.9% oxygen by volume,
a. how many liters of air are needed for complete combustion of 25.0 L of octane vapor, $C_8H_{18}$?
b. what volume of each product is produced?

**48.** Methanol, $CH_3OH$, is made by causing carbon monoxide and hydrogen gases to react at high temperature and pressure. If $4.50 \times 10^2$ mL CO and $8.25 \times 10^2$ mL $H_2$ are mixed,
a. which reactant is present in excess?
b. how much of that reactant remains after the reaction?
c. what volume of $CH_3OH$ is produced, assuming the same pressure?

**49.** Calculate the pressure, in atmospheres, exerted by each of the following:
a. 2.50 L HF containing 1.35 mol at 320.0 K
b. 4.75 L $NO_2$ containing 0.86 mol at 300.0 K
c. $5.50 \times 10^4$ mL $CO_2$ containing 2.15 mol at 57°C

**50.** Calculate the volume, in liters, occupied by each of the following:
a. 2.00 mol $H_2$ at 300.0 K and 1.25 atm
b. 0.425 mol $NH_3$ at 37°C and 0.724 atm
c. 4.00 g $O_2$ at 57°C and 0.888 atm

**51.** Determine the number of moles of gas contained in each of the following:
a. 1.25 L at 250.0 K and 1.06 atm
b. 0.80 L at 27°C and 0.925 atm
c. $7.50 \times 10^2$ mL at –50.0°C and 0.921 atm

**52.** Find the mass of each of the following.
a. 5.60 L $O_2$ at 1.75 atm and 250.0 K
b. 3.50 L $NH_3$ at 0.921 atm and 27°C
c. 125 mL $SO_2$ at 0.822 atm and –5°C

## *Diffusion and Effusion*

**SECTION 4 REVIEW**

**53.** Describe in your own words the process of diffusion.

**54.** At a given temperature, what factor determines the rates at which different molecules undergo diffusion and effusion?

**55.** Ammonia, $NH_3$, and alcohol, $C_2H_6O$, are released together across a room. Which will you smell first?

## PRACTICE PROBLEMS

**56.** Quantitatively compare the rates of effusion for the following pairs of gases at the same temperature and pressure:
a. hydrogen and nitrogen
b. fluorine and chlorine

**57.** What is the ratio of the average velocity of hydrogen molecules to that of neon atoms at the same temperature and pressure?

**58.** At a certain temperature and pressure, chlorine molecules have an average velocity of 324 m/s. What is the average velocity of sulfur dioxide molecules under the same conditions?

## MIXED REVIEW

**59.** A mixture of three gases, A, B, and C, is at a total pressure of 6.11 atm. The partial pressure of gas A is 1.68 atm; that of gas B is 3.89 atm. What is the partial pressure of gas C?

**60.** A child receives a balloon filled with 2.30 L of helium from a vendor at an amusement park. The temperature outside is 311 K. What will the volume of the balloon be when the child brings it home to an air-conditioned house at 295 K? Assume that the pressure stays the same.

**61.** A sample of argon gas occupies a volume of 295 mL at 36°C. What volume will the gas occupy at 55°C, assuming constant pressure?

**62.** A sample of carbon dioxide gas occupies 638 mL at 0.893 atm and 12°C. What will the pressure be at a volume of 881 mL and a temperature of 18°C?

**63.** At 84°C, a gas in a container exerts a pressure of 0.503 atm. Assuming the size of the container has not changed, at what temperature in Celsius degrees would the pressure be 1.20 atm?

**64.** A weather balloon at Earth's surface has a volume of 4.00 L at 304 K and 755 mm Hg. If the balloon is released and the volume reaches 4.08 L at 728 mm Hg, what is the temperature?

**65.** A gas has a pressure of 4.62 atm when its volume is 2.33 L. If the temperature remains constant, what will the pressure be when the volume is changed to 1.03 L? Express the final pressure in torrs.

**66.** At a deep-sea station that is 200. m below the surface of the Pacific Ocean, workers live in a highly pressurized environment. How many liters of gas at STP must be compressed on the surface to fill the underwater environment with $2.00 \times 10^7$ L of gas at 20.0 atm? Assume that temperature remains constant.

**67.** An unknown gas effuses at 0.850 times the effusion rate of nitrogen dioxide, $NO_2$. Estimate the molar mass of the unknown gas.

**68.** A container holds 265 mL of chlorine gas, $Cl_2$. If the gas sample is at STP, what is its mass?

**69.** Suppose that 3.11 mol of carbon dioxide is at a pressure of 0.820 atm and a temperature of 39°C. What is the volume of the sample, in liters?

**70.** Compare the rates of diffusion of carbon monoxide, CO, and sulfur trioxide, $SO_3$.

**71.** A gas sample that has a mass of 0.993 g occupies 0.570 L. Given that the temperature is 281 K and the pressure is 1.44 atm, what is the molar mass of the gas?

**72.** How many moles of helium gas would it take to fill a balloon with a volume of 1000.0 $cm^3$ when the temperature is 32°C and the atmospheric pressure is 752 mm Hg?

**73.** A gas sample is collected at 16°C and 0.982 atm. If the sample has a mass of 7.40 g and a volume of 3.96 L, find the volume of the gas at STP and the molar mass.

## CRITICAL THINKING

**74. Applying Models**
a. Why do we say the graph in **Figure 7** illustrates an inverse relationship?
b. Why do we say the data plotted in **Figure 9** indicates a direct relationship?

**75. Inferring Conclusions** If all gases behaved as ideal gases under all conditions of temperature and pressure, solid or liquid forms of these substances would not exist. Explain.

**76. Relating Ideas** Pressure is defined as force per unit area. Yet Torricelli found that the diameter of the barometer dish and the surface area of contact between the mercury in the tube and in the dish did not affect the height of mercury that was supported. Explain this seemingly inconsistent observation in view of the relationship between pressure and surface area.

**77. Evaluating Methods** In solving a problem, what types of conditions involving temperature, pressure, volume, or number of moles would allow you to use
a. the combined gas law?
b. the ideal gas law?

**78. Evaluating Ideas** Gay-Lussac's law of combining volumes holds true for relative volumes at any proportionate size. Use Avogadro's law to explain why this proportionality exists.

**79. Interpreting Graphics** The graph below shows velocity distribution curves for the same gas under two different conditions, A and B. Compare the behavior of the gas under conditions A and B in relation to each of the following:
a. temperature
b. average kinetic energy
c. average molecular velocity
d. gas volume
e. gas pressure

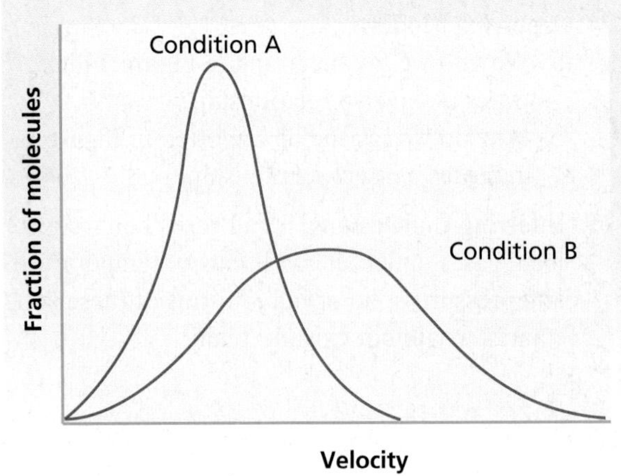


**80. Interpreting Concepts** The diagrams below represent equal volumes of four different gases.

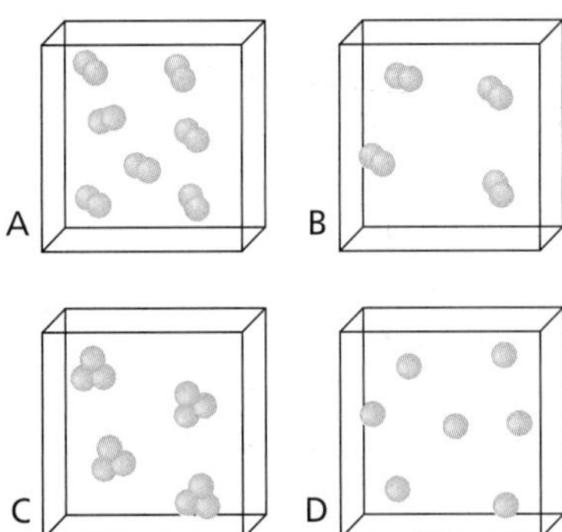


Use the diagrams to answer the following questions:
a. Are these gases at the same temperature and pressure? How do you know?
b. If the molar mass of gas B is 38 g/mol and that of gas C is 46 g/mol, which gas sample is denser?
c. To make the densities of gas samples B and C equal, which gas should expand in volume?
d. If the densities of gas samples A and C are equal, what is the relationship between their molar masses?

## RESEARCH & WRITING

**81.** Design and conduct a meteorological study to examine the interrelationships between barometric pressure, temperature, humidity, and other weather variables. Prepare a report explaining your results.

**82.** Conduct library research on attempts made to approach absolute zero and on the interesting properties that materials exhibit near that temperature. Write a report on your findings.

**83.** How do scuba divers use the laws and principles that describe the behavior of gases to their advantage? What precautions do they take to prevent the bends?

**84.** Explain the processes involved in the liquefaction of gases. Name some substances that are gases under normal room conditions and that are typically used in the liquid form. Explain why this is so.

85. Write a summary describing how Gay-Lussac's work on combining volumes relates to Avogadro's study of gases. Explain how certain conclusions about gases followed logically from consideration of the work of both scientists.

## USING THE HANDBOOK

86. Review the melting point data in the properties tables for each group of the *Elements Handbook*. What elements on the periodic table exist as gases at room temperature?
87. Review in the *Elements Handbook* the listing of the top 10 chemicals produced in the United States. Which of the top 10 chemicals are gases?
88. Most elements from Groups 1, 2, and 13 will react with water, acids, or bases to produce hydrogen gas. Review the common reactions information in the *Elements Handbook* and answer the following questions:
   a. What is the equation for the reaction of barium with water?
   b. What is the equation for the reaction between cesium and hydrochloric acid?
   c. What is the equation for the reaction of gallium with hydrofluoric acid?
   d. What mass of barium would be needed to react with excess water to produce 10.1 L $H_2$ at STP?
   e. What masses of cesium and hydrochloric acid would be required to produce 10.1 L $H_2$ at STP?
89. Group 1 metals react with oxygen to produce oxides, peroxides, or superoxides. Review the equations for these common reactions in the *Elements Handbook*, and answer the following:
   a. How do oxides, peroxides, and superoxides differ?
   b. What mass of product will be formed from a reaction of 5.00 L $O_2$ with excess sodium? The reaction occurs at 27°C and 1 atm.

## ALTERNATIVE ASSESSMENT

90. The air pressure of car tires should be checked regularly for safety reasons and for prevention of uneven tire wear. Find out the units of measurement on a typical tire gauge, and determine how gauge pressure relates to atmospheric pressure.
91. During a typical day, record every instance in which you encounter the diffusion or effusion of gases (for example, when smelling perfume).
92. **Performance** Qualitatively compare the molecular masses of various gases by noting how long it takes you to smell them from a fixed distance. Work only with materials that are not dangerous, such as flavor extracts, fruit peels, and onions.
93. **Performance** Design an experiment to gather data to verify the ideal gas law. If your teacher approves of your plan, carry it out. Illustrate your data with a graph, and determine if the data are consistent with the ideal gas law.

**extension**

**Graphing Calculator**
**Using the Ideal Gas Law**

Go to **go.hrw.com** for a graphing calculator exercise that asks you to use the ideal gas law.

**Keyword: HC6GASX**

# *Math Tutor* ALGEBRAIC REARRANGEMENTS OF GAS LAWS

When you solve problems in chemistry, it's usually a bad idea to just start entering numbers into a calculator. Instead, doing a little pencil-and-paper work beforehand will help you eliminate errors. When using the gas laws, you do not need to memorize all of the equations because they are easily derived from the equation for the combined gas law, $\frac{P_1V_1}{T_1} = \frac{P_2V_2}{T_2}$. Study the table below. In each of Boyle's, Charles's, and Gay-Lussac's laws, one of the quantities—*T*, *P*, or *V*—does not change. By simply eliminating that factor from the equation, you obtain the equation for one particular gas law.

| Gas law | Held constant | Cancellation | Result |
|---|---|---|---|
| Combined gas law | none | $\frac{P_1V_1}{T_1} = \frac{P_2V_2}{T_2}$ | $\frac{P_1V_1}{T_1} = \frac{P_2V_2}{T_2}$ |
| Boyle's law | temperature | $\frac{P_1V_1}{\cancel{T_1}} = \frac{P_2V_2}{\cancel{T_2}}$ | $P_1V_1 = P_2V_2$ |
| Charles's law | pressure | $\frac{\cancel{P_1}V_1}{T_1} = \frac{\cancel{P_2}V_2}{T_2}$ | $\frac{V_1}{T_1} = \frac{V_2}{T_2}$ |
| Gay-Lussac's law | volume | $\frac{P_1\cancel{V_1}}{T_1} = \frac{P_2\cancel{V_2}}{T_2}$ | $\frac{P_1}{T_1} = \frac{P_2}{T_2}$ |

The conditions stated in the problem should make clear which factors change and which are held constant. This information will tell you which law's equation you need to use.

## SAMPLE

**A cylinder of nitrogen gas has a volume of 35.00 L at a pressure of 11.50 atm. What pressure will the nitrogen have if the contents of the cylinder are allowed to flow into a sealed reaction chamber whose volume is 140.0 L, and if the temperature remains constant?**

Start with the combined gas law, and cancel the temperature, which does not change.

$$\frac{P_1V_1}{\cancel{T_1}} = \frac{P_2V_2}{\cancel{T_2}};\ P_1V_1 = P_2V_2$$

You want to know the new pressure in the chamber, so solve for $P_2$.

$$\frac{P_1V_1}{V_2} = \frac{P_2\cancel{V_2}}{\cancel{V_2}};\ \frac{P_1V_1}{V_2} = P_2$$

The resulting equation to use in solving the problem is $P_2 = \frac{P_1V_1}{V_2} = \frac{(11.50 \text{ atm})(35.00 \text{ L})}{140.0 \text{ L}}$ = 2.875 atm.

## PRACTICE PROBLEMS

1. A sample of gas has a pressure $P_1$ at a temperature $T_1$. Write the equation that you would use to find the temperature, $T_2$ at which the gas has a pressure of $P_2$.

2. An ideal gas occupies a volume of 785 mL at a pressure of 0.879 atm. What volume will the gas occupy at a pressure of 0.994 atm?

# Standardized Test Prep

Answer the following items on a separate piece of paper.

**MULTIPLE CHOICE**

**1.** Pressure can be measured in
**A.** grams. **C.** pascals.
**B.** meters. **D.** liters.

**2.** A sample of oxygen gas has a volume of 150 mL when its pressure is 0.923 atm. If the pressure is increased to 0.987 atm and the temperature remains constant, what will the new volume be?
**A.** 140 mL **C.** 200 mL
**B.** 160 mL **D.** 240 mL

**3.** What is the pressure exerted by a 0.500 mol sample of nitrogen in a 10.0 L container at 20°C?
**A.** 1.2 kPa **C.** 0.10 kPa
**B.** 10 kPa **D.** 120 kPa

**4.** A sample of gas in a closed container at a temperature of 100.0°C and 3.0 atm is heated to 300.0°C. What is the pressure of the gas at the higher temperature?
**A.** 35 atm **C.** 59 atm
**B.** 4.6 atm **D.** 9.0 atm

**5.** An unknown gas effuses twice as fast as $CH_4$. What is the molar mass of the gas?
**A.** 64 g/mol **C.** 8 g/mol
**B.** 32 g/mol **D.** 4 g/mol

**6.** If 3 L $N_2$ and 3 L $H_2$ are mixed and react according to the equation below, how many liters of unreacted gas remain? Assume temperature and pressure remain constant.

$$N_2(g) + 3H_2(g) \longrightarrow 2NH_3(g)$$

**A.** 4 L **C.** 2 L
**B.** 3 L **D.** 1 L

**7.** Avogadro's law states that
**A.** equal numbers of moles of gases at the same conditions occupy equal volumes, regardless of the identity of the gases.
**B.** at constant pressure, gas volume is directly proportional to absolute temperature.
**C.** the volume of a gas is inversely proportional to its amount in moles.
**D.** at constant temperature, gas volume is inversely proportional to pressure.

**SHORT ANSWER**

**8.** Give a molecular explanation for the observation that the pressure of a gas increases when the gas volume is decreased.

**9.** The graph below shows a plot of volume versus pressure for a particular gas sample at constant temperature. Answer the following questions by referring to the graph. No calculation is necessary.
a. What is the volume of this gas sample at standard pressure?
b. What is the volume of this gas sample at 4.0 atm pressure?
c. At what pressure would this gas sample occupy a volume of 5.0 L?

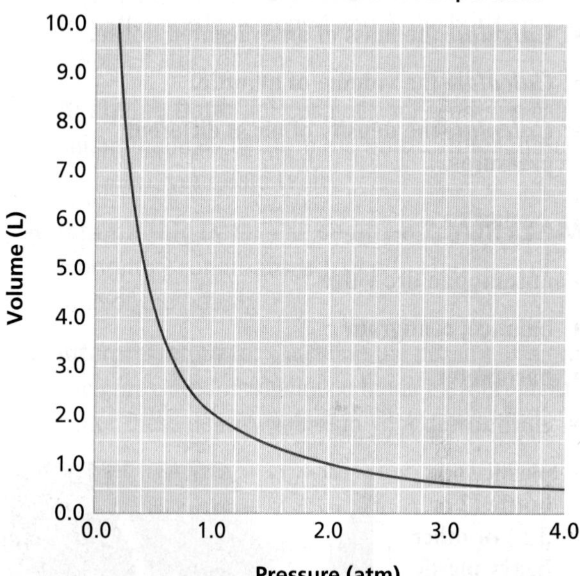


**EXTENDED RESPONSE**

**10.** Refer to the plot in question 9. Suppose the same gas sample were heated to a higher temperature and a new graph of *V* versus *P* were plotted. Would the new plot be identical to this one? If not, how would it differ?

**Test TIP** If you are permitted to, draw a line through each incorrect answer choice as you eliminate it.

**34.** Sodium metal reacts violently with water to form NaOH and release hydrogen gas. Suppose that 10.0 g of Na react completely with 1.00 L of water and the final solution volume is 1.00 L.
a. What is the molar mass of NaOH?
b. Write a balanced equation for the reaction.
c. What is the molarity of the NaOH solution formed by the reaction?

**35.** In cars, ethylene glycol, $C_2H_6O_2$, is used as a coolant and antifreeze. A mechanic fills a radiator with 6.5 kg of ethylene glycol and 1.5 kg of water.
a. What is the molar mass of ethylene glycol?
b. What is the molality of the water in the solution?

**36.** Plot a solubility graph for $AgNO_3$ from the following data, with grams of solute (by increments of 50) per 100 g of $H_2O$ on the vertical axis and with temperature in °C on the horizontal axis.

| Grams solute per 100 g $H_2O$ | Temperature (°C) |
|---|---|
| 122 | 0 |
| 216 | 30 |
| 311 | 40 |
| 440 | 60 |
| 585 | 80 |
| 733 | 100 |

a. How does the solubility of $AgNO_3$ vary with the temperature of the water?
b. Estimate the solubility of $AgNO_3$ at 35°C, 55°C, and 75°C.
c. At what temperature would the solubility of $AgNO_3$ be 275 g per 100 g of $H_2O$?
d. If 100 g of $AgNO_3$ were added to 100 g of $H_2O$ at 10°C, would the resulting solution be saturated or unsaturated? What would occur if 325 g of $AgNO_3$ were added to 100 g of $H_2O$ at 35°C?

**37.** If a saturated solution of $KNO_3$ in 100. g of $H_2O$ at 60°C is cooled to 20°C, approximately how many grams of the solute will precipitate out of the solution? (Use **Table 4.**)

**38.** a. Suppose you wanted to dissolve 294.3 g of $H_2SO_4$ in 1.000 kg of $H_2O$.
(1) What is the solute?
(2) What is the solvent?
(3) What is the molality of this solution?
b. What is the molality of a solution of 63.0 g $HNO_3$ in 0.250 kg $H_2O$?

## CRITICAL THINKING

**39. Predicting Outcomes** You have been investigating the nature of suspensions, colloids, and solutions and have collected the following observational data on four unknown samples. From the data, infer whether each sample is a solution, suspension, or colloid.

**DATA TABLE 1** *Samples*

| Sample | Color | Clarity (clear or cloudy) | Settle out | Tyndall effect |
|---|---|---|---|---|
| 1 | green | clear | no | no |
| 2 | blue | cloudy | yes | no |
| 3 | colorless | clear | no | yes |
| 4 | white | cloudy | no | yes |

Based on your inferences in Data Table 1, you decide to conduct one more test of the particles. You filter the samples and then reexamine the filtrate. You obtain the data found in Data Table 2. Infer the classifications of the filtrate based on the data in Data Table 2.

**DATA TABLE 2** *Filtrate of Samples*

| Sample | Color | Clarity (clear or cloudy) | On filter paper | Tyndall effect |
|---|---|---|---|---|
| 1 | green | clear | nothing | no |
| 2 | blue | cloudy | gray solid | yes |
| 3 | colorless | clear | none | yes |
| 4 | colorless | clear | white solid | no |

## USING THE HANDBOOK

**40.** Review the information on alloys in the Elements Handbook.

a. Why is aluminum such an important component of alloys?

b. What metals make up bronze?

c. What metals make up brass?

d. What is steel?

e. What is the composition of the mixture called *cast iron?*

**41.** **Table 5A** of the *Elements Handbook* contains carbon monoxide concentration data expressed as parts per million (ppm). The OSHA (Occupational Safety and Health Administration) limit for worker exposure to CO is 200 ppm for an eight-hour period.

a. At what concentration do harmful effects occur in less than one hour?

b. By what factor does the concentration in item (a) exceed the maximum limit set by OSHA?

## RESEARCH & WRITING

**42.** Find out about the chemistry of emulsifying agents. How do these substances affect the dissolution of immiscible substances such as oil and water? As part of your research on this topic, find out why eggs are an emulsifying agent for baking mixtures.

## ALTERNATIVE ASSESSMENT

**43.** Make a comparison of the electrolyte concentration in various brands of sports drinks. Using the labeling information for sugar, calculate the molarity of sugar in each product or brand. Construct a poster to show the results of your analysis of the product labels.

**44.** Write a set of instructions on how to prepare a solution that is 1 M $CuSO_4$ using $CuSO_4 \cdot 5H_2O$ as the solute. How do the instructions differ if the solute is anhydrous $CuSO_4$? Your instructions should include a list of all materials needed.

extension

**Graphing Calculator**

**Solubility vs. Temperature**

Go to **go.hrw.com** for a graphing calculator exercise that asks you to graph the solubility versus temperatures for NaCl and $KNO_3$.

**Keyword:** HC6SLNX

# Math Tutor CALCULATING SOLUTION CONCENTRATION

You can use the relationship below to calculate the concentration in molarity of any solution.

$$\text{molarity of solution (M)} = \frac{\text{moles of solute (mol)}}{\text{volume of solution (L)}}$$

Suppose you dissolve 20.00 g of NaOH in some water and dilute the solution to a volume of 250.0 mL (0.2500 L). You don't know the molarity of this solution until you know how many moles of NaOH were dissolved. You know that the number of moles of a substance can be found by dividing the mass of the substance by the mass of 1 mol (molar mass) of the substance. The molar mass of NaOH is 40.00, so the number of moles of NaOH dissolved is

$$20.00\text{ g NaOH} \times \frac{1\text{ mol NaOH}}{40.00\text{ g NaOH}} = 0.5000\text{ mol NaOH}$$

Now you know that the solution has 0.5000 mol NaOH dissolved in 0.2500 L of solution, so you can calculate molarity.

$$\text{molarity of NaOH} \times \frac{\text{mol NaOH}}{\text{L solution}} = \frac{0.5000\text{ mol NaOH}}{0.2500\text{ L solution}} = 2.000\text{ mol/L} = 2.000\text{ M NaOH}$$

## Problem-Solving *TIPS*

- Remember that balances measure mass, not moles, so you often have to convert between mass and moles of solute when making or using solutions.

## SAMPLE

**A 0.5000 L volume of a solution contains 36.49 g of magnesium chloride, $MgCl_2$. What is the molarity of the solution?**

You know the volume of the solution, but you need to find the number of moles of the solute $MgCl_2$ by the following conversion.

$$\text{mass } MgCl_2 \times \frac{1\text{ mol } MgCl_2}{\text{molar mass } MgCl_2} = \text{mol } MgCl_2$$

$$36.49\text{ g } \cancel{MgCl_2} \times \frac{1\text{ mol } MgCl_2}{95.20\text{ g } \cancel{MgCl_2}} = 0.3833\text{ mol } MgCl_2$$

Now you can calculate mol $MgCl_2$ per liter of solution (molarity).

$$\frac{0.3833\text{ mol } MgCl_2}{0.5000\text{ L solution}} = 0.7666\text{ M } MgCl_2$$

## PRACTICE PROBLEMS

1. What is the molarity of a solution that contains 0.0350 mol of sodium sulfate, $Na_2SO_4$, dissolved in 50.0 mL of solution?

2. What is the molarity of a solution that contains 45.00 g of cadmium nitrate, $Cd(NO_3)_2$, dissolved in 400.0 mL of solution?

# Standardized Test Prep

**Answer the following items on a separate piece of paper.**

**MULTIPLE CHOICE**

**1.** Water is an excellent solvent because
**A.** it is a covalent compound.
**B.** it is a nonconductor of electricity.
**C.** its molecules are quite polar.
**D.** it is a clear, colorless liquid.

**2.** Two liquids are likely to be immiscible if
**A.** both have polar molecules.
**B.** both have nonpolar molecules.
**C.** one is polar and the other is nonpolar.
**D.** one is water and the other is methyl alcohol, $CH_3OH$.

**3.** The solubility of a gas in a liquid would be increased by an
**A.** addition of an electrolyte.
**B.** addition of an emulsifier.
**C.** agitation of the solution.
**D.** increase in its partial pressure.

**4.** Which of the following types of compounds is most likely to be a strong electrolyte?
**A.** a polar compound
**B.** a nonpolar compound
**C.** a covalent compound
**D.** an ionic compound

**5.** A saturated solution can become supersaturated under which of the following conditions?
**A.** It contains electrolytes.
**B.** The solution is heated and then allowed to cool.
**C.** More solvent is added.
**D.** More solute is added.

**6.** Molarity is expressed in units of
**A.** moles of solute per liter of solution.
**B.** liters of solution per mole of solute.
**C.** moles of solute per liter of solvent.
**D.** liters of solvent per mole of solute.

**7.** What mass of NaOH is contained in 2.5 L of a 0.010 M solution?
**A.** 0.010 g
**B.** 1.0 g
**C.** 2.5 g
**D.** 0.40 g

**8.** Which one of the following statements is false?
**A.** Gases are generally more soluble in water under high pressures than under low pressures.
**B.** As temperature increases, the solubilities of some solids in water increase and the solubilities of other solids in water decrease.
**C.** Water dissolves many ionic solutes because of its ability to hydrate ions in solution.
**D.** Many solids dissolve more quickly in a cold solvent than in a warm solvent.

**SHORT ANSWER**

**9.** Several experiments are carried out to determine the solubility of cadmium iodide, $CdI_2$, in water. In each experiment, a measured mass of $CdI_2$ is added to 100 g of water at 25°C and the mixture is stirred. Any undissolved $CdI_2$ is then filtered off and dried, and its mass is determined. Results for several such experiments are shown in the table below. What is the solubility of $CdI_2$ in water at this temperature?

| Mass of $CdI_2$ added, g | Mass of undissolved $CdI_2$ recovered, g |
|---|---|
| 17.9 | 0.0 |
| 38.2 | 0.0 |
| 53.6 | 0.0 |
| 79.3 | 0.0 |
| 93.6 | 7.4 |
| 104.3 | 18.1 |

**EXTENDED RESPONSE**

**10.** Explain why oil and water do not mix.

**11.** Write a set of instructions on how to prepare a solution that is 0.100 M KBr, using solid KBr (molar mass 119 g/mol) as the solute. Your instructions should include a list of all materials and equipment needed.

**Test TIP** Allow a few minutes at the end of the test-taking period to check for careless mistakes, such as marking two answers for a single question.

SEE PRE-LAB
PAPER CHROMATOGRAPHY

# Separation of Pen Inks by Paper Chromatography

## OBJECTIVES

- ***Demonstrate*** **proficiency in qualitatively separating mixtures using paper chromatography.**
- ***Determine*** **the $R_f$ factor(s) for each component of each tested ink.**
- ***Explain*** **how the inks are separated by paper chromatography.**
- ***Observe*** **the separation of a mixture by the method of paper chromatography.**

## MATERIALS

- **12 cm circular chromatography paper or filter paper**
- **distilled water**
- **filter paper wick, 2 cm equilateral triangle**
- **isopropanol**
- **numbered pens, each with a different black ink, 4**
- **pencil**
- **petri dish with lid**
- **scissors**

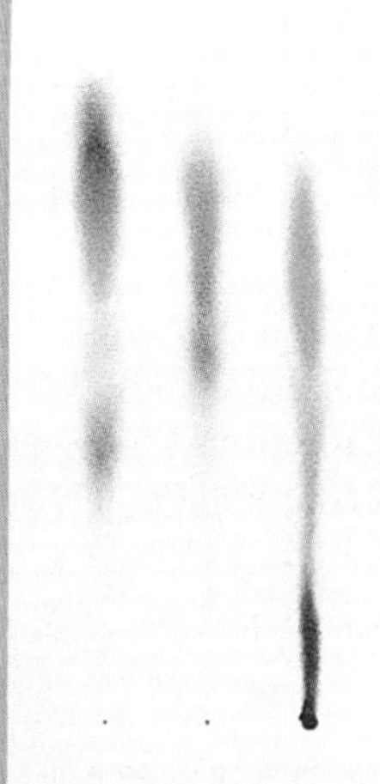

**FIGURE A** Paper chromatography reveals the different colored dyes that black ink contains.

## BACKGROUND

### Paper Chromatography

Details on this technique can be found in the Pre-Laboratory Procedure "Paper Chromatography" on page 848.

### Writing Inks

Most ballpoint pen inks are complex mixtures, containing pigments or dyes that can be separated by paper chromatography, as shown in **Figure A.**

Black inks can contain three or more colors; the number of colors depends on the manufacturer. Each ink formulation has a characteristic pattern that uniquely identifies it.

In this experiment you will develop radial paper chromatograms for four black ballpoint pen inks, using water as solvent. You will then repeat this process using isopropanol as the solvent. You will then measure the distance traveled by each of the individual ink components and the distance traveled by the solvent front. Finally, you will use these measurements to calculate the $R_f$ factor for each component.

## SAFETY

For review of safety, please see **Safety in the Chemistry Laboratory** in the front of your book.

## PREPARATION

1. Determine the formula, structure, polarity, density, and volatility at room temperature for water and isopropanol. The following titles are sources that provide general information on specific elements and compounds: *CRC Handbook of Chemistry and Physics, McGraw-Hill Dictionary of Chemical Terms,* and *Merck Index.*

2. Prepare two data tables, one for the chromatogram made with water and one for the chromatogram made with isopropanol. Record the pen number you are testing. In your data tables, create columns for each color in which to record the distance and $R_f$ value. Your teacher can provide you with sample data tables. Leave room below each data table to record the distance that the solvent reaches.

## PROCEDURE

### Part A: Prepare a chromatogram using water as the solvent

1. Construct an apparatus for paper chromatography as described in the Pre-Laboratory Procedure on page 848. You will make only four dots. You will use ballpoint pens rather than micropipets to spot your paper.

2. After 15 min or when the water is about 1 cm from the outside edge of the paper, remove the paper from the Petri dish and allow the chromatogram to dry. Record in the data table the colors that have separated from each of the four different black inks.

### Part B: Prepare a chromatogram using isopropanol as the solvent

3. Repeat Procedure steps 1 to 2, replacing the water in the Petri dish with isopropanol.

### Part C: Determine $R_f$ values for each component

4. After the chromatogram is dry, use a pencil to mark the point where the solvent front stopped.

5. With a ruler, measure the distance from the initial ink spot to your mark, and record this distance on your data table.

6. Make a small dot with your pencil in the center of each color band.

7. With a ruler, measure the distance from the initial ink spot to each dot separately, and record each distance on your data table.

8. Divide each value recorded in Procedure step 7 by the value recorded in Procedure step 5. The result is the $R_f$ value for that component. Record the $R_f$ values in your data table. Tape or staple the chromatogram to your data table.

## CLEANUP AND DISPOSAL

9. The water may be poured down the sink. Chromatograms and other pieces of filter paper may be discarded in the trash. The isopropanol solution should be placed in the waste disposal container designated by your teacher. Clean up your equipment and lab station. Thoroughly wash your hands after completing the lab session and cleanup.

## ANALYSIS AND INTERPRETATION

1. **Evaluating Conclusions:** Is the color in each pen the result of a single dye or multiple dyes? Justify your answer.

2. **Relating Ideas:** What can be said about the properties of a component ink that has an $R_f$ value of 0.50?

3. **Analyzing Methods:** Suggest a reason for stopping the process when the solvent front is 1 cm from the edge of the filter paper rather than when it is even with the edge of the paper.

4. **Predicting Outcomes:** Predict the results of forgetting to remove the chromatogram from the water in the petri dish until the next day.

## CONCLUSIONS

1. **Analyzing Results:** Compare the $R_f$ values for the colors from pen number 2 when water was the solvent and the $R_f$ values obtained when isopropanol was the solvent. Explain why they differ.

2. **Evaluating Methods:** Would you consider isopropanol a better choice for the solvent than water? Why or why not?

3. **Analyzing Conclusions:** Are the properties of the component that traveled the farthest in the water chromatogram likely to be similar to the properties of the component that traveled the farthest in the isopropanol chromatogram? Explain your reasoning.

4. **Inferring Conclusions:** What can you conclude about the composition of the inks in ballpoint pens from your chromatogram?

CHAPTER 13

# Ions in Aqueous Solutions and Colligative Properties

*These formations were made by the precipitation of ionic compounds from an aqueous solution.*

Cyanotrichite Crystals

# Compounds in Aqueous Solutions

SC C.6.12 Use solubility rules to write net ionic equations for precipitation reactions in aqueous solution

SECTION 1

## Objectives

- Write equations for the dissolution of soluble ionic compounds in water.
- Predict whether a precipitate will form when solutions of soluble ionic compounds are combined, and write net ionic equations for precipitation reactions.
- Compare dissociation of ionic compounds with ionization of molecular compounds.
- Draw the structure of the hydronium ion, and explain why it is used to represent the hydrogen ion in solution.
- Distinguish between strong electrolytes and weak electrolytes.

As you have learned, solid compounds can be ionic or molecular. In an ionic solid, a crystal structure is made up of charged particles held together by ionic attractions. In a molecular solid, molecules are composed of covalently bonded atoms. The solid is held together by noncovalent, intermolecular forces. When they dissolve in water, ionic compounds and molecular compounds behave differently.

## Dissociation

When a compound that is made of ions dissolves in water, the ions separate from one another, as shown in **Figure 1.** *This separation of ions that occurs when an ionic compound dissolves is called* **dissociation.** For example, dissociation of sodium chloride and calcium chloride in water can be represented by the following equations. (As usual, (*s*) indicates a solid species, and (*aq*) indicates a species in an aqueous solution. Note that each equation is balanced for charge as well as for atoms.)

$$NaCl(s) \xrightarrow{H_2O} Na^+(aq) + Cl^-(aq)$$

$$CaCl_2(s) \xrightarrow{H_2O} Ca^{2+}(aq) + 2Cl^-(aq)$$

Notice the number of ions produced per formula unit in the equations above. One formula unit of sodium chloride gives two ions in solution, whereas one formula unit of calcium chloride gives three ions in solution.

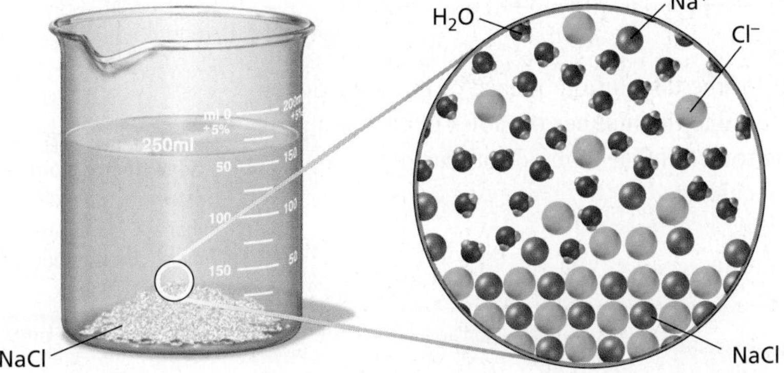


**FIGURE 1** When NaCl dissolves in water, the ions separate as they leave the crystal.

Assuming 100% dissociation, a solution that contains 1 mol of sodium chloride contains 1 mol of $Na^+$ ions and 1 mol of $Cl^-$ ions. In this book, you can assume 100% dissociation for all soluble ionic compounds. The dissociation of NaCl can be represented as follows.

$$\underset{1\text{ mol}}{NaCl(s)} \xrightarrow{H_2O} \underset{1\text{ mol}}{Na^+(aq)} + \underset{1\text{ mol}}{Cl^-(aq)}$$

A solution that contains 1 mol of calcium chloride contains 1 mol of $Ca^{2+}$ ions and 2 mol of $Cl^-$ ions—a total of 3 mol of ions.

$$\underset{1\text{ mol}}{CaCl_2(s)} \xrightarrow{H_2O} \underset{1\text{ mol}}{Ca^{2+}(aq)} + \underset{2\text{ mol}}{2Cl^-(aq)}$$

## SAMPLE PROBLEM A

**Write the equation for the dissolution of aluminum sulfate, $Al_2(SO_4)_3$, in water. How many moles of aluminum ions and sulfate ions are produced by dissolving 1 mol of aluminum sulfate? What is the total number of moles of ions produced by dissolving 1 mol of aluminum sulfate?**

### SOLUTION

**1 *ANALYZE***

**Given:** amount of solute = 1 mol $Al_2(SO_4)_3$
solvent identity = water

**Unknown:** **a.** moles of aluminum ions and sulfate ions
**b.** total number of moles of solute ions produced

**2 *PLAN***

The coefficients in the balanced dissociation equation will reveal the mole relationships, so you can use the equation to determine the number of moles of solute ions produced.

$$Al_2(SO_4)_3(s) \xrightarrow{H_2O} 2Al^{3+}(aq) + 3SO_4^{2-}(aq)$$

**3 *COMPUTE***

**a.** 1 mol $Al_2(SO_4)_3 \rightarrow$ 2 mol $Al^{3+}$ + 3 mol $SO_4^{2-}$
**b.** 2 mol $Al^{3+}$ + 3 mol $SO_4^{2-}$ = 5 mol of solute ions

**4 *EVALUATE***

The equation is correctly balanced. Because one formula unit of $Al_2(SO_4)_3$ produces 5 ions, 1 mol of $Al_2(SO_4)_3$ produces 5 mol of ions.

### PRACTICE

*Answers in Appendix E*

1. Write the equation for the dissolution of each of the following in water, and then determine the number of moles of each ion produced as well as the total number of moles of ions produced.
   **a.** 1 mol ammonium chloride
   **b.** 1 mol sodium sulfide
   **c.** 0.5 mol barium nitrate

**extension**

Go to **go.hrw.com** for more practice problems that ask you to calculate moles of ions produced in dissociation.

**Keyword: HC6IONX**

### Faraday Provides a Spark

Although Michael Faraday is best remembered for his work in electromagnetism, he began his career as Humphry Davy's laboratory assistant at the Royal Institution in London and went on to be the professor of chemistry there for over 30 years. In the 1830s, Faraday devised several ingenious experiments to determine whether the current in an electrolytic solution is dependent solely on the contact of the battery's poles with the solution. In a typical setup, one of the poles was separated from the solution, and electricity was permitted to enter the solution by way of a spark. In all cases, Faraday observed current in the electrolytic cell despite one or both of the poles not being in direct contact with the electrolytic solution. In 1833, he made the hypothesis that the process of electrolysis was due to the intrinsic properties of the metals in solution and the effect of current on these properties.

Although the battery's poles were, in fact, later shown to play a part in the current, Faraday had established the active role of the electrolytic solution in electrolysis. And in realizing that electricity affected the chemical nature of the solution, he anticipated the ideas of oxidation and reduction despite that the concepts of electrons and ions were unknown at the time.

### Faraday's Legacy

Faraday continued to study the role of the electrolytic solution, or electrolyte, as he named it, in electrolysis. He also coined most of the other modern terms of electrolysis, including *electrode, ion, anode, cathode, anion,* and *cation.* These investigations culminated in the discovery of his basic laws of electrolysis.

Still valid today, these principles put electrolysis on a quantitative footing, leading to our current understanding of the phenomenon. They also bolstered the atomic theory, which was still seriously contested by many chemists at the time. And perhaps most important, Faraday's experiments inspired his successors to further clarify the chemical nature of solutions. This ultimately led to Svante Arrhenius's theory of electrolytic dissociation and the evolution of a new division in the chemical field, known today as *physical chemistry.*

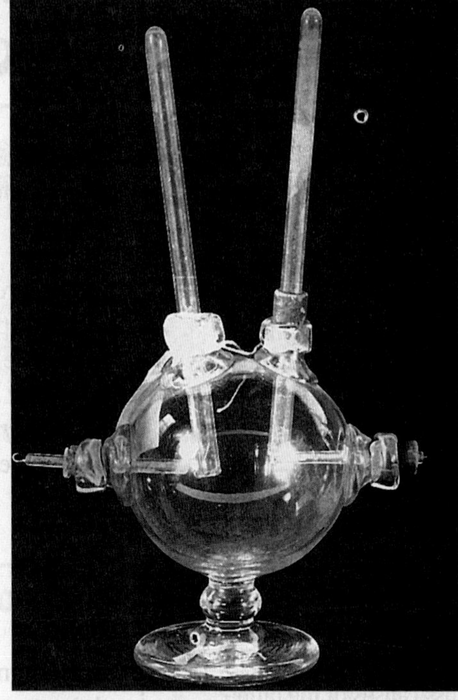

▲ *Michael Faraday used this instrument in his studies of electrolysis.*

### Questions

1. To which scientist does this feature give the most credit for the initial understanding of the basic nature of electrolysis? Briefly summarize his contributions in this area.

2. How are amounts of hydrogen and oxygen gas made from the electrolytic decomposition of water related to the chemical formula of water?

SCILINKS.
**www.scilinks.org**
**Topic:** Electrolysis
**Code:** HC60479

## MIXED REVIEW

35. Given 0.01 *m* aqueous solutions of each of the following, arrange the solutions in order of increasing change in the freezing point of the solution.
    a. NaI
    b. $CaCl_2$
    c. $K_3PO_4$
    d. $C_6H_{12}O_6$ (glucose)
36. What is the molal concentration of an aqueous calcium chloride solution that freezes at –2.43°C?
37. a. Write the balanced formula equation that shows the possible products of a double-displacement reaction between calcium nitrate and sodium chloride.
    b. Using **Table 1,** determine whether there is a precipitate.
    c. Does this reaction occur?
38. Write a balanced equation to show what occurs when hydrogen bromide dissolves and reacts with water. Include a hydronium ion in the equation.
39. Write the equation for the dissolution of each of the following in water, and then indicate the total number of moles of solute ions formed.
    a. 0.275 mol of potassium sulfide
    b. 0.15 mol of aluminum sulfate
40. Calculate the expected change in the boiling point of water in a solution made up of 131.2 g of silver nitrate, $AgNO_3$, in 2.00 kg of water.
41. Nitrous acid, $HNO_2$, is a weak electrolyte. Nitric acid, $HNO_3$, is a strong electrolyte. Write equations to represent the ionization of each in water. Include the hydronium ion, and show the appropriate kind of arrow in each equation.
42. Find the boiling point of an aqueous solution containing a nonelectrolyte that freezes at –6.51°C.
43. Write a balanced equation for the dissolution of sodium carbonate, $Na_2CO_3$, in water. Find the number of moles of each ion produced when 0.20 mol of sodium carbonate dissolves. Then, find the total number of moles of ions.
44. Given the reaction below and the information in **Table 1,** write the net ionic equation for the reaction.
    potassium phosphate (*aq*) + lead (II) nitrate (*aq*)
45. Find the expected freezing point of a water solution that contains 268 g of aluminum nitrate, $Al(NO_3)_3$, in 8.50 kg of water.

## CRITICAL THINKING

46. **Applying Models**
    a. You are conducting a freezing-point determination in the laboratory by using an aqueous solution of $KNO_3$. The observed freezing point of the solution is −1.15°C. Using a pure water sample, you recorded the freezing point of the pure solvent on the same thermometer as 0.25°C. Determine the molal concentration of $KNO_3$. Assume that there are no forces of attraction between ions.
    b. You are not satisfied with the result in part (a) because you suspect that you should not ignore the effect of ion interaction. You take a 10.00 mL sample of the solution. After carefully evaporating the water from the solution, you obtain 0.415 g $KNO_3$. Determine the actual molal concentration of $KNO_3$ and the percentage difference between the concentration observed in the freezing-point determination and the actual concentration of $KNO_3$. Assume that the solution's density is 1.00 g/mL.
47. **Analyzing Information** The observed freezing-point depression for electrolyte solutions is sometimes less than the calculated value. Why does this occur? Is the difference greater for concentrated solutions or dilute solutions?
48. **Analyzing Information** The osmotic pressure of a dilute solution can be calculated as follows:

    $\pi = MRT$
    $\pi$ = osmotic pressure
    $M$ = concentration in moles per liter
    $R$ = ideal gas constant
    $T$ = absolute temperature of the solution

    How does the osmotic-pressure equation compare with the ideal gas law?

TABLE 2

| Solvent |
|---|
| Acetic ac |
| Camphor |
| Ether |
| Naphthal |
| Phenol |
| Water |

## USING THE HANDBOOK

**49.** Common reactions for Group 13 elements are found in the *Elements Handbook.* Review this material, and answer the following:
   a. Write net ionic equations for each of the example reactions shown on page 809.
   b. Which reactions did not change when written in net ionic form? Why?

**50.** Common reactions for Group 14 elements are found in the *Elements Handbook.* Review this material, and answer the following:
   a. Write net ionic equations for each of the example reactions shown on page 813.
   b. Which reactions did not change when written in net ionic form? Why?

## RESEARCH & WRITING

**51.** Find out how much salt a large northern city, such as New York City or Chicago, uses on its streets in a typical winter. What environmental problems result from this use of salt? What substitutes for salt are being used to melt ice and snow?

**52.** Research the role of electrolytes and electrolytic solutions in your body. Find out how electrolytes work in the functioning of nerves and muscles. What are some of the health problems that can arise from an imbalance of electrolytes in body fluids?

## ALTERNATIVE ASSESSMENT

**53. Performance** Determine the freezing point of four different mixtures of water and ethylene glycol (use commercial antifreeze). What mixture has the lowest freezing point?

**54. Performance** Find the optimum mixture of salt and ice for reducing the temperature of the chilling bath for an ice-cream freezer. Use your data to write a set of instructions on how to prepare the chilling bath for making ice cream.

**55. Performance** Using a low-voltage dry cell, assemble a conductivity apparatus. Secure several unknown aqueous solutions of equal molality from your instructor, and use the apparatus to distinguish the electrolytes from the nonelectrolytes. Among those identified as electrolytes, rank their relative strengths as conductors from good to poor.

**56. Performance** Using equal volumes of the unknown solutions from the preceding activity, explain how you could use the freezing-point depression concept to distinguish the electrolytes from the nonelectrolytes. Explain how you could determine the number of ions contained per molecule among the solutes identified as electrolytes. Design and conduct an experiment to test your theories.

# Math Tutor BOILING AND FREEZING POINTS OF SOLUTIONS

The presence of a nonvolatile solute causes the freezing point of a solution to be lower and the boiling point to be higher than those of the pure solvent. The freezing-point depression, $\Delta t_f$, is the amount that the freezing point is lowered. It is calculated by using the formula $\Delta t_f = K_f m$. The boiling-point elevation, $\Delta t_b$, is the amount that the boiling point is elevated. It is found by using the equation $\Delta t_b = K_b m$. To determine $\Delta t_f$ or $\Delta t_b$, you need to know its *molal* concentration, *m* (moles of solute per kilogram of solvent). You also need to know the molal freezing-point constant, $K_f$, or the molal boiling-point constant, $K_b$. The values for $K_f$ and $K_b$ depend on the solvent and are given in **Table 2.** When these equations are used for electrolytes, the molality represents the total number of moles of ions in solution.

## Problem-Solving *TIPS*

- Make sure that you find the molal concentration, not the molar concentration.
- For electrolytes, calculate the total number of moles of ions in solution.

## SAMPLE

**What is the theoretical boiling point of a solution of 247 g of potassium chloride, KCl, dissolved in 2.90 kg of water? Potassium chloride is a strong electrolyte.**

First, determine the molality of the KCl that dissolved.

$$\text{mass of solute (g)} \times \frac{\text{1 mol solute}}{\text{molar mass of solute (g)}} = \text{amount of solute (mol)}$$

$$247 \text{ g KCl} \times \frac{\text{1 mol KCl}}{74.55 \text{ g KCl}} = 3.31 \text{ mol KCl}$$

$$\text{molality KCl}(m) = \frac{\text{mol solute particles}}{\text{mass of solvent (kg)}} = \frac{3.31 \text{ mol KCl}}{2.90 \text{ kg } H_2O} = 1.14\ m \text{ KCl}$$

Because KCl is an electrolyte, the total moles of ions in solution must now be determined. The equation $KCl(s) \longrightarrow K^+(aq) + Cl^-(aq)$ shows that 1 mol KCl will yield 2 mol of ions.

To find the total molality of particles in solution, multiply the molality of the solute by the moles of ions produced by the dissociation: $2 \times 1.14\ m$ KCl = 2.28 *m*.

Next, use the equation $\Delta t_b = K_b m$, where $K_b$ for water is 0.51°C/*m* and the value for *m* is 2.28.

$$\Delta t_b = (0.51°C/m)(2.28\ m) = 1.16°C$$

The new boiling point is equal to the sum of the boiling point of the solvent and $\Delta t_b$.

$$\text{boiling point of solution} = 100°C + 1.16°C = 101.16°C$$

## PRACTICE PROBLEMS

1. What is the freezing point of a solution containing 28.0 g of the strong electrolyte calcium chloride, $CaCl_2$, dissolved in 295 g of water?

2. What is the boiling point of a solution composed of 850 g of ethylene glycol, $C_2H_6O_2$, mixed with 1100 g of water?

# Standardized Test Prep

**Answer the following items on a separate piece of paper.**

**MULTIPLE CHOICE**

**1.** Acetic acid is a weak electrolyte because it
**A.** is miscible with water.
**B.** forms hydronium and hydroxide ions in aqueous solution.
**C.** lowers the freezing point of water.
**D.** ionizes only slightly in aqueous solution.

**2.** Which of the following solutions would contain the highest concentration of hydronium ions, $H_3O^+$?
**A.** 0.10 M HCl
**B.** 0.10 M HF
**C.** 0.10 M $CH_3COOH$
**D.** 0.10 M NaCl

**3.** Which of the following is the best representation of the precipitation reaction that occurs when aqueous solutions of sodium carbonate and calcium chloride are mixed?
**A.** $Na^+(aq) + Cl^-(aq) \longrightarrow 2NaCl(s)$
**B.** $2Na^+(aq) + CO_3^{2-}(aq) + Ca^{2+}(aq) + 2Cl^-(aq) \longrightarrow CaCO_3(s) + 2NaCl(s)$
**C.** $Ca^{2+}(aq) + CO_3^{2-}(aq) \longrightarrow CaCO_3(s)$
**D.** No precipitation reaction occurs.

**4.** Which of the following is *not* a colligative property?
**A.** molality
**B.** vapor-pressure lowering
**C.** boiling-point elevation
**D.** osmotic pressure

**5.** Solution A contains 0.1 mol of sucrose, $C_{12}H_{22}O_{11}$, dissolved in 500 g of water. Solution B contains 0.1 mol of sodium chloride, NaCl, in 500 g of water. Which of the following statements about these solutions is true?
**A.** Both solutions have the same vapor pressure.
**B.** Solution A would boil at a higher temperature than solution B would.
**C.** Solution A would freeze at a higher temperature than solution B would.
**D.** Both solutions would boil at the same temperature.

The table below shows the freezing points of solutions of three nonvolatile solutes, X, Y, and Z, in water. Refer to the table to answer items 6 and 7. The $K_f$ for water is $-1.86°C/m$.

| Solute | Solute (mol) | Water (g) | Freezing point (°C) |
|---|---|---|---|
| X | 1.00 | 1000 | −5.58 |
| Y | 1.00 | 1000 | −1.86 |
| Z | 1.00 | 1000 | −3.72 |

**6.** Which of the following statements is *not* true?
**A.** All three solutes are nonelectrolytes.
**B.** Solute X could be $Ca(NO_3)_2$.
**C.** Solute Y could be sucrose.
**D.** Solute Z could be KCl.

**7.** Which of the solutions described in the table would have the highest boiling point?
**A.** the solution of solute X
**B.** the solution of solute Y
**C.** the solution of solute Z
**D.** All three solutions would have the same boiling point.

**SHORT ANSWER**

**8.** An aqueous solution of an unknown quantity of a nonelectrolyte solute is found to have a freezing point of −0.58°C. What is the molal concentration of the solution?

**9.** Give the names and formulas of two strong electrolytes.

**EXTENDED RESPONSE**

**10.** Write the formula equation, the overall ionic equation, and the net ionic equation for the precipitation reaction that occurs when solutions of zinc chloride, $ZnCl_2$, and sodium sulfide, $Na_2S$, are mixed.

**11.** Distinguish between dissociation and ionization. Write one chemical equation to illustrate each of these terms.

**Test TIP** Before choosing an answer to a question, try to answer the question without looking at the answer choices on the test.

# Testing Water for Ions

## OBJECTIVES

- ***Observe*** **chemical reactions involving aqueous solutions of ions.**
- ***Relate*** **observations of chemical properties to the presence of ions.**
- ***Infer*** **whether an ion is present in a water sample.**
- ***Apply*** **concepts concerning aqueous solutions of ions.**

## MATERIALS

- **24-well microplate lid**
- **fine-tipped dropper bulbs, labeled, with solutions, 10**
- **overhead projector (optional)**
- **paper towels**
- **solution 1: reference (all ions)**
- **solution 2: distilled water (no ions)**
- **solution 3: tap water (may have ions)**
- **solution 4: bottled spring water (may have ions)**
- **solution 5: local river or lake water (may have ions)**
- **solution 6: solution X, prepared by your teacher (may have ions)**
- **solution A: NaSCN solution (test for $Fe^{3+}$)**
- **solution B: $Na_2C_2O_4$ solution (test for $Ca^{2+}$)**
- **solution C: $AgNO_3$ solution (test for $Cl^-$)**
- **solution D: $Sr(NO_3)_2$ solution (test for $SO_4^{2-}$)**
- **white paper**

## BACKGROUND

The physical and chemical properties of aqueous solutions are affected by small amounts of dissolved ions. For example, if a water sample has enough $Mg^{2+}$ or $Ca^{2+}$ ions, it does not create lather when soap is added. This is common in places where there are many minerals in the water (hard water). Other ions, such as $Pb^{2+}$ and $Co^{2+}$, can accumulate in body tissues; therefore, solutions of these ions are poisonous.

Because some sources of water may contain harmful or unwanted substances, it is important to find out what ions are present. In this experiment, you will test various water samples for the presence of four common, nontoxic ions: $Fe^{3+}$, $Ca^{2+}$, $Cl^-$, and $SO_4^{2-}$. Some of the samples may contain these ions in very small concentrations, so make very careful observations.

## SAFETY

For review of safety, please see **Safety in the Chemistry Laboratory** in the front of your book.

## PREPARATION

1. Create a data table in your lab notebook following your teacher's instructions. Record all of your observations in your data table.
2. Place the 24-well microplate lid in front of you on a white background. Label the columns and rows as instructed by your teacher. The coordinates will designate the individual circles. For example, the circle in the top right corner would be 1-D.

## PROCEDURE

1. Obtain labeled dropper bulbs containing the six different solutions from your teacher.

2. Place a drop of the solution from bulb 1 into circles 1-A, 1-B, 1-C, and 1-D (the top row). Solution 1 contains all four of the dissolved ions, so these drops will show what a **positive** test for each ion looks like. **Be careful to keep the solutions in the appropriate circles. Any spills will cause poor results.**

3. Place a drop of the solution from bulb 2 into each of the circles in row 2. This solution is distilled water and should not contain any of the ions. It will show what a **negative** test looks like.

4. Place a drop from bulb 3 into each of the circles in row 3 and a drop from bulb 4 into each of the circles in row 4. Follow the same procedure for bulb 5 (into row 5) and bulb 6 (into row 6). These solutions may or may not contain ions. The materials list gives contents of each bulb.

5. Now that each circle contains a solution to be analyzed, use the solutions in bulbs A–D to test for the presence of the ions. Bulb A contains NaSCN, sodium thiocyanate, which reacts with any $Fe^{3+}$ to form the complex ion $Fe(SCN)^{2+}$, which results in a deep red solution. Bulb B contains $Na_2C_2O_4$, sodium oxalate, which reacts with $Ca^{2+}$ ions. Bulb C contains $AgNO_3$, silver nitrate, which reacts with $Cl^-$ ions. Bulb D contains $Sr(NO_3)_2$, strontium nitrate, which reacts with $SO_4^{2-}$ ions. The contents of bulbs B–D react with the specified ion to yield insoluble precipitates.

6. **Holding the tip of bulb A 1 to 2 cm above the drop of water to be tested,** add one drop of solution A to the drop of reference solution in circle 1-A and one drop to the distilled water in circle 2-A. Circle 1-A should show a positive test, and circle 2-A should show a negative test. In your data table, record your observations about what the positive and negative tests look like.

7. Use the NaSCN solution in bulb A to test the rest of the water drops in column A to determine whether they contain the $Fe^{3+}$ ion. Record your observations in your data table. For each of the tests in which the ion was present, specify whether it seemed to be at a high, moderate, or low concentration.

8. Follow the procedure used for bulb A with bulbs B, C, and D to test for the other ions. Record your observations about the test results. Specify whether the solutions contained $Ca^{2+}$, $Cl^-$, or $SO_4^{2-}$ and whether the ions seemed to be present at a high, moderate, or low concentration. A black background may be useful for these three tests.

9. If some of the results are difficult to discern, place your microplate on an overhead projector. Examine the drops for signs of cloudiness. Looking at the drops from the side, keep your line of vision 10° to 15° above the plane of the lid. Compare each drop tested with the control drops in row 2. If any sign of cloudiness is detected in a test sample, it is due to the Tyndall effect and is a positive test result. Record your results.

## CLEANUP AND DISPOSAL

10. Clean all equipment and your lab station. Return equipment to its proper place. Dispose of chemicals and solutions in the containers designated by your teacher. Do not pour any chemicals down the drain or in the trash unless your teacher directs you to do so. Wash your hands thoroughly before you leave the lab and after all work is finished.

## ANALYSIS AND INTERPRETATION

1. **Organizing Ideas:** Describe what each positive test looked like. Write the balanced chemical equations and net ionic equations for each of the positive tests.

## CONCLUSIONS

1. **Organizing Conclusions:** List the solutions that you tested and the ions that you found in each solution. Include notes on whether the concentration of each ion was high, moderate, or low based on your observations.

2. **Predicting Outcomes:** Using your test results, predict which water sample would be the "hardest." Explain your reasoning.

CHAPTER 14

# *Acids and Bases*

*Acids and bases change the color of compounds called* indicators.

Hydrangeas

# Properties of Acids and Bases

SECTION 1

## OBJECTIVES

- List five general properties of aqueous acids and bases.
- Name common binary acids and oxyacids, given their chemical formulas.
- List five acids commonly used in industry and the laboratory, and give two properties of each.
- Define *acid* and *base* according to Arrhenius's theory of ionization.
- Explain the differences between strong and weak acids and bases.

SC **C.6.5** Summarize the properties of salts, acids, and bases; **C.6.6** Distinguish between strong and weak common acids and bases; **C.6.7** Represent common acids and bases by their names and formulas

How many foods can you think of that are sour? Chances are that almost all the foods you thought of, like those in **Figure 1a,** owe their sour taste to an acid. Sour milk contains *lactic acid.* Vinegar, which can be produced by fermenting juices, contains *acetic acid. Phosphoric acid* gives a tart flavor to many carbonated beverages. Most fruits contain some kind of acid. Lemons, oranges, grapefruits, and other citrus fruits contain *citric acid.* Apples contain *malic acid,* and grape juice contains *tartaric acid.*

Many substances known as bases are commonly found in household products, such as those in **Figure 1b.** Household ammonia is an ammonia-water solution that is useful for all types of general cleaning. Sodium hydroxide, NaOH, known by the common name *lye,* is present in some commercial cleaners. Milk of magnesia is a suspension in water of magnesium hydroxide, $Mg(OH)_2$, which is not very water-soluble. It is used as an antacid to relieve discomfort caused by excess hydrochloric acid in the stomach. Aluminum hydroxide, $Al(OH)_3$, and sodium hydrogen carbonate, $NaHCO_3$, are also bases commonly found in antacids.

(a)

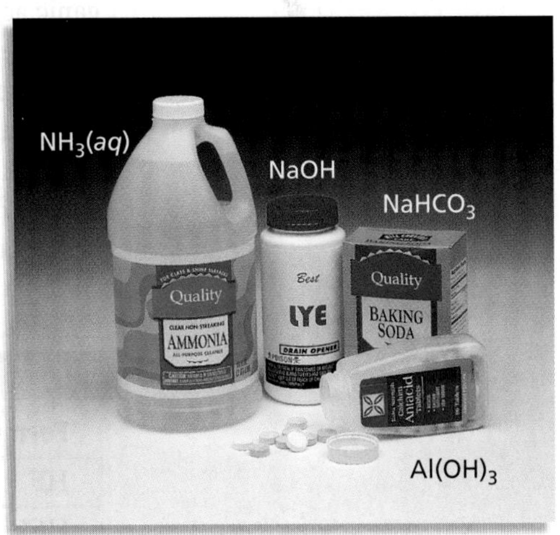


(b)

**FIGURE 1** (a) Fruits and fruit juices contain acids such as citric acid and ascorbic acid. Carbonated beverages contain benzoic acid, phosphoric acid, and carbonic acid. (b) Many household cleaners contain bases such as ammonia and sodium hydroxide. Antacids contain bases such as aluminum hydroxide.

# QuickLAB

Wear safety goggles, gloves and an apron.

## Household Acids and Bases

### Question

**Which of the household substances are acids, and which are bases?**

### Procedure

Record all your results in a data table.

1. To make an acid-base indicator, extract juice from red cabbage. First, cut up some red cabbage and place it in a large beaker. Add enough water so that the beaker is half full. Then, bring the mixture to a boil. Let it cool, and then pour off and save the cabbage juice. This solution is an acid-base indicator.
2. Assemble foods, beverages, and cleaning products to be tested.
3. If the substance being tested is a liquid, pour about 5 mL into a small beaker. If it is a solid, place a small amount into a beaker, and moisten it with about 5 mL of water.
4. Add a drop or two of the red cabbage juice to the solution being tested, and note the color. The solution will turn red if it is acidic and green if it is basic.

### Discussion

1. Are the cleaning products acids, bases, or neither?
2. What are acid/base characteristics of foods and beverages?
3. Did you find consumer warning labels on basic or acidic products?

### Materials

- **dishwashing liquid, dishwasher detergent, laundry detergent, laundry stain remover, fabric softener, and bleach**
- **mayonnaise, baking powder, baking soda, white vinegar, cider vinegar, lemon juice, soft drinks, mineral water, and milk**
- **fresh red cabbage**
- **hot plate**
- **beaker, 500 mL or larger**
- **beakers, 50 mL**
- **spatula**
- **tap water**
- **tongs**

*Red cabbage, which contains an anthocyanin pigment, can be made into an acid-base indicator.*

www.scilinks.org
**Topic:** Household Acids and Bases
**Code:** HC60762

3. *Dilute aqueous solutions of bases feel slippery.* You encounter this property of aqueous bases whenever you wash with soap.
4. *Bases react with acids to produce salts and water.* The properties of a base disappear with the addition of an equivalent amount of an acid. It could also be said that "neutralization" of the base occurs when these two substances react to produce a salt and water.
5. *Bases conduct electric current.* Like acids, bases form ions in aqueous solutions and are thus electrolytes.

## Arrhenius Acids and Bases

Svante Arrhenius, a Swedish chemist who lived from 1859 to 1927, understood that aqueous solutions of acids and bases conducted electric current. Arrhenius therefore theorized that acids and bases must produce ions in solution. *An* **Arrhenius acid** *is a chemical compound that increases the concentration of hydrogen ions, $H^+$, in aqueous solution.* In other words, an acid will ionize in solution, increasing the number of hydrogen ions present. *An* **Arrhenius base** *is a substance that increases the concentration of hydroxide ions, $OH^-$, in aqueous solution.* Some bases are ionic hydroxides. These bases dissociate in solution to release hydroxide ions into the solution. Other bases are substances that react with water to remove a hydrogen ion, leaving hydroxide ions in the solution.

### Aqueous Solutions of Acids

The acids described by Arrhenius are molecular compounds with ionizable hydrogen atoms. Their water solutions are known as *aqueous acids*. All aqueous acids are electrolytes.

Because acid molecules are sufficiently polar, water molecules attract one or more of their hydrogen ions. Negatively charged anions are left behind. As explained in Chapter 13, the hydrogen ion in aqueous solution is best represented as $H_3O^+$, the hydronium ion. The ionization of an $HNO_3$ molecule is shown by the following equation. **Figure 6** also shows how the hydronium ion forms when nitric acid reacts with water.

$$HNO_3(l) + H_2O(l) \longrightarrow H_3O^+(aq) + NO_3^-(aq)$$

Similarly, ionization of a hydrogen chloride molecule in hydrochloric acid can be represented in the following way.

$$HCl(g) + H_2O(l) \longrightarrow H_3O^+(aq) + Cl^-(aq)$$

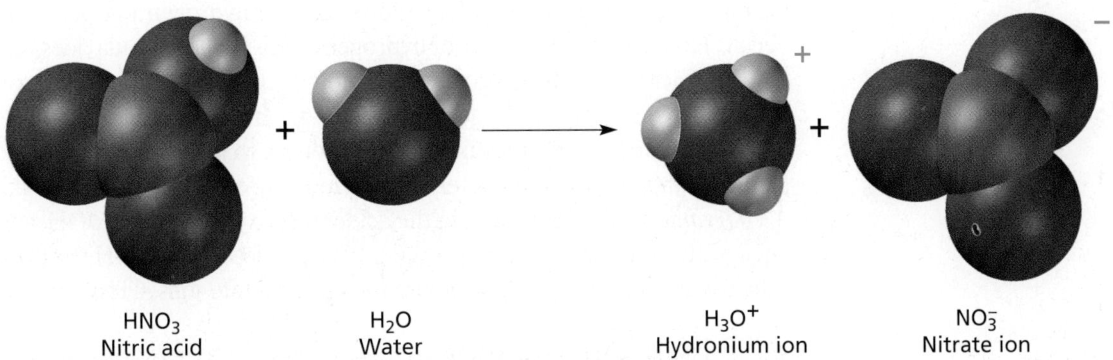


**FIGURE 6** Arrhenius's observations form the basis of a definition of acids. Arrhenius acids, such as the nitric acid shown here, produce hydronium ions in aqueous solution.

**TABLE 3 Common Aqueous Acids**

| Strong acids | Weak acids |
|---|---|
| $HI + H_2O \longrightarrow H_3O^+ + I^-$ | $HSO_4^- + H_2O \rightleftharpoons H_3O^+ + SO_4^{2-}$ |
| $HClO_4 + H_2O \longrightarrow H_3O^+ + ClO_4^-$ | $H_3PO_4 + H_2O \rightleftharpoons H_3O^+ + H_2PO_4^-$ |
| $HBr + H_2O \longrightarrow H_3O^+ + Br^-$ | $HF + H_2O \rightleftharpoons H_3O^+ + F^-$ |
| $HCl + H_2O \longrightarrow H_3O^+ + Cl^-$ | $CH_3COOH + H_2O \rightleftharpoons H_3O^+ + CH_3COO^-$ |
| $H_2SO_4 + H_2O \longrightarrow H_3O^+ + HSO_4^-$ | $H_2CO_3 + H_2O \rightleftharpoons H_3O^+ + HCO_3^-$ |
| $HClO_3 + H_2O \longrightarrow H_3O^+ + ClO_3^-$ | $H_2S + H_2O \rightleftharpoons H_3O^+ + HS^-$ |
| | $HCN + H_2O \rightleftharpoons H_3O^+ + CN^-$ |
| | $HCO_3^- + H_2O \rightleftharpoons H_3O^+ + CO_3^{2-}$ |

## Strength of Acids

*A* **strong acid** *is one that ionizes completely in aqueous solution.* A strong acid is a strong electrolyte. Perchloric acid, $HClO_4$, hydrochloric acid, HCl, and nitric acid, $HNO_3$, are examples of strong acids. In water, 100% of the acid molecules are ionized. The strength of an acid depends on the polarity of the bond between hydrogen and the element to which it is bonded and the ease with which that bond can be broken. Acid strength increases with increasing polarity and decreasing bond energy.

*An acid that releases few hydrogen ions in aqueous solution is a* **weak acid.** The aqueous solution of a weak acid contains hydronium ions, anions, and dissolved acid molecules. Hydrocyanic acid is an example of a weak acid. In aqueous solution, both the ionization of HCN and the reverse reaction occur simultaneously. In a 1 M solution of HCN there will be only two $H^+$ ions and two $CN^-$ ions out of 100,000 molecules. The other 99,998 molecules remain as HCN.

$$HCN(aq) + H_2O(l) \rightleftharpoons H_3O^+(aq) + CN^-(aq)$$

Common aqueous acids are listed in **Table 3.** Each strong acid ionizes completely in aqueous solution to give up one hydrogen ion per molecule. Notice that the number of hydrogen atoms in the formula does not indicate acid strength. Molecules with multiple hydrogen atoms may not readily give up each hydrogen. The fact that phosphoric acid has three hydrogen atoms per molecule does not mean that it is a strong acid. None of these ionize completely in solution, so phosphoric acid is weak.

*Organic acids,* which contain the acidic carboxyl group —COOH, are generally weak acids. For example, acetic acid, $CH_3COOH$, ionizes slightly in water to give hydronium ions and acetate ions, $CH_3COO^-$.

$$CH_3COOH(aq) + H_2O(l) \rightleftharpoons H_3O^+(aq) + CH_3COO^-(aq)$$

A molecule of acetic acid contains four hydrogen atoms. However, only one of the hydrogen atoms is ionizable. The hydrogen atom in the carboxyl group in acetic acid is the one that is "acidic" and forms the hydronium ion. This acidic hydrogen can be seen in the structural diagram in **Figure 7.**

```
   H  O
   |  ||
H–C–C–O–H
   |        \ acidic hydrogen
   H
```

**FIGURE 7** Acetic acid contains four hydrogen atoms, but only one of them is "acidic" and forms the hydronium ion in solution.

## Aqueous Solutions of Bases

Most bases are ionic compounds containing metal cations and the hydroxide anion, $OH^-$. Because these bases are ionic, they dissociate when dissolved in water. When a base completely dissociates in water to yield aqueous $OH^-$ ions, the solution is referred to as strongly basic. Sodium hydroxide, NaOH, is a common laboratory base. It is water-soluble and dissociates as shown by the equation below.

$$NaOH(s) \xrightarrow{H_2O} Na^+(aq) + OH^-(aq)$$

You will remember from Chapter 5 that Group 1 elements are the alkali metals. This group gets its name from the fact that the hydroxides of Li, Na, K, Rb, and Cs all form alkaline (basic) solutions.

Not all bases are ionic compounds. A base commonly used in household cleaners is ammonia, $NH_3$, which is molecular. Ammonia is a base because it produces hydroxide ions when it reacts with water molecules, as shown in the equation below.

$$NH_3(aq) + H_2O(l) \rightleftharpoons NH_4^+(aq) + OH^-(aq)$$

**extension**

**Chemistry in Action**

Go to **go.hrw.com** for a full-length article on drain cleaners.

**Keyword: HC6ACDX**

## Strength of Bases

As with acids, the strength of a base also depends on the extent to which the base dissociates, or adds hydroxide ions to the solution. For example, potassium hydroxide, KOH, is a strong base because it completely dissociates into its ions in dilute aqueous solutions.

$$KOH(s) \xrightarrow{H_2O} K^+(aq) + OH^-(aq)$$

*Strong bases* are strong electrolytes, just as strong acids are strong electrolytes. **Table 4** lists some strong bases.

**TABLE 4 Common Aqueous Bases**

| Strong bases | Weak bases |
|---|---|
| $Ca(OH)_2 \longrightarrow Ca^{2+} + 2OH^-$ | $NH_3 + H_2O \rightleftharpoons NH_4^+ + OH^-$ |
| $Sr(OH)_2 \longrightarrow Sr^{2+} + 2OH^-$ | $C_6H_5NH_2 + H_2O \rightleftharpoons C_6H_5NH_3^+ + OH^-$ |
| $Ba(OH)_2 \longrightarrow Ba^{2+} + 2OH^-$ | |
| $NaOH \longrightarrow Na^+ + OH^-$ | |
| $KOH \longrightarrow K^+ + OH^-$ | |
| $RbOH \longrightarrow Rb^+ + OH^-$ | |
| $CsOH \longrightarrow Cs^+ + OH^-$ | |

**FIGURE 8** The hydroxides of most *d*-block metals are nearly insoluble in water, as is shown by the gelatinous precipitate, copper(II) hydroxide, $Cu(OH)_2$, in the beaker on the right.

Bases that are not very soluble do not produce a large number of hydroxide ions when added to water. Some metal hydroxides, such as $Cu(OH)_2$, are not very soluble in water, as seen in **Figure 8.** They cannot produce strongly alkaline solutions. The alkalinity of aqueous solutions depends on the concentration of $OH^-$ ions in solution. It is unrelated to the number of hydroxide ions in the undissolved compound.

Now consider ammonia, which is highly soluble but is a weak electrolyte. The concentration of $OH^-$ ions in an ammonia solution is relatively low. Ammonia is therefore a *weak base*. Many organic compounds that contain nitrogen atoms are also weak bases. For example, codeine, $C_{18}H_{21}NO_3$, a pain reliever and common cough suppressant found in prescription cough medicine, is a weak base.

## SECTION REVIEW

1. **a.** What are five general properties of aqueous acids?

   **b.** Name some common substances that have one or more of these properties.

2. Name the following acids: a. HBrO b. $HBrO_3$.

3. **a.** What are five general properties of aqueous bases?

   **b.** Name some common substances that have one or more of these properties.

4. **a.** Why are strong acids also strong electrolytes?

   **b.** Is every strong electrolyte also a strong acid?

**Critical Thinking**

5. **RELATING IDEAS** A classmate states, "All compounds containing H atoms are acids, and all compounds containing OH groups are bases." Do you agree? Give examples.

## CROSS-DISCIPLINARY CONNECTION

# Acid Water—A Hidden Menace

Many people are unaware of the pH of the tap water in their home until they are confronted with such phenomena as a blue ring materializing around a porcelain sink drain, a water heater suddenly giving out, or tropical fish that keep dying. Each of these events could be due to acidic water. Acidic water can also cause the amount of lead in the water to rise.

The possibility of lead poisoning from home water supplies is a concern. Many older homes still have lead pipes in their plumbing, while most modern homes use copper piping. Copper pipe joints, however, are often sealed with lead-containing solder. Highly acidic water can leach out both the lead from the solder joints and copper from the pipes themselves, which turns the sink drain blue. In addition, people who are in the habit of filling their tea kettles and coffee pots in the morning without letting the tap run awhile first could be adding copper and lead ions to their tea or coffee.

Lead poisoning is of particular concern in young children. The absorption rate of lead in the intestinal tract of a child is much higher than in that of an adult, and lead poisoning can permanently impair a child's rapidly growing nervous system. The good news is that lead poisoning and other effects of acidic water in the home can be easily prevented by following these tips:

1. Monitor the pH of your water on a regular basis, especially if you have well water. This can easily be done with pH test kits (see photograph) that are sold in hardware or pet stores—many tropical fish are intolerant of water with a pH that is either too high (basic) or too low (acidic). The pH of municipal water supplies is already regulated, but regularly checking your water's pH yourself is a good idea.
2. In the morning, let your water tap run for about half a minute before you fill your kettle or drink the water. If the water is acidic, the first flush of water will have the highest concentration of lead and copper ions.
3. Install an alkali-injection pump, a low-cost, low-maintenance solution that can save your plumbing and lessen the risk of lead poisoning from your own water supply. The pump injects a small amount of an alkali (usually potassium carbonate or sodium carbonate) into your water-pressure tank each time your well's pump starts. This effectively neutralizes the acidity of your water.

### Questions

1. What is the source of lead contamination in water in the home?
2. Does the use of copper water pipes ensure that your household water is free from lead?
3. Why does lead poisoning affect children more severely than it affects adults?

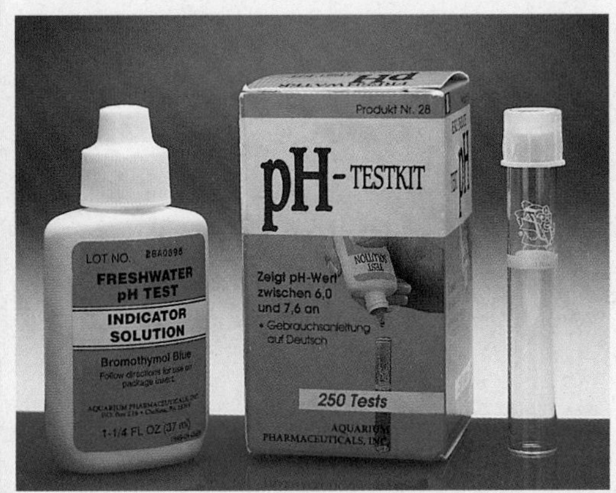


◄*The pH of your home's water supply can be easily monitored using a test kit, such as the one shown here.*

SCILINKS.
www.scilinks.org
**Topic:** Acid Water
**Code:** HC60011

SECTION 2

# Acid-Base Theories

**C.6.5** Summarize the properties of salts, acids, and bases

## OBJECTIVES

- Define and recognize *Brønsted-Lowry acids* and *bases.*
- Define a *Lewis acid* and a *Lewis base.*
- Name compounds that are acids under the Lewis definition but are not acids under the Brønsted-Lowry definition.

For most uses, scientists found the Arrhenius definition of acids and bases to be adequate. However, as scientists further investigated acid-base behavior, they found that some substances acted as acids or bases when they were not in a water solution. Because the Arrhenius definition requires that the substances be aqueous, the definitions of acids and bases had to be revised.

## Brønsted-Lowry Acids and Bases

In 1923, the Danish chemist J. N. Brønsted and the English chemist T. M. Lowry independently expanded the Arrhenius acid definition. *A* **Brønsted-Lowry acid** *is a molecule or ion that is a proton donor.* Because $H^+$ is a proton, all acids as defined by Arrhenius donate protons to water and are Brønsted-Lowry acids as well. Substances other than molecules, such as certain ions, can also donate protons. Such substances are not Arrhenius acids but are included in the category of Brønsted-Lowry acids.

Hydrogen chloride acts as a Brønsted-Lowry acid when it reacts with ammonia. The HCl transfers protons to $NH_3$ much as it does in water.

$$HCl + NH_3 \longrightarrow NH_4^+ + Cl^-$$

A proton is transferred from the hydrogen chloride molecule, HCl, to the ammonia molecule, $NH_3$. The ammonium ion, $NH_4^+$, is formed. Electron-dot formulas show the similarity of this reaction to the reaction of HCl with water.

$$\mathrm{H{:}\ddot{\underset{..}{Cl}}{:}} + \mathrm{H{:}\ddot{\underset{..}{O}}{:}\atop H} \longrightarrow \left[\mathrm{H{:}\ddot{\underset{..}{O}}{:}H \atop H}\right]^+ + \mathrm{{:}\ddot{\underset{..}{Cl}}{:}^-}$$

$$\mathrm{H{:}\ddot{\underset{..}{Cl}}{:}} + \mathrm{H{:}\ddot{N}{:}H \atop H} \longrightarrow \left[\mathrm{{H \atop H{:}\ddot{\underset{..}{N}}{:}H} \atop H}\right]^+ + \mathrm{{:}\ddot{\underset{..}{Cl}}{:}^-}$$

In both reactions, hydrogen chloride is a Brønsted-Lowry acid.

Water can also act as a Brønsted-Lowry acid. Consider, for example, the following reaction, in which the water molecule donates a proton to the ammonia molecule.

$$H_2O(l) + NH_3(aq) \rightleftharpoons NH_4^+(aq) + OH^-(aq)$$

$$\mathrm{H{:}\ddot{\underset{..}{O}}{:}\atop H} + \mathrm{H{:}\ddot{N}{:}H \atop H} \rightleftharpoons \left[\mathrm{{H \atop H{:}\ddot{\underset{..}{N}}{:}H} \atop H}\right]^+ + \left[\mathrm{{:}\ddot{\underset{..}{O}}{:} \atop H}\right]^-$$

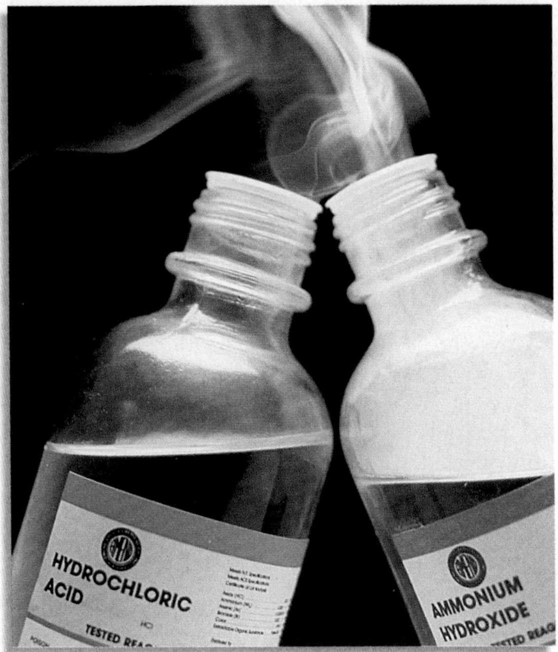


**FIGURE 9** Hydrogen chloride gas escapes from a hydrochloric acid solution and combines with ammonia gas that has escaped from an aqueous ammonia solution. The resulting cloud is solid ammonium chloride that is dispersed in air.

*A* **Brønsted-Lowry base** *is a molecule or ion that is a proton acceptor.* In the reaction between hydrochloric acid and ammonia, ammonia accepts a proton from the hydrochloric acid. It is a Brønsted-Lowry base. The Arrhenius hydroxide bases, such as NaOH, are not, strictly speaking, Brønsted-Lowry bases. Instead, it is the $OH^-$ ion produced in solution that is the Brønsted-Lowry base. It is the species that can accept a proton.

*In a* **Brønsted-Lowry acid-base reaction,** *protons are transferred from one reactant (the acid) to another (the base).* **Figure 9** shows the reaction between the Brønsted-Lowry acid HCl and the Brønsted-Lowry base $NH_3$.

## Monoprotic and Polyprotic Acids

*An acid that can donate only one proton (hydrogen ion) per molecule is known as a* **monoprotic acid.** Perchloric acid, $HClO_4$, hydrochloric acid, HCl, and nitric acid, $HNO_3$, are all monoprotic. The following equation shows how a molecule of the monoprotic acid HCl donates a proton to a water molecule. The HCl ionizes to form $H_3O^+$ ions and $Cl^-$ ions. The $Cl^-$ has no hydrogens to lose, so HCl has only one ionization step.

$$HCl(g) + H_2O(l) \longrightarrow H_3O^+(aq) + Cl^-(aq)$$

A **polyprotic acid** *is an acid that can donate more than one proton per molecule.* Sulfuric acid, $H_2SO_4$, and phosphoric acid, $H_3PO_4$, are examples of polyprotic acids. The ionization of a polyprotic acid occurs in stages. The acid loses its hydrogen ions one at a time. Sulfuric acid ionizes in two stages. In its first ionization, sulfuric acid is a strong acid. It is completely converted to hydrogen sulfate ions, $HSO_4^-$.

$$H_2SO_4(l) + H_2O(l) \longrightarrow H_3O^+(aq) + HSO_4^-(aq)$$

The hydrogen sulfate ion is itself a weak acid. It establishes the following equilibrium in solution.

$$HSO_4^-(aq) + H_2O(l) \rightleftarrows H_3O^+(aq) + SO_4^{2-}(aq)$$

All stages of ionization of a polyprotic acid occur in the same solution. Sulfuric acid solutions therefore contain $H_3O^+$, $HSO_4^-$, and $SO_4^{2-}$ ions. Note that in sulfuric acid solutions, there are many more hydrogen sulfate and hydronium ions than there are sulfate ions.

Sulfuric acid is the type of polyprotic acid that *can donate two protons per molecule, and it is therefore known as a* **diprotic acid.** Ionizations of a monoprotic acid and a diprotic acid are shown in **Figure 10.**

Phosphoric acid is the type of polyprotic acid known as a **triprotic acid**—*an acid able to donate three protons per molecule.* The equations for these reactions are shown below.

$$H_3PO_4(aq) + H_2O(l) \rightleftarrows H_3O^+(aq) + H_2PO_4^-(aq)$$
$$H_2PO_4^-(aq) + H_2O(l) \rightleftarrows H_3O^+(aq) + HPO_4^{2-}(aq)$$
$$HPO_4^{2-}(aq) + H_2O(l) \rightleftarrows H_3O^+(aq) + PO_4^{3-}(aq)$$

**FIGURE 10** Hydrochloric acid, HCl, is a strong monoprotic acid. A dilute HCl solution contains hydronium ions and chloride ions. Sulfuric acid, $H_2SO_4$, is a strong diprotic acid. A dilute $H_2SO_4$ solution contains hydrogen sulfate ions from the first ionization, sulfate ions from the second ionization, and hydronium ions from both ionizations.

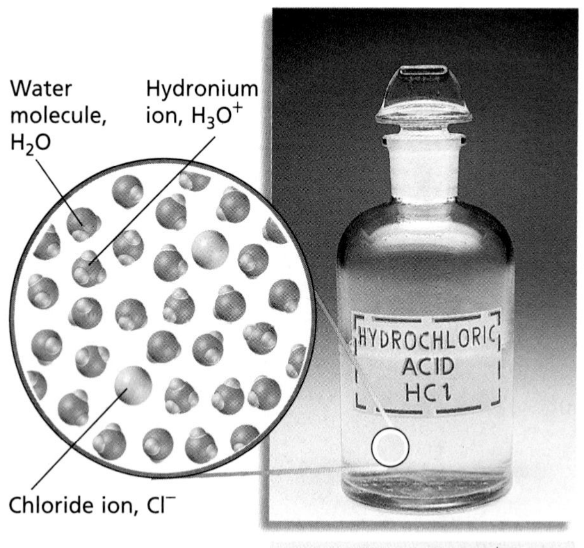


$HCl + H_2O \longrightarrow H_3O^+ + Cl^-$

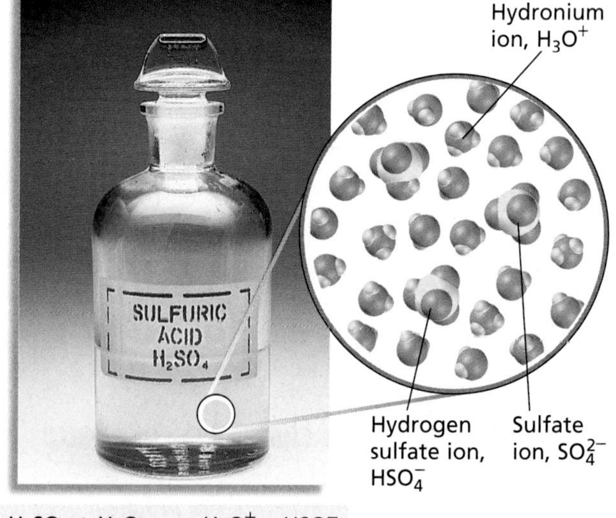


$H_2SO_4 + H_2O \longrightarrow H_3O^+ + HSO_4^-$
$HSO_4^- + H_2O \rightleftarrows H_3O^+ + SO_4^{2-}$

A solution of phosphoric acid contains $H_3O^+$, $H_3PO_4$, $H_2PO_4^-$, $HPO_4^{2-}$, and $PO_4^{3-}$. As with most polyprotic acids, the concentration of ions formed in the first ionization is the greatest. There are lesser concentrations of the respective ions from each succeeding ionization. Phosphoric acid is a weak acid in each step of its ionization.

## Lewis Acids and Bases

The Arrhenius and Brønsted-Lowry definitions describe most acids and bases. Both definitions assume that the acid contains or produces hydrogen ions. A third acid classification, based on bonding and structure, includes, as acids, substances that do not contain hydrogen at all. This definition of acids was introduced in 1923 by G. N. Lewis, the American chemist whose name was given to electron-dot structures. Lewis's definition emphasizes the role of electron pairs in acid-base reactions. *A* **Lewis acid** *is an atom, ion, or molecule that accepts an electron pair to form a covalent bond.*

The Lewis definition is the broadest of the three acid definitions you have read about so far. It applies to any species that can accept an electron pair to form a covalent bond with another species. A bare proton (hydrogen ion) is a Lewis acid in reactions in which it forms a covalent bond, as shown below.

$$H^+(aq) + :NH_3(aq) \longrightarrow [H{-}NH_3]^+(aq) \text{ or } [NH_4]^+(aq)$$

The formula for a Lewis acid need not include hydrogen. Even a silver ion can be a Lewis acid, accepting electron pairs from ammonia to form covalent bonds.

$$Ag^+(aq) + 2:NH_3(aq) \longrightarrow [H_3N{-}Ag{-}NH_3]^+(aq) \text{ or } [Ag(NH_3)_2]^+$$

Any compound in which the central atom has three valence electrons and forms three covalent bonds can react as a Lewis acid. It does so by accepting a pair of electrons to form a fourth covalent bond, completing an electron octet. Boron trifluoride, for example, is an excellent Lewis acid. It forms a fourth covalent bond with many molecules and ions. Its reaction with a fluoride ion is shown below.

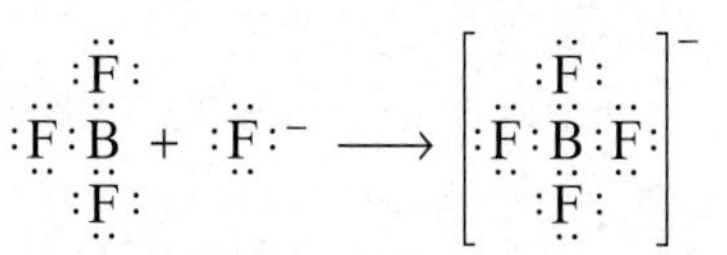

$$\begin{array}{c}:\ddot{F}:\\ :\ddot{F}:B\\ :\ddot{F}:\end{array} + :\ddot{F}:^- \longrightarrow \left[\begin{array}{c}:\ddot{F}:\\ :\ddot{F}:B:\ddot{F}:\\ :\ddot{F}:\end{array}\right]^-$$

$$BF_3(aq) + F^-(aq) \longrightarrow BF_4^-(aq)$$

**TABLE 5 Acid-Base Definitions**

| Type | Acid | Base |
|---|---|---|
| Arrhenius | $H^+$ or $H_3O^+$ producer | $OH^-$ producer |
| Brønsted-Lowry | proton ($H^+$) donor | proton ($H^+$) acceptor |
| Lewis | electron-pair acceptor | electron-pair donor |

The Lewis definition of acids can apply to species in any phase. For example, boron trifluoride is a Lewis acid in the gas-phase combination with ammonia.

$$BF_3 + :NH_3 \longrightarrow F_3B:NH_3$$

*A* **Lewis base** *is an atom, ion, or molecule that donates an electron pair to form a covalent bond.* An anion is a Lewis base in a reaction in which it forms a covalent bond by donating an electron pair. In the example of boron trifluoride reacting with the fluoride anion, $F^-$ donates an electron pair to boron trifluoride. $F^-$ acts as a Lewis base.

$$BF_3(aq) + :\ddot{F}:^-(aq) \longrightarrow BF_4^-(aq)$$

*A* **Lewis acid-base reaction** *is the formation of one or more covalent bonds between an electron-pair donor and an electron-pair acceptor.*

Note that although the three acid-base definitions differ, many compounds may be categorized as acids or bases according to all three descriptions. For example, ammonia is an Arrhenius base because $OH^-$ ions are created when ammonia is in solution, it is a Brønsted-Lowry base because it accepts a proton in an acid-base reaction, and it is a Lewis base in all reactions in which it donates its lone pair to form a covalent bond. A comparison of the three acid-base definitions is given in **Table 5.**

## SECTION REVIEW

1. Label each reactant in the reaction below as a proton donor or a proton acceptor and as acidic or basic.

$$H_2CO_3 + H_2O \rightleftharpoons HCO_3^- + H_3O^+$$

2. For the reaction below, label each reactant as an electron pair acceptor or electron pair donor and as a Lewis acid or a Lewis base.

$$AlCl_3 + Cl^- \longrightarrow AlCl_4^-$$

**Critical Thinking**

3. **ANALYZING INFORMATION** For the following three reactions, identify the reactants that are Arrhenius bases, Brønsted-Lowry bases, and/or Lewis bases. State which type(s) of bases each reactant is. Explain your answers.

   **a.** $NaOH(s) \longrightarrow Na^+(aq) + OH^-(aq)$

   **b.** $HF(aq) + H_2O(l) \longrightarrow F^-(aq) + H_3O^+(aq)$

   **c.** $H^+(aq) + NH_3(aq) \longrightarrow NH_4^+(aq)$

# Acid-Base Reactions

SECTION 3

**C.4.2** Predict the products of acid-base neutralization and combustion reactions; **C.6.6** Distinguish between strong and weak common acids and bases

In the previous sections, you learned about three acid-base theories: Arrhenius, Brønsted-Lowry, and Lewis. The Brønsted-Lowry theory is especially useful for describing acid-base reactions that take place in aqueous solutions. This section will use the Brønsted-Lowry description to explore reactions between acids and bases.

## Objectives

- Describe a conjugate acid, a conjugate base, and an amphoteric compound.
- Explain the process of neutralization.
- Define *acid rain,* give examples of compounds that can cause acid rain, and describe effects of acid rain.

## Conjugate Acids and Bases

The Brønsted-Lowry definitions of acids and bases provide a basis for studying proton-transfer reactions. Suppose that a Brønsted-Lowry acid gives up a proton; the remaining ion or molecule can re-accept that proton and can act as a base. Such a base is known as a conjugate base. Thus, *the species that remains after a Brønsted-Lowry acid has given up a proton is the* **conjugate base** *of that acid.* For example, the fluoride ion is the conjugate base of hydrofluoric acid.

$$\underset{\text{acid}}{HF(aq)} + H_2O(l) \rightleftharpoons \underset{\text{conjugate base}}{F^-(aq)} + H_3O^+(aq)$$

In this reaction, the water molecule is a Brønsted-Lowry base. It accepts a proton from HF to form $H_3O^+$, which is an acid. The hydronium ion is the conjugate acid of water. *The species that is formed when a Brønsted-Lowry base gains a proton is the* **conjugate acid** *of that base.*

$$HF(aq) + \underset{\text{base}}{H_2O(l)} \rightleftharpoons F^-(aq) + \underset{\text{conjugate acid}}{H_3O^+(aq)}$$

In general, Brønsted-Lowry acid-base reactions are equilibrium systems meaning that both the forward and reverse reactions occur. They involve two acid-base pairs, known as conjugate acid-base pairs.

$$\underset{\text{acid}_1}{HF(aq)} + \underset{\text{base}_2}{H_2O(l)} \rightleftharpoons \underset{\text{base}_1}{F^-(aq)} + \underset{\text{acid}_2}{H_3O^+(aq)}$$

The subscripts designate the two conjugate acid-base pairs: (1) HF and $F^-$ and (2) $H_3O^+$ and $H_2O$. In every conjugate acid-base pair, the acid has one more proton than its conjugate base.

## Strength of Conjugate Acids and Bases

The extent of the reaction between a Brønsted-Lowry acid and base depends on the relative strengths of the acids and bases involved. Consider the following example. Hydrochloric acid is a strong acid. It gives up protons readily. Therefore, the $Cl^-$ ion has little tendency to attract and retain a proton. Consequently, the $Cl^-$ ion is an extremely weak base.

$$\underset{\text{stronger acid}}{HCl(g)} + \underset{\text{stronger base}}{H_2O(l)} \longrightarrow \underset{\text{weaker acid}}{H_3O^+(aq)} + \underset{\text{weaker base}}{Cl^-(aq)}$$

This observation leads to an important conclusion: *the stronger an acid is, the weaker its conjugate base; the stronger a base is, the weaker its conjugate acid.*

This concept allows strengths of different acids and bases to be compared to predict the outcome of a reaction. As an example, consider the reaction of perchloric acid, $HClO_4$, and water.

$$\underset{\text{stronger acid}}{HClO_4(aq)} + \underset{\text{stronger base}}{H_2O(l)} \longrightarrow \underset{\text{weaker acid}}{H_3O^+(aq)} + \underset{\text{weaker base}}{ClO_4^-(aq)}$$

The hydronium ion is too weak an acid to compete successfully with perchloric acid in donating a proton; $HClO_4$ is the stronger acid. In this reaction, the perchlorate ion, $ClO_4^-$, and $H_2O$ are both bases. Because $HClO_4$ is a very strong acid, $ClO_4^-$ is an extremely weak base. Therefore, $H_2O$ competes more strongly than $ClO_4^-$ to acquire a proton. The reaction proceeds such that the stronger acid reacts with the stronger base to produce the weaker acid and base.

Now consider a comparable reaction between water and acetic acid.

$$\underset{\text{weaker acid}}{CH_3COOH(aq)} + \underset{\text{weaker base}}{H_2O(l)} \longleftarrow \underset{\text{stronger acid}}{H_3O^+(aq)} + \underset{\text{stronger base}}{CH_3COO^-(aq)}$$

The $H_3O^+$ ion concentration in this solution is much lower than it was in the $HClO_4$ solution because acetic acid is a weak acid. The $CH_3COOH$ molecule does not compete successfully with the $H_3O^+$ ion in donating protons to a base. The acetate ion, $CH_3COO^-$, is a stronger base than $H_2O$. Therefore, the $H_2O$ molecule does not compete successfully with the $CH_3COO^-$ ion in accepting a proton. The $H_3O^+$ ion is the stronger acid, and the $CH_3COO^-$ ion is the stronger base. Thus, the reverse reaction (to the left) is more favorable.

Note that in the reactions for both perchloric acid and acetic acid, the favored direction is toward the weaker acid and the weaker base. This observation leads to a second important general conclusion: *proton-transfer reactions favor the production of the weaker acid and the weaker base.* For an acid-base reaction to form products completely, the reactants must be much stronger as acids and bases than the products.

By comparing many different acids and bases, a table of relative strengths, such as **Table 6,** can be assembled. Note that a very strong acid, such as $HClO_4$, has a very weak conjugate base, $ClO_4^-$. The

**CROSS-DISCIPLINARY**

### "It's a Bitter Pill"

Have you ever wondered about the origin of the saying, "It's a bitter pill to swallow"? This saying is used to describe a situation that is difficult to accept. Many medications contain bases, and a bitter taste is a property of bases. So, many medications actually have a bitter taste. If you look at the chemical formulas of the components of medications, you will see that they often contain nitrogen. One such component is caffeine, which acts as a stimulant on the central nervous and respiratory systems. Its molecular formula is $C_8H_{10}O_2N_4$. Like ammonia, caffeine has basic properties because it has a nitrogen that can accept a proton.

**TABLE 6 Relative Strengths of Acids and Bases**

| Conjugate acid | Formula | Conjugate base | Formula |
|---|---|---|---|
| hydriodic acid* | $HI$ | iodide ion | $I^-$ |
| perchloric acid* | $HClO_4$ | perchlorate ion | $ClO_4^-$ |
| hydrobromic acid* | $HBr$ | bromide ion | $Br^-$ |
| hydrochloric acid* | $HCl$ | chloride ion | $Cl^-$ |
| sulfuric acid* | $H_2SO_4$ | hydrogen sulfate ion | $HSO_4^-$ |
| chloric acid* | $HClO_3$ | chlorate ion | $ClO_3^-$ |
| nitric acid* | $HNO_3$ | nitrate ion | $NO_3^-$ |
| hydronium ion | $H_3O^+$ | water | $H_2O$ |
| chlorous acid | $HClO_2$ | chlorite ion | $ClO_2^-$ |
| hydrogen sulfate ion | $HSO_4^-$ | sulfate ion | $SO_4^{2-}$ |
| phosphoric acid | $H_3PO_4$ | dihydrogen phosphate ion | $H_2PO_4^-$ |
| hydrofluoric acid | $HF$ | fluoride ion | $F^-$ |
| acetic acid | $CH_3COOH$ | acetate ion | $CH_3COO^-$ |
| carbonic acid | $H_2CO_3$ | hydrogen carbonate ion | $HCO_3^-$ |
| hydrosulfuric acid | $H_2S$ | hydrosulfide ion | $HS^-$ |
| dihydrogen phosphate ion | $H_2PO_4^-$ | hydrogen phosphate ion | $HPO_4^{2-}$ |
| hypochlorous acid | $HClO$ | hypochlorite ion | $ClO^-$ |
| ammonium ion | $NH_4^+$ | ammonia | $NH_3$ |
| hydrogen carbonate ion | $HCO_3^-$ | carbonate ion | $CO_3^{2-}$ |
| hydrogen phosphate ion | $HPO_4^{2-}$ | phosphate ion | $PO_4^{3-}$ |
| water | $H_2O$ | hydroxide ion | $OH^-$ |
| ammonia | $NH_3$ | amide ion† | $NH_2^-$ |
| hydrogen | $H_2$ | hydride ion† | $H^-$ |

Increasing acid strength (upward) — Increasing base strength (downward)

* Strong acids
† Strong bases

strongest base listed in the table, the hydride ion, $H^-$, has the weakest conjugate acid, $H_2$. In aqueous solutions, all of the strong acids are 100% ionized, forming hydronium ions along with their anion. The acids below hydronium ion in **Table 6** do not ionize 100% in water. Water is a very weak acid, but it will react as an acid if a very strong base, such as hydride ion, is present. Such a reaction is illustrated in **Figure 11.**

## Amphoteric Compounds

You have probably noticed that water can be either an acid or a base. *Any species that can react as either an acid or a base is described as* **amphoteric.** For example, consider the first ionization of sulfuric acid, in which water acts as a base.

**FIGURE 11** Calcium hydride, $CaH_2$, reacts vigorously with water to produce hydrogen gas.

$$CaH_2(s) + 2H_2O(l) \longrightarrow Ca(OH)_2(aq) + 2H_2(g)$$

$$\underset{\text{acid}_1}{H_2SO_4(aq)} + \underset{\text{base}_2}{H_2O(l)} \longrightarrow \underset{\text{acid}_2}{H_3O^+(aq)} + \underset{\text{base}_1}{HSO_4^-(aq)}$$

However, water acts as an acid in the following reaction.

$$\underset{\text{base}_1}{NH_3(g)} + \underset{\text{acid}_2}{H_2O(l)} \rightleftarrows \underset{\text{acid}_1}{NH_4^+(aq)} + \underset{\text{base}_2}{OH^-(aq)}$$

Thus, water can act as either an acid or a base and is amphoteric. Such a substance acts as either an acid or a base depending on the strength of the acid or base with which it is reacting. For example, if water reacts with a compound that is a stronger acid than water, water acts as a base. If water reacts with a molecule that is a weaker acid than water, water will act as an acid and the other molecule will act as a base.

**FIGURE 12** Each oxyacid of chlorine contains one chlorine atom and one hydrogen atom. They differ in the number of oxygen atoms they contain. The effect of the changing O—H bond polarity can be seen in the increasing acid strength from hypochlorous acid to perchloric acid.

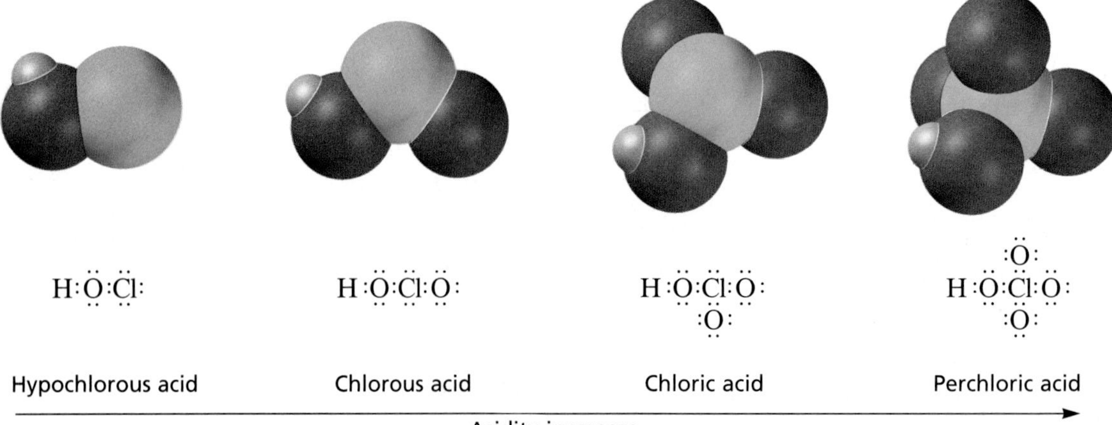

## –OH in a Molecule

Molecular compounds containing –OH groups can be acidic or amphoteric. The covalently bonded –OH group in an acid is referred to as a *hydroxyl group*. For the compound to be acidic, a water molecule must be able to attract a hydrogen atom from a hydroxyl group. This occurs more easily when the O–H bond is very polar. Any feature of a molecule that increases the polarity of the O–H bond increases the acidity of a molecular compound. The small, more-electronegative atoms of nonmetals at the upper right in the periodic table form compounds with acidic hydroxyl groups. All oxyacids are molecular electrolytes that contain one or more of these O–H bonds. Such compounds include chloric and perchloric acids.

**Figure 12** shows the electron-dot formulas of the four oxyacids of chlorine. Notice that all of the oxygen atoms are bonded to the chlorine atom. Each hydrogen atom is bonded to an oxygen atom. Aqueous solutions of these molecules are acids because the O–H bonds are broken as the hydrogen is pulled away by water molecules.

The behavior of a compound is affected by the number of oxygen atoms bonded to the atom connected to the –OH group. The larger the number of such oxygen atoms is, the more acidic the compound is. The electronegative oxygen atoms draw electron density away from the O–H bond and make it more polar. For example, chromium forms three different compounds containing –OH groups, as shown below.

| *basic* | *amphoteric* | *acidic* |
|---|---|---|
| $Cr(OH)_2$ | $Cr(OH)_3$ | $H_2CrO_4$ |
| chromium(II) hydroxide | chromium(III) hydroxide | chromic acid |

Notice that as the number of oxygen atoms increases, so does the acidity of the compound.

Consider also the compounds shown in **Figure 13.** In acetic acid, but not in ethanol, a second oxygen atom is bonded to the carbon atom connected to the –OH group. That explains why acetic acid is acidic but ethanol is not, even though the same elements form each compound.

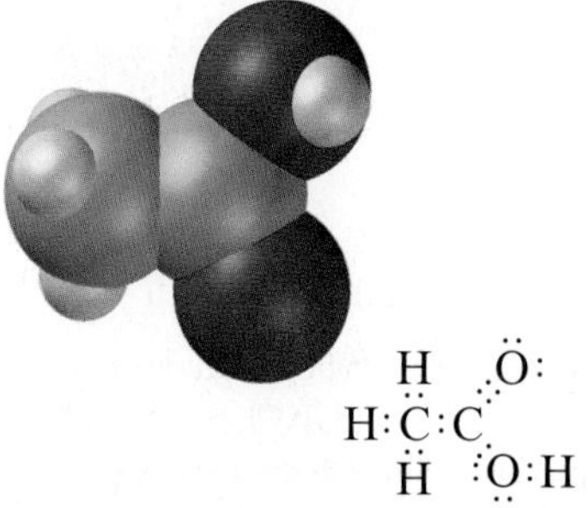

**(a)** $CH_3COOH$
Acetic acid

H H
H:C:C:O:H
H H

**(b)** $C_2H_5OH$
Ethanol

**FIGURE 13** (a) Acetic acid is acidic. The second oxygen atom on the carbon draws electron density away from the –OH group, making the O–H bond more polar. (b) Ethanol is essentially neutral. It has no second oxygen atom, so the O–H bond is less polar than in acetic acid, and is a much weaker acid.

# Neutralization Reactions

There are many common examples of acidic compounds reacting with basic compounds, each neutralizing the other. Sodium bicarbonate, $NaHCO_3$, and tartaric acid, $H_2C_4H_4O_6$, are two components in baking powder. When water is added, the two compounds produce carbon dioxide. The escaping carbon dioxide causes foods, such as biscuits, to rise. Another example is an antacid soothing an overly acidic stomach by neutralizing the stomach acid.

## Strong Acid-Strong Base Neutralization

An acid-base reaction occurs in aqueous solution between hydrochloric acid, a strong acid that completely ionizes to produce $H_3O^+$, and sodium hydroxide, a strong base that completely dissociates to produce $OH^-$. The formula equation for this reaction is written as follows.



$$HCl(aq) + NaOH(aq) \longrightarrow NaCl(aq) + H_2O(l)$$

In an aqueous solution containing 1 mol of sodium hydroxide, NaOH dissociates as represented by the following equation.

$$NaOH(aq) \longrightarrow Na^+(aq) + OH^-(aq)$$

A solution containing 1 mol of hydrochloric acid ionizes as represented by the following equation.

$$HCl(aq) + H_2O(l) \longrightarrow H_3O^+(aq) + Cl^-(aq)$$

If the two solutions are mixed, as in **Figure 14,** a reaction occurs between the aqueous $H_3O^+$ and $OH^-$ ions. Notice that sodium chloride, NaCl, and water are produced. The overall ionic equation is shown below.

$$H_3O^+(aq) + Cl^-(aq) + Na^+(aq) + OH^-(aq) \longrightarrow Na^+(aq) + Cl^-(aq) + 2H_2O(l)$$

**FIGURE 14** When aqueous hydrochloric acid, HCl, reacts with aqueous sodium hydroxide, NaOH, the reaction produces aqueous sodium chloride, NaCl. Ions that are present in each solution are represented by the models.

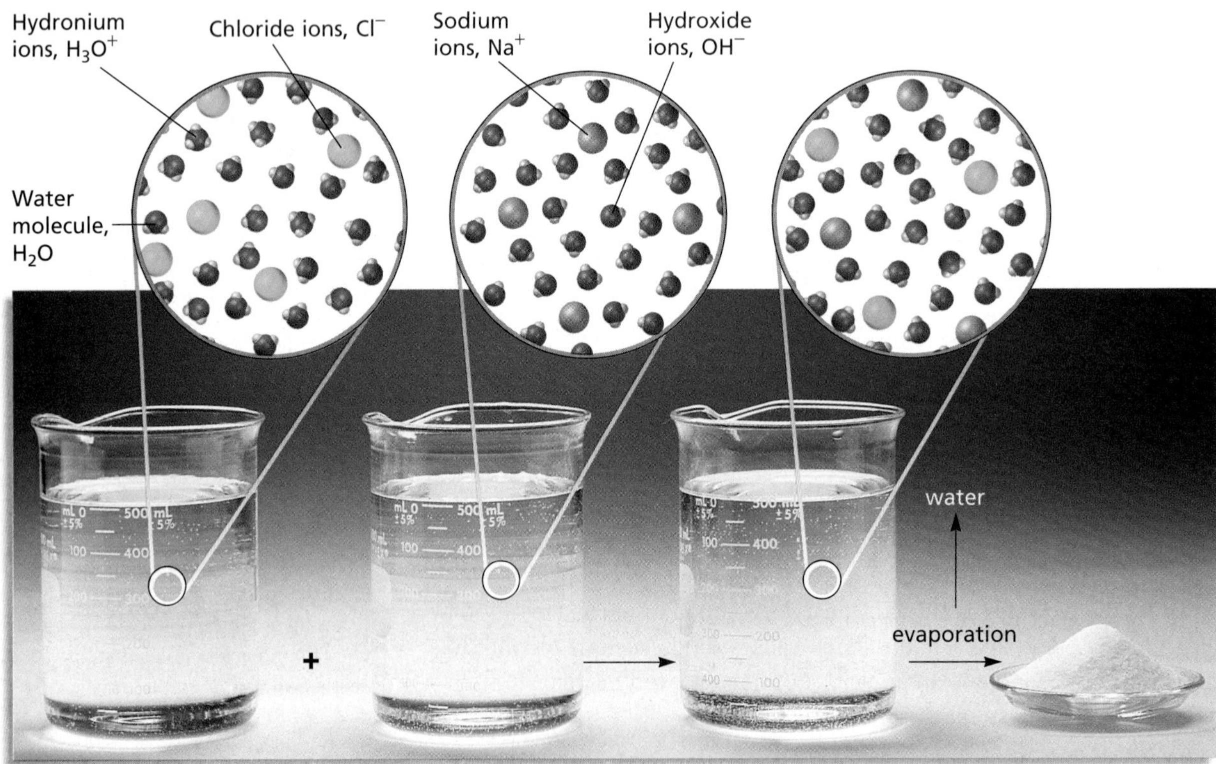

Because they appear on both sides of the overall ionic equation, $Na^+$ and $Cl^-$ are spectator ions. The only participants in the reaction are the hydronium ion and the hydroxide ion, as shown in the following net ionic equation.

$$H_3O^+(aq) + OH^-(aq) \longrightarrow 2H_2O(l)$$

There are equal numbers of $H_3O^+$ and $OH^-$ ions in this reaction, and they are fully converted to water. In aqueous solutions, **neutralization** *is the reaction of hydronium ions and hydroxide ions to form water molecules.*

Notice that water is not the only product of a neutralization. A salt is also produced. *A* **salt** *is an ionic compound composed of a cation from a base and an anion from an acid.*

## Acid Rain

Many industrial processes produce gases such as NO, $NO_2$, $CO_2$, $SO_2$, and $SO_3$. These compounds can dissolve in atmospheric water to produce acidic solutions that fall to the ground in the form of rain or snow. For example, sulfur from the burning of oil and coal forms sulfur dioxide, $SO_2$. The $SO_2$ is then converted to $SO_3$, sulfur trioxide, which reacts with water in the atmosphere to produce sulfuric acid, as shown below.

$$SO_3(g) + H_2O(l) \longrightarrow H_2SO_4(aq)$$

Rainwater is normally slightly acidic, but sometimes rain is very acidic and is called *acid rain.* **Figure 15** shows a forest that was damaged by severe acid rain. Acid rain can erode statues and affect ecosystems, such as water environments and forests. In the 1970s, scientists found that acid rain was causing the fish populations in some lakes and streams to decline. When fish are completely eliminated from lakes and streams because of acid rain, the biodiversity of the ecosystem decreases. Because of amendments to the Clean Air Act in 1990, a limit was set on the amount of $SO_2$ that power plants are permitted to emit. This limit has decreased but not eliminated acid rain in the United States.

**FIGURE 15** Acid precipitation causes extensive environmental damage.

## SECTION REVIEW

1. Complete and balance the equations for the following acid-base reactions:
   a. $H_2CO_3 + Sr(OH)_2 \longrightarrow$
   b. $HClO_4 + NaOH \longrightarrow$
   c. $HBr + Ba(OH)_2 \longrightarrow$
   d. $NaHCO_3 + H_2SO_4 \longrightarrow$
2. Consider the equation for acetic acid plus water.
   $$CH_3COOH + H_2O \longrightarrow CH_3COO^- + H_3O^+$$
   a. Refer to **Table 6** to compare the strengths of the two acids in the equation. Do the same for the two bases.
   b. Determine which direction—forward or reverse—is favored in the reaction.

### Critical Thinking

3. **INFERRING RELATIONSHIPS** Explain how the presence of several oxygen atoms in a compound containing an –OH group can make the compound acidic.

# CHAPTER HIGHLIGHTS

## Properties of Acids and Bases

**Vocabulary**
binary acid
oxyacid
Arrhenius acid
Arrhenius base
strong acid
weak acid

- Acids have a sour taste and react with active metals. Acids change the colors of acid-base indicators, react with bases to produce salts and water, and conduct electricity in aqueous solutions.
- Bases have a bitter taste, feel slippery to the skin in dilute aqueous solutions, change the colors of acid-base indicators, react with acids to produce salts and water, and conduct electricity in aqueous solution.
- An Arrhenius acid contains hydrogen and ionizes in aqueous solution to form hydrogen ions. An Arrhenius base produces hydroxide ions in aqueous solution.
- The strength of an Arrhenius acid or base is determined by the extent to which the acid or base ionizes or dissociates in aqueous solutions.

## Acid-Base Theories

**Vocabulary**
Brønsted-Lowry acid
Brønsted-Lowry base
Brønsted-Lowry acid-base reaction
monoprotic acid
polyprotic acid
diprotic acid
triprotic acid
Lewis acid
Lewis base
Lewis acid-base reaction

- A Brønsted-Lowry acid is a proton donor. A Brønsted-Lowry base is a proton acceptor.
- A Lewis acid is an electron-pair acceptor. A Lewis base is an electron-pair donor.
- Acids are described as monoprotic, diprotic, or triprotic depending on whether they can donate one, two, or three protons per molecule, respectively, in aqueous solutions. Polyprotic acids include both diprotic and triprotic acids.

## Acid-Base Reactions

**Vocabulary**
conjugate base
conjugate acid
amphoteric
neutralization
salt

- In every Brønsted-Lowry acid-base reaction, there are two conjugate acid-base pairs.
- A strong acid has a weak conjugate base; a strong base has a weak conjugate acid.
- Proton-transfer reactions favor the production of the weaker acid and weaker base.
- The acidic or basic behavior of a molecule containing $-OH$ groups depends on the electronegativity of other atoms in the molecule and on the number of oxygen atoms bonded to the atom that is connected to the $-OH$ group.
- A neutralization reaction produces water and an ionic compound called a *salt.*
- Acid rain can create severe ecological problems.

## *Properties of Acids and Bases*

### SECTION 1 REVIEW

1. Compare the general properties of acids with the general properties of bases.
2. a. Distinguish between binary acids and oxyacids in terms of their component elements and the systems used in naming them.
   b. Give three examples of each type of acid.
3. Identify and describe the characteristic properties of five common acids used in industry. Give some examples of the typical uses of each.
4. Although $HCl(aq)$ exhibits properties of an Arrhenius acid, pure HCl gas and HCl dissolved in a nonpolar solvent exhibit none of the properties of an Arrhenius acid. Explain why.
5. a. What distinguishes strong acids from weak acids?
   b. Give two examples each of strong acids and weak acids.
6. $H_3PO_4$, which contains three hydrogen atoms per molecule, is a weak acid, whereas HCl, which contains only one hydrogen atom per molecule, is a strong acid. Explain why.
7. a. What determines the strength of an Arrhenius base?
   b. Give one example each of an aqueous solution of a strong base and an aqueous solution of a weak base.

### PRACTICE PROBLEMS

8. Name each of the following binary acids:
   a. HCl
   b. $H_2S$
9. Name each of the following oxyacids:
   a. $HNO_3$
   b. $H_2SO_3$
   c. $HClO_3$
   d. $HNO_2$
10. Write formulas for the following binary acids:
    a. hydrofluoric acid
    b. hydriodic acid
11. Write formulas for the following oxyacids:
    a. perbromic acid
    b. chlorous acid
    c. phosphoric acid
    d. hypochlorous acid

## *Acid-Base Theories*

### SECTION 2 REVIEW

12. Distinguish between a monoprotic, a diprotic, and a triprotic acid. Give an example of each.
13. Which of the three acid definitions is the broadest? Explain.

### PRACTICE PROBLEMS

14. a. Write the balanced equations that describe the two-step ionization of sulfuric acid in a dilute aqueous solution.
    b. How do the degrees of ionization in the two steps compare?
15. Dilute $HCl(aq)$ and $KOH(aq)$ are mixed in chemically equivalent quantities. Write the following:
    a. formula equation for the reaction
    b. overall ionic equation
    c. net ionic equation
16. Repeat item 15, but mix $H_3PO_4(aq)$ and $NaOH(aq)$.
17. Write the formula equation and net ionic equation for each of the following reactions:
    a. $Zn(s) + HCl(aq) \longrightarrow$
    b. $Al(s) + H_2SO_4(aq) \longrightarrow$
18. Write the formula equation and net ionic equation for the reaction between $Ca(s)$ and $HCl(aq)$.

## *Acid-Base Reactions*

### SECTION 3 REVIEW

19. Define and give an equation to illustrate each of the following substances:
    a. a conjugate base
    b. a conjugate acid
20. a. What is the relationship between the strength of an acid and the strength of its conjugate base?
    b. What is the relationship between the strength of a base and the strength of its conjugate acid?

21. a. What trend is there in the favored direction of proton-transfer reactions?
b. What determines the extent to which a proton-transfer reaction occurs?

22. a. What is meant by the term *amphoteric?*
b. Give an example of a substance or ion that has amphoteric characteristics.

23. For each reaction listed, identify the proton donor or acid and the proton acceptor or base. Label each conjugate acid-base pair.
a. $CH_3COOH(aq) + H_2O(l) \rightleftharpoons H_3O^+(aq) + CH_3COO^-(aq)$
b. $HCO_3^-(aq) + H_2O(l) \rightleftharpoons H_2CO_3(aq) + OH^-(aq)$
c. $HNO_3 + SO_4^{2-} \longrightarrow HSO_4^- + NO_3^-$

24. Using the information given in **Table 6,** determine the following relative to HF, $H_2S$, $HNO_3$, and $CH_3COOH$:
a. strongest acid
b. weakest acid
c. strongest conjugate base among the four conjugate bases produced by the acids listed
d. weakest conjugate base among the four conjugate bases produced by the acids listed

25. Explain why the conjugate base of a strong acid is a weak base and the conjugate acid of a strong base is a weak acid.

## PRACTICE PROBLEMS

26. Complete the following neutralization reactions. Balance each reaction, and then write the overall ionic and net ionic equation for each.
a. $HCl(aq) + NaOH(aq) \longrightarrow$
b. $HNO_3(aq) + KOH(aq) \longrightarrow$
c. $Ca(OH)_2(aq) + HNO_3(aq) \longrightarrow$
d. $Mg(OH)_2(aq) + HCl(aq) \longrightarrow$

27. Write the formula equation, the overall ionic equation, and the net ionic equation for the neutralization reaction involving aqueous solutions of $H_3PO_4$ and $Mg(OH)_2$. Assume that the solutions are sufficiently dilute so that no precipitates form.

28. Write the balanced chemical equation for each of the following reactions between water and the non-metallic oxide to form an acid.
a. $CO_2(g) + H_2O(l) \longrightarrow$
b. $SO_3(g) + H_2O(l) \longrightarrow$
c. $N_2O_5(g) + H_2O(l) \longrightarrow$

29. Write the formula equation, the overall ionic equation, and the net ionic equation for a neutralization reaction that would form each of the following salts.
a. $RbClO_4$
b. $BaSO_4$
c. $CaCl_2$
d. $K_2SO_4$

30. Zinc reacts with 100.0 mL of 6.00 M cold, aqueous sulfuric acid through single replacement.
a. How many grams of zinc sulfate can be produced?
b. How many liters of hydrogen gas could be released at STP?

31. A 211 g sample of barium carbonate, $BaCO_3$, reacts with a solution of nitric acid to give barium nitrate, carbon dioxide and water. If the acid is present in excess, what mass and volume of dry carbon dioxide gas at STP will be produced?

32. A seashell that is composed largely of calcium carbonate reacts with a solution of HCl. As a result, 1500 mL of dry $CO_2$ gas at STP is produced. The other products are $CaCl_2$ and $H_2O$.
a. How many grams of $CaCO_3$ are consumed in the reaction?
b. What volume of 2.00 M HCl solution is used in this reaction?

33. *Acid precipitation* is the term generally used to describe rain or snow that is more acidic than it normally is. One cause of acid precipitation is the formation of sulfuric and nitric acids from various sulfur and nitrogen oxides produced in volcanic eruptions, forest fires, and thunderstorms. In a typical volcanic eruption, for example, $3.50 \times 10^8$ kg $SO_2$ may be produced. If this amount of $SO_2$ were converted to $H_2SO_4$ according to the two-step process given below, how many kilograms of $H_2SO_4$ would be produced from such an eruption?

$$SO_2 + \frac{1}{2}O_2 \longrightarrow SO_3$$

$$SO_3 + H_2O \longrightarrow H_2SO_4$$

## MIXED REVIEW

**34.** Suppose that dilute $HNO_3(aq)$ and $LiOH(aq)$ are mixed in chemically equivalent quantities. Write the following for the resulting reaction:
a. formula equation
b. overall ionic equation
c. net ionic equation

**35.** Write the balanced chemical equation for the reaction between hydrochloric acid and magnesium metal.

**36.** Write equations for the three-step ionization of phosphoric acid, $H_3PO_4$. Compare the degree of ionization for the three steps.

**37.** Name or give the molecular formula for each of the following acids:
a. HF
b. acetic acid
c. phosphorous acid
d. $HClO_4$
e. $H_3PO_4$
f. hydrobromic acid
g. HClO
h. $H_2CO_3$
i. sulfuric acid

## CRITICAL THINKING

**38. Analyzing Conclusions** In the 18th century, Antoine Lavoisier experimented with oxides, such as $CO_2$ and $SO_2$. He observed that they formed acidic solutions. His observations led him to infer that to exhibit acidic behavior, a substance must contain oxygen. However, today that inference is known to be incorrect. Provide evidence to refute Lavoisier's conclusion.

## USING THE HANDBOOK

**39.** Group 16 of the *Elements Handbook* contains a section covering the acid-base chemistry of oxides. Review this material, and answer the following questions:
a. What types of compounds form acidic oxides?
b. What is an acid anhydride?
c. What are three examples of compounds that are classified as acid anhydrides?
d. What types of compounds form basic oxides? Why are they basic oxides?

**40.** a. Look at Table 7A in the *Elements Handbook.* What periodic trends regarding the acid-base character of oxides do you notice?
b. How is the nature of the product affected by the concentrations of the reactants?

## RESEARCH & WRITING

**41.** Explain how sulfuric acid production serves as a measure of a country's economy. Write a report on your findings.

**42. Performance** Conduct library research to find out about the buffering of solutions. Include information on why solutions are buffered and what kinds of materials used as buffers. Write a brief report on your findings.

**43.** Obtain some pH paper from your teacher. Determine whether the soil around your house is acidic or basic. Find one type of plant that would grow well in the type of soil around your home and one that would not grow well.

## ALTERNATIVE ASSESSMENT

**44.** Antacids are designed to neutralize excess hydrochloric acid secreted by the stomach during digestion. Carbonates, bicarbonates, and hydroxides are the active ingredients in the most widely used antacids. These ingredients act to drive the neutralization reactions. Examine the labels of several common antacids, and identify the active ingredients.

**45.** Design an experiment that compares three brands of antacids in terms of the speed of symptom relief and amount of acid neutralized.

# Math Tutor WRITING EQUATIONS FOR IONIC REACTIONS

Many chemical reactions that occur in water solutions are reactions involving ions. Soluble ionic compounds dissociate into ions when they dissolve, and some molecular compounds, including acids, ionize when they dissolve. An ionic equation represents the species actually present more accurately than an equation that uses full formulas.

## Problem-Solving TIPS

- All dissolved substances in ionic reactions are dissociated into ions. Therefore, soluble ionic compounds are shown as the separated ions in the full ionic equation. Strong acids and bases are also shown as the separated ions in the full ionic equation because they are 100% ionized.
- Ions that do not take part in the reaction are called *spectator ions.* In other words, spectator ions stay in solution and will be labeled "(*aq*)" on both sides of the equation. Eliminating spectator ions reduces the "clutter" of the full ionic equation and produces a net ionic equation that shows only the species that actually react.

### SAMPLE 1

**Write the net ionic equation for the reaction of aqueous ammonium sulfate and aqueous barium nitrate to produce a precipitate of barium sulfate. The balanced formula equation is**

$$\mathbf{(NH_4)_2SO_4(\mathit{aq}) + Ba(NO_3)_2(\mathit{aq}) \longrightarrow 2NH_4NO_3(\mathit{aq}) + BaSO_4(\mathit{s})}$$

Rewrite the equation in full ionic form; because ammonium sulfate and barium nitrate are soluble, they are written as separated ions:

$$2NH_4^+(aq) + SO_4^{2-}(aq) + Ba^{2+}(aq) + 2NO_3^-(aq) \longrightarrow 2NH_4^+(aq) + 2NO_3^-(aq) + BaSO_4(s)$$

Eliminating spectator ions, $NH_4^+$ and $NO_3^-$, yields the net ionic equation:

$$SO_4^{2-}(aq) + Ba^{2+}(aq) \longrightarrow BaSO_4(s)$$

### SAMPLE 2

**Write full and net ionic equations for the reaction that occurs when hydrochloric acid solution is combined with silver nitrate solution.**

Hydrochloric acid is a strong acid, so it is completely ionized in solution. Silver nitrate is a soluble ionic compound, so its ions are separated in solution. Although most chlorides are soluble, silver chloride is not, so silver chloride will precipitate. The balanced formula equation is

$$HCl(aq) + AgNO_3(aq) \longrightarrow AgCl(s) + HNO_3(aq)$$

The full ionic equation is

$$H_3O^+(aq) + Cl^-(aq) + Ag^+(aq) + NO_3^-(aq) \longrightarrow H_3O^+(aq) + NO_3^-(aq) + AgCl(s)$$

Eliminate spectator ions to obtain the net ionic equation:

$$Cl^-(aq) + Ag^+(aq) \longrightarrow AgCl(s)$$

### PRACTICE PROBLEMS

1. Aqueous copper(II) sulfate reacts with aqueous sodium sulfide to produce a black precipitate of copper(II) sulfide. Write the formula equation, the full ionic equation, and the net ionic equation for this reaction.

2. Write full and net ionic equations for the reaction that occurs when a solution of cadmium chloride, $CdCl_2$, is mixed with a solution of sodium carbonate, $Na_2CO_3$. Cadmium carbonate is insoluble.

# Standardized Test Prep

**Answer the following items on a separate piece of paper.**

## MULTIPLE CHOICE

**1.** Which of the following is *not* a characteristic of an acid?
**A.** An acid changes the color of an indicator.
**B.** An acid has a bitter taste.
**C.** An acid ionizes in water.
**D.** An acid produces hydronium ions in water.

**2.** When an acid reacts with an active metal,
**A.** the hydronium ion concentration increases.
**B.** the metal forms anions.
**C.** hydrogen gas is produced.
**D.** carbon dioxide gas is produced.

**3.** Which of the following is a Brønsted-Lowry base?
**A.** an electron pair donor
**B.** an electron pair acceptor
**C.** a proton donor
**D.** a proton acceptor

**4.** Which acid is the most commonly produced industrial chemical?
**A.** hydrochloric acid
**B.** acetic acid
**C.** nitric acid
**D.** sulfuric acid

**5.** Which of the following is a conjugate pair?
**A.** $H^+$ and $OH^-$
**B.** $NH_2^-$ and $NH_4^+$
**C.** HCl and $Cl^-$
**D.** $H_2SO_4$ and $SO_4^{2-}$

**6.** What is the formula for acetic acid?
**A.** $CH_3COOH$
**B.** $HNO_3$
**C.** $HClO_4$
**D.** HCN

**7.** Which of the following species is the conjugate acid of another species in the list?
**A.** $PO_4^{3-}$
**B.** $H_3PO_4$
**C.** $H_2O$
**D.** $H_2PO_4^-$

**8.** Identify the salt that forms when a solution of $H_2SO_4$ is titrated with a solution of $Ca(OH)_2$.
**A.** calcium sulfate
**B.** calcium hydroxide
**C.** calcium oxide
**D.** calcium phosphate

**9.** Which of the following statements is true for the reaction below?

$$HF(aq) + HPO_4^{2-}(aq) \rightleftharpoons F^-(aq) + H_2PO_4^-(aq)$$

**A.** HF is the base.
**B.** $HPO_4^{2-}$ is the acid.
**C.** $F^-$ is the conjugate base.
**D.** $H_2PO_4^-$ is the conjugate base.

## SHORT ANSWER

**10.** How does a strong acid differ from a weak acid? Give one example of each.

**11.** Identify the conjugate acid-base pairs in the following reaction:

$$HClO_2(aq) + NH_3(aq) \rightleftharpoons ClO_2^-(aq) + NH_4^+(aq)$$

## EXTENDED RESPONSE

**12.** Phosphoric acid, $H_3PO_4$, has three hydrogen atoms and is classified as a triprotic acid. Acetic acid, $CH_3COOH$, has four hydrogen atoms and is classified as a monoprotic acid. Explain the difference, and justify your explanation by drawing the Lewis structure for both acids.

**13.** Write the full equation, ionic equation, and net ionic equation for the neutralization reaction between ammonia and sulfuric acid. Identify the spectator ion(s).

**Test TIP** Double check (with a calculator, if permitted) all mathematical computations involved in answering a question.

# Is It an Acid or a Base?

## OBJECTIVES

- ***Design*** **an experiment to solve a chemical problem.**
- ***Relate*** **observations of chemical properties to identify unknowns.**
- ***Infer*** **a conclusion from experimental data.**
- ***Apply*** **acid-base concepts.**

## MATERIALS

- **24-well microplate or 24 small test tubes**
- **labeled pipets containing solutions numbered 1–8**
- **toothpicks**

**For other supplies, check with your teacher.**

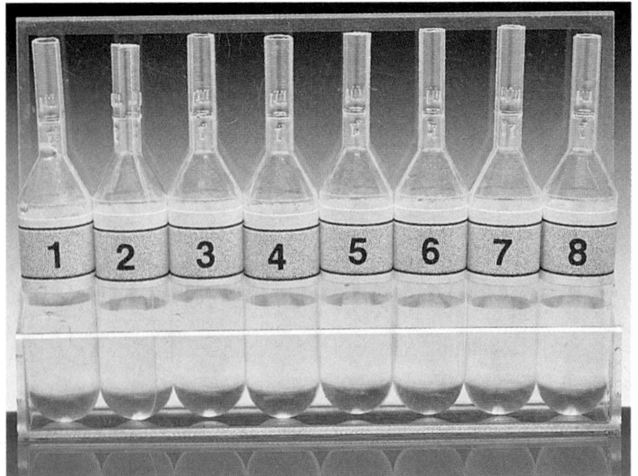


## BACKGROUND

When scientists uncover a problem that they need to solve, they think carefully about the problem and then use their knowledge and experience to develop a plan for solving it. In this experiment, you will be given a set of eight colorless solutions. Four of them are acidic solutions (dilute hydrochloric acid), and four are basic solutions (dilute sodium hydroxide). The concentrations of both the acidic and the basic solutions are 0.1 M, 0.2 M, 0.4 M, and 0.8 M. Phenolphthalein has been added to the acidic solutions.

First, write a procedure to determine which solutions are acidic and which are basic. Then, carry out your procedure. Next, develop and carry out procedure that allows you to list the acidic and basic solutions in order from lowest to highest concentration. As you plan your procedures, consider the properties of acids and bases that are discussed in Chapter 14. Predict what will happen to a solution of each type and concentration when you do each test. Then, compare your predictions with what actually happens. You will have limited amounts of the unknown solutions to work with, so use them carefully. Ask your teacher what additional supplies (if any) will be available to you.

## SAFETY

For review of safety, please see **Safety in the Chemistry Laboratory** in the front of your book.

## PREPARATION

1. Make two data tables in your lab notebook. For Data Table 1, make two columns, one labeled "Acids" and the other labeled "Bases."

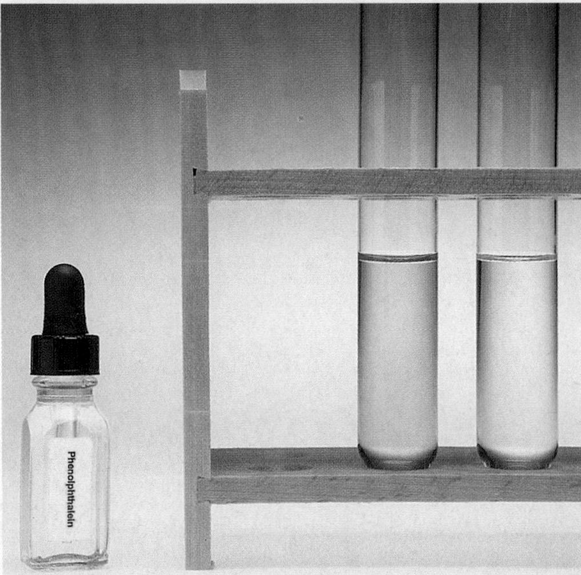


FIGURE A After adding phenolphthalein indicator, you can more easily determine which solution is acidic and which solution is basic.

You will record the numbers of the unknown solutions in the proper column as you identify them.

For Data Table 2, make three columns, with the headings "Concentration," "HCl," and "NaOH." Record the concentration of each solution as you test it, and then record the concentrations of HCl and NaOH present in the solution.

2. In your lab notebook, write the steps that you will use to determine which solutions are acids and which solutions are bases. Figure A shows one test that you can use to make this determination.

3. Ask your teacher to approve your plan and to give you any additional supplies that you will need.

## PROCEDURE

1. Carry out your plan for determining which solutions are acids and which are bases. As you perform your tests, avoid letting the tips of the storage pipets come into contact with other chemicals. Squeeze drops out of the pipets onto the 24-well plate, and then use these drops for your tests. Record all observations in your lab notebook, and then record your results in your first data table.

2. In your lab notebook, write your procedure for determining the concentrations of the solutions. Ask your teacher to approve your plan, and request any additional supplies that you will need.

3. Carry out your procedure for determining the concentrations of the solutions. Record all observations in your lab notebook, and record your results in the second data table.

## CLEANUP AND DISPOSAL

4. Clean all equipment and your lab station. Return equipment to its proper place. Dispose of chemicals and solutions in the containers designated by your teacher. Do not pour any chemicals down the drain or in the trash unless your teacher directs you to do so. Wash your hands thoroughly before you leave the lab and after all work is finished.

## CONCLUSIONS

1. **Analyzing Conclusions:** List the numbers of the solutions and their concentrations.

2. **Analyzing Conclusions:** Describe the test results that led you to identify some solutions as acids and others as bases. Explain how you determined the concentrations of the unknown solutions.

## EXTENSIONS

1. **Evaluating Methods:** Compare your results with those of another lab group. Do you think that your teacher gave both groups the same set of solutions? (For example, is your solution 1 the same as the other group's solution 1?) Explain your reasoning.

2. **Applying Conclusions:** Imagine that you are helping clean out the school's chemical storeroom. You find a spill of a clear liquid coming from a large, unlabeled reagent bottle. What tests would you do to quickly determine if the substance is acidic or basic?

CHAPTER 15

# Acid-Base Titration and pH

*Many of the foods we eat, such as tomatoes, are acidic.*

Heirloom Tomatoes

# Aqueous Solutions and the Concept of pH

**C.6.8** Use the hydronium or hydroxide ion concentration to determine the pH and pOH of aqueous solutions

## OBJECTIVES

- Describe the self-ionization of water.
- Define *pH,* and give the pH of a neutral solution at 25°C.
- Explain and use the pH scale.
- Given $[H_3O^+]$ or $[OH^-]$, find pH.
- Given pH, find $[H_3O^+]$ or $[OH^-]$.

## Hydronium Ions and Hydroxide Ions

You have already seen that acids and bases form hydronium ions and hydroxide ions, respectively, in aqueous solutions. However, these ions formed from the solute are not the only such ions present in an aqueous solution. Hydronium ions and hydroxide ions are also provided by the solvent, water.

### Self-Ionization of Water

Careful electrical conductivity experiments have shown that pure water is an extremely weak electrolyte. Water undergoes self-ionization, as shown in the model in **Figure 1.** *In the* **self-ionization of water,** *two water molecules produce a hydronium ion and a hydroxide ion by transfer of a proton.* The following equilibrium takes place.

$$H_2O(l) + H_2O(l) \rightleftharpoons H_3O^+(aq) + OH^-(aq)$$

Conductivity measurements show that concentrations of $H_3O^+$ and $OH^-$ in pure water are each only $1.0 \times 10^{-7}$ mol/L of water at 25°C.

There is a standard notation to represent concentration in moles per liter. The formula of the particular ion or molecule is enclosed in brackets, [ ]. For example, the symbol $[H_3O^+]$ means "hydronium ion concentration in moles per liter," or "molar hydronium ion concentration." In water at 25°C, $[H_3O^+] = 1.0 \times 10^{-7}$ M and $[OH^-] = 1.0 \times 10^{-7}$ M.

The mathematical product of $[H_3O^+]$ and $[OH^-]$ remains constant in water and dilute aqueous solutions at constant temperature. This

SCILINKS. www.scilinks.org
Topic: pH
Code: HC61129

**FIGURE 1** Water undergoes self-ionization to a slight extent. A proton is transferred from one water molecule to another. A hydronium ion, $H_3O^+$, and a hydroxide ion, $OH^-$, are produced.

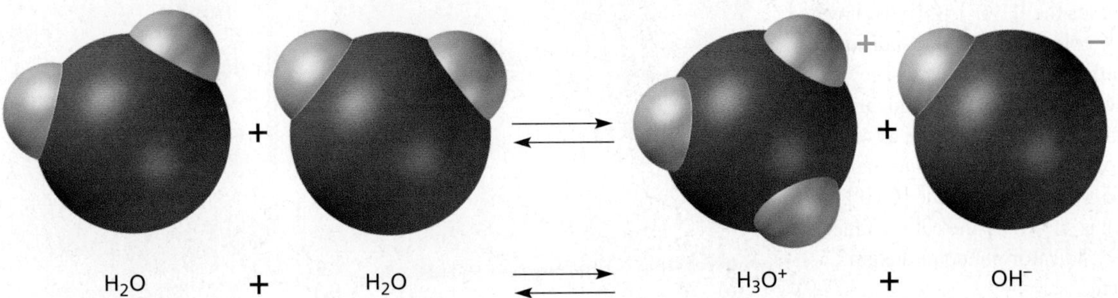

**TABLE 1 $K_w$ at Selected Temperatures**

| Temperature (°C) | $K_w$ |
|---|---|
| 0 | $1.2 \times 10^{-15}$ |
| 10 | $3.0 \times 10^{-15}$ |
| 25 | $1.0 \times 10^{-14}$ |
| 50 | $5.3 \times 10^{-14}$ |

constant mathematical product is called the *ionization constant of water*, $K_w$, and is expressed by the following equation.

$$K_w = [H_3O^+][OH^-]$$

For example, in water and dilute aqueous solutions at 25°C, the following relationship is valid.

$$K_w = [H_3O^+][OH^-] = (1.0 \times 10^{-7})(1.0 \times 10^{-7}) = 1.0 \times 10^{-14}$$

The ionization of water increases as temperature increases. Therefore, the ion product, $K_w$, also increases as temperature increases, as shown in **Table 1.** However, at any given temperature $K_w$ is always a constant value. The value $1.0 \times 10^{-14}$ is assumed to be constant within the ordinary range of room temperatures. In this chapter, you can assume that these conditions are present unless otherwise stated.

## Neutral, Acidic, and Basic Solutions

Because the hydronium ion and hydroxide ion concentrations are the same in pure water, it is *neutral.* In fact, any solution in which $[H_3O^+] = [OH^-]$ is neutral. Recall from Chapter 14 that acids increase the concentration of $H_3O^+$ in aqueous solutions, as shown in **Figure 2a.** Solutions in which the $[H_3O^+]$ is greater than the $[OH^-]$ are *acidic.* Bases increase the concentration of $OH^-$ in aqueous solutions, as shown in **Figure 2b.** In *basic* solutions, the $[OH^-]$ is greater than the $[H_3O^+]$.

As stated earlier, the $[H_3O^+]$ and the $[OH^-]$ of a neutral solution at 25°C both equal $1.0 \times 10^{-7}$ M. Therefore, if the $[H_3O^+]$ is increased to greater than $1.0 \times 10^{-7}$ M, the solution becomes acidic. A solution containing $1.0 \times 10^{-5}$ mol $H_3O^+$ ion/L at 25°C is acidic because $1.0 \times 10^{-5}$ is greater than $1.0 \times 10^{-7}$. If the $[OH^-]$ is increased to greater than $1.0 \times 10^{-7}$ M, the solution becomes basic. A solution containing $1.0 \times 10^{-4}$ mol $OH^-$ ions/L at 25°C is basic because $1.0 \times 10^{-4}$ is greater than $1.0 \times 10^{-7}$.

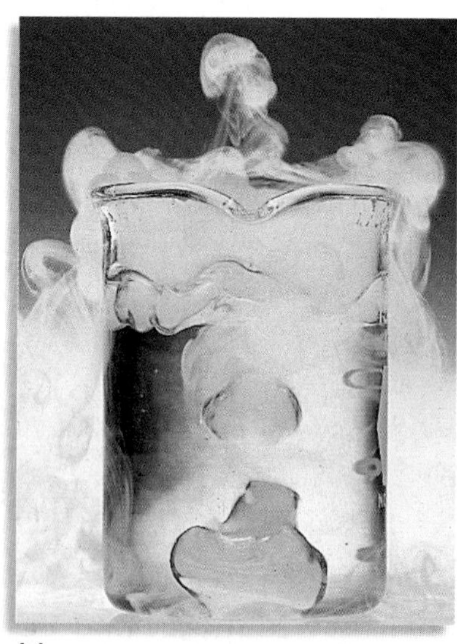

(a)

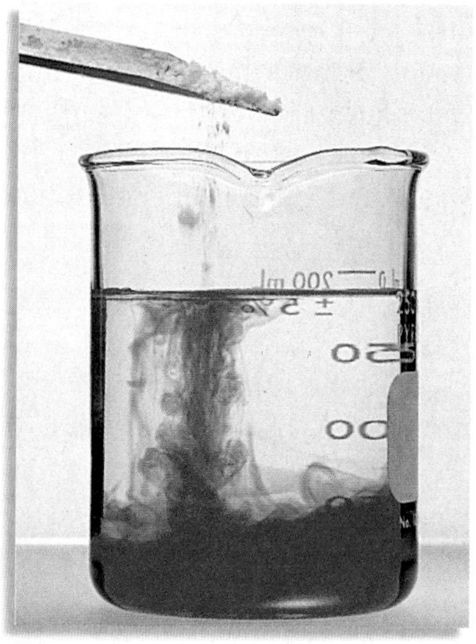

(b)

**FIGURE 2** (a) Addition of dry ice, carbon dioxide, to water increases the $[H_3O^+]$, which is shown by the color change of the indicator bromthymol blue to yellow. The white mist is formed by condensation of water vapor because the dry ice is cold. (b) Addition of sodium peroxide to water increases the $[OH^-]$, which is shown by the color change of the indicator phenolphthalein to pink.

## Calculating $[H_3O^+]$ and $[OH^-]$

Recall that strong acids and bases are considered completely ionized or dissociated in weak aqueous solutions. A review of strong acids and bases is given in **Table 2.** Because NaOH is a strong base, 1 mol of it will yield 1 mol of $OH^-$ in an aqueous solution.

$$\underset{1\text{ mol}}{NaOH(s)} \xrightarrow{H_2O} \underset{1\text{ mol}}{Na^+(aq)} + \underset{1\text{ mol}}{OH^-(aq)}$$

Therefore, a $1.0 \times 10^{-2}$ M NaOH solution has an $[OH^-]$ of $1.0 \times 10^{-2}$ M, as shown by the following.

$$\frac{1.0 \times 10^{-2}\text{ mol NaOH}}{1\text{ L solution}} \times \frac{1\text{ mol } OH^-}{1\text{ mol NaOH}} = \frac{1.0 \times 10^{-2}\text{ mol } OH^-}{1\text{ L solution}}$$
$$= 1.0 \times 10^{-2}\text{ M } OH^-$$

Notice that the $[OH^-]$ is greater than $1.0 \times 10^{-7}$ M. This solution is basic.

Because the $K_w$ of an aqueous solution is a relatively constant $1.0 \times 10^{-14}$ at ordinary room temperatures, the concentration of either ion can be determined if the concentration of the other ion is known. The $[H_3O^+]$ of this solution is calculated as follows.

$$K_w = [H_3O^+][OH^-] = 1.0 \times 10^{-14}$$
$$[H_3O^+] = \frac{1.0 \times 10^{-14}}{[OH^-]} = \frac{1.0 \times 10^{-14}}{1.0 \times 10^{-2}} = 1.0 \times 10^{-12}\text{ M}$$

The $[OH^-]$, $1.0 \times 10^{-2}$ M, is greater than the $[H_3O^+]$, $1.0 \times 10^{-12}$ M, as is true for all basic solutions.

Now consider a $2.0 \times 10^{-4}$ M HCl solution. Because HCl is a strong acid, the $[H_3O^+]$ is $2.0 \times 10^{-4}$ M, as shown by the following.

$$\underset{1\text{ mol}}{HCl(g)} + \underset{1\text{ mol}}{H_2O(l)} \longrightarrow \underset{1\text{ mol}}{H_3O^+(aq)} + \underset{1\text{ mol}}{Cl^-(aq)}$$

$$\frac{2.0 \times 10^{-4}\text{ mol HCl}}{1\text{ L solution}} \times \frac{1\text{ mol } H_3O^+}{1\text{ mol HCl}} = \frac{2.0 \times 10^{-4}\text{ mol } H_3O^+}{1\text{ L solution}}$$
$$= 2.0 \times 10^{-4}\text{ M } H_3O^+$$

Notice that the $[H_3O^+]$ is greater than $1.0 \times 10^{-7}$ M. This solution is acidic. The $[OH^-]$ of this solution is calculated as follows.

$$K_w = [H_3O^+][OH^-] = 1.0 \times 10^{-14}$$
$$[OH^-] = \frac{1.0 \times 10^{-14}}{[H_3O^+]} = \frac{1.0 \times 10^{-14}}{2.0 \times 10^{-4}} = 5.0 \times 10^{-10}\text{ M}$$

The $[H_3O^+]$ is greater than the $[OH^-]$ for all acidic solutions.

You may have realized that in order for $K_w$ to remain constant, an increase in either the $[H_3O^+]$ or the $[OH^-]$ in an aqueous solution causes a decrease in the concentration of the other ion. Sample Problem A also shows calculation of the $[H_3O^+]$ and $[OH^-]$ of an acidic solution.

**TABLE 2 Common Strong Acids and Bases**

| Strong Acids | Strong Bases |
|---|---|
| HCl | LiOH |
| HBr | NaOH |
| HI | KOH |
| $HClO_4$ | RbOH |
| $HClO_3$ | CsOH |
| $HNO_3$ | $Ca(OH)_2$ |
| $H_2SO_4$ | $Sr(OH)_2$ |
| | $Ba(OH)_2$ |

## SAMPLE PROBLEM E

For more help, go to the *Math Tutor* at the end of this chapter.

**The pH of a solution is measured and determined to be 7.52.**
**a. What is the hydronium ion concentration?**
**b. What is the hydroxide ion concentration?**
**c. Is the solution acidic or basic?**

### SOLUTION

1 ***ANALYZE*** **Given:** pH of the solution = 7.52
**Unknown:** **a.** $[H_3O^+]$ **b.** $[OH^-]$ **c.** Is the solution acidic or basic?

2 ***PLAN***

$$pH \longrightarrow [H_3O^+] \longrightarrow [OH^-]$$

This problem is very similar to previous pH problems. You will need to substitute values into the $pH = -\log [H_3O^+]$ equation and use a calculator. Once the $[H_3O^+]$ is determined, the ion-product constant $[H_3O^+][OH^-] = 1.0 \times 10^{-14}$ may be used to calculate $[OH^-]$.

3 ***COMPUTE*** **a.** $pH = -\log [H_3O^+]$
$\log [H_3O^+] = -pH$
$[H_3O^+] = \text{antilog}(-pH) = \text{antilog}(-7.52) = 1.0 \times 10^{-7.52} = 3.0 \times 10^{-8}\ M\ H_3O^+$

On most calculators, this is entered in one of the following two ways.

7 . 5 2 +/- 2nd $10^x$ *or* 7 . 5 2 +/- 2nd LOG

**b.** $[H_3O^+][OH^-] = 1.0 \times 10^{-14}$

$$[OH^-] = \frac{1.0 \times 10^{-14}}{[H_3O^+]}$$

$$= \frac{1.0 \times 10^{-14}}{3.0 \times 10^{-8}} = 3.3 \times 10^{-7}\ M\ OH^-$$

**c.** A pH of 7.52 is slightly greater than a pH of 7. This means that the solution is slightly basic.

4 ***EVALUATE*** Because the solution is slightly basic, a hydroxide ion concentration slightly larger than $10^{-7}$ M is predicted. A hydronium ion concentration slightly less than $10^{-7}$ M is also predicted. The answers agree with these predictions.

### PRACTICE

*Answers in Appendix E*

1. The pH of a solution is determined to be 5.0. What is the hydronium ion concentration of this solution?
2. The pH of a solution is determined to be 12.0. What is the hydronium ion concentration of this solution?
3. The pH of an aqueous solution is measured as 1.50. Calculate the $[H_3O^+]$ and the $[OH^-]$.
4. The pH of an aqueous solution is 3.67. Determine $[H_3O^+]$.

**extension**

Go to **go.hrw.com** for more practice problems that ask you to calculate hydronium ion concentration.

**Keyword: HC6ABTX**

**TABLE 5 Relationship of $[H_3O^+]$ to $[OH^-]$ and pH (at 25°C)**

| Solution | $[H_3O^+]$ | $[OH^-]$ | pH |
|---|---|---|---|
| $1.0 \times 10^{-2}$ M KOH | $1.0 \times 10^{-12}$ | $1.0 \times 10^{-2}$ | 12.00 |
| $1.0 \times 10^{-2}$ M $NH_3$ | $2.4 \times 10^{-11}$ | $4.2 \times 10^{-4}$ | 10.63 |
| Pure $H_2O$ | $1.0 \times 10^{-7}$ | $1.0 \times 10^{-7}$ | 7.00 |
| $1.0 \times 10^{-3}$ M HCl | $1.0 \times 10^{-3}$ | $1.0 \times 10^{-11}$ | 3.00 |
| $1.0 \times 10^{-1}$ M $CH_3COOH$ | $1.3 \times 10^{-3}$ | $7.5 \times 10^{-12}$ | 2.87 |

## pH Calculations and the Strength of Acids and Bases

So far, we have discussed the pH of solutions that contain only strong acids or strong bases. We must also consider weak acids and weak bases. **Table 5** lists the $[H_3O^+]$, the $[OH^-]$, and the pH for several solutions.

KOH, the solute in the first solution listed, is a soluble ionic compound and a strong base. The molarity of a KOH solution directly indicates the $[OH^-]$, and the $[H_3O^+]$ can be calculated. Once the $[H_3O^+]$ is known, the pH can be calculated as in Sample Problem C. If the pH of this solution is measured experimentally, it will be the same as this calculated value. Methods for experimentally determining the pH of solutions will be presented in Section 2. Hydrochloric acid, HCl, is a strong acid, and similar calculations can be made for solutions that contain HCl.

Solutions of weak acids, such as acetic acid, $CH_3COOH$, present a different problem. The $[H_3O^+]$ cannot be calculated directly from the molar concentration because not all of the acetic acid molecules are ionized. The same problem occurs for weak bases such as ammonia, $NH_3$. The pH of these solutions must be measured experimentally. The $[H_3O^+]$ and $[OH^-]$ can then be calculated from the measured pH values.

extension

**CROSS-DISCIPLINARY**

Go to **go.hrw.com** for a full-length article on how buffers maintain the acid-base balance in blood.

**Keyword: HC6ABTX**

## SECTION REVIEW

1. What is the concentration of hydronium and hydroxide ions in pure water at 25°C?
2. Why does the pH scale generally range from 0 to 14 in aqueous solutions?
3. Why does a pH of 7 represent a neutral solution at 25°C?
4. A solution contains $4.5 \times 10^{-3}$ M HCl. Determine the following for the solution:
   **a.** $[H_3O^+]$ **b.** $[OH^-]$ **c.** pH
5. A $Ca(OH)_2$ solution has a pH of 8.0. Determine the following for the solution:
   **a.** $[H_3O^+]$ **b.** $[OH^-]$ **c.** $[Ca(OH)_2]$

**Critical Thinking**

6. **PREDICTING OUTCOMES** Arrange the following solutions in order from lowest to highest pH: 0.10 M HCl, 0.10 M $H_2SO_4$, and 0.10 M HF.

# CROSS-DISCIPLINARY CONNECTION

## Liming Streams

In 1987, Dr. Ken Simmons tested some rainbow trout in the waters of north-central Massachusetts' Whetstone Brook. He placed the trout in cages in the brook so that their behavior and survival could be monitored. Three days later, they were dead. Acid rain had lowered the pH level of the water to a point at which the trout simply could not survive.

Acid rain begins with the fossil fuels that we burn to power our cars and factories. Those fuels release combustion products that contain sulfur and nitrogen that combine with the water vapor in the atmosphere and turn the vapor acidic. The pH level of normal rainwater is about 5.5, but levels as low as 4.3 have been recorded.

Acid rain lowers the brook's pH level, which significantly affects most of the organisms living in the brook. Some fish, such as the rainbow trout, simply die. Other species, such as Whetstone's brown trout, will not spawn in acidic waters.

In 1987, brown trout did not spawn in Whetstone Brook. The pH level of the brook averaged 5.97 that year. The population of all the trout dropped significantly. In 1989, Dr. Simmons and other researchers instituted an experiment to decrease the acidity of the stream. They created a system to continuously add calcium carbonate, or limestone, in measured amounts to part of the brook. The limestone, which was ground into a powder, immediately reacted with the acid, which raised the pH level of the water.

The experiment lasted three years and managed to raise the average pH level of the stream from 5.97 to 6.54, which met the scientists' goal.

▲ *Biologists studied trout to determine the effectiveness of liming Whetstone Brook to raise the pH.*

At the same time, the concentration of aluminum ion, which is toxic to trout, in the limed area decreased, while it increased in untreated parts of the brook.

The success of the project was most convincingly demonstrated by the stream's residents. The population of brook trout increased; the mortality rate of brown trout decreased, and for the first time in years, fish actually began to move into the stream from its source, the Millers River. In 1991, Dr. Simmons again tested rainbow trout in the waters of the Whetstone. This time, they all survived.

"We clearly don't view it as a solution," says Dr. Simmons. "It's a band-aid approach, but we need data to make intelligent management decisions as to how useful or harmful liming could be. And I think that is the key thing this study has shown. It has provided us with information that we can use."

### Questions

1. Describe two possible benefits of adding measured amounts of $CaCO_3$, a base, to an acidified stream.
2. What elements are responsible for acid rain? How do they get into rainwater?

# Determining pH and Titrations

SECTION 2

**C.6.4** Carry out calculations to find the concentration of solutions in terms of molarity and percent weight (mass)

## OBJECTIVES

- Describe how an acid-base indicator functions.
- Explain how to carry out an acid-base titration.
- Calculate the molarity of a solution from titration data.

## Indicators and pH Meters

An approximate value for the pH of a solution can be obtained using acid-base indicators. **Acid-base indicators** *are compounds whose colors are sensitive to pH.* In other words, the color of an indicator changes as the pH of a solution changes.

Indicators change colors because they are either weak acids or weak bases. In solution, a weak-acid indicator (H*In*) can be represented by the equation below, which is modeled in **Figure 4.**

$$HIn \rightleftharpoons H^+ + In^-$$

($In^-$ is the symbol of the anion part of the indicator.) Because the reaction is reversable, both H*In* and $In^-$ are present. The colors displayed result from the fact that H*In* and $In^-$ are different colors.

In acidic solutions, any $In^-$ ions that are present act as Brønsted bases and accept protons from the acid. The indicator is then present in largely nonionized form, H*In*. The indicator has its acid-indicating color, as shown for litmus in **Figure 4.**

In basic solutions, the $OH^-$ ions from the base combine with the $H^+$ ions produced by the indicator. The indicator molecules further ionize to offset the loss of $H^+$ ions. The indicator is thus present largely in the form of its anion, $In^-$. The solution now displays the base-indicating color, which for litmus is blue.

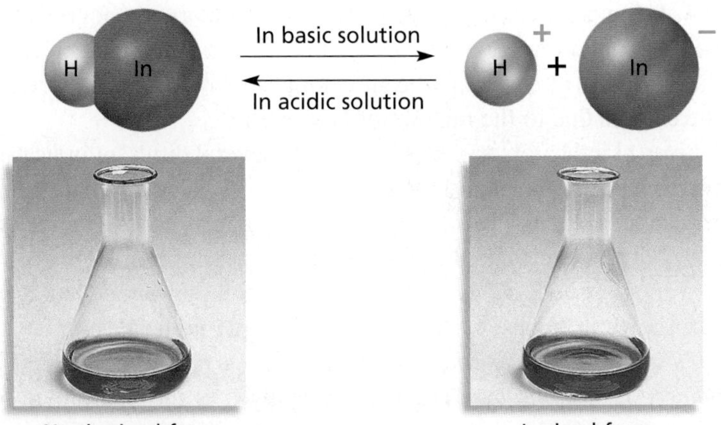


**FIGURE 4** Basic solutions shift the equilibrium of litmus to the right. The ionized form, $In^-$, then predominates, and the litmus turns blue. Acidic solutions shift the equilibrium of the indicator litmus to the left. The nonionized form, H*In*, predominates, and the litmus turns red.

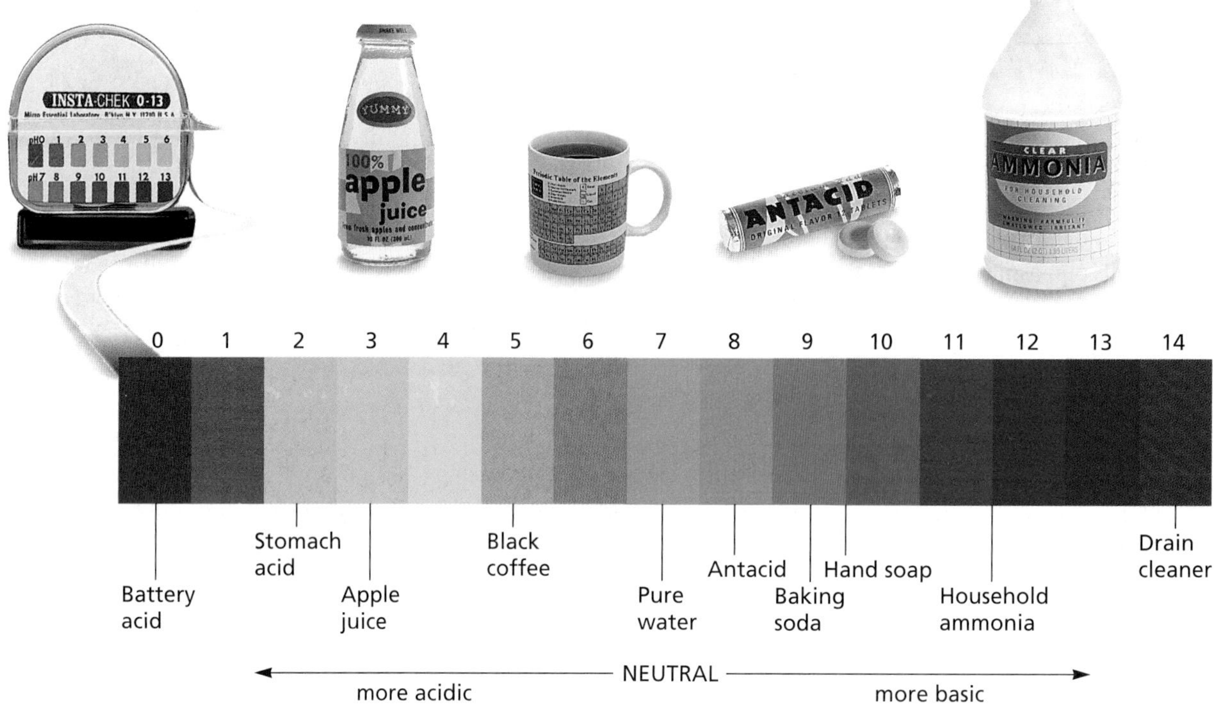


**FIGURE 5** The pH of a solution can be determined by comparing the color it turns pH paper with the scale of the paper. The colors of pH paper at various pH values are shown, as are the pH values for some common materials.

Indicators come in many different colors. The exact pH range over which an indicator changes color also varies. *The pH range over which an indicator changes color is called its* **transition interval. Table 6** gives the color changes and transition intervals for a number of common acid-base indicators.

Different indicators change color at different pH values. The color depends on the relative amounts of H*In* and $In^-$ at a given pH. Methyl red changes from red to yellow between pH 4.4 and 6.2. At pH 4.4, the indicator exists mostly as H*In* molecules, which appear red in the solution. Above pH 6.2, the indicator exists mostly as $In^-$ ions, which appear yellow. A similar situation exists with other indicators. Phenol red at 6.4 or below is yellow as H*In*. Above 8.0, it is in the $In^-$ form, which is red. In the transition interval, significant amounts of both forms are present, so the color is due to the mixture of H*In* and $In^-$.

Universal indicators are made by mixing several different indicators. Paper soaked in universal indicator solution is called pH paper. This paper can turn almost any color of the rainbow and provides a fairly accurate way of distinguishing the pH of solutions, as shown in **Figure 5.**

If a more precise value for the pH of a solution is needed, a pH meter, shown in **Figure 6,** should be used. *A* **pH meter** *determines the pH of a solution by measuring the voltage between the two electrodes that are placed in the solution.* The voltage changes as the hydronium ion concentration in the solution changes.

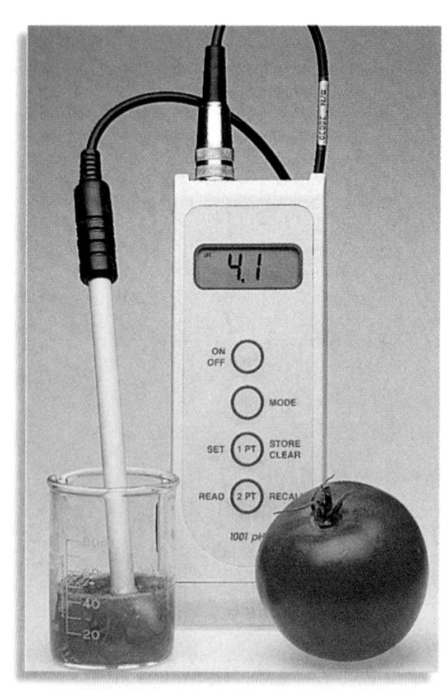


**FIGURE 6** A pH meter precisely measures the pH of a solution.

## TABLE 6 Color Ranges of Various Indicators Used in Titrations

| Titration type | Indicator | Acid color | Transition color | Base color |
|---|---|---|---|---|
| **Strong acid/ strong base** | methyl red (4.4–6.2) |  | | |
| | bromthymol blue (6.2–7.6) |  | | |
| **Strong acid/ weak base** | methyl orange (3.1–4.4) |  | | |
| | bromphenol blue (3.0–4.6) |  | | |
| **Weak acid/ strong base** | phenolphthalein (8.0–10.0) |  | | |
| | phenol red (6.4–8.0) | 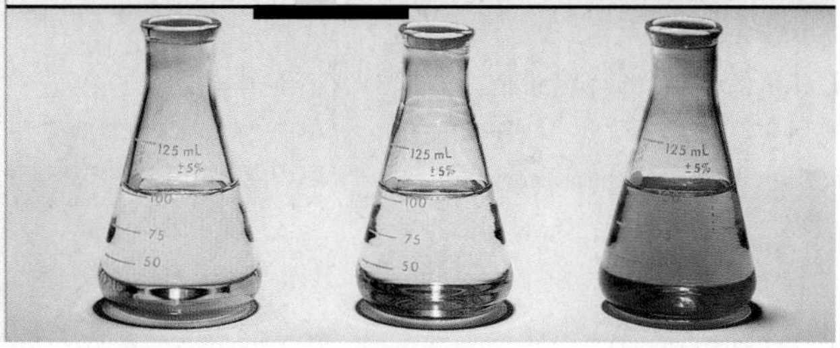 | | |

pH scales: 3 4 5 6 7 8 9 10 11; 0 1 2 3 4 5 6 7 8; 4 5 6 7 8 9 10 11 12

# QuickLAB  Wear safety goggles and an apron.

## *Testing the pH of Rainwater*

### Materials

- rainwater
- distilled water
- 500 mL jars
- thin, transparent metric ruler (± 0.1 cm)
- pH test paper: narrow range, ± 0.2–0.3, or pH meter

### Question

**Do you have acid precipitation in your area?**

### Procedure

Record all of your results in a data table.

1. Each time it rains, set out five clean jars to collect the rainwater. If the rain continues for more than 24 hours, put out new containers at the end of each 24-hour period until the rain stops. (The same procedure can be used with snow if the snow is allowed to melt before measurements are taken. You may need to use larger containers if a heavy snowfall is expected.)
2. After the rain stops or at the end of each 24-hour period, use a thin, plastic ruler to measure the depth of the water to the nearest 0.1 cm with a thin plastic ruler. Using the pH paper, test the water to determine its pH to the nearest 0.2 to 0.3.
3. Record the following information:
   - **a.** the date and time the collection started
   - **b.** the date and time the collection ended
   - **c.** the location where the collection was made (town and state)
   - **d.** the amount of rainfall in centimeters
   - **e.** the pH of the rainwater
4. Find the average pH of each collection that you have made for each rainfall, and record it in the data table.
5. Collect samples on at least five different days. The more samples you collect, the more informative your data will be.
6. For comparison, determine the pH of pure water by testing five samples of distilled water with pH paper. Record your results in a separate data table, and then calculate an average pH for distilled water.

### Discussion

1. What is the pH of distilled water?
2. What is the pH of normal rainwater? How do you explain any differences between the pH readings?
3. What are the drawbacks of using a ruler to measure the depth of collected water? How could you increase the precision of your measurement?
4. Does the amount of rainfall or the time of day the sample is taken have an effect on its pH? Try to explain any variability among samples.
5. What conclusion can you draw from this investigation? Explain how your data support your conclusion.

## Titration

As you know, neutralization reactions occur between acids and bases. The $OH^-$ ion acquires a proton from the $H_3O^+$ ion, forming two molecules of water. The following equation summarizes this reaction.

$$H_3O^+(aq) + OH^-(aq) \longrightarrow 2H_2O(l)$$

This equation shows that one mol of hydronium ions and one mol of hydroxide ions are chemically equivalent amounts. They combine in a one-to-one mole ratio. Neutralization occurs when hydronium ions and hydroxide ions are supplied in equal numbers by reactants, as shown in **Figure 7.**

One liter of a 0.10 M HCl solution contains 0.10 mol of hydronium ions. Now suppose that 0.10 mol of solid NaOH is added to 1 L of 0.10 M HCl solution. The NaOH dissolves and supplies 0.10 mol of hydroxide ions to the solution. HCl and NaOH are present in chemically equivalent amounts. Hydronium and hydroxide ions, which are present in equal numbers, combine until the product $[H_3O^+]\ [OH^-]$ returns to the value of $1 \times 10^{-14}$. NaCl, the salt produced in the reaction, is the product of this neutralization of a strong acid and a strong base. The resulting solution is neutral.

Because acids and bases react, the progressive addition of an acid to a base (or a base to an acid) can be used to compare the concentrations of the acid and the base. **Titration** *is the controlled addition and measurement of the amount of a solution of known concentration required to react completely with a measured amount of a solution of unknown concentration.* Titration provides a sensitive means of determining the chemically equivalent amounts of acid and base.

**FIGURE 7** The solution on the left turns pH paper red because it is acidic. The solution on the right turns pH paper blue because it is basic. When equal numbers of $H_3O^+$ and $OH^-$ from the acidic and basic solutions react, the resulting solution is neutral. The neutral solution turns pH paper green.

## Equivalence Point

*The point at which the two solutions used in a titration are present in chemically equivalent amounts is the* **equivalence point.** Indicators and pH meters can be used to determine the equivalence point. The pH will change rapidly as the equivalence point is approached. If an indicator is used, it must change color over a range that includes the pH of the equivalence point, as shown in **Figure 8.** *The point in a titration at which an indicator changes color is called the* **end point** *of the indicator.*

Some indicators, such as litmus, change color at about pH 7. However, the color-change interval for litmus is broad, pH 5.5–8.0. This broad range makes it difficult to determine an accurate pH. Bromthymol blue is better because it has a smaller transition interval, pH 6.2–7.6 (see **Table 6**). Indicators that undergo transition at about pH 7 are used to determine the equivalence point of strong-acid/strong-base titrations because the neutralization of strong acids with strong bases produces a salt solution with a pH of 7.

Indicators that change color at pH lower than 7 are useful in determining the equivalence point of strong-acid/weak-base titrations. Methyl orange is an example of this type. The equivalence point of a strong-acid/weak-base titration is acidic because the salt formed is itself a weak acid. Thus the salt solution has a pH lower than 7 at the equivalence point.

Indicators that change color at pH higher than 7 are useful in determining the equivalence point of weak-acid/strong-base titrations. Phenolphthalein is an example. These reactions produce salt solutions whose pH is greater than 7. This occurs because the salt formed is a weak base.

You may be wondering what type of indicator is used to determine the equivalence point of weak-acid/weak-base titrations. The surprising answer is "none at all." The pH at the equivalence point of a weak-acid/weak-base titration could be acidic, basic, or neutral, depending on

### CAREERS in Chemistry

#### Analytical Chemist

The primary job of an analytical chemist is to obtain information by making precise measurements. Analytical chemists often use sophisticated, state-of-the-art instruments to analyze for barely detectable amounts of materials. In addition to collecting data, analytical chemists must process the data and communicate their findings with others. These findings must be the result of careful and reproducible work, strict accountability, and control of the samples. Although analytical chemists work in all areas of chemistry, one important area is environmental chemistry, which involves analyzing air, water, and soil samples. The results of these tests are used by regulatory agencies such as the Environmental Protection Agency.

(a)

(b)

**FIGURE 8** Indicators change color at the end point of a titration. Phenolphthalein (a) turns pink and methyl red (b) turns red at the end point of these titrations with a base.

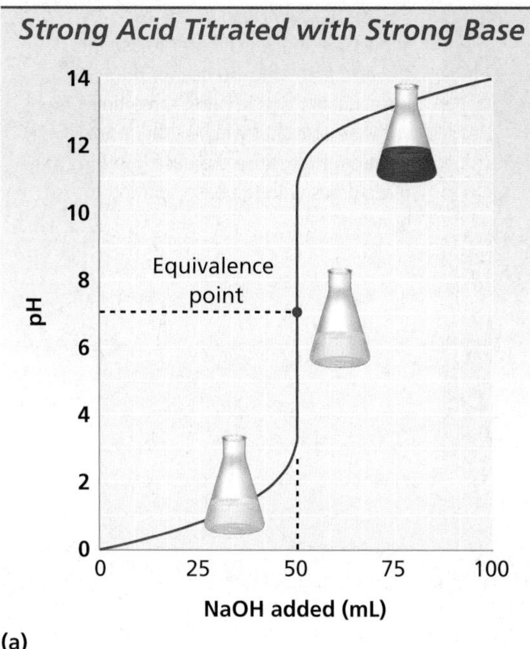


(a)

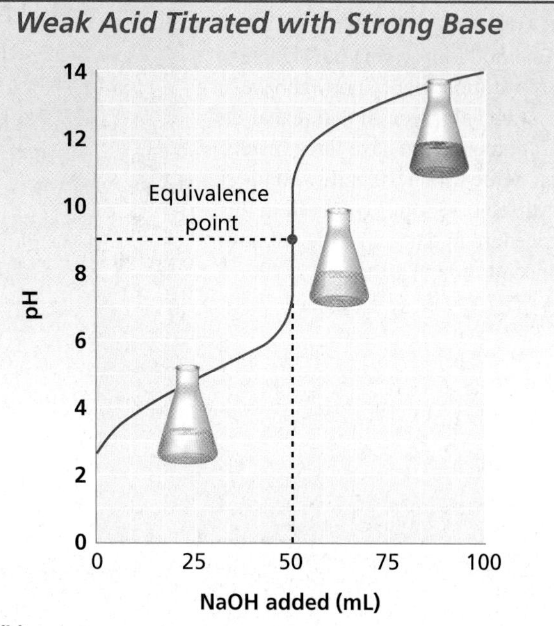


(b)

**FIGURE 9** (a) When a strong acid, such as 50.0 mL of 1.00 M HCl, is titrated with a strong base, such as 1.00 M NaOH, the equivalence point occurs at pH 7.00. (b) When a weak acid, such as 50.0 mL of 1.00 M $CH_3COOH$, is titrated with a strong base, such as 1.00 M NaOH, the initial pH is higher and the equivalence point occurs at a pH above 7.00.

the relative acid-base strengths. Since the pH value does not change dramatically as the equivalence point is approached, it is not practical to carry out weak-acid/weak-base titrations.

In a titration, successive additions of an aqueous base are made to a measured volume of an aqueous acid. As base is added, the pH changes from a lower numerical value to a higher one. The change in pH occurs slowly at first, then rapidly through the equivalence point, and then slowly again as the solution becomes more basic. Near the equivalence point, one drop can cause a pH change of 3 to 5 pH units! Typical pH curves for strong-acid/strong-base and weak-acid/strong-base titrations are shown in **Figure 9.**

## Molarity and Titration

**Figure 10** shows the proper method of carrying out a titration. If the concentration of one solution is known precisely, the concentration of the other solution in a titration can be calculated from the chemically equivalent volumes. *The solution that contains the precisely known concentration of a solute is known as a* **standard solution.** It is often called simply the "known" solution.

To be certain of the concentration of the known solution, that solution must first be compared with a solution of a primary standard. *A* **primary standard** *is a highly purified solid compound used to check the concentration of the known solution in a titration.* The known solution is prepared first to give approximately the desired concentration. The known solution concentration is then determined precisely by titrating a carefully measured quantity of the primary standard.

**FIGURE 10** Following is the proper method for carrying out an acid-base titration. To be sure you have an accurate value, you should repeat the titration until you have three results that agree within 0.05 mL. A standardized base solution is used in this procedure to determine the unknown concentration of an acid.

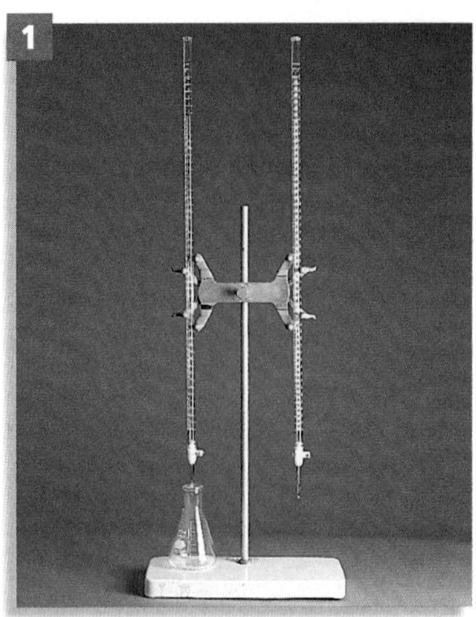

First set up two clean burets as shown. Decide which buret to use for the acid and which to use for the base. Rinse the acid buret three times with the acid that will be used in the titration. Then, rinse the base buret three times with the base solution to be used.

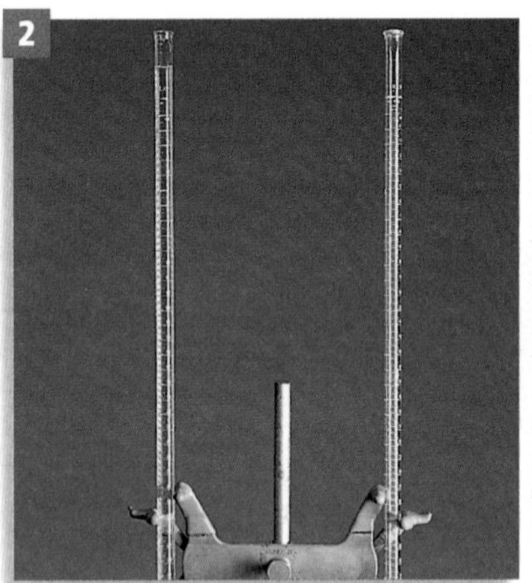

Fill the first buret to a point above the 0 mL calibration mark with the acid of unknown concentration.

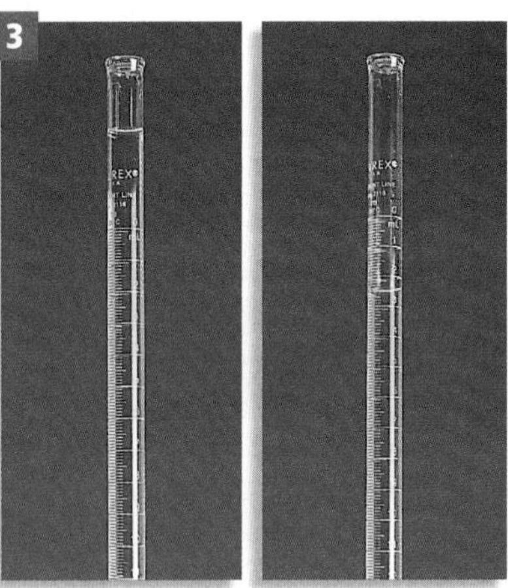

Release some acid from the buret to remove any air bubbles from the tip and to lower the volume to the calibrated portion of the buret.

Record the volume of the acid in the buret to the nearest 0.01 mL as the initial volume. Remember to read the volume at the bottom of the meniscus.

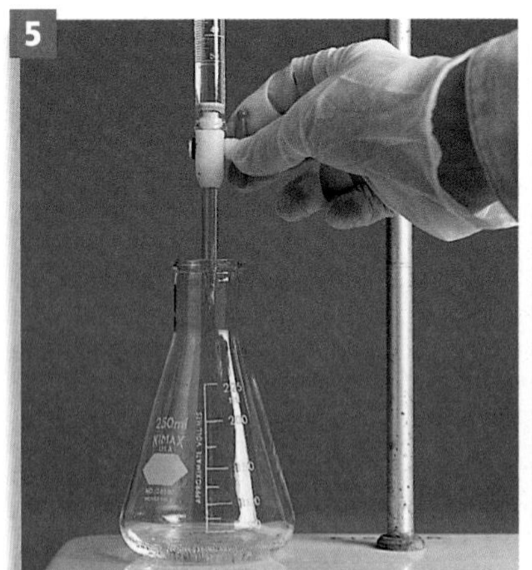

Allow approximately the volume of acid that was determined by your teacher or lab procedure to flow into a clean Erlenmeyer flask.

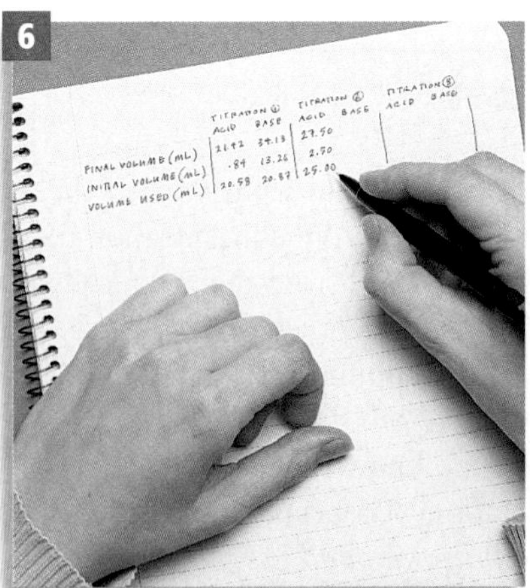


Subtract the initial volume reading on the buret from the final reading. This is the exact volume of the acid released into the flask. Record it to the nearest 0.01 mL.

Add three drops of the appropriate indicator (in this case phenolphthalein) to the flask.

Fill the other buret with the standard base solution to a point above the calibration mark. The concentration of the standard base is known to a certain degree of precision because the base was previously titrated with an exact mass of solid acid, which is the primary standard.

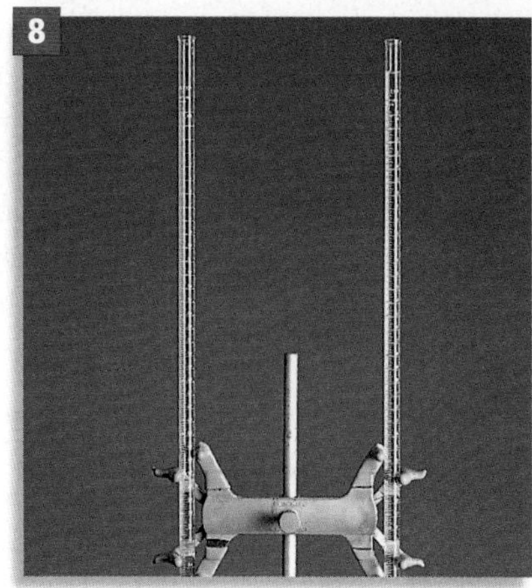

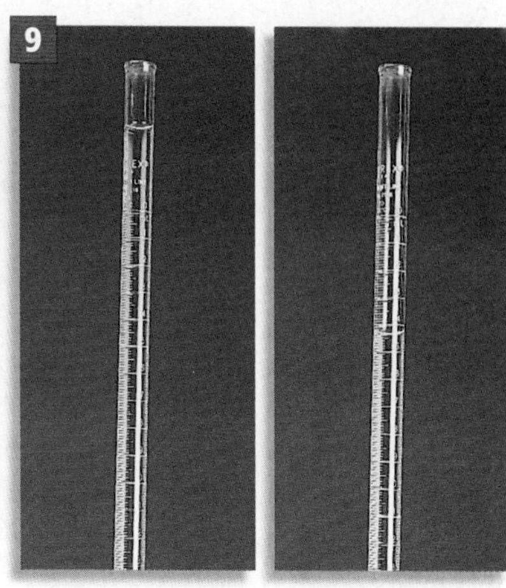

Release some base from the buret to remove any air bubbles and to lower the volume to the calibrated portion of the buret.

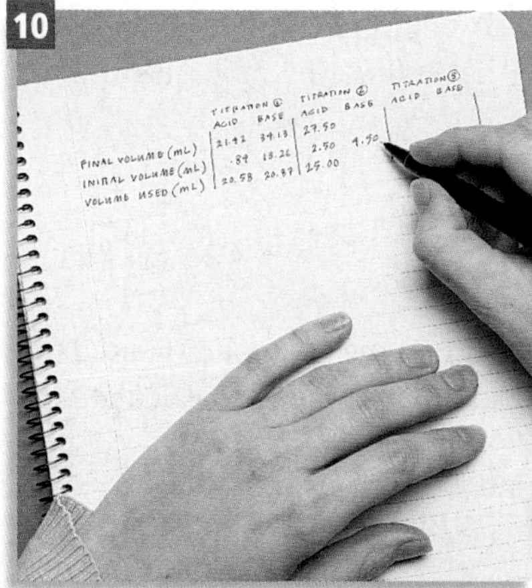

Record the volume of the base to the nearest 0.01 mL as your initial volume. Remember to read the volume at the bottom of the meniscus.

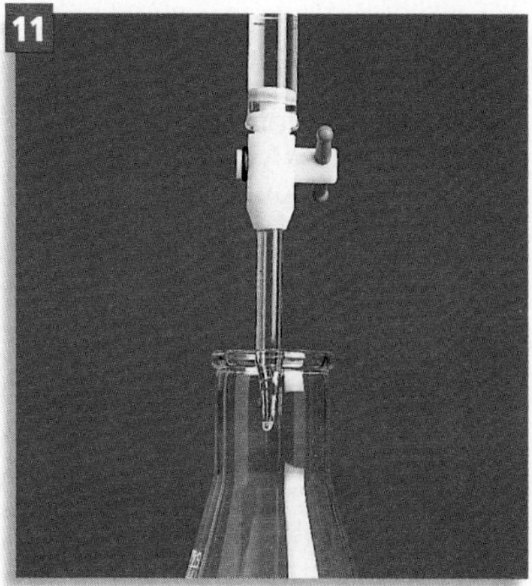

Place the Erlenmeyer flask under the base buret as shown. Notice that the tip of the buret extends into the mouth of the flask.

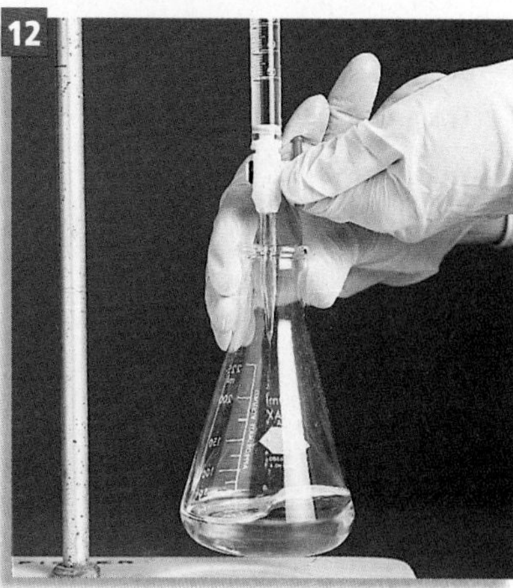

Slowly release base from the buret into the flask while constantly swirling the contents of the flask. The pink color of the indicator should fade with swirling.

The titration is nearing the end point when the pink color stays for longer periods of time. At this point, add base drop by drop.

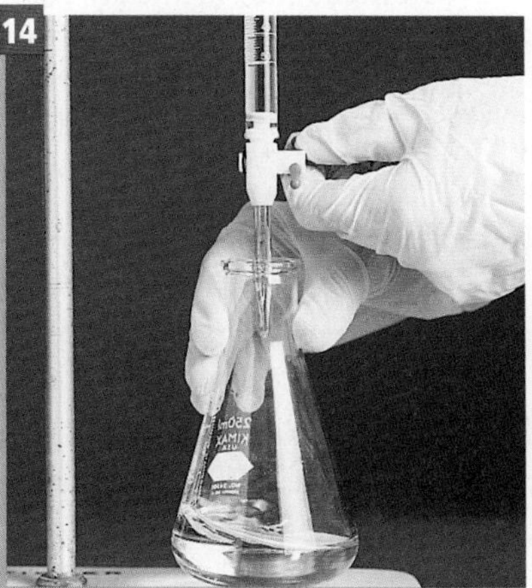

The equivalence point is reached when a very light pink color remains after 30 seconds of swirling.

Subtract the initial volume reading on the buret from the final reading. This is the exact volume of the base released into the flask. Record it to the nearest 0.01 mL.

The known solution can be used to determine the molarity of another solution by titration. Suppose 20.0 mL of $5.00 \times 10^{-3}$ M NaOH is required to reach the end point in the titration of 10.0 mL of HCl of unknown concentration. How can these titration data be used to determine the molarity of the acidic solution?

Begin with the balanced neutralization reaction equation. From the equation, determine the chemically equivalent amounts of HCl and NaOH.

$$\underset{1\text{ mol}}{\mathrm{HCl}(aq)} + \underset{1\text{ mol}}{\mathrm{NaOH}(aq)} \longrightarrow \underset{1\text{ mol}}{\mathrm{NaCl}(aq)} + \underset{1\text{ mol}}{\mathrm{H_2O}(l)}$$

Calculate the number of moles of NaOH used in the titration.

$$\frac{5.00 \times 10^{-3}\text{ mol NaOH}}{1\text{ L}} \times \frac{1\text{ L}}{1000\text{ mL}} \times 20.0\text{ mL} = 1.00 \times 10^{-4}\text{ mol NaOH used}$$

Because 1 mol of NaOH is needed to neutralize 1 mol of HCl, the amount of HCl in the titration must be $1.00 \times 10^{-4}$ mol. This is confirmed by the following equation.

$$1.00 \times 10^{-4}\text{ mol NaOH} \times \frac{1\text{ mol HCl}}{1\text{ mol NaOH}} = 1.00 \times 10^{-4}\text{ mol HCl}$$

This amount of acid must be in the 10.0 mL of the HCl solution used for the titration. The molarity of the HCl solution can now be calculated.

$$\frac{1.00 \times 10^{-4}\text{ mol HCl}}{10.0\text{ mL}} \times \frac{1000\text{ mL}}{1\text{ L}} = \frac{1.00 \times 10^{-2}\text{ mol HCl}}{1\text{ L}}$$

$$= 1.00 \times 10^{-2}\text{ M HCl}$$

Sample Problem F illustrates the following four steps.

1. Start with the balanced equation for the neutralization reaction, and determine the chemically equivalent amounts of the acid and base.
2. Determine the moles of acid (or base) from the known solution used during the titration.
3. Determine the moles of solute of the unknown solution used during the titration.
4. Determine the molarity of the unknown solution.

## SAMPLE PROBLEM F

**In a titration, 27.4 mL of 0.0154 M $Ba(OH)_2$ is added to a 20.0 mL sample of HCl solution of unknown concentration until the equivalence point is reached. What is the molarity of the acid solution?**

### SOLUTION

**1** ***ANALYZE***

**Given:** volume and concentration of known solution = 27.4 mL of 0.0154 M $Ba(OH)_2$
volume of unknown HCl solution = 20.0 mL

**Unknown:** molarity of acid solution

**2 PLAN**

1. balanced neutralization equation ⟶ chemically equivalent amounts

$$\underset{1\text{ mol}}{Ba(OH)_2} + \underset{2\text{ mol}}{2HCl} \longrightarrow \underset{1\text{ mol}}{BaCl_2} + \underset{2\text{ mol}}{2H_2O}$$

2. volume of known basic solution used (mL) ⟶ amount of base used (mol)

$$\frac{\text{mol } Ba(OH)_2}{1\text{ L}} \times \text{mL of } Ba(OH)_2 \text{ solution} \times \frac{1\text{ L}}{1000\text{ mL}} = \text{mol } Ba(OH)_2$$

3. moles of base used, mole ratio ⟶ moles of acid used from unknown solution

$$\text{mol } Ba(OH)_2 \times \frac{2\text{ mol HCl}}{1\text{ mol } Ba(OH)_2} \text{ in known solution} = \text{mol HCl in unknown solution}$$

4. volume of unknown, moles of solute in unknown ⟶ molarity of unknown

$$\frac{\text{amount of solute in unknown solution (mol)}}{\text{volume of unknown solution (mL)}} \times \frac{1000\text{ mL}}{1\text{ L}} = \text{molarity of unknown solution}$$

**3 COMPUTE**

1. The mole ratio from the equation is 1 mol $Ba(OH)_2$ for every 2 mol HCl.

2. $$\frac{0.0154\text{ mol } Ba(OH)_2}{1\text{ L}} \times \frac{1\text{ L}}{1000\text{ mL}} \times 27.4\text{ mL} = 4.22 \times 10^{-4}\text{ mol } Ba(OH)_2$$

3. $$4.22 \times 10^{-4}\text{ mol } Ba(OH)_2 \times \frac{2\text{ mol HCl}}{1\text{ mol } Ba(OH)_2} = 8.44 \times 10^{-4}\text{ mol HCl}$$

4. $$\frac{8.44 \times 10^{-4}\text{ mol HCl}}{20.0\text{ mL}} \times \frac{1000\text{ mL}}{1\text{ L}} = \frac{4.22 \times 10^{-2}\text{ mol HCl}}{1\text{ L}} = 4.22 \times 10^{-2}\text{ M HCl}$$

**PRACTICE**

*Answers in Appendix E*

1. A 15.5 mL sample of 0.215 M KOH solution required 21.2 mL of aqueous acetic acid solution in a titration experiment. Calculate the molarity of the acetic acid solution.

2. By titration, 17.6 mL of aqueous $H_2SO_4$ neutralized 27.4 mL of 0.0165 M LiOH solution. What was the molarity of the aqueous acid solution?

**extension**

Go to **go.hrw.com** for more practice problems that ask you to calculate molarities of acidic or basic solutions.

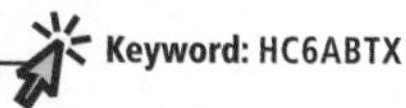


## SECTION REVIEW

1. Name an appropriate indicator for titrating the following:

   **a.** a strong acid and a weak base

   **b.** a strong base and a weak acid

2. If 20.0 mL of 0.0100 M aqueous HCl is required to neutralize 30.0 mL of an aqueous solution of NaOH, determine the molarity of the NaOH solution.

3. Suppose that 20.0 mL of 0.010 M $Ca(OH)_2$ is required to neutralize 12.0 mL of aqueous HCl solution. What is the molarity of the HCl solution?

**Critical Thinking**

4. **PREDICTING OUTCOMES** Sketch the titration curve for 50.0 mL of 0.10 M $NH_3$ that is titrated with 0.10 M HCl.

# CHAPTER HIGHLIGHTS

## Aqueous Solutions and the Concept of pH

**Vocabulary**
self-ionization of water
pH
pOH

- Pure water undergoes self-ionization to give $1.0 \times 10^{-7}$ M $H_3O^+$ and $1.0 \times 10^{-7}$ M $OH^-$ at 25°C.
- $pH = -\log[H_3O^+]$; $pOH = -\log[OH^-]$; at 25°C, pH + pOH = 14.0.
- At 25°C, acids have a pH of less than 7, bases have a pH of greater than 7, and neutral solutions have a pH of 7.
- If a solution contains a strong acid or a strong base, the $[H_3O^+]$, $[OH^-]$, and pH can be calculated from the molarity of the solution. If a solution contains a weak acid or a weak base, the $[H_3O^+]$ and the $[OH^-]$ must be calculated from an experimentally measured pH.

## Determining pH and Titrations

**Vocabulary**
acid-base indicators
transition interval
pH meter
titration
equivalence point
end point
standard solution
primary standard

- The pH of a solution can be measured using either a pH meter or acid-base indicators.
- Titration uses a solution of known concentration to determine the concentration of a solution of unknown concentration.
- To determine the end point of a titration, one should choose indicators that change color over ranges that include the pH of the equivalence point.
- When the molarity and volume of a known solution used in a titration are known, then the molarity of a given volume of an unknown solution can be found.

For more practice, go to the Problem Bank in Appendix D.

## Aqueous Solutions and the Concept of pH

### SECTION 1 REVIEW

1. Why is pure water a very weak electric conductor?
2. What does it mean when the formula of a particular ion or molecule is enclosed in brackets?
3. a. What is the $[H_3O^+]$ of pure water at 25°C?
   b. Is this true at all temperatures? Why or why not?
4. a. What is always true about the $[H_3O^+]$ value of acidic solutions?
   b. What is true about the $[H_3O^+]$ value of acidic solutions at 25°C?
5. a. Describe what is meant by the pH of a solution.
   b. Write the equation for determining pH.
   c. Explain and illustrate what is meant by the common logarithm of a number.
6. Identify each of the following solutions that are at 25°C as acidic, basic, or neutral:
   a. $[H_3O^+] = 1.0 \times 10^{-7}$ M
   b. $[H_3O^+] = 1.0 \times 10^{-10}$ M
   c. $[OH^-] = 1.0 \times 10^{-7}$ M
   d. $[OH^-] = 1.0 \times 10^{-11}$ M
   e. $[H_3O^+] = [OH^-]$
   f. pH = 3.0
   g. pH = 13.0
7. Arrange the following common substances in order of increasing pH:
   a. eggs
   b. apples
   c. tomatoes
   d. milk
   e. bananas
   f. potatoes
   g. lemons
   h. milk of magnesia
   i. sea water

### PRACTICE PROBLEMS

8. Calculate the $[H_3O^+]$ and $[OH^-]$ for each of the following. (Hint: See Sample Problem A.)
   a. 0.030 M HCl
   b. $1.0 \times 10^{-4}$ M NaOH
   c. $5.0 \times 10^{-3}$ M $HNO_3$
   d. 0.010 M $Ca(OH)_2$
9. Determine the pH of each of the following solutions. (Hint: See Sample Problem B.)
   a. $1.0 \times 10^{-2}$ M HCl
   b. $1.0 \times 10^{-3}$ M $HNO_3$
   c. $1.0 \times 10^{-5}$ M HI
   d. $1.0 \times 10^{-4}$ M HBr
10. Given the following $[OH^-]$ values, determine the pH of each solution.
    a. $1.0 \times 10^{-6}$ M
    b. $1.0 \times 10^{-9}$ M
    c. $1.0 \times 10^{-2}$ M
    d. $1.0 \times 10^{-7}$ M
11. Determine the pH of each solution.
    a. $1.0 \times 10^{-2}$ M NaOH
    b. $1.0 \times 10^{-3}$ M KOH
    c. $1.0 \times 10^{-4}$ M LiOH
12. Determine the pH of solutions with each of the following $[H_3O^+]$. (Hint: See Sample Problem C.)
    a. $2.0 \times 10^{-5}$ M
    b. $4.7 \times 10^{-7}$ M
    c. $3.8 \times 10^{-3}$ M
13. Given the following pH values, determine the $[H_3O^+]$ for each solution. (Hint: See Sample Problem D.)
    a. 3.0
    b. 7.00
    c. 11.0
    d. 5.0
14. Given the following pH values, determine the $[OH^-]$ for each solution.
    a. 7.00
    b. 11.00
    c. 4.00
    d. 6.00
15. Determine $[H_3O^+]$ for solutions with the following pH values. (Hint: See Sample Problem E.)
    a. 4.23
    b. 7.65
    c. 9.48
16. A nitric acid solution is found to have a pH of 2.70. Determine each of the following:
    a. $[H_3O^+]$
    b. $[OH^-]$
    c. the number of moles of $HNO_3$ required to prepare 5.50 L of this solution
    d. the mass of $HNO_3$ in the solution in part (c)
    e. the milliliters of concentrated acid needed to prepare the solution in part (c) (Concentrated nitric acid is 69.5% $HNO_3$ by mass and has a density of 1.42 g/mL.)

## *Determining pH and Titrations*

### SECTION 2 REVIEW

**17.** What is meant by the transition interval of an indicator?

**18.** Explain how changes in pH affect the color of an indicator.

**19.** a. Without using an indicator, how can you determine the equivalence point of a titration experiment or the pH of a solution?
b. What can be observed about the rate of change of the pH of a solution near the end point of a titration?

**20.** a. What is meant by the end point of a titration?
b. What is the role of an indicator in the titration process?
c. On what basis is an indicator selected for a particular titration experiment?

**21.** For each of the four possible types of acid-base titration combinations (strong-strong, strong-weak, etc.), indicate the approximate pH at the end point. Also name a suitable indicator for detecting that end point.

**22.** Use **Figures 9(a)** and **9(b)** to sketch the pH curve of a strong acid being titrated by a weak base.

**23.** An unknown solution is colorless when tested with phenolphthalein but causes the indicator phenol red to turn red. Use this information to find the approximate pH of this solution.

### PRACTICE PROBLEMS

**24.** For each of the following acid-base titration combinations, determine the number of moles of the first substance listed that would be the chemically equivalent amount of the second substance.
a. NaOH with 1.0 mol HCl
b. $HNO_3$ with 0.75 mol KOH
c. $Ba(OH)_2$ with 0.20 mol HF
d. $H_2SO_4$ with 0.90 mol $Mg(OH)_2$

**25.** Suppose that 15.0 mL of $2.50 \times 10^{-2}$ M aqueous $H_2SO_4$ is required to neutralize 10.0 mL of an aqueous solution of KOH. What is the molarity of the KOH solution? (Hint: See Sample Problem F.)

**26.** In a titration experiment, a 12.5 mL sample of $1.75 \times 10^{-2}$ M $Ba(OH)_2$ just neutralized 14.5 mL of $HNO_3$ solution. Calculate the molarity of the $HNO_3$ solution.

## MIXED REVIEW

**27.** a. What is the $[OH^-]$ of a $4.0 \times 10^{-4}$ M solution of $Ca(OH)_2$?
b. What is the $[H_3O^+]$ of the solution?

**28.** Given the following $[H_3O^+]$ values, determine the pH of each solution.
a. $1.0 \times 10^{-7}$ M
b. $1.0 \times 10^{-3}$ M
c. $1.0 \times 10^{-12}$ M
d. $1.0 \times 10^{-5}$ M

**29.** What is the $[H_3O^+]$ for a solution that has a pH of 6.0?

**30.** Suppose that a $5.0 \times 10^{-5}$ M solution of $Ba(OH)_2$ is prepared. What is the pH of the solution?

**31.** a. Calculate the pH of a solution that has an $[H_3O^+]$ of $8.4 \times 10^{-11}$ M.
b. Calculate the $[H_3O^+]$ of a solution that has a pH of 2.50.

**32.** a. What is the concentration of $OH^-$ in a $5.4 \times 10^{-5}$ M solution of magnesium hydroxide, $Mg(OH)_2$?
b. Calculate the concentration of $H_3O^+$ for this solution.

**33.** a. Calculate the molarity of $H_3O^+$ in a solution that has a pH of 8.90.
b. Calculate the concentration of $OH^-$ for this solution.

**34.** What is the pH of a solution in which $[OH^-]$ equals $6.9 \times 10^{-10}$ M?

**35.** In a titration, 25.9 mL of $3.4 \times 10^{-3}$ M $Ba(OH)_2$ neutralized 16.6 mL of HCl solution. What is the molarity of the HCl solution?

**36.** Find the molarity of a $Ca(OH)_2$ solution given that 428 mL of the solution is neutralized in a titration by 115 mL of $6.7 \times 10^{-3}$ M $HNO_3$.

**37.** Suppose that 10.1 mL of $HNO_3$ is neutralized by 71.4 mL of a $4.2 \times 10^{-3}$ M solution of KOH in a titration. Calculate the concentration of the $HNO_3$ solution.

## CRITICAL THINKING

**38. Interpreting Graphics** The following titration curve resulted from the titration of an unknown acid with 0.10 M NaOH. Analyze the curve. Make inferences related to the type of acidic solution titrated.

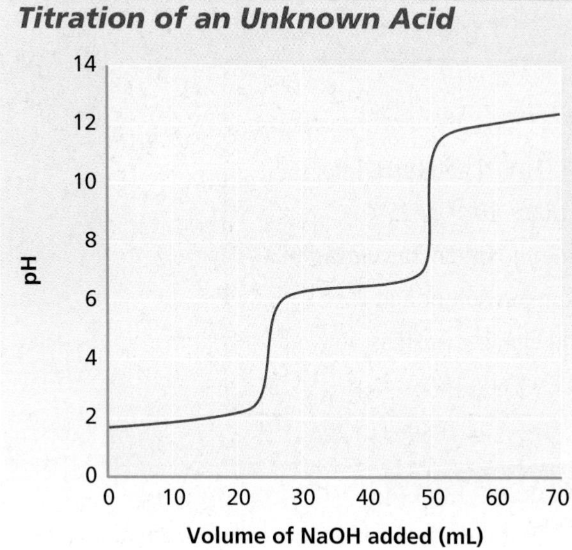


## USING THE HANDBOOK

**39.** The normal pH of blood is about 7.4. When the pH shifts above or below that level, the results are acidosis or alkalosis. Review the section on blood pH in Group 14 of the *Elements Handbook,* and answer the following.

a. What chemical species keep $H_3O^+$ in blood at the appropriate pH?

b. What condition results when there is an excess of $CO_2$ in the blood?

c. What is hyperventilation and how does it affect blood pH?

## RESEARCH & WRITING

**40.** Examine the labels of at least five brands of shampoo. Note what is written there, if anything, regarding the pH of the shampoo. Do library research to find out why such pH ranges are chosen and why other ranges might be harmful to hair or eyes.

**41.** Acid rain is an environmental issue that crosses state and national boundaries. Conduct library research on this topic and write a brief report. Include a description of the areas in the United States affected by acid rain, and the geographical source of the sulfur and nitrogen oxides that are responsible for acid rain in each region.

## ALTERNATIVE ASSESSMENT

**42. Performance** Use pH paper to determine the approximate pH of various brands of orange juice, which contains citric acid.

**43. Performance** Design and conduct an experiment to extract possible acid-base indicators from sources such as red cabbage, berries, and flower petals. Use known acidic, basic, and neutral solutions to test the action of each indicator that you are able to isolate.

extension

**Graphing Calculator**
**Acid-Base Titration**

Go to **go.hrw.com** for a graphing calculator exercise that asks you to graph acid-base titration curves.

# Math Tutor USING LOGARITHMS AND pH

When you work with acids and bases, you often need to state the hydronium ion concentration, $[H_3O^+]$, of a solution. One simple way is to use the negative logarithm of $[H_3O^+]$. This quantity is called *pH*. For example, pure water has a $[H_3O^+]$ of $1.00 \times 10^{-7}$ M. So, the pH of pure water is $-\log(1.00 \times 10^{-7}\ M) = 7.00$. A solution of 0.1 M HCl has a pH of 1.00 or $pH = -\log(1 \times 10^{-1}) = 1.00$. The term *pOH* is also used for the negative logarithm of the hydroxide ion concentration, $[OH^-]$. The pOH of pure water is also 7.00.

## Problem-Solving *TIPS*

- For pure water at 25°C, $[H_3O^+] = [OH^-] = 1.00 \times 10^{-7}$ M.
- The ionization constant of water, $K_w$, is the product of $[H_3O^+]$ and $[OH^-]$, so
  $K_w = [H_3O^+][OH^-] = (1.00 \times 10^{-7})(1.00 \times 10^{-7}) = 1.00 \times 10^{-14}$ at 25°C.
- If you know either $[H_3O^+]$ or $[OH^-]$, you can determine the other concentration.
- In terms of pH and pOH, pH + pOH = 14.00 for an aqueous solution at 25°C.
- Because pH calculations involve scientific notation and changes in signs, you should always check to see if answers make sense.

### SAMPLE 1

**What is the pH of a 0.0046 M solution of KOH?**

KOH is completely dissociated into equal numbers of $K^+(aq)$ and $OH^-(aq)$. The concentration of $OH^-$ is the same as the concentration of dissolved KOH, 0.0046 M. So, $[OH^-] = 4.6 \times 10^{-3}$ M, and $pOH = -\log(4.6 \times 10^{-3}\ M) = 2.34$.

For an aqueous solution at 25°C, pH + pOH = 14.00, so pH + 2.34 = 14.00.

Therefore, the pH of 0.0046 M KOH solution = 14.00 − 2.34 = 11.66.

### SAMPLE 2

**What is the hydronium ion concentration, $[H_3O^+]$, of a solution with a pH of 4.08? What is the pOH of the solution?**

In this solution,

$$\log [H_3O^+] = -4.08$$

$[H_3O^+] = \text{antilog}(-4.08) = 0.000\ 083\ M = 8.3 \times 10^{-5}$ M

The pOH of the solution is 14.00 − pH = 14.00 − 4.08 = 9.92.

### PRACTICE PROBLEMS

1. What is the pH of a 0.000 85 M solution of nitric acid, $HNO_3$, which is a strong acid?

2. What is the hydroxide ion concentration of an aqueous solution that has a pH of 9.95?

# Standardized Test Prep

**Answer the following items on a separate piece of paper.**

**MULTIPLE CHOICE**

**1.** Distilled water contains
**A.** $H_2O$.
**B.** $H_3O^+$.
**C.** $OH^-$.
**D.** All of the above

**2.** What is the pH of a 0.0010 M $HNO_3$?
**A.** 1.0
**B.** 3.0
**C.** 4.0
**D.** 5.0

**3.** Which of the following solutions would have a pH value greater than 7?
**A.** $[OH^-] = 2.4 \times 10^{-2}$ M
**B.** $[H_3O^+] = 1.53 \times 10^{-2}$ M
**C.** 0.0001 M HCl
**D.** $[OH^-] = 4.4 \times 10^{-9}$ M

**4.** If the pH of a solution of the strong base NaOH is known, which property of the solution can be calculated?
**A.** molar concentration
**B.** $[OH^-]$
**C.** $[H_3O^+]$
**D.** All of the above

**5.** A neutral aqueous solution
**A.** has a 7.0 M $H_3O^+$ concentration.
**B.** contains neither hydronium ions nor hydroxide ions.
**C.** has an equal number of hydronium ions and hydroxide ions.
**D.** None of the above

**6.** Identify the salt that forms when a solution of $H_2SO_4$ is titrated with a solution of $Ca(OH)_2$.
**A.** calcium sulfate
**B.** calcium hydroxide
**C.** calcium oxide
**D.** calcium phosphate

**7.** The pH of a solution is 6.32. What is the pOH?
**A.** 6.32
**B.** $4.8 \times 10^{-7}$
**C.** 7.68
**D.** $2.1 \times 10^{-8}$

**8.** The $K_w$ value for water can be affected by
**A.** dissolving a salt in the solution.
**B.** changes in temperature.
**C.** changes in the hydroxide ion concentration.
**D.** the presence of a strong acid.

**9.** Which of the pH levels listed below is the most acidic?
**A.** pH = 1
**B.** pH = 5
**C.** pH = 9
**D.** pH = 13

**SHORT ANSWER**

**10.** A solution has a pH of 4.75. What is the hydronium ion concentration? Is the solution acidic or basic?

**11.** A weak acid that is used as an indicator is added to a strong acid solution before titration of the strong acid with a strong base. Why doesn't the weak acid affect the value calculated for the concentration of the acid?

**EXTENDED RESPONSE**

**12.** The hydroxide ion concentration in a solution is $1.6 \times 10^{-11}$ M. What are the $[H_3O^+]$, the pH, and the pOH of the solution?

**13.** Write the balanced equation and the net ionic equation that represent the reaction that takes place when milk of magnesia (magnesium hydroxide) reacts with hydrochloric acid in your stomach.

**Test TIP** If you do not understand a question, try to reword it. But be careful not to change its meaning.

# How Much Calcium Carbonate Is in an Eggshell?

## OBJECTIVES

- ***Determine*** **the amount of calcium carbonate present in an eggshell.**
- ***Relate*** **experimental titration measurements to a balanced chemical equation.**
- ***Infer*** **a conclusion from experimental data.**
- ***Apply*** **reaction stoichiometry concepts.**

## MATERIALS

- **1.00 M HCl**
- **1.00 M NaOH**
- **10 mL graduated cylinder**
- **50 mL micro solution bottle or small Erlenmeyer flask**
- **100 mL beaker**
- **balance**
- **desiccator (optional)**
- **distilled water**
- **drying oven**
- **eggshell**
- **forceps**
- **mortar and pestle**
- **phenolphthalein solution**
- **thin-stemmed pipets or medicine droppers, 3**
- **weighing paper**

## BACKGROUND

The calcium carbonate content of eggshells can be easily determined by means of an acid/base back-titration. In this experiment, a strong acid will react with calcium carbonate in eggshells. Then, the amount of unreacted acid will be determined by titration with a strong base.

## SAFETY

For review of safety, please see **Safety in the Chemistry Laboratory** in the front of your book.

## PREPARATION

1. Wash an empty eggshell with distilled water and carefully peel all the membranes from its inside. Place *all* of the shell in a premassed beaker and dry the shell in the drying oven at 110°C for about 15 min.
2. Copy data and calculations tables from your teacher.
3. Put exactly 5.0 mL of water in the 10.0 mL graduated cylinder. Record this volume in your data table. Label the first pipet "Acid." To calibrate the pipet, fill it with water. **Do not use this pipet for the base solution.** Holding the pipet vertically, add 20 drops of water to the cylinder. Record the new volume of water in the graduated cylinder in the first data table under Trial 1.
4. Without emptying the graduated cylinder, add an additional 20 drops from the pipet. Record the new volume for Trial 2. Repeat this procedure once more for Trial 3.

5. Repeat Preparation steps 3 and 4 for the second pipet. Label this pipet "Base." **Do not use this pipet for the acid solution.**

6. Make sure that the three trials produce data that are similar to one another. If one is greatly different from the others, perform Preparation steps 3–5 again.

7. Remove the beaker containing the eggshell from the oven. Cool them in a desiccator. Record the mass of the entire eggshell in the second table. Place half of the shell into the clean mortar, and grind the shell into a very fine powder.

## PROCEDURE

1. Measure the mass of a piece of weighing paper. Transfer about 0.1 g of ground eggshell to a piece of weighing paper, and measure the eggshell's mass as accurately as possible. Record the mass in the second data table. Place this eggshell sample into a clean, 50 mL micro solution bottle (or Erlenmeyer flask).

2. Fill the acid pipet with 1.00 M HCl acid solution, and then empty the pipet into an extra 100 mL beaker. Label the beaker "Waste." Fill the base pipet with the 1.00 M NaOH base solution, and then empty the pipet into the waste beaker.

3. Fill the acid pipet once more with 1.00 M HCl. Holding the acid pipet vertically, add exactly 150 drops of 1.00 M HCl to the bottle or flask that contains the eggshell. Swirl the flask gently for 3 to 4 min. Observe the reaction taking place. Wash down the sides of the flask with about 10 mL of distilled water. Using a third pipet, add two drops of phenolphthalein solution.

4. Fill the base pipet with the 1.00 M NaOH. Slowly add NaOH from the base pipet into the bottle or flask that contains the eggshell reaction mixture, counting and recording the drops added. Stop adding base when the mixture remains a faint pink color, even after it is swirled gently. **Be sure to add the base drop by drop, and be certain the drops end up in the reaction mixture and not on the walls of the bottle or flask.** Record in the second data table the number of drops of base used.

## CLEANUP AND DISPOSAL

5. Clean all equipment and your lab station. Dispose of chemicals and solutions as directed by your teacher. Wash your hands thoroughly before you leave the lab.

## ANALYSIS AND INTERPRETATION

1. **Organizing Ideas:** The calcium carbonate in the eggshell sample undergoes a double-displacement reaction with the HCl in step 3. Write a balanced chemical equation for this reaction. (Hint: The gas evolved was $CO_2$.)

2. **Organizing Ideas:** Write the balanced chemical equation for the acid/base neutralization of the excess unreacted HCl with the NaOH.

3. **Organizing Data:** Calculate the volume of each drop in milliliters. Then convert the number of drops of HCl into volume in milliliters. Record this volume in your data table. Repeat this step for the drops of NaOH.

4. **Organizing Data:** Using the relationship between the molarity and volume of acid and the molarity and volume of base needed to neutralize it, calculate the number of moles of the HCl solution that was neutralized by the NaOH, and record it in your table. (Hint: This relationship was discussed in Section 2.)

5. **Analyzing Results:** Calculate the number of moles of HCl that reacted with the $CaCO_3$ and record both in your table.

## CONCLUSIONS

1. **Organizing Data:** Use the balanced equation for the reaction to calculate the number of moles of $CaCO_3$ that reacted with the HCl, and record this number in your table.

2. **Organizing Data:** Use the periodic table to calculate the molar mass of $CaCO_3$. Then, use the number of moles of $CaCO_3$ to calculate the mass of $CaCO_3$ in your eggshell sample. Record this mass in your data table. Using the mass of $CaCO_3$, calculate the percentage of $CaCO_3$ in your eggshell and record it in your data table.

CHAPTER 16

# Reaction Energy

*Many chemical reactions give off or take in energy as heat.*

Kilauea volcano erupting, Hawaii Island

# Thermochemistry

SC **C.4.3** Analyze the energy changes (endothermic or exothermic) associated with chemical reactions

SECTION 1

## Objectives

- Define *temperature* and state the units in which it is measured.
- Define *heat* and state its units.
- Perform specific-heat calculations.
- Explain enthalpy change, enthalpy of reaction, enthalpy of formation, and enthalpy of combustion.
- Solve problems involving enthalpies of reaction, enthalpies of formation, and enthalpies of combustion.

Virtually every chemical reaction is accompanied by a change in energy. Chemical reactions usually absorb or release energy as heat. You learned in Chapter 10 that energy is also absorbed or released in physical changes, such as melting a solid or condensing a vapor. **Thermochemistry** *is the study of the transfers of energy as heat that accompany chemical reactions and physical changes.*

## Heat and Temperature

*The energy absorbed or released as heat in a chemical or physical change is measured in a* **calorimeter.** In one kind of calorimeter, known quantities of reactants are sealed in a reaction chamber, which is immersed in a known quantity of water in an insulated vessel. Therefore, the energy given off (or absorbed) during the reaction is equal to the energy absorbed (or given off) by the known quantity of water. The amount of energy is determined from the temperature change of the known mass of surrounding water. The data collected from calorimetry experiments are temperature changes because energy cannot be measured directly; but temperature, which is affected by the transfer of energy as heat, is directly measurable. To see why this is so, let us look at the definitions of heat and temperature and at how temperature is measured.

**Temperature** *is a measure of the average kinetic energy of the particles in a sample of matter.* The greater the kinetic energy of the particles in a sample, the higher the temperature is and the hotter it feels. To assign a numerical value to temperature, it is necessary to define a temperature scale. For calculations in thermochemistry, we use the Celsius and Kelvin scales. Celsius and Kelvin temperatures are related by the following equation.

$$K = 273.15 + {}^\circ C$$

For most calculations in this book, 273.15 is rounded to 273.

The ability to measure temperature is thus based on energy transfer. The amount of energy transferred as heat is usually measured in joules. *A* **joule** *is the SI unit of heat as well as all other forms of energy.* The joule, abbreviated J, is derived from the units for force and length.

$$N \times m = \frac{kg \times m^2}{s^2}$$

SCILINKS.
www.scilinks.org
**Topic:** Heat/Temperature
**Code:** HC60726

**FIGURE 1** The direction of energy transfer is determined by the temperature differences between the objects within a system. The energy is transferred as heat from the hotter brass bar to the cooler water. This energy transfer will continue until the bar and the water reach the same temperature.

**Heat** *can be thought of as the energy transferred between samples of matter because of a difference in their temperatures.* Energy transferred as heat always moves spontaneously from matter at a higher temperature to matter at a lower temperature, as shown in **Figure 1.** The temperature of the cool water in the beaker increases as energy flows into it. Likewise, the temperature of the hot brass bar decreases as energy flows away from it. When the temperature of the water equals the temperature of the brass bar, energy is no longer transferred as heat within the system.

## Specific Heat

The quantity of energy transferred as heat during a temperature change depends on the nature of the material changing temperature, the mass of the material changing temperature, and the size of the temperature change. One gram of iron heated to 100.0°C and cooled to 50.0°C in a calorimeter transfers 22.5 J of energy to the surrounding water. But one gram of silver transfers 11.8 J of energy under the same conditions. The difference depends on the metals' differing capacities for absorbing this energy. A quantity called specific heat can be used to compare heat absorption capacities for different materials. **Specific heat** *is the amount of energy required to raise the temperature of one gram of a substance by one Celsius degree (1°C) or one kelvin (1 K)*(because the sizes of the degree divisions on both scales are equal). Values of specific heat can be given in units of joules per gram per Celsius degree, J/(g•°C), joules per gram per kelvin, J/(g•K), or calories per gram per Celsius degree, cal/(g•°C). **Table 1** gives the specific heats of some common substances. Notice the extremely high specific heat of water, one of the highest of most common substances.

Specific heat is usually measured under constant pressure conditions, so its symbol, $c_p$, contains a subscripted $p$ as a reminder to the reader.

**TABLE 1 Specific Heats of Some Common Substances at 298.15 K**

| Substance | Specific heat J/(g•K) |
|---|---|
| Water (*l*) | 4.18 |
| Water (*s*) | 2.06 |
| Water (*g*) | 1.87 |
| Ammonia (*g*) | 2.09 |
| Benzene (*l*) | 1.74 |
| Ethanol (*l*) | 2.44 |
| Ethanol (*g*) | 1.42 |
| Aluminum (*s*) | 0.897 |
| Calcium (*s*) | 0.647 |
| Carbon, graphite (*s*) | 0.709 |
| Copper (*s*) | 0.385 |
| Gold (*s*) | 0.129 |
| Iron (*s*) | 0.449 |
| Mercury (*l*) | 0.140 |
| Lead (*s*) | 0.129 |

In the following mathematical equation, $c_p$ is the specific heat at a given pressure, $q$ is the energy lost or gained, $m$ is the mass of the sample, and $\Delta T$ represents the difference between the initial and final temperatures.

$$c_p = \frac{q}{m \times \Delta T}$$

This equation can be rearranged to give an equation that can be used to find the quantity of energy gained or lost with a change in temperature.

$$q = c_p \times m \times \Delta T$$

## SAMPLE PROBLEM A

**A 4.0 g sample of glass was heated from 274 K to 314 K, a temperature increase of 40. K, and was found to have absorbed 32 J of energy as heat.**

**a. What is the specific heat of this type of glass?**

**b. How much energy will the same glass sample gain when it is heated from 314 K to 344 K?**

### SOLUTION

**1** *ANALYZE* **Given:** $m = 4.0$ g

$\Delta T = 40.$ K

$q = 32$ J

**Unknown:** $c_p$ in J/(g•K)

**2 PLAN**

**a.** The specific heat, $c_p$, of the glass is calculated using the equation given for specific heat.

$$c_p = \frac{q}{m \times \Delta T}$$

**b.** The rearranged specific heat equation is used to find the energy gained when the glass was heated.

$$q = c_p \times m \times \Delta T$$

**3 COMPUTE**

**a.** $$\frac{32\ \text{J}}{(4.0\ \text{g})(40.\ \text{K})} = 0.20\ \text{J/(g•K)}$$

**b.** $$\frac{0.20\ \text{J}}{(\text{g•K})}(4.0\ \text{g})(344\ \text{K} - 314\ \text{K})$$

$$\frac{0.20\ \text{J}}{(\text{g•K})}(4.0\ \text{g})(30\ \text{K}) = 24\ \text{J}$$

**4 EVALUATE** The units combine or cancel correctly to give the specific heat in J/(g•K) and the energy in J.

**PRACTICE** *Answers in Appendix E*

1. Determine the specific heat of a material if a 35 g sample absorbed 96 J as it was heated from 293 K to 313 K.
2. If 980 kJ of energy are added to 6.2 L of water at 291 K, what will the final temperature of the water be?

Go to **go.hrw.com** for more practice problems that ask you to calculate using specific heat.

**Keyword: HC6NRGX**

## Enthalpy of Reaction

The energy absorbed as heat during a chemical reaction at constant pressure is represented by $\Delta H$. The $H$ is the symbol for a quantity called *enthalpy.* It is not practical to talk just about enthalpy as a quantity, because we have no way to directly measure the enthalpy of a system. Only *changes* in enthalpy can be measured. The Greek letter Δ ("delta") stands for "change in." Therefore, $\Delta H$ is read as "change in enthalpy." *An* **enthalpy change** *is the amount of energy absorbed by a system as heat during a process at constant pressure.* The enthalpy change is always the difference between the enthalpies of the products and the reactants. The following equation expresses an enthalpy change for a reaction.

$$\Delta H = H_{products} - H_{reactants}$$

*The* **enthalpy of reaction** *is the quantity of energy transferred as heat during a chemical reaction.* You can think of enthalpy of reaction as the difference between the stored energy of the reactants and the products. Enthalpy of reaction is sometimes called "heat of reaction."

If a mixture of hydrogen and oxygen is ignited, water will form and energy will be released explosively. The energy that is released comes from the reactants as they form products. Because energy is released, the reaction is *exothermic,* and the energy of the product, water, must be less than the energy of the reactants. The following chemical equation for this reaction indicates that when 2 mol of hydrogen gas at room temperature are burned, 1 mol of oxygen gas is consumed and 2 mol of water vapor are formed.

$$2H_2(g) + O_2(g) \longrightarrow 2H_2O(g)$$

The equation does not tell you that energy is evolved as heat during the reaction. Experiments have shown that 483.6 kJ of energy are evolved when 2 mol of gaseous water are formed from its elements at 298.15 K.

Modifying the chemical equation to show the amount of energy as heat released during the reaction gives the following expression.

$$2H_2(g) + O_2(g) \longrightarrow 2H_2O(g) + 483.6 \text{ kJ}$$

This expression is an example of a **thermochemical equation,** *an equation that includes the quantity of energy released or absorbed as heat during the reaction as written.* In any thermochemical equation, we must always interpret the coefficients as *numbers of moles* and never as *numbers of molecules.* The quantity of energy released as heat in this or any other reaction depends on the amounts of reactants and products. The quantity of energy as heat released during the formation of water from $H_2$ and $O_2$ is proportional to the quantity of water formed. Producing twice as much water vapor would require twice as many moles of reactants and would release 2 × 483.6 kJ of energy as heat, as shown in the following thermochemical equation (which is simply the previous thermochemical equation, multiplied by two).

$$4H_2(g) + 2O_2(g) \longrightarrow 4H_2O(g) + 967.2 \text{ kJ}$$

Producing one-half as much water would require one-half as many moles of reactants and would release only one-half as much energy, or $\frac{1}{2} \times 483.6$ kJ. The thermochemical equation for this reaction would be as follows.

$$H_2(g) + \tfrac{1}{2}O_2(g) \longrightarrow H_2O(g) + 241.8 \text{ kJ}$$

The situation is reversed in an *endothermic* reaction because products have a larger enthalpy than reactants. The decomposition of water vapor is endothermic; it is the reverse of the reaction that forms water vapor. The amount of energy as heat absorbed by water molecules to form hydrogen and oxygen equals the amount of energy as heat released when the elements combine to form the water. This is to be expected because the difference between the energy of reactants and products is unchanged. Enthalpy now appears on the reactant side of the thermochemical equation that follows, indicating that it is an endothermic reaction.

**FIGURE 2** In an exothermic chemical reaction, the enthalpy change is negative, meaning energy is released from the system as heat.

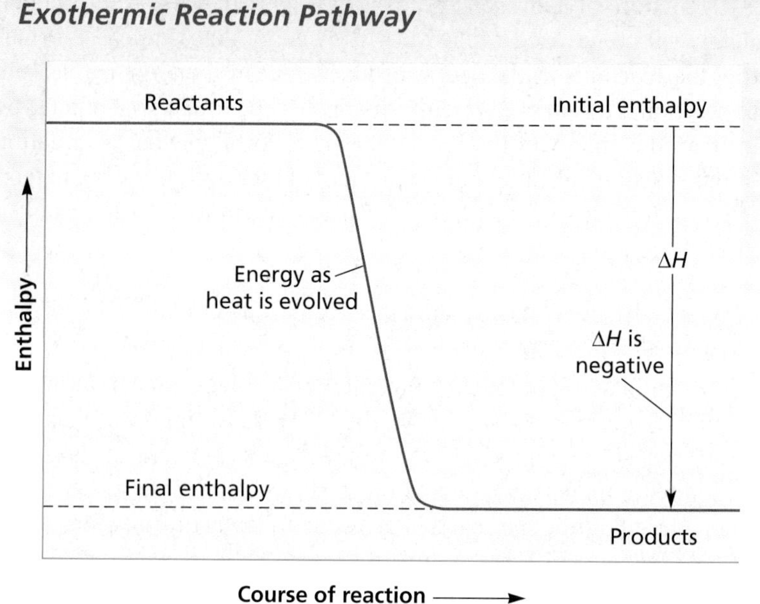


$$2H_2O(g) + 483.6 \text{ kJ} \longrightarrow 2H_2(g) + O_2(g)$$

The physical states of reactants and products must always be included in thermochemical equations because they influence the overall amount of energy as heat gained or lost. For example, the energy needed for the decomposition of water would be greater than 483.6 kJ if we started with ice, because extra energy would be needed to melt the ice and to change the liquid into a vapor.

Thermochemical equations are usually written by designating the value of $\Delta H$ rather than writing the energy as a reactant or product. For an exothermic reaction, $\Delta H$ is always negative because the system loses energy. So, the thermochemical equation for the exothermic formation of 2 mol of gaseous water from its elements now has the following form.

$$2H_2(g) + O_2(g) \longrightarrow 2H_2O(g) \quad \Delta H = -483.6 \text{ kJ}$$

**Figure 2** graphically shows the course of an exothermic reaction. The initial enthalpy of the reactants is greater than the final enthalpy of the products. This means energy as heat is evolved, or given off, during the reaction; this is described as a negative enthalpy change.

For an endothermic reaction, $\Delta H$ is always positive because the system gains energy. Thus, the endothermic decomposition of 2 mol of gaseous water has the following thermochemical equation.

$$2H_2O(g) \longrightarrow 2H_2(g) + O_2(g) \quad \Delta H = +483.6 \text{ kJ}$$

The course of an endothermic reaction is illustrated in **Figure 3.** Energy as heat is absorbed in this reaction, meaning that the initial enthalpy of

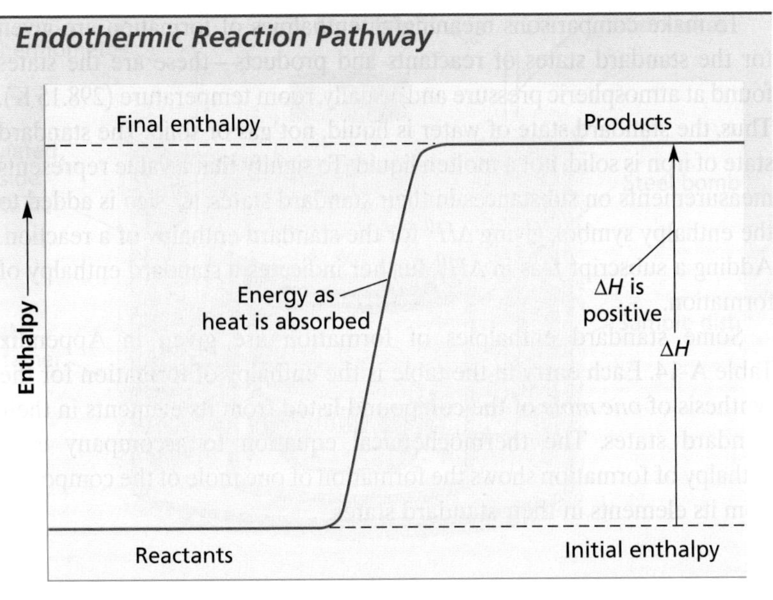


**FIGURE 3** In an endothermic chemical reaction, the enthalpy change is positive because energy is absorbed into the system as heat.

the reactants is lower than the final enthalpy of the products. In this case, $\Delta H$ is designated as positive.

Keep in mind the following when using thermochemical equations.

1. The coefficients in a balanced thermochemical equation represent the numbers of *moles* of reactants and products and never the numbers of *molecules.* This allows us to write these coefficients as fractions rather than whole numbers when necessary.
2. The physical state of the product or reactant involved in a reaction is an important factor and therefore must be included in the thermochemical equation.
3. The change in enthalpy represented by a thermochemical equation is directly proportional to the number of moles of substances undergoing a change. For example, if 2 mol of water are decomposed, twice as much enthalpy, 483.6 kJ, is needed than for the decomposition of 1 mol of water.
4. The value of the enthalpy change, $\Delta H$, is usually not significantly influenced by changing temperature.

## Enthalpy of Formation

The formation of water from hydrogen and oxygen is a composition reaction—the formation of a compound from its elements in their standard form. Thermochemical data are often recorded as the enthalpies of such composition reactions. *The* **molar enthalpy of formation** *is the enthalpy change that occurs when one mole of a compound is formed from its elements in their standard state at 25°C and 1 atm.*

In order to calculate the change in enthalpy for this reaction, we can use the combustion reactions of the elements, carbon and hydrogen, and of methane.

$$C(s) + O_2(g) \longrightarrow CO_2(g) \qquad \Delta H_c^0 = -393.5 \text{ kJ}$$

$$H_2(g) + \tfrac{1}{2}O_2(g) \longrightarrow H_2O(l) \qquad \Delta H_c^0 = -285.8 \text{ kJ}$$

$$CH_4(g) + 2O_2(g) \longrightarrow CO_2(g) + 2H_2O(l) \qquad \Delta H_c^0 = -890.8 \text{ kJ}$$

The general principles for combining thermochemical equations follow.

1. If a reaction is reversed, the sign of $\Delta H$ is also reversed.
2. Multiply the coefficients of the known equations so that when added together they give the desired thermochemical equation. Multiply the $\Delta H$ by the same factor as the corresponding equation.

In this case, reverse the combustion equation for methane, and remember to change the sign of $\Delta H$ from negative to positive. This will change the exothermic reaction to an endothermic one.

$$CO_2(g) + 2H_2O(l) \longrightarrow CH_4(g) + 2O_2(g) \quad \Delta H^0 = +890.8 \text{ kJ}$$

Now we notice that 2 moles of water are used as a reactant; therefore, 2 moles of water will be needed as a product. In the combustion reaction for hydrogen as it is written, it only produces one mole of water. We must multiply the coefficients of this combustion reaction and the value of $\Delta H$ by 2 in order to obtain the desired quantity of water.

$$2H_2(g) + O_2(g) \longrightarrow 2H_2O(l) \quad \Delta H_c^0 = 2(-285.8 \text{ kJ})$$

We are now ready to add the three equations together using Hess's law to give the enthalpy of formation for methane and the balanced equation.

$$C(s) + \cancel{O_2(g)} \longrightarrow \cancel{CO_2(g)} \qquad \Delta H_c^0 = -393.5 \text{ kJ}$$

$$2H_2(g) + \cancel{O_2(g)} \longrightarrow \cancel{2H_2O(l)} \qquad \Delta H_c^0 = 2(-285.8 \text{ kJ})$$

$$\underline{\cancel{CO_2(g)} + \cancel{2H_2O(l)} \longrightarrow CH_4(g) + \cancel{2O_2(g)} \qquad \Delta H^0 = +890.8 \text{ kJ}}$$

$$C(s) + 2H_2(g) \longrightarrow CH_4(g) \qquad \Delta H_f^0 = -74.3 \text{ kJ}$$

Hess's law says that the enthalpy difference between reactants and products is independent of pathway. Therefore, any enthalpy of reaction may be calculated using enthalpies of formation for all the substances in the reaction of interest, without knowing anything else about how the reaction occurs. Mathematically, the overall equation for enthalpy change will be in the form of the equation shown below.

$$\Delta H^0 = \text{sum of } [(\Delta H_f^0 \text{ of products}) \times (\text{mol of products})] - \text{sum of } [(\Delta H_f^0 \text{ of reactants}) \times (\text{mol of reactants})]$$

An example using Hess's law is shown in **Sample Problem B.**

## SAMPLE PROBLEM B

For more help, go to the **Math Tutor** at the end of this chapter.

**Calculate the enthalpy of reaction for the combustion of nitrogen monoxide gas, NO, to form nitrogen dioxide gas, $NO_2$, as given in the following thermochemical equation.**

$$NO(g) + \frac{1}{2}O_2(g) \longrightarrow NO_2(g)$$

**Use the enthalpy-of-formation data in Appendix Table A-14. Solve by combining the known thermochemical equations. Verify the result by using the general equation for finding enthalpies of reaction from enthalpies of formation.**

### SOLUTION

**1 ANALYZE**

Given: $\frac{1}{2}N_2(g) + \frac{1}{2}O_2(g) \longrightarrow NO(g) \qquad \Delta H_f^0 = +90.29\ \text{kJ}$

$\frac{1}{2}N_2(g) + O_2(g) \longrightarrow NO_2(g) \qquad \Delta H_f^0 = +33.2\ \text{kJ}$

Unknown: $\Delta H^0$ for $NO(g) + \frac{1}{2}O_2(g) \longrightarrow NO_2(g)$

**2 PLAN**

$\Delta H$ can be found by adding the $\Delta H$s of the component reactions as specified in Hess's law. The desired equation has $NO(g)$ and $\frac{1}{2}O_2(g)$ as reactants and $NO_2(g)$ as the product.

$$NO(g) + \frac{1}{2}O_2(g) \longrightarrow NO_2(g)$$

We need an equation with NO as a reactant. Reversing the first reaction for the formation of NO from its elements and the sign of $\Delta H$ yields the following thermochemical equation.

$$NO(g) \longrightarrow \frac{1}{2}N_2(g) + \frac{1}{2}O_2(g) \qquad \Delta H^0 = -90.29\ \text{kJ}$$

The other equation should have $NO_2$ as a product, so we can retain the second equation for the formation of $NO_2$ from its elements as it stands.

$$\frac{1}{2}N_2(g) + O_2(g) \longrightarrow NO_2(g) \qquad \Delta H_f^0 = +33.2\ \text{kJ}$$

**3 COMPUTE**

$$NO(g) \longrightarrow \cancel{\frac{1}{2}N_2(g)} + \cancel{\frac{1}{2}O_2(g)} \qquad \Delta H^0 = -90.29\ \text{kJ}$$

$$\cancel{\frac{1}{2}N_2(g)} + O_2(g) \longrightarrow NO_2(g) \qquad \Delta H_f^0 = +33.2\ \text{kJ}$$

$$NO(g) + \frac{1}{2}O_2(g) \longrightarrow NO_2(g) \qquad \Delta H^0 = -57.1\ \text{kJ}$$

Note the cancellation of the $\frac{1}{2}N_2(g)$ and the partial cancellation of the $O_2(g)$.

**4 EVALUATE**

The unnecessary reactants and products cancel to give the desired equation.
The general relationship between the enthalpy of a reaction and the enthalpies of formation of the reactants and products is described in the following word equation.

$$\Delta H^0 = \text{sum of } [(\Delta H_f^0 \text{ of products}) \times (\text{mol of products})] - \text{sum of } [(\Delta H_f^0 \text{ of reactants}) \times (\text{mol of reactants})]$$

SECTION 2

# Driving Force of Reactions

## Objectives

- Explain the relationship between enthalpy change and the tendency of a reaction to occur.
- Explain the relationship between entropy change and the tendency of a reaction to occur.
- Discuss the concept of free energy, and explain how the value of this quantity is calculated and interpreted.
- Describe the use of free energy change to determine the tendency of a reaction to occur.

**C.4.10** Explain the role of collision frequency, the energy of collisions, and the orientation of molecules in reaction rates

The change in energy of a reaction system is one of two factors that allow chemists to predict whether a reaction will occur spontaneously and to explain how it occurs. The randomness of the particles in a system is the second factor affecting whether a reaction will occur spontaneously.

## Enthalpy and Reaction Tendency

The great majority of chemical reactions in nature are exothermic. As these reactions proceed, energy is liberated and the products have less energy than the original reactants. The products are also more resistant to change, more stable, than the original reactants. The tendency throughout nature is for a reaction to proceed in a direction that leads to a lower energy state.

We might think that endothermic reactions, in which energy is absorbed, cannot occur spontaneously because the products are at higher potential energy and are less stable than the original reactants. They would be expected to proceed only with the assistance of an outside influence, such as continued heating. However, some endothermic reactions *do* occur spontaneously. We conclude that something other than enthalpy change must help determine whether a reaction will occur.

## Entropy and Reaction Tendency

A naturally occurring endothermic process is melting. An ice cube melts spontaneously at room temperature as energy is transferred from the warm air to the ice. The well-ordered arrangement of water molecules in the ice crystal is lost, and the less-ordered liquid phase of higher energy content is formed. A system that can go from one state to another without a decrease in enthalpy does so with an increase in entropy.

Look at the physical states of the reactants in the chemical equation for the decomposition of ammonium nitrate.

$$2NH_4NO_3(s) \longrightarrow 2N_2(g) + 4H_2O(l) + O_2(g)$$

www.scilinks.org
**Topic:** Entropy
**Code:** HC60523

On the left side are 2 mol of solid ammonium nitrate. The right-hand side of the equation shows 3 mol of gaseous molecules plus 4 mol of a liquid. The arrangement of particles on the right-hand side of the equation is more random than the arrangement on the left side of the equation and hence is less ordered. **Figures 6a** and **6b** show the reactant and products of this decomposition reaction.

These examples illustrate that there is a tendency in nature to proceed in a direction that increases the randomness of a system. A random system is one that lacks a regular arrangement of its parts. This tendency toward randomness is called entropy. **Entropy,** *S*, can be defined in a simple qualitative way as *a measure of the degree of randomness of the particles, such as molecules, in a system.* To understand the concept of entropy, consider solids, liquids, and gases. In a solid, the particles are fixed in position in their small regions of space, but they are vibrating back and forth. Even so, we can determine with fair precision the location of the particles. The degree of randomness is low, so the entropy is low. When the solid melts, the particles are still very close together, but they can move about somewhat. The system is more random, and it is more difficult to describe the location of the particles. The entropy is higher. When the liquid evaporates, the particles are moving rapidly and are also much farther apart. Locating an individual particle is much more difficult, and the system is much more random. The entropy of the gas is still higher than that of the liquid. A general but not absolute rule is that the entropy of liquids is larger than that of solids and the entropy of gases is larger than that of liquids. But this rule must be used with caution. For example, the entropy of liquid mercury is much less than that of some solids.

The entropy of a pure crystalline solid is zero at absolute zero. As energy is added, the randomness of the molecular motion increases. Measurements of energy absorbed and calculations are used to determine the absolute entropy or standard molar entropy, and values are then recorded in tables. These molar values are reported as kJ/(mol•K). Entropy change, which can also be measured, is defined as the difference between the entropy of the products and the reactants. Therefore, an increase in entropy is represented by a positive value for $\Delta S$, and a decrease in entropy is represented by a negative value for $\Delta S$.

The process of forming a solution almost always involves an increase in entropy because there is an increase in randomness. This is true for mixing gases, dissolving a liquid in another liquid, and dissolving a solid in a liquid.

(a)

(b)

**FIGURE 6** When ammonium nitrate, $NH_4NO_3$, decomposes, the entropy of the reaction system increases as (a) one solid reactant becomes (b) two gaseous products and one liquid product.

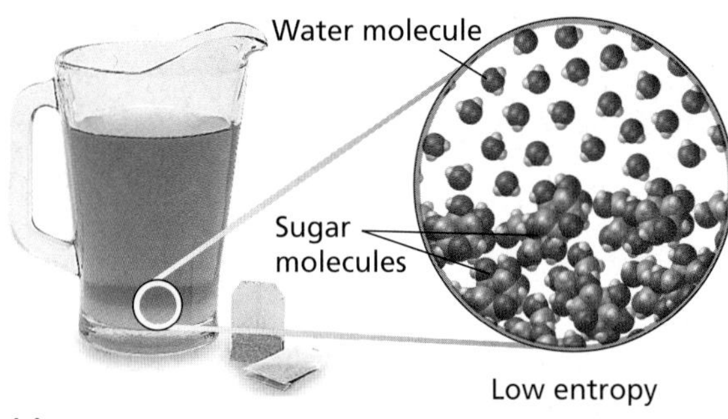

(a)

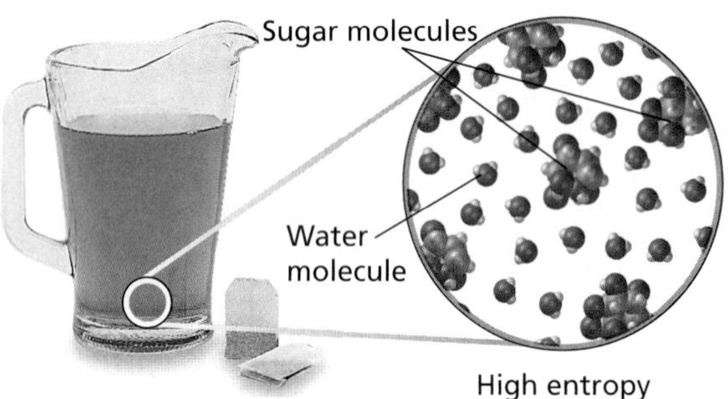

(b)

**FIGURE 7** When a solid dissolves in a liquid, the entropy of the system increases.

**Figure 7** illustrates the entropy change that takes place when solid sugar is dissolved in tea (an aqueous solution). In the sugar-water system shown in **Figure 7a,** the solid sugar has just been added to the tea, but most of it has not yet dissolved. The entropy is low because the majority of the sugar molecules are in one region at the bottom of the pitcher and the majority of the water molecules can be found everywhere else in the pitcher. After the sugar dissolves in the tea, shown in **Figure 7b,** the sugar molecules are thoroughly mixed throughout the tea solution. Sugar molecules and water molecules might be found anywhere in the solution, so the entropy, the randomness, of the system increases. This would give $\Delta S$ a positive value for this solid-liquid system. You can imagine the same series of events happening for a system of gases mixing with each other or a system of liquids mixing. In each case, $\Delta S$ would have a positive value once the solution was formed.

**extension**

**CROSS-DISCIPLINARY**

Go to **go.hrw.com** for a full-length article on free-energy changes related to ATP in the body.

**Keyword: HC6NRGX**

## Free Energy

Processes in nature are driven in two directions: toward least enthalpy and toward largest entropy. When these two oppose each other, the dominant factor determines the direction of change. As a way to predict which factor will dominate for a given system, a function has been defined to relate the enthalpy and entropy factors at a given temperature and constant pressure. *This combined enthalpy-entropy function is called the* **free energy,** *G, of the system;* it is also called *Gibbs free energy.* This function simultaneously assesses the tendencies for enthalpy and entropy to change. Natural processes proceed in the direction that lowers the free energy of a system.

Only the *change* in free energy can be measured. It can be defined in terms of changes in enthalpy and entropy. *At a constant pressure and temperature, the* **free-energy change,** *$\Delta G$, of a system is defined as the difference between the change in enthalpy, $\Delta H$, and the product of the Kelvin temperature and the entropy change, which is defined as $T\Delta S$.*

$$\Delta G^0 = \Delta H^0 - T\Delta S^0$$

Note that this expression is for substances in their standard states. The product $T\Delta S$ and the quantities $\Delta G$ and $\Delta H$ have the same units, usually kJ. The units of $\Delta S$ for use in this equation are usually kJ/K. If $\Delta G < 0$, the reaction is spontaneous.

$\Delta H$ and $\Delta S$ in the free-energy equation can have positive or negative values. This leads to four possible combinations of terms.

**Table 2** on the next page shows that if $\Delta H$ is negative and $\Delta S$ is positive, then both terms on the right in the free energy equation are negative. Both factors contribute to the process's being spontaneous. Therefore, $\Delta G$ will always be negative, and the reaction is definitely spontaneous. On the other hand, if $\Delta H$ is positive (endothermic process) and $\Delta S$ is negative (decrease in randomness), then the reaction as written is not spontaneous. When the enthalpy and entropy changes are operating in different directions, sometimes one will predominate and sometimes the other will predominate. There are reactions in which the enthalpy change is negative and the entropy change is negative. The enthalpy factor leads to a spontaneous process, but the negative entropy change opposes this. This is true in the following reaction. The entropy decreases because there is a decrease in moles of gas.

$$C_2H_4(g) + H_2(g) \longrightarrow C_2H_6(g)$$

There is a fairly large decrease in entropy, $\Delta S^0 = -0.1207$ kJ/(mol•K). However, the reaction is strongly exothermic, with a $\Delta H^0 = -136.9$ kJ/mol. The reaction proceeds because the enthalpy term predominates.

$$\Delta G^0 = \Delta H^0 - T\Delta S^0 = -136.9 \text{ kJ/mol} - 298 \text{ K}[-0.1207 \text{ kJ/(mol•K)}]$$
$$= -100.9 \text{ kJ/mol}$$

We can contrast this with the common commercial process for the manufacture of syngas, a mixture of CO and $H_2$. (This gas mixture is the starting point for the synthesis of a number of large-volume commercial chemicals, such as methanol, $CH_3OH$.)

$$CH_4(g) + H_2O(g) \longrightarrow CO(g) + 3H_2(g)$$

This reaction is endothermic, with $\Delta H^0 = +206.1$ kJ/mol and $\Delta S^0 = +0.215$ kJ/(mol•K), at standard conditions. The resulting $\Delta G$ is positive at room temperature. This tells us that the reaction will not occur at room temperature even though the entropy change is favorable.

$$\Delta G^0 = \Delta H^0 - T\Delta S^0 = +206.1 \text{ kJ/mol} - 298 \text{ K}[+0.215 \text{ kJ/(mol•K)}]$$
$$= +142.0 \text{ kJ/mol}$$

**TABLE 2 *Relating Enthalpy, Entropy, and Free-Energy Changes to Reaction Occurrence***

| $\Delta H$ | $\Delta S$ | $\Delta G$ |
|---|---|---|
| – value (exothermic) | + value (more random) | always negative |
| – value (exothermic) | – value (less random) | negative at *lower* temperatures |
| + value (endothermic) | + value (more random) | negative at *higher* temperatures |
| + value (endothermic) | – value (less random) | never negative |

## Chemistry in Action

### Diamonds Are Forever?

Carbon occurs in different forms, two of which are graphite and diamond. Using thermodynamic data, the change in free energy for diamond converting to graphite under standard thermodynamic conditions is –3 kJ/mol. That is, since ΔG is negative for this reaction, diamond should spontaneously change to graphite at 25°C and 1 atm. So, why doesn't all of our diamond jewelry change to graphite? The reaction rate is too slow for this spontaneous change to be observed. Therefore, at 25°C and 1 atm, although diamonds are not "forever," they will last a very long time.

## SAMPLE PROBLEM D

**For the reaction $NH_4Cl(s) \longrightarrow NH_3(g) + HCl(g)$, at 298.15 K, $\Delta H^0 = 176$ kJ/mol and $\Delta S^0 = 0.285$ kJ/(mol•K). Calculate $\Delta G^0$, and tell whether this reaction is spontaneous in the forward direction at 298.15 K.**

### SOLUTION

**1 ANALYZE** Given: $\Delta H^0 = 176$ kJ/mol at 298.15 K

$\Delta S^0 = 0.285$ kJ/(mol•K) at 298.15 K

Unknown: $\Delta G^0$ at 298.15 K

**2 PLAN**

$$\Delta S, \Delta H, T \rightarrow \Delta G$$

The value of $\Delta G$ can be calculated according to the following equation.

$$\Delta G^0 = \Delta H^0 - T\Delta S^0$$

**3 COMPUTE**

$$\begin{aligned} \Delta G^0 &= 176 \text{ kJ/mol} - 298 \text{ K } [0.285 \text{ kJ/(mol•K)}] \\ &= 176 \text{ kJ/mol} - 84.9 \text{ kJ/mol} \\ &= 91 \text{ kJ/mol} \end{aligned}$$

**4 EVALUATE** The answer is reasonably close to an estimated value of 110, calculated as $200 - (300 \times 0.3)$. The positive value of $\Delta G$ shows that this reaction does not occur naturally at 298.15 K.

### PRACTICE

*Answers in Appendix E*

1. For the vaporization reaction $Br_2(l) \longrightarrow Br_2(g)$, $\Delta H^0 = 31.0$ kJ/mol and $\Delta S^0 = 93.0$ J/(mol•K). At what temperature will this process be spontaneous?

Go to **go.hrw.com** for more practice problems that ask you to determine spontaneity based on free-energy changes.

**Keyword: HC6NRGX**

## SECTION REVIEW

1. What kind of enthalpy change favors a spontaneous reaction?
2. What is entropy, and how does it relate to spontaneity of reactions?
3. List several changes that result in an entropy increase.
4. Define *free energy*, and explain how its change is calculated.
5. Explain the relationship between free-energy change and spontaneity of reactions.
6. In the reaction in Sample Problem D, why does the entropy increase?

**Critical Thinking**

7. **APPLYING MODELS** Most biological enzymes become denatured when they are heated and lose their ability to catalyze reactions. This process (original enzyme $\longrightarrow$ denatured enzyme) is endothermic and spontaneous. Which structure, the original enzyme or the denatured enzyme, is more ordered? Explain your reasoning using thermodynamic concepts.

# CHAPTER HIGHLIGHTS

## Thermochemistry

**Vocabulary**
thermochemistry
calorimeter
temperature
joule
heat
specific heat
enthalpy change
enthalpy of reaction
thermochemical equation
molar enthalpy of formation
enthalpy of combustion
Hess's law

- Thermochemistry is the study of the changes in energy that accompany chemical reactions and physical changes.
- A thermochemical equation is an equation that includes the quantity of energy released or absorbed as heat during the reaction as written.
- An enthalpy change is the amount of energy absorbed as heat by a system in a process carried out at constant pressure.
- The enthalpy of reaction is the enthalpy change that occurs during a chemical reaction.
- The enthalpy change is negative for exothermic reactions and positive for endothermic reactions.
- Compounds with highly negative enthalpies of formation tend to be stable; compounds with highly positive or only slightly negative enthalpies of formation tend to be unstable.
- The standard molar enthalpy of formation is the enthalpy change that occurs when one mole of a compound is formed from its elements in their standard states at 25°C and 1 atm.
- The enthalpy change that occurs in a combustion reaction is called the enthalpy of combustion.
- Enthalpies of reaction can be calculated by using enthalpies of formation of reactants and products.

## Driving Force of Reactions

**Vocabulary**
entropy
free energy
free-energy change

- The tendency throughout nature is for a reaction to proceed in the direction that leads to a lower energy state.
- Entropy is a measure of the randomness of a system.
- Free-energy change combines the effects of entropy and enthalpy changes and temperature of a system, and it is a measure of the overall tendency toward natural change.
- A reaction is spontaneous if it is accompanied by a decrease in free energy. It is not spontaneous if there is an increase in free energy.

# CHAPTER REVIEW

For more practice, go to the Problem Bank in Appendix D.

## Thermochemistry

### SECTION 1 REVIEW

1. How does the enthalpy of the products of a reaction system compare with the enthalpy of the reactants when the reaction is
   a. endothermic?
   b. exothermic?
2. a. Distinguish between enthalpies of reaction, formation, and combustion.
   b. On what basis are enthalpies of formation and combustion defined?
3. Write the equation that can be used to calculate the enthalpy of reaction from enthalpies of formation.
4. What factors affect the value of $\Delta H$ in a reaction system?
5. State Hess's law. How is it used?
6. Describe a combustion calorimeter. What information can it give?

### PRACTICE PROBLEMS

7. How much energy is needed to raise the temperature of a 55 g sample of aluminum from 22.4°C to 94.6°C? Refer to **Table 1** for the specific heat of aluminum. (Hint: See Sample Problem A.)
8. If 3.5 kJ of energy are added to a 28.2 g sample of iron at 20°C, what is the final temperature of the iron in kelvins? Refer to **Table 1** for the specific heat of iron.
9. You need 70.2 J to raise the temperature of 34.0 g of ammonia, $NH_3(g)$, from 23.0°C to 24.0°C. Calculate the specific heat of ammonia.
10. Calculate $c_p$ for indium metal, given that 1.0 mol In absorbs 53 J while increasing in temperature from 297.5 K to 299.5 K.
11. For each equation listed below, determine the $\Delta H$ and type of reaction (endothermic or exothermic).
    a. $C(s) + O_2(g) \longrightarrow CO_2(g) + 393.51$ kJ
    b. $CH_4(g) + 2O_2(g) \longrightarrow CO_2(g) + 2H_2O(l) + 890.31$ kJ
    c. $CaCO_3(s) + 176$ kJ $\longrightarrow CaO(s) + CO_2(g)$
    d. $H_2O(g) \longrightarrow H_2O(l) + 44.02$ kJ
12. Rewrite each equation below with the $\Delta H$ value included with either the reactants or the products, and identify the reaction as endothermic or exothermic.
    a. $H_2(g) + O_2(g) \longrightarrow H_2O(l)$; $\Delta H^0 = -285.83$ kJ
    b. $2Mg(s) + O_2(g) \longrightarrow 2MgO(s)$; $\Delta H^0 = -1200$ kJ
    c. $I_2(s) \longrightarrow I_2(g)$; $\Delta H^0 = +62.4$ kJ
    d. $3CO(g) + Fe_2O_3(s) \longrightarrow 2Fe(s) + 3CO_2(g)$; $\Delta H^0 = -24.7$ kJ
13. Use Appendix Table A-14 to write the reaction illustrating the formation of each of the following compounds from its elements. Write the $\Delta H$ as part of each equation, and indicate the $\Delta H$ for the reverse reaction.
    a. $CaCl_2(s)$
    b. $C_2H_2(g)$ (ethyne, or acetylene)
    c. $SO_2(g)$
14. The reaction $2Fe_2O_3(s) + 3C(s) \longrightarrow 4Fe(s) + 3CO_2(g)$ is involved in the smelting of iron. Use $\Delta H_f$ values given in Appendix Table A-14 to calculate the enthalpy change during the production of 1 mol of iron.
15. Use enthalpy-of-formation data given in Appendix Table A-14 to calculate the enthalpy of reaction for each of the following. Solve each by combining the known thermochemical equations. Verify each result by using the general equation for finding enthalpies of reaction from enthalpies of formation. (Hint: See Sample Problem B.)
    a. $CaCO_3(s) \longrightarrow CaO(s) + CO_2(g)$
    b. $Ca(OH)_2(s) \longrightarrow CaO(s) + H_2O(g)$
    c. $Fe_2O_3(s) + 3CO(g) \longrightarrow 2Fe(s) + 3CO_2(g)$
16. For glucose, $C_6H_{12}O_6(s)$, $\Delta H_f = -1263$ kJ/mol. Calculate the enthalpy change when 1 mol of $C_6H_{12}O_6(s)$ combusts to form $CO_2(g)$ and $H_2O(l)$.
17. Calculate the standard enthalpies of reaction for combustion reactions in which ethane, $C_2H_6$, and benzene, $C_6H_6$, are the respective reactants and $CO_2(g)$ and $H_2O(l)$ are the products in each. Solve each by combining the known thermochemical equations using the $\Delta H_f$ values in

Appendix Table A-14. Verify the result by using the general equation for finding enthalpies of reaction from enthalpies of formation.

a. $C_2H_6(g) + O_2(g) \longrightarrow$

b. $C_6H_6(l) + O_2(g) \longrightarrow$

**18.** The enthalpy of formation of ethanol, $C_2H_5OH$, is –277.0 kJ/mol at 298.15 K. Calculate the enthalpy of combustion of one mole of ethanol, assuming that the products are $CO_2(g)$ and $H_2O(l)$. (Hint: See Sample Problem C.)

## *Driving Force of Reactions*

### SECTION 2 REVIEW

**19.** Would entropy increase or decrease for changes in state in which the reactant is a gas or liquid and the product is a solid? What sign would the entropy change have?

**20.** How does an increase in temperature affect the entropy of a system?

**21.** What combination of $\Delta H$ and $\Delta S$ values always produces a negative free-energy change?

**22.** Explain the relationship between temperature and the tendency for reactions to occur spontaneously.

### PRACTICE PROBLEMS

**23.** A reaction has $\Delta H = -356$ kJ and $\Delta S = -36$ J/K. Calculate $\Delta G$ at 25°C to confirm that the reaction is spontaneous.

**24.** A reaction has $\Delta H = 98$ kJ and $\Delta S = 292$ J/K. Investigate the spontaneity of the reaction at room temperature. Would increasing the temperature have any effect on the spontaneity of the reaction?

**25.** A reaction has $\Delta H = -76$ kJ and $\Delta S = -117$ J/K. Calculate $\Delta G$ for the reaction at 298.15 K. Is the reaction spontaneous?

**26.** The gas-phase reaction of $H_2$ with $CO_2$ to produce $H_2O$ and CO has $\Delta H = 11$ kJ and $\Delta S = 41$ J/K. Is the reaction spontaneous at 298.15 K? What is $\Delta G$?

**27.** Based on the following values, compute $\Delta G$ values for each reaction and predict whether the reaction will occur spontaneously. (Hint: See Sample Problem D.)

a. $\Delta H = +125$ kJ, T = 293 K, $\Delta S = 0.0350$ kJ/K

b. $\Delta H = -85.2$ kJ, T = 127°C, $\Delta S = 0.125$ kJ/K

c. $\Delta H = -275$kJ, T = 773 K, $\Delta S = 0.450$ kJ/K

**28.** The $\Delta S^0$ for the reaction shown, at 298.15 K, is 0.003 00 kJ/(mol•K). Calculate the $\Delta G^0$ for this reaction, and determine whether it will occur spontaneously at 298.15 K.

$$C(s) + O_2(g) \longrightarrow CO_2(g) + 393.51 \text{ kJ}$$

### MIXED REVIEW

**29.** When graphite reacts with hydrogen at 300 K, $\Delta H$ is –74.8 kJ and $\Delta S$ is –0.0809 kJ/K. Will this reaction occur spontaneously?

**30.** How might you change reaction conditions to induce an endothermic reaction that does not occur naturally?

**31.** The diagram below represents an interpretation of Hess's law for the following reaction.

$$Sn(s) + 2Cl_2(g) \longrightarrow SnCl_4(l)$$

Use the diagram to determine $\Delta H$ for each step and the net reaction.

$Sn(s) + Cl_2(g) \longrightarrow SnCl_2(s)$ $\quad \Delta H = ?$

$SnCl_2(l) + Cl_2(g) \longrightarrow SnCl_4(s)$ $\quad \Delta H = ?$

$Sn(s) + 2Cl_2(g) \longrightarrow SnCl_4(l)$ $\quad \Delta H = ?$

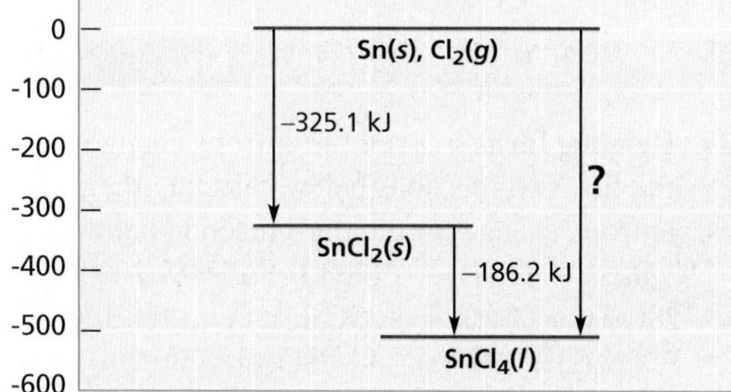


**32.** The standard enthalpy of formation for sulfur dioxide gas is –296.8 kJ/mol. Calculate the amount of energy given off in kJ when 30.0 g of $SO_2(g)$ is formed from its elements.

33. The thermite reaction used in some welding applications has the following enthalpy and entropy changes at 298.15 K. Assuming $\Delta S$ and $\Delta H$ are constant, calculate $\Delta G$ at 448 K.
$Fe_2O_3 + 2Al(s) \longrightarrow 2Fe(s) + Al_2O_3(s)$
$\Delta H^0 = -851.5$ kJ $\Delta S^0 = -38.5$ J/K

34. Rewrite each equation below with the $\Delta H$ value included in either the reactants or products, and identify the reaction as endothermic or exothermic.
    a. $2SO_2(g) + O_2(g) \longrightarrow 2SO_3(g)$; $\Delta H = -197.8$ kJ
    b. $2NO_2(g) \longrightarrow 2NO(g) + O_2(g)$; $\Delta H = +114.2$ kJ
    c. $C_2H_4(g) + 3O_2(g) \longrightarrow 2CO_2(g) + 2H_2O(l)$; $\Delta H = -1411.0$ kJ

35. Calculate the change in enthalpy for the following reaction.
$$4FeO(s) + O_2(g) \longrightarrow 2Fe_2O_3(s)$$
Use the enthalpy-of-formation data listed in Appendix Table A-14.

36. The reaction to synthesize methanol ($CH_3OH$) industrially is
$$CO(g) + 2H_2(g) \longrightarrow CH_3OH(g).$$
The $\Delta H^0_{reaction} = -90.7$ kJ and the $\Delta S^0_{reaction} = -220.8$ J/K. At what temperatures is the reaction nonspontaneous?

37. What is the main characteristic of a calorimeter in a bomb calorimeter experiment, and why is this characteristic essential?

## CRITICAL THINKING

38. **Relating Ideas** Given the entropy change for the first two reactions below, calculate the entropy change for the third reaction below.
$$S_8(s) + 8O_2(s) \longrightarrow 8SO_2(g) \ \Delta S = 89 \text{ J/K}$$
$$2SO_2(s) + O_2(s) \longrightarrow 2SO_3(g) \ \Delta S = -188 \text{ J/K}$$
$$S_8(s) + 12O_2(s) \longrightarrow 8SO_3(g) \ \Delta S = ?$$

39. **Interpreting Concepts** Look at the two pictures below. Which picture appears to have more order? Why? Are there any similarities between the amount of order the marbles have and the entropy of particles?

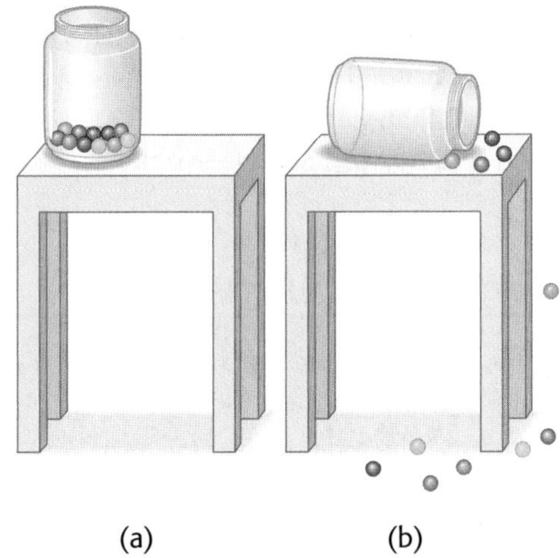


40. **Inferring Conclusions** A reaction is endothermic and has a $\Delta H = 8$ kJ. This reaction occurs spontaneously at 25°C. What must be true about the entropy change?

41. **Inferring Conclusions** If both $\Delta H$ and $\Delta S$ are negative, how does temperature affect spontaneity?

42. **Inferring Relationships** If the reaction $X \longrightarrow Y$ is spontaneous, what can be said about the reaction $Y \longrightarrow X$?

43. **Interpreting Concepts** Absolute enthalpy cannot be determined; only change in energy can be measured. However, absolute entropy can be determined. Explain why an absolute entropy can be determined.

## RESEARCH & WRITING

**44.** Obtain information on alternative units of measure used to express values of energy as heat and other forms of energy. Also, find out how the quantities relate to SI units. Include information specifically on English units, such as the British thermal unit (BTU), and on typical BTU ratings of household appliances. Calculate how these ratings would be expressed in joules instead.

## ALTERNATIVE ASSESSMENT

**45. Performance** Design a simple calorimeter investigation to determine the molar enthalpy of fusion of water. Use the following materials: a large plastic-foam cup with cover, a thermometer, a balance, water at room temperature, and an ice cube. Allow your teacher to review your design. Then carry out the investigation, and write a laboratory report including your calculations and a comparison of your quantitative results with known values. Try to account for any disagreements between the experimental and actual values.

**46. Performance** Design an experiment to measure the molar heat capacities of zinc and copper. If your teacher approves the design, obtain the materials needed and conduct the experiment. When you are finished, compare your experimental values with those from a chemical handbook or other reference source.

**47. Performance** Develop a procedure to measure the $\Delta H$ of the reaction shown below. If your teacher approves your procedure, test your procedure by measuring the $\Delta H$ value of the reaction. Determine the accuracy of your method by comparing your $\Delta H$ with the accepted $\Delta H$ value.

$$CH_3COONa(s) \longrightarrow Na^+(aq) + CH_3COO^-(aq)$$

**Graphing Calculator**
**Free-Energy Changes**
Go to **go.hrw.com** for a graphing calculator exercise that asks you to calculate and graph free-energy (ΔG) changes.

**Keyword: HC6NRGX**

# Math Tutor HESS'S LAW

You may have seen a popular comic strip in which a little boy takes a long, twisting path between the school-bus stop and home. No matter which path the boy takes, the result is always the same: He goes from the bus stop to the door of his house. Hess's law covers a similar situation in thermochemistry. No matter which or how many steps occur in the process of changing one or more substances into one or more other substances, the overall change in enthalpy is always the same. Hess's law can be used, for example, to predict the enthalpy change, $\Delta H^0$, of a reaction without actually carrying out the reaction.

## SAMPLE

**Determine $\Delta H$ for the burning of carbon disulfide in oxygen.**

$$CS_2(l) + 3O_2(g) \longrightarrow CO_2(g) + 2SO_2(g) \;\; \Delta H^0 = ?$$

Use the following information:

$$C(s) + O_2(g) \longrightarrow CO_2(g) \;\; \Delta H_f^0 = -393.5 \text{ kJ/mol}$$
$$S(s) + O_2(g) \longrightarrow SO_2(g) \;\; \Delta H_f^0 = -296.8 \text{ kJ/mol}$$
$$C(s) + 2S(s) \longrightarrow CS_2(l) \;\; \Delta H_f^0 = 87.9 \text{ kJ/mol}$$

Rearrange the given equations in a way that will put the reactants of the above equation on the left and the products on the right.

1. $\cancel{C(s)} + O_2(g) \longrightarrow CO_2(g)$ $\quad \Delta H_f^0 = -393.5$ kJ/mol
2. $\cancel{2S(s)} + 2O_2(g) \longrightarrow 2SO_2(g)$ $\quad \Delta H^0 = 2(-296.8$ kJ$)$
3. $CS_2(l) \longrightarrow \cancel{C(s)} + \cancel{2S(s)}$ $\quad \Delta H^0 = -87.9$ kJ

**SUM:** $CS_2(l) + 3O_2(g) \longrightarrow CO_2(g) + 2SO_2(g)$

Notice that equation 2 is double the original equation $S(s) + O_2(g) \longrightarrow SO_2(g)$. The reason for this is that $2SO_2$ are needed on the product side to match the $2SO_2$ in $CS_2(l) + 3O_2(g) \longrightarrow CO_2(g) + 2SO_2(g)$. The third equation is the reverse of the original, putting $CS_2$ on the reactant side of the final equation. The sign of $\Delta H$ is likewise reversed. The value of $\Delta H^0$ is the sum of the $\Delta H^0$ values for the three added equations.

$\Delta H^0 = -393.5 \text{ kJ} + 2(-296.8 \text{ kJ}) + (-87.9 \text{ kJ})$

$\Delta H^0 = -1075.0 \text{ kJ}$

## PRACTICE PROBLEMS

**1.** Calculate $\Delta H^0$ for the complete oxidation of sulfur to sulfur trioxide.

$$S(s) + \tfrac{3}{2}O_2(g) \longrightarrow SO_3(g)$$

Use the following information.

$S(s) + O_2(g) \longrightarrow SO_2(g)$ $\quad \Delta H_f^0 = -296.8$ kJ/mol

$SO_2(g) + \tfrac{1}{2}O_2(g) \longrightarrow SO_3(g)$ $\quad \Delta H_f^0 = -99.2$ kJ/mol

**2.** Calculate $\Delta H^0$ for the reaction in which zinc sulfide ore is roasted to obtain zinc oxide.

$$ZnS(s) + \tfrac{3}{2}O_2(g) \longrightarrow ZnO(s) + SO_2(g)$$

Use the following information.

$Zn(s) + \tfrac{1}{2}O_2(g) \longrightarrow ZnO(s)$ $\quad \Delta H_f^0 = -348.0$ kJ/mol

$Zn(s) + S(s) \longrightarrow ZnS(s)$ $\quad \Delta H_f^0 = -203.0$ kJ/mol

$S(s) + O_2(g) \longrightarrow SO_2(g)$ $\quad \Delta H_f^0 = -296.8$ kJ/mol

# Standardized Test Prep

**Answer the following items on a separate piece of paper.**

## MULTIPLE CHOICE

**1.** Which of the following two conditions will favor a spontaneous reaction?

**A.** an increase in entropy and a decrease in enthalpy
**B.** an increase in entropy and an increase in enthalpy
**C.** a decrease in entropy and a decrease in enthalpy
**D.** a decrease in entropy and an increase in enthalpy

**2.** The gasification of coal is a method of producing methane by the following reaction.

$$C(s) + 2H_2(g) \longrightarrow CH_4(g) \qquad \Delta H = ?$$

Find $\Delta H$ by using the enthalpy changes in the following combustion reactions

$$C(s) + O_2(g) \longrightarrow CO_2(g) \qquad \Delta H = -394 \text{ kJ}$$
$$H_2(g) + \tfrac{1}{2}O_2(g) \longrightarrow H_2O(l) \qquad \Delta H = -286 \text{ kJ}$$
$$CH_4(g) + 2O_2(g) \longrightarrow CO_2(g) + 2H_2O(l) \qquad \Delta H = -891 \text{ kJ}$$

**A.** 75 kJ
**B.** –75 kJ
**C.** 1856 kJ
**D.** –1856 kJ

**3.** Two metals of equal mass but different specific heats absorb the same amount of heat. Which metal undergoes the smaller change in temperature?

**A.** The metal with the higher specific heat.
**B.** The metal with the lower specific heat.
**C.** Both undergo the same change in temperature.
**D.** Cannot determine from the information given.

**4.** Which of the following processes has a negative $\Delta S$?

**A.** evaporating 1 mol of a liquid
**B.** raising the temperature of 1 L of water from 295 K to 350 K
**C.** freezing of 1 mol of a liquid
**D.** None of the above

**5.** At a constant pressure, the following reaction is exothermic: $2NO_2(g) \longrightarrow N_2O_4(g)$. Which of the following statements is true about the reaction (as written)?

**A.** The reaction is always spontaneous.
**B.** The reaction is spontaneous at low temperatures, but not at high temperatures.
**C.** The reaction is spontaneous at high temperatures, but not at low temperatures.
**D.** The reaction is never spontaneous.

## SHORT ANSWER

**6.** For a reaction in which a diatomic molecule dissociates into atoms, what are the signs of $\Delta S$ and $\Delta H$? Explain your answer. You may use the reaction $N_2(g) \longrightarrow 2N(g)$ as an example of such a reaction.

## EXTENDED RESPONSE

**7.** For certain molecules, enthalpies of formation can be determined from combustion data. Using the diagram below, calculate the enthalpy of formation of methane gas, $CH_4(g)$, and the enthalpies for two of the combustion reactions listed below.

Combustion reactions:

$$C(s) + O_2(g) \longrightarrow CO_2(g) \qquad \Delta H = -393.5 \text{ kJ}$$
$$H_2(g) + \tfrac{1}{2}O_2(g) \longrightarrow H_2O(l) \qquad \Delta H = ?$$
$$CH_4(g) + 2O_2(g) \longrightarrow CO_2(g) + 2H_2O(l) \qquad \Delta H = ?$$

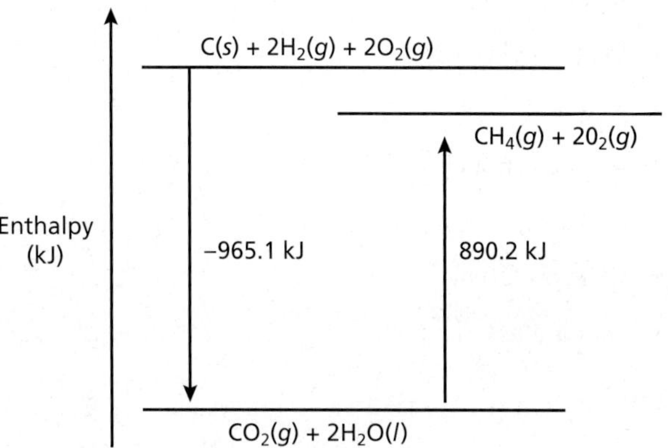


**Test TIP** Always read the question before looking at the answer choices.

SEE PRE-LAB
CALORIMETRY

# Calorimetry and Hess's Law

## OBJECTIVES

- ***Demonstrate* proficiency in the use of calorimeters and related equipment.**
- ***Relate* temperature changes to enthalpy changes.**
- ***Determine* enthalpies of reaction for several reactions.**
- ***Demonstrate* that enthalpies of reactions can be additive.**

## MATERIALS

- **4 g NaOH pellets**
- **50 mL 1.0 M HCl acid solution**
- **50 mL 1.0 M NaOH solution**
- **100 mL 0.50 M HCl solution**
- **100 mL graduated cylinder**
- **balance**
- **distilled water**
- **forceps**
- **glass stirring rod**
- **gloves**
- **plastic-foam cups (or calorimeter)**
- **spatula**
- **thermometer**
- **watch glass**

## BACKGROUND

Hess's law states that the overall enthalpy change in a reaction is equal to the sum of the enthalpy changes in the individual steps in the process. In this experiment, you will use a calorimeter to measure the energy released in three chemical reactions. From your experimental data, you will verify Hess's law.

## SAFETY

For review of safety, please see **Safety in the Chemistry Laboratory** in the front of your book.

## PREPARATION

1. Prepare a data table in which to record the total volumes of liquid, initial temperature, and final temperature of the three reactions you will carry out, as well as the mass of the empty watch glass and the watch glass plus NaOH pellets.
2. Gently insert the thermometer into the plastic foam cup held upside down. **Thermometers break easily, so be careful with them, and do not use them to stir a solution.**

## PROCEDURE

### Reaction 1: Dissolving NaOH

1. Pour 100 mL of distilled water into your calorimeter. Record the water temperature to the nearest 0.1°C.
2. Weigh a clean and dry watch glass to the nearest 0.01 g. Wearing gloves and using forceps, place about 2 g of NaOH pellets on the watch glass. Measure and record the mass of the watch glass and the pellets to the nearest 0.01 g. **It is important that this step be done quickly: NaOH absorbs moisture from the air.**

3. Immediately place the NaOH pellets in the calorimeter cup, and gently stir the solution with a stirring rod. **Do not stir with a thermometer.** Place the lid on the calorimeter. Watch the thermometer, and record the highest temperature in your data table.

4. Be sure to clean all equipment and rinse it with distilled water before continuing.

### Reaction 2: NaOH and HCl in Solution

5. Pour 50 mL of 1.0 M HCl into your calorimeter. Record the temperature of the HCl solution to the nearest 0.1°C.

6. Pour 50 mL of 1.0 M NaOH into a graduated cylinder. **For this step only, rinse the thermometer, and measure the temperature of the NaOH solution in the graduated cylinder to the nearest 0.1°C. Record the temperature, and then replace the thermometer in the calorimeter.**

7. Pour the NaOH solution into the calorimeter cup, and stir gently. Place the lid on the calorimeter. Watch the thermometer and record the highest temperature.

8. Pour the solution in the container designated by your teacher. Clean and rinse all equipment before continuing with the procedure.

### Reaction 3: Solid NaOH and HCl in Solution

9. Pour 100 mL of 0.50 M HCl into your calorimeter. Record the temperature of the HCl solution to the nearest 0.1°C.

10. Measure the mass of a clean and dry watch glass, and record the mass. Wear gloves, and using forceps, obtain approximately 2 g of NaOH pellets. Place them on the watch glass, and record the total mass. **As in step 2, it is important that this step be done quickly.**

11. Immediately place the NaOH pellets in the calorimeter, and gently stir the solution. Place the lid on the calorimeter. Watch the thermometer, and record the highest temperature. When finished with this reaction, pour the solution into the container designated by your teacher for disposal of basic solutions.

## CLEANUP AND DISPOSAL

12. Check with your teacher for the proper disposal procedures. Always wash your hands thoroughly after cleaning up the lab area and equipment.

## ANALYSIS AND INTERPRETATION

1. **Organizing Ideas:** Write a balanced chemical equation for each of the three reactions that you performed. (Hint: Be sure to include the physical states of matter for all substances.)

2. **Organizing Ideas:** Write the equation for the total reaction by adding two of the equations from item 1 and then canceling out substances that appear in the same form on both sides of the new equation.

3. **Organizing Data:** Calculate the change in temperature for each of the reactions.

4. **Organizing Data:** Assuming that the density of the water and the solutions is 1.00 g/mL, calculate the mass of liquid present for each of the reactions.

5. **Analyzing Results:** Using the calorimeter equation, calculate the energy as heat released by each reaction. (Hint: Use the specific heat of water in your calculations.)

$$c_{p,H_2O} = 4.184 \text{ J/g} \cdot {}^\circ\text{C}$$

$$\text{heat} = m \times \Delta t \times c_{p,H_2O}$$

6. **Organizing Data:** Calculate the moles of NaOH used in each of the reactions.

7. **Analyzing Results:** Calculate the $\Delta H$ value in kJ/mol of NaOH for each of the three reactions.

8. **Organizing Ideas:** Using your answer to Analysis and Interpretation item 2 and your knowledge of Hess's law, explain how the enthalpies for the three reactions should be mathematically related.

CHAPTER 17

# Reaction Kinetics

*Chemists can determine the rates at which chemical reactions occur.*

The Thermite Reaction

# The Reaction Process

SECTION 1

C.4.6 Explain the role of activation energy and the effects of temperature, particle size, stirring, concentration, and catalysts in reaction rates

## OBJECTIVES

- Explain the concept of reaction mechanism.
- Use the collision theory to interpret chemical reactions.
- Define *activated complex.*
- Relate activation energy to enthalpy of reaction.

By studying many types of experiments, chemists have found that chemical reactions occur at widely differing rates. For example, in the presence of air, iron rusts very slowly, whereas the methane in natural gas burns rapidly. The speed of a chemical reaction depends on the energy pathway that a reaction follows and the changes that take place on the molecular level when substances interact. In this chapter, you will study the factors that affect how fast chemical reactions take place.

## Reaction Mechanisms

If you mix aqueous solutions of HCl and NaOH, an extremely rapid neutralization reaction occurs, as shown in **Figure 1.**

$$H_3O^+(aq) + Cl^-(aq) + Na^+(aq) + OH^-(aq) \longrightarrow 2H_2O(l) + Na^+(aq) + Cl^-(aq)$$

The reaction is practically instantaneous; the rate is limited only by the speed with which the $H_3O^+$ and $OH^-$ ions can diffuse through the water to meet each other. On the other hand, reactions between ions of the same charge and between molecular substances are not instantaneous. Negative ions repel each other, as do positive ions. The electron clouds of molecules also repel each other strongly at very short distances. Therefore, only ions or molecules with very high kinetic energy can overcome repulsive forces and get close enough to react. In this section, we will limit our discussion to reactions between molecules.

Colorless hydrogen gas consists of pairs of hydrogen atoms bonded together as diatomic molecules, $H_2$. Violet-colored iodine vapor is also diatomic, consisting of pairs of iodine atoms bonded together as $I_2$ molecules. A chemical reaction between these two gases at elevated temperatures produces hydrogen iodide, HI, a colorless gas. Hydrogen iodide molecules, in turn, tend to decompose and re-form hydrogen and iodine molecules, producing the violet gas shown in **Figure 2.** The following chemical equations describe these two reactions.

$$H_2(g) + I_2(g) \longrightarrow 2HI(g)$$

$$2HI(g) \longrightarrow H_2(g) + I_2(g)$$

Such equations indicate only which molecular species disappear as a result of the reactions and which species are produced. They do not show the **reaction mechanism,** *the step-by-step sequence of reactions by which the overall chemical change occurs.*

**FIGURE 1** As NaOH solution is poured into HCl solution, a very rapid neutralization reaction occurs. Excess NaOH turns the phenolphthalein indicator pink.

# *Quick*LAB

Wear safety goggles and an apron.

## *Factors Influencing Reaction Rate*

### Question

**How do the type of reactants, surface area of reactants, concentration of reactants, and catalysts affect the rates of chemical reactions?**

### Procedure

Remove all combustible material from the work area. Wear safety goggles and an apron. Record all your results in a data table.

1. Add 10 mL of vinegar to each of three test tubes. To one test tube, add a 3 cm piece of magnesium ribbon; to a second, add a 3 cm zinc strip; and to a third, add a 3 cm copper strip. (All metals should be the same width.) If necessary, polish the metals with sandpaper until they are shiny.
2. Using tongs, hold a paper clip in the hottest part of the burner flame for 30 s. Repeat with a ball of steel wool 2 cm in diameter.
3. To one test tube, add 10 mL of vinegar; to a second, add 5 mL of vinegar plus 5 mL of water; and to a third, add 2.5 mL of vinegar plus 7.5 mL of water. To each of the three test tubes, add a 3 cm piece of magnesium ribbon.
4. Using tongs, hold a sugar cube and try to ignite it with a match. Then try to ignite it in a burner flame. Rub paper ash on a second cube, and try to ignite it with a match.

### Discussion

1. What are the rate-influencing factors in each step of the procedure?
2. What were the results from each step of the procedure? How do you interpret each result?

### Materials

- **Bunsen burner**
- **paper ash**
- **copper foil strip**
- **graduated cylinder, 10 mL**
- **magnesium ribbon**
- **matches**
- **paper clip**
- **sandpaper**
- **steel wool**
- **2 sugar cubes**
- **white vinegar**
- **zinc strip**
- **6 test tubes, 16 × 150 mm**
- **tongs**

## SECTION REVIEW

1. What is studied in the branch of chemistry that is known as chemical kinetics?
2. List five important factors that influence the rate of chemical reactions.
3. What is a catalyst? Explain the effect of a catalyst on the rate of chemical reactions. How does a catalyst influence the activation energy required by a particular reaction?
4. What is meant by a rate law for a chemical reaction? Explain the conditions under which a rate law can be written from a chemical equation. When can a rate law not be written from a single step?

**Critical Thinking**

5. **RELATING IDEAS** Using the ideas of reaction kinetics, explain the purpose of food refrigeration.

# Chemistry in Action

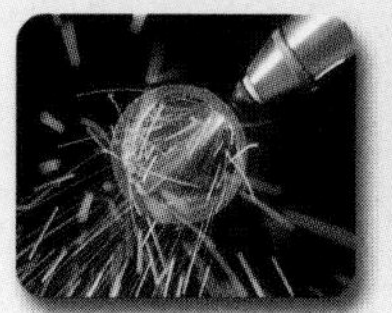
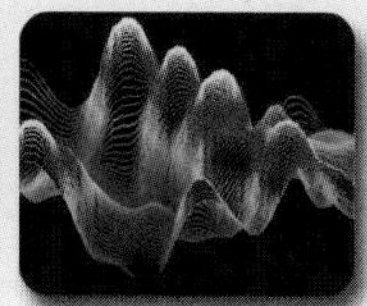
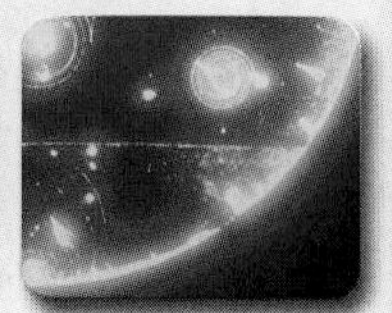

## Catalytic Converters

To see an important example of *heterogeneous catalysis*, you do not need to look any farther than the streets near your home. The *catalytic converter,* an important part of a vehicle's exhaust system, uses metal catalysts to reduce harmful gaseous pollutants.

In an automobile engine, hydrocarbon molecules in gasoline or diesel fuel undergo a combustion reaction with oxygen from air to make carbon dioxide, $CO_2$, and water. The correct stoichiometric ratio of fuel to oxygen is required for the fuel to be completely burned in the reaction. Additional reaction products are formed when not enough oxygen or excess oxygen is present. These products include carbon monoxide, CO, and $NO_x$ compounds, such as nitric oxide, NO, and nitrogen dioxide, $NO_2$. There is also leftover unburned fuel, which is called a volatile organic compound (VOC).

The Clean Air Act, enacted in 1990, regulates automobile emissions of CO, $NO_x$, and VOCs. Without a catalytic converter, a car would release all of the byproducts of incomplete combustion into the atmosphere. In addition to being harmful themselves, $NO_x$ compounds, CO, and VOCs react with sunlight to make ozone, $O_3$. In the lower atmosphere, ozone is a major part of photochemical smog. $NO_x$ gases can also mix with rainwater to produce acid rain.

Catalytic converters use precious metal catalysts to change the gases coming from the engine into less harmful gases. A combination of rhodium and platinum, and sometimes palladium, is used to convert nitrogen compounds back into $N_2$ and $O_2$. This combination also converts CO into $CO_2$ and converts VOCs into $CO_2$ and water. The catalysts need $O_2$ from the air and temperatures above approximately 500°F to work properly. The temperatures are achieved from the normal operation of the car engine. However, until the car engine reaches the temperatures needed for the catalysts to work, CO, $NO_x$, and VOCs will be released into the air by the automobile.

The interior structure of a catalytic converter is usually made of a ceramic honeycomb with a surface coating of metal catalyst particles. The honeycomb has many holes for the gases to pass through and provides a large surface area for the metal to be deposited on. A large surface area is needed to maximize the reactions that occur during heterogeneous catalysis because the transformation of the gas molecules occurs at the surface of the metal.

Up to 90% of CO, $NO_x$, and VOCs are typically eliminated from automobile exhaust by a catalytic converter. Although catalytic converters are beneficial to our environment, they could still be improved.

▲ *The ceramic honeycomb inside a catalytic converter is coated with a metal catalyst.*

Catalysts that work at lower temperatures would reduce an automobile's emission during the first few minutes of operation. Other gases that are emitted by cars may also pose problems for the environment. Nitrous oxide, $N_2O$, can be formed from the incomplete reduction of $NO_x$ in catalytic converters. Unlike the $NO_x$ gases, $N_2O$ can travel to the upper atmosphere, where it can destroy ozone. As a greenhouse gas, $N_2O$ is more that 300 times more potent than $CO_2$.

### Questions

1. Why do you think a heterogeneous catalyst is used instead of homogeneous catalyst in a catalytic converter?
2. Nitrous oxide, $N_2O$, actually has beneficial uses, despite its role as a greenhouse gas. Can you name a beneficial use of $N_2O$?

# CHAPTER HIGHLIGHTS

## *The Reaction Process*

**Vocabulary**

reaction mechanism
intermediate
homogenous reaction
collision theory
activation energy
activated complex

- The step-by-step process by which an overall chemical reaction occurs is called the *reaction mechanism.*
- In order for chemical reactions to occur, the particles of the reactants must collide.
- Activation energy is needed to merge valence electrons and to loosen bonds sufficiently for molecules to react.
- An activated complex is formed when an effective collision between molecules of reactants raises the internal energy to the minimum level necessary for a reaction to occur.

## *Reaction Rate*

**Vocabulary**

reaction rate
chemical kinetics
heterogeneous reactions
catalyst
catalysis
homogeneous catalyst
heterogeneous catalyst
rate law
order
rate-determining step

- The rate of reaction is influenced by the following factors: nature of reactants, surface area, temperature, concentration of reactants, and the presence of catalysts.
- The rates at which chemical reactions occur can sometimes be experimentally measured and expressed in terms of mathematical equations called *rate laws.*
- Rate laws are determined by studying how reaction rate depends on concentration.

## The Reaction Process

### SECTION 1 REVIEW

1. a. What is the collision theory?
   b. According to this theory, what two conditions must be met for a collision between reactant molecules to be effective in producing new chemical species?
2. a. What condition must be met for an activated complex to result from the collision of reactant particles?
   b. Where, in terms of energy, does the activated complex occur along a typical reaction pathway?
3. In a reversible reaction, how does the activation energy required for the exothermic change compare with the activation energy required for the endothermic change?
4. Would you expect the following equation to represent the mechanism by which propane, $C_3H_8$, burns? Why or why not?
   $C_3H_8(g) + 5O_2(g) \longrightarrow 3CO_2(g) + 4H_2O(g)$
5. The decomposition of nitrogen dioxide $2NO_2 \longrightarrow 2NO + O_2$ occurs in a two-step sequence at elevated temperatures. The first step is $NO_2 \longrightarrow NO + O$. Predict a possible second step that, when combined with the first step, gives the complete reaction.

### PRACTICE PROBLEMS

6. For each of the energy diagrams provided below, label the reactants, products, $\Delta E$, $E_a$, and $E_a'$. Also determine the values of $\Delta E$ for the forward and reverse reactions, and determine the values of $E_a$ and $E_a'$. (Hint: See Sample Problem A.)

a.

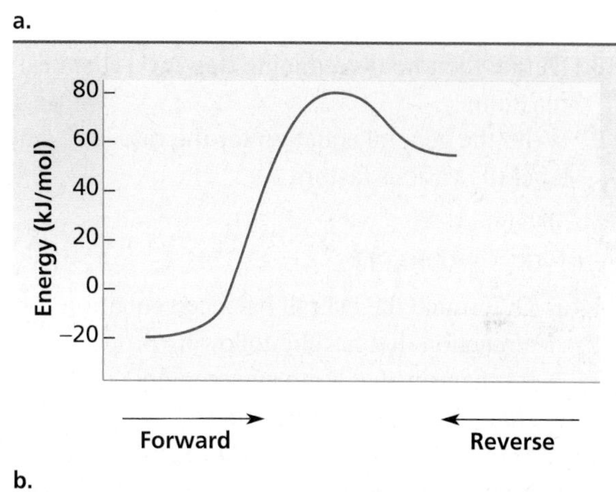


b.

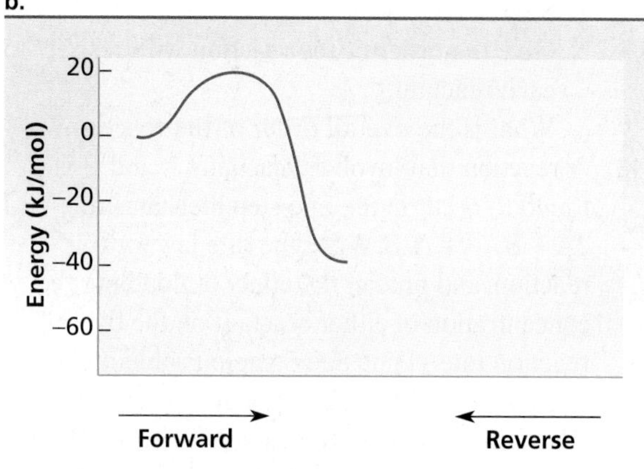


c.

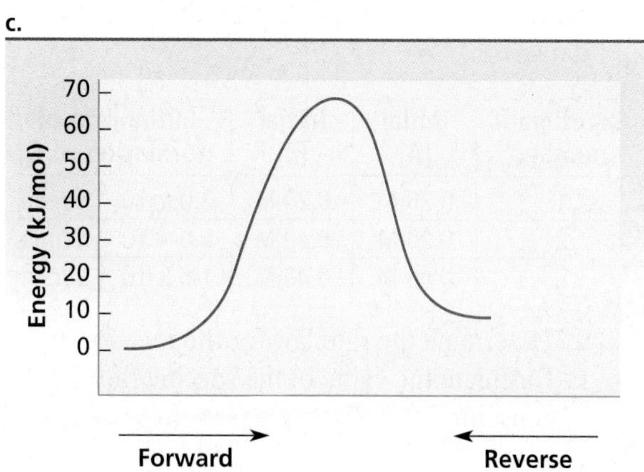

**7.** Draw and label energy diagrams that depict the following reactions, and determine all remaining values. Place the reactants at energy level zero.
a. $\Delta E_{forward} = -10$ kJ/mol $E_a' = 40$ kJ/mol
b. $\Delta E_{forward} = -95$ kJ/mol $E_a = 20$ kJ/mol
c. $\Delta E_{reverse} = -40$ kJ/mol $E_a' = 30$ kJ/mol

## *Reaction Rate*

### SECTION 2 REVIEW

**8.** Define the rate-determining step for a chemical reaction.

**9.** Write the general equation for the rate law, and label the various factors.

### PRACTICE PROBLEMS

**10.** a. Determine the overall balanced equation for a reaction that has the following proposed mechanism, and write an acceptable rate law. (Hint: See Sample Problem C.)
**Step 1:** $B_2 + B_2 \longrightarrow E_3 + D$ slow
**Step 2:** $E_3 + A \longrightarrow B_2 + C_2$ fast
b. Give the order of the reaction with respect to each reactant.
c. What is the overall order of the reaction?

**11.** A reaction that involves reactants A and B is found to occur in the one-step mechanism: $2A + B \longrightarrow A_2B$. Write the rate law for this reaction, and predict the effect of doubling the concentration of either reactant on the overall reaction rate. (Hint: See Sample Problem C.)

**12.** A chemical reaction is expressed by the balanced chemical equation $A + 2B \longrightarrow C$. Three reaction-rate experiments yield the following data.

| Experiment number | Initial [A] | Initial [B] | Initial rate of formation of C |
|---|---|---|---|
| 1 | 0.20 M | 0.20 M | $2.0 \times 10^{-4}$ M/min |
| 2 | 0.20 M | 0.40 M | $8.0 \times 10^{-4}$ M/min |
| 3 | 0.40 M | 0.40 M | $1.6 \times 10^{-3}$ M/min |

a. Determine the rate law for the reaction.
b. Calculate the value of the specific rate constant.
c. If the initial concentrations of both A and B are 0.30 M, at what initial rate is C formed?
d. What is the order of the reaction with respect to A?
e. What is the order of the reaction with respect to B?

## MIXED REVIEW

**13.** Draw and label energy diagrams that depict the following reactions, and determine all remaining values. Place the reactants at energy level zero.
a. $\Delta E = +30$ kJ/mol $E_a' = 20$ kJ/mol
b. $\Delta E = -30$ kJ/mol $E_a = 20$ kJ/mol

**14.** A particular reaction is found to have the following rate law.

$$R = k[A][B]^2$$

How is the rate affected by each of the following changes?
a. The initial concentration of A is cut in half.
b. The initial concentration of B is tripled.
c. The concentration of A is doubled, but the concentration of B is cut in half.
d. A catalyst is added.

**15.** For each of the following pairs, choose the substance or process that you would expect to react more rapidly.
a. granulated sugar or powdered sugar
b. zinc in HCl at 298.15 K or zinc in HCl at 320 K
c. 5 g of thick platinum wire or 5 g of thin platinum wire

**16.** The following data relate to the reaction $A + B \longrightarrow C$. Find the order with respect to each reactant.

| [A] (M) | [B] (M) | Rate (M/s) |
|---|---|---|
| 0.08 | 0.06 | 0.012 |
| 0.08 | 0.03 | 0.006 |
| 0.04 | 0.06 | 0.003 |

## CRITICAL THINKING

17. **Predicting Outcomes** The balanced equation for a rapid homogeneous reaction between two gases is as follows: $4A + B \longrightarrow 2C + 2D$. Because the simultaneous collision of four molecules of one reactant with one molecule of the other reactant is extremely improbable, what would you predict about the nature of the reaction mechanism for this reaction system?

18. **Evaluating Ideas**
    a. How can you justify calling the reaction pathway that is shown in **Figure 4** the minimum-energy pathway for reaction?
    b. What significance is associated with the maximum-energy region of this minimum-energy pathway?

19. **Applying Models** Explain why there is a danger of explosion in places such as coal mines, sawmills, and grain elevators, where large amounts of dry, powdered combustible materials are present.

20. **Evaluating Methods** What property would you measure to determine the reaction rate for the following reaction? Justify your choice.

$$2NO_2(g) \longrightarrow N_2O_4(g)$$

## RESEARCH & WRITING

21. Look for situations around your house in which processes are speeded up by an increase in temperature or slowed down by a decrease in temperature. Make a list, and discuss the different processes.

## ALTERNATIVE ASSESSMENT

22. Boilers are sometimes used to heat large buildings. Deposits of $CaCO_3$, $MgCO_3$, and $FeCO_3$ can hinder the boiler operation. Aqueous solutions of hydrochloric acid are commonly used to remove these deposits. The general equation for the reaction is written below.

$$MCO_3(s) + 2H_3O^+(aq) \longrightarrow M^{2+}(aq) + 3H_2O(l) + CO_2(g)$$

In the equation, M stands for Ca, Mg, or Fe. Design an experiment to determine the effect of various HCl concentrations on the rates of this reaction. Present your design to the class.

**extension**

**Graphing Calculator**
**Reaction Orders**

Go to **go.hrw.com** for a graphing calculator exercise that asks you to calculate the order of a reaction from the reaction rates and concentrations.

Keyword: HC6RXKX

# Math Tutor WRITING RATE LAWS

Factors such as surface area and temperature affect the rate of reactions because they affect the frequency and energy of collisions between particles. The concentrations of reactants can also affect the frequency of collisions. If other factors are kept constant, the rates of most chemical reactions will be determined by the concentrations of reactants. Thus, it is possible to write an equation called a *rate law* that relates the rate of a reaction to the concentrations of reactants.

## SAMPLE

**Fluorine gas reacts with chlorine dioxide according to the following equation.**

$$F_2(g) + 2ClO_2(g) \longrightarrow 2FClO_2(g)$$

**Use the following experimental data to write a rate law for this reaction.**

| Trial | Concentration of $F_2$ | Concentration of $ClO_2$ | Rate (mol/L•s) |
|---|---|---|---|
| 1 | 0.10 *M* | 0.10 *M* | $1.1 \times 10^{-3}$ |
| 2 | 0.20 *M* | 0.10 *M* | $2.2 \times 10^{-3}$ |
| 3 | 0.10 *M* | 0.20 *M* | $2.2 \times 10^{-3}$ |
| 4 | 0.20 *M* | 0.20 *M* | $4.4 \times 10^{-3}$ |

To write the rate law, first examine the data to see how the rate of reaction changes as the concentrations of the reactants change.

- When $[F_2]$ doubles and $[ClO_2]$ remains constant, the rate of reaction doubles from $1.1 \times 10^{-3}$ mol/L•s to $2.2 \times 10^{-3}$ mol/L•s. So, the rate is directly proportional to $[F_2]$, or $R \propto [F_2]$.
- When $[ClO_2]$ doubles and $[F_2]$ remains constant, the rate of reaction also doubles from $1.1 \times 10^{-3}$ mol/L•s to $2.2 \times 10^{-3}$ mol/L•s. So, the rate is directly proportional to $[ClO_2]$, or $R \propto [ClO_2]$.
- Because rate is proportional to both $[F_2]$ and $[ClO_2]$, you can write the rate law $R = k[F_2][ClO_2]$. The data from Trial 4 help confirm the rate law because when both $[F_2]$ and $[ClO_2]$ double, the rate increases by a factor of four, from $1.1 \times 10^{-3}$ mol/L•s to $4.4 \times 10^{-3}$ mol/L•s.

## PRACTICE PROBLEMS

**1.** Nitrogen monoxide and oxygen react to produce nitrogen dioxide according to the following equation:

$$O_2(g) + 2NO(g) \longrightarrow 2NO_2(g)$$

Use the data in the following table to write a rate law for this reaction.

| Trial | $[O_2]$ | [NO] | Reaction Rate (mol/L•s) |
|---|---|---|---|
| 1 | $1.20 \times 10^{-2}$ *M* | $1.40 \times 10^{-2}$ *M* | $3.30 \times 10^{-3}$ |
| 2 | $2.40 \times 10^{-2}$ *M* | $1.40 \times 10^{-2}$ *M* | $6.60 \times 10^{-3}$ |
| 3 | $1.20 \times 10^{-2}$ *M* | $2.80 \times 10^{-2}$ *M* | $1.32 \times 10^{-2}$ |

**2.** Hydrogen reacts with ethyne, $C_2H_2$, to produce ethane, $C_2H_6$, as shown below:

$$2H_2(g) + C_2H_2(g) \longrightarrow C_2H_6(g)$$

Use the data in the following table to write a rate law for this reaction.

| Trial | $[H_2]$ | $[C_2H_2]$ | Reaction Rate (mol/L•min) |
|---|---|---|---|
| 1 | 0.20 *M* | 0.20 *M* | $1.5 \times 10^{-4}$ |
| 2 | 0.40 *M* | 0.20 *M* | $3.0 \times 10^{-4}$ |
| 3 | 0.20 *M* | 0.40 *M* | $1.5 \times 10^{-4}$ |

# Standardized Test Prep

**Answer the following items on a separate piece of paper.**

**MULTIPLE CHOICE**

**1.** The sequence of steps that occurs in a reaction process is called the
**A.** order of the reaction.
**B.** rate law.
**C.** overall reaction.
**D.** reaction mechanism.

**2.** To be effective, a collision requires
**A.** enough energy only.
**B.** favorable orientation only.
**C.** enough energy and a favorable orientation.
**D.** a reaction mechanism.

**3.** How does the energy of the activated complex compare with the energies of the reactants and products?
**A.** It is lower than both the energy of the reactants and the energy of the products.
**B.** It is lower than the energy of the reactants but higher than the energy of the products.
**C.** It is higher than the energy of the reactants but lower than the energy of the products.
**D.** It is higher than both the energy of the reactants and the energy of the products.

**4.** If a collision between molecules is very gentle, the molecules are
**A.** more likely to be oriented favorably.
**B.** less likely to be oriented favorably.
**C.** likely to react.
**D.** likely to rebound without reacting.

**5.** A species that changes the rate of a reaction but is neither consumed nor changed is
**A.** a catalyst.
**B.** an activated complex.
**C.** an intermediate.
**D.** a reactant.

**6.** A rate law relates
**A.** reaction rate and temperature.
**B.** reaction rate and concentration.
**C.** temperature and concentration.
**D.** energy and concentration.

**7.** In a graph of how energy changes with reaction progress, the activated complex appears at the
**A.** left end of the curve.
**B.** right end of the curve.
**C.** bottom of the curve.
**D.** peak of the curve.

**8.** The slowest step in a mechanism is called
**A.** the rate-determining step.
**B.** the uncatalyzed reaction.
**C.** the activation step.
**D.** None of the above

**9.** A certain reaction is zero order in reactant A and second order in reactant B. What happens to the reaction rate when the concentrations of both reactants are doubled?
**A.** The reaction rate remains the same.
**B.** The reaction increases by a factor of two.
**C.** The reaction rate increases by a factor of four.
**D.** The reaction rate increases by a factor of eight.

**SHORT ANSWER**

**10.** Two molecules collide but bounce apart unchanged. What two reasons could account for their failure to react?

**11.** Sketch a diagram that shows how the energy changes with the progress of an endothermic reaction. Label the curve "Reactants," "Products," and "Activated complex." On the same diagram, sketch a second curve to show the change caused by a catalyst.

**EXTENDED RESPONSE**

**12.** Suggest ways of measuring the concentration of a reactant or product in a reaction mixture.

**13.** Why are reaction orders not always equal to the coefficients in a balanced chemical equation?

**Test TIP** Sometimes, only one part of a graph or table is needed to answer a question. In such cases, focus on only the information that is required to answer the question.

# Rate of a Chemical Reaction

## OBJECTIVES

- ***Prepare*** **and** ***observe*** **several different reaction mixtures.**
- ***Demonstrate*** **proficiency in measuring reaction rates.**
- ***Relate*** **experimental results to a rate law that can be used to predict the results of various combinations of reactants.**

## MATERIALS

- **8-well microscale reaction strips, 2**
- **distilled or deionized water**
- **fine-tipped dropper bulbs or small microtip pipets, 3**
- **solution A**
- **solution B**
- **stopwatch or clock with second hand**

## BACKGROUND

In this experiment, you will determine the rate of the reaction whose net equation is written as follows:

$$3Na_2S_2O_5(aq) + 2KIO_3(aq) + 3H_2O(l) \xrightarrow{H^+} 2KI(aq) + 6NaHSO_4(aq)$$

One way to study the rate of this reaction is to observe how fast $Na_2S_2O_5$ is used up. After all the $Na_2S_2O_5$ solution has reacted, the concentration of iodine, $I_2$, an intermediate in the reaction, increases. A starch indicator solution, added to the reaction mixture, will change from clear to a blue-black color in the presence of $I_2$.

In the procedure, the concentrations of the reactants are given in terms of drops of solution A and drops of solution B. Solution A contains $Na_2S_2O_5$, the starch indicator solution, and dilute sulfuric acid to supply the hydrogen ions needed to catalyze the reaction. Solution B contains $KIO_3$. You will run the reaction with several different concentrations of the reactants and record the time it takes for the blue-black color to appear.

## SAFETY

For review of safety, please see the **Safety in the Chemistry Laboratory** in the front of your book.

## PREPARATION

1. Prepare a data table with six rows and six columns. Label the boxes in the first row of the second through sixth columns "Well 1," "Well 2," "Well 3," "Well 4," and "Well 5." In the first column, label the boxes in the second through sixth rows "Time reaction began," "Time reaction stopped," "Drops of solution A," "Drops of solution B," and "Drops of $H_2O$."

2. Obtain three dropper bulbs or small microtip pipets, and label them "A," "B," and "$H_2O$."

3. Fill the bulb or pipet A with solution A, the bulb or pipet B with solution B, and the bulb or pipet for $H_2O$ with distilled water.

## PROCEDURE

1. Using the first 8-well strip, place five drops of solution A into each of the first five wells. Record the number of drops in the appropriate places in your data table. **For the best results, try to make all drops about the same size.**

2. In the second 8-well reaction strip, place one drop of solution B in the first well, two drops in the second well, three drops in the third well, four drops in the fourth well, and five drops in the fifth well. Record the number of drops in your data table.

3. In the second 8-well strip that contains drops of solution B, add four drops of water to the first well, three drops to the second well, two drops to the third well, and one drop to the fourth well. Do not add any water to the fifth well.

4. Carefully invert the second strip. The surface tension should keep the solutions from falling out of the wells. Place the strip well-to-well on top of the first strip, as shown in Figure A.

5. Hold the strips tightly together as shown in Figure A, and record the exact time, or set the stopwatch, as you shake the strips once. This procedure should mix the upper solutions with each of the corresponding lower ones.

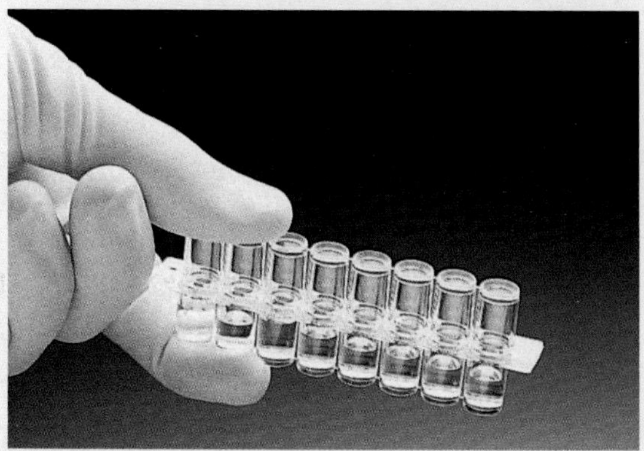

FIGURE A

6. Observe the lower wells. Note the sequence in which the solutions react, and record the number of seconds it takes for each solution to turn a blue-black color.

## CLEANUP AND DISPOSAL

7. Dispose of the solutions in the container designated by your teacher. Wash your hands thoroughly after cleaning up the area and equipment.

## ANALYSIS AND INTERPRETATION

1. **Organizing Data:** Calculate the time elapsed for the complete reaction of each combination of solutions A and B.

2. **Evaluating Data:** Make a graph of your results. Label the *x*-axis "Number of drops of solution B." Label the *y*-axis "Time elapsed." Make a similar graph for drops of solution B versus rate (1/time elapsed).

3. **Analyzing Information:** Which mixture reacted the fastest? Which mixture reacted the slowest?

4. **Evaluating Methods:** Why was it important to add the drops of water to the wells that contained fewer than five drops of solution B? (Hint: Figure out the total number of drops in each of the reaction wells.)

## CONCLUSIONS

1. **Evaluating Conclusions:** Which of the following variables that can affect the rate of a reaction is tested in this experiment: temperature, catalyst, concentration, surface area, or nature of reactants? Explain your answer.

2. **Applying Ideas:** Use your data and graphs to determine the relationship between the concentration of solution B and the rate of the reaction. Describe this relationship in terms of a rate law.

## EXTENSIONS

1. **Predicting Outcomes:** What combination of drops of solutions A and B would you use if you wanted the reaction to last exactly 2.5 min?

# CHAPTER 18

# *Chemical Equilibrium*

*The creation of stalactites and stalagmites is the result of a reversible chemical reaction.*

Carlsbad Caverns, New Mexico

# The Nature of Chemical Equilibrium

SECTION 1

## Objectives

- Define *chemical equilibrium.*
- Explain the nature of the equilibrium constant.
- Write chemical equilibrium expressions and carry out calculations involving them.

**C.4.9** Summarize the concept of chemical equilibrium and Le Châtelier's principle

In systems that are in equilibrium, opposing processes occur at the same time and at the same rate. For example, when an excess of sugar is placed in water, some sugar molecules go into solution, and others remain undissolved. At equilibrium, molecules of sugar are crystallizing at the same rate that molecules from the crystal are dissolving. The rate of evaporation of a liquid in a closed vessel can eventually be equaled by the rate of condensation of its vapor. The resulting equilibrium vapor pressure is a characteristic of the liquid at the prevailing temperature. The preceding examples are physical equilibria. In this chapter, we will expand on the concept of equilibrium to include chemical reactions. You will learn how a system at equilibrium responds when equilibrium conditions are altered by changing concentration, pressure, and temperature.

## Reversible Reactions

Theoretically, every reaction can proceed in two directions, forward and reverse. Thus, essentially all chemical reactions are considered to be reversible under suitable conditions. *A chemical reaction in which the products can react to re-form the reactants is called a* **reversible reaction.**

Mercury(II) oxide decomposes when heated.

$$2HgO(s) \xrightarrow{\Delta} 2Hg(l) + O_2(g)$$

Mercury and oxygen combine to form mercury(II) oxide when heated gently.

$$2Hg(l) + O_2(g) \xrightarrow{\Delta} 2HgO(s)$$

**FIGURE 1** When heated, mercury(II) oxide decomposes into its elements, mercury and oxygen. Liquid mercury reacts with oxygen to re-form mercury(II) oxide. Together these reactions represent a reversible chemical process.

**Figure 1** shows both of these reactions taking place. Suppose mercury(II) oxide is heated in a closed container from which neither the mercury nor the oxygen can escape. Once decomposition has begun, the mercury and oxygen released can recombine to form mercury(II) oxide again. Thus, both reactions can proceed at the same time. Under these conditions, the rate of the synthesis reaction will eventually equal that of the decomposition reaction. At equilibrium, mercury and oxygen will combine to form mercury(II) oxide at the same rate that mercury(II) oxide decomposes into mercury and oxygen. The amounts of mercury(II) oxide, mercury, and oxygen can then be expected to remain constant as long as these conditions persist. At this point, a state of dynamic equilibrium has been reached between the two chemical reactions. Both reactions continue, but there is no net change in the composition of the system. *A reversible chemical reaction is in* **chemical equilibrium** *when the rate of its forward reaction equals the rate of its reverse reaction and the concentrations of its products and reactants remain unchanged.* The chemical equation for the reaction at equilibrium is written using double arrows to indicate the overall reversibility of the reaction.

$$2HgO(s) \rightleftharpoons 2Hg(l) + O_2(g)$$

## Equilibrium, a Dynamic State

Many chemical reactions are reversible under ordinary conditions of temperature and concentration. They will reach a state of equilibrium unless at least one of the substances involved escapes or is removed from the reaction system. In some cases, however, the forward reaction is so predominant that essentially all reactants will react to form products. Here, the products of the forward reaction are favored, meaning that at equilibrium there is a much higher concentration of products than of reactants. Hence, we can say that the equilibrium "lies to the right," because products predominate, and products conventionally are written on the right-hand side of a chemical equation. An example of such a system is the formation of sulfur trioxide from sulfur dioxide and oxygen.

$$2SO_2(g) + O_2(g) \rightleftharpoons 2SO_3(g)$$

Notice that the equation is written showing an inequality of the two arrow lengths. The forward reaction is represented by the longer arrow to imply that the product is favored in this reaction.

In other cases, the forward reaction is barely under way when the rate of the reverse reaction becomes equal to that of the forward reaction, and equilibrium is established. In these cases, the amounts of reactants remain high and the amounts of products are low. Here we say that the equilibrium "lies to the left," because the reactants are the predominant species. An example of such a system is the acid-base reaction between carbonic acid and water.

$$H_2CO_3(aq) + H_2O(l) \rightleftharpoons H_3O^+(aq) + HCO_3^-(aq)$$

In still other cases, both forward and reverse reactions occur to nearly the same extent before chemical equilibrium is established. Neither reaction is favored, and considerable concentrations of both reactants and products are present at equilibrium. An example is the dissociation of sulfurous acid in water.

$$H_2SO_3(aq) + H_2O(l) \rightleftharpoons H_3O^+(aq) + HSO_3^-(aq)$$

Chemical reactions ordinarily are used to convert available reactants into more desirable products. Chemists try to convert as much of these reactants as possible into products. The extent to which reactants are converted to products is indicated by the numerical value of the equilibrium constant.

## The Equilibrium Expression

Suppose two substances, A and B, react to form products C and D. In turn, C and D react to produce A and B. Under appropriate conditions, equilibrium occurs for this reversible reaction. This hypothetical equilibrium reaction is described by the following general equation.

$$n\text{A} + m\text{B} \rightleftharpoons x\text{C} + y\text{D}$$

Initially, the concentrations of C and D are zero and those of A and B are maximum. **Figure 2** shows that over time the rate of the forward reaction decreases as A and B are used up. Meanwhile, the rate of the reverse reaction increases as C and D are formed. When these two reaction rates become equal, equilibrium is established. The individual concentrations of A, B, C, and D undergo no further change if conditions remain the same.

After equilibrium is attained, the concentrations of products and reactants remain constant, so a ratio of their concentrations should also

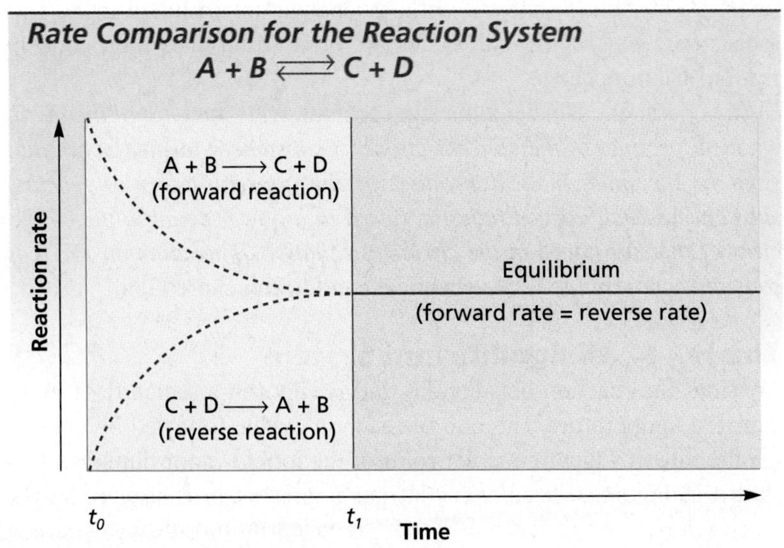


**FIGURE 2** Shown are reaction rates for the hypothetical equilibrium reaction system $A + B \rightleftharpoons C + D$. From the time A and B are mixed together at $t_0$, the rate of the forward reaction declines and the rate of the reverse reaction increases until both forward and reverse reaction rates are equal at $t_1$, when the equilibrium condition begins.

remain constant. The ratio of the mathematical product $[C]^x \times [D]^y$ to the mathematical product $[A]^n \times [B]^m$ for this reaction has a definite value at a given temperature. It is the equilibrium constant of the reaction and is designated by the letter $K$. The following equation describes the equilibrium constant for the hypothetical equilibrium system. The brackets ([ ]) indicate the concentration of each substance as expressed in mol/L. The superscripts are the coefficients of each substance in the balanced chemical equation.

$$K = \frac{[C]^x[D]^y}{[A]^n[B]^m}$$

The concentrations of substances on the right side of the chemical equation appear in the numerator of the ratio, with each concentration raised to a power equal to the coefficient of that substance in the balanced chemical equation. These substances are the products of the forward reaction. The concentrations of substances on the left side of the chemical equation are in the denominator of the ratio, with each concentration raised to a power equal to the coefficient of that substance in the balanced chemical equation. These substances are the reactants of the forward reaction. The constant $K$ is independent of the initial concentrations. It is, however, dependent on the temperature of the system.

## The Equilibrium Constant

The numerical value of $K$ for a particular equilibrium system is obtained experimentally. The chemist must analyze the equilibrium mixture and determine the concentrations of all substances. The value of $K$ for a given equilibrium reaction at a given temperature shows the extent to which the reactants are converted into the products of the reaction. If the value of $K$ is small, the forward reaction occurs only very slightly before equilibrium is established, and the reactants are favored. A large value of $K$ indicates an equilibrium in which the original reactants are largely converted to products. Only the concentrations of substances that can actually change are included in $K$. This means that *pure* solids and liquids are omitted because their concentrations cannot change.

In general, then, *the* **equilibrium constant,** *K, is the ratio of the mathematical product of the concentrations of substances formed at equilibrium to the mathematical product of the concentrations of reacting substances. Each concentration is raised to a power equal to the coefficient of that substance in the chemical equation. The equation for K is sometimes referred to as the* **chemical equilibrium expression.**

## The $H_2$, $I_2$, HI Equilibrium System

Consider the reaction between $H_2$ and $I_2$ vapor in a sealed flask at an elevated temperature. The rate of reaction can be followed by observing the rate at which the violet color of the iodine vapor diminishes, as shown in **Figure 3.** If colorless $H_2$ gas is present in excess, we might expect that the reaction would continue until all of the $I_2$ is used up. The violet color of the tube would decrease in intensity until all of the iodine reacts. At that time, the tube would be colorless, because both HI and the excess $H_2$ are colorless gases.

In actuality, the color fades to a constant intensity but does not disappear completely because the reaction is reversible. Hydrogen iodide decomposes to re-form hydrogen and iodine. The rate of this reverse reaction increases as the concentration of hydrogen iodide increases. The rate of the forward reaction decreases accordingly. The concentrations of hydrogen and iodine decrease as they react. As the rates of the opposing reactions become equal, equilibrium is established. The constant color achieved indicates that equilibrium exists among hydrogen, iodine, and hydrogen iodide. The net chemical equation for the reaction system at equilibrium follows.

$$H_2(g) + I_2(g) \rightleftarrows 2HI(g)$$

From this chemical equation, the following chemical equilibrium expression can be written. The concentration of HI is raised to the power of 2 because the coefficient of HI in the balanced chemical equation is 2.

$$K = \frac{[HI]^2}{[H_2][I_2]}$$

Chemists have carefully measured the concentrations of $H_2$, $I_2$, and HI in equilibrium mixtures at various temperatures. In some experiments, the flasks were filled with hydrogen iodide at known pressure. The flasks were held at fixed temperatures until equilibrium was established. In other experiments, hydrogen and iodine were the original substances. Experimental data, together with the calculated values for $K$, are listed in **Table 1.** Experiments 1 and 2 began with hydrogen iodide. Experiments 3 and 4 began with hydrogen and iodine. Note the close agreement obtained for the numerical values of the equilibrium constant in all cases.

At 425°C, the equilibrium constant for this equilibrium reaction system has the average value of 54.34. This value for $K$ is constant for any system of $H_2$, $I_2$, and HI at equilibrium at this temperature. If the

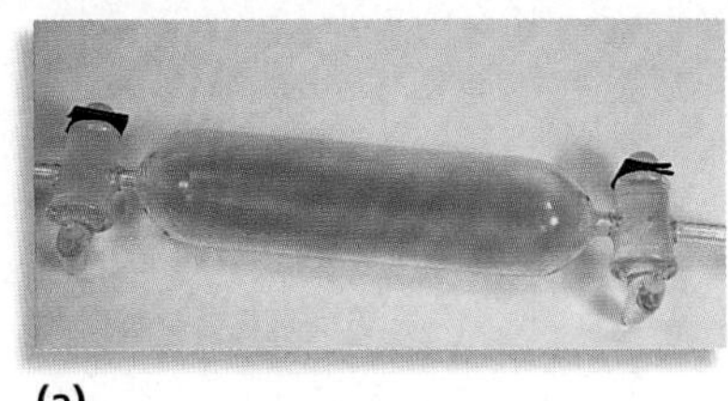

(a)

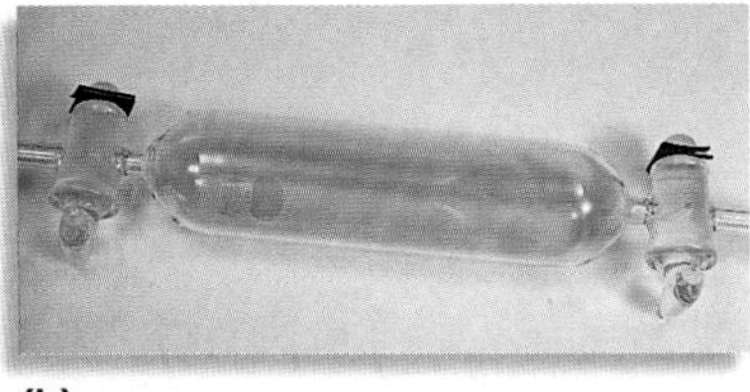

(b)

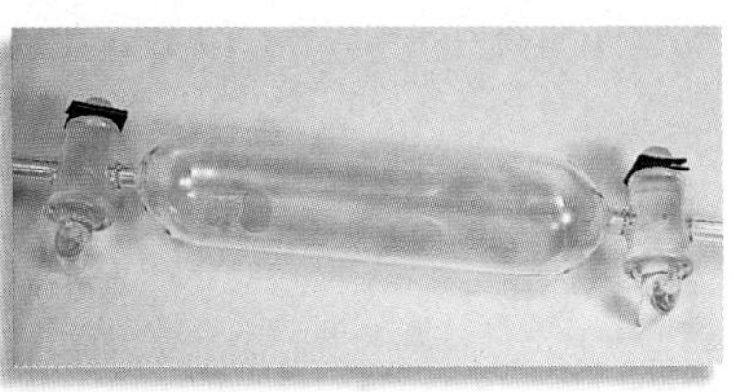

(c)

**FIGURE 3** Hydrogen iodide gas is produced from gaseous hydrogen and iodine. The violet color of iodine gas (a) becomes fainter as the reaction consumes the iodine (b). The violet does not disappear but reaches a constant intensity when the reaction reaches equilibrium (c).

**TABLE 1** ***Typical Equilibrium Concentrations of $H_2$, $I_2$, and HI in mol/L at 425°C***

| Experiment | $[H_2]$ | $[I_2]$ | $[HI]$ | $K = \frac{[HI]^2}{[H_2][I_2]}$ |
|---|---|---|---|---|
| 1 | $0.4953 \times 10^{-3}$ | $0.4953 \times 10^{-3}$ | $3.655 \times 10^{-3}$ | 54.46 |
| 2 | $1.141 \times 10^{-3}$ | $1.141 \times 10^{-3}$ | $8.410 \times 10^{-3}$ | 54.33 |
| 3 | $3.560 \times 10^{-3}$ | $1.250 \times 10^{-3}$ | $15.59 \times 10^{-3}$ | 54.62 |
| 4 | $2.252 \times 10^{-3}$ | $2.336 \times 10^{-3}$ | $16.85 \times 10^{-3}$ | 53.97 |

calculation for $K$ yields a different result, there must be a reason. Either the $H_2$, $I_2$, and HI system has not reached equilibrium or the system is not at 425°C.

The balanced chemical equation for an equilibrium system is necessary to write the expression for the equilibrium constant. The data in **Table 1** show that the validity of this expression is confirmed when the actual values of the equilibrium concentrations of reactants and products are determined experimentally. The values of $K$ are calculated from these concentrations. No information concerning the kinetics of the reacting systems is required.

Once the value of the equilibrium constant is known, the equilibrium-constant expression can be used to calculate concentrations of reactants or products at equilibrium. Suppose an equilibrium system at 425°C is found to contain 0.015 mol/L each of $H_2$ and $I_2$. To find the concentration of HI in this system, rearrange the chemical equilibrium expression as shown in the two equations that follow.

$$K = \frac{[HI]^2}{[H_2][I_2]}$$

$$[HI] = \sqrt{K[H_2][I_2]}$$

Using the known $K$ value and the given concentrations for $H_2$ and $I_2$, solve the equation for [HI].

$$[HI] = \sqrt{0.015 \times 0.015 \times 54.34}$$

$$[HI] = 0.11 \text{ mol/L}$$

## SAMPLE PROBLEM A

For more help, go to the *Math Tutor* at the end of this chapter.

**An equilibrium mixture of $N_2$, $O_2$, and NO gases at 1500 K is determined to consist of $6.4 \times 10^{-3}$ mol/L of $N_2$, $1.7 \times 10^{-3}$ mol/L of $O_2$, and $1.1 \times 10^{-5}$ mol/L of NO. What is the equilibrium constant for the system at this temperature?**

### SOLUTION

**1 ANALYZE**

**Given:** $[N_2] = 6.4 \times 10^{-3}$ mol/L
$[O_2] = 1.7 \times 10^{-3}$ mol/L
$[NO] = 1.1 \times 10^{-5}$ mol/L

**Unknown:** $K$

**2 PLAN**

The balanced chemical equation is $N_2(g) + O_2(g) \rightleftharpoons 2NO(g)$.

The chemical equilibrium expression is $K = \dfrac{[NO]^2}{[N_2][O_2]}$.

**3 COMPUTE**

Substitute the given values for the concentrations into the equilibrium expression.

$$K = \frac{(1.1 \times 10^{-5} \text{ mol/L})^2}{(6.4 \times 10^{-3} \text{ mol/L})(1.7 \times 10^{-3} \text{ mol/L})} = 1.1 \times 10^{-5}$$

**4 EVALUATE** The value of $K$ is small, which is consistent with more $N_2$ and $O_2$ being present at equilibrium than NO. The answer has the correct number of significant figures and is close to an estimated value of

$8 \times 10^{-6}$, calculated as $\dfrac{(1 \times 10^{-5})^2}{(6 \times 10^{-3})(2 \times 10^{-3})}$.

**PRACTICE** *Answers in Appendix E*

1. At equilibrium a mixture of $N_2$, $H_2$, and $NH_3$ gas at 500°C is determined to consist of 0.602 mol/L of $N_2$, 0.420 mol/L of $H_2$, and 0.113 mol/L of $NH_3$. What is the equilibrium constant for the reaction $N_2(g) + 3H_2(g) \rightleftharpoons 2NH_3(g)$ at this temperature?

2. The reaction $AB_2C(g) \rightleftharpoons B_2(g) + AC(g)$ reached equilibrium at 900 K in a 5.00 L vessel. At equilibrium 0.084 mol of $AB_2C$, 0.035 mol of $B_2$, and 0.059 mol of AC were detected. What is the equilibrium constant at this temperature for this system? (Don't forget to convert amounts to concentrations.)

3. A reaction between gaseous sulfur dioxide and oxygen gas to produce gaseous sulfur trioxide takes place at 600°C. At that temperature, the concentration of $SO_2$ is found to be 1.50 mol/L, the concentration of $O_2$ is 1.25 mol/L, and the concentration of $SO_3$ is 3.50 mol/L. Using the balanced chemical equation, calculate the equilibrium constant for this system.

**extension**

Go to **go.hrw.com** for more practice problems that ask you to calculate equilibrium constants.

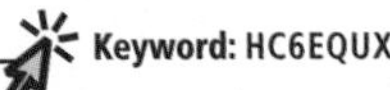


## SECTION REVIEW

1. What is meant by *chemical equilibrium*?
2. What is an equilibrium constant?
3. How does the value of an equilibrium constant relate to the relative quantities of reactants and products at equilibrium?
4. What is meant by a *chemical equilibrium expression*?
5. Hydrochloric acid, HCl, is a strong acid that dissociates completely in water to form $H_3O^+$ and $Cl^-$. Would you expect the value of $K$ for the reaction $HCl(aq) + H_2O(l) \rightleftharpoons H_3O^+(aq) + Cl^-(aq)$ to be $1 \times 10^{-2}$, $1 \times 10^{-5}$, or "very large"? Justify your answer.
6. Write the chemical equilibrium expression for the reaction $4HCl(g) + O_2(g) \rightleftharpoons 2Cl_2(g) + 2H_2O(g)$.
7. At equilibrium at 2500 K, $[HCl] = 0.0625$ mol/L and $[H_2] = [Cl_2] = 0.00450$ mol/L for the reaction $H_2(g) + Cl_2(g) \rightleftharpoons 2HCl(g)$. Find the value of $K$.
8. An equilibrium mixture at 425°C is found to consist of $1.83 \times 10^{-3}$ mol/L of $H_2$, $3.13 \times 10^{-3}$ mol/L of $I_2$, and $1.77 \times 10^{-2}$ mol/L of HI. Calculate the equilibrium constant, $K$, for the reaction $H_2(g) + I_2(g) \rightleftharpoons 2HI(g)$.
9. For the reaction $H_2(g) + I_2(g) \rightleftharpoons 2HI(g)$ at 425°C, calculate [HI], given $[H_2] = [I_2] = 4.79 \times 10^{-4}$ mol/L and $K = 54.3$.

### Critical Thinking

10. **INFERRING RELATIONSHIPS** Use the data from Experiment 1 in **Table 1** to calculate the value of $K$ for the reaction $2HI(g) \rightleftharpoons H_2(g) + I_2(g)$. Do you see a relationship between the value you obtained and the value in the table?

# HISTORICAL CHEMISTRY

## Fixing the Nitrogen Problem

### Historical Perspective

Each year, the chemical industry synthesizes tons of nitrogenous fertilizers, increasing agricultural production around the globe. But prior to 1915, humans had to rely solely on natural resources for fertilizer, and the dwindling supply of these materials caused widespread fear of world starvation. A crisis was averted, however, through the discovery of an answer to the "nitrogen problem," a term used at the time to describe the shortage of useful nitrogen despite its abundance in the atmosphere.

### The Malthusian Threat

In 1798, Thomas Malthus published his famous "Essay on Population," a report predicting that the world's food supplies could not keep up with the growing human population and that famine, death, and misery were inevitable. Malthus's warning seemed to be echoed in the 1840s by the great Irish potato famine. In fact, the rest of Europe likely would have suffered serious food shortages as well had crop yields per acre not been increased through the use of fertilizers containing nitrogen.

Few living things can utilize the gas that forms 78% of the atmosphere; they need nitrogen that has been combined with other elements, or "fixed," to survive.

But soil often lacks sufficient amounts of the organisms that fix nitrogen for plants, so fertilizers containing usable nitrogen compounds are added. In 1898, two-thirds of the world's supply of these compounds came from Chile, where beds of sodium nitrate, or Chile saltpeter, were abundant. But, as the chemist William Crookes emphasized in his speech to the British Association that year, these reserves

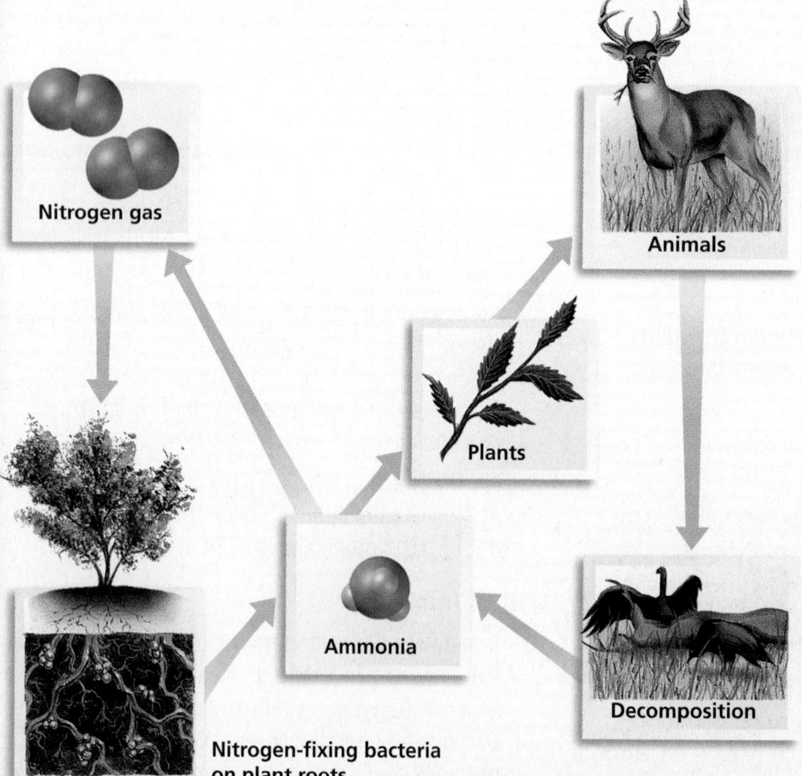


*◀Nitrogen is released when living things die and also from animal wastes and plant material. Some bacteria are able to break the bond holding the nitrogen molecule together, freeing the nitrogen atoms to combine with hydrogen to form ammonia. Plants can absorb the nitrogen in this form from the soil. Animals then benefit from the nitrogen by eating the plants.*

were limited; it was up to his colleagues to discover alternatives and prevent Malthus's dire forecast from coming true.

### The Haber-Nernst Controversy

As early as the 1890s, chemists had shown that ammonia, a practical source of fixed nitrogen, could be synthesized at high temperatures and at atmospheric pressure from elemental hydrogen and nitrogen. The problem was that the end product was present in such minute amounts that the process was not industrially practical.

In 1904, the German chemist Fritz Haber seemed to confirm this assessment. He tried reacting hydrogen and nitrogen at temperatures of up to 1020°C using pure iron as well as other metals as a catalyst. He found that the amount of ammonia was a mere 0.005% to 0.012% at equilibrium.

Haber had apparently closed the door on the synthesis of ammonia from its elements. But in 1906, Walther Nernst, using his new heat theorem, calculated the reaction's theoretical ammonia concentration at equilibria corresponding to several pressures. He found that his value at atmospheric pressure disagreed significantly with Haber's, and he publicly challenged Haber's values.

Haber was convinced that he was right. He ran the reaction at increased pressure to attain an amount of ammonia that could be measured more accurately.

Haber and his assistants confirmed their original findings, and Nernst later conceded a mathematical error. But more important, the new round of experiments indicated that a reasonable amount of ammonia might be attained at pressures of 200 atm (20,000 kPa) using a uranium or osmium catalyst.

### Scaling Up

Large-scale equipment that could withstand such high pressures was unheard of at the time, and osmium and uranium were far too scarce to be cost-effective for industry. Nevertheless, in 1909, the German firm BASF bought the rights to Haber's findings and put its gifted chemical engineer Karl Bosch in charge of creating an industrial-scale system that would make the process profitable.

After nearly five years, Bosch and the company's chief chemist, Alwin Mittasch, succeeded in developing a suitable reactor that could handle the reaction's high pressures. They also discovered that a catalyst of iron containing small amounts of impurities was an effective replacement for the rare metals used by Haber.

▲ *Today, ammonia is produced on an industrial scale in plants like this one.*

### An Eerie Epilogue

By September 1913, BASF was producing 20 metric tons of ammonia a day using the Haber-Bosch process. Eventually, enough ammonia was produced by the chemical industry to free Germany and the world of dependence on Chile saltpeter for fertilizer. Chemists had thwarted the Malthusian threat. Yet, the victory proved bittersweet; the new ammonia synthesis also became the basis of the production of nitric acid, used to make many of the explosives employed in the wars that rocked Europe and the rest of the globe in the first half of the twentieth century.

### Questions

1. What is the major use for ammonia?
2. What did Haber find when he tried to synthesize ammonia at increased pressure?

SECTION 2

# Shifting Equilibrium

## OBJECTIVES

- Discuss the factors that disturb equilibrium.
- Discuss conditions under which reactions go to completion.
- Describe the common-ion effect.

 C.4.9 Summarize the concept of chemical equilibrium and Le Châtelier's principle

In systems that have attained chemical equilibrium, the relative amounts of reactants and products stay the same. But changes in pressure, concentration, or temperature can alter the equilibrium position and thereby change the relative amounts of reactants and products. By shifting an equilibrium in the desired direction, chemists can often improve the yield of the product they are seeking.

## Predicting the Direction of Shift

In 1888, the French chemist Henri Louis Le Châtelier developed a principle that provides a means of predicting the influence of stress factors on equilibrium systems. Le Châtelier's principle states that *if a system at equilibrium is subjected to a stress, the equilibrium is shifted in the direction that tends to relieve the stress.* This principle is true for all dynamic equilibria, chemical as well as physical. Changes in pressure, concentration, and temperature illustrate Le Châtelier's principle.

### Changes in Pressure

A change in pressure affects only equilibrium systems in which gases are involved. For changes in pressure to affect the system, the *total* number of moles of gas on the left side of the equation must be different from the *total* number of moles of gas on the right side of the equation.

Let us consider the Haber process for the synthesis of ammonia. Note that there is a total of four molecules of gas on the reactant side of the equation and two molecules of gas on the product side of the equation.

$$N_2(g) + 3H_2(g) \rightleftarrows 2NH_3(g)$$

First, consider an increase in pressure as the applied stress. Can the system shift in a way that reduces the stress? Yes. An increase in pressure causes increases in the concentrations of all species. The system can reduce the number of molecules, and hence the total pressure, by shifting the equilibrium to the right. For each four molecules of reactants, nitrogen and hydrogen, there are two molecules of product, ammonia. By producing more $NH_3$, and using up $N_2$ and $H_2$, the system can reduce the total number of molecules. This leads to a decrease in pressure. Although the new equilibrium pressure is still higher than before, it is not as high as the pressure caused by the initial stress.

An increase in pressure on confined gases causes an increase in the concentrations of these gases. Even though changes in pressure may

shift the equilibrium position, they do not affect the value of the equilibrium constant.

Ammonia produced in the Haber process is continuously removed by condensing it to liquid ammonia. This condensation removes most of the product from the gas phase in which the reaction occurs. The resulting decrease in the partial pressure of $NH_3$ gas in the reaction vessel is a stress and is the same as a decrease in product concentration, which shifts the equilibrium to the right.

The introduction of an inert gas, such as helium, into the reaction vessel for the synthesis of ammonia increases the total pressure in the vessel. But it does not change the partial pressures of the reaction gases present. Therefore, increasing pressure by adding a gas that is not a reactant or a product *cannot* affect the equilibrium position of the reaction system.

## Changes in Concentration

An increase in the concentration of a reactant is a stress on the equilibrium system. Consider the following hypothetical reaction.

$$A + B \rightleftharpoons C + D$$

An increase in the concentration of A creates a stress. To relieve the stress, some of the added A reacts with B to form products C and D. The equilibrium is reestablished with a higher concentration of A than before the addition but a lower concentration of B. **Figure 4** illustrates the effect on a system in equilibrium produced by increasing the concentration of a reactant. Similarly, an increase in the concentration of B drives the reaction to the right. An increase in the concentration of either C or D shifts the equilibrium to the left. A decrease in the concentration of C or D has the same effect on the position of the equilibrium as does an increase in the concentration of A or B; the equilibrium shifts to the right.

Changes in concentration have no effect on the value of the equilibrium constant. Although concentrations of both reactants and products do change, the new concentrations give the same value of the equilibrium constant when equilibrium is reestablished.

Many chemical processes involve heterogeneous reactions in which reactants or products are in different phases. The concentrations of pure solids and liquids do not change, and by convention are not written in the equilibrium expression. Also, when a solvent such as water, in a system involving acids and bases, is in an equilibrium equation, it is not included in the equilibrium expression. In Chapter 15, the expression for $K_w$ used this convention and the concentration of water is not included in the expression. The reaction representing the self-ionization of water is

$$2H_2O(l) \rightleftharpoons H_3O^+(aq) + OH^-(aq)$$

and the equation for $K_w$ is $K_w = [H_3O^+][OH^-]$.

The following equation describes the equilibrium system established by the decomposition of solid calcium carbonate.

$$CaCO_3(s) \rightleftharpoons CaO(s) + CO_2(g)$$

**(a) at equilibrium**

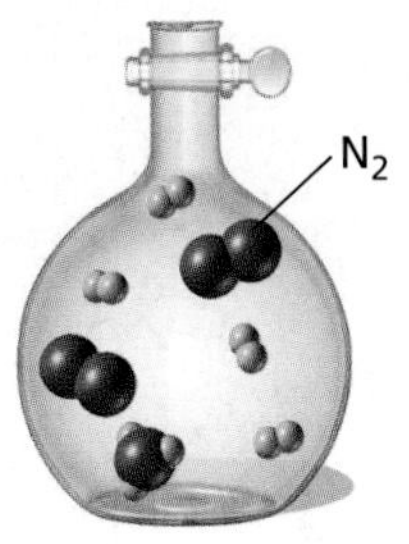


**(b) stressed (not at equilibrium)**

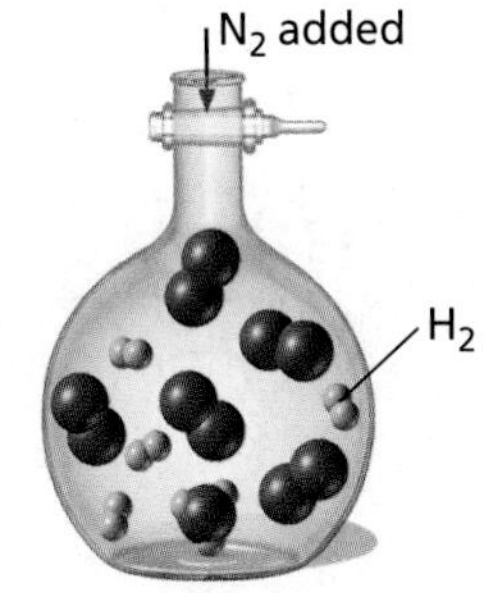


**(c) at new equilibrium**

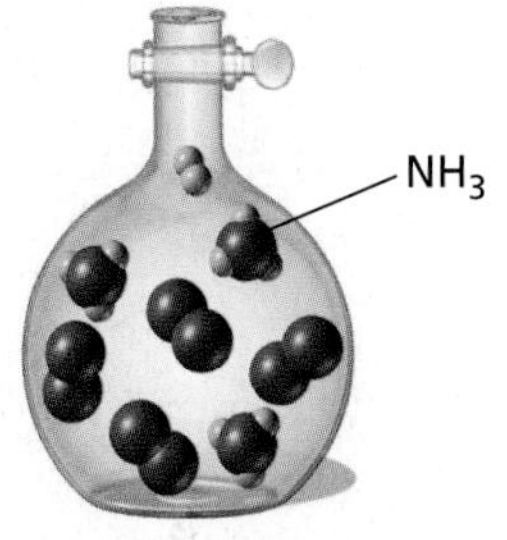


$$N_2(g) + 3H_2(g) \rightleftharpoons 2NH_3(g)$$

**FIGURE 4** (a) $N_2$, $H_2$, and $NH_3$ are in equilibrium within a closed system. (b) Addition of more $N_2$ causes a stress on the initial equilibrium. (c) The new equilibrium position for this system has a higher concentration of $N_2$, a lower concentration of $H_2$, and a higher concentration of $NH_3$ than initially.

The products are a solid and a gas. Because both $CaCO_3$ and CaO are solids, they are not in the equilibrium constant expression. This leads to the following expression for the equilibrium constant.

$$K = [CO_2]$$

Carbon dioxide is the only substance in the system that appears in the equilibrium expression. Because the total number of moles of gas on the left side of the equation is different from the total number of moles on the right side of the equation, pressure changes will affect the equilibrium. High pressure favors the reverse reaction, which causes $CO_2$ molecules to react with the solid CaO to form solid $CaCO_3$. Low pressure favors the formation of $CO_2$ from the decomposition of $CaCO_3$. Because both CaO and $CaCO_3$ are solids, changing their amounts will not change the equilibrium concentration of $CO_2$.

## Changes in Temperature

Reversible reactions are exothermic in one direction and endothermic in the other. Remember, equilibrium constants are for a given temperature because changing the temperature changes the relative amounts of reactants and products.

Increasing the temperature is, in effect, the addition of enery in the form of heat. According to Le Châtelier's principle, the stress of the added heat will be lessened by shifting the equilibrium in the direction that removes heat (lowers the temperature). This means that energy must be absorbed so the reaction that is endothermic occurs until a new equilibrium is established. Likewise, the removal of energy as a result of lowering the temperature causes the exothermic reaction to take place.

The synthesis of ammonia by the Haber process is exothermic, as indicated by the energy as heat shown on the product side of the equation.

$$N_2(g) + 3H_2(g) \rightleftharpoons 2NH_3(g) + 92\ \text{kJ}$$

A high temperature favors the decomposition of ammonia, the endothermic reaction. But at low temperatures, the forward reaction is too slow to be commercially useful. The temperature used represents a compromise between kinetic and equilibrium requirements. It is high enough that equilibrium is established rapidly but low enough that the equilibrium concentration of ammonia is significant. Moderate temperature (about 500°C) and very high pressure (700–1000 atm) produce a satisfactory yield of ammonia.

The production of colorless dinitrogen tetroxide gas, $N_2O_4$, from dark red-brown $NO_2$ gas is also an exothermic reaction. **Figure 5** shows how temperature affects the equilibrium of this system. **Figure 5b** shows the $NO_2/N_2O_4$ equilibrium mixture at 25°C. When the temperature of the system is lowered to 0°C, the system experiences a stress (removal of energy as heat). To counteract this stress, the system shifts to the right, or in the direction of the exothermic reaction. This shift increases the amount of colorless $N_2O_4$ gas and decreases the amount of brown $NO_2$ gas, as shown in **Figure 5a.** Because more $N_2O_4$ is present, $K$ is increased. When the system is heated to 100°C, the added energy is the stress, and the equi-

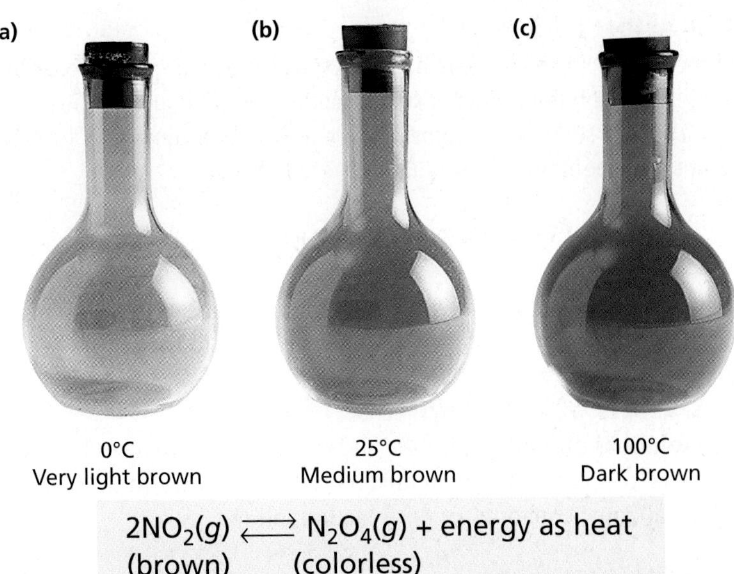


**FIGURE 5** Different temperatures can cause an equilibrium system to shift and seek a new equilibrium position.

librium shifts to the left, or in the direction of the endothermic reaction. This shift decreases the amount of colorless $N_2O_4$ gas and increases the amount of brown $NO_2$ gas, as shown in **Figure 5c.** Because less $N_2O_4$ gas is present, $K$ is decreased. The change in temperature changes the value of $K$. For any system in which the forward reaction is an exothermic reaction, increasing the temperature decreases the value of $K$.

For an endothermic reaction, such as the decomposition of calcium carbonate, energy as heat shows up on the reactant side of the equation.

$$556 \text{ kJ} + CaCO_3(s) \rightleftharpoons CaO(s) + CO_2(g)$$

An increase in temperature caused by adding energy to the system causes the value of $K$ to increase and the equilibrium to shift to the right.

Catalysts speed up the rate of reactions. So what happens to equilibrium concentrations if a catalyst is present? Nothing! When a catalyst is added to an equilibrium system, it speeds up both the forward and reverse reactions. The equilibrium concentrations are achieved faster, but the concentrations and $K$ remain the same.

## Reactions That Go to Completion

Some reactions involving compounds formed by the chemical interaction of ions in solutions appear to go to completion in the sense that the ions are almost completely removed from solution. The extent to which reacting ions are removed from solution depends on the solubility of the compound formed and, if the compound is soluble, on the degree of ionization. Thus, a product that escapes as a gas, precipitates as a solid, or is only slightly ionized effectively removes from solution the bulk of the reacting ions that compose it. Consider some specific examples of situations in which such ionic reactions go to completion.

## Formation of a Gas

Reactions that form a gas as a product are one example of reactions that go to completion. When a strong acid is added to an aqueous solution of baking soda, or sodium bicarbonate, carbon dioxide is formed. The net ionic equation shows that ions are removed.

$$H_3O^+ + HCO_3^- \longrightarrow 2H_2O(l) + CO_2(g)$$

This reaction goes practically to completion because one of the products, $CO_2$, escapes as a gas if the container is open to the air.

## Formation of a Precipitate

When solutions of sodium chloride and silver nitrate are mixed, a white precipitate of silver chloride immediately forms, as shown in **Figure 6.** The overall ionic equation for this reaction follows.

$$Na^+(aq) + Cl^-(aq) + Ag^+(aq) + NO_3^-(aq) \longrightarrow Na^+(aq) + NO_3^-(aq) + AgCl(s)$$

If chemically equivalent amounts of the two solutes are mixed, only $Na^+$ ions and $NO_3^-$ ions remain in solution in appreciable quantities. Almost all of the $Ag^+$ ions and $Cl^-$ ions combine and separate from the solution as a precipitate of AgCl. The reason is that AgCl is only very slightly soluble in water. The solution is now a saturated solution of AgCl. The reaction thus effectively goes to completion because an essentially insoluble product is formed.

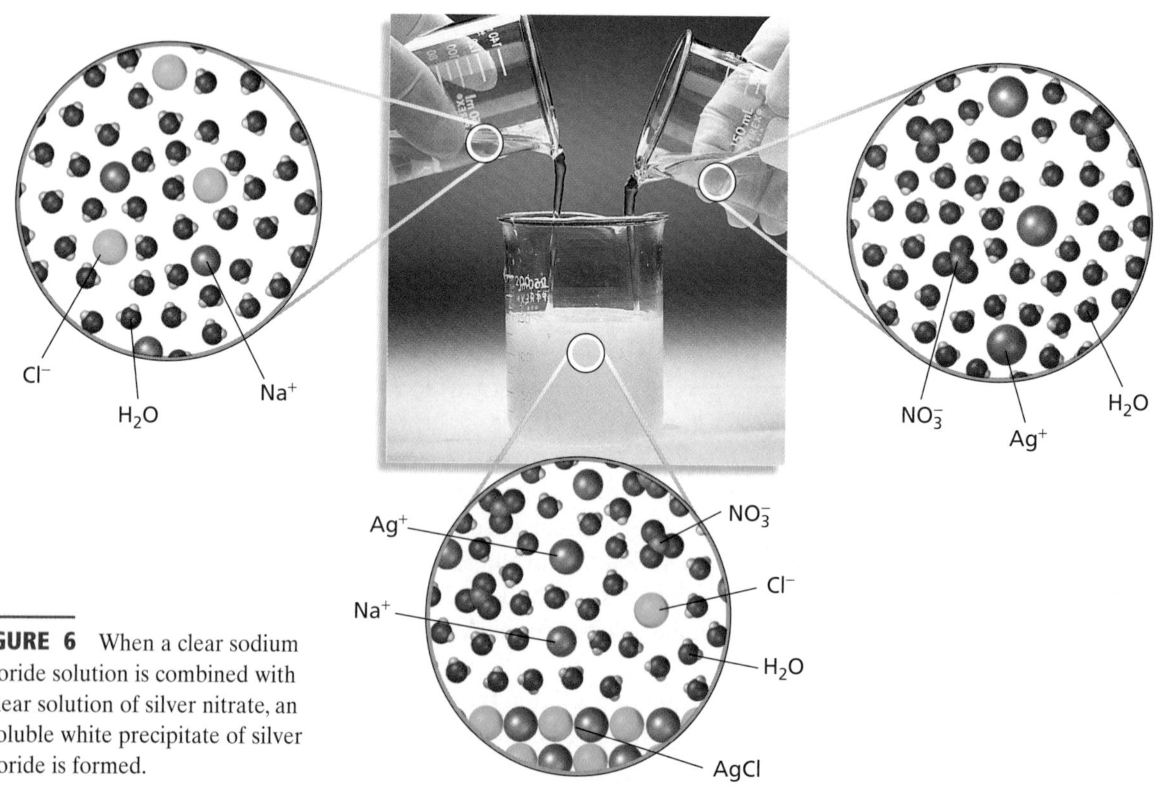


**FIGURE 6** When a clear sodium chloride solution is combined with a clear solution of silver nitrate, an insoluble white precipitate of silver chloride is formed.

### Formation of a Slightly Ionized Product

Neutralization reactions between $H_3O^+$ ions from aqueous acids and $OH^-$ ions from aqueous bases result in the formation of water molecules, which are only slightly ionized. A reaction between HCl and NaOH illustrates this process. Aqueous HCl supplies $H_3O^+$ ions and $Cl^-$ ions to the solution, and aqueous NaOH supplies $Na^+$ ions and $OH^-$ ions, as shown in the following overall ionic equation.

$$H_3O^+(aq) + Cl^-(aq) + Na^+(aq) + OH^-(aq) \longrightarrow Na^+(aq) + Cl^-(aq) + 2H_2O(l)$$

Neglecting the spectator ions, the net ionic equation is as follows.

$$H_3O^+(aq) + OH^-(aq) \longrightarrow 2H_2O(l)$$

Because it is only slightly ionized, the water exists almost entirely as molecules. Thus, hydronium ions and hydroxide ions are almost entirely removed from the solution. The reaction effectively goes to completion because the product is only slightly ionized.

**CROSS-DISCIPLINARY**

Go to **go.hrw.com** for a full-length article on equilibrium reactions and caves.

**Keyword: HC6EQUX**

## Common-Ion Effect

An equilibrium reaction may be driven in the desired direction by applying Le Châtelier's principle. Suppose hydrogen chloride gas is bubbled into a saturated solution of sodium chloride. Hydrogen chloride is extremely soluble in water, and it is completely ionized.

$$HCl(g) + H_2O(l) \longrightarrow H_3O^+(aq) + Cl^-(aq)$$

The equilibrium for a saturated solution of sodium chloride is described by the following equation.

$$NaCl(s) \rightleftarrows Na^+(aq) + Cl^-(aq)$$

As the hydrogen chloride dissolves in sufficient quantity, it increases the concentration of $Cl^-$ ions in the solution, which is a stress on the equilibrium system. The system can compensate, according to Le Châtelier's principle, by combining some of the added $Cl^-$ ions with an equivalent amount of $Na^+$ ions. This causes some solid NaCl to precipitate out, relieving the stress of added chloride. The new equilibrium has a greater concentration of $Cl^-$ ions but a decreased concentration of $Na^+$ ions. However, the product of $[Na^+]$ and $[Cl^-]$ still has the same value as before. *This phenomenon, in which the addition of an ion common to two solutes brings about precipitation or reduced ionization, is an example of the* **common-ion effect.**

The common-ion effect is also observed when one ion species of a weak electrolyte is added in excess to a solution. Acetic acid, $CH_3COOH$, is such an electrolyte. A 0.1 M $CH_3COOH$ solution is only about 1.3% ionized as hydronium ions and acetate ions, $CH_3COO^-$. The ionic equilibrium is shown by the following equation.

$$CH_3COOH(aq) + H_2O(l) \rightleftharpoons H_3O^+(aq) + CH_3COO^-(aq)$$

Addition of sodium acetate, $NaCH_3COO$ (an ionic salt that is soluble in water), to a solution containing acetic acid increases the acetate ion concentration. The equilibrium then shifts in the direction that uses up some of the added acetate ions in accordance with Le Châtelier's principle. More molecules of acetic acid are formed, and the concentration of hydronium ions is reduced. In general, the addition of a salt with an ion in common with the weak electrolyte reduces the ionization of the electrolyte. **Figure 7** shows a 0.25 M $CH_3COOH$ solution on the left that has a pH of about 2.7. Mixing that with the 0.10 M $NaCH_3COO$ solution in the center produces the solution on the right, which has a pH of about 4.5, indicating lower $[H_3O^+]$ and thus lowered acetic acid ionization.

**FIGURE 7** The solution of $CH_3COOH$ on the left is combined with the solution of $NaCH_3COO$ in the center. Both contain the common ion, $CH_3COO^-$. They produce the solution on the right, which is only slightly acidic due to the decreased ionization of the acid. The colors of the solutions are due to the addition of an acid-base indicator.

## SECTION REVIEW

1. Name three ways the chemical equilibrium can be disturbed.
2. Describe three situations in which ionic reactions go to completion.
3. Describe the common-ion effect.
4. Identify the common ion in each of the following situations.
   **a.** 5 g of NaCl is added to a 2.0 M solution of HCl
   **b.** 50 mL of 1.0 M $NaCH_3COO$ is added to 1.0 M $CH_3COOH$
   **c.** 1 g of $NH_4Cl$ is added to 100 mL of aqueous $NH_3$
5. Predict the effect that decreasing pressure would have on each of the following reaction systems at equilibrium.
   **a.** $H_2(g) + Cl_2(g) \rightleftharpoons 2HCl(g)$
   **b.** $NH_4Cl(s) \rightleftharpoons NH_3(g) + HCl(g)$
   **c.** $2H_2O_2(aq) \rightleftharpoons 2H_2O(l) + O_2(g)$
   **d.** $3O_2(g) \rightleftharpoons 2O_3(g)$

**Critical Thinking**

6. **PREDICTING OUTCOMES** Carbon dioxide and water react to form bicarbonate ion and hydronium ion. Hyperventilation (rapid breathing) causes more carbon dioxide to be exhaled than normal. How will hyperventilation affect the pH of blood? Explain.

# Equilibria of Acids, Bases, and Salts

SECTION 3

**C.4.9** Summarize the concept of chemical equilibrium and Le Châtelier's principle

## Objectives

- Explain the concept of acid ionization constants, and write acid ionization equilibrium expressions.
- Review the ionization constant of water.
- Explain buffering.
- Compare cation and anion hydrolysis.

## Ionization Constant of a Weak Acid

About 1.3% of the solute molecules in a 0.1 M acetic acid solution are ionized at room temperature. The remaining 98.7% of the acetic acid molecules, $CH_3COOH$, remain nonionized. Thus, the solution contains three species of particles in equilibrium: $CH_3COOH$ molecules, $H_3O^+$ ions, and acetate ions, $CH_3COO^-$. From the equilibrium equation for the ionization of acetic acid, the equilibrium constant equation can be written.

$$CH_3COOH + H_2O \rightleftharpoons H_3O^+ + CH_3COO^-$$

$$K = \frac{[H_3O^+][CH_3COO^-]}{[CH_3COOH][H_2O]}$$

Notice that the concentration of water is not included in the equilibrium expression. The reason is that water is the solvent, and water molecules greatly exceed the number of acetic acid molecules. Without introducing a measurable error, one can assume that the molar concentration of $H_2O$ molecules remains constant in such a solution. Thus, because both $K$ and $[H_2O]$ are constant, the product $K[H_2O]$ is constant.

$$K[H_2O] = \frac{[H_3O^+][CH_3COO^-]}{[CH_3COOH]}$$

The left side of the equation can be simplified by setting $K[H_2O] = K_a$.

$$K_a = \frac{[H_3O^+][CH_3COO^-]}{[CH_3COOH]}$$

*The term $K_a$ is called the* **acid ionization constant.** The acid ionization constant, $K_a$, like the equilibrium constant, $K$, is constant for a specified temperature but has a new value for each new temperature.

The acid ionization constant for a weak acid represents a small value. To determine the numerical value of the ionization constant for acetic acid at a specific temperature, the equilibrium concentrations of $H_3O^+$ ions, $CH_3COO^-$ ions, and $CH_3COOH$ molecules must be known. The ionization of a molecule of $CH_3COOH$ in water yields one $H_3O^+$ ion and one $CH_3COO^-$ ion. These concentrations can, therefore, be found experimentally by measuring the pH of the solution.

**TABLE 2 Ionization of Acetic Acid**

| Molarity | % ionized | $[H_3O^+]$ | $[CH_3COOH]$ | $K_a$ |
|---|---|---|---|---|
| 0.100 | 1.33 | 0.00133 | 0.0987 | $1.79 \times 10^{-5}$ |
| 0.0500 | 1.89 | 0.000945 | 0.0491 | $1.82 \times 10^{-5}$ |
| 0.0100 | 4.17 | 0.000417 | 0.00958 | $1.81 \times 10^{-5}$ |
| 0.00500 | 5.86 | 0.000293 | 0.00471 | $1.82 \times 10^{-5}$ |
| 0.00100 | 12.6 | 0.000126 | 0.000874 | $1.82 \times 10^{-5}$ |

Ionization data and constants for some dilute acetic acid solutions at 25°C are given in **Table 2.** Notice that the numerical value of $K_a$ is almost identical for each solution molarity shown. The numerical value of $K_a$ for $CH_3COOH$ at 25°C can be determined by substituting numerical values for concentration into the equilibrium equation.

$$K_a = \frac{[H_3O^+][CH_3COO^-]}{[CH_3COOH]}$$

At constant temperature, an increase in the concentration of $CH_3COO^-$ ions through the addition of sodium acetate, $NaCH_3COO$, disturbs the equilibrium, as predicted by Le Châtelier's principle. This disturbance causes a decrease in $[H_3O^+]$ and an increase in $[CH_3COOH]$. Eventually, the equilibrium is reestablished with the *same* value of $K_a$. But there is a higher concentration of nonionized acetic acid molecules and a lower concentration of $H_3O^+$ ions than before the extra $CH_3COO^-$ was added. Changes in the hydronium ion concentration affect pH. In this example, the reduction in $[H_3O^+]$ means an increase in the pH of the solution.

(a)

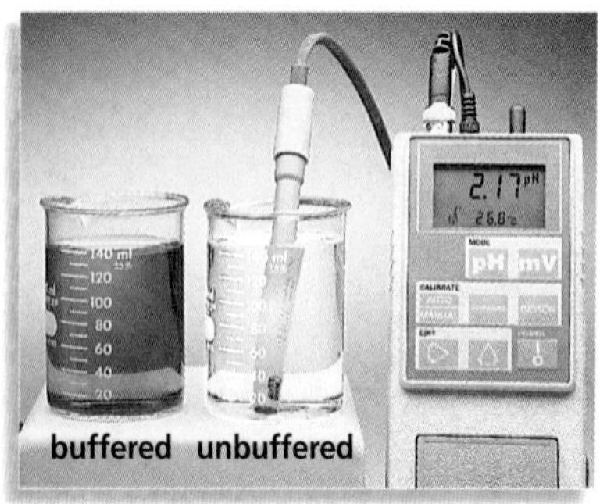

(b)

**FIGURE 8** (a) The beaker on the left contains a buffered solution and an indicator with a pH of about 5. The beaker on the right contains mostly water with a trace amount of acid and an indicator. The pH meter shows a pH of 5.00 for this solution. (b) After 5 mL of 0.10 M HCl is added to both beakers, the beaker on the left does not change color, indicating no substantial change in its pH. However, the beaker on the right undergoes a definite color change, and the pH meter shows a pH of 2.17.

## Buffers

The solution just described contains both a weak acid, $CH_3COOH$, and a salt of the weak acid, $NaCH_3COO$. The solution can react with either an acid or a base. When small amounts of acids or bases are added, the pH of the solution remains nearly constant. The weak acid and the common ion, $CH_3COO^-$, act as a "buffer" against significant changes in the pH of the solution. *Because it can resist changes in pH, this solution is a* **buffered solution. Figure 8** shows how a buffered and a nonbuffered solution react to the addition of an acid.

Suppose a small amount of acid is added to the acetic acid–sodium acetate solution. Acetate ions react with most of the added hydronium ions to form nonionized acetic acid molecules.

$$CH_3COO^-(aq) + H_3O^+(aq) \longrightarrow CH_3COOH(aq) + H_2O(l)$$

The hydronium ion concentration and the pH of the solution remain practically unchanged.

Suppose a small amount of a base is added to the original solution. The $OH^-$ ions of the base react with and remove hydronium ions to form nonionized water molecules. Acetic acid molecules then ionize and mostly replace the hydronium ions neutralized by the added $OH^-$ ions.

$$CH_3COOH(aq) + H_2O(l) \longrightarrow H_3O^+(aq) + CH_3COO^-(aq)$$

The pH of the solution again remains practically unchanged.

A solution of a weak base containing a salt of the base behaves in a similar manner. The hydroxide ion concentration and the pH of the solution remain essentially constant with small additions of acids or bases. Suppose a base is added to an aqueous solution of ammonia that also contains ammonium chloride. Ammonium ions donate a proton to the added hydroxide ions to form nonionized water molecules.

$$NH_4^+(aq) + OH^-(aq) \longrightarrow NH_3(aq) + H_2O(l)$$

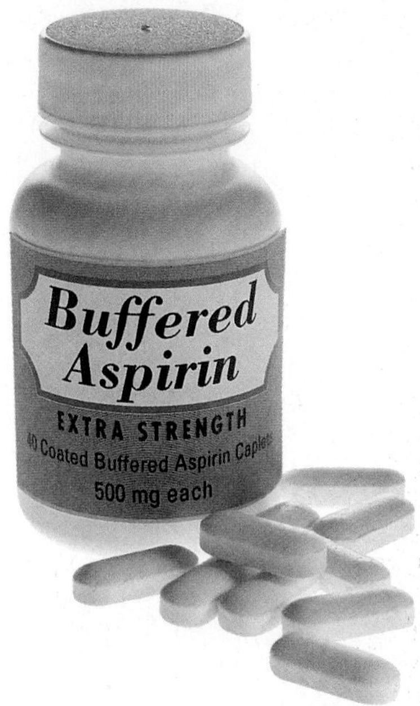


**FIGURE 9** Many consumer products are buffered to protect the body from potentially harmful pH changes.

If a small amount of an acid is added to the solution instead, hydroxide ions from the solution accept protons from the added hydronium ions to form nonionized water molecules. Ammonia molecules in the solution then ionize and mostly replace the hydroxide ions neutralized by added $H_3O^+$.

$$NH_3(aq) + H_2O(l) \longrightarrow NH_4^+(aq) + OH^-(aq)$$

Buffer action has many important applications in chemistry and physiology. Human blood is naturally buffered to maintain a pH of between 7.3 and 7.5. This is essential because large changes in pH would lead to serious disturbances of normal body functions. **Figure 9** shows an example of one of the many medicines buffered to prevent large and potentially damaging changes in pH.

## Ionization Constant of Water

Recall from Chapter 15 that the self-ionization of water is an equilibrium reaction.

$$H_2O(l) + H_2O(l) \rightleftarrows H_3O^+(aq) + OH^-(aq)$$

Equilibrium is established with a very low concentration of $H_3O^+$ and $OH^-$ ions. The expression for the equilibrium constant, $K_w = [H_3O^+][OH^-]$, is derived from the balanced chemical equation. The numerical value of $K_w$, obtained experimentally, is $1.0 \times 10^{-14}$ at 25°C.

# Hydrolysis of Salts

Salts are formed during neutralization reactions between acids and bases. When a salt dissolves in water, it produces positive ions (cations) of the base from which it was formed and negative ions (anions) of the acid from which it was formed. Therefore, the solution might be expected to be neutral. The aqueous solutions of some salts, such as NaCl and $KNO_3$, are neutral, having a pH of 7. However, when sodium carbonate dissolves in water, the resulting solution turns red litmus paper blue, indicating a pH greater than 7. Ammonium chloride produces an aqueous solution that turns blue litmus paper red, indicating a pH less than 7. Salts formed from the combination of strong or weak acids and bases are shown in **Figure 10.**

The variation in pH values can be accounted for by examining the ions formed when each of these salts dissociates. If the ions formed are from weak acids or bases, they react chemically with the water molecules, and the pH of the solution will have a value other than 7. *A reaction between water molecules and ions of a dissolved salt is* **hydrolysis.** If the anions react with water, the process is anion hydrolysis and results in a more basic solution. If the cations react with water molecules, the process is cation hydrolysis and results in a more acidic solution.

## Anion Hydrolysis

In the Brønsted sense, the anion of the salt is the conjugate base of the acid from which it was formed. It is also a proton acceptor. If the acid is weak, its conjugate base (the anion) will be strong enough to remove pro-

(a)

(b)

(c)

(d)

**FIGURE 10** The universal indicator shows that the pH of salt solutions varies, depending on the strength of the acid and the base that formed the salt. (a) NaCl is formed from a strong acid and a strong base; the color of the indicator shows the pH is neutral. (b) The indicator shows the pH of the sodium acetate solution is basic. This was formed from a strong base and a weak acid. (c) The strong acid and weak base combination in ammonium chloride produces an acidic solution, as shown by the reddish tint of the indicator. (d) The weak acid and weak base that form ammonium acetate are of comparable strength. A solution of ammonium acetate is essentially neutral.

tons from some water molecules, proton donors, to form $OH^-$ ions. An equilibrium is established in which the net effect of the anion hydrolysis is an increase in the hydroxide ion concentration, $[OH^-]$, of the solution.

The equilibrium equation for a typical weak acid in water, HA, forming hydronium ion and an anion, $A^-$, is as follows.

$$HA(aq) + H_2O(l) \rightleftharpoons H_3O^+(aq) + A^-(aq)$$

From this equation, the generalized expression for $K_a$ can be written. Note that as before, water does not appear in the general equilibrium equation.

$$K_a = \frac{[H_3O^+][A^-]}{[HA]}$$

The hydrolysis reaction between water and the anion, $A^-$, that is produced by the ionization of the weak acid, HA, is represented by the general equilibrium equation that follows.

$$A^-(aq) + H_2O(l) \rightleftharpoons HA(aq) + OH^-(aq)$$

Neutral water has equal concentrations of $H_3O^+$ and $OH^-$. Since HA is a weak acid, the anion $A^-$ has a strong attraction for protons. Adding $A^-$ to water in effect attracts (removes) $H_3O^+$ in water to form HA. This causes $OH^-$ to increase relative to $H_3O^+$ as represented in the equation above. The lower the value of $K_a$, the stronger the attraction $A^-$ will have for protons and the larger the concentration of $OH^-$. In other words, the weaker the acid, HA, the stronger its conjugate base, $A^-$.

Aqueous solutions of sodium carbonate are strongly basic. The sodium ions, $Na^+$, in sodium carbonate do not undergo hydrolysis in aqueous solution, but the carbonate ions, $CO_3^{2-}$, react as a Brønsted base. A $CO_3^{2-}$ anion acquires a proton from a water molecule to form the weak Brønsted acid, $HCO_3^-$, and the $OH^-$ ion.

$$CO_3^{2-}(aq) + H_2O(l) \rightleftharpoons HCO_3^-(aq) + OH^-(aq)$$

The $OH^-$ ion concentration increases until equilibrium is established. Consequently, the $H_3O^+$ ion concentration decreases so that the product $[H_3O^+][OH^-]$ remains equal to the ionization constant, $K_w$, of water at the temperature of the solution. Thus, the pH is *higher* than 7, and the solution is basic.

## Cation Hydrolysis

In the Brønsted sense, the cation of the salt is the conjugate acid of the base from which it was formed. It is also a proton donor. If the base is weak, the cation is an acid strong enough to donate a proton to a water molecule, a proton acceptor, to form $H_3O^+$ ions. An equilibrium is established in which the net effect of the cation hydrolysis is an increase in the hydronium ion concentration, $[H_3O^+]$, of the solution.

**CROSS-DISCIPLINARY**

### Blood Buffers

Blood normally has a pH of 7.4. If the pH of blood in a human rises above 7.8 or falls below 7.0, this change in pH is usually fatal. The primary buffer in blood is the carbonic acid–bicarbonate ion system, $CO_2(g) + H_2O(l) \rightleftharpoons H_2CO_3(aq) + HCO_3^-(aq)$. A condition called *respiratory acidosis* causes the pH to drop. It is the result of *hypoventilation,* or slowed breathing, the opposite of hyperventilation. Hypoventilation can be caused by congestive heart failure, pneumonia, or narcotics. Because breathing is slowed, carbon dioxide accumulates and its concentration rises. This change causes a shift in the equilibrium to the right due to Le Châtelier's principle, and the blood becomes more acidic because of the higher concentration of carbonic acid.

The following equilibrium equation for a typical weak base, B, is used to derive the generalized expression for $K_b$, the base dissociation constant.

$$B(aq) + H_2O(l) \rightleftharpoons BH^+(aq) + OH^-(aq)$$

$$K_b = \frac{[BH^+][OH^-]}{[B]}$$

The hydrolysis reaction between water and the cation, $BH^+$, produced by the dissociation of the weak base, B, is represented by the general equilibrium equation that follows.

$$BH^+(aq) + H_2O(l) \rightleftharpoons H_3O^+(aq) + B(aq)$$

In the forward reaction, the cation $BH^+$ donates a proton to the water molecule to form the hydronium ion. Because $H_3O^+$ ions are formed, the solution must become more acidic, as shown in the equation above. The extent of $H_3O^+$ ion formation depends on the relative strength of the base B. The weaker the base, the greater the concentration of $H_3O^+$ ions will be. Therefore, the weaker the base, the stronger its conjugate acid.

Ammonium chloride, $NH_4Cl$, dissociates in water to produce $NH_4^+$ ions and $Cl^-$ ions. Chloride ions are the conjugate base of the strong acid HCl, so they do not hydrolyze in water. Ammonium ions, however, are the conjugate acid of a weak base, $NH_3$. Ammonium ions donate protons to water molecules. Equilibrium is established with an increased $[H_3O^+]$, so the pH is *lower* than 7.

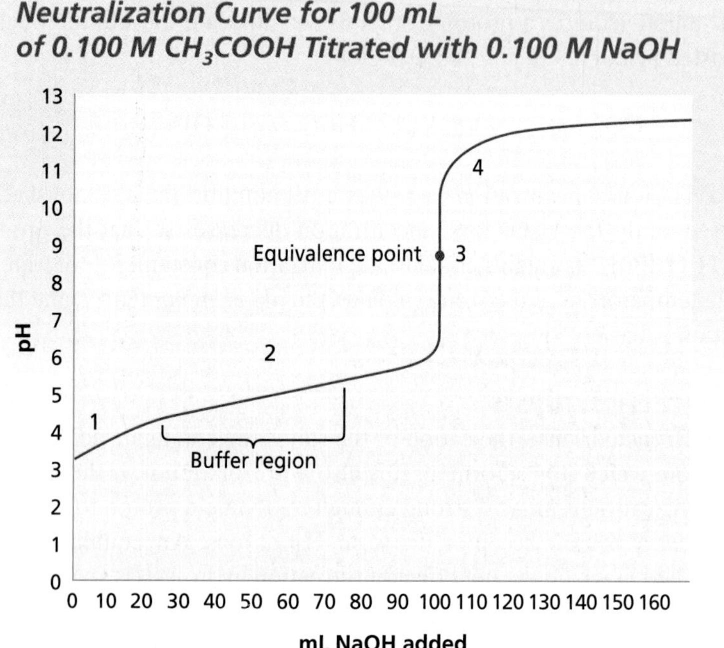


**FIGURE 11** At point *1* on the titration curve, only acetic acid is present. The pH depends on the weak acid alone. At *2* there is a mixture of $CH_3COOH$ and $CH_3COO^-$. Adding NaOH changes the pH slowly. At point *3* all acid has been converted to $CH_3COO^-$. This hydrolyzes to produce a slightly basic solution. At *4* the pH is due to the excess $OH^-$ that has been added.

## Hydrolysis in Acid-Base Reactions

Hydrolysis can help explain why the end point of a neutralization reaction can occur at a pH other than 7. The hydrolysis properties of salts are determined by the relative strengths of the acids and bases from which the salts were formed. Salts can be placed in four general categories, depending on their hydrolysis properties: strong acid–strong base, strong acid–weak base, weak acid–strong base, and weak acid–weak base.

Salts of strong acids and strong bases produce neutral solutions because neither the cation of a strong base nor the anion of a strong acid hydrolyzes appreciably in aqueous solutions. HCl(*aq*) is a strong acid, and NaOH(*aq*) is a strong base. Neither the $Na^+$ cation of the strong base nor the $Cl^-$ anion of the strong acid undergoes hydrolysis in water solutions. Therefore, aqueous solutions of NaCl are neutral. Similarly, $KNO_3$ is the salt of the strong acid $HNO_3$ and the strong base KOH. Measurements show that the pH of an aqueous $KNO_3$ solution is always very close to 7.

The aqueous solutions of salts formed from reactions between weak acids and strong bases are basic at the equivalence point, as shown in **Figure 11.** Anions of the dissolved salt are hydrolyzed by the water molecules, and the pH of the solution is raised, indicating that the hydroxide-ion concentration has increased. Aqueous solutions of sodium acetate, $NaCH_3COO$, are basic. The acetate ions, $CH_3COO^-$, undergo hydrolysis because they are the anions of the weak acid acetic acid. The cations of the salt are from a strong base, NaOH, and do not hydrolyze, because NaOH is 100% dissociated.

**Figure 12** shows that salts of strong acids and weak bases are acidic at the equivalence point. Cations of the dissolved salt are hydrolyzed in

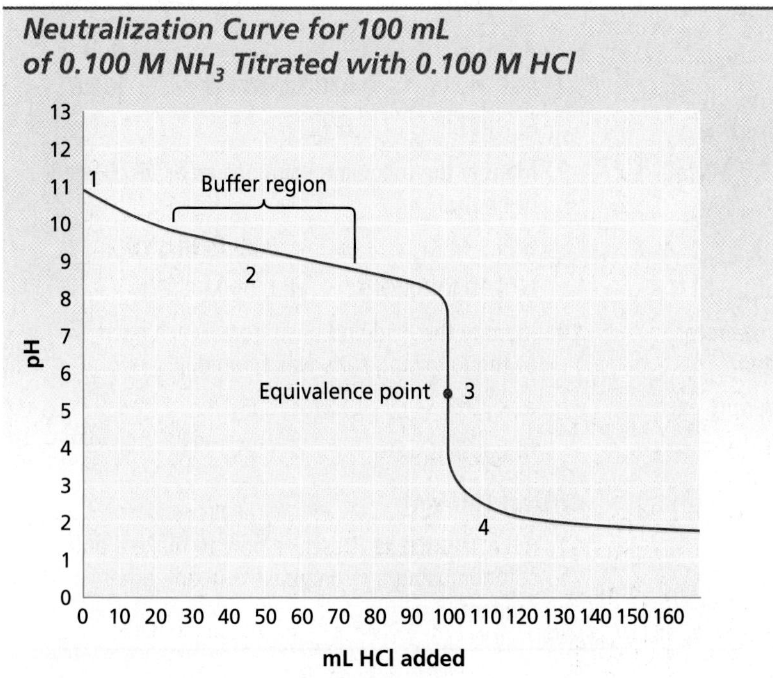


**FIGURE 12** At point *1* on the titration curve, only aqueous ammonia is present. The pH is determined by the base alone. At *2* there is a mixture of $NH_3$ and $NH_4^+$. Adding HCl changes the pH slowly. At point *3* all aqueous ammonia has been converted to $NH_4^+$. At *4* the pH is determined by the excess $H_3O^+$ that is being added.

the water solvent, and the pH of the solution is lowered, indicating that the hydronium ion concentration has increased. In this case, the cations of the salt undergo hydrolysis because they are the positive ions from a weak base. The anions of the salt are the negative ions from a strong acid and do not hydrolyze appreciably. Ammonium chloride, $NH_4Cl$, is a salt that produces an acidic solution.

Salts of weak acids and weak bases can produce either acidic, neutral, or basic aqueous solutions, depending on the salt dissolved. This is because both ions of the dissolved salt are hydrolyzed extensively. If both ions are hydrolyzed equally, the solution remains neutral. The ions in ammonium acetate, $NH_4CH_3COO$, hydrolyze equally, producing a neutral solution, as shown in **Figure 10d** on page 608.

In salts formed from a weak acid and weak base, the cation and anion both undergo hydrolysis. For example, when aluminum sulfide is placed in water, $Al^{3+}$ reacts with $OH^-$ forming $Al(OH)_3$, and $S^{2-}$ reacts with $H^+$ forming $H_2S$. The reaction is symbolized by the following chemical equation.

$$Al_2S_3(s) + 6H_2O(l) \longrightarrow 2Al(OH)_3(s) + 3H_2S(g)$$

Since $Al(OH)_3$ is a precipitate and $H_2S$ is a gas, both are removed from solution.

## SECTION REVIEW

1. What is meant by an *acid ionization constant*?
2. How is an acid ionization equilibrium expression written?
3. What is meant by the term *buffered solution*?
4. Which of the following combinations of solutions would form buffers when they are mixed?
   **a.** 50 mL of 1.0 M HCl and 50 mL of 1.0 M NaCl
   **b.** 25 mL of 0.5 M $HNO_2$ and 50 mL of 1.0 M $NaNO_2$
   **c.** 25 mL of 1.0 M $HNO_2$ and 25 mL of 1.0 M NaCl
5. What is meant by the *ion product constant* for water? What is the value of this constant?
6. For each of the following reactions, identify each conjugate acid-base pair.
   **a.** $H_2CO_3 + H_2O \rightleftharpoons HCO_3^- + H_3O^+$
   **b.** $H_2O + H_2O \rightleftharpoons H_3O^+ + OH^-$
   **c.** $H_2S + NH_3 \rightleftharpoons HS^- + NH_4^+$
   **d.** $H_2PO_4^- + H_2O \rightleftharpoons H_3PO_4 + OH^-$
7. What is hydrolysis? Compare cation and anion hydrolysis.
8. Which of the following ions hydrolyze in aqueous solution?
   **a.** $NO_3^-$ **b.** $F^-$ **c.** $NH_4^+$ **d.** $K^+$ **e.** $CH_3COO^-$ **f.** $SO_4^{2-}$ **g.** $CO_3^{2-}$ **h.** $PO_4^{3-}$
9. Identify the following solutions as acidic, basic, or neutral.
   **a.** 0.5 M KI **b.** 0.10 M $Ba(OH)_2$ **c.** 0.25 M $NH_4NO_3$ **d.** 0.05 M $K_2CO_3$
10. Identify the acid and base from which each of the following salts was formed.
   **a.** $K_2CrO_4$ **b.** $Ca(CH_3COO)_2$ **c.** $CaF_2$ **d.** $(NH_4)_2SO_4$

### Critical Thinking

11. **RELATING IDEAS** Describe how to make a buffer solution using a strong base and one other reagent.

# Solubility Equilibrium

SECTION 4

C.4.9 Summarize the concept of chemical equilibrium and Le Châtelier's principle

## Objectives

- Explain what is meant by *solubility product constants,* and calculate their values.
- Calculate solubilities using solubility product constants.
- Carry out calculations to predict whether precipitates will form when solutions are combined.

Ionic solids dissolve in water until they are in equilibrium with their ions. An equilibrium expression can be written from the balanced chemical equation of the solid's dissociation. Concentrations of the ions can be determined from the balanced chemical equation and solubility data. The ion concentrations can then be used to determine the value of the equilibrium constant. The numerical value for the equilibrium constant can be used to predict whether precipitation occurs when solutions of various concentrations are combined.

## Solubility Product

A saturated solution contains the maximum amount of solute possible at a given temperature in equilibrium with an undissolved excess of the substance. A saturated solution is not necessarily a concentrated solution. The concentration may be high or low, depending on the solubility of the solute.

A general rule is often used to express solubilities qualitatively. By this rule, a substance is said to be *soluble* if the solubility is *greater than* 1 g per 100 g of water and slightly soluble if less than that. Even substances we have previously referred to as "insoluble" are slightly soluble. We will describe the degree of solubility with an equilibrium constant.

The equilibrium principles developed in this chapter apply to all saturated solutions of slightly soluble salts. Silver chloride is an example of a slightly soluble salt. Its solution reaches saturation when the $Ag^+$ and $Cl^-$ concentrations are $1.3 \times 10^{-5}$ M, or about $2 \times 10^{-4}$ g of AgCl in 100 mL. When mixed, all $Ag^+$ and $Cl^-$ ions in excess of this concentration eventually precipitate as AgCl.

Consider the equilibrium system in a saturated solution of silver chloride containing an excess of the solid AgCl. This system is represented by the following equilibrium equation and equilibrium-constant expression.

$$AgCl(s) \rightleftharpoons Ag^+(aq) + Cl^-(aq)$$

The equation represents a heterogeneous reaction, as described on page 599. Once again, we follow the convention of writing the equilibrium expression without including the solid species. Therefore, [AgCl] does not appear in the final expression. The resulting equilibrium expression gives the solubility product constant $K_{sp}$. *The* **solubility product constant** *of a substance is the product of the molar concentra-*

*tions of its ions in a saturated solution, each raised to the power that is the coefficient of that ion in the balanced chemical equation.*

$$K_{sp} = [Ag^+][Cl^-]$$

This equation is the solubility equilibrium expression for the reaction. It expresses the fact that the solubility product constant, $K_{sp}$, of AgCl is the product of the molar concentrations of its ions in a saturated solution.

Calcium fluoride is another slightly soluble salt. The equilibrium in a saturated $CaF_2$ solution is described by the following equation.

$$CaF_2(s) \rightleftharpoons Ca^{2+}(aq) + 2F^-(aq)$$

The solubility product constant has the following form.

$$K_{sp} = [Ca^{2+}][F^-]^2$$

Notice that $K_{sp}$ is the product of the molar concentration of $Ca^{2+}$ ions and the molar concentration of $F^-$ ions squared, as required by the balanced chemical equilibrium expression.

The numerical value of $K_{sp}$ can be determined from solubility data. These data indicate that a maximum of $1.9 \times 10^{-4}$ g of AgCl can dissolve in 100. g of water at 25°C. One mole of AgCl has a mass of 143.32 g. The solubility of AgCl can therefore be expressed in moles per liter of water, which is very nearly equal to moles per liter of solution.

$$\frac{1.9 \times 10^{-4} \cancel{\text{g AgCl}}}{100. \cancel{\text{g } H_2O}} \times \frac{1 \cancel{\text{g } H_2O}}{1 \cancel{\text{mL } H_2O}} \times \frac{1000 \cancel{\text{mL}}}{1 \text{ L}} \times \frac{1 \text{ mol AgCl}}{143.32 \cancel{\text{g AgCl}}}$$
$$= 1.3 \times 10^{-5} \text{ mol/L}$$

Silver chloride dissociates in solution, contributing equal numbers of $Ag^+$ and $Cl^-$ ions. The ion concentrations in the saturated solution are therefore $1.3 \times 10^{-5}$ mol/L.

$$[Ag^+] = 1.3 \times 10^{-5}$$
$$[Cl^-] = 1.3 \times 10^{-5}$$

and

$$K_{sp} = [Ag^+][Cl^-]$$
$$K_{sp} = (1.3 \times 10^{-5})(1.3 \times 10^{-5})$$
$$K_{sp} = (1.3 \times 10^{-5})^2$$
$$K_{sp} = 1.7 \times 10^{-10}$$

This result is the solubility product constant of AgCl at 25°C.

The solubility of $CaF_2$ is $8.6 \times 10^{-3}$ g/100 g of water at 25°C. Expressed in moles per liter, as before, this concentration becomes $1.1 \times 10^{-3}$ mol/L. $CaF_2$ dissociates in solution to yield twice as many $F^-$ ions as

$Ca^{2+}$ ions. The ion concentrations in the saturated solution are $1.1 \times 10^{-3}$ for the calcium ion and $2(1.1 \times 10^{-3})$, or $2.2 \times 10^{-3}$, for the fluoride ion. Note that at equilibrium at 25°C, $[Ca^{2+}]$ equals the solubility of $1.1 \times 10^{-3}$ mol/L but $[F^-]$ equals twice the solubility, or $2.2 \times 10^{-3}$ mol/L. The number of moles of positive and negative ions per mole of compound must always be accounted for when using $K_{sp}$ and solubilities.

$$K_{sp} = [Ca^{2+}][F^-]^2$$

$$K_{sp} = (1.1 \times 10^{-3})(2.2 \times 10^{-3})^2$$

$$K_{sp} = 5.3 \times 10^{-9}$$

Thus, the solubility product constant of $CaF_2$ is $5.3 \times 10^{-9}$ at 25°C.

It is difficult to measure very small concentrations of a solute with precision. For this reason, solubility data from different sources may report different values of $K_{sp}$ for a substance. Thus, calculations of $K_{sp}$ ordinarily should be limited to two significant figures. Representative values of $K_{sp}$ at 25°C for some slightly soluble compounds are listed in **Table 3.** Assume that all data used in $K_{sp}$ calculations have been taken at 25°C unless otherwise specified.

At this point, you should note the difference between the solubility of a given solid and its solubility product constant. Remember that the *solubility product constant* is an equilibrium constant representing the product of the molar concentrations of its ions in a saturated solution. It

**TABLE 3 Solubility Product Constants, $K_{sp}$, at 25°C**

| Salt | Ion product | $K_{sp}$ | Salt | Ion product | $K_{sp}$ |
|---|---|---|---|---|---|
| $AgCH_3COO$ | $[Ag^+][CH_3COO^-]$ | $1.9 \times 10^{-3}$ | $CuCl$ | $[Cu^+][Cl^-]$ | $1.2 \times 10^{-6}$ |
| $AgBr$ | $[Ag^+][Br^-]$ | $5.0 \times 10^{-13}$ | $CuS$ | $[Cu^{2+}][S^{2-}]$ | $6.3 \times 10^{-36}$ |
| $Ag_2CO_3$ | $[Ag^+]^2[CO_3^{2-}]$ | $8.1 \times 10^{-12}$ | $FeS$ | $[Fe^{2+}][S^{2-}]$ | $6.3 \times 10^{-18}$ |
| $AgCl$ | $[Ag^+][Cl^-]$ | $1.8 \times 10^{-10}$ | $Fe(OH)_2$ | $[Fe^{2+}][OH^-]^2$ | $8.0 \times 10^{-16}$ |
| $AgI$ | $[Ag^+][I^-]$ | $8.3 \times 10^{-17}$ | $Fe(OH)_3$ | $[Fe^{3+}][OH^-]^3$ | $4 \times 10^{-38}$ |
| $Ag_2S$ | $[Ag^+]^2[S^{2-}]$ | $6.3 \times 10^{-50}$ | $HgS$ | $[Hg^{2+}][S^{2-}]$ | $1.6 \times 10^{-52}$ |
| $Al(OH)_3$ | $[Al^{3+}][OH^-]^3$ | $1.3 \times 10^{-33}$ | $MgCO_3$ | $[Mg^{2+}][CO_3^{2-}]$ | $3.5 \times 10^{-8}$ |
| $BaCO_3$ | $[Ba^{2+}][CO_3^{2-}]$ | $5.1 \times 10^{-9}$ | $Mg(OH)_2$ | $[Mg^{2+}][OH^-]^2$ | $1.8 \times 10^{-11}$ |
| $BaSO_4$ | $[Ba^{2+}][SO_4^{2-}]$ | $1.1 \times 10^{-10}$ | $MnS$ | $[Mn^{2+}][S^{2-}]$ | $2.5 \times 10^{-13}$ |
| $CdS$ | $[Cd^{2+}][S^{2-}]$ | $8.0 \times 10^{-27}$ | $PbCl_2$ | $[Pb^{2+}][Cl^-]^2$ | $1.6 \times 10^{-5}$ |
| $CaCO_3$ | $[Ca^{2+}][CO_3^{2-}]$ | $2.8 \times 10^{-9}$ | $PbCrO_4$ | $[Pb^{2+}][CrO_4^{2-}]$ | $2.8 \times 10^{-13}$ |
| $CaF_2$ | $[Ca^{2+}][F^-]^2$ | $5.3 \times 10^{-9}$ | $PbSO_4$ | $[Pb^{2+}][SO_4^{2-}]$ | $1.6 \times 10^{-8}$ |
| $Ca(OH)_2$ | $[Ca^{2+}][OH^-]^2$ | $5.5 \times 10^{-6}$ | $PbS$ | $[Pb^{2+}][S^{2-}]$ | $8.0 \times 10^{-28}$ |
| $CaSO_4$ | $[Ca^{2+}][SO_4^{2-}]$ | $9.1 \times 10^{-6}$ | $SnS$ | $[Sn^{2+}][S^{2-}]$ | $1.0 \times 10^{-25}$ |
| $CoCO_3$ | $[Co^{2+}][CO_3^{2-}]$ | $1.4 \times 10^{-13}$ | $SrSO_4$ | $[Sr^{2+}][SO_4^{2-}]$ | $3.2 \times 10^{-7}$ |
| $CoS$ | $[Co^{2+}][S^{2-}]$ | $4.0 \times 10^{-21}$ | $ZnS$ | $[Zn^{2+}][S^{2-}]$ | $1.6 \times 10^{-24}$ |

has only one value for a given solid at a given temperature. The *solubility* of a solid is an equilibrium position that represents the amount of the solid required to form a saturated solution with a specific amount of solvent. It has an infinite number of possible values at a given temperature and is dependent on other conditions, such as the presence of a common ion.

## SAMPLE PROBLEM B

**Calculate the solubility product constant, $K_{sp}$, for copper(I) chloride, CuCl, given that the solubility of this compound at 25°C is $1.08 \times 10^{-2}$ g/100. g $H_2O$.**

### SOLUTION

**1 ANALYZE**

**Given:** solubility of CuCl = $1.08 \times 10^{-2}$ g CuCl/100. g $H_2O$

**Unknown:** $K_{sp}$

**2 PLAN**

Start by converting the solubility of CuCl in g/100. g $H_2O$ to mol/L. You will need the molar mass of CuCl to get moles CuCl from grams CuCl. Then use the solubility of the $[Cu^+]$ and $[Cl^-]$ ions in the $K_{sp}$ expression and solve for $K_{sp}$.

$$\frac{\text{g CuCl}}{100.\text{ g H}_2\text{O}} \times \frac{1\text{ g H}_2\text{O}}{1\text{ mL H}_2\text{O}} \times \frac{1000\text{ mL}}{1\text{ L}} \times \frac{1\text{ mol CuCl}}{\text{g CuCl}} = \text{solubility in mol/L}$$

$$\text{CuCl}(s) \rightleftharpoons \text{Cu}^+(aq) + \text{Cl}^-(aq)$$

$$K_{sp} = [\text{Cu}^+][\text{Cl}^-]$$

$$[\text{Cu}^+] = [\text{Cl}^-] = \text{solubility in mol/L}$$

**3 COMPUTE**

The molar mass of CuCl is 99.0 g/mol.

$$\text{solubility} = \frac{1.08 \times 10^{-2}\text{ g CuCl}}{100.\text{ g H}_2\text{O}} \times \frac{1\text{ g H}_2\text{O}}{1\text{ mL}} \times \frac{1000\text{ mL}}{1\text{L}} \times \frac{1\text{ mol CuCl}}{99.0\text{ g CuCl}} =$$

$$1.09 \times 10^{-3}\text{ mol/L CuCl}$$

$$[\text{Cu}^+] = [\text{Cl}^-] = 1.09 \times 10^{-3}\text{ mol/L}$$

$$K_{sp} = (1.09 \times 10^{-3})(1.09 \times 10^{-3}) = 1.19 \times 10^{-6}$$

**4 EVALUATE**

The answer contains the proper number of significant figures and is close to the $K_{sp}$ value given in **Table 3.**

### PRACTICE

*Answers in Appendix E*

1. Calculate the solubility product constant, $K_{sp}$, of lead(II) chloride, $PbCl_2$, which has a solubility of 1.0 g/100. g $H_2O$ at 20°C.
2. A 5.0 gram sample of $Ag_2SO_4$ will dissolve in 1.0 L of water. Calculate the solubility product constant for this salt.

**extension**

Go to **go.hrw.com** for more practice problems that ask you to calculate solubility product constants.

**Keyword: HC6EQUX**

## Calculating Solubilities

Once known, the solubility product constant can be used to determine the solubility of a slightly soluble salt. Suppose you wish to know how many moles of barium carbonate, $BaCO_3$, can be dissolved in 1 L of water at 25°C. From **Table 3,** $K_{sp}$ for $BaCO_3$ has the numerical value $5.1 \times 10^{-9}$. The equilibrium equation is written as follows.

$$BaCO_3(s) \rightleftharpoons Ba^{2+}(aq) + CO_3^{2-}(aq)$$

Given the value for $K_{sp}$, we can write the solubility equilibrium expression as follows.

$$K_{sp} = [Ba^{2+}][CO_3^{2-}] = 5.1 \times 10^{-9}$$

Therefore, $BaCO_3$ dissolves until the product of the molar concentrations of $Ba^{2+}$ ions and $CO_3^{2-}$ ions equals $5.1 \times 10^{-9}$. The solubility equilibrium equation shows that $Ba^{2+}$ ions and $CO_3^{2-}$ ions enter the solution in equal numbers as the salt dissolves. Thus, they have the same concentration. Let $[Ba^{2+}] = x$. Then $[CO_3^{2-}] = x$ also.

$$[Ba^{2+}][CO_3^{2-}] = K_{sp} = 5.1 \times 10^{-9}$$

$$(x)(x) = x^2 = 5.1 \times 10^{-9}$$

$$x = \sqrt{5.1 \times 10^{-9}}$$

The molar solubility of $BaCO_3$ is $7.1 \times 10^{-5}$ mol/L.

Thus, the solution concentration is $7.1 \times 10^{-5}$ M for $Ba^{2+}$ ions and $7.1 \times 10^{-5}$ M for $CO_3^{2-}$ ions.

### SAMPLE PROBLEM C

**Calculate the solubility of silver bromide, AgBr, in mol/L, using the $K_{sp}$ value for this compound listed in Table 3.**

#### SOLUTION

**1 ANALYZE**

**Given:** $K_{sp} = 5.0 \times 10^{-13}$
**Unknown:** solubility of AgBr

**2 PLAN**

$$AgBr \rightleftharpoons Ag^{+}(aq) + Br^{-}(aq)$$

$$K_{sp} = [Ag^{+}][Br^{-}]$$

$[Ag^{+}] = [Br^{-}]$, so let $[Ag^{+}] = x$ and $[Br^{-}] = x$

**3 COMPUTE**

$$K_{sp} = [Ag^{+}][Br^{-}]$$

$$K_{sp} = x^2$$

$$x^2 = 5.0 \times 10^{-13}$$

$$x = \sqrt{5.0 \times 10^{-13}}$$

Solubility of AgBr $= \sqrt{5.0 \times 10^{-13}} = 7.1 \times 10^{-7}$ mol/L

**4 EVALUATE** The answer has the proper number of significant figures and is close to an estimated value of $7.0 \times 10^{-7}$ calculated as $\sqrt{49 \times 10^{-14}}$.

**PRACTICE** *Answers in Appendix E*

1. Calculate the solubility of cadmium sulfide, CdS, in mol/L, given the $K_{sp}$ value listed in **Table 3.**
2. Determine the concentration of strontium ions in a saturated solution of strontium sulfate, $SrSO_4$, if the $K_{sp}$ for $SrSO_4$ is $3.2 \times 10^{-7}$.

**extension**

Go to **go.hrw.com** for more practice problems that ask you to calculate solubilities.

# Precipitation Calculations

In an earlier example, $BaCO_3$ served as the source of both $Ba^{2+}$ and $CO_3^{2-}$ ions. Because each mole of $BaCO_3$ yields one mole of $Ba^{2+}$ ions and one mole of $CO_3^{2-}$ ions, the concentrations of the two ions were equal. However, the equilibrium condition does not require that the two ion concentrations be equal. Equilibrium will still be established so that the ion product $[Ba^{2+}][CO_3^{2-}]$ does not exceed the value of $K_{sp}$ for the system.

Similarly, if the ion product $[Ca^{2+}][F^-]^2$ is less than the value of $K_{sp}$ at a particular temperature, the solution is unsaturated. If the ion product is greater than the value for $K_{sp}$, $CaF_2$ precipitates. This precipitation reduces the concentrations of $Ca^{2+}$ and $F^-$ ions until equilibrium is established.

Suppose that unequal quantities of $BaCl_2$ and $Na_2CO_3$ are dissolved in water and that the solutions are mixed. If the ion product $[Ba^{2+}][CO_3^{2-}]$ exceeds the $K_{sp}$ of $BaCO_3$, a precipitate of $BaCO_3$ forms. After precipitation, the ion concentrations are such that $[Ba^{2+}][CO_3^{2-}]$ equals the $K_{sp}$.

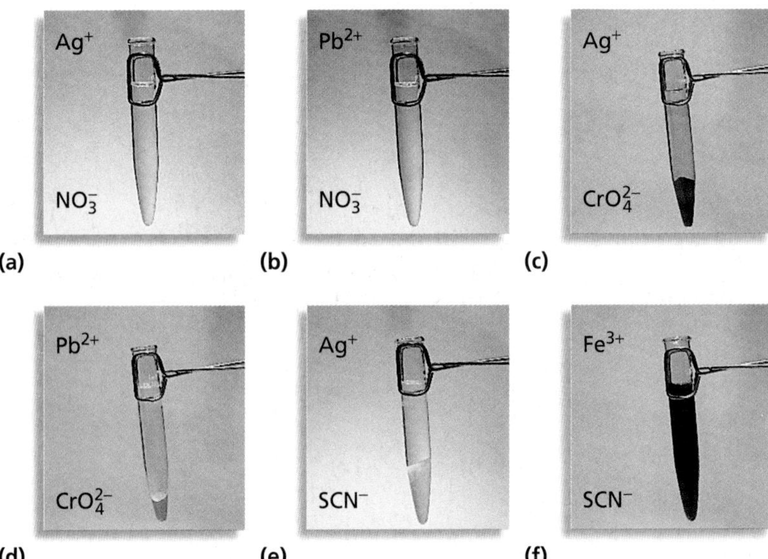


**FIGURE 13** Nitrate salts of $Ag^+$ (a) and $Pb^{2+}$ (b) are soluble. When chromate ions, $CrO_4^{2-}$, combine with $Ag^+$ (c) or $Pb^{2+}$ (d), a slightly soluble salt forms. Thiocyanate ions, $SCN^-$, can form a slightly soluble salt with $Ag^+$ (e) or a soluble salt with $Fe^{3+}$ (f).

Substances differ greatly in their tendencies to form precipitates when mixed in moderate concentrations. The photos in **Figure 13** show the behavior of some anions in the presence of certain cations. Note that some of the combinations have produced precipitates and some have not. The solubility product can be used to predict whether a precipitate forms when two solutions are mixed.

## SAMPLE PROBLEM D

**Will a precipitate form if 20.0 mL of 0.010 M $BaCl_2$ is mixed with 20.0 mL of 0.0050 M $Na_2SO_4$?**

### SOLUTION

**1 ANALYZE**

**Given:** concentration of $BaCl_2$ = 0.010 M
volume of $BaCl_2$ = 20.0 mL
concentration of $Na_2SO_4$ = 0.0050 M
volume of $Na_2SO_4$ = 20.0 mL

**Unknown:** whether a precipitate forms

**2 PLAN**

The two possible new pairings of ions are NaCl and $BaSO_4$. Of these, only $BaSO_4$ is a slightly soluble salt. It will precipitate if the ion product $[Ba^{2+}][SO_4^{2-}]$ in the mixed solution exceeds $K_{sp}$ for $BaSO_4$. From the list of solubility products in **Table 3,** the $K_{sp}$ is found to be $1.1 \times 10^{-10}$. The solubility equilibrium equation follows.

$$BaSO_4(s) \rightleftharpoons Ba^{2+}(aq) + SO_4^{2-}(aq)$$

The solubility equilibrium expression is written as follows.

$$K_{sp} = [Ba^{2+}][SO_4^{2-}] = 1.1 \times 10^{-10}$$

First $[Ba^{2+}]$ and $[SO_4^{2-}]$ in the above solution must be found. Then the ion product is calculated and compared with the $K_{sp}$.

**3 COMPUTE**

Calculate the mole quantities of $Ba^{2+}$ and $SO_4^{2-}$ ions.

$$0.020\ \cancel{L} \times \frac{0.010\ \text{mol Ba}^{2+}}{1\ \cancel{L}} = 0.000\ 20\ \text{mol Ba}^{2+}$$

$$0.020\ \cancel{L} \times \frac{0.0050\ \text{mol SO}_4^{2-}}{1\ \cancel{L}} = 0.000\ 10\ \text{mol SO}_4^{2-}$$

Calculate the total volume of solution containing $Ba^{2+}$ and $SO_4^{2-}$ ions.

$$0.020\ \text{L} + 0.020\ \text{L} = 0.040\ \text{L}$$

Calculate the $Ba^{2+}$ and $SO_4^{2-}$ ion concentrations in the combined solution.

$$\frac{0.000\ 20\ \text{mol Ba}^{2+}}{0.040\ \text{L}} = 5.0 \times 10^{-3}\ \text{mol/L Ba}^{2+}$$

$$\frac{0.000\ 10\ \text{mol SO}_4^{2-}}{0.040\ \text{L}} = 2.5 \times 10^{-3}\ \text{mol/L SO}_4^{2-}$$

Calculate the ion product.

$$[Ba^{2+}][SO_4^{2-}] = (5.0 \times 10^{-3})(2.5 \times 10^{-3})$$
$$= 1.2 \times 10^{-5}$$

The ion product, $1.2 \times 10^{-5}$, is greater than the value of $K_{sp}$, $1.1 \times 10^{-10}$, so precipitation occurs.

**4 EVALUATE** The answer contains the appropriate number of significant figures and is close to an estimated value of $1 \times 10^{-5}$, calculated as $(5 \times 10^{-3})(2 \times 10^{-3})$; because $10^{-5} > 10^{-10}$, precipitation should occur.

**PRACTICE** *Answers in Appendix E*

1. Does a precipitate form when 100. mL of 0.0025 M $AgNO_3$ and 150. mL of 0.0020 M NaBr solutions are mixed?
2. Does a precipitate form when 20. mL of 0.038 M $Pb(NO_3)_2$ and 30. mL of 0.018 M KCl solutions are mixed?

Go to **go.hrw.com** for more practice problems that ask you to perform precipitation calculations.

**Keyword: HC6EQUX**

## Limitations on the Use of $K_{sp}$

The solubility product principle can be very useful when applied to solutions of slightly soluble substances. It *cannot* be applied to solutions of soluble substances. This is because the positive and negative ions attract each other, and this attraction becomes appreciable when the ions are close together. Sometimes it is necessary to consider two equilibria simultaneously. For example, if either ion hydrolyzes, the salt will be more soluble than predicted when only the solubility product constant is used. The solubility product is also sensitive to changes in solution temperature to the extent that the solubility of the dissolved substance is affected by such changes. All of these factors limit the conditions under which the solubility product principle can be applied.

## SECTION REVIEW

1. What is a solubility product constant? How are such constants determined?
2. How are solubility product constants used to calculate solubilities?
3. What is an ion product?
4. How are calculations to predict possible precipitation carried out?
5. What is the value of $K_{sp}$ for $Ag_2SO_4$ if 5.40 g is soluble in 1.00 L of water?
6. Determine whether a precipitate will form if 20.0 mL of $1.00 \times 10^{-7}$ M $AgNO_3$ is mixed with 20.0 mL of $2.00 \times 10^{-9}$ M NaCl at 25°C.

**Critical Thinking**

7. **ANALYZING DATA** A solution is 0.20 M in each of the following: $Ca(NO_3)_2$, $Cr(NO_3)_3$, and $La(NO_3)_3$. Solid NaF is added to the solution until the $[F^-]$ of the solution is $1.0 \times 10^{-4}$ M. Given the values of $K_{sp}$ below, describe what will happen.
$CaF_2 = 3.9 \times 10^{-11}$; $CrF_3 = 6.6 \times 10^{-11}$; and $LaF_3 = 4.0 \times 10^{-17}$

# CHAPTER HIGHLIGHTS

## The Nature of Chemical Equilibrium

**Vocabulary**
reversible reaction
chemical equilibrium
equilibrium constant
chemical equilibrium expression

- A reaction system in which the forward and reverse reactions occur simultaneously and at the same rate is said to be at *equilibrium.* Both reactions continue, but there is no net change in the composition of the system.
- At equilibrium, the ratio of the product of the molar concentrations of substances formed to the product of the molar concentrations of reactants, each raised to the appropriate power, has a definite numerical value, $K$, which is the equilibrium constant at a given temperature.

## Shifting Equilibrium

**Vocabulary**
common-ion effect

- According to Le Châtelier's principle, when a stress (a change in concentration, pressure, or temperature) is applied to a system at equilibrium, the equilibrium is shifted in the direction that relieves the stress.
- The common-ion effect is recognized when a solution containing ions such as those of a reactant or a product in an equilibrium system is added to the system. Le Châtelier's principle explains the response of the system to the stress.

## Equilibria of Acids, Bases, and Salts

**Vocabulary**
acid ionization constant
buffered solution
hydrolysis

- The equilibrium expression for the ionization constant of the weak acid HA follows.

$$K_a = \frac{[H_3O^+][A^-]}{[HA]}$$

- Salts formed from strong bases and weak acids produce aqueous solutions that are basic because of *anion hydrolysis.*
- Salts formed from strong acids and weak bases produce aqueous solutions that are acidic because of *cation hydrolysis.*
- Salts formed from strong acids and strong bases do not hydrolyze in water, and their solutions are neutral.
- Salts formed from weak acids and weak bases may produce neutral, acidic, or basic solutions, depending on the relative amounts of cation and anion hydrolysis.

## Solubility Equilibrium

**Vocabulary**
solubility product constant

- Ions of salts that are slightly soluble form saturated aqueous solutions at low concentrations. The solubility equilibrium expression for such salts yields a constant—the solubility product constant, $K_{sp}$.

*For more practice, go to the Problem Bank in Appendix D.*

## *The Nature of Chemical Equilibrium*

### SECTION 1 REVIEW

**1.** Describe and explain how the concentrations of A, B, C, and D change from the time when A and B are first combined to the point at which equilibrium is established for the reaction $A + B \rightleftharpoons C + D$.

**2.** a. Write the general expression for an equilibrium constant based on the equation $nA + mB + \ldots \rightleftharpoons xC + yD + \ldots$

b. What information is provided by the value of $K$ for a given equilibrium system at a specified temperature?

**3.** In general, which reaction is favored (forward or reverse) if the value of $K$ at a specified temperature is

a. very small?

b. very large?

### PRACTICE PROBLEMS

**4.** Determine the value of the equilibrium constant for each reaction given, assuming that the equilibrium concentrations are found to be those specified. (Concentrations are in mol/L.) (Hint: See Sample Problem A.)

a. $A + B \rightleftharpoons C$; $[A] = 2.0$; $[B] = 3.0$; $[C] = 4.0$

b. $D + 2E \rightleftharpoons F + 3G$; $[D] = 1.5$; $[E] = 2.0$; $[F] = 1.8$; $[G] = 1.2$

c. $N_2(g) + 3H_2(g) \rightleftharpoons 2NH_3(g)$; $[N_2] = 0.45$; $[H_2] = 0.14$; $[NH_3] = 0.62$

**5.** An equilibrium mixture at a specific temperature is found to consist of $1.2 \times 10^{-3}$ mol/L HCl, $3.8 \times 10^{-4}$ mol/L $O_2$, $5.8 \times 10^{-2}$ mol/L $H_2O$, and $5.8 \times 10^{-2}$ mol/L $Cl_2$ according to the following:

$$4HCl(g) + O_2(g) \rightleftharpoons 2H_2O(g) + 2Cl_2(g).$$

Determine the value of the equilibrium constant for this system.

**6.** At 450°C, the value of the equilibrium constant for the following system is $6.59 \times 10^{-3}$. If $[NH_3] = 1.23 \times 10^{-4}$ M and $[H_2] = 2.75 \times 10^{-2}$ M at equilibrium, determine the concentration of $N_2$ at that point.

$$N_2(g) + 3H_2(g) \rightleftharpoons 2NH_3(g)$$

**7.** The value of the equilibrium constant for the reaction below is 40.0 at a specified temperature. What would be the value of that constant for the reverse reaction under the same conditions?

$$H_2(g) + I_2(g) \rightleftharpoons 2HI(g)$$

## *Shifting Equilibrium*

### SECTION 2 REVIEW

**8.** Predict whether each of the following pressure changes would favor the forward or reverse reaction.

$$2NO(g) + O_2(g) \rightleftharpoons 2NO_2(g)$$

a. increased pressure

b. decreased pressure

**9.** In heterogeneous reaction systems, what types of substances do not appear in the equilibrium constant expression? Why?

**10.** Explain the effect of a catalyst on an equilibrium system.

**11.** Predict the effect of each of the following on the indicated equilibrium system in terms of the direction of equilibrium shift (forward, reverse, or neither).

$$H_2(g) + Cl_2(g) \rightleftharpoons 2HCl(g) + 184 \text{ kJ}$$

a. addition of $Cl_2$

b. removal of HCl

c. increased pressure

d. decreased temperature

e. removal of $H_2$

f. decreased pressure

g. addition of a catalyst

h. increased temperature

i. decreased system volume

**12.** How would the changes in (a) through (i) of item 11 affect the new equilibrium concentration of HCl and the value of $K$ at the new equilibrium?

**13.** Explain why changes in the concentrations of the reactants and products at equilibrium have no impact on the value of the equilibrium constant.

**14.** What relative pressure (high or low) would result in the production of the maximum level of $CO_2$ according to the following equation? Why?

$$2CO(g) + O_2(g) \rightleftharpoons 2CO_2(g)$$

**15.** What relative conditions (reactant concentrations, pressure, and temperature) would favor a high equilibrium concentration of the underlined substance in each of the following equilibrium systems?

a. $2CO(g) + O_2(g) \rightleftharpoons \underline{2CO_2(g)} + 167\text{ kJ}$

b. $Cu^{2+}(aq) + 4NH_3(aq) \rightleftharpoons \underline{Cu(NH_3)_4^{2+}(aq)} + 42\text{ kJ}$

c. $2HI(g) + 12.6\text{ kJ} \rightleftharpoons H_2(g) + \underline{I_2(g)}$

d. $4HCl(g) + O_2(g) \rightleftharpoons 2H_2O(g) + \underline{2Cl_2(g)} + 113\text{ kJ}$

e. $PCl_5(g) + 88\text{ kJ} \rightleftharpoons PCl_3(g) + \underline{Cl_2(g)}$

**16.** The reaction between hemoglobin, Hb, and oxygen, $O_2$, in red blood cells is responsible for transporting $O_2$ to body tissues. This process can be represented by the following equilibrium reaction:

$$Hb(aq) + O_2(g) \rightleftharpoons HbO_2(aq)$$

What will happen to the concentration of oxygenated hemoglobin, $HbO_2$, at high altitude, where the pressure of oxygen is 0.1 atm instead of 0.2 atm, as it is at sea level?

**17.** What two factors determine the extent to which reacting ions are removed from solution?

**18.** Identify the three conditions under which ionic reactions can run to completion, and write an equation for each.

## *Equilibria of Acids, Bases, and Salts*

### SECTION 3 REVIEW

**19.** a. Write the ion product constant expression for water.

b. What is the value of this constant at 25°C?

**20.** List and distinguish between the four general categories of salts, based on their hydrolysis properties, and give an example of each.

**21.** Explain why the pH of a solution containing both acetic acid and sodium acetate is higher than that of a solution containing the same concentration of acetic acid alone.

**22.** The ionization constant, $K_a$, for acetic acid is $1.8 \times 10^{-5}$ at 25°C. Explain the significance of this value.

**23.** a. From the development of $K_a$ described in Section 3, show how you would express an ionization constant, $K_b$, for the weak base $NH_3$.

b. In this case, $K_b = 1.8 \times 10^{-5}$. What is the significance of this numerical value to equilibrium?

## *Solubility Equilibrium*

### SECTION 4 REVIEW

**24.** Explain why a saturated solution is not necessarily a concentrated solution.

**25.** What rule of thumb is used to distinguish between soluble and slightly soluble substances?

**26.** What is the relative ion concentration of an ionic substance typically involved in solubility equilibrium systems?

**27.** What is the relationship between $K_{sp}$ and the product of the ion concentrations in terms of determining whether a solution of those ions is saturated?

### PRACTICE PROBLEMS

**28.** The ionic substance EJ dissociates to form $E^{2+}$ and $J^{2-}$ ions. The solubility of EJ is $8.45 \times 10^{-6}$ mol/L. What is the value of the solubility product constant? (Hint: See Sample Problem B.)

**29.** Calculate the solubility product constant $K_{sp}$ for each of the following, based on the solubility information provided:

a. $BaSO_4 = 2.4 \times 10^{-4}$ g/100. g $H_2O$ at 20°C

b. $Ca(OH)_2 = 0.173$ g/100. g $H_2O$ at 20°C

**30.** Calculate the molar solubility of a substance MN that ionizes to form $M^{2+}$ and $N^{2-}$ ions, given that $K_{sp} = 8.1 \times 10^{-6}$. (Hint: See Sample Problem C.)

**31.** Use the $K_{sp}$ values given in **Table 3** to evaluate the solubility of each of the following in moles per liter.

a. AgBr

b. CoS

**32.** Complete each of the following relative to the reaction that occurs when 25.0 mL of 0.0500 M $Pb(NO_3)_2$ is combined with 25.0 mL of 0.0400 M $Na_2SO_4$ if equilibrium is reached at 25°C.

a. Write the solubility equilibrium equation at 25°C.

b. Write the solubility equilibrium expression for the net reaction.

**33.** The ionic substance $T_3U_2$ ionizes to form $T^{2+}$ and $U^{3-}$ ions. The solubility of $T_3U_2$ is $3.8 \times 10^{-10}$ mol/L. What is the value of the solubility product constant?

**34.** A solution of AgI contains $2.7 \times 10^{-10}$ mol/L $Ag^+$. What is the maximum $I^-$ concentration that can exist in this solution?

**35.** Calculate whether a precipitate will form if 0.35 L of 0.0044 M $Ca(NO_3)_2$ and 0.17 L of 0.000 39 M NaOH are mixed at 25°C. (See **Table 3** for $K_{sp}$ values.) (Hint: See Sample Problem D.)

**36.** Determine whether a precipitate will form if 1.70 g of solid $AgNO_3$ and 14.5 g of solid NaCl are dissolved in 200. mL of water to form a solution at 25°C.

**37.** If $2.50 \times 10^{-2}$ g of solid $Fe(NO_3)_3$ is added to 100. mL of a $1.0 \times 10^{-4}$ M NaOH solution, will a precipitate form?

## MIXED REVIEW

**38.** Calcium carbonate is only slightly soluble in water.

a. Write the equilibrium equation for calcium carbonate in solution.

b. Write the solubility product constant expression, $K_{sp}$, for the equilibrium in a saturated solution of $CaCO_3$.

**39.** Calculate the concentration of $Hg^{2+}$ ions in a saturated solution of HgS(*s*). How many $Hg^{2+}$ ions are in 1000 L of the solution?

**40.** Calculate the equilibrium constant, *K*, for the following reaction at 900°C.

$$H_2(g) + CO_2(g) \rightleftharpoons H_2O(g) + CO(g)$$

The components were analyzed, and it was found that $[H_2] = 0.061$ mol/L, $[CO_2] = 0.16$ mol/L, $[H_2O] = 0.11$ mol/L, and $[CO] = 0.14$ mol/L.

**41.** A solution in equilibrium with solid barium phosphate is found to have a barium ion concentration of $5.0 \times 10^{-4}$ M and a $K_{sp}$ of $3.4 \times 10^{-23}$. Calculate the concentration of phosphate ion.

**42.** At 25°C, the value of *K* is $1.7 \times 10^{-13}$ for the following reaction.

$$2N_2O(g) + O_2(g) \rightleftharpoons 4NO(g)$$

It is determined that $[N_2O] = 0.0035$ mol/L and $[O_2] = 0.0027$ mol/L. Using this information, what is the concentration of NO(*g*) at equilibrium?

**43.** Tooth enamel is composed of the mineral hydroxyapatite, $Ca_5(PO_4)_3OH$, which has a $K_{sp}$ of $6.8 \times 10^{-37}$. The molar solubility of hydroxyapatite is $2.7 \times 10^{-5}$ mol/L. When hydroxyapatite is reacted with fluoride, the $OH^-$ is replaced with the $F^-$ ion on the mineral, forming fluorapatite, $Ca_5(PO_4)_3F$. (The latter is harder and less susceptible to cavities.) The $K_{sp}$ of fluorapatite is $1 \times 10^{-60}$. Calculate the molar solubility of fluorapatite in water. Given your calculations, can you support the fluoridation of drinking water?

**44.** Determine if a precipitate will form when 0.96 g $Na_2CO_3$ is combined with 0.20 g $BaBr_2$ in a 10. L solution ($K_{sp} = 2.8 \times 10^{-9}$).

**45.** For the formation of ammonia, the equilibrium constant is calculated to be $5.2 \times 10^{-5}$ at 25°C. After analysis, it is determined that $[N_2] = 2.00$ M and $[H_2] = 0.80$ M. How many grams of ammonia are in the 10. L reaction vessel at equilibrium? Use the following equilibrium equation.

$$N_2(g) + 3H_2(g) \rightleftharpoons 2NH_3(g)$$

## CRITICAL THINKING

**46. Relating Ideas** Let *s* equal the solubility, in mol/L, of $AB_2$. In terms of *s*, what is the molar concentration of A? of B? What is the $K_{sp}$ of $AB_2$?

47. **Predicting Outcomes** When gasoline burns in an automobile engine, nitric oxide is formed from oxygen and nitrogen. Nitric oxide is a major air pollutant. High temperatures such as those found in a combustion engine are needed for the following reaction:

$$N_2(g) + O_2(g) \rightleftharpoons 2NO(g)$$

*K* for the reaction is 0.01 at 2000°C. If 4.0 mol of $N_2$, 0.1 mol of $O_2$, and 0.08 mol of NO are placed in a 1.0 L vessel at 2000°C, predict which reaction will be favored.

## USING THE HANDBOOK

48. An equilibrium system helps maintain the pH of the blood. Review the material on the carbon dioxide–bicarbonate ion equilibrium system in Group 14 of the *Elements Handbook,* and answer the following.
    a. Write the equation for the equilibrium system that responds to changes in $H_3O^+$ concentration.
    b. Use Le Châtelier's principle to explain how hyperventilation affects this system.
    c. How does this system maintain pH when acid is added?
49. The reactions used to confirm the presence of transition metal ions often involve the formation of precipitates. Review the analytical tests for the transition metals in the *Elements Handbook.* Use that information and **Table 3** to determine the minimum concentration of $Zn^{2+}$ needed to produce a precipitate that confirms the presence of Zn. Assume enough sulfide ion reagent is added to the unknown solution in the test tube to produce a sulfide ion concentration of $1.4 \times 10^{-20}$ M.

## RESEARCH & WRITING

50. Find photos of several examples of stalagmites and stalactites in various caves. Investigate the equilibrium processes involved in the formation of stalagmites and stalactites.
51. Carry out library research on the use of catalysts in industrial processes. Explain what types of catalysts are used for specific processes, such as the Haber process.

## ALTERNATIVE ASSESSMENT

52. Research nitrogen narcosis in the library. What causes nitrogen narcosis, and how does it relate to Le Châtelier's principle?

extension

**Graphing Calculator Chemical Equilibrium**

Go to **go.hrw.com** for a graphing calculator exercise that asks you to calculate the percent ionization for an acid equilibrium.

# *Math Tutor* DETERMINING EQUILIBRIUM CONSTANTS

For a given temperature, you can write a mathematical equation that describes the equilibrium of a reaction in terms of concentration. The equation defines an equilibrium constant, *K*, as a function of the concentrations of products and reactants at equilibrium.

Consider an equilibrium process in which reactants A and B form products C and D.

$$nA + mB \rightleftharpoons xC + yD$$

The terms *n, m, x,* and *y* are the coefficients of the balanced equation.

$$K = \frac{[C]^x[D]^y}{[A]^n[B]^m}$$

## Problem-Solving TIPS

- Always use a balanced chemical equation to write an equilibrium-constant equation.
- To write an equation, place the product concentrations in the numerator and the reactant concentrations in the denominator. Raise each substance's concentration to the power equal to the substance's coefficient in the balanced chemical equation.
- The concentration of any solid or pure liquid that takes part in the reaction is left out because these concentrations never change.

## SAMPLE

**Write an equation for the equilibrium constant of the reaction in which nitrogen monoxide changes to dinitrogen monoxide and nitrogen dioxide.**

To write an equation for an equilibrium constant, you must start with a balanced chemical equation for the equilibrium reaction. By writing the formulas of the compounds mentioned in the description, you get the unbalanced equilibrium equation $NO(g) \rightleftharpoons N_2O(g) + NO_2(g)$.

Balancing the equation requires a coefficient of 3 in front of NO, giving $3NO(g) \rightleftharpoons N_2O(g) + NO_2(g)$. Next, write an equilibrium equation. Remember, each concentration in the equilibrium equation is raised to a power equal to its coefficient in the balanced chemical equation. The product concentrations, $[N_2O]$ and $[NO_2]$, are placed in the numerator. The coefficient of each of the products is 1, so the exponent of each concentration is 1. There is only one reactant, so its concentration, [NO], is written in the denominator. Its coefficient is 3 in the balanced chemical equation, so the concentration of NO is raised to the third power. The exponents with a value of 1 do not have to be written. The resulting equation is

$$K = \frac{[N_2O]^1[NO_2]^1}{[NO]^3} = \frac{[N_2O][NO_2]}{[NO]^3}$$

## PRACTICE PROBLEMS

1. Write equations for the equilibrium constant of each of the following hypothetical reactions:
   a. $A(aq) + 2B(aq) \rightleftharpoons AB_2(aq)$
   b. $2DE_2(g) \rightleftharpoons D_2(g) + 2E_2(g)$

2. Use the equilibrium concentrations below to calculate the equilibrium constant for the following decomposition reaction:
   $$2BrF_5(g) \rightleftharpoons Br_2(g) + 5F_2(g)$$
   $[BrF_5] = 0.000137$ mol/L, $[Br_2] = 0.00050$ mol/L, and $[F_2] = 0.0025$ mol/L

# Standardized Test Prep

Answer the following items on a separate piece of paper.

**MULTIPLE CHOICE**

**1.** A chemical reaction is in equilibrium when
**A.** forward and reverse reactions have ceased.
**B.** the equilibrium constant equals 1.
**C.** forward and reverse reaction rates are equal.
**D.** No reactants remain.

**2.** Which change can cause the value of the equilibrium constant to change?
**A.** temperature
**B.** concentration of a reactant
**C.** concentration of a product
**D.** None of the above

**3.** Consider the following reaction:

$$2C(s) + O_2(g) \rightleftharpoons 2CO(g)$$

The equilibrium constant expression for this reaction is

**A.** $\frac{[CO]^2}{[O_2]}$.
**B.** $\frac{[CO]^2}{[O_2][C]^2}$.
**C.** $\frac{2[CO]}{[O_2][2C]}$.
**D.** $\frac{[CO]}{[O_2]^2}$.

**4.** The solubility product of cadmium carbonate, $CdCO_3$, is $1.0 \times 10^{-12}$. In a saturated solution of this salt, the concentration of $Cd^{2+}(aq)$ ions is
**A.** $5.0 \times 10^{-13}$ mol/L.
**B.** $1.0 \times 10^{-12}$ mol/L.
**C.** $1.0 \times 10^{-6}$ mol/L.
**D.** $5.0 \times 10^{-7}$ mol/L.

**5.** Consider the following equation for an equilibrium system:

$$2PbS(s) + 3O_2(g) + C(s) \rightleftharpoons 2Pb(s) + CO_2(g) + 2SO_2(g)$$

Which concentration(s) would be included in the denominator of the equilibrium constant expression?
**A.** $Pb(s)$, $CO_2(g)$, and $SO_2(g)$
**B.** $PbS(s)$, $O_2(g)$, and $C(s)$
**C.** $O_2(g)$, $Pb(s)$, $CO_2(g)$, and $SO_2(g)$
**D.** $O_2(g)$

**6.** If an exothermic reaction has reached equilibrium, then increasing the temperature will
**A.** favor the forward reaction.
**B.** favor the reverse reaction.
**C.** favor both the forward and reverse reactions.
**D.** have no effect on the equilibrium.

**7.** Le Châtelier's principle states that
**A.** at equilibrium, the forward and reverse reaction rates are equal.
**B.** stresses include changes in concentrations, pressure, and temperature.
**C.** to relieve stress, solids and solvents are omitted from equilibrium constant expressions.
**D.** chemical equilibria respond to reduce applied stress.

**SHORT ANSWER**

**8.** Describe the conditions that would allow you to conclusively determine that a solution is saturated. You can use only visual observation and cannot add anything to the solution.

**9.** The graph below shows the neutralization curve for 100 mL of 0.100 M acid with 0.100 M base. Which letter represents the equivalence point? What type of acid and base produced this curve?

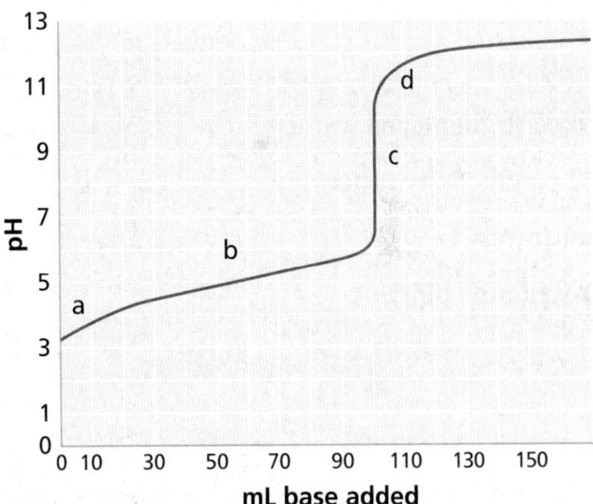


**EXTENDED RESPONSE**

**10.** Explain how the same buffer can resist a change in pH when either an acid or a base is added. Give an example.

**Test TIP** Keeping a positive attitude during any test will help you focus on the test and likely improve your score.

# Measuring $K_a$ for Acetic Acid

## OBJECTIVES

- *Compare* the conductivities of solutions of known and unknown hydronium ion concentrations.
- *Relate* conductivity to the concentration of ions in solution.
- *Explain* the validity of the procedure on the basis of the definitions of strong and weak acids.
- *Compute* the numerical value of $K_a$ for acetic acid.

## MATERIALS

- 1.0 M acetic acid, $CH_3COOH$
- 1.0 M hydrochloric acid, HCl
- 24-well plate
- distilled or deionized water
- LED conductivity testers
- paper towels
- thin-stemmed pipets

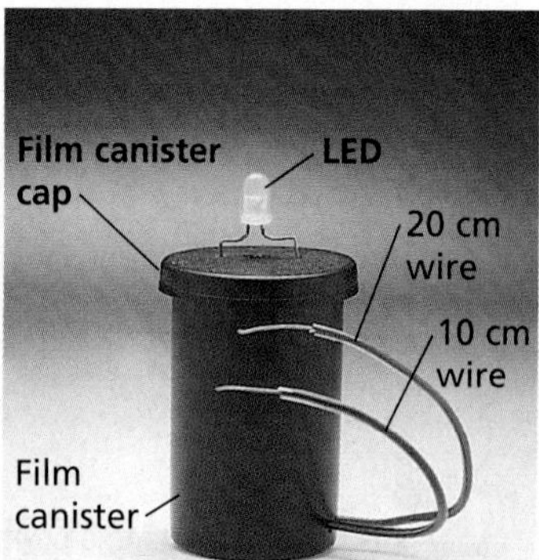


Teacher-made LED conductivity tester

## BACKGROUND

The acid dissociation constant, $K_a$, is a measure of the strength of an acid. Strong acids are completely ionized in water. Because weak acids are only partly ionized, they have a characteristic $K_a$ value. Properties that depend on the ability of a substance to ionize, such as conductivity and colligative properties, can be used to measure $K_a$. In this experiment, you will compare the conductivity of a 1.0 M solution of acetic acid, $CH_3COOH$, a weak acid, with the conductivities of solutions of varying concentrations of hydrochloric acid, HCl, a strong acid. From the comparisons you make, you will be able to estimate the concentration of hydronium ions in the acetic acid solution and calculate its $K_a$.

## SAFETY

For review of safety, please see **Safety in the Chemistry Laboratory** in the front of your book.

## PREPARATION

1. Create a table with two columns for recording your observations. Head the first column "HCl concentration." A wide second column can be headed "Observations and comparisons."

## PROCEDURE

1. Obtain samples of 1.0 M HCl solution and 1.0 M $CH_3COOH$ solution.
2. Place 20 drops of HCl in one well of a 24-well plate. Place 20 drops of $CH_3COOH$ in an adjacent well. Label the location of each sample.
3. Test the HCl and $CH_3COOH$ with the conductivity tester. Note the relative intensity of the

tester light for each solution. After testing, rinse the tester probes with distilled water. Remove any excess moisture with a paper towel.

4. Place 18 drops of distilled water in each of six wells in your 24-well plate. Add 2 drops of 1.0 M HCl to the first well to make a total of 20 drops of solution. Mix the contents of this well thoroughly by picking the contents up in a pipet and returning them to the well.

5. Repeat this procedure by taking 2 drops of the previous dilution and placing it in the next well containing 18 drops of water. Return any unused solution in the pipet to the well from which it was taken. Mix the new solution with a new pipet. (You now have 1.0 M HCl in the well from Procedure step 2, 0.10 M HCl in the first dilution well, and 0.010 M HCl in the second dilution.)

6. Continue diluting in this manner until you have six successive dilutions. The $[H_3O^+]$ should now range from 1.0 M to $1.0 \times 10^{-6}$ M. Write the concentrations in the first column of your data table.

7. Using the conductivity tester, test the cells containing HCl in order from most concentrated to least concentrated. Note the brightness of the tester bulb, and compare it with the brightness of the bulb when it was placed in the acetic acid solution. (Retest the acetic acid well any time for comparison.) After each test, rinse the tester probes with distilled water, and use a paper towel to remove any excess moisture. When the brightness produced by one of the HCl solutions is about the same as that produced by the acetic acid, you can infer that the two solutions have about the same hydronium ion concentration and that the pH of the HCl solution is equal to the pH of the acetic acid. If the glow from the bulb is too faint to see, turn off the lights or build a light shield around your conductivity tester bulb.

8. Record the results of your observations by noting which HCl concentration causes the intensity of the bulb to most closely match that of the bulb when it is in acetic acid. (Hint: If the conductivity of no single HCl concentration matches that of the acetic acid, then estimate the value between the two concentrations that match the best.)

## CLEANUP AND DISPOSAL

9. Clean your lab station. Clean all equipment, and return it to its proper place. Dispose of chemicals and solutions in containers designated by your teacher. Do not pour any chemicals down the drain or throw anything in the trash unless your teacher directs you to do so. Wash your hands thoroughly after all work is finished and before you leave the lab.

## ANALYSIS AND INTERPRETATION

1. **Resolving Discrepancies:** How did the conductivity of the 1.0 M HCl solution compare with that of the 1.0 M $CH_3COOH$ solution? Why do you think this was so?

2. **Organizing Data:** What is the $H_3O^+$ concentration of the HCl solution that most closely matched the conductivity of the acetic acid?

3. **Drawing Conclusions:** What was the $H_3O^+$ concentration of the 1.0 M $CH_3COOH$ solution? Why?

## CONCLUSIONS

1. **Applying Models:** The acid ionization expression for $CH_3COOH$ is the following:

$$K_a = \frac{[H_3O^+][CH_3COO^-]}{[CH_3COOH]}$$

Use your answer to Analysis and Interpretation item 3 to calculate $K_a$ for the acetic acid solution.

2. **Applying Models:** Explain how it is possible for solutions of HCl and $CH_3COOH$ to show the same conductivity but have different concentrations.

## EXTENSIONS

1. **Evaluating Methods:** Compare the $K_a$ value that you calculated with the value found on page 606 of your text. Calculate the percent error for this experiment.

2. **Predicting Outcomes:** Lactic acid ($HOOCCHOHCH_3$) has a $K_a$ of $1.4 \times 10^{-4}$. Predict whether a solution of lactic acid would cause the conductivity tester to glow brighter or dimmer than a solution of acetic acid with the same concentration. How noticeable would the difference be?

CHAPTER 19

# Oxidation-Reduction Reactions

*Copper oxidizes in air to form the green patina you see on this building.*

Columbus Tower, San Francisco

# Oxidation and Reduction

SECTION 1

## OBJECTIVES

- Assign oxidation numbers to reactant and product species.
- Define *oxidation* and *reduction.*
- Explain what an oxidation-reduction reaction (redox reaction) is.

SC **C.4.7** Summarize the oxidation and reduction processes (including oxidizing and reducing agents)

Oxidation-reduction reactions involve a transfer of electrons. Oxidation involves the loss of electrons, whereas reduction involves the gain of electrons. Reduction and oxidation half-reactions must occur simultaneously. These processes can be identified through the understanding and use of oxidation numbers (oxidation states).

## Oxidation States

Oxidation states were defined in Chapter 7. The oxidation number assigned to an element in a molecule is based on the distribution of electrons in that molecule. The rules by which oxidation numbers are assigned were given in Chapter 7. These rules are summarized in **Table 1.**

**TABLE 1 *Rules for Assigning Oxidation Numbers***

| Rule | Example |
|---|---|
| 1. The oxidation number of any pure element is 0. | The oxidation number of Na(*s*) is 0. |
| 2. The oxidation number of a monatomic ion equals the charge on the ion. | The oxidation number of $Cl^-$ is –1. |
| 3. The more electronegative element in a binary compound is assigned the number equal to the charge it would have if it were an ion. | The oxidation number of O in NO is –2. |
| 4. The oxidation number of fluorine in a compound is always –1. | The oxidation number of F in LiF is –1. |
| 5. Oxygen has an oxidation number of –2 unless it is combined with F, in which it is +1 or +2, or it is in a peroxide, in which it is –1. | The oxidation number of O in $NO_2$ is –2. |
| 6. Hydrogen's oxidation state in most of its compounds is +1 unless it is combined with a metal, in which case it is –1. | The oxidation number of H in LiH is –1. |
| 7. In compounds, Group 1 and 2 elements and aluminum have oxidation numbers of +1, +2, and +3, respectively. | The oxidation number of Ca in $CaCO_3$ is +2. |
| 8. The sum of the oxidation numbers of all atoms in a neutral compound is 0. | The oxidation number of C in $CaCO_3$ is +4. |
| 9. The sum of the oxidation numbers of all atoms in a polyatomic ion equals the charge of the ion. | The oxidation number of P in $H_2PO_4^-$ is +5. |

FIGURE 1 The color of solutions containing chromium compounds changes with the oxidation state of chromium.

Chromium provides a very visual example of oxidation numbers. Different oxidation states of chromium have dramatically different colors, as can be seen in **Figure 1.** Solutions with the same oxidation state show less dramatic differences. The chromium(II) chloride solution is blue, chromium(III) chloride solution is green, potassium chromate solution is yellow, and potassium dichromate solution is orange.

## Oxidation

FIGURE 2 Sodium and chlorine react violently to form NaCl. The synthesis of NaCl from its elements illustrates the oxidation-reduction process.

*Processes in which the atoms or ions of an element experience an increase in oxidation state are* **oxidation** *processes.* The combustion of metallic sodium in an atmosphere of chlorine gas is shown in **Figure 2.** The sodium ions and chloride ions produced during this strongly exothermic reaction form a cubic crystal lattice in which sodium cations are ionically bonded to chloride anions. The chemical equation for this reaction is written as follows.

$$2\text{Na}(s) + \text{Cl}_2(g) \longrightarrow 2\text{NaCl}(s)$$

The formation of sodium ions illustrates an oxidation process because each sodium atom loses an electron to become a sodium ion. The oxidation state is represented by placing an oxidation number above the symbol of the atom and the ion.

$$\overset{0}{\text{Na}} \longrightarrow \overset{+1}{\text{Na}^+} + e^-$$

The oxidation state of sodium has changed from 0, its elemental state, to the +1 state of the ion (Rules 1 and 7, **Table 1**). *A species whose oxidation number increases is* **oxidized.** The sodium atom is *oxidized* to a sodium ion.

## Reduction

*Processes in which the oxidation state of an element decreases are* **reduction** *processes.* Consider the behavior of chlorine in its reaction with sodium. Each chlorine atom accepts an electron and becomes a chloride ion. The oxidation state of chlorine decreases from 0 to –1 for the chloride ion (Rules 1 and 2, **Table 1**).

$$\overset{0}{Cl_2} + 2e^- \longrightarrow 2\overset{-1}{Cl^-}$$

*A species that undergoes a decrease in oxidation state is* **reduced.** The chlorine atom is reduced to the chloride ion.

**FIGURE 3** Copper is oxidized and nitrogen dioxide is produced when this penny is placed in a concentrated nitric acid solution.

## Oxidation and Reduction as a Process

Electrons are released in oxidation and acquired in reduction. Therefore, for oxidation to occur during a chemical reaction, reduction must also occur. Furthermore, the number of electrons produced in oxidation must equal the number of electrons acquired in reduction. This makes sense when you recall that electrons are negatively charged and that for charge to be conserved, the number of electrons lost must equal the number of electrons gained. You learned in Chapter 8 that mass is conserved in any chemical reaction. Therefore, the masses of the elements that undergo oxidation and reduction and the electrons that are exchanged are conserved.

A transfer of electrons causes changes in the oxidation states of one or more elements. *Any chemical process in which elements undergo changes in oxidation number is an* **oxidation-reduction reaction.** This name is often shortened to **redox reaction.** An example of a redox reaction can be seen in **Figure 3,** in which copper is being oxidized and $NO_3^-$ from nitric acid is being reduced. *The part of the reaction involving oxidation or reduction alone can be written as a* **half-reaction.** The overall equation for a redox reaction is the sum of two half-reactions. Because the number of electrons involved is the same for oxidation and reduction, they cancel each other out and do not appear in the overall chemical equation. Equations for the reaction between nitric acid and copper illustrate the relationship between half-reactions and the overall redox reaction.

$$\overset{0}{Cu} \longrightarrow \overset{+2}{Cu^{2+}} + 2e^- \qquad \text{(oxidation half-reaction)}$$

$$2\overset{+5\,-2}{NO_3^-} + 2e^- + 4\overset{+1}{H^+} \longrightarrow 2\overset{+4\,-2}{NO_2} + 2\overset{+1\,-2}{H_2O} \qquad \text{(reduction half-reaction)}$$

$$\overset{0}{Cu} + 2\overset{+5}{NO_3^-} + 4H^+ \longrightarrow \overset{+2}{Cu^{2+}} + 2\overset{+4}{NO_2} + 2H_2O \qquad \text{(redox reaction)}$$

Notice that electrons lost in oxidation appear on the product side of the oxidation half-reaction. Electrons are gained in reduction and

# Chemistry in Action

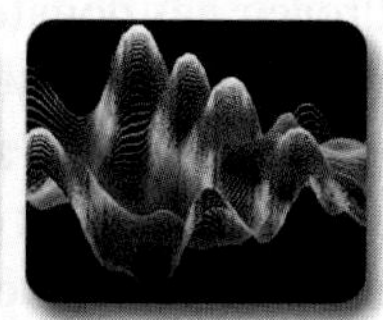
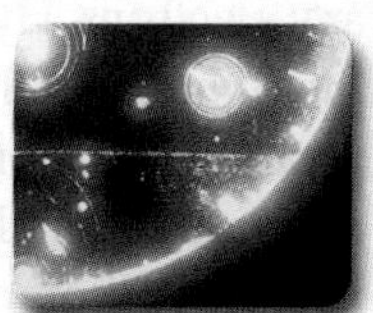

## Skunk-Spray Remedy

Have you ever given your pet a tomato juice bath to get rid of the smell of skunk spray on its coat? Chemistry has a much better way of conquering skunk spray.

Paul Krebaum, the inventor of a new "deskunking" formula, says that while working as a materials engineer, he constantly had to deal with the less-than-pleasant smell of the hydrogen sulfide gas that was released from one of his experiments. Venting off the gas only partially solved the problem. A better solution would be to eliminate the smell entirely.

Mr. Krebaum rifled through his old chemistry books and found that hydrogen peroxide could oxidize these sulfur-containing compounds to much less smelly components. He immediately whipped up a hydrogen peroxide mixture, and it worked like a charm.

The equation below shows that hydrogen sulfide reacts with $H_2O_2$ to form sulfate compounds that do not have a bad odor.

$$2NaOH + 4H_2O_2 + H_2S \longrightarrow Na_2SO_4 + 6H_2O$$

"The receptors that are in your nose are sensitive to sulfur in its low oxidation state," says Mr. Krebaum. "However, they are not sensitive to sulfur in its high oxidation state."

Some time later, a friend of Mr. Krebaum's complained to him that a skunk had sprayed his pet.

▲*Skunk spray gets its odor from chemicals called* mercaptans.

Because the odor in a skunk's spray also comes from compounds containing sulfur in a low oxidation state, Mr. Krebaum thought his solution might also work on this age-old problem. He mixed up a milder version to try out on the pet: 1 qt of a 3% hydrogen peroxide solution, 1/4 cup of baking soda, and 1 tsp of liquid soap. His friend tried it out, and the result was one wet and unhappy—but much less smelly—pet.

Mr. Krebaum says that the hydrogen peroxide in the remedy actually oxidizes the compounds, while the baking soda reduces the acidity of the mixture and the soap helps to wash out the greasy skunk spray. This reaction can be seen in the following equation. The symbol *R* represents all the other elements in the sulfur-containing compound that is in skunk spray.

$$RSH + 3H_2O_2 + NaHCO_3 \longrightarrow RSO_3Na + 4H_2O + CO_2$$

The pet should be thoroughly washed with the mixture, and care should be taken to avoid the eyes. If the mixture is left on for a few minutes—long enough for the reaction to occur—and then rinsed away with tap water, the smell will disappear.

The formula does not bleach or cause any other negative side effects. Mr. Krebaum does have one warning: Mix the formula just before using it, because the mixture breaks down quickly. The reaction releases oxygen, so the formula should not be kept in a sealed container. Pressure will build up, and the lid could eventually blow off. For this reason, bottles of "Krebaum's Skunkinator" will not be appearing on drugstore shelves any time soon.

### Questions

1. How did Paul Krebaum's research into the properties of $H_2S$ result in a benefit to dog owners?
2. What are some possible packaging designs that Paul Krebaum could have used if he had wanted to sell his formula?

# Balancing Redox Equations

**C.4.7** Summarize the oxidation and reduction processes (including oxidizing and reducing agents)

SECTION 2

*OBJECTIVES*

- Explain what must be conserved in redox equations.
- Balance redox equations by using the half-reaction method.

Equations for simple redox reactions can be balanced by inspection, which you learned to do in Chapter 8. Most redox equations, however, require more systematic methods. The equation-balancing process requires the use of oxidation numbers. In a balanced equation, both charge and mass are conserved. Although oxidation and reduction half-reactions occur together, their reaction equations are balanced separately and then combined to give the balanced redox-reaction equation.

## Half-Reaction Method

The *half-reaction method,* or ion-electron method, for balancing redox equations consists of seven steps. Oxidation numbers are assigned to all atoms and polyatomic ions to determine which species are part of the redox process. The oxidation and reduction equations are balanced separately for mass and charge. They are then added together to produce a complete balanced equation. These seven steps are applied to balance the reaction of hydrogen sulfide and nitric acid. Sulfuric acid, nitrogen dioxide, and water are the products of the reaction.

**1.** *Write the formula equation if it is not given in the problem. Then write the ionic equation.*

Formula equation: $H_2S + HNO_3 \longrightarrow H_2SO_4 + NO_2 + H_2O$

Ionic equation: $H_2S + H^+ + NO_3^- \longrightarrow 2H^+ + SO_4^{2-} + NO_2 + H_2O$

**2.** *Assign oxidation numbers. Delete substances containing only elements that do not change oxidation state.*

$$\overset{+1\,-2}{H_2S} + \overset{+1}{H^+} + \overset{+5\,-2}{NO_3^-} \longrightarrow 2\overset{+1}{H^+} + \overset{+6\,-2}{SO_4^{2-}} + \overset{+4\,-2}{NO_2} + \overset{+1\,-2}{H_2O}$$

The sulfur changes oxidation state from −2 to +6. The nitrogen changes oxidation state from +5 to +4. The other substances are deleted.

$$\overset{+1\,-2}{H_2S} + \overset{+5\,-2}{NO_3^-} \longrightarrow \overset{+6\,-2}{SO_4^{2-}} + \overset{+4\,-2}{NO_2}$$

The remaining species are used in step 3.

extension

**CROSS-DISCIPLINARY**

Go to **go.hrw.com** for a full-length article on redox reactions in photosynthesis.

**Keyword: HC6OXRX**

3. *Write the half-reaction for oxidation.* In this example, the sulfur is being oxidized.

$$\overset{-2}{H_2S} \longrightarrow \overset{+6}{SO_4^{2-}}$$

- *Balance the atoms.* To balance the oxygen in this half-reaction, $H_2O$ must be added to the left side. This gives 10 extra hydrogen atoms on that side of the equation. Therefore, 10 hydrogen ions are added to the right side. In basic solution, $OH^-$ ions and water may be used to balance atoms.

$$\overset{-2}{H_2S} + 4H_2O \longrightarrow \overset{+6}{SO_4^{2-}} + 10H^+$$

- *Balance the charge.* Electrons are added to the side having the greater positive net charge. The left side of the equation has no net charge; the right side has a net charge of 8+. For the charges to balance, each side must have the same net charge. Therefore, 8 electrons are added to the product side so that it has no charge and balances with the reactant side of the equation. Notice that the oxidation of sulfur from a state of –2 to +6 indicates a loss of 8 electrons.

$$\overset{-2}{H_2S} + 4H_2O \longrightarrow \overset{+6}{SO_4^{2-}} + 10H^+ + 8e^-$$

The oxidation half-reaction is now balanced.

4. *Write the half-reaction for reduction.* In this example, nitrogen is being reduced from a +5 state to a +4 state.

$$\overset{+5}{NO_3^-} \longrightarrow \overset{+4}{NO_2}$$

- *Balance the atoms.* $H_2O$ must be added to the product side of the reaction to balance the oxygen atoms. Therefore, two hydrogen ions must be added to the reactant side to balance the hydrogen atoms.

$$\overset{+5}{NO_3^-} + 2H^+ \longrightarrow \overset{+4}{NO_2} + H_2O$$

- *Balance the charge.* Electrons are added to the side having the greater positive net charge. The left side of the equation has a net charge of 1+. Therefore, 1 electron must be added to this side to balance the charge.

$$\overset{+5}{NO_3^-} + 2H^+ + e^- \longrightarrow \overset{+4}{NO_2} + H_2O$$

The reduction half-reaction is now balanced.

5. *Conserve charge by adjusting the coefficients in front of the electrons so that the number lost in oxidation equals the number gained in reduction.* Write the ratio of the number of electrons lost to the number of electrons gained.

$$\frac{e^- \text{ lost in oxidation}}{e^- \text{ gained in reduction}} = \frac{8}{1}$$

This ratio is already in its lowest terms. If it were not, it would need to be reduced. Multiply the oxidation half-reaction by 1 (it remains unchanged) and the reduction half-reaction by 8. The number of electrons lost now equals the number of electrons gained.

$$1\left(\overset{-2}{H_2S} + 4H_2O \longrightarrow \overset{+6}{SO_4^{2-}} + 10H^+ + 8e^-\right)$$

$$8\left(\overset{+5}{NO_3^-} + 2H^+ + e^- \longrightarrow \overset{+4}{NO_2} + H_2O\right)$$

**6.** *Combine the half-reactions, and cancel out anything common to both sides of the equation.*

$$\overset{-2}{H_2S} + 4H_2O \longrightarrow \overset{+6}{SO_4^{2-}} + 10H^+ + 8e^-$$

$$8\overset{+5}{NO_3^-} + 16H^+ + 8e^- \longrightarrow 8\overset{+4}{NO_2} + 8H_2O$$

$$8\overset{+5}{NO_3^-} + \overset{6}{\cancel{16}}H^+ + \cancel{8e^-} + \overset{-2}{H_2S} + \cancel{4H_2O} \longrightarrow$$

$$8\overset{+4}{NO_2} + \overset{4}{\cancel{8}}H_2O + \overset{+6}{SO_4^{2-}} + \cancel{10}H^+ + \cancel{8e^-}$$

Each side of the above equation has $10H^+$, $8e^-$, and $4H_2O$. These cancel each other out and do not appear in the balanced equation.

$$8\overset{+5}{NO_3^-} + \overset{-2}{H_2S} + 6H^+ \longrightarrow 8\overset{+4}{NO_2} + 4H_2O + \overset{+6}{SO_4^{2-}}$$

**7.** *Combine ions to form the compounds shown in the original formula equation. Check to ensure that all other ions balance.* The $NO_3^-$ ion appeared as nitric acid in the original equation. There are only 6 hydrogen ions to pair with the 8 nitrate ions. Therefore, 2 hydrogen ions must be added to complete this formula. If 2 hydrogen ions are added to the left side of the equation, 2 hydrogen ions must also be added to the right side of the equation.

$$8HNO_3 + H_2S \longrightarrow 8NO_2 + 4H_2O + SO_4^{2-} + 2H^+$$

The sulfate ion appeared as sulfuric acid in the original equation. The hydrogen ions added to the right side are used to complete the formula for sulfuric acid.

$$8HNO_3 + H_2S \longrightarrow 8NO_2 + 4H_2O + H_2SO_4$$

A final check must be made to ensure that all elements are correctly balanced.

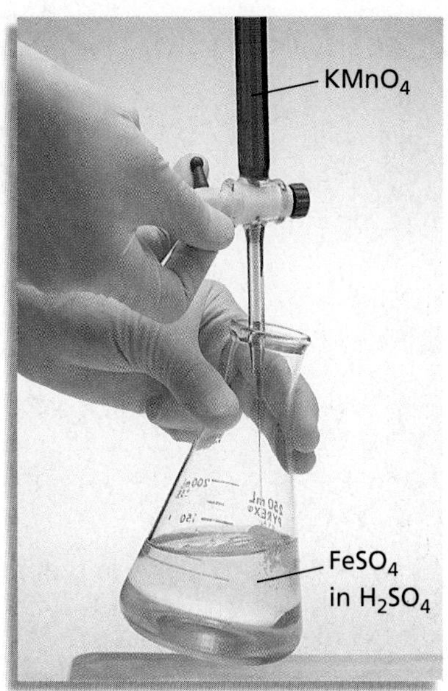


**FIGURE 4** As a $KMnO_4$ solution is titrated into an acidic solution of $FeSO_4$, deep purple $MnO_4^-$ ions are reduced to colorless $Mn^{2+}$ ions. When all $Fe^{2+}$ ions are oxidized, $MnO_4^-$ ions are no longer reduced to colorless $Mn^{2+}$ ions. Thus, the first faint appearance of the $MnO_4^-$ color indicates the end point of the titration.

## SAMPLE PROBLEM A

*For more help, go to the* ***Math Tutor*** *at the end of this chapter.*

**Write a balanced equation for the reaction shown in Figure 4. A deep purple solution of potassium permanganate is titrated with a colorless solution of iron(II) sulfate and sulfuric acid. The products are iron(III) sulfate, manganese(II) sulfate, potassium sulfate, and water—all of which are colorless.**

**SOLUTION** 1. *Write the formula equation if it is not given in the problem. Then write the ionic equation.*

$$KMnO_4 + FeSO_4 + H_2SO_4 \longrightarrow Fe_2(SO_4)_3 + MnSO_4 + K_2SO_4 + H_2O$$

$$K^+ + MnO_4^- + Fe^{2+} + SO_4^{2-} + 2H^+ + SO_4^{2-} \longrightarrow$$
$$2Fe^{3+} + 3SO_4^{2-} + Mn^{2+} + SO_4^{2-} + 2K^+ + SO_4^{2-} + H_2O$$

2. *Assign oxidation numbers to each element and ion. Delete substances containing an element that does not change oxidation state.*

$$\overset{+1}{K^+} + \overset{+7\ -2}{MnO_4^-} + \overset{+2}{Fe^{2+}} + \overset{+6\ -2}{SO_4^{2-}} + \overset{+1}{2H^+} + \overset{+6\ -2}{SO_4^{2-}} \longrightarrow$$
$$\overset{+3}{2Fe^{3+}} + \overset{+6\ -2}{3SO_4^{2-}} + \overset{+2}{Mn^{2+}} + \overset{+6\ -2}{SO_4^{2-}} + \overset{+1}{2K^+} + \overset{+6\ -2}{SO_4^{2-}} + \overset{+1\ -2}{H_2O}$$

Only ions or molecules whose oxidation numbers change are retained.

$$\overset{+7\ -2}{MnO_4^-} + \overset{+2}{Fe^{2+}} \longrightarrow \overset{+3}{Fe^{3+}} + \overset{+2}{Mn^{2+}}$$

3. *Write the half-reaction for oxidation.* The iron shows the increase in oxidation number. Therefore, it is oxidized.

$$\overset{+2}{Fe^{2+}} \longrightarrow \overset{+3}{Fe^{3+}}$$

- *Balance the mass.* The mass is already balanced.
- *Balance the charge.*

$$\overset{+2}{Fe^{2+}} \longrightarrow \overset{+3}{Fe^{3+}} + e^-$$

4. *Write the half-reaction for reduction.* Manganese shows a change in oxidation number from +7 to +2. It is reduced.

$$\overset{+7}{MnO_4^-} \longrightarrow \overset{+2}{Mn^{2+}}$$

- *Balance the mass.* Water and hydrogen ions must be added to balance the oxygen atoms in the permanganate ion.

$$\overset{+7}{MnO_4^-} + 8H^+ \longrightarrow \overset{+2}{Mn^{2+}} + 4H_2O$$

- *Balance the charge.*

$$\overset{+7}{MnO_4^-} + 8H^+ + 5e^- \longrightarrow \overset{+2}{Mn^{2+}} + 4H_2O$$

5. *Adjust the coefficients to conserve charge.*

$$\frac{e^- \text{ lost in oxidation}}{e^- \text{ gained in reduction}} = \frac{1}{5}$$

$$5(Fe^{2+} \longrightarrow Fe^{3+} + e^-)$$
$$1(MnO_4^- + 8H^+ + 5e^- \longrightarrow Mn^{2+} + 4H_2O)$$

6. *Combine the half-reactions and cancel.*

$$5Fe^{2+} \longrightarrow 5Fe^{3+} + 5e^-$$
$$MnO_4^- + 8H^+ + 5e^- \longrightarrow Mn^{2+} + 4H_2O$$

$$MnO_4^- + 5Fe^{2+} + 8H^+ + \cancel{5e^-} \longrightarrow Mn^{2+} + 5Fe^{3+} + 4H_2O + \cancel{5e^-}$$

7. *Combine ions to form compounds from the original equation.* The iron(III) product appears in the original equation as $Fe_2(SO_4)_3$. Every iron(III) sulfate molecule requires two iron ions. Therefore, the entire equation must be multiplied by 2 to provide an even number of iron ions.

$$2(5Fe^{2+} + MnO_4^- + 8H^+ \longrightarrow 5Fe^{3+} + Mn^{2+} + 4H_2O)$$
$$10Fe^{2+} + 2MnO_4^- + 16H^+ \longrightarrow 10Fe^{3+} + 2Mn^{2+} + 8H_2O$$

The iron(II), iron(III), manganese(II), and 2 hydrogen ions in the original equation are paired with sulfate ions. Iron(II) sulfate requires 10 sulfate ions, and sulfuric acid requires 8 sulfate ions. To balance the equation, 18 sulfate ions must be added to each side. On the product side, 15 of these ions form iron(III) sulfate, and 2 of them form manganese(II) sulfate. That leaves 1 sulfate ion unaccounted for. The permanganate ion requires the addition of 2 potassium ions to each side. These 2 potassium ions form potassium sulfate on the product side of the reaction.

$$10FeSO_4 + 2KMnO_4 + 8H_2SO_4 \longrightarrow 5Fe_2(SO_4)_3 + 2MnSO_4 + K_2SO_4 + 8H_2O$$

Final inspection shows that atoms and charges are balanced.

**PRACTICE**

*Answers in Appendix E*

1. Copper reacts with hot, concentrated sulfuric acid to form copper(II) sulfate, sulfur dioxide, and water. Write and balance the equation for this reaction.

2. Write and balance the equation for the reaction between nitric acid and potassium iodide. The products are potassium nitrate, iodine, nitrogen monoxide, and water.

Go to **go.hrw.com** for more practice problems that ask you to balance redox equations.

**Keyword: HC6OXRX**

## SECTION REVIEW

1. What two quantities are conserved in redox equations?

2. Why do we add $H^+$ and $H_2O$ to some half-reactions and $OH^-$ and $H_2O$ to others?

3. Balance the following redox reaction:
   $Na_2SnO_2 + Bi(OH)_3 \longrightarrow Bi + Na_2SnO_3 + H_2O$

**Critical Thinking**

4. **RELATING IDEAS** When heated, elemental phosphorus, $P_4$, produces phosphine, $PH_3$, and phosphoric acid, $H_3PO_4$. How many grams of phosphine are produced if 56 g $P_4$ have reacted?

# QuickLAB

Wear safety goggles and an apron.

## Redox Reactions

### Materials

- aluminum foil
- beaker, 250 mL
- 1 M copper(II) chloride solution, $CuCl_2$
- 3% hydrogen peroxide
- manganese dioxide
- metric ruler
- scissors
- test-tube clamp
- test tube, 16 × 150 mm
- wooden splint

### Procedure

Record all of your results in a data table.

1. Put 10 mL of hydrogen peroxide in a test tube, and add a small amount of manganese dioxide (equal to the size of about half a pea). What is the result?
2. Insert a glowing wooden splint into the test tube (see diagram). What is the result? If oxygen is produced, a glowing wooden splint inserted into the test tube will glow brighter.
3. Fill the 250 mL beaker halfway with the copper(II) chloride solution.
4. Cut foil into 2 cm × 12 cm strips.
5. Add the aluminum strips to the copper(II) chloride solution. Use a glass rod to stir the mixture, and observe for 12 to 15 minutes. What is the result?

### Discussion

1. Write balanced equations showing what happened in each of the reactions.
2. Write a conclusion for the two experiments.

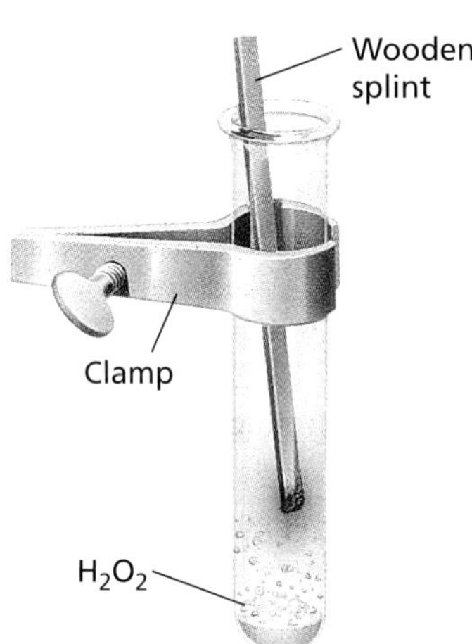


## Disproportionation

Some substances can be both reduced and oxidized easily. For example, peroxide ions, $O_2^{2-}$, have a relatively unstable covalent bond between the two oxygen atoms. The electron-dot formula is written as follows.

$$\left[:\ddot{\underset{..}{O}}:\ddot{\underset{..}{O}}:\right]^{2-}$$

Each oxygen atom has an oxidation number of −1. The peroxide ion structure represents an intermediate oxidation state between $O_2$ and $O^{2-}$. Therefore, the peroxide ion is highly reactive.

Hydrogen peroxide, $H_2O_2$, is a covalent compound. It decomposes into water and molecular oxygen, as shown in the equation below.

$$2H_2\overset{-1}{O}_2 \longrightarrow 2H_2\overset{-2}{O} + \overset{0}{O}_2$$

**FIGURE 6** A bombardier beetle can repel large predators such as frogs with a chemical defense mechanism that uses the disproportionation of hydrogen peroxide.

Notice that in this reaction, hydrogen peroxide is both oxidized and reduced. Oxygen atoms that become part of gaseous oxygen molecules are oxidized. The oxidation number of these oxygen atoms increases from –1 to 0. Oxygen atoms that become part of water are reduced. The oxidation number of these oxygen atoms decreases from –1 to –2. *A process in which a substance acts as both an oxidizing agent and a reducing agent is called* **disproportionation.** A substance that undergoes disproportionation is both *self-oxidizing* and *self-reducing.*

The bombardier beetle defends itself by spraying its enemies with an unpleasant hot chemical mixture, as shown in **Figure 6.** The catalyzed disproportionation of hydrogen peroxide produces hot oxygen gas. This gas gives the insect an ability to eject irritating chemicals from its abdomen with explosive force.

## SECTION REVIEW

1. Describe the chemical activity of the alkali metals and of the halogens on the basis of oxidizing and reducing strength.

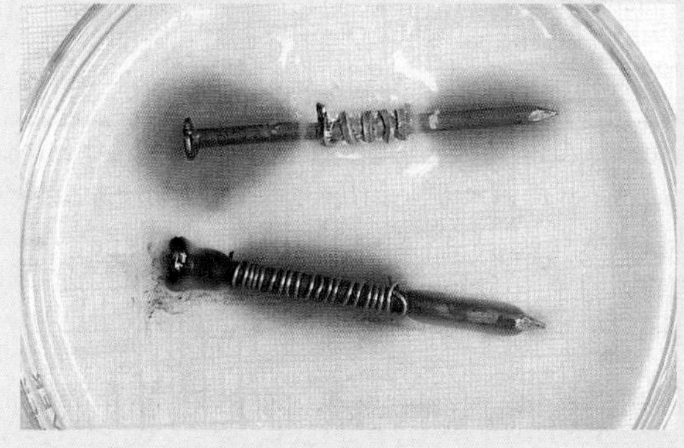

2. The photo on the left depicts two redox reactions. Both nails are in a sulfuric acid solution. Answer the following questions:
   **a.** When zinc is wrapped around an iron nail, is the iron or zinc oxidized?
   **b.** When copper is wrapped around an iron nail, is the iron or copper oxidized?
3. Would $Cl_2$ be reduced by $I^-$? Explain.
4. Which is the stronger oxidizing agent in each of the following pairs: $Cu^{2+}$ or $Al^{3+}$, $I_2$ or S, $F_2$ or $Li^+$?
5. What is meant by *disproportionation*?

### Critical Thinking

6. **ORGANIZING IDEAS** In general, where in the periodic table are the elements found that in elemental form are the strongest oxidizing agents? Explain.

# CHAPTER HIGHLIGHTS

## Oxidation and Reduction

**Vocabulary**
oxidation
oxidized
reduction
reduced
oxidation-reduction reaction
redox reaction
half-reaction

- Oxidation numbers are assigned by the set of rules listed in **Table 1.** Oxidation numbers are based on the distribution of electrons in a molecule.
- Oxidation-reduction reactions consist of two half-reactions that must occur simultaneously.
- Oxidation-reduction reactions are identified by examining the changes in the oxidation numbers of atoms in the reactants and products.
- Oxidation involves the loss of electrons, and reduction involves the gain of electrons.
- A species whose oxidation number increases is oxidized. A species whose oxidation number decreases is reduced.

## Balancing Redox Equations

- Charge and mass are conserved in a balanced redox equation.
- In the half-reaction method for balancing equations, the atoms and charge of oxidation and reduction equations are balanced separately. Then, they are combined to give a complete balanced equation.
- In a half-reaction, the charge on the reactant side must equal the charge on the product side, but these charges do not need to be zero.
- For the half-reaction method, the atoms in each half-reaction are balanced by adding $H^+$ ions and $H_2O$ molecules in acidic solutions. If the solution is basic, $OH^-$ ions and $H_2O$ molecules are added to balance the atoms in each half-reaction.
- The number of electrons lost in the oxidation half-reaction must equal the number of electrons gained in the reduction half-reaction. The two half-reactions must be multiplied by appropriate factors to ensure that the same number of electrons are transferred.

## Oxidizing and Reducing Agents

**Vocabulary**
reducing agent
oxidizing agent
disproportionation

- The substance that is *reduced* in redox reactions is the *oxidizing agent* because it *acquires* electrons from the substance that is oxidized.
- The substance that is *oxidized* in a redox reaction is the *reducing agent* because it *supplies* the electrons to the substance that is reduced.
- Strong reducing agents are substances that easily give up electrons.
- Disproportionation is a process in which a substance is both an oxidizing agent and a reducing agent.

For more practice, go to the Problem Bank in Appendix D.

## Oxidation and Reduction

### SECTION 1 REVIEW

1. a. Distinguish between the processes of oxidation and reduction.
   b. Write an equation to illustrate each process.
2. Which of the following are redox reactions?
   a. $2Na + Cl_2 \longrightarrow 2NaCl$
   b. $C + O_2 \longrightarrow CO_2$
   c. $2H_2O \longrightarrow 2H_2 + O_2$
   d. $NaCl + AgNO_3 \longrightarrow AgCl + NaNO_3$
   e. $NH_3 + HCl \longrightarrow NH_4^+ + Cl^-$
   f. $2KClO_3 \longrightarrow 2KCl + 3O_2$
   g. $H_2 + Cl_2 \longrightarrow 2HCl$
   h. $H_2SO_4 + 2KOH \longrightarrow K_2SO_4 + 2H_2O$
   i. $Zn + CuSO_4 \longrightarrow ZnSO_4 + Cu$
3. For each oxidation-reduction reaction in the previous question, identify what is oxidized and what is reduced.

### PRACTICE PROBLEMS

4. Each of the following atom/ion pairs undergoes the oxidation number change indicated below. For each pair, determine whether oxidation or reduction has occurred, and then write the electronic equation indicating the corresponding number of electrons lost or gained.
   a. $K \longrightarrow K^+$
   b. $S \longrightarrow S^{2-}$
   c. $Mg \longrightarrow Mg^{2+}$
   d. $F^- \longrightarrow F_2$
   e. $H_2 \longrightarrow H^+$
   f. $O_2 \longrightarrow O^{2-}$
   g. $Fe^{3+} \longrightarrow Fe^{2+}$
   h. $Mn^{2+} \longrightarrow MnO_4^-$
5. Identify the following reactions as redox or nonredox:
   a. $2NH_4Cl(aq) + Ca(OH)_2(aq) \longrightarrow 2NH_3(aq) + 2H_2O(l) + CaCl_2(aq)$
   b. $2HNO_3(aq) + 3H_2S(g) \longrightarrow 2NO(g) + 4H_2O(l) + 3S(s)$
   c. $[Be(H_2O)_4]^{2+}(aq) + H_2O(l) \longrightarrow H_3O^+(aq) + [Be(H_2O)_3OH]^+(aq)$
6. Arrange the following in order of increasing oxidation number of the xenon atom: $CsXeF_8$, Xe, $XeF_2$, $XeOF_2$, $XeO_3$, and XeF.
7. Determine the oxidation number of each atom indicated in the following:
   a. $H_2$
   b. $H_2O$
   c. Al
   d. MgO
   e. $Al_2S_3$
   f. $HNO_3$
   g. $H_2SO_4$
   h. $Ca(OH)_2$
   i. $Fe(NO_3)_2$
   j. $O_2$

## Balancing Redox Equations

### SECTION 2 REVIEW

8. Label the following half-reactions as either reduction or oxidation half-reactions.
   a. $H_2S \longrightarrow S + 2e^- + 2H^+$
   b. $SO_2 + 4e^- + 2H_2O \longrightarrow S + 4OH^-$
   c. $ClO_3^- + 6H^+ + 6e^- \longrightarrow Cl^- + 3H_2O$
   d. $Mn(CN)_6^{4-} \longrightarrow Mn(CN)_6^{3-} + e^-$
9. What are the oxidation states of the elements that changed oxidation states in the half-reactions in the above question?
10. Balance the equation for the following reaction in a basic solution. Give balanced equations for both half-reactions and the balanced equation for the overall reaction.
    $KMnO_4 + NaIO_3 \longrightarrow MnO_2 + NaIO_4$

### PRACTICE PROBLEMS

11. For each requested step, use the half-reaction method to balance the oxidation-reduction equation below. (Hint: See Sample Problem A.)
    $$K + H_2O \longrightarrow KOH + H_2$$
    a. Write the ionic equation, and assign oxidation numbers to all atoms to determine what is oxidized and what is reduced.
    b. Write the equation for the reduction, and balance it for both atoms and charge.
    c. Write the equation for the oxidation, and balance it for both atoms and charge.
    d. Multiply the coefficients of the oxidation and reduction equations so that the number of electrons lost equals the number of electrons gained. Add the two equations.
    e. Add species as necessary to balance the overall formula equation.

**12.** Use the method in the previous problem to balance each of the reactions below.
a. $HI + HNO_2 \longrightarrow NO + I_2 + H_2O$
b. $FeCl_3 + H_2S \longrightarrow FeCl_2 + HCl + S$

**13.** Balance the equation for the reaction in which hot, concentrated sulfuric acid reacts with zinc to form zinc sulfate, hydrogen sulfide, and water.

## *Oxidizing and Reducing Agents*

### SECTION 3 REVIEW

**14.** a. Identify the most active reducing agent among all common elements.
b. Why are all of the elements in its group in the periodic table very active reducing agents?
c. Identify the most active oxidizing agent among the common elements.

**15.** Use **Table 3** to identify the strongest and weakest reducing agents among the substances listed within each of the following groupings:
a. Ca, Ag, Sn, $Cl^-$
b. Fe, Hg, Al, $Br^-$
c. $F^-$, Pb, $Mn^{2+}$, Na

**16.** Use **Table 3** to respond to each of the following:
a. Would Al be oxidized by $Ni^{2+}$?
b. Would Cu be oxidized by $Ag^+$?
c. Would Pb be oxidized by $Na^+$?
d. Would $F_2$ be reduced by $Cl^-$?
e. Would $Br_2$ be reduced by $Cl^-$?

## MIXED REVIEW

**17.** Identify the following reactions as redox or nonredox:
a. $Mg(s) + ZnCl_2(aq) \longrightarrow Zn(s) + MgCl_2(aq)$
b. $2H_2(g) + OF_2(g) \longrightarrow H_2O(g) + 2HF(g)$
c. $2KI(aq) + Pb(NO_3)_2(aq) \longrightarrow PbI_2(s) + 2KNO_3(aq)$
d. $CaO(s) + H_2O(l) \longrightarrow Ca(OH)_2(aq)$
e. $3CuCl_2(aq) + 2(NH_4)_3PO_4(aq) \longrightarrow 6NH_4Cl(aq) + Cu_3(PO_4)_2(s)$
f. $CH_4(g) + 2O_2(g) \longrightarrow CO_2(g) + 2H_2O(g)$

**18.** Arrange the following in order of decreasing oxidation number of the nitrogen atom: $N_2$, $NH_3$, $N_2O_4$, $N_2O$, $N_2H_4$, and $NO_3^-$.

**19.** Balance the following redox equations:
a. $SbCl_5 + KI \longrightarrow KCl + I_2 + SbCl_3$
b. $Ca(OH)_2 + NaOH + ClO_2 + C \longrightarrow NaClO_2 + CaCO_3 + H_2O$

**20.** Balance the following equations in basic solution:
a. $PbO_2 + KCl \longrightarrow KClO + KPb(OH)_3$
b. $KMnO_4 + KIO_3 \longrightarrow MnO_2 + KIO_4$
c. $K_2MnO_4 \longrightarrow MnO_2 + KMnO_4$

**21.** Balance the following equations in acidic solution:
a. $MnO_4^- + Cl^- \longrightarrow Mn^{2+} + HClO$
b. $NO_3^- + I_2 \longrightarrow IO_3^- + NO_2$
c. $NO_2^- \longrightarrow NO + NO_3^-$

## CRITICAL THINKING

**22. Interpreting Graphics** Given the activity table below, determine whether a reaction will occur or not. If the reaction will occur, give the products.

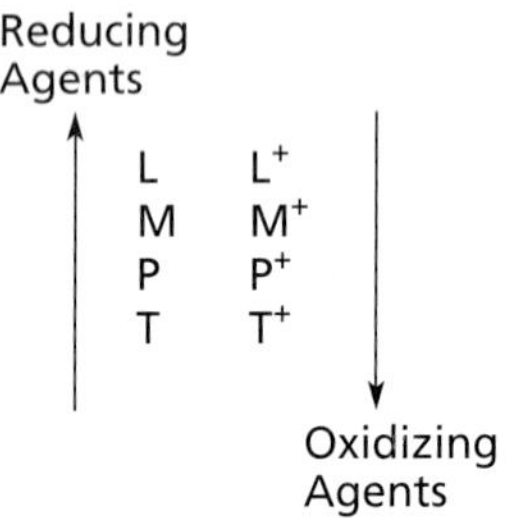


a. L and $M^+$
b. P and $M^+$
c. P and $T^+$

**23. Drawing Conclusions** A substance has an element in one of its highest possible oxidation states. Is this substance more likely to be an oxidizing agent or a reducing agent? Explain your reasoning.

24. **Drawing Conclusions** Use **Table 3** to decide if a redox reaction would occur between the two species, and if so, write the balanced equation. Explain your reasoning.
   a. $Cl_2$ and $Br_2$
   b. $Sn^{2+}$ and Zn

25. **Drawing Conclusions** An element that disproportionates must have at least how many different oxidation states? Explain your reasoning.

## USING THE HANDBOOK

26. Several reactions of aluminum are shown in the common reactions section for Group 13 of the *Elements Handbook*. Use these reactions to answer the following:
   a. Which of the five reactions shown are oxidation-reduction reactions? How do you know?
   b. For each redox reaction you listed in item **a,** identify what is oxidized and what is reduced.
   c. Write half-reactions for each equation you listed in item **a.**

27. Aluminum is described in Group 13 of the *Elements Handbook* as a self-protecting metal. This property of aluminum results from a redox reaction.
   a. Write the redox equation for the oxidation of aluminum.
   b. Write the half-reactions for this reaction, and show the number of electrons transferred.
   c. What problems are associated with the buildup of aluminum oxide on electrical wiring made of aluminum?

## RESEARCH & WRITING

28. Oxidizing agents are used in the cleaning industry. Research three different oxidizing agents used in this area, and write a report on the advantages and disadvantages of these compounds.

29. Oxidizing and reducing agents play important roles in biological systems. Research the role of one of these agents in a biological process. Write a report describing the process and the role of oxidation and reduction.

## ALTERNATIVE ASSESSMENT

30. Boilers are used to convert water to steam in electric power plants. Dissolved oxygen in the water promotes corrosion of the steel used in boiler parts. Explain how dissolved oxygen is removed from the water in boilers.

31. **Performance** For one day, record situations that show evidence of oxidation-reduction reactions. Identify the reactants and the products, and determine whether there is proof that a chemical reaction has taken place.

# Math Tutor BALANCING REDOX EQUATIONS

A redox equation must conserve both mass and charge. So, to balance a redox equation, you must balance both atoms and charge (electrons). The problem-solving tips and sample below show how to balance an equation for a redox reaction in *basic* solution.

## Problem-Solving TIPS

To balance redox equations for reactions in *basic* solution:

- Add $OH^-$ and $H_2O$ to balance oxygen and hydrogen in the redox half-reactions.
- Add $OH^-$ ions to the side of the equation that needs oxygen atoms. Make sure you add enough $OH^-$ ions so that the number of oxygen atoms added is twice the number needed.
- Then, add enough $H_2O$ molecules to the other side of the equation to balance the hydrogen atoms.

## SAMPLE

**The following unbalanced equation represents a redox reaction that takes place in a basic solution containing KOH. Balance the redox equation.**

$$Br_2(l) + KOH(aq) \longrightarrow KBr(aq) + KBrO_3(aq)$$

Write the full ionic equation, assign oxidation numbers, and eliminate species whose oxidation numbers do not change. The result is the following equation:

$$\overset{0}{Br_2} \longrightarrow \overset{-1}{Br^-} + \overset{+5}{BrO_3^-}$$

Divide this equation into half-reactions. Note that $Br_2$ is the reactant in both half-reactions.

Reduction: $Br_2 \longrightarrow Br^-$ Oxidation: $Br_2 \longrightarrow BrO_3^-$

Add $H_2O$ and $OH^-$ to balance atoms in basic solution. Then, add electrons to balance charge.

Reduction: $Br_2 + 2e^- \longrightarrow 2Br^-$ (no need to add $H_2O$ or $OH^-$)

Oxidation: $12OH^- + Br_2 \longrightarrow 2BrO_3^- + 6H_2O + 10e^-$

To balance transferred electrons, you must multiply the reduction half-reaction by 5 so that both reactions have $10e^-$.

$$5 \times (Br_2 + 2e^- \longrightarrow 2Br^-) = 5Br_2 + 10e^- \longrightarrow 10Br^-$$

Combining the two half-reactions gives

$$5Br_2 + 12OH^- + Br_2 + 10e^- \longrightarrow 10Br^- + 2BrO_3^- + 6H_2O + 10e^-$$

Canceling common species gives

$$6Br_2 + 12OH^- \longrightarrow 10Br^- + 2BrO_3^- + 6H_2O$$

Returning the potassium ions to the equation gives

$$6Br_2 + 12KOH \longrightarrow 10KBr + 2KBrO_3 + 6H_2O, \text{ or } 3Br_2 + 6KOH \longrightarrow 5KBr + KBrO_3 + 3H_2O$$

## PRACTICE PROBLEMS

**1.** Balance the following equation for a redox reaction that takes place in basic solution:
$MnO_2(s) + NaClO_3(aq) + NaOH(aq) \longrightarrow NaMnO_4(aq) + NaCl(aq) + H_2O(l)$

**2.** Balance the following equation for a redox reaction that takes place in basic solution:
$N_2O(g) + KClO(aq) + KOH(aq) \longrightarrow KCl(aq) + KNO_2(aq) + H_2O(l)$

# Standardized Test Prep

**Answer the following items on a separate piece of paper.**

**MULTIPLE CHOICE**

**1.** In the following reaction, which species is reduced?

$$2K + Br_2 \longrightarrow 2K^+ + 2Br^-$$

**A.** K
**B.** $Br_2$
**C.** All of the above
**D.** None of the above

**2.** The oxidation number of the sulfur atom in the $SO_4^{2-}$ ion is

**A.** +2.
**B.** −2.
**C.** +6.
**D.** +4.

**3.** A half-reaction

**A.** involves a change in the oxidation state of an element.
**B.** always contains $H_2O$ molecules.
**C.** always contains $H^+$ ions.
**D.** All of the above

**4.** In the following reaction, which is the oxidizing agent?

$$AgNO_2 + Cl_2 + 2KOH \longrightarrow AgNO_3 + 2KCl + H_2O$$

**A.** $AgNO_2$
**B.** $Cl_2$
**C.** KOH
**D.** KCl

**5.** What are the oxidation states (in increasing order) of the element that undergoes disproportionation in the following reaction:

$$Cl_2 + H_2O \longrightarrow HCl + HOCl$$

**A.** −1, 0, +2
**B.** −1, 0, +1
**C.** −2, −1, 0
**D.** None of the above

**6.** Which reaction is a redox reaction?

**A.** $Al_2O_3 + 6HCl \longrightarrow 2AlCl_3 + 3H_2O$
**B.** $2HCO_3^- \longrightarrow CO_2 + CO_3^{2-} + H_2O$
**C.** $SiBr_4 + 3H_2O \longrightarrow H_2SiO_3 + 4HBr$
**D.** $H_2O + PbO_2 + NaOH + KCl \longrightarrow KClO + NaPb(OH)_3$

**7.** Arrange the following in order of increasing oxidation number of the sulfur atom: $S_2O_3^{2-}$, $S_4O_6^{2-}$, $HSO_4^-$, and $H_2S$.

**A.** $H_2S$, $S_2O_3^{2-}$, $S_4O_6^{2-}$, $HSO_4^-$
**B.** $S_2O_3^{2-}$, $H_2S$, $S_4O_6^{2-}$, $HSO_4^-$
**C.** $H_2S$, $S_2O_3^{2-}$, $HSO_4^-$, $S_4O_6^{2-}$
**D.** $HSO_4^-$, $S_2O_3^{2-}$, $S_4O_6^{2-}$, $H_2S$

**8.** Which answer contains the correct information about the following reaction:

$$2Pb(NO_3)_2 \longrightarrow 2PbO + 4NO_2 + O_2$$

**A.** This reaction is a decomposition reaction and not a redox reaction.
**B.** This reaction is a redox reaction in which the lead is reduced and the oxygen is oxidized.
**C.** This reaction is a disproportionation reaction.
**D.** This reaction is a redox reaction in which the nitrogen is reduced and the oxygen is oxidized.

**SHORT ANSWER**

**9.** Determine the oxidation numbers for Cu in the superconductor $YBa_2Cu_3O_7$. Yttrium (Y) has an oxidation number of +3. (Cu does not have oxidation numbers greater than +3.) Give only integer oxidation numbers.

**10.** What is an oxidizing agent?

**EXTENDED RESPONSE**

**11.** B, F, K, and L are four unknown reducing agents that oxidize to singly charged cations. Using the following information, construct a table showing the relative strengths of the oxidizing and reducing agents. Data: F reduces $K^+$, $B^+$, and $L^+$. $B^+$ oxidizes K and F, but not L.

**12.** Balance the equation for the following reaction in basic solution:

$$ClO_2 \longrightarrow KClO_3 + KClO_2$$

Give the balanced equation for each half-reaction and for the overall reaction. Give the oxidizing agent and the reducing agent.

**Test TIP** If you are short on time, quickly scan the unanswered questions to see which might be easiest to answer.

# Reduction of Manganese in Permanganate Ion

## OBJECTIVES

- ***Demonstrate*** **proficiency in performing redox titrations and recognizing end points of a redox reaction.**
- ***Write*** **a balanced oxidation-reduction equation for a redox reaction.**
- ***Determine*** **the concentration of a solution by using stoichiometry and volume data from a titration.**

## MATERIALS

- **0.0200 M $KMnO_4$**
- **1.0 M $H_2SO_4$**
- **100 mL graduated cylinder**
- **125 mL Erlenmeyer flasks, 4**
- **250 mL beakers, 2**
- **400 mL beaker**
- **burets, 2**
- **distilled water**
- **double buret clamp**
- **$FeSO_4$ solution**
- **ring stand**
- **wash bottle**

## BACKGROUND

In Chapter 15, you studied acid-base titrations in which an unknown amount of acid is titrated with a carefully measured amount of base. In this procedure, a similar approach called a *redox titration* is used. In a redox titration, the reducing agent, $Fe^{2+}$, is oxidized to $Fe^{3+}$ by the oxidizing agent, $MnO_4^-$. When this process occurs, the Mn in $MnO_4^-$ changes from a +7 to a +2 oxidation state and has a noticeably different color. You can use this color change to signify a redox reaction "end point." When the reaction is complete, any excess $MnO_4^-$ added to the reaction mixture will give the solution a pink or purple color. The volume data from the titration, the known molarity of the $KMnO_4$ solution, and the mole ratio from the balanced redox equation will give you the information you need to calculate the molarity of the $FeSO_4$ solution.

## SAFETY

For review of safety, please see **Safety in the Chemistry Laboratory** in the front of your book.

## PREPARATION

1. In your lab notebook, prepare a data table like the one shown on the next page.
2. Clean two 50 mL burets with a buret brush and distilled water. Rinse each buret at least three times with distilled water to remove contaminants.
3. Label one 250 mL beaker "0.0200 M $KMnO_4$" and the other "$FeSO_4$." Label three of the flasks "1," "2," and "3." Label the 400 mL beaker "Waste." Label one buret "$KMnO_4$" and the other "$FeSO_4$."

**DATA TABLE**

| Trial | Initial $KMnO_4$ volume (mL) | Final $KMnO_4$ volume (mL) | Initial $FeSO_4$ volume (mL) | Final $FeSO_4$ volume (mL) |
|---|---|---|---|---|
| 1 | | | | |
| 2 | | | | |
| 3 | | | | |

4. Measure approximately 75 mL of 0.0200 M $KMnO_4$, and pour it into the appropriately labeled beaker. Obtain approximately 75 mL of $FeSO_4$ solution, and pour it into the appropriately labeled beaker.

5. Rinse one buret three times with a few milliliters of 0.0200 M $KMnO_4$ from the appropriately labeled beaker. Collect these rinses in the waste beaker. Rinse the other buret three times with small amounts of $FeSO_4$ solution from the appropriately labeled beaker. Collect these rinses in the waste beaker.

6. Set up the burets as instructed by your teacher. Fill one buret with approximately 50 mL of 0.0200 M $KMnO_4$ from the beaker, and fill the other buret with approximately 50 mL of the $FeSO_4$ solution from the other beaker.

7. With the waste beaker underneath its tip, open the $KMnO_4$ buret long enough to be sure the buret tip is filled. Repeat the process for the $FeSO_4$ buret.

8. Add 50 mL of distilled water to one of the 125 mL Erlenmeyer flasks, and add one drop of 0.0200 M $KMnO_4$ to the flask. Set this mixture aside to use as a color standard. It can be compared with the titration mixture to determine the end point.

## PROCEDURE

1. Record in your data table the initial buret readings for both solutions. Add 10 mL of the hydrated iron(II) sulfate solution, $FeSO_4{\bullet}7H_2O$, to the flask labeled "1." Add 5 mL of 1 M $H_2SO_4$ to the $FeSO_4$ solution in this flask. The acid will help keep the $Fe^{2+}$ ions in the reduced state, which will allow you time to titrate.

2. Slowly add $KMnO_4$ from the buret to the $FeSO_4$ in the flask while swirling the flask. When the color of the solution matches the color standard you prepared in Preparation step 8, record in your data table the final readings of the burets.

3. Empty the titration flask into the waste beaker. Repeat the titration procedure in steps 1 and 2 with the flasks labeled "2" and "3."

## CLEANUP AND DISPOSAL

4. Dispose of the contents of the waste beaker in the container designated by your teacher. Also, pour the color-standard flask into this container. Wash your hands thoroughly after cleaning up the area and equipment.

## ANALYSIS AND INTERPRETATION

1. **Organizing Ideas:** Write the balanced equation for the redox reaction of $FeSO_4$ and $KMnO_4$.

2. **Evaluating Data:** Calculate the number of moles of $MnO_4^-$ reduced in each trial.

3. **Analyzing Information:** Calculate the number of moles of $Fe^{2+}$ oxidized in each trial.

4. **Applying Conclusions:** Calculate the average concentration (molarity) of the iron(II) sulfate solution.

## EXTENSIONS

1. **Designing Experiments:** What possible sources of error can you identify with this procedure? If you can think of ways to eliminate them, ask your teacher to approve your plan, and run the procedure again.

# CHAPTER 20

# *Electrochemistry*

*Electrochemical reactions provide energy in all kinds of applications.*

Artist's rendering of the *Mars Rover*

# Introduction to Electrochemistry

SECTION 1

C.4.8 Illustrate the uses of electrochemistry (including electrolytic cells, voltaic cells, and the production of metals from ore by electrolysis)

## OBJECTIVES

- Identify parts of an electrochemical cell and their functions.
- Write electrode half reactions for cathodes and anodes.

Oxidation-reduction reactions involve energy changes. Because these reactions involve electron transfer, the net *release* or net *absorption* of energy can occur in the form of electrical energy rather than as heat. This property allows for a great many practical applications of redox reactions. *The branch of chemistry that deals with electricity-related applications of oxidation-reduction reactions is called* **electrochemistry.**

## Electrochemical Cells

Oxidation-reduction reactions involve a transfer of electrons. If the two substances are in contact with one another, a transfer of energy as heat accompanies the electron transfer. In **Figure 1** a zinc strip is in contact with a copper(II) sulfate solution. The zinc strip loses electrons to the copper(II) ions in solution. Copper(II) ions accept the electrons and fall out of solution as copper atoms. As electrons are transferred between zinc atoms and copper(II) ions, energy is released as heat, as indicated by the rise in temperature.

SCILINKS.
www.scilinks.org
Topic: Electrochemical Cells
Code: HC60478

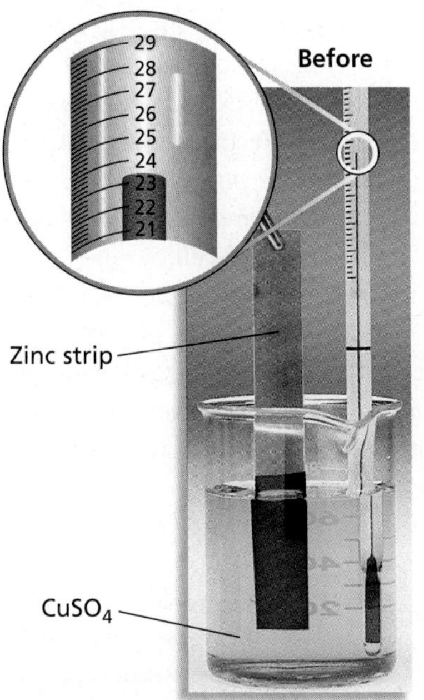


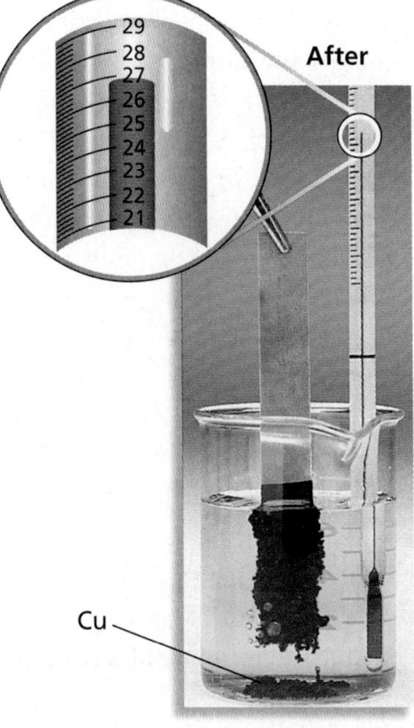


**FIGURE 1** Energy as heat given off when electrons are transferred directly from Zn atoms to $Cu^{2+}$ ions causes the temperature of the aqueous $CuSO_4$ solution to rise.

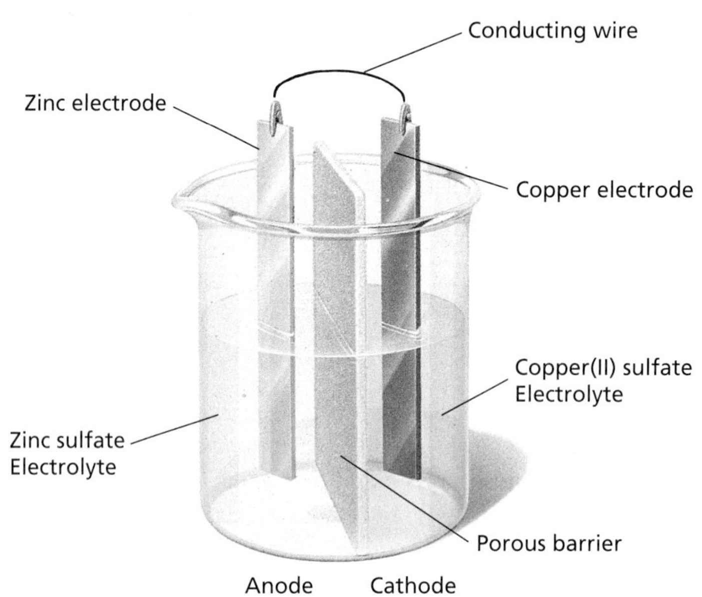


**FIGURE 2** An electrochemical cell consists of two electrodes. Each electrode is in contact with an electrolyte; the electrode and the electrolyte make up a half-cell. The two electrodes are connected by a wire, and a porous barrier separates the two electrolytes.

If, however, we separate the substance that is oxidized from the substance that is reduced, the electron transfer is accompanied by a transfer of electrical energy instead of energy as heat. One means of separating oxidation and reduction half-reactions is with a *porous barrier,* or *salt bridge.* This barrier prevents the metal atoms of one half-reaction from mixing with the ions of the other half-reaction. Ions in the two solutions can move through the porous barrier, which keeps a charge from building up on the electrodes. Electrons can be transferred from one side to the other through an external connecting wire. Electric current moves in a closed loop path, or *circuit,* so this movement of electrons through the wire is balanced by the movement of ions in solution.

Altering the system in **Figure 1** as just described would simply involve separating the copper and zinc, as shown in **Figure 2.** The Zn strip is in an aqueous solution of $ZnSO_4$. The Cu strip is in an aqueous solution of $CuSO_4$. Both solutions conduct electricity, so, as you learned in Chapter 12, they are classified as electrolytes. *An* **electrode** *is a conductor used to establish electrical contact with a nonmetallic part of a circuit, such as an electrolyte.* In **Figure 2,** the Zn and Cu strips are electrodes. *A single electrode immersed in a solution of its ions is a* **half-cell.**

## The Half-Cells

In the half-cell that contains the Zn electrode in aqueous $ZnSO_4$ solution, the half-reaction is $Zn(s) \longrightarrow Zn^{2+}(aq) + 2e^-$. The Zn metal loses two electrons to form $Zn^{2+}$ ions in solution, and therefore oxidation is taking place in this half-cell. *The electrode where oxidation occurs is called the* **anode.** In the half-cell that contains the Cu electrode in aqueous $CuSO_4$ solution, the half-reaction is $Cu^{2+}(aq) + 2e^- \longrightarrow Cu(s)$. In this half-reaction, the $Cu^{2+}$ ions in solution gain electrons to become Cu solid; that is, reduction is taking place. *The electrode where reduction occurs is called the* **cathode.**

Recall from Chapter 19 that these two half-reactions cannot occur separately. Both oxidation and reduction must occur in an electrochemical reaction. The two half-cells taken together make an electrochemical cell. In the Zn/Cu electrochemical cell, the electrons move from the Zn electrode through the wire and down the Cu electrode to the $Cu^{2+}$ ions at the electrode-solution interface. The $Cu^{2+}$ ions are reduced to solid Cu, and the resulting Cu atoms attach themselves to the surface of the Cu electrode. For this reaction, charge is carried through the barrier by a combination of $Zn^{2+}(aq)$ ions moving from the anode to the cathode and the $SO_4^{2-}(aq)$ ions moving from the cathode to the anode.

SCILINKS. www.scilinks.org
Topic: Electrical Energy
Code: HC60475

## The Complete Cell

An electrochemical cell may be represented by the following notation:

anode electrode | anode solution || cathode solution | cathode electrode

The double line represents the salt bridge, or porous barrier, between the two half-cells. For the present cell, the cell notation is

$$Zn(s)\,|\,Zn^{2+}(aq)\,||\,Cu^{2+}(aq)\,|\,Cu(s).$$

The electrochemical reaction can be found by adding the anode half-reaction to the cathode half-reaction. This overall (or net) reaction is the following redox reaction:

$$Zn(s) + Cu^{2+}(aq) \longrightarrow Zn^{2+}(aq) + Cu(s)$$

Although the two half-reactions occur at the same time, they occur at different places in the cell. Thus, for the reaction to proceed, electrons must pass through the wire that connects the two half-cells.

An electrochemical cell that consists of the Zn and Cu reaction described above is called the *Daniell Cell,* named for the English chemist John Frederick Daniell. The Daniell Cell can generate enough electricity to light up the light bulb shown in **Figure 3.** In electrochemical cells, either a chemical reaction produces electrical energy or an electric current produces a chemical change.

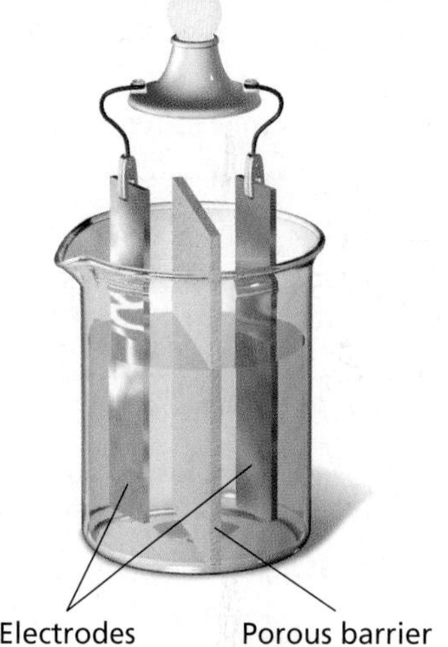


**FIGURE 3** The light bulb is powered by the reaction in this cell.

## SECTION REVIEW

1. Why is the use of a salt bridge or porous barrier necessary in an electrochemical cell?
2. Given the $Cu^{2+}(aq)\,|\,Cu(s)$ and $Mg^{2+}(aq)\,|\,Mg(s)$ half-reactions, where $Cu^{2+}(aq)\,|\,Cu(s)$ is the cathode reaction,
   **a.** write the overall reaction.
   **b.** write the cell notation.
3. Write the half-reaction in which $I^-(aq)$ changes to $I_2(s)$. Would this reaction occur at the anode or cathode?

**Critical Thinking**

4. **RELATING IDEAS** Is the net chemical result of an electrochemical cell a redox reaction? Explain your answer.

SECTION 2

# Voltaic Cells

## OBJECTIVES

- Describe the operation of voltaic cells, including dry cells, lead-acid batteries, and fuel cells.
- Identify conditions that lead to corrosion and ways to prevent it.
- Describe the relationship between voltage and the movement of electrons.
- Calculate cell voltage/potentials from a table of standard electrode potentials.

**C.4.8** Illustrate the uses of electrochemistry (including electrolytic cells, voltaic cells, and the production of metals from ore by electrolysis)

**Voltaic cells** *use spontaneous oxidation-reduction reactions to convert chemical energy into electrical energy.* Voltaic cells are also called *galvanic cells.* The most common application of voltaic cells is in batteries.

## How Voltaic Cells Work

**Figure 4** shows an example of a voltaic cell: the Zn || Cu electrochemical cell discussed in the previous section.

Electrons given up at the anode pass along the external connecting wire to the cathode. The movement of electrons through the wire must be balanced by the movement of ions in the solution. Thus, in **Figure 4,** sulfate ions in the $CuSO_4$ solution can move through the barrier into the $ZnSO_4$ solution.

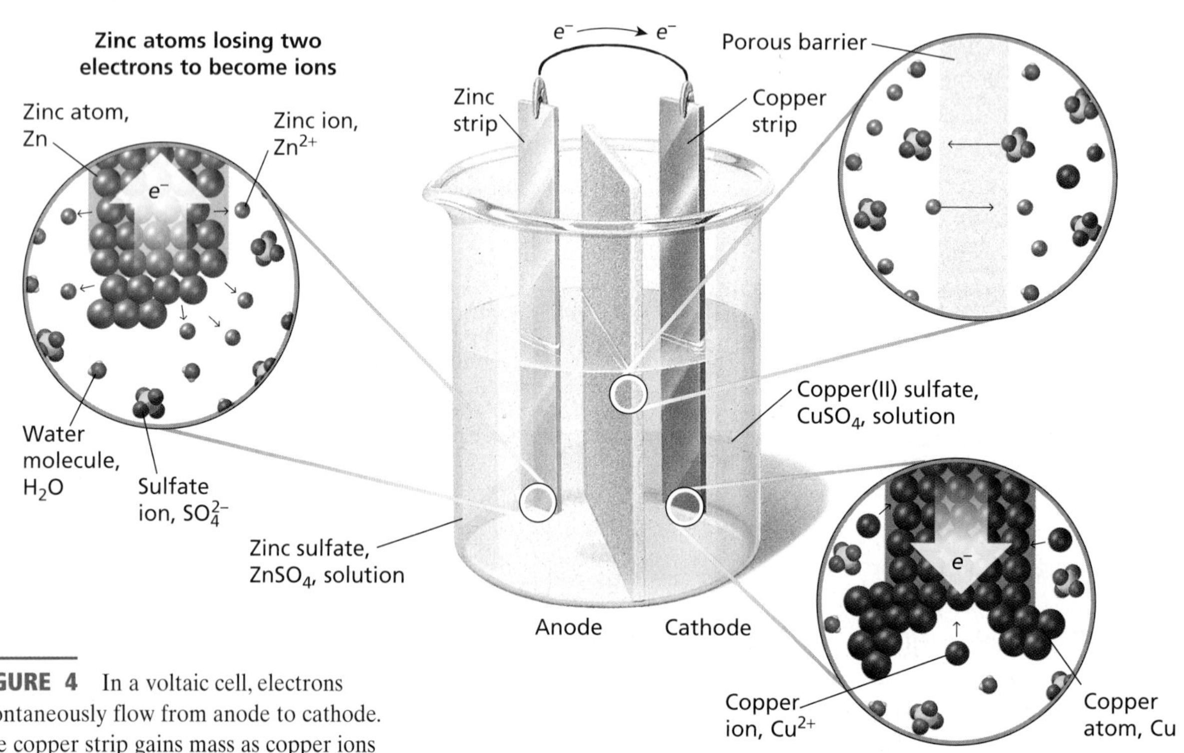


**FIGURE 4** In a voltaic cell, electrons spontaneously flow from anode to cathode. The copper strip gains mass as copper ions become copper atoms. The zinc strip loses mass as the zinc atoms become zinc ions.

The dry cells pictured in **Figure 5** are common sources of electrical energy. Like the wet cell previously described, dry cells are voltaic cells. The three most common types of dry cells are the zinc-carbon battery, the alkaline battery, and the mercury battery. They differ in the substances being oxidized and reduced.

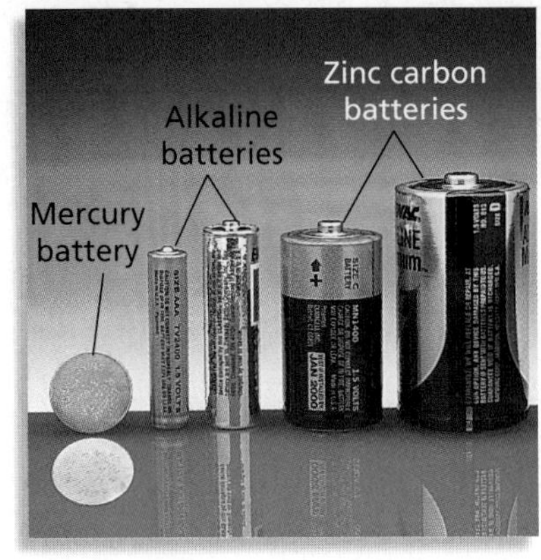


**FIGURE 5** Many common batteries are simple voltaic dry cells.

## Zinc-Carbon Dry Cells

Batteries such as those used in flashlights are zinc-carbon dry cells. These cells consist of a zinc container, which serves as the anode, filled with a moist paste of $MnO_2$, carbon black, $NH_4Cl$, and $ZnCl_2$, as illustrated in **Figure 6a.** When the external circuit is closed, zinc atoms are oxidized at the negative electrode, or anode.

$$\overset{0}{Zn}(s) \longrightarrow \overset{+2}{Zn^{2+}}(aq) + 2e^-$$

Electrons move across the circuit and reenter the cell through the carbon rod. The carbon rod is the cathode or positive electrode. Here $MnO_2$ is reduced in the presence of $H_2O$ according to the following half-reaction.

$$2\overset{+4}{Mn}O_2(s) + H_2O(l) + 2e^- \longrightarrow \overset{+3}{Mn_2}O_3(s) + 2OH^-(aq)$$

## Alkaline Batteries

The batteries found in a portable compact disc player or other small electronic device are frequently alkaline dry cells. These cells do not have a carbon rod cathode, as in the zinc-carbon cell. The absence of the carbon rod allows them to be smaller. **Figure 6b** shows a model of an alkaline battery. This cell uses a paste of Zn metal and potassium hydroxide instead of a solid metal anode. The half-reaction at the anode is as follows.

$$\overset{0}{Zn}(s) + 2OH^-(aq) \longrightarrow \overset{+2}{Zn}(OH)_2(s) + 2e^-$$

The reduction half-reaction, the reaction at the cathode, is exactly the same as that for the zinc-carbon dry cell.

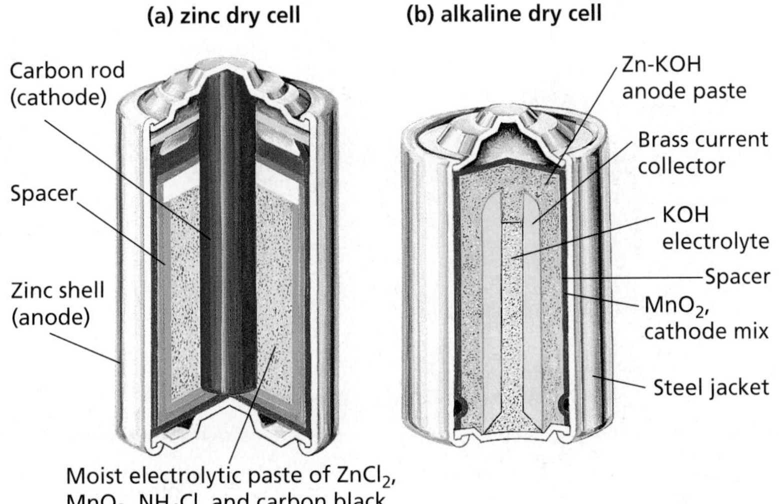


**FIGURE 6** (a) In a zinc dry cell, zinc is oxidized to $Zn^{2+}$ at the anode, and manganese(IV) is reduced to manganese(III) at the cathode. (b) KOH makes the electrolyte paste in this battery basic. Thus, it is called an alkaline dry cell.

**FIGURE 7** It is important that mercury batteries be recycled and not just discarded because mercury is a poisonous substance.

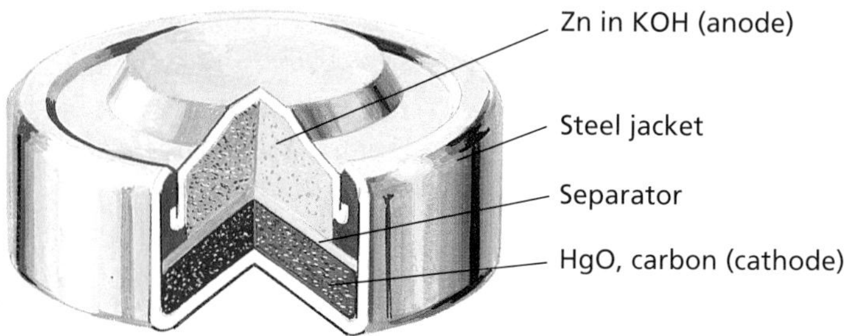


## Mercury Batteries

The tiny batteries found in hearing aids, calculators, and camera flashes are mercury batteries, as shown in **Figure 7.** The anode half-reaction is identical to that found in the alkaline dry cell. However, the cathode, or reduction, half-reaction is different. The cathode half-reaction is described by the following equation.

$$\overset{+2}{Hg}O(s) + H_2O(l) + 2e^- \longrightarrow \overset{0}{Hg}(l) + 2OH^-(aq)$$

## Fuel Cells

A fuel cell is a voltaic cell in which the reactants are being continuously supplied and the products are being continuously removed. Therefore, unlike a battery, a fuel cell could, in principle, work forever, changing chemical energy into electrical energy.

Fuel cells based on the reactions listed below and shown in **Figure 8** are used in the United States space program.

SCILINKS. www.scilinks.org **Topic:** Fuel Cells **Code:** HC60625

$$\text{Cathode: } O_2(g) + 2H_2O(l) + 4e^- \longrightarrow 4OH^-(aq)$$

$$\text{Anode: } 2H_2(g) + 4OH^-(aq) \longrightarrow 4e^- + 4H_2O(l)$$

$$\text{Net reaction: } 2H_2 + O_2 \longrightarrow 2H_2O$$

Fuel cells are very efficient and have very low emissions.

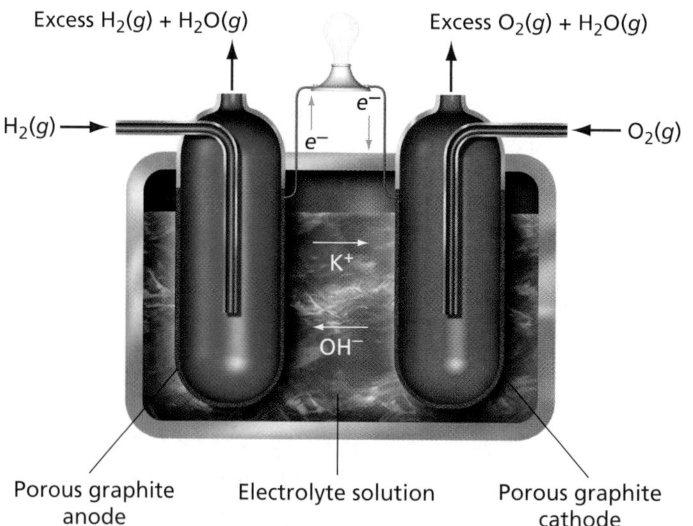


**FIGURE 8** The reactions in this fuel cell take place at carbon electrodes that contain metal catalysts. The water formed is removed as a gas.

## Corrosion and Its Prevention

Corrosion is an electrochemical process that has a large economic impact. Approximately 20% of all the iron and steel produced is used to repair or replace corroded structures. One of the metals most commonly affected by corrosion is iron. Rust, hydrated iron(III) oxide, forms by the following overall reaction.

$$4Fe(s) + 3O_2(g) + xH_2O(l) \longrightarrow 2Fe_2O_3{\bullet}xH_2O(s)$$

The amount of hydration of the iron oxide, reflected by the coefficient $x$ in the equation above, varies, and affects the color of the rust formed.

The mechanism for the corrosion of iron contains the following electrochemical reactions.

$$\text{Anode: } Fe(s) \longrightarrow Fe^{2+}(aq) + 2e^-$$

$$\text{Cathode: } O_2(g) + 2H_2O(l) + 4e^- \longrightarrow 4OH^-(aq)$$

The anode and cathode reactions occur at different regions of the metal surface. The electric circuit is completed by electron flow through the metal itself, which acts like the wire in an electrochemical cell. The water on the surface of the metal serves as the salt bridge. Thus, for corrosion to occur, water and oxygen must be present with the iron.

As shown in **Figure 9,** when the iron is exposed to water and oxygen, the iron metal at the anodic site is oxidized to $Fe^{2+}$ ions. The electrons released at this site travel along the metal (like the wire of a cell) to the cathodic region, where oxygen is reduced. The $Fe^{2+}$ ions travel along the moisture toward the cathodic regions. At the cathode, the $Fe^{2+}$ ions are further oxidized to $Fe^{3+}$ ions and form rust, which is hydrated iron oxide, $Fe_2O_3{\bullet}xH_2O$.

$$2Fe^{2+}(aq) + (3 + x)H_2O(l) \longrightarrow Fe_2O_3{\bullet}xH_2O(s) + 6H^+(aq) + 2e^-$$

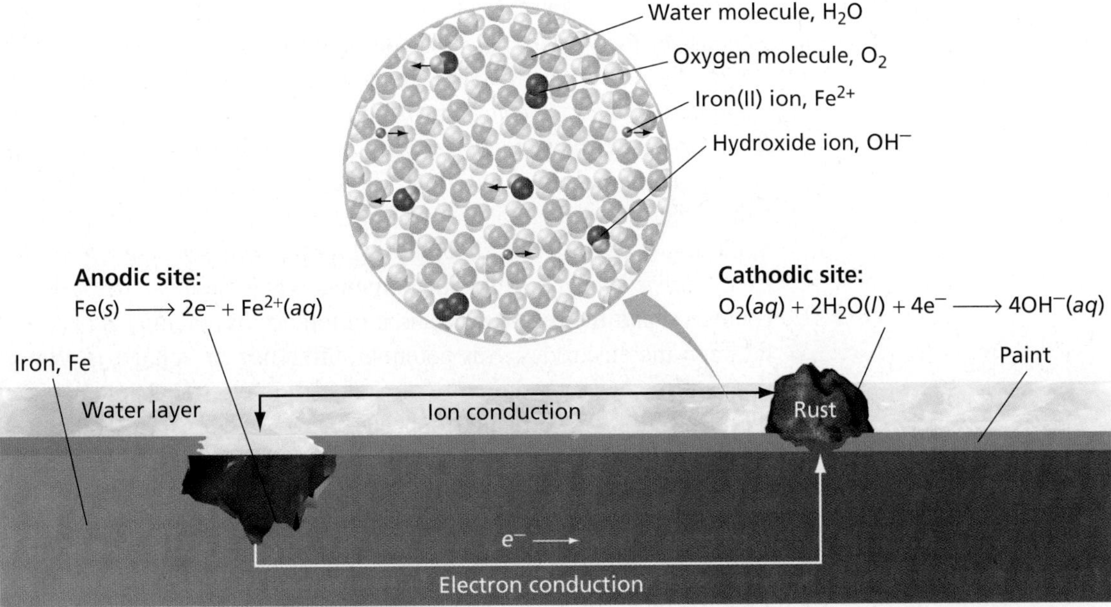


**FIGURE 9** The cathodic reaction happens where the $O_2$ concentration is high. The anodic reaction happens in a region where the $O_2$ concentration is low, such as a pit in the metal.

The presence of salt or high acidity speed the corrosion process, because the movement of electrons is facilitated by the extra ions present.

How can corrosion be prevented? One way, which makes use of electrochemical properties of metals, is to coat steel with zinc in a process called *galvanizing*. Zinc is more easily oxidized than iron; therefore, zinc will react before the iron is oxidized. This is called *cathodic protection,* and the more easily oxidized metal used is called a *sacrificial anode.*

The Alaskan oil pipeline, shown in **Figure 10,** is an example of steel that is cathodically protected. However, instead of coating, zinc is connected to the pipe by a wire. The zinc will oxidize before the iron in the steel does. As the zinc anode corrodes, it gives electrons to the cathode, the steel, and as the zinc anode does so, it prevents the steel from corroding. As the zinc dissolves, it needs to be replaced. As long as zinc metal that is able to corrode is present, the steel will be protected from corrosion.

**FIGURE 10** The Alaskan pipeline is cathodically protected by a parallel zinc cable.

## Electrical Potential

In a voltaic cell, the oxidizing agent at the cathode pulls the electrons through the wire away from the reducing agent at the anode. The "pull," or driving force on the electrons, is called the *electric potential.* Electric potential, or voltage, is expressed in units of volts (V), which is the potential energy per unit charge. Current is the movement of the electrons and is expressed in units of amperes, or amps (A).

Electrical potential is analogous to gravitational potential. Just as water flows from a position of higher gravitational potential to a position of lower gravitational potential, electrons flow from higher electric potential to lower electrical potential.

**extension**

**Careers in Chemistry**

Go to **go.hrw.com** for a full-length article on careers in chemical engineering.

**Keyword: HC6ELEX**

### Electrode Potentials

Reconsider the voltaic cell shown in **Figure 4.** There are two electrodes, Zn and Cu. These two metals each have different tendencies for accepting electrons. *This tendency for the half-reaction of either copper or zinc to occur as a reduction half-reaction in an electrochemical cell can be quantified as a* **reduction potential.** There are two half-cells in **Figure 4:** a strip of zinc placed in a solution of $ZnSO_4$ and a strip of copper placed in a solution of $CuSO_4$. *The difference in potential between an electrode and its solution is known as* **electrode potential.** When these two half-cells are connected and the reaction begins, a difference in potential is observed between the electrodes. This potential difference, or voltage, is proportional to the energy required to move a certain electric charge between the electrodes. A voltmeter connected across the Zn||Cu voltaic cell measures a potential difference of about 1.10 V when the solution concentrations of $Zn^{2+}$ and $Cu^{2+}$ ions are each 1 M.

The potential difference measured across the complete voltaic cell is easily measured and equals the sum of the electrode potentials for the two half-reactions. But an individual electrode potential cannot be measured directly. This is because there can be no transfer of electrons unless both the anode and the cathode are connected to form a complete circuit. A relative value for the potential of a half-reaction can be determined by connecting it to a standard half-cell as a reference. This standard half-cell, shown in **Figure 11,** is called a standard hydrogen electrode, or SHE. It consists of a platinum electrode dipped into a 1.00 M acid solution surrounded by hydrogen gas at 1 atm pressure and 25°C. Other electrodes are ranked according to their ability to reduce hydrogen under these conditions.

The anodic reaction for the standard hydrogen electrode is described by the forward half-reaction in the following equilibrium equation.

$$\overset{0}{H_2}(g) \rightleftharpoons \overset{+1}{2H^+}(aq) + 2e^-$$

The cathodic half-reaction is the reverse. An arbitrary potential of 0.00 V is assigned to both of these half-reactions. *The potential of a half-cell under standard conditions measured relative to the standard hydrogen electrode is a* **standard electrode potential,** $E^0$. Electrode potentials are expressed as *potentials for reduction.* These reduction potentials provide a reliable indication of the tendency of a substance to be reduced. **Figure 12** shows how the SHE is used to find the electrode potentials of the zinc and copper half-cells. Half-reactions for some common electrodes and their standard electrode potentials are listed in **Table 1** on the next page.

Effective oxidizing agents, such as $Cu^{2+}$ and $F_2$, have positive $E^0$ values. Half-reactions with negative reduction potentials prefer oxidation over reduction. Negative $E^0$ values indicate that the metal or other electrode is more willing to give up electrons than hydrogen. Effective reducing agents, such as Li and Zn, have negative $E^0$ values.

When a half-reaction is written as an oxidation reaction, the sign of its electrode potential is reversed, as shown for the oxidation and reduction half-reactions for zinc.

$$Zn^{2+} + 2e^- \longrightarrow Zn \qquad E^0 = -0.76 \text{ V}$$
$$Zn \longrightarrow Zn^{2+} + 2e^- \qquad E^0 = +0.76 \text{ V}$$

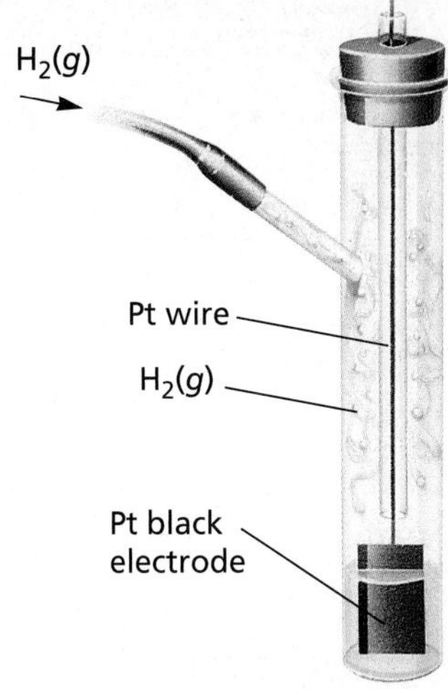


**FIGURE 11** A hydrogen electrode is the standard reference electrode for measuring electrode potentials. The electrode surface in contact with the solution is actually a layer of hydrogen adsorbed onto the surface of the platinum.

**FIGURE 12** The electrode potentials of zinc and copper half-cells are measured by coupling them with a standard hydrogen electrode.

**TABLE 1 *Standard Reduction Potentials***

| Half-cell reaction | Standard electrode potential, $E^0$ (in volts) | Half-cell reaction | Standard electrode potential, $E^0$ (in volts) |
|---|---|---|---|
| $F_2 + 2e^- \rightleftarrows 2F^-$ | +2.87 | $Fe^{3+} + 3e^- \rightleftarrows Fe$ | −0.04 |
| $MnO_4^- + 8H^+ + 5e^- \rightleftarrows Mn^{2+} + 4H_2O$ | +1.49 | $Pb^{2+} + 2e^- \rightleftarrows Pb$ | −0.13 |
| $Au^{3+} + 3e^- \rightleftarrows Au$ | +1.42 | $Sn^{2+} + 2e^- \rightleftarrows Sn$ | −0.14 |
| $Cl_2 + 2e^- \rightleftarrows 2Cl^-$ | +1.36 | $Ni^{2+} + 2e^- \rightleftarrows Ni$ | −0.23 |
| $Cr_2O_7^{2-} + 14H^+ + 6e^- \rightleftarrows 2Cr^{3+} + 7H_2O$ | +1.33 | $Co^{2+} + 2e^- \rightleftarrows Co$ | −0.28 |
| $MnO_2 + 4H^+ + 2e^- \rightleftarrows Mn^{2+} + 2H_2O$ | +1.21 | $Cd^{2+} + 2e^- \rightleftarrows Cd$ | −0.40 |
| $Br_2 + 2e^- \rightleftarrows 2Br^-$ | +1.07 | $Fe^{2+} + 2e^- \rightleftarrows Fe$ | −0.41 |
| $Hg^{2+} + 2e^- \rightleftarrows Hg$ | +0.85 | $S + 2e^- \rightleftarrows S^{2-}$ | −0.51 |
| $Ag^+ + e^- \rightleftarrows Ag$ | +0.80 | $Cr^{3+} + 3e^- \rightleftarrows Cr$ | −0.74 |
| $Hg_2^{2+} + 2e^- \rightleftarrows 2Hg$ | +0.80 | $Zn^{2+} + 2e^- \rightleftarrows Zn$ | −0.76 |
| $Fe^{3+} + e^- \rightleftarrows Fe^{2+}$ | +0.77 | $Al^{3+} + 3e^- \rightleftarrows Al$ | −1.66 |
| $MnO_4^- + e^- \rightleftarrows MnO_4^{2-}$ | +0.56 | $Mg^{2+} + 2e^- \rightleftarrows Mg$ | −2.37 |
| $I_2 + 2e^- \rightleftarrows 2I^-$ | +0.54 | $Na^+ + e^- \rightleftarrows Na$ | −2.71 |
| $Cu^{2+} + 2e^- \rightleftarrows Cu$ | +0.34 | $Ca^{2+} + 2e^- \rightleftarrows Ca$ | −2.76 |
| $Cu^{2+} + e^- \rightleftarrows Cu^+$ | +0.16 | $Ba^{2+} + 2e^- \rightleftarrows Ba$ | −2.90 |
| $S + 2H^+(aq) + 2e^- \rightleftarrows H_2S(aq)$ | +0.14 | $K^+ + e^- \rightleftarrows K$ | −2.93 |
| $2H^+(aq) + 2e^- \rightleftarrows H_2$ | 0.00 | $Li^+ + e^- \rightleftarrows Li$ | −3.04 |

The potential difference across the zinc/hydrogen cell is −0.76 V, so zinc is considered to have an electrode potential of −0.76. The negative number indicates that electrons flow from the zinc electrode, where zinc is oxidized, to the hydrogen electrode, where aqueous hydrogen ions are reduced.

A copper half-cell coupled with the standard hydrogen electrode gives a potential difference measurement of +0.34 V. This positive number indicates that $Cu^{2+}(aq)$ ions are more readily reduced than $H^+(aq)$ ions.

Standard electrode potentials can be used to predict if a redox reaction will occur spontaneously. A spontaneous reaction will have a positive value for $E^0_{cell}$, which is calculated using the following equation.

$$E^0_{cell} = E^0_{cathode} - E^0_{anode}$$

The half-reaction that has the more negative standard reduction potential will be the anode. Oxidation occurs at the anode, so the anode half-cell reaction will be the reverse of the reduction reaction found in **Table 1.** For this reason, the total potential of a cell is calculated by *subtracting* the standard reduction potential for the reaction at the anode ($E^0_{anode}$) from the standard reduction potential for the reaction at the cathode ($E^0_{cathode}$).

## SAMPLE PROBLEM A

*For more help, go to the **Math Tutor** at the end of this chapter.*

**Write the overall cell reaction, and calculate the cell potential for a voltaic cell consisting of the following half-cells: an iron (Fe) electrode in a solution of $Fe(NO_3)_3$ and a silver (Ag) electrode in a solution of $AgNO_3$.**

### SOLUTION

**1 ANALYZE**

**Given:** A half-cell consists of Fe(*s*) with $Fe(NO_3)_3(aq)$ and a second half-cell consists of Ag(*s*) with $AgNO_3(aq)$.

**Unknown:** $E^0_{cell}$

**2 PLAN**

1. Look up $E^0$ for each half-reaction (written as reductions) in Table 1.

$Fe^{3+}(aq) + 3e^- \longrightarrow Fe(s)$ $E^0 = -0.04$ V $\qquad Ag^+(aq) + e^- \longrightarrow Ag(s)$ $E^0 = +0.80$ V

2. Determine the cathode and anode.

Fe in $Fe(NO_3)_3$ is the anode because it has a lower reduction potential than Ag. Ag in $Ag(NO_3)$ is therefore the cathode.

**3 COMPUTE**

1. Determine the overall cell reaction. Multiply the Ag half-reaction by 3 so that the number of electrons lost in that half-reaction equals the number of electrons gained in the oxidation of iron. Reverse the iron half-reaction to be an oxidation half-reaction.

$$3Ag^+(aq) + Fe(s) \longrightarrow 3Ag(s) + Fe^{3+}(aq)$$

2. Calculate the cell potential by $E^0_{cell} = E^0_{cathode} - E^0_{anode}$. Note that when a half-reaction is multiplied by a constant, the $E^0$ value is not multiplied by that constant but remains the same.

$$E^0_{cell} = E^0_{cathode} - E^0_{anode} = +0.80 \text{ V} - (-0.04 \text{ V}) = +0.84 \text{ V}$$

**4 EVALUATE**

The calculated value for $E^0_{cell}$ is positive, which confirms that it is a voltaic cell, as the problem states.

### PRACTICE

*Answers in Appendix E*

1. For each pair of half-cells, determine the overall electrochemical reaction that proceeds spontaneously and the $E^0$ value.

a. $Cr_2O_7^{2-}/Cr^{3+}$ and $Ni^{2+}/Ni$

b. SHE and $Fe^{2+}/Fe^{3+}$

**extension**

Go to **go.hrw.com** for more practice problems that ask you to calculate cell potential.

**Keyword: HC6ELEX**

## SECTION REVIEW

1. What is a voltaic cell?
2. What is electrode potential, and how is it used to calculate information about an electrochemical cell?
3. Given the $Na^+/Na$ and $K^+/K$ half-cells, determine the overall electrochemical reaction that proceeds spontaneously and the $E^0$ value.
4. Given the $MnO_2/Mn^{2+}$ and $Cr^{3+}/Cr$ half-cells, determine the overall electrochemical reaction that occurs spontaneously and the $E^0$ value.

**Critical Thinking**

5. **EVALUATING IDEAS** A sacrificial anode is allowed to corrode. Why is use of a sacrificial anode considered to be a way to prevent corrosion?

# Chemistry in Action

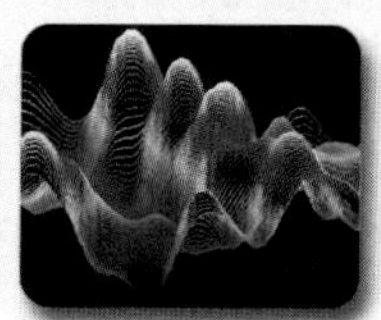
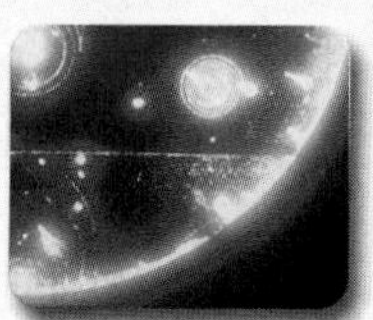

## Fuel-Cell Cars

The car of the future is quiet, has low emissions, and requires less maintenance than cars of today do. These are the promises of fuel-cell cars. The development of fuel-cell cars has been pushed by state and federal programs, legislation, and funding. There are a number of issues that need to be resolved before the large-scale manufacture of fuel-cell cars becomes feasible. These include the fuel-storage capacity of the car, and the fueling infrastructure.

The technology currently favored for automobiles is the proton-exchange membrane (PEM) fuel cell. The system works by combining hydrogen with oxygen taken from the outside air. The movement of the electrons (produced by the redox reaction) along an external route generates electricity, which is used eventually to turn the car wheels. The process is two to three times more efficient than that of the internal-combustion engine, and the only products are water and a moderate amount of energy as heat. In most cases, a traditional car battery is used to operate the car's electrical system.

In principle, fuel cells can run on any hydrogen-rich fuel. Several candidate fuels that can power fuel cells are being investigated: methanol, ethanol, natural gas, gasoline, and liquid or compressed hydrogen. If the fuel is not hydrogen gas, the engine needs to include a reformer that can convert the other fuel (such as methanol) to hydrogen.

▲*Eventually, fuel-cell cars such as this one may replace gasoline-powered cars.*

The range of fuel-cell powered cars is limited by the amount of fuel that can be stored in the storage tank. Current storage now limits the cars to around 100 miles before refueling. Researchers in this area are looking into carbon-adsorption systems, which are refrigerated and pressurized tanks that can store large amounts of hydrogen. Hydrogen is very combustible, but safe hydrogen tanks have been developed. So today, the experts do not have any more concern about the safety of hydrogen storage then they do about gasoline storage.

However, the landscape is not yet dotted with hydrogen refueling stations. Current experimental users such as governmental institutions must have their own hydrogen refueling stations. Auto companies say there needs to be a consumer infrastructure for the hydrogen fuel-cell cars before consumers will buy. On the other hand, possible developers of such hydrogen stations say that there needs to be a demand before the infrastructure can form.

The use of fuels such as methanol solves the storage and fuel infrastructure problem, because these fuels can be stored similar to the way gasoline is stored. Therefore, these fuels can be sold at current gasoline stations.

One should also consider the emissions and energy use involved in making and delivering the hydrogen fuel in addition to the emissions from the hydrogen fuel cell. Producing hydrogen fuel itself could involve substantial emissions. Even so, fuel-cell cars are still more efficient and have greater environmental benefits than the internal-combustion cars of today.

Currently, all major car companies are developing and researching fuel-cell cars. Most companies have prototype cars and some cars are in use by governmental institutions. Which type will ultimately succeed in the mass market is yet unknown. Experts agree, though, that for zero-emission cars, hydrogen is the only major fuel option that has been identified to date.

### Questions

1. Fuel cells that use hydrogen as fuel produce water and moderate amounts of energy in the form of heat as the only emissions. What kinds of negative effects might cars that use hydrogen-rich fuels have on the environment?

2. In the PEM fuel cell, the hydrogen ions are produced at which electrode: the anode or cathode?

# Electrolytic Cells



**C.4.8** Illustrate the uses of electrochemistry (including electrolytic cells, voltaic cells, and the production of metals from ore by electrolysis)

## *Objectives*

- Describe the nature of electrolytic cells.
- Describe the process of electrolysis in the decomposition of water and in production of metals.
- Explain the process of electroplating.
- Describe the chemistry of a rechargeable cell.

Some oxidation-reduction reactions do not occur spontaneously but can be driven by electrical energy. *If electrical energy is required to produce a redox reaction and bring about a chemical change in an electrochemical cell, it is an* **electrolytic cell.** Most commercial uses of redox reactions make use of electrolytic cells.

## How Electrolytic Cells Work

A comparison of electrolytic and voltaic cells can be seen in **Figure 13.** The voltaic cell shown in **Figure 13** has a copper cathode and a zinc anode. If a battery is connected so that the positive terminal contacts the copper electrode and the negative terminal contacts the zinc electrode, the electrons move in the opposite direction. The battery forces the cell to reverse its reaction; the zinc electrode becomes the cathode, and the copper electrode becomes the anode. The half-reaction at the anode, in which copper metal is oxidized, can be written as follows:

$$\overset{0}{Cu} \longrightarrow \overset{+2}{Cu^{2+}} + 2e^-$$

The reduction half-reaction of zinc at the cathode is written as follows:

$$\overset{+2}{Zn^{2+}} + 2e^- \longrightarrow \overset{0}{Zn}$$

**Voltaic Cell**

$e^-$ → $e^-$

Zinc strip

Copper strip

Zinc sulfate, $ZnSO_4$, solution

Copper(II) sulfate, $CuSO_4$, solution

Anode

Cathode

**FIGURE 13** The direction in which the electrons move reverses if a voltaic cell is connected to a direct current source to become an electrolytic cell.

There are two important differences between the voltaic cell and the electrolytic cell.

1. The anode and cathode of an electrolytic cell are connected to a battery or other direct-current source, whereas a voltaic cell serves as a source of electrical energy.
2. Electrolytic cells are those in which electrical energy from an external source causes *nonspontaneous* redox reactions to occur. Voltaic cells are those in which *spontaneous* redox reactions produce electricity. In an electrolytic cell, electrical energy is converted to chemical energy; in a voltaic cell, chemical energy is converted to electrical energy.

## Electroplating

*An electrolytic process in which a metal ion is reduced and a solid metal is deposited on a surface is called* **electroplating.** An electroplating cell contains a solution of a salt of the plating metal, an object to be plated (the cathode), and a piece of the plating metal (the anode). A silver-plating cell contains a solution of a soluble silver salt and a silver anode. The cathode is the object to be plated. The silver anode is connected to the positive electrode of a battery or to some other source of direct current. The object to be plated is connected to the negative electrode.

A cell in which silver is being electroplated onto a bracelet can be seen in **Figure 14.** Silver ions are reduced at the cathode according to the following half-reaction and deposited as metallic silver when electrons flow through the circuit.

$$\overset{+1}{Ag^+} + e^- \longrightarrow \overset{0}{Ag}$$

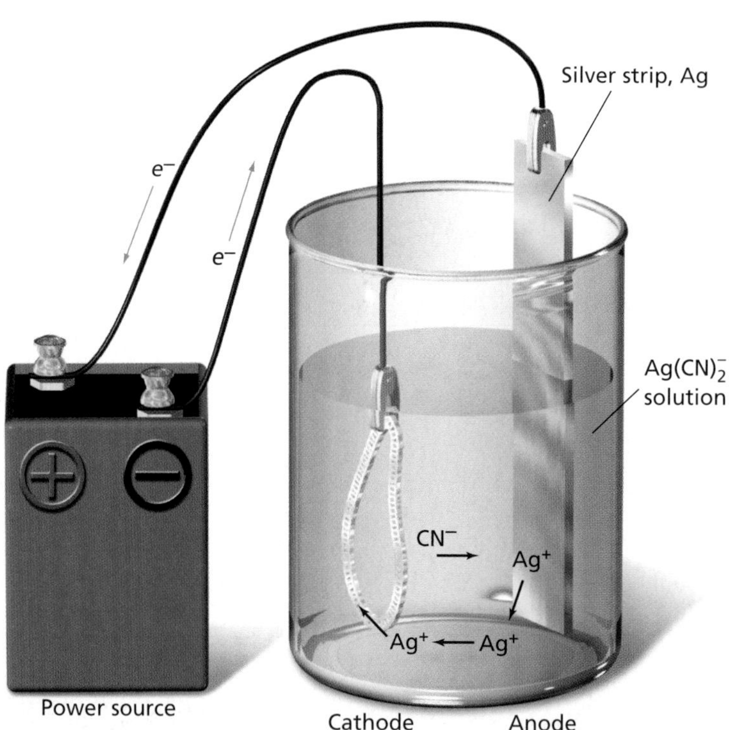


**FIGURE 14** The bracelet in this cell is being coated with a thin layer of silver. Silver ions are replaced in the solution as the pure silver anode dissolves.

Meanwhile, metallic silver is oxidized at the anode according to the following half-reaction.

$$\overset{0}{Ag} \longrightarrow \overset{+1}{Ag^+} + e^-$$

In effect, silver is transferred from the anode to the cathode of the cell.

## Rechargeable Cells

A rechargeable cell combines the oxidation-reduction chemistry of both voltaic cells and electrolytic cells. When a rechargeable cell converts chemical energy to electrical energy, it operates as a voltaic cell. But when the cell is recharged, it operates as an electrolytic cell, converting electrical energy to chemical energy.

The standard 12 V automobile battery, shown in **Figure 15,** is a set of six rechargeable cells. The anode in each cell is lead submerged in a solution of $H_2SO_4$. The anode half-reaction is described below.

$$Pb(s) + SO_4^{2-}(aq) \longrightarrow PbSO_4(s) + 2e^-$$

At the cathode, $PbO_2$ is reduced according to the following equation.

$$PbO_2(s) + 4H^+(aq) + SO_4^{2-}(aq) + 2e^- \longrightarrow PbSO_4(s) + 2H_2O(l)$$

The net oxidation-reduction reaction for the discharge cycle is:

$$Pb(s) + PbO_2(s) + 2H_2SO_4(aq) \longrightarrow 2PbSO_4(s) + 2H_2O(l)$$

A car's battery produces the electric energy needed to start its engine. Sulfuric acid, present as its ions, is consumed, and lead(II) sulfate accumulates as a white powder on the electrodes. Once the car is running, the half-reactions are reversed by a voltage produced by the alternator. The Pb, $PbO_2$, and $H_2SO_4$ are regenerated. A battery can be recharged as long as all reactants necessary for the electrolytic reaction are present, and all reactions are reversible.

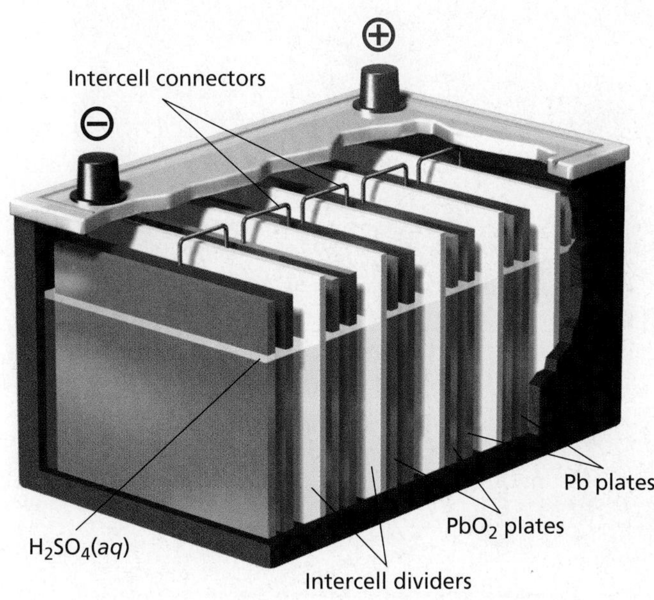


**FIGURE 15** The rechargeable cells of a car battery produce electricity from reactions between lead(IV) oxide, lead, and sulfuric acid.

# Electrolysis

Electroplating and recharging a battery are examples of electrolysis. **Electrolysis** *is the process of passing a current through a cell for which the cell potential is negative and causing an oxidation-reduction reaction to occur.* That is, electrical energy is used to force a nonspontaneous chemical reaction to occur. For this cell reaction to occur, the external voltage must be greater than the potential that would be produced by the spontaneous reverse cell reaction.

Electrolysis is of great industrial importance. It is used to purify many metals from the ores in which they are found chemically combined in Earth's crust.

## Electrolysis of Water

The electrolysis of water, shown in **Figure 16,** leads to the cell reaction in which water is broken down into its elements, $H_2$ and $O_2$. Recall that hydrogen gas and oxygen gas combine spontaneously to form water and are used to power fuel cells, which produce electricity. Therefore, the reverse process (electrolysis of water) is nonspontaneous and requires electrical energy. The following half-reactions occur at the anode and cathode.

$$\text{Anode: } 6H_2O(l) \longrightarrow 4e^- + O_2(g) + 4H_3O^+(aq)$$

$$\text{Cathode: } 4H_2O(l) + 4e^- \longrightarrow 2H_2(g) + 4OH^-(aq)$$

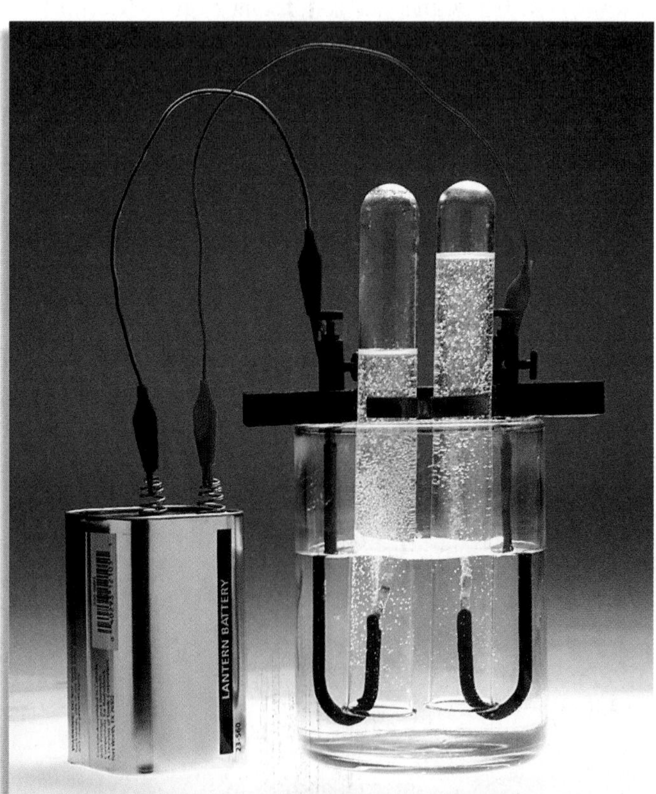


**FIGURE 16** Electrical energy from the battery is used to break down water. Hydrogen forms at the cathode (left tube), and oxygen forms at the anode (right tube).

## Aluminum Production by Electrolysis

Aluminum is the most abundant metal in Earth's crust. It is a relatively reactive metal; therefore, in nature, it is found as its oxide in an ore called *bauxite.* Aluminum is now very useful commercially, but it was not until 1886 that a process to obtain pure aluminum metal was discovered. Charles M. Hall (from the United States) and Paul Héroult (from France) simultaneously, but independently, determined a practical method for producing aluminum; it is an electrolytic process called the Hall-Héroult process.

Bauxite ore contains not only aluminum oxide ($Al_2O_3$), but oxides of iron, silicon, and titanium. Therefore, the aluminum oxide (called alumina) must first be separated from the other compounds in the ore. The pure hydrated alumina ($Al_2O_3 \cdot nH_2O$) is obtained by treating bauxite with sodium hydroxide, which dissolves the alumina but does not dissolve the other compounds in the ore. The alumina solution is then separated from the remaining solid compounds and reprecipitated to obtain pure alumina. The purified alumina is dissolved in molten cryolite, $Na_3AlF_6$, at 970°C in an electrochemical cell, and the aluminum ions are reduced to aluminum metal. The liquid aluminum is denser than the molten cryolite and alumina; therefore, the molten aluminum metal settles to the bottom of the cell and is drained off periodically.

The electrolytic solution contains a large number of aluminum-containing ions, and the chemistry of the electrochemical reaction is not completely understood. Scientists still debate the exact species that participate in the half-reactions; but the overall cell reaction is

$$2Al_2O_3(l) + 3C(s) \longrightarrow 4Al(l) + 3CO_2(g),$$

where carbon is the anode and steel is the cathode in the cell.

The aluminum metal produced in this process is 99.5% pure. The Hall-Héroult process made the production of aluminum economically feasible. However, this process is the largest single user of electrical energy in the United States—nearly 5% of the national total. Recycling aluminum saves almost 95% of the cost of production. Aluminum recycling is one of the most economically worthwhile recycling programs that has been developed.

### Chemistry in Action

**Sodium Production by Electrolysis**

Sodium is such a reactive metal that preparing it through a chemical process can be dangerous. Today, sodium is produced mainly by the electrolysis of molten sodium chloride. The melting point of sodium chloride is about 800°C; but mixing it with solid calcium chloride lowers the melting point to around 600°C. This mixture is introduced into an electrolytic cell called the Downs Cell to retrieve the sodium metal, and the lower melting point allows the cell to use less electrical energy to run.

## SECTION REVIEW

1. Describe an electrolytic cell.
2. Explain the process of electroplating.
3. What is a rechargeable cell?
4. Give an example of how electrolytic cells are used in industry.

**Critical Thinking**

5. **APPLYING CONCEPTS** Copper ore contains zinc metal, which is oxidized along with Cu during the electrolytic purification process. However, the $Zn^{2+}$ ions are not then reduced when the $Cu^{2+}$ ions are reduced to Cu at the cathode to obtain purified copper metal. Explain how Zn can be oxidized with Cu, but their ions not be reduced together.

# CHAPTER HIGHLIGHTS

## Introduction to Electrochemistry

**Vocabulary**
electrochemistry
electrode
half-cell
anode
cathode

- Electrochemistry is the branch of chemistry that deals with electricity-related applications of redox reactions.
- The electrode immersed in an electrolyte solution is a half-cell.
- The anode is the electrode where oxidation takes place. The cathode is the electrode where reduction occurs.
- The cell consists of electrodes connected by a wire along which the electron travels and a salt bridge (or porous barrier) through which ions transfer to balance the charge.
- An electrochemical cell is a system of electrodes and electrolytes in which either chemical reactions produce electrical energy or electric current produces chemical change.

## Voltaic Cells

**Vocabulary**
voltaic cell
reduction potential
electrode potential
standard electrode potential

- A voltaic cell, sometimes called a galvanic cell, uses a spontaneous redox reaction to produce electrical energy. Examples of voltaic cells are batteries and fuel cells.
- Fuel cells are voltaic cells in which the reactants are continuously supplied and the products are continuously removed.
- The potential difference must be measured across a complete cell because no transfer of electrons can occur unless both the anode and cathode are connected to form a complete circuit. Thus, the standard electrode potential for a half-cell is measured against the standard hydrogen electrode (SHE).
- Standard reduction potentials, $E^0$, are stated as reduction half-reactions. Effective oxidizing agents have positive $E^0$ values, while effective reducing agents have negative $E^0$ values.
- A voltaic cell has an $E^0_{cell}$ value that is positive.
- Corrosion occurs when iron is exposed to oxygen and water. One of the best methods to prevent corrosion is by the use of sacrificial anodes.

## Electrolytic Cells

**Vocabulary**
electrolytic cell
electroplating
electrolysis

- Electrolytic cells are cells in which electrical energy from an external source causes a nonspontaneous reaction to occur.
- An electrolytic cell has an $E^0_{cell}$ value that is negative.
- Electrolysis has great economic impact. Applications of electrolytic cells are electroplating of metallic surfaces, rechargeable batteries, aluminum production, and purification of metals.

# CHAPTER REVIEW

For more practice, go to the Problem Bank in Appendix D.

## *Introduction to Electrochemistry*

### SECTION 1 REVIEW

1. In the half-cell $Zn^{2+}(aq) + 2e^- \longrightarrow Zn(s)$, what is the electrode and is this half-reaction an anodic reaction or a cathodic reaction?
2. What role does the porous barrier play?
3. For each of the following pairs of half-cells, write the overall reaction and the cell notation. Assume the first half-cell given in each pair is the cathodic half-cell.
   a. $Ag^+/Ag$, $Co^{2+}/Co$
   b. $Au^{3+}/Au$, $Zn^{2+}/Zn$
   c. $Hg^{2+}/Hg$, $K^+/K$
4. Describe the components of an electrochemical cell and how the electrical charge travels through these components.

## *Voltaic Cells*

### SECTION 2 REVIEW

5. Describe a voltaic cell, and give two examples of a voltaic cell.
6. What is the essential advantage of a fuel cell over batteries in the generation of electrical energy?
7. Explain why corrosion is a voltaic cell.
8. Discuss the advantages and disadvantages of corrosion-prevention methods.
9. Which half reaction would more likely be an oxidation reaction: one with a standard reduction potential of –0.42 V, or one with a standard reduction potential of +0.42 V?
10. Why are dry-cell batteries called *dry cells,* even though their chemistry involves water?
11. a. Explain what is meant by the potential difference between the two electrodes in an electrochemical cell.
    b. How is this potential difference measured? What units are used?
12. The standard hydrogen electrode is assigned an electrode potential of 0.00 V. Explain why this voltage is assigned.
13. a. What information is provided by the standard reduction potential of a given half-cell?
    b. What does the relative value of the reduction potential of a given half-reaction indicate about its oxidation-reduction tendency?
14. When the cell $Ba(s)\,|\,Ba^{2+}(aq)\,||\,Sn^{2+}(aq)\,|\,Sn(s)$ is running, what observations can be made?

### PRACTICE PROBLEMS

15. For each of the following pairs of half-cells, determine the overall electrochemical reaction that proceeds spontaneously:
    a. $Na^+/Na$, $Ni^{2+}/Ni$
    b. $F_2/F^-$, $S/H_2S$
    c. $Br_2/Br^-$, $Cr^{3+}/Cr$
    d. $MnO_4^-/Mn^{2+}$, $Co^{2+}/Co$
16. Determine the values of $E^0$ for the cells in the previous problem.
17. Suppose chemists had chosen to make the $I_2 + 2e^- \longrightarrow 2I^-$ half-cell the standard electrode and had assigned it a potential of zero volts.
    a. What would be the $E^0$ value for the $Br_2 + 2e^- \longrightarrow 2Br^-$ half-cell?
    b. What would be the $E^0$ value for the $Al^{3+} + 3e^- \longrightarrow Al$ half-cell?
    c. How much change would be observed in the $E^0$ value for the reaction involving $Br_2 + I^-$ if the $I_2$ half-cell is the standard?
18. If a strip of Ni were dipped into a solution of $AgNO_3$, what would be expected to occur? Explain, using $E^0$ values and equations.

## *Electrolytic Cells*

### SECTION 3 REVIEW

19. What reaction happens at the cathode in an electrolysis process?
20. Explain why water cannot be used in the electrochemical cell during the production of aluminum.
21. Calculate the voltage of a cell in which the overall reaction is the electrolysis of aqueous cadmium chloride into its elements.
22. According to electrochemical data, can Ni be plated onto a zinc metal object using a nickel nitrate solution? Explain.

23. Distinguish between a voltaic cell and an electrolytic cell in terms of the nature of the reaction involved.

24. a. What is electroplating?
    b. Identify the anode and cathode in such a process.

## MIXED REVIEW

25. Predict whether each of the following reactions will occur spontaneously as written by determining the $E^0$ value for potential reaction. Write and balance the overall equation for each reaction that does occur spontaneously.
    a. $Mg + Sn^{2+} \longrightarrow$
    b. $K + Al^{3+} \longrightarrow$
    c. $Li^+ + Zn \longrightarrow$
    d. $Cu + Cl_2 \longrightarrow$

26. Why is it possible for alkaline batteries to be smaller than zinc-carbon dry cells?

27. Draw a diagram of a voltaic cell whose two half-reactions consist of Ag in $AgNO_3$ and Ni in $NiSO_4$. Identify the anode and cathode, and indicate the directions in which the electrons and ions are moving.

28. Can a solution of $Sn(NO_3)_2$ be stored in an aluminum container? Explain, using $E^0$ values.

29. A voltaic cell is made up of a cadmium electrode in a solution of $CdSO_4$ and a zinc electrode in a solution of $ZnSO_4$. The two half-cells are separated by a porous barrier.
    a. Which is the cathode, and which is the anode?
    b. In which direction are the electrons flowing?
    c. Write balanced equations for the two half-reactions, and write a net equation for the combined reaction.

30. Would the following pair of electrodes make a good battery? Explain.
    $Cd \longrightarrow Cd^{2+} + 2e^-$
    $Fe \longrightarrow Fe^{2+} + 2e^-$

31. a. What would happen if an aluminum spoon were used to stir a solution of $Zn(NO_3)_2$?
    b. Could a strip of Zn be used to stir a solution of $Al(NO_3)_3$? Explain, using $E^0$ values.

32. How do the redox reactions for each of the following types of batteries differ?
    a. zinc-carbon
    b. alkaline
    c. mercury

33. a. Why are some standard reduction potentials positive and some negative?
    b. Compare the $E^0$ value for a metal with the reactivity of that metal.

## CRITICAL THINKING

34. **Applying Models** Explain how the oxidation-reduction chemistry of both the voltaic cell and the electrolytic cell are combined in the chemistry of rechargeable cells.

35. **Applying Ideas** In lead-acid batteries, such as your car battery, the degree of discharge of the battery can be determined by measuring the density of the battery fluid. Explain how this is possible.

36. **Applying Ideas** In lead-acid batteries, the battery cannot be recharged indefinitely. Explain why not.

37. **Interpreting Graphics** A voltaic cell is pictured below. Identify the species that is oxidized if current is allowed to flow.

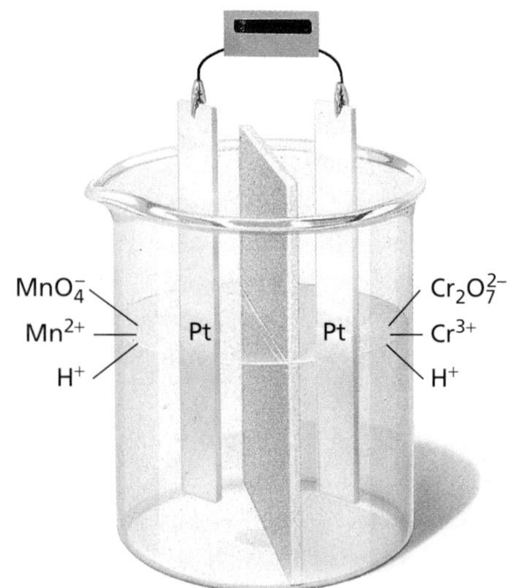

## USING THE HANDBOOK

**38.** Aluminum is described in Group 13 of the *Elements Handbook* as a self-protecting metal, and can be used in preventing corrosion of iron structures. Using electrochemical data, explain how aluminum protects iron structures.

## RESEARCH & WRITING

**39.** Go to the library, and find out about the electroplating industry in the United States. What are the top three metals used for plating, and how many metric tons of each are used for electroplating each year in the United States?

**40.** Investigate the types of batteries being considered for electric cars. Write a report on the advantages and disadvantages of these types of batteries.

## ALTERNATIVE ASSESSMENT

**41.** **Performance** Take an inventory of the types of batteries used in your home. Find out the voltage supplied by each battery and what electrochemical reaction each uses. Suggest why that electrochemical reaction is used in each case.

**42.** In our portable society, batteries have become a necessary power supply. As consumers, we want to purchase batteries that will last as long as possible. Advertisements tell us that some batteries last longer than others, but do they really? Design an investigation to answer the question. Is there a difference in longevity between the major brands of AA batteries? Add a cost-effectiveness component to your design.

**43.** When someone who has a silver filling in a tooth bites down on an aluminum gum wrapper, saliva acts as an electrolyte. The system is an electrochemical cell that produces a small jolt of pain. Explain what occurs, using half-cell reactions and $E^0$ values.

extension

**Graphing Calculator Equilibrium Constant for an Electrochemical Cell**

Go to **go.hrw.com** for a graphing calculator exercise that asks you to calculate an equilibrium constant for an electrochemical cell.

Keyword: HC6ELEX

# Math Tutor CALCULATING CELL POTENTIALS

You have learned that electrons are transferred in all oxidation-reduction reactions. Electrons from a substance being oxidized are transferred to another substance being reduced. A voltaic cell is a simple device that physically separates the oxidation reaction from the reduction reaction, thus forcing electrons released during oxidation to travel through a wire to reach the site of reduction. If a device, such as a light bulb or motor, is placed in the circuit, the moving electrons can perform useful work.

The potential, or voltage, of a given voltaic cell depends on how strongly the oxidation process tends to give up electrons in addition to how strongly the reduction process tends to take them. The greater these two combined tendencies, the higher the potential of the cell. A potential has been measured for each half-reaction, as you can see in **Table 1** on p. 664. In a voltaic cell, the process with the more-negative reduction potential will proceed as the oxidation reaction at the anode of the cell. The more positive reaction will proceed as reduction at the cathode. The following example shows you how to determine the potentials of different kinds of voltaic cells.

## Problem-Solving *TIPS*

- In a voltaic cell, the process that has the more negative reduction potential will proceed as the oxidation reaction at the anode of the cell.

## SAMPLE

**Calculate the potential of a voltaic cell in which $Hg^{2+}$ ions are reduced to Hg metal while Zn metal is oxidized to $Zn^{2+}$ ions.**

Reduction takes place at the cathode, so the cathode half-reaction is

$$Hg^{2+}(aq) + 2e^- \longrightarrow Hg(l)$$

Oxidation takes place at the anode, so the anode half-reaction is

$$Zn(s) \longrightarrow Zn^{2+}(aq) + 2e^-$$

To use the equation for cell potential, rewrite the anode half-reaction as a reduction reaction, $Zn^{2+}(aq) + 2e^- \longrightarrow Zn(s)$.

Use **Table 1** on page 664 to find the standard reduction potential for each half-reaction. Then, calculate the cell potential.

$$Hg^{2+}(aq) + 2e^- \longrightarrow Hg(l)\ E^0_{cathode} = +0.85\ V$$

$$Zn^{2+}(aq) + 2e^- \longrightarrow Zn(s)\ E^0_{anode} = -0.76\ V$$

$$E^0_{cell} = E^0_{cathode} - E^0_{anode} = +0.85\ V - (-0.76\ V) = 1.61\ V$$

## PRACTICE PROBLEMS

1. Calculate the potential of a voltaic cell in which aluminum metal is oxidized to $Al^{3+}$ ions while $Cu^{2+}$ ions are reduced to $Cu^+$ ions.

2. Calculate the potential of a cell in which the reaction is $Pb(s) + Br_2(l) \longrightarrow Pb^{2+}(aq) + 2Br^-(aq)$.

# Standardized Test Prep

**Answer the following items on a separate piece of paper.**

**MULTIPLE CHOICE**

**1.** The electrode at which reduction occurs is
**A.** always the anode.
**B.** always the cathode.
**C.** either the anode or the cathode.
**D.** always the half-cell.

**2.** Refer to the table of standard reduction potentials below. A voltaic cell contains a strip of zinc metal in a solution containing zinc ions in one half-cell. The second is a strip of tin metal in a solution containing tin ions. When this cell operates,
**A.** Sn is oxidized and $Zn^{2+}$ is reduced.
**B.** Sn is reduced and $Zn^{2+}$ is oxidized.
**C.** $Sn^{2+}$ is oxidized and Zn is reduced.
**D.** $Sn^{2+}$ is reduced and Zn is oxidized.

**3.** When a rechargeable cell is being recharged, the cell acts as a(n)
**A.** fuel cell.
**B.** electrolytic cell.
**C.** voltaic cell.
**D.** Leclanche cell.

**4.** Refer to the table of standard reduction potentials below. The standard potential of the cell $Sn | Sn^{2+} || Cr^{3+} | Cr$ is –0.60 V. What is the standard reduction potential of the $Cr^{3+}/Cr$ electrode?
**A.** +0.88 V
**B.** +0.74 V
**C.** –0.88 V
**D.** –0.74 V

| Half-cell reaction | Standard reduction potential, $E^0$ (in volts) |
|---|---|
| $Au^{3+} + 3e^- \rightleftharpoons Au$ | +1.50 |
| $Cu^{2+} + 2e^- \rightleftharpoons Cu$ | +0.34 |
| $Fe^{2+} + 2e^- \rightleftharpoons Fe$ | –0.41 |
| $Sn^{2+} + 2e^- \rightleftharpoons Sn$ | –0.14 |
| $Zn^{2+} + 2e^- \rightleftharpoons Zn$ | –0.76 |
| $Mg^{2+} + 2e^- \rightleftharpoons Mg$ | –2.37 |

**5.** Refer to the table of reduction potentials below. Which metal, Zn or Au, can reduce $Sn^{2+}$ ions to Sn metal when placed in an aqueous solution of $Sn^{2+}$ ions?
**A.** Zn
**B.** Au
**C.** Both Zn and Au can reduce $Sn^{2+}$ ions
**D.** Neither Zn or Au can reduce $Sn^{2+}$ ions

**6.** When silver is electroplated onto another metal, $Ag^+$ is
**A.** oxidized at the anode.
**B.** reduced at the anode.
**C.** oxidized at the cathode.
**D.** reduced at the cathode.

**7.** Which metal would best provide cathodic protection from corrosion for an iron bridge?
**A.** Au
**B.** Sn
**C.** Cu
**D.** Mg

**SHORT ANSWER**

**8.** In the production of aluminum by the Hall-Héroult process, is the aluminum metal produced at the cathode or the anode?

**9.** The reduction potential for nitric acid is 0.96 V (reduction half-reaction is $NO_3^- + 4H^+ + 3e^- \longrightarrow NO + 2H_2O$). If gold (Au) is placed in a beaker of 1 M nitric acid, will the gold dissolve?

**EXTENDED RESPONSE**

**10.** Given a voltaic cell consisting of a gold electrode in a gold nitrate solution in one half-cell and a zinc electrode in a zinc nitrate solution in the other half-cell, what occurs once the wire is connected to both electrodes?

**11.** If pure water is placed in a beaker with wires connected to a cathode and anode and electrical voltage is applied, will electrolysis of water occur? Explain your answer.

**Test TIP** Remember that if you can eliminate two of the four answer choices, your chances of choosing the correct answer choice will double.

# Voltaic Cells

## OBJECTIVES

- *Construct* a Cu-Zn voltaic cell.
- *Design* and construct two other voltaic cells.
- *Measure* the potential of the voltaic cells.
- *Evaluate* cells by comparing the measured cell voltages with the voltages calculated from standard reduction potentials.

## MATERIALS

- 0.5 M $Al_2(SO_4)_3$, 75 mL
- 0.5 M $CuSO_4$, 75 mL
- 0.5 M $ZnSO_4$, 75 mL
- Aluminum strip, 1 cm × 8 cm
- Copper strip, 1 cm × 8 cm
- Zinc strip, 1 cm × 8 cm
- Distilled water
- 100 mL graduated cylinder
- Emery cloth
- 150 mL beakers, 3
- Salt bridge
- Voltmeter
- Wires with alligator clips, 2

## BACKGROUND

In voltaic cells, oxidation and reduction half-reactions take place in separate half-cells, which can consist of a metal electrode immersed in a solution of its metal ions. The electrical potential, or voltage, that develops between the electrodes is a measure of the combined reducing strength of one reactant and oxidizing strength of the other reactant.

## SAFETY

For review of safety, please see **Safety in the Chemistry Laboratory** in the front of your book.

## PREPARATION

1. Follow your teacher's instructions to create the data table that you will use to record your data for three voltaic cells.
2. Remove any oxide coating from strips of aluminum, copper, and zinc by rubbing them with an emery cloth. Keep the metal strips dry until you are ready to use them.
3. Label three 150 mL beakers "$Al_2(SO_4)_3$," "$CuSO_4$," and "$ZnSO_4$."

## PROCEDURE

1. Pour 75 mL of 0.5 M $ZnSO_4$ into the $ZnSO_4$ beaker and 75 mL of 0.5 M $CuSO_4$ into the $CuSO_4$ beaker.
2. Place one end of the salt bridge into the $CuSO_4$ solution and the other end into the $ZnSO_4$ solution.
3. Place a zinc strip into the zinc solution and a copper strip into the copper solution.

4. Using the alligator clips, connect one wire to one end of the zinc strip and the second wire to the copper strip. Take the free end of the wire attached to the zinc strip, and connect it to one terminal on the voltmeter. Take the free end of the wire attached to the copper strip, and connect it to the other terminal on the voltmeter. The needle on the voltmeter should move to the right. If your voltmeter's needle points to the left, reverse the way the wires are connected to the terminals of the voltmeter. Immediately record the voltage reading in your data table, and disconnect the circuit.

5. Record the concentration of the solutions and sketch a diagram of your electrochemical cell.

6. Rinse the copper and zinc strips with a *very small* amount of distilled water. Collect the rinse from the copper strip in the $CuSO_4$ beaker and the rinse from the zinc strip in the $ZnSO_4$ beaker. Rinse each end of the salt bridge into the corresponding beaker.

7. Use the table of standard reduction potentials in the textbook to calculate the standard voltages for the other cells you can build using copper, zinc, or aluminum. Build these cells and measure their potentials following steps 1–6.

## CLEANUP AND DISPOSAL

8. Clean all apparatus and your lab station. Wash your hands. Place the pieces of metal in the containers designated by your teacher. Each solution should be poured in its own separate disposal container. Do not mix the contents of the beakers.

## ANALYSIS AND INTERPRETATION

1. **Organizing Ideas:** For each cell that you constructed, write the equations for the two half-cell reactions. Obtain the standard half-cell potentials for the half-reactions from **Table 1,** and write these $E^0$ values after the equations.

2. **Organizing Ideas:** For each cell you tested, combine the two half-reactions to obtain the equation for the net reaction.

3. **Organizing Ideas:** Use the $E^0$ values for the half-reactions to determine the $E^0$ for each cell.

4. **Resolving Discrepancies:** Compare the actual cell voltages you measured with the standard cell voltages in item 3. Explain why you would expect a difference.

## CONCLUSIONS

1. **Inferring Conclusions:** Based on the voltages that you measured, which cell produces the most energy?

2. **Applying Ideas:** On the basis of your data, which metal is the strongest reducing agent? Which metal ion is the strongest oxidizing agent?

3. **Applying Ideas:** Indicate the direction of electron flow in each of your cell diagrams.

## EXTENSIONS

1. **Predicting Outcomes:** Describe how and why the reactions would stop if the cells had been left connected.

2. **Designing Experiments:** Design a method that could use several of the electrochemical cells you constructed to generate more voltage than any individual cell provided. (Hint: consider what would happen if you linked an Al-Zn cell and a Zn-Cu cell. If your teacher approves your plan, test your idea.)

CHAPTER 21

# Nuclear Chemistry

*High temperature plasmas are being studied as potential sources of fusion energy.*

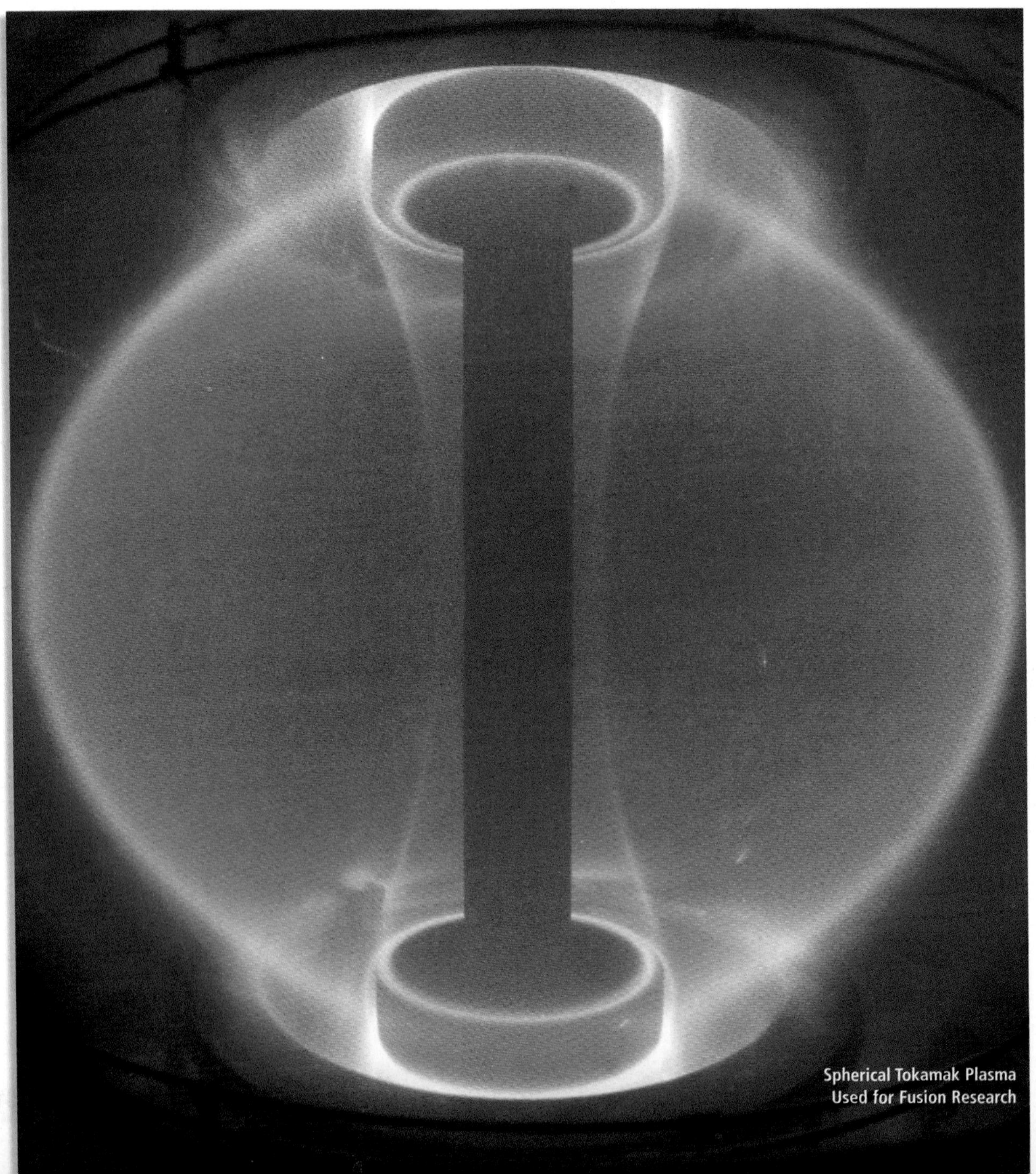

# The Nucleus

SECTION 1

C.2.8 Analyze a decay series chart to determine the products of successive nuclear reactions and write nuclear equations for disintegration of specified nuclides

## OBJECTIVES

- Explain what a nuclide is, and describe the different ways nuclides can be represented.
- Define and relate the terms *mass defect* and *nuclear binding energy.*
- Explain the relationship between number of nucleons and stability of nuclei.
- Explain why nuclear reactions occur, and know how to balance a nuclear equation.

Atomic nuclei are made of *protons and neutrons, which are collectively called* **nucleons.** In nuclear chemistry, *an atom is referred to as a* **nuclide** *and is identified by the number of protons and neutrons in its nucleus.* Nuclides can be represented in two ways. When a symbol such as $^{228}_{88}Ra$ is used, the superscript is the mass number and the subscript is the atomic number. The same nuclide can also be written as radium-228, where the mass number is written following the element name.

## Mass Defect and Nuclear Stability

Because an atom is made of protons, neutrons, and electrons, you might expect the mass of an atom to be the same as the mass of an equal number of isolated protons, neutrons, and electrons. However, this is not the case. Let's consider a $^{4}_{2}He$ atom as an example. The combined mass of two protons, two neutrons, and two electrons is calculated below.

$$\begin{aligned}
&\text{2 protons:} \quad (2 \times 1.007\,276 \text{ amu}) = 2.014\,552 \text{ amu}\\
&\text{2 neutrons:} \quad (2 \times 1.008\,665 \text{ amu}) = 2.017\,330 \text{ amu}\\
&\text{2 electrons:} \quad (2 \times 0.000\,548\,6 \text{ amu}) = \underline{0.001\,097 \text{ amu}}\\
&\qquad\qquad \text{total combined mass: } 4.032\,979 \text{ amu}
\end{aligned}$$

However, the atomic mass of a $^{4}_{2}He$ atom has been measured to be 4.002 602 amu. The measured mass, 4.002 602 amu, is 0.030 377 amu *less* than the combined mass, 4.032 979 amu, calculated above. *This difference between the mass of an atom and the sum of the masses of its protons, neutrons, and electrons is called the* **mass defect.**

### Nuclear Binding Energy

What causes the loss in mass? According to Albert Einstein's equation $E = mc^2$, mass can be converted to energy, and energy to mass. The mass defect is caused by the conversion of mass to energy upon formation of the nucleus. The mass units of the mass defect can be converted to energy units by using Einstein's equation. First, convert 0.030 377 amu to kilograms to match the mass units for energy, kg•m$^2$/s$^2$.

$$0.030\,377 \text{ amu} \times \frac{1.6605 \times 10^{-27} \text{ kg}}{1 \text{ amu}} = 5.0441 \times 10^{-29} \text{ kg}$$

**FIGURE 1** This graph shows the relationship between binding energy per nucleon and mass number. The binding energy per nucleon is a measure of the stability of a nucleus.

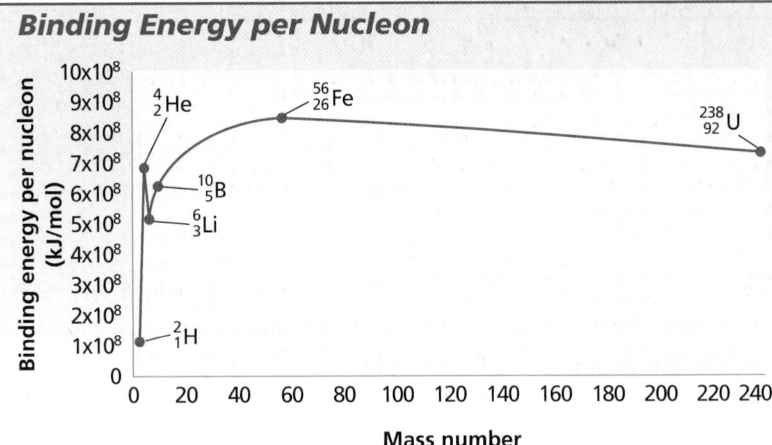


**CROSS-DISCIPLINARY**

**Quarks**

Many subatomic particles have been identified. Leptons and quarks are the elementary particles of matter. The electron is a lepton. Protons and neutrons are made of quarks. There are six types of quarks that differ in mass and charge. They are named *up, down, strange, charm, bottom,* and *top.* Protons consist of two *up* quarks and one *down* quark, and neutrons consist of two *down* quarks and one *up* quark. Although individual quarks have not been isolated, their existence explains the patterns of nuclear binding and decay.

The energy equivalent can now be calculated.

$$E = mc^2$$

$$E = (5.0441 \times 10^{-29}\ \text{kg})(3.00 \times 10^{8}\ \text{m/s})^2$$

$$= 4.54 \times 10^{-12}\ \text{kg•m}^2/\text{s}^2 = 4.54 \times 10^{-12}\ \text{J}$$

This is the **nuclear binding energy,** *the energy released when a nucleus is formed from nucleons*. This energy can also be thought of as the energy required to hold the nucleus together. Therefore, the nuclear binding energy is also a measure of the stability of a nucleus.

### Binding Energy per Nucleon

The binding energy per nucleon is used to compare the stability of different nuclides, as shown in **Figure 1.** The *binding energy per nucleon* is the binding energy of the nucleus divided by the number of nucleons it contains. The higher the binding energy per nucleon, the more tightly the nucleons are held together. Elements with intermediate atomic masses have the greatest binding energies per nucleon and are therefore the most stable.

## Nucleons and Nuclear Stability

Stable nuclides have certain characteristics. When the number of protons in stable nuclei is plotted against the number of neutrons, as shown in **Figure 2,** a pattern is observed. The neutron-proton ratios of stable nuclides cluster in a narrow band referred to as the *band of stability.* Among atoms having low atomic numbers, the most stable nuclei are those with a neutron-proton ratio of approximately 1:1. For example, $^{4}_{2}$He, a stable isotope of helium with two neutrons and two protons, has a neutron-proton ratio of 1:1. As the atomic number increases, the stable neutron-proton ratio increases to about 1.5:1. For example, $^{206}_{82}$Pb, with 124 neutrons and 82 protons, has a neutron-proton ratio of 1.51:1.

This trend can be explained by the relationship between the nuclear force and the electrostatic forces between protons. A proton in a nucleus repels all other protons through electrostatic repulsion, but the short

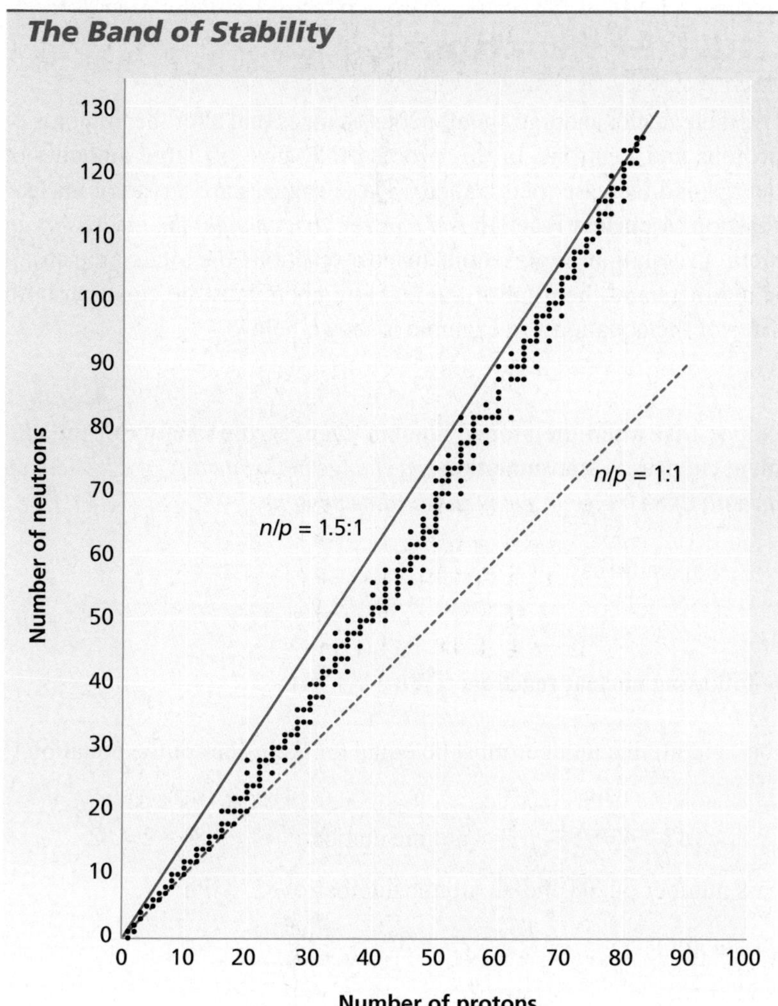


**FIGURE 2** The neutron-proton ratios of stable nuclides cluster together in a region known as the band of stability. As the number of protons increases, the ratio increases from 1:1 to about 1.5:1.

range of the nuclear force allows them to attract only protons very close to them, as shown in **Figure 3.** As the number of protons in a nucleus increases, the repulsive electrostatic force between protons increases faster than the nuclear force. More neutrons are required to increase the nuclear force and stabilize the nucleus. Beyond the atomic number 83, bismuth, the repulsive force of the protons is so great that no stable nuclides exist.

Stable nuclei tend to have even numbers of nucleons. Of the stable nuclides, more than half have even numbers of both protons and neutrons. Only five nuclides have odd numbers of both. This indicates that stability of a nucleus is greatest when the nucleons—like electrons—are paired.

The most stable nuclides are those having 2, 8, 20, 28, 50, 82, or 126 protons, neutrons, or total nucleons. This extra stability at certain numbers supports a theory that nucleons—like electrons—exist at certain energy levels. According to the **nuclear shell model,** *nucleons exist in different energy levels, or shells, in the nucleus. The numbers of nucleons that represent completed nuclear energy levels—2, 8, 20, 28, 50, 82, and 126—are called* **magic numbers.**

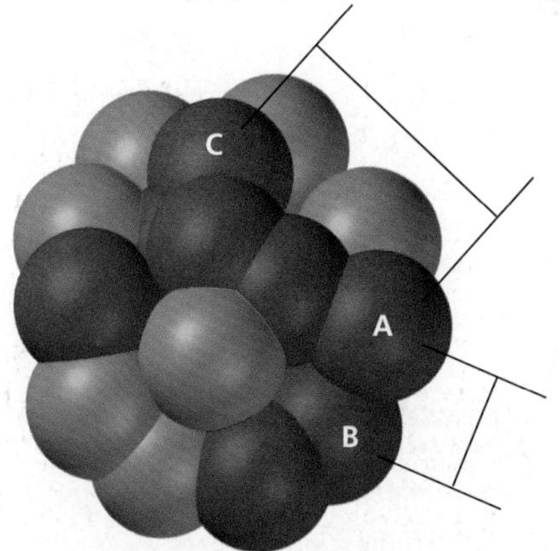


**FIGURE 3** Proton A attracts proton B through the nuclear force but repels it through the electrostatic force. Proton A mainly repels proton C through the electrostatic force because the nuclear force reaches only a few nucleon diameters.

## Nuclear Reactions

Unstable nuclei undergo spontaneous changes that alter the numbers of protons and neutrons. In this process, they give off large amounts of energy and increase their stability. These changes are a type of nuclear reaction. *A* **nuclear reaction** *is a reaction that changes the nucleus of an atom.* In equations representing nuclear reactions, the total of the atomic numbers and the total of the mass numbers must be equal on both sides of the equation. An example is shown below.

$$^{9}_{4}\text{Be} + ^{4}_{2}\text{He} \longrightarrow ^{12}_{6}\text{C} + ^{1}_{0}n$$

Notice that when the atomic number changes, the identity of the element changes. *A* **transmutation** *is a change in the identity of a nucleus as a result of a change in the number of its protons.*

### SAMPLE PROBLEM A

**Identify the product that balances the following nuclear reaction:** $^{212}_{84}\text{Po} \longrightarrow ^{4}_{2}\text{He} + \underline{\ ?\ }$

**SOLUTION**

1. The total mass number and atomic number must be equal on both sides of the equation.

$$^{212}_{84}\text{Po} \longrightarrow ^{4}_{2}\text{He} + \underline{\ ?\ }$$

mass number: $212 - 4 = 208$ atomic number: $84 - 2 = 82$

2. The nuclide has a mass number of 208 and an atomic number of 82, $^{208}_{82}\text{Pb}$.
3. The balanced nuclear equation is $^{212}_{84}\text{Po} \longrightarrow ^{4}_{2}\text{He} + ^{208}_{82}\text{Pb}$

**PRACTICE** *Answers in Appendix E*

Using $^{1}_{0}n$ to represent a neutron and $^{0}_{-1}e$ to represent an electron, complete the following nuclear equations:

1. $^{253}_{99}\text{Es} + ^{4}_{2}\text{He} \longrightarrow ^{1}_{0}n + \underline{\ ?\ }$
2. $^{142}_{61}\text{Pm} + \underline{\ ?\ } \longrightarrow ^{142}_{60}\text{Nd}$

**extension**

Go to **go.hrw.com** for more practice problems that ask you to complete nuclear equations.

### SECTION REVIEW

1. Define mass defect.
2. How is nuclear stability related to the neutron-proton ratio?
3. Complete and balance the following nuclear equations:

   a. $^{187}_{75}\text{Re} + \underline{\ ?\ } \longrightarrow ^{188}_{75}\text{Re} + ^{1}_{1}\text{H}$

   b. $^{9}_{4}\text{Be} + ^{4}_{2}\text{He} \longrightarrow \underline{\ ?\ } + ^{1}_{0}n$

   c. $^{22}_{11}\text{Na} + \underline{\ ?\ } \longrightarrow ^{22}_{10}\text{Ne}$

**Critical Thinking**

4. **INTERPRETING GRAPHICS** Examine **Figure 2,** and predict if $^{9}_{3}\text{Li}$ is a stable isotope of lithium. Explain your answer.

# Radioactive Decay

**C.2.6** Explain the concept of half-life, its use in determining the age of materials, and its significance to nuclear waste disposal

## OBJECTIVES

- Define and relate the terms *radioactive decay* and *nuclear radiation.*
- Describe the different types of radioactive decay and their effects on the nucleus.
- Define the term *half-life,* and explain how it relates to the stability of a nucleus.
- Define and relate the terms *decay series, parent nuclide,* and *daughter nuclide.*
- Explain how artificial radioactive nuclides are made, and discuss their significance.

In 1896, Henri Becquerel was studying the possible connection between light emission of some uranium compounds after exposure to sunlight and X-ray emission. He wrapped a photographic plate in a lightproof covering and placed a uranium compound on top of it. He then placed them in sunlight. The photographic plate was exposed even though it was protected from visible light, suggesting exposure by X rays. When he tried to repeat his experiment, cloudy weather prevented him from placing the experiment in sunlight. To his surprise, the plate was still exposed. This meant that sunlight was not needed to produce the rays that exposed the plate. The rays were produced by radioactive decay. **Radioactive decay** *is the spontaneous disintegration of a nucleus into a slightly lighter nucleus, accompanied by emission of particles, electromagnetic radiation, or both.* The radiation that exposed the plate was **nuclear radiation,** *particles or electromagnetic radiation emitted from the nucleus during radioactive decay.*

Uranium is a **radioactive nuclide,** *an unstable nucleus that undergoes radioactive decay*. Studies by Marie Curie and Pierre Curie found that of the elements known in 1896, only uranium and thorium were radioactive. In 1898, the Curies discovered two new radioactive metallic elements, polonium and radium. Since that time, many other radioactive nuclides have been identified. In fact, all of the nuclides beyond atomic number 83 are unstable and thus radioactive.

## Types of Radioactive Decay

A nuclide's type and rate of decay depend on the nucleon content and energy level of the nucleus. Some common types of radioactive nuclide emissions are summarized in **Table 1.**

SCINKS.
www.scilinks.org
**Topic:** Radioactive Decay
**Code:** HC61254

**TABLE 1** ***Radioactive Nuclide Emissions***

| Type | Symbol | Charge | Mass (amu) |
|---|---|---|---|
| Alpha particle | ${}^{4}_{2}He$ | 2+ | 4.001 5062 |
| Beta particle | ${}^{0}_{-1}\beta$ | 1− | 0.000 5486 |
| Positron | ${}^{0}_{+1}\beta$ | 1+ | 0.000 5486 |
| Gamma ray | $\gamma$ | 0 | 0 |

process that fuels our sun and the stars. Creating and maintaining a fusion reaction is more complex and expensive than performing fission. Both fission and fusion release enormous amounts of energy that can be converted into energy as heat and electrical energy, and both produce **nuclear waste.** Fission produces more waste than fusion. As new processes are developed to use energy from fission and fusion, a more vexing question arises: how to contain, store, and dispose of nuclear waste.

### Containment of Nuclear Waste

Every radioactive substance has a half-life, which is the amount of time needed for half of a given material to decay. Radioactive waste from medical research, for example, usually has a half-life that is a few months or less. Some of the waste that is produced in a nuclear reactor will take hundreds of thousands of years to decay, and it needs to be contained so that living organisms can be shielded from radioactivity. There are two main types of containment: on-site storage and off-site disposal.

### Storage of Nuclear Waste

The most common form of nuclear waste is spent fuel rods from nuclear power plants. These fuel rods can be contained above the ground by placing them in water pools or in dry casks. Each nuclear reactor in the United States has large pools of water where spent rods can be stored, and some of the radioactive materials will decay. When these pools are full, the rods are moved to dry casks, which are usually made of concrete and steel. Both storage pools and casks are meant for only temporary storage before the waste is moved to permanent underground storage facilities.

### Disposal of Nuclear Waste

Disposal of nuclear waste is done with the intention of never retrieving the materials. Because of this, building disposal sites takes careful planning. Currently, there are 131 disposal sites in 39 states around the United States. The U. S. Department of Energy is developing a new site near Las Vegas, Nevada, called Yucca Mountain, for the permanent disposal of much of this waste. Nuclear waste could be transported there by truck and train beginning in 2017. This plan is controversial—some organizations oppose the idea of the disposal site, and others have proposed alternate plans.

## SECTION REVIEW

1. What is required to shield alpha particles? Why are these materials effective?
2. **a.** What is the average exposure of people living in the United States to environmental background radiation?

   **b.** How does this relate to the maximum permissible dose?
3. What device is used to measure the radiation exposure of people working with radiation?
4. Explain why nuclear radiation can be used to preserve food.

**Critical Thinking**

5. **INFERRING CONCLUSIONS** Explain how nuclear waste is contained, stored, and disposed of, and how each method affects the environment.

# Nuclear Fission and Nuclear Fusion

**SECTION 4**

## OBJECTIVES

- Define *nuclear fission, chain reaction,* and *nuclear fusion,* and distinguish between them.
- Explain how a fission reaction is used to generate power.
- Discuss the possible benefits and the current difficulty of controlling fusion reactions.

**C.2.4** Compare the nuclear reactions of fission and fusion to chemical reactions (including the parts of the atom involved and the relative amounts of energy released)

## Nuclear Fission

Review **Figure 1,** which shows that nuclei of intermediate mass are the most stable. *In* **nuclear fission,** *a very heavy nucleus splits into more-stable nuclei of intermediate mass.* This process releases enormous amounts of energy. Nuclear fission can occur spontaneously or when nuclei are bombarded by particles. When uranium-235 is bombarded with slow neutrons, a uranium nucleus can capture one of the neutrons, making it very unstable. The nucleus splits into medium-mass nuclei with the emission of more neutrons. The mass of the products is less than the mass of the reactants. The missing mass is converted to energy.

### Nuclear Chain Reaction

When fission of an atom bombarded by neutrons produces more neutrons, a chain reaction can occur. *A* **chain reaction** *is a reaction in which the material that starts the reaction is also one of the products and can start another reaction.* As shown in **Figure 14,** two or three neutrons can be given off when uranium-235 fission occurs. These neutrons can cause the fission of other uranium-235 nuclei. Again neutrons are emitted, which

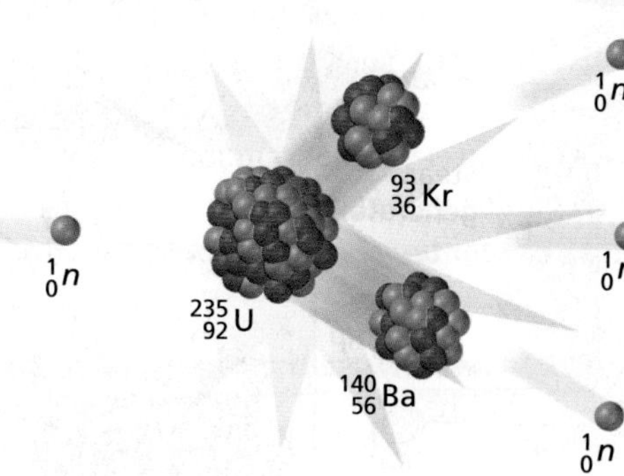


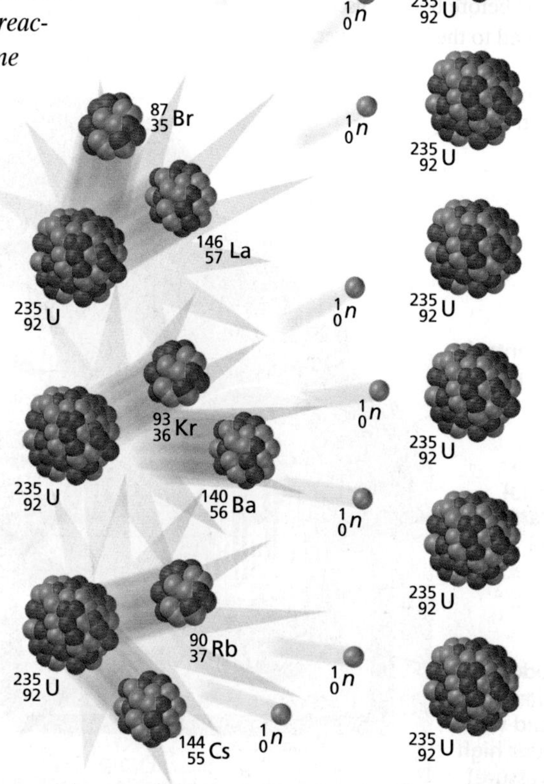


**FIGURE 14** Fission induction of uranium-235 by bombardment with neutrons can lead to a chain reaction when a critical mass of uranium-235 is present.

World War II prevented Lise
ceiving the Nobel Prize in
ining nuclear fission.

very of this unexpected phenomenon,
named nuclear fission, the talented Hahn
he 1944 Nobel Prize in chemistry. Because
tics, however, Lise Meitner did not receive
ing award in physics. She was not properly
il well after her death in 1968 for her role
process that she first explained and

of element did Fermi expect to find when
sorbed a neutron and then ejected a beta

the products of uranium disintegrations?

LINKS.
www.scilinks.org
**Topic:** Enrico Fermi
**Code:** HC60521

# CHAPTER HIGHLIGHTS

## The Nucleus

**Vocabulary**

- nucleon
- nuclide
- mass defect
- nuclear binding energy
- nuclear shell model
- magic numbers
- nuclear reaction
- transmutation

- The difference between the sum of the masses of the nucleons and electrons in an atom and the actual mass of an atom is the mass defect, or nuclear binding energy.
- Nuclear stability tends to be greatest when nucleons are paired, when there are magic numbers of nucleons, and when there are certain neutron-proton ratios.
- Nuclear reactions, which are represented by nuclear equations, can involve the transmutation of nuclides.

## Radioactive Decay

**Vocabulary**

- radioactive decay
- nuclear radiation
- radioactive nuclide
- alpha particle
- beta particle
- positron
- electron capture
- gamma ray
- half-life
- decay series
- parent nuclide
- daughter nuclide
- artificial transmutation
- transuranium element

- Radioactive nuclides become more stable by radioactive decay.
- Alpha, beta, positron, and gamma emission, and electron capture are types of radioactive decay. The type of decay is related to the nucleon content and the energy level of the nucleus.
- The half-life of a radioactive nuclide is the length of time that it takes for half of a given number of atoms of the nuclide to decay.
- Artificial transmutations are used to produce artificial radioactive nuclides, which include the transuranium elements.

## Nuclear Radiation

**Vocabulary**

- roentgen
- rem
- film badge
- Geiger-Müller counter
- scintillation counter
- radioactive dating
- radioactive tracer
- nuclear waste

- Alpha particles, beta particles, and gamma rays have different penetrating abilities and shielding requirements.
- Film badges, Geiger-Müller counters, and scintillation detectors are used to detect radiation.
- Everyone is exposed to environmental background radiation.
- Radioactive nuclides have many uses, including radioactive dating, disease detection, and therapy.
- Nuclear waste must be contained, stored, and disposed of in a way that minimizes harm to people or the environment.

## Nuclear Fission and Nuclear Fusion

**Vocabulary**

- nuclear fission
- chain reaction
- critical mass
- nuclear reactor
- nuclear power plant
- shielding
- control rod
- moderator
- nuclear fusion

- Nuclear fission and nuclear fusion are nuclear reactions in which the splitting and fusing of nuclei produce more stable nuclei and release enormous amounts of energy.
- Controlled fission reactions produce energy and radioactive nuclides.
- Fusion reactions produce the sun's energy in the form of heat and light. If fusion reactions could be controlled, they would produce more usable energy per gram of fuel than fission reactions.



RY

ed to produce fission reactions.

d not know enough chemistry to separate
ıranium disintegration from one another."

erlin

ents caught the attention of a physicist in
ner. Knowing that she could not perform
of chemically separating radionuclides
persuaded a colleague, radiochemist Otto
er explain Fermi's results. Joined by expert
t Fritz Strassman, Meitner's team began
utron-induced uranium decay at the end

et, Meitner's team, as well as all other sci-
ne, operated under two false assumptions.
d the makeup of the bombarded nuclei. In
action that had been observed, the result-
never differed from the original by more
ons or neutrons. Thus, scientists assumed
ts of neutron bombardment were radioiso-
ts that were at most a few places in the
efore or beyond the atoms being bombard-
d presumed in hypothesizing the

## The Nucleus

### SECTION 1 REVIEW

1. a. How does mass defect relate to nuclear binding energy?
   b. How does binding energy per nucleon vary with mass number?
   c. How does binding energy per nucleon affect the stability of a nucleus?
2. Describe three ways in which the number of protons and the number of neutrons in a nucleus affect the stability of the nucleus.

### PRACTICE PROBLEMS

3. The mass of a $^{20}_{10}Ne$ atom is 19.992 44 amu. Calculate the atom's mass defect.
4. The mass of a $^{7}_{3}Li$ atom is 7.016 00 amu. Calculate the atom's mass defect.
5. Calculate the nuclear binding energy of one lithium-6 atom. The measured atomic mass of lithium-6 is 6.015 amu.
6. Calculate the binding energies of the following two nuclei, and indicate which nucleus releases more energy when formed. You will need information from the periodic table and the text.
   a. atomic mass 34.988011 amu, $^{35}_{19}K$
   b. atomic mass 22.989767 amu, $^{23}_{11}Na$
7. a. What is the binding energy per nucleon for each nucleus in the previous problem?
   b. Which nucleus is more stable?
8. The mass of $^{7}_{3}Li$ is 7.016 00 amu. Calculate the binding energy per nucleon for $^{7}_{3}Li$.
9. Calculate the neutron-proton ratios for the following nuclides:
   a. $^{12}_{6}C$  c. $^{206}_{82}Pb$
   b. $^{3}_{1}H$  d. $^{134}_{50}Sn$
10. a. Locate the nuclides in problem 9 on the graph in **Figure 2.** Which ones lie within the band of stability?
    b. For the stable nuclides, determine whether their neutron-proton ratio tends toward 1:1 or 1.5:1.
11. Balance the following nuclear equations. (Hint: See Sample Problem A.)
    a. $^{43}_{19}K \longrightarrow ^{43}_{20}Ca + \underline{\ ?\ }$
    b. $^{233}_{92}U \longrightarrow ^{229}_{90}Th + \underline{\ ?\ }$
    c. $^{11}_{6}C + \underline{\ ?\ } \longrightarrow ^{11}_{5}B$
    d. $^{13}_{7}N \longrightarrow ^{0}_{+1}\beta + \underline{\ ?\ }$
12. Write the nuclear equation for the release of an alpha particle by $^{210}_{84}Po$.
13. Write the nuclear equation for the release of a beta particle by $^{210}_{82}Pb$.

## Radioactive Decay

### SECTION 2 REVIEW

14. Where on the periodic table are most of the natural radioactive nuclides located?
15. What changes in atomic number and mass number occur in each of the following types of radioactive decay?
    a. alpha emission
    b. beta emission
    c. positron emission
    d. electron capture
16. Which types of radioactive decay cause the transmutation of a nuclide? (Hint: Review the definition of *transmutation.*)
17. Explain how beta emission, positron emission, and electron capture affect the neutron-proton ratio.
18. Write the nuclear reactions that show particle conversion for the following types of radioactive decay:
    a. beta emission
    b. positron emission
    c. electron capture
19. Compare electrons, beta particles, and positrons.
20. a. What are gamma rays?
    b. How do scientists think gamma rays are produced?
21. How does the half-life of a nuclide relate to the stability of the nuclide?
22. List the three parent nuclides of the natural decay series.

23. How are artificial radioactive isotopes produced?
24. Neutrons are more effective for bombarding atomic nuclei than protons or alpha particles are. Why?
25. Why are all of the transuranium elements radioactive? (Hint: See Section 1.)

**PRACTICE PROBLEMS**

26. The half-life of plutonium-239 is 24 110 years. Of an original mass of 100.g, how much plutonium-239 remains after 96 440 years? (Hint: See Sample Problem B.)
27. The half-life of thorium-227 is 18.72 days. How many days are required for three-fourths of a given amount of thorium-227 to decay?
28. Exactly $\frac{1}{16}$ of a given amount of protactinium-234 remains after 26.76 hours. What is the half-life of protactinium-234?
29. How many milligrams of a 15.0 mg sample of radium-226 remain after 6396 years? The half-life of radium-226 is 1599 years.

# Nuclear Radiation

**SECTION 3 REVIEW**

30. Why can a radioactive material affect photographic film even though the film is well wrapped in black paper?
31. How does the penetrating ability of gamma rays compare with that of alpha particles and beta particles?
32. How does nuclear radiation damage biological tissue?
33. Explain how film badges, Geiger-Müller counters, and scintillation detectors are used to detect radiation and measure radiation exposure.
34. How is the age of an object that contains a radioactive nuclide estimated?

# Nuclear Fission and Nuclear Fusion

**SECTION 4 REVIEW**

35. How is the fission of a uranium-235 nucleus induced?
36. How does the fission of uranium-235 produce a chain reaction?
37. Describe the purposes of the five major components of a nuclear power plant.
38. Describe the reaction that produces the sun's energy.
39. What is one problem that must be overcome before controlled fusion reactions that produce energy are a reality?

## MIXED REVIEW

40. Balance the following nuclear reactions:
    a. $^{239}_{93}\text{Np} \longrightarrow {}^{0}_{-1}\beta + \underline{\ ?\ }$
    b. $^{9}_{4}\text{Be} + {}^{4}_{2}\text{He} \longrightarrow \underline{\ ?\ }$
    c. $^{32}_{15}\text{P} + \underline{\ ?\ } \longrightarrow {}^{33}_{15}\text{P}$
    d. $^{236}_{92}\text{U} \longrightarrow {}^{94}_{36}\text{Kr} + \underline{\ ?\ } + 3{}^{1}_{0}n$
41. After 4797 years, how much of the original 0.250 g of radium-226 remains? The half-life of radium-226 is 1599 years.
42. The parent nuclide of the thorium decay series is $^{232}_{90}\text{Th}$. The first four decays are as follows: alpha emission, beta emission, beta emission, and alpha emission. Write the nuclear equations for this series of emissions.
43. The half-life of radium-224 is 3.66 days. What was the original mass of radium-224 if 0.0500 g remains after 7.32 days?
44. Calculate the neutron-proton ratios for the following nuclides, and determine where they lie in relation to the band of stability.
    a. $^{235}_{92}\text{U}$
    b. $^{16}_{8}\text{O}$
    c. $^{56}_{26}\text{Fe}$
    d. $^{156}_{60}\text{Nd}$
45. Calculate the binding energy per nucleon of $^{238}_{92}\text{U}$ in joules. The atomic mass of a $^{238}_{92}\text{U}$ nucleus is 238.050 784 amu.

**46.** The energy released by the formation of a nucleus of $^{56}_{26}Fe$ is $7.89 \times 10^{-11}$ J. Use Einstein's equation, $E = mc^2$, to determine how much mass is lost (in kilograms) in this process.

**47.** Calculate the binding energy for one mole of deuterium atoms. The measured mass of deuterium is 2.0140 amu.

## CRITICAL THINKING

**48.** Why do we compare binding energy per nuclear particle of different nuclides instead of the total binding energy per nucleus of different nuclides?

**49.** Why is the constant rate of decay of radioactive nuclei so important in radioactive dating?

**50.** Which of the following nuclides of carbon is more likely to be stable? State reasons for your answer.

a. $^{11}_{6}C$ b. $^{12}_{6}C$

**51.** Which of the following nuclides of iron is more likely to be stable? State reasons for your answer.

a. $^{56}_{26}Fe$ b. $^{59}_{26}Fe$

**52.** Use the data in the table shown to determine the following:

a. the isotopes that would be best for dating ancient rocks

b. the isotopes that could be used as tracers

State reasons for your answers.

| Element | Half-Life |
|---|---|
| potassium-40 | $1.28 \times 10^9$ y |
| potassium-42 | 12.36 h |
| uranium-238 | $4.468 \times 10^9$ y |
| uranium-239 | 23.47 min |

## RESEARCH & WRITING

**53.** Investigate the history of the Manhattan Project.

**54.** Research the 1986 nuclear reactor accident at Chernobyl, Ukraine. What factors combined to cause the accident?

**55.** Find out about the various fusion-energy research projects that are being conducted in the United States and other parts of the world. What obstacles in finding an economical method of producing energy must still be overcome?

## ALTERNATIVE ASSESSMENT

**56.** Using the library, research the medical uses of radioactive isotopes such as cobalt-60 and technetium-99. Evaluate the benefits and risks of using radioisotopes in the diagnosis and treatment of medical conditions. Report your findings to the class.

**Graphing Calculator**
**Half-Lives**

Go to **go.hrw.com** for a graphing calculator exercise that asks you to determine the amount of a radioactive isotope based on its half-life.

**Keyword:** HC6NUCX

# Math Tutor CALCULATING WITH HALF-LIFE

The rate at which a sample of a radioactive nuclide decays is expressed in terms of half-life. This quantity is the time required for half of the atoms of a sample of a given nuclide to decay. For example, it takes 37.2 min for half of the nuclei of chlorine-38 to decay to argon-38. After 37.2 min, 0.50 g of a 1.0 g sample of chlorine-38 will remain and there will be 0.50 g of argon-38. After two half-lives (74.4 min), the fraction of chlorine-38 that remains will be $\frac{1}{2}$ of $\frac{1}{2}$, or $\frac{1}{4}$.

After $n$ half-lives, the fraction of a radioactive nuclide that remains is $\left(\frac{1}{2}\right)^n$, or $2^{-n}$.

If you know the amount of nuclide that was present initially and the amount of nuclide that remains, you can determine the number of half-lives that have passed.

## Problem-Solving TIPS

- Familiarize yourself with the values of some common powers of two ($2^n$, $n = 1, 2, 3, 4, 5, 6$, etc). This will allow you to determine the number of half-lives quickly.

### SAMPLE 1

**The half-life of polonium-218 is 3.04 min. A sample of polonium contains 0.00558 g of $^{218}_{84}Po$. What mass of $^{218}_{84}Po$ will remain after 18.24 min?**

First, you must determine the number of half-lives that have passed in 18.24 min.

$$\text{number of half-lives} = \frac{\text{time elapsed}}{\text{half-life}} = \frac{18.24\text{ min}}{3.04\text{ min}} = 6.00\text{ half-lives}$$

Then, to determine the mass of polonium-218 remaining, apply the following relationship.

$$\text{mass remaining} = \text{starting mass} \times \text{fraction remaining}$$

$$\text{mass } ^{218}_{84}\text{Po remaining} = 0.00558\text{ g} \times \left(\frac{1}{2}\right)^6 = 0.00558\text{ g} \times \frac{1}{64} = 8.72 \times 10^{-5}\text{ g } ^{218}_{84}\text{Po}$$

### SAMPLE 2

**The half-life of potassium-40 is $1.3 \times 10^9$ years. A volcanic rock contains $\frac{1}{8}$ of the amount of potassium-40 found in newly formed rocks. When was the rock formed?**

First, determine the number of half-lives that have passed.

$$\text{fraction remaining} = \frac{1}{8} = \left(\frac{1}{2}\right) \times \left(\frac{1}{2}\right) \times \left(\frac{1}{2}\right)$$

Therefore, three half-lives have passed. The time since the rock was formed is 3 half-lives $\times \left(1.3 \times 10^9 \frac{\text{y}}{\text{half-life}}\right) = 3.9 \times 10^9$ y.

### PRACTICE PROBLEMS

1. A sample of chromium contains $8.9 \times 10^{-5}$ g of the radioactive nuclide chromium-51, which has a half-life of 28 days. What mass of chromium-51 will remain in the sample after 168 days?

2. The half-life of lead-202 is 53 000 years. A sample of lead contains only $\frac{1}{256}$ of the expected amount of lead-202. How old is the lead sample?

# Standardized Test Prep

**Answer the following items on a separate piece of paper.**

**MULTIPLE CHOICE**

**1.** Complete the following nuclear equation:
$\underline{?} \longrightarrow {}^{187}_{76}\text{Os} + {}^{0}_{-1}\beta$

**A.** ${}^{187}_{77}\text{Os}$
**B.** ${}^{187}_{75}\text{Os}$
**C.** ${}^{187}_{77}\text{Ir}$
**D.** ${}^{187}_{75}\text{Re}$

**2.** The mass of the nucleus is

**A.** greater than the mass of the protons and neutrons that make up the nucleus.
**B.** equal to the mass of the protons and neutrons that make up the nucleus.
**C.** less than the mass of the protons and neutrons that make up the nucleus.
**D.** converted to energy.

**3.** Which type of radiation has the most penetrating ability?

**A.** an alpha particle
**B.** a beta particle
**C.** a gamma ray
**D.** a neutron

**4.** Which two particles have the same mass but opposite charge?

**A.** a beta particle and a positron
**B.** a neutron and a proton
**C.** a proton and an electron
**D.** an alpha particle and a proton

**5.** Which of the following nuclear equations is correctly balanced?

**A.** ${}^{37}_{18}\text{Ar} + {}^{0}_{-1}e \longrightarrow {}^{37}_{17}\text{Cl}$
**B.** ${}^{6}_{3}\text{Li} + 2{}^{1}_{0}n \longrightarrow {}^{4}_{2}\text{He} + {}^{3}_{1}\text{H}$
**C.** ${}^{254}_{99}\text{Es} + {}^{4}_{2}\text{He} \longrightarrow {}^{258}_{101}\text{Md} + 2{}^{1}_{0}n$
**D.** ${}^{14}_{7}\text{N} + {}^{4}_{2}\text{He} \longrightarrow {}^{17}_{8}\text{O} + {}^{2}_{1}\text{H}$

**6.** Gamma rays

**A.** have the same energy as beta particles do.
**B.** are visible light.
**C.** have no charge and no mass.
**D.** are not a form of electromagnetic radiation.

**7.** Which of the following nuclides is radioactive?

**A.** ${}^{40}_{20}\text{Ca}$
**B.** ${}^{226}_{88}\text{Ra}$
**C.** ${}^{12}_{6}\text{C}$
**D.** ${}^{206}_{82}\text{Pb}$

**8.** The half-life of thorium-234 is 24 days. If you have a 42.0 g sample of thorium-24, how much will remain after 72 days?

**A.** 42.0 g
**B.** 21.0 g
**C.** 10.5 g
**D.** 5.25 g

**9.** It takes 5.2 min for a 4.0 g sample of francium-210 to decay until only 1.0 g is left. What is the half-life of francium-210?

**A.** 1.3 min
**B.** 2.6 min
**C.** 5.2 min
**D.** 7.8 min

**SHORT ANSWER**

**10.** Write the nuclear equation that represents the process in which a neutron in the nucleus is changed to a proton with the emission of a beta particle.

**11.** Describe a positron, and write its nuclear symbol.

**EXTENDED RESPONSE**

**12.** Explain the difference between nuclear fission and nuclear fusion, and explain the energy changes that accompany each process.

**13.** What is meant by the term *mass defect*?

**Test TIP** Keeping a positive attitude during any test will help you focus on the test and likely improve your score.

CHAPTER LAB

# Simulation of Nuclear Decay Using Pennies and Paper

## OBJECTIVES

- ***Infer*** **that the rate of decay can be simulated by a random process.**
- ***Compare*** **the numbers of pennies that are showing heads with the number showing tails.**
- ***Create*** **a string plot that represents nuclear decay.**
- ***Relate*** **observations to the rate of nuclear decay.**
- ***Graph*** **the data.**
- ***Compare*** **the results of the two simulation procedures.**

## MATERIALS

- **colored paper or cloth strips, approximately 65 cm × 2.5 cm (2 strips)**
- **graph paper**
- **one sheet of stiff poster board, 70 cm × 60 cm**
- **pennies or other objects supplied by your teacher (100)**
- **scissors, tape, meter stick, pencil, and string**
- **shoe box with lid**

## BACKGROUND

Radioactive isotopes are unstable. All radioactive matter decays, or breaks down, in a predictable pattern. Radioactive isotopes release radiation as they disintegrate into daughter isotopes.

The rate of decay is a measure of how fast an isotope changes into its daughter isotope. The rate of radioactive decay is conveniently characterized by the isotope's half-life, the period of time it takes one-half of the original material to decay. Half-lives vary from billions of years to fractions of a second.

## SAFETY

For a review of safety, please see **Safety in the Chemistry Laboratory** in the front of your book.

## PREPARATION

1. For Part A, make a data table that has at least 10 rows in your lab notebook by using the format described by your teacher.

## PROCEDURE

### Part A: Simulating radioactive decay with pennies

1. Place 100 pennies into the shoe box so that the head sides are up. The pennies will represent atoms. Record 100 in the "Unchanged atoms" column and 0 in the "Changed atoms" column.
2. With the lid on the box, shake the box up and down 5 times. We will count each shaking period as being equivalent to 10 s.
3. Open the lid, and remove all of the pennies that have the tails side up. These pennies represent the changed atoms.

4. Count the number of pennies remaining in the box. Record this number in the 10 s row of the "Unchanged atoms" column. Count the number of changed atoms (the pennies that you removed from the box), and record the number table in the 10 s row.

5. Each lab partner should predict how many times steps 2–4 will need to be repeated until only one unchanged atom remains. Record the time that each lab partner predicted. Remember that each shaking period is counted as 10 s, so four shaking periods would be recorded as 40 s.

6. Repeat steps 2–4 by counting and recording each time until only 1 (or 0) penny with the head side up remains.

**Part B: Simulating decay with paper**

7. Draw an *y*-axis and *x*-axis on the poster board so that they are about 5 cm from the left side and the bottom edge respectively. Label the *x*-axis as "Time" and the *y*-axis as "Amount of material."

8. Along the *x*-axis, draw marks every 10 cm from the *y*-axis line. Label the first mark "0" and the next mark "1," and so on. Each mark represents 1 minute.

9. Place one of the colored strips vertically with its lower edge centered on the 0 mark of the *x*-axis. Tape the strip in place.

10. Fold the other colored strip in half, and cut it in the middle. Place one-half of the strip so that it is centered on the next mark, and tape the strip in place.

11. Fold the remaining piece of the strip in half, and cut it exactly in the middle.

12. Place one of the pieces so that it is centered on the next mark, and tape the piece in place.

13. Repeat steps 11 and 12, and each time, tape the first piece vertically at the next *x*-axis mark. Continue until you have at least 8 strips taped along the *x*-axis.

14. Use the string to join the tops of each strip of paper to make a continuous curve.

## CLEANUP AND DISPOSAL

15. Return the pennies and box to your teacher. Dispose of the poster board, strips, and string as instructed by your teacher. Clean up your lab station.

## ANALYSIS AND INTERPRETATION

**Part A**

1. **Predicting Outcomes:** How long did it take to have only 1 penny (0 pennies) left in the box? How close was your prediction in step 5?

2. **Analyzing Data:** Make a graph of your data on a piece of graph paper. Label the *x*-axis "Time" and the *y*-axis "Unchanged atoms." Plot the number of unchanged atoms versus time. Draw a smooth curve through the data points.

3. **Analyzing Results:** Each trial was comparable to a 10 s period of time. How long did it take for half of your pennies to be removed from the box? What is the half-life of the process?

4. **Interpreting Graphics:** Use your graph to determine the time it takes to have only 25% of the unchanged atoms remaining. In your experiment, how many pennies remained in the box at that time?

**Part B**

5. **Analyzing Results:** How many half lives have passed after 4 minutes?

6. **Interpreting Graphics:** Using the string plot, determine how many minutes it took until only 20% of the original material remained.

## CONCLUSIONS

1. **Inferring Conclusions:** If you started with a paper strip that was twice as long, would the half-life change?

2. **Inferring Conclusions:** Is there a relationship between the graph from Part A and the string plot from Part B?

# CHAPTER 22

# *Organic Chemistry*

*Nanotubes and buckminsterfullerene balls are molecules that contain repeated hexagons of carbon atoms. The rainbow pattern is a graph of electron distribution around the molecules.*

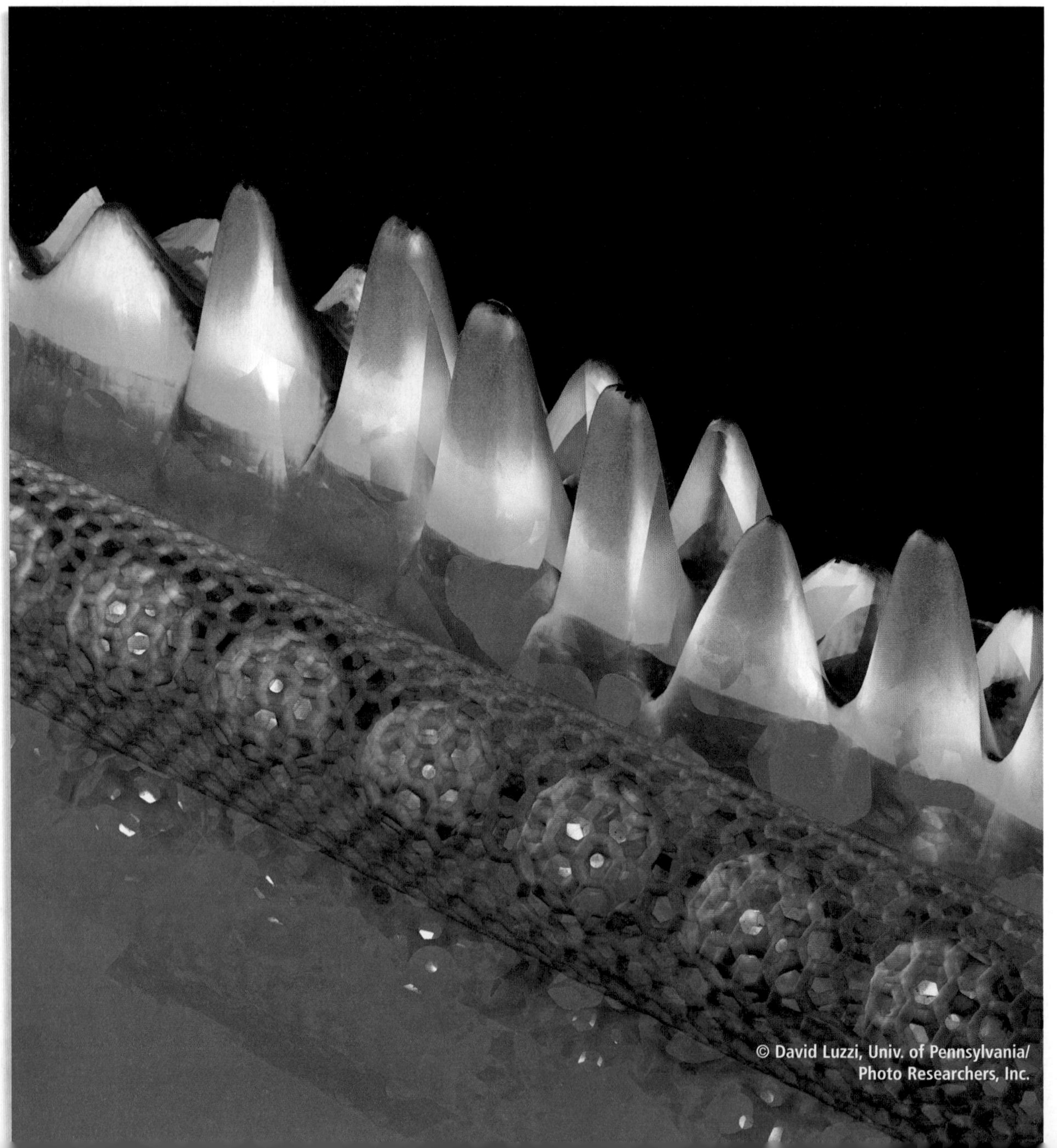

# Organic Compounds

SECTION 1

 **C.3.4** Explain the unique bonding characteristics of carbon that have resulted in the formation of a large variety of organic structures

**All** organic compounds contain carbon atoms. However, not all carbon-containing compounds are classified as organic. There are a few exceptions, such as $Na_2CO_3$, CO, and $CO_2$, that are considered inorganic. **Organic compounds,** then, can be defined as *covalently bonded compounds containing carbon, excluding carbonates and oxides.* **Figure 1** shows a few familiar items that contain organic compounds.

## Carbon Bonding and the Diversity of Organic Compounds

The diversity of organic compounds results from the uniqueness of carbon's structure and bonding. Carbon's electronic structure allows it to bind to itself to form chains and rings, to bind covalently to other elements, and to bind to itself and other elements in different arrangements.

### Objectives

- Explain how the structure and bonding of carbon lead to the diversity and number of organic compounds.
- Compare the use of molecular and structural formulas to represent organic compounds.
- Compare structural and geometric isomers of organic compounds.

**FIGURE 1** Aspirin, polyethylene in plastic bags, citric acid in fruit, and amino acids in animals are all examples of organic compounds.

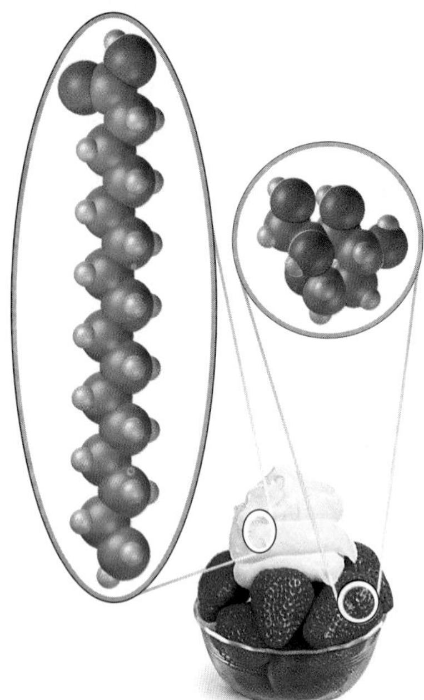

FIGURE 2 Compare the shape of a fatty acid found in cream with that of fructose, found in fruit. In the fatty acid, the carbon atoms are in chains. In fructose, carbon atoms form a ring.

## Carbon-Carbon Bonding

Carbon atoms are unique in their ability to form long chains and rings of covalently bonded atoms. This type of bonding is known as **catenation,** *the covalent bonding of an element to itself to form chains or rings.* In addition, carbon atoms in these structures can be linked by single, double, or triple covalent bonds. Examples of molecules containing carbon-atom rings and chains are shown in **Figure 2.**

## Carbon Bonding to Other Elements

Besides binding to other carbon atoms, carbon atoms bind readily to elements with similar electronegativities. Organic compounds consist of carbon and these other elements. **Hydrocarbons** *are composed of only carbon and hydrogen; they are the simplest organic compounds.* Other organic compounds contain hydrocarbon backbones to which other elements, primarily O, N, S, and the halogens, are attached. **Figure 3** shows a molecule in which carbon atoms are bound to other elements.

## Arrangement of Atoms

The bonding capabilities of carbon also allow for different arrangements of atoms. This means that some compounds may contain the same atoms but have different properties because the atoms are arranged differently. For example, the molecular formula $C_2H_6O$ represents both ethanol and dimethyl ether. *Compounds that have the same molecular formula but different structures are called* **isomers.**

FIGURE 3 In firefly luciferin, carbon atoms bind to hydrogen, oxygen, nitrogen, and sulfur. Luciferin is responsible for the light emitted from the tail of a firefly.

# Structural Formulas

Organic chemists use structural formulas to represent organic compounds. *A* **structural formula** *indicates the number and types of atoms present in a molecule and also shows the bonding arrangement of the atoms.* An example of a structural formula for an isomer of $C_4H_{10}$ is the following.

$$
\begin{array}{ccccccc}
 & \mathrm{H} & & \mathrm{H} & & \mathrm{H} & \\
 & | & & | & & | & \\
\mathrm{H-} & \mathrm{C} & \text{---} & \mathrm{C} & \text{---} & \mathrm{C} & \mathrm{-H} \\
 & | & & | & & | & \\
 & \mathrm{H} & & \mathrm{H-C-H} & & \mathrm{H} & \\
 & & & | & & & \\
 & & & \mathrm{H} & & &
\end{array}
$$

Structural formulas are sometimes condensed to make them easier to read. In one type of condensed structure, hydrogen single covalent bonds are not shown. The hydrogen atoms are understood to bind to the atom they are written beside. The following structural and condensed structural formulas represent the same molecule.

$$
\begin{array}{ccccccc}
 & \mathrm{H} & & \mathrm{H} & & \mathrm{H} & \\
 & | & & | & & | & \\
\mathrm{H-} & \mathrm{C} & \text{---} & \mathrm{C} & \text{---} & \mathrm{C} & \mathrm{-H} \\
 & | & & | & & | & \\
 & \mathrm{H} & & \mathrm{H-C-H} & & \mathrm{H} & \\
 & & & | & & & \\
 & & & \mathrm{H} & & &
\end{array}
\quad \text{is the same as} \quad
\begin{array}{c}
\mathrm{CH_3-CH-CH_3} \\
| \\
\mathrm{CH_3}
\end{array}
$$

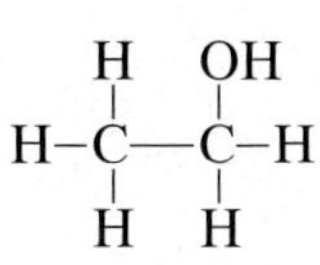


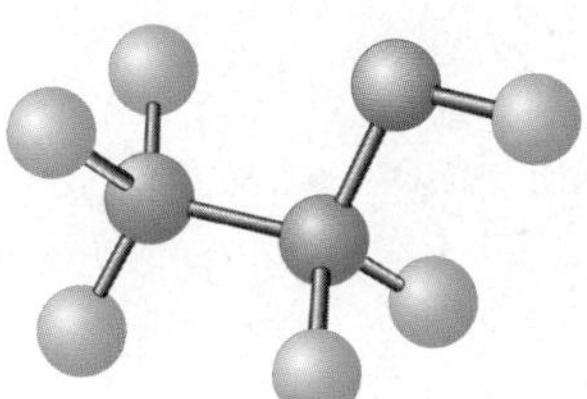
Ball-and-stick model

Space-filling model

**FIGURE 4** The structure of ethanol can be represented in different ways. Ball-and-stick and space-filling models represent the three-dimensional shape of the molecule.

Remember that the structural formula does not accurately show the three-dimensional shape of the molecule. Three-dimensional shape is depicted with drawings or models, as shown for ethanol in **Figure 4.**

## Isomers

You have learned that isomers are compounds that have the same molecular formula but different structural formulas. Isomers can be further classified by structure and geometry.

### Structural Isomers

**Structural isomers,** *also called "constitutional isomers," are isomers in which the atoms are bonded together in different orders.* For example, the atoms of the molecular formula $C_4H_{10}$ can be arranged in two different ways.

```
     H  H  H  H
     |  |  |  |
  H–C–C–C–C–H
     |  |  |  |
     H  H  H  H
```

butane

```
     H       H       H
     |       |       |
  H–C———C———C–H
     |       |       |
     H   H–C–H   H
             |
             H
```

methylpropane

Notice that the formula for butane shows a continuous chain of four carbon atoms. The chain may be bent or twisted, but it is continuous. The formula of methylpropane shows a continuous chain of three carbon atoms, with the fourth carbon atom attached to the second carbon atom of the chain.

Structural isomers can have different physical or chemical properties. For example, butane and methylpropane have different melting points, boiling points, and densities, as shown in **Table 1.**

**TABLE 1** ***Physical Properties of the Structural Isomers Butane and 2-Methylpropane***

| | Melting point (°C) | Boiling point (°C) | Density at 20°C (g/mL) |
|---|---|---|---|
| butane | –138.4 | –0.5 | 0.5788 |
| 2-methylpropane | –159.4 | –11.633 | 0.549 |

extension

**Chemical Content**

Go to **go.hrw.com** for another version of this content. See the chapters "Carbon and Hydrocarbons" and "Other Organic Compounds."

**Keyword: HC6ORGX**

**FIGURE 5** Males of the Iowa strain of the European corn borer respond most strongly to mixtures of the female sex attractant pheromone that are 96% *cis* isomer. But males of the New York strain respond most strongly to mixtures containing 97% *trans* isomer.

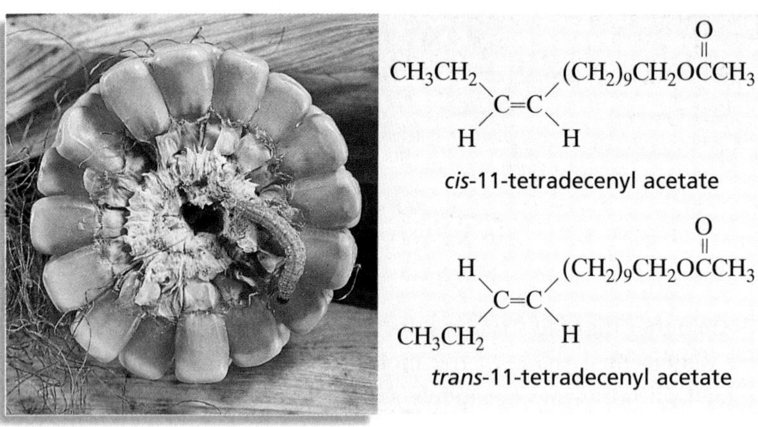


## Geometric Isomers

**Geometric isomers** *are isomers in which the order of atom bonding is the same but the arrangement of atoms in space is different.* Consider the molecule 1,2-dichloroethene, which contains a double bond. The double bond prevents free rotation and holds groups to either side of the molecule. This means there can be two different 1,2-dichloroethene geometric isomers, as shown below.

$$\underset{cis}{\begin{array}{ccc} Cl & & Cl \\ & C{=}C & \\ H & & H \end{array}} \qquad \underset{trans}{\begin{array}{ccc} H & & Cl \\ & C{=}C & \\ Cl & & H \end{array}}$$

The geometric isomer with the two chlorine atoms on the same side of the molecule is called *cis.* The isomer with the chlorine atoms on opposite sides of the molecule is called *trans.* **Figure 5** shows an example of geometric isomers that occur in nature.

## SECTION REVIEW

1. Which of the following represent the same molecule?

   **a.**
   $$\begin{array}{ccccccccccc} & & H & & H & & H & & H & & H \\ & & | & & | & & | & & | & & | \\ H & - & C & - & C & - & C & - & C & - & C & - H \\ & & | & & | & & | & & | & & | \\ & & H & & H & & H & & H & & H \end{array}$$

   **b.** $CH_3-CH_2-CH_2-CH_3$

   **c.**
   $$\begin{array}{l} CH_3-CH_2-CH_2 \\ \qquad\qquad\quad | \\ \qquad\qquad\; CH_2 \\ \qquad\qquad\quad | \\ \qquad\qquad\; CH_3 \end{array}$$

   **d.** $C_5H_{12}$

2. What are three characteristics of carbon that contribute to the diversity of organic compounds?
3. Define the term *isomer,* and distinguish between structural and geometric isomers.
4. Which of the following types of molecular representations can be used to show differences between isomers? Explain why each can or cannot.
   **a.** molecular formula
   **b.** structural formula
   **c.** three-dimensional drawing or model

### Critical Thinking

5. **INTERPRETING CONCEPTS** Can molecules that have molecular formulas $C_4H_{10}$ and $C_4H_{10}O$ be isomers of one another? Why or why not?

# Historical Chemistry

## The Beginnings of Organic Chemistry

Today, "organic chemistry" refers to the study of carbon compounds. However, organic chemistry was originally thought of as unique among all chemical sciences, because it emphasized the study of compounds that came from living organisms. Chemists of the early 19th century viewed organic compounds as fundamentally different from inorganic compounds, such as rocks and minerals, because organic compounds seemed to come only from living things. But because living organisms are built from carbon-containing molecules, organic chemistry later came to mean the study of carbon compounds, including those that are manufactured artificially.

Like modern researchers, early chemists were interested in the workings of the body. They tried to characterize the chemicals in blood, tissue, and urine. Urea, the molecule that the human body excretes to get rid of ammonia waste, was first isolated from urine in 1773. Although scientists could successfully isolate urea and other organic compounds, they did not know how to synthesize—that is, make from other, simpler chemicals—organic compounds. This tended to confirm a commonly-held belief, called *vitalism,* that organic compounds could only be made inside living organisms with the help of a special life force known as the "vital force."

▲ *Friedrich Wöhler was the first to synthesize an organic compound from inorganic chemicals.*

In 1828, the young German chemist Friedrich Wöhler announced that he had been able to make urea from inorganic chemicals. Wöhler had been attempting to prepare ammonium cyanate, $NH_4OCN$, from inorganic compounds, such as silver cyanate and ammonium chloride. But Wöhler unintentionally synthesized urea as a byproduct of the reactions that he carried out! Wöhler made an exciting discovery—the first example of organic synthesis—by using the same principles of qualitative analysis used by chemists today.

The remainder of the 19th century saw the syntheses of many other organic compounds. In 1845, acetic acid was prepared in several steps from charcoal. Many other organic molecules, such as dyes and glucose (blood sugar), were synthesized in the last half of the 19th century. Gradually, as more natural products were prepared in chemistry laboratories, the concept of vitalism was abandoned.

Today, urea, acetic acid, and many other organic chemicals are produced in huge quantities. Organic chemists can synthesize complex drug molecules, such as penicillin and taxol, which were once available only from natural sources. Using methods of organic synthesis, chemists can also prepare completely new drugs, polymers, flavors, and dyes that are not present in nature.

### Questions

1. What do people usually mean by the term *organic* when they use it to describe food, such as fruits and vegetables?
2. Think of three things that you use in your everyday life and that an organic chemist might be able to make.

SECTION 2

# Hydrocarbons

## OBJECTIVES

- Distinguish among the structures of alkanes, alkenes, alkynes, and aromatic hydrocarbons.
- Write structural formulas and names for alkanes, alkenes, and alkynes.
- Relate properties of different types of hydrocarbons to their structures.

**C.3.5** Illustrate the structural formulas and names of simple hydrocarbons (including alkanes and their isomers and benzene rings)

Hydrocarbons are compounds that contain only carbon and hydrogen. They make up the simplest class of organic compounds. All other organic compounds can be viewed as hydrocarbons in which one or more hydrogen atoms have been replaced by other atoms or groups of atoms.

Hydrocarbons are grouped mainly by the type of bonding between carbon atoms. **Saturated hydrocarbons** *are hydrocarbons in which each carbon atom in the molecule forms four single covalent bonds with other atoms.*

## Alkanes

*Hydrocarbons that contain only single bonds are* **alkanes.** In **Table 2,** the molecular formulas, structural formulas, and space-filling models are given for alkanes with one to four carbon atoms. If you examine the molecular formulas for successive alkanes in **Table 2,** you will see a clear pattern. Each member of the series differs from the preceding one by one carbon atom and two hydrogen atoms. For example, propane, $C_3H_8$, differs from ethane, $C_2H_6$, by one carbon atom and two hydrogen atoms, a $-CH_2-$ group.

SCILINKS.
www.scilinks.org
**Topic:** Alkanes
**Code:** HC60045

```
  H H              H H H
  | |              | | |
H-C-C-H          H-C-C-C-H
  | |              | | |
  H H              H H H
 ethane           propane
```

Compounds that differ in this fashion belong to a *homologous series.* A homologous series is one in which adjacent members differ by a constant unit. It is not necessary to remember the molecular formulas for all members of a homologous series. Instead, a general molecular formula can be used to determine the formulas. Look at the molecular formulas for ethane and propane, $C_2H_6$ and $C_3H_8$. They both fit the formula $C_nH_{2n+2}$. For ethane, $n = 2$, so there are two carbon atoms and $(2 \times 2) + 2 = 6$ hydrogen atoms. For propane, $n = 3$, so there are three carbon atoms and $(2 \times 3) + 2 = 8$ hydrogen atoms. Now consider a molecule for which we do not know the molecular formula. Suppose a member of this series has 30 carbon atoms in its molecules. Then $n = 30$, and there are $(2 \times 30) + 2 = 62$ hydrogen atoms. The formula is $C_{30}H_{62}$.

**TABLE 2 *Alkanes with One to Four Carbon Atoms***

| Molecular formulas | Structural formulas | Space-filling models |
|---|---|---|
| $CH_4$ | 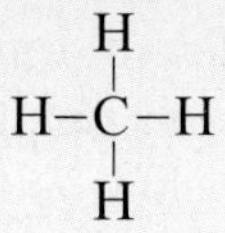 methane | 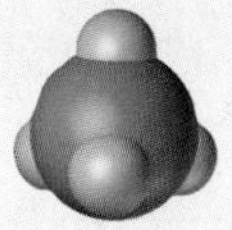 |
| $C_2H_6$ | 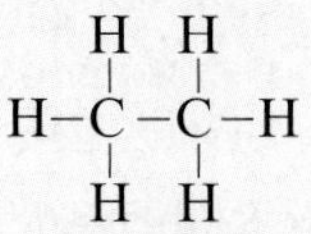 ethane | 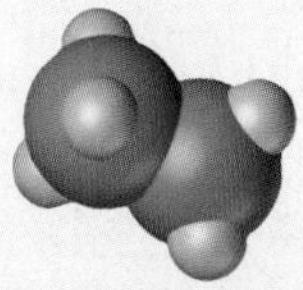 |
| $C_3H_8$ | 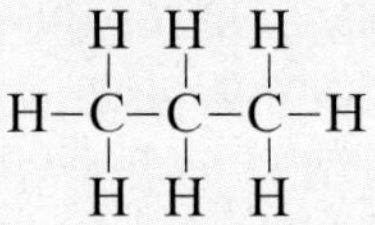 propane | 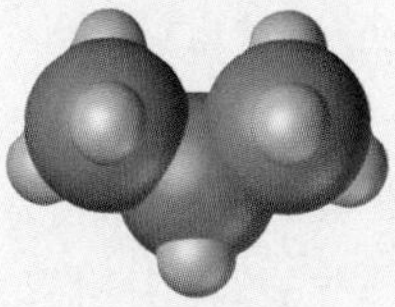 |
| $C_4H_{10}$ | 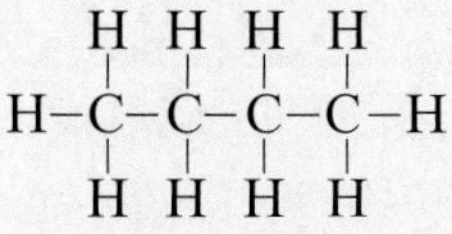 butane | 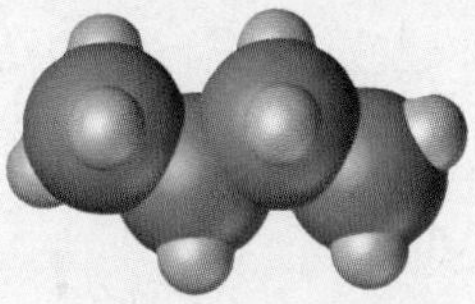 |
| | 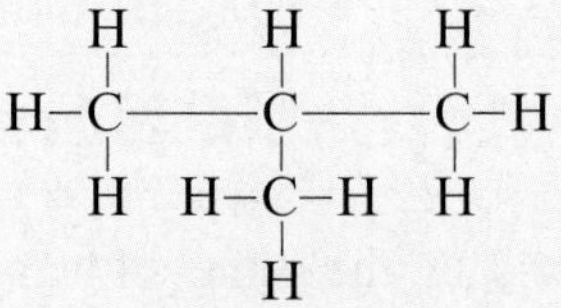 methylpropane |  |

Notice that for alkanes with three or fewer carbon atoms, only one molecular structure is possible. However, in alkanes with more than three carbon atoms, the chains can be straight or branched. Thus, alkanes with four or more carbon atoms have structural isomers. There are two possible structural isomers for alkanes with four carbon atoms, butane and 2-methylpropane.

The number of structural isomers increases greatly as the number of carbon atoms in alkanes increases. There are three isomeric $C_5H_{12}$ alkanes, five isomeric $C_6H_{14}$ alkanes, and nine isomeric $C_7H_{16}$ alkanes. There are nearly 37 million possible isomers of $C_{25}H_{52}$, though most have never been prepared or isolated.

## Cycloalkanes

**Cycloalkanes** *are alkanes in which the carbon atoms are arranged in a ring, or cyclic, structure.* The structural formulas for cycloalkanes are often drawn in a simplified form. In these skeletal representations, such as the one below on the right, it is understood that there is a carbon atom at each corner and enough hydrogen atoms to complete the four bonds to each carbon atom.

$$\begin{array}{c} CH_2 \\ CH_2 \quad\quad CH_2 \\ CH_2-CH_2 \end{array} \quad \textit{or} \quad \text{(pentagon)}$$

cyclopentane    cyclopentane

The general structure for cycloalkanes, $C_nH_{2n}$, shows that they have $2 \times n$ hydrogen atoms, two fewer hydrogen atoms than noncyclic alkanes, $C_nH_{2n+2}$, have. This is because cycloalkanes have no free ends where a carbon atom is attached to three hydrogen atoms. Another example, of a four-carbon alkane and cycloalkane, is shown below.

$$\begin{array}{ccccccccc} & H & & H & & H & & H & \\ & | & & | & & | & & | & \\ H- & C & - & C & - & C & - & C & -H \\ & | & & | & & | & & | & \\ & H & & H & & H & & H & \end{array} \qquad \begin{array}{ccccc} & H & & H & \\ & | & & | & \\ H- & C & - & C & -H \\ & | & & | & \\ H- & C & - & C & -H \\ & | & & | & \\ & H & & H & \end{array}$$

butane $C_4H_{10}$    cyclobutane $C_4H_8$

**TABLE 3 Carbon-Atom Chain Prefixes**

| Number of carbon atoms | Prefix |
|---|---|
| 1 | meth- |
| 2 | eth- |
| 3 | prop- |
| 4 | but- |
| 5 | pent- |
| 6 | hex- |
| 7 | hept- |
| 8 | oct- |
| 9 | non- |
| 10 | dec- |

## Systematic Names of Alkanes

Historically, the names of many organic compounds were derived from the sources in which they were found. As more organic compounds were discovered, a systematic naming method became necessary. The systematic method used primarily in this book was developed by the International Union of Pure and Applied Chemistry, IUPAC.

### Unbranched-Chain Alkane Nomenclature

To name an unbranched alkane, find the prefix in **Table 3** that corresponds to the number of carbon atoms in the chain of the hydrocarbon. Then add the suffix *-ane* to the prefix. An example is shown below.

$$\overset{1}{C}H_3-\overset{2}{C}H_2-\overset{3}{C}H_2-\overset{4}{C}H_2-\overset{5}{C}H_2-\overset{6}{C}H_2-\overset{7}{C}H_3$$

heptane

The molecule has a chain seven carbon atoms long, so the prefix *hept-* is added to the suffix *-ane* to form *heptane.*

**TABLE 4 Some Straight-Chain Alkyl Groups**

| Alkane | Name | Alkyl group | Name |
|---|---|---|---|
| $CH_4$ | methane | $-CH_3$ | methyl |
| $CH_3-CH_3$ | ethane | $-CH_2-CH_3$ | ethyl |
| $CH_3-CH_2-CH_3$ | propane | $-CH_2-CH_2-CH_3$ | propyl |
| $CH_3-CH_2-CH_2-CH_3$ | butane | $-CH_2-CH_2-CH_2-CH_3$ | butyl |
| $CH_3-CH_2-CH_2-CH_2-CH_3$ | pentane | $-CH_2-CH_2-CH_2-CH_2-CH_3$ | pentyl |

## Branched-Chain Alkane Nomenclature

The naming of branched-chain alkanes also follows a systematic method. The hydrocarbon branches of alkanes are alkyl groups. **Alkyl groups** *are groups of atoms that are formed when one hydrogen atom is removed from an alkane molecule*. Alkyl groups are named by replacing the suffix *-ane* of the parent alkane with the suffix *-yl*. Some examples are shown in **Table 4.** Alkyl group names are used when naming branched-chain alkanes. We will only present the method for naming simple branched-chain alkanes with only straight-chain alkyl groups. Consider the following molecule.

```
               CH3 CH3
                |   |
CH3-CH2-CH2-CH-CH-CH-CH2-CH3
                     |
                     CH-CH3
                     |
                     CH3
```

To name this molecule, locate the parent hydrocarbon. The parent hydrocarbon is the longest continuous chain that contains the most straight-chain branches. In this molecule, there are two chains that are eight carbon atoms long. The parent hydrocarbon is the chain that contains the most straight-chain branches. Do not be tricked by the way the molecule is drawn. The longest chain may be shown bent.

```
               CH3 CH3
                |   |
CH3-CH2-CH2-CH-CH-CH-CH2-CH3
                     |
                     CH-CH3
                     |
                     CH3
```

***NOT***

```
               CH3 CH3
                |   |
CH3-CH2-CH2-CH-CH-CH-CH2-CH3
                     |
                     CH-CH3
                     |
                     CH3
```

To name the parent hydrocarbon, add the suffix *-ane* to the prefix *oct-* (for a carbon-atom chain with eight carbon atoms) to form *octane.* Now identify and name the alkyl groups.

$$\begin{array}{c} \quad\quad\quad\quad\quad\ CH_3\ \ CH_3 \\ \quad\quad\quad\quad\quad\ |\quad\ \ | \\ CH_3-CH_2-CH_2-CH-CH-CH-CH_2-CH_3 \\ \quad\quad\quad\quad\quad\quad\quad\quad\quad\ \ | \\ \quad\quad\quad\quad\quad\quad\quad\quad\quad\ \ CH-CH_3 \\ \quad\quad\quad\quad\quad\quad\quad\quad\quad\ \ | \\ \quad\quad\quad\quad\quad\quad\quad\quad\quad\ \ CH_3 \end{array}$$

The three $-CH_3$ groups are methyl groups. The $-CH_2-CH_3$ group is an ethyl group. Arrange the names in alphabetical order in front of the name of the parent hydrocarbon.

**ethyl methyl**octane



### Petroleum Engineer

Petroleum engineers search for underground reservoirs of oil or natural gas. They then work with other scientists and engineers to develop and oversee drilling and production operations. Petroleum engineers are also responsible for developing technology and methods to increase the amount of oil or gas obtained and to lower the cost of drilling and production operations. In addition to possessing a broad range of engineering expertise (chemical, mechanical, or electrical) a petroleum engineer must also apply the basic sciences of chemistry, geology, physics, and mathematics.

To show that there are three methyl groups present, attach the prefix *tri-* to the name *methyl* to form *trimethyl.*

ethyl **tri**methyloctane

Now we need to show the locations of the alkyl groups on the parent hydrocarbon. Number the octane chain so that the alkyl groups have the lowest numbers possible.

$$\begin{array}{c} \quad\quad\quad\quad\quad\ CH_3\ \ CH_3 \\ \quad\quad\quad\quad\quad\ |\quad\ \ | \\ \overset{8}{C}H_3-\overset{7}{C}H_2-\overset{6}{C}H_2-\overset{5}{C}H-\overset{4}{C}H-\overset{3}{C}H-CH_2-CH_3 \\ \quad\quad\quad\quad\quad\quad\quad\quad\quad\ \ | \\ \quad\quad\quad\quad\quad\quad\quad\quad\quad\ \ {}_2CH-CH_3 \\ \quad\quad\quad\quad\quad\quad\quad\quad\quad\ \ | \\ \quad\quad\quad\quad\quad\quad\quad\quad\quad\ \ {}_1CH_3 \end{array}$$

***NOT***

$$\begin{array}{c} \quad\quad\quad\quad\quad\ CH_3\ \ CH_3 \\ \quad\quad\quad\quad\quad\ |\quad\ \ | \\ \overset{1}{C}H_3-\overset{2}{C}H_2-\overset{3}{C}H_2-\overset{4}{C}H-\overset{5}{C}H-\overset{6}{C}H-CH_2-CH_3 \\ \quad\quad\quad\quad\quad\quad\quad\quad\quad\ \ | \\ \quad\quad\quad\quad\quad\quad\quad\quad\quad\ \ {}_7CH-CH_3 \\ \quad\quad\quad\quad\quad\quad\quad\quad\quad\ \ | \\ \quad\quad\quad\quad\quad\quad\quad\quad\quad\ \ {}_8CH_3 \end{array}$$

Place the location numbers of *each* of the alkyl groups in front of its name. Separate the numbers from the names of the alkyl groups with hyphens. The ethyl group is on carbon *3*.

**3-**ethyl trimethyloctane

Because there are three methyl groups, there will be three numbers, separated by commas, in front of *trimethyl.*

3-ethyl**-2,4,5-**trimethyloctane

The full name is 3-ethyl-2,4,5-trimethyloctane.

The procedure for naming simple branched-chain alkanes can be summarized as shown in the list on the next page.

**Alkane Nomenclature**

1. **Name the parent hydrocarbon.** Find the longest continuous chain of carbon atoms that have straight-chain branches. Add the suffix *-ane* to the prefix corresponding to the number of carbon atoms in the chain.
2. **Add the names of the alkyl groups.** Add the names of the alkyl groups in front of the name of the parent hydrocarbon in alphabetical order. When there is more than one branch of the same alkyl group present, attach the appropriate numerical prefix to the name: *di* = 2, *tri* = 3, *tetra* = 4, and so on. Do so after the names have been put in alphabetical order.
3. **Number the carbon atoms in the parent hydrocarbon.** If one or more alkyl groups are present, number the carbon atoms in the continuous chain to give the lowest numbers possible in the name. If there are two equivalent lowest positions with two different alkyl groups, give the lowest number to the alkyl group that comes first in the name. (This will be the alkyl group that is first in alphabetical order, *before* any prefixes are attached.)
4. **Insert position numbers.** Put the position numbers of each alkyl group in front of the name of that alkyl group.
5. **Punctuate the name.** Use hyphens to separate the position numbers from the names. If there is more than one number in front of a name, use commas to separate the numbers.

## SAMPLE PROBLEM A

**Name the following simple branched-chain alkane:**

$$\begin{array}{l} CH_3-\underset{\displaystyle CH_3}{\underset{|}{CH}}-CH_2-\underset{\displaystyle CH_3}{\underset{|}{CH}}-\underset{\displaystyle CH_3}{\underset{|}{CH}}-CH_3 \end{array}$$

**SOLUTION** 1. Identify and name the parent hydrocarbon.

$$\begin{array}{l} CH_3-\underset{\displaystyle CH_3}{\underset{|}{CH}}-CH_2-\underset{\displaystyle CH_3}{\underset{|}{CH}}-\underset{\displaystyle CH_3}{\underset{|}{CH}}-CH_3 \end{array}$$

Because the longest continuous chain contains six carbon atoms, the parent hydrocarbon is *hexane.*

2. Identify and name the alkyl groups attached to the chain.

$$\begin{array}{l} CH_3-\underset{\displaystyle CH_3}{\underset{|}{CH}}-CH_2-\underset{\displaystyle CH_3}{\underset{|}{CH}}-\underset{\displaystyle CH_3}{\underset{|}{CH}}-CH_3 \end{array}$$

There is only one type of alkyl group, with one carbon atom. Alkyl groups with one carbon atom are methyl groups. Add the name *methyl* in front of the name of the continuous chain. Add the prefix *tri-* to show that there are three methyl groups present.

**trimethyl**hexane

## Unsaturated Hydrocarbons

Hydrocarbons that do not contain the maximum amount of hydrogen are referred to as *unsaturated.* **Unsaturated hydrocarbons** *are hydrocarbons in which not all carbon atoms have four single covalent bonds.* An unsaturated hydrocarbon has one or more double bonds or triple bonds. Carbon atoms can easily form double and triple bonds to other carbon atoms, so multiple bonds between carbon atoms are common in organic compounds.

### Alkenes

**Alkenes** *are hydrocarbons that contain double covalent bonds.* Some examples of alkenes are given in **Table 7.** Notice that because alkenes have a double bond, the simplest alkene, ethene, has two carbon atoms.

Carbon atoms linked by double bonds cannot bind as many atoms as those that are linked by only single bonds. An alkene with one double bond has two fewer hydrogen atoms than the corresponding alkane.

```
   H  H  H                      H
   |  |  |                      |
H—C—C—C—H             H—C=C—C—H
   |  |  |                |  |  |
   H  H  H                H  H  H
    C3H8                   C3H6
```

$C_3H_8$ $\qquad$ $C_3H_6$

Thus, the general formula for noncyclic alkenes with one double bond is $C_nH_{2n}$.

Because alkenes have a double bond, they can have geometric isomers, as shown in the examples below.

```
 H          H             H          CH3
   \      /                 \      /
    C=C                      C=C
   /      \                 /      \
CH3        CH3           CH3        H
```

*cis*-2-butene $\qquad$ *trans*-2-butene

**TABLE 7 *Structures of Alkenes***

| | ethene | propene | *trans*-2-butene | *cis*-2-butene |
|---|---|---|---|---|
| **Structural formula** | H(H)C=C(H)H | H(CH₃)C=C(H)H | H(CH₃)C=C(CH₃)H | H(CH₃)C=C(H)CH₃ |
| **Ball-and-stick model** | | | | |

## Systematic Names of Alkenes

The rules for naming a simple alkene are similar to those for naming an alkane. The parent hydrocarbon is the longest continuous chain of carbon atoms *that contains the double bond*.

$$\begin{array}{c} \quad CH_2{-}CH_3 \\ | \\ CH_2{=}C{-}CH_2{-}CH_2{-}CH_3 \end{array} \quad \textbf{\textit{NOT}} \quad \begin{array}{c} \quad CH_2{-}CH_3 \\ | \\ CH_2{=}C{-}CH_2{-}CH_2{-}CH_3 \end{array}$$

**pentene** hexane

The carbon atoms in the chain are numbered so that the first carbon atom in the double bond has the lowest number.

$$\begin{array}{c} CH_2{-}CH_3 \\ | \\ \overset{1}{C}H_2{=}\overset{2}{C}{-}\overset{3}{C}H_2{-}\overset{4}{C}H_2{-}\overset{5}{C}H_3 \end{array}$$

**1**-pentene

The position number and name of the alkyl group are placed in front of the double-bond position number. This alkyl group has two carbon atoms, an ethyl group. It is on the second carbon atom of the parent hydrocarbon.

**2-ethyl-**1-pentene

If there is more than one double bond, the suffix is modified to indicate the number of double bonds: 2 = *-adiene*, 3 = *-atriene*, and so on.

$$CH_2{=}CH{-}CH_2{-}CH{=}CH_2$$

1,4-pentadiene

The procedure for naming alkenes can be summarized as follows.

**Alkene Nomenclature**

**Use the rules for alkane nomenclature on page 721, with the following exceptions.**

1. **Name the parent hydrocarbon.** Locate the longest continuous chain that *contains the double bond(s)*. If there is only one double bond, add the suffix *-ene* to the prefix corresponding to the number of carbon atoms in this chain. If there is more than one double bond, modify the suffix to indicate the number of double bonds. For example, 2 = *-adiene,* 3 = *-atriene,* and so on.
2. **Add the names of the alkyl groups.**
3. **Number the carbon atoms in the parent hydrocarbon.** Number the carbon atoms in the chain so that the first carbon atom in the double bond nearest the end of the chain has the lowest number. If numbering from both ends gives equivalent positions for two double bonds, then number from the end nearest the first alkyl group.
4. **Insert position numbers.** Place double-bond position numbers immediately before the name of the parent hydrocarbon alkene. Place alkyl group position numbers immediately before the name of the corresponding alkyl group.
5. **Punctuate the name.**

## Chemistry in Action

### Carbon Allotropes

Carbon occurs in several different bonding patterns, called *allotropes,* which have very different properties. Diamond is a colorless, crystalline solid form of carbon, in which each atom is tetrahedrally bonded to four others in a network fashion. This three-dimensional bonding makes diamond the hardest material known.

Graphite is a soft, black, crystalline form of carbon that is a fair conductor of electricity. The carbon atoms in graphite are bonded together in layers. Within each layer, each atom is bonded to three other carbon atoms. But because adjacent layers are held together only by very weak London dispersion forces, graphite is very soft.

Diamond and graphite have been known for thousands of years. In the mid-1980s, a new solid allotropic form of carbon known as a *fullerene,* or, informally, "Buckyball," was discovered in the soot that forms when carbon-containing materials are burned with limited oxygen. The structure of a fullerene consists of a near-spherical cage of carbon atoms. The most stable fullerene is $C_{60}$, the structure of which resembles the design of a soccer ball.

## SAMPLE PROBLEM B

**Name the following alkene.**

$$\begin{array}{l} \qquad\quad CH_3 \\ \qquad\quad\;\, | \\ CH_3{-}CH{-}C{=}CH_2 \\ \qquad\qquad\;\;\, | \\ \qquad\qquad\; CH_2{-}CH_3 \end{array}$$

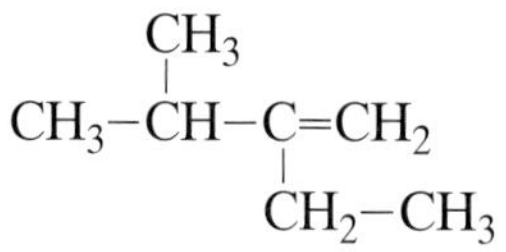

**SOLUTION**

1. Identify and name the parent hydrocarbon.

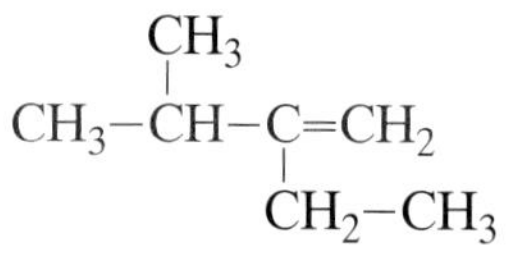

$$\begin{array}{l} \qquad\quad CH_3 \\ \qquad\quad\;\, | \\ CH_3{-}CH{-}C{=}CH_2 \\ \qquad\qquad\;\;\, | \\ \qquad\qquad\; CH_2{-}CH_3 \end{array}$$

The parent hydrocarbon has four carbon atoms and one double bond, so it is named *butene.*

2. Identify and name the alkyl groups.

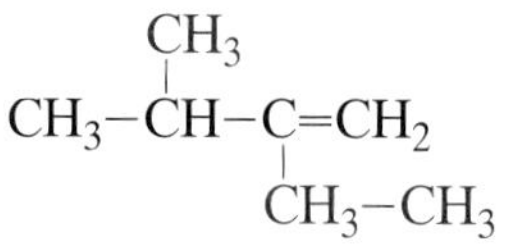

$$\begin{array}{l} \qquad\quad CH_3 \\ \qquad\quad\;\, | \\ CH_3{-}CH{-}C{=}CH_2 \\ \qquad\qquad\;\;\, | \\ \qquad\qquad\; CH_3{-}CH_3 \end{array}$$

The alkyl groups are *ethyl* and *methyl.*
Place their names in front of the name of the parent hydrocarbon in alphabetical order.

**ethyl methyl** butene

3. Number the carbon chain to give the double bond the lowest position.

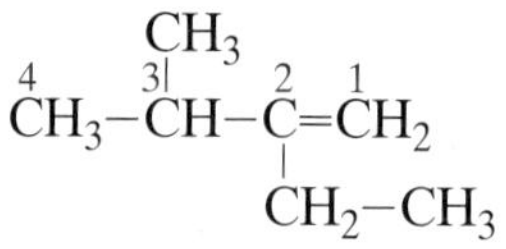

$$\begin{array}{l} \qquad\quad CH_3 \\ \;\,4 \qquad\; 3| \qquad\; 2 \quad\; 1 \\ CH_3{-}CH{-}C{=}CH_2 \\ \qquad\qquad\;\;\, | \\ \qquad\qquad\; CH_2{-}CH_3 \end{array}$$

Place the position number of the double bond in front of butene. Place the position numbers of the alkyl groups in front of each alkyl group. Separate the numbers from the name with hyphens. The full name is 2-ethyl-3-methyl-1-butene.

**PRACTICE**

*Answers in Appendix E*

Name the following alkenes:

1. $CH_3{-}CH_2{-}CH_2{-}CH{=}CH{-}CH_3$

2. 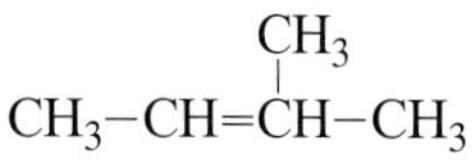
$$\begin{array}{l} \qquad\qquad\quad CH_3 \\ \qquad\qquad\quad\;\, | \\ CH_3{-}CH{=}CH{-}CH_3 \end{array}$$

3.
$$\begin{array}{l} \qquad\quad CH_3 \\ \qquad\quad\;\, | \\ CH_3{-}CH{-}CH{=}CH{-}CH_2{-}CH_3 \end{array}$$

4. 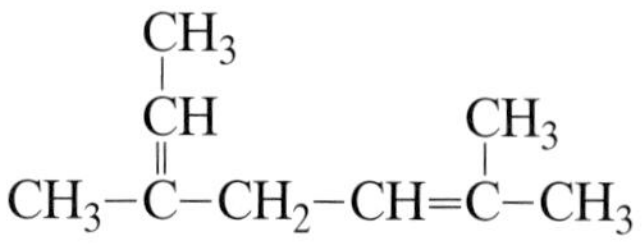
$$\begin{array}{l} \qquad\quad CH_3 \\ \qquad\quad\;\, | \\ \qquad\quad CH \qquad\qquad\quad CH_3 \\ \qquad\quad\;\, \| \qquad\qquad\qquad\;\, | \\ CH_3{-}C{-}CH_2{-}CH{=}C{-}CH_3 \end{array}$$

**extension**

Go to **go.hrw.com** for more practice problems that ask you to name alkenes.

Keyword: HC6ORGX

**FIGURE 8** α-farnesene is a solid alkene found in the natural wax covering of apples. Can you determine the IUPAC name for this large alkene?

## Properties and Uses of Alkenes

Alkenes are nonpolar and show trends in properties similar to those of alkanes in boiling points and physical states. For example, α-farnesene has 15 carbon atoms and 4 double bonds, as shown in **Figure 8.** This large alkene is a solid at room temperature and atmospheric pressure. It is found in the natural wax covering of apples. Ethene, the smallest alkene, is a gas. Ethene is commonly called *ethylene.*

Ethene is the hydrocarbon commercially produced in the greatest quantity in the United States. It is used in the synthesis of many plastics and commercially important alcohols. Ethene is also an important plant hormone. Induction of flowering and fruit ripening, as shown in **Figure 9,** are effects of ethene hormone action that can be manipulated by commercial growers.

## Alkynes

*Hydrocarbons with triple covalent bonds are* **alkynes.** Like the double bond of alkenes, the triple bond of alkynes requires that the simplest alkyne has two carbon atoms.

$$H{-}C{\equiv}C{-}H$$

ethyne

The general formula for the alkynes is $C_nH_{2n-2}$. Alkynes have four fewer hydrogen atoms than the corresponding alkanes and two fewer hydrogen atoms than the corresponding alkenes. The simplest alkyne is ethyne, more commonly known as *acetylene.*

| $H_3C{-}CH_3$ (H–C–C–H with H above and below each C) | $H_2C{=}CH_2$ | $H{-}C{\equiv}C{-}H$ |
|---|---|---|
| $C_2H_6$ | $C_2H_4$ | $C_2H_2$ |

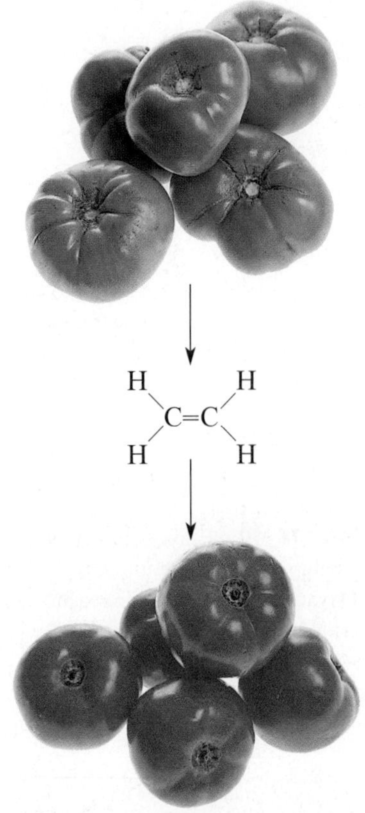


**FIGURE 9** Ethene is a plant hormone that triggers fruit ripening. At ordinary conditions, ethene is a gas.

## Systematic Naming of Alkynes

Alkyne nomenclature is almost the same as alkene nomenclature. The only difference is that the *-ene* suffix of the corresponding alkene is replaced with *-yne*. A complete list of rules follows.

**Alkyne Nomenclature**

**Use the rules for alkane nomenclature on page 721, with the following exceptions.**

1. **Name the parent hydrocarbon.** Locate the longest continuous chain that *contains the triple bond(s)*. If there is only one triple bond, add the suffix *-yne*. If there is more than one triple bond, modify the suffix. For example, 2 = *-adiyne*, 3 = *-atriyne*, and so on.
2. **Add the names of the alkyl groups.**
3. **Number the carbon atoms in the parent hydrocarbon.** Number the carbon atoms in the chain so that the first carbon atom in the triple bond nearest the end of the chain has the lowest number.
4. **Insert position numbers.** Place the position numbers of the triple bond immediately before the name of the parent hydrocarbon alkyne. Place alkyl group position numbers immediately before the name of the corresponding alkyl group.
5. **Punctuate the name.**

**extension**

**Chemistry in Action**

Go to **go.hrw.com** for a full-length article on synthetic diamonds.

**Keyword: HC6ORGX**

Two examples of correctly named alkynes are given below.

$$CH_3{-}CH_2{-}CH_2{-}C{\equiv}CH$$

1-pentyne

$$CH{\equiv}C{-}\underset{\displaystyle CH_3}{\underset{|}{CH}}{-}CH_3$$

3-methyl-1-butyne

## Properties and Uses of Alkynes

Alkynes are nonpolar and exhibit the same trends in boiling points and physical state as other hydrocarbons. The smallest alkyne, ethyne, is a gas. The combustion of ethyne when it is mixed with pure oxygen produces the intense heat of welding torches, as shown in **Figure 10.** The common name of ethyne is *acetylene,* and these welding torches are commonly called oxyacetylene torches.

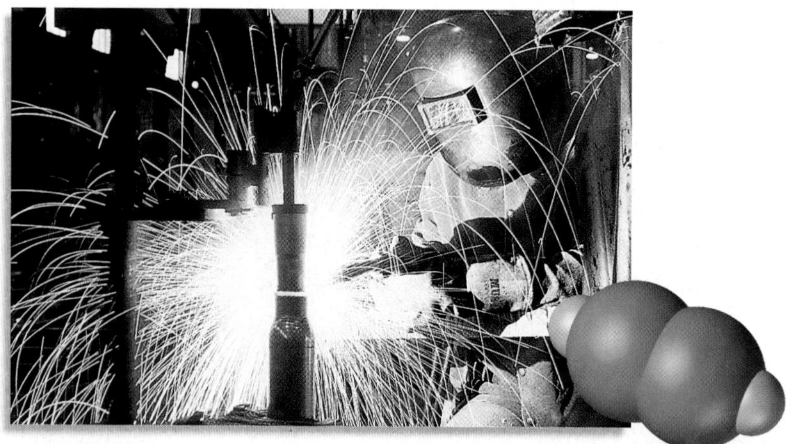

**FIGURE 10** Ethyne is the fuel used in oxyacetylene torches. Oxyacetylene torches can reach temperatures of over 3000°C.

## Aromatic Hydrocarbons

**Aromatic hydrocarbons** *are hydrocarbons that have six-membered carbon rings and delocalized electrons.* **Benzene** *is the primary aromatic hydrocarbon.* The molecular formula of benzene is $C_6H_6$. One possible structural formula is a six-carbon atom ring with three double bonds.

SciLINKS.
www.scilinks.org
**Topic:** Aromatic Compounds
**Code:** HC60095

However, benzene does not behave chemically like an alkene. The entire molecule lies in the same plane, as shown in **Figure 11.** Benzene contains resonance hybrid bonds, and the structure of the benzene ring allows electrons to be spread through delocalized *p*-orbitals over the whole ring. The structural and skeletal formulas below show benzene as a resonance hybrid, representing the delocalization of electrons.

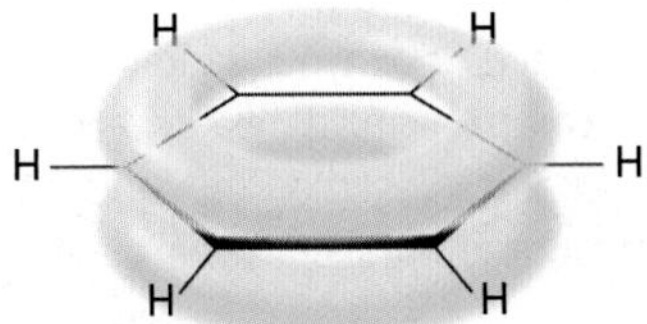

**FIGURE 11** Electron orbitals in benzene overlap to form continuous *p*-orbitals that allow the delocalized electrons to spread uniformly over the entire ring.

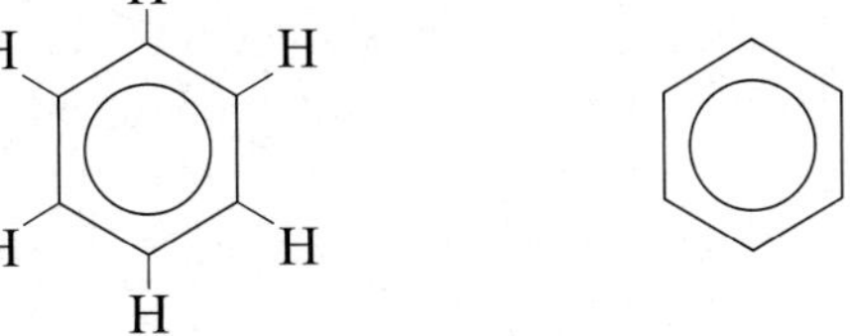

Aromatic hydrocarbons can be thought of as derivatives of benzene. The simplest have one benzene ring, as shown in the following example.

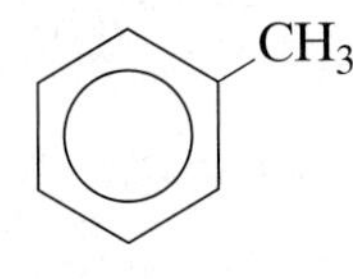


methylbenzene

## SECTION REVIEW

1. List the basic structural features that characterize each of the following hydrocarbons:
   **a.** alkanes
   **b.** alkenes
   **c.** alkynes
   **d.** aromatic hydrocarbons
2. Draw all of the condensed structural formulas that can represent $C_5H_{12}$.
3. Give the systematic name for each compound in your answers to item 2.
4. Give examples of a property or use of three hydrocarbons.
5. Name the following compounds:
   **a.** $CH_3{-}CH_2$ $CH_3$ (attached to the second and third carbons of) $CH_3{-}CH{-}CH{-}CH_2{-}CH_3$
   **b.** $CH_2{=}CH{-}CH{=}CH_2$
   **c.** $CH_3{-}C{\equiv}C{-}CH_2{-}CH_3$

**Critical Thinking**

6. **ANALYZING INFORMATION** Write the structural formulas for an alkane, an alkene, and an alkyne that have five carbon atoms each. Why are these three hydrocarbons not considered isomers?

## SECTION 3

# Functional Groups

### OBJECTIVES

- Define "functional group" and explain why functional groups are important.
- Identify alcohols, alkyl halides, ethers, aldehydes, ketones, carboxylic acids, esters, and amines based on the functional group present in each.
- Explain the relationships between the properties and structures of compounds with various functional groups.

**C.3.7** Classify organic compounds in terms of their functional group

A **functional group** *is an atom or group of atoms that is responsible for the specific properties of an organic compound.* A given functional group undergoes the same types of chemical reactions in every molecule in which it is found. Therefore, compounds that contain the same functional group can be classified together.

## Classes of Organic Compounds

A functional group gives an organic compound properties that are very different from those of the corresponding hydrocarbon. The compounds in **Table 8** have four carbon atoms, but they have very different physical properties due to their different functional groups. Some functional groups and their characteristic general formulas are shown in **Table 9.**

**TABLE 8** ***Comparing Classes of Organic Compounds***

| Name | Structural Formula | Melting Point (°C) | Boiling Point (°C) | Density (g/mol) |
|---|---|---|---|---|
| Butane | H H H H<br>H–C–C–C–C–H<br>H H H H | −138.4 | −0.5 | 0.5788 |
| 1-Butanol | H H H H<br>HO–C–C–C–C–H<br>H H H H | −89.5 | 117.2 | 0.8098 |
| Butanoic acid | O H H H<br>HO–C–C–C–C–H (C=O)<br>H H H | −4.5 | 163.5 | 0.9577 |
| 2-Butanone | H O H H<br>H–C–C–C–C–H (C=O)<br>H H H | −86.3 | 79.6 | 0.8054 |
| Diethyl ether | H H H H<br>H–C–C–O–C–C–H<br>H H H H | −116.2 | 34.5 | 0.7138 |

**TABLE 9 Classes of Organic Compounds**

| Class | Functional group | General formula |
|---|---|---|
| alcohol | $-\text{OH}$ | $R-\text{OH}$ |
| alkyl halide | $-X$ ($X = \text{F, Cl, Br, I}$) | $R-X$ |
| ether | $-\text{O}-$ | $R-\text{O}-R'$ |
| aldehyde | $-\overset{\text{O}}{\overset{\Vert}{\text{C}}}-\text{H}$ | $R-\overset{\text{O}}{\overset{\Vert}{\text{C}}}-\text{H}$ |
| ketone | $-\overset{\text{O}}{\overset{\Vert}{\text{C}}}-$ | $R-\overset{\text{O}}{\overset{\Vert}{\text{C}}}-R'$ |
| amine | $-\underset{\vert}{\text{N}}-$ | $R-\underset{R'}{\underset{\vert}{\text{N}}}-R''$ |
| carboxylic acid | $-\overset{\text{O}}{\overset{\Vert}{\text{C}}}-\text{OH}$ | $R-\overset{\text{O}}{\overset{\Vert}{\text{C}}}-\text{OH}$ |
| ester | $-\overset{\text{O}}{\overset{\Vert}{\text{C}}}-\text{O}-$ | $R-\overset{\text{O}}{\overset{\Vert}{\text{C}}}-\text{O}-R'$ |

SCILINKS.
**www.scilinks.org**
**Topic:** Alcohols
**Code:** HC60038

## Alcohols

**Alcohols** *are organic compounds that contain one or more hydroxyl groups.* The general formula for a class of organic compounds consists of the functional group and the letter *R,* which stands for the rest of the molecule. The general formula for alcohols is $R-\text{OH}$.

Hydrogen bonding in alcohols can also explain other properties and uses of alcohols. Cold creams, lipsticks, body lotions, and similar products generally include 1,2,3-propanetriol, commonly called glycerol, to keep them moist. A model for glycerol is shown in **Figure 12.** Multiple hydroxyl groups allow glycerol to form many hydrogen bonds with water molecules.

Alcohols are sometimes used today as alternative fuels and as octane enhancers in fuel for automobiles. Ethanol is combined with gasoline, for example, in a one-to-nine ratio to produce gasohol. Some experts have promoted the use of gasohol as a fuel for automobiles because it burns more cleanly and efficiently. However, there are also disadvantages. The combustion of ethanol produces only about 60% as much energy per gram as the combustion of gasoline does. The presence of ethanol also causes increased water absorption in the fuel.

**FIGURE 12** Glycerol contains three hydroxyl groups. This structure allows it to form multiple hydrogen bonds with water. Glycerol is added as a moisturizer to skin products.

## Alkyl Halides

**Alkyl halides** *are organic compounds in which one or more halogen atoms—fluorine, chlorine, bromine, or iodine—are substituted for one or more hydrogen atoms in a hydrocarbon.* Because $-X$ is often used to represent any halogen, an alkyl halide may be represented by the general formula $R{-}X$.

Alkyl halides are some of the most widely used organic chemicals. A family of alkyl halides that has received widespread attention in recent years is the chlorofluorocarbons, or CFCs. *CFCs* are alkyl halides that contain both chlorine and fluorine. The formulas for two widely used CFCs, Freon-11 and Freon-12, are shown below.

```
   Cl                  F
   |                   |
F—C—Cl             Cl—C—F
   |                   |
   Cl                  Cl
```

trichlorofluoromethane (Freon-11) dichlorodifluoromethane (Freon-12)

CFCs, which have been used as liquid refrigerants, contribute to the destruction of ozone in the upper atmosphere. When released into the atmosphere, CFCs can break down and release free chlorine atoms.

$$CCl_2F_2 \xrightarrow{\text{solar radiation}} Cl + CClF_2$$

The released chlorine atoms attack molecules of ozone, $O_3$, found in the upper atmosphere. The ozone is converted to diatomic oxygen.

$$Cl + O_3 \longrightarrow ClO + O_2$$

Chlorine atoms are eventually regenerated in various ways, including the reaction of ClO with O.

$$ClO + O \longrightarrow Cl + O_2$$

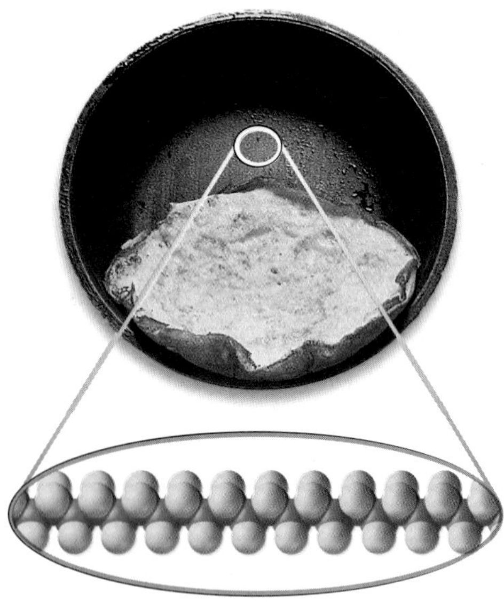

**FIGURE 13** The nonstick coating on this pan is made of Teflon, an alkyl halide.

This makes it possible for a single chlorine atom to destroy thousands of ozone molecules. Because CFCs are a major cause of ozone depletion, more than 100 nations signed an agreement in 1987 to reduce the amount of CFCs produced.

Another alkyl halide is tetrafluoroethene, $C_2F_4$. It is joined in long chains to make a material with the trade name Teflon®. Because of the unreactive carbon-fluorine bond, Teflon is inactive and stable to about 325°C. It also has a low coefficient of friction, which means that other objects slide smoothly over its surface. These properties enable Teflon to be used in heat-resistant machine parts that cannot be lubricated. It is also used in making utensils with "nonstick" surfaces, such as the frying pan in **Figure 13.**

## Ethers

**Ethers** *are organic compounds in which two hydrocarbon groups are bonded to the same atom of oxygen.* They can be represented by the general formula $R{-}O{-}R'$. In this formula, $R'$ may be the same hydrocarbon group as $R$ or a different one. Like alkanes, ethers are not very reactive compounds, so they are commonly used as solvents.

**FIGURE 14** Many common odors and flavors come from aldehydes and ketones.

## Aldehydes and Ketones

Aldehydes and ketones contain the *carbonyl group,* shown below.

$$-\overset{\overset{\displaystyle O}{\|}}{C}-$$

The difference between aldehydes and ketones is the location of the carbonyl group. **Aldehydes** *are organic compounds in which the carbonyl group is attached to a carbon atom at the end of a carbon-atom chain.* **Ketones** *are organic compounds in which the carbonyl group is attached to carbon atoms within the chain.* These differences can be seen in their general formulas, shown below.

$$R-\overset{\overset{\displaystyle O}{\|}}{C}-H \qquad\qquad R-\overset{\overset{\displaystyle O}{\|}}{C}-R'$$

aldehyde ketone

Aldehydes and ketones are often responsible for odors and flavors. **Figure 14** gives some examples.

## Amines

**Amines** *are organic compounds that can be considered to be derivatives of ammonia, $NH_3$.* Amines are common in nature. They often form during the breakdown of proteins in animal cells.

The unshared electron pair on the nitrogen atom makes amines act as weak bases in aqueous solutions, as shown below.

$$R-\underset{\underset{\displaystyle R'}{|}}{\ddot{N}}-R'' + H-O-H \rightleftharpoons R-\overset{\overset{\displaystyle H^+}{|}}{\underset{\underset{\displaystyle R'}{|}}{N}}-R'' + OH^-$$

extension

**Chemical Content**

Go to **go.hrw.com** for more information on functional groups.

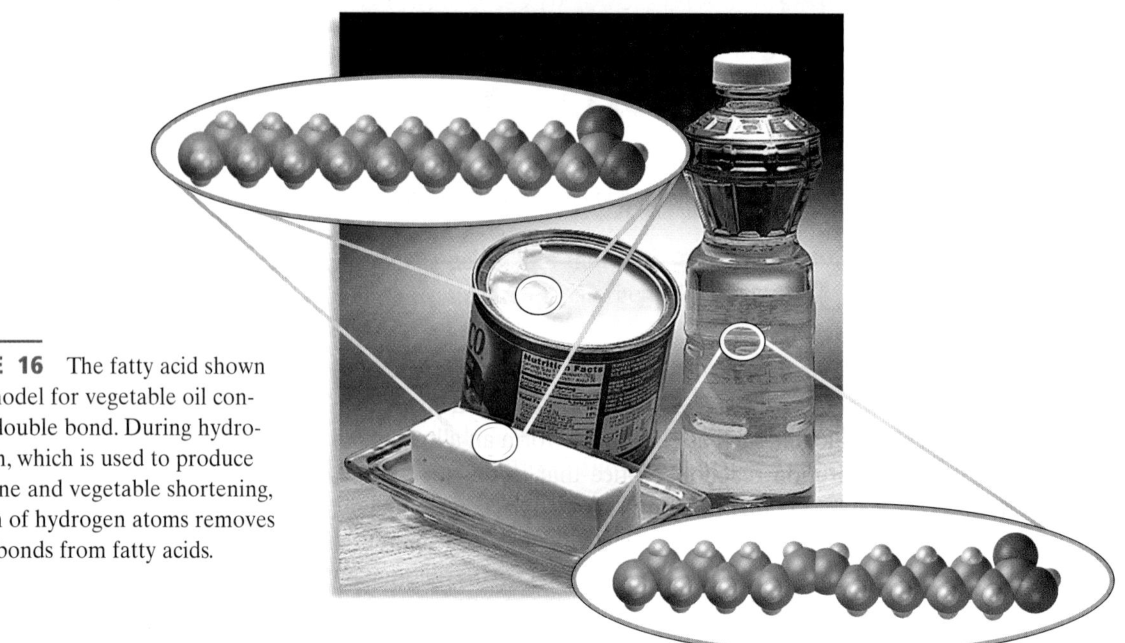

**FIGURE 16** The fatty acid shown in the model for vegetable oil contains a double bond. During hydrogenation, which is used to produce margarine and vegetable shortening, addition of hydrogen atoms removes double bonds from fatty acids.

$$\left(-\mathrm{CH_2-CH{=}CH-CH_2-CH{=}CH-CH_2}-\right) + \mathrm{H_2} \xrightarrow{\text{catalyst}} \left(-\mathrm{CH_2-CH{=}CH-CH_2-CH_2-CH_2-CH_2}-\right)$$

The molecule still consists of long chains of carbon atoms, but it contains far fewer double bonds. The conversion of these double bonds to single bonds changes the material from an oil, which is a liquid, into a fat, which is a solid. When you see the word *hydrogenated* on a food product, you know that an oil has been converted to a fat by this process. Examples of an oil and hydrogenated fats are shown in **Figure 16.**

## Condensation Reactions

*A* **condensation reaction** *is one in which two molecules or parts of the same molecule combine.* A small molecule, such as water, is usually removed during the reaction. An example is the reaction between two amino acids, which contain both amine and carboxyl groups. One hydrogen from the amine group of one amino acid combines with the hydroxyl from the carboxyl group of the other amino acid to form a molecule of water. When repeated many times, this reaction forms a protein molecule.

$$\underset{\text{amino acid}}{\mathrm{H-NH-CH}(R)\mathrm{-C({=}O)-OH}} + \underset{\text{amino acid}}{\mathrm{H-NH-CH}(R')\mathrm{-C({=}O)-OH}} \longrightarrow \underset{\text{dipeptide}}{\mathrm{H-NH-CH}(R)\mathrm{-C({=}O)-NH-CH}(R')\mathrm{-C({=}O)-OH}} + \underset{\text{water}}{\mathrm{H_2O}}$$

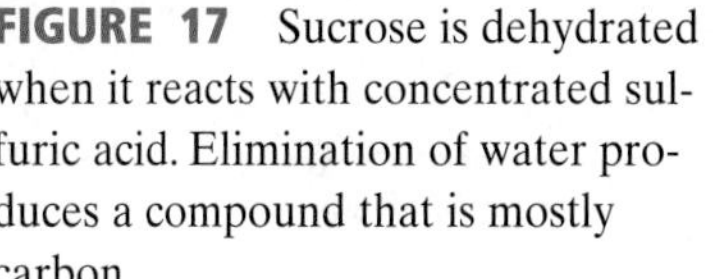

**FIGURE 17** Sucrose is dehydrated when it reacts with concentrated sulfuric acid. Elimination of water produces a compound that is mostly carbon.

## Elimination Reactions

*An* **elimination reaction** *is one in which a simple molecule, such as water or ammonia, is formed from adjacent carbon atoms of a larger molecule.* A simple example of an elimination reaction is the heating of ethanol in the presence of concentrated sulfuric acid. Under these conditions, a hydrogen atom bonded to one carbon atom and a hydroxyl group bonded to the second carbon atom are removed from the ethanol molecule. A molecule of water is formed as a result.

$$\begin{array}{c} \text{H}\ \ \text{OH} \\ |\quad\ | \\ \text{H}-\text{C}-\text{C}-\text{H} \\ |\quad\ | \\ \text{H}\ \ \text{H} \\ \text{ethanol} \end{array} \xrightarrow[\Delta]{H_2SO_4} \begin{array}{c} \\ \\ \text{H}-\text{C}=\text{C}-\text{H} \\ |\quad\ | \\ \text{H}\ \ \text{H} \\ \text{ethene} \end{array} + \begin{array}{c} \\ \\ H_2O \\ \\ \\ \text{water} \end{array}$$

Another example of an elimination reaction is the dehydration of sucrose with concentrated sulfuric acid, shown in **Figure 17.**

## Polymers

**Polymers** *are large molecules made of many small units joined to each other through organic reactions. The small units are* **monomers.** A polymer can be made from identical or different monomers. *A polymer made from two or more different monomers is a* **copolymer.**

Polymers are all around us. The foods we eat and clothes we wear are made of polymers. Some of the most common natural polymers include starch, cellulose, and proteins. Some synthetic polymers may be familiar to you as plastics and synthetic fibers.

Chemistry in Action

Go to **go.hrw.com** for a full-length article on high-barrier plastics.

**Keyword: HC6ORGX**

## Addition Polymers

An *addition polymer* is a polymer formed by addition reactions between monomers that contain a double bond. For example, molecules of ethene can polymerize with each other to form polyethene, commonly called polyethylene.

$$\underset{\text{ethene}}{n\,CH_2{=}CH_2} \xrightarrow{\text{catalyst}} \underset{\text{polyethylene}}{\left(CH_2{-}CH_2\right)_n}$$

The letter *n* shows that the addition reaction can be repeated multiple times to form a polymer *n* monomers long. In fact, this reaction can be repeated hundreds or thousands of times.

### Forms of Polyethylene and Related Polymers

Various forms of polyethylene, shown in **Figure 18,** have different molecular structures. High-density polyethylene (HDPE) is a linear polymer. It has a high density because linear molecules can pack together closely. One use of HDPE is in plastic containers such as milk and juice bottles because HDPE tends to remain stiff and rigid.

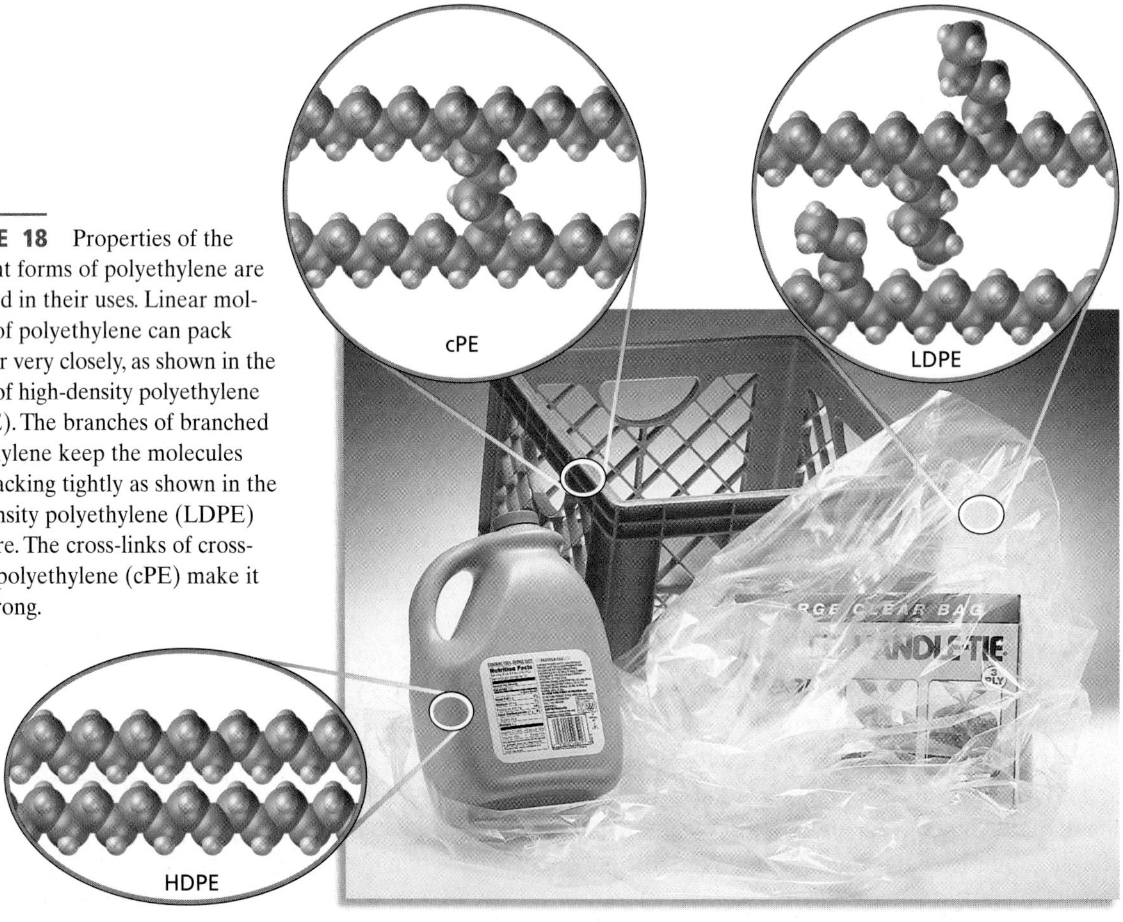

**FIGURE 18** Properties of the different forms of polyethylene are reflected in their uses. Linear molecules of polyethylene can pack together very closely, as shown in the model of high-density polyethylene (HDPE). The branches of branched polyethylene keep the molecules from packing tightly as shown in the low-density polyethylene (LDPE) structure. The cross-links of cross-linked polyethylene (cPE) make it very strong.

## Condensation Polymers

A *condensation polymer* is a polymer formed by condensation reactions. Monomers of condensation polymers must contain two functional groups. This allows each monomer to link with two other monomers by condensation reactions. Condensation polymers are usually copolymers with two monomers in an alternating order.

### Polyamides and Polyesters

One example of a condensation polymer is shown below. A carboxylic acid with two carboxyl groups, adipic acid, and an amine with two amine groups, hexanediamine, react with each other to form water.

$$n\,\mathrm{H{-}\overset{H}{\underset{|}{N}}{-}CH_2{-}CH_2{-}CH_2{-}CH_2{-}CH_2{-}CH_2{-}\overset{H}{\underset{|}{N}}{-}H} + n\,\mathrm{HO{-}\overset{O}{\overset{\|}{C}}{-}CH_2{-}CH_2{-}CH_2{-}CH_2{-}\overset{O}{\overset{\|}{C}}{-}OH} \longrightarrow$$

hexanediamine / adipic acid

$$\left(\mathrm{\overset{H}{\underset{|}{N}}{-}CH_2{-}CH_2{-}CH_2{-}CH_2{-}CH_2{-}CH_2{-}\overset{H}{\underset{|}{N}}{-}\overset{O}{\overset{\|}{C}}{-}CH_2{-}CH_2{-}CH_2{-}CH_2{-}\overset{O}{\overset{\|}{C}}}\right)_n + n\,H_2O$$

nylon 66 / water

The product is a polyamide and contains the adipic acid monomer and the hexanediamine monomer. This copolymer is known as nylon 66 because each of the monomers contains six carbon atoms. Nylon 66 is one of the most widely used of all synthetic polymers.

Polyesters are another common type of condensation polymer. They are formed from dialcohols and dicarboxylic acids, which undergo a condensation reaction to form an ester group, linking the alcohol end of a monomer to the acid end of a monomer. Polyesters have many uses, such as in tires, in food packaging, and as fibers in permanent press fabrics.

## SECTION REVIEW

1. Can an addition reaction occur between chlorine and ethane? Why or why not?
2. Does an addition reaction increase or decrease the saturation of a molecule?
3. The condensation reaction between two amino acids has a water molecule as one product. Which functional groups are the sources of the atoms in the water molecule?
4. Explain how elimination reactions could be considered the opposite of addition reactions.
5. Why can a molecule that has only one functional group *not* undergo a condensation reaction to form a polymer?
6. Would it be possible to have an addition polymer synthesized from a monomer that has only single bonds? Why or why not?

**Critical Thinking**

7. **APPLYING MODELS** Polyvinyl chloride (PVC) is a polymer that is widely used in pipes and flooring. It is an addition polymer made from chloroethene, commonly known as *vinyl chloride.*
   **a.** Draw the structure of vinyl chloride. Then, look up the structure or check it with your teacher.
   **b.** Write the reaction for the polymerization of vinyl chloride to form polyvinyl chloride (PVC).

# CHAPTER HIGHLIGHTS

## Organic Compounds

**Vocabulary**
organic compound
catenation
hydrocarbon
isomer
structural formula
structural isomer
geometric isomer

- The ability of carbon to bond to other elements and to allow different arrangements of atoms contributes to the diversity of carbon compounds.
- Isomers are compounds that have the same molecular formula but different structures. In structural isomers, the atoms are bonded together in different orders. In geometric isomers, the order of atom bonding is the same, but the atoms are oriented differently in space.

## Hydrocarbons

**Vocabulary**
saturated hydrocarbon
alkane
cycloalkane
alkyl group
natural gas
petroleum
unsaturated hydrocarbon
alkene
alkyne
aromatic hydrocarbon
benzene

- Alkanes are saturated hydrocarbons; they contain only single bonds. Physical trends in alkanes correspond to trends in alkane size and amount of branching.
- Organic compounds are named according to a systematic method.
- Unsaturated hydrocarbons have one or more multiple carbon-carbon bonds: these include alkenes, alkynes, and aromatic hydrocarbons.

## Functional Groups

**Vocabulary**
functional group
alcohol
alkyl halide
ether
aldehyde
ketone
amine
carboxylic acid
ester

- Functional groups are responsible for the properties of the organic compound that contains the functional group.
- Alcohols contain the hydroxyl functional group.
- Alkyl halides contain one or more halogen atoms.
- Two alkyl groups are joined to an oxygen atom in ethers.
- Both aldehydes and ketones contain the carbonyl group.
- Amines are derivatives of ammonia.
- Carboxylic acids contain carboxyl groups.
- In esters, the hydrogen atom of a carboxylic acid group has been replaced with an alkyl group.

## Organic Reactions

**Vocabulary**
substitution reaction
addition reaction
condensation reaction
elimination reaction
polymer
monomer
copolymer

- In substitution reactions, an atom or group of atoms is replaced. In addition reactions, an atom or group of atoms is added to a double or triple bond.
- In a condensation reaction, two molecules combine. In an elimination reaction, a small molecule forms from a large molecule.
- Polymers are large molecules made of many repeating units called *monomers.* A copolymer consists of two or more different monomers.

# CHAPTER REVIEW

## *Organic Compounds*

### SECTION 1 REVIEW

**1.** a. What is catenation?
b. How does catenation contribute to the diversity of organic compounds?

**2.** a. What information about a compound is provided by a structural formula?
b. How are structural formulas used in organic chemistry?

**3.** Can molecules with the molecular formulas $C_4H_{10}$ and $C_4H_{10}O$ be structural isomers of one another? Why or why not?

**4.** Can molecules with only single bonds (and no rings) have geometric isomers? Why or why not?

## *Hydrocarbons*

### SECTION 2 REVIEW

**5.** What are hydrocarbons, and what is their importance?

**6.** a. What do the terms *saturated* and *unsaturated* mean when applied to hydrocarbons?
b. What other meanings do these terms have in chemistry?
c. Classify alkenes, alkanes, alkynes, and aromatic hydrocarbons as either saturated or unsaturated.

**7.** Classify each of the following as an alkane, alkene, alkyne, or aromatic hydrocarbon.

a. Benzene ring with $CH_2{-}CH_3$ substituents (meta positions)

b. $CH_3{-}CH{=}CH_2$

c. $CH{\equiv}C{-}CH(CH_3){-}CH_2{-}CH_3$

d. $CH_3{-}CH(CH_3){-}CH_2{-}CH_2{-}CH_2{-}CH_2{-}CH_3$

**8.** Give the general formula for the members of the following:
a. alkane series
b. alkene series
c. alkyne series

**9.** a. What is a homologous series?
b. By what method are straight-chain hydrocarbons named?
c. Name the straight-chain alkane with the molecular formula $C_{10}H_{22}$

**10.** What are cycloalkanes?

**11.** a. What trend occurs in the boiling points of alkanes?
b. How would you explain this trend?
c. How is the trend in alkane boiling points used in petroleum fractional distillation?

**12.** Give examples of ethene's commercial uses.

**13.** Give one use for ethyne.

**14.** What is the name of the parent hydrocarbon of simple aromatic hydrocarbons?

### PRACTICE PROBLEMS

**15.** Name the following molecules. (Hint: See Sample Problem A.)

a. $CH_3{-}CH_2{-}CH_2{-}CH_2{-}CH_2{-}CH_2{-}CH_3$

b. $CH_3{-}C(CH_3)_2{-}CH_2{-}CH(CH_3){-}CH{-}CH_3$

c. $CH_3{-}C(CH_3)_2{-}CH_2{-}CH_2{-}CH(CH_2{-}CH_2{-}CH_2{-}CH_3){-}CH_2{-}CH_2{-}CH_2{-}CH_3$

**16.** Give the complete, uncondensed, structural formula for each of the following alkanes. (Hint: See Sample Problem A.)
a. decane
b. 3,3-dimethylpentane

**17.** Give the condensed structural formula for 2,2,4,4-tetramethylpentane.

**18.** For each of the following, determine whether the alkane is named correctly. If it is not, give the correct name.
a. 1-methylpropane
b. nonane
c. 4-methylhexane
d. 4-ethyl-2-methylhexane

**19.** Name the following alkenes. (Hint: See Sample Problem B.)

a. $CH_2{=}CH{-}CH_2{-}CH_2{-}CH_3$

b. 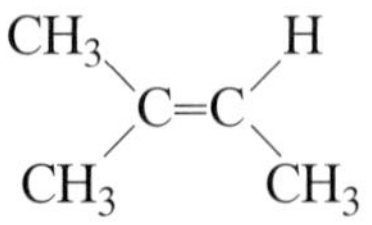 $(CH_3)_2C{=}C(H)CH_3$ (structure: $CH_3$ and $CH_3$ on the left carbon; H and $CH_3$ on the right carbon)

c. $CH_2{=}CH{-}C(CH_3)(CH_2CH_3){-}CH_2{-}CH_3$ (structure: central C bearing $CH_3$ above and $CH_2{-}CH_3$ below)

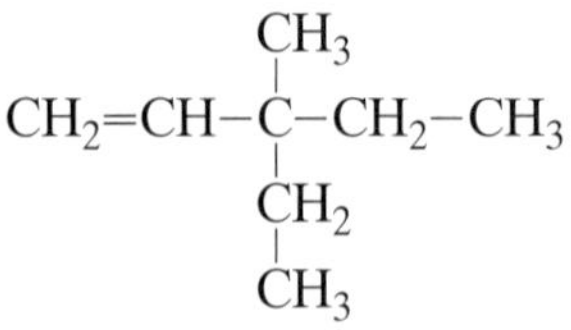

d. 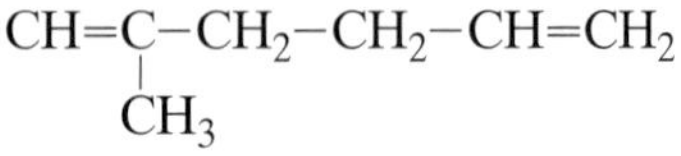 $CH{=}C(CH_3){-}CH_2{-}CH_2{-}CH{=}CH_2$

**20.** Name the following alkynes:

a. $CH{\equiv}C{-}CH_3$

b. 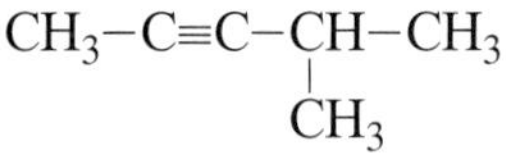 $CH_3{-}C{\equiv}C{-}CH(CH_3){-}CH_3$

c. $CH_3{-}CH(CH_3){-}C{\equiv}C{-}CH(CH_3){-}CH_3$

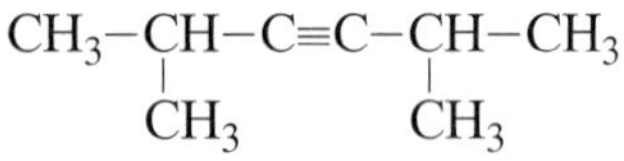

d. $CH{\equiv}C{-}CH_2{-}CH_2{-}CH_2{-}C{\equiv}CH$

## Functional Groups

### SECTION 3 REVIEW

**21.** Write the general formula for each of the following:
a. alcohol
b. ether
c. alkyl halide

**22.** Based on the boiling points of water and methanol, in which would you expect to observe a greater degree of hydrogen bonding? Explain your answer.

**23.** a. Why is glycerol used in moisturizing skin lotions?
b. How does this relate to the chemical structure of glycerol?

**24.** Write the general formula for each of the following:
a. aldehyde
b. ketone
c. carboxylic acid
d. ester
e. amine

**25.** Aldehydes and ketones both contain the same functional group. Why are they classified as separate classes of organic compounds?

**26.** How are esters related to carboxylic acids?

**27.** What element do amines contain besides carbon and hydrogen?

**28.** Explain why an amine acts as a base.

**29.** What classes of organic compounds contain oxygen?

## Organic Reactions

### SECTION 4 REVIEW

**30.** What type of chemical reaction would you expect to occur between 2-octene and hydrogen bromide, HBr?

**31.** How many molecules of chlorine, $Cl_2$, can be added to a molecule of 1-propene? a molecule of 1-propyne?

**32.** Compare substitution and addition reactions.

**33.** In a chemical reaction, two small molecules are joined and a water molecule is produced. What type of reaction took place?

**34.** What are two reactions by which polymers can be formed?

**35.** What is the structural requirement for a molecule to be a monomer in an addition polymer?

**36.** Which of the following reactions is a substitution reaction?

a. $CH_2{=}CH_2 + Cl_2 \longrightarrow Cl{-}CH_2{-}CH_2{-}Cl$

b. $CH_3{-}CH_2{-}CH_2{-}CH_3 + Cl_2 \longrightarrow Cl{-}CH_2{-}CH_2{-}CH_2{-}CH_3 + HCl$

c. 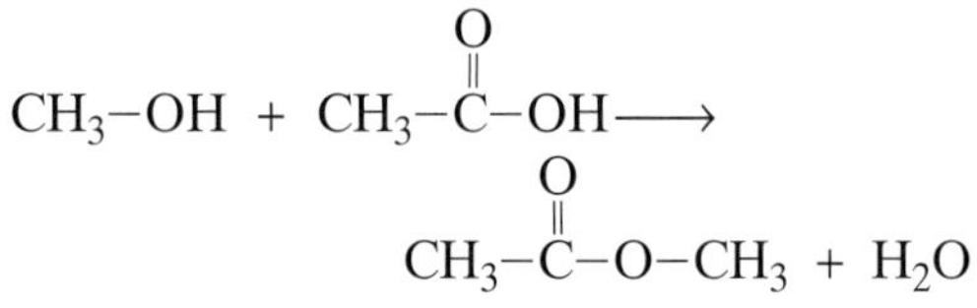 $CH_3{-}OH + CH_3{-}C({=}O){-}OH \longrightarrow CH_3{-}C({=}O){-}O{-}CH_3 + H_2O$

**37.** Which of the following reactions is an addition reaction?

a. 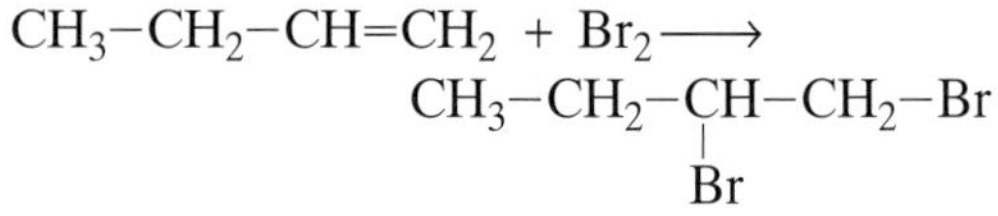 $CH_3{-}CH_2{-}CH{=}CH_2 + Br_2 \longrightarrow CH_3{-}CH_2{-}CH(Br){-}CH_2{-}Br$

b. Cyclohexanol (OH) $\xrightarrow[\text{heat}]{85\%\ H_3PO_4}$ cyclohexene + $H_2O$

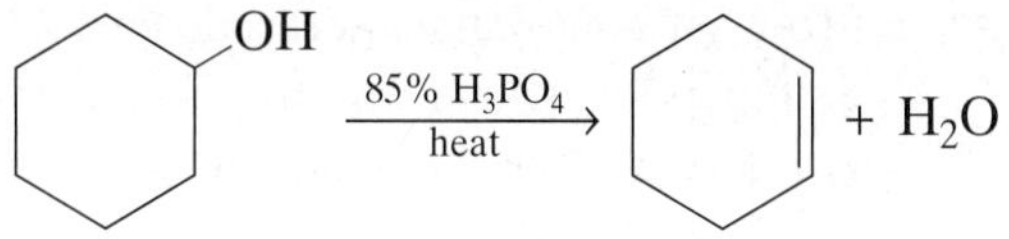

c. $CH_3-\overset{\overset{\large O}{\|}}{C}-OH + CH_3-OH \longrightarrow CH_3-\overset{\overset{\large O}{\|}}{C}-O-CH_3 + H_2O$

**38.** Which of the following reactions is a condensation reaction?

a. $CH_3C{\equiv}CH + HBr \xrightarrow{\text{ether}} CH_3-\overset{\overset{\large Br}{|}}{C}{=}CH_2$

b. Cyclohexene $+ Br_2 \xrightarrow{CCl_4}$ 1,2-dibromocyclohexane (Br, Br)

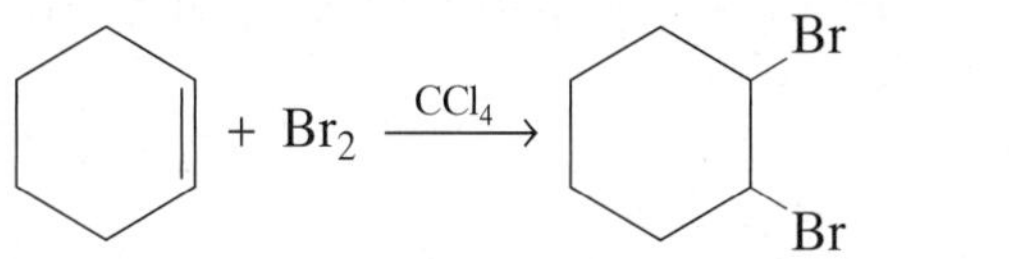

c. $CH_3-CH_2-OH + CH_3-CH_2-OH \xrightarrow{H_2SO_4} CH_3-CH_2-O-CH_2-CH_3 + H_2O$

**39.** Which of the following reactions is an elimination reaction?

a. $CH_2{=}CH-CH_2-CH_3 + Cl_2 \longrightarrow Cl-CH_2-\underset{\underset{\large Cl}{|}}{CH}-CH_2-CH_3$

b. $CH_3-\overset{\overset{\large OH}{|}}{CH}-CH_3 \xrightarrow{H_3O^+} CH_3-CH{=}CH_2 + H_2O$

c. $CH_3CH_3 + Cl_2 \xrightarrow[\text{heat}]{\text{light or}} CH_3CH_2Cl + HCl$

## MIXED REVIEW

**40.** Classify each of the following reactions as an elimination reaction or a condensation reaction:

a. $CH_3-\overset{\overset{\large Br}{|}}{C}{=}CH_2 + NaNH_2 \longrightarrow CH_3C{\equiv}CH + NaBr + NH_3$

b. $CH_3-CH_2-\overset{\overset{\large OH}{|}}{CH}-CH_3 \xrightarrow[\text{heat}]{85\%\ H_3PO_4} CH_3-CH{=}CH-CH_3 + H_2O$

c. $CH_3-CH_2-OH + CH_3-\overset{\overset{\large O}{\|}}{C}-OH \longrightarrow CH_3-CH_2-O-\overset{\overset{\large O}{\|}}{C}-CH_3 + H_2O$

d. $C_6H_5-\overset{\overset{\large O}{\|}}{C}H + CH_3-\overset{\overset{\large O}{\|}}{C}-CH_3 \xrightarrow{OH^-} C_6H_5-CH{=}CH-\overset{\overset{\large O}{\|}}{C}-CH_3 + H_2O$

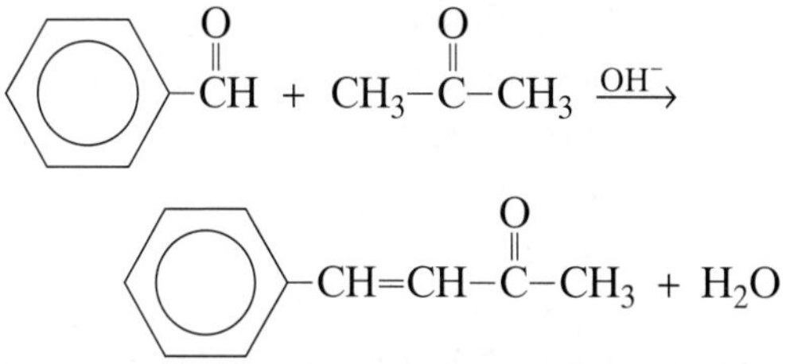

**41.** Classify each of the following reactions as a substitution reaction or an addition reaction:

a. $CH_3-CH_2-CH_2-CH_2-OH + HCl \xrightarrow[\text{heat}]{ZnCl_2} CH_3-CH_2-CH_2-CH_2-Cl + H_2O$

b. $CH_2{=}CH_2 + HBr \xrightarrow[25°C]{\text{ether}} CH_3-CH_2-Br$

c. $CH{\equiv}CH + HCl \xrightarrow{HgCl_2} CH_2{=}CH-Cl$

d. 1-Methylcyclohexene ($CH_3$) + HBr $\xrightarrow{\text{ether}}$ 1-bromo-1-methylcyclohexane ($CH_3$, Br)

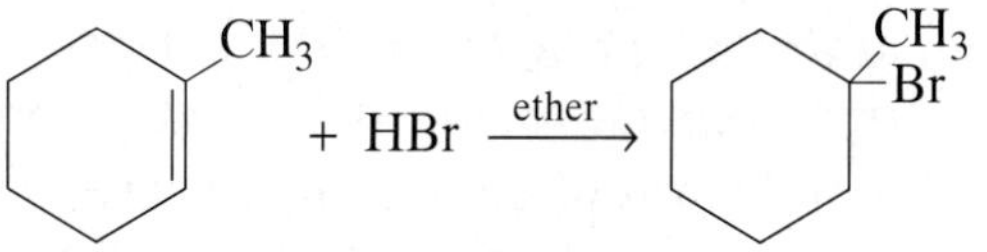

**42.** Identify each of the following reactions as an addition, substitution, elimination, or condensation reaction:

a. $CH_3-\overset{\overset{\large O}{\|}}{C}-OH + CH_3-\overset{\overset{\large OH}{|}}{CH}-CH_3 \longrightarrow CH_3-\overset{\overset{\large O}{\|}}{C}-O-\overset{\overset{\large CH_3}{|}}{CH}-CH_3 + H_2O$

b. $CH_2{=}CH-CH_3 + Cl_2 \longrightarrow Cl-CH_2-\underset{\underset{\large Cl}{|}}{CH}-CH_3$

c. Cyclohexane $+ Cl_2 \xrightarrow[\text{heat}]{\text{light or}}$ chlorocyclohexane (Cl) + HCl

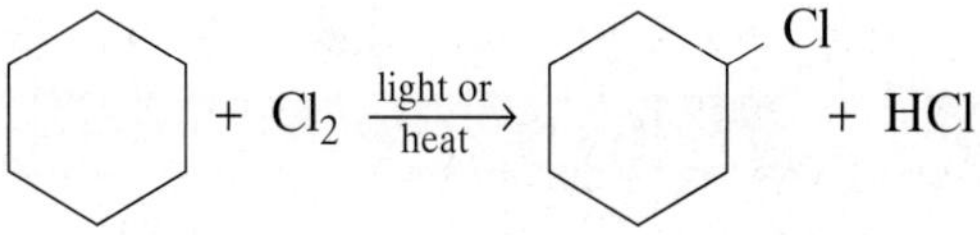

d. 1-Methylcyclohexanol ($CH_3$, OH) $\xrightarrow[50°C]{H_3O^+,\ THF}$ 1-methylcyclohexene ($CH_3$) + $H_2O$

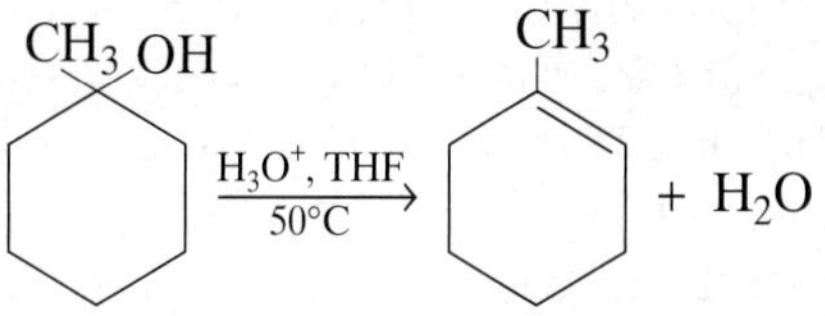

**43.** Give the molecular formula for each type of hydrocarbon if it contains seven carbon atoms.
a. an alkane
b. an alkene
c. an alkyne

**44.** a. Alkyne nomenclature is very similar to the nomenclature of what other group of hydrocarbons?
b. How do these nomenclatures differ?

**45.** a. What are delocalized electrons?
b. What is their effect on the reactivity of aromatic hydrocarbons?

## CRITICAL THINKING

**46. Inferring Conclusions** Why are organic compounds with covalent bonds usually less stable when heated than inorganic compounds with ionic bonds?

**47. Inferring Relationships** The element that appears in the greatest number of compounds is hydrogen. The element found in the second greatest number of compounds is carbon. Why are there more hydrogen compounds than carbon compounds?

**48. Relating Ideas** As the number of carbon atoms in an alkane molecule increases, does the percentage by mass of hydrogen increase, decrease, or remain the same?

**49. Applying Ideas** How does ethylene glycol protect radiator fluid in an automobile from both freezing in the winter and boiling over in the summer?

## USING THE HANDBOOK

**50.** The top 10 chemicals produced in the United States are listed in Table 7B of the *Elements Handbook*. Review this material, and answer the following:
a. Which of the top ten compounds are organic?
b. Write structural formulas for the compounds you listed in item (a).
c. To what homologous series do each of these compounds belong?

**51.** The reaction of methane with oxygen produces two different oxides of carbon. Review this material in the *Elements Handbook*, and answer the following:
a. What condition determines whether the product of the methane reaction is $CO_2$ or CO?
b. If a home heating system is fueled by natural gas, what difference does it make if the combustion produces $CO_2$ or CO?

**52.** Silicon is similar to carbon in forming long-chain compounds. Review the material on silicon in the *Elements Handbook* and answer the following.
a. How does a long-chain silicon compound differ in composition from a long-chain carbon compound?
b. The simplest alkane is methane. Methyl groups are found in all alkanes. What is a common subunit of a silicate? What is the geometry of that subunit?

**53.** Mercury in the environment poses a hazard to living things. Review the section on mercury poisoning in the *Elements Handbook*.
a. Draw a structural formula for the organic mercury compound described in that section.
b. What is the IUPAC name for this compound?

## RESEARCH & WRITING

**54.** *Chemical and Engineering News* publishes a list once a year of the top 50 chemicals. Find out which chemicals on the current year's list are hydrocarbons, and report your findings to the class.

**55.** Consult reference materials at the library, and read about products made from hydrocarbons. Keep a list of the number of petroleum-related products you use in a single day.

**56.** The widespread use of synthetic polymers in modern society has led to a number of new environmental problems. Find out what some of these problems are and what can be done to reduce them.

## ALTERNATIVE ASSESSMENT

57. **Performance** Models are often used to visualize the three-dimensional shape of molecules. Using gumdrops as atoms and toothpicks to bond them together, construct models of different hydrocarbons. Use large gumdrops for carbon and smaller gumdrops for hydrogen.

58. **Performance** Using your gumdrop models, demonstrate why alkenes can have geometric isomers, while alkanes (except cycloalkanes) cannot.

59. **Performance** Devise a set of experiments to study how well biodegradable plastics break down. If your teacher approves your plan, conduct an experiment to test the procedure on products labeled "biodegradable."

60. **Performance** Your teacher will make available unlabeled samples of benzoic acid, ethyl alcohol, and hexanediamine. Develop an experiment to identify each. If your teacher approves your plan, identify the unknown substances.

61. Keep a list of the food you consume in a single day. Compare the content labels from those foods, and then list the most commonly used chemicals in them. With the aid of your teacher and some reference books, try to classify the organic chemicals by their functional groups.

62. As a class or small group, research the preservatives used in various foods. Examine their chemical structures. Determine a way to test for organic functional groups of possibly hazardous preservatives.

**extension**

**Graphing Calculator**

**Formulas of Hydrocarbons**

Go to **go.hrw.com** for a graphing calculator exercise that asks you to find the formula of any straight-chain hydrocarbon, given the number of carbon atoms and the number of double bonds in the compound.

**Keyword:** HC6ORGX

# *Math Tutor* CALCULATING EMPIRICAL FORMULAS

An empirical formula shows the simplest whole-number ratio among the elements in a compound. For example, the simplest ratio among the atoms in benzene, $C_6H_6$, can be expressed by the empirical formula CH (or $C_1H_1$). Empirical formulas may be calculated from simple analytical data, as shown in the example below.

## Problem-Solving *TIPS*

- Sometimes, you can deduce the mole ratios of the elements in a compound just by examining the moles of each element. If not, divide the moles of each element by the moles of the least abundant element in the compound.

## SAMPLE

**Find the empirical formula of acetone, a common organic solvent, whose composition by mass is 62.04% carbon, 10.41% hydrogen, and 27.55% oxygen.**

The easiest way to calculate an empirical formula from percentage composition is to consider a 100.00 g sample of the compound. In this case, a 100.00 g sample would contain 62.04 g of carbon, 10.41 g of hydrogen, and 27.55 g of oxygen. Convert each mass to moles so that you can compare the mole ratio of the three elements.

$$62.04 \text{ g C} \times \frac{1 \text{ mol C}}{12.01 \text{ g C}} = 5.166 \text{ mol C}$$

$$10.41 \text{ g H} \times \frac{1 \text{ mol H}}{1.008 \text{ g H}} = 10.33 \text{ mol H}$$

$$27.55 \text{ g O} \times \frac{1 \text{ mol O}}{16.00 \text{ g O}} = 1.722 \text{ mol O}$$

$$\frac{5.166 \text{ mol C}}{1.722} : \frac{10.33 \text{ mol H}}{1.722} : \frac{1.722 \text{ mol O}}{1.722}$$

$$3.000 \text{ mol C} : 5.999 \text{ mol H} : 1.000 \text{ mol O}$$

As you can see, the empirical formula of this compound is $C_3H_6O$.

## PRACTICE PROBLEMS

1. Urea was the first organic compound to be synthesized in the laboratory. Urea's composition by mass is 20.00% carbon, 6.71% hydrogen, 46.65% nitrogen, and 26.64% oxygen. What is the empirical formula of urea?
2. An organic compound sometimes used in the manufacture of perfumes is 29.78% carbon, 4.17% hydrogen, and 66.05% bromine, by mass. What is the empirical formula of this compound?
3. The composition by mass of lactic acid is 40.00% carbon, 6.71% hydrogen, and 53.28% oxygen. What is the empirical formula of lactic acid?

# Standardized Test Prep

**Answer the following items on a separate piece of paper.**

**MULTIPLE CHOICE**

**1.** Which of the following hydrocarbons must be an alkane?
**A.** $C_2H_2$
**B.** $C_5H_{10}$
**C.** $C_7H_{12}$
**D.** $C_{14}H_{30}$

**2.** A hydrocarbon with the formula $C_8H_{18}$ is called
**A.** octene.
**B.** octyne.
**C.** octane.
**D.** propane.

**3.** During a condensation polymerization reaction,
**A.** single bonds replace all double bonds that are present in the monomer.
**B.** water is often produced.
**C.** alcohol groups are formed.
**D.** an aldehyde group is changed to a ketone group.

**4.** In naming an organic compound, we
**A.** should remember that naming the locations of all functional groups is optional.
**B.** do not consider the number of carbon atoms in the molecule as a factor.
**C.** begin by identifying and naming the longest hydrocarbon chain.
**D.** ignore side chains when we name the molecule.

**5.** Which of the following compounds cannot have different isomers?
**A.** $C_7H_{16}$
**B.** $C_5H_{10}$
**C.** $C_3H_8$
**D.** $C_6H_{12}O_6$

**6.** Compounds that differ only in the order in which the atoms are bonded together are called
**A.** condensation polymers.
**B.** addition polymers.
**C.** structural isomers.
**D.** geometric isomers.

**7.** Examine the following structural formula:

```
            H
            |
          H-C-H
   H        |       H H
   |        |       | |
 H-C--------C-------C-C-H
   |        |       | |
   H        |       H H
          H-C-H
            |
            H
```

The correct name for this compound is
**A.** 2,2-dimethylbutane.
**B.** 1,1,1-trimethylpropane.
**C.** 2-ethyl-2-methylpropane.
**D.** 3,3-dimethylbutane.

**8.** Organic functional groups
**A.** give characteristic properties to compounds that contain them.
**B.** always contain oxygen.
**C.** always contain a double or triple bond.
**D.** are present in every organic compound.

**SHORT ANSWER**

**9.** What feature must be present in a compound for it to undergo an addition reaction?

**10.** Organic compounds of what class contain only two elements?

**EXTENDED RESPONSE**

**11.** Describe the difference between substitution and addition reactions. Your answer should mention the degree of saturation of the organic compound.

**12.** Explain why some alkanes are gases, others are liquids, and still others are solids at room temperature.

**Test TIP** If you become short on time, quickly scan the unanswered questions to see which might be easiest to answer.

# Polymers and Toy Balls

## OBJECTIVES

- ***Synthesize*** **two different polymers.**
- ***Prepare*** **a small toy ball from each polymer.**
- ***Observe*** **the similarities and differences between the two types of balls.**
- ***Measure*** **the density of each polymer.**
- ***Compare*** **the bounce height of the two balls.**

## MATERIALS

- **2 L beaker, or plastic bucket or tub**
- **3 mL 50% ethanol solution**
- **5 oz paper cups, 2**
- **10 mL 5% acetic acid solution (vinegar)**
- **25 mL graduated cylinder**
- **10 mL graduated cylinder**
- **10 mL liquid latex**
- **12 mL sodium silicate solution**
- **distilled water**
- **gloves**
- **meterstick**
- **paper towels**
- **wooden stick**

## BACKGROUND

What polymers make the best toy balls? Two possibilities are latex rubber and a polymer produced from ethanol and sodium silicate. Latex rubber is a polymer of covalently bonded atoms.

The polymer formed from ethanol, $C_2H_5OH$, and a solution of sodium silicate, $Na_2Si_3O_7$, also has covalent bonds. It is known as *water glass* because it dissolves in water.

In this experiment, you will synthesize rubber and the ethanol silicate polymer and test their properties.

## SAFETY

For review of safety, please see **Safety in the Chemistry Laboratory** in the front of your book.

## PREPARATION

1. **Organizing Data:** Create a data table in your lab notebook in which the columns are labeled "Trial," "Height (cm)," "Mass (g)," and "Diameter (cm)." Create three rows (Trials 1, 2, and 3) in your table.

## PROCEDURE

1. Fill the 2 L beaker, bucket, or tub about half-full with distilled water.
2. Using a clean 25 mL graduated cylinder, measure 10 mL of liquid latex and pour it into one of the paper cups.
3. Thoroughly clean the 25 mL graduated cylinder with soap and water, and then rinse it with distilled water.

4. Measure 10 mL of distilled water. Pour it into the paper cup with the latex.

5. Measure 10 mL of the 5% acetic acid solution, and pour it into the paper cup with the latex and water.

6. Immediately stir the mixture with the wooden stick.

7. As you continue stirring, a polymer lump will form around the wooden stick. Pull the stick with the polymer lump from the paper cup, and immerse the lump in the 2 L beaker, bucket, or tub.

8. While wearing gloves, gently pull the lump from the wooden stick. Be sure to keep the lump immersed under the water.

9. Keep the latex rubber underwater, and use your gloved hands to mold the lump into a ball. Then, squeeze the lump several times to remove any unused chemicals. You may remove the latex rubber from the water as you roll it in your hands to smooth the ball.

10. Set aside the latex rubber ball to dry. While it is drying, proceed to step 11.

11. In a clean 25 mL graduated cylinder, measure 12 mL of sodium silicate solution, and pour it into the other paper cup.

12. In a clean 10 mL graduated cylinder, measure 3 mL of 50% ethanol. Pour the ethanol into the paper cup with the sodium silicate, and mix with the wooden stick until a solid substance is formed.

13. While wearing gloves, remove the polymer that forms and place it in the palm of one hand. Gently press it with the palms of both hands until a ball that does not crumble is formed. This step takes a little time and patience. The liquid that comes out of the ball is a combination of ethanol and water. Occasionally, moisten the ball by letting a small amount of water from a faucet run over it. When the ball no longer crumbles, you are ready to go to the next step.

14. Observe as many physical properties of the balls as possible, and record your observations in your lab notebook.

15. Drop each ball several times, and record your observations.

16. Drop one ball from a height of 1 m, and measure its bounce. Perform three trials for each ball.

17. Measure the diameter and mass of each ball.

## CLEANUP AND DISPOSAL

18. Dispose of any extra solutions in the containers indicated by your teacher. Clean up your lab area. Remember to wash your hands thoroughly when your lab work is finished.

## ANALYSIS AND INTERPRETATION

1. **Analyzing Information:** List at least three of your observations of the properties of the two balls.

2. **Organizing Data:** Calculate the average height of the bounce for each type of ball.

3. **Organizing Data:** Calculate the volume for each ball. Even though the balls may not be perfectly spherical, assume that they are. (Hint: The volume of a sphere is equal to $\frac{4}{3} \times \pi \times r^3$, where $r$ is the radius of the sphere, which is one-half of the diameter.) Then, calculate the density of each ball, using your mass measurements.

## CONCLUSIONS

1. **Inferring Conclusions:** Which polymer would you recommend to a toy company for making new toy balls? Explain your reasoning.

2. **Evaluating Viewpoints:** What are some other possible practical applications for each of the polymers you made?

## EXTENSIONS

1. **Predicting Outcomes:** Explain why you would not be able to measure the volumes of the balls by submerging them in water.

CHAPTER 23

# Biological Chemistry

*Chemical reactions occur in all living organisms.*

Honeybee Pollinating a Poppy

# Carbohydrates and Lipids

SECTION 1

## OBJECTIVES

- Describe the structural characteristics of simple carbohydrates and complex carbohydrates.
- Explain the role of carbohydrates in living systems.
- Describe the structural characteristics of lipid molecules.
- Identify the functions of lipids in living cells.

**C.3.6** Identify the basic structure of common polymers (including proteins, nucleic acids, plastics, and starches)

Biochemistry is the study of the chemicals and reactions that occur in living things. Biochemical compounds are often large and complex organic molecules, but their chemistry is similar to that of the smaller organic molecules you studied in Chapter 22. Now you will study many important biochemical molecules and learn why they are needed to stay healthy. Two of the most common types of molecules that you may know about are *carbohydrates* and *lipids*. These molecules are important parts of the food that you eat and provide most of the energy that your body needs.

## Carbohydrates

*Sugars, starches,* and *cellulose* belong to the large group of biochemical molecules called carbohydrates. **Carbohydrates** *are molecules that are composed of carbon, hydrogen, and oxygen atoms in a 1:2:1 ratio, and provide nutrients to the cells of living things.* They are produced by plants through a process called *photosynthesis.* Cellulose provides structure and support for plants and starch stores energy in plants. Because animals cannot make all of their own carbohydrates, they must get them from food. Carbohydrates provide nearly all of the energy that is available in most plant-derived food.

### Monosaccharides

*A* **monosaccharide** *is a simple sugar that is the basic subunit of a carbohydrate.* A single monosaccharide molecule contains three to seven carbon atoms. Monosaccharide compounds are typically sweet-tasting, white solids at room temperature. Because they have polar, hydroxyl (−OH) groups in their molecular structures, they are very soluble in water. The most common monosaccharides are *glucose* (also called *dextrose*) and *fructose.* Although both of these monosaccharides have the formula $C_6(H_2O)_6$, their structural formulas differ. As **Figure 1** shows, glucose in a water solution forms a ring made up of five carbon atoms and one oxygen atom, and fructose in a water solution forms a ring made up of four carbon atoms and one oxygen atom. Notice that both compounds have five −OH groups in their structures.

**FIGURE 1** Glucose and fructose both have 6 C, 12 H, and 6 O atoms. The arrangement of the C, H, and O atoms determines the shape and properties of each sugar.

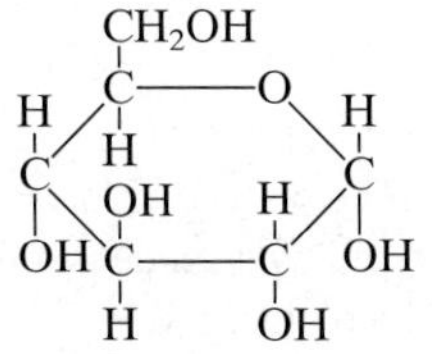

$CH_2OH$ C O H H C H C OH H OH C C OH H OH

**glucose**

$CH_2OH$ O H C C H OH HO C C $CH_2OH$ OH H

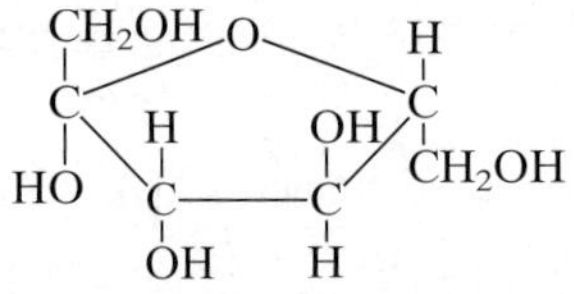

**fructose**

Glucose is the most abundant monosaccharide in nature. It is also the most important monosaccharide nutritionally for animals because glucose provides energy for cellular activities. The carbohydrates we eat are broken down into glucose, which may be used immediately by cells or stored in the liver as glycogen for later use. Glucose is also found in some fruits, corn, and the sap of plants.

Fructose, also called *fruit sugar,* is found in most fruits and in honey. The sweetest naturally occurring sugar, fructose is sweeter than table sugar. Because of its sweetness, fructose is sometimes used as a low-calorie sweetener because less fructose is needed to produce the same sweetness that table sugar does.

**FIGURE 2** Most of the sugar produced throughout the world comes from sugar beets such as those shown here, or from sugar cane.

## Disaccharides

Generally, when someone asks for "sugar," the person is asking for the disaccharide *sucrose*, $C_{12}H_{22}O_{11}$. *A* **disaccharide** *is a sugar that consists of two monosaccharide units that are joined together.* Like monosaccharides, disaccharides have polar hydroxy groups in their molecular structures and therefore are water soluble. A molecule of sucrose forms when a glucose molecule bonds to a fructose molecule. Commercially available sugar comes from sugar cane or sugar beets, such as those shown in **Figure 2.** Another important disaccharide is *lactose*, or milk sugar. Lactose is made up of a sugar called *galactose* and glucose. Human milk is 7 to 8% lactose, but cow's milk is only 4% to 5% lactose. Infant formula may be enriched with lactose to simulate human milk.

## Carbohydrate Reactions

Carbohydrates undergo two important kinds of reactions: condensation reactions and hydrolysis reactions. *A* **condensation reaction** *is a reaction in which two molecules or parts of the same molecule combine.* **Figure 3** shows a condensation reaction in which a molecule of glucose combines with a molecule of fructose to yield a molecule of sucrose. Note that in this reaction a molecule of water is also formed.

Disaccharides and longer-chain polysaccharides can be broken down into smaller sugar units by hydrolysis. **Hydrolysis** *is a chemical reaction between water and another substance to form two or more new substances.* Sucrose will undergo a hydrolysis reaction with water, forming glucose and fructose. This hydrolysis, or "water-splitting," reaction occurs in many common processes, such as in the making of jams and jellies.

**FIGURE 3** The disaccharide sucrose is formed by a condensation reaction between glucose and fructose.

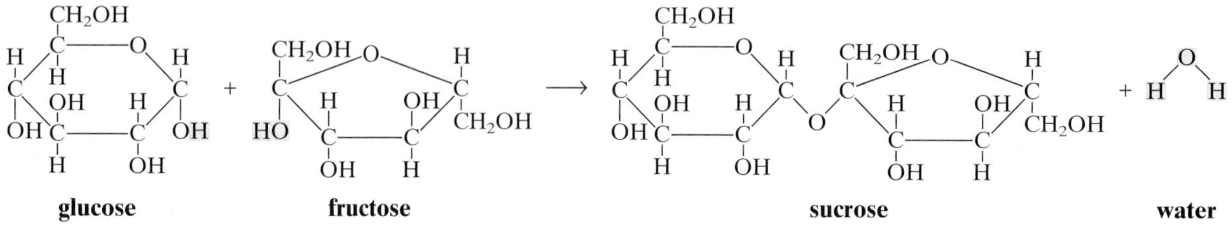

**glucose** + **fructose** → **sucrose** + **water**

Cooking sucrose with high acid foods, such as berries and fruits, causes it to break down into a mixture of equal parts of glucose and fructose. This new mixture provides the sweet taste in jams and jellies, which is sweeter than the starting sugar. When lactose is broken down, glucose and galactose are formed. Some people do not produce the enzyme needed to break down the milk sugar in dairy products. This condition is called *lactose intolerance*. People who have this can become ill when they drink milk or eat foods that have milk in them.

## Polysaccharides

When many monosaccharides or disaccharides combine in a series of condensation reactions, they form a polysaccharide. *A* **polysaccharide** *is a carbohydrate made up of long chains of simple sugars.* Cellulose, starch, and glycogen are *polymers* of glucose, or polysaccharides, that contain many glucose monomer units.

As shown in **Figure 4,** the glucose molecules in cellulose chains are arranged in such a way that hydrogen bonds link the hydroxy groups of adjacent glucose molecules to form insoluble fibrous sheets. These sheets of cellulose are the basic component of plant cell walls. More than 50% of the total organic matter in the world is cellulose. People cannot digest cellulose, but when we eat fiber, which is cellulose, it speeds the movement of food through the digestive tract. Microorganisms that can digest cellulose are present in the digestive tracts of some animals. Cows and other ruminants have a special stomach chamber that holds the plants they eat for long periods of time, during which these micro-organisms can break down the cellulose into glucose.

Starch is the storage form of glucose in plants. Starch from foods such as potatoes and cereal grains makes up about two-thirds of the food eaten by people throughout the world. Starch in food is broken down into glucose during digestion. Glucose is broken down further in metabolic reactions that will be discussed later in this chapter.

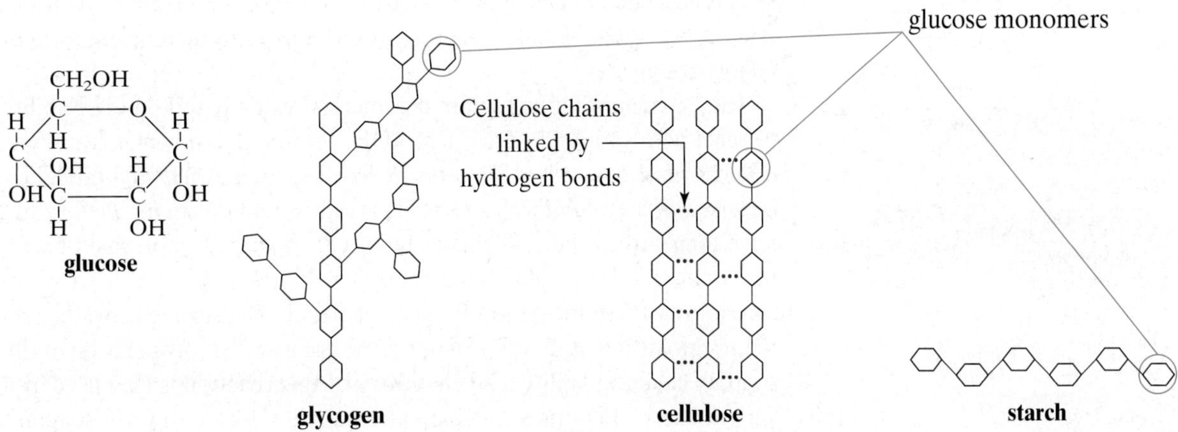


**FIGURE 4** Glucose is the monosaccharide subunit for glycogen, cellulose, and starch. Notice that these three polymers differ in their arrangement of glucose monomers.

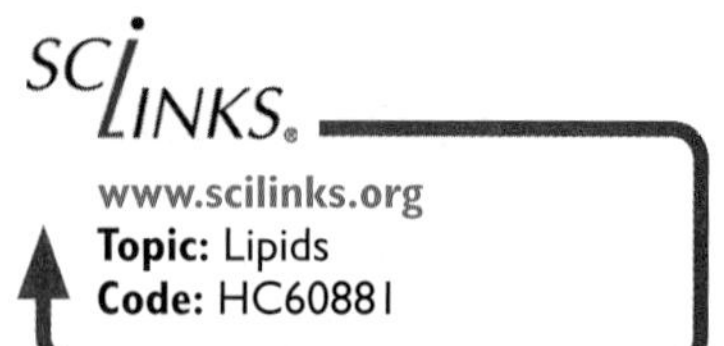


## Lipids

Lipids are another important class of nutrients in our diet. They are found in dairy products, grains, meats, and oils. *A* **lipid** *is a type of biochemical that does not dissolve in water, has a high percentage of C and H atoms, and is soluble in nonpolar solvents.* As a class, lipids are not nearly as similar to each other as carbohydrates are. Long-chain fatty acids, phospholipids, steroids, and cholesterol are all lipids.

### Fatty Acids and Triglycerides

**Fatty acids** *consist of a long, nonpolar hydrocarbon "tail" and a polar carboxylic acid functional group at the "head."* Fatty acids are the simplest lipid molecules. They have *hydrophilic* polar heads, but their hydrocarbon chains make them insoluble in water. Fatty acids can also be saturated or unsaturated. *Saturated fatty acids* have no carbon-carbon double bonds, while *unsaturated fatty acids* have one or more double bonds in the hydrocarbon chain. The lipid shown below is oleic acid, which is unsaturated.

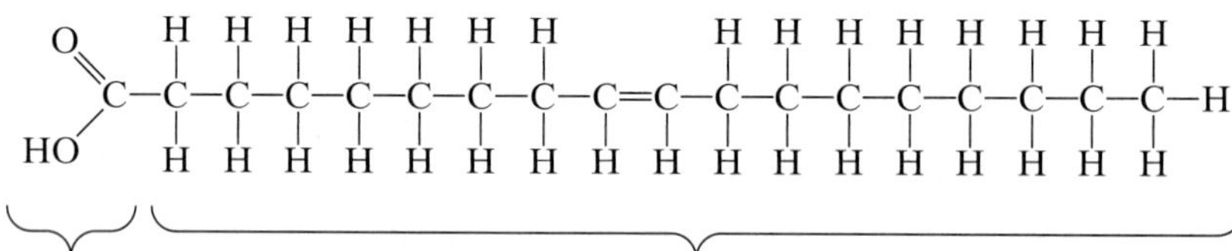


*Triglycerides* are the major component of the fats and oils in your diet. They are formed by condensation reactions in which three fatty acid molecules bond to one glycerol (a type of alcohol) molecule. Fats, such as butter and lard, come from animals, while oils come from plant sources, such as coconuts, peanuts, corn, and olives, as shown in **Figure 5.** Because they have a large amount of saturated fatty acids, fats are solids at room temperature. Oils have more unsaturated fatty acids than fats, and are liquids. Like other animals, humans make fat, which is stored in *adipose* tissue until it is needed as an energy source. Fat has about twice as much energy per gram as carbohydrates or proteins do. Thus, fat is an efficient form of energy storage.

**FIGURE 5** Fats, such as lard and butter, are obtained from animals. Oils are found in many different plants.

Fats have another important commercial value based on their ability to react with sodium hydroxide, NaOH, commonly known as *lye. When a fat combines with NaOH, an acid-base reaction called* **saponification** *occurs, and a salt and water form.* This salt is made from molecules that have long carboxylic acid chains and is called *soap*. A molecule of soap has a charged ionic head and a nonpolar hydrocarbon tail. This structure allows the ionic head of a soap molecule to dissolve in water and the nonpolar tail to dissolve in nonpolar greases. This property gives the soap its cleaning ability. The chemistry of this reaction is also used as a way of classifying lipids. Lipids that react with a base to form soap are called *saponifiable lipids*, which include fats, oils, and fatty acids.

## Other Important Lipids

*Compound saponifiable lipids* play an important role in biochemical processes. These lipids are structurally similar to triglycerides in that at least one fatty acid is bonded to the central glycerol or glycerol-like unit. These molecules may also have phosphate groups, sugar units, or nitrogen-containing groups. Phospholipids, shown in **Figure 6,** are compound saponifiable lipids and are the main structural component of cell membranes. Phospholipids are arranged in a *bilayer,* or double layer, at the surface of the cell. As **Figure 6** shows, the hydrophilic heads of the phospholipids are on the outside surfaces of the bilayer. The heads are in contact with water-containing solutions inside of the cell and surrounding the cell. The hydrophobic tails point toward the interior of the membrane, away from water-containing solutions. The cell membrane forms a boundary between the cell and its external environment. Only certain substances may pass through the cell membrane. This enables the cell to maintain a stable internal environment.

*Nonsaponifiable* lipids are nonpolar compounds that do not form soap. They include *steroids,* many *vitamins,* and *bile acids. Cholesterol* is a steroid present in animal cell membranes and is a precursor of many hormones.

SCILINKS®
www.scilinks.org
**Topic:** Function of the Cell Membrane
**Code:** HC60627

**FIGURE 6**

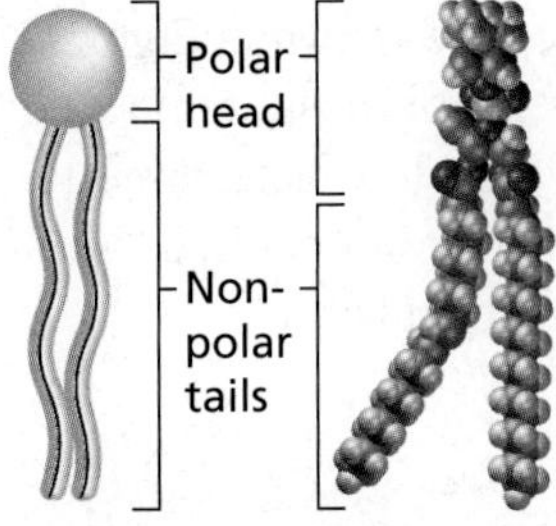


A phospholipid's "head" is polar, and its two fatty "tails" are nonpolar.

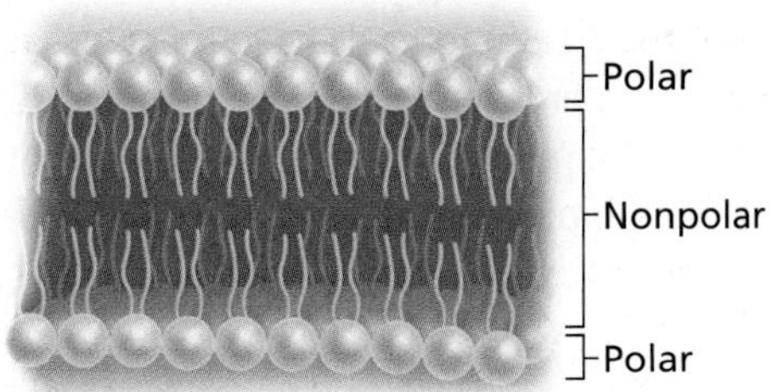


Phospholipids are arranged in a bilayer, with the hydrophilic heads pointing outward and the hydrophobic tails pointing inward.

## SECTION REVIEW

1. Describe two functions of carbohydrates in living systems.
2. Carbohydrates make up about 2% of the mass of the human body, yet we need about 1 tsp of glucose every 15 min to maintain energy for our cells. Where does all of this glucose come from?
3. What is the difference between saponifiable and nonsaponifiable lipids?

### Critical Thinking

4. **ANALYZING RELATIONSHIPS** Glucose is soluble in water. Why is cellulose, which is made up of glucose, insoluble in water?
5. **EVALUATING IDEAS** Carbohydrates make up about 90% of the mass of cotton. Why don't humans include cotton in their diet?

SECTION 2

# Amino Acids and Proteins

## Objectives

- Describe the basic structure of amino acids and the formation of polypeptides.
- Determine the significance of amino acid side chains to the three-dimensional structure of a protein and the function of a protein.
- Describe the functions of proteins in cells.
- Identify the effects of enzymes on biological molecules.

SC **C.4.6** Explain the role of activation energy and the effects of temperature, particle size, stirring, concentration, and catalysts in reaction rates

Amino acid molecules are the basic building blocks of proteins. Although only 20 types of amino acids are found in human proteins, more than 700 types of amino acids occur in nature. The human body can synthesize only 11 of the 20 amino acids as needed. The other nine, called the *essential amino acids,* have to be supplied by the food that we eat.

## Amino Acids

**Amino acids** *are organic molecules that contain two functional groups: a basic* $-NH_2$ *amino group and an acidic* $-COOH$ *carboxylic acid group.* All of the 20 amino acids have the general structure shown in **Figure 7.** The "R" represents a side chain that is different for each amino acid. The R-groups of the amino acids present in a protein determine the protein's biological activity. The structures of four amino acids—cysteine, valine, glutamic acid, and histidine—are shown below.

**FIGURE 7** Amino acids have the same basic structure. The *R* represents a side chain.

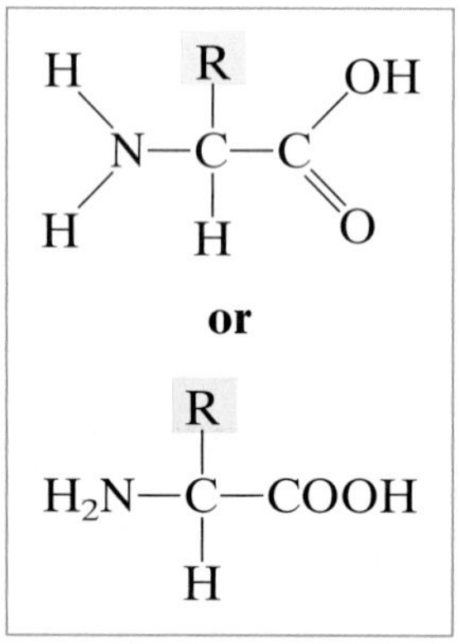

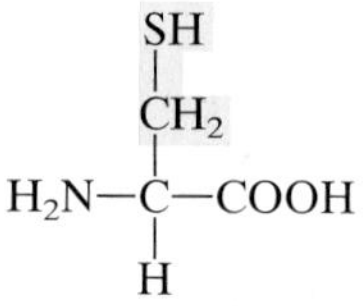

H, H, N, R, C, H, C, OH, O

or

R, $H_2N-C-COOH$, H

SH, $CH_2$, $H_2N-C-COOH$, H

**cysteine**

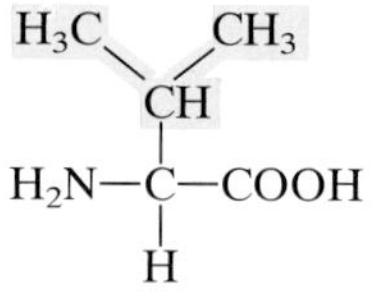

$H_3C$, $CH_3$, CH, $H_2N-C-COOH$, H

**valine**

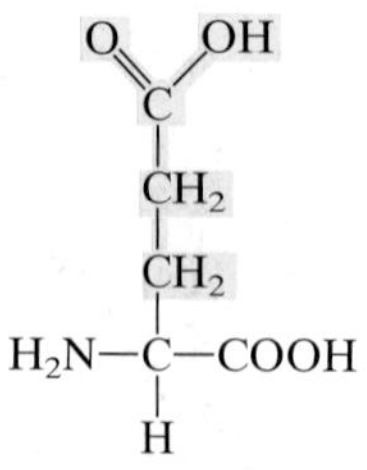

O, OH, C, $CH_2$, $CH_2$, $H_2N-C-COOH$, H

**glutamic acid**

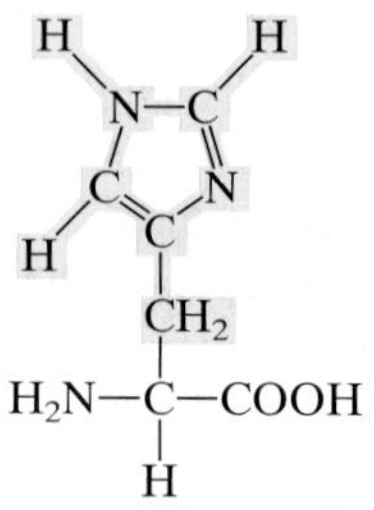

H, H, N, C, C, N, C, H, $CH_2$, $H_2N-C-COOH$, H

**histidine**

### Amino Acid Reactions

Two amino acids can react with each other in an acid-base reaction similar to those discussed in Chapter 14. The basic amino group of one amino acid reacts with the acidic carboxylic acid group of another amino acid, forming a *peptide,* and a molecule of water is lost. This reaction, shown below, is classified as a condensation reaction because the two amino acid molecules join together, and water is formed. The bond formed is called a *peptide bond,* and the product is a *dipeptide* because it is made up of two amino acid units. Longer chains are called *polypeptides,* and chains of 50 or more amino acids are called *proteins.*

**peptide bond**

$$H_2N\text{—}CHR\text{—}COOH + H_2N\text{—}CHR\text{—}COOH \longrightarrow H_2N\text{—}CHR\text{—}C(=O)\text{—}NH\text{—}CHR\text{—}COOH + H_2O$$

**dipeptide**

Peptide bonds can be broken by enzymes called *proteases.* These enzymes are found in cells and tissues where they aid in the digestion of proteins from food, or where they degrade unneeded or damaged proteins.

## Proteins

Proteins are found in all living cells and are the most complex and varied class of biochemical molecules. *A* **protein** *is an organic biological polymer that is made up of polypeptide chains of 50 or more amino acids and is an important building block of all cells.* The name *protein* comes from the Greek *proteios,* which means "of first importance." This name was chosen to show the importance of proteins in living things.

Proteins are the second most common molecules found in the human body (after water) and make up about 10% to 20% of the mass of a cell. Made up of specific sequences of amino acids, proteins have molecular masses that range from 6000 to more than 9 million atomic mass units. About 9000 different protein molecules are found in cells in the human body. Nitrogen accounts for about 15% of the mass of a protein molecule, which makes the structure of a protein quite different from that of a carbohydrate or lipid. Most proteins also contain sulfur, and some contain phosphorus or other elements, such as iron, zinc, and copper.

The importance of proteins in living things comes from their many different functions. Besides being the body's main food source for nitrogen and sulfur, proteins have many important catalytic, structural, regulatory, and antibody defense functions. Some different kinds of proteins are *keratin,* which is the main component of hair and fingernails; *enzymes,* which catalyze biochemical reactions; *hemoglobin*, which carries oxygen in the blood; *insulin*, which regulates glucose levels; and *antibodies*, which protect the body from foreign substances.

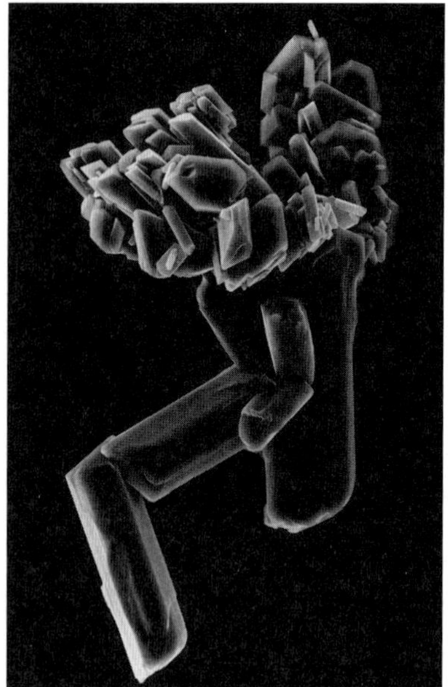

**FIGURE 8** A scanning electron micrograph showing crystals of the amino acid glycine, one of the building blocks of proteins.

## Arrangement of Amino Acids in Peptides and Proteins

Each peptide, polypeptide, or protein is made up of a special sequence of amino acids. A simple set of three-letter abbreviations is used to represent each amino acid in these kinds of molecules. For example, the dipeptide from glycine, shown in **Figure 8,** and glutamic acid would be written as Gly–Glu. The dipeptide Glu–Gly is an isomer of Gly–Glu. Both have the same numbers of C, H, O, and N atoms but in a different order. For the tripeptide Val–Asp–His, made up of valine, asparagine, and histidine, there are five isomers. There are 120 possible isomers for a pentapeptide of five different amino acids. Even though there are only 20 types of amino acids in proteins found in the human body, an incredibly large number of polypeptide and protein molecules are possible. Even for a small protein made up of 100 amino acids, the number of possible combinations of the 20 amino acids is $20^{100}$! Polypeptide and protein function depend not only on the kinds and number of amino acids but also on their order. Later, you will see that even the difference of only one amino acid in a polypeptide or protein chain can cause a big change in a protein's activity in a cell.

## Amino Acid Side-Chain Reactions

The properties of amino acids—and ultimately polypeptides and proteins—depend on the properties of the side chains present. For example, the side chain of *glutamic acid* is acidic, and the side chain of *histidine* is basic. The side chains of *asparagine* and several other amino acids are polar. In addition, both glutamic acid and asparagine can form hydrogen bonds, shown in **Figure 9.** Some amino acid side chains can form ionic or covalent bonds with other side chains. *Cysteine* is a unique amino acid, because the $-SH$ group in cysteine can form a covalent bond with another cysteine side chain. **Figure 9** shows that two cysteine units—at different points on a protein molecule—can bond to form a *disulfide bridge.* Such bonding can link two separate polypeptides or can cause one long protein to bond onto itself to form a loop. In fact, curly hair is a result of the presence of many disulfide bridges in hair protein.

**FIGURE 9** Three kinds of interactions between side chains on a polypeptide molecule are shown here. These interactions help determine the shape of a protein.

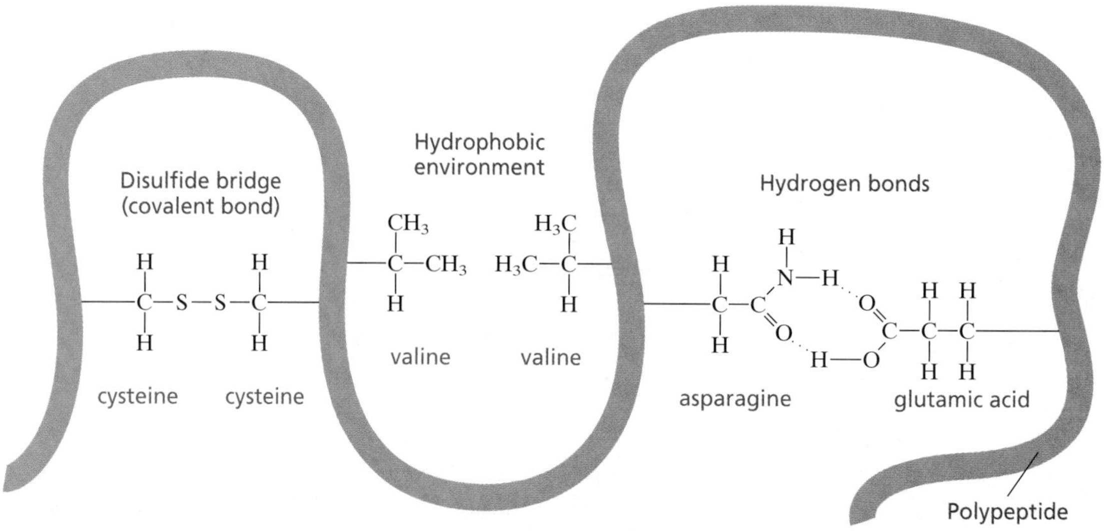

## Shape and Structure of Protein Molecules

The interaction of amino acid side chains determines the shape and structure of proteins, which in turn are important to the proteins' biological functions. In a polypeptide chain or protein, the sequence of the amino acids is called the *primary* (1°) *structure.* The *secondary* (2°) *structure* describes how the chain is coiled or otherwise arranged in space. For example, the alpha ($\alpha$) helix is a secondary structure that resembles a coiled spring. Another type of secondary structure is the beta ($\beta$) pleated sheet, which has accordion-like folds. Both of these secondary structures form because hydrogen bonding occurs between a hydrogen atom attached to the nitrogen atom in one peptide bond and the oxygen atom of another peptide bond farther down the backbone of the protein.

In a protein, the amino acid side chains project out in such a way that they often interact with other side chains located at various positions along the protein backbone. These interactions give the protein its characteristic three-dimensional shape, which is called its *tertiary* (3°) *structure*. The side-chain interactions can include hydrogen bonding, salt bridges, and cysteine-cysteine disulfide bonds. Hydrophobic interactions that occur between nonpolar side chains also contribute to a protein's tertiary structure. Because nonpolar side groups are repulsed by the water found in cells and body fluids, these groups tend to be found in the interior of the protein, where contact with water is minimal. Polar and ionic side chains tend to be on the protein surface, where they are in contact with water. In some proteins, different polypeptides, each of which has its own 3° structure, come together. In the case of hemoglobin, four different polypeptides make up the *quaternary* (4°) *structure*. The four structural levels of proteins are shown in **Figure 10.**

**FIGURE 10**

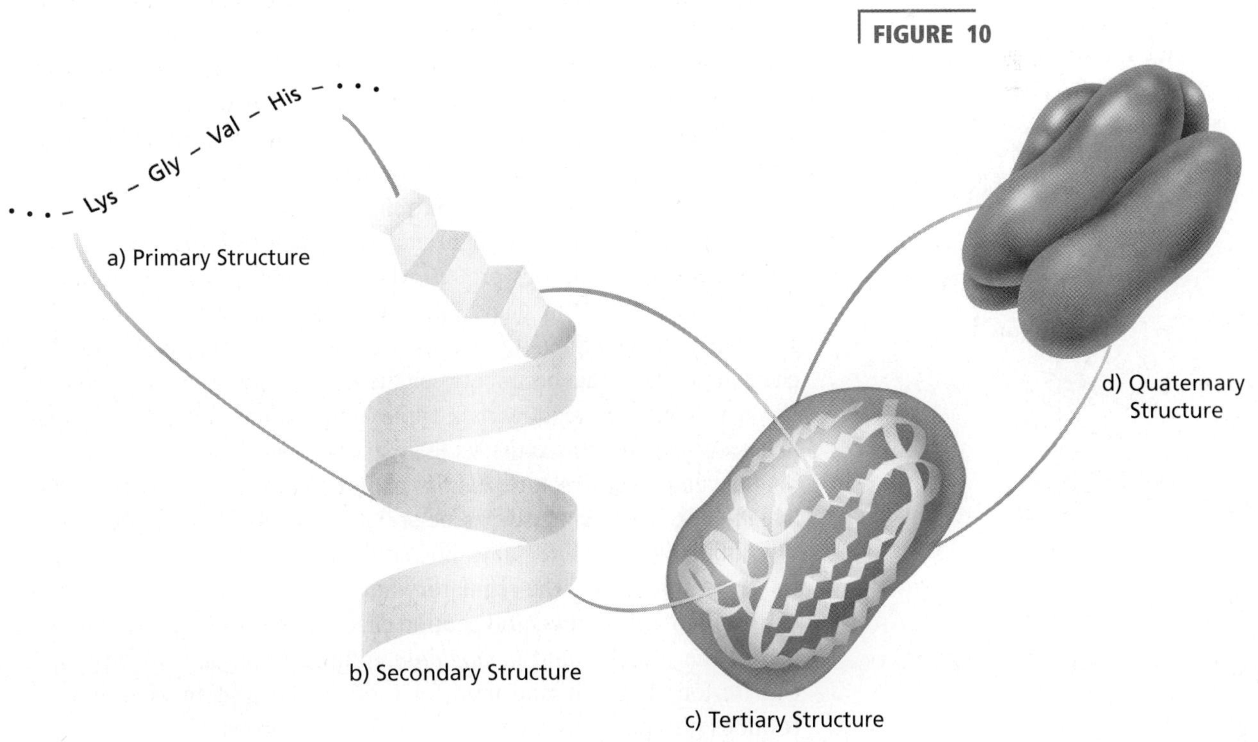

**TABLE 1** ***Biological Functions of Proteins***

| Type of Protein | Function | Examples |
|---|---|---|
| Storage | storage of amino acids | *Casein* protein in milk supplies amino acids for baby mammals. Egg white protein, or *ovalbumin,* is a source of amino acids for developing embryos. Plants store proteins in seeds. |
| Transport | transport of substances | Proteins transport molecules across cell membranes. *Hemoglobin* in blood transports oxygen. |
| Structural | support | Spiders produce silk fibers, which are proteins, to make webs. *Collagen* and *elastin* give connective tissues strength and flexibility. *Keratin* is found in hair, feathers, horns, hooves, and nails. |
| Contractile | movement | *Actin* and *myosin* fibers cause movement in muscles. Contractile fibers in cilia and flagella help propel single-celled organisms. |
| Enzymatic | catalysis of chemical reactions | Enzymes break down large molecules in food within the digestive system. |
| Hormonal | coordination of processes in an organism | Pancreatic insulin helps regulate blood-sugar levels. |
| Receptor | response of cell to chemical stimuli | Nerve cell membranes have chemical receptors that detect chemical signals released by other nerve cells. |
| Defensive | protection against disease | Antibodies attack pathogenic viruses and bacteria. |

## Biological Functions of Proteins

From **Table 1,** you can see that almost everything that occurs in a living organism depends on one or more proteins. Scientists have discovered that the specific function of a protein is related to the protein's shape. The shape of a protein can generally be described as fibrous or globular. *Fibrous proteins* are insoluble in water and are long, thin, and physically strong. *Globular proteins* are generally soluble in water and are twisted and folded into a globe-like shape.

Fibrous proteins give strength and protection to structures in living things. *Keratin* is a fibrous protein whose secondary structure is almost entirely alpha helical in shape. The keratin in nails and hooves is much stiffer than the keratin in fur or wool because of the large number of side-chain interactions that occur between the nail and hoof proteins. *Collagen,* found in bone and tendons, is a triple helix of three intertwined alpha helices, which gives these tissues their strength. *Fibrin* found in silk has a beta-pleated sheet structure. *Elastins* in blood tissue, *fibrins* in blood clots, and *myosins* found in muscle tissue are other kinds of fibrous proteins.

Globular proteins regulate body functions, catalyze reactions, and transport substances. The regulatory hormone *insulin* is a small protein of 51 amino acids in two polypeptide chains. *Myoglobin* transports oxygen in the muscles, and *hemoglobin* transports oxygen in the blood. *Casein,* found in milk and used for food, is also a globular protein. It contains phosphorus, which is needed for bone growth.

## Amino Acid Substitution

A protein's amino acid sequence determines its three-dimensional structure, which in turn determines its function. Even a single substitution of one amino acid for another can change the shape and function of a protein. For example, the genetic disease sickle cell anemia can happen when one amino acid—glutamic acid—is replaced by a molecule of valine. This change in only 1 of 146 amino acids in one of the two protein chains in the hemoglobin molecule causes a major change in the shape of the molecule. This change in the shape of the hemoglobin molecule causes the red blood cells to sickle when oxygen levels are relatively low (as is the case in most body tissues). The sickled cells tend to clog small blood vessels, which prevents the transport of enough oxygen to tissue cells. As a result, people who have sickle cell anemia suffer from shortness of breath. **Figure 11** shows the shape of normal red blood cells and sickled cells. The sickle cell gene is more common in some groups of people than it is in others. In areas where the disease malaria is common, scientists have discovered that sickled cells are more resistant to malarial infection than other cells are. So, people who have sickle cell anemia are more resistant to malaria than other people are.

**FIGURE 11**

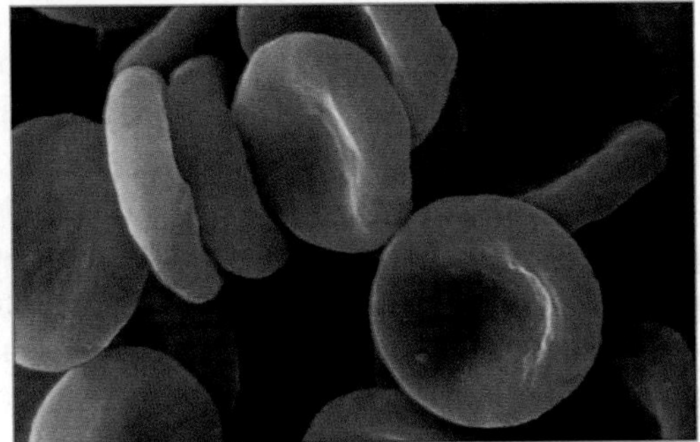

(a) The round, flat shape of healthy red blood cells shows they have normal hemoglobin molecules.

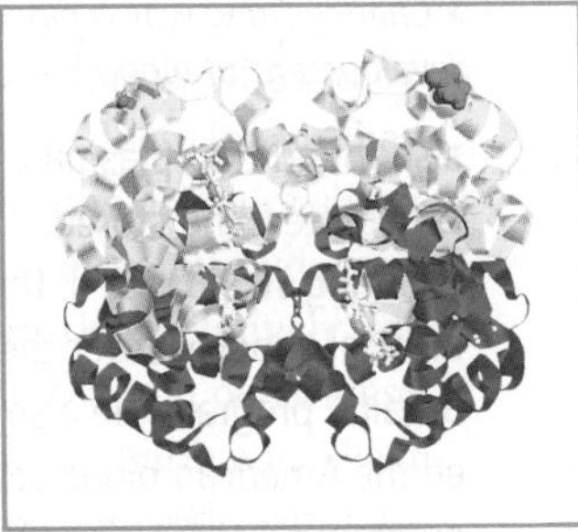

(b) Hemoglobin consists of four polypeptide chains; the area where the change in sickle cell hemoglobin occurs is shown in green.

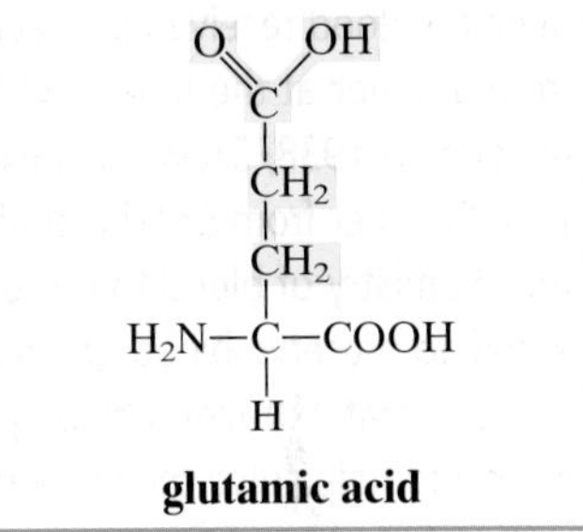


(c) Each of the chains is a polymer of 141 or 146 amino acid units, such as the glutamic acid monomer shown here.

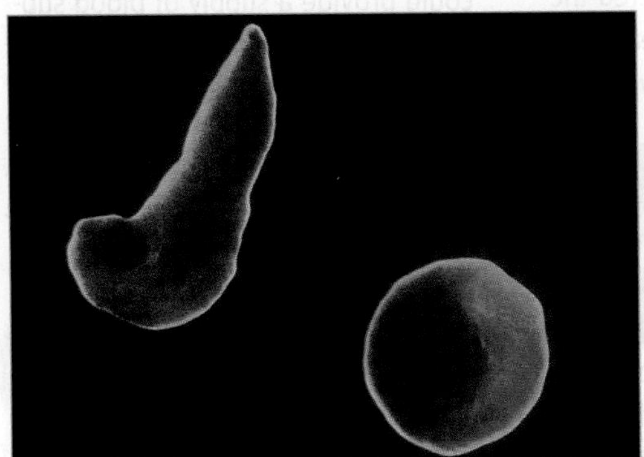

(d) Because of their shape, sickle cells clog small blood vessels.

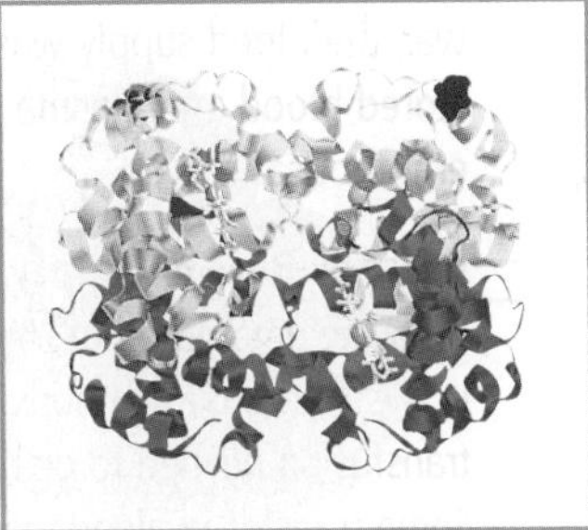

(e) A genetic mutation causes one glutamic acid to be replaced by valine in the hemoglobin molecules, as shown in red.

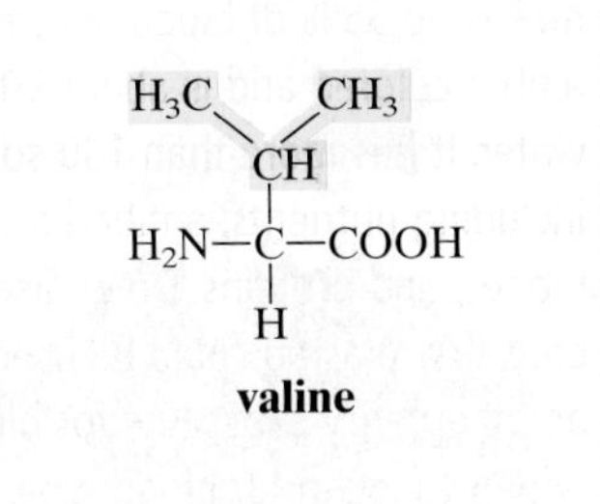


(f) The sickle shape of the cell comes from the different shape of the hemoglobin caused by the substitution of one valine for one glutamic acid in the 146 amino acids.

reaction just discussed. The shape of the enzyme is such that a molecule of hydrogen peroxide can fit into the enzyme at a specific part of the enzyme molecule, called the *active site*. The resulting compound is called the *enzyme-substrate complex*. In the enzyme-substrate complex, hydrogen-oxygen bonds break, and oxygen-oxygen bonds form. Then, the enzyme releases the products and is ready to react with another substrate molecule. This model of enzyme action is called the *lock and key model*.

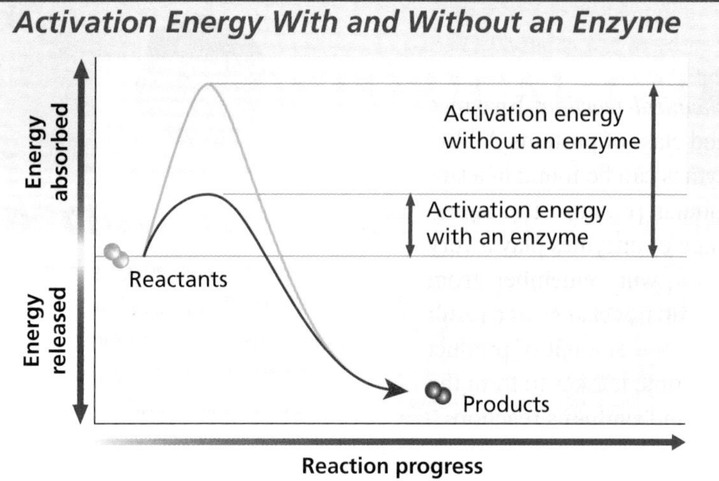


**FIGURE 13** Enzymes decrease the activation energy of a chemical reaction. However, the energy change from reactants to products is the same for both the catalyzed and the non-catalyzed reaction.

## Enzymes and Reaction Rates

The presence of an enzyme in a chemical reaction can increase the rate of a reaction by a factor of up to $10^{20}$. In Chapter 17, you saw that a reaction can occur when two atoms or molecules collide. But only collisions that have enough energy to overcome the *activation energy* and have the proper orientation change reactants into products. As you can see from the graph in **Figure 13,** an enzyme that catalyzes a chemical reaction causes an increase in the rate of the reaction by reducing the activation energy. The enzyme lowers the activation energy by forming the enzyme-substrate complex, which makes breaking bonds in the reactants and forming new bonds in the products easier. Even though the reaction is faster, the net amount of energy required for the reaction or released by the reaction is not changed by the action of an enzyme.

**FIGURE 14** Most enzymes have maximum activity within a narrow temperature range. Denaturation in many occurs at temperatures above 50°C and causes a decrease in activity.

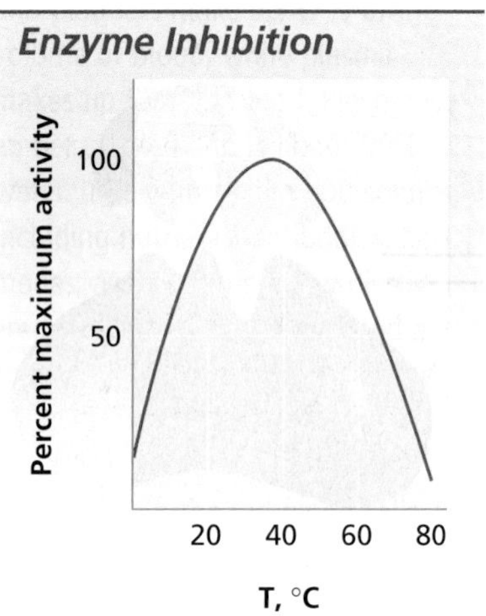


## Temperature and Enzyme Activity

Proteins, including enzymes, are also affected by changes in temperature. The graph in **Figure 14** shows the relatively narrow range of temperatures within which enzymes typically have maximum activity. Enzymes in the human body work optimally at the normal body temperature of 37°C (98.6°F). At temperatures above 50°C to 60°C enzymes typically show a decline in activity. High heat can denature, or alter, the shape of a protein, which in turn alters the protein's function. **Denaturation** *is a change in a protein's characteristic three-dimensional shape due to changes of its secondary, tertiary, and quaternary structure.* If you have ever cooked an egg, you have caused protein denaturation. The white of an egg is a solution of the protein albumin. When the egg is placed in a hot frying pan, a dramatic change takes place and the semitransparent solution turns into a white solid. Because the primary structure is retained in denaturation, the nutritional value of the egg white is not affected. However, the process is not reversable. Cooling a fried egg does not reverse the denaturation. When food is cooked, the three-dimensional structure of the protein is altered, making the food easier to digest.

## pH and Enzyme Activity

Enzymes also typically have maximum activity within a relatively narrow range of pH. The optimal pH for normal cell enzyme functions is almost neutral, about 7.3 to 7.4. Changes in pH can cause changes in protein structure and shape. For example, adding acid or base can interfere with the side-chain interactions and thus change the shape of a protein. Most enzymes become *inactivated,* or no longer work, because of denaturation when the pH changes. When milk sours (because lactic acid has formed), it curdles, and curds of the protein casein form. Yogurt is made by growing acid-producing bacteria in milk, which causes the casein to denature, giving yogurt its consistency.

The digestion of dietary protein by enzymes begins in the stomach. When food is swallowed, the stomach lining produces HCl and *pre-enzymes,* inactive forms of protein-digesting enzymes. These pre-enzymes travel from the stomach lining into the stomach before they become activated by the stomach's low pH of 1.5 to 2.0. This process is important because it prevents the active form of the enzymes from digesting the stomach lining. A layer of mucus protects the lining of the stomach from the enzymes it contains. Once activated, the enzymes catalyze the breakdown of the proteins in food into shorter polypeptide segments. *Pepsin* is a stomach enzyme found in adults. The partially digested protein in food travels into the small intestine, where the pH is 7 to 8. Under these conditions, the enzyme *trypsin* becomes active. It catalyzes the hydrolysis of the polypeptide segments into amino acids, which are absorbed through the intestinal wall and enter the bloodstream. The body uses these newly acquired amino acids to make other amino acids and new protein molecules. **Figure 15** shows how the protein in raw fish looks before and after it is soaked in acidic lime juice. Because the acidic lime juice denatures protein in the fish, the acid-treated fish looks very different.

**FIGURE 15** The fish treated with lime has turned white because the acidic lime juice denatures the protein in raw fish.

## SECTION REVIEW

1. Which elements do amino acids and proteins have in common with carbohydrates and lipids?
2. What is the difference between an amino acid and a protein?
3. Explain the difference between fibrous proteins and globular proteins.
4. Why are only small amounts of enzymes found in the body?

### Critical Thinking

5. **RELATING IDEAS** Explain how the ball-like structure of globular proteins allows them to be water soluble.
6. **INFERRING CONCLUSIONS** If an essential amino acid is in short supply in the diet, it can become a limiting reactant in building any protein that contains the amino acid. Explain why, under these conditions, the only way that the cell could make that protein would be to degrade one of its proteins that contain the limiting amino acid.

SECTION 3

# Metabolism

## Objectives

- Describe the role of ATP in cells.
- Explain how energy is released by metabolic reactions.
- Summarize the relationship between anabolism and catabolism.

**Metabolism** *is the sum of all the chemical processes that occur in an organism.* Complex molecules are broken down into smaller ones through *catabolism,* and simple molecules are used to build bigger ones through a process called *anabolism.* A *metabolic pathway* is a series of linked chemical reactions that occur within a cell and result in a specific product or products. The major metabolic pathways for most organisms are similar. So, one can study the basic metabolic pathways in simple organisms to get information about the reactions in organisms that are more complex, including humans.

## ATP: Energy for the Cell

SCILINKS.
www.scilinks.org
**Topic:** Exothermic and Endothermic Reactions
**Code:** HC60555

Just as it takes energy to run a chemical factory, cells require energy to make the proteins, carbohydrates, lipids, and nucleic acids that are necessary for life. In addition, the body needs energy as heat to keep warm, mechanical energy to move muscles and pump blood, and electrical energy to move ions across cell membranes. The original source for almost all of the energy needed by living systems is the sun. **Autotrophs,** such as plants, algae, and photosynthetic bacteria, can use sunlight, water, and $CO_2$ to make carbon-containing biomolecules, including carbohydrates. This process is called *photosynthesis* and occurs in the cells of plants and algae, such as those shown in **Figure 16,** within structures called *chloroplasts*. Chloroplasts contain *chlorophyll,* an organic molecule that absorbs solar energy. This energy is captured immediately in two compounds, one of which is **adenosine triphosphate (ATP). ATP** *is an energy storage molecule that plant cells use to make carbohydrates.* The other compound, known as *NADPH,* is also used in carbohydrate-forming reactions.

**FIGURE 16** The cells of algae and green plants contain chlorophyll, the green pigment that absorbs light energy from the sun.

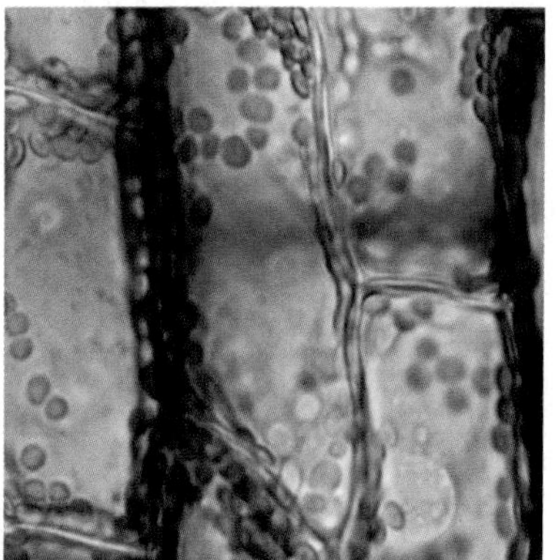

Unlike plants, animals cannot use the sun's energy to convert $CO_2$ into food. Animals must get the energy that they need to sustain life by consuming plants and other animals. *Living things, including most microorganisms, which depend on plants or other animals for food, are called* **heterotrophs.** Heterotrophs use the energy released when complex molecules react to form simpler products to drive chemical reactions in cells. The carbohydrates, lipids, and amino acids that heterotrophs consume undergo several energy-yielding reactions as they break down into simpler molecules. Some of this energy is stored in the ATP molecules, which cells use to drive a wide variety of metabolic reactions.

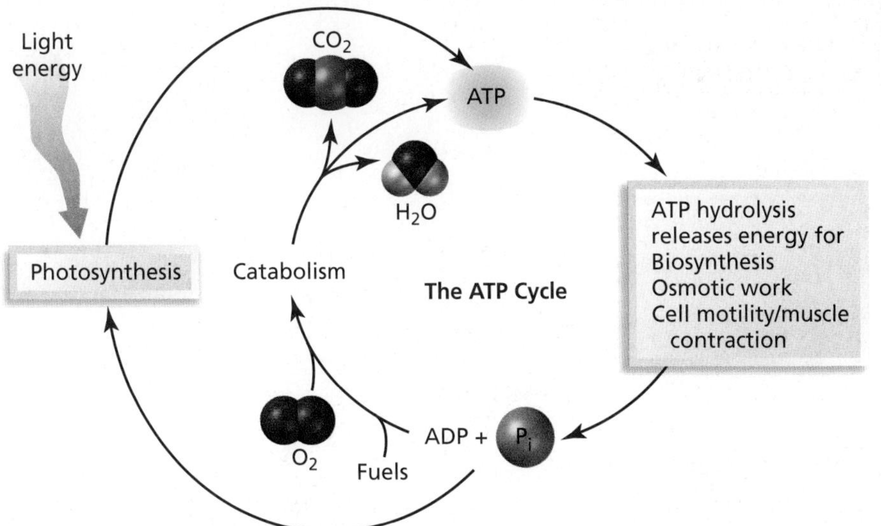


**FIGURE 17** ATP is formed by photosynthesis or catabolism. Cell activities that require energy are powered by ATP hydrolysis. "$P_i$" represents a phosphate.

## Energy Activities

The cycle between ATP and *ADP, adenosine diphosphate,* is the primary energy exchange mechanism in the body. **Figure 17** provides an overview of the ATP cycle in cells. In this energy cycle, ATP is the molecule that serves to carry energy from energy-storing molecules, carbohydrates, lipids, and proteins to specific energy-requiring processes in cells. When ATP is hydrolyzed to ADP, energy is released to power the cell's activities. The molecular structures of ATP and ADP are closely related, as shown in **Figure 18.**

The difference in the number of phosphate groups between ATP and ADP molecules is the key to the energy exchange in metabolic reactions. The chemical equation below shows the hydrolysis reaction by which ATP is converted into ADP and a phosphate group (represented by the gold-colored ball in **Figure 17**). The free energy for this reaction is –31 kJ, which is the amount of energy available to do work.

$$ATP^{4-}(aq) + H_2O(l) \longrightarrow ADP^{3-}(aq) + H_2PO_4^-(aq)\ \Delta G = -31\ kJ$$

**FIGURE 18** The hydrolysis of ATP produces ADP and releases energy.

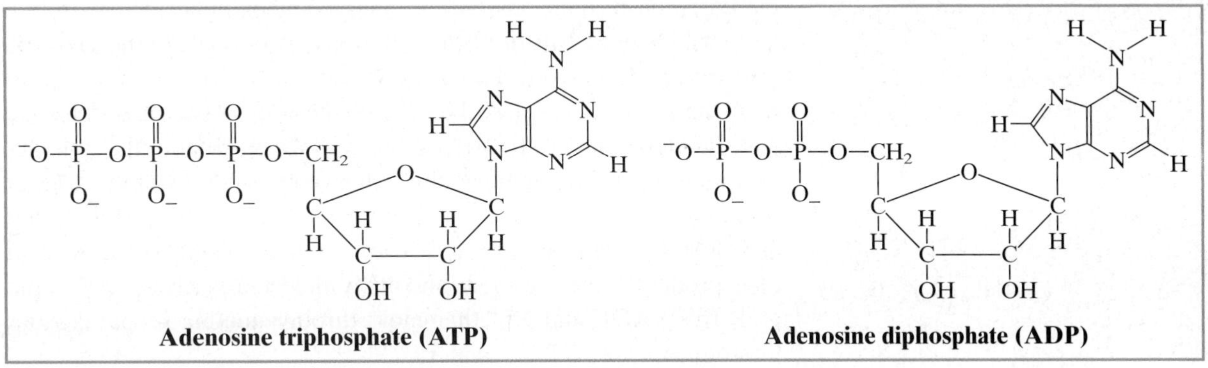

**Adenosine triphosphate (ATP)**

**Adenosine diphosphate (ADP)**

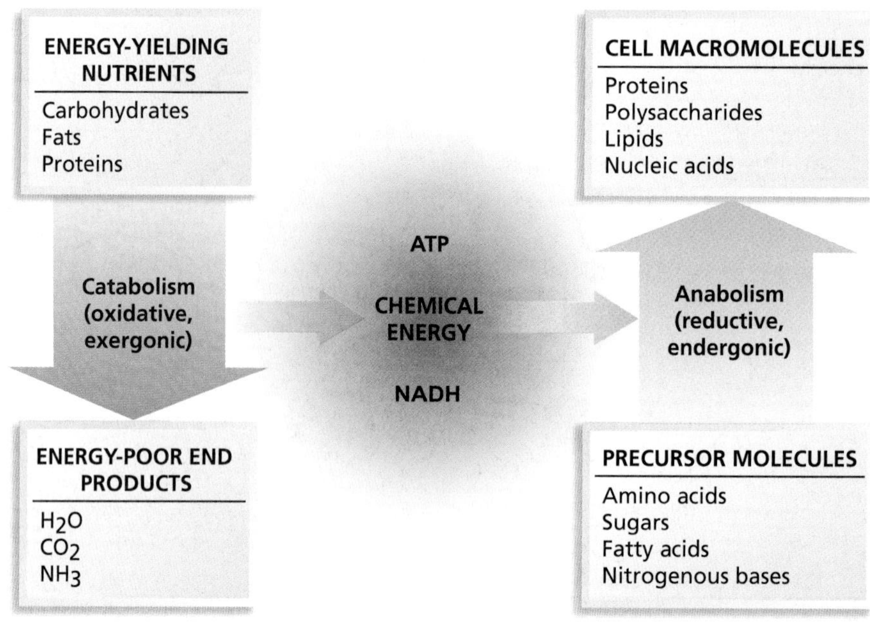


**FIGURE 19** Catabolic pathways release free energy in the form of ATP and NADH. Anabolic pathways consume energy released by catabolic pathways.

SCILINKS®
www.scilinks.org
**Topic:** Food as Fuel
**Code:** HC60591

## Catabolism

The energy that your body needs to maintain its temperature and drive its biochemical reactions is provided through *catabolic* processes. **Figure 19** illustrates the relationship between the pathways of catabolism and anabolism. **Catabolism** *is the part of metabolism in which complex compounds break down into simpler ones and is accompanied by the release of energy.* First, enzymes break down the complex compounds in food—carbohydrates, fats, and proteins—into simpler molecules.

Carbohydrate digestion begins in the mouth, where the enzyme *amylase* in saliva begins to break down polysaccharides. The food then passes through the esophagus, then the stomach, and into the small intestine. Here, additional enzymes are secreted to complete the hydrolysis of carbohydrates to form glucose and other monosaccharides.

Digestion of fats occurs only in the small intestine. Protein digestion begins in the stomach and is completed in the small intestine. During the digestion of both fats and proteins, complex molecules hydrolyze into simpler ones. Fats are broken down into fatty acids and glycerol. Proteins are broken down into amino acids.

These products are absorbed across the wall of the small intestine into the blood and are transported to cells. Once in the cells, each glucose molecule is broken down through glycolysis into two molecules of pyruvate, which enter the mitochondria and feed into a complex series of reactions called the *citric acid cycle,* or *Krebs cycle*. The citric acid cycle produces carbon dioxide and other molecules, such as NADH and ATP. This NADH and ATP then move through another set of reactions to produce more ATP and water.

The amount of energy released in catabolism depends on the amount of ATP that is made as the products of digestion are oxidized. The catabolism of 1 glucose molecule generally may produce up to a total of 36 ATP molecules. This accounts for about 40% of the energy released by the complete oxidation of glucose. Most of the energy not converted to ATP is lost by the body as energy in the form of heat. **Table 2** shows how much ATP is needed for some daily activities.

**TABLE 2** ***Approximate "Cost" of Daily Activities***

| Activity | Energy required (kJ) | ATP required (mol) |
|---|---|---|
| Running | 1120 | 56 |
| Swimming | 840 | 42 |
| Bicycling | 1400 | 70 |
| Walking | 560 | 28 |

## Anabolism

Cells use the simple molecules that result from the breakdown of food to make larger, more complex molecules. Energy released during catabolism powers the synthesis of new molecules as well as the active transport of ions and molecules across cell membranes. *Anabolic* processes are the energy-consuming pathways by which cells produce the molecules that they need for sustaining life and for growth and repair. *The conversion of small biomolecules into larger ones is called* **anabolism.**

In an anabolic pathway, small precursor molecules are converted into complex molecules, including lipids, polysaccharides, proteins, and nucleic acids. Energy from ATP and NADH is necessary for these biosynthesis reactions to occur. **Figure 19** illustrates that catabolism and anabolism occur simultaneously and that ATP and NADH serve as chemical "links" between the two processes.

One important anabolic pathway that is common to animals, plants, fungi, and microorganisms is *gluconeogenesis*. As the name implies, glucose is synthesized in this pathway from non-carbohydrate substances, including lactate, pyruvate, glycerol, and most of the amino acids. In mammals, glucose from the blood is the fuel source for the brain and nervous system as well as for the kidney medulla, red blood cells, and embryonic tissues.

### SECTION REVIEW

1. List four ways in which the body uses energy.
2. What is the total energy (in kilojoules) stored in the 36 ATP molecules that are made from the metabolism of 1 molecule of glucose in skeletal tissue?
3. The teeth break large pieces of food into smaller ones. However, this process is not considered part of digestion. Explain why.
4. How does the digestion of fat in a strip of ham differ from the digestion of starch in a piece of toast?
5. Why are diets that are severely restrictive in carbohydrate intake potentially dangerous to a person's health?

**Critical Thinking**

6. **RELATING CONCEPTS** When a molecule of glucose is oxidized, only about 40% of the energy is captured in ATP molecules, and the rest is lost as energy in the form of heat. What do you think would happen if this energy remained in the body as heat?

SECTION 4

# Nucleic Acids

**C.3.6** Identify the basic structure of common polymers (including proteins, nucleic acids, plastics, and starches)

## *Objectives*

- Describe the structure of the nucleic acids DNA and RNA.
- Explain the functions of DNA and RNA in the cell.
- Describe applications of modern gene technology.

Nucleic acids contain all of the genetic information of an organism. They are the means by which a living organism stores and conveys instructional information for all of its activities. They are also the means by which an organism can reproduce. The two nucleic acids found in organisms are *deoxyribonucleic acid (DNA)* and *ribonucleic acid (RNA)*.

## Nucleic Acid Structure

*A* **nucleic acid** *is an organic compound, either RNA or DNA, whose molecules carry genetic information and is made up of one or two chains of monomer units called* nucleotides. However, unlike the monomer units in polysaccharides and polypeptides, each nucleotide monomer can be further hydrolyzed into three different molecules. A nucleotide molecule is composed of a five-carbon sugar unit that is bonded to both a phosphate group and a cyclic organic base containing nitrogen.

The sugar unit in DNA is deoxyribose, and the sugar unit in RNA is ribose. The diagram below shows the sugar-phosphate arrangement in three nucleotides.

```
—phosphate—sugar—phosphate—sugar—phosphate—sugar—
             |                 |                 |
            base              base              base
```

The five nitrogenous bases found in nucleic acids are shown in **Figure 20.** *Adenine* (A), *guanine* (G), and *cytosine* (C) are found in both DNA and RNA. *Thymine* (T) is found only in DNA, and *uracil* (U) is found only in RNA.

**FIGURE 20** There are five common nitrogenous bases. Thymine (T), cytosine (C), and uracil (U) have a single six-member ring. Adenine (A) and guanine (G) have a six-member ring connected to a five-member ring.

**adenine** **guanine** **cytosine** **thymine** **uracil**

## DNA: Deoxyribonucleic Acid

Every single instruction for all of the traits that you have inherited and all of the life processes that occur in your cells is contained in your DNA. It is no wonder then that DNA molecules are the largest molecules found in cells. Living organisms vary widely in the size and number of DNA molecules in their cells. Some bacterial cells contain only 1 DNA molecule, while human cells contain 46 relatively large DNA molecules. The DNA in each human cell is about 2 m long. This DNA is divided and packed into the cell's 46 *chromosomes.* An average cell is only about 6 $\mu$m in diameter and contains many organelles and structures. To fit in a cell, DNA must undergo extensive twisting, coiling, folding, and wrapping.

SCILINKS.
www.scilinks.org
**Topic:** DNA
**Code:** HC60418
**Topic:** DNA Replication
**Code:** HC60420

The Swedish scientist Friedrich Miescher first extracted DNA from cells in 1868, but its three-dimensional structure was not discovered until 1953. Using the X-ray data of Maurice Wilkins and Rosalind Franklin, James Watson of the United States and Francis Crick of England proposed that DNA was a double helix. In this structure, which has been confirmed by numerous methods, two strands of the sugar-phosphate backbone are wound around each other, and the nitrogenous bases point inward, as shown in **Figure 21.** The sequence of these nitrogenous bases along the phosphate-sugar backbone in DNA forms the code responsible for transferring genetic information. The three-dimensional DNA molecule is similar to a twisted ladder. The sides of the ladder are the sugar-phosphate backbone, and the rungs are base pairs of A–T (adenine-thymine) or G–C (guanine-cytosine) bases extending between the two backbones. Hydrogen bonding between these pairs of nitrogenous bases holds the rungs of the ladder together.

**FIGURE 21** Hydrogen bonding between base pairs makes the three-dimensional structure of DNA stable. Base pairing occurs between adenine and thymine or guanine and cytosine, keeping the distance between the strands constant.

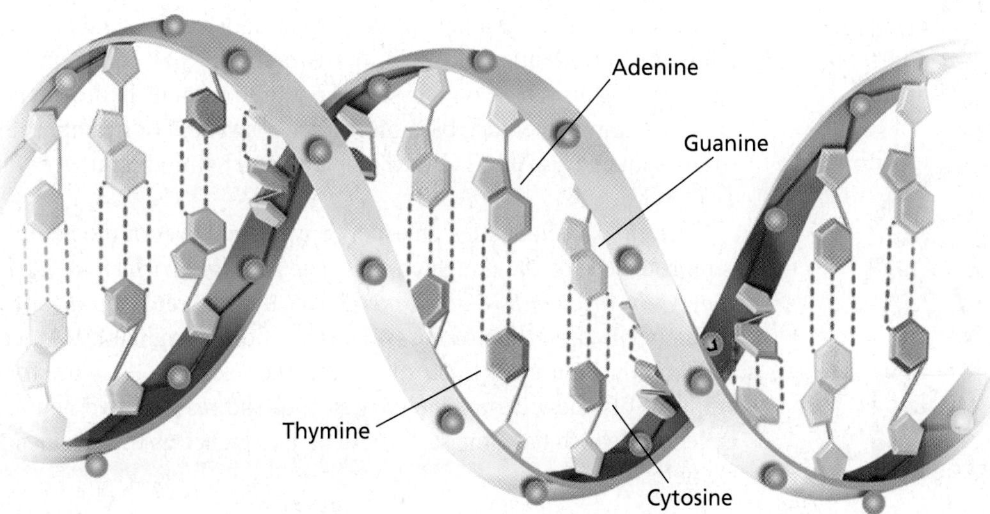

FIGURE 22 The double helix of DNA can be seen by using scanning tunneling microscopy (STM).

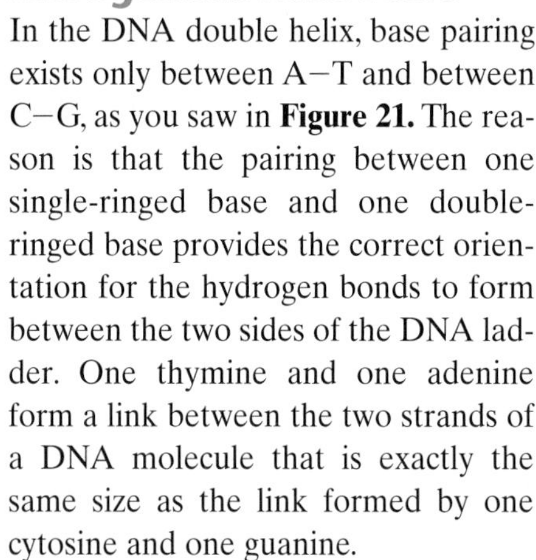

## Nitrogenous Base Pairs

In the DNA double helix, base pairing exists only between A–T and between C–G, as you saw in **Figure 21.** The reason is that the pairing between one single-ringed base and one double-ringed base provides the correct orientation for the hydrogen bonds to form between the two sides of the DNA ladder. One thymine and one adenine form a link between the two strands of a DNA molecule that is exactly the same size as the link formed by one cytosine and one guanine.

The double-helix configuration of DNA, shown in **Figure 22,** can be seen by using a scanning tunneling microscope (STM). The discovery of the relative quantities of the nitrogenous bases A, T, G, and C present in DNA was the key to determining the three-dimensional molecular structure. Analysis of DNA from different organisms reveals that the amounts of A and T are the same and that the amounts of G and C are the same for all members of the same species. In humans, DNA is about 30% A, 30% T, 20% G, and 20% C.

The interaction between base pairs accounts for the ability of DNA to replicate, as you will see in the next section. Just as combinations of the 26 letters of the alphabet form words that tell a story in a novel, combinations of the four-letter alphabet of A, T, G, and C form the *genes* that define our heredity. Each gene is a section of DNA that contains a specific sequence of four bases (A, G, T, and C) and encodes instructions for protein synthesis. Researchers using the Human Genome Project data predict that the human body contains about 20 000 to 25 000 genes. Laboratory verification of this count will require many more years.

**Historical Chemistry**

Go to **go.hrw.com** for full-length article on the discovery of the structure of DNA.

**Keyword: HC6BIOX**

## DNA Replication

Like the two sides of a zipper, the two strands of the double helix of DNA are not identical. Instead, the two strands are complements of each other. Thus, a base on one strand is paired through hydrogen bonding to its complementary base on the other strand. For example, if one strand sequence is AGCTC, the complementary strand sequence will be TCGAG.

Each time a cell divides, an exact copy of the DNA of the parent cell is reproduced for the daughter cells. *The process by which an identical copy of the original DNA is formed is called* **DNA replication.** As replication begins, a portion of the two strands of the original DNA unzips, as shown in **Figure 23.** Each strand can then act as a template for the synthesis of a new, complementary strand. The result is two new DNA molecules, which have the same base pair sequence as the original double helix.

FIGURE 23 DNA replicates when its double helix unwinds and becomes single stranded. The single strands are used as a template for the formation of new complementary strands.

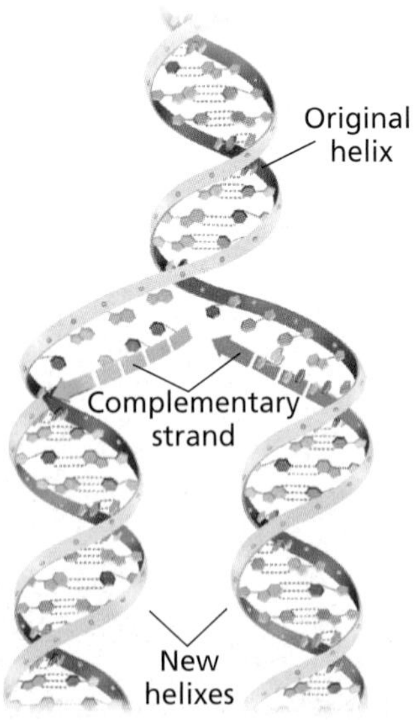

## RNA: Ribonucleic Acid

RNA molecules are responsible for the synthesis of proteins, which in turn control the operation and function of the cell. RNA differs from DNA in four basic ways: (1) the sugar unit in the backbone of RNA is ribose rather than deoxyribose, (2) RNA contains the base uracil, U, instead of thymine, which occurs in DNA, (3) RNA is a single-stranded molecule rather than a double-stranded helix like DNA, and (4) RNA molecules typically consist of 75 to a few thousand nucleotide units rather than the millions that exist in DNA. Even though RNA is much smaller than DNA, RNA is still large enough to twist, coil, bend, and fold back onto itself. In fact, it is not uncommon for up to 50% of an RNA molecule to have a double-helix structure. The reason is that the base sequences along the helical regions of the RNA strand are complementary, which makes hydrogen bonding between bases possible.

### Synthesis of RNA

RNA is synthesized in the nucleus of eukaryotic cells, where DNA and protein molecules actually help synthesize specific RNA molecules. RNA can also be seen by STM, as shown in **Figure 24.** As RNA is synthesized, some information contained in the DNA is transferred to the RNA molecules. Like the genetic information of DNA, the genetic information of RNA is carried in its nucleotide sequence. One type of RNA molecule is called *messenger RNA* (mRNA) because it carries the instructions for making proteins out into the cytosol, where proteins are produced on *ribosomes. A* **ribosome** *is a cell organelle that is composed of RNA and protein. Ribosomes are the main site of protein production in cells.* The DNA template is also used to make two other types of RNA molecules: *ribosomal RNA* (rRNA) and *transfer RNA* (tRNA). Both of these types of RNA also leave the nucleus and come together in the ribosome where they help synthesize proteins. Ribosomal RNA becomes part of the structure of the ribosome, and tRNA is used to transfer amino acids into the ribosome. Only mRNA carries the coded genetic information that is translated into proteins.

DNA supplies all of the information necessary for RNA to be used to make the proteins needed by the body. The portion of DNA that holds the specific genetic code for a single, specific mRNA molecule is a gene. As you learned previously, each gene is a section of the DNA chain that contains a specific sequence of the bases A, G, T, and C. A gene has the information necessary in this sequence to direct RNA to produce several proteins that have specific functions.

**FIGURE 24** Scanning tunneling micrograph of RNA strands being transcribed in a cell.

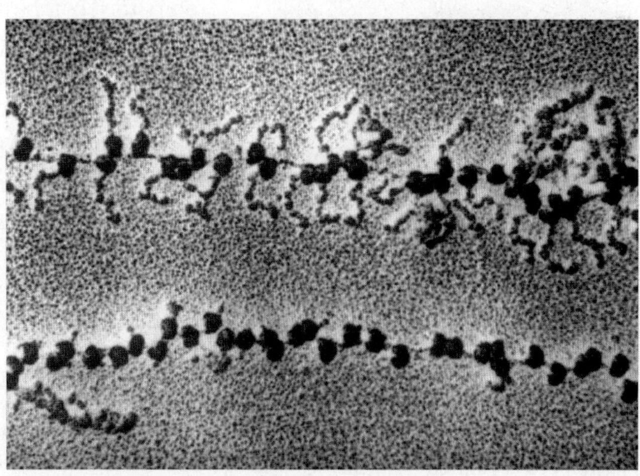

CAREERS in Chemistry

**Forensic Chemist**

A forensic chemist applies scientific methodology to physical evidence. Forensic chemists focus on analyzing evidence that has been collected at a crime scene. They then report any conclusions that they can draw from the analysis. Understanding evidence requires knowledge of biology, materials science, and genetics in addition to chemistry. Because forensic chemists are often asked to testify in court, they need to be comfortable speaking in public and able to give clear and concise explanations to those who do not have a background in science.

### RNA and Protein Synthesis

RNA is made from DNA in a process that is similar to how DNA replicates itself. At a gene, a portion of DNA unwinds and RNA is assembled using the same complementary base pairs as DNA except that uracil replaces the thymine. When a signal to stop is received, the RNA is released. As in DNA replication, the RNA sequence that forms has the complementary base pairs of the DNA gene. The DNA sequence below would form the complementary RNA sequence shown.

DNA strand: C C C C A C C C T A C G G T G
RNA strand: G G G G U G G G A U G C C A C

A sequence of three bases in mRNA codes for a specific amino acid. Thus, the sequence CAG codes for glutamic acid, and GUC codes for valine. There are 64 ($4^3$) unique combinations of three-base sequences made from four bases. Because only 20 amino acids require codes, some of the amino acids have more than one code. For example, leucine is coded by six three-base sequences: UUA, UUG, CUU, CUC, CUA, and CUG. The genetic code is universal, meaning that the same three-base sequence always codes for the same amino acid regardless of whether the organism is a bacterium or a human. The "stop" signal in the gene is also a three-base code: UAG, UAA, or UGA.

## Technology and Genetic Engineering

The discovery of DNA's function in life has provided new options for the production of food, medical diagnosis and treatments, and increased understanding of genetic disorders. Scientists in the field of genetic engineering study how manipulation of an organism's genetic material can modify the proteins that are produced and the changes that result in the organism. Although the selective breeding of plants and animals has been practiced for hundreds of years, today genetic engineering refers to recombinant DNA technology that is used for cloning and the creation of new forms of life. Because the technique is so powerful, it is controversial and must be used responsibly.

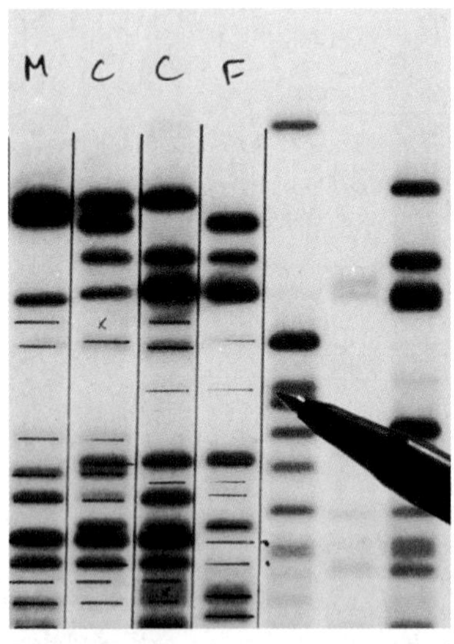


**FIGURE 25** A DNA autoradiograph shows the pattern of DNA fragments of an organism after they have been separated from each other by electrophoresis.

### DNA Fingerprinting

One of the most visible uses of molecular technology is DNA fingerprinting. DNA is unique to an individual except for identical twins. This technology is used in criminal investigations and victim identification. Often there are only very small samples available, such as a single drop of blood or one strand of hair. The technique of the *polymerase chain reaction* (PCR) may be used to copy a DNA sample to supply sufficient DNA for identification. The processes of electrophoresis and autoradiography may be used to compare DNA from a sample with the DNA of a known individual to confirm identification, as **Figure 25** shows. DNA technology can also be used to test paternity or to trace heredity.

## Cloning

One meaning of the word **cloning** *is the process of making an exact copy of an organism*. One example of a natural occurrence of cloning, the formation of identical twins, is the result of a chance splitting of the embryonic cells very early in the growth of a zygote. Artificial cloning, using stem cells from animals or meristem cells from plants, can produce identical replicas of the parent cells or, under specialized conditions, a complete organism that is identical to the original organism. The orchid shown in **Figure 26** is a clone of its parent plant. Cloning of plants may hold promise for increasing the yields of crops. Recently, scientists at Pennsylvania State University cloned cocoa plants from cocoa flowers. When cocoa trees are planted from seed, as many as 50% do not mature with the desired characteristics. By planting young trees that are clones of plants with desirable characteristics, farmers may be able to increase their cocoa production.

**FIGURE 26** Growers can produce many orchids by artificial cloning of the meristem tissue of a single orchid plant.

The first animal to be cloned, a sheep named Dolly, was born in 1996 in Scotland. Dolly was euthanized in 2003 because of lung disease. She had also been diagnosed with arthritis. Both diseases are normally found in sheep older than Dolly was.

## Recombinant DNA Technology

Recombinant DNA technology has been used to insert DNA from one organism into another. One technique involves splicing a gene from one organism's DNA into a molecule of DNA from another organism. *Escherichia coli,* a bacterium found in animal intestinal tracts, are often used by biologists as cellular factories for the production or manufacture of DNA fragments cloned from other organisms. In some instances, *E. coli* can even be used to produce protein from DNA cloned from other organisms.

One of the first applications of genetic engineering was the synthesis of human insulin. Previously, most diabetics had to use either pig or cow insulin. But insulin from animals is not exactly the same as human insulin. Today, most insulin used is produced in bacteria and harvested. Human growth hormone is also commercially produced by using recombinant DNA technology.

## SECTION REVIEW

1. What sugar is present in DNA? What sugar is present in RNA?
2. Explain why the two strands of the DNA double helix are said to be complementary instead of identical.
3. Describe how DNA uses the genetic code to control the synthesis of proteins.
4. Why is a very small trace of blood enough for DNA fingerprinting?

### Critical Thinking

5. **INTERPRET AND APPLY** Is it possible to specify 20 amino acids by using only two base pairs instead of three for coding?
6. **DRAWING CONCLUSIONS** Why is the arrangement of base pairs that is found in DNA ideal for holding the double helix of DNA together?

# CHAPTER HIGHLIGHTS

## Carbohydrates and Lipids

**Vocabulary**
carbohydrate
monosaccharide
disaccharide
condensation reaction
hydrolysis
polysaccharide
lipid
fatty acid
saponification

- Carbohydrates are nutrients that are produced by plants and are made up of carbon, oxygen, and hydrogen.
- Monosaccharides are the simplest carbohydrates. Carbohydrates made of two monosaccharides are called *disaccharides,* and carbohydrates made of more than two monosaccharides are called *polysaccharides.*
- Carbohydrates undergo condensation reactions and hydrolysis reactions.
- Lipids are a varied group of biochemical molecules that have a high percentage of C and H atoms.

## Amino Acids and Proteins

**Vocabulary**
amino acid
protein
enzyme
denaturation

- Amino acid molecules are the basic building blocks of proteins.
- Proteins are biopolymers, each of which has a unique sequence of the acid monomer molecules.
- The specific function of a protein is related to the shape of the protein.
- Side-chain interactions between amino acids result in secondary, tertiary, and quaternary protein structures.

## Metabolism

**Vocabulary**
metabolism
autotroph
adenosine triphosphate (ATP)
heterotroph
adenosine diphosphate (ADP)
catabolism
anabolism

- ATP is a high-energy storage compound that the body uses to store and provide energy for life.
- The metabolic pathways involve both the conversion of ATP to ADP and the conversion of ADP to ATP.
- Metabolic pathways are classified as two types: catabolism and anabolism.
- Catabolism includes reactions in which large molecules are changed into simpler molecules. These reactions release energy.
- Anabolic processes are energy-consuming pathways by which cells produce the molecules needed for growth and repair.

## Nucleic Acids

**Vocabulary**
nucleic acid
DNA replication
cloning

- Deoxyribonucleic acid (DNA) and ribonucleic acid (RNA) are nucleic acids, the compounds by which living organisms can reproduce themselves.
- Nucleic acids are polymers of monomer units called *nucleotides.*
- The two strands of the double helix of DNA are complementary to each other, not identical. These strands are held together by hydrogen bonding of the base pairs.
- RNA is used as a template to produce proteins in the cell.

## Carbohydrates and Lipids

### SECTION 1 REVIEW

1. Describe the general chemical formula of carbohydrates.
2. Name two examples from each of the following classes of carbohydrates: monosaccharides, disaccharides, and polysaccharides.
3. What different roles do the polysaccharides starch and cellulose play in plant systems?
4. What word is used to describe fatty acids that contain at least one double bond?
5. Why are some triglycerides liquid, while others are solid?
6. What reagents are used to make soaps?

### PRACTICE PROBLEMS

7. Draw the structural formula for glucose.
8. Using structural formulas, write the equation showing the formation of maltose, which is the disaccharide made of two glucose units.
9. Write the equation representing the formation of a soap molecule from stearic acid, $C_{17}H_{35}COOH$, and sodium hydroxide.

## Amino Acids and Proteins

### SECTION 2 REVIEW

10. Describe the structure of an amino acid. Then, explain how amino acids become linked together to form a protein.
11. Circle and identify the carboxylic acid groups and the amino groups in the following molecule:

```
           O  H         O  H
           ‖  |         ‖  |
NH2—CH—C—N—CH—C—N—CH—COOH
     |           |           |
    CH2         CH—OH       CH2
     |           |           |
    COOH        CH3         C—NH2
                             ‖
                             O
```

12. Can two types of enzymes contain the same number and kinds of amino acids? Explain.
13. What happens when a protein is denatured?
14. Explain the cause of the genetic disease sickle cell anemia.
15. Why is the water solubility of fibrous proteins so different from that of globular proteins?

### PRACTICE PROBLEMS

16. Draw the structures of two dipeptides made up of glycine and valine.
17. How many different tripeptides can be formed from two molecules of glycine and one molecule of cysteine? Write all of the structures by using the three-letter codes Gly and Cys.

## Metabolism

### SECTION 3 REVIEW

18. What chemical gains the metabolic energy that is released as glucose is broken down in the body?
19. What does *ATP* stand for? What is the role of ATP in living things?
20. Describe the steps that occur in the digestion of fats.
21. Review the following diagram of catabolism.

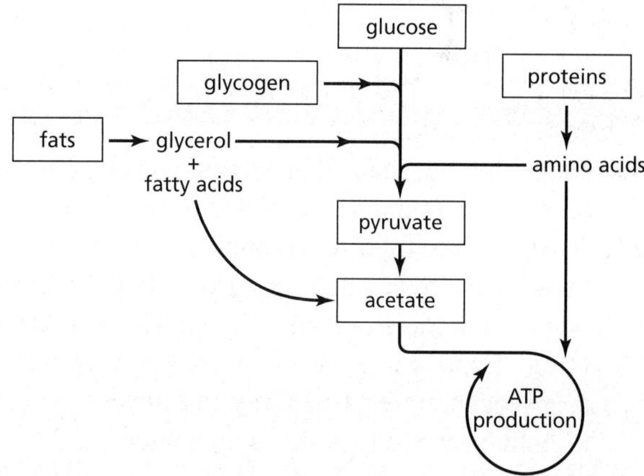


According to the diagram, what could happen in the cell when glucose and glycogen reserves are nearly gone?

### PRACTICE PROBLEMS

22. Draw the structure of ATP. Circle the bond that breaks when ADP forms.

## *Nucleic Acids*

### SECTION 4 REVIEW

**23.** What are the three components of a nucleotide?

**24.** How are the two polynucleotide chains of DNA held together?

**25.** Describe in general terms the process of DNA replication.

**26.** What are the main differences between DNA and RNA?

**27.** Describe the similarities and differences between the three kinds of RNA molecules.

**28.** What is a ribosome? What is the function of a ribosome in a cell?

### PRACTICE PROBLEMS

**29.** The following sequence of bases might be found on the gene that codes for oxytocin, the human pituitary hormone:
TACACAATGTAAGTTTTGACGGGGGAC-CCTATC

a. What is the sequence of bases on the complementary strand of DNA?

b. What is the sequence of bases that would occur on a strand of mRNA that was transcribed from the oxytocin DNA sequence?

## MIXED REVIEW

**30.** Name the four main elements that make up compounds found in living organisms.

**31.** In each of the following groups, one of the items does not belong in the group. Identify the odd item in the group and explain why it is different. Explain how the other items are related.

a. glycogen, starch, fructose, and cellulose

b. amino acids, dipeptides, polypeptides, and proteins

c. fats, oils, and fatty acids

d. cytosine, adenine, and guanine

**32.** What is the human body's *storage* form of each of the following?

a. glucose

b. lipids

c. protein

**33.** Is each of the following statements about proteins and triglycerides true or false?

a. Both contain the amide functional group.

b. Both are a part of a major class of biochemical molecules.

c. Both hydrolyze in order to enter the metabolic pathway in humans.

**34.** Circle the hydrophobic part in each of the figures shown below.

a.
```
H3C     CH3
   \   /
    CH
    |
H2N—C—COOH
    |
    H
```

b.
```
HO    O
  \  //
   C
   |
 H—C—H
   |
 H—C—H
   |
 H—C—H
   |
 H—C—H
   |
 H—C—H
   |
 H—C—H
   |
 H—C—H
   |
 H—C
   ||
 H—C
   |
 H—C—H
   |
 H—C—H
   |
 H—C—H
   |
 H—C—H
   |
 H—C—H
   |
 H—C—H
   |
 H—C—H
   |
 H—C—H
   |
   H
```

35. Both celery and potato chips are composed of molecules that are polymers of glucose. Explain why celery is a good snack for people on a diet while potato chips are not.

36. Carbohydrates, fats, and proteins can provide energy for an organism.
    a. Which class of substances most rapidly provides energy?
    b. Which class can be used as a building material in the human body?
    c. Which is the most efficient as an energy storage system?

37. Describe the basic structure of the cell membrane. What is the cell membrane's main function?

## CRITICAL THINKING

38. **Interpreting Concepts** A diet that consists primarily of corn can result in a protein-deficiency disease called *kwashiorkor*. What does this information indicate about the protein content of corn?

39. **Inferring Relationships** Explain how a similar reaction forms three kinds of biological polymers: polysaccharides, polypeptides, and nucleic acids.

40. **Evaluating Ideas** Some diets recommend severely restricting or eliminating the intake of carbohydrates. Why is it not a good idea to eliminate all carbohydrates from the diet?

41. **Using Analogies** Explain why the model of enzyme action is called the "lock and key" model.

## RESEARCH & WRITING

42. Conduct library research about how Olestra® decreases fat and caloric content of potato chips. What are the advantages and disadvantages of Olestra in food products?

43. Write a summary discussing what you have learned about the four major classes of organic compounds found in living things—carbohydrates, lipids, proteins, and nucleic acids. Include a description of how these organic molecules are used by the body.

## ALTERNATIVE ASSESSMENT

44. Amylase, the enzyme present in the mouth, catalyzes the digestion of starch. The pH of the mouth is almost neutral.
    a. Do you think that amylase is active in the stomach after you swallow the food? Why or why not?
    b. Design an experiment you could perform to test your answer to item a. Note: A common test for the presence of starch is the addition of tincture of iodine, which will produce a blue color if starch is present.

# Math Tutor INTERPRETATION OF THE GENETIC CODE

In protein synthesis, the DNA sequence of bases is transcribed onto messenger RNA (mRNA). The mRNA base sequence is the complement of the DNA sequence except that uracil takes the place of thymine as the complement of adenine.

## Problem-Solving TIPS

- Find the first base of the mRNA triplet along the left side of the table.
- Follow that row to the right until you are beneath the second base of the triplet.
- Move up or down in the square that corresponds to the second base until you are even, on the right side of the chart, with the third base of the triplet.

**The Genetic Code (mRNA)**

| First base | Second base: U | Second base: C | Second base: A | Second base: G | Third base |
|---|---|---|---|---|---|
| U | UUU Phenylalanine | UCU Serine | UAU Tyrosine | UGU Cysteine | U |
| U | UUC Phenylalanine | UCC Serine | UAC Tyrosine | UGC Cysteine | C |
| U | UUA Leucine | UCA Serine | UAA Stop | UGA—Stop | A |
| U | UUG Leucine | UCG Serine | UAG Stop | UGG—Tryptophan | G |
| C | CUU Leucine | CCU Proline | CAU Histidine | CGU Arginine | U |
| C | CUC Leucine | CCC Proline | CAC Histidine | CGC Arginine | C |
| C | CUA Leucine | CCA Proline | CAA Glutamine | CGA Arginine | A |
| C | CUG Leucine | CCG Proline | CAG Glutamine | CGG Arginine | G |
| A | AUU Isoleucine | ACU Threonine | AAU Asparagine | AGU Serine | U |
| A | AUC Isoleucine | ACC Threonine | AAC Asparagine | AGC Serine | C |
| A | AUA Isoleucine | ACA Threonine | AAA Lysine | AGA Arginine | A |
| A | AUG—Start | ACG Threonine | AAG Lysine | AGG Arginine | G |
| G | GUU Valine | GCU Alanine | GAU Aspartic acid | GGU Glycine | U |
| G | GUC Valine | GCC Alanine | GAC Aspartic acid | GGC Glycine | C |
| G | GUA Valine | GCA Alanine | GAA Glutamic acid | GGA Glycine | A |
| G | GUG Valine | GCG Alanine | GAG Glutamic acid | GGG Glycine | G |

## SAMPLE

**What sequence of amino acids will be incorporated into protein as a result of the mRNA sequence UUACCCGAGAAGUCC?**

Divide the sequence into groups of three to clearly see the separate codons.

UUACCCGAGAAGUCC = UUA | CCC | GAG | AAG | UCC

Now, use the table to determine the match between codons and amino acids.

| UUA | CCC | GAG | AAG | UCC |
|---|---|---|---|---|
| leucine | proline | glutamic acid | lysine | serine |

## PRACTICE PROBLEMS

1. What amino acid sequence will be added to a protein as a result of the mRNA sequence UUACACGACUAUAAUUGG?

2. What amino acid sequence will be added to a protein as a result of the mRNA sequence CUAACCGGGUGAGCUUCU?

# Standardized Test Prep

**Answer the following items on a separate piece of paper.**

**MULTIPLE CHOICE**

**1.** Which of the following statements about enzymes is true?
**A.** Enzymes can be biological catalysts.
**B.** Enzymes increase the speed of a chemical reaction.
**C.** Enzymes are highly specific.
**D.** All of the above

**2.** Which of the following statements about denaturing is true?
**A.** Denaturing occurs when a protein unfolds.
**B.** Denaturing occurs when a carbohydrate is heated.
**C.** Denaturing does not affect the tertiary structure of an enzyme.
**D.** Denaturing increases the rate of a chemical reaction.

**3.** The process in which molecules in a cell break down to produce smaller molecules and energy is called
**A.** glycogenesis.
**B.** biosynthesis.
**C.** catabolism.
**D.** metabolism.

**4.** Which of the following is partially digested by saliva in the mouth?
**A.** glucose
**B.** starch
**C.** fat
**D.** protein

**5.** In the human body, the storage form of
**A.** glucose is maltose.
**B.** triglycerides is protein.
**C.** carbohydrates is glycogen.
**D.** nucleic acids is amino acids.

**6.** The purpose of insulin is to
**A.** regulate glucose levels in the body.
**B.** catalyze the oxidation of fatty acids.
**C.** stimulate RNA production.
**D.** initiate DNA replication.

**7.** Which of the following statements about fats is true?
**A.** Fats serve as a reserve supply of energy.
**B.** Fats are stored in the adipose tissue.
**C.** Fats act as insulators.
**D.** All of the above

**8.** When carbohydrates are unavailable or unable to provide the energy needs of the body,
**A.** glucose is converted to glycogen.
**B.** proteins or fats are used for energy.
**C.** amino acids form proteins.
**D.** All of the above

**9.** Which of the following statements is true?
**A.** RNA contains the base uracil rather than thymine, which occurs in DNA.
**B.** Both RNA and DNA are double-stranded helixes.
**C.** The ribose sugar unit is in the backbone of DNA.
**D.** None of the above

**SHORT ANSWER**

**10.** Draw a simple dipeptide, and label the functional groups and peptide linkage.

**11.** Describe the shape of the DNA molecule, and discuss how the DNA molecule is held in this shape.

**EXTENDED RESPONSE**

**12.** The body has numerous energy reserves. What are they, and where are they found in the body? Which of these reserves provides the greatest source of quick energy?

**13.** Explain how it is possible to denature a protein without breaking the polypeptide chain.

**Test TIP** If a question or an answer choice contains an unfamiliar term, try to break the word into parts to determine its meaning.

# GROUP 1
# ALKALI METALS

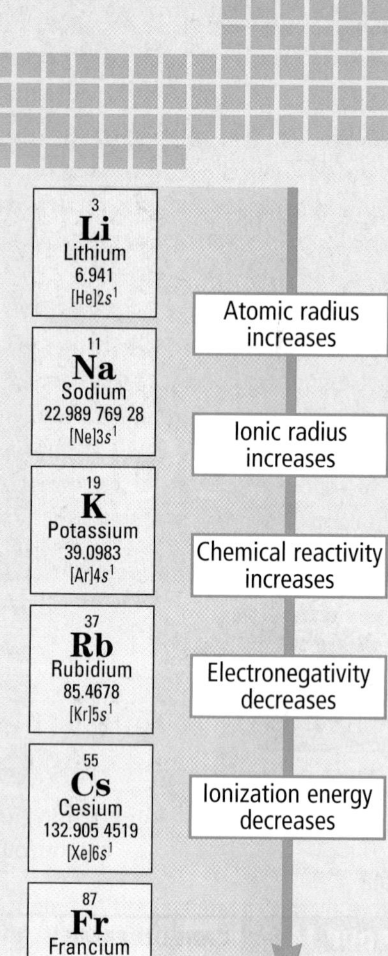


## CHARACTERISTICS

- do not occur in nature as free elements
- are reactive metals and are obtained by reducing the 1+ ions in their natural compounds
- are stored under kerosene or other hydrocarbon solvent because they react with water vapor or oxygen in air
- consist of atoms with one electron in the outermost energy level
- form colorless ions in solution, each of which has a 1+ charge
- form ionic compounds
- form water-soluble bases
- are strong reducing agents
- consist of atoms that have low ionization energies
- are good heat and electrical conductors
- are ductile, malleable, and soft enough to be cut with a knife
- have a silvery luster, low density, and low melting point

*Lithium was discovered in 1817. It is found in most igneous rocks and is used in batteries as an anode because it has a very low reduction potential. Lithium is soft and is stored in oil or kerosene to prevent it from reacting with the air.*

*Sodium derives its name from the word soda. It was first isolated in 1807 from the electrolysis of caustic soda, NaOH. Sodium is soft enough to be cut with a knife. It is shiny until it reacts with oxygen, which causes the surface to lose its luster.*

*Potassium was first isolated in 1807 from the electrolysis of caustic potash, KOH.*

## COMMON REACTIONS

**With Water to Form Bases and Hydrogen Gas**

*Example:* $2Na(s) + 2H_2O(l) \longrightarrow 2NaOH(aq) + H_2(g)$

Li, K, Rb, and Cs also follow this pattern.

**With Acids to Form Salts and Hydrogen Gas**

*Example:* $2Na(s) + 2HCl(aq) \longrightarrow 2NaCl(aq) + H_2(g)$

Li, K, Rb, and Cs also follow this pattern.

**With Halogens to Form Salts**

*Example:* $2Na(s) + F_2(g) \longrightarrow 2NaF(s)$

Li, K, Rb, and Cs also follow this pattern in reacting with $F_2$, $Cl_2$, $Br_2$, and $I_2$.

**With Oxygen to Form Oxides, Peroxides, or Superoxides**

*Lithium forms an oxide.*

$4Li(s) + O_2(g) \longrightarrow 2Li_2O(s)$

*Sodium also forms a peroxide.*

$2Na(s) + O_2(g) \longrightarrow Na_2O_2(s)$

*Alkali metals with higher molecular masses can also form superoxides.*

$K(s) + O_2(g) \longrightarrow KO_2(s)$

Rb and Cs also follow this pattern.

**Alkali-Metal Oxides with Water to Form Bases**

Oxides of Na, K, Rb, and Cs can be prepared indirectly. These basic anhydrides form hydroxides in water.

*Example:* $K_2O(s) + H_2O(l) \longrightarrow 2KOH(aq)$

Li, Na, Rb, and Cs also follow this pattern.

*A small piece of potassium dropped into water will react explosively, releasing $H_2$ to form a strongly basic hydroxide solution. The energy of the reaction ignites the hydrogen gas that is produced.*

*Sodium reacts vigorously with chlorine to produce NaCl. Most salts of Group 1 metals are white crystalline compounds.*

## ANALYTICAL TEST

Alkali metals are easily detected by flame tests because each metal imparts a characteristic color to a flame.

When sodium and potassium are both present in a sample, the yellow color of the sodium masks the violet color of the potassium. The violet color can be seen only when the combined sodium-potassium flame is viewed through a cobalt-blue glass. The glass blocks the yellow flame of sodium and makes it possible to see the violet flame of potassium.

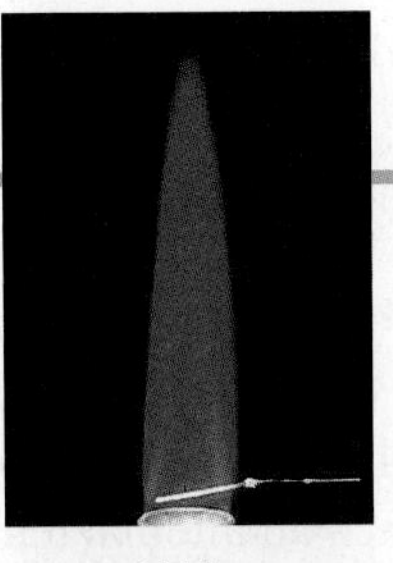

*Lithium*

*Sodium*

*Potassium*

*Rubidium*

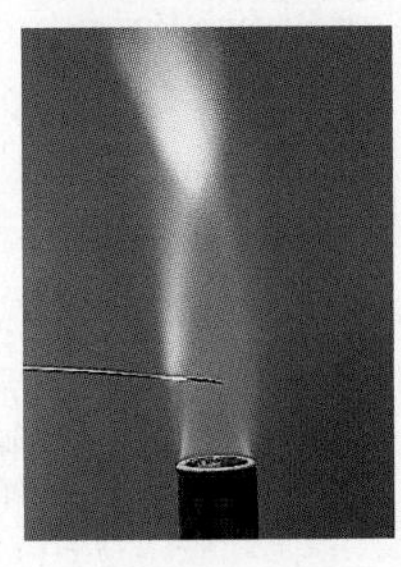

*Cesium*

## PROPERTIES OF THE GROUP 1 ELEMENTS

| | Li | Na | K | Rb | Cs | Fr |
|---|---|---|---|---|---|---|
| Melting point (°C) | 180.5 | 97.8 | 63.25 | 38.89 | 28.5 | 27 |
| Boiling point (°C) | 1342 | 882.9 | 760 | 691 | 668 | 677 |
| Density (g/cm$^3$) | 0.534 | 0.971 | 0.862 | 1.53 | 1.87 | — |
| Ionization energy (kJ/mol) | 520 | 496 | 419 | 403 | 376 | — |
| Atomic radius (pm) | 152 | 186 | 227 | 248 | 265 | 270 |
| Ionic radius (pm) | 76 | 102 | 138 | 152 | 167 | 180 |
| Common oxidation number in compounds | +1 | +1 | +1 | +1 | +1 | — |
| Crystal structure | bcc* | bcc | bcc | bcc | bcc | — |
| Hardness (Mohs' scale) | 0.6 | 0.4 | 0.5 | 0.3 | 0.2 | — |

*body-centered cubic

## APPLICATION *Technology*

### Sodium Vapor Lighting

The flame test for sodium shows two bright lines at 589.0 and 589.6 nm, which is the yellow range of the emission spectrum. Sodium can be vaporized at high temperatures in a sealed tube and made to give off light using two electrodes connected to a power source. Sodium vapor lighting is often used along highways and in parking lots because it provides good illumination while using less energy than other types of lighting.

Sodium vapor lighting comes in both low-pressure and high-pressure bulbs. Low-pressure lamps reach an internal temperature of 270°C to vaporize the sodium under a pressure of about 1 Pa. High-pressure lamps contain mercury and xenon in addition to sodium. These substances reach an internal temperature of 1100°C under a pressure of about 100 000 Pa. The high-pressure lamp provides a higher light intensity. The design of both types of lamps must take into account the high reactivity of sodium, which increases at high temperatures. Because ordinary glass will react with sodium at 250°C, a special sodium-resistant glass is used for low-pressure lamps. High-pressure lamps use an aluminum oxide material for the column containing the sodium, mercury, and xenon. Both types of lamps contain tungsten electrodes.

The light intensity per watt for sodium vapor lamps far exceeds that of fluorescent lamps, high-pressure mercury vapor lamps, tungsten halogen lamps, and incandescent bulbs.

APPLICATION **Health**

## Electrolyte Balance in the Body

The elements of Group 1 are important to a person's diet and body maintenance because they form ionic compounds. These compounds are present in the body as solutions of the ions. All ions carry an electric charge, so they are electrolyte solutes. Two of the most important electrolyte solutes found in the body are $K^+$ and $Na^+$ ions. Both ions facilitate the transmission of nerve impulses and control the amount of water retained by cells.

*During situations where the body is losing water rapidly through intense sweating or diarrhea for a prolonged period (more than 5 hours), a sports drink can hydrate the body and restore electrolyte balance.*

**TABLE 1A Sodium-Potassium Concentration in Body Fluids**

| Cation | Inside cells (mmol/L) | Outside cells or in plasma (mmol/L) |
|---|---|---|
| $Na^+$ | 12 | 145 |
| $K^+$ | 140 | 4 |

The sodium and potassium ion concentrations in body fluids are shown in Table 1A. Sodium ions are found primarily in the fluid outside cells, while potassium ions are largely found in the fluid inside cells. Anions are present in the fluids to balance the electrical charge of the $Na^+$ and $K^+$ cations.

Abnormal electrolyte concentrations in blood serum can indicate the presence of disease. The ion concentrations that vary as a result of disease are $Na^+$, $K^+$, $Cl^-$, and $HCO_3^-$. Sodium ion concentration is a good indicator of the water balance between blood and tissue cells. Unusual potassium ion levels can indicate kidney or gastrointestinal problems. Chloride ion is the anion that balances the positive charge of the sodium ion in the fluid outside the cells. It also diffuses into a cell to maintain normal electrolyte balance when hydrogen carbonate ions diffuse out of the cell into the blood. Table 1B shows medical conditions associated with electrolyte imbalances.

**TABLE 1B Electrolyte Imbalances**

| Electrolyte | Normal range (mmol/L) | Causes of imbalance | |
|---|---|---|---|
| | | Excess | Deficiency |
| Sodium, $Na^+$ | 135–145 | hypernatremia (increased urine excretion; excess water loss) | hyponatremia (dehydration; diabetes-related low blood pH; vomiting; diarrhea) |
| Potassium, $K^+$ | 3.5–5.0 | hyperkalemia (renal failure; low blood pH) | hypokalemia (gastrointestinal conditions) |
| Hydrogen carbonate, $HCO_3^-$ | 24–30 | hypercapnia (high blood pH; hypoventilation) | hypocapnia (low blood pH; hyperventilation; dehydration) |
| Chloride, $Cl^-$ | 100–106 | hyperchloremia (anemia; heart conditions; dehydration) | hypochloremia (acute infection; burns; hypoventilation) |

### Sodium-Potassium Pump in the Cell Membrane

The process of active transport allows a cell to maintain its proper electrolyte balance. To keep the ion concentrations at the proper levels shown in Table 1B, a sodium-potassium pump embedded in the cell membrane shuttles sodium ions out of the cell across the cell membrane. A model for the action of the sodium-potassium pump is shown below.

### Nerve Impulses and Ion Concentration

The difference in $Na^+$ and $K^+$ concentrations inside and outside nerve cell membranes is essential for the normal operation of the nervous system. This unequal concentration of ions creates a voltage across nerve cell membranes. When a nerve cell is stimulated, sodium ions diffuse into the cell from the surrounding fluid, raising voltage across the nerve cell membrane from –70 mV to nearly +60 mV. Potassium ions then diffuse out of the cell into the surrounding fluid, restoring the voltage across the nerve cell membrane to –70 mV. This voltage fluctuation initiates the transmission of a nerve impulse. The amount of $Na^+$ inside the cell has increased slightly, and the amount of $K^+$ outside the cell has decreased. But the sodium-potassium pump will restore these ions to their proper concentrations.

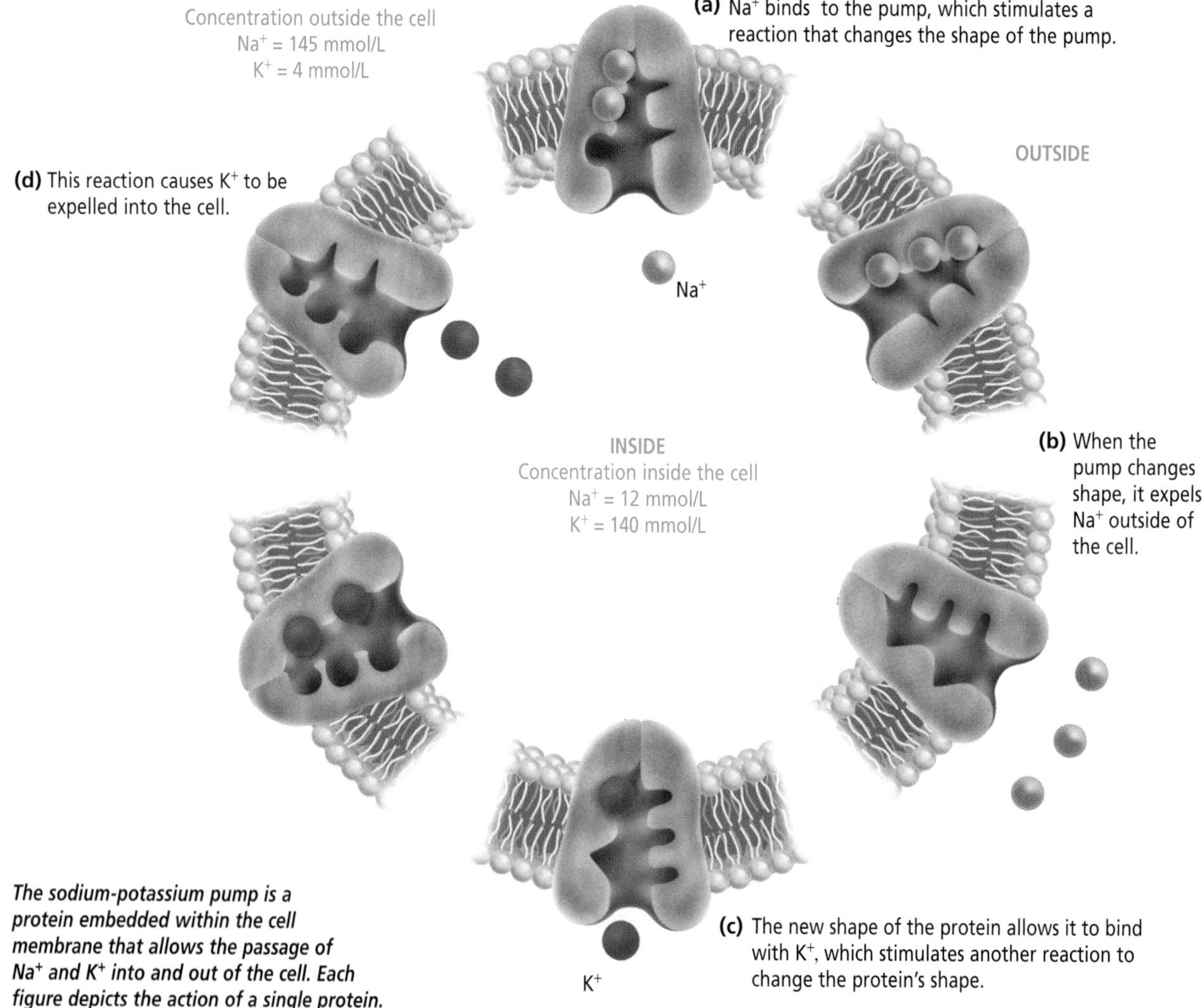


*The sodium-potassium pump is a protein embedded within the cell membrane that allows the passage of $Na^+$ and $K^+$ into and out of the cell. Each figure depicts the action of a single protein.*

## *What's your sodium IQ?*

Though sodium is an important mineral in your body, a diet that is high in sodium is one of several factors linked to high blood pressure, also known as hypertension. High $Na^+$ levels cause water retention, which results in increased blood pressure. Sodium is not the direct cause of all hypertension, but reducing sodium levels in the diet can affect individuals with a condition known as salt-sensitive hypertension. Therefore, the Dietary Guidelines for Americans recommend consuming salt and sodium in moderation. Test your knowledge about sodium in foods with the questions below.

**1.** Which of the following condiments do you think has the lowest salt content?
a. mustard c. catsup e. vinegar
b. steak sauce d. pickles

**2.** One-fourth of a teaspoon of salt contains about _____ of sodium.
a. 10 mg c. 500 mg e. 1 kg
b. 100 g d. 500 g

**3.** According to FDA regulations for food product labels, a food labeled *salt-free* must contain less than _____ mg of sodium ion per serving.
a. 100 c. 0.001 e. 0.00005
b. 5 d. 0.005

**4.** The Nutrition Facts label for a particular food reads "Sodium 15 mg." This is the amount of sodium ion per _____.
a. package c. serving e. RDA
b. teaspoon d. ounce

**5.** The recommended average daily intake of sodium ion for adults is 2400 mg. For a low-sodium diet the intake should be ______.
a. 200 mg c. 750 mg e. 150 mg
b. 2000 mg d. 500 mg

**6.** Each of the following ingredients can be found in the ingredients lists for some common food products. Which ones indicate that the product contains sodium?
a. trisodium phosphate d. sodium sulfate
b. sodium bicarbonate e. MSG
c. sodium benzoate f. baking soda

**7.** Which of the following spices is NOT a salt substitute?
a. caraway seeds c. ginger
b. dill d. onion salt

**8.** Most salt in the average American diet comes from salting foods too heavily at the dinner table.
a. true b. false

**9.** Which of the following foods are high in sodium?
a. potato chips c. doughnuts e. figs
b. pizza d. banana

**10.** Your body requires about 200 mg of sodium ion, or 500 mg of salt, per day. Why do these numbers differ?

*Answers* 1. e; 2. c; 3. b; 4. c; 5. c; 6. all of them; 7. d; 8. b, processed foods can contain very high levels of sodium; 9. a, b, c; 10. Salt is not pure sodium.

# GROUP 2
# ALKALINE EARTH METALS

## CHARACTERISTICS

- do not occur naturally as free elements
- occur most commonly as the carbonates, phosphates, silicates, and sulfates
- occur naturally as compounds that are either insoluble or only slightly soluble in water
- consist of atoms that contain two electrons in their outermost energy level
- consist of atoms that tend to lose two electrons per atom, forming ions with a 2+ charge
- are less reactive than alkali metals
- form ionic compounds primarily
- react with water to form bases and hydrogen gas
- are good heat and electrical conductors
- are ductile and malleable
- have a silvery luster
- include the naturally radioactive element radium

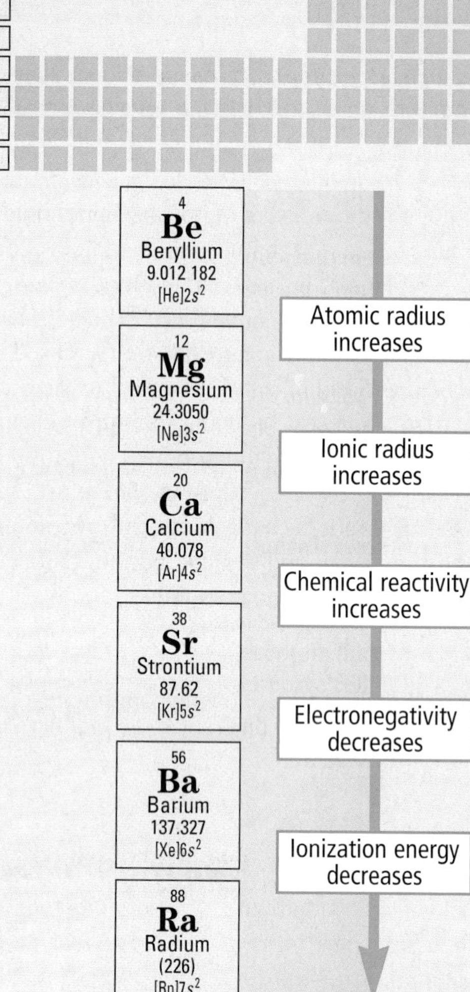


*Calcium carbonate is a major component of marble.*

*Beryllium is found in the mineral compound beryl. Beryl crystals include the dark green emerald and the blue-green aquamarine. The colors of these gems come from other metal impurities.*

*The mineral dolomite, $CaCO_3 \cdot MgCO_3$, is a natural source of both calcium and magnesium.*

## COMMON REACTIONS

**With Water to Form Bases and Hydrogen Gas**

*Example:* $Mg(s) + 2H_2O(l) \longrightarrow Mg(OH)_2(aq) + H_2(g)$

Ca, Sr, and Ba also follow this pattern.

**With Acids to Form Salts and Hydrogen Gas**

*Example:* $Mg(s) + 2HCl(aq) \longrightarrow MgCl_2(aq) + H_2(g)$

Be, Ca, Sr, and Ba also follow this pattern.

**With Halogens to Form Salts**

*Example:* $Mg(s) + F_2(g) \longrightarrow MgF_2(s)$

Ca, Sr, and Ba also follow this pattern in reacting with $F_2$, $Cl_2$, $Br_2$, and $I_2$.

Calcium reacts with water to form hydrogen gas.

**With Oxygen to Form Oxides or Peroxides**

*Magnesium forms an oxide.*

$2Mg(s) + O_2(g) \longrightarrow 2MgO(s)$

Be and Ca also follow this pattern.

*Strontium also forms a peroxide.*

$Sr(s) + O_2(g) \longrightarrow SrO_2(s)$

Ba also reacts in this way.

**With Hydrogen to Form Hydrides**

*Example:* $Mg(s) + H_2(g) \longrightarrow MgH_2(s)$

Ca, Sr, and Ba also follow this pattern.

**With Nitrogen to Form Nitrides**

*Example:* $3Mg(s) + N_2(g) \longrightarrow Mg_3N_2(s)$

Be and Ca also follow this pattern.

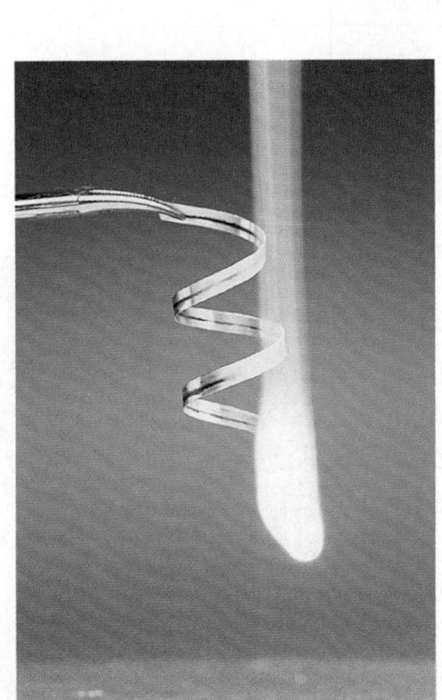

Magnesium burns in air to form MgO and $Mg_3N_2$.

Magnesium reacts with HCl to produce $MgCl_2(aq)$.

## ANALYTICAL TEST

Flame tests can be used to identify three of the alkaline earth elements. The colors of both calcium and strontium can be masked by the presence of barium, which produces a green flame.

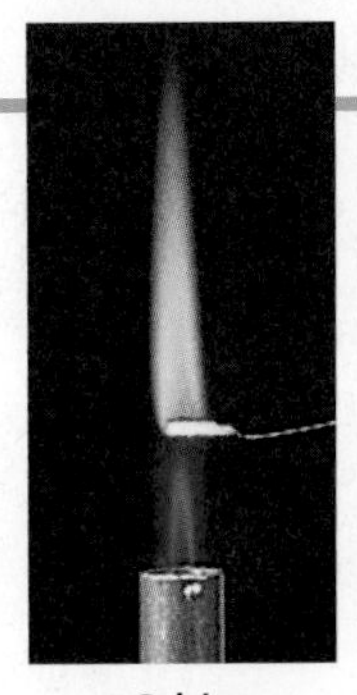

Calcium

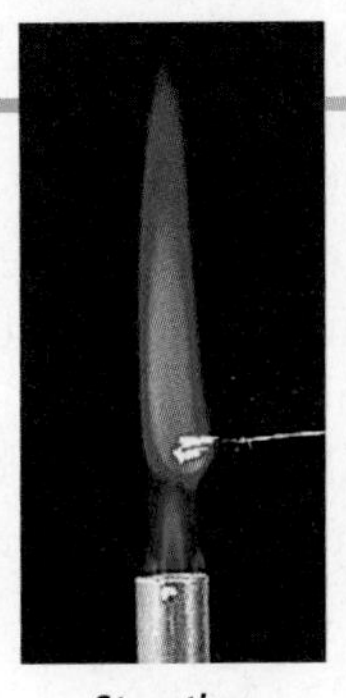

Strontium

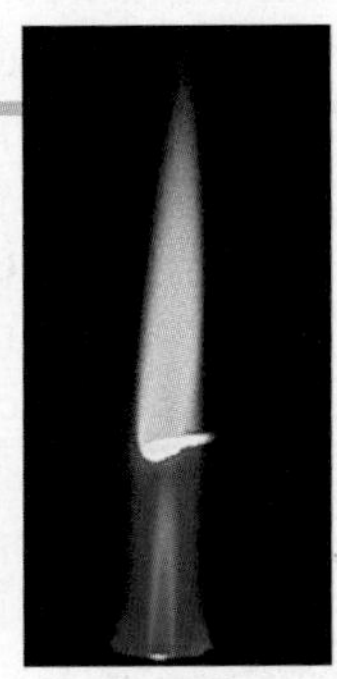

Barium

**PROPERTIES OF THE GROUP 2 ELEMENTS**

| | Be | Mg | Ca | Sr | Ba | Ra |
|---|---|---|---|---|---|---|
| Melting point (°C) | 1278 ± 5 | 649 | 839 ± 2 | 769 | 725 | 700 |
| Boiling point (°C) | 2467 | 1090 | 1484 | 1384 | 1640 | 1140 |
| Density (g/cm$^3$) | 1.85 | 1.74 | 1.54 | 2.6 | 3.51 | 5 |
| Ionization energy (kJ/mol) | 900 | 738 | 590 | 550 | 503 | 509 |
| Atomic radius (pm) | 112 | 160 | 197 | 215 | 222 | 220 |
| Ionic radius (pm) | 45 | 72 | 100 | 118 | 136 | 148 |
| Common oxidation number in compounds | +2 | +2 | +2 | +2 | +2 | +2 |
| Crystal structure | hcp* | hcp | fcc** | fcc | bcc | bcc |
| Hardness (Mohs' scale) | 4.0 | 2.0 | 1.5 | 1.8 | 1.5 | — |

*hexagonal close-packed **face-centered cubic

## APPLICATION *Technology*

### Fireworks

Fireworks are made from pyrotechnics—chemical substances that produce light and smoke when they are ignited. Pyrotechnics are also used in flares, smoke bombs, explosives, and matches. An aerial fireworks device is a rocket made of a cylinder, chemicals inside the cylinder, and fuses attached to the cylinder. The illustration on the right shows how the device works. The lift charge at the bottom of the cylinder consists of a small amount of black gunpowder. When the side fuse ignites the gunpowder, it explodes like a small bomb. The gunpowder consists of potassium nitrate, charcoal, and sulfur. When these three chemicals react with one another, they produce gases. In this case, the gases produced are carbon monoxide, carbon dioxide, sulfur dioxide, and nitrogen monoxide. These hot gases expand very rapidly, providing the thrust that lifts the rocket into the sky.

About the time the shell reaches its maximum altitude and minimum speed, the time fuse ignites the chemicals contained in the cylinder. The chemicals inside the cylinder determine the color of the burst.

*The cylinder of a multiple-burst rocket contains separate reaction chambers connected by fuses. A common fuse ignites the propellant and the time-delay fuse in the first reaction chamber.*

### Chemical Composition and Color

One of the characteristics of fireworks that we enjoy most is their variety of rich colors. These colors are created in much the same way as the colors produced during a flame test. In a fireworks device, the chloride salt is heated to a high temperature, causing the excited atoms to give off a burst of light. The color of light produced depends on the metal used. The decomposition of barium chloride, $BaCl_2$, for example, produces a burst of green light, whereas strontium chloride, $SrCl_2$, releases red light.

People who design fireworks combine artistry with a technical knowledge of chemical properties. They have found ways to combine different colors within a single cylinder and to make parts of the cylinder explode at different times. Fireworks designers have a technical knowledge of projectile motion that is used to determine the height, direction, and angle at which a fireworks device will explode to produce a fan, fountain, flower, stream, comet, spider, star, or other shape.

### Strontium and the Visible Spectrum

When heated, some metallic elements and their compounds emit light at specific wavelengths that are characteristic of the element or compound. Visible light includes wavelengths between about 400 and 700 nanometers. The figure below shows the emission spectrum for strontium. When heated, strontium gives off the maximum amount of visible light at about 700 nanometers, which falls in the red-light region of the visible spectrum.

*The emission spectrum for strontium shows strong bands in the red region of the visible light spectrum.*



### Flares

Flares operate on a chemical principle that is different from that of fireworks. A typical flare consists of finely divided magnesium metal and an oxidizing agent. When the flare is ignited, the oxidizing agent reacts with the magnesium metal to produce magnesium oxide. This reaction releases so much energy that it produces a glow like that of the filaments in a light bulb. The brilliant white light produced by the flare is caused by billions of tiny particles of magnesium that glow when they react. If slightly larger particles of magnesium metal are used in the flare, the system glows for a longer period of time because the particles' reaction with the oxidizing agent is slower.

A colored flare can be thought of as a combination of a white flare and a chemical that produces colored light when burned. For example, a red flare can be made from magnesium metal, an oxidizing agent, and a compound of strontium. When the flare is ignited, the oxidizing agent and magnesium metal react, heating the magnesium to white-hot temperatures. The energy from this reaction causes the strontium compound to give off its characteristic red color.

*A flare is made up of billions of reacting magnesium particles.*

For safety reasons, some fireworks manufacturers store their products in metal sheds separated by sand banks. Also, people who work with fireworks are advised to wear cotton clothing because cotton is less likely than other fabrics to develop a static charge, which can cause a spark and accidentally ignite fireworks.

APPLICATION *Health*

## Calcium: An Essential Mineral in the Diet

Calcium is the most abundant mineral in the body. It is the mineral that makes up a good portion of the teeth and the bone mass of the body. A small percentage of calcium in the body is used in the reactions by which cells communicate and in the regulation of certain body processes. Calcium is so important to normal body functioning that if the calcium level of the blood falls far below normal, hormones signal the release of calcium from bone and signal the gastrointestinal tract to absorb more calcium during the digestion process.

A prolonged diet that is low in calcium is linked to a disease characterized by a decrease in bone mass, a condition called osteoporosis. Reduced bone mass results in brittle bones that fracture easily. Osteoporosis generally occurs later in life and is more prevalent in females. However, because you achieve peak bone mass during the late teens or early twenties, it is critical that your diet meet the recommended requirements to increase your peak bone mass. The recommended dietary intake for calcium is 1000 mg per day. Maintaining that level in the diet along with regular exercise through adulthood are thought to reduce the rate of bone loss later in life. Excess calcium in the diet (consuming more than 2500 mg daily) can interfere with the absorption of other minerals.

*Dairy products are generally good sources of calcium.*

## Magnesium: An Essential Mineral in the Diet

Though magnesium has several functions in the body, one of the more important functions is its role in the absorption of calcium by cells. Magnesium, like sodium and potassium, is involved in the transmission of nerve impulses. Like calcium, magnesium is a component of bone.

A major source of magnesium in the diet is plants. Magnesium is the central atom in the green plant pigment chlorophyll. The structure of chlorophyll in plants is somewhat similar to the structure of heme—the oxygen-carrying molecule in animals. (See page 816 for the heme structure.)

**TABLE 2A Good Sources of Calcium in the Diet**

| Food | Serving size | Calcium present (mg) |
|---|---|---|
| Broccoli | 6.3 oz | 82 |
| Cheddar cheese | 1 oz | 204 |
| Cheese pizza, frozen | pizza for one | 375 |
| Milk, low-fat 1% | 8 oz | 300 |
| Tofu, regular | 4 oz | 130 |
| Vegetable pizza, frozen | pizza for one | 500 |
| Yogurt, low-fat | 8 oz | 415 |
| Yogurt, plain whole milk | 8 oz | 274 |

Spinach is a good source of magnesium. Magnesium is the central atom in the green plant pigment chlorophyll. The chlorophyll structure is shown on the right.

The recommended dietary intake of magnesium is 400 mg per day. This is equivalent to just 4 oz of bran cereal. Because magnesium levels are easily maintained by a normal diet, it is unusual for anyone to have a magnesium deficiency. Most magnesium deficiencies are the result of factors that decrease magnesium absorption. People with gastrointestinal disorders, alcohol abusers, and the critically ill are most likely to have these types of absorption problems.

Excess magnesium in the diet is excreted by the kidneys, so there are no cumulative toxic effects.



## TABLE 2B Good Sources of Magnesium in the Diet

| Food | Serving size | Magnesium present (mg) |
|---|---|---|
| Barley, raw | 1 cup | 244 |
| Beef, broiled sirloin | 4 oz | 36 |
| Cabbage, raw | 1 med. head | 134 |
| Cashews, dry-roasted | 1 oz | 74 |
| Chicken, roasted breast | 4 oz | 31 |
| Lima beans, boiled | 1/2 cup | 63 |
| Oatmeal | 1 oz | 39 |
| Potato, baked | 7.1 oz | 115 |
| Prunes, dried | 4 oz | 51 |
| Rice bran | 8 oz | 648 |
| Salmon, canned | 4 oz | 39 |
| Spinach, raw | 10 oz | 161 |

# GROUPS 3–12
# TRANSITION METALS

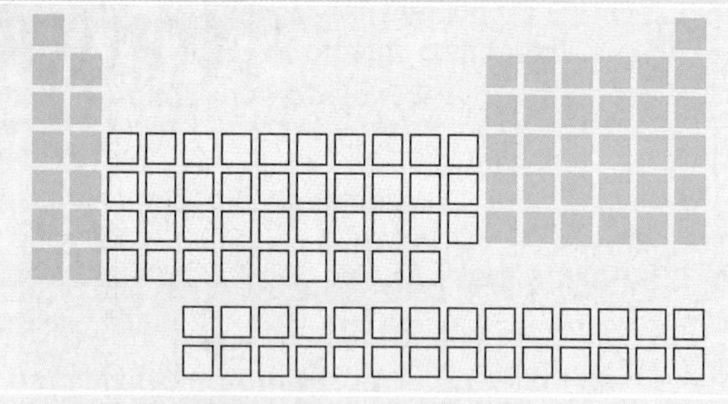

## CHARACTERISTICS

- consist of metals in Groups 3 through 12
- contain one or two electrons in their outermost energy level
- are usually harder and more brittle than metals in Groups 1 and 2
- have higher melting and boiling points than metals in Groups 1 and 2
- are good heat and electrical conductors
- are malleable and ductile
- have a silvery luster, except copper and gold
- include radioactive elements with numbers 89 through 112
- include mercury, the only liquid metal at room temperature
- have chemical properties that differ from each other
- tend to have two or more common oxidation states
- often form colored compounds
- may form complex ions

*Iron ore is obtained from surface mines. Hematite, $Fe_2O_3$, is the most common iron ore.*

*Copper ores are also obtained from surface mines. Copper ore is shown here.*

*Gold, silver, platinum, palladium, iridium, rhodium, ruthenium, and osmium are sometimes referred to as the noble metals because they are not very reactive. These metals are found in coins, jewelry, and metal sculptures.*

## COMMON REACTIONS

Because this region of the periodic table is so large, you would expect great variety in the types of reaction characteristics of transition metals. For example, copper oxidizes in air to form the green patina you see on the Statue of Liberty. Copper reacts with concentrated $HNO_3$ but not with dilute $HNO_3$. Zinc, on the other hand, reacts readily with dilute HCl. Iron oxidizes in air to form rust, but chromium is generally unreactive in air. Some common reactions for transition elements are shown by the following.

**May form two or more different ions**

*Example:* $Fe(s) \longrightarrow Fe^{2+}(aq) + 2e^-$

*Example:* $Fe(s) \longrightarrow Fe^{3+}(aq) + 3e^-$

**May react with oxygen to form oxides**

*Example:* $4Cr(s) + 3O_2(g) \longrightarrow 2Cr_2O_3(s)$

*Example:* $2Cu(s) + O_2(g) \longrightarrow 2CuO(s)$

**May react with halogens to form halides**

*Example:* $Ni(s) + Cl_2(g) \longrightarrow NiCl_2(s)$

**May form complex ions**

See examples in the lower right.

*Copper reacts with oxygen in air.*

*Copper reacts with concentrated nitric acid.*

*Zinc reacts with dilute hydrochloric acid.*

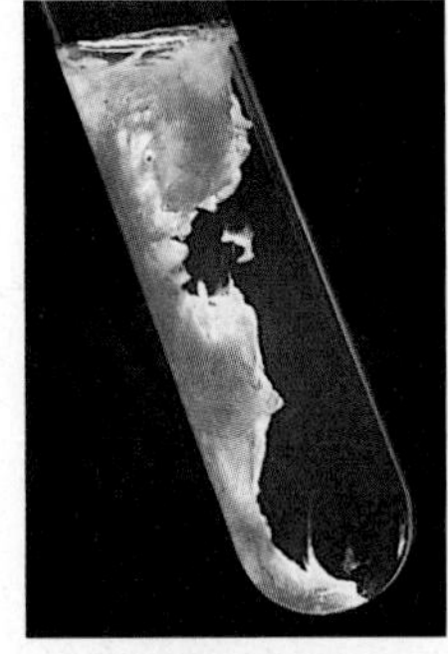

*Soluble iron(III) salts form insoluble $Fe(OH)_3$ when they are reacted with a hydroxide base.*

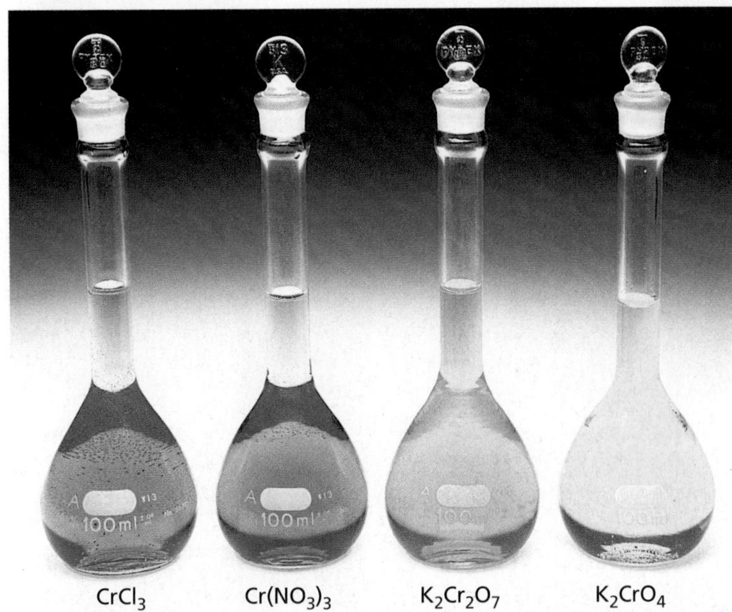


*Chromium has several common oxidation states, represented here by aqueous solutions of its compounds. The violet and green solutions contain chromium in the +3 state, and the yellow and orange solutions contain chromium in the +6 oxidation state.*

*Complex ions belong to a class of compounds called coordination compounds. Coordination compounds show great variety in colors. Several transition-metal coordination compounds are shown.*

## ANALYTICAL TEST

Flame tests are not commonly used to identify transition metals. The presence of a certain transition-metal ion in a solution is sometimes obvious from the solution's color. Some transition-metal ions can be more accurately identified using a procedure called qualitative analysis. **Qualitative analysis** *is the identification of ions by their characteristic reactions.* The transition-metal ions most often identified through qualitative analysis include copper, nickel, zinc, chromium, iron cobalt, cadmium, manganese, and tin. Most tests to identify the presence of an ion in a mixture involve causing the ion to precipitate out of solution. Some of the more dramatic precipitation reactions for transition metals are shown.

*Some transition metal ions can be identified by characteristic colors of their salt solutions.*

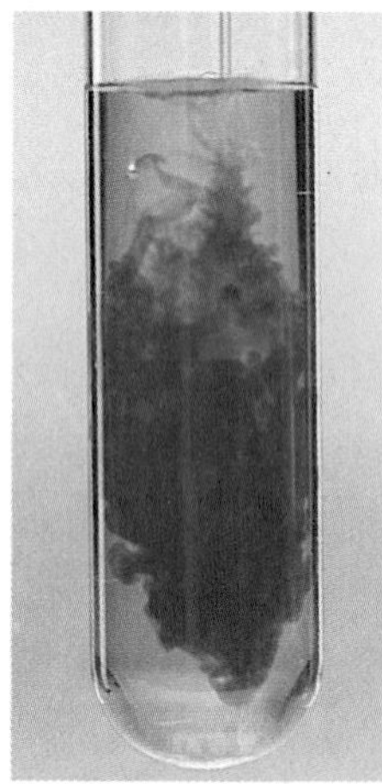

*Copper (formation of $[Cu(NH_3)_4](OH)_2$)*

*Cadmium (formation of CdS)*

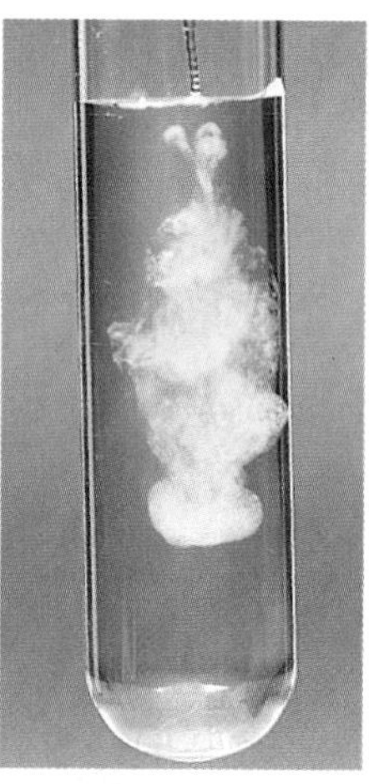

*Zinc (formation of ZnS)*

*Chromium (formation of $PbCrO_4$)*

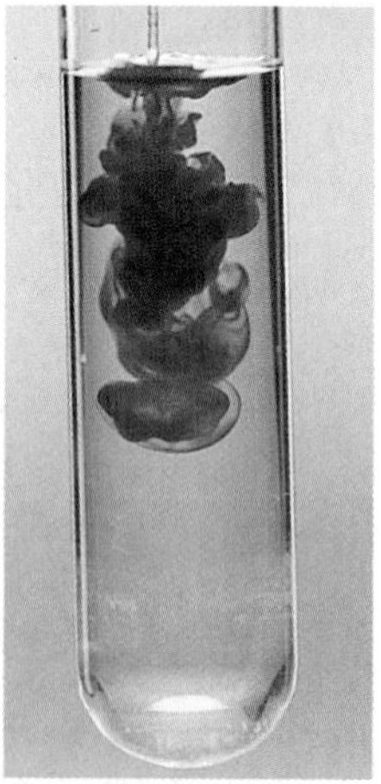

*Iron (formation of $[Fe(SCN)]^{2+}$)*

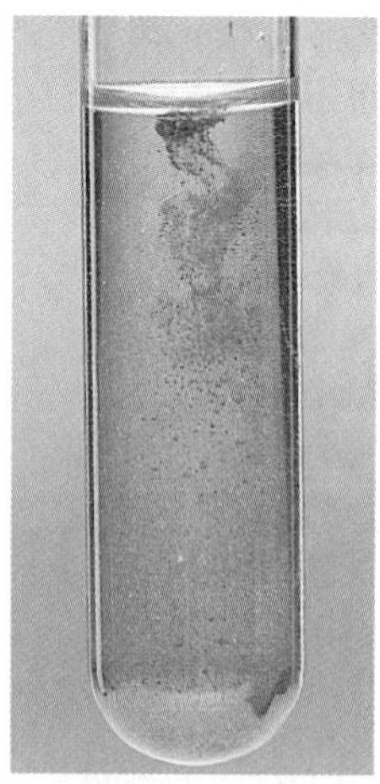

*Manganese (formation of $MnO_4^-$)*

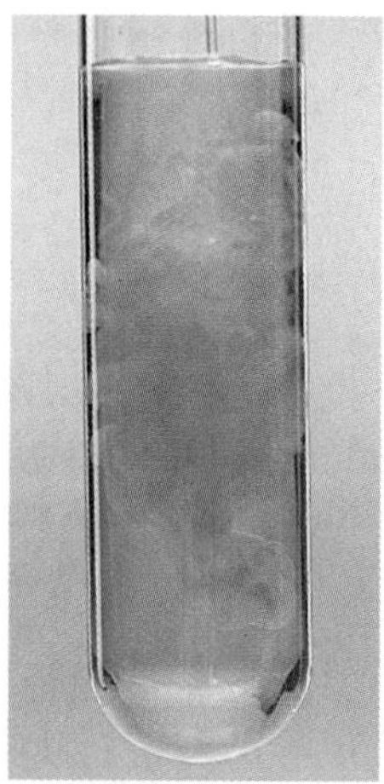

*Nickel (formation of a nickel dimethylglyoxime complex)*

**PROPERTIES OF SOME TRANSITION METALS**

| | Cr | Fe | Co | Ni | Cu | Zn | Ag | Au | Hg |
|---|---|---|---|---|---|---|---|---|---|
| Melting point (°C) | 1857 ± 20 | 1535 | 1495 | 1455 | 1083 | 420 | 962 | 1064 | −38.8 |
| Boiling point (°C) | 2672 | 2750 | 2870 | 2732 | 2567 | 907 | 2212 | 2808 ± 2 | 356.6 |
| Density (g/cm$^3$) | 7.20 | 7.86 | 8.9 | 8.92 | 8.96 | 7.14 | 10.5 | 19.3 | 13.5 |
| Ionization energy (kJ/mol) | 653 | 762 | 760 | 737 | 746 | 906 | 731 | 890 | 1007 |
| Atomic radius (pm) | 128 | 126 | 125 | 124 | 128 | 134 | 144 | 144 | 151 |
| Common oxidation numbers | +2, +3, +6 | +2, +3 | +2, +3 | +2 | +1, +2 | +2 | +1 | +1, +3 | +1, +2 |

## APPLICATION *Geology*

### Gemstones and Color

A gemstone is a mineral that can be cut and polished to make gems for an ornament or piece of jewelry. At one time, all gemstones were naturally occurring minerals mined from Earth's crust. Today, however, chemists can duplicate natural processes to produce artificial gemstones. Amethyst, emerald, jade, opal, ruby, sapphire, and topaz occur naturally and can also be produced synthetically.

The color of a gemstone is determined by the presence of small amounts of one or more transition metals. For example, aluminum oxide, $Al_2O_3$, often occurs naturally as corundum—a clear, colorless mineral. However, if as few as 1 to 2% of the aluminum ions, $Al^{3+}$, are replaced by chromium ions, $Cr^{3+}$, the corundum takes on a reddish color and is known as ruby. If a small fraction of aluminum ions in corundum are replaced by $Fe^{3+}$ and $Ti^{3+}$, the corundum has a greenish color and is known as emerald. In another variation, if vanadium ions, $V^{3+}$, replace a few $Al^{3+}$ ions in corundum, the result is a gemstone known as alexandrite. This gemstone appears green in reflected natural light and red in transmitted or artificial light.

Table 3A lists transition metals that are responsible for the colors of various gemstones. The table provides only a general overview, however, as most naturally occurring gemstones occur in a range of hues, depending on the exact composition of the stone.

#### Artificial Gemstones

In 1902, the French chemist Auguste Verneuil found a way to melt a mixture of aluminum oxide and chromium salts and then cool the mixture very slowly to produce large crystals of reddish aluminum oxide—rubies.

*Sapphire*

*Ruby*

*Peridot*

*Garnet*

**TABLE 3A Transition Metals and Gemstone Colors**

| Gemstone | Color | Element |
|---|---|---|
| Amethyst | purple | iron |
| Aquamarine | blue | iron |
| Emerald | green | iron/titanium |
| Garnet | red | iron |
| Peridot | yellow-green | iron |
| Ruby | red | chromium |
| Sapphire | blue | iron/titanium |
| Spinel | colorless to red to black | varies |
| Turquoise | blue | copper |

Verneuil's method, although somewhat modified, is still the one most widely used today for the manufacture of colored gemstones. When magnesium oxide is substituted for aluminum oxide, a colorless spinel-like product is formed. The addition of various transition metals then adds a tint to the spinel that results in the formation of synthetic emerald, aquamarine, tourmaline, or other gemstones. Synthetic gems look very much like their natural counterparts.

Synthetic sapphire

Synthetic ruby

## APPLICATION *Technology*

### Alloys

An alloy is a mixture of a metal and one or more other elements. In most cases, the second component of the mixture is also a metal.

Alloys are desirable because mixtures of elements usually have properties different from and often superior to the properties of individual metals. For example, many alloys that contain iron are harder, stronger, and more resistant to oxidation than iron itself.

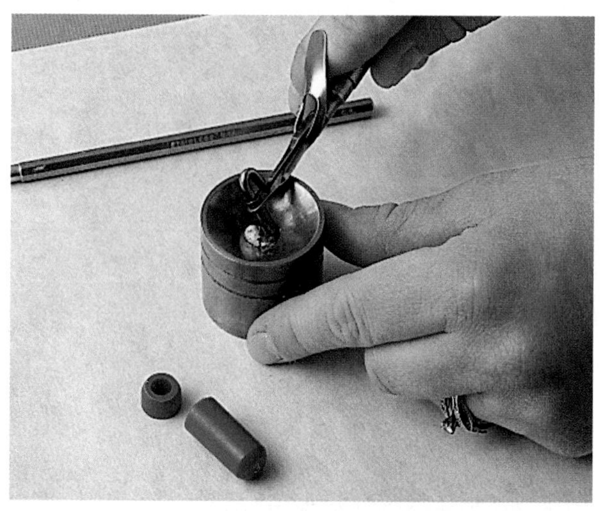

*Amalgams are alloys that contain mercury. They are soft and pliable when first produced, but later become solid and hard. Dental fillings were once made of an amalgam of mercury and silver. Concerns about the possible toxicity of mercury led to the development of other filling materials.*

**Cast Iron and Steel**

The term *steel* applies to any alloy consisting of iron and less than 1.5% carbon, and often other elements. When iron ore is treated with carbon in the form of coke to extract pure iron metal, some of the carbon also reacts with the iron to produce a form of iron carbide known as cementite. The reaction can be represented by the following equation.

$$3Fe + C \longrightarrow Fe_3C$$

Cast iron is a mixture that consists of some pure iron, known as ferrite, some cementite, and some carbon atoms trapped within the crystalline structure of the iron and cementite. The rate at which cast iron is cooled changes the proportion of these three components. If the cast iron is cooled slowly, the ferrite and cementite tend to separate from each other, forming a banded product that is tough but not very hard. However, if the cast iron is cooled quickly, the components of the original mixture cannot separate from each other, forming a product that is both tough and hard.

***Stainless steel, which is hard and resists corrosion, is made of iron and chromium (12–30%). The properties of stainless steel make it a suitable alloy for making cutlery and utensils.***

**TABLE 3B Composition and Uses of Some Alloys**

| Name of alloy | Composition | Uses |
|---|---|---|
| Brass | copper with up to 50% zinc, some lead, and a small amount of tin | inexpensive jewelry; hose nozzles and couplings; piping; stamping dies |
| Bronze | copper with up to 12% tin | coins and medals; heavy gears; tools; electrical hardware |
| Coin metal | copper: 75%<br>nickel: 25% | United States coins |
| Duralumin | aluminum: 95%<br>copper: 4%<br>magnesium: 0.5%<br>manganese: <1% | aircraft, boats, railroad cars, and machinery because of its high strength and resistance to corrosion |
| Nichrome | nickel: 80–85%<br>chromium: 15–20% | heating elements in toasters, electric heaters, etc. |
| Phosphor bronze | bronze with a small amount of phosphorus | springs, electrical springs, boat propellers |
| Solder | lead: 50%, tin: 50%<br>or<br>tin: 98%, silver: 2% | joining two metals to each other<br><br>joining copper pipes |
| Sterling silver | silver: 92.5%<br>copper: 7.5% | jewelry, art objects, flatware |
| Type metal | lead: 75–95%<br>antimony: 2–18%<br>tin: trace | used to make type for printing because it expands as it cools |

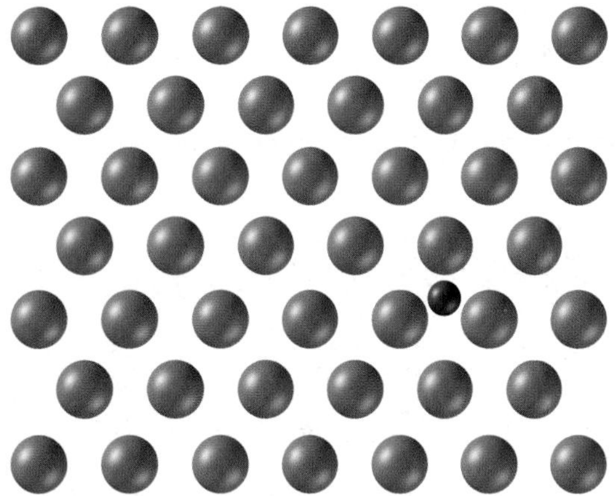

***Interstitial crystal***
*A smaller atom or ion fits into a small space between particles in the array.*

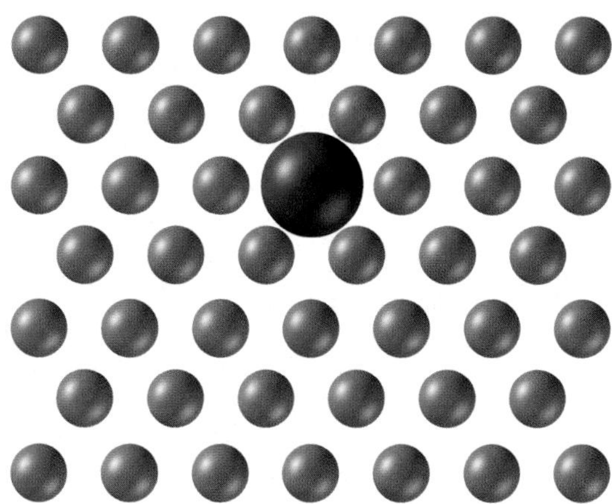

***Substitutional crystal***
*A larger atom or ion is substituted for a particle in the array.*

**Structures and Preparation of Alloys**

Alloys generally crystallize in one of two ways, depending on relative sizes of atoms. If the atoms of one of the metals present are small enough to fit into the spaces between the atoms of the second metal, they form an alloy with an interstitial structure (*inter* means "between," and *stitial* means "to stand"). If atoms of the two metals are of similar size or if one is larger, the atoms of one metal can substitute for the atoms of the second metal in its crystalline structure. Such alloys are substitutional alloys. Models for both types of crystals are shown above.

Techniques for making alloys depend on the metals used in the mixture. In some cases, the two metals can simply be melted together to form a mixture. The composition of the mixture often varies within a range, evidence that the final product is indeed a mixture and not a compound. In other cases, one metal may be melted first and the second dissolved in it. Brass is prepared in this way. If copper and zinc were heated together to a high temperature, zinc (bp 907°C) would evaporate before copper (mp 1084°C) melted. Therefore, the copper is melted first, and the zinc is added to it.

***Brass has a high luster and resembles gold when cleaned and polished. A brass object can be coated with a varnish to prevent reactions of the alloy with air and water.***

***Sterling silver is more widely used than pure silver because it is stronger and more durable.***

## APPLICATION *The Environment*

### Mercury Poisoning

Mercury is the only metal that is liquid at room temperature. It has a very high density compared with most other common transition metals and has a very large surface tension and high vapor pressure. Mercury and many of its compounds must be handled with extreme care because they are highly toxic. Mercury spills are especially hazardous because the droplets scatter easily and are often undetected during cleanup. These droplets release toxic vapors into the air.

Overexposure to mercury vapor or its compounds can occur by absorption through the skin, respiratory tract, or digestive tract. Mercury is a cumulative poison, which means that its concentration in the body increases as exposure increases.

Mercury that enters the body damages the kidneys, heart, and brain. The action of mercury on the brain affects the nervous system. Symptoms of mercury poisoning include numbness, tunnel vision, garbled speech, bleeding and inflammation of the gums, muscle spasms, anemia, and emotional disorders, such as depression, irritability, and personality changes. The saying "mad as a hatter" probably came about because of mercury poisoning. Mercury salts were once routinely used to process the felt used in hats. Hatters often displayed the nerve and mental impairments associated with overexposure to mercury.

#### Methylmercury in Freshwater Ecosystems

Mercury, Hg, can be found in our environment and in our food supply. Fortunately, the body has some protective mechanisms to deal with trace amounts of mercury. However, levels of mercury and of methylmercury, $(CH_3)Hg^+$, are increasing in the environment due to mercury mining operations and runoff from the application of pesticides and fungicides.

Mercury is easily converted to methylmercury by bacteria. Methylmercury is more readily absorbed by cells than mercury itself. As a result, methylmercury accumulates in the food chain as shown in the diagram below. A serious incident of methylmercury poisoning occurred in Japan in the 1950s. People living in Minamata, Japan, were exposed to high levels of methylmercury from eating shellfish.

In the United States, there is concern about mercury levels in fish from some freshwater lakes. Though environmental regulations have reduced the level of lake pollutants, it takes time to see a reduction in the concentration of an accumulated poison.

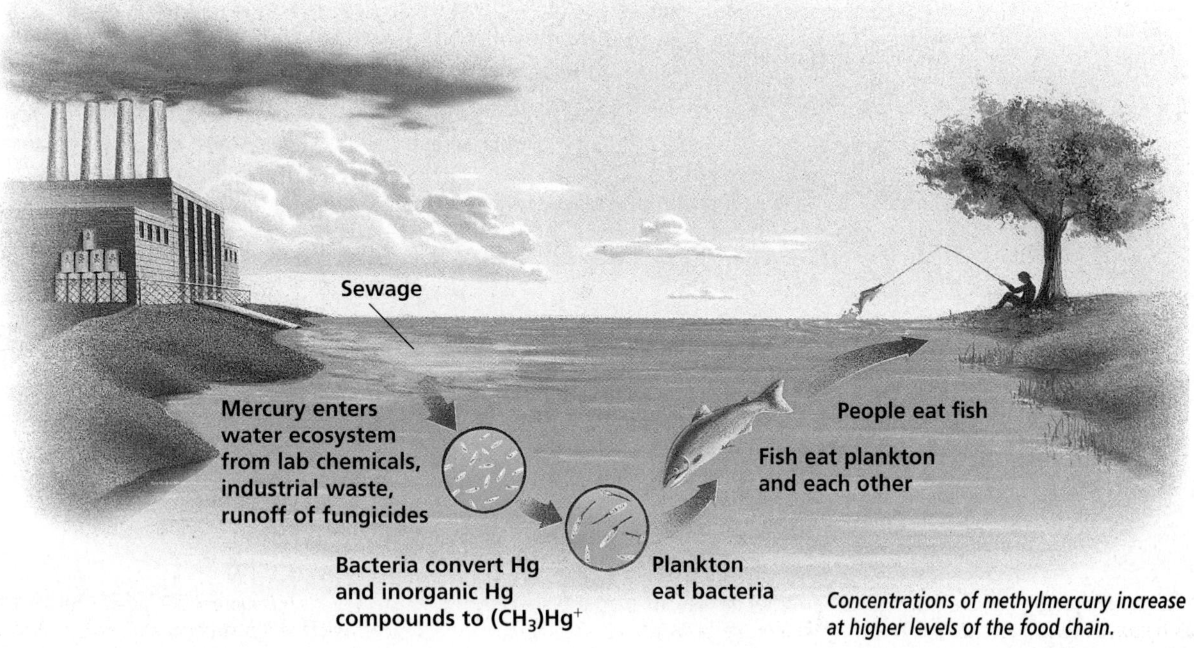


*Concentrations of methylmercury increase at higher levels of the food chain.*

## APPLICATION *Health*

### Elements in the Body

The four most abundant elements in the body (oxygen, carbon, hydrogen, and nitrogen) are the major components of organic biomolecules, such as carbohydrates, proteins, fats, and nucleic acids. Other elements compose a dietary category of compounds called minerals. Minerals are considered the inorganic elements of the body. Minerals fall into two categories—the major minerals and the trace minerals, or trace elements, as they are sometimes called. Notice in the periodic table below that most elements in the trace elements category of minerals are transition metals.

Trace elements are minerals with dietary daily requirements of 100 mg or less. They are found in foods derived from both plants and animals. Though these elements are present in very small quantities, they perform a variety of essential functions in the body, as shown in Table 3C on the next page.

**Abundance of Elements in the Body (by mass)**

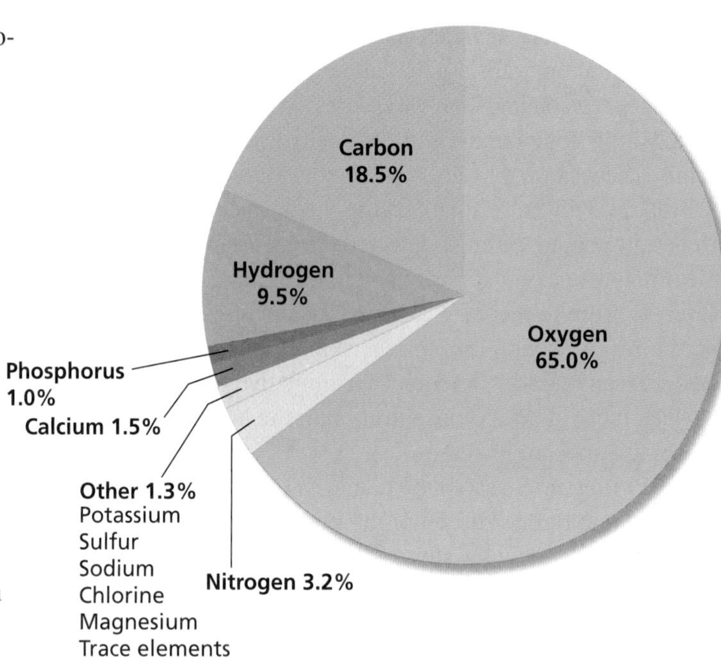


Elements in organic matter

Major minerals

Trace elements

| Group 1 | Group 2 | Group 3 | Group 4 | Group 5 | Group 6 | Group 7 | Group 8 | Group 9 | Group 10 | Group 11 | Group 12 | Group 13 | Group 14 | Group 15 | Group 16 | Group 17 | Group 18 |
|---|---|---|---|---|---|---|---|---|---|---|---|---|---|---|---|---|---|
| 1 H | | | | | | | | | | | | | | | | | 2 He |
| 3 Li | 4 Be | | | | | | | | | | | 5 B | 6 C | 7 N | 8 O | 9 F | 10 Ne |
| 11 Na | 12 Mg | | | | | | | | | | | 13 Al | 14 Si | 15 P | 16 S | 17 Cl | 18 Ar |
| 19 K | 20 Ca | 21 Sc | 22 Ti | 23 V | 24 Cr | 25 Mn | 26 Fe | 27 Co | 28 Ni | 29 Cu | 30 Zn | 31 Ga | 32 Ge | 33 As | 34 Se | 35 Br | 36 Kr |
| 37 Rb | 38 Sr | 39 Y | 40 Zr | 41 Nb | 42 Mo | 43 Tc | 44 Ru | 45 Rh | 46 Pd | 47 Ag | 48 Cd | 49 In | 50 Sn | 51 Sb | 52 Te | 53 I | 54 Xe |
| 55 Cs | 56 Ba | 57 La | 72 Hf | 73 Ta | 74 W | 75 Re | 76 Os | 77 Ir | 78 Pt | 79 Au | 80 Hg | 81 Tl | 82 Pb | 83 Bi | 84 Po | 85 At | 86 Rn |
| 87 Fr | 88 Ra | 89 Ac | | | | | | | | | | | | | | | |

**TABLE 3C Transition Metal Trace Elements**

| Transition metal | Function |
|---|---|
| Vanadium, Cadmium | function not fully determined, but linked to a reduced growth rate and impaired reproduction |
| Chromium | needed for glucose transport to cells |
| Manganese | used in the enzyme reactions that synthesize cholesterol and metabolize carbohydrates |
| Iron | central atom in the heme molecule—a component of hemoglobin, which binds oxygen in the blood for transport to cells |
| Cobalt | a component of vitamin $B_{12}$ |
| Nickel | enzyme cofactor in the metabolism of fatty acids and amino acids |
| Copper | a major component of an enzyme that functions to protect cells from damage |
| Zinc | needed for tissue growth and repair and as an enzyme cofactor |
| Molybdenum | enzyme cofactor in the production of uric acid |

## Role of Iron

Most iron in the body is in hemoglobin. $Fe^{3+}$ is the central ion in the heme molecule, which is a component of the proteins hemoglobin and myoglobin. Hemoglobin in red blood cells transports oxygen to cells and picks up carbon dioxide as waste. Myoglobin is a protein that stores oxygen to be used in muscle contraction. Iron is also in the proteins of the electron transport system and the immune system.

Mechanisms of the body control the rate of iron absorption from food in the diet. When iron reserves are low, chemical signals stimulate cells of the intestines to absorb more iron during digestion. If the diet is low in iron, causing a deficiency, hemoglobin production stops and a condition called iron-deficiency anemia results. The blood cells produced during this state are stunted and unable to deliver adequate oxygen to cells. As a result, a person with iron-deficiency anemia feels tired and weak and has difficulty maintaining normal body temperature. The recommended daily intake of iron is 15 mg. The recommended level doubles for pregnant women. Iron supplements are for people who do not get enough iron in their daily diets. Table 3D lists some foods that are good sources of iron in the diet. Too much iron can be toxic because the body stores iron once it is absorbed. Abusing iron supplements can cause severe liver and heart damage.

**TABLE 3D Sources of Iron in Foods**

| Food | Serving size | Iron present (mg) |
|---|---|---|
| Beef roast (lean cut) | 4 oz | 3.55 |
| Beef, T-bone steak (lean cut) | 4 oz | 3.40 |
| Beef, ground (hamburger) | 4 oz | 2.78 |
| Broccoli | 6.3 oz | 1.50 |
| Chicken, breast | 4 oz | 1.35 |
| Chicken, giblets | 4 oz | 7.30 |
| Oatmeal, instant enriched | 1 pkg | 8.35 |
| Pita bread, white enriched | 6 1/2 in. diameter | 1.40 |
| Pork roast | 4 oz | 1.15 |
| Prunes | 4 oz | 2.00 |
| Raisins | 4 oz | 1.88 |

# GROUP 13
# BORON FAMILY

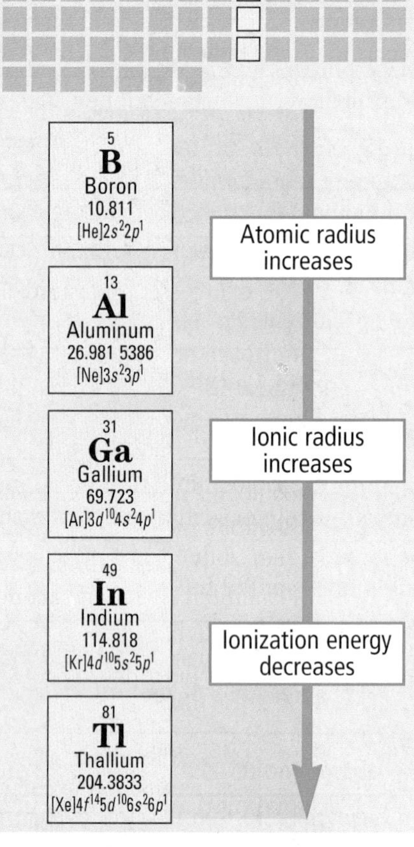


## CHARACTERISTICS

- do not occur in nature as free elements
- are scarce in nature (except aluminum, which is the most abundant metallic element)
- consist of atoms that have three electrons in their outer energy level
- are metallic solids (except boron, which is a solid metalloid)
- are soft and have low melting points (except boron, which is hard and has a high melting point)
- are chemically reactive at moderate temperatures (except boron)

*Boron is a covalent solid. Other members of the family are metallic solids.*

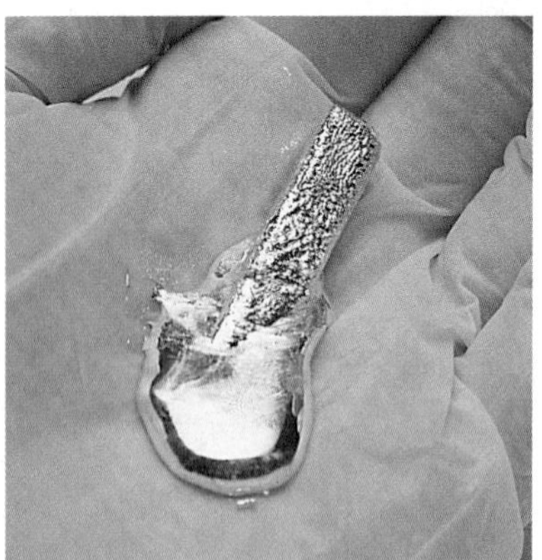

*The warmth of a person's hand will melt gallium. Gallium metal has the lowest melting point (29.77°C) of any metal except mercury.*

*Aluminum is the most abundant metal in Earth's crust. It exists in nature as an ore called bauxite.*

## COMMON REACTIONS

The reaction chemistry of boron differs greatly from that of the other members of this family. Pure boron is a covalent network solid, whereas the other members of the family are metallic crystals in pure form. Boron resembles silicon more closely than it resembles the other members of its family.

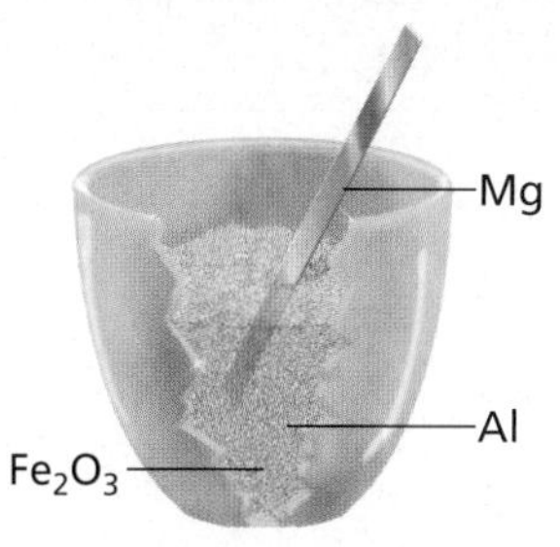


*A mixture of powdered aluminum and iron(III) oxide is called thermite. Al reacts with $Fe_2O_3$ using Mg ribbon as a fuse to provide activation energy. The energy produced by the thermite reaction is sufficient to produce molten iron as a product.*

**With Strong Bases to Form Hydrogen Gas and a Salt**

*Example:* $2Al(s) + 2NaOH(aq) + 2H_2O(l) \longrightarrow 2NaAlO_2(aq) + 3H_2(g)$

Ga also follows this pattern.

**With Dilute Acids to Form Hydrogen Gas and a Salt**

*Example:* $2Al(s) + 6HCl(aq) \longrightarrow 2AlCl_3(aq) + 3H_2(g)$

Ga, In, and Tl follow this pattern in reacting with dilute HF, HCl, HBr, and HI.

**With Halogens to Form Halides**

*Example:* $2Al(s) + 3Cl_2(g) \longrightarrow 2AlCl_3(s)$

B, Al, Ga, In, and Tl also follow this pattern in reacting with $F_2$, $Cl_2$, $Br_2$, and $I_2$ (except $BF_3$).

**With Oxygen to Form Oxides**

*Example:* $4Al(s) + 3O_2(g) \longrightarrow 2Al_2O_3(s)$

Ga, In, and Tl also follow this pattern.

## ANALYTICAL TEST

Other than atomic absorption spectroscopy, there is no simple analytical test for all the members of the boron family.

*The confirmatory test for the presence of aluminum in qualitative analysis is the red color formed by aluminum and the organic compound aluminon, $C_{22}H_{23}N_3O_9$.*

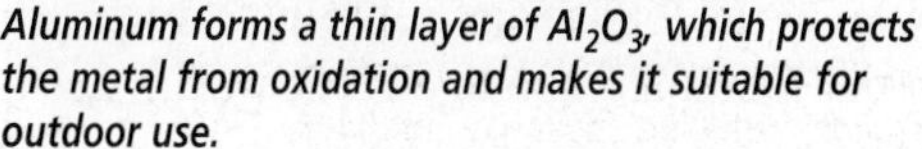

*Aluminum forms a thin layer of $Al_2O_3$, which protects the metal from oxidation and makes it suitable for outdoor use.*

**PROPERTIES OF THE GROUP 13 ELEMENTS**

| | B | Al | Ga | In | Tl |
|---|---|---|---|---|---|
| Melting point (°C) | 2300 | 660.37 | 29.77 | 156.61 | 303.5 |
| Boiling point (°C) | 2550 | 2467 | 2403 | 2080 | 1457 |
| Density (g/cm$^3$) | 2.34 | 2.702 | 5.904 | 7.31 | 11.85 |
| Ionization energy (kJ/mol) | 801 | 578 | 579 | 558 | 589 |
| Atomic radius (pm) | 85 | 143 | 135 | 167 | 170 |
| Ionic radius (pm) | — | 54 | 62 | 80 | 89 |
| Common oxidation number in compounds | +3 | +3 | +1, +3 | +1, +3 | +1, +3 |
| Crystal structure | monoclinic | fcc | orthorhombic | fcc | hcp |
| Hardness (Mohs' scale) | 9.3 | 2.75 | 1.5 | 1.2 | 1.2 |

## APPLICATION *Technology*

### Aluminum

Chemically, aluminum is much more active than copper, and it belongs to the category of *self-protecting metals*. These metals are oxidized when exposed to oxygen in the air and form a hard, protective metal oxide on the surface. The oxidation of aluminum is shown by the following reaction.

$$4Al(s) + 3O_2(g) \longrightarrow 2Al_2O_3(s)$$

This oxide coating protects the underlying metal from further reaction with oxygen or other substances. Self-protecting metals are valuable in themselves or when used to coat iron and steel to keep them from corroding.

Aluminum is a very good conductor of electric current. Many years ago, most high-voltage electric power lines were made of copper. Although copper is a better conductor of electricity than aluminum, copper is heavier and more expensive. Today more than 90% of high-voltage transmission lines are made of relatively pure aluminum. The aluminum wire does not have to be self-supporting because steel cable is incorporated to bear the weight of the wire in the long spans between towers.

*These high-voltage transmission lines are made of aluminum supported with steel cables.*

In the 1960s, aluminum electric wiring was used in many houses and other buildings. Over time, however, because the aluminum oxidized, $Al_2O_3$ built up and increased electric resistance at points where wires connected to outlets, switches, and other metals. As current flowed through the extra resistance, enough energy as heat was generated to cause a fire. Though some homes have been rewired, aluminum wiring is still prevalent in many homes.

## Aluminum Alloys

Because aluminum has a low density and is inexpensive, it is used to construct aircraft, boats, sports equipment, and other lightweight, high-strength objects. The pure metal is not strong, so it is mixed with small quantities of other metals—usually manganese, copper, magnesium, zinc, or silicon—to produce strong low-density alloys. Typically, 80% of a modern aircraft frame consists of aluminum alloy.

Aluminum and its alloys are good heat conductors. An alloy of aluminum and manganese is used to make cookware. High-quality pots and pans made of stainless steel may have a plate of aluminum on the bottom to help conduct energy as heat quickly to the interior.

Automobile radiators made of aluminum conduct energy as heat as hot coolant from the engine enters the bottom of the radiator. The coolant is deflected into several channels. These channels are covered by thin vanes of aluminum, which conduct energy away from the coolant and transfer it to the cooler air rushing past. By the time the coolant reaches the top of the radiator, its temperature has dropped so that when it flows back into the engine it can absorb more energy as heat. To keep the process efficient, the outside of a radiator should be kept unobstructed and free of dirt buildup.

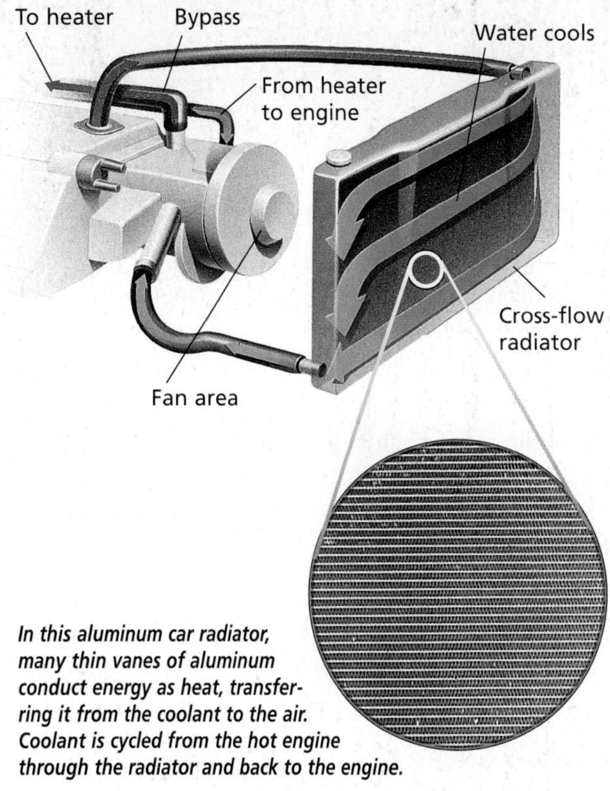


*In this aluminum car radiator, many thin vanes of aluminum conduct energy as heat, transferring it from the coolant to the air. Coolant is cycled from the hot engine through the radiator and back to the engine.*

**TABLE 4A Alloys of Aluminum and Their Uses**

| Principal alloying element(s)* | Characteristics | Application examples |
|---|---|---|
| Manganese | moderately strong, easily worked | cookware, roofing, storage tanks, lawn furniture |
| Copper | strong, easily formed | aircraft structural parts; large, thin structural panels |
| Magnesium | strong, resists corrosion, easy to weld | parts for boats and ships, outdoor decorative objects, tall poles |
| Zinc and magnesium | very strong, resists corrosion | aircraft structural parts, vehicle parts, anything that needs high strength and low weight |
| Silicon | expands little on heating and cooling | aluminum castings |
| Magnesium and silicon | resists corrosion, easily formed | exposed parts of buildings, bridges |

* All these alloys have small amounts of other elements.

# GROUP 14
# CARBON FAMILY

## CHARACTERISTICS

- include a nonmetal (carbon), two metalloids (silicon and germanium), and two metals (tin and lead)
- vary greatly in both physical and chemical properties
- occur in nature in both combined and elemental forms
- consist of atoms that contain four electrons in the outermost energy level
- are relatively unreactive
- tend to form covalent compounds (tin and lead also form ionic compounds)

| Atomic number | Symbol | Name | Atomic mass | Electron configuration |
|---|---|---|---|---|
| 6 | C | Carbon | 12.0107 | [He]$2s^2 2p^2$ |
| 14 | Si | Silicon | 28.0855 | [Ne]$3s^2 3p^2$ |
| 32 | Ge | Germanium | 72.64 | [Ar]$3d^{10} 4s^2 4p^2$ |
| 50 | Sn | Tin | 118.710 | [Kr]$4d^{10} 5s^2 5p^2$ |
| 82 | Pb | Lead | 207.2 | [Xe]$4f^{14} 5d^{10} 6s^2 6p^2$ |

Atomic radius increases

Ionization energy decreases

*Lead has a low reactivity and is resistant to corrosion. It is very soft, highly ductile, and malleable. Lead is toxic and, like mercury, it is a cumulative poison.*

*Silicon has a luster but does not exhibit metallic properties. Most silicon in nature is a silicon oxide, which occurs in sand and quartz, which is shown here.*

*Tin, which is shown on the right, is a self-protecting metal like lead, but unlike lead it has a high luster. Tin occurs in nature in cassiterite ore, which is shown above.*

## COMMON REACTIONS

**With Oxygen to Form Oxides**

*Example:* $Sn(s) + O_2(g) \longrightarrow SnO_2(s)$

Pb follows this pattern, as do C, Si, and Ge at high temperatures.

**With Acids to Form Salts and Hydrogen Gas**

Only the metallic elements of this group react slowly with aqueous acids.

*Example:* $Sn(s) + 2HCl(aq) \longrightarrow SnCl_2(aq) + H_2(g)$

Both Sn and Pb can also react to form tin(IV) and lead(IV) salts, respectively.

**With Halogens to Form Halides**

*Example:* $Sn(s) + 2Cl_2(g) \longrightarrow SnCl_4(s)$

Si, Ge, and Pb follow this pattern, reacting with $F_2$, $Cl_2$, $Br_2$, and $I_2$.

## ANALYTICAL TEST

Ionic compounds of tin and lead can be identified in aqueous solutions by adding a solution containing sulfide ions. The formation of a yellow precipitate indicates the presence of $Sn^{4+}$, and the formation of a black precipitate indicates the presence of $Pb^{2+}$.

$$Sn^{4+}(aq) + 2S^{2-}(aq) \longrightarrow SnS_2(s)$$
$$Pb^{2+}(aq) + S^{2-}(aq) \longrightarrow PbS(s)$$

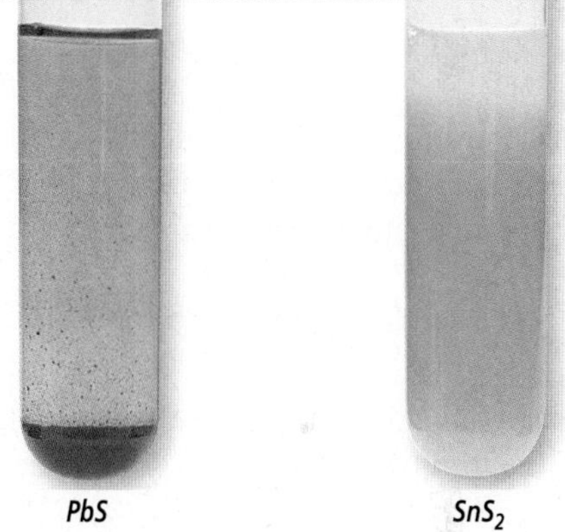

PbS $SnS_2$

## PROPERTIES OF THE GROUP 14 ELEMENTS

| | C | Si | Ge | Sn | Pb |
|---|---|---|---|---|---|
| Melting point (°C) | 3500/3652* | 1410 | 937.4 | 231.88 | 327.502 |
| Boiling point (°C) | 4827 | 2355 | 2830 | 2260 | 1740 |
| Density ($g/cm^3$) | 3.51/2.25* | 2.33 ± 0.01 | 5.323 | 7.28 | 11.343 |
| Ionization energy (kJ/mol) | 1086 | 787 | 762 | 709 | 716 |
| Atomic radius (pm) | 77 | 118 | 122 | 140 | 175 |
| Ionic radius (pm) | 260 ($C^{4-}$ ion) | — | — | 118 ($Sn^{2+}$ ion) | 119 ($Pb^{2+}$ ion) |
| Common oxidation number in compounds | +4, −4 | +4 | +2, +4 | +2, +4 | +2, +4 |
| Crystal structure | cubic/hexagonal* | cubic | cubic | tetragonal | fcc |
| Hardness (Mohs' scale) | 10/0.5* | 6.5 | 6.0 | 1.5 | 1.5 |

* The data are for two allotropic forms: diamond/graphite.

## APPLICATION Chemical Industry

### Carbon and the Reduction of Iron Ore

Some metals, especially iron, are separated from their ores through reduction reactions in a blast furnace. The blast furnace gets its name from the fact that air or pure oxygen is blown into the furnace, where it oxidizes carbon to form carbon monoxide, CO. Carbon and its compounds are important reactants in this process.

What happens inside the blast furnace to recover the iron from its ore? The actual chemical changes that occur are complex. A simplified explanation begins with the reaction of oxygen in hot air with coke, a form of carbon. Some of the coke burns to form carbon dioxide.

$$C(s) + O_2(g) \longrightarrow CO_2(g)$$

As the concentration of oxygen is decreased, the carbon dioxide comes in contact with pieces of hot coke and is reduced to carbon monoxide.

$$CO_2(g) + C(s) \longrightarrow 2CO(g)$$

The carbon monoxide now acts as a reducing agent to reduce the iron oxides in the ore to metallic iron.

$$Fe_2O_3(s) + 3CO(g) \longrightarrow 2Fe(l) + 3CO_2(g)$$

The reduction is thought to occur in steps as the temperature in the furnace increases. The following are some of the possible steps.

$$Fe_2O_3 \longrightarrow Fe_3O_4 \longrightarrow FeO \longrightarrow Fe$$

The white-hot liquid iron collects in the bottom of the furnace and is removed every four or five hours. The iron may be cast in molds or converted to steel in another process.

Limestone, present in the center of the furnace, decomposes to form calcium oxide and carbon dioxide.

$$CaCO_3(s) \longrightarrow CaO(s) + CO_2(g)$$

The calcium oxide then combines with silica, a silicon compound, to form calcium silicate slag.

The relatively high carbon content of iron produced in a blast furnace makes the metal hard but brittle. It also has other impurities, like sulfur and phosphorus, that cause the recovered iron to be brittle. The conversion of iron to steel is essentially a purification process in which impurities are removed by oxidation. This purification process is carried out in another kind of furnace at very high temperatures. All steel contains 0.02 to 1.5% carbon. In fact, steels are graded by their carbon content. Low-carbon steels typically contain 0.02 to 0.3% carbon. Medium-carbon steels typically contain 0.03 to 0.7% carbon. High-carbon steels contain 0.7 to 1.5% carbon.

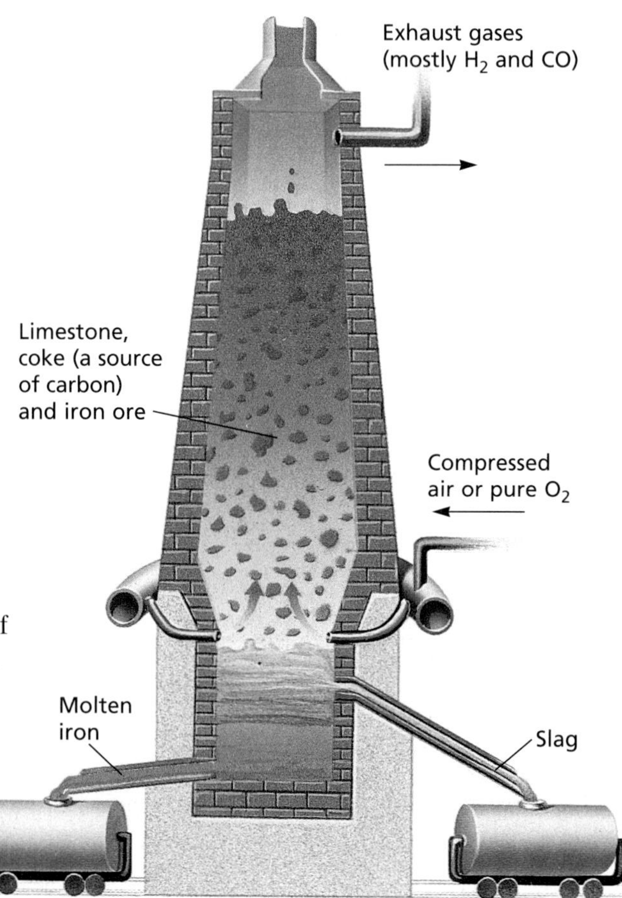


*Molten iron flowing from the bottom of a blast furnace has been reduced from its ore through a series of reactions at high temperatures in different regions of the furnace.*

## Carbon Dioxide

Carbon dioxide is a colorless gas with a faintly irritating odor and a slightly sour taste. The sour taste is the result of the formation of carbonic acid when $CO_2$ dissolves in the water in saliva. It is a stable gas that does not burn or support combustion. At temperatures lower than 31°C and at pressures higher than 72.9 atm, $CO_2$ condenses to the liquid form. A phase diagram for $CO_2$ is found in the chapter review section of Chapter 10. At normal atmospheric pressure, solid $CO_2$ (dry ice) sublimes at −78.5°C. The linear arrangement of carbon dioxide molecules makes them nonpolar.

$CO_2$ is produced by the burning of organic fuels and from respiration processes in most living things. Most $CO_2$ released into the atmosphere is used by plants during photosynthesis. Recall that photosynthesis is the process by which green plants and some forms of algae and bacteria make food. During photosynthesis, $CO_2$ reacts with $H_2O$, using the energy from sunlight. The relationships among the various processes on Earth that convert carbon to carbon dioxide are summarized in the diagram of the carbon cycle, which is pictured below.

## Carbon Monoxide

Carbon monoxide is a poisonous gas produced naturally by decaying plants, certain types of algae, volcanic eruptions, and the oxidation of methane in the atmosphere.

Because CO is colorless, odorless, and tasteless, it is difficult to detect. It is slightly less dense than air and slightly soluble in water. Its main chemical uses are in the reduction of iron, described on page 814, and the production of organic compounds, such as methanol.

$$CO(g) + 2H_2(g) \longrightarrow CH_3OH(l)$$

Carbon monoxide is also produced during the incomplete combustion of organic fuels. Incomplete combustion of methane occurs when the supply of oxygen is limited.

$$2CH_4(g) + 3O_2(g) \longrightarrow 2CO(g) + 4H_2O(g)$$

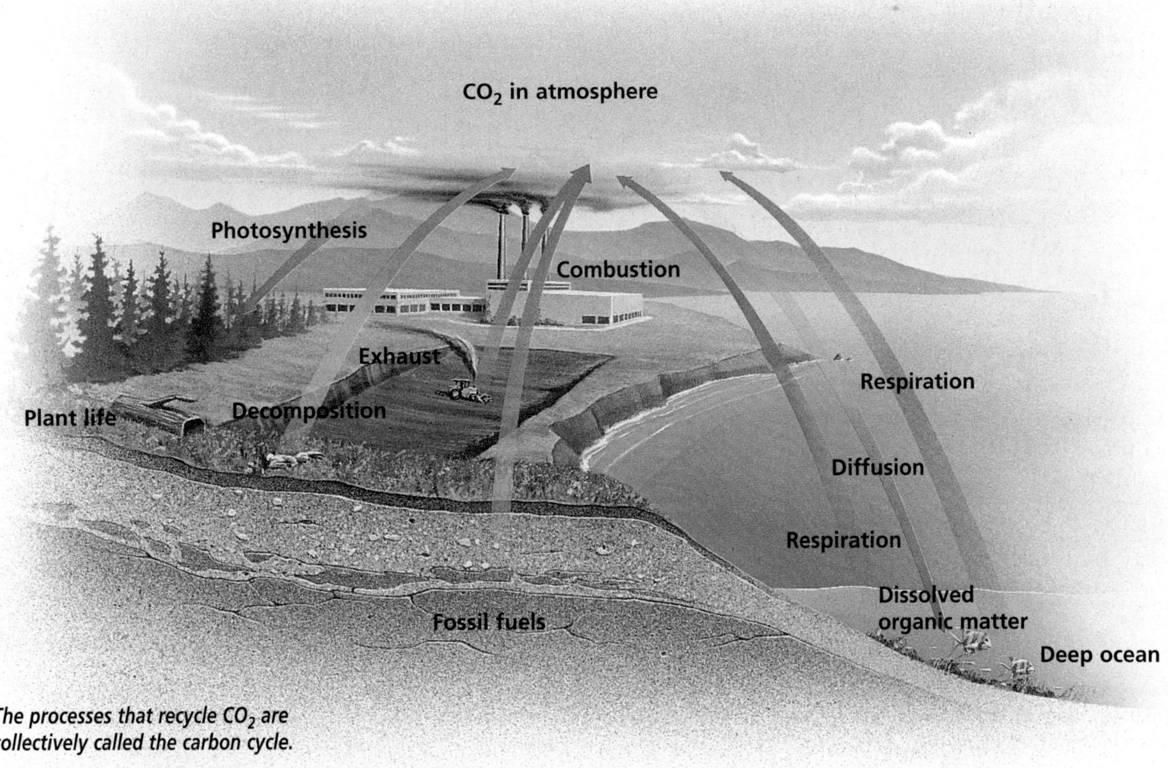


*The processes that recycle $CO_2$ are collectively called the carbon cycle.*

## APPLICATION *Biochemistry*

### Carbon Dioxide and Respiration

Many organisms, including humans, carry out cellular respiration. In this process, cells break down food molecules and release the energy used to build those molecules during photosynthesis. Glucose, $C_6H_{12}O_6$, is a common substance broken down in respiration. The following chemical equation expresses this process.

$$C_6H_{12}O_6 + 6O_2 \longrightarrow 6CO_2 + 6H_2O + \text{energy}$$

In humans and most other vertebrate animals, the oxygen needed for this reaction is delivered to cells by hemoglobin found in red blood cells. Oxygen binds with hemoglobin as blood passes through capillaries in the lungs, as represented by the following reaction.

$$\text{Hb} + O_2 \longrightarrow \text{HbO}_2$$

Hb represents the hemoglobin molecule, and $HbO_2$ represents oxyhemoglobin, which is hemoglobin with bound oxygen. When the red blood cells pass through capillaries near cells that have depleted their oxygen supply through respiration, the reaction reverses and oxyhemoglobin gives up its oxygen.

$$\text{HbO}_2 \longrightarrow \text{Hb} + O_2$$

Carbon dioxide produced during respiration is a waste product that must be expelled from an organism. Various things happen when $CO_2$ enters the blood. Seven percent dissolves in the plasma, about 23% binds loosely to hemoglobin, and the remaining 70% reacts reversibly with water in plasma to form hydrogen carbonate, $HCO_3^-$ ions. To form $HCO_3^-$ ions, $CO_2$ first combines with $H_2O$ to form carbonic acid, $H_2CO_3$, in a reversible reaction.

$$CO_2(aq) + H_2O(l) \rightleftharpoons H_2CO_3(aq)$$

The dissolved carbonic acid ionizes to $HCO_3^-$ ions and aqueous $H^+$ ions in the form of $H_3O^+$.

$$H_2CO_3(aq) + H_2O \rightleftharpoons H_3O^+(aq) + HCO_3^-(aq)$$

The combined equilibrium reaction follows.

$$CO_2(aq) + 2H_2O(l) \rightleftharpoons H_3O^+(aq) + HCO_3^-(aq)$$

When the blood reaches the lungs, the reaction reverses and the blood releases $CO_2$, which is then exhaled to the surroundings.

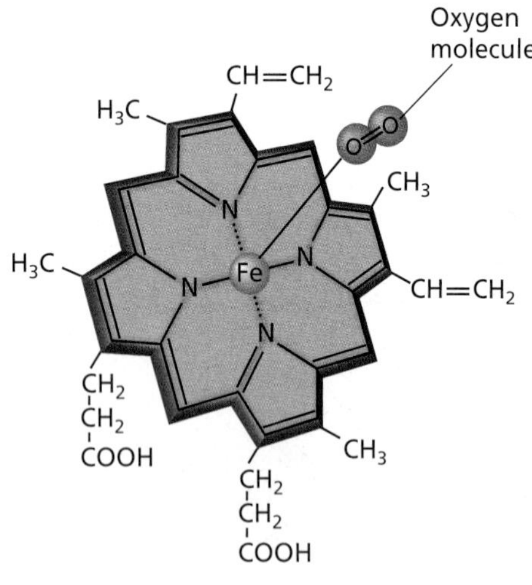


Heme

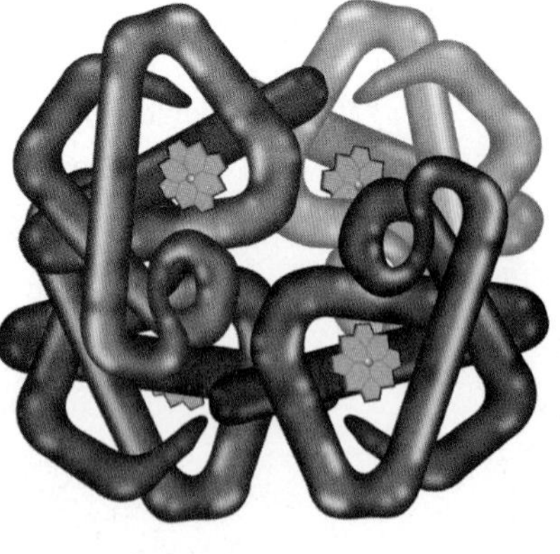

Hemoglobin (protein)

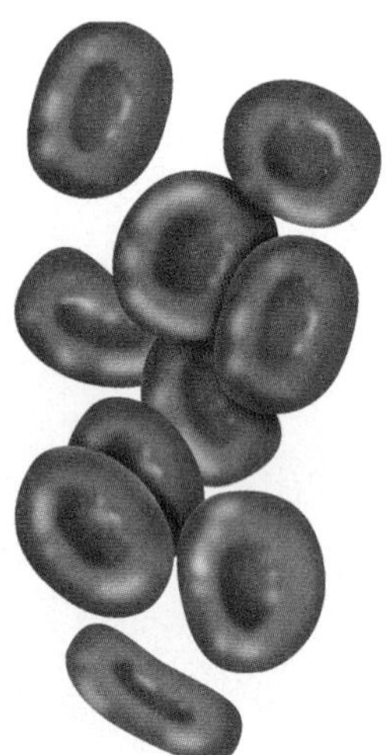

Red blood cells

***The oxygen carrier molecule, heme, is a component of the more-complex protein hemoglobin. Note that each hemoglobin molecule has four heme subunits. Hemoglobin is a component of red blood cells.***

**Exchange of $CO_2$ and $O_2$ in the Lungs**

Why does $CO_2$ leave the blood as it passes through the lung's capillaries, and why does $O_2$ enter the blood? The exchange is caused by the difference in concentrations of $CO_2$ and $O_2$ in the blood and in the atmosphere. Oxygen is 21% of the atmosphere. Although the amount of $CO_2$ varies from place to place, it averages about 0.033% of the atmosphere. Thus, $O_2$ is about 640 times more concentrated in the atmosphere than is $CO_2$.

Substances tend to diffuse from regions of higher concentration toward regions of lower concentration. Thus, when blood reaches the capillaries of the lung, $O_2$ from the air diffuses into the blood, where its pressure is only 40 mm Hg, while $CO_2$ diffuses out of the blood, where its pressure is 45 mm Hg, and into the air. The diagram below summarizes the process.

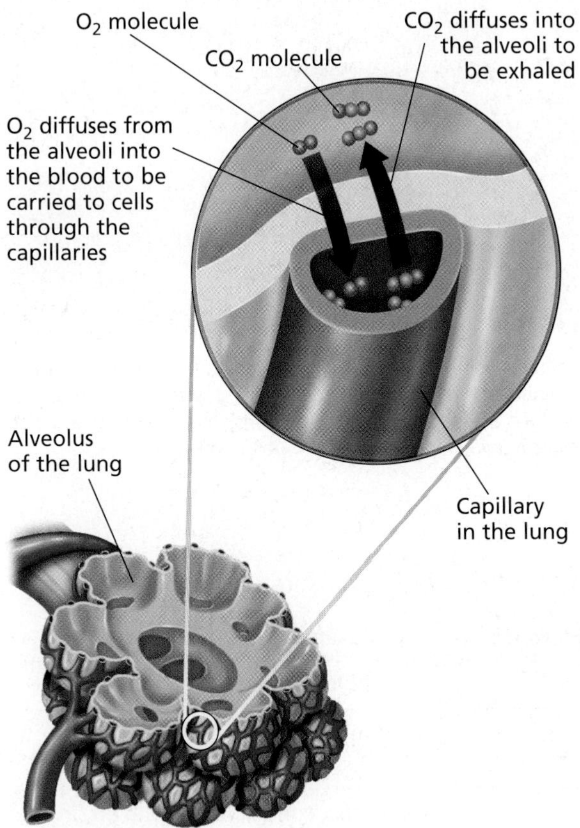


*The pressure of $O_2$ in the blood entering the lung is much lower than it is in the atmosphere. As a result, $O_2$ diffuses into the blood. The opposite situation exists for $CO_2$, so it diffuses from the blood into the air. Note that blood leaving the lung still contains a significant concentration of $CO_2$.*

**Acidosis and Alkalosis**

In humans, blood is maintained between pH 7.3 and 7.5. The pH of blood is dependent on the concentration of $CO_2$ in the blood. Look again at this equilibrium system.

$$CO_2(aq) + 2H_2O(l) \rightleftharpoons H_3O^+(aq) + HCO_3^-(aq)$$

Notice that the right side of the equation contains the $H_3O^+$ ion, which determines the pH of the blood. If excess $H_3O^+$ enters the blood from tissues, the reverse reaction is favored. Excess $H_3O^+$ combines with $HCO_3^-$ to produce more $CO_2$ and $H_2O$. If the $H_3O^+$ concentration begins to fall, the forward reaction is favored, producing additional $H_3O^+$ and $HCO_3^-$. To keep $H_3O^+$ in balance, adequate amounts of both $CO_2$ and $HCO_3^-$ must be present. If something occurs that changes these conditions, a person can become very ill and can even die.

Hyperventilation occurs when a person breathes too rapidly for an extended time. Too much $CO_2$ is eliminated, causing the reverse reaction to be favored, and $H_3O^+$ and $HCO_3^-$ are used up. As a result, the person develops a condition known as alkalosis because the pH of the blood rises to an abnormal alkaline level. The person begins to feel lightheaded and faint, and, unless treatment is provided, he or she may fall into a coma. Alkalosis is treated by having the victim breathe air that is rich in $CO_2$. One way to accomplish this is to have the person breathe with a bag held tightly over the nose and mouth. Alkalosis is also caused by fever, infection, intoxication, hysteria, and prolonged vomiting.

The reverse of alkalosis is a condition known as acidosis. This condition is often caused by a depletion of $HCO_3^-$ ions from the blood, which can occur as a result of kidney dysfunction. The kidney controls the excretion of $HCO_3^-$ ions. If there are too few $HCO_3^-$ ions in solution, the forward reaction is favored and $H_3O^+$ ions accumulate, which lowers the blood's pH. Acidosis can also result from the body's inability to expel $CO_2$, which can occur during pneumonia, emphysema, and other respiratory disorders. Perhaps the single most common cause of acidosis is uncontrolled diabetes, in which acids normally excreted in the urinary system are instead retained by the body.

## APPLICATION *The Environment*

### Carbon Monoxide Poisoning

Standing on a street corner in any major city exposes a person to above-normal concentrations of carbon monoxide from automobile exhaust. Carbon monoxide also reacts with hemoglobin. The following reaction takes place in the capillaries of the lung.

$$\text{Hb} + \text{CO} \longrightarrow \text{HbCO}$$

Unlike $CO_2$ or $O_2$, CO binds strongly to hemoglobin. Carboxyhemoglobin, HbCO, is 200 times more stable than oxyhemoglobin, $HbO_2$. So as blood circulates, more and more CO molecules bind to hemoglobin, reducing the amount of $O_2$ bond sites available for transport. Eventually, CO occupies so many hemoglobin binding sites that cells die from lack of oxygen. Symptoms of carbon monoxide poisoning include headache, mental confusion, dizziness, weakness, nausea, loss of muscular control, and decreased heart rate and respiratory rate. The victim loses consciousness and will die without treatment.

If the condition is caught in time, a victim of carbon monoxide poisoning can be revived by breathing pure oxygen. This treatment causes carboxyhemoglobin to be converted slowly to oxyhemoglobin according to the following chemical equation.

$$O_2 + \text{HbCO} \longrightarrow \text{CO} + \text{HbO}_2$$

Mild carbon monoxide poisoning usually does not have long-term effects. In severe cases, cells are destroyed. Damage to brain cells is irreversible.

The level of danger posed by carbon monoxide depends on two factors: the concentration of the gas in the air and the amount of time that a person is exposed to the gas. Table 5A shows the effects of increasing levels of carbon monoxide in the bloodstream. These effects vary considerably depending on a person's activity level and metabolic rate.

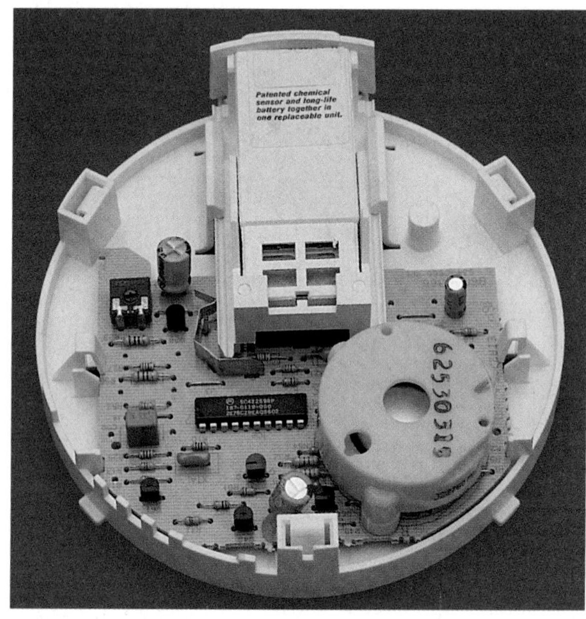


*Carbon monoxide detectors are now available to reduce the risk of poisoning from defective home heating systems. The Consumer Products Safety Commission recommends that all homes have a CO detector with a UL label.*

**TABLE 5A Symptoms of CO Poisoning at Increasing Levels of CO Exposure and Concentration**

| Concentration of CO in air (ppm)* | Hemoglobin molecules as HbCO | Visible effects |
|---|---|---|
| 100 for 1 hour or less | 10% or less | no visible symptoms |
| 500 for 1 hour or less | 20% | mild to throbbing headache, some dizziness, impaired perception |
| 500 for an extended period of time | 30–50% | headache, confusion, nausea, dizziness, muscular weakness, fainting |
| 1000 for 1 hour or less | 50–80% | coma, convulsions, respiratory failure, death |

* ppm is parts per million

## APPLICATION Biochemistry

### Macromolecules

Large organic polymers are called macromolecules (the prefix *macro* means "large"). Macromolecules play important roles in living systems. Most macromolecules essential to life belong to four main classes, three of which we know as nutrients in food:

1. **Proteins** Hair, tendons, ligaments, and silk are made of protein. Other proteins act as hormones, transport substances throughout the body, and fight infections. Enzymes are proteins that control the body's chemical reactions. Proteins provide energy, yielding 17 kJ/g.
2. **Carbohydrates** Sugars, starches, and cellulose are carbohydrates. Carbohydrates are sources of energy, yielding 17 kJ/g.
3. **Lipids** Fats, oils, waxes, and steroids are lipids, nonpolar substances that do not dissolve in water. Fats are sources of energy, yielding 38 kJ/g.
4. **Nucleic acids** DNA and RNA are nucleic acids. In most organisms, DNA is used to store hereditary information and RNA helps to assemble proteins.

#### Proteins

Proteins are macromolecules formed by condensation reactions between amino acid monomers. Proteins contain carbon, oxygen, hydrogen, nitrogen, and usually some sulfur.

All amino acids have a carboxyl group, —COOH, and an amino group, $—NH_2$, attached to a central carbon atom, which is also attached to hydrogen, —H. Amino acids differ from one another at the fourth bond site of the central carbon, which is attached to a group of atoms (called an *R* group). *R* groups differ from one amino acid to another, as shown in the structures for several amino acids below. The proteins of all organisms contain a set of 20 common amino acids. The reaction that links amino acids is a condensation reaction, which is described in Chapter 22.

Each protein has its own unique sequence of amino acids. A complex organism has at least several thousand different proteins, each with a special structure and function. For instance, *insulin,* a hormone that helps the body regulate the level of sugar in the blood, is made up of two linked chains.

***Amino acids have the same general structure. These examples show some of the variations within this class of compounds.***

$R-CH(NH_2)-COOH$

General structure

$CH_3-CH(NH_2)-COOH$

Alanine

$H_2N-C(=O)-CH_2-CH(NH_2)-COOH$

Asparagine

$H_2N-C(=O)-CH_2-CH_2-CH(NH_2)-COOH$

Glutamine

$CH_3CH_2-CH(CH_3)-CH(NH_2)-COOH$

Isoleucine

$H-CH(CH_3)-CH_2-CH(NH_2)-COOH$ (with $CH_3$ above and below the first C)

Leucine

$CH_3-S-CH_2-CH_2-CH(NH_2)-COOH$

Methionine

$C_6H_5-CH_2-CH(NH_2)-COOH$

Phenylalanine

$CH_3-CH(OH)-CH(NH_2)-COOH$

Threonine

$HO-C_6H_4-CH_2-CH(NH_2)-COOH$

Tyrosine

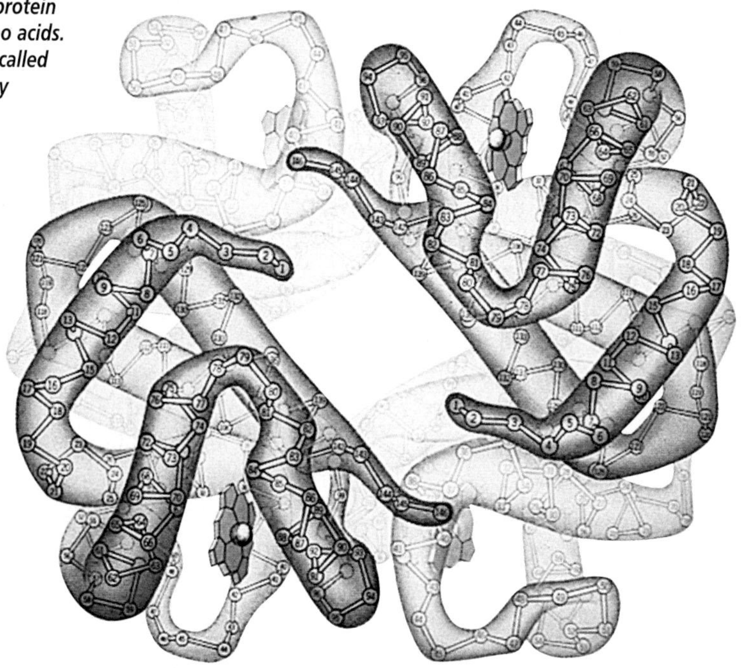

*Hemoglobin is a complex protein made of hundreds of amino acids. Its 3-dimensional shape is called a tertiary structure. Tertiary structures break down when a protein is denatured.*

The chains are held together by S—S bonds between sulfur atoms in two cysteine amino acids. Insulin is one of the smaller proteins, containing only 51 amino acids. In contrast, hemoglobin, which carries oxygen in the blood, is a large protein consisting of four long chains with the complicated three-dimensional structures shown above. Proteins can lose their shape with increases in temperature or changes in the chemical composition of their environment. When they are returned to normal surroundings, they may fold or coil up again and re-form their original structure.

Changing even one amino acid can change a protein's structure and function. For example, the difference between normal hemoglobin and the hemoglobin that causes sickle cell anemia is just one amino acid substituted for another.

**Enzymes**

You learned how enzymes alter reaction rates in Chapter 17. Some enzymes cannot bind to their substrates without the help of additional molecules. These may be *minerals,* such as calcium or iron ions, or helper molecules called *coenzymes* that play accessory roles in enzyme-catalyzed reactions. Many vitamins are coenzymes or parts of coenzymes.

*Vitamins* are organic molecules that we cannot manufacture and hence need to eat in small amounts.

OH
HO O
=O
HO OH

Vitamin C, $C_6H_8O_6$
Water-soluble

$CH_3$ $CH_3$ $CH_3$ $CH_3$
OH
$CH_3$

Vitamin A, $C_{20}H_{30}O$
Fat-soluble

You can see why we need vitamins and minerals in our diet—to enable our enzymes to work. You can also see why we need only small amounts of them. Minerals and coenzymes are not destroyed in biochemical reactions. Like enzymes, coenzymes and minerals can be used over and over again.

Temperature and pH have the most significant effects on the rates of reactions catalyzed by enzymes. Most enzymes work best in a solution of approximately neutral pH. Most body cells have a pH of 7.4. However, some enzymes function only in acidic or basic environments. For example, pepsin, the collective

## APPLICATION Chemical Industry

### Silicon and Silicates

Silicon is as important in the mineral world as carbon is in living systems. Silicon dioxide and silicates make up about 87% of Earth's crust. Silicates are a class of compounds containing silicon, oxygen, one or more metals, and possibly hydrogen. Many mineral compounds are silicates. Sand is probably the most familiar silicate.

Glasses consist of 75% silicate. Borosilicate glass is the special heat-resistant glass used in making laboratory beakers and flasks. The addition of 5% boron oxide to the glass increases the softening temperature of the glass. Because boron and silicon atoms have roughly similar radii, these atoms can be substituted for one another to make borosilicate glass.

Asbestos is the name given to a class of fibrous magnesium silicate minerals. Asbestos is very strong and flexible, and it does not burn, so it was widely used as a heat-insulating material.

It is now known that asbestos is a carcinogen. When handled, asbestos releases dust particles that are easily inhaled and can cause lung cancer. Asbestos materials found in older homes and buildings should be removed by firms licensed by the Environmental Protection Agency (EPA).

### Silicones

Silicones are a class of organic silicon polymers composed of silicon, carbon, oxygen, and hydrogen. The silicon chain is held together by bonding with the oxygen atoms. Each silicon atom is also bonded to different hydrocarbon groups to create a variety of silicone structures.

Silicones are widely used for their adhesive and protective properties. They have good electric insulating properties and are water-repellent. Some silicones have the character of oils or greases, so they are used as lubricants. Silicones are also used in automobile and furniture polishes as protective agents.

*Silicon has the ability to form long chain compounds by bonding with oxygen. The $SiO_4$ subunit in this silicate is tetrahedral.*

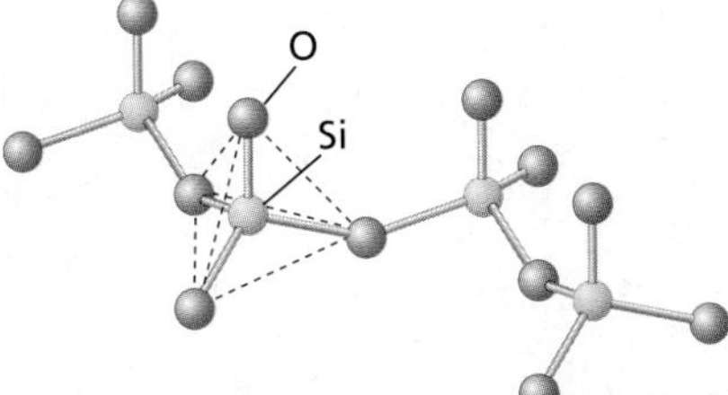


*Silicones also have a tetrahedral structure. How does this structure differ from that of a silicate?*

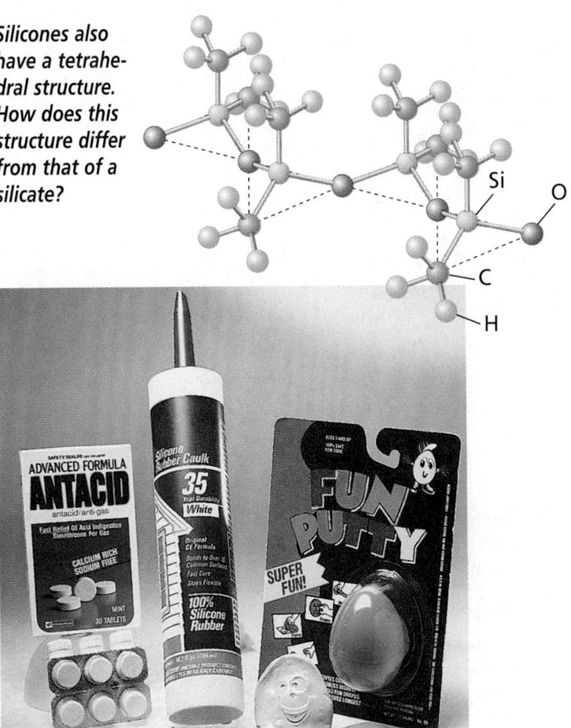

*Silicates exist in a variety of mineral forms, including mica.*

*Because of their protective properties, silicones are used in a number of consumer products, from cosmetics to caulkings.*

## APPLICATION *Technology*

### Semiconductors

When electrons can move freely through a material, the material is a conductor. The electrons in metals are loosely held and require little additional energy to move from one vacant orbital to the next. A set of overlapping orbitals is called a *conduction band.* Because electrons can easily jump to the conduction band, metals conduct electricity when only a very small voltage is applied.

Semiconductors conduct a current if the voltage applied is large enough to excite the outer-level electrons of their atoms into the higher energy levels. With semiconductors, more energy, and thus a higher voltage, is required to cause conduction. By contrast, nonmetals are insulators because they do not conduct at ordinary voltages. Too much energy is needed to raise their outer electrons into conduction bands.

Semiconductor devices include transistors; diodes, including light-emitting diodes (LEDs); some lasers; and photovoltaic cells ("solar" cells). Though silicon is the basis of most semiconductor devices in the computer industry, pure silicon has little use as a semiconductor. Instead, small amounts of impurities are added to increase its conductive properties. Adding impurities to silicon is called *doping,* and the substances added are *dopants.* The dopant is usually incorporated into just the surface layer of a silicon chip. Typical dopants include the Group 15 elements phosphorus and arsenic and the Group 13 elements boron, aluminum, gallium, and indium.

A silicon atom has four electrons in its outer energy level whereas Group 13 atoms have three and Group 15 atoms have five. Adding boron to silicon creates a mix of atoms having four valence electrons and atoms having three valence electrons. Boron atoms form only three bonds with silicon, whereas silicon forms four bonds with other silicon atoms. The unbonded spot between a silicon atom

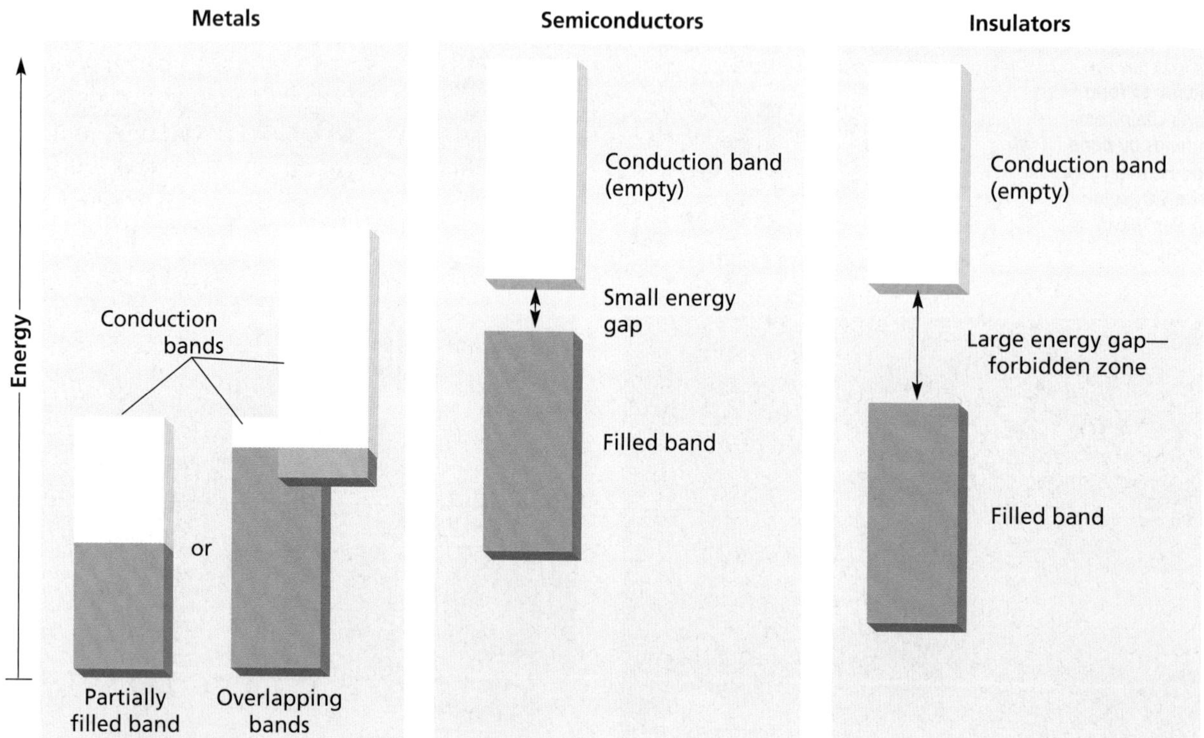


***This model shows the difference in the levels of energy required to excite electrons into the conduction band in metals, semiconductors, and insulators. The forbidden zone is too great an energy gap in insulators for these elements to function as conductors. The energy gap for semiconductors is small enough that it can be crossed under certain conditions.***

Dopants
Semiconductor elements
Forms semiconductor compounds

| Group 1 | Group 2 | Group 3 | Group 4 | Group 5 | Group 6 | Group 7 | Group 8 | Group 9 | Group 10 | Group 11 | Group 12 | Group 13 | Group 14 | Group 15 | Group 16 | Group 17 | Group 18 |
|---|---|---|---|---|---|---|---|---|---|---|---|---|---|---|---|---|---|
| 1 H | | | | | | | | | | | | | | | | | 2 He |
| 3 Li | 4 Be | | | | | | | | | | | 5 B | 6 C | 7 N | 8 O | 9 F | 10 Ne |
| 11 Na | 12 Mg | | | | | | | | | | | 13 Al | 14 Si | 15 P | 16 S | 17 Cl | 18 Ar |
| 19 K | 20 Ca | 21 Sc | 22 Ti | 23 V | 24 Cr | 25 Mn | 26 Fe | 27 Co | 28 Ni | 29 Cu | 30 Zn | 31 Ga | 32 Ge | 33 As | 34 Se | 35 Br | 36 Kr |
| 37 Rb | 38 Sr | 39 Y | 40 Zr | 41 Nb | 42 Mo | 43 Tc | 44 Ru | 45 Rh | 46 Pd | 47 Ag | 48 Cd | 49 In | 50 Sn | 51 Sb | 52 Te | 53 I | 54 Xe |
| 55 Cs | 56 Ba | 57 La | 72 Hf | 73 Ta | 74 W | 75 Re | 76 Os | 77 Ir | 78 Pt | 79 Au | 80 Hg | 81 Tl | 82 Pb | 83 Bi | 84 Po | 85 At | 86 Rn |
| 87 Fr | 88 Ra | 89 Ac | | | | | | | | | | | | | | | |

***Semiconductor elements and dopants fall in the metalloid region of the periodic table. Semiconductor compounds often contain metals.***

and a boron atom is a hole that a free electron can occupy. Because this hole "attracts" an electron, it is viewed as if it were positively charged. Semiconductors that are doped with boron, aluminum, or gallium are *p-type semiconductors,* the *p* standing for "positive." P-type semiconductors conduct electricity better than pure silicon because they provide spaces that moving electrons can occupy as they flow through the material.

Doping silicon with phosphorus or arsenic produces the opposite effect. When phosphorus is added to silicon, it forms four bonds to silicon atoms and has a nonbonding electron left over. This extra electron is free to move through the material when a voltage is applied, thus increasing its conductivity compared with pure silicon. These extra electrons have a negative charge. Therefore, the material is an *n-type semiconductor*. Compare these two types of semiconductors in the models below.

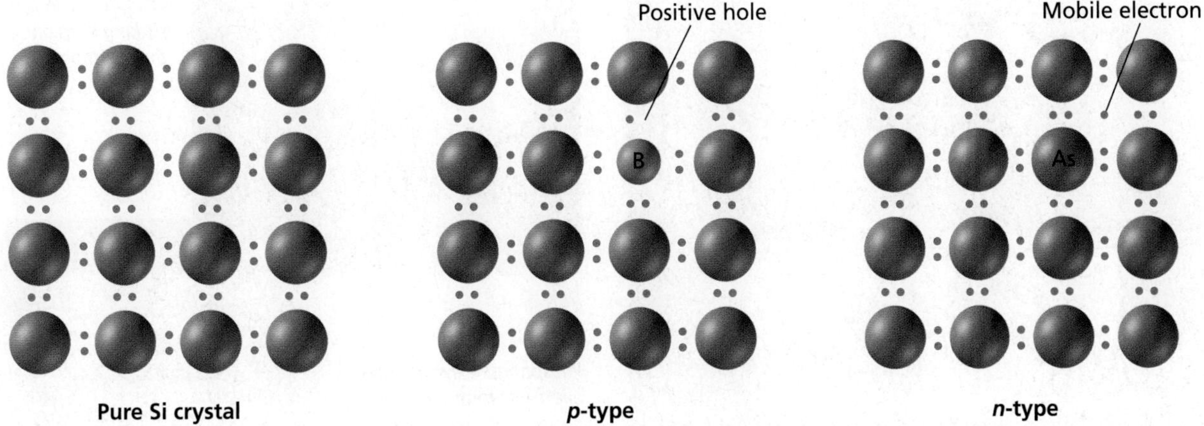


***Each silicon atom in the pure crystal is surrounded by four pairs of electrons. The p-type semiconductor model contains an atom of boron with a hole that an electron can occupy. The n-type semiconductor model contains an atom of arsenic, which provides the extra electron that can move through the crystal.***

# GROUP 15
# NITROGEN FAMILY

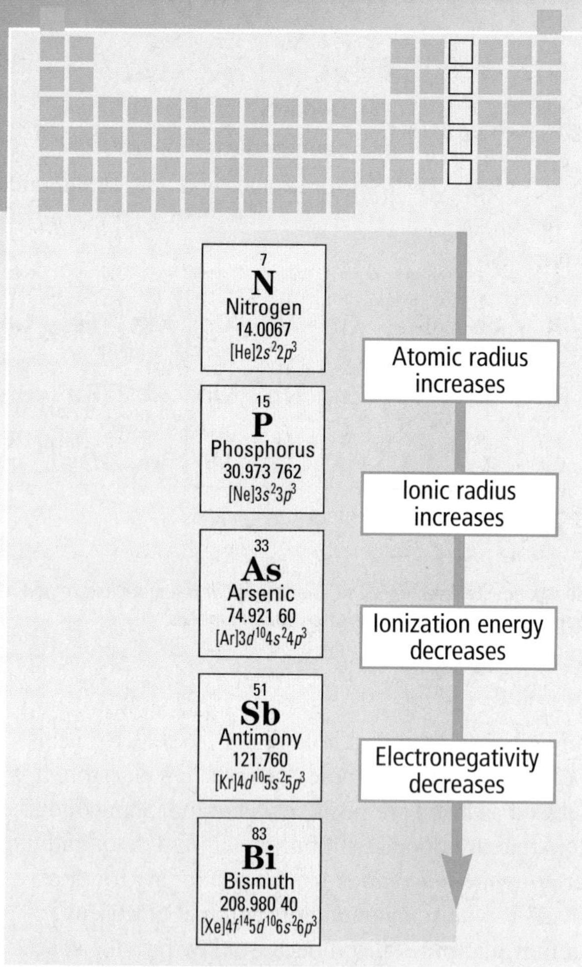

## CHARACTERISTICS

- consist of two nonmetals (nitrogen and phosphorus), two metalloids (arsenic and antimony), and one metal (bismuth)
- Nitrogen is most commonly found as atmospheric $N_2$; phosphorus as phosphate rock; and arsenic, antimony, and bismuth as sulfides or oxides. Antimony and bismuth are also found as free elements.
- range from very abundant elements (nitrogen and phosphorus) to relatively rare elements (arsenic, antimony, and bismuth)
- consist of atoms that contain five electrons in their outermost energy level
- tend to form covalent compounds, most commonly with oxidation numbers of +3 or +5
- exist in two or more allotropic forms, except nitrogen and bismuth
- are solids at room temperature, except nitrogen

| Atomic number | Symbol | Name | Atomic mass | Electron configuration |
|---|---|---|---|---|
| 7 | N | Nitrogen | 14.0067 | $[He]2s^22p^3$ |
| 15 | P | Phosphorus | 30.973 762 | $[Ne]3s^23p^3$ |
| 33 | As | Arsenic | 74.921 60 | $[Ar]3d^{10}4s^24p^3$ |
| 51 | Sb | Antimony | 121.760 | $[Kr]4d^{10}5s^25p^3$ |
| 83 | Bi | Bismuth | 208.980 40 | $[Xe]4f^{14}5d^{10}6s^26p^3$ |

Atomic radius increases

Ionic radius increases

Ionization energy decreases

Electronegativity decreases

*You can see the contrast in physical properties among the elements of this family. Arsenic, antimony, and bismuth are shown.*

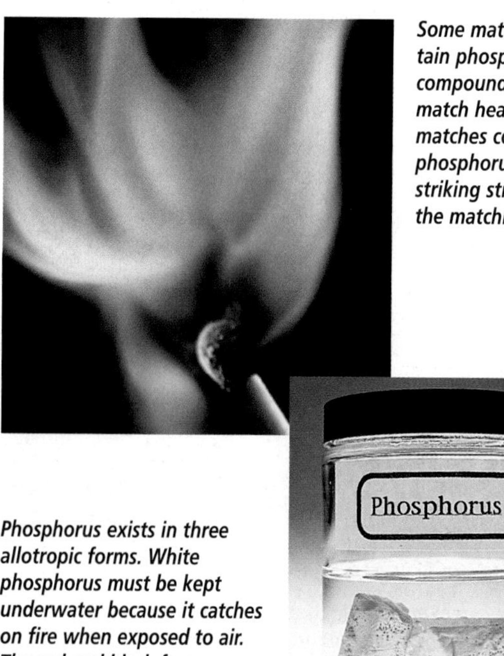


*Some matches contain phosphorus compounds in the match head. Safety matches contain phosphorus in the striking strip on the matchbox.*

*Phosphorus exists in three allotropic forms. White phosphorus must be kept underwater because it catches on fire when exposed to air. The red and black forms are stable in air.*

## COMMON REACTIONS

**With Oxygen to Form Oxides**

*Example:* $P_4(s) + 5O_2(g) \longrightarrow P_4O_{10}(s)$

As, Sb, and Bi follow this reaction pattern, but as monatomic elements. N reacts to form NO and $NO_2$. It also reacts as $N_2$ to form $N_2O_3$ and $N_2O_5$.

**With Metals to Form Binary Compounds**

*Example:* $3Mg(s) + N_2(g) \longrightarrow Mg_3N_2(s)$

## ANALYTICAL TEST

There are no simple analytical tests for the presence of nitrogen or phosphorus compounds in a sample. Antimony produces a pale green color in a flame test, and arsenic produces a light blue color. Arsenic, antimony, and bismuth are recognized in qualitative analyses by their characteristic sulfide colors.

*Formation of sulfides is the confirmatory qualitative analysis test for the presence of bismuth, antimony, and arsenic.*

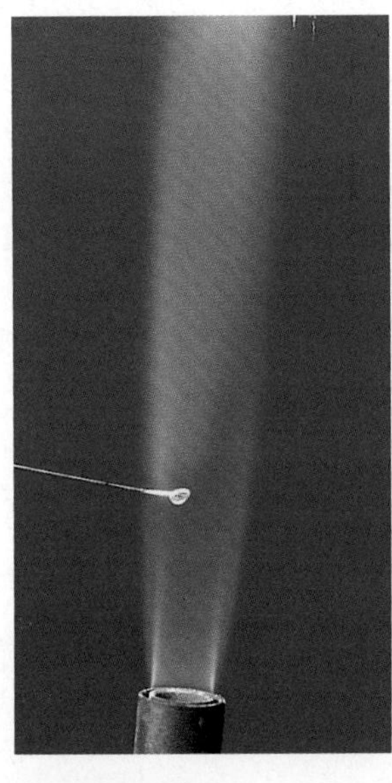

*Arsenic flame test*

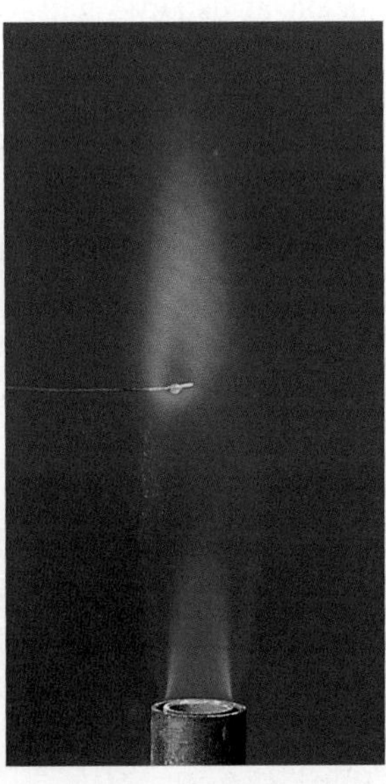

*Antimony flame test*

## PROPERTIES OF THE GROUP 15 ELEMENTS

| | N | P* | As | Sb | Bi |
|---|---|---|---|---|---|
| Melting point (°C) | –209.86 | 44.1 | 817 (28 atm) | 630.5 | 271.3 |
| Boiling point (°C) | –195.8 | 280 | 613 (sublimes) | 1750 | 1560 ± 5 |
| Density ($g/cm^3$) | $1.25 \times 10^{-3}$ | 1.82 | 5.727 | 6.684 | 9.80 |
| Ionization energy (kJ/mol) | 1402 | 1012 | 947 | 834 | 703 |
| Atomic radius (pm) | 75 | 110 | 120 | 140 | 150 |
| Ionic radius (pm) | 146 ($N^{3-}$) | 212 ($P^{3-}$) | — | 76 ($Sb^{3+}$) | 103 ($Bi^{3+}$) |
| Common oxidation number in compounds | –3, +3, +5 | –3, +3, +5 | +3, +5 | +3, +5 | +3 |
| Crystal structure† | cubic (as a solid) | cubic | rhombohedral | hcp | rhombohedral |
| Hardness (Mohs' scale) | none (gas) | — | 3.5 | 3.0 | 2.25 |

* Data given apply to white phosphorus.

† Crystal structures are for the most common allotropes.

APPLICATION **Biology**

## Plants and Nitrogen

All organisms, including plants, require certain elements to survive and grow. These elements include carbon, hydrogen, oxygen, nitrogen, phosphorus, potassium, sulfur, and several other elements needed in small amounts. An organism needs nitrogen to synthesize structural proteins, enzymes, and the nucleic acids DNA and RNA.

Carbon, hydrogen, and oxygen are available to plants from carbon dioxide in the air and from water in both the air and the soil. Nitrogen is necessary for plants' survival. Although nitrogen gas, $N_2$, makes up 78% of air, most plants cannot take nitrogen out of the air and incorporate it into their cells, because the strong triple covalent bond in $N_2$ is not easily broken. Plants need nitrogen in the form of a compound that they can take in and use. The process of using atmospheric $N_2$ to make $NH_3$ is called *nitrogen fixation*. Several kinds of nitrogen-fixing bacteria live in the soil and in the root nodules of plants called legumes. Legumes obtain the nitrogen they need through a symbiotic relationship with nitrogen-fixing bacteria. Legumes include peas, beans, clover, alfalfa, and locust trees. The bacteria convert nitrogen into ammonia, $NH_3$, which is then absorbed by the host plants.

Because wheat, rice, corn, and potatoes cannot perform the same feat as legumes, these plants depend on nitrogen-fixing bacteria in the soil. Soil bacteria convert $NH_3$ into nitrate ions, $NO_3^-$, the form of nitrogen that can be absorbed and used by plants. These plants also often need nitrogen fertilizers to supplement the work of the bacteria. Besides supplying nitrogen, fertilizers are manufactured to contain phosphorus, potassium, and trace minerals.

*Nitrogen-fixing bacteria,* Rhizobium, *live in these small nodules that grow on the roots of soybeans.*

*Soybeans are legumes that live in a symbiotic relationship with nitrogen-fixing bacteria.*

## APPLICATION Chemical Industry

### Fertilizers

Fertilizers can supply nitrogen to plants in the form of ammonium sulfate, ammonium nitrate, and urea, all of which are made from $NH_3$. Now you know why there is such a demand for ammonia. Though some soils contain sufficient concentrations of phosphorus and potassium, most soils need additional nitrogen for adequate plant growth. Ammonia, ammonium nitrate, or urea can fill that need.

Most fertilizers contain all three major plant nutrients N, P, and K, and are called *complete fertilizers.* A typical complete fertilizer might contain ammonium nitrate or sodium nitrate to provide nitrogen. Calcium dihydrogen phosphate, $Ca(H_2PO_4)_2$, or the anhydrous form of phosphoric acid, $P_4O_{10}$, can provide phosphorus. Potassium chloride, KCl, or potassium oxide, $K_2O$, can provide potassium.

The proportion of each major nutrient in a fertilizer is indicated by a set of three numbers printed on the container. These numbers are the N-P-K formula of the fertilizer and indicate the percentage of N, P, and K, respectively. A fertilizer graded as 6-12-6, for example, contains 6% nitrogen, 12% phosphorus, and 6% potassium by weight.

Nitrogen stimulates overall plant growth. Phosphorus promotes root growth and flowering. Potassium regulates the structures in leaves that allow $CO_2$ to enter the leaf and $O_2$ and $H_2O$ to exit. Fertilizers are available in N-P-K formulas best suited for their intended use. For example, plants that produce large amounts of carbohydrates (sugars) need more potassium than most other types of plants. Grain crops need higher concentrations of phosphorus. Lawn fertilizers applied in the spring are generally high in nitrogen to stimulate shoot growth in grasses. Lawn fertilizers applied in the fall of the year should have a higher phosphorus content to stimulate root growth during the winter.

**TABLE 6A Some Commercial Fertilizers and Uses**

| Fertilizer composition (N-P-K) | Uses |
|---|---|
| **1-2-1 ratio**<br>10-20-10 15-30-15 | early-spring application for trees and shrubs with flowers and fruit; general-purpose feedings of the following: cucumbers, peppers, tomatoes |
| **3-1-2 ratio**<br>12-4-8 15-5-10 21-7-4 16-4-8 20-5-10 | lawns and general-purpose feedings of the following: trees, shrubs, most berries, apple trees, grapes, vines, walnut trees, broccoli, cabbage, carrots, onions |
| **High nitrogen**<br>33-0-0 21-0-0 40-4-4 36-6-6 | pecan trees, lawns, early feedings of corn |
| **Balanced**<br>13-13-13 | general purpose feeding of the following: broccoli, cabbage, melons, potatoes |
| **Special purpose: acid-loving flowering shrubs**<br>12-10-4 | azaleas, rhododendrons, camellias, gardenias |
| **Special purpose**<br>18-24-16 | roses |
| **Special purpose: flowering**<br>12-55-6 | flowering plants and shrubs (annuals and perennials) |
| **Special purpose: root growth**<br>5-20-10 | starter fertilizer for transplants |

# GROUP 16
# OXYGEN FAMILY

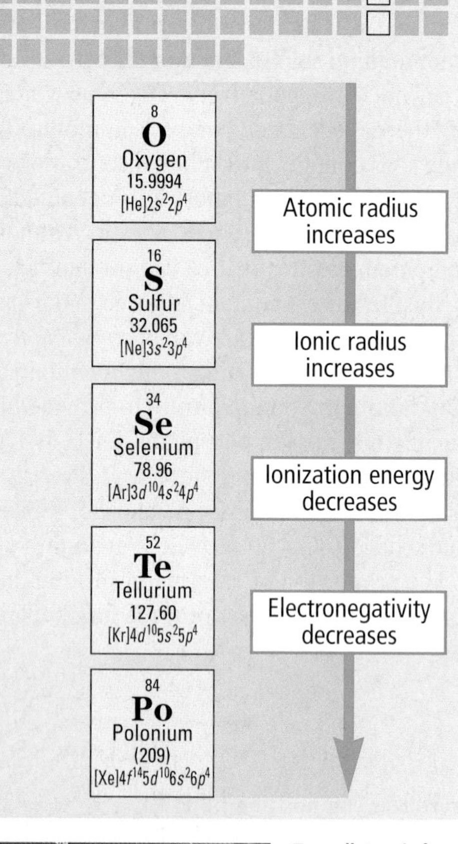


## CHARACTERISTICS

- occur naturally as free elements and in combined states
- consist of three nonmetals (oxygen, sulfur, and selenium), one metalloid (tellurium), and one metal (polonium)
- consist of atoms that have six electrons in their outermost energy level
- tend to form covalent compounds with other elements
- exist in several allotropic forms
- tend to exist as diatomic and polyatomic molecules, such as $O_2$, $O_3$, $S_6$, $S_8$, and $Se_8$
- commonly exist in compounds with the –2 oxidation state but often exhibit other oxidation states

*Sulfur is found naturally in underground deposits and in the steam vents near volcanoes.*

*Sulfur exists in combined forms in many minerals. Iron pyrite, $FeS_2$, black galena, PbS, and yellow orpiment, $As_2S_3$, are shown.*

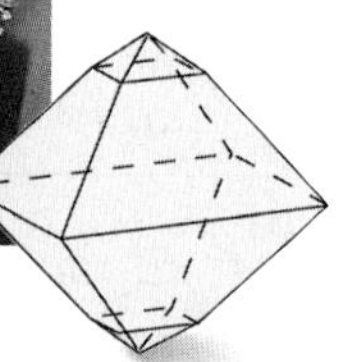

*Orthorhombic*

*Two allotropic forms of sulfur are orthorhombic and monoclinic. Each has a different crystal structure.*

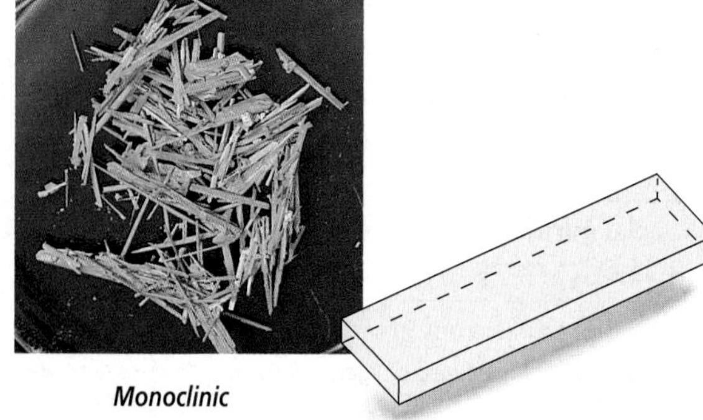

*Monoclinic*

## COMMON REACTIONS

**With Metals to Form Binary Compounds**
*Example:* $8Mg(s) + S_8(l) \longrightarrow 8MgS(s)$
$O_2$, Se, and Te follow this pattern in reacting with Na, K, Ca, Mg, and Al.

**With Oxygen to Form Oxides**
*Example:* $Se(s) + O_2(g) \longrightarrow SeO_2(s)$
S, Te, and Po follow this pattern. S, Se, and Te can form $SO_3$, $SeO_3$, and $TeO_3$.

**With Halogens to Form Binary Compounds**
*Example:* $S_8(l) + 8Cl_2(g) \longrightarrow 8SCl_2(l)$
O, Se, Te, and Po follow this pattern in reacting with $F_2$, $Cl_2$, $Br_2$, and $I_2$.

**With Hydrogen to Form Binary Compounds**
$2H_2(g) + O_2(g) \longrightarrow 2H_2O(l)$

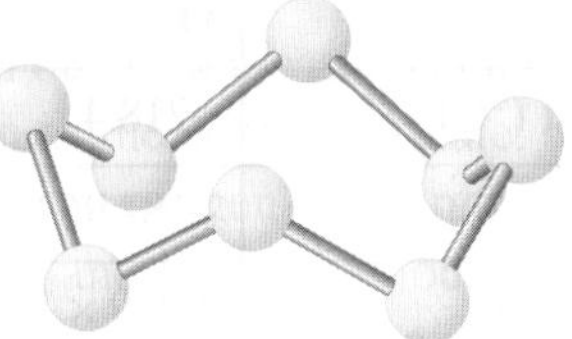

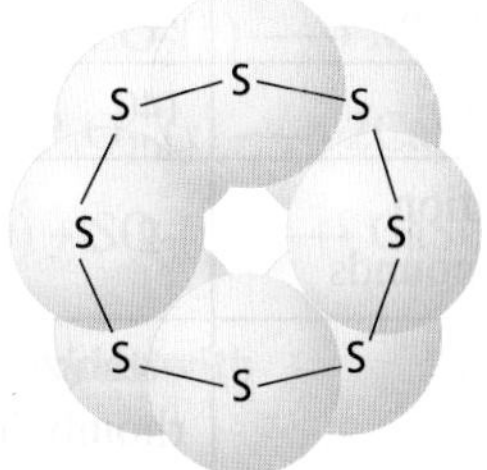


*Sulfur exists as $S_8$ molecules in which the atoms are bonded in a ring, as shown by the ball-and-stick and space-filling models.*

## ANALYTICAL TEST

There is no simple analytical test to identify all elements of this family. Selenium and tellurium can be identified by flame tests. A light blue flame is characteristic of selenium, and a green flame is characteristic of tellurium. Oxygen can be identified by the splint test, in which a glowing splint bursts into flame when thrust into oxygen. Elemental sulfur is typically identified by its physical characteristics, especially its color and its properties when heated. It melts to form a viscous brown liquid and burns with a blue flame.

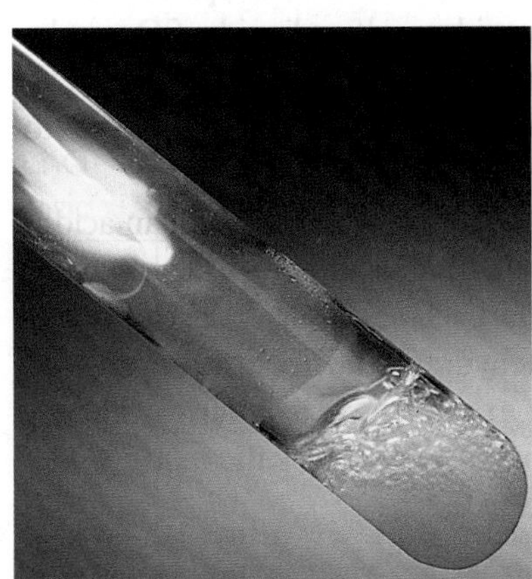

*A glowing splint thrust into oxygen bursts into a bright flame.*

*Sulfur burns with a characteristically deep blue flame.*

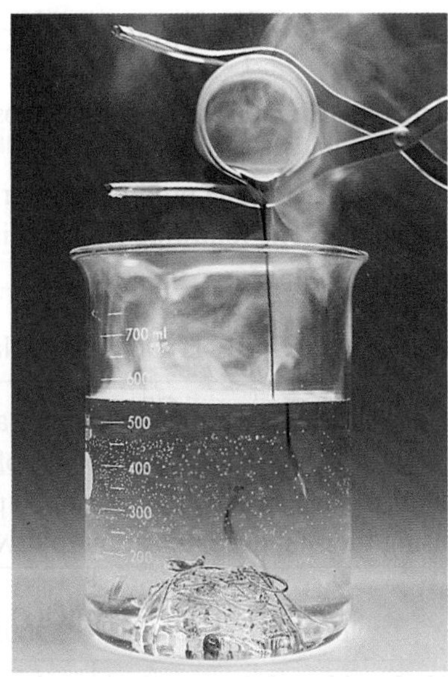


*Molten sulfur returns to its orthorhombic form upon cooling.*

## APPLICATION The Environment

### Ozone

Ozone, $O_3$, is an allotrope of oxygen that is important for life on Earth. Like $O_2$, $O_3$ is a gas at room temperature. However, unlike $O_2$, $O_3$ is a poisonous bluish gas with an irritating odor at high concentrations. The triatomic ozone molecule is angular (bent) with a bond angle of about 116.5°. The O—O bonds in ozone are shorter and stronger than a single bond, but longer and weaker than a double bond. The ozone molecule is best represented by two resonance hybrid structures.

$$:\ddot{O}\!=\!\ddot{O}\!-\!\ddot{O}: \longleftrightarrow :\ddot{O}\!-\!\ddot{O}\!=\!\ddot{O}:$$

Ozone forms naturally in Earth's atmosphere more than 24 km above the Earth's surface in a layer called the stratosphere. There, $O_2$ molecules absorb energy from ultraviolet light and split into free oxygen atoms.

$$O_2(g) \xrightarrow{\text{ultraviolet light}} 2O$$

A free oxygen atom has an unpaired electron and is highly reactive. A chemical species that has one or more unpaired or unshared electrons is referred to as a *free radical*. A free radical is a short-lived fragment of a molecule. The oxygen free radical can react with a molecule of $O_2$ to produce an ozone molecule.

$$O + O_2(g) \longrightarrow O_3(g)$$

A molecule of $O_3$ can then absorb ultraviolet light and split to produce $O_2$ and a free oxygen atom.

$$O_3(g) \xrightarrow{\text{ultraviolet light}} O_2(g) + O$$

The production and breakdown of ozone in the stratosphere are examples of *photochemical* processes, in which light causes a chemical reaction.

In this way, $O_3$ is constantly formed and destroyed in the stratosphere, and its concentration is determined by the balance among these reactions. The breakdown of ozone absorbs the sun's intense ultraviolet light in the range of wavelengths between 290 nm and 320 nm. Light of these wavelengths damages and kills living cells, so if these wavelengths were to reach Earth's surface in large amounts, life would be impossible. Even now, the normal amount of ultraviolet light reaching Earth's surface is a major cause of skin cancer and the damage to DNA molecules that causes mutations. One life-form that is very sensitive to ultraviolet radiation is the phytoplankton in the oceans. These organisms carry out photosynthesis and are the first level of oceanic food webs.

#### Ozone and Air Pollution

Ozone in the lower atmosphere is a harmful pollutant. Ozone is highly reactive and can oxidize organic compounds. The products of these reactions are harmful substances that, when mixed with air, water vapor, and dust, make up *photochemical smog*. This mixture is the smog typically found in cities.

Typically, ozone is produced in a complex series of reactions involving unburned hydrocarbons and nitrogen oxides given off from engines in the form of exhaust and from fuel-burning power plants. When fuel burns explosively in the cylinder of an internal-combustion engine, some of the nitrogen in the cylinder also combines with oxygen to form NO, a very reactive nitrogen oxide free radical.

$$N_2(g) + O_2(g) \longrightarrow 2NO$$

When the free radical reaches the air, it reacts with oxygen to produce $NO_2$ radicals, which react with water in the air to produce $HNO_3$.

$$2NO + O_2(g) \longrightarrow 2NO_2$$
$$3NO_2 + H_2O(l) \longrightarrow NO + 2HNO_3(aq)$$

In sunlight, nitrogen dioxide decomposes to give nitric oxide and an atom of oxygen. Note that the NO produced is free to undergo the previous reaction once more.

$$NO_2 \xrightarrow{\text{sunlight}} NO + O$$

Just as it is in the stratosphere, a free oxygen atom in the lower atmosphere is highly reactive and reacts with a molecule of diatomic oxygen to form ozone.

$$O + O_2(g) \longrightarrow O_3(g)$$

## APPLICATION Chemical Industry

### Sulfuric Acid

Sulfuric acid is the so-called "king of chemicals" because it is produced in the largest volume in the United States. It is produced by the contact process. This process starts with the production of $SO_2$ by burning sulfur or roasting iron pyrite, $FeS_2$. The purified sulfur dioxide is mixed with air and passed through hot iron pipes containing a catalyst. The contact between the catalyst, $SO_2$, and $O_2$ produces sulfur trioxide, $SO_3$, and gives the contact process its name. $SO_3$ is dissolved in concentrated $H_2SO_4$ to produce pyrosulfuric acid, $H_2S_2O_7$.

$$SO_3(g) + H_2SO_4(aq) \longrightarrow H_2S_2O_7(aq)$$

The pyrosulfuric acid is then diluted with water to produce sulfuric acid.

$$H_2S_2O_7(aq) + H_2O(l) \longrightarrow 2H_2SO_4(aq)$$

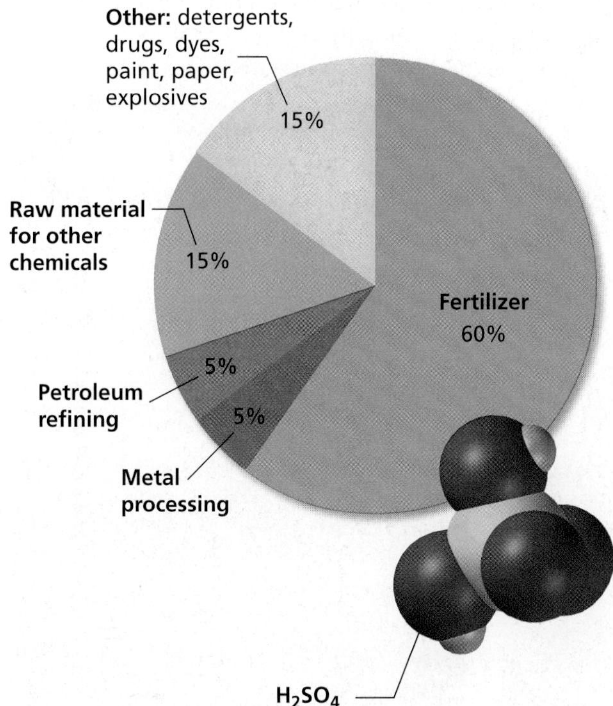


*Important uses of the U.S. supply of sulfuric acid*

**Properties and Uses of Sulfuric Acid**

Concentrated sulfuric acid is a good oxidizing agent. During the oxidation process, sulfur is reduced from +6 to +4 or −2. The change in oxidation state for a reaction depends on the concentration of the acid and on the nature of the reducing agent used in the reaction.

Sulfuric acid is also an important dehydrating agent. Gases that do not react with $H_2SO_4$ can be dried by being bubbled through concentrated sulfuric acid. Organic compounds, like sucrose, are dehydrated to leave carbon, as shown by the following reaction.

$$C_{12}H_{22}O_{11}(s) + 11H_2SO_4(aq) \longrightarrow 12C(s) + 11H_2SO_4{\cdot}H_2O(l)$$

The decomposition of sucrose proceeds rapidly, as shown in Figure 17 on page 737.

About 60% of the sulfuric acid produced in this country is used to make superphosphate, which is a mixture of phosphate compounds used in fertilizers.

**TABLE 7B Top Ten Chemicals Produced in the U.S.**

| Rank | Chemical | Physical state | Formula |
|---|---|---|---|
| 1 | sulfuric acid | *l* | $H_2SO_4$ |
| 2 | nitrogen | *g* | $N_2$ |
| 3 | oxygen | *g* | $O_2$ |
| 4 | ethylene | *g* | $C_2H_4$ |
| 5 | calcium oxide (lime) | *s* | CaO |
| 6 | ammonia | *g* | $NH_3$ |
| 7 | phosphoric acid | *l* | $H_3PO_4$ |
| 8 | sodium hydroxide | *s* | NaOH |
| 9 | propylene | *g* | $C_3H_6$ |
| 10 | chlorine | *g* | $Cl_2$ |

# GROUP 17
# HALOGEN FAMILY

## CHARACTERISTICS

- are all nonmetals and occur in combined form in nature, mainly as metal halides
- are found in the rocks of Earth's crust and dissolved in sea water
- range from fluorine, the 13th most abundant element, to astatine, which is one of the rarest elements
- exist at room temperature as a gas ($F_2$ and $Cl_2$), a liquid ($Br_2$), and a solid ($I_2$ and At)
- consist of atoms that have seven electrons in their outermost energy level
- tend to gain one electron to form a halide, $X^-$ ion, but also share electrons and have positive oxidation states
- are reactive, with fluorine being the most reactive of all nonmetals

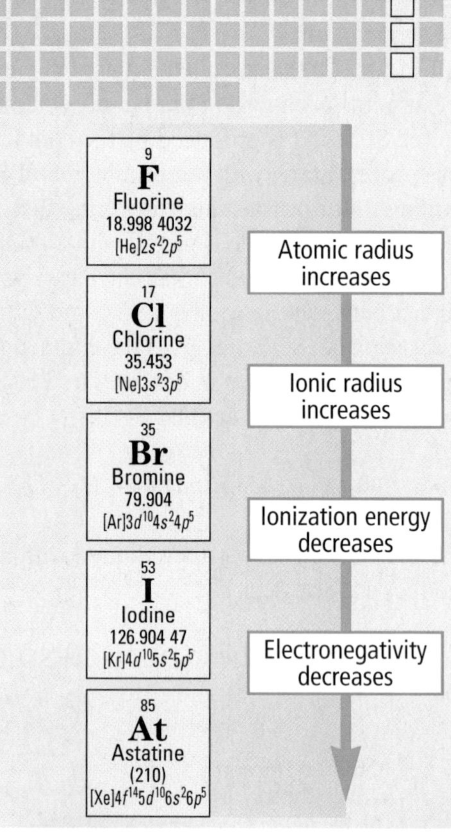

*Halogens are the only family that contains elements representing all three states of matter at room temperature. Chlorine is a yellowish green gas; bromine is a reddish brown liquid; and iodine is a purple-black solid.*

*Iodine sublimes to produce a violet vapor that recrystallizes on the bottom of the evaporating dish filled with ice.*

## COMMON REACTIONS*

**With Metals to Form Halides**

*Example:* $Mg(s) + Cl_2(g) \longrightarrow MgCl_2(s)$

*Example:* $Sn(s) + 2F_2(g) \longrightarrow SnF_4(s)$

The halide formula depends on the oxidation state of the metal.

**With Hydrogen to Form Hydrogen Halides**

*Example:* $H_2(g) + F_2(g) \rightarrow 2HF(g)$

$Cl_2$, $Br_2$, and $I_2$ also follow this pattern.

**With Nonmetals and Metalloids to Form Halides**

*Example:* $Si(s) + 2Cl_2(g) \longrightarrow SiCl_4(s)$

*Example:* $N_2(g) + 3F_2(g) \longrightarrow 2NF_3(g)$

*Example:* $P_4(s) + 6Br_2(l) \longrightarrow 4PBr_3(s)$

The formula of the halide depends on the oxidation state of the metalloid or nonmetal.

**With Other Halogens to Form Interhalogen Compounds**

*Example:* $Br_2(l) + 3F_2(g) \longrightarrow 2BrF_3(l)$

* Chemists assume that astatine undergoes similar reactions, but few chemical tests have been made.

***Chlorine combines readily with iron wool, which ignites in chlorine gas to form $FeCl_3$.***

***Hydrofluoric acid is used to etch patterns into glass.***

***Shown here from left to right are precipitates of AgCl, AgBr, and AgI.***

## ANALYTICAL TEST

As with most elements, the presence of each of the halogens can be determined by atomic absorption spectroscopy. Fluorides react with concentrated sulfuric acid, $H_2SO_4$, to release hydrogen fluoride gas. Three of the halide ions can be identified in solution by their reactions with silver nitrate.

$Cl^-(aq) + Ag^+(aq) \longrightarrow AgCl(s)$

$Br^-(aq) + Ag^+(aq) \longrightarrow AgBr(s)$

$I^-(aq) + Ag^+(aq) \longrightarrow AgI(s)$

## PROPERTIES OF THE GROUP 17 ELEMENTS

| | F | Cl | Br | I | At |
|---|---|---|---|---|---|
| Melting point (°C) | –219.62 | –100.98 | –7.2 | 113.5 | 302 |
| Boiling point (°C) | –188.14 | –34.6 | 58.78 | 184.35 | 337 |
| Density ($g/cm^3$) | $1.69 \times 10^{-3}$ | $3.214 \times 10^{-3}$ | 3.119 | 4.93 | not known |
| Ionization energy (kJ/mol) | 1681 | 1251 | 1140 | 1008 | — |
| Atomic radius (pm) | 72 | 100 | 114 | 133 | 140 |
| Ionic radius (pm) | 133 | 181 | 196 | 220 | — |
| Common oxidation number in compounds | –1 | –1, +1, +3, +5, +7 | –1, +1, +3, +5, +7 | –1, +1, +3, +5, +7 | –1, +5 |
| Crystal structure | cubic | orthorhombic | orthorhombic | orthorhombic | not known |

## APPLICATION *The Environment*

### Chlorine in Water Treatment

For more than a century, communities have treated their water to prevent disease. A treatment process widely used in the United States is chlorination. All halogens kill bacteria and other microorganisms. Chlorine, however, is the only halogen acceptable for large-scale treatment of public water supplies.

When chlorine is added to water, the following reaction produces HCl and hypochlorous acid, HOCl.

$$Cl_2(g) + H_2O(l) \longrightarrow HCl(aq) + HOCl(aq)$$

Hypochlorous acid is a weak acid that ionizes to give hydrogen ions and hypochlorite ions, $OCl^-$.

$$HOCl(aq) + H_2O(l) \longrightarrow H_3O^+(aq) + OCl^-(aq)$$

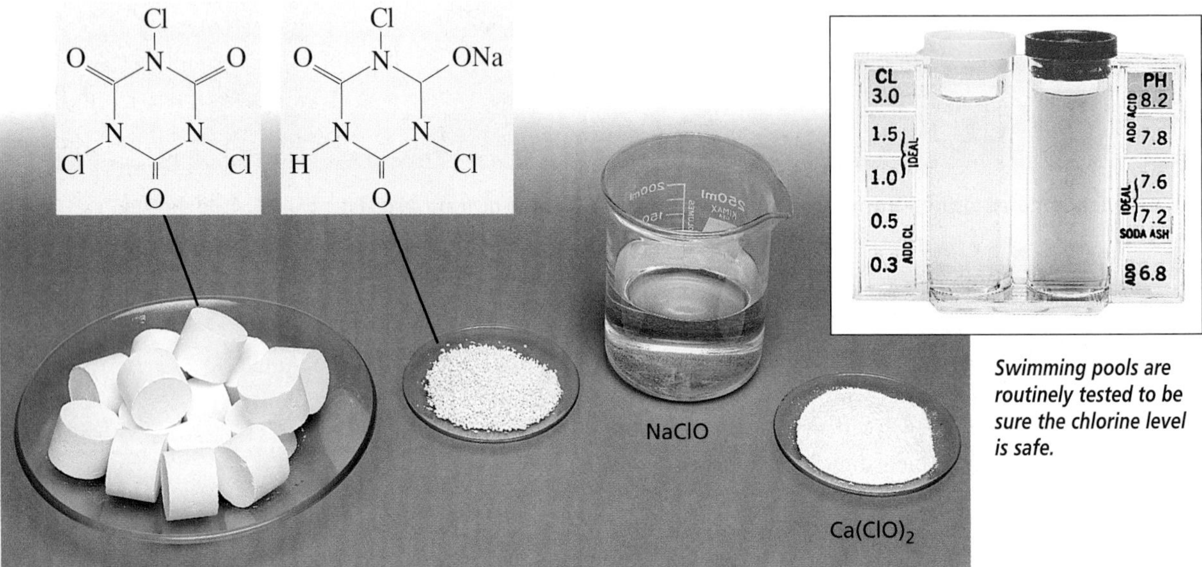


*Swimming pools are routinely tested to be sure the chlorine level is safe.*

*The "chlorine" used in swimming pools is really the compounds shown above and not chlorine at all.*

The $OCl^-$ ions are strong oxidizing agents that can destroy microorganisms.

In some water-treatment plants, calcium hypochlorite, $Ca(ClO)_2$, a salt of hypochlorous acid, is added to water to provide $OCl^-$ ions. Similar treatments are used in swimming pools.

Nearly a hundred cities in the United States and thousands of communities in Europe use chlorine in the form of chlorine dioxide, $ClO_2$, as their primary means of disinfecting water. The main drawback to the use of $ClO_2$ is that it is unstable and cannot be stored. Instead, $ClO_2$ must be prepared on location by one of the following reactions involving sodium chlorite, $NaClO_2$.

$$10NaClO_2(aq) + 5H_2SO_4(aq) \longrightarrow 8ClO_2(g) + 5Na_2SO_4(aq) + 2HCl(aq) + 4H_2O(l)$$

$$2NaClO_2(aq) + Cl_2(g) \longrightarrow 2ClO_2(g) + 2NaCl(aq)$$

The expense of using $ClO_2$ makes it less desirable than $Cl_2$ in water-treatment systems unless there are other considerations. For example, the use of $ClO_2$ is likely to result in purified water with less of the aftertaste and odor associated with water purified by $Cl_2$.

## Fluoride and Tooth Decay

In the 1940s, scientists noticed that people living in communities that have natural water supplies with high concentrations of fluoride ions, $F^-$, have significantly lower rates of dental caries (tooth decay) than most of the population.

In June 1944, a study on the effects of water fluoridation began in two Michigan cities, Muskegon and Grand Rapids, where the natural level of fluoride in drinking water was low (about 0.05 ppm). In Grand Rapids, sodium fluoride, NaF, was added to the drinking water to raise levels to 1.0 ppm. In Muskegon, no fluoride was added. Also included in the study was Aurora, Illinois, a city that was similar to Grand Rapids and Muskegon, except that it had a natural $F^-$ concentration of 1.2 ppm in the water supply. After 10 years, the rate of tooth decay in Grand Rapids had dropped far below that in Muskegon and was about the same as it was in Aurora.

Tooth enamel is made of a strong, rocklike material consisting mostly of calcium hydroxyphosphate, $Ca_5(PO_4)_3(OH)$, also known as apatite. Apatite is an insoluble and very hard compound—ideal for tooth enamel. Sometimes, however, saliva becomes more acidic, particularly after a person eats a high-sugar meal. Acids ionize to produce hydronium ions, which react with the hydroxide ion, $OH^-$, in the apatite to form water. The loss of $OH^-$ causes the apatite to dissolve.

$$Ca_5(PO_4)_3(OH)(s) + H_3O^+(aq) \longrightarrow 5Ca^{2+}(aq) + 3PO_4^{3-}(aq) + 2H_2O(l)$$

Saliva supplies more $OH^-$ ions, and new apatite is formed, but slowly.

If fluoride ions are present in saliva, some fluorapatite, $Ca_5(PO_4)_3F$, also forms.

$$5Ca^{2+}(aq) + 3PO_4^{3-}(aq) + F^-(aq) \longrightarrow Ca_5(PO_4)_3F(s)$$

Fluorapatite resists attack by acids, so the tooth enamel resists decay better than enamel containing no fluoride.

When the beneficial effect of fluoride had been established, public health authorities proposed that fluoride compounds be added to water supplies in low-fluoride communities. Fluoridation started in the 1950s, and by 1965, nearly every medical and dental association in the United States had endorsed fluoridation of water supplies. In the past decade, however, that trend slowed as opposition to fluoridation grew.

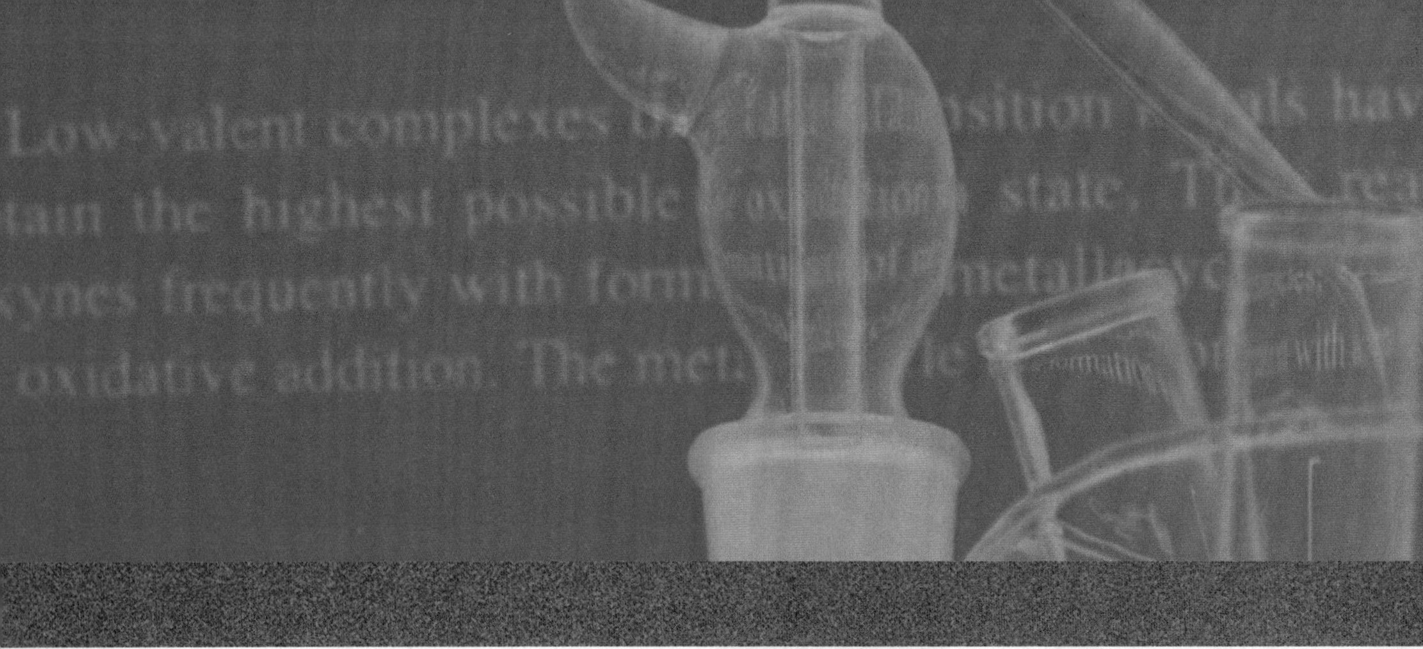

# *Preparing for Chemistry Lab*

Performing experiments in the chemistry laboratory provides you with the opportunity to learn important lab techniques and observe interesting chemical reactions. Taking the time to prepare for your lab activity will help ensure that you understand the procedures you are to follow and that your experiment runs smoothly and safely. You can prepare for each lab activity by reviewing the lab preparation tips below.

- Read the experiment thoroughly, and familiarize yourself with what you will do at each step in the procedure. If there is any part of the experiment that you do not understand, ask your teacher before you start the experiment.
- Do any assigned pre-lab exercises. These will generally cover any calculations or important observations that you will make.
- Prepare data tables ahead of time. If you have the data table ready before you begin, you will be able to record your observations as they happen, in the appropriate spaces.
- Review the materials list for the experiment. Make sure that you have all the items you need to perform the experiment. If you are missing any items or if any items are broken or unusable, let your teacher know before you begin the lab.
- Review all safety guidelines and safety icons at the beginning of each experiment. Read "Safety in the Chemistry Laboratory" in the front of your book for a complete explanation of the safety rules that you should follow in the lab.
- Know where the emergency eyewash station, safety shower, and fire extinguisher are located, and be sure you know how to use them. If you cannot locate the lab safety equipment or you do not know how to use any equipment, ask your teacher for help.
- Know the proper disposal procedures for the experiment. Your teacher will tell you what to do with any substances that need to be disposed of.

# Pre-Laboratory Procedures

The Pre-Laboratory Procedures help you develop solid laboratory skills before you do an actual experiment.

# Volumetric Analysis

**Volumetric analysis, the quantitative determination of the concentration of a solution, is achieved by adding a substance of known concentration to a substance of unknown concentration until the reaction between them is complete. The most common application of volumetric analysis is titration.**

**A buret is used in titrations. The solution with the known concentration is usually in the buret. The solution with the unknown concentration is usually in the Erlenmeyer flask. A few drops of a visual indicator are also added to the flask. The solution in the buret is then added to the flask until the indicator changes color, which signals that the reaction between the two solutions is complete. Then, the volumetric data obtained and the balanced chemical equation for the reaction are used to calculate the unknown concentration.**

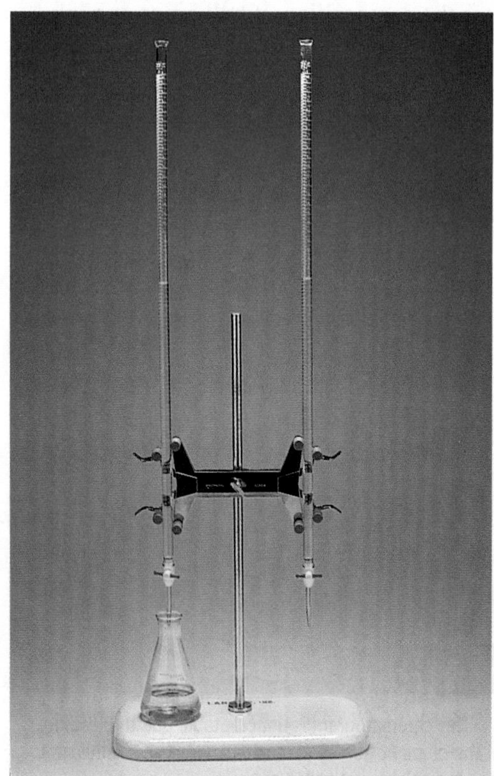

FIGURE A

## GENERAL SAFETY

Always wear safety goggles and a lab apron to protect your eyes and clothing. If you get a chemical in your eyes, immediately flush the chemical out at the eyewash station while calling to your teacher. Know the location of the emergency lab shower and eyewash station and the procedure for using them.

The general setup for a titration is shown in Figure A. The steps for setting up this technique follow.

## ASSEMBLING THE APPARATUS

1. Attach a buret clamp to a ring stand.
2. Thoroughly wash and rinse a buret. If water droplets cling to the walls of the buret, wash it again and gently scrub the inside walls with a buret brush.
3. Attach the buret to one side of the buret clamp.
4. Place an Erlenmeyer flask for waste solutions under the buret tip, as shown in Figure A.

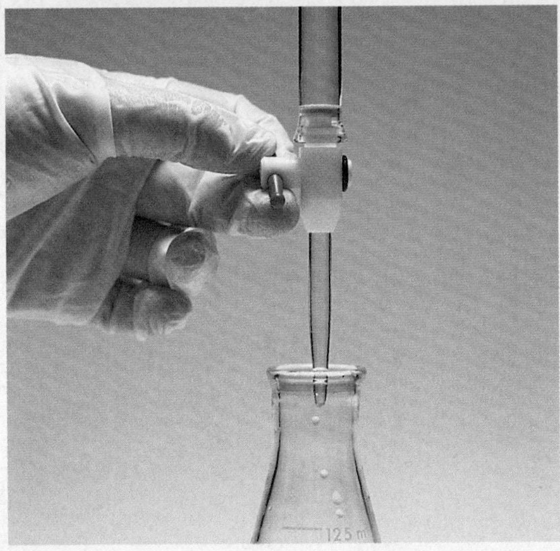

FIGURE B

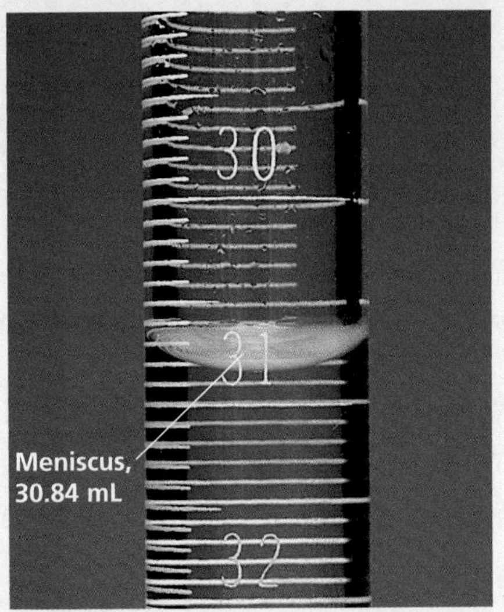


FIGURE C

## OPERATING THE STOPCOCK

1. The stopcock should be operated with the left hand. This method gives better control but may prove awkward at first for right-handed students. The handle should be moved with the thumb and first two fingers of the left hand, as shown in Figure B.

2. Rotate the stopcock back and forth. It should move freely and easily. If it sticks or will not move, ask your teacher for assistance. Turn the stopcock to the closed position. Use a wash bottle to add 10 mL of distilled water to the buret. Rotate the stopcock to the open position. The water should come out in a steady stream. If no water comes out or if the stream of water is blocked, ask your teacher to check the stopcock for clogs.

## FILLING THE BURET

1. To fill the buret, place a funnel in the top of the buret. Slowly and carefully pour the solution of known concentration from a beaker into the funnel. Open the stopcock, and allow some of the solution to drain into the waste beaker. Then, add enough solution to the buret to raise the level above the zero mark, but do not allow the solution to overflow.

## READING THE BURET

1. Drain the buret until the bottom of the meniscus is on the zero mark or within the calibrated portion of the buret. If the solution level is not at zero, record the exact reading. If you start from the zero mark, your final buret reading will equal the amount of solution added. Remember, burets can be read to the second decimal place. Burets are designed to read the volume of liquid delivered to the flask, so numbers increase as you read downward from the top. For example, the meniscus in Figure C is at 30.84 mL, not 31.16 mL.

2. Replace the waste beaker with an Erlenmeyer flask containing a measured amount of the solution of unknown concentration.

Experiment 15 is an example of a back-titration applied to an acid-base reaction; it can be performed on a larger scale if micropipets are replaced with burets.

PRE-LABORATORY PROCEDURE

# Calorimetry

**Calorimetry, the measurement of the transfer of energy as heat, allows chemists to determine thermal constants, such as the specific heat of metals and the enthalpy of solution.**

**When two substances at different temperatures touch one another, energy as heat flows from the warmer substance to the cooler substance until the two substances are at the same temperature. The amount of energy transferred is measured in joules. (One joule equals 4.184 calories.)**

**A device used to measure the transfer of energy as heat is a calorimeter. Calorimeters vary in construction depending on the purpose and the accuracy of the energy measurement required. No calorimeter is a perfect insulator; some energy is always lost to the surroundings as heat. Therefore, every calorimeter must be calibrated to obtain its calorimeter constant.**

## GENERAL SAFETY

Always wear safety goggles and a lab apron to protect your eyes and clothing. If you get a chemical in your eyes, immediately flush the chemical out at the eyewash station while calling to your teacher. Know the location of the emergency lab shower and eyewash station and the procedure for using them.

Turn off hot plates and other heat sources when not in use. Do not touch a hot plate after it has just been turned off; it is probably hotter than you think. Use tongs when handling heated containers. Never hold or touch containers with your hands while heating them.

The general setup for a calorimeter made from plastic-foam cups is shown in Figure A. The steps for constructing this setup follow.

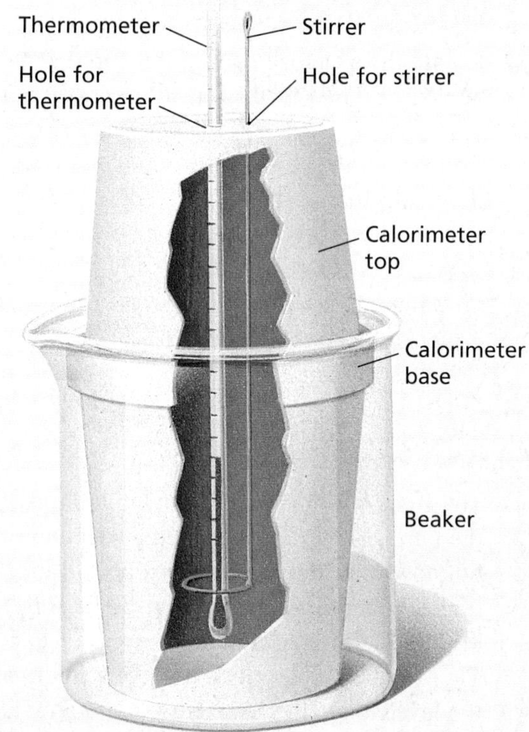


**FIGURE A** Position the hole for the stirrer so that the thermometer is in the center of the wire ring.

## CONSTRUCTING THE CALORIMETER

1. Trim the lip of one plastic-foam cup, and use that cup as the top of your calorimeter. The other cup will be used as the base.
2. Use the pointed end of a pencil to gently make a hole in the center of the calorimeter top. The hole should be large enough to insert a thermometer. Make a hole for the wire stirrer. As you can see in Figure A, this hole should be positioned so that the wire stirrer can be raised and lowered without interfering with the thermometer.
3. Place the calorimeter in a beaker to prevent it from tipping over.

## CALIBRATING A PLASTIC-FOAM CUP CALORIMETER

1. Measure 50 mL of distilled water in a graduated cylinder. Pour it into the calorimeter. Measure and record the temperature of the water in the plastic-foam cup.
2. Pour another 50 mL of distilled water into a beaker. Set the beaker on a hot plate, and warm the water to about 60°C, as shown in Figure B. Measure and record the temperature of the water.
3. Immediately pour the warm water into the cup, as shown in Figure C. Cover the cup, and move the stirrer gently up and down to mix the contents thoroughly. **Take care not to break the thermometer.**

**FIGURE B** Heat the distilled water to approximately 60°C.

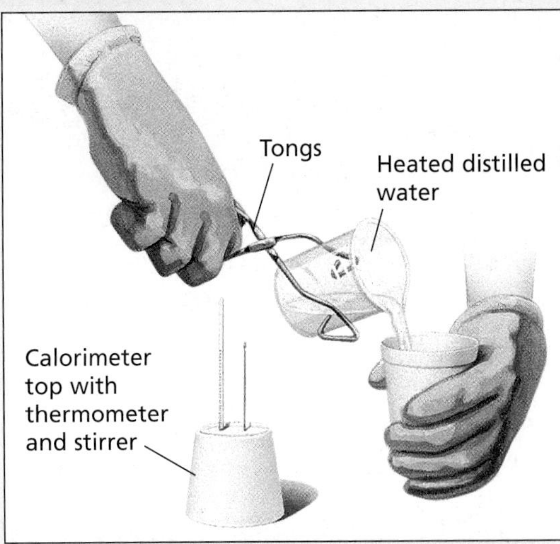


**FIGURE C** When transferring warm water from the beaker to the calorimeter, hold the bottom of the calorimeter steady so it does not tip over.

4. Watch the thermometer, and record the highest temperature attained (usually after about 30 s).
5. Empty the calorimeter.
6. The derivation of the equation to find the calorimeter constant starts with the following relationship.

   *Energy lost by the warm water = Energy gained by the cool water + Energy gained by the calorimeter*

   $$q_{warm\ H_2O} = q_{cool\ H_2O} + q_{calorimeter}$$

   The energy lost as heat by the warm water is calculated by the following equation.

   $$q_{warm\ H_2O} = mass_{warm\ H_2O} \times 4.184\ \text{J/g}{\bullet}{}^\circ\text{C} \times \Delta t$$

   The energy gained as heat by the calorimeter system equals the energy lost as heat by the warm water. You can use the following equation to calculate the calorimeter constant C′ for your calorimeter.

   $$q_{calorimeter} = q_{warm\ H_2O} = (mass_{cool\ H_2O})(4.184\ \text{J/g}{\bullet}{}^\circ\text{C})(\Delta t_{cool\ H_2O}) + C'(\Delta t_{cool\ H_2O})$$

   Substitute the data from your calibration, and solve for C′.

## TABLE A-1 SI MEASUREMENT

### Metric Prefixes

| Prefix | Symbol | Factor of Base Unit |
|---|---|---|
| **giga** | G | 1 000 000 000 |
| **mega** | M | 1 000 000 |
| **kilo** | k | 1 000 |
| **hecto** | h | 100 |
| **deka** | da | 10 |
| **deci** | d | 0.1 |
| **centi** | c | 0.01 |
| **milli** | m | 0.001 |
| **micro** | μ | 0.000 001 |
| **nano** | n | 0.000 000 001 |
| **pico** | p | 0.000 000 000 001 |

### Mass

| | |
|---|---|
| **1 kilogram (kg)** | = SI base unit of mass |
| **1 gram (g)** | = 0.001 kg |
| **1 milligram (mg)** | = 0.000 001 kg |
| **1 microgram (μg)** | = 0.000 000 001 kg |

### Length

| | |
|---|---|
| **1 kilometer (km)** | = 1 000 m |
| **1 meter (m)** | = SI base unit of length |
| **1 centimeter (cm)** | = 0.01 m |
| **1 millimeter (mm)** | = 0.001 m |
| **1 micrometer (μm)** | = 0.000 001 m |
| **1 nanometer (nm)** | = 0.000 000 001 m |
| **1 picometer (pm)** | = 0.000 000 000 001 m |

### Area

| | |
|---|---|
| **1 square kilometer (km$^2$)** | = 100 hectares (ha) |
| **1 hectare (ha)** | = 10 000 square meters (m$^2$) |
| **1 square meter (m$^2$)** | = 10 000 square centimeters (cm$^2$) |
| **1 square centimeter (cm$^2$)** | = 100 square millimeters (mm$^2$) |

### Volume

| | |
|---|---|
| **1 liter (L)** | = common unit for liquid volume (not SI) |
| **1 cubic meter (m$^3$)** | = 1000 L |
| **1 kiloliter (kL)** | = 1000 L |
| **1 milliliter (mL)** | = 0.001 L |
| **1 milliliter (mL)** | = 1 cubic centimeter (cm$^3$) |

## TABLE A-2 UNIT SYMBOLS

| | | |
|---|---|---|
| **amu** | = | atomic mass unit (mass) |
| **atm** | = | atmosphere (pressure, non-SI) |
| **Bq** | = | becquerel (nuclear activity) |
| **°C** | = | degree Celsius (temperature) |
| **J** | = | joule (energy) |
| **K** | = | kelvin (temperature, thermodynamic) |
| **mol** | = | mole (quantity) |
| **M** | = | molarity (concentration) |
| **N** | = | newton (force) |
| **Pa** | = | pascal (pressure) |
| **s** | = | second (time) |
| **V** | = | volt (electric potential difference) |

## TABLE A-3 SYMBOLS

| Symbol | | Meaning |
|---|---|---|
| $\alpha$ | = | helium nucleus (also ${}^{4}_{2}He$) emission from radioactive materials |
| $\beta$ | = | electron (also ${}^{0}_{-1}e$) emission from radioactive materials |
| $\gamma$ | = | high-energy photon emission from radioactive materials |
| $\Delta$ | = | change in a given quantity (e.g., $\Delta H$ for change in enthalpy) |
| $c$ | = | speed of light in vacuum |
| $c_p$ | = | specific heat capacity (at constant pressure) |
| $D$ | = | density |
| $E_a$ | = | activation energy |
| $E^0$ | = | standard electrode potential |
| $E^0$ cell | = | standard potential of an electrochemical cell |
| $G$ | = | Gibbs free energy |
| $\Delta G^0$ | = | standard free energy of reaction |
| $\Delta G^0{}_f$ | = | standard molar free energy of formation |
| $H$ | = | enthalpy |
| $\Delta H^0$ | = | standard enthalpy of reaction |
| $\Delta H^0{}_f$ | = | standard molar enthalpy of formation |
| $K_a$ | = | ionization constant (acid) |
| $K_b$ | = | dissociation constant (base) |
| $K_{eq}$ | = | equilibrium constant |
| $K_{sp}$ | = | solubility-product constant |
| $KE$ | = | kinetic energy |
| $m$ | = | mass |
| $N_A$ | = | Avogadro's number |
| $n$ | = | number of moles |
| $P$ | = | pressure |
| pH | = | measure of acidity ($-\log[H_3O^+]$) |
| $R$ | = | ideal gas law constant |
| $S$ | = | entropy |
| $S^0$ | = | standard molar entropy |
| $T$ | = | temperature (thermodynamic, in kelvins) |
| $t$ | = | temperature (± degrees Celsius) |
| $V$ | = | volume |
| $v$ | = | velocity |

## TABLE A-4 PHYSICAL CONSTANTS

| Quantity | Symbol | Value |
|---|---|---|
| **Atomic mass unit** | amu | $1.660\ 5389 \times 10^{-27}$ kg |
| **Avogadro's number** | $N_A$ | $6.022\ 142 \times 10^{23}$/mol |
| **Electron rest mass** | $m_e$ | $9.109\ 3826 \times 10^{-31}$ kg<br>$5.4858 \times 10^{-4}$ amu |
| **Ideal gas law constant** | $R$ | 8.314 L • kPa/(mol • K)<br>0.0821 L • atm/(mol • K) |
| **Molar volume of ideal gas at STP** | $V_M$ | 22.414 10 L/mol |
| **Neutron rest mass** | $m_n$ | $1.674\ 9273 \times 10^{-27}$ kg<br>1.008 665 amu |
| **Normal boiling point of water** | $T_b$ | 373.15 K = 100.0°C |
| **Normal freezing point of water** | $T_f$ | 273.15 K = 0.00°C |
| **Planck's constant** | $h$ | $6.626\ 069 \times 10^{-34}$ J • s |
| **Proton rest mass** | $m_p$ | $1.672\ 6217 \times 10^{-27}$ kg<br>1.007 276 amu |
| **Speed of light in a vacuum** | $c$ | $2.997\ 924\ 58 \times 10^{8}$ m/s |
| **Temperature of triple point of water** | | 273.16 K = 0.01°C |

## TABLE A-5 ENTHALPY OF COMBUSTION

| Substance | Formula | State | $\Delta H_c$ |
|---|---|---|---|
| **hydrogen** | $H_2$ | *g* | –285.8 |
| **graphite** | C | *s* | –393.5 |
| **carbon monoxide** | CO | *g* | –283.0 |
| **methane** | $CH_4$ | *g* | –890.8 |
| **ethane** | $C_2H_6$ | *g* | –1560.7 |
| **propane** | $C_3H_8$ | *g* | –2219.2 |
| **butane** | $C_4H_{10}$ | *g* | –2877.6 |
| **pentane** | $C_5H_{12}$ | *g* | –3535.6 |
| **hexane** | $C_6H_{14}$ | *l* | –4163.2 |
| **heptane** | $C_7H_{16}$ | *l* | –4817.0 |
| **octane** | $C_8H_{18}$ | *l* | –5470.5 |
| **ethene (ethylene)** | $C_2H_4$ | *g* | –1411.2 |
| **propene (propylene)** | $C_3H_6$ | *g* | –2058.0 |
| **ethyne (acetylene)** | $C_2H_2$ | *g* | –1301.1 |
| **benzene** | $C_6H_6$ | *l* | –3267.6 |
| **toluene** | $C_7H_8$ | *l* | –3910.3 |
| **naphthalene** | $C_{10}H_8$ | *s* | –5156.3 |
| **anthracene** | $C_{14}H_{10}$ | *s* | –7163.0 |
| **methanol** | $CH_3OH$ | *l* | –726.1 |
| **ethanol** | $C_2H_5OH$ | *l* | –1366.8 |
| **ether** | $(C_2H_5)_2O$ | *l* | –2751.1 |
| **formaldehyde** | $CH_2O$ | *g* | –570.7 |
| **glucose** | $C_6H_{12}O_6$ | *s* | –2803.0 |
| **sucrose** | $C_{12}H_{22}O_{11}$ | *s* | –5640.9 |

$\Delta H_c$ = enthalpy of combustion of the given substance. All values of $\Delta H_c$ are expressed as kJ/mol of substance oxidized to $H_2O(l)$ and/or $CO_2(g)$ at constant pressure and 25°C.
*s* = solid, *l* = liquid, *g* = gas

## TABLE A-6 THE ELEMENTS—SYMBOLS, ATOMIC NUMBERS, AND ATOMIC MASSES

| Name of element | Symbol | Atomic number | Atomic mass |
|---|---|---|---|
| **actinium** | Ac | 89 | [227] |
| **aluminum** | Al | 13 | 26.9815386 |
| **americium** | Am | 95 | [243] |
| **antimony** | Sb | 51 | 121.760 |
| **argon** | Ar | 18 | 39.948 |
| **arsenic** | As | 33 | 74.92160 |
| **astatine** | At | 85 | [210] |
| **barium** | Ba | 56 | 137.327 |
| **berkelium** | Bk | 97 | [247] |
| **beryllium** | Be | 4 | 9.012182 |
| **bismuth** | Bi | 83 | 208.98040 |
| **bohrium** | Bh | 107 | [264] |
| **boron** | B | 5 | 10.811 |
| **bromine** | Br | 35 | 79.904 |
| **cadmium** | Cd | 48 | 112.411 |
| **calcium** | Ca | 20 | 40.078 |
| **californium** | Cf | 98 | [251] |
| **carbon** | C | 6 | 12.0107 |
| **cerium** | Ce | 58 | 140.116 |
| **cesium** | Cs | 55 | 132.9054519 |
| **chlorine** | Cl | 17 | 35.453 |
| **chromium** | Cr | 24 | 51.9961 |
| **cobalt** | Co | 27 | 58.933195 |
| **copper** | Cu | 29 | 63.546 |
| **curium** | Cm | 96 | [247] |
| **darmstadtium** | Ds | 110 | [271] |
| **dubnium** | Db | 105 | [262] |
| **dysprosium** | Dy | 66 | 162.500 |
| **einsteinium** | Es | 99 | [252] |
| **erbium** | Er | 68 | 167.259 |
| **europium** | Eu | 63 | 151.964 |
| **fermium** | Fm | 100 | [257] |
| **fluorine** | F | 9 | 18.9984032 |
| **francium** | Fr | 87 | [223] |
| **gadolinium** | Gd | 64 | 157.25 |
| **gallium** | Ga | 31 | 69.723 |
| **germanium** | Ge | 32 | 72.64 |
| **gold** | Au | 79 | 196.966569 |
| **hafnium** | Hf | 72 | 178.49 |
| **hassium** | Hs | 108 | [277] |
| **helium** | He | 2 | 4.00260 |
| **holmium** | Ho | 67 | 164.93032 |
| **hydrogen** | H | 1 | 1.00794 |
| **indium** | In | 49 | 114.818 |
| **iodine** | I | 53 | 126.90447 |
| **iridium** | Ir | 77 | 192.217 |

## TABLE A-6 CONTINUED

| Name of element | Symbol | Atomic number | Atomic mass |
|---|---|---|---|
| **iron** | Fe | 26 | 55.845 |
| **krypton** | Kr | 36 | 83.798 |
| **lanthanum** | La | 57 | 138.90547 |
| **lawrencium** | Lr | 103 | [262] |
| **lead** | Pb | 82 | 207.2 |
| **lithium** | Li | 3 | 6.941 |
| **lutetium** | Lu | 71 | 174.967 |
| **magnesium** | Mg | 12 | 24.3050 |
| **manganese** | Mn | 25 | 54.938045 |
| **meitnerium** | Mt | 109 | [268] |
| **mendelevium** | Md | 101 | [258] |
| **mercury** | Hg | 80 | 200.59 |
| **molybdenum** | Mo | 42 | 95.94 |
| **neodymium** | Nd | 60 | 144.242 |
| **neon** | Ne | 10 | 20.1797 |
| **neptunium** | Np | 93 | [237] |
| **nickel** | Ni | 28 | 58.6934 |
| **niobium** | Nb | 41 | 92.90638 |
| **nitrogen** | N | 7 | 14.0067 |
| **nobelium** | No | 102 | [259] |
| **osmium** | Os | 76 | 190.23 |
| **oxygen** | O | 8 | 15.9994 |
| **palladium** | Pd | 46 | 106.42 |
| **phosphorus** | P | 15 | 30.973762 |
| **platinum** | Pt | 78 | 195.084 |
| **plutonium** | Pu | 94 | [244] |
| **polonium** | Po | 84 | [209] |
| **potassium** | K | 19 | 39.0983 |
| **praseodymium** | Pr | 59 | 140.90765 |
| **promethium** | Pm | 61 | [145] |
| **protactinium** | Pa | 91 | 231.03588 |
| **radium** | Ra | 88 | [226] |
| **radon** | Rn | 86 | [222] |
| **rhenium** | Re | 75 | 186.207 |
| **rhodium** | Rh | 45 | 102.90550 |
| **roentgenium** | Rg | 111 | [272] |
| **rubidium** | Rb | 37 | 85.4678 |
| **ruthenium** | Ru | 44 | 101.07 |
| **rutherfordium** | Rf | 104 | [261] |
| **samarium** | Sm | 62 | 150.36 |
| **scandium** | Sc | 21 | 44.955912 |
| **seaborgium** | Sg | 106 | [266] |
| **selenium** | Se | 34 | 78.96 |
| **silicon** | Si | 14 | 28.0855 |
| **silver** | Ag | 47 | 107.8682 |
| **sodium** | Na | 11 | 22.98976928 |
| **strontium** | Sr | 38 | 87.62 |
| **sulfur** | S | 16 | 32.065 |
| **tantalum** | Ta | 73 | 180.94788 |
| **technetium** | Tc | 43 | [98] |
| **tellurium** | Te | 52 | 127.60 |
| **terbium** | Tb | 65 | 158.92535 |
| **thallium** | Tl | 81 | 204.3833 |
| **thorium** | Th | 90 | 232.03806 |
| **thulium** | Tm | 69 | 168.93421 |
| **tin** | Sn | 50 | 118.710 |
| **titanium** | Ti | 22 | 47.867 |
| **tungsten** | W | 74 | 183.84 |
| **uranium** | U | 92 | 238.02891 |
| **vanadium** | V | 23 | 50.9415 |
| **xenon** | Xe | 54 | 131.293 |
| **ytterbium** | Yb | 70 | 173.04 |
| **yttrium** | Y | 39 | 88.90585 |
| **zinc** | Zn | 30 | 65.409 |
| **zirconium** | Zr | 40 | 91.224 |

A value given in brackets denotes the mass number of the most stable or most common isotope. The atomic masses of most of these elements are believed to have an error no greater than ±1 in the last digit given.

# Study Skills for Chemistry Table of Contents

# Study Skills for Chemistry

## Succeeding in Your Chemistry Class

Your success in this course will depend on your ability to apply some basic study skills to learning the material. Studying chemistry can be difficult, but you can make it easier using simple strategies for dealing with the concepts and problems. Becoming skilled in using these strategies will be your keys to success in this and many other courses.

### ▶ Reading the Text

- **Read the assigned material before class** so that the class lecture makes sense. Use a dictionary to help you build and interpret vocabulary. Remember that, while reading, one of your tasks is to figure out what information is important.

  Working together with others using Paired Reading and Discussion strategies can help you decide what is important and clarify the material. (For more discussion, see Other Reading Strategies on page 876.)
- **Select a quiet setting** away from distractions so that you can concentrate on what you are reading.
- **Have a pencil and paper nearby to jot down notes and questions** you may have. Be sure to get these questions answered in class. Power Notes (see page 871) can help you organize the notes you take and prepare you for class.
- **Use the Objectives in the beginning of each section as a list of what you need to know from the section.** Teachers generally make their tests based on the text objectives or their own objectives. Using the objectives to focus your reading can make your learning more efficient.

  Using the K/W/L strategy (see page 874) can help you relate new material to what you already know and what you need to learn.

### ▶ Taking Notes in Class

- **Be prepared to take notes during class.** Have your materials organized in a notebook. Separate sheets of paper can be easily lost.
- **Don't write down everything your teacher says.** Try to tell which parts of the lecture are important and which are not. Reading the text before class will help in this. You will not be able to write down everything, so you must try to write down only the important things.
- **Recopying notes later is a waste of time** and does not help you learn material for a test. Do

it right the first time. Organize your notes as you are writing them down so that you can make sense of your notes when you review them without needing to recopy them.

## ▶ Reviewing Class Notes

- **Review your notes as soon as possible after class.** Write down any questions you may have about the material covered that day. Be sure to get these questions answered during the next class. You can work with friends to use strategies such as Paired Summarizing and L.I.N.K. (See page 878.)
- **Do not wait until the test to review.** By then you will have forgotten a good portion of the material.
- **Be selective about what you memorize.** You cannot memorize everything in a chapter. First of all, it is too time consuming. Second, memorizing and understanding are not the same thing. Memorizing topics as they appear in your notes or text does not guarantee that you will be able to correctly answer questions that require understanding of those topics. You should only memorize material that you understand. Concept Maps and other Reading Organizers, Sequencing/Pattern Puzzles, and Prediction Guides can help you understand key ideas and major concepts. (See pages 868, 875, and 877.)

## ▶ Working Problems

In addition to understanding the concepts, the ability to solve problems will be a key to your success in chemistry. You will probably spend a lot of time working problems in class and at home. The ability to solve chemistry problems is a skill, and like any skill, it requires practice.

- **Always review the Sample Problems in the chapter.** The Sample Problems in the text provide road maps for solving certain types of problems. Cover the solution while trying to work the problem yourself.
- **The problems in the Chapter Review are similar to the Sample Problems.** If you can relate an assigned problem to one of the Sample Problems in the chapter, it shows that you understand the material.
- **The four steps: Analyze, Plan, Compute, and Evaluate should be the steps you go through when working assigned problems.** These steps will allow you to organize your thoughts and help you develop your problem-solving skills.
- **Never spend more than 15 minutes trying to solve a problem.** If you have not been able to come up with a plan for the solution after 15 minutes, additional time spent will only cause you to become frustrated. What do you do? Get help! See your teacher or a classmate. Find out what it is that you do not understand.
- **Do not try to memorize the Sample Problems; spend your time trying to understand how the solution develops.** Memorizing a particular sample problem will not ensure that you understand it well enough to solve a similar problem.
- **Always look at your answer and ask yourself if it is reasonable and makes sense.** Check to be sure you have the correct units and numbers of significant figures.

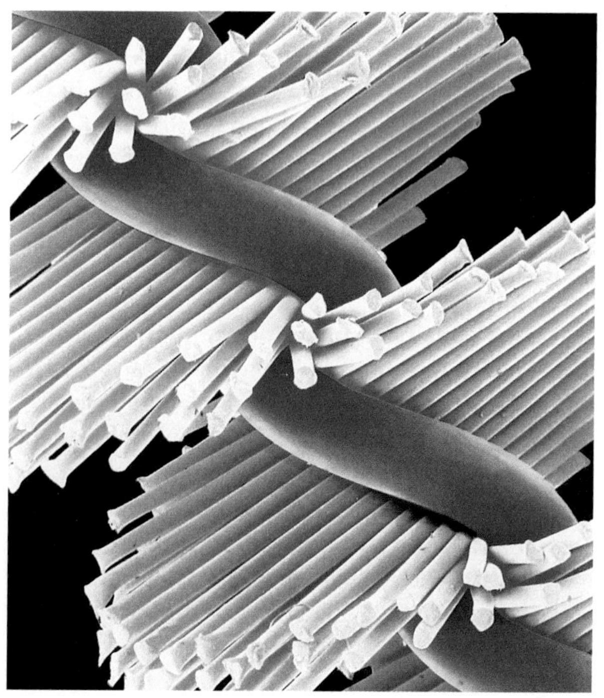

## ▶ Completing Homework

Your teacher will probably assign questions and problems from the Section Reviews and Chapter Reviews or assign *Modern Chemistry* Daily Homework. The purpose of these assignments is to review what you have covered in class and to see if you can use the information to answer questions or solve problems. As in reviewing class notes, do your homework as soon after class as possible while the topics are still fresh in your mind. Do not wait until late at night, when you are more likely to be tired and to become frustrated.

## ▶ Preparing for and Taking Exams

### Reviewing for an exam

- **Don't panic and don't cram! It takes longer to learn if you are under pressure.** If you have followed the strategies listed here and reviewed along the way, studying for the exam should be less stressful.
- **When looking over your notes and concept maps, recite ideas out loud.** There are two reasons for reciting:
  1. You are hearing the information, which is effective in helping you learn.
  2. If you cannot recite the ideas, it should be a clue that you do not understand the material, and you should begin rereading or reviewing the material again.
- **Studying with a friend provides a good opportunity for recitation.** If you can explain ideas to your study partner, you know the material.

### Taking an exam

- **Get plenty of rest before the exam so that you can think clearly.** If you have been awake all night studying, you are less likely to succeed than if you had gotten a full night of rest.
- **Start with the questions you know.** If you get stuck on a question, save it for later. As time passes and you work through the exam, you may recall the information you need to answer a difficult question or solve a difficult problem.

Good luck!

## Making Concept Maps

Making concept maps can help you decide what material in a chapter is important and how to efficiently learn that material. A concept map presents key ideas, meanings, and relationships for the concepts being studied. It can be thought of as a visual road map of the chapter. Learning happens efficiently when you use concept maps because you work with only the key ideas and how they fit together.

The concept map shown as **Map A** was made from vocabulary terms in Chapter 1. Vocabulary terms are generally labels for concepts, and concepts are generally nouns. In a concept map, linking words are used to form propositions that connect concepts and give them meaning in context. For example, on the map below, "matter is described by physical properties" is a proposition.

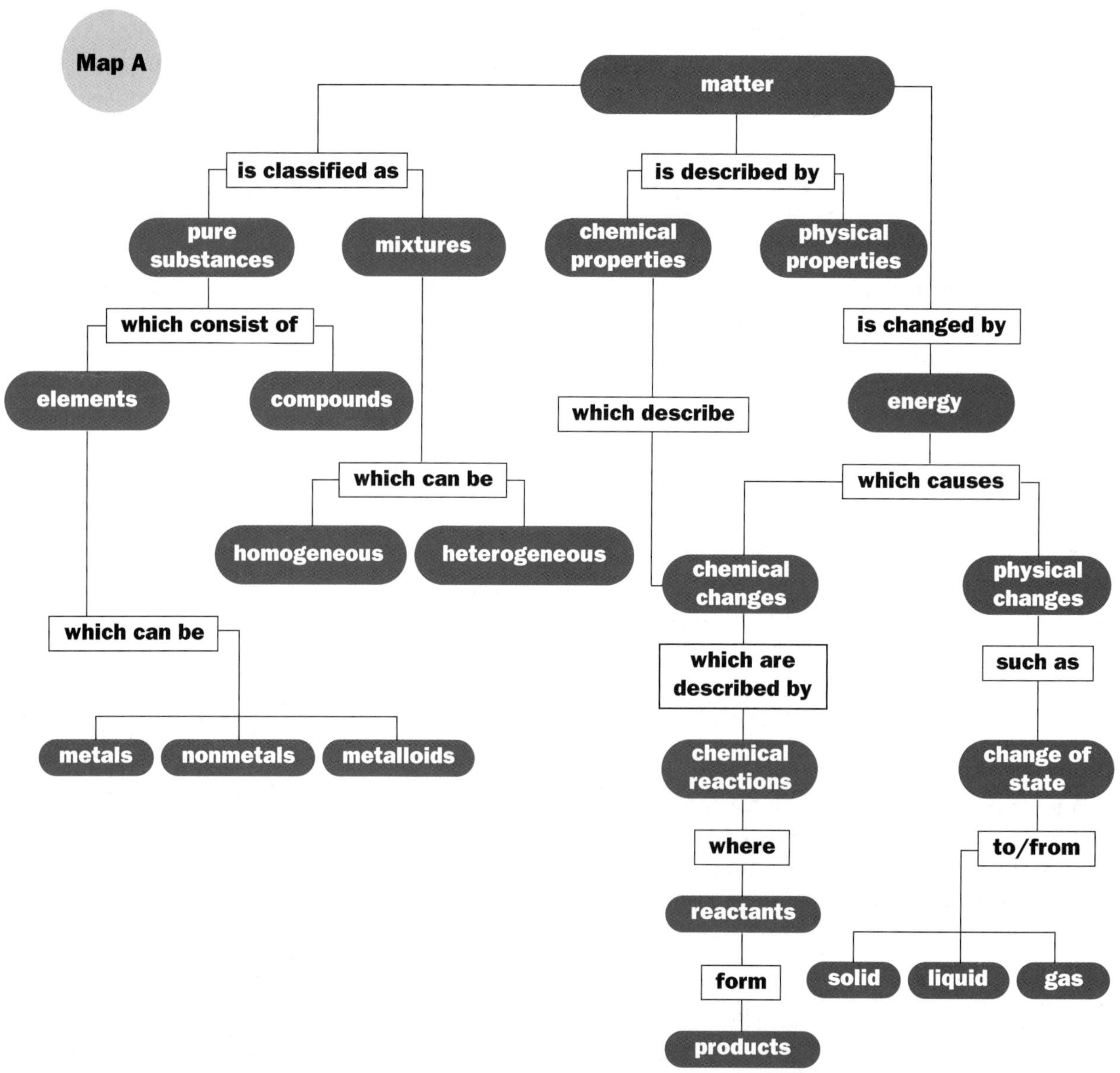

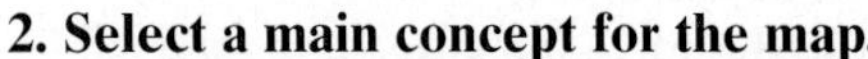

Studies show that people are better able to remember materials presented visually. A concept map is better than an outline because you can see the relationships among many ideas. Because outlines are linear, there is no way of linking the ideas from various sections of the outline. Read through the map to become familiar with the information presented. Then look at the map in relation to all of the text pages in Chapter 1; which gives a better picture of the important concepts—the map or the full chapter?

## ▶ To Make a Concept Map

**1. List all the important concepts.**
We'll use some of the boldfaced and italicized terms from Chapter 1, Section 2.

| | |
|---|---|
| matter | mixture |
| compound | pure substance |
| element | |
| homogenous mixture | |
| heterogeneous mixture | |

- From this list, group similar concepts together. For example, one way to group these concepts would be into two groups—one that is related to mixtures and one that is related to pure substances.

| | |
|---|---|
| *mixture* | *pure substance* |
| heterogeneous mixture | compound |
| homogeneous mixture | element |

**2. Select a main concept for the map.**
We will use *matter* as the main concept for this map.

**3. Build the map by placing the concepts according to their importance under the main concept, *matter.***
One way of arranging the concepts is shown in **Map B.**

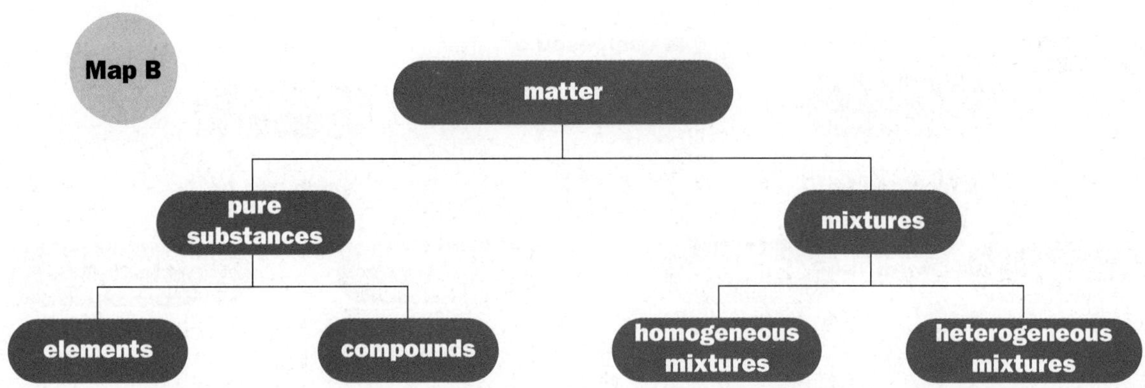

**4. Add linking words to give meaning to the arrangement of concepts.**

When adding the links, be sure that each proposition makes sense. To distinguish concepts from links, place your concepts in circles, ovals, or rectangles, as shown in the maps. Then make cross-links. Cross-links are made of propositions and lines connecting concepts across the map. Links that apply in only one direction are indicated with an arrowhead. **Map C** is a finished map covering the main ideas listed in Step 1.

Making maps might seem difficult at first, but the process forces you to think about the meanings and relationships among the concepts. If you do not understand those relationships, you can get help early on.

Practice mapping by making concept maps about topics you know. For example, if you know a lot about a particular sport, such as basketball, or if you have a particular hobby, such as playing a musical instrument, you can use that topic to make a practice map. By perfecting your skills with information that you know very well, you will begin to feel more confident about making maps from the information in a chapter.

Remember, the time you devote to mapping will pay off when it is time to review for an exam.

**Practice**

**1.** Classify each of the following as either a concept or linking word(s).

**a.** classification ______

**b.** is classified as ______

**c.** forms ______

**d.** is described by ______

**e.** reaction ______

**f.** reacts with ______

**g.** metal ______

**h.** defines ______

**2.** Write three propositions from the information in **Map A.** ______

______

______

______

**3.** List two cross-links shown on **Map C.**

______

______

______

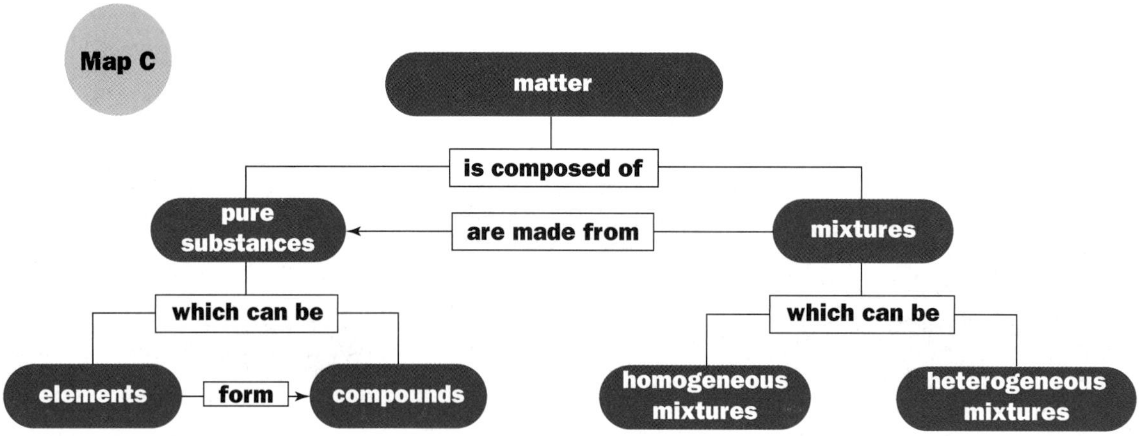

Map C

matter

is composed of

pure substances

are made from

mixtures

which can be

elements

form

compounds

which can be

homogeneous mixtures

heterogeneous mixtures

## Making Power Notes

Power notes help you organize the chemical concepts you are studying by distinguishing main ideas from details. Similar to outlines, power notes are linear in form and provide you with a framework of important concepts. Power notes are easier to use than outlines because their structure is simpler. Using the power notes numbering system you assign a *1* to each main idea and a *2, 3,* or *4* to each detail.

Power notes are an invaluable asset to the learning process, and they can be used frequently throughout your chemistry course. You can use power notes to organize ideas while reading your text or to restructure your class notes for studying purposes.

To learn to make power notes, practice first by using single-word concepts and a subject you are especially interested in, such as animals, sports, or movies. As you become comfortable with structuring power notes, integrate their use into your study of chemistry. For an easier transition, start with a few boldfaced or italicized terms. Later you can strengthen your notes by expanding these single-word concepts into more-detailed phrases and sentences. Use the following general format to help you structure your power notes.

**Power 1: Main idea**
**Power 2: Detail or support for power 1**
**Power 3: Detail or support for power 2**
**Power 4: Detail or support for power 3**

1. **Pick a Power 1 word from the text.**
   The text you choose does not have to come straight from your chemistry textbook. You may be making power notes from your lecture notes or from an outside source. We'll use the term *atom* found in Chapter 3, Section 2 of your textbook.

   **Power 1: Atom**

2. **Using the text, select some Power 2 words to support your Power 1 word.**
   We'll use the terms *nucleus* and *electrons,* which are two parts of an atom.

   **Power 1: Atom**
   **Power 2: Nucleus**
   **Power 2: Electrons**

3. **Select some Power 3 words to support your Power 2 words.**
   We'll use the terms *positively charged* and *negatively charged,* two terms that describe the Power 2 words.

   **Power 1: Atom**
   **Power 2: Nucleus**
   **Power 3: Positively charged**
   **Power 2: Electrons**
   **Power 3: Negatively charged**

**4. Continue to add powers to support and detail the main idea as necessary.**
There are no restrictions on how many power numbers you can use in your notes. If you have a main idea that requires a lot of support, add more powers to help you extend and organize your ideas. Be sure that words having the same power number have a similar relationship to the power above. Power 1 terms do not have to be related to each other. You can use power notes to organize the material in an entire section or chapter of your text. Doing so will provide you with an invaluable study guide for your classroom quizzes and tests.

**Power 1:** Atom
  **Power 2:** Nucleus
    **Power 3:** Positively charged
    **Power 3:** Protons
      **Power 4:** Positively charged
    **Power 3:** Neutrons
      **Power 4:** No charge
  **Power 2:** Electrons
    **Power 3:** Negatively charged

**Practice**

**1.** Use a periodic table and the power notes structure below to organize the following terms: *alkaline-earth metals, nonmetals, calcium, sodium, halogens, metals, alkali metals, chlorine, barium,* and *iodine.*

1 ______________________________
  2 ____________________________
    3 __________________________
  2 ____________________________
    3 __________________________
    3 __________________________
1 ______________________________
  2 ____________________________
    3 __________________________
    3 __________________________

## Making Two-Column Notes

Two-column notes can be used to learn and review definitions of vocabulary terms, examples of multiple-step processes, or details of specific concepts. The two-column-note strategy is simple: write the term, main idea, step-by-step process, or concept in the left-hand column, and the definition, example, or detail on the right.

One strategy for using two-column notes is to organize main ideas and their details. The main ideas from your reading are written in the left-hand column of your paper and can be written as questions, key words, or a combination of both. Details describing these main ideas are then written in the right-hand column of your paper.

1. **Identify the main ideas.** The main ideas for a chapter are listed in the section objectives. However, you decide which ideas to include in your notes. For example, the table below shows some main ideas from the objectives in Chapter 5, Section 2.
   - Describe the locations in the periodic table and the general properties of the alkali metals, alkaline-earth metals, the halogens, and the noble gases.
2. **Divide a blank sheet of paper into two columns and write the main ideas in the left-hand column.** Summarize your ideas using quick phrases that are easy for you to understand and remember. Decide how many details you need for each main idea, and write that number in parentheses under the main idea.
3. **Write the detail notes in the right-hand column.** Be sure you list as many details as you designated in the main-idea column. The table below shows some details that correspond to the main ideas in Chapter 5, Section 2.

The two-column method of review is perfect whether you use it to study for a short quiz or for a test on the material in an entire chapter. Just cover the information in the right-hand column with a sheet of paper, and after reciting what you know, uncover the notes to check your answers. Then ask yourself what else you know about that topic. Linking ideas in this way will help you to gain a more complete picture of chemistry.

| Main Idea | Detail Notes |
|---|---|
| • Alkali metals<br>(4 details) | • Group 1<br>• highly reactive<br>• $ns^1$ electron configuration<br>• soft, silvery |
| • Alkaline-earth metals<br>(4 details) | • Group 2<br>• reactive<br>• $ns^2$ electron configuration<br>• harder than alkali metals |
| • Halogens (3 details) | • Group 17<br>• reactive<br>• nonmetallic |
| • Noble gases (3 details) | • Group 18<br>• low reactivity<br>• stable $ns^2np^6$ configuration |

## Using the K/W/L Strategy

The K/W/L strategy stands for "what I **K**now—what I **W**ant to know—what I **L**earned." You start by brainstorming about the subject matter before reading the assigned material. Relating new ideas and concepts to those you have learned previously will help you better understand and apply the new knowledge you obtain. The section objectives throughout your textbook are ideal for using the K/W/L strategy.

1. **Read the section objectives.** You may also want to scan headings, boldfaced terms, and illustrations before reading. Here are two of the objectives from Chapter 1, Section 2 to use as an example.
   - Explain the gas, liquid, and solid states in terms of particles.
   - Distinguish between a mixture and a pure substance.
2. **Divide a sheet of paper into three columns, and label the columns "What I Know," "What I Want to Know," and "What I Learned."**
3. **Brainstorm about what you know about the information in the objectives, and write these ideas in the first column.** Because this chart is designed primarily to help you integrate your own knowledge with new information, it is not necessary to write complete sentences.
4. **Think about what you want to know about the information in the objectives, and write these ideas in the second column.** Include information from both the section objectives and any other objectives your teacher has given you.
5. **While reading the section or afterwards, use the third column to write down the information you learned.** While reading, pay close attention to any information about the topics you wrote in the "What I Want to Know" column. If you do not find all of the answers you are looking for, you may need to reread the section or reference a second source. Be sure to ask your teacher if you still cannot find the information after reading the section a second time.

It is also important to review your brainstormed ideas when you have completed reading the section. Compare your ideas in the first column with the information you wrote down in the third column. If you find that some of your brainstormed ideas are incorrect, cross them out. It is extremely important to identify and correct any misconceptions you had prior to reading before you begin studying for your test.

| What I Know | What I Want to Know | What I Learned |
|---|---|---|
| • gas has no definite shape or volume<br>• liquid has no definite shape, but has definite volume<br>• solid has definite shape and volume<br>• mixture is combination of substances<br>• pure substance has only one component | • how gas, liquid, and solid states are related to particles<br>• how mixtures and pure substances are different | • molecules in solid and liquid states are close together, but are far apart in gas state<br>• molecules in solid state have fixed positions, but molecules in liquid and gas states can flow<br>• mixtures are combinations of pure substances<br>• pure substances have fixed compositions and definite properties |

## Using Sequencing/Pattern Puzzles

You can use pattern puzzles to help you remember sequential information. Pattern puzzles are not just a tool for memorization. They also promote a greater understanding of a variety of chemical processes, from the steps in solving a mass-mass stoichiometry problem to the procedure for making a solution of specified molarity.

1. **Write down the steps of a process in your own words.** For an example, we will use the process for converting the amount of a substance in moles to mass in grams. (See Sample Problem B on page 84.) On a sheet of notebook paper, write down one step per line, and do not number the steps. Also, do not copy the process straight from your textbook.

   Writing the steps in your own words promotes a more thorough understanding of the process. You may want to divide longer steps into two or three shorter steps.

- List the given and unknown information.
- Look at the periodic table to determine the molar mass of the substance.
- Write the correct conversion factor to convert moles to grams.
- Multiply the amount of substance by the conversion factor.
- Solve the equation and check your answer.

2. **Cut the sheet of paper into strips with only one step per strip of paper.** Shuffle the strips of paper so that they are out of sequence.

- Look at the periodic table to determine the molar mass of the substance.
- Solve the equation and check your answer.
- List the given and unknown information.
- Multiply the amount of substance by the conversion factor.
- Write the correct conversion factor to convert moles to grams.

3. **Place the strips in their proper sequence.** Confirm the order of the process by checking your text or your class notes.

- List the given and unknown information.
- Look at the periodic table to determine the molar mass of the substance.
- Write the correct conversion factor to convert moles to grams.
- Multiply the amount of substance by the conversion factor.
- Solve the equation and check your answer.

Pattern puzzles are especially helpful when you are studying for your chemistry tests. Before tests, use your puzzles to practice sequencing and to review the steps of chemistry processes. You and a classmate can also take turns creating your own pattern puzzles of different chemical processes and putting each other's puzzles in the correct sequence. Studying with a classmate in this manner will help make studying fun and will enable you to help each other.

## Other Reading Strategies

### ▶ Brainstorming

Brainstorming is a strategy that helps you recognize and evaluate the knowledge you already have before you start reading. It works well individually or in groups. When you brainstorm, you start with a central term or idea, then quickly list all the words, phrases, and other ideas that you think are related to it.

Because there are no "right" or "wrong" answers, you can use the list as a basis for classifying terms, developing a general explanation, or speculating about new relationships. For example, you might brainstorm a list of terms related to the word *element* before you read Chapter 1, Section 2. The list might include gold, metals, chemicals, silver, carbon, oxygen, and water. As you read the textbook, you might decide that some of the terms you listed are *not* elements. Later, you might use that information to help you distinguish between elements and compounds.

### ▶ Building/Interpreting Vocabulary

Using a dictionary to look up the meanings of prefixes and suffixes as well as word origins and meanings helps you build your vocabulary and interpret what you read. If you know the meaning of prefixes like *kilo-* (one thousand) and *milli-* (one thousandth), you have a good idea what kilograms, kilometers, milligrams, and millimeters are and how they are different. (See page 35 for a list of SI Prefixes.)

Knowledge of prefixes, suffixes, and word origins can help you understand the meaning of new words. For example, if you know the suffix *-protic* comes from the same word as *proton,* it will help you understand what monoprotic and polyprotic acids are (see page 479).

### ▶ Reading Hints

Reading hints help you identify and bookmark important charts, tables, and illustrations for easy reference. For example, you may want to use a self-adhesive note to bookmark the periodic table on pages 140–141 or on the inside back cover of your book so you can easily locate it and use it for reference as you study different aspects of chemistry and solve problems involving elements and compounds.

### ▶ Interpreting Graphic Sources of Information

Charts, tables, photographs, diagrams, and other illustrations are graphic, or visual, sources of information. The labels and captions, together with the illustrations help you make connections between the words and the ideas presented in the text.

### ▶ Reading Response Logs

Keeping a reading response log helps you interpret what you read and gives you a chance to express your reactions and opinions about what you have read. Draw a vertical line down the center of a piece of paper. In the left-hand column, write down or make notes about passages you read to which you have reactions, thoughts, feelings, questions, or associations. In the right-hand column, write what those reactions, thoughts, feelings, questions, or associations are. For example, you might keep a reading response log when studying about Nuclear Energy in Chapter 21.

## Other Studying Strategies

### ▶ Comparing and Contrasting

Comparing and contrasting is a strategy that helps you note similarities and differences between two or more objects or events. When you determine similarities, you are comparing. When you determine differences, you are contrasting.

You can use comparing and contrasting to help you classify objects or properties, differentiate between similar concepts, and speculate about new relationships. For example, as you read Chapter 1 you might begin to make a table in which you compare and contrast metals, nonmetals, and metalloids. As you continue to learn about these substances in Chapters 4 and 5, you can add to your table, giving you a better understanding of the similarities and differences among elements.

### ▶ Identifying Cause and Effect

Identifying causes and effects as you read helps you understand the material and builds logical reasoning skills. An effect is an event or the result of some action. A cause is the reason the event or action occurred. Signal words, such as *because, so, since, therefore, as a result,* and *depends on,* indicate a cause-and-effect relationship.

You can use arrows to show cause and effect. For example, you might write this cause-and-effect relationship as you read Chapter 11, Section 2: At constant pressure, increase in temperature (cause) $\rightarrow$ increase in gas volume (effect).

### ▶ Making a Prediction Guide

A prediction guide is a list of statements about which you express and try to justify your opinions based on your current knowledge. After reading the material, you re-evaluate your opinion in light of what you learned. Using prediction guides helps you evaluate your knowledge, identify assumptions you may have that could lead to mistaken conclusions, and form an idea of expected results.

1. **Read the statements your teacher writes on the board.** For example, look at the five statements from Dalton's theory listed on page 68 of your textbook.
2. **Decide whether you think each statement is true or false and discuss reasons why you think so.**
3. **After reading the section, re-evaluate your opinion of each statement. Discuss why your opinion changed or remained the same. Find passages in the text that account for the change of reinforcement of your opinions.** For example, you might have agreed with all five statements from Dalton's theory before reading the text. Then, after reading about atoms and subatomic particles, you might have changed your opinion about the first statement.

## Cooperative Learning Techniques

### ▶ Reading with a Partner

Reading with a partner is a strategy that can help you understand what you read and point out where more explanation is needed.

1. **First read the text silently by yourself. Use self-adhesive notes to mark those parts of the text that you do not understand.** For example, you might have difficulty with some of the material about quantum numbers in Section 2 of Chapter 4, while another student understands quantum numbers but has trouble with electron configurations in Section 3.
2. **Work with a partner to discuss the passages each of you marked.** Take turns listening and trying to clarify the difficult passages for each other. Together, study the related tables and illustrations and explain to each other how they relate to the text.
3. **For concepts that need further explanation, work together to formulate questions for class discussion or for your teacher to answer.**

### ▶ Using L.I.N.K.

The L.I.N.K. strategy stands for **L**ist, **I**nquire, **N**otes, **K**now. It is similar to the K/W/L strategy, but you work as a class or in groups.

1. **Brainstorm all the words, phrases, and ideas associated with the term your teacher provides.** Volunteers can keep track of contributions on the board or on a separate sheet of paper.
2. **Your teacher will direct you in a class or group discussion about the words and ideas listed.** Now is the time to inquire, or ask your teacher and other students for clarification of the listed ideas.
3. **At the end of the discussion, make notes about everything you can remember.** Look over your notes to see if you have left anything out.
4. **See what you now know about the given concept based on your own experience and the discussion.**

### ▶ Summarizing/Paired Summarizing

A summary is a brief statement of main ideas or important concepts. Making a summary of what you have read provides you with a way to review what you have learned, see what information needs further clarification, and helps you make connections to previously studied material.

Paired summarizing helps strengthen your ability to read, listen, and understand. It is especially useful when a section of text has several subdivisions, each dealing with different concepts, such as Chapter 2, Section 3 in your textbook.

1. **First read the material silently by yourself.**
2. **Then you and your partner take turns being the "listener" and the "reteller."** The reteller summarizes the material for the listener, who does not interrupt until the reteller has finished. If necessary, the reteller may consult the text, and the listener may ask for clarification. The listener then states any inaccuracies or omissions made by the reteller.
3. **Work together to refine the summary.** Make sure the summary states the important ideas in a clear and concise manner.

### ▶ Discussing Ideas

Discussing ideas with a partner or in a group before you read is a strategy that can help you broaden your knowledge base and decide what concepts to focus on as you are reading. Discussing ideas after you have read a section or chapter can help you check your understanding, clarify difficult concepts, and lead you to speculate about new ideas.

APPENDIX C

# Graphing Calculator Technology

Charts, graphs, and data analysis are essential elements of chemistry. To be successful in your study of chemistry, you must know how to make and interpret graphs and must understand the relationships between different variables.

Your graphing calculator can be a powerful tool for analyzing chemical data. In addition to using your calculator to organize and graph data, you can program your calculator to perform specialized functions.

In the text, you can use your graphing calculator to help solve the Chapter Review exercises. In addition, specific Graphing Calculator exercises referred to in the Chapter Reviews will help you explore the capabilities of your calculator while enhancing your understanding of mathematical relationships that are important in chemistry. The CBL 2™ and LabPro® probeware experiments will enable you to become adept at analyzing experimental data.

## Graphing Calculator Exercises

The **go.hrw.com** site provides downloadable programs for the TI-83 Plus and the TI-84 Plus graphing calculator families. These programs include data sets to analyze. Using these programs will improve your ability to handle scientific data.

You will learn to use your calculator to graph data. Then, you will interpret the graphs and will extract the information required to answer the questions in the exercises. You will gain experience with simple linear relationships, such as the relationship between energy and temperature, and complex relationships, such as the relationship between pH and titrant volume, which is represented by a titration curve.

To solve the Graphing Calculator exercises in the Chapter Reviews and to download the programs, you will need

- a graphing calculator (TI-83 Plus or TI-84 Plus)
- appropriate TI Connectivity computer-to-calculator cable and TI Connect™ software
- a computer that has Internet access

The detailed instructions on how to download the calculator programs can be found at **go.hrw.com** (keyword **HC6 CALC**).

## Calculator-Based Laboratories

Analyzing your data properly is as important as using good experimental technique in the chemistry lab. Your results will be meaningless if you do not know how to interpret them. The Calculator-Based Laboratory 2™ (CBL 2™) data-collection interface by Texas Instruments and the Vernier LabPro® data-collection interface by Vernier Software & Technology can simplify the process of obtaining and analyzing experimental data.

The data-collection interface mimics expensive electronic laboratory equipment and allows you to collect real experimental data that are stored directly onto your calculator. As a result, you will not have to record and graph your data manually. Instead, your data are automatically tabulated, and you can view real-time graphs. Consequently, you have more time to interpret your experimental results. The interface and probes allow you to collect experimental data, and with the DataMate™ App the information coming from the probes is automatically recognized.

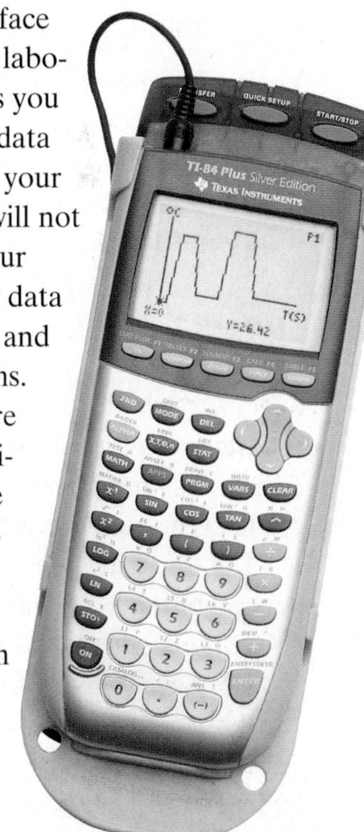

The CBL 2™ set-up is shown above. In some labs, you will use a temperature sensor, a pressure sensor, a voltage sensor, and a colorimeter to collect data. You will then analyze the data on your calculator to obtain the results of your experiment. To perform the calculator-based probeware experiments, you will need

- a graphing calculator (TI-83 Plus or TI-84 Plus)
- the CBL 2™ or LabPro® data collection interface
- the appropriate Texas Instruments or Vernier probe for the experiment
- the probeware experiment

The probeware experiments are available at **go.hrw.com** (keyword **HC6 CBL**). For additional information about the CBL 2 and LabPro hardware or software, visit **education.ti.com** or **www.vernier.com**

## Making the Most of your Calculator

In addition to organizing and graphing scientific data, Texas Instruments calculators have other applications that are available for use in chemistry.

The Periodic Table App provides an electronic version of the periodic table as well as information about the elements.

The Science Tool App provides various physical constants and allows you to convert between different units and to determine the number of significant figures for calculations.

Additional information about these and other applications for your calculator is available at **education.ti.com.** These applications are standard for some models of TI calculators and can be obtained from Texas Instruments and downloaded onto other models.

### Troubleshooting

- Calculator instructions in the *Modern Chemistry* program are written for the TI-84 Plus. You may use other graphing calculators, but some of the programs and instructions may require minor adjustments.
- Calculator-based probeware experiments are written for the CBL 2™ and LabPro® interfaces. Older versions of the experiments for the original CBL are available at **go.hrw.com.**
- The DataMate™ App is not compatible with the original CBL™ system. For more information and user manuals for the CBL 2™ and the CBL™ systems, visit **education.ti.com/guides**
- If you have problems loading programs or applications onto your calculator, you may need to clear programs or other data from your calculator's memory.
- Always make sure that you are downloading the version of the software that is correct for your calculator and that you have the latest operating system for your calculator and your CBL 2™.
- If you need additional help, Texas Instruments and Vernier Software & Technology can provide technical support. Contact TI at **education.ti.com** or 1-800-TI-CARES and Vernier at **info@vernnier.com** or 1-888-837-6437.

**go.hrw.com**
Keyword: **HC6 CALC**
This Web site contains links for downloading programs and applications that you will need for the Graphing Calculator exercises.

# APPENDIX D

# Problem Bank

## Conversions: Chap. 2, Sec. 2

### Converting Simple SI Units

1. State the following measured quantities in the units indicated.
   a. 5.2 cm of magnesium ribbon in millimeters
   b. 0.049 kg of sulfur in grams
   c. 1.60 mL of ethanol in microliters
   d. 0.0025 g of vitamin A in micrograms
   e. 0.020 kg of tin in milligrams
   f. 3 kL of saline solution in liters
2. State the following measured quantities in the units indicated.
   a. 150 mg of aspirin in grams
   b. 2500 mL of hydrochloric acid in liters
   c. 0.5 g of sodium in kilograms
   d. 55 L of carbon dioxide gas in kiloliters
   e. 35 mm in centimeters
   f. 8740 m in kilometers
   g. 209 nm in millimeters
   h. 500 000 $\mu$g in kilograms
3. The greatest distance between Earth and the sun during Earth's revolution is 152 million kilometers. What is this distance in megameters?
4. How many milliliters of water will it take to fill a 2.00 L bottle that already contains 1.87 L of water?
5. A piece of copper wire is 150 cm long. How long is the wire in millimeters? How many 50 mm segments of wire can be cut from the length?
6. The ladle at an iron foundry can hold 8500 kg of molten iron; 646 metric tons of iron are needed to make rails. How many ladlefuls of iron will it take to make 646 metric tons of iron? (1 metric ton = 1000 kg)

### Converting Derived SI Units

7. State the following measured quantities in the units indicated.
   a. 310 000 $cm^3$ of concrete in cubic meters
   b. 6.5 $m^2$ of steel sheet in square centimeters
   c. 0.035 $m^3$ of chlorine gas in cubic centimeters
   d. 0.49 $cm^2$ of copper in square millimeters
   e. 1200 $dm^3$ of acetic acid solution in cubic meters
   f. 87.5 $mm^3$ of actinium in cubic centimeters
   g. 250 000 $cm^2$ of polyethylene sheet in square meters
8. How many palisade cells from plant leaves would fit in a volume of 1.0 $cm^3$ of cells if the average volume of a palisade cell is 0.0147 $mm^3$?

### Mixed Review

9. Convert each of the following quantities to the required unit.
   a. 12.75 Mm to kilometers
   b. 277 cm to meters
   c. 30 560 $m^2$ to hectares (1 ha = 10 000 $m^2$)
   d. 81.9 $cm^2$ to square meters
   e. 300 000 km to megameters
10. Convert each of the following quantities to the required unit.
    a. 0.62 km to meters
    b. 3857 g to milligrams
    c. 0.0036 mL to microliters
    d. 0.342 metric tons to kg (1 metric ton = 1000 kg)
    e. 68.71 kL to liters
11. Convert each of the following quantities to the required unit.
    a. 856 mg to kilograms
    b. 1 210 000 $\mu$g to kilograms
    c. 6598 $\mu$L to cubic centimeters (1 mL = 1 $cm^3$)
    d. 80 600 nm to millimeters
    e. 10.74 $cm^3$ to liters
12. Convert each of the following quantities to the required unit.
    a. 7.93 L to cubic centimeters
    b. 0.0059 km to centimeters
    c. 4.19 L to cubic decimeters
    d. 7.48 $m^2$ to square centimeters
    e. 0.197 $m^3$ to liters
13. An automobile uses 0.05 mL of oil for each kilometer it is driven. How much oil in liters is consumed if the automobile is driven 20 000 km?
14. How many microliters are there in a volume of 370 $mm^3$ of cobra venom?
15. A baker uses 1.5 tsp of vanilla extract in each cake. How much vanilla extract in liters should the baker order to make 800 cakes? (1 tsp = 5 mL)
16. A person drinks eight glasses of water each day, and each glass contains 300 mL. How many liters of water will that person consume in a year? What is the mass of this volume of water in kilograms? (Assume one year has 365 days and the density of water is 1.00 kg/L.)
17. At the equator Earth rotates with a velocity of about 465 m/s.

**a.** What is this velocity in kilometers per hour?
**b.** What is this velocity in kilometers per day?

**18.** A chemistry teacher needs to determine what quantity of sodium hydroxide to order. If each student will use 130 g and there are 60 students, how many kilograms of sodium hydroxide should the teacher order?

**19.** The teacher in item 18 also needs to order plastic tubing. If each of the 60 students needs 750 mm of tubing, what length of tubing in meters should the teacher order?

**20.** Convert the following to the required units.
**a.** 550 $\mu$L/h to milliliters per day
**b.** 9.00 metric tons/h to kilograms per minute
**c.** 3.72 L/h to cubic centimeters per minute
**d.** 6.12 km/h to meters per second

**21.** Express the following in the units indicated.
**a.** 2.97 kg/L as grams per cubic centimeter
**b.** 4128 g/dm$^2$ as kilograms per square centimeter
**c.** 5.27 g/cm$^3$ as kilograms per cubic decimeter
**d.** 6.91 kg/m$^3$ as milligrams per cubic millimeter

**22.** A gas has a density of 5.56 g/L.
**a.** What volume in milliliters would 4.17 g of this gas occupy?
**b.** What would be the mass in kilograms of 1 m$^3$ of this gas?

**23.** The average density of living matter on Earth's land areas is 0.10 g/cm$^2$. What mass of living matter in kilograms would occupy an area of 0.125 ha?

**24.** A textbook measures 250. mm long, 224 mm wide, and 50.0 mm thick. It has a mass of 2.94 kg.
**a.** What is the volume of the book in cubic meters?
**b.** What is the density of the book in grams per cubic centimeter?
**c.** What is the area of one cover in square meters?

**25.** A glass dropper delivers liquid so that 25 drops equal 1.00 mL.
**a.** What is the volume of one drop in milliliters?
**b.** How many milliliters are in 37 drops?
**c.** How many drops would be required to get 0.68 L?

**26.** Express each of the following in kilograms and grams.
**a.** 504 700 mg
**b.** 9 200 000 $\mu$g
**c.** 122 mg
**d.** 7195 cg

**27.** Express each of the following in liters and milliliters.
**a.** 582 cm$^3$
**b.** 0.0025 m$^3$
**c.** 1.18 dm$^3$
**d.** 32 900 $\mu$L

**28.** Express each of the following in grams per liter and kilograms per cubic meter.
**a.** 1.37 g/cm$^3$
**b.** 0.692 kg/dm$^3$
**c.** 5.2 kg/L
**d.** 38 000 g/m$^3$
**e.** 5.79 mg/mm$^3$
**f.** 1.1 $\mu$g/mL

**29.** An industrial chemical reaction is run for 30.0 h and produces 648.0 kg of product. What is the average rate of product production in the stated units?
**a.** grams per minute
**b.** kilograms per day
**c.** milligrams per millisecond

**30.** What is the speed of a car in meters per second when it is moving at 100. km/h?

**31.** A heater gives off energy as heat at a rate of 330 kJ/min. What is the rate of energy output in kilocalories per hour? (1 cal = 4.184 J)

**32.** The instructions on a package of fertilizer tell you to apply it at the rate of 62 g/m$^2$. How much fertilizer in kilograms would you need to apply to 1.0 ha? (1 ha = 10 000 m$^2$)

**33.** A water tank leaks water at the rate of 3.9 mL/h. If the tank is not repaired, what volume of water in liters will it leak in a year? Show your setup for solving this. Hint: Use one conversion factor to convert hours to days and another to convert days to years, and assume that one year has 365 days.

**34.** A nurse plans to give flu injections of 50 $\mu$L each from a bottle containing 2.0 mL of vaccine. How many doses are in the bottle?

## Significant Figures: Chap. 2, Sec. 2

**35.** Determine the number of significant figures in the following measurements.
**a.** 640 cm$^3$
**b.** 200.0 mL
**c.** 0.5200 g
**d.** 1.005 kg
**e.** 10 000 L
**f.** 20.900 cm
**g.** 0.000 000 56 g/L
**h.** 0.040 02 kg/m$^3$
**i.** 790 001 cm$^2$
**j.** 665.000 kg•m/s$^2$

**36.** Perform the following calculations, and express the result in the correct units and number of significant figures.
**a.** 47.0 m ÷ 2.2 s
**b.** 140 cm × 35 cm
**c.** 5.88 kg ÷ 200 m$^3$
**d.** 0.00 50 m$^2$ × 0.042 m
**e.** 300.3 L ÷ 180. s
**f.** 33.00 cm$^2$ × 2.70 cm
**g.** 35 000 kJ ÷ 0.250 min

**37.** Perform the following calculations and express the results in the correct units and number of significant figures.
**a.** 22.0 m + 5.28 m + 15.5 m
**b.** 0.042 kg + 1.229 kg + 0.502 kg
**c.** 170 cm$^2$ + 3.5 cm$^2$ − 28 cm$^2$
**d.** 0.003 L + 0.0048 L + 0.100 L
**e.** 24.50 dL + 4.30 dL + 10.2 dL
**f.** 3200 mg + 325 mg − 688 mg
**g.** 14 000 kg + 8000 kg + 590 kg

### Mixed Review

**38.** Determine the number of significant figures in the following measurements.
**a.** 0.0120 m
**b.** 100.5 mL
**c.** 101 g
**d.** 350 cm$^2$
**e.** 0.97 km
**f.** 1000 kg
**g.** 180. mm
**h.** 0.4936 L
**i.** 0.020 700 s

**39.** Round the following quantities to the specified number of significant figures.
**a.** 5 487 129 m to three significant figures
**b.** 0.013 479 265 mL to six significant figures

**c.** 31 947.972 $cm^2$ to four significant figures
**d.** 192.6739 $m^2$ to five significant figures
**e.** 786.9164 cm to two significant figures
**f.** 389 277 600 J to six significant figures
**g.** 225 834.762 $cm^3$ to seven significant figures

**40.** Perform the following calculations, and express the answer in the correct units and number of significant figures.
**a.** 651 cm × 75 cm
**b.** 7.835 kg ÷ 2.5 L
**c.** 14.75 L ÷ 1.20 s
**d.** 360 cm × 51 cm × 9.07 cm
**e.** 5.18 m × 0.77 m × 10.22 m
**f.** 34.95 g ÷ 11.169 $cm^3$

**41.** Perform the following calculations, and express the answer in the correct units and number of significant figures.
**a.** 7.945 J + 82.3 J − 0.02 J
**b.** 0.0012 m − 0.000 45 m − 0.000 11 m
**c.** 500 g + 432 g + 2 g
**d.** 31.2 kPa + 0.0035 kPa − 0.147 kPa
**e.** 312 dL − 31.2 dL − 3.12 dL
**f.** 1701 kg + 50 kg + 43 kg

**42.** A rectangle measures 87.59 cm by 35.1 mm. Express its area with the proper number of significant figures in the specified unit.
**a.** in $cm^2$
**b.** in $mm^2$
**c.** in $m^2$

**43.** A box measures 900. mm by 31.5 mm by 6.3 cm. State its volume with the proper number of significant figures in the specified unit.
**a.** in $cm^3$
**b.** in $m^3$
**c.** in $mm^3$

**44.** A 125 mL sample of liquid has a mass of 0.16 kg. What is the density of the liquid in the following measurements?
**a.** $kg/m^3$
**b.** g/mL
**c.** $kg/dm^3$

**45.** Perform the following calculations, and express the results in the correct units and with the proper number of significant figures.
**a.** 13.75 mm × 10.1 mm × 0.91 mm
**b.** 89.4 $cm^2$ × 4.8 cm
**c.** 14.9 $m^3$ ÷ 3.0 $m^2$
**d.** 6.975 m × 30 m × 21.5 m

**46.** What is the volume of a region of space that measures 752 m × 319 m × 110 m? Give your answer in the correct unit and with the proper number of significant figures.

**47.** Perform the following calculations, and express the results in the correct units and with the proper number of significant figures.
**a.** 7.382 g + 1.21 g + 4.7923 g
**b.** 51.3 mg + 83 mg − 34.2 mg
**c.** 0.007 L − 0.0037 L + 0.012 L
**d.** 253.05 $cm^2$ + 33.9 $cm^2$ + 28 $cm^2$
**e.** 14.77 kg + 0.086 kg − 0.391 kg
**f.** 319 mL + 13.75 mL + 20. mL

**48.** A container measures 30.5 mm × 202 mm × 153 mm. When it is full of a liquid, it has a mass of 1.33 kg. When it is empty, it has a mass of 0.30 kg. What is the density of the liquid in kilograms per liter?

**49.** If 7.76 km of wire has a mass of 3.3 kg, what is the mass of the wire in g/m? What length in meters would have a mass of 1.0 g?

**50.** A container of plant food recommends an application rate of 52 kg/ha. If the container holds 10 kg of plant food, how many square meters will it cover? (1 ha = 10 000 $m^2$)

**51.** A chemical process produces 974 550 kJ of energy as heat in 37.0 min. What is the rate in kilojoules per minute? What is the rate in kilojoules per second?

**52.** A water pipe fills a container that measures 189 cm × 307 cm × 272 cm in 97 s.
**a.** What is the volume of the container in cubic meters?
**b.** What is the rate of flow in the pipe in liters per minute?
**c.** What is the rate of flow in cubic meters per hour?

**53.** Perform the following calculations, and express the results in the correct units and with the proper number of significant figures. Note, in problems with multiple steps, it is better to perform the entire calculation and then round to significant figures.
**a.** (0.054 kg + 1.33 kg) × 5.4 $m^2$
**b.** 67.35 $cm^2$ ÷ (1.401 cm − 0.399 cm)
**c.** 4.198 kg × (1019 $m^2$ − 40 $m^2$) ÷ (54.2 s × 31.3 s)
**d.** 3.14159 m × (4.17 m + 2.150 m)
**e.** 690 000 m ÷ (5.022 h − 4.31 h)
**f.** (6.23 cm + 3.111 cm − 0.05 cm) × 14.99 cm

## Scientific Notation: Chap. 2, Sec. 3

### Converting Quantities to Scientific Notation

**54.** Express the following quantities in scientific notation.
**a.** 8 800 000 000 m
**b.** 0.0015 kg
**c.** 0.000 000 000 06 $kg/m^3$
**d.** 8 002 000 Hz
**e.** 0.009 003 A
**f.** 70 000 000 000 000 000 km
**g.** 6028 L
**h.** 0.2105 g
**i.** 600 005 000 kJ/h
**j.** 33.8 $m^2$

### Calculating with Quantities in Scientific Notation

**55.** Carry out the following calculations. Express the results in scientific notation and with the correct number of significant figures.
**a.** $4.74 \times 10^4$ km + $7.71 \times 10^3$ km + $1.05 \times 10^3$ km
**b.** $2.75 \times 10^{-4}$ m + $8.03 \times 10^{-5}$ m + $2.122 \times 10^{-3}$ m
**c.** $4.0 \times 10^{-5}$ $m^3$ + $6.85 \times 10^{-6}$ $m^3$ − $1.05 \times 10^{-5}$ $m^3$
**d.** $3.15 \times 10^2$ mg + $3.15 \times 10^3$ mg + $3.15 \times 10^4$ mg
**e.** $3.01 \times 10^{22}$ atoms + $1.19 \times 10^{23}$ atoms + $9.80 \times 10^{21}$ atoms
**f.** $6.85 \times 10^7$ nm + $4.0229 \times 10^8$ nm − $8.38 \times 10^6$ nm

56. Carry out the following computations, and express the result in scientific notation.
**a.** $7.20 \times 10^3$ cm $\times$ $8.08 \times 10^3$ cm
**b.** $3.7 \times 10^4$ mm $\times$ $6.6 \times 10^4$ mm $\times$ $9.89 \times 10^3$ mm
**c.** $8.27 \times 10^2$ m $\times$ $2.5 \times 10^{-3}$ m $\times$ $3.00 \times 10^{-4}$ m
**d.** $4.44 \times 10^{-35}$ m $\times$ $5.55 \times 10^{19}$ m $\times$ $7.69 \times 10^{-12}$ kg
**e.** $6.55 \times 10^4$ dm $\times$ $7.89 \times 10^9$ dm $\times$ $4.01893 \times 10^5$ dm

57. Carry out the following computations, and express the result in scientific notation.
**a.** $2.290 \times 10^7$ cm $\div$ $4.33 \times 10^3$ s
**b.** $1.788 \times 10^{-5}$ L $\div$ $7.111 \times 10^{-3}$ $m^2$
**c.** $5.515 \times 10^4$ L $\div$ $6.04 \times 10^3$ km
**d.** $3.29 \times 10^{-4}$ km $\div$ $1.48 \times 10^{-2}$ min
**e.** $4.73 \times 10^{-4}$ g $\div$ ($2.08 \times 10^{-3}$ km $\times$ $5.60 \times 10^{-4}$ km)

## Mixed Review

58. Express the following quantities in scientific notation.
**a.** 158 000 km
**b.** 0.000 009 782 L
**c.** 837 100 000 $cm^3$
**d.** 6 500 000 000 $mm^2$
**e.** 0.005 93 g
**f.** 0.000 000 006 13 m
**g.** 12 552 000 J
**h.** 0.000 008 004 g/L
**i.** 0.010 995 kg
**j.** 1 050 000 000 Hz

59. Perform the following calculations, and express the result in scientific notation with the correct number of significant figures.
**a.** $2.48 \times 10^2$ kg + $9.17 \times 10^3$ kg + $7.2 \times 10^1$ kg
**b.** $4.07 \times 10^{-5}$ mg + $3.966 \times 10^{-4}$ mg + $7.1 \times 10^{-2}$ mg
**c.** $1.39 \times 10^4$ $m^3$ + $6.52 \times 10^2$ $m^3$ − $4.8 \times 10^3$ $m^3$
**d.** $7.70 \times 10^{-9}$ m − $3.95 \times 10^{-8}$ m + $1.88 \times 10^{-7}$ m
**e.** $1.111 \times 10^5$ J + $5.82 \times 10^4$ J + $3.01 \times 10^6$ J
**f.** $9.81 \times 10^{27}$ molecules + $3.18 \times 10^{25}$ molecules − $2.09 \times 10^{26}$ molecules
**g.** $1.36 \times 10^7$ cm + $3.456 \times 10^6$ cm − $1.01 \times 10^7$ cm + $5.122 \times 10^5$ cm

60. Perform the following computations, and express the result in scientific notation with the correct number of significant figures.
**a.** $1.54 \times 10^{-1}$ L $\div$ $2.36 \times 10^{-4}$ s
**b.** $3.890 \times 10^4$ mm $\times$ $4.71 \times 10^2$ $mm^2$
**c.** $9.571 \times 10^3$ kg $\div$ $3.82 \times 10^{-1}$ $m^2$
**d.** $8.33 \times 10^3$ km $\div$ $1.97 \times 10^2$ s
**e.** $9.36 \times 10^2$ m $\times$ $3.82 \times 10^3$ m $\times$ $9.01 \times 10^{-1}$ m
**f.** $6.377 \times 10^4$ J $\div$ $7.35 \times 10^{-3}$ s

61. Your electric company charges you for the electric energy you use, measured in kilowatt-hours (kWh). One kWh is equivalent to 3 600 000 J. Express this quantity in scientific notation.

62. The pressure in the deepest part of the ocean is 11 200 000 Pa. Express this pressure in scientific notation.

63. Convert 1.5 km to millimeters, and express the result in scientific notation.

64. Light travels at a speed of about 300 000 km/s.
**a.** Express this value in scientific notation.
**b.** Convert this value to meters per hour.
**c.** What distance in centimeters does light travel in 1 $\mu$s?

65. There are $7.11 \times 10^{24}$ molecules in 100.0 $cm^3$ of a certain substance.
**a.** What is the number of molecules in 1.09 $cm^3$ of the substance?
**b.** What would be the number of molecules in $2.24 \times 10^4$ $cm^3$ of the substance?
**c.** What number of molecules are in $9.01 \times 10^{-6}$ $cm^3$ of the substance?

66. The number of transistors on a particular integrated circuit is 3 578 000, and the integrated circuit measures 9.5 mm $\times$ 8.2 mm.
**a.** What is the area occupied by each transistor?
**b.** Using your answer from (a), how many transistors could be formed on a silicon sheet that measures 353 mm $\times$ 265 mm?

67. A solution has 0.0501 g of a substance in 1.00 L. Express this concentration in grams per microliter.

68. Cesium atoms are the largest of the naturally occurring elements. They have a diameter of $5.30 \times 10^{-10}$ m. Calculate the number of cesium atoms that would have to be lined up to give a row of cesium atoms 2.54 cm (1 in.) long.

69. The neutron has a volume of approximately $1.4 \times 10^{-44}$ $m^3$ and a mass of $1.675 \times 10^{-24}$ g. Calculate the density of the neutron in g/$m^3$. What is the mass of 1.0 $cm^3$ of neutrons in kilograms?

70. The pits in a compact disc are some of the smallest things ever mass-produced mechanically by humans. These pits represent the 1s and 0s of digital information on a compact disc. These pits are only $1.6 \times 10^{-8}$ m deep (1/4 the wavelength of red laser light). How many of these pits would have to be stacked on top of each other to make a hole 0.305 m deep?

71. 22 400 mL of oxygen gas contains $6.022 \times 10^{23}$ oxygen molecules at 0°C and standard atmospheric pressure.
**a.** How many oxygen molecules are in 0.100 mL of gas?
**b.** How many oxygen molecules are in 1.00 L of gas?
**c.** What is the average space in milliliters occupied by one oxygen molecule?

72. The mass of the atmosphere is calculated to be $5.136 \times 10^{18}$ kg, and there are 6 500 000 000 people living on Earth. Calculate the following values.
**a.** The mass of atmosphere in kilograms per person.
**b.** The mass of atmosphere in metric tons per person.
**c.** If the number of people increases to 9 500 000 000, what is the mass in kilograms per person?

73. The mass of the sun is $1.989 \times 10^{30}$ kg, and the mass of Earth is $5.974 \times 10^{24}$ kilograms. How many Earths would be needed to equal the mass of the sun?

74. A new landfill has dimensions of 2.3 km $\times$ 1.4 km $\times$ 0.15 km.

a. What is the volume in cubic kilometer?
b. What is the volume in cubic meters?
c. If 250 000 000 objects averaging 0.060 $m^3$ each are placed into the landfill each year, how many years will it take to fill the landfill?

75. A dietary calorie (C) is exactly equal to 1000 cal. If your daily intake of food gives you 2400 C, what is your intake in joules per day? (1 cal = 4.184 J)

## Four Steps for Solving Quantitative Problems: Chap. 2, Sec. 3

76. Gasoline has a density of 0.73 g/$cm^3$. How many liters of gasoline would be required to increase the mass of an automobile from 1271 kg to 1305 kg?
77. A swimming pool measures 9.0 m long by 3.5 m wide by 1.75 m deep. What mass of water in metric tons (1 metric ton = 1000 kg) does the pool contain when filled? The density of the water in the pool is 0.997 g/$cm^3$.
78. A tightly packed box of crackers contains 250 g of crackers and measures 7.0 cm × 17.0 cm × 19.0 cm. What is the average density in kilograms per liter of the crackers in the package? Assume that the unused volume is negligible.

## Mixed Review

*Solve these problems by using the Four Steps for Solving Quantitative Problems.*

79. The aluminum foil on a certain roll has a total area of 18.5 $m^2$ and a mass of 1275 g. Using a density of 2.7 g per cubic centimeter for aluminum, determine the thickness in millimeters of the aluminum foil.
80. If a liquid has a density of 1.17 g/$cm^3$, how many liters of the liquid have a mass of 3.75 kg?
81. A stack of 500 sheets of paper measuring 28 cm × 21 cm is 44.5 mm high and has a mass of 2090 g. What is the density of the paper in grams per cubic centimeter?
82. A triangular-shaped piece of a metal has a mass of 6.58 g. The triangle is 0.560 mm thick and measures 36.4 mm on the base and 30.1 mm in height. What is the density of the metal in grams per cubic centimeter?
83. A packing crate measures 0.40 m × 0.40 m × 0.25 m. You must fill the crate with boxes of cookies that each measure 22.0 cm × 12.0 cm × 5.0 cm. How many boxes of cookies can fit into the crate?
84. Calculate the unknown quantities in the following table. Use the following relationships for volumes of the various shapes.

Volume of a cube = $l \times l \times l$
Volume of a rectangle = $l \times w \times h$
Volume of a sphere = $4/3\pi r^3$
Volume of a cylinder = $\pi r^2 \times h$

| *D* | *m* | *V* | *Shape* | *Dimensions* |
|---|---|---|---|---|
| a. 2.27 g/$cm^3$ | 3.93 kg | ? L | cube | ? m × ? m × ? m |
| b. 1.85 g/$cm^3$ | ? g | ? $cm^3$ | rectangle | 33 mm × 21 mm × 7.2 mm |
| c. 3.21 g/L | ? kg | ? $dm^3$ | sphere | 3.30 m diameter |
| d. ? g/$cm^3$ | 497 g | ? $m^3$ | cylinder | 7.5 cm diameter × 12 cm |
| e. 0.92 g/$cm^3$ | ? kg | ? $cm^3$ | rectangle | 3.5 m × 1.2 m × 0.65 m |

85. When a sample of a metal alloy that has a mass of 9.65 g is placed into a graduated cylinder containing water, the volume reading in the cylinder increases from 16.0 mL to 19.5 mL. What is the density of the alloy sample in grams per cubic centimeter?
86. Pure gold can be made into extremely thin sheets called gold leaf. Suppose that 50. kg of gold is made into gold leaf having an area of 3620 $m^2$. The density of gold is 19.3 g/$cm^3$.
    a. How thick in micrometers is the gold leaf?
    b. A gold atom has a radius of $1.44 \times 10^{-10}$ m. How many atoms thick is the gold leaf?
87. A chemical plant process requires that a cylindrical reaction tank be filled with a certain liquid in 238 s. The tank is 1.2 m in diameter and 4.6 m high. What flow rate in liters per minute is required to fill the reaction tank in the specified time?
88. The radioactive decay of 2.8 g of plutonium-238 generates 1.0 joule of energy as heat every second. Plutonium has a density of 19.86 g/$cm^3$. How many calories (1 cal = 4.184 J) of energy as heat will a rectangular piece of plutonium that is 4.5 cm × 3.05 cm × 15 cm generate per hour?
89. The mass of Earth is $5.974 \times 10^{24}$ kg. Assume that Earth is a sphere of diameter $1.28 \times 10^4$ km and calculate the average density of Earth in g/$cm^3$.
90. What volume of magnesium in cubic centimeters would have the same mass as 1.82 $dm^3$ of platinum? The density of magnesium is 1.74 g/$cm^3$, and the density of platinum is 21.45 g/$cm^3$.
91. A roll of transparent tape has 66 m of tape on it. If an average of 5.0 cm of tape is needed each time the tape is used, how many uses can you get from a case of tape containing 24 rolls?
92. An automobile can travel 38 km on 4.0 L of gasoline. If the automobile is driven 75% of the days in a year and the average distance traveled each day is 86 km, how many liters of gasoline will be consumed in one year (assume the year has 365 days)?
93. A hose delivers water to a swimming pool that measures 9.0 m long by 3.5 m wide by 1.75 m deep. It requires 97 h to fill the pool. At what rate in liters per minute will the hose fill the pool?
94. Automobile batteries are filled with a solution of sulfuric acid, which has a density of 1.285 g/$cm^3$. The solution used to fill the battery is 38% (by mass)

sulfuric acid. How many grams of sulfuric acid are present in 500 mL of battery acid?

## Mole Concept: Chap. 3, Sec. 3; Chap. 7, Sec. 3

### Problems Involving Atoms and Elements

**95.** Calculate the number of moles in each of the following masses.
**a.** 64.1 g of aluminum
**b.** 28.1 g of silicon
**c.** 0.255 g of sulfur
**d.** 850.5 g of zinc

**96.** Calculate the mass of each of the following amounts.
**a.** 1.22 mol sodium
**b.** 14.5 mol copper
**c.** 0.275 mol mercury
**d.** $9.37 \times 10^{-3}$ mol magnesium

**97.** Calculate the amount in moles in each of the following quantities.
**a.** $3.01 \times 10^{23}$ atoms of rubidium
**b.** $8.08 \times 10^{22}$ atoms of krypton
**c.** 5 700 000 000 atoms of lead
**d.** $2.997 \times 10^{25}$ atoms of vanadium

**98.** Calculate the number of atoms in each of the following amounts.
**a.** 1.004 mol bismuth
**b.** 2.5 mol manganese
**c.** 0.000 0002 mol helium
**d.** 32.6 mol strontium

**99.** Calculate the number of atoms in each of the following masses.
**a.** 54.0 g of aluminum
**b.** 69.45 g of lanthanum
**c.** 0.697 g of gallium
**d.** 0.000 000 020 g beryllium

**100.** Calculate the mass of the following numbers of atoms.
**a.** $6.022 \times 10^{24}$ atoms of tantalum
**b.** $3.01 \times 10^{21}$ atoms of cobalt
**c.** $1.506 \times 10^{24}$ atoms of argon
**d.** $1.20 \times 10^{25}$ atoms of helium

### Problems Involving Molecules, Formula Units, and Ions

**101.** Calculate the number of moles in each of the following masses.
**a.** 3.00 g of boron tribromide, $BBr_3$
**b.** 0.472 g of sodium fluoride, NaF
**c.** $7.50 \times 10^2$ g of methanol, $CH_3OH$
**d.** 50.0 g of calcium chlorate, $Ca(ClO_3)_2$

**102.** Determine the mass of each of the following amounts.
**a.** 1.366 mol of $NH_3$
**b.** 0.120 mol of glucose, $C_6H_{12}O_6$
**c.** 6.94 mol barium chloride, $BaCl_2$
**d.** 0.005 mol of propane, $C_3H_8$

**103.** Calculate the number of molecules in each of the following amounts.
**a.** 4.99 mol of methane, $CH_4$
**b.** 0.005 20 mol of nitrogen gas, $N_2$
**c.** 1.05 mol of phosphorus trichloride, $PCl_3$
**d.** $3.5 \times 10^{-5}$ mol of vitamin C, ascorbic acid, $C_6H_8O_6$

**104.** Calculate the number of formula units in the following amounts.
**a.** 1.25 mol of potassium bromide, KBr
**b.** 5.00 mol of magnesium chloride, $MgCl_2$
**c.** 0.025 mol of sodium carbonate, $Na_2CO_3$
**d.** $6.82 \times 10^{-6}$ mol of lead(II) nitrate, $Pb(NO_3)_2$

**105.** Calculate the amount in moles of the following numbers of molecules or formula units.
**a.** $3.34 \times 10^{34}$ formula units of $Cu(OH)_2$
**b.** $1.17 \times 10^{16}$ molecules of $H_2S$
**c.** $5.47 \times 10^{21}$ formula units of nickel(II) sulfate, $NiSO_4$
**d.** $7.66 \times 10^{19}$ molecules of hydrogen peroxide, $H_2O_2$

**106.** Calculate the mass of each of the following quantities.
**a.** $2.41 \times 10^{24}$ molecules of hydrogen, $H_2$
**b.** $5.00 \times 10^{21}$ formula units of aluminum hydroxide, $Al(OH)_3$
**c.** $8.25 \times 10^{22}$ molecules of bromine pentafluoride, $BrF_5$
**d.** $1.20 \times 10^{23}$ formula units of sodium oxalate, $Na_2C_2O_4$

**107.** Calculate the number of molecules or formula units in each of the following masses.
**a.** 22.9 g of sodium sulfide, $Na_2S$
**b.** 0.272 g of nickel(II) nitrate, $Ni(NO_3)_2$
**c.** 260 mg of acrylonitrile, $CH_2CHCN$

### Mixed Review

**108.** Calculate the number of moles in each of the following masses.
**a.** 0.039 g of palladium
**b.** 8200 g of iron
**c.** 0.0073 kg of tantalum
**d.** 0.006 55 g of antimony
**e.** 5.64 kg of barium

**109.** Calculate the mass in grams of each of the following amounts.
**a.** 1.002 mol of chromium
**b.** 550 mol of aluminum
**c.** $4.08 \times 10^{-8}$ mol of neon
**d.** 7 mol of titanium
**e.** 0.0086 mol of xenon
**f.** $3.29 \times 10^4$ mol of lithium

**110.** Calculate the number of atoms in each of the following amounts.
**a.** 17.0 mol of germanium
**b.** 0.6144 mol of copper
**c.** 3.02 mol of tin
**d.** $2.0 \times 10^6$ mol of carbon
**e.** 0.0019 mol of zirconium
**f.** $3.227 \times 10^{-10}$ mol of potassium

**111.** Calculate the number of moles in each of the following quantities.
**a.** $6.022 \times 10^{24}$ atoms of cobalt
**b.** $1.06 \times 10^{23}$ atoms of tungsten
**c.** $3.008 \times 10^{19}$ atoms of silver

**d.** 950 000 000 atoms of plutonium
**e.** $4.61 \times 10^{17}$ atoms of radon
**f.** 8 trillion atoms of cerium

**112.** Calculate the number of atoms in each of the following masses.
**a.** 0.0082 g of gold
**b.** 812 g of molybdenum
**c.** $2.00 \times 10^2$ mg of americium
**d.** 10.09 kg of neon
**e.** 0.705 mg of bismuth
**f.** 37 $\mu$g of uranium

**113.** Calculate the mass of each of the following.
**a.** $8.22 \times 10^{23}$ atoms of rubidium
**b.** 4.05 Avogadro's constants of manganese atoms
**c.** $9.96 \times 10^{26}$ atoms of tellurium
**d.** 0.000 025 Avogadro's constants of rhodium atoms
**e.** 88 300 000 000 000 atoms of radium
**f.** $2.94 \times 10^{17}$ atoms of hafnium

**114.** Calculate the number of moles in each of the following masses.
**a.** 45.0 g of acetic acid, $CH_3COOH$
**b.** 7.04 g of lead(II) nitrate, $Pb(NO_3)_2$
**c.** 5000 kg of iron(III) oxide, $Fe_2O_3$
**d.** 12.0 mg of ethylamine, $C_2H_5NH_2$
**e.** 0.003 22 g of stearic acid, $C_{17}H_{35}COOH$
**f.** 50.0 kg of ammonium sulfate, $(NH_4)_2SO_4$

**115.** Calculate the mass of each of the following amounts.
**a.** 3.00 mol of selenium oxybromide, $SeOBr_2$
**b.** 488 mol of calcium carbonate, $CaCO_3$
**c.** 0.0091 mol of retinoic acid, $C_{20}H_{28}O_2$
**d.** $6.00 \times 10^{-8}$ mol of nicotine, $C_{10}H_{14}N_2$
**e.** 2.50 mol of strontium nitrate, $Sr(NO_3)_2$
**f.** $3.50 \times 10^{-6}$ mol of uranium hexafluoride, $UF_6$

**116.** Calculate the number of molecules or formula units in each of the following amounts.
**a.** 4.27 mol of tungsten(VI) oxide, $WO_3$
**b.** 0.003 00 mol of strontium nitrate, $Sr(NO_3)_2$
**c.** 72.5 mol of toluene, $C_6H_5CH_3$
**d.** $5.11 \times 10^{-7}$ mol of $\alpha$-tocopherol (vitamin E), $C_{29}H_{50}O_2$
**e.** 1500 mol of hydrazine, $N_2H_4$
**f.** 0.989 mol of nitrobenzene $C_6H_5NO_2$

**117.** Calculate the number of molecules or formula units in each of the following masses.
**a.** 285 g of iron(III) phosphate, $FePO_4$
**b.** 0.0084 g of $C_5H_5N$
**c.** 85 mg of 2-methyl-1-propanol, $(CH_3)_2CHCH_2OH$
**d.** $4.6 \times 10^{-4}$ g of mercury(II) acetate, $Hg(C_2H_3O_2)_2$
**e.** 0.0067 g of lithium carbonate, $Li_2CO_3$

**118.** Calculate the mass of each of the following quantities.
**a.** $8.39 \times 10^{23}$ molecules of fluorine, $F_2$
**b.** $6.82 \times 10^{24}$ formula units of beryllium sulfate, $BeSO_4$
**c.** $7.004 \times 10^{26}$ molecules of chloroform, $CHCl_3$
**d.** 31 billion formula units of chromium(III) formate, $Cr(CHO_2)_3$
**e.** $6.3 \times 10^{18}$ molecules of nitric acid, $HNO_3$
**f.** $8.37 \times 10^{25}$ molecules of freon 114, $C_2Cl_2F_4$

**119.** Precious metals are commonly measured in troy ounces. A troy ounce is equivalent to 31.1 g. How many moles are in a troy ounce of gold? How many moles are in a troy ounce of platinum? of silver?

**120.** A chemist needs 22.0 g of phenol, $C_6H_5OH$, for an experiment. How many moles of phenol is this?

**121.** A student needs 0.015 mol of iodine crystals, $I_2$, for an experiment. What mass of iodine crystals should the student obtain?

**122.** The weight of a diamond is given in carats. One carat is equivalent to 200. mg. A pure diamond is made up entirely of carbon atoms. How many carbon atoms make up a 1.00 carat diamond?

**123.** 8.00 g of calcium chloride, $CaCl_2$, is dissolved in 1.000 kg of water.
**a.** How many moles of $CaCl_2$ are in solution? How many moles of water are present?
**b.** Assume that the ionic compound, $CaCl_2$, separates completely into $Ca^{2+}$ and $Cl^-$ ions when it dissolves in water. How many moles of each ion are present in the solution?

**124.** How many moles are in each of the following masses?
**a.** 453.6 g (1.000 pound) of sucrose (table sugar), $C_{12}H_{22}O_{11}$
**b.** 1.000 pound of table salt, NaCl

**125.** When the ionic compound $NH_4Cl$ dissolves in water, it breaks into one ammonium ion, $NH_4^+$, and one chloride ion, $Cl^-$. If you dissolved 10.7 g of $NH_4Cl$ in water, how many moles of ions would be in solution?

**126.** What is the total amount in moles of atoms in a jar that contains $2.41 \times 10^{24}$ atoms of chromium, $1.51 \times 10^{23}$ atoms of nickel, and $3.01 \times 10^{23}$ atoms of copper?

**127.** The density of liquid water is 0.997 g/mL at 25°C.
**a.** Calculate the mass of 250.0 mL (about a cupful) of water.
**b.** How many moles of water are in 250.0 mL of water? Hint: Use the result of (a).
**c.** Calculate the volume that would be occupied by 2.000 mol of water at 25°C.
**d.** What mass of water is 2.000 mol of water?

**128.** An Avogadro's constant (1 mol) of sugar molecules has a mass of 342 g, but an Avogadro's constant (1 mol) of water molecules has a mass of only 18 g. Explain why there is such a difference between the mass of 1 mol of sugar and the mass of 1 mol of water.

**129.** Calculate the mass of aluminum that would have the same number of atoms as 6.35 g of cadmium.

**130.** A chemist weighs a steel cylinder of compressed oxygen, $O_2$, and finds that it has a mass of 1027.8 g. After some of the oxygen is used in an experiment, the cylinder has a mass of 1023.2 g. How many moles of oxygen gas are used in the experiment?

**131.** Suppose that you could decompose 0.250 mol of $Ag_2S$ into its elements.
**a.** How many moles of silver would you have? How many moles of sulfur would you have?
**b.** How many moles of $Ag_2S$ are there in 38.8 g of $Ag_2S$? How many moles of silver and sulfur would be produced from this amount of $Ag_2S$?
**c.** Calculate the masses of silver and sulfur produced in (b).

## Percentage Composition: Chap. 7, Sec. 3

**132.** Determine the percentage composition of each of the following compounds.
**a.** sodium oxalate, $Na_2C_2O_4$
**b.** ethanol, $C_2H_5OH$
**c.** aluminum oxide, $Al_2O_3$
**d.** potassium sulfate, $K_2SO_4$

**133.** Suppose that a laboratory analysis of white powder showed 42.59% Na, 12.02% C, and 44.99% oxygen. Would you report that the compound is sodium oxalate or sodium carbonate? (Use 43.38% Na, 11.33% C, and 45.29% O for sodium carbonate, and 34.31% Na, 17.93% C, and 47.76% O for sodium oxalate.)

**134.** Calculate the mass of the given element in each of the following compounds.
**a.** bromine in 50.0 g potassium bromide, KBr
**b.** chromium in 1.00 kg sodium dichromate, $Na_2Cr_2O_7$
**c.** nitrogen in 85.0 mg of the amino acid lysine, $C_6H_{14}N_2O_2$
**d.** cobalt in 2.84 g cobalt(II) acetate, $Co(C_2H_3O_2)_2$

### Hydrates

**135.** Calculate the percentage of water in each of the following hydrates.
**a.** sodium carbonate decahydrate, $Na_2CO_3{\bullet}10H_2O$
**b.** nickel(II) iodide hexahydrate, $NiI_2{\bullet}6H_2O$
**c.** ammonium hexacyanoferrate(III) trihydrate (commonly called ammonium ferricyanide), $(NH_4)_2Fe(CN)_6{\bullet}3H_2O$
**d.** aluminum bromide hexahydrate

### Mixed Review

**136.** Write formulas for the following compounds and determine the percentage composition of each.
**a.** nitric acid
**b.** ammonia
**c.** mercury(II) sulfate
**d.** antimony(V) fluoride

**137.** Calculate the percentage composition of the following compounds.
**a.** lithium bromide, LiBr
**b.** anthracene, $C_{14}H_{10}$
**c.** ammonium nitrate, $NH_4NO_3$
**d.** nitrous acid, $HNO_2$
**e.** silver sulfide, $Ag_2S$
**f.** iron(II) thiocyanate, $Fe(SCN)_2$
**g.** lithium acetate
**h.** nickel(II) formate

**138.** Calculate the percentage of the given element in each of the following compounds.
**a.** nitrogen in urea, $NH_2CONH_2$
**b.** sulfur in sulfuryl chloride, $SO_2Cl_2$
**c.** thallium in thallium(III) oxide, $Tl_2O_3$
**d.** oxygen in potassium chlorate, $KClO_3$
**e.** bromine in calcium bromide, $CaBr_2$
**f.** tin in tin(IV) oxide, $SnO_2$

**139.** Calculate the mass of the given element in each of the following quantities.
**a.** oxygen in 4.00 g of manganese dioxide, $MnO_2$
**b.** aluminum in 50.0 metric tons of aluminum oxide, $Al_2O_3$
**c.** silver in 325 g silver cyanide, AgCN
**d.** gold in 0.780 g of gold(III) selenide, $Au_2Se_3$
**e.** selenium in 683 g sodium selenite, $Na_2SeO_3$
**f.** chlorine in $5.0 \times 10^4$ g of 1,1-dichloropropane, $CHCl_2CH_2CH_3$

**140.** Calculate the percentage of water in each of the following hydrates.
**a.** strontium chloride hexahydrate, $SrCl_2{\bullet}6H_2O$
**b.** zinc sulfate heptahydrate, $ZnSO_4{\bullet}7H_2O$
**c.** calcium fluorophosphate dihydrate, $CaFPO_3{\bullet}2H_2O$
**d.** beryllium nitrate trihydrate, $Be(NO_3)_2{\bullet}3H_2O$

**141.** Calculate the percentage of the given element in each of the following hydrates. You must first determine the formulas of the hydrates.
**a.** nickel in nickel(II) acetate tetrahydrate
**b.** chromium in sodium chromate tetrahydrate
**c.** cerium in cerium(IV) sulfate tetrahydrate

**142.** Cinnabar is a mineral that is mined in order to produce mercury. Cinnabar is mercury(II) sulfide, HgS. What mass of mercury can be obtained from 50.0 kg of cinnabar?

**143.** The minerals malachite, $Cu_2(OH)_2CO_3$, and chalcopyrite, $CuFeS_2$, can be mined to obtain copper metal. How much copper could be obtained from $1.00 \times 10^3$ kg of each? Which of the two has the greater copper content?

**144.** Calculate the percentage of the given element in each of the following hydrates.
**a.** vanadium in vanadium oxysulfate dihydrate, $VOSO_4{\bullet}2H_2O$
**b.** tin in potassium stannate trihydrate, $K_2SnO_3{\bullet}3H_2O$
**c.** chlorine in calcium chlorate dihydrate, $CaClO_3{\bullet}2H_2O$

**145.** Heating copper sulfate pentahydrate will evaporate the water from the crystals, leaving anhydrous copper sulfate, a white powder. *Anhydrous* means "without water." What mass of anhydrous $CuSO_4$ would be produced by heating 500.0 g of $CuSO_4{\bullet}5H_2O$?

**146.** Silver metal may be precipitated from a solution of silver nitrate by placing a copper strip into the solution. What mass of $AgNO_3$ would you dissolve in water in order to get 1.00 g of silver?

**147.** A sample of $Ag_2S$ has a mass of 62.4 g. What mass of each element could be obtained by decomposing this sample?

**148.** A quantity of epsom salts, magnesium sulfate heptahydrate, $MgSO_4{\bullet}7H_2O$, is heated until all the water is driven off. The sample loses 11.8 g in the process. What was the mass of the original sample?

**149.** The process of manufacturing sulfuric acid begins with the burning of sulfur. What mass of sulfur would have to be burned in order to produce 1.00 kg of $H_2SO_4$? Assume that all of the sulfur ends up in the sulfuric acid.

## Empirical Formulas: Chap. 7, Sec. 4

**150.** Determine the empirical formula for compounds that have the following analyses.
  **a.** 28.4% copper, 71.6% bromine
  **b.** 39.0% potassium, 12.0% carbon, 1.01% hydrogen, and 47.9% oxygen
  **c.** 77.3% silver, 7.4% phosphorus, 15.3% oxygen
  **d.** 0.57% hydrogen, 72.1% iodine, 27.3% oxygen

**151.** Determine the simplest formula for compounds that have the following analyses. The data may not be exact.
  **a.** 36.2% aluminum and 63.8% sulfur
  **b.** 93.5% niobium and 6.50% oxygen
  **c.** 57.6% strontium, 13.8% phosphorus, and 28.6% oxygen
  **d.** 28.5% iron, 48.6% oxygen, and 22.9% sulfur

**152.** Determine the molecular formula of each of the following unknown substances.
  **a.** empirical formula $CH_2$
  experimental molar mass 28 g/mol
  **b.** empirical formula $B_2H_5$
  experimental molar mass 54 g/mol
  **c.** empirical formula $C_2HCl$
  experimental molar mass 179 g/mol
  **d.** empirical formula $C_6H_8O$
  experimental molar mass 290 g/mol
  **e.** empirical formula $C_3H_2O$
  experimental molar mass 216 g/mol

### Mixed Review

**153.** Determine the empirical formula for compounds that have the following analyses.
  **a.** 66.0% barium and 34.0% chlorine
  **b.** 80.38% bismuth, 18.46% oxygen, and 1.16% hydrogen
  **c.** 12.67% aluminum, 19.73% nitrogen, and 67.60% oxygen
  **d.** 35.64% zinc, 26.18% carbon, 34.88% oxygen, and 3.30% hydrogen
  **e.** 2.8% hydrogen, 9.8% nitrogen, 20.5% nickel, 44.5% oxygen, and 22.4% sulfur
  **f.** 8.09% carbon, 0.34% hydrogen, 10.78% oxygen, and 80.78% bromine

**154.** Sometimes, instead of percentage composition, you will have the composition of a sample by mass. Using the actual mass of the sample, determine the empirical formula for compounds that have the following analyses.
  **a.** a 0.858 g sample of an unknown substance is composed of 0.537 g of copper and 0.321 g of fluorine
  **b.** a 13.07 g sample of an unknown substance is composed of 9.48 g of barium, 1.66 g of carbon, and 1.93 g of nitrogen
  **c.** a 0.025 g sample of an unknown substance is composed of 0.0091 g manganese, 0.0106 g oxygen, and 0.0053 g sulfur

**155.** Determine the empirical formula for compounds that have the following analyses.
  **a.** a 0.0082 g sample contains 0.0015 g of nickel and 0.0067 g of iodine
  **b.** a 0.470 g sample contains 0.144 g of manganese, 0.074 g of nitrogen, and 0.252 g of oxygen
  **c.** a 3.880 g sample contains 0.691 g of magnesium, 1.824 g of sulfur, and 1.365 g of oxygen
  **d.** a 46.25 g sample contains 14.77 g of potassium, 9.06 g of oxygen, and 22.42 g of tin

**156.** Determine the empirical formula for compounds that have the following analyses:
  **a.** 60.9% As and 39.1% S
  **b.** 76.89% Re and 23.12% O
  **c.** 5.04% H, 35.00% N, and 59.96% O
  **d.** 24.3% Fe, 33.9% Cr, and 41.8% O
  **e.** 54.03% C, 37.81% N, and 8.16% H
  **f.** 55.81% C, 3.90% H, 29.43% F, and 10.85% N

**157.** Determine the molecular formulas for compounds having the following empirical formulas and molar masses.
  **a.** $C_2H_4S$; experimental molar mass 179
  **b.** $C_2H_4O$; experimental molar mass 176
  **c.** $C_2H_3O_2$; experimental molar mass 119
  **d.** $C_2H_2O$, experimental molar mass 254

**158.** Use the experimental molar mass to determine the molecular formula for compounds having the following analyses.
  **a.** 41.39% carbon, 3.47% hydrogen, and 55.14% oxygen; experimental molar mass 116.07
  **b.** 54.53% carbon, 9.15% hydrogen, and 36.32% oxygen; experimental molar mass 88
  **c.** 64.27% carbon, 7.19% hydrogen, and 28.54% oxygen; experimental molar mass 168.19

**159.** A 0.400 g sample of a white powder contains 0.141 g of potassium, 0.115 g of sulfur, and 0.144 g of oxygen. What is the empirical formula for the compound?

**160.** A 10.64 g sample of a lead compound is analyzed and found to be made up of 9.65 g of lead and 0.99 g of oxygen. Determine the empirical formula for this compound.

**161.** A 2.65 g sample of a salmon-colored powder contains 0.70 g of chromium, 0.65 g of sulfur, and 1.30 g of oxygen. The molar mass is 392.2. What is the formula of the compound?

**162.** Ninhydrin is a compound that reacts with amino acids and proteins to produce a dark-colored complex. It is used by forensic chemists and detectives to see fingerprints that might otherwise be invisible. Ninhydrin's composition is 60.68% carbon, 3.40% hydrogen, and 35.92% oxygen. What is the empirical formula for ninhydrin?

**163.** Histamine is a substance that is released by cells in response to injury, infection, stings, and materials that cause allergic responses, such as pollen. Histamine causes dilation of blood vessels and swelling due to accumulation of fluid in the tissues. People sometimes take *anti*histamine drugs to counteract the effects of histamine. A sample of histamine having a mass of 385 mg is composed of 208 mg of carbon, 31 mg of hydrogen, and 146 mg of nitrogen. The molar mass of histamine is 111 g/mol. What is the molecular formula for histamine?

**164.** You analyze two substances in the laboratory and discover that each has the empirical formula $CH_2O$. You can easily see that they are different substances because one is a liquid with a sharp, biting odor and the other is an odorless, crystalline solid. How can you account for the fact that both have the same empirical formula?

## Stoichiometry: Chap. 9, Sec. 1–2

**165.** How many moles of sodium will react with water to produce 4.0 mol of hydrogen in the following reaction?

$$2Na(s) + 2H_2O(l) \rightarrow 2NaOH(aq) + H_2(g)$$

**166.** How many moles of lithium chloride will be formed by the reaction of chlorine with 0.046 mol of lithium bromide in the following reaction?

$$2LiBr(aq) + Cl_2(g) \rightarrow 2LiCl(aq) + Br_2(l)$$

**167.** Aluminum will react with sulfuric acid in the following reaction.

$$2Al(s) + 3H_2SO_4(l) \rightarrow Al_2(SO_4)_3(aq) + 3H_2(g)$$

**a.** How many moles of $H_2SO_4$ will react with 18 mol Al?
**b.** How many moles of each product will be produced?

**168.** Propane burns in excess oxygen according to the following reaction.

$$C_3H_8 + 5O_2 \rightarrow 3CO_2 + 4H_2O$$

**a.** How many moles each of $CO_2$ and $H_2O$ are formed from 3.85 mol of propane?
**b.** If 0.647 mol of oxygen are used in the burning of propane, how many moles each of $CO_2$ and $H_2O$ are produced? How many moles of $C_3H_8$ are consumed?

**169.** Phosphorus burns in air to produce a phosphorus oxide in the following reaction:

$$4P(s) + 5O_2(g) \rightarrow P_4O_{10}(s)$$

**a.** What mass of phosphorus will be needed to produce 3.25 mol of $P_4O_{10}$?
**b.** If 0.489 mol of phosphorus burns, what mass of oxygen is used? What mass of $P_4O_{10}$ is produced?

**170.** Hydrogen peroxide breaks down, releasing oxygen, in the following reaction.

$$2H_2O_2(aq) \rightarrow 2H_2O(l) + O_2(g)$$

**a.** What mass of oxygen is produced when 1.840 mol of $H_2O_2$ decompose?
**b.** What mass of water is produced when 5.0 mol $O_2$ is produced by this reaction?

**171.** Sodium carbonate reacts with nitric acid according to the following equation:

$$Na_2CO_3(s) + 2HNO_3 \rightarrow 2NaNO_3 + CO_2 + H_2O$$

**a.** How many moles of $Na_2CO_3$ are required to produce 100.0 g of $NaNO_3$?
**b.** If 7.50 g of $Na_2CO_3$ reacts, how many moles of $CO_2$ are produced?

**172.** Hydrogen is generated by passing hot steam over iron, which oxidizes to form $Fe_3O_4$, in the following equation:

$$3Fe(s) + 4H_2O(g) \rightarrow 4H_2(g) + Fe_3O_4(s)$$

**a.** If 625 g of $Fe_3O_4$ is produced in the reaction, how many moles of hydrogen are produced at the same time?
**b.** How many moles of iron would be needed to generate 27 g of hydrogen?

**173.** Calculate the mass of silver bromide produced from 22.5 g of silver nitrate in the following reaction:

$$2AgNO_3(aq) + MgBr_2(aq) \rightarrow 2AgBr(s) + Mg(NO_3)_2(aq)$$

**174.** What mass of acetylene, $C_2H_2$, will be produced from the reaction of 90. g of calcium carbide, $CaC_2$, with water in the following reaction?

$$CaC_2(s) + 2H_2O(l) \rightarrow C_2H_2(g) + Ca(OH)_2(s)$$

**175.** Chlorine gas can be produced in the laboratory by adding concentrated hydrochloric acid to manganese(IV) oxide in the following reaction:

$$MnO_2(s) + 4HCl(aq) \rightarrow MnCl_2(aq) + 2H_2O(l) + Cl_2(g)$$

**a.** Calculate the mass of $MnO_2$ needed to produce 25.0 g of $Cl_2$.
**b.** What mass of $MnCl_2$ is produced when 0.091 g of $Cl_2$ is generated?

### Mixed Review

**176.** How many moles of ammonium sulfate can be made from the reaction of 30.0 mol of $NH_3$ with $H_2SO_4$ according to the following equation:

$$2NH_3 + H_2SO_4 \rightarrow (NH_4)_2SO_4$$

**177.** In a very violent reaction called a thermite reaction, aluminum metal reacts with iron(III) oxide to form iron metal and aluminum oxide according to the following equation:

$$Fe_2O_3 + 2Al \rightarrow 2Fe + Al_2O_3$$

**a.** What mass of Al will react with 150 g of $Fe_2O_3$?
**b.** If 0.905 mol $Al_2O_3$ is produced in the reaction, what mass of Fe is produced?
**c.** How many moles of $Fe_2O_3$ will react with 99.0 g of Al?

**178.** The reaction $N_2(g) + 3H_2(g) \rightarrow 2NH_3(g)$ is used to produce ammonia commercially. If 1.40 g of $N_2$ are used in the reaction, how many grams of $H_2$ will be needed?

**179.** What mass of sulfuric acid, $H_2SO_4$, is required to react with 1.27 g of potassium hydroxide, KOH? The products of this reaction are potassium sulfate and water.

**180.** Ammonium hydrogen phosphate, $(NH_4)_2HPO_4$, a common fertilizer; is made from reacting phosphoric acid, $H_3PO_4$, with ammonia.
**a.** Write the equation for this reaction.
**b.** If 10.00 g of ammonia react, how many moles of fertilizer will be produced?

**c.** What mass of ammonia will react with 2800 kg of $H_3PO_4$?

**181.** The following reaction shows the synthesis of zinc citrate, a ingredient in toothpaste, from zinc carbonate and citric acid:

$$3ZnCO_3(s) + 2C_6H_8O_7(aq) \rightarrow Zn_3(C_6H_5O_7)_2(aq) + 3H_2O(l) + 3CO_2(g)$$

**a.** How many moles of $ZnCO_3$ and $C_6H_8O_7$ are required to produce 30.0 mol of $Zn_3(C_6H_5O_7)_2$?

**b.** What quantities, in kilograms, of $H_2O$ and $CO_2$ are produced by the reaction of 500. mol of citric acid?

**182.** Methyl butanoate, an oily substance with a strong fruity fragrance can be made by reacting butanoic acid with methanol according to the following equation:

$$C_3H_7COOH + CH_3OH \rightarrow C_3H_7COOCH_3 + H_2O$$

**a.** What mass of methyl butanoate is produced from the reaction of 52.5 g of butanoic acid?

**b.** In order to purify methyl butanoate, water must be removed. What mass of water is produced from the reaction of 5800. g of methanol?

**183.** Ammonium nitrate decomposes to yield nitrogen gas, water, and oxygen gas in the following reaction:

$$2NH_4NO_3 \rightarrow 2N_2 + O_2 + 4H_2O$$

**a.** How many moles of nitrogen gas are produced when 36.0 g of $NH_4NO_3$ reacts?

**b.** If 7.35 mol of $H_2O$ are produced in this reaction, what mass of $NH_4NO_3$ reacted?

**184.** Lead(II) nitrate reacts with potassium iodide to produce lead(II) iodide and potassium nitrate. If 1.23 mg of lead nitrate are consumed, what is the mass of the potassium nitrate produced?

**185.** A car battery produces electrical energy with the following chemical reaction:

$$Pb(s) + PbO_2(s) + 2H_2SO_4(aq) \rightarrow 2PbSO_4(s) + 2H_2O(l)$$

If the battery loses 0.34 kg of lead in this reaction, how many moles of lead(II) sulfate are produced?

**186.** In a space shuttle, the $CO_2$ that the crew exhales is removed from the air by a reaction within canisters of lithium hydroxide. On average, each astronaut exhales about 20.0 mol of $CO_2$ daily. What mass of water will be produced when this amount reacts with LiOH? The other product of the reaction is $Li_2CO_3$.

**187.** Water is sometimes removed from the products of a reaction by placing them in a closed container with excess $P_4O_{10}$. Water is absorbed by the following reaction:

$$P_4O_{10} + 6H_2O \rightarrow 4H_3PO_4$$

**a.** What mass of water can be absorbed by $1.00 \times 10^2$ g of $P_4O_{10}$?

**b.** If the $P_4O_{10}$ in the container absorbs 0.614 mol of water, what mass of $H_3PO_4$ is produced?

**c.** If the mass of the container of $P_4O_{10}$ increases from 56.64 g to 63.70 g, how many moles of water are absorbed?

**188.** Ethanol, $C_2H_5OH$, is considered a clean fuel because it burns in oxygen to produce carbon dioxide and water with few trace pollutants. If 95.0 g of $H_2O$ are produced during the combustion of ethanol, how many grams of ethanol were present at the beginning of the reaction?

**189.** Sulfur dioxide is one of the major contributors to acid rain. Sulfur dioxide can react with oxygen and water in the atmosphere to form sulfuric acid, as shown in the following equation:

$$2H_2O(l) + O_2(g) + 2SO_2(g) \rightarrow 2H_2SO_4(aq)$$

If 50.0 g of sulfur dioxide from pollutants reacts with water and oxygen found in the air, how many grams of sulfuric acid can be produced? How many grams of oxygen are used in the process?

**190.** When heated, sodium bicarbonate, $NaHCO_3$, decomposes into sodium carbonate, $Na_2CO_3$, water, and carbon dioxide. If 5.00 g of $NaHCO_3$ decomposes, what is the mass of the carbon dioxide produced?

**191.** A reaction between hydrazine, $N_2H_4$, and dinitrogen tetroxide, $N_2O_4$, has been used to launch rockets into space. The reaction produces nitrogen gas and water vapor.

**a.** Write a balanced chemical equation for this reaction.

**b.** What is the mole ratio of $N_2O_4$ to $N_2$?

**c.** How many moles of $N_2$ will be produced if 20 000 mol of $N_2H_4$ are used by a rocket?

**d.** How many grams of $H_2O$ are made when 450. kg of $N_2O_4$ are consumed?

**192.** Joseph Priestley is credited with the discovery of oxygen. He produced $O_2$ by heating mercury(II) oxide, HgO, to decompose it into its elements. How many moles of oxygen could Priestley have produced if he had decomposed 517.84 g of mercury oxide?

**193.** Iron(III) chloride, $FeCl_3$, can be made by the reaction of iron with chlorine gas. How much iron, in grams, will be needed to completely react with 58.0 g of $Cl_2$?

**194.** Sodium sulfide and cadmium nitrate undergo a double-displacement reaction as shown by the following equation:

$$Na_2S + Cd(NO_3)_2 \rightarrow 2NaNO_3 + CdS$$

What is the mass, in milligrams, of cadmium sulfide that can be made from 5.00 mg of sodium sulfide?

**195.** Potassium permanganate and glycerin react explosively according to the following equation:

$$14KMnO_4 + 4C_3H_5(OH)_3 \rightarrow 7K_2CO_3 + 7Mn_2O_3 + 5CO_2 + 16H_2O$$

**a.** How many moles of carbon dioxide can be produced from 4.44 mol of $KMnO_4$?

**b.** If 5.21 g of $H_2O$ are produced, how many moles of glycerin, $C_3H_5(OH)_3$, were used?

**c.** If 3.39 mol of potassium carbonate are made, how many grams of manganese(III) oxide are also made?

**d.** How many grams of glycerin will be needed to react with 50.0 g of $KMnO_4$? How many grams of $CO_2$ will be produced in the same reaction?

**196.** Calcium carbonate found in limestone and marble reacts with hydrochloric acid to form calcium chloride, carbon dioxide, and water according to the following equation:

$$CaCO_3(s) + 2HCl(aq) \rightarrow CaCl_2(aq) + CO_2(g) + H_2O(l)$$

**a.** What mass of HCl will be needed to produce $5.00 \times 10^3$ kg of $CaCl_2$?

**b.** What mass of $CO_2$ could be produced from the reaction of 750 g of $CaCO_3$?

**197.** The fuel used to power the booster rockets on the space shuttle is a mixture of aluminum metal and ammonium perchlorate. The following balanced equation represents the reaction of these two ingredients:

$$3Al(s) + 3NH_4ClO_4(s) \rightarrow Al_2O_3(s) + AlCl_3(g) + 3NO(g) + 6H_2O(g)$$

**a.** If $1.50 \times 10^5$ g of Al react, what mass of $NH_4ClO_4$, in grams, is required?

**b.** If aluminum reacts with 620 kg of $NH_4ClO_4$, what mass of nitrogen monoxide is produced?

**198.** Phosphoric acid is typically produced by the action of sulfuric acid on rock that has a high content of calcium phosphate according to the following equation:

$$3H_2SO_4 + Ca_3(PO_4)_2 + 6H_2O \rightarrow 3[CaSO_4{\bullet}2H_2O] + 2H_3PO_4$$

**a.** If $2.50 \times 10^5$ kg of $H_2SO_4$ react, how many moles of $H_3PO_4$ can be made?

**b.** What mass of calcium sulfate dihydrate is produced by the reaction of 400. kg of calcium phosphate?

**c.** If the rock being used contains 78.8% $Ca_3(PO_4)_2$, how many metric tons of $H_3PO_4$ can be produced from 68 metric tons of rock?

**199.** Rusting of iron occurs in the presence of moisture according to the following equation:

$$4Fe(s) + 3O_2(g) \rightarrow 2Fe_2O_3(s)$$

Suppose that 3.19% of a heap of steel scrap with a mass of 1650 kg rusts in a year. What mass will the heap have after one year of rusting?

## Limiting Reactants: Chap. 9, Sec. 3

**200.** Aluminum oxidizes according to the following equation:

$$4Al + 3O_2 \rightarrow 2Al_2O_3$$

Powdered Al (0.048 mol) is placed into a container containing 0.030 mol $O_2$. What is the limiting reactant?

**201.** A process by which zirconium metal can be produced from the mineral zirconium(IV) orthosilicate, $ZrSiO_4$, starts by reacting it with chlorine gas to form zirconium(IV) chloride:

$$ZrSiO_4 + 2Cl_2 \rightarrow ZrCl_4 + SiO_2 + O_2$$

What mass of $ZrCl_4$ can be produced if 862 g of $ZrSiO_4$ and 950. g of $Cl_2$ are available? You must first determine the limiting reactant.

### Mixed Review

**202.** Heating zinc sulfide in the presence of oxygen yields the following:

$$ZnS + O_2 \rightarrow ZnO + SO_2$$

If 1.72 mol of ZnS is heated in the presence of 3.04 mol of $O_2$, which reactant will be used up? Balance the equation first.

**203.** Use the following equation for the oxidation of aluminum in the following problems:

$$4Al + 3O_2 \rightarrow 2Al_2O_3$$

**a.** Which reactant is limiting if 0.32 mol Al and 0.26 mol $O_2$ are available?

**b.** How many moles of $Al_2O_3$ are formed from the reaction of $6.38 \times 10^{-3}$ mol of $O_2$ and $9.15 \times 10^{-3}$ mol of Al?

**c.** If 3.17 g of Al and 2.55 g of $O_2$ are available, which reactant is limiting?

**204.** In the production of copper from ore containing copper(II) sulfide, the ore is first roasted to change it to the oxide according to the following equation:

$$2CuS + 3O_2 \rightarrow 2CuO + 2SO_2$$

**a.** If 100 g of CuS and 56 g of $O_2$ are available, which reactant is limiting?

**b.** What mass of CuO can be formed from the reaction of 18.7 g of CuS and 12.0 g of $O_2$?

**205.** A reaction such as the one shown here is often used to demonstrate a single-displacement reaction:

$$3CuSO_4(aq) + 2Fe(s) \rightarrow 3Cu(s) + Fe_2(SO_4)_3(aq)$$

If you place 0.092 mol of iron filings in a solution containing 0.158 mol of $CuSO_4$, what is the limiting reactant? How many moles of Cu will be formed?

**206.** In the reaction $BaCO_3 + 2HNO_3 \rightarrow Ba(NO_3)_2 + CO_2 + H_2O$, what mass of $Ba(NO_3)_2$ can be formed by combining 55 g $BaCO_3$ and 26 g $HNO_3$?

**207.** Bromine replaces iodine in magnesium iodide by the following process:

$$MgI_2 + Br_2 \rightarrow MgBr_2 + I_2$$

**a.** Which is the excess reactant when 560 g of $MgI_2$ and 360 g of $Br_2$ react, and what mass remains?

**b.** What mass of $I_2$ is formed in the same process?

**208.** Nickel replaces silver from silver nitrate in solution according to the following equation:

$$2AgNO_3 + Ni \rightarrow 2Ag + Ni(NO_3)_2$$

**a.** If you have 22.9 g of Ni and 112 g of $AgNO_3$, which reactant is in excess?

**b.** What mass of nickel(II) nitrate would be produced given the quantities above?

**209.** Carbon disulfide, $CS_2$, is an important industrial substance. Its fumes can burn explosively in air to form sulfur dioxide and carbon dioxide:

$$CS_2(g) + O_2(g) \rightarrow SO_2(g) + CO_2(g)$$

If 1.60 mol of $CS_2$ burns with 5.60 mol of $O_2$, how many moles of the excess reactant will still be present when the reaction is over?

**210.** Although poisonous, mercury compounds were once used to kill bacteria in wounds and on the skin. One was called "ammoniated mercury" and is made from mercury(II) chloride according to the following equation:

$$HgCl_2(aq) + 2NH_3(aq) \rightarrow Hg(NH_2)Cl(s) + NH_4Cl(aq)$$

a. What mass of $Hg(NH_2)Cl$ could be produced from 0.91 g of $HgCl_2$ assuming plenty of ammonia is available?
b. What mass of $Hg(NH_2)Cl$ could be produced from 0.91 g of $HgCl_2$ and 0.15 g of $NH_3$ in solution?

**211.** Aluminum chips are sometimes added to sodium hydroxide-based drain cleaners because they react to generate hydrogen gas which bubbles and helps loosen material in the drain. The equation follows:

$$Al(s) + NaOH(aq) + H_2O(l) \rightarrow NaAlO_2(aq) + H_2(g)$$

a. Balance the equation.
b. How many moles of $H_2$ can be generated from 0.57 mol Al and 0.37 mol NaOH in excess water?
c. Which reactant should be limiting in order for the mixture to be most effective as a drain cleaner? Explain your choice.

**212.** Copper is changed to copper(II) ions by nitric acid according to the following equation:

$$4HNO_3 + Cu \rightarrow Cu(NO_3)_2 + 2NO_2 + 2H_2O$$

a. How many moles each of $HNO_3$ and Cu must react in order to produce 0.0845 mol of $NO_2$?
b. If 5.94 g of Cu and 23.23 g of $HNO_3$ are combined, which reactant is in excess?

**213.** One industrial process for producing nitric acid begins with the following reaction:

$$4NH_3 + 5O_2 \rightarrow 4NO + 6H_2O$$

a. If 2.90 mol $NH_3$ and 3.75 mol $O_2$ are available, how many moles of each product are formed?
b. Which reactant is limiting if $4.20 \times 10^4$ g of $NH_3$ and $1.31 \times 10^5$ g of $O_2$ are available?
c. What mass of NO is formed in the reaction of 869 kg of $NH_3$ and 2480 kg $O_2$?

**214.** Acetaldehyde, $CH_3CHO$, is manufactured by the reaction of ethanol with copper(II) oxide according to the following equation:

$$CH_3CH_2OH + CuO \rightarrow CH_3CHO + H_2O + Cu$$

What mass of acetaldehyde can be produced by the reaction between 620 g of ethanol and 1020 g of CuO? What mass of which reactant will be left over?

**215.** Hydrogen bromide can be produced by a reaction among bromine, sulfur dioxide, and water as follows:

$$SO_2 + Br_2 + H_2O \rightarrow 2HBr + H_2SO_4$$

If 250 g of $SO_2$ and 650 g of $Br_2$ react in the presence of excess water, what mass of HBr will be formed?

**216.** Sulfur dioxide can be produced in the laboratory by the reaction of hydrochloric acid and a sulfite salt such as sodium sulfite:

$$Na_2SO_3 + 2HCl \rightarrow 2NaCl + SO_2 + H_2O$$

What mass of $SO_2$ can be made from 25.0 g of $Na_2SO_3$ and 22.0 g of HCl?

**217.** The rare-earth metal terbium is produced from terbium(III) fluoride and calcium metal by the following single-displacement reaction:

$$2TbF_3 + 3Ca \rightarrow 3CaF_2 + 2Tb$$

a. Given 27.5 g of $TbF_3$ and 6.96 g of Ca, how many grams of terbium could be produced?
b. How many grams of the excess reactant is left over?

## Percentage Yield: Chap. 9, Sec. 3

**218.** Calculate the percentage yield in each of the following cases.
a. theoretical yield is 50.0 g of product; actual yield is 41.9 g
b. theoretical yield is 290 kg of product; actual yield is 270 kg
c. theoretical yield is $6.05 \times 10^4$ kg of product; actual yield is $4.18 \times 10^4$ kg
d. theoretical yield is 0.00192 g of product; actual yield is 0.00089 g

**219.** In the commercial production of the element arsenic, arsenic(III) oxide is heated with carbon, which reduces the oxide to the metal according to the following equation:

$$2As_2O_3 + 3C \rightarrow 3CO_2 + 4As$$

a. If 8.87 g of $As_2O_3$ is used in the reaction and 5.33 g of As is produced, what is the percentage yield?
b. If 67 g of carbon is used up in a different reaction and 425 g of As is produced, calculate the percentage yield of this reaction.

### Mixed Review

**220.** Ethyl acetate is a sweet-smelling solvent used in varnishes and fingernail-polish remover. It is produced industrially by heating acetic acid and ethanol together in the presence of sulfuric acid, which is added to speed up the reaction. The ethyl acetate is distilled off as it is formed. The equation for the process is as follows:

$$\underset{\textit{acetic acid}}{CH_3COOH} + \underset{\textit{ethanol}}{CH_3CH_2OH} \xrightarrow{H_2SO_4} \underset{\textit{ethyl acetate}}{CH_3COOCH_2CH_3} + H_2O$$

Determine the percentage yield in the following cases.
a. 68.3 g of ethyl acetate should be produced but only 43.9 g is recovered.
b. 0.0419 mol of ethyl acetate is produced but 0.0722 mol is expected. (Hint: Percentage yield can also be calculated by dividing the actual yield in moles by the theoretical yield in moles.)
c. 4.29 mol of ethanol is reacted with excess acetic acid, but only 2.98 mol of ethyl acetate is produced.
d. A mixture of 0.58 mol ethanol and 0.82 mol acetic acid is reacted and 0.46 mol ethyl acetate is produced. (Hint: What is the limiting reactant?)

**221.** Assume the following hypothetical reaction takes place:

$$2A + 7B \rightarrow 4C + 3D$$

Calculate the percentage yield in each of the following cases.
a. The reaction of 0.0251 mol of A produces 0.0349 mol of C.

**b.** The reaction of 1.19 mol of A produces 1.41 mol of D.
**c.** The reaction of 189 mol of B produces 39 mol of D.
**d.** The reaction of 3500 mol of B produces 1700 mol of C.

**222.** Elemental phosphorus can be produced by heating calcium phosphate from rocks with silica sand ($SiO_2$) and carbon in the form of coke. The following reaction takes place:

$$Ca_3(PO_4)_2 + 3SiO_2 + 5C \rightarrow 3CaSiO_3 + 2P + 5CO$$

**a.** If 57 mol of $Ca_3(PO_4)_2$ is used and 101 mol of $CaSiO_3$ is obtained, what is the percentage yield?
**b.** Determine the percentage yield obtained if 1280 mol of carbon is consumed and 622 mol of $CaSiO_3$ is produced.
**c.** The engineer in charge of this process expects a yield of 81.5%. If $1.4 \times 10^5$ mol of $Ca_3(PO_4)_2$ is used, how many moles of phosphorus will be produced?

**223.** Tungsten (W) can be produced from its oxide by reacting the oxide with hydrogen at a high temperature according to the following equation:

$$WO_3 + 3H_2 \rightarrow W + 3H_2O$$

**a.** What is the percentage yield if 56.9 g of $WO_3$ yields 41.4 g of tungsten?
**b.** How many moles of tungsten will be produced from 3.72 g of $WO_3$ if the yield is 92.0%?
**c.** A chemist carries out this reaction and obtains 11.4 g of tungsten. If the percentage yield is 89.4%, what mass of $WO_3$ was used?

**224.** Carbon tetrachloride, $CCl_4$, is a solvent that was once used in large quantities in dry cleaning. Because it is a dense liquid that does not burn, it was also used in fire extinguishers. Unfortunately, its use was discontinued because it was found to be a carcinogen. It was manufactured by the following reaction:

$$CS_2 + 3Cl_2 \rightarrow CCl_4 + S_2Cl_2$$

The reaction was economical because the byproduct disulfur dichloride, $S_2Cl_2$, could be used by industry in the manufacture of rubber products and other materials.

**a.** What is the percentage yield of $CCl_4$ if 719 kg is produced from the reaction of 410. kg of $CS_2$?
**b.** If 67.5 g of $Cl_2$ are used in the reaction and 39.5 g of $S_2Cl_2$ is produced, what is the percentage yield?
**c.** If the percentage yield of the industrial process is 83.3%, how many kilograms of $CS_2$ should be reacted to obtain $5.00 \times 10^4$ kg of $CCl_4$? How many kilograms of $S_2Cl_2$ will be produced, assuming the same yield for that product?

**225.** Nitrogen dioxide, $NO_2$, can be converted to dinitrogen pentoxide, $N_2O_5$, by reacting it with ozone, $O_3$. The reaction of $NO_2$ takes place according to the following equation:

$$2NO_2(g) + O_3(g) \rightarrow N_2O_5(s \text{ or } g) + O_2(g)$$

**a.** Calculate the percentage yield for a reaction in which 0.38 g of $NO_2$ reacts and 0.36 g of $N_2O_5$ is recovered.
**b.** What mass of $N_2O_5$ will result from the reaction of 6.0 mol of $NO_2$ if there is a 61.1% yield in the reaction?

**226.** In the past, hydrogen chloride, HCl, was made using the *salt-cake* method as shown in the following equation:

$$2NaCl(s) + H_2SO_4(aq) \rightarrow Na_2SO_4(s) + 2HCl(g)$$

If 30.0 g of NaCl and 0.250 mol of $H_2SO_4$ are available, and 14.6 g of HCl is made, what is the percentage yield?

**227.** Cyanide compounds such as sodium cyanide, NaCN, are especially useful in gold refining because they will react with gold to form a stable compound that can then be separated and broken down to retrieve the gold. Ore containing only small quantities of gold can be used in this form of "chemical mining." The equation for the reaction follows:

$$4Au + 8NaCN + 2H_2O + O_2 \rightarrow 4NaAu(CN)_2 + 4NaOH$$

**a.** What percentage yield is obtained if 410 g of gold produces 540 g of $NaAu(CN)_2$?
**b.** Assuming a 79.6% yield in the conversion of gold to $NaAu(CN)_2$, what mass of gold would produce 1.00 kg of $NaAu(CN)_2$?
**c.** Given the conditions in (b), what mass of gold ore that is 0.001% gold would be needed to produce 1.00 kg of $NaAu(CN)_2$?

**228.** Diiodine pentoxide is useful in devices such as respirators because it reacts with the dangerous gas carbon monoxide, CO, to produce relatively harmless $CO_2$ according to the following equation:

$$I_2O_5 + 5CO \rightarrow I_2 + 5CO_2$$

**a.** In testing a respirator, 2.00 g of carbon monoxide gas is passed through diiodine pentoxide. Upon analyzing the results, it is found that 3.17 g of $I_2$ was produced. Calculate the percentage yield of the reaction.
**b.** Assuming that the yield in (a) resulted because some of the CO did not react, calculate the mass of CO that passed through.

**229.** Sodium hypochlorite, NaClO, the main ingredient in household bleach, is produced by bubbling chlorine gas through a strong lye (sodium hydroxide, NaOH) solution. The following equation shows the reaction that occurs:

$$2NaOH(aq) + Cl_2(g) \rightarrow NaCl(aq) + NaClO(aq) + H_2O(l)$$

**a.** What is the percentage yield of the reaction if 1.2 kg of $Cl_2$ reacts to form 0.90 kg of NaClO?
**b.** If a plant operator wants to make 25 metric tons of NaClO per day at a yield of 91.8%, how many metric tons of chlorine gas must be on hand each day?
**c.** What mass of NaCl is formed per mole of chlorine gas at a yield of 81.8%?
**d.** At what rate in kg per hour must NaOH be replenished if the reaction produces 370 kg/h of NaClO at a yield of 79.5%? Assume that all of the NaOH reacts to produce this yield.

**230.** Magnesium burns in oxygen to form magnesium oxide. However, when magnesium burns in air, which is only about one-fifth oxygen, side reactions form other products, such as magnesium nitride, $Mg_3N_2$.

a. Write a balanced equation for the burning of magnesium in oxygen.
b. If enough magnesium burns in air to produce 2.04 g of magnesium oxide but only 1.79 g is obtained, what is the percentage yield?
c. Magnesium will react with pure nitrogen to form the nitride, $Mg_3N_2$. Write a balanced equation for this reaction.
d. If 0.097 mol of Mg react with nitrogen and 0.027 mol of $Mg_3N_2$ is produced, what is the percentage yield of the reaction?

**231.** Some alcohols can be converted to organic acids by using sodium dichromate and sulfuric acid. The following equation shows the reaction of 1-propanol to propanoic acid:

$$3CH_3CH_2CH_2OH + 2Na_2Cr_2O_7 + 8H_2SO_4 \rightarrow 3CH_3CH_2COOH + 2Cr_2(SO_4)_3 + 2Na_2SO_4 + 11H_2O$$

a. If 0.89 g of 1-propanol reacts and 0.88 g of propanoic acid is produced, what is the percentage yield?
b. A chemist uses this reaction to obtain 1.50 mol of propanoic acid. The reaction consumes 136 g of propanol. Calculate the percentage yield.
c. Some 1-propanol of uncertain purity is used in the reaction. If 116 g of $Na_2Cr_2O_7$ are consumed in the reaction and 28.1 g of propanoic acid are produced, what is the percentage yield?

**232.** Acrylonitrile, $C_3H_3N(g)$, is an important ingredient in the production of various fibers and plastics. Acrylonitrile is produced from the following reaction:

$$C_3H_6(g) + NH_3(g) + O_2(g) \rightarrow C_3H_3N(g) + H_2O(g)$$

If 850. g of $C_3H_6$ is mixed with 300. g of $NH_3$ and unlimited $O_2$, to produce 850. g of acrylonitrile, what is the percentage yield? You must first balance the equation.

**233.** Methanol, $CH_3OH$, is frequently used in race cars as fuel. It is produced as the sole product of the combination of carbon monoxide gas and hydrogen gas.
a. If 430. kg of hydrogen react, what mass of methanol could be produced?
b. If $3.12 \times 10^3$ kg of methanol are actually produced, what is the percentage yield?

**234.** The compound, $C_6H_{16}N_2$, is one of the starting materials in the production of nylon. It can be prepared from the following reaction involving adipic acid, $C_6H_{10}O_4$:

$$C_6H_{10}O_4(l) + 2NH_3(g) + 4H_2(g) \rightarrow C_6H_{16}N_2(l) + 4H_2O$$

What is the percentage yield if 750. g of adipic acid results in the production of 578 g of $C_6H_{16}N_2$?

**235.** Plants convert carbon dioxide to oxygen during photosynthesis according to the following equation:

$$CO_2 + H_2O \rightarrow C_6H_{12}O_6 + O_2$$

Balance this equation, and calculate how much oxygen would be produced if $1.37 \times 10^4$ g of carbon dioxide reacts with a percentage yield of 63.4%.

**236.** Lime, CaO, is frequently added to streams and lakes which have been polluted by acid rain. The calcium oxide reacts with the water to form a base that can neutralize the acid as shown in the following reaction:

$$CaO(s) + H_2O(l) \rightarrow Ca(OH)_2(s)$$

If $2.67 \times 10^2$ mol of base are needed to neutralize the acid in a lake, and the above reaction has a percentage yield of 54.3%, what is the mass, in kilograms, of lime that must be added to the lake?

## Gas Laws: Chap. 11, Sec. 2

### Boyle's Law

*In each of the following problems, assume that the temperature and molar quantity of gas do not change.*

**237.** Calculate the unknown quantity in each of the following measurements of gases.

| $P_1$ | $V_1$ | $P_2$ | $V_2$ |
|---|---|---|---|
| **a.** 3.0 atm | 25 mL | 6.0 atm | ? mL |
| **b.** 99.97 kPa | 550. mL | ? kPa | 275 mL |
| **c.** 0.89 atm | ? L | 3.56 atm | 20.0 L |
| **d.** ? kPa | 800. mL | 500. kPa | 160. mL |
| **e.** 0.040 atm | ? L | 250 atm | $1.0 \times 10^{-2}$ L |

**238.** A sample of neon gas occupies a volume of 2.8 L at 1.8 atm. What will its volume be at 1.2 atm?

**239.** To what pressure would you have to compress 48.0 L of oxygen gas at 99.3 kPa in order to reduce its volume to 16.0 L?

**240.** A chemist collects 59.0 mL of sulfur dioxide gas on a day when the atmospheric pressure is 0.989 atm. On the next day, the pressure has changed to 0.967 atm. What will the volume of the $SO_2$ gas be on the second day?

**241.** 2.2 L of hydrogen at 6.5 atm pressure is used to fill a balloon at a final pressure of 1.15 atm. What is its final volume?

### Charles's Law

*In each of the following problems, assume that the pressure and molar quantity of gas do not change.*

**242.** Calculate the unknown quantity in each of the following measurements of gases:

| $V_1$ | $T_1$ | $V_2$ | $T_2$ |
|---|---|---|---|
| **a.** 40.0 mL | 280. K | ? mL | 350. K |
| **b.** 0.606 L | 300. K | 0.404 L | ? K |
| **c.** ? mL | 292 K | 250. mL | 365 K |
| **d.** 100. mL | ? K | 125 mL | 305 K |
| **e.** 0.0024 L | 22°C | ? L | −14°C |

**243.** A balloon full of air has a volume of 2.75 L at a temperature of 18°C. What is the balloon's volume at 45°C?

**244.** A sample of argon has a volume of 0.43 mL at 24°C. At what temperature in degrees Celsius will it have a volume of 0.57 mL?

## Gay-Lussac's Law

*In each of the following problems, assume that the volume and molar quantity of gas do not change.*

**245.** Calculate the unknown quantity in each of the following measurements of gases.

| $P_1$ | $T_1$ | $P_2$ | $T_2$ |
|---|---|---|---|
| **a.** 1.50 atm | 273 K | ? atm | 410 K |
| **b.** 0.208 atm | 300. K | 0.156 atm | ? K |
| **c.** ? kPa | 52°C | 99.7 kPa | 77°C |
| **d.** 5.20 atm | ?°C | 4.16 atm | −13°C |
| **e.** $8.33 \times 10^{-4}$ atm | −84°C | $3.92 \times 10^{-3}$ atm | ? °C |

**246.** A cylinder of compressed gas has a pressure of 4.882 atm on one day. The next day, the same cylinder of gas has a pressure of 4.690 atm, and its temperature is 8°C. What was the temperature on the previous day in °C?

**247.** A mylar balloon is filled with helium gas to a pressure of 107 kPa when the temperature is 22°C. If the temperature changes to 45°C, what will be the pressure of the helium in the balloon?

## The Combined Gas Law

*In each of the following problems, it is assumed that the molar quantity of gas does not change.*

**248.** Calculate the unknown quantity in each of the following measurements of gases.

| $P_1$ | $V_1$ | $T_1$ | $P_2$ | $V_2$ | $T_2$ |
|---|---|---|---|---|---|
| **a.** 99.3 kPa | 225 mL | 15°C | 102.8 kPa | ? mL | 24°C |
| **b.** 0.959 atm | 3.50 L | 45°C | ? atm | 3.70 L | 37°C |
| **c.** 0.0036 atm | 62 mL | 373 K | 0.0029 atm | 64 mL | ? K |
| **d.** 100. kPa | 43.2 mL | 19°C | 101.3 kPa | ? mL | 0°C |

**249.** A student collects 450. mL of $HCl(g)$ hydrogen chloride gas at a pressure of 100. kPa and a temperature of 17°C. What is the volume of the HCl at 0°C and 101.3 kPa?

## Dalton's Law of Partial Pressures

**250.** A chemist collects a sample of $H_2S(g)$ over water at a temperature of 27°C. The total pressure of the gas that has displaced a volume of 15 mL of water is 207.33 kPa. What is the pressure of the $H_2S$ gas collected?

*In each of the following problems, assume that the molar quantity of gas does not change.*

**251.** Some hydrogen is collected over water at 10°C and 105.5 kPa pressure. The total volume of the sample was 1.93 L. Calculate the volume of the hydrogen corrected to STP.

**252.** One student carries out a reaction that gives off methane gas and obtains a total volume by water displacement of 338 mL at a temperature of 19°C and a pressure of 0.9566 atm. Another student does the identical experiment on another day at a temperature of 26°C and a pressure of 0.989 atm. Which student collected more $CH_4$?

## Mixed Review

*In each of the following problems, assume that the molar quantity of gas does not change.*

**253.** Calculate the unknown quantity in each of the following measurements of gases.

| $P_1$ | $V_1$ | $P_2$ | $V_2$ |
|---|---|---|---|
| **a.** 127.3 kPa | 796 $cm^3$ | ? kPa | 965 $cm^3$ |
| **b.** $7.1 \times 10^2$ atm | ? mL | $9.6 \times 10^{-1}$ atm | $3.7 \times 10^3$ mL |
| **c.** ? kPa | 1.77 L | 30.79 kPa | 2.44 L |
| **d.** 114 kPa | 2.93 $dm^3$ | $4.93 \times 10^4$ kPa | ? $dm^3$ |
| **e.** 1.00 atm | 120. mL | ? atm | 97.0 mL |
| **f.** 0.77 atm | 3.6 $m^3$ | 1.90 atm | ? $m^3$ |

**254.** A gas cylinder contains 0.722 $m^3$ of hydrogen gas at a pressure of 10.6 atm. If the gas is used to fill a balloon at a pressure of 0.96 atm, what is the volume in $m^3$ of the filled balloon?

**255.** A weather balloon has a maximum volume of $7.50 \times 10^3$ L. The balloon contains 195 L of helium gas at a pressure of 0.993 atm. What will be the pressure when the balloon is at maximum volume?

**256.** A rubber ball contains $5.70 \times 10^{-1}$ $dm^3$ of gas at a pressure of 1.05 atm. What volume will the gas occupy at 7.47 atm?

**257.** Calculate the unknown quantity in each of the following measurements of gases.

| $V_1$ | $T_1$ | $V_2$ | $T_2$ |
|---|---|---|---|
| **a.** 26.5 mL | ? K | 32.9 mL | 290. K |
| **b.** ? $dm^3$ | 100.°C | 0.83 $dm^3$ | 29°C |
| **c.** $7.44 \times 10^4$ $mm^3$ | 870.°C | $2.59 \times 10^2$ $mm^3$ | ? °C |
| **d.** $5.63 \times 10^{-2}$ L | 132 K | ? L | 190. K |
| **e.** ? $cm^3$ | 243 K | 819 $cm^3$ | 409 K |
| **f.** 679 $m^3$ | −3°C | ? $m^3$ | −246°C |

**258.** A bubble of carbon dioxide gas in some unbaked bread dough has a volume of 1.15 $cm^3$ at a temperature of 22°C. What volume will the bubble have when the bread is baked and the bubble reaches a temperature of 99°C?

**259.** A perfectly elastic balloon contains 6.75 $dm^3$ of air at a temperature of 40.°C. What is the temperature if the balloon has a volume of 5.03 $dm^3$?

**260.** Calculate the unknown quantity in each of the following measurements of gases.

| $P_1$ | $T_1$ | $P_2$ | $T_2$ |
|---|---|---|---|
| **a.** 0.777 atm | ?°C | 5.6 atm | 192°C |
| **b.** 152 kPa | 302 K | ? kPa | 11 K |
| **c.** ? atm | −76°C | 3.97 atm | 27°C |
| **d.** 395 atm | 46°C | 706 atm | ?°C |
| **e.** ? atm | −37°C | 350. atm | 2050°C |
| **f.** 0.39 atm | 263 K | 0.058 atm | ? K |

**261.** A 2 L bottle containing only air is sealed at a temperature of 22°C and a pressure of 0.982 atm. The bottle is placed in a freezer and allowed to cool to −3°C. What is the pressure in the bottle?

**262.** The pressure in a car tire is 2.50 atm at a temperature of 33°C . What would the pressure be if the tire were allowed to cool to 0°C? Assume that the tire does not change volume.

**263.** A container filled with helium gas has a pressure of 127.5 kPa at a temperature of 290. K. What is the temperature when the pressure is 3.51 kPa?

**264.** Calculate the unknown quantity in each of the following measurements of gases.

| $P_1$ | $V_1$ | $T_1$ | $P_2$ | $V_2$ | $T_2$ |
|---|---|---|---|---|---|
| **a.** 1.03 atm | 1.65 L | 19°C | 0.920 atm | ? L | 46°C |
| **b.** 107.0 kPa | 3.79 $dm^3$ | 73°C | ? kPa | 7.58 $dm^3$ | 217°C |
| **c.** 0.029 atm | 249 mL | ? K | 0.098 atm | 197 mL | 293 K |
| **d.** 113 kPa | ? $mm^3$ | 12°C | 149 kPa | $3.18 \times 10^3$ $mm^3$ | −18°C |
| **e.** 1.15 atm | 0.93 $m^3$ | −22°C | 1.01 atm | 0.85 $m^3$ | ?°C |
| **f.** ? atm | 156 $cm^3$ | 195 K | 2.25 atm | 468 $cm^3$ | 585 K |

**265.** A scientist has a sample of gas that was collected several days earlier. The sample has a volume of 392 $cm^3$ at a pressure of 0.987 atm and a temperature of 21°C. On the day the gas was collected, the temperature was 13°C and the pressure was 0.992 atm. What volume did the gas have on the day it was collected?

**266.** Hydrogen gas is collected by water displacement. Total volume collected is 0.461 L at a temperature of 17°C and a pressure of 0.989 atm. What is the pressure of dry hydrogen gas collected?

**267.** One container with a volume of 1.00 L contains argon at a pressure of 1.77 atm, and a second container of 1.50 L volume contains argon at a pressure of 0.487 atm. They are then connected to each other so that the pressure can become equal in both containers. What is the equalized pressure? Hint: Each sample of gas now occupies the total space. Dalton's law of partial pressures applies here.

**268.** Oxygen gas is collected over water at a temperature of 10.°C and a pressure of 1.02 atm. The volume of gas plus water vapor collected is 293 mL. What volume of oxygen at STP was collected?

**269.** A 500 mL bottle is partially filled with water so that the total volume of gases (water vapor and air) remaining in the bottle is 325 $cm^3$, measured at 20.°C and 101.3 kPa. The bottle is sealed and taken to a mountaintop where the pressure is 76.24 kPa and the temperature is 10°C. If the bottle is upside down and the seal leaks, how much water will leak out? The key to this problem is to determine the pressure in the 325 $cm^3$ space when the bottle is at the top of the mountain.

**270.** An air thermometer can be constructed by using a glass bubble attached to a piece of small-diameter glass tubing. The tubing contains a small amount of colored water that rises when the temperature increases and the trapped air expands. You want a 0.20 $cm^3$ change in volume to equal a 1°C change in temperature. What total volume of air at 20.°C should be trapped in the apparatus below the liquid?

**271.** A sample of nitrogen gas is collected over water, yielding a total volume of 62.25 mL at a temperature of 22°C and a total pressure of 97.7 kPa. At what pressure will the nitrogen alone occupy a volume of 50.00 mL at the same temperature?

**272.** The theoretical yield of a reaction that gives off nitrogen trifluoride gas is 844 mL at STP. What total volume of $NF_3$ plus water vapor will be collected over water at 25°C and a total pressure of 1.017 atm?

**273.** A weather balloon is inflated with 2.94 kL of helium at a location where the pressure is 1.06 atm and the temperature is 32°C. What will be the volume of the balloon at an altitude where the pressure is 0.092 atm and the temperature is −35°C?

**274.** The safety limit for a certain can of aerosol spray is 95°C. If the pressure of the gas in the can is 2.96 atm when it is 17°C, what will the pressure be at the safety limit?

**275.** A chemistry student collects a sample of ammonia gas at a temperature of 39°C. Later, the student measures the volume of the ammonia as 108 mL, but its temperature is now 21°C. What was the volume of the ammonia when it was collected?

**276.** A quantity of $CO_2$ gas occupies a volume of 624 L at a pressure of 1.40 atm. If this $CO_2$ is pumped into a gas cylinder that has a volume of 80.0 L, what pressure will the $CO_2$ exert on the cylinder?

## The Ideal Gas Law: Chap. 11, Sec. 3

**277.** Use the ideal-gas-law equation to calculate the unknown quantity in each of the following sets of measurements. You will need to convert Celsius temperatures to Kelvin temperatures and volume units to liters.

| *P* | *V* | *n* | *T* |
|---|---|---|---|
| **a.** 1.09 atm | ? L | 0.0881 mol | 302 K |
| **b.** 94.9 kPa | 0.0350 L | ? mol | 55°C |
| **c.** ? kPa | 15.7 L | 0.815 mol | −20.°C |
| **d.** 0.500 atm | 629 mL | 0.0337 mol | ? K |
| **e.** 0.950 atm | ? L | 0.0818 mol | 19°C |
| **f.** 107 kPa | 39.0 mL | ? mol | 27°C |

**278.** A student collects 425 mL of oxygen at a temperature of 24°C and a pressure of 0.899 atm. How many moles of oxygen did the student collect?

### Applications of the Ideal Gas Law

**279.** A sample of an unknown gas has a mass of 0.116 g. It occupies a volume of 25.0 mL at a temperature of 127°C and has a pressure of 155.3 kPa. Calculate the molar mass of the gas.

**280.** Determine the mass of $CO_2$ gas that has a volume of 7.10 L at a pressure of 1.11 atm and a temperature of 31°C. Hint: Solve the equation for *m*, and calculate the molar mass using the chemical formula and the periodic table.

**281.** What is the density of silicon tetrafluoride gas at 72°C and a pressure of 144.5 kPa?

**282.** At what temperature will nitrogen gas have a density of 1.13 g/L at a pressure of 1.09 atm?

### Mixed Review

**283.** Use the ideal-gas-law equation to calculate the unknown quantity in each of the following sets of measurements.

| *P* | *V* | *n* | *t* |
|---|---|---|---|
| **a.** 0.0477 atm | 15 200 L | ? mol | −15°C |
| **b.** ? kPa | 0.119 mL | 0.000 350 mol | 0°C |
| **c.** 500.0 kPa | 250. mL | 0.120 mol | ?°C |
| **d.** 19.5 atm | ? | $4.7 \times 10^4$ mol | 300.°C |

**284.** Use the ideal-gas-law equation to calculate the unknown quantity in each of the following sets of measurements.

| *P* | *V* | *m* | *M* | *t* |
|---|---|---|---|---|
| **a.** 0.955 atm | 3.77 L | 8.23 g | ? g/mol | 25°C |
| **b.** 105.0 kPa | 50.0 mL | ? g | 48.02 g/mol | 0°C |
| **c.** 0.782 atm | ? L | $3.20 \times 10^{-3}$ g | 2.02 g/mol | −5°C |
| **d.** ? atm | 2.00 L | 7.19 g | 159.8 g/mol | 185°C |
| **e.** 107.2 kPa | 26.1 mL | 0.414 g | ? g/mol | 45°C |

**285.** Determine the volume of one mole of an ideal gas at 25°C and 0.915 kPa.

**286.** Calculate the unknown quantity in each of the following sets of measurements.

| *P* | *Molar Mass* | *Density* | *t* |
|---|---|---|---|
| **a.** 1.12 atm | ? g/mol | 2.40 g/L | 2°C |
| **b.** 7.50 atm | 30.07 g/mol | ? g/L | 20.°C |
| **c.** 97.4 kPa | 104.09 g/mol | 4.37 g/L | ? °C |
| **d.** ? atm | 77.95 g/mol | 6.27 g/L | 66°C |

**287.** What pressure in atmospheres will 1.36 kg of $N_2O$ gas exert when it is compressed in a 25.0 L cylinder and is stored in an outdoor shed where the temperature can reach 59°C during the summer?

**288.** Aluminum chloride sublimes at high temperatures. What density will the vapor have at 225°C and 0.939 atm pressure?

**289.** An unknown gas has a density of 0.0262 g/mL at a pressure of 0.918 atm and a temperature of 10.°C. What is the molar mass of the gas?

**290.** A large balloon contains 11.7 g of helium. What volume will the helium occupy at an altitude of 10 000 m, where the atmospheric pressure is 0.262 atm and the temperature is −50.°C?

**291.** A student collects ethane by water displacement at a temperature of 15°C (vapor pressure of water is 1.5988 kPa) and a total pressure of 100.0 kPa. The volume of the collection bottle is 245 mL. How many moles of ethane are in the bottle?

**292.** A reaction yields 3.75 L of nitrogen monoxide. The volume is measured at 19°C and at a pressure of 1.10 atm. What mass of NO was produced by the reaction?

**293.** A reaction has a theoretical yield of 8.83 g of ammonia. The reaction gives off 10.24 L of ammonia measured at 52°C and 105.3 kPa. What was the percent yield of the reaction?

**294.** An unknown gas has a density of 0.405 g/L at a pressure of 0.889 atm and a temperature of 7°C. Calculate its molar mass.

**295.** A paper label has been lost from an old tank of compressed gas. To help identify the unknown gas, you must calculate its molar mass. It is known that the tank has a capacity of 90.0 L and weighs 39.2 kg when empty. You find its current mass to be 50.5 kg. The gauge shows a pressure of 1780 kPa when the temperature is 18°C. What is the molar mass of the gas in the cylinder?

**296.** What is the pressure inside a tank that has a volume of $1.20 \times 10^3$ L and contains 12.0 kg of HCl gas at a temperature of 18°C?

**297.** What pressure in kPa is exerted at a temperature of 20.°C by compressed neon gas that has a density of 2.70 g/L?

**298.** A tank with a volume of 658 mL contains 1.50 g of neon gas. The maximum safe pressure that the tank can withstand is $4.50 \times 10^2$ kPa. At what temperature will the tank have that pressure?

**299.** The atmospheric pressure on Mars is about 6.75 millibars (1 bar = 100 kPa = 0.9869 atm), and the nighttime temperature can be about −75°C on the same day that the daytime temperature goes up to −8°C. What volume would a bag containing 1.00 g of $H_2$ gas have at both the daytime and nighttime temperatures?

**300.** What is the pressure in kPa of 3.95 mol of $Cl_2$ gas if it is compressed in a cylinder with a volume of 850. mL at a temperature of 15°C?

**301.** What volume in mL will 0.00660 mol of hydrogen gas occupy at a pressure of 0.907 atm and a temperature of 9°C?

**302.** What volume will 8.47 kg of sulfur dioxide gas occupy at a pressure of 89.4 kPa and a temperature of 40.°C?

**303.** A cylinder contains 908 g of compressed helium. It is to be used to inflate a balloon to a final pressure of 128.3 kPa at a temperature of 2°C. What will the volume of the balloon be under these conditions?

**304.** The density of dry air at 27°C and 100.0 kPa is 1.162 g/L. Use this information to calculate the molar mass of air (calculate as if air were a pure substance).

## Stoichiometry of Gases: Chap. 11, Sec. 3

**305.** In one method of manufacturing nitric acid, ammonia is oxidized to nitrogen monoxide and water:

$$4NH_3(g) + 5O_2(g) \rightarrow 4NO(g) + 6H_2O(l)$$

What volume of oxygen will be used in a reaction of 2800 L of $NH_3$? What volume of NO will be produced? All volumes are measured under the same conditions.

**306.** Fluorine gas reacts violently with water to produce hydrogen fluoride and ozone according to the following equation:

$$3F_2(g) + 3H_2O(l) \rightarrow 6HF(g) + O_3(g)$$

What volumes of $O_3$ and HF gas would be produced by the complete reaction of $3.60 \times 10^4$ mL of fluorine gas? All gases are measured under the same conditions.

**307.** A sample of ethanol burns in $O_2$ to form $CO_2$ and $H_2O$ according to the following equation:

$$C_2H_5OH + 3O_2 \rightarrow 2CO_2 + 3H_2O$$

If the combustion uses 55.8 mL of oxygen measured at 2.26 atm and 40.°C, what volume of $CO_2$ is produced when measured at STP?

**308.** Dinitrogen pentoxide decomposes into nitrogen dioxide and oxygen. If 5.00 L of $N_2O_5$ reacts at STP, what volume of $NO_2$ is produced when measured at 64.5°C and 1.76 atm?

**309.** Complete the table below using the following equation, which represents a reaction that produces aluminum chloride:

$$2Al(s) + 3Cl_2(g) \rightarrow 2AlCl_3(s)$$

| *Mass Al* | *Volume $Cl_2$* | *Conditions* | *Mass $AlCl_3$* |
|---|---|---|---|
| **a.** excess | ? L | STP | 7.15 g |
| **b.** 19.4 g | ? L | STP | NA |
| **c.** 1.559 kg | ? L | 20.°C and 0.945 atm | NA |
| **d.** excess | 920. L | STP | ? g |
| **e.** ? g | 1.049 mL | 37°C and 5.00 atm | NA |
| **f.** 500.00 kg | ? $m^3$ | 15°C and 83.0 kPa | NA |

### Mixed Review

**310.** The industrial production of ammonia proceeds according to the following equation:

$$N_2(g) + 3H_2(g) \rightarrow 2NH_3(g)$$

**a.** What volume of nitrogen at STP is needed to react with 57.0 mL of hydrogen measured at STP?

**b.** What volume of $NH_3$ at STP can be produced from the complete reaction of $6.39 \times 10^4$ L of hydrogen?

**c.** If 20.0 mol of nitrogen is available, what volume of $NH_3$ at STP can be produced?

**d.** What volume of $H_2$ at STP will be needed to produce 800. L of ammonia, measured at 55°C and 0.900 atm?

**311.** Propane burns according to the following equation:

$$C_3H_8(g) + 5O_2(g) \rightarrow 3CO_2(g) + 4H_2O(g)$$

**a.** What volume of water vapor measured at 250.°C and 1.00 atm is produced when 3.0 L of propane at STP is burned?

**b.** What volume of oxygen at 20.°C and 102.6 kPa is used if 640. L of $CO_2$ is produced? The $CO_2$ is also measured at 20.°C and 102.6 kPa.

**c.** If 465 mL of oxygen at STP is used in the reaction, what volume of $CO_2$, measured at 37°C and 0.973 atm, is produced?

**d.** When 2.50 L of $C_3H_8$ at STP burns, what total volume of gaseous products is formed? The volume of the products is measured at 175°C and 1.14 atm.

**312.** Carbon monoxide will burn in air to produce $CO_2$ according to the following equation:

$$2CO(g) + O_2(g) \rightarrow 2CO_2(g)$$

What volume of oxygen at STP will be needed to react with 3500. L of CO measured at 20.°C and a pressure of 0.953 atm?

**313.** Silicon tetrafluoride gas can be produced by the action of HF on silica according to the following equation:

$$SiO_2(s) + 4HF(g) \rightarrow SiF_4(g) + 2H_2O(l)$$

1.00 L of HF gas under pressure at 3.48 atm and a temperature of 25°C reacts completely with $SiO_2$ to form $SiF_4$. What volume of $SiF_4$, measured at 15°C and 0.940 atm, is produced by this reaction?

**314.** One method used in the eighteenth century to generate hydrogen was to pass steam through red-hot steel tubes. The following reaction takes place:

$$3Fe(s) + 4H_2O(g) \rightarrow Fe_3O_4(s) + 4H_2(g)$$

**a.** What volume of hydrogen at STP can be produced by the reaction of 6.28 g of iron?
**b.** What mass of iron will react with 500. L of steam at 250.°C and 1.00 atm pressure?
**c.** If 285 g of $Fe_3O_4$ are formed, what volume of hydrogen, measured at 20.°C and 1.06 atm, is produced?

**315.** Sodium reacts vigorously with water to produce hydrogen and sodium hydroxide according to the following equation:

$$2Na(s) + 2H_2O(l) \rightarrow 2NaOH(aq) + H_2(g)$$

If 0.027 g of sodium reacts with excess water, what volume of hydrogen at STP is formed?

**316.** Diethyl ether burns in air according to the following equation:

$$C_4H_{10}O(l) + 6O_2(g) \rightarrow 4CO_2(g) + 5H_2O(l)$$

If 7.15 L of $CO_2$ is produced at a temperature of 125°C and a pressure of 1.02 atm, what volume of oxygen, measured at STP, was consumed and what mass of diethyl ether was burned?

**317.** When nitroglycerin detonates, it produces large volumes of hot gases almost instantly according to the following equation:

$$4C_3H_5N_3O_9(l) \rightarrow 6N_2(g) + 12CO_2(g) + 10H_2O(g) + O_2(g)$$

**a.** When 0.100 mol of nitroglycerin explodes, what volume of each gas measured at STP is produced?
**b.** What total volume of gases is produced at 300.°C and 1.00 atm when 10.0 g of nitroglycerin explodes?

**318.** Dinitrogen monoxide can be prepared by heating ammonium nitrate, which decomposes according to the following equation:

$$NH_4NO_3(s) \rightarrow N_2O(g) + 2H_2O(l)$$

What mass of ammonium nitrate should be decomposed in order to produce 250. mL of $N_2O$, measured at STP?

**319.** Phosphine, $PH_3$, is the phosphorus analogue to ammonia, $NH_3$. It can be produced by the reaction between calcium phosphide and water according to the following equation:

$$Ca_3P_2(s) + 6H_2O(l) \rightarrow 3Ca(OH)_2(s \text{ and } aq) + 2PH_3(g)$$

What volume of phosphine, measured at 18°C and 102.4 kPa, is produced by the reaction of 8.46 g of $Ca_3P_2$?

**320.** In one method of producing aluminum chloride, HCl gas is passed over aluminum and the following reaction takes place:

$$2Al(s) + 6HCl(g) \rightarrow 2AlCl_3(g) + 3H_2(g)$$

What mass of Al should be on hand in order to produce $6.0 \times 10^3$ kg of $AlCl_3$? What volume of compressed HCl at 4.71 atm and a temperature of 43°C should be on hand at the same time?

**321.** Urea, $(NH_2)_2CO$, is an important fertilizer that is manufactured by the following reaction:

$$2NH_3(g) + CO_2(g) \rightarrow (NH_2)_2CO(s) + H_2O(g)$$

What volume of $NH_3$ at STP will be needed to produce $8.50 \times 10^4$ kg of urea if there is an 89.5% yield in the process?

**322.** An obsolete method of generating oxygen in the laboratory involves the decomposition of barium peroxide by the following equation:

$$2BaO_2(s) \rightarrow 2BaO(s) + O_2(g)$$

What mass of $BaO_2$ reacted if 265 mL of $O_2$ is collected by water displacement at 0.975 atm and 10.°C?

**323.** It is possible to generate chlorine gas by dripping concentrated HCl solution onto solid potassium permanganate according to the following equation:

$$2KMnO_4(aq) + 16HCl(aq) \rightarrow 2KCl(aq) + 2MnCl_2(aq) + 8H_2O(l) + 5Cl_2(g)$$

If excess HCl is dripped onto 15.0 g of $KMnO_4$, what volume of $Cl_2$ will be produced? The $Cl_2$ is measured at 15°C and 0.959 atm.

**324.** Ammonia can be oxidized in the presence of a platinum catalyst according to the following equation:

$$4NH_3(g) + 5O_2(g) \rightarrow 4NO(g) + 6H_2O(l)$$

The NO that is produced reacts almost immediately with additional oxygen according to the following equation:

$$2NO(g) + O_2(g) \rightarrow 2NO_2(g)$$

If 35.0 kL of oxygen at STP react in the first reaction, what volume of $NH_3$ at STP reacts with it? What volume of $NO_2$ at STP will be formed in the second reaction, assuming there is excess oxygen that was not used up in the first reaction?

**325.** Oxygen can be generated in the laboratory by heating potassium chlorate. The reaction is represented by the following equation:

$$2KClO_3(s) \rightarrow 2KCl(s) + 3O_2(g)$$

What mass of $KClO_3$ must be used in order to generate 5.00 L of $O_2$, measured at STP?

**326.** One of the reactions in the Solvay process is used to make sodium hydrogen carbonate. It occurs when carbon dioxide and ammonia are passed through concentrated salt brine. The following equation represents the reaction:

$$NaCl(aq) + H_2O(l) + CO_2(g) + NH_3(g) \rightarrow NaHCO_3(s) + NH_4Cl(aq)$$

**a.** What volume of $NH_3$ at 25°C and 1.00 atm pressure will be required if 38 000 L of $CO_2$, measured under the same conditions, react to form $NaHCO_3$?
**b.** What mass of $NaHCO_3$ can be formed when the gases in (a) react with NaCl?
**c.** If this reaction forms 46.0 kg of $NaHCO_3$, what volume of $NH_3$, measured at STP, reacted?
**d.** What volume of $CO_2$, compressed in a tank at 5.50 atm and a temperature of 42°C, will be needed to produce 100.00 kg of $NaHCO_3$?

**327.** The combustion of butane is represented in the following equation:

$$2C_4H_{10}(g) + 13O_2(g) \rightarrow 8CO_2(g) + 10H_2O(l)$$

**a.** If 4.74 g of butane react with excess oxygen, what volume of $CO_2$, measured at 150.°C and 1.14 atm, will be formed?
**b.** What volume of oxygen, measured at 0.980 atm and 75°C, will be consumed by the complete combustion of 0.500 g of butane?
**c.** A butane-fueled torch has a mass of 876.2 g. After burning for some time, the torch has a mass of 859.3 g. What volume of $CO_2$, at STP, was formed while the torch burned?
**d.** What mass of $H_2O$ is produced when butane burns and produces 3720 L of $CO_2$, measured at 35°C and 0.993 atm pressure?

## Concentration of Solutions: Chap. 12, Sec. 3

### Percentage Concentration

**328.** What is the percentage concentration of 75.0 g of ethanol dissolved in 500.0 g of water?

**329.** A chemist dissolves 3.50 g of potassium iodate and 6.23 g of potassium hydroxide in 805.05 g of water. What is the percentage concentration of each solute in the solution?

**330.** A student wants to make a 5.00% solution of rubidium chloride using 0.377 g of the substance. What mass of water will be needed to make the solution?

**331.** What mass of lithium nitrate would have to be dissolved in 30.0 g of water in order to make an 18.0% solution?

### Molarity

**332.** Determine the molarity of a solution prepared by dissolving 141.6 g of citric acid, $C_3H_5O(COOH)_3$, in water and then diluting the resulting solution to 3500.0 mL.

**333.** What is the molarity of a salt solution made by dissolving 280.0 mg of NaCl in 2.00 mL of water? Assume the final volume is the same as the volume of the water.

**334.** What is the molarity of a solution that contains 390.0 g of acetic acid, $CH_3COOH$, dissolved in enough acetone to make 1000.0 mL of solution?

**335.** What mass of glucose, $C_6H_{12}O_6$, would be required to prepare $5.000 \times 10^3$ L of a 0.215 M solution?

**336.** What mass of magnesium bromide would be required to prepare 720. mL of a 0.0939 M aqueous solution?

**337.** What mass of ammonium chloride is dissolved in 300. mL of a 0.875 M solution?

### Molality

**338.** Determine the molality of a solution of 560 g of acetone, $CH_3COCH_3$, in 620 g of water.

**339.** What is the molality of a solution of 12.9 g of fructose, $C_6H_{12}O_6$, in 31.0 g of water?

**340.** How many moles of 2-butanol, $CH_3CHOHCH_2CH_3$, must be dissolved in 125 g of ethanol in order to produce a 12.0 *m* 2-butanol solution? What mass of 2-butanol is this?

### Mixed Review

**341.** Complete the table below by determining the missing quantity in each example. All solutions are aqueous. Any quantity that is not applicable to a given solution is marked NA.

| *Solution Made* | *Mass of Solute Used* | *Quantity of Solution Made* | *Quantity of Solvent Used* |
|---|---|---|---|
| **a.** 12.0% $KMnO_4$ | ? g $KMnO_4$ | 500.0 g | ? g $H_2O$ |
| **b.** 0.60 M $BaCl_2$ | ? g $BaCl_2$ | 1.750 L | NA |
| **c.** 6.20 *m* glycerol, $HOCH_2CHOHCH_2OH$ | ? g glycerol | NA | 800.0 g $H_2O$ |
| **d.** ? M $K_2Cr_2O_7$ | 12.27 g $K_2Cr_2O_7$ | 650. mL | NA |
| **e.** ? *m* $CaCl_2$ | 288 g $CaCl_2$ | NA | 2.04 kg $H_2O$ |
| **f.** 0.160 M NaCl | ? g NaCl | 25.0 mL | NA |
| **g.** 2.00 *m* glucose, $C_6H_{12}O_6$ | ? g glucose | ? g solution | 1.50 kg $H_2O$ |

**342.** How many moles of $H_2SO_4$ are in 2.50 L of a 4.25 M aqueous solution?

**343.** Determine the molal concentration of 71.5 g of linoleic acid, $C_{18}H_{32}O_2$, in 525 g of hexane, $C_6H_{14}$.

**344.** You have a solution that is 16.2% sodium thiosulfate, $Na_2S_2O_3$, by mass.
**a.** What mass of sodium thiosulfate is in 80.0 g of solution?
**b.** How many moles of sodium thiosulfate are in 80.0 g of solution?
**c.** If 80.0 g of the sodium thiosulfate solution is diluted to 250.0 mL with water, what is the molarity of the resulting solution?

345. What mass of anhydrous cobalt(II) chloride would be needed in order to make 650.00 mL of a 4.00 M cobalt(II) chloride solution?

346. A student wants to make a 0.150 M aqueous solution of silver nitrate, $AgNO_3$, and has a bottle containing 11.27 g of silver nitrate. What should be the final volume of the solution?

347. What mass of urea, $NH_2CONH_2$, must be dissolved in 2250 g of water in order to prepare a 1.50 *m* solution?

348. What mass of barium nitrate is dissolved in 21.29 mL of a 3.38 M solution?

349. Describe what you would do to prepare 100.0 g of a 3.5% solution of ammonium sulfate in water.

350. What mass of anhydrous calcium chloride should be dissolved in 590.0 g of water in order to produce a 0.82 *m* solution?

351. How many moles of ammonia are in 0.250 L of a 5.00 M aqueous ammonia solution? If this solution were diluted to 1.000 L, what would be the molarity of the resulting solution?

352. What is the molar mass of a solute if 62.0 g of the solute in 125 g of water produce a 5.3 *m* solution?

353. A saline solution is 0.9% NaCl. What masses of NaCl and water would be required to prepare 50. L of this saline solution? Assume that the density of water is 1.000 g/mL and that the NaCl does not add to the volume of the solution.

354. A student weighs an empty beaker on a balance and finds its mass to be 68.60 g. The student weighs the beaker again after adding water and finds the new mass to be 115.12 g. A mass of 4.08 g of glucose is then dissolved in the water. What is the percentage concentration of glucose in the solution?

355. The density of ethyl acetate at 20°C is 0.902 g/mL. What volume of ethyl acetate at 20°C would be required to prepare a 2.0% solution of cellulose nitrate using 25 g of cellulose nitrate?

356. Aqueous cadmium chloride reacts with sodium sulfide to produce bright-yellow cadmium sulfide. Write the balanced equation for this reaction and answer the following questions.
   **a.** How many moles of $CdCl_2$ are in 50.00 mL of a 3.91 M solution?
   **b.** If the solution in (a) reacted with excess sodium sulfide, how many moles of CdS would be formed?
   **c.** What mass of CdS would be formed?

357. What mass of $H_2SO_4$ is contained in 60.00 mL of a 5.85 M solution of sulfuric acid?

358. A truck carrying 22.5 kL of 6.83 M aqueous hydrochloric acid used to clean brick and masonry has overturned. The authorities plan to neutralize the acid with sodium carbonate. How many moles of HCl will have to be neutralized?

359. A chemist wants to produce 12.00 g of barium sulfate by reacting a 0.600 M $BaCl_2$ solution with excess $H_2SO_4$, as shown in the reaction below. What volume of the $BaCl_2$ solution should be used?

$$BaCl_2 + H_2SO_4 \rightarrow BaSO_4 + 2HCl$$

360. Many substances are hydrates. Whenever you make a solution, it is important to know whether or not the solute you are using is a hydrate and, if it is a hydrate, how many molecules of water are present per formula unit of the substance. This water must be taken into account when weighing out the solute. Something else to remember when making aqueous solutions from hydrates is that once the hydrate is dissolved, the water of hydration is considered to be part of the solvent. A common hydrate used in the chemistry laboratory is copper sulfate pentahydrate, $CuSO_4{\bullet}5H_2O$. Describe how you would make each of the following solutions using $CuSO_4{\bullet}5H_2O$. Specify masses and volumes as needed.
   **a.** 100. g of a 6.00% solution of $CuSO_4$
   **b.** 1.00 L of a 0.800 M solution of $CuSO_4$
   **c.** a 3.5 *m* solution of $CuSO_4$ in 1.0 kg of water

361. What mass of calcium chloride hexahydrate is required in order to make 700.0 mL of a 2.50 M solution?

362. What mass of the amino acid arginine, $C_6H_{14}N_4O_2$, would be required to make 1.250 L of a 0.00205 M solution?

363. How much water would you have to add to 2.402 kg of nickel(II) sulfate hexahydrate in order to prepare a 25.00% solution?

364. What mass of potassium aluminum sulfate dodecahydrate, $KAl(SO_4)_2{\bullet}12H_2O$, would be needed to prepare 35.00 g of a 15.00% $KAl(SO_4)_2$ solution? What mass of water would be added to make this solution?

## Dilutions: Chap. 12, Sec. 3

365. Complete the table below by calculating the missing value in each row.

| *Molarity of Stock Solution* | *Volume of Stock Solution* | *Molarity of Dilute Solution* | *Volume of Dilute Solution* |
|---|---|---|---|
| **a.** 0.500 M KBr | 20.00 mL | ? M KBr | 100.00 mL |
| **b.** 1.00 M LiOH | ? mL | 0.075 M LiOH | 500.00 mL |
| **c.** ? M HI | 5.00 mL | 0.0493 M HI | 100.00 mL |
| **d.** 12.0 M HCl | 0.250 L | 1.8 M HCl | ? L |
| **e.** 7.44 M $NH_3$ | ? mL | 0.093 M $NH_3$ | 4.00 L |

366. What volume of water would be added to 16.5 mL of a 0.0813 M solution of sodium borate in order to get a 0.0200 M solution?

### Mixed Review

367. What is the molarity of a solution of ammonium chloride prepared by diluting 50.00 mL of a 3.79 M $NH_4Cl$ solution to 2.00 L?

**368.** A student takes a sample of KOH solution and dilutes it with 100.00 mL of water. The student determines that the diluted solution is 0.046 M KOH, but has forgotten to record the volume of the original sample. The concentration of the original solution is 2.09 M. What was the volume of the original sample?

**369.** A chemist wants to prepare a stock solution of $H_2SO_4$ so that samples of 20.00 mL will produce a solution with a concentration of 0.50 M when added to 100.0 mL of water.
   **a.** What should the molarity of the stock solution be?
   **b.** If the chemist wants to prepare 5.00 L of the stock solution from concentrated $H_2SO_4$, which is 18.0 M, what volume of concentrated acid should be used?
   **c.** The density of 18.0 M $H_2SO_4$ is 1.84 g/mL. What mass of concentrated $H_2SO_4$ should be used to make the stock solution in (b)?

**370.** To what volume should 1.19 mL of an 8.00 M acetic acid solution be diluted in order to obtain a final solution that is 1.50 M?

**371.** What volume of a 5.75 M formic acid solution should be used to prepare 2.00 L of a 1.00 M formic acid solution?

**372.** A 25.00 mL sample of ammonium nitrate solution produces a 0.186 M solution when diluted with 50.00 mL of water. What is the molarity of the stock solution?

**373.** Given a solution of known percentage concentration by mass, a laboratory worker can often measure out a calculated mass of the solution in order to obtain a certain mass of solute. Sometimes, though, it is impractical to use the mass of a solution, especially with fuming solutions, such as concentrated HCl and concentrated $HNO_3$. Measuring these solutions by volume is much more practical. In order to determine the volume that should be measured, a worker would need to know the density of the solution. This information usually appears on the label of the solution bottle.
   **a.** Concentrated hydrochloric acid is 36% HCl by mass and has a density of 1.18 g/mL. What is the volume of 1.0 kg of this HCl solution? What volume contains 1.0 g of HCl? What volume contains 1.0 mol of HCl?
   **b.** The density of concentrated nitric acid is 1.42 g/mL, and its concentration is 71% $HNO_3$ by mass. What volume of concentrated $HNO_3$ would be needed to prepare 10.0 L of a 2.00 M solution of $HNO_3$?
   **c.** What volume of concentrated HCl solution would be needed to prepare 4.50 L of 3.0 M HCl? See (a) for data.

**374.** A 3.8 M solution of $FeSO_4$ solution is diluted to eight times its original volume. What is the molarity of the diluted solution?

**375.** A chemist prepares 480. mL of a 2.50 M solution of $K_2Cr_2O_7$ in water. A week later, the chemist wants to use the solution, but the stopper has been left off the flask and 39 mL of water has evaporated. What is the new molarity of the solution?

**376.** You must write out procedures for a group of lab technicians. One test they will perform requires 25.00 mL of a 1.22 M solution of acetic acid. You decide to use a 6.45 M acetic acid solution that you have on hand. What procedure should the technicians use in order to get the solution they need?

**377.** A chemical test has determined the concentration of a solution of an unknown substance to be 2.41 M. A 100.0 mL volume of the solution is evaporated to dryness, leaving 9.56 g of crystals of the unknown solute. Calculate the molar mass of the unknown substance.

**378.** Tincture of iodine can be prepared by dissolving 34 g of $I_2$ and 25 g of KI in 25 mL of distilled water and diluting the solution to 500. mL with ethanol. What is the molarity of $I_2$ in the solution?

**379.** Phosphoric acid is commonly supplied as an 85% solution. What mass of this solution would be required to prepare 600.0 mL of a 2.80 M phosphoric acid solution?

**380.** Commercially available concentrated sulfuric acid is 18.0 M $H_2SO_4$. What volume of concentrated $H_2SO_4$ would you use in order to make 3.00 L of a 4.0 M stock solution?

**381.** Describe how to prepare 1.00 L of a 0.495 M solution of urea, $NH_2CONH_2$, starting with a 3.07 M stock solution.

**382.** Honey is a solution consisting almost entirely of a mixture of the hexose sugars fructose and glucose; both sugars have the formula $C_6H_{12}O_6$, but they differ in molecular structure.
   **a.** A sample of honey is found to be 76.2% $C_6H_{12}O_6$ by mass. What is the molality of the hexose sugars in honey? Consider the sugars to be equivalent.
   **b.** The density of the honey sample is 1.42 g/mL. What mass of hexose sugars are in 1.00 L of honey? What is the molarity of the mixed hexose sugars in honey?

**383.** Industrial chemicals used in manufacturing are almost never pure, and the content of the material may vary from one batch to the next. For these reasons, a sample is taken from each shipment and sent to a laboratory, where its makeup is determined. This procedure is called assaying. Once the content of a material is known, engineers adjust the manufacturing process to account for the degree of purity of the starting chemicals.

Suppose you have just received a shipment of sodium carbonate, $Na_2CO_3$. You weigh out 50.00 g of the material, dissolve it in water, and dilute the solution to 1.000 L. You remove 10.00 mL from the solution and dilute it to 50.00 mL. By measuring the amount of a second substance that reacts with $Na_2CO_3$, you determine that the concentration of sodium carbonate in the diluted solution is 0.0890 M. Calculate the percentage of $Na_2CO_3$ in the original batch of material. The molar mass of $Na_2CO_3$ is 105.99 g. (Hint: Determine the number of moles in the original solution and convert to mass of $Na_2CO_3$.)

**384.** A student wants to prepare 0.600 L of a stock solution of copper(II) chloride so that 20.0 mL of the stock solution diluted by adding 130.0 mL of water will yield a 0.250 M solution. What mass of $CuCl_2$ should be used to make the stock solution?

**385.** You have a bottle containing a 2.15 M $BaCl_2$ solution. You must tell other students how to dilute this solution to get various volumes of a 0.65 M $BaCl_2$ solution. By what factor will you tell them to dilute the stock solution? In other words, when a student removes any volume, $V$, of the stock solution, how many times $V$ of water should be added to dilute to 0.65 M?

**386.** You have a bottle containing an 18.2% solution of strontium nitrate (density = 1.02 g/mL).

**a.** What mass of strontium nitrate is dissolved in 80.0 mL of this solution?

**b.** How many moles of strontium nitrate are dissolved in 80.0 mL of the solution?

**c.** If 80.0 mL of this solution is diluted with 420.0 mL of water, what is the molarity of the solution?

## Colligative Properties: Chap. 13, Sec. 2

**387.** Determine the freezing point of a solution of 60.0 g of glucose, $C_6H_{12}O_6$, dissolved in 80.0 g of water.

**388.** What is the freezing point of a solution of 645 g of urea, $H_2NCONH_2$, dissolved in 980. g of water?

**389.** What is the expected boiling point of a brine solution containing 30.00 g of KBr dissolved in 100.00 g of water?

**390.** What is the expected boiling point of a $CaCl_2$ solution containing 385 g of $CaCl_2$ dissolved in $1.230 \times 10^3$ g of water?

**391.** A solution of 0.827 g of an unknown non-electrolyte compound in 2.500 g of water has a freezing point of −10.18°C. Calculate the molar mass of the compound.

**392.** A 0.171 g sample of an unknown organic compound is dissolved in ether. The solution has a total mass of 2.470 g. The boiling point of the solution is found to be 36.43°C. What is the molar mass of the organic compound?

### Mixed Review

*In each of the following problems, assume that the solute is a nonelectrolyte unless otherwise stated.*

**393.** Calculate the freezing point and boiling point of a solution of 383 g of glucose dissolved in 400. g of water.

**394.** Determine the boiling point of a solution of 72.4 g of glycerol dissolved in 122.5 g of water.

**395.** What is the boiling point of a solution of 30.20 g of ethylene glycol, $HOCH_2CH_2OH$, in 88.40 g of phenol?

**396.** What mass of ethanol, $CH_3CH_2OH$, should be dissolved in 450. g of water to obtain a freezing point of − 4.5°C?

**397.** Calculate the molar mass of a nonelectrolyte that lowers the freezing point of 25.00 g of water to − 3.9°C when 4.27 g of the substance is dissolved in the water.

**398.** What is the freezing point of a solution of 1.17 g of 1-naphthol, $C_{10}H_8O$, dissolved in 2.00 mL of benzene at 20°C? The density of benzene at 20°C is 0.876 g/mL. $K_f$ for benzene is − 5.12°C/$m$, and benzene's normal freezing point is 5.53°C.

**399.** The boiling point of a solution containing 10.44 g of an unknown nonelectrolyte in 50.00 g of acetic acid is 159.2°C. What is the molar mass of the solute?

**400.** A 0.0355 g sample of an unknown molecular compound is dissolved in 1.000 g of liquid camphor at 200.0°C. Upon cooling, the camphor freezes at 157.7°C. Calculate the molar mass of the unknown compound.

**401.** Determine the boiling point of a solution of 22.5 g of fructose, $C_6H_{12}O_6$, in 294 g of phenol.

**402.** Ethylene glycol, $HOCH_2CH_2OH$, is effective as an antifreeze, but it also raises the boiling temperature of automobile coolant, which helps prevent loss of coolant when the weather is hot.

**a.** What is the freezing point of a 50.0% solution of ethylene glycol in water?

**b.** What is the boiling point of the same 50.0% solution?

**403.** The value of $K_f$ for cyclohexane is − 20.0°C/$m$, and its normal freezing point is 6.6°C. A mass of 1.604 g of a waxy solid dissolved in 10.000 g of cyclohexane results in a freezing point of − 4.4°C. Calculate the molar mass of the solid.

**404.** What is the expected freezing point of an aqueous solution of 2.62 kg of nitric acid, $HNO_3$, in a solution with a total mass of 5.91 kg? Assume that the nitric acid is completely ionized.

**405.** An unknown organic compound is mixed with 0.5190 g of naphthalene crystals to give a mixture having a total mass of 0.5959 g. The mixture is heated until the naphthalene melts and the unknown substance dissolves. Upon cooling, the solution freezes at a temperature of 74.8°C. What is the molar mass of the unknown compound?

**406.** What is the boiling point of a solution of 8.69 g of the electrolyte sodium acetate, $NaCH_3COO$, dissolved in 15.00 g of water?

**407.** What is the expected freezing point of a solution of 110.5 g of $H_2SO_4$ in 225 g of water? Assume sulfuric acid completely dissociates in water.

**408.** A compound called pyrene has the empirical formula $C_8H_5$. When 4.04 g of pyrene is dissolved in 10.00 g of benzene, the boiling point of the solution is 85.1°C. Calculate the molar mass of pyrene and determine its molecular formula. The molal boiling-point constant for benzene is 2.53°C/$m$. Its normal boiling point is 80.1°C.

**409.** What mass of $CaCl_2$, when dissolved in 100.00 g of water, gives an expected freezing point of − 5.0°C; $CaCl_2$ is ionic? What mass of glucose would give the same result?

**410.** A compound has the empirical formula $CH_2O$. When 0.0866 g is dissolved in 1.000 g of ether, the solution's boiling point is 36.5°C. Determine the molecular formula of this substance.

**411.** What is the freezing point of a 28.6% (by mass) aqueous solution of HCl? Assume the HCl is 100% ionized.

**412.** What mass of ethylene glycol, $HOCH_2CH_2OH$, must be dissolved in 4.510 kg of water to result in a freezing point of − 18.0°C? What is the boiling point of the same solution?

**413.** A water solution containing 2.00 g of an unknown molecular substance dissolved in 10.00 g of water has a freezing point of − 4.0°C.

**a.** Calculate the molality of the solution.

**b.** When 2.00 g of the substance is dissolved in acetone instead of in water, the boiling point of the solution is 58.9°C. The normal boiling point of acetone is 56.00°C, and its $K_b$ is 1.71°C/*m*. Calculate the molality of the solution from this data.

**414.** A chemist wants to prepare a solution with a freezing point of − 22.0°C and has 100.00 g of glycerol on hand. What mass of water should the chemist mix with the glycerol?

**415.** An unknown carbohydrate compound has the empirical formula $CH_2O$. A solution consisting of 0.515 g of the carbohydrate dissolved in 1.717 g of acetic acid freezes at 8.8°C. What is the molar mass of the carbohydrate? What is its molecular formula?

**416.** An unknown organic compound has the empirical formula $C_2H_2O$. A solution of 3.775 g of the unknown compound dissolved in 12.00 g of water is cooled until it freezes at a temperature of − 4.72°C. Determine the molar mass and the molecular formula of the compound.

## pH: Chap. 15, Sec. 1

**417.** The hydroxide ion concentration of an aqueous solution is $6.4 \times 10^{-5}$ M. What is the hydronium ion concentration?

**418.** Calculate the $H_3O^+$ and $OH^-$ concentrations in a $7.50 \times 10^{-4}$ M solution of $HNO_3$, a strong acid.

**419.** Determine the pH of a 0.001 18 M solution of HBr.

**420.** **a.** What is the pH of a solution that has a hydronium ion concentration of 1.0 M?

**b.** What is the pH of a 2.0 M solution of HCl, assuming the acid remains 100% ionized?

**c.** What is the theoretical pH of a 10. M solution of HCl?

**421.** What is the pH of a solution with the following hydroxide ion concentrations?

**a.** $1 \times 10^{-5}$ M

**b.** $5 \times 10^{-8}$ M

**c.** $2.90 \times 10^{-11}$ M

**422.** What are the pOH and hydroxide ion concentration of a solution with a pH of 8.92?

**423.** What are the pOH values of solutions with the following hydronium ion concentrations?

**a.** $2.51 \times 10^{-13}$ M

**b.** $4.3 \times 10^{-3}$ M

**c.** $9.1 \times 10^{-6}$ M

**d.** 0.070 M

**424.** A solution is prepared by dissolving 3.50 g of sodium hydroxide in water and adding water until the total volume of the solution is 2.50 L. What are the $OH^-$ and $H_3O^+$ concentrations?

**425.** If 1.00 L of a potassium hydroxide solution with a pH of 12.90 is diluted to 2.00 L, what is the pH of the resulting solution?

## Mixed Review

**426.** Calculate the $H_3O^+$ and $OH^-$ concentrations in the following solutions. Each is either a strong acid or a strong base.

**a.** 0.05 M sodium hydroxide

**b.** 0.0025 M sulfuric acid

**c.** 0.013 M lithium hydroxide

**d.** 0.150 M nitric acid

**e.** 0.0200 M calcium hydroxide

**f.** 0.390 M perchloric acid

**427.** What is the pH of each solution in item 426?

**428.** Calculate $[H_3O^+]$ and $[OH^-]$ in a 0.160 M solution of potassium hydroxide. Assume that the solute is 100% dissociated at this concentration.

**429.** The pH of an aqueous solution of NaOH is 12.9. What is the molarity of the solution?

**430.** What is the pH of a 0.001 25 M HBr solution? If 175 mL of this solution is diluted to a total volume of 3.00 L, what is the pH of the diluted solution?

**431.** What is the pH of a 0.0001 M solution of NaOH? What is the pH of a 0.0005 M solution of NaOH?

**432.** A solution is prepared using 15.0 mL of 1.0 M HCl and 20.0 mL of 0.50 M $HNO_3$. The final volume of the solution is 1.25 L. Answer the following questions:

**a.** What are the $[H_3O^+]$ and $[OH^-]$ in the final solution?

**b.** What is the pH of the final solution?

**433.** A container is labeled 500.0 mL of 0.001 57 M nitric acid solution. A chemist finds that the container was not sealed and that some evaporation has taken place. The volume of solution is now 447.0 mL.

**a.** What was the original pH of the solution?

**b.** What is the pH of the solution now?

**434.** Calculate the hydroxide ion concentration in an aqueous solution that has a 0.000 35 M hydronium ion concentration.

**435.** A solution of sodium hydroxide has a pH of 12.14. If 50.00 mL of the solution is diluted to 2.000 L with water, what is the pH of the diluted solution?

**436.** An acetic acid solution has a pH of 4.0. What are the $[H_3O^+]$ and $[OH^-]$ in this solution?

**437.** What is the pH of a 0.000 460 M solution of $Ca(OH)_2$?

**438.** A solution of strontium hydroxide with a pH of 11.4 is to be prepared. What mass of strontium hydroxide would be required to make 1.00 L of this solution?

**439.** A solution of $NH_3$ has a pH of 11.00. What are the concentrations of hydronium and hydroxide ions in this solution?

**440.** Acetic acid does not completely ionize in solution. Percent ionization of a substance dissolved in water is equal to the moles of ions produced as a percentage of the moles of ions that would be produced if the substance were completely ionized. Calculate the percent ionization of acetic acid in the following solutions.
**a.** 1.0 M acetic acid solution with a pH of 2.40
**b.** 0.10 M acetic acid solution with a pH of 2.90
**c.** 0.010 M acetic acid solution with a pH of 3.40

**441.** Calculate the pH of a solution that contains 5.00 g of $HNO_3$ in 2.00 L of solution.

**442.** A solution of HCl has a pH of 1.50. Determine the pH of the solutions made in each of the following ways.
**a.** 1.00 mL of the solution is diluted to 1000. mL with water.
**b.** 25.00 mL is diluted to 200. mL with distilled water.
**c.** 18.83 mL of the solution is diluted to 4.000 L with distilled water.
**d.** 1.50 L is diluted to 20.0 kL with distilled water.

**443.** An aqueous solution contains 10 000 times more hydronium ions than hydroxide ions. What is the concentration of each ion?

**444.** A potassium hydroxide solution has a pH of 12.90. Enough acid is added to react with half of the $OH^-$ ions present. What is the pH of the resulting solution? Assume that the products of the neutralization have no effect on pH and that the amount of additional water produced is negligible.

**445.** A hydrochloric acid solution has a pH of 1.70. What is the $[H_3O^+]$ in this solution? Considering that HCl is a strong acid, what is the HCl concentration of the solution?

**446.** What is the molarity of a solution of the strong base $Ca(OH)_2$ in a solution that has a pH of 10.80?

**447.** You have a 1.00 M solution of the strong acid, HCl. What is the pH of this solution? You need a solution of pH 4.00. To what volume would you dilute 1.00 L of the HCl solution to get this pH? To what volume would you dilute 1.00 L of the pH 4.00 solution to get a solution of pH 6.00? To what volume would you dilute 1.00 L of the pH 4.00 solution to get a solution of pH 8.00?

**448.** A solution of chloric acid, $HClO_3$, a strong acid, has a pH of 1.28. How many moles of NaOH would be required to react completely with the $HClO_3$ in 1.00 L of the solution? What mass of NaOH is required?

**449.** A solution of the weak base $NH_3$ has a pH of 11.90. How many moles of HCl would have to be added to 1.00 L of the ammonia to react with all of the $OH^-$ ions present at pH 11.90?

**450.** The pH of a citric acid solution is 3.15. What are the $[H_3O^+]$ and $[OH^-]$ in this solution?

## Titrations: Chap. 15, Sec. 2

*In each of the following problems, the acids and bases react in a mole ratio of 1 mol base : 1 mol acid.*

**451.** A student titrates a 20.00 mL sample of a solution of HBr with unknown molarity. The titration requires 20.05 mL of a 0.1819 M solution of NaOH. What is the molarity of the HBr solution?

**452.** Vinegar can be assayed to determine its acetic acid content. Determine the molarity of acetic acid in a 15.00 mL sample of vinegar that requires 22.70 mL of a 0.550 M solution of NaOH to reach the equivalence point.

**453.** A 20.00 mL sample of a solution of $Sr(OH)_2$ is titrated to the equivalence point with 43.03 mL of 0.1159 M HCl. What is the molarity of the $Sr(OH)_2$ solution?

**454.** A 35.00 mL sample of ammonia solution is titrated to the equivalence point with 54.95 mL of a 0.400 M sulfuric acid solution. What is the molarity of the ammonia solution?

*In the problems below, assume that impurities are not acidic or basic and that they do not react in an acid-base titration.*

**455.** A supply of glacial acetic acid has absorbed water from the air. It must be assayed to determine the actual percentage of acetic acid. 2.000 g of the acid is diluted to 100.00 mL, and 20.00 mL is titrated with a solution of sodium hydroxide. The base solution has a concentration of 0.218 M, and 28.25 mL is used in the titration. Calculate the percentage of acetic acid in the original sample. Write the titration equation to get the mole ratio.

**456.** A shipment of crude sodium carbonate must be assayed for its $Na_2CO_3$ content. You receive a small jar containing a sample from the shipment and weigh out 9.709 g into a flask, where it is dissolved in water and diluted to 1.0000 L with distilled water. A 10.00 mL sample is taken from the flask and titrated to the equivalence point with 16.90 mL of a 0.1022 M HCl solution. Determine the percentage of $Na_2CO_3$ in the sample. Write the titration equation to get the mole ratio.

### Mixed Review

**457.** A 50.00 mL sample of a potassium hydroxide is titrated with a 0.8186 M HCl solution. The titration requires 27.87 mL of the HCl solution to reach the equivalence point. What is the molarity of the KOH solution?

**458.** A 15.00 mL sample of acetic acid is titrated with 34.13 mL of 0.9940 M NaOH. Determine the molarity of the acetic acid.

**459.** A 12.00 mL sample of an ammonia solution is titrated with 1.499 M $HNO_3$ solution. A total of 19.48 mL of acid is required to reach the equivalence point. What is the molarity of the ammonia solution?

**460.** A certain acid and base react in a 1:1 ratio.
**a.** If the acid and base solutions are of equal concentration, what volume of acid will titrate a 20.00 mL sample of the base?
**b.** If the acid is twice as concentrated as the base, what volume of acid will be required to titrate 20.00 mL of the base?
**c.** How much acid will be required if the base is four times as concentrated as the acid, and 20.00 mL of base is used?

**461.** A 10.00 mL sample of a solution of hydrofluoric acid, HF, is diluted to 500.00 mL. A 20.00 mL sample of the diluted solution requires 13.51 mL of a 0.1500 M NaOH solution to be titrated to the equivalence point. What is the molarity of the original HF solution?

**462.** A solution of oxalic acid, a diprotic acid, is used to titrate a 16.22 mL sample of a 0.5030 M KOH solution. If the titration requires 18.41 mL of the oxalic acid solution, what is its molarity?

**463.** A $H_2SO_4$ solution of unknown molarity is titrated with a 1.209 M NaOH solution. The titration requires 42.27 mL of the NaOH solution to reach the equivalent point with 25.00 mL of the $H_2SO_4$ solution. What is the molarity of the acid solution?

**464.** Potassium hydrogen phthalate, $KHC_8H_4O_4$, is a solid acidic substance that reacts in a 1:1 mole ratio with bases that have one hydroxide ion. Suppose that 0.7025 g of potassium hydrogen phthalate is titrated to the equivalence point by 20.18 mL of a KOH solution. What is the molarity of the KOH solution?

**465.** A solution of citric acid, a triprotic acid, is titrated with a sodium hydroxide solution. A 20.00 mL sample of the citric acid solution requires 17.03 mL of a 2.025 M solution of NaOH to reach the equivalence point. What is the molarity of the acid solution?

**466.** A flask contains 41.04 mL of a solution of potassium hydroxide. The solution is titrated and reaches an equivalence point when 21.65 mL of a 0.6515 M solution of $HNO_3$ is added. Calculate the molarity of the base solution.

**467.** A bottle is labeled 2.00 M $H_2SO_4$. You decide to titrate a 20.00 mL sample with a 1.85 M NaOH solution. What volume of NaOH solution would you expect to use if the label is correct?

**468.** What volume of a 0.5200 M solution of $H_2SO_4$ would be needed to titrate 100.00 mL of a 0.1225 M solution of $Sr(OH)_2$?

**469.** A sample of a crude grade of KOH is sent to the lab to be tested for KOH content. A 4.005 g sample is dissolved and diluted to 200.00 mL with water. A 25.00 mL sample of the solution is titrated with a 0.4388 M HCl solution and requires 19.93 mL to reach the equivalence point. How many moles of KOH were in the 4.005 g sample? What mass of KOH is this? What is the percent of KOH in the crude material?

**470.** What mass of magnesium hydroxide would be required for the magnesium hydroxide to react to the equivalence point with 558 mL of 3.18 M hydrochloric acid?

**471.** An ammonia solution of unknown concentration is titrated with a solution of hydrochloric acid. The HCl solution is 1.25 M, and 5.19 mL are required to titrate 12.61 mL of the ammonia solution. What is the molarity of the ammonia solution?

**472.** What volume of 2.811 M oxalic acid solution is needed to react to the equivalence point with a 5.090 g sample of material that is 92.10% NaOH? Oxalic acid is a diprotic acid.

**473.** Standard solutions of accurately known concentration are available in most laboratories. These solutions are used to titrate other solutions to determine their concentrations. Once the concentration of the other solutions are accurately known, they may be used to titrate solutions of unknowns.

The molarity of a solution of HCl is determined by titrating the solution with an accurately known solution of $Ba(OH)_2$, which has a molar concentration of 0.1529 M. A volume of 43.09 mL of the $Ba(OH)_2$ solution titrates 26.06 mL of the acid solution. The acid solution is in turn used to titrate 15.00 mL of a solution of rubidium hydroxide. The titration requires 27.05 mL of the acid.
**a.** What is the molarity of the HCl solution?
**b.** What is the molarity of the RbOH solution?

**474.** A truck containing 2800 kg of a 6.0 M hydrochloric acid has been in an accident and is in danger of spilling its load. What mass of $Ca(OH)_2$ should be sent to the scene in order to neutralize all of the acid in case the tank bursts? The density of the 6.0 M HCl solution is 1.10 g/mL.

**475.** A 1.00 mL sample of a fairly concentrated nitric acid solution is diluted to 200.00 mL. A 10.00 mL sample of the diluted solution requires 23.94 mL of a 0.0177 M solution of $Ba(OH)_2$ to be titrated to the equivalence point. Determine the molarity of the original nitric acid solution.

**476.** What volume of 4.494 M $H_2SO_4$ solution would be required to react to the equivalence point with 7.2280 g of LiOH(*s*)?

## Thermochemistry: Chap. 16, Sec. 1

**477.** Calculate the reaction enthalpy for the following reaction:

$$5CO_2(g) + Si_3N_4(s) \rightarrow 3SiO(s) + 2N_2O(g) + 5CO(g)$$

Use the following equations and data:

(1) $CO(g) + SiO_2(s) \rightarrow SiO(g) + CO_2(g)$

(2) $8CO_2(g) + Si_3N_4(s) \rightarrow 3SiO_2(s) + 2N_2O(g) + 8CO(g)$

$\Delta H_{reaction\ 1} = +520.9$ kJ

$\Delta H_{reaction\ 2} = +461.05$ kJ

*Determine $\Delta H$ for each of the following three reactions.*

**478.** The following reaction is used to make CaO from limestone:

$$CaCO_3(s) \rightarrow CaO(s) + CO_2(g)$$

**479.** The following reaction represents the oxidation of FeO to $Fe_2O_3$:

$$2FeO(s) + O_2(g) \rightarrow Fe_2O_3(s)$$

**480.** The following reaction of ammonia and hydrogen fluoride produces ammonium fluoride:

$$NH_3(g) + HF(g) \rightarrow NH_4F(s)$$

**481.** Calculate the free energy change, $\Delta G$, for the combustion of hydrogen sulfide according to the following chemical equation. Assume reactants and products are at 25°C:

$$H_2S(g) + O_2(g) \rightarrow H_2O(l) + SO_2(g)$$

$\Delta H_{reaction} = -562.1$ kJ/mol

$\Delta S_{reaction} = -0.09278$ kJ/mol•K

**482.** Calculate the free energy change for the decomposition of sodium chlorate. Assume reactants and products are at 25°C:

$$NaClO_3(s) \rightarrow NaCl(s) + O_2(g)$$

$\Delta H_{reaction} = -19.1$ kJ/mol

$\Delta S_{reaction} = -0.1768$ kJ/mol•K

**483.** Calculate the free energy change for the combustion of 1 mol of ethane. Assume reactants and products are at 25°C:

$$C_2H_6(g) + O_2(g) \rightarrow 2CO_2(g) + 3H_2O(l)$$

$\Delta H_{reaction} = -1561$ kJ/mol

$\Delta S_{reaction} = -0.4084$ kJ/mol•K

## Mixed Review

**484.** Calculate $\Delta H$ for the reaction of fluorine with water:

$$F_2(g) + H_2O(l) \rightarrow 2HF(g) + O_2(g)$$

**485.** Calculate $\Delta H$ for the reaction of calcium oxide and sulfur trioxide:

$$CaO(s) + SO_3(g) \rightarrow CaSO_4(s)$$

Use the following equations and data:

$$H_2O(l) + SO_3(g) \rightarrow H_2SO_4(l)$$

$\Delta H = -132.5$ kJ/mol

$$H_2SO_4(l) + Ca(s) \rightarrow CaSO_4(s) + H_2(g)$$

$\Delta H = -602.5$ kJ/mol

$$Ca(s) + O_2(g) \rightarrow CaO(s)$$

$\Delta H = -634.9$ kJ/mol

$$H_2(g) + O_2(g) \rightarrow H_2O(l)$$

$\Delta H = -285.8$ kJ/mol

**486.** Calculate $\Delta H$ for the reaction of sodium oxide with sulfur dioxide:

$$Na_2O(s) + SO_2(g) \rightarrow Na_2SO_3(s)$$

**487.** Use enthalpies of combustion to calculate $\Delta H$ for the oxidation of 1-butanol to make butanoic acid:

$$C_4H_9OH(l) + O_2(g) \rightarrow C_3H_7COOH(l) + H_2O(l)$$

Combustion of butanol:

$$C_4H_9OH(l) + 6O_2(g) \rightarrow 4CO_2(g) + 5H_2O(l)$$

$\Delta H_c = -2675.9$ kJ/mol

Combustion of butanoic acid:

$$C_3H_7COOH(l) + 5O_2(g) \rightarrow 4CO_2(g) + 4H_2O(l)$$

$\Delta H_c = -2183.6$ kJ/mol

**488.** Determine the free energy change for the reduction of CuO with hydrogen. Products and reactants are at 25°C.

$$CuO(s) + H_2(g) \rightarrow Cu(s) + H_2O(l)$$

$\Delta H = -128.5$ kJ/mol
$\Delta S = -70.1$ J/mol•K

**489.** Calculate the enthalpy change at 25°C for the reaction of sodium iodide and chlorine. Use only the data given.

$$NaI(s) + Cl_2(g) \rightarrow NaCl(s) + I_2(l)$$

$\Delta S = -79.9$ J/mol•K
$\Delta G = -98.0$ kJ/mol

**490.** The element bromine can be produced by the reaction of hydrogen bromide and manganese(IV) oxide:

$$4HBr(g) + MnO_2(s) \rightarrow MnBr_2(s) + 2H_2O(l) + Br_2(l)$$

$\Delta H$ for the reaction is $-291.3$ kJ/mol at 25°C. Use this value and the following values of $\Delta H_f^0$ to calculate $\Delta H_f^0$ of $MnBr_2(s)$.

$\Delta H^0_{f HBr} = -36.29$ kJ/mol
$\Delta H^0_{f MnO_2} = -520.0$ kJ/mol
$\Delta H^0_{f H_2O} = -285.8$ kJ/mol
$\Delta H^0_{f Br_2} = 0.00$ kJ/mol

**491.** Calculate the change in entropy, $\Delta S$, at 25°C for the reaction of calcium carbide with water to produce acetylene gas:

$$CaC_2(s) + 2H_2O(l) \rightarrow C_2H_2(g) + Ca(OH)_2(s)$$

$\Delta G = -147.7$ kJ/mol
$\Delta H = -125.6$ kJ/mol

**492.** Calculate the free energy change for the explosive decomposition of ammonium nitrate at 25°C. Note that $H_2O$ is a gas in this reaction:

$$NH_4NO_3(s) \rightarrow N_2O(g) + 2H_2O(g)$$

$\Delta S = 446.4$ J/mol•K

**493.** In locations where natural gas, which is mostly methane, is not available, many people burn propane, which is delivered by truck and stored in a tank under pressure.

**a.** Write the chemical equations for the complete combustion of 1 mol of methane, $CH_4$, and 1 mol of propane, $C_3H_8$.

**b.** Calculate the enthalpy change for each reaction to determine the amount of energy as heat evolved by burning 1 mol of each fuel.

**c.** Using the molar enthalpies of combustion you calculated, determine the energy output per kilogram of each fuel. Which fuel yields more energy per unit mass?

**494.** The hydration of acetylene to form acetaldehyde is shown in the following equation:

$$C_2H_2(g) + H_2O(l) \rightarrow CH_3CHO(l)$$

Use enthalpies of combustion for $C_2H_2$ and $CH_3CHO$ to compute the enthalpy of the above reaction.

$$C_2H_2(g) + 2O_2(g) \rightarrow 2CO_2(g) + H_2O(l)$$

$\Delta H = -1299.6$ kJ/mol

$$CH_3CHO(l) + 2O_2(g) \rightarrow 2CO_2(g) + 2H_2O(l)$$

$\Delta H = -1166.9$ kJ/mol

**495.** Calculate the enthalpy for the combustion of decane. $\Delta H_f^0$ for liquid decane is $-300.9$ kJ/mol.

$$C_{10}H_{22}(l) + 15O_2(g) \rightarrow 10CO_2(g) + 11H_2O(l)$$

**496.** Find the enthalpy of the reaction of magnesium oxide with hydrogen chloride:

$$MgO(s) + 2HCl(g) \rightarrow MgCl_2(s) + H_2O(l)$$

Use the following equations and data.

$$Mg(s) + 2HCl(g) \rightarrow MgCl_2(s) + H_2(g)$$

$\Delta H = -456.9$ kJ/mol

$$Mg(s) + O_2(g) \rightarrow MgO(s)$$

$\Delta H = -601.6$ kJ/mol

$$H_2O(l) \rightarrow H_2(g) + O_2(g)$$

$\Delta H = +285.8$ kJ/mol

**497.** What is the free energy change for the following reaction at 25°C?

$$2NaOH(s) + 2Na(s) \xrightarrow{\Delta} 2\,Na_2O(s) + H_2(g)$$

$\Delta S = 10.6$ J/mol•K $\qquad \Delta H^0_{f\,NaOH} = -425.9$ kJ/mol

**498.** The following equation represents the reaction between gaseous HCl and gaseous ammonia to form solid ammonium chloride:

$$NH_3(g) + HCl(g) \rightarrow NH_4Cl(s)$$

Calculate the entropy change in J/mol•K for the reaction of hydrogen chloride and ammonia at 25°C using the following data and the table following item 500.

$\Delta G = -91.2$ kJ/mol

**499.** The production of steel from iron involves the removal of many impurities in the iron ore. The following equations show some of the purifying reactions. Calculate the enthalpy for each reaction. Use the table following item 500 and the data given below.

**a.** $3C(s) + Fe_2O_3(s) \rightarrow 3CO(g) + 2Fe(s)$
$\Delta H^0_{f\,CO(g)} = -110.53$ kJ/mol

**b.** $3Mn(s) + Fe_2O_3(s) \rightarrow 3MnO(s) + 2Fe(s)$
$\Delta H^0_{f\,MnO(s)} = -384.9$ kJ/mol

**c.** $12P(s) + 10Fe_2O_3(s) \rightarrow 3P_4O_{10}(s) + 20Fe(s)$
$\Delta H^0_{f\,P_4O_{10}(s)} = -3009.9$ kJ/mol

**d.** $3Si(s) + 2Fe_2O_3(s) \rightarrow 3SiO_2(s) + 4Fe(s)$
$\Delta H^0_{f\,SiO_2(s)} = -910.9$ kJ/mol

**e.** $3S(s) + 2Fe_2O_3(s) \rightarrow 3SO_2(g) + 4Fe(s)$

## Equilibrium: Chap. 18, Sec. 1

**500.** Calculate the equilibrium constants for the following hypothetical reactions. Assume that all components of the reactions are gaseous.

**a.** $A \rightleftarrows C + D$

*For problems 498–499*

| *Substance* | $\Delta H_f^0$ *(kj/mol)* | *Substance* | $\Delta H_f^0$ *(kj/mol)* |
|---|---|---|---|
| $NH_3(g)$ | −45.9 | $HF(g)$ | −273.3 |
| $NH_4Cl(s)$ | −314.4 | $H_2O(g)$ | −241.82 |
| $NH_4F(s)$ | −125 | $H_2O(l)$ | −285.8 |
| $NH_4NO_3(s)$ | −365.56 | $H_2O_2(l)$ | −187.8 |
| $Br_2(l)$ | 0.00 | $H_2SO_4(l)$ | −813.989 |
| $CaCO_3(s)$ | −1207.6 | $FeO(s)$ | −825.5 |
| $CaO(s)$ | −634.9 | $Fe_2O_3(s)$ | −1118.4 |
| $CH_4(g)$ | −74.9 | $MnO_2(s)$ | −520.0 |
| $C_3H_8(g)$ | −104.7 | $N_2O(g)$ | +82.1 |
| $CO_2(g)$ | −393.5 | $O_2(g)$ | 0.00 |
| $F_2(g)$ | 0.00 | $Na_2O(s)$ | −414.2 |
| $H_2(g)$ | 0.00 | $Na_2SO_3(s)$ | −1101 |
| $HBr(g)$ | −36.29 | $SO_2(g)$ | −296.8 |
| $HCl(g)$ | −92.3 | $SO_3(g)$ | −395.7 |

At equilibrium, the concentration of A is $2.24 \times 10^{-2}$ M and the concentrations of both C and D are $6.41 \times 10^{-3}$ M.

**b.** $A + B \rightleftarrows C + D$

At equilibrium, the concentrations of both A and B are $3.23 \times 10^{-5}$ M and the concentrations of both C and D are $1.27 \times 10^{-2}$ M.

**c.** $A + B \rightleftarrows 2C$

At equilibrium, the concentrations of both A and B are $7.02 \times 10^{-3}$ M and the concentration of C is $2.16 \times 10^{-2}$ M.

**d.** $2A \rightleftarrows 2C + D$

At equilibrium, the concentration of A is $6.59 \times 10^{-4}$ M. The concentration of C is $4.06 \times 10^{-3}$ M, and the concentration of D is $2.03 \times 10^{-3}$ M.

**e.** $A + B \rightleftarrows C + D + E$

At equilibrium, the concentrations of both A and B are $3.73 \times 10^{-4}$ M and the concentrations of C, D, and E are $9.35 \times 10^{-4}$ M.

**f.** $2A + B \rightleftarrows 2C$

At equilibrium, the concentration of A is $5.50 \times 10^{-3}$ M, the concentration of B is $2.25 \times 10^{-3}$, and the concentration of C is $1.02 \times 10^{-2}$ M.

**501.** Calculate the concentration of product D in the following hypothetical reaction:

$$2A(g) \rightleftarrows 2C(g) + D(g)$$

At equilibrium, the concentration of A is $1.88 \times 10^{-1}$ M, the concentration of C is 6.56 M, and the equilibrium constant is $2.403 \times 10^2$.

**502.** At a temperature of 700 K, the equilibrium constant is $3.164 \times 10^3$ for the following reaction system for the hydrogenation of ethene, $C_2H_4$, to ethane, $C_2H_6$:

$$C_2H_4(g) + H_2(g) \rightleftarrows C_2H_6(g)$$

What will be the equilibrium concentration of ethene if the concentration of $H_2$ is 0.0619 M and the concentration of $C_2H_6$ is 1.055 M?

## Mixed Review

**503.** Using the reaction $A + 2B \rightleftarrows C + 2D$, determine the equilibrium constant if the following equilibrium concentrations are found. All components are gases.

$[A] = 0.0567$ M

$[B] = 0.1171$ M

$[C] = 0.000\ 3378$ M

$[D] = 0.000\ 6756$ M

**504.** In the reaction $2A \rightleftarrows 2C + 2D$, determine the equilibrium constant when the following equilibrium concentrations are found. All components are gases.

$[A] = 0.1077$ M

$[C] = 0.000\ 4104$ M

$[D] = 0.000\ 4104$ M

**505.** Calculate the equilibrium constant for the following reaction. Note the phases of the components.

$$2A(g) + B(s) \rightleftarrows C(g) + D(g)$$

The equilibrium concentrations of the components are

$[A] = 0.0922$ M

$[C] = 4.11 \times 10^{-4}$ M

$[D] = 8.22 \times 10^{-4}$ M

**506.** The equilibrium constant of the following reaction for the decomposition of phosgene at 25°C is $4.282 \times 10^{-2}$.

$$COCl_2(g) \rightleftarrows CO(g) + Cl_2(g)$$

**a.** What is the concentration of $COCl_2$ when the concentrations of both CO and $Cl_2$ are $5.90 \times 10^{-3}$ M?

**b.** When the equilibrium concentration of $COCl_2$ is 0.003 70 M, what are the concentrations of CO and $Cl_2$? Assume the concentrations are equal.

**507.** Consider the following hypothetical reaction.

$$A(g) + B(s) \rightleftarrows C(g) + D(s)$$

**a.** If $K = 1$ for this reaction at 500 K, what can you say about the concentrations of A and C at equilibrium?

**b.** If raising the temperature of the reaction results in an equilibrium with a higher concentration of C than A, how will the value of $K$ change?

**508.** The following reaction occurs when steam is passed over hot carbon. The mixture of gases it generates is called *water gas* and is useful as an industrial fuel and as a source of hydrogen for the production of ammonia.

$$C(s) + H_2O(g) \rightleftarrows CO(g) + H_2(g)$$

The equilibrium constant for this reaction is $4.251 \times 10^{-2}$ at 800 K. If the equilibrium concentration of $H_2O(g)$ is 0.1990 M, what concentrations of CO and $H_2$ would you expect to find?

**509.** When nitrogen monoxide gas comes in contact with air, it oxidizes to the brown gas nitrogen dioxide according to the following equation:

$$2NO(g) + O_2(g) \rightleftarrows 2NO_2(g)$$

**a.** The equilibrium constant for this reaction at 500 K is $1.671 \times 10^4$. What concentration of $NO_2$ is present at equilibrium if $[NO] = 6.200 \times 10^{-2}$ M and $[O_2] = 8.305 \times 10^{-3}$ M?

**b.** At 1000 K, the equilibrium constant, $K$, for the same reaction is $1.315 \times 10^{-2}$. What will be the concentration of $NO_2$ at 1000 K given the same concentrations of NO and $O_2$ as were in (a)?

**510.** Consider the following hypothetical reaction, for which $K = 1$ at 300 K:

$$A(g) + B(g) \rightleftarrows 2C(g)$$

**a.** If the reaction begins with equal concentrations of A and B and a zero concentration of C, what can you say about the relative concentrations of the components at equilibrium?

**b.** Additional C is introduced at equilibrium, and the temperature remains constant. When equilibrium is restored, how will the concentrations of all components have changed? How will $K$ have changed?

**511.** The equilibrium constant for the following reaction of hydrogen gas and bromine gas at 25°C is $5.628 \times 10^{18}$:

$$H_2(g) + Br_2(g) \rightleftarrows 2HBr(g)$$

**a.** Write the equilibrium expression for this reaction.

**b.** Assume that equimolar amounts of $H_2$ and $Br_2$ were present at the beginning. Calculate the equilibrium concentration of $H_2$ if the concentration of HBr is 0.500 M.

**c.** If equal amounts of $H_2$ and $Br_2$ react, which reaction component will be present in the greatest concentration at equilibrium? Explain your reasoning.

**512.** The following reaction reaches an equilibrium state:

$$N_2F_4(g) \rightleftarrows 2NF_2(g)$$

At equilibrium at 25°C the concentration of $N_2F_4$ is found to be 0.9989 M and the concentration of $NF_2$ is $1.131 \times 10^{-3}$ M. Calculate the equilibrium constant of the reaction.

**513.** The equilibrium between dinitrogen tetroxide and nitrogen dioxide is represented by the following equation:

$$N_2O_4(g) \rightleftarrows 2NO_2(g)$$

A student places a mixture of the two gases into a closed gas tube and allows the reaction to reach equilibrium at 25°C. At equilibrium, the concentration of $N_2O_4$ is found to be $5.95 \times 10^{-1}$ M and the concentration of $NO_2$ is found to be $5.24 \times 10^{-2}$ M. What is the equilibrium constant of the reaction?

**514.** Consider the following equilibrium system:

$$NaCN(s) + HCl(g) \rightleftarrows HCN(g) + NaCl(s)$$

**a.** Write a complete expression for the equilibrium constant of this system.

**b.** The equilibrium constant for this reaction is $2.405 \times 10^6$. What is the concentration of HCl remaining when the concentration of HCN is 0.8959 M?

**515.** The following reaction is used in the industrial production of hydrogen gas:

$$CH_4(g) + H_2O(g) \rightleftarrows CO(g) + 3H_2(g)$$

The equilibrium constant of this reaction at 298 K (25°C) is $3.896 \times 10^{-27}$, but at 1100 K the constant is $3.112 \times 10^{2}$.

**a.** What do these equilibrium constants tell you about the progress of the reaction at the two temperatures?

**b.** Suppose the reaction mixture is sampled at 1100 K and found to contain 1.56 M of hydrogen, $3.70 \times 10^{-2}$ M of methane, and $8.27 \times 10^{-1}$ M of gaseous $H_2O$. What concentration of carbon monoxide would you expect to find?

**516.** Dinitrogen tetroxide, $N_2O_4$, is soluble in cyclohexane, a common nonpolar solvent. While in solution, $N_2O_4$ can break down into $NO_2$ according to the following equation:

$$N_2O_4(cyclohexane) \rightleftarrows NO_2(cyclohexane)$$

At 20°C, the following concentrations were observed for this equilibrium reaction:

$[N_2O_4] = 2.55 \times 10^{-3}$ M

$[NO_2] = 10.4 \times 10^{-3}$ M

What is the value of the equilibrium constant for this reaction? Note: the chemical equation must be balanced first.

**517.** The reaction given in item 516 also occurs when the dinitrogen tetroxide and nitrogen dioxide are dissolved in carbon tetrachloride, $CCl_4$, another nonpolar solvent.

$$N_2O_4(CCl_4) \rightleftarrows NO_2(CCl_4)$$

The following experimental data were obtained at 20°C:

$[N_2O_4] = 2.67 \times 10^{-3}$ M

$[NO_2] = 10.2 \times 10^{-3}$ M

Calculate the value of the equilibrium constant for this reaction occurring in carbon tetrachloride.

## Equilibrium of Acids and Bases $K_a$ and $K_b$: Chap. 18, Sec. 3

**518.** At 25°C, a 0.025 M solution of formic acid, HCOOH, is found to have a hydronium ion concentration of $2.03 \times 10^{-3}$ M. Calculate the ionization constant of formic acid.

**519.** The pH of a 0.400 M solution of iodic acid, $HIO_3$, is 0.726 at 25°C. What is the $K_a$ at this temperature?

**520.** The pH of a 0.150 M solution of hypochlorous acid, HClO, is found to be 4.55 at 25°C. Calculate the $K_a$ for HClO at this temperature.

**521.** The compound propylamine, $CH_3CH_2CH_2NH_2$, is a weak base. At equilibrium, a 0.039 M solution of propylamine has an $OH^-$ concentration of $3.74 \times 10^{-3}$ M. Calculate the pH of this solution and $K_b$ for propylamine.

**522.** The $K_a$ of nitrous acid is $4.6 \times 10^{-4}$ at 25°C. Calculate the $[H_3O^+]$ of a 0.0450 M nitrous acid solution.

## Mixed Review

**523.** Hydrazoic acid, $HN_3$, is a weak acid. The $[H_3O^+]$ of a 0.102 M solution of hydrazoic acid is $1.39 \times 10^{-3}$ M. Determine the pH of this solution, and calculate $K_a$ at 25°C for $HN_3$.

**524.** Bromoacetic acid, $BrCH_2COOH$, is a moderately weak acid. A 0.200 M solution of bromoacetic acid has a $H_3O^+$ concentration of 0.0192 M. Determine the pH of this solution and the $K_a$ of bromoacetic acid at 25°C.

**525.** A base, B, dissociates in water according to the following equation:

$$B + H_2O \rightleftarrows BH^+ + OH^-$$

Complete the following table for base solutions with the characteristics given.

| *Initial [B]* | *[B] at Equilibrium* | *[OH⁻]* | $K_b$ | $[H_3O^+]$ | *pH* |
|---|---|---|---|---|---|
| **a.** 0.400 M | NA | $2.70 \times 10^{-4}$ M | ? | ? M | ? |
| **b.** 0.005 50 M | ? M | $8.45 \times 10^{-4}$ M | ? | NA | ? |
| **c.** 0.0350 M | ? M | ? M | ? | ? M | 11.29 |
| **d.** ? M | 0.006 28 M | 0.000 92 M | ? | NA | ? |

**526.** The solubility of benzoic acid, $C_6H_5COOH$, in water at 25°C is 2.9 g/L. The pH of this saturated solution is 2.92. Determine $K_a$ at 25°C for benzoic acid. (Hint: first calculate the initial concentration of benzoic acid.)

**527.** A 0.006 50 M solution of ethanolamine, $H_2NCH_2CH_2OH$, has a pH of 10.64 at 25°C. Calculate the $K_b$ of ethanolamine. What concentration of undissociated ethanolamine remains at equilibrium?

**528.** The weak acid hydrogen selenide, $H_2Se$, has two hydrogen atoms that can form hydronium ions. The second ionization is so small that the concentration of the resulting $H_3O^+$ is insignificant. If the $[H_3O^+]$ of a 0.060 M solution of $H_2Se$ is $2.72 \times 10^{-3}$ M at 25°C, what is the $K_a$ of the first ionization?

**529.** Pyridine, $C_5H_5N$, is a very weak base. Its $K_b$ at 25°C is $1.78 \times 10^{-9}$. Calculate the $[OH^-]$ and pH of a 0.140 M solution. Assume that the concentration of pyridine at equilibrium is equal to its initial concentration because so little pyridine is dissociated.

**530.** A solution of a monoprotic acid, HA, at equilibrium is found to have a 0.0208 M concentration of nonionized acid. The pH of the acid solution is 2.17. Calculate the initial acid concentration and $K_a$ for this acid.

**531.** Pyruvic acid, $CH_3COCOOH$, is an important intermediate in the metabolism of carbohydrates in the cells of the body. A solution made by dissolving 438 mg of pyruvic acid in 10.00 mL of water is found to have a pH of 1.34 at 25°C. Calculate $K_a$ for pyruvic acid.

532. The $[H_3O^+]$ of a solution of acetoacetic acid, $CH_3COCH_2COOH$, is $4.38 \times 10^{-3}$ M at 25°C. The concentration of nonionized acid is 0.0731 M at equilibrium. Calculate $K_a$ for acetoacetic acid at 25°C.

533. The $K_a$ of 2-chloropropanoic acid, $CH_3CHClCOOH$, is $1.48 \times 10^{-3}$. Calculate the $[H_3O^+]$ and the pH of a 0.116 M solution of 2-chloropropionic acid. Let $x = [H_3O^+]$. The degree of ionization of the acid is too large to ignore. If your set up is correct, you will have a quadratic equation to solve.

534. Sulfuric acid ionizes in two steps in water solution. For the first ionization shown in the following equation, the $K_a$ is so large that in moderately dilute solution the ionization can be considered 100%.

$$H_2SO_4 + H_2O \rightarrow H_3O^+ + HSO_4^-$$

The second ionization is fairly strong, and $K_a = 1.3 \times 10^{-2}$:

$$HSO_4^- + H_2O \rightleftarrows H_3O^+ + SO_4^{2-}$$

Calculate the total $[H_3O^+]$ and pH of a 0.0788 M $H_2SO_4$ solution. Hint: If the first ionization is 100%, what will $[HSO_4^-]$ and $[H_3O^+]$ be? Remember to account for the already existing concentration of $H_3O^+$ in the second ionization. Let $x = [SO_4^{2-}]$.

535. The hydronium ion concentration of a 0.100 M solution of cyanic acid, HOCN, is found to be $5.74 \times 10^{-3}$ M at 25°C. Calculate the ionization constant of cyanic acid. What is the pH of this solution?

536. A solution of hydrogen cyanide, HCN, has a 0.025 M concentration. The cyanide ion concentration is found to be $3.16 \times 10^{-6}$ M.
   **a.** What is the hydronium ion concentration of this solution?
   **b.** What is the pH of this solution?
   **c.** What is the concentration of nonionized HCN in the solution? Be sure to use the correct number of significant figures.
   **d.** Calculate the ionization constant of HCN.
   **e.** How would you characterize the strength of HCN as an acid?
   **f.** Determine the $[H_3O^+]$ for a 0.085 M solution of HCN.

537. A 1.20 M solution of dichloroacetic acid, $CCl_2HCOOH$, at 25°C has a hydronium ion concentration of 0.182 M.
   **a.** What is the pH of this solution?
   **b.** What is the $K_a$ of dichloroacetic acid at 25°C?
   **c.** What is the concentration of nonionized dichloroacetic acid in this solution?
   **d.** What can you say about the strength of dichloroacetic acid?

538. Phenol, $C_6H_5OH$, is a very weak acid. The pH of a 0.215 M solution of phenol at 25°C is found to be 5.61. Calculate the $K_a$ for phenol.

539. A solution of the simplest amino acid, glycine ($NH_2CH_2COOH$), is prepared by dissolving 3.75 g in 250.0 mL of water at 25°C. The pH of this solution is found to be 0.890.
   **a.** Calculate the molarity of the glycine solution.
   **b.** Calculate the $K_a$ for glycine.

540. Trimethylamine, $(CH_3)_3N$, dissociates in water the same way that $NH_3$ does—by accepting a proton from a water molecule. The $[OH^-]$ of a 0.0750 M solution of trimethylamine at 25°C is $2.32 \times 10^{-3}$ M. Calculate the pH of this solution and the $K_b$ of trimethylamine.

541. Dimethylamine, $(CH_3)_2NH$, is a weak base similar to the trimethylamine in item 540. A $5.00 \times 10^{-3}$ M solution of dimethylamine has a pH of 11.20 at 25°C. Calculate the $K_b$ of dimethylamine. Compare this $K_b$ with the $K_b$ for trimethylamine that you calculated in item 540. Which substance is the stronger base?

542. Hydrazine dissociates in water solution according to the following equations:

$$H_2NNH_2 + H_2O(l) \rightleftarrows H_2NNH_3^+(aq) + OH^-(aq)$$
$$H_2NNH_3^+(aq) + H_2O(l) \rightleftarrows H_3NNH_3^{2+}(aq) + OH^-(aq)$$

The $K_b$ of this second dissociation is $8.9 \times 10^{-16}$, so it contributes almost no hydroxide ions in solution and can be ignored here.
   **a.** The pH of a 0.120 M solution of hydrazine at 25°C is 10.50. Calculate $K_b$ for the first ionization of hydrazine. Assume that the original concentration of $H_2NNH_2$ does not change.
   **b.** Make the same assumption as you did in (a) and calculate the $[OH^-]$ of a 0.020 M solution.
   **c.** Calculate the pH of the solution in (b).

## Equilibrium of Salts, $K_{sp}$: Chap. 18, Sec. 4

543. Silver bromate, $AgBrO_3$, is slightly soluble in water. A saturated solution is found to contain 0.276 g $AgBrO_3$ dissolved in 150.0 mL of water. Calculate $K_{sp}$ for silver bromate.

544. 2.50 L of a saturated solution of calcium fluoride leaves a residue of 0.0427 g of $CaF_2$ when evaporated to dryness. Calculate the $K_{sp}$ of $CaF_2$.

545. The $K_{sp}$ of calcium sulfate, $CaSO_4$, is $9.1 \times 10^{-6}$. What is the molar concentration of $CaSO_4$ in a saturated solution?

546. A salt has the formula $X_2Y$, and its $K_{sp}$ is $4.25 \times 10^{-7}$.
   **a.** What is the molarity of a saturated solution of the salt?
   **b.** What is the molarity of a solution of AZ if its $K_{sp}$ is the same value?

*In each of the following problems, include the calculated ion product with your answer.*

547. Will a precipitate of $Ca(OH)_2$ form when 320. mL of a 0.046 M solution of NaOH mixes with 400. mL of a 0.085 M $CaCl_2$ solution? $K_{sp}$ of $Ca(OH)_2$ is $5.5 \times 10^{-6}$.

548. 20.00 mL of a 0.077 M solution of silver nitrate, $AgNO_3$, is mixed with 30.00 mL of a 0.043 M solution of sodium acetate, $NaC_2H_3O_2$. Does a precipitate form? The $K_{sp}$ of $AgC_2H_3O_2$ is $2.5 \times 10^{-3}$.

549. If you mix 100. mL of 0.036 M $Pb(C_2H_3O_2)_2$ with 50. mL of 0.074 M NaCl, will a precipitate of $PbCl_2$ form? The $K_{sp}$ of $PbCl_2$ is $1.9 \times 10^{-4}$.

**550.** If 20.00 mL of a 0.0090 M solution of $(NH_4)_2S$ is mixed with 120.00 mL of a 0.0082 M solution of $Al(NO_3)_3$, does a precipitate form? The $K_{sp}$ of $Al_2S_3$ is $2.00 \times 10^{-7}$.

## Mixed Review

**551.** The molar concentration of a saturated calcium chromate, $CaCrO_4$, solution is 0.010 M at 25°C. What is the $K_{sp}$ of calcium chromate?

**552.** A 10.00 mL sample of a saturated lead selenate solution is found to contain 0.00136 g of dissolved $PbSeO_4$ at 25°C. Determine the $K_{sp}$ of lead selenate.

**553.** A 22.50 mL sample of a saturated copper(I) thiocyanate, CuSCN, solution at 25°C is found to have a $4.0 \times 10^{-6}$ M concentration.
**a.** Determine the $K_{sp}$ of CuSCN.
**b.** What mass of CuSCN would be dissolved in $1.0 \times 10^3$ L of solution?

**554.** A saturated solution of silver dichromate, $Ag_2Cr_2O_7$, has a concentration of $3.684 \times 10^{-3}$ M. Calculate the $K_{sp}$ of silver dichromate.

**555.** The $K_{sp}$ of barium sulfite, $BaSO_3$, at 25°C is $8.0 \times 10^{-7}$.
**a.** What is the molar concentration of a saturated solution of $BaSO_3$?
**b.** What mass of $BaSO_3$ would dissolve in 500. mL of water?

**556.** The $K_{sp}$ of lead(II) chloride at 25°C is $1.9 \times 10^{-4}$. What is the molar concentration of a saturated solution at 25°C?

**557.** The $K_{sp}$ of barium carbonate at 25°C is $1.2 \times 10^{-8}$.
**a.** What is the molar concentration of a saturated solution of $BaCO_3$ at 25°C?
**b.** What volume of water would be needed to dissolve 0.10 g of barium carbonate?

**558.** The $K_{sp}$ of $SrSO_4$ is $3.2 \times 10^{-7}$ at 25°C.
**a.** What is the molar concentration of a saturated $SrSO_4$ solution?
**b.** If 20.0 L of a saturated solution of $SrSO_4$ were evaporated to dryness, what mass of $SrSO_4$ would remain?

**559.** The $K_{sp}$ of strontium sulfite, $SrSO_3$, is $4.0 \times 10^{-8}$ at 25°C. If 1.0000 g of $SrSO_3$ is stirred in 5.0 L of water until the solution is saturated and then filtered, what mass of $SrSO_3$ would remain?

**560.** The $K_{sp}$ of manganese(II) arsenate is $1.9 \times 10^{-11}$ at 25°C. What is the molar concentration of $Mn_3(AsO_4)_2$ in a saturated solution? Note that five ions are produced from the dissociation of $Mn_3(AsO_4)_2$.

**561.** Suppose that 30.0 mL of a 0.0050 M solution of $Sr(NO_3)_2$ is mixed with 20.0 mL of a 0.010 M solution of $K_2SO_4$ at 25°C. The $K_{sp}$ of $SrSO_4$ is $3.2 \times 10^{-7}$.
**a.** What is the ion product of the ions that can potentially form a precipitate?
**b.** Does a precipitate form?

**562.** Lead(II) bromide, $PbBr_2$, is slightly soluble in water. Its $K_{sp}$ is $6.3 \times 10^{-6}$ at 25°C. Suppose that 120. mL of a 0.0035 M solution of $MgBr_2$ is mixed with 180. mL of a 0.0024 M $Pb(C_2H_3O_2)_2$ solution at 25°C.
**a.** What is the ion product of $Br^-$ and $Pb^{2+}$ in the mixed solution?
**b.** Does a precipitate form?

**563.** The $K_{sp}$ of $Mg(OH)_2$ at 25°C is $1.5 \times 10^{-11}$.
**a.** Write the equilibrium equation for the dissociation of $Mg(OH)_2$.
**b.** What volume of water would be required to dissolve 0.10 g of $Mg(OH)_2$?
**c.** Considering that magnesium hydroxide is essentially insoluble, why is it possible to titrate a suspension of $Mg(OH)_2$ to an equivalence point with a strong acid such as HCl?

**564.** Lithium carbonate is somewhat soluble in water; its $K_{sp}$ at 25°C is $2.51 \times 10^{-2}$.
**a.** What is the molar concentration of a saturated $Li_2CO_3$ solution?
**b.** What mass of $Li_2CO_3$ would you dissolve in order to make 3440 mL of saturated solution?

**565.** A 50.00 mL sample of a saturated solution of barium hydroxide, $Ba(OH)_2$, is titrated to the equivalence point by 31.61 mL of a 0.3417 M solution of HCl. Determine the $K_{sp}$ of $Ba(OH)_2$.

**566.** Calculate the $K_{sp}$ for salts represented by QR that dissociate into two ions, $Q^+$ and $R^-$, in each of the following solutions:
**a.** saturated solution of QR is 1.0 M
**b.** saturated solution of QR is 0.50 M
**c.** saturated solution of QR is 0.1 M
**d.** saturated solution of QR is 0.001 M

**567.** Suppose that salts QR, $X_2Y$, $KL_2$, $A_3Z$, and $D_2E_3$ form saturated solutions that are 0.02 M in concentration. Calculate $K_{sp}$ for each of these salts.

**568.** The $K_{sp}$ at 25°C of silver bromide is $5.0 \times 10^{-13}$. What is the molar concentration of a saturated AgBr solution? What mass of silver bromide would dissolve in 10.0 L of saturated solution at 25°C?

**569.** The $K_{sp}$ at 25°C for calcium hydroxide is $5.5 \times 10^{-6}$.
**a.** Calculate the molarity of a saturated $Ca(OH)_2$ solution.
**b.** What is the $OH^-$ concentration of this solution?
**c.** What is the pH of the saturated solution?

**570.** The $K_{sp}$ of magnesium carbonate is $3.5 \times 10^{-8}$ at 25°C. What mass of $MgCO_3$ would dissolve in 4.00 L of water at 25°C?

# Redox Equations: Chap. 19, Sec. 2

## Reactions in Acidic Solution

*Balance the following redox equations. Assume that all reactions take place in an acid environment where $H^+$ and $H_2O$ are readily available.*

**571.** $Fe + SnCl_4 \rightarrow FeCl_3 + SnCl_2$

**572.** $H_2O_2 + FeSO_4 + H_2SO_4 \rightarrow Fe_2(SO_4)_3 + H_2O$

**573.** $CuS + HNO_3 \rightarrow Cu(NO_3)_2 + NO + S + H_2O$

**574.** $K_2Cr_2O_7 + HI \rightarrow CrI_3 + KI + I_2 + H_2O$

## Reactions in Basic Solution

*Balance the following redox equations. Assume that all reactions take place in a basic environment where $OH^-$ and $H_2O$ are readily available.*

**575.** $CO_2 + NH_2OH \rightarrow CO + N_2 + H_2O$

**576.** $Bi(OH)_3 + K_2SnO_2 \rightarrow Bi + K_2SnO_3$
(Both of the potassium-tin-oxygen compounds dissociate into potassium ions and tin-oxygen ions.)

## Mixed Review

*Balance each of the following redox equations. Unless stated otherwise, assume that the reaction occurs in acidic solution.*

**577.** $Mg + N_2 \rightarrow Mg_3N_2$

**578.** $SO_2 + Br_2 + H_2O \rightarrow HBr + H_2SO_4$

**579.** $H_2S + Cl_2 \rightarrow S + HCl$

**580.** $PbO_2 + HBr \rightarrow PbBr_2 + Br_2 + H_2O$

**581.** $S + HNO_3 \rightarrow NO_2 + H_2SO_4 + H_2O$

**582.** $NaIO_3 + N_2H_4 + HCl \rightarrow N_2 + NaICl_2 + H_2O$ ($N_2H_4$ is hydrazine; do not separate it into ions.)

**583.** $MnO_2 + H_2O_2 + HCl \rightarrow MnCl_2 + O_2 + H_2O$

**584.** $AsH_3 + NaClO_3 \rightarrow H_3AsO_4 + NaCl$ ($AsH_3$ is arsine, the arsenic analogue of ammonia, $NH_3$.)

**585.** $K_2Cr_2O_7 + H_2C_2O_4 + HCl \rightarrow CrCl_3 + CO_2 + KCl + H_2O$ ($H_2C_2O_4$ is oxalic acid; it can be treated as $2H^+ + C_2O_4^{2-}$.)

**586.** $Hg(NO_3)_2 \xrightarrow{heat} HgO + NO_2 + O_2$ (The reaction is not in solution.)

**587.** $HAuCl_4 + N_2H_4 \rightarrow Au + N_2 + HCl$ ($HAuCl_4$ can be considered as $H^+ + AuCl_4^-$.)

**588.** $Sb_2(SO_4)_3 + KMnO_4 + H_2O \rightarrow H_3SbO_4 + K_2SO_4 + MnSO_4 + H_2SO_4$

**589.** $Mn(NO_3)_2 + NaBiO_3 + HNO_3 \rightarrow Bi(NO_3)_2 + HMnO_4 + NaNO_3 + H_2O$

**590.** $H_3AsO_4 + Zn + HCl \rightarrow AsH_3 + ZnCl_2 + H_2O$

**591.** $KClO_3 + HCl \rightarrow Cl_2 + H_2O + KCl$

**592.** The same reactants as in item 591 can combine in the following way when more $KClO_3$ is present. Balance the equation.

$$KClO_3 + HCl \rightarrow Cl_2 + ClO_2 + H_2O + KCl$$

**593.** $MnCl_3 + H_2O \rightarrow MnCl_2 + MnO_2 + HCl$

**594.** $NaOH + H_2O + Al \rightarrow NaAl(OH)_4 + H_2$ in basic solution

**595.** $Br_2 + Ca(OH)_2 \rightarrow CaBr_2 + Ca(BrO_3)_2 + H_2O$ in basic solution

**596.** $N_2O + NaClO + NaOH \rightarrow NaCl + NaNO_2 + H_2O$ in basic solution

**597.** Balance the following reaction, which can be used to prepare bromine in the laboratory:

$$HBr + MnO_2 \rightarrow MnBr_2 + H_2O + Br_2$$

**598.** The following reaction occurs when gold is dissolved in *aqua regia.* Balance the equation.

$$Au + HCl + HNO_3 \rightarrow HAuCl_4 + NO + H_2O$$

## Electrochemistry: Chap. 20, Sec. 2

*Use the reduction potentials in the table on page 915 to determine whether the following reactions are spontaneous as written. Report the $E^0_{cell}$ for the reactions.*

**599.** $Cu^{2+} + Fe \rightarrow Fe^{2+} + Cu$

**600.** $Pb^{2+} + Fe^{2+} \rightarrow Fe^{3+} + Pb$

**601.** $Mn^{2+} + 4H_2O + Sn^{2+} \rightarrow MnO_4^- + 8H^+ + Sn$

**602.** $MnO_4^{2-} + Cl_2 \rightarrow MnO_4^- + 2Cl^-$

**603.** $Hg_2^{2+} + 2MnO_4^{2-} \rightarrow 2Hg + 2MnO_4^-$

**604.** $2Li^+ + Pb \rightarrow 2Li + Pb^{2+}$

**605.** $Br_2 + 2Cl^- \rightarrow 2Br^- + Cl_2$

**606.** $S + 2I^- \rightarrow S^{2-} + I_2$

*If a cell is constructed in which the following pairs of reactions are possible, what would be the cathode reaction, the anode reaction, and the overall cell voltage?*

**607.** $Ca^{2+} + 2e^- \rightleftarrows Ca$
$Fe^{3+} + 3e^- \rightleftarrows Fe$

**608.** $Ag^+ + e^- \rightleftarrows Ag$
$S + 2H^+ + 2e^- \rightleftarrows H_2S$

**609.** $Fe^{3+} + e^- \rightleftarrows Fe^{2+}$
$Sn^{2+} + 2e^- \rightleftarrows Sn$

**610.** $Cu^{2+} + 2e^- \rightleftarrows Cu$
$Au^{3+} + 3e^- \rightleftarrows Au$

## Mixed Review

*Use reduction potentials to determine whether the reactions in the following 10 problems are spontaneous.*

**611.** $Ba + Sn^{2+} \rightarrow Ba^{2+} + Sn$

**612.** $Ni + Hg^{2+} \rightarrow Ni^{2+} + Hg$

**613.** $2Cr^{3+} + 7\ H_2O + 6Fe^{3+} \rightarrow Cr_2O_7^{2-} + 14H^+ + 6Fe^{2+}$

**614.** $Cl_2 + Sn \rightarrow 2Cl^- + Sn^{2+}$

**615.** $Al + 3Ag^+ \rightarrow Al^{3+} + 3Ag$

**616.** $Hg_2^{2+} + S^{2-} \rightarrow 2Hg + S$

**617.** $Ba + 2Ag^+ \rightarrow Ba^{2+} + 2Ag$

**618.** $2I^- + Ca^{2+} \rightarrow I_2 + Ca$

**619.** $Zn + 2MnO_4^- \rightarrow Zn^{2+} + 2MnO_4^{2-}$

**620.** $2Cr^{3+} + 3Mg^{2+} + 7H_2O \rightarrow Cr_2O_7^{2-} + 14H^+ + 3Mg$

*In the following problems, you are given a pair of reduction half-reactions. If a cell were constructed in which the pairs of half-reactions were possible, what would be the balanced equation for the overall cell reaction that would occur? Write the half-reactions that occur at the cathode and anode, and calculate the cell voltage.*

**621.** $Cl_2 + 2e^- \rightleftarrows 2Cl^-$

$Ni^{2+} + 2e^- \rightleftarrows Ni$

**622.** $Fe^{3+} + 3e^- \rightleftarrows Fe$

$Hg^{2+} + 2e^- \rightleftarrows Hg$

**623.** $MnO_4^- + e^- \rightleftarrows MnO_4^{2-}$

$Al^{3+} + 3e^- \rightleftarrows Al$

**624.** $MnO_4^- + 8H^+ + 5e^- \rightleftarrows Mn^{2+} + 4H_2O$

$S + 2H^+ + 2e^- \rightleftarrows H_2S$

**625.** $Ca^{2+} + 2e^- \rightleftarrows Ca$

$Li^+ + e^- \rightleftarrows Li$

**626.** $Br_2 + 2e^- \rightleftarrows 2Br^-$

$MnO_4^- + 8H^+ + 5e^- \rightleftarrows Mn^{2+} + 4H_2O$

**627.** $Sn^{2+} + 2e^- \rightleftarrows Sn$

$Fe^{3+} + e^- \rightleftarrows Fe^{2+}$

**628.** $Zn^{2+} + 2e^- \rightleftarrows Zn$

$Cr_2O_7^{2-} + 14H^+ + 6e^- \rightleftarrows 2Cr^{3+} + 7H_2O$

**629.** $Ba^{2+} + 2e^- \rightleftarrows Ba$

$Ca^{2+} + 2e^- \rightleftarrows Ca$

**630.** $Hg_2^{2+} + 2e^- \rightleftarrows 2Hg$

$Cd^{2+} + 2e^- \rightleftarrows Cd$

*For problems 599–606*

| ***Reduction Half-reaction*** | ***Standard Electrode Potential, $E^0$ (in volts)*** | ***Reduction Half-reaction*** | ***Standard Electrode Potential, $E^0$ (in volts)*** |
|---|---|---|---|
| $MnO_4^- + 8H^+ + 5e^- \rightleftarrows Mn^{2+} + 4H_2O$ | +1.50 | $Fe^{3+} + 3e^- \rightleftarrows Fe$ | −0.04 |
| $Au^{3+} + 3e^- \rightleftarrows Au$ | +1.50 | $Pb^{2+} + 2e^- \rightleftarrows Pb$ | −0.13 |
| $Cl_2 + 2e^- \rightleftarrows 2Cl^-$ | +1.36 | $Sn^{2+} + 2e^- \rightleftarrows Sn$ | −0.14 |
| $Cr_2O_7^{2-} + 14H^+ + 6e^- \rightleftarrows 2Cr^{3+} + 7H_2O$ | +1.23 | $Ni^{2+} + 2e^- \rightleftarrows Ni$ | −0.26 |
| $MnO_2 + 4H^+ + 2e^- \rightleftarrows Mn^{2+} + 2H_2O$ | +1.22 | $Cd^{2+} + 2e^- \rightleftarrows Cd$ | −0.40 |
| $Br_2 + 2e^- \rightleftarrows 2Br^-$ | +1.07 | $Fe^{2+} + 2e^- \rightleftarrows Fe$ | −0.45 |
| $Hg^{2+} + 2e^- \rightleftarrows Hg$ | +0.85 | $S + 2e^- \rightleftarrows S^{2-}$ | −0.48 |
| $Ag^+ + e^- \rightleftarrows Ag$ | +0.80 | $Zn^{2+} + 2e^- \rightleftarrows Zn$ | −0.76 |
| $Hg_2^{2+} + 2e^- \rightleftarrows 2Hg$ | +0.80 | $Al^{3+} + 3e^- \rightleftarrows Al$ | −1.66 |
| $Fe^{3+} + e^- \rightleftarrows Fe^{2+}$ | +0.77 | $Mg^{2+} + 2e^- \rightleftarrows Mg$ | −2.37 |
| $MnO_4^- + e^- \rightleftarrows MnO_4^{2-}$ | +0.56 | $Na^+ + e^- \rightleftarrows Na$ | −2.71 |
| $I_2 + 2e^- \rightleftarrows 2I^-$ | +0.54 | $Ca^{2+} + 2e^- \rightleftarrows Ca$ | −2.87 |
| $Cu^{2+} + 2e^- \rightleftarrows Cu$ | +0.34 | $Ba^{2+} + 2e^- \rightleftarrows Ba$ | −2.91 |
| $S + 2H^+(aq) + 2e^- \rightleftarrows H_2S(aq)$ | +0.14 | $K^+ + e^- \rightleftarrows K$ | −2.93 |
| $2H^+(aq) + 2e^- \rightleftarrows H_2$ | 0.00 | $Li^+ + e^- \rightleftarrows Li$ | −3.04 |

# Selected Answers

## Matter and Change

### Math Tutor Practice

1. a. 5 significant figures
   b. 4 significant figures
2. a. 4.21 g/cm$^3$
   b. 16.5 g

## Measurements and Calculations

### Practice Problems A

1. 2.75 g/cm$^3$
2. 1.14 g
3. 5.60 mL

### Practice Problems B

1. 1645 cm, 0.01645 km
2. 0.000 014 g

### Practice Problems C

1. −17%
2. 2.7%

### Practice Problems D

1. a. 5
   b. 6
   c. 4
   d. 1
   e. 5
   f. 6
2. a. 7000 cm
   b. 7000. cm
   c. 7000.00 cm

### Practice Problems E

1. 2.156 g
2. 85.6 cm
3. 1.00 µm2
4. 440 g

### Practice Problems F

1. 9.69 mL
2. 1.67 g/cm$^3$
3. $5.12 \times 10^{11}$ mm
4. $5.2 \times 10^3$ s

### Math Tutor Practice

1. a. $7.45 \times 10^{-5}$ g
   b. $5.984102 \times 10^6$ nm
2. a. $-9.11 \times 10^3$
   b. $8.25 \times 10^{-2}$

## Atoms: The Building Blocks of Matter

### Practice Problems A

1. 35 protons, 35 electrons, 45 neutrons
2. $^{13}_{6}C$
3. phosphorus-30

### Practice Problems B

1. 126 g Fe
2. 14.7 g K
3. 0.310 g Na
4. 957 g Ni

### Practice Problems C

1. 0.125 mol Ca
2. $1.83 \times 10^{-7}$ mol Au
3. $8.18 \times 10^{-3}$

### Practice Problems D

1. $2.49 \times 10^{-12}$ mol Pb
2. $4.2 \times 10^{-21}$ mol Sn
3. $1.66 \times 10^{24}$ atoms Al

### Practice Problems E

1. $7.3 \times 10^{-7}$ g Ni
2. $7.51 \times 10^{22}$ atoms S
3. 66 g Au

### Math Tutor Practice

1. a. 2.25 g
   b. 59 300 L
2. a. $7.2 \times 10^1$ $\mu$g
   b. $3.98 \times 10^3$ km

## Arrangement of Electrons in Atoms

### Practice Problems A

1. 7, 7, $\underset{1s}{\uparrow\downarrow}$ $\underset{2s}{\uparrow\downarrow}$ $\underbrace{\uparrow\ \uparrow\ \uparrow}_{2p}$
2. 9, 2

### Practice Problems B

1. a. $1s^22s^22p^63s^23p^63d^{10}4s^24p^64d^{10}5s^25p^5$, [Kr]$4d^{10}5s^25p^5$, 46
   b. 27, 26, 1
2. a. [Kr]$4d^{10}5s^25p^2$, 2
   b. 10, germanium

3. a. $1s^22s^22p^63s^23p^63d^54s^2$
   b. manganese
4. a. 9, $1s^22s^22p^63s^23p^6$
   b. argon

### Practice Problems C

1. a. $1s^22s^22p^63s^23p^63d^{10}4s^24p^6 4d^{10}5s^25p^66s^2$, $[Xe]6s^2$
   b. Be, Mg, Ca, Sr
2. a. $[Xe]4f^{14}5d^{10}6s^1$
   b. Au, Cs, Pt

### Math Tutor Practice

1. 85.47 amu
2. 28.1 amu

## The Periodic Law

### Practice Problems A

1. Group 1, fifth period, *s* block
2. a. $ns^2$
   b. $1s^22s^22p^63s^23p^64s^2$
   c. Ca, $[Ar]4s^2$

### Practice Problems B

1. fourth period, *d* block, Group 10
2. $4d^{10}5s^2$

### Practice Problems C

1. a. $3s^23p^5$
   b. chlorine, nonmetal
2. a. fourth period, *p* block, Group 15
   b. arsenic, metalloid

### Practice Problems D

1. a. *p* block, second period, Group 17, halogens, fluorine, nonmetal, high reactivity
   b. *d* block, fourth period, Group 11, transition elements, copper, metal, low reactivity

### Practice Problems E

1. Li; F
2. All of the elements are in Group 2. Of the four, barium has the highest atomic number and is farthest down the group. Therefore, barium has the largest atomic radius because atomic radii increase down a group.
3. All of the elements are in Period 3. Of the four, silicon has the largest atomic number and therefore is the farthest to the right on the periodic table. Therefore, silicon has the smallest atomic radius because atomic radii decrease from *left to right* across a period.

### Practice Problems F

1. a. Q is in the *p* block, R is in the *s* block, T is in the *p* block, and X is in the *p* block.
   b. Q and R, and X and T are in the same period. Q and T are in the same group.
   c. Q would have the highest ionization energy, and R would have the lowest.
   d. R
   e. R

### Practice Problems G

1. a. All are in the *p* block. E, J, and M are in the same period, and E, G, and L are in the same group.
   b. E should have the highest electron affinity; E, G, and L are most likely to form 1– ions; E should have the highest electronegativity.
   c. The ionic radius would be larger.
   d. E, G, and L

### Math Tutor Practice

1. a. $1s^22s^22p^63s^23p^1$
   b. $1s^22s^22p^6$
   c. $1s^22s^22p^63s^23p^63d^{10}4s^24p^6 4d^{10}5s^25p^2$
   d. $1s^22s^22p^63s^23p^64s^1$
2. a. $[Ne]3s^23p^2$
   b. $[Kr]5s^1$
   c. $[Kr]4d^{10}5s^25p^3$
   d. $[Ar]3d^{10}4s^24p^3$

## Chemical Bonding

### Practice Problems A

See table below.

### Practice Problems C

1. $\mathrm{H}:\ddot{\mathrm{N}}:\mathrm{H}$ (with H below N, two dots below N) or H–$\ddot{\mathrm{N}}$–H (with H bonded below N)
2. $\mathrm{H}:\ddot{\underset{..}{\mathrm{S}}}:\mathrm{H}$ or $\mathrm{H}-\ddot{\underset{..}{\mathrm{S}}}-\mathrm{H}$

| Bonding between chlorine and | Electronegativity difference | Bond type | More-negative atom |
|---|---|---|---|
| calcium | 3.0 – 1.0 = 2.0 | ionic | chlorine |
| oxygen | 3.5 – 3.0 = 0.5 | polar-covalent | oxygen |
| bromine | 3.0 – 2.8 = 0.2 | nonpolar-covalent | chlorine |

3. H:Si:H or H–Si–H (each Si bonded to four H atoms)

4. :F:P:F: or :F–P–F: with :F: below P

### Practice Problems D

1. $\ddot{O}=C=\ddot{O}$
2. $H-C\equiv N:$

### Practice Problems E

1. **a.** linear
   **b.** tetrahedral
   **c.** tetrahedral

### Practice Problems F

1. **a.** bent or angular
   **b.** trigonal-pyramidal

### Math Tutor Practice

1. **a.** ·Si· (four dots)
   **b.** Sr· (two dots)
2. **a.** H
   H:S: (with lone pairs)
   **b.** :O:
   H:C:O:H

## Chemical Formulas and Chemical Compounds

### Practice Problems A

1. **a.** KI
   **b.** $MgCl_2$
   **c.** $Na_2S$
   **d.** $Al_2S_3$
   **e.** AlN
2. **a.** silver chloride
   **b.** zinc oxide
   **c.** calcium bromide
   **d.** strontium fluoride
   **e.** barium oxide
   **f.** calcium chloride

### Practice Problems B

1. **a.** $CuBr_2$, copper(II) bromide
   **b.** FeO, iron(II) oxide
   **c.** $PbCl_2$, lead(II) chloride
   **d.** HgS, mercury(II) sulfide
   **e.** $SnF_2$, tin(II) fluoride
   **f.** $Fe_2O_3$, iron(III) oxide
2. **a.** copper(II) oxide
   **b.** cobalt(III) fluoride
   **c.** tin(IV) iodide
   **d.** iron(II) sulfide

### Practice Problems C

1. **a.** NaI
   **b.** $CaCl_2$
   **c.** $K_2S$
   **d.** $LiNO_3$
   **e.** $CuSO_4$
   **f.** $Na_2CO_3$
   **g.** $Ca(NO_2)_2$
   **h.** $KClO_4$
2. **a.** silver oxide
   **b.** calcium hydroxide
   **c.** potassium chlorate
   **d.** ammonium hydroxide
   **e.** iron(III) chromate
   **f.** potassium hypochlorite

### Practice Problems D

1. **a.** sulfur trioxide
   **b.** iodine trichloride
   **c.** phosphorus pentabromide
2. **a.** $CI_4$
   **b.** $PCl_3$
   **c.** $N_2O_3$

### Practice Problem E

**a.** +1, −1
**b.** +4, −1
**c.** +3, −1
**d.** +4, −2
**e.** +1, +5, −2
**f.** +1, −1
**g.** +5, −2
**h.** +1, +5, −2
**i.** +5, −2
**j.** +2, −1

### Practice Problem F

**a.** 98.09 amu
**b.** 164.10 amu
**c.** 94.97 amu
**d.** 95.21 amu

### Practice Problems G

1. **a.** 2 mol Al, 3 mol S
   **b.** 1 mol Na, 1 mol N, 3 mol O
   **c.** 1 mol Ba, 2 mol O, 2 mol H
2. **a.** 150.17 g/mol
   **b.** 85.00 g/mol
   **c.** 171.35 g/mol

### Practice Problems I

1. **a.** 0.0499 mol
   **b.** 61 mol
2. **a.** $1.53 \times 10^{23}$ molecules
   **b.** $2.20 \times 10^{23}$ molecules
3. 1170 g

### Practice Problems K

1. **a.** 74.51% Pb, 25.49% Cl
   **b.** 52.55% Ba, 10.72% N, 36.73% O
2. 43.85% $H_2O$
3. 96.0 g O; 6.00 mol O

### Practice Problems M

1. FeS
2. $K_2Cr_2O_7$
3. $CaBr_2$

### Practice Problems N

1. $C_6H_6$
2. $H_2O_2$

### Math Tutor Practice

1. 43.38% Na, 11.33% C, 45.29% O
2. 61.13% I

## Chemical Equations and Reactions

### Practice Problems B

1. **a.** calcium + sulfur ⟶ calcium sulfide; $8Ca(s) + S_8(s) \longrightarrow 8CaS(s)$

   **b.** hydrogen + fluorine ⟶ hydrogen fluoride; $H_2(g) + F_2(g) \longrightarrow 2HF(g)$

   **c.** aluminum + zinc chloride ⟶ zinc + aluminum chloride; $2Al(s) + 3ZnCl_2(aq) \longrightarrow 3Zn(s) + 2AlCl_3(aq)$

2. **a.** Liquid carbon disulfide reacts with oxygen gas to produce carbon dioxide gas and sulfur dioxide gas.

   **b.** Aqueous solutions of sodium chloride and silver nitrate react to produce aqueous sodium nitrate and a precipitate of silver chloride.

3. $N_2H_4(l) + O_2(g) \longrightarrow N_2(g) + 2H_2O(l)$

### Practice Problems C

1. **a.** Word: magnesium + hydrochloric acid ⟶ magnesium chloride + hydrogen
   Formula: $Mg(s) + HCl(aq) \longrightarrow MgCl_2(aq) + H_2(g)$
   Balanced: $Mg(s) + 2HCl(aq) \longrightarrow MgCl_2(aq) + H_2(g)$

   **b.** Word: nitric acid + magnesium hydroxide ⟶ magnesium nitrate + water
   Formula: $HNO_3(aq) + Mg(OH)_2(s) \longrightarrow Mg(NO_3)_2(aq) + H_2O(l)$
   Balanced: $2HNO_3(aq) + Mg(OH)_2(s) \longrightarrow Mg(NO_3)_2(aq) + 2H_2O(l)$

2. $Ca(s) + 2H_2O(l) \longrightarrow Ca(OH)_2(aq) + H_2(g)$

### Practice Problems E

1. **a.** $2Na(s) + Cl_2(g) \longrightarrow 2NaCl(s)$

   **b.** $Cu(s) + 2AgNO_3(aq) \longrightarrow Cu(NO_3)_2(aq) + 2Ag(s)$

   **c.** $Fe_2O_3(s) + 3CO(g) \longrightarrow 2Fe(s) + 3CO_2(g)$

### Practice Problems F

1. **a.**no

   **b.** no

   **c.** yes; $Cd(s) + 2HBr(aq) \longrightarrow CdBr_2(aq) + H_2(g)$

   **d.** yes; $Mg(s) + 2H_2O(g) \longrightarrow Mg(OH)_2(aq) + H_2(g)$

2. Pb
3. Mn

### Math Tutor Practice

1. $C_3H_8 + 5O_2 \longrightarrow 3CO_2 + 4H_2O$
2. **a.** $2KI(aq) + Cl_2(g) \longrightarrow 2KCl(aq) + I_2(s)$

   **b.** $2Al(s) + 3H_2SO_4(aq) \longrightarrow Al_2(SO_4)_3(aq) + 3H_2(g)$

## Stoichiometry

### Practice Problems A

1. 4 mol $NH_3$
2. 10. mol $KClO_3$

### Practice Problems C

1. 80.6 g MgO
2. 300 g $C_6H_{12}O_6$

### Practice Problems D

1. 7.81 mol HgO
2. 7.81 mol Hg

### Practice Problems E

1. **a.** 60.0 g $NH_4NO_3$

   **b.** 27.0 g $H_2O$

2. 339 g Ag
3. 2.6 kg Al

### Practice Problems F

1. **a.** $H_2O_2$

   **b.** 0.500 mol $N_2H_4$

   **c.** 0.250 mol $N_2$, 1.00 mol $H_2O$

### Practice Problems G

1. **a.** Zn

   **b.** 0.75 mol $S_8$ remains

   **c.** 2.00 mol ZnS

2. **a.** carbon

   **b.** 2.40 mol $H_2$ and 2.40 mol CO

   **c.** 4.85 g $H_2$ and 67.2 g CO

### Practice Problems H

1. 79.7%
2. 3.70 g Cu

### Math Tutor Practice

1. 24.48 mol $SO_3$
2. 30.75 g $O_2$

## States of Matter

### Practice Problems A

1. 169 kJ
2. $2.19 \times 10^5$ g

### Math Tutor Practice

1. 11.65 kJ/mol
2. 74.7 kJ

**b.** exothermic; The energy of the reactants is greater than the energy of the products.

**2. a.**

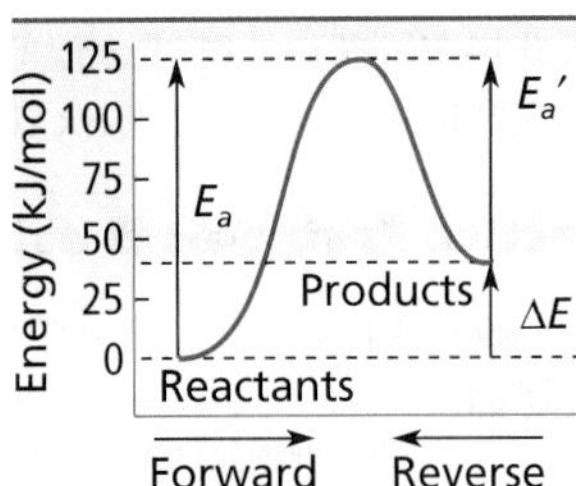


**b.** $\Delta E_{forward} = 39$ kJ/mol
$\Delta E_{reverse} = -39$ kJ/mol
**c.** endothermic; The energy of the products is greater that the energy of the products

**3. a.**

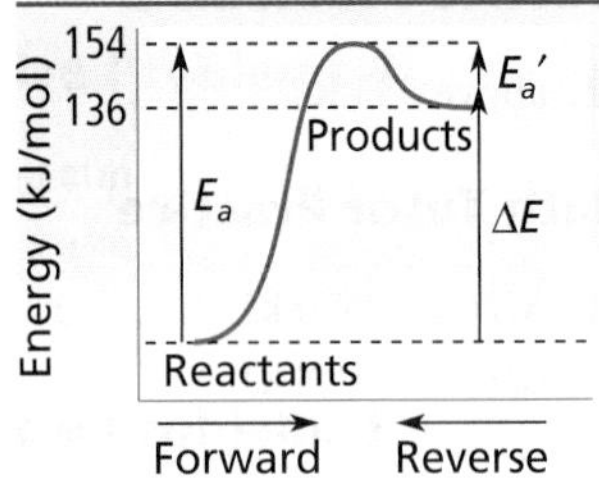


**b.** $E_a$ (reverse) = 18 kJ/mol

### Practice Problems B

1. rate = $k[A]^2$
2. 27

### Practice Problems E

1. $R = k[L][M]^2$
2. $R = k[NO_2]^2$

### Math Tutor Practice

1. $R = k[O_2][NO]_2$
2. $R = k[H_2]$; Students should observe that changing the concentration of $C_2H_2$ has no effect on the rate. The rate depends on only the concentration of hydrogen.

## Chemical Equilibrium

### Practice Problems A

1. 0.286
2. $4.9 \times 10^{-3}$
3. 4.36

### Practice Problems B

1. $1.9 \times 10^{-4}$
2. $1.6 \times 10^{-5}$

### Practice Problems C

1. $8.9 \times 10^{-14}$ mol/L
2. $5.7 \times 10^{-4}$ mol/L

### Practice Problems D

1. AgBr precipitates.
2. $PbCl_2$ does *not* precipitate.

### Math Tutor Practice

1. **a.** $K = \frac{[AB_2]}{[A][B]^2}$

   **b.** $K = \frac{[D_2][E_2]^2}{[DE_2]^2}$
2. $K = 2.6 \times 10^{-9}$

## Oxidation-Reduction Reactions

### Practice Problems A

1. $Cu + 2H_2SO_4 \longrightarrow CuSO_4 + SO_2 + 2H_2O$
2. $8HNO_3 + 6KI \longrightarrow 6KNO_3 + 3I_2 + 2NO + 4H_2O$

### Math Tutor Practice

1. $2MnO_2 + NaClO_3 + 2NaOH \longrightarrow 2NaMnO_4 + NaCl + H_2O$
2. $N_2O + 2KClO + 2KOH \longrightarrow 2KCl + 2KNO_2 + H_2O$

## Electrochemistry

### Practice Problems A

1. **a.** $Cr_2O_7^{2-} + 14H^+ + 3Ni \longrightarrow 2Cr^{3+} + 3Ni^{2+} + 7H_2O$;
   $E^0 = 1.33 - (-0.23) = 1.56$ V

   **b.** $2Fe^{3+} + H_2 \longrightarrow 2Fe^{2+} + 2H^+$;
   $E^0 = 0.77 - 0.0 = 0.77$ V

### Math Tutor Practice

1. $E^0 = 1.82$ V
2. $E^0 = 1.20$ V

## Nuclear Chemistry

### Practice Problems A

1. ${}^{253}_{99}Es + {}^{4}_{2}He \longrightarrow {}^{1}_{0}n + {}^{256}_{101}Md$
2. ${}^{142}_{61}Pm + {}^{0}_{-1}e \longrightarrow {}^{142}_{60}Nd$

### Practice Problems B

1. 0.25 mg
2. 6396 years
3. 7.648 days
4. 0.00977 mg
5. $4.46 \times 10^9$ years

### Math Tutor Practice

1. $1.4 \times 10^{-6}$ g chromium-51
2. 8 half-lives or 420 000 years (expressed with 2 significant figures)

## Organic Chemistry

### Practice Problems A

1. methylbutane
2. 3-ethyl-4-methylhexane

### Practice Problems B

1. 2-hexene
2. 2-methyl-2-butene *or* methyl-2-butene
3. 2-methyl-3-hexene
4. 2,5-dimethyl-2,5-heptadiene

### Math Tutor Practice

1. $CH_4N_2O$
2. $C_3H_5Br$
3. $CH_2O$

## Biological Chemistry

### Math Tutor Practice

1. leucine–histidine–aspartic acid–tyrosine–asparagine–tryptophan
2. leucine–threonine–glycine; The codon UGA is a stop codon, so no more amino acids will be added.

# GLOSSARY

## A

**absolute zero** the temperature at which molecular energy is at a minimum (0 K on the Kelvin scale or –273.15 °C on the Celsius scale) (371)

**accuracy** a description of how close a measurement is to the true value of the quantity measured (44)

**acid-base indicator** a substance that changes in color depending on the pH of the solution that the substance is in (511)

**acid ionization constant** the term $K_a$ (605)

**actinide** any of the series of heavy radioactive elements that extends from thorium (atomic number 90) through lawrencium (atomic number 103) on the periodic table (136)

**activated complex** a molecule in an unstable state intermediate to the reactants and the products in the chemical reaction (565)

**activation energy** the minimum amount of energy required to start a chemical reaction (564)

**activity series** a series of elements that have similar properties and that are arranged in descending order of chemical activity; examples of activity series include metals and halogens (285)

**actual yield** the measured amount of a product of a reaction (317)

**addition reaction** a reaction in which an atom or molecule is added to an unsaturated molecule (735)

**adensosine diphosphate (ADP)** an organic molecule that is involved in energy metabolism; composed of a nitrogenous base, a sugar, and two phosphate groups (767)

**adenosine triphosphate (ATP)** an organic molecule that acts as the main energy source for cell processes; composed of a nitrogenous base, a sugar, and three phosphate groups (766)

**alcohol** an organic compound that contains one or more hydroxyl groups attached to carbon atoms (731)

**aldehyde** an organic compound that contains the carbonyl group, —CHO (733)

**alkali metal** one of the elements of Group 1 of the periodic table (lithium, sodium, potassium, rubidium, cesium, and francium) (142)

**alkaline-earth metal** one of the elements of Group 2 of the periodic table (beryllium, magnesium, calcium, strontium, barium, and radium) (142)

**alkane** a hydrocarbon characterized by a straight or branched carbon chain that contains only single bonds (716)

**alkene** a hydrocarbon that contains one or more double bonds (724)

**alkyl group** a group of atoms that forms when one hydrogen atom is removed from an alkane molecule (719)

**alkyl halide** a compound formed from an alkyl group and a halogen (fluorine, chlorine, bromine, or iodine) (732)

**alkyne** a hydrocarbon that contains one or more triple bonds (727)

**alpha particle** a positively charged atom that is released in the disintegration of radioactive elements and that consists of two protons and two neutrons (686)

**amine** an organic compound that can be considered to be a derivative of ammonia (733)

**amino acid** any one of 20 different organic molecules that contain a carboxyl and an amino group and that combine to form proteins (756)

**amorphous solid** a solid in which the particles are not arranged with periodicity or order (338)

**amphoteric** describes a substance, such as water, that has the properties of an acid and the properties of a base (485)

**anabolism** the metabolic synthesis of proteins, fats, and other large biomolecules from smaller molecules; requires energy in the form of ATP (769)

**angular momentum quantum number** the quantum number that indicates the shape of an orbital (107)

**anion** an ion that has a negative charge (159)

**anode** the electrode on whose surface oxidation takes place; anions migrate toward the anode, and electrons leave the system from the anode (656)

**aromatic hydrocarbon** a member of the class of hydrocarbons (of which benzene is the first member) that consists of assemblages of cyclic conjugated carbon atoms and that is characterized by large resonance energies (729)

**Arrhenius acid** a substance that increases the concentration of hydronium ions in aqueous solution (473)

**Arrhenius base** a substance that increases the concentration of hydroxide ions in aqueous solution (473)

**artificial transmutation** the transformation of atoms of one element into atoms of another element as a result of a nuclear reaction, such as bombardment with neutrons (691)

**atmosphere of pressure** the pressure of Earth's atmosphere at sea level; exactly equivalent to 760 mm Hg (364)

**atom** the smallest unit of an element that maintains the chemical properties of that element (6, 72)

**atomic mass unit** a unit of mass that describes the mass of an atom or molecule; it is exactly 1/12 of the mass of a carbon atom with mass number 12 (abbreviation, amu) (80)

**atomic number** the number of protons in the nucleus of an atom; the atomic number is the same for all atoms of an element (77)

**atomic radius** one-half of the distance between the center of identical atoms that are not bonded together (150)

**Aufbau principle** the principle that states that the structure of each successive element is obtained by adding one proton to the nucleus of the atom and one electron to the lowest-energy orbital that is available (111)

**autotroph** an organism that produces its own nutrients from inorganic substances or from the environment instead of consuming other organisms (766)

**average atomic mass** the weighted average of the masses of all naturally occurring isotopes of an element (81)

**Avogadro's law** the law that states that equal volumes of gases at the same temperature and pressure contain equal numbers of molecules (379)

**Avogadro's number** $6.02 \times 10^{23}$, the number of atoms or molecules in 1 mol (83)

## B

**barometer** an instrument that measures atmospheric pressure (363)

**benzene** the simplest aromatic hydrocarbon (729)

**beta particle** a charged electron emitted during certain types of radioactive decay, such as beta decay (686)

**binary acid** an acid that does not contain oxygen, such as hydrofluoric acid (468)

**binary compound** a compound composed of two different elements (222)

**boiling** the conversion of a liquid to a vapor within the liquid as well as at the surface of the liquid at a specific temperature and pressure; occurs when the vapor pressure of the liquid equals the atmospheric pressure (344)

**boiling point** the temperature and pressure at which a liquid and a gas are in equilibrium (344)

**boiling-point elevation** the difference between the boiling point of a liquid in pure state and the boiling point of the liquid in solution; the increase depends on the amount of solute particles present (450)

**bond energy** the energy required to break the bonds in 1 mol of a chemical compound (181)

**Boyle's law** the law that states that for a fixed amount of gas at a constant temperature, the volume of the gas increases as the pressure of the gas decreases and the volume of the gas decreases as the pressure of the gas increases (370)

**Brønsted-Lowry acid** a substance that donates a proton to another substance (478)

**Brønsted-Lowry acid-base reaction** the transfer of protons from one reactant (the acid) to another (the base) (479)

**Brønsted-Lowry base** a substance that accepts a proton (479)

**buffered solution** a solution that can resist changes in pH when an acid or a base is added to it; a buffer (606)

## C

**calorimeter** a device used to measure the energy as heat absorbed or released in a chemical or physical change (531)

**capillary action** the attraction of the surface of a liquid to the surface of a solid, which causes the liquid to rise or fall (335)

**carbohydrate** any organic compound that is made of carbon, hydrogen, and oxygen and that provides nutrients to the cells of living things (751)

**carboxylic acid** an organic acid that contains the carboxyl functional group (734)

**catabolism** the chemical decomposition of complex biological substances, such as carbohydrates, proteins, and glycogen, accompanied by the release of energy (768)

**catalysis** the acceleration of a chemical reaction by a catalyst (570)

**catalyst** a substance that changes the rate of a chemical reaction without being consumed or changed significantly (570)

**catenation** the binding of an element to itself to form chains or rings (712)

**cathode** the electrode on whose surface reduction takes place (656)

**cation** an ion that has a positive charge (159)

**chain reaction** a reaction in which the material that starts the reaction is also one of the products and can start another reaction (697)

**change of state** the change of a substance from one physical state to another (8)

**Charles's law** the law that states that for a fixed amount of gas at a constant pressure, the volume of the gas increases as the temperature of the gas increases and the volume of the gas decreases as the temperature of the gas decreases (372)

**chemical** any substance that has a defined composition (4)

**chemical bond** the attractive force that holds atoms or ions together (175)

**chemical change** a change that occurs when one or more substances change into entirely new substances with different properties (9)

**chemical equation** a representation of a chemical reaction that uses symbols to show the relationship between the reactants and the products (261)

**chemical equilibrium** a state of balance in which the rate of a forward reaction equals the rate of the reverse reaction and the concentrations of products and reactants remain unchanged (590)

**chemical equilibrium expression** the equation for the equilibrium constant, $K_{eq}$ (592)

**chemical formula** a combination of chemical symbols and numbers to represent a substance (178)

**chemical kinetics** the area of chemistry that is the study of reaction rates and reaction mechanisms (568)

**chemical property** a property of matter that describes a substance's ability to participate in chemical reactions (8)

**chemical reaction** the process by which one or more substances change to produce one or more different substances (9)

**chemistry** the scientific study of the composition, structure, and properties of matter and the changes that matter undergoes (3)

**clone** an organism that is produced by asexual reproduction and that is genetically identical to its parent; to make a genetic duplicate (775)

**coefficient** a small whole number that appears as a factor in front of a formula in a chemical equation (263)

**colligative property** a property that is determined by the number of particles present in a system but that is independent of the properties of the particles themselves (446)

**collision theory** the theory that states that the number of new compounds formed in a chemical reaction is equal to the number of molecules that collide, multiplied by a factor that corrects for low-energy collisions (562)

**colloid** a mixture consisting of tiny particles that are intermediate in size between those in solutions and those in suspensions and that are suspended in a liquid, solid, or gas (403)

**combined gas law** the relationship between the pressure, volume, and temperature of a fixed amount of gas (374)

**combustion reaction** the oxidation reaction of an element or compound, in which energy as heat is released (283)

**common-ion effect** the phenomenon in which the addition of an ion common to two solutes brings about precipitation or reduces ionization (603)

**composition stoichiometry** calculations involving the mass relationships of elements in compounds (299)

**compound** a substance made up of atoms of two or more different elements joined by chemical bonds (7)

**concentration** the amount of a particular substance in a given quantity of a mixture, solution, or ore (418)

**condensation** the change of state from a gas to a liquid (342)

**condensation reaction** a chemical reaction in which two or more molecules combine to produce water or another simple molecule (736, 752)

**conjugate acid** an acid that forms when a base gains a proton (483)

**conjugate base** a base that forms when an acid loses a proton (483)

**continuous spectrum** the uninterrupted broad band of all colors (wavelengths) emitted by incandescent solids (100)

**control rod** a neutron-absorbing rod that helps control a nuclear reaction by limiting the number of free neutrons (698)

**conversion factor** a ratio that is derived from the equality of two different units and that can be used to convert from one unit to the other (40)

**copolymer** a polymer made from two different monomers (737)

**covalent bond** a bond formed when atoms share one or more pairs of electrons (175)

**critical mass** the minimum mass of a fissionable isotope that provides the number of neutrons needed to sustain a chain reaction (698)

**critical point** the temperature and pressure at which the gas and liquid states of a substance become identical and form one phase (347)

**critical pressure** the lowest pressure at which a substance can exist as a liquid at the critical temperature (348)

**critical temperature** the temperature above which a substance cannot exist in the liquid state (347)

**crystal** a solid whose atoms, ions, or molecules are arranged in a regular, repeating pattern (338)

**crystal structure** the arrangement of atoms, ions, or molecules in a regular way to form a crystal (339)

**crystalline solid** a solid that consists of crystals (338)

**cycloalkane** a saturated carbon chain that forms a loop or a ring (718)

## D

**Dalton's law of partial pressures** the law that states that the total pressure of a mixture of gases is equal to the sum of the partial pressures of the component gases (365)

**daughter nuclide** a nuclide produced by the radioactive decay of another nuclide (690)

**decay series** a series of radioactive nuclides produced by successive radioactive decay until a stable nuclide is reached (690)

**decomposition reaction** a reaction in which a single compound breaks down to form two or more simpler substances (279)

**denature** to change irreversibly the structure or shape—and thus the solubility and other properties—of a protein by heating, shaking, or treating the protein with acid, alkali, or other species (764)

**density** the ratio of the mass of a substance to the volume of the substance; often expressed as grams per cubic centimeter for solids and liquids and as grams per liter for gases (38)

**deposition** the change of state from a gas directly to a solid (346)

**derived unit** a unit of measure that is a combination of other measurements (36)

**diffusion** the movement of particles from regions of higher density to regions of lower density (331)

**dimensional analysis** a mathematical technique for studying dimensions of physical quantities (40)

**dipole** a molecule or a part of a molecule that contains both positively and negatively charged regions (204)

**diprotic acid** an acid that has two ionizable hydrogen atoms in each molecule, such as sulfuric acid (480)

**direct proportion** the relationship between two variables whose ratio is a constant value (55)

**disaccharide** a sugar formed from two monosaccharides (752)

**disproportionation** the process by which a substance is transformed into two or more dissimilar substances, usually by simultaneous oxidation and reduction (645)

**dissociation** the separating of a molecule into simpler molecules, atoms, radicals, or ions (435)

**DNA replication** the process of making a copy of DNA (772)

**double-displacement reaction** a reaction in which a gas, a solid precipitate, or a molecular compound forms from the apparent exchange of atoms or ions between two compounds (282)

**ductility** the ability of a substance to be hammered thin or drawn out into a wire (196)

## E

**effervescence** a bubbling of a liquid caused by the rapid escape of a gas rather than by boiling (413)

**effusion** the passage of a gas under pressure through a tiny opening (332)

**elastic collision** a collision between ideally elastic bodies in which the final and initial kinetic energies are the same (329)

**electrochemistry** the branch of chemistry that is the study of the relationship between electric forces and chemical reactions (655)

**electrode** a conductor used to establish electrical contact with a nonmetallic part of a circuit, such as an electrolyte (656)

**electrode potential** the difference in potential between an electrode and its solution (662)

**electrolysis** the process in which an electric current is used to produce a chemical reaction, such as the decomposition of water (279, 670)

**electrolyte** a substance that dissolves in water to give a solution that conducts an electric current (405)

**electrolytic cell** an electrochemical device in which electrolysis takes place when an electric current is in the device (667)

**electromagnetic radiation** the radiation associated with an electric and magnetic field; it varies periodically and travels at the speed of light (97)

**electromagnetic spectrum** all of the frequencies or wavelengths of electromagnetic radiation (97)

**electron affinity** the energy needed to remove an electron from a negative ion to form a neutral atom or molecule (157)

**electron capture** the process in which an inner orbital electron is captured by the nucleus of the atom that contains the electron (687)

**electron configuration** the arrangement of electrons in an atom (111)

**electron-dot notation** an electron-configuration notation in which only the valence electrons of an atom of the a particular element are shown, indicated by dots placed around the element's symbol (184)

**electronegativity** a measure of the ability of an atom in a chemical compound to attract electrons (161)

**electroplating** the electrolytic process of plating or coating an object with a metal (668)

**element** a substance that cannot be separated or broken down into simpler substances by chemical means; all atoms of an element have the same atomic number (6)

**elimination reaction** a reaction in which a simple molecule, such as water or ammonia, is removed and a new compound is produced (737)

**emission-line spectrum** a diagram or graph that indicates the degree to which a substance emits radiant energy with respect to wavelength (100)

**empirical formula** a chemical formula that shows the composition of a compound in terms of the relative numbers and kinds of atoms in the simplest ratio (245)

**end point** the point in a titration at which a marked color change takes place (516)

**enthalpy change** the amount of energy released or absorbed as heat by a system during a process at constant pressure (534)

**enthalpy of combustion** the energy released as heat by the complete combustion of a specific amount of a substance at constant pressure or constant volume (539)

**enthalpy of reaction** the amount of energy released or absorbed as heat during a chemical reaction (534)

**enthalpy of solution** the amount of energy released or absorbed as heat when a specific amount of solute dissolves in a solvent (416)

**entropy** a measure of the randomness or disorder of a system (547)

**enzyme** a type of protein that speeds up metabolic reactions in plants and animals without being permanently changed or destroyed (763)

**equilibrium** in chemistry, the state in which a chemical process and the reverse chemical process occur at the same rate such that the concentrations of reactants and products do not change; in physics, the state in which the net force on an object is zero (342)

**equilibrium constant** a number that relates the concentrations of starting materials and products of a reversible chemical reaction to one another at a given temperature (592)

**equilibrium vapor pressure** the vapor pressure of a system at equilibrium (343)

**equivalence point** the point at which the two solutions used in a titration are present in chemically equivalent amounts (516)

**ester** an organic compound formed by combining an organic acid with an alcohol such that water is eliminated (734)

**ether** an organic compound in which two carbon atoms bond to the same oxygen atom (732)

**evaporation** the change of state from a liquid to a gas (335)

**excess reactant** the substance that is not used up completely in a reaction (312)

**excited state** a state in which an atom has more energy than it does at its ground state (100)

**extensive property** a property that depends on the extent or size of a system (7)

**family** a vertical column of the periodic table (17)

**fatty acid** an organic acid that is contained in lipids, such as fats or oils (754)

**film badge** a device that measures the approximate amount of radiation received in a given period of time by people who work with radiation (694)

**fluid** a nonsolid state of matter in which the atoms or molecules are free to move past each other, as in a gas or liquid (333)

**formula equation** a representation of the reactants and products of a chemical reaction by their symbols or formulas (264)

**formula mass** the sum of the average atomic masses of all atoms represented in the formula of any molecule, formula unit, or ion (237)

**formula unit** the collection of atoms corresponding to an ionic compound's formula such that the molar mass of the compound is the same as the mass of 1 mol of formula units (190)

**free energy** the energy in a system that is available for work; a system's capacity to do useful work (548)

**free-energy change** the difference between the change in enthalpy, $\Delta H$, and the product of the Kelvin temperature and the entropy change, which is defined as $T\Delta S$, at a constant pressure and temperature (548)

**freezing** the change of state in which a liquid becomes a solid as energy as heat is removed (336)

**freezing point** the temperature at which a solid and liquid are in equilibrium at 1 atm pressure; the temperature at which a liquid substance freezes (345)

**freezing-point depression** the difference between the freezing points of a pure solvent and a solution, which is directly proportional to the amount of solute present (448)

**frequency** the number of cycles or vibrations per unit of time; *also* the number of waves produced in a given amount of time (98)

**functional group** the portion of a molecule that is active in a chemical reaction and that determines the properties of many organic compounds (730)

**gamma ray** the high-energy photon emitted by a nucleus during fission and radioactive decay (687)

**gas** a form of matter that does not have a definite volume or shape (8)

**Gay-Lussac's law** the law that states that the volume occupied by a gas at a constant pressure is directly proportional to the absolute temperature (373)

**Gay-Lussac's law of combining volumes of gases** the law that states that the volumes of gases involved in a chemical change can be represented by a ratio of small whole numbers (378)

**Geiger-Müller counter** an instrument that detects and measures the intensity of radiation by counting the number of electric pulses that pass between the anode and the cathode in a tube filled with gas (694)

**geometric isomer** a compound that exists in two or more geometrically different configurations (714)

**Graham's law of effusion** the law that states that the rates of effusion of gases at the same temperature and pressure are inversely proportional to the square roots of their molar masses (387)

**ground state** the lowest energy state of a quantized system (100)

**group** a vertical column of elements in the periodic table; elements in a group share chemical properties (17)

**half-cell** a single electrode immersed in a solution of its ions (656)

**half-life** the time required for half of a sample of a radioactive isotope to break down by radioactive decay to form a daughter isotope (688)

**half-reaction** the part of a reaction that involves only oxidation or reduction (633)

**halogen** one of the elements of Group 17 (fluorine, chlorine, bromine, iodine, and astatine); halogens combine with most metals to form salts (147)

**heat** the energy transferred between objects that are at different temperatures; energy is always transferred from higher-temperature objects to lower-temperature objects until thermal equilibrium is reached (532)

**Heisenberg uncertainty principle** the principle that states that determining both the position and velocity of an electron or any other particle simultaneously is impossible (105)

**Henry's law** the law that states that at constant temperature, the solubility of a gas in a liquid is directly proportional to the partial pressure of the gas on the surface of the liquid (413)

**Hess's law** the overall enthalpy change in a reaction is equal to the sum of the enthalpy changes for the individual steps in the process (539)

**heterogeneous** composed of dissimilar components (12)

**heterogeneous catalyst** a catalyst that is in a different phase from the phase of the reactants (570)

**heterogeneous reaction** a reaction in which the reactants are in two different phases (568)

**heterotroph** an organism that obtains organic food molecules by eating other organisms or their byproducts and that cannot synthesize organic compounds from inorganic materials (766)

**homogeneous** describes something that has a uniform structure or composition throughout (12)

**homogeneous catalyst** a catalyst that is in the same phase as the reactants are (570)

**homogeneous reaction** a reaction in which all of the reactants and products are in the same phase (562)

**Hund's rule** the rule that states that for an atom in the ground state, the number of unpaired electrons is the maximum possible and these unpaired electrons have the same spin (112)

**hybrid orbitals** orbitals that have the properties to explain the geometry of chemical bonds between atoms (202)

**hybridization** the mixing of two or more atomic orbitals of the same atom to produce new orbitals; hybridization represents the mixing of higher- and lower-energy orbitals to form orbitals of intermediate energy (201)

**hydration** the strong affinity of water molecules for particles of dissolved or suspended substances that causes electrolytic dissociation (411)

**hydrocarbon** an organic compound composed only of carbon and hydrogen (712)

**hydrogen bond** the intermolecular force occurring when a hydrogen atom that is bonded to a highly electronegative atom of one molecule is attracted to two unshared electrons of another molecule (206)

**hydrolysis** a chemical reaction between water and another substance to form two or more new substances; a reaction between water and a salt to create an acid or a base (608, 752)

**hydronium ion** an ion consisting of a proton combined with a molecule of water; $H_3O^+$ (441)

**hypothesis** an explanation that is based on prior scientific research or observations and that can be tested (30)

**ideal gas** an imaginary gas whose particles are infinitely small and do not interact with each other (329)

**ideal gas constant** the proportionality constant that appears in the equation of state for 1 mol of an ideal gas; $R = 0.082\,057\,84$ L • atm/mol • K (384)

**ideal gas law** the law that states the mathematical relationship of pressure ($P$), volume ($V$), temperature ($T$), the gas constant ($R$), and the number of moles of a gas ($n$); $PV = nRT$ (383)

**immiscible** describes two or more liquids that do not mix with each other (412)

**intensive property** a property that does not depend on the amount of matter present, such as pressure, temperature, or density (7)

**intermediate** a substance that forms in a middle stage of a chemical reaction and is considered a stepping stone between the parent substance and the final product (562)

**inverse proportion** the relationship between two variables whose product is constant (56)

**ion** an atom, radical, or molecule that has gained or lost one or more electrons and has a negative or positive charge (153)

**ionic bond** a force that attracts electrons from one atom to another, which transforms a neutral atom into an ion (175)

**ionic compound** a compound composed of ions bound together by electrostatic attraction (190)

**ionization** the process of adding or removing electrons from an atom or molecule, which gives the atom or molecule a net charge (153, 441)

**ionization energy** the energy required to remove an electron from an atom or ion (abbreviation, IE) (153)

**isomer** one of two or more compounds that have the same chemical composition but different structures (712)

**isotope** an atom that has the same number of protons (or the same atomic number) as other atoms of the same element do but that has a different number of neutrons (and thus a different atomic mass) (78)

**joule** the unit used to express energy; equivalent to the amount of work done by a force of 1 N acting through a distance of 1 m in the direction of the force (abbreviation, J) (531)

**ketone** an organic compound in which a carbonyl group is attached to two alkyl groups; obtained by the oxidation of secondary alcohols (733)

**kinetic-molecular theory** a theory that explains that the behavior of physical systems depends on the combined actions of the molecules constituting the system (329)

**lanthanide** a member of the rare-earth series of elements, whose atomic numbers range from 58 (cerium) to 71 (lutetium) (136)

**lattice energy** the energy associated with constructing a crystal lattice relative to the energy of all constituent atoms separated by infinite distances (192)

**law of conservation of mass** the law that states that mass cannot be created or destroyed in ordinary chemical and physical changes (68)

**law of definite proportions** the law that states that a chemical compound always contains the same elements in exactly the same proportions by weight or mass (68)

**law of multiple proportions** the law that states that when two elements combine to form two or more compounds, the mass of one element that combines with a given mass of the other is in the ratio of small whole numbers (68)

**Lewis acid** an atom, ion, or molecule that accepts a pair of electrons (481)

**Lewis acid-base reaction** the formation of one or more covalent bonds between an electron-pair donor and an electron-pair acceptor (482)

**Lewis base** an atom, ion, or molecule that donates a pair of electrons (482)

**Lewis structure** a structural formula in which electrons are represented by dots; dot pairs or dashes between two atomic symbols represent pairs in covalent bonds (185)

**limiting reactant** the substance that controls the quantity of product that can form in a chemical reaction (312)

**lipid** a type of biochemical that does not dissolve in water, including fats and steroids; lipids store energy and make up cell membranes (754)

**liquid** the state of matter that has a definite volume but not a definite shape (8)

**London dispersion force** the intermolecular attraction resulting from the uneven distribution of electrons and the creation of temporary dipoles (207)

## M

**magic numbers** the numbers (2, 8, 20, 28, 50, 82, and 126) that represent the number of particles in an extra stable atomic nucleus that has completed shells of protons and neutrons (683)

**magnetic quantum number** the quantum number that corresponds to the alignment of the angular momentum component with a magnetic field (108)

**main-group element** an element in the *s*-block or *p*-block of the periodic table (146)

**malleability** the ability of a substance to be hammered or beaten into a sheet (196)

**mass** a measure of the amount of matter in an object (6)

**mass defect** the difference between the mass of an atom and the sum of the masses of the atom's protons, neutrons, and electrons (681)

**mass number** the sum of the numbers of protons and neutrons that make up the nucleus of an atom (78)

**matter** anything that has mass and takes up space (6)

**melting** the change of state in which a solid becomes a liquid by adding energy as heat or changing pressure (338)

**melting point** the temperature and pressure at which a solid becomes a liquid (338)

**metabolism** the sum of all chemical processes that occur in an organism (766)

**metal** an element that is shiny and that conducts heat and electricity well (18)

**metallic bond** a bond formed by the attraction between positively charged metal ions and the electrons around them (195)

**metalloid** an element that has properties of both metals and nonmetals; sometimes referred to as a semiconductor (19)

**millimeters of mercury** a unit of pressure (364)

**miscible** describes two or more liquids that can dissolve into each other in various proportions (412)

**mixture** a combination of two or more substances that are not chemically combined (11)

**model** a pattern, plan, representation, or description designed to show the structure or workings of an object, system, or concept (31)

**moderator** a material that slows the velocity of neutrons so that they may be absorbed by the nuclei (698)

**molal boiling-point constant** a quantity calculated to represent the boiling-point elevation of a 1-molal solution of a nonvolatile, nonelectrolyte solution (450)

**molal freezing-point constant** a quantity calculated to represent the freezing-point depression of a 1-molal solution of a nonvolatile, nonelectrolyte solute (448)

**molality** the concentration of a solution expressed in moles of solute per kilogram of solvent (422)

**molar enthalpy of formation** the amount of energy as heat resulting from the formation of 1 mol of a substance at constant pressure (537)

**molar enthalpy of fusion** the amount of energy as heat required to change 1 mol of a substance from solid to liquid at constant temperature and pressure (346)

**molar enthalpy of vaporization** the amount of energy as heat required to evaporate 1 mol of a liquid at constant pressure and temperature (345)

**molar mass** the mass in grams of 1 mol of a substance (83)

**molarity** a concentration unit of a solution expressed as moles of solute dissolved per liter of solution (418)

**mole** the SI base unit used to measure the amount of a substance whose number of particles is the same as the number of atoms of carbon in exactly 12 g of carbon-12 (83)

**mole ratio** a conversion factor that relates the amounts in moles of any two substances involved in a chemical reaction (300)

**molecular compound** a chemical compound whose simplest units are molecules (178)

**molecular formula** a chemical formula that shows the number and kinds of atoms in a molecule, but not the arrangement of the atoms (178)

**molecule** a group of atoms that are held together by chemical forces; a molecule is the smallest unit of matter that can exist by itself and retain all of a substance's chemical properties (178)

**monatomic ion** an ion formed from a single atom (220)

**monomer** a simple molecule that can combine with other like or unlike molecules to make a polymer (737)

**monoprotic acid** an acid that can donate only one proton to a base (479)

**monosaccharide** a simple sugar that is the basic subunit of a carbohydrate (751)

**multiple bond** a bond in which the atoms share more than one pair of electrons, such as a double bond or a triple bond (187)

**natural gas** a mixture of gaseous hydrocarbons located under the surface of Earth, often near petroleum deposits; used as a fuel (723)

**net ionic equation** an equation that includes only those compounds and ions that undergo a chemical change in a reaction in an aqueous solution (439)

**neutralization** the reaction of the ions that characterize acids (hydronium ions) and the ions that characterize bases (hydroxide ions) to form water molecules and a salt (489)

**newton** the SI unit for force; the force that will increase the speed of a 1 kg mass by 1 m/s each second that the force is applied (abbreviation, N) (362)

**noble gas** one of the elements of Group 18 of the periodic table (helium, neon, argon, krypton, xenon, and radon); noble gases are unreactive (117)

**noble-gas configuration** an outer main energy level fully occupied, in most cases, by eight electrons (118)

**nomenclature** a naming system (222)

**nonelectrolyte** a liquid or solid substance or mixture that does not allow an electric current (406)

**nonmetal** an element that conducts heat and electricity poorly and that does not form positive ions in an electrolytic solution (19)

**nonpolar covalent bond** a covalent bond in which the bonding electrons are equally attracted to both bonded atoms (176)

**nonvolatile substance** a substance that has little tendency to become a gas under existing conditions (446)

**nuclear binding energy** the energy released when a nucleus is formed from nucleons (682)

**nuclear fission** the splitting of the nucleus of a large atom into two or more fragments; releases additional neutrons and energy (697)

**nuclear forces** the interaction that binds protons and neutrons, protons and protons, and neutrons and neutrons together in a nucleus (76)

**nuclear fusion** the combination of the nuclei of small atoms to form a larger nucleus; releases energy (699)

**nuclear power plant** a facility that uses heat from nuclear reactors to produce electrical energy (698)

**nuclear radiation** the particles that are released from the nucleus during radioactive decay, such as neutrons, electrons, and photons (685)

**nuclear reaction** a reaction that affects the nucleus of an atom (684)

**nuclear reactor** a device that uses controlled nuclear reactions to produce energy or nuclides (698)

**nuclear shell model** a model which represents nucleons as existing in different energy levels, or shells, in the nucleus (683)

**nuclear waste** waste that contains radioisotopes (696)

**nucleic acid** an organic compound, either RNA or DNA, whose molecules are made up of one or two chains of nucleotides and carry genetic information (770)

**nucleon** a proton or neutron (681)

**nuclide** an atom that is identified by the number of protons and neutrons in its nucleus (79, 681)

## O

**orbital** a region in an atom where there is a high probability of finding electrons (106)

**order** in chemistry, a classification of chemical reactions that depends on the number of molecules that appear to enter into the reaction (572)

**organic compound** a covalently bonded compound that contains carbon, excluding carbonates and oxides (711)

**osmosis** the diffusion of water or another solvent from a more dilute solution (of a solute) to a more concentrated solution (of the solute) through a membrane that is permeable to the solvent (452)

**osmotic pressure** the external pressure that must be applied to stop osmosis (452)

**oxidation** a reaction that removes one or more electrons from a substance such that the substance's valence or oxidation state increases (632)

**oxidation number** the number of electrons that must be added to or removed from an atom in a combined state to convert the atom into the elemental form (232)

**oxidation state** the condition of an atom expressed by the number of electrons that the atom needs to reach its elemental form (232)

**oxidation-reduction reaction** any chemical change in which one species is oxidized (loses electrons) and another species is reduced (gains electrons); also called *redox reaction* (633)

**oxidized** describes an element that has lost electrons and that has increased its oxidation number (632)

**oxidizing agent** the substance that gains electrons in an oxidation-reduction reaction and that is reduced (642)

**oxyacid** an acid that is a compound of hydrogen, oxygen, and a third element, usually a nonmetal (469)

**oxyanion** a polyatomic ion that contains oxygen (225)

## P

**parent nuclide** a radionuclide that yields a specific daughter nuclide as a later member of a radioactive series (690)

**partial pressure** the pressure of each gas in a mixture (365)

**pascal** the SI unit of pressure; equal to the force of 1 N exerted over an area of 1 $m^2$ (abbreviation, Pa) (364)

**Pauli exclusion principle** the principle that states that two particles of a certain class cannot be in exactly the same energy state (112)

**percentage composition** the percentage by mass of each element in a compound (243)

**percentage error** a figure that is calculated by subtracting the accepted value from the experimental value, dividing the difference by the accepted value, and then multiplying by 100 (45)

**percentage yield** the ratio of the actual yield to the theoretical yield, multiplied by 100 (317)

**period** in chemistry, a horizontal row of elements in the periodic table (17)

**periodic law** the law that states that the repeating chemical and physical properties of elements change periodically with the atomic numbers of the elements (135)

**periodic table** an arrangement of the elements in order of their atomic numbers such that elements with similar properties fall in the same column, or group (135)

**petroleum** a liquid mixture of complex hydrocarbon compounds; used widely as a fuel source (723)

**pH** a value that is used to express the acidity or alkalinity (basicity) of a system; each whole number on the scale indicates a tenfold change in acidity; a pH of 7 is neutral, a pH of less than 7 is acidic, and a pH of greater than 7 is basic (503)

**pH meter** a device used to determine the pH of a solution by measuring the voltage between the two electrodes that are placed in the solution (512)

**phase** in chemistry, one of the four states or conditions in which a substance can exist: solid, liquid, gas, or plasma; a part of matter that is uniform (342)

**phase diagram** a graph of the relationship between the physical state of a substance and the temperature and pressure of the substance (347)

**photoelectric effect** the emission of electrons from a material when light of certain frequencies shines on the surface of the material (99)

**photon** a unit or quantum of light; a particle of electromagnetic radiation that has zero rest mass and carries a quantum of energy (100)

**physical change** a change of matter from one form to another without a change in chemical properties (7)

**physical property** a characteristic of a substance that does not involve a chemical change, such as density, color, or hardness (7)

**plasma** in physical science, a state of matter that starts as a gas and then becomes ionized; it consists of free-moving ions and electrons, it takes on an electric charge, and its properties differ from those of a solid, liquid, or gas (8)

**pOH** the negative of the common logarithm of the hydroxide ion concentration of a solution (503)

**polar** describes a molecule in which the positive and negative charges are separated (176)

**polar covalent bond** a covalent bond in which a pair of electrons shared by two atoms is held more closely by one atom (176)

**polyatomic ion** an ion made of two or more atoms (194)

**polymer** a large molecule that is formed by more than five monomers, or small units (737)

**polyprotic acid** an acid that can donate more than one proton per molecule (479)

**polysaccharide** one of the carbohydrates made up of long chains of simple sugars; polysaccharides include starch, cellulose, and glycogen (753)

**positron** a particle that has the same mass and spin as an electron but that has a positive charge (686)

**precipitate** a solid that is produced as a result of a chemical reaction in solution (262)

**precision** the exactness of a measurement (44)

**pressure** the amount of force exerted per unit area of a surface (361)

**primary standard** a highly purified solid compound used to check the concentration of a known solution in a titration (517)

**principal quantum number** the quantum number that indicates the energy and orbital of an electron in an atom (107)

**product** a substance that forms in a chemical reaction (9)

**protein** an organic compound that is made of one or more chains of amino acids and that is a principal component of all cells (757)

**pure substance** a sample of matter, either a single element or a single compound, that has definite chemical and physical properties (13)

## Q

**quantity** something that has magnitude, size, or amount (33)

**quantum** the basic unit of electromagnetic energy; it characterizes the wave properties of electrons (99)

**quantum number** a number that specifies certain properties of electrons (107)

**quantum theory** the study of the structure and behavior of the atom and of subatomic particles from the view that all energy comes in tiny, indivisible bundles (105)

## R

**radioactive dating** the process by which the approximate age of an object is determined based on the amount of certain radioactive nuclides present (695)

**radioactive decay** the disintegration of an unstable atomic nucleus into one or more different nuclides, accompanied by the emission of radiation, the nuclear capture or ejection of electrons, or fission (685)

**radioactive nuclide** a nuclide that contains isotopes that decay and that emit radiation (685)

**radioactive tracer** a radioactive material that is added to a substance so that its distribution can be detected later (695)

**rate law** the expression that shows how the rate of formation of product depends on the concentration of all species other than the solvent that take part in a reaction (572)

**rate-determining step** in a multistep chemical reaction, the step that has the lowest velocity, which determines the rate of the overall reaction (576)

**reactant** a substance or molecule that participates in a chemical reaction (9)

**reaction mechanism** the way in which a chemical reaction takes place; expressed in a series of chemical equations (561)

**reaction rate** the rate at which a chemical reaction takes place; measured by the rate of formation of the product or the rate of disappearance of the reactants (568)

**reaction stoichiometry** calculations involving the mass relationships between reactants and products in a chemical reaction (299)

**real gas** a gas that does not behave completely like a hypothetical ideal gas because of the interactions between the gas molecules (332)

**redox reaction** [see *oxidation-reduction reaction*] (633)

**reduced** describes a substance that has gained electrons, lost an oxygen atom, or gained a hydrogen atom (633)

**reducing agent** a substance that has the potential to reduce another substance (642)

**reduction** a chemical change in which electrons are gained, either by the removal of oxygen, the addition of hydrogen, or the addition of electrons (633)

**reduction potential** the decrease in voltage that takes place when a positive ion becomes less positive or neutral or when a neutral atom becomes negative ion (662)

**rem** the quantity of ionizing radiation that does as much damage to human tissue as 1 roentgen of high-voltage X rays does (693)

**resonance** the bonding in molecules or ions that cannot be correctly represented by a single Lewis structure (189)

**reversible reaction** a chemical reaction in which the products re-form the original reactants (266, 589)

**roentgen** a unit of radiation dose of X rays or gamma rays that is equal to the amount of radiation that will produce $2.58 \times 10^{-4}$ of ions per kilogram of air at atmospheric pressure (693)

## S

**salt** an ionic compound that forms when a metal atom or a positive radical replaces the hydrogen of an acid (231, 489)

**saponification** a chemical reaction in which esters of fatty acids react with a strong base to produce glycerol and a fatty acid salt; the process that is used to make soap (754)

**saturated hydrocarbon** an organic compound formed only by carbon and hydrogen linked by single bonds (716)

**saturated solution** a solution that cannot dissolve any more solute under the given conditions (409)

**scientific method** a series of steps followed to solve problems, including collecting data, formulating a hypothesis, testing the hypothesis, and stating conclusions (29)

**scientific notation** a method of expressing a quantity as a number multiplied by 10 to the appropriate power (50)

**scintillation counter** an instrument that converts scintillating light into an electrical signal for detecting and measuring radiation (694)

**self-ionization of water** a process in which two water molecules produce a hydronium ion and a hydroxide ion by transfer of a proton (499)

**semipermeable membrane** a membrane that permits the passage of only certain molecules (452)

**shielding** a radiation-absorbing material that is used to decrease radiation leakage from nuclear reactors (698)

**SI** Le **S**ystème **I**nternational d'Unités, or the International System of Units, which is the measurement system that is accepted worldwide (33)

**significant figure** a prescribed decimal place that determines the amount of rounding off to be done based on the precision of the measurement (46)

**single bond** a covalent bond in which two atoms share one pair of electrons (185)

**single-displacement reaction** a reaction in which one element or radical takes the place of another element or radical in a compound (281)

**solid** the state of matter in which the volume and shape of a substance are fixed (8)

**solubility** the ability of one substance to dissolve in another at a given temperature and pressure; expressed in terms of the amount of solute that will dissolve in a given amount of solvent to produce a saturated solution (410)

**solubility product constant** the equilibrium constant for a solid that is in equilibrium with the solid's dissolved ions (613)

**soluble** capable of dissolving in a particular solvent (401)

**solute** in a solution, the substance that dissolves in the solvent (402)

**solution** a homogeneous mixture of two or more substances uniformly dispersed throughout a single phase (402)

**solution equilibrium** the physical state in which the opposing processes of dissolution and crystallization of a solute occur at equal rates (408)

**solvated** describes a solute molecule that is surrounded by solvent molecules (415)

**solvent** in a solution, the substance in which the solute dissolves (402)

**specific heat** the quantity of heat required to raise a unit mass of homogeneous material 1 K or 1°C in a specified way given constant pressure and volume (532)

**spectator ions** ions that are present in a solution in which a reaction is taking place but that do not participate in the reaction (439)

**spin quantum number** the quantum number that describes the intrinsic angular momentum of a particle (110)

**standard electrode potential** the potential developed by a metal or other material immersed in an electrolyte solution relative to the potential of the hydrogen electrode, which is set at zero (663)

**standard solution** a solution of known concentration, expressed in terms of the amount of solute in a given amount of solvent or solution (517)

**standard temperature and pressure** for a gas, the temperature of 0°C and the pressure 1.00 atm (364)

**strong acid** an acid that ionizes completely in a solvent (474)

**strong electrolyte** a compound that completely or largely dissociates in an aqueous solution, such as soluble mineral salts (442)

**structural formula** a formula that indicates the location of the atoms, groups, or ions relative to one another in a molecule and that indicates the number and location of chemical bonds (185, 712)

**structural isomers** two or more compounds that have the same number and kinds of atoms and the same molecular weight but that differ in the order in which the atoms are attached to one another (713)

**sublimation** the process in which a solid changes directly into a gas (the term is sometimes also used for the reverse process) (346)

**substitution reaction** a reaction in which one or more atoms replace another atom or group of atoms in a molecule (735)

**supercooled liquid** a liquid that is cooled below its normal freezing point without solidifying (338)

**supersaturated solution** a solution that holds more dissolved solute than is required to reach equilibrium at a given temperature (409)

**surface tension** the force that acts on the surface of a liquid and that tends to minimize the area of the surface (335)

**suspension** a mixture in which particles of a material are more or less evenly dispersed throughout a liquid or gas (403)

**synthesis reaction** a reaction in which two or more substances combine to form a new compound (276)

**system** a set of particles or interacting components considered to be a distinct physical entity for the purpose of study (29)

## T

**temperature** a measure of how hot (or cold) something is; specifically, a measure of the average kinetic energy of the particles in an object (531)

**theoretical yield** the maximum amount of product that can be produced from a given amount of reactant (317)

**theory** an explanation for some phenomenon that is based on observation, experimentation, and reasoning (31)

**thermochemical equation** an equation that includes the quantity of energy as heat released or absorbed during the reaction as written (535)

**thermochemistry** the branch of chemistry that is the study of the energy changes that accompany chemical reactions and changes of state (531)

**titration** a method to determine the concentration of a substance in solution by adding a solution of known volume and concentration until the reaction is completed, which is usually indicated by a change in color (515)

**transition element** one of the metals that can use the inner shell before using the outer shell to bond (144)

**transition interval** the range in concentration over which a variation in a chemical indicator can be observed (512)

**transmutation** the transformation of atoms of one element into atoms of a different element as a result of a nuclear reaction (684)

**transuranium element** a synthetic element whose an atomic number is greater than that of uranium (atomic number 92) (692)

**triple point** the temperature and pressure conditions at which the solid, liquid, and gaseous phases of a substance coexist at equilibrium (347)

**triprotic acid** an acid that has three ionizable protons per molecule, such as phosphoric acid (480)

**unit cell** the smallest portion of a crystal lattice that shows the three-dimensional pattern of the entire lattice (339)

**unsaturated hydrocarbon** a hydrocarbon that has available valence bonds, usually from double or triple bonds with carbon (724)

**unsaturated solution** a solution that contains less solute than a saturated solution does and that is able to dissolve additional solute (409)

**valence electron** an electron that is found in the outermost shell of an atom and that determines the atom's chemical properties (160)

**vaporization** the process by which a liquid or solid changes to a gas (335)

**volatile liquid** a liquid that evaporates readily or at a low temperature (343)

**voltaic cell** a primary cell that consists of two electrodes made of different metals immersed in an electrolyte; used to generate voltage (658)

**volume** a measure of the size of a body or region in three-dimensional space (37)

**VSEPR theory** a theory that predicts some molecular shapes based on the idea that pairs of valence electrons surrounding an atom repel each other (197)

**wavelength** the distance from any point on a wave to an identical point on the next wave (97)

**weak acid** an acid that releases few hydrogen ions in aqueous solution (474)

**weak electrolyte** a compound that dissociates only to a small extent in aqueous solution (443)

**weight** a measure of the gravitational force exerted on an object; its value can change with the location of the object in the universe (35)

**word equation** an equation in which the reactants and products in a chemical reaction are represented by words (263)

# INDEX

Page references followed by *f* refer to figures. Page references followed by *t* refer to tables.

## A

## D



## E

## F

## M

## P

## T

## Acknowledgments, continued

## Staff Credits

The people who contributed to **Modern Chemistry** are listed below. They represent editorial, design, inventory, multimedia production, manufacturing, marketing, permissions, and production.

Brigitta Arden, Wesley M. Bain, Juan Baquera, Kimberly Barr, Angela Beckmann, Ed Blake, Sara Butler, Soojinn Choi, Lana Cox, Eddie Dawson, Julie Dervin, Michelle Dike, Lydia Doty, Paul Draper, Sam Dudgeon, James Foster, Jeff Galvez, Leigh Ann García, Diana Goetting, Mark Grayson, Armin Gutzmer, Wilonda Ieans, Jevara Jackson, Stephanie Janda, Simon Key, Jane A. Kirschman, Cathy Kuhles, Ivania Quant Lee, Laura Likon, Jenifer Limb, Denise Mahoney, Carol Martin, Sean McCormick, Richard Metzger, Jessica Mraz, Cathy Murphy, Mercedes Newman, Micah Newman, Cathy Paré, Nanda Patel, Jenny Patton, Peter D. Reid, Sara Rider, Michael Rinella, Jeff Robinson, Mike Roche, Tara Ross, Teresa Ruiz, Beth Sample, Margaret Sanchez, Kay Selke, Chris Smith, Victoria Smith, Dawn Marie Spinozza, Sherry Sprague, Christine Stanford, Jeff Streber, JoAnn Stringer, Jeannie Taylor, David Trevino, Bob Tucek, Kira J. Watkins, Holly Whittaker, Patty Zepeda, and Sara Zettner.

## Photo Credits

**Abbreviations used: (t) top, (b) bottom, (c) center, (l) left, (r) right, (bkgd) background**

**All photos, unless otherwise noted, by Sam Dudgeon/HRW. Cover:** W. P. Wergin/E. F. Erbe; Electron Microscope Unit; ARS-USDA. **CBL calculator icon:** Andy Christiansen/HRW. **Historical Chemistry feature icons:** (bkgd), Charles D. Winters. **Cross-Disciplinary Connection feature icons:** (l), © Digital Art/CORBIS; (c), PhotoDisc/gettyimages; (r), © Dr. Dennis Kunkel/Visuals Unlimited. **Careers in Chemistry feature icons:** (l), © Kaluzny-Thatcher/Getty Images; (c), © LWA-Stephen Welstead/CORBIS; (r), © Roger Tully/Getty Images. **Chemistry in Action feature icons:** (l), © Maximilian Stock Ltd/Photo Researchers, Inc.; (c), Lawrence Berkeley Laboratory/Science Source/Photo Researchers, Inc.; (r), Omikron/Photo Researchers, Inc. **Table of Contents:** v (bl), © Ed Bock/CORBIS; vi (tl), Sinclair Stammers/Photo Researchers, Inc.; vi (cl), © National Institute of Standards & Technology/Photo Researchers, Inc.; vi (bl), © Eurelios/Phototake; vii (tl), © Silvestre Machado/SuperStock; vii (cl), © NOAO/Photo Researchers, Inc.; vii (bl), Alfred Pasieka/Science Photo Library/Photo Researchers, Inc.; viii (tl), Phil Degginger/Bruce Coleman, Inc.; viii (bl), Richard Megna/Fundamental Photographs; viii (cl), Robert Burch/Bruce Coleman, Inc.; ix (tl), Andy Goldsworthy. Courtesy of the artist and Galerie Lelong, New York.; ix (cl), Pictor International/ImageState/Alamy; ix (bl), © Stephen Simpson/Getty Images; x (tl), J & L Weber/Peter Arnold, Inc.; x (tlc), Richard B. Swint, M. D./The Texas Collection, Baylor Unversity, Waco, Texas; x (blc), © Sandra Ivany/FoodPix/Getty Images; x (bl), © Paul Chesley/Getty Images; xi (tlc), Greg Edmonds/Earth Images; xi (blc), © SuperStock/PictureQuest; xi (bl), Jet Propulsion Laboratory/NASA; xii (tl), EFDA-JET/Photo Researchers, Inc.; xii (cl), © David Luzzi, Univ. of Pennsylvania/Photo Researchers, Inc.; xii (bl), Dr. Jeremy Burgess/Photo Researchers, Inc.; xiii (bl), J & L Weber/Peter Arnold, Inc. **Chapter 1:** 2 (c), Sinclair Stammers/Photo Researchers, Inc.; 3 (br), Volker Steger/Peter Arnold, Inc.; 5 (tr), © Jon Feingersh/CORBIS; 13 (bl), Tom Pantages Photography; 15 (c), James Lyle/Texas A&M University; 18 (bc), Bruce Iverson; 20 (t), C. Bradley Simmons/Bruce Coleman, Inc. **Chapter 2:** 28 (c), © National Institute of Standards & Technology/Photo Researchers, Inc. **Chapter 3:** 66 (c), © Eurelios/Phototake; 68 (tl), Grant Heilman Photography, Inc.; 70 (cr), IBM Corporation/Research Division/Almaden Research Center; 83 (tr, cr, br), Dennis Fagan/HRW. **Chapter 4:** 96 (c), © Silvestre Machado/SuperStock; 100 (cl), © SuperStock; 105 (tl), Polytechnic Institute of Brooklyn; 105 (tr), Atlas of optical phenomena by Michel Cagnet, Maurice Francon & Jean Claude Thrierr. Published by Springer-Verlag in 1962. © Springer-Verlag; 114 (bl), Reprinted with permission from Nature (No. 1196, Vol. 46). Copyright 1892 Macmillian Magazines Limited; 115 (tl), Elliott & Fry, photographers, courtesy AIP Emilio Segrè Visual Archives, WF Meggers Gallery of Nobel Laureates; 130 (c), PhotoTake. **Chapter 5:** 132 (c), © NOAO/Photo Researchers, Inc.; 133 (br), © SuperStock; 142 (bl), Dr. E. R. Degginger/Color-Pic, Inc.; 142 (br), Breck P. Kent/Animals Animals/Earth Scenes; 144 (bl), Alfred Pasieka/Peter Arnold, Inc.; 145 (cr), NASA; 147 (bl, cl), Dr. E. R. Degginger/Color-Pic, Inc. **Chapter 6:** 174 (c), Alfred Pasieka/Science Photo Library/Photo Researchers, Inc.; 190 (bl), Bruce Iverson; 196 (tl), Photri; 206 (bc), Photri. **Chapter 7:** 218 (c), Phil Degginger/Bruce Coleman, Inc. **Chapter 8:** 260 (c), Robert Burch/Bruce Coleman, Inc.; 272 (tr), L. S. Stepanowicz/Visuals Unlimited; 288 (all), Institute of Structural Macrokinetics and Materials Science (ISMAN); 296 (bl), Tom Pantages Photography. **Chapter 9:** 298 (c), Richard Megna/Fundamental Photographs; 302 (tr), © Stefano Bianchetti/CORBIS. **Chapter 10:** 328 (c), Andy Goldsworthy. Courtesy of the artist and Galerie Lelong, New York.; 334 (tl), Dennis Fagan/HRW; 335 (cr), © Harold & Esther Edgerton Foundation, 2006, Courtesy of Palm Press, Inc.; 336 (cl), Dr. E. R. Degginger/Color-Pic, Inc.; 337 (br), Photonica; 338 (cl), PhotoTake;

339 (tr, cl), PhotoTake; 339 (c, cr, br, tl, tc), Breck P. Kent/Animals Animals/Earth Scenes; 341 (tr), Dr. E. R. Degginger/Color-Pic, Inc. **Chapter 11:** 360 (c), Pictor International/ImageState/Alamy; 361 (all), Dennis Fagan/HRW; 362 (b), NASA/SIPA Press; 368 (bl), © Royalty Free/CORBIS; 376 (bl), © Bettmann/CORBIS; 377 (t), © James Schwabel/Panoramic Images; 377 (c), © Leo L. Larson/Panoramic Images; 398 (bc), age fotostock/Rick Gomez. **Chapter 12:** 400 (c), © Stephen Simpson/Getty Images; 401 (bl), Courtesy Dr. C. W. Dill, Texas A&M University-Corpus Christi Bell Library; 403 (tl), © Neal Mishler/Getty Images; 404 (cl), Richard Haynes/HRW; 408 (bl), Peter Van Steen/HRW Photo. **Chapter 13:** 434 (c), J & L Weber/Peter Arnold, Inc.; 445 (tr), © Hulton Archive/Getty Images; 456 (tl), Lawrence Stepanowicz/Bruce Coleman, Inc. **Chapter 14:** 466 (c), Richard B. Swint, M.D./The Texas Collection, Baylor Unversity, Waco, Texas; 467 (br), Peter Van Steen/HRW Photo; 479 (tc), Photo Researchers, Inc.; 489 (cr), © Thomas Nilsen/Photo Researchers, Inc. **Chapter 15:** 498 (c), © Sandra Ivany/FoodPix/Getty Images; 500 (bl, br), Richard Megna/Fundamental Photographs; 510 (c), Massachusetts Division of Fisheries & Wildlife; 511 (bl, br), Jerry Mason/Science Photo Library/Photo Researchers, Inc.; 512 (bl), Photo Researchers, Inc.; 513 (all), Peter Van Steen/HRW Photo; 516 (bl, br), Richard Megna/Fundamental Photographs **Chapter 16:** 530 (c), © Paul Chesley/Getty Images **Chapter 17:** 562 (tl), Larry Stepanowicz; 573 (br), © Robert Harding World Imagery/Alamy Photos; 579 (bl), Dorling Kindersley Limited courtesy of the Science Museum, London/Corbis **Chapter 18:** 588 (c), David Muench/CORBIS; 593 (all), Dr. E. R. Degginger/Color-Pic, Inc.; 597 (tr), Steve McCutcheon/Visuals Unlimited; 608 (all), Dennis Fagan/HRW; 618 (all), John King/HRW **Chapter 19:** 630 (c), © SuperStock/PictureQuest; 633 (tr), Richard Megna/Fundamental Photographs; 636 (c), Renee Lynn/Photo Researchers, Inc.; 645 (bc), Richard L. Carlton/Photo Researchers, Inc.; 645 (tc), Thomas Eisner and Daniel Aneshansley, Cornell University. **Chapter 20:** 654 (c), Jet Propulsion Laboratory/NASA; 662 (tl), Adam Jones/Visuals Unlimited; 666 (c), Getty/NewsCom. **Chapter 21:** 680 (c), EFDA-JET/Photo Researchers, Inc. ; 693 (b), Fermilab National Accelerator Laboratory; 695 (tr), 1991 Peter Berndt, M.D., P.A. All Rights Reserved; 699 (t), © Roger Ressmeyer/CORBIS; 700 (bc), AIP Emilio Segrè Visual Archives; 701 (tr), AIP Emilio Segrè Visual Archives; 708 (cl), Peter Van Steen/HRW. **Chapter 22:** 710 (c), © David Luzzi, Univ. of Pennsylvania/Photo Researchers, Inc.; 712 (bl), Gregory K. Scott/Photo Researchers, Inc.; 714 (tc), Runk/Schoenberger/Grant Heilman Photography, Inc.; 715 (c), © Science Photo Library/Photo Researchers, Inc.; 723 (tr), © David Spindel/SuperStock; 723 (br), © Keith Wood/Getty Images; 728 (br), © Kevin Anderson/Getty Images; 734 (tl), Seth Joel/Science Photo Library/Photo Researchers, Inc.; 748 (bc), Charles Cecil/Visuals Unlimited; 748 (bl), Tom Pix/Peter Arnold, Inc. **Chapter 23:** 750 (c), Dr. Jeremy Burgess/Photo Researchers, Inc.; 752 (cl), © Richard Hamilton Smith/CORBIS; 754 (bl), Stephanie Friedman/HRW; 757 (tr), Dr. Jeremy Burgess/Photo Researchers, Inc.; 761 (bl), © Gopal Murti/Phototake; 761 (cl), © Microworks/Phototake; 762 (bl), National Portrait Gallery, Smithsonian Institution/Art Resource, NY; 765 (cr), Andy Christiansen/HRW; 766 (bl), © Barry Runk/STAN/Grant Heilman Photography, Inc.; 772 (tc), W. Schonert, GSI Biophysik, Darmstadt, Germany; 773 (br), © Kiseleva and Donald Fawcett/Visuals Unlimited; 774 (bl), David Parker/Photo Researchers, Inc.; 775 (tr), Charles Marden Fitch. **Elements Handbook:** 784–785 (bkgd), Yoav Levy/Phototake; 784 (bl, bc), Tom Pantages Photography; 784 (br), Breck P. Kent/Animals Animals/Earth Scenes; 787 (cl, cr, bc), Lester Bergman/The Bergman Collection; 787 (bl, br), Dr. E. R. Degginger/Color-Pic, Inc.; 788 (all), Phi-Lo Photo; 789 (cl), John Langford/HRW; 791 (bl), PhotoTake; 792 (bl), Dr. E. R. Degginger/Color-Pic, Inc.; 792 (bc), Carl Frank/Photo Researchers, Inc.; 792 (br), Gary Retherford/Photo Researchers, Inc.; 792 (cl), Breck P. Kent/Animals Animals/Earth Scenes; 793 (bl, bc), PhotoTake; 793 (br), Larry Stepanowicz; 794 (cr), © Mauritius/SuperStock; 795 (b), Stuart Craig Jr./Bruce Coleman, Inc.; 795 (bc), PhotoTake; 796 (tr), © Chris Rogers/Rainbow; 797 (tl), Dr. E. R. Degginger/Color-Pic, Inc.; 798 (br), © Brent Cavedo/SuperStock; 798 (tr), © Thomas Del Brase/Getty Images; 798 (cr), Larry Stepanowicz; 798 (bc), Ken Lucas/Visuals Unlimited; 798 (bl), © Bettmann/CORBIS; 799 (tl), David R. Frazier Photolibrary; 799 (cr), L. S. Stepanowicz/Visuals Unlimited; 801 (all), Tom Pantages Photography; 802 (tr, tl), Larry Stepanowicz; 802 (br), Tom Pantages Photography; 803 (tr), © Dan McCoy/Rainbow; 804 (bl), © Hank Morgan/Rainbow; 804 (br), Dan Rubin/The Stock Shop/Medichrome; 808 (br), Visuals Unlimited; 808 (bc), Arthur Hill/Visuals Unlimited; 809 (br), Tom Pantages Photography; 810 (cr), © CoCo McCoy/Rainbow; 811 (cr), Tom Pantages Photography; 812 (bl), J & L Weber/Peter Arnold, Inc.; 818 (cr), Tom Pantages Photography; 820 (tc), Irving Geis/Science Source/Photo Researchers, Inc.; 828 (bc), © Myron Jay Dorf/CORBIS; 829 (c, cr), Dr. E. R. Degginger/Color-Pic, Inc.; 830 (br), © George Glod/SuperStock; 830 (bl), © Peter Beck/CORBIS; 832 (cl), Heather Angel/Natural Visions; 832 (cr, br), Dr. E. R. Degginger/Color-Pic, Inc.; 839 (bl), Tom Tracy/The Stock Shop/Medichrome. **Reference:** 842-843 (bkgd), Yoav Levy/Phototake; 843 (t), Photri; 864 (c), © Stephen Simpson/Getty Images; 866 (br), Science Photo Library/Photo Researchers, Inc.; 867 (c), Photo Researchers, Inc.; 869 (cr), Bruce Iverson; 871 (br), © Ed Bock/CORBIS; 875 (br), Phil Degginger/Bruce Coleman, Inc.; 878 (c), J & L Weber/Peter Arnold, Inc.

**Photos by Charles D. Winters:** xi (tl), xiii (bc), 3 (bl), 7 (br), 8 (bl), 10 (t), 12 (tl, tc), 13 (br), 14 (all), 18 (bl, br), 19 (all), 26 (bl), 38 (tl), 73 (tr), 94 (bl), 142 (tl, cl), 144 (bc, br), 147 (cr, br), 224 (b), 231 (t), 239 (tr), 258 (bl), 261 (br), 262 (all), 270 (cl), 277 (all), 280 (tc), 281 (br), 316 (br), 334 (bl, bc, br), 335 (bl, bc), 337 (bc), 358 (bl), 366 (tc), 371 (all), 401 (cl), 406 (all), 413 (all), 437 (t), 438 (b), 444 (b, c), 467 (bl), 470 (bl, br), 471 (br), 472 (br), 476 (tc), 477 (br), 480 (all), 486 (tc), 488 (b), 496 (bl), 497 (tl), 512 (cl, cr, tr, tc, tl), 528 (bl), 532 (all), 547 (all), 560 (c), 561 (br), 569 (all), 570 (cl), 587 (bl), 589 (br), 602 (bc), 604 (cl), 606 (tl, cl), 628 (bl, br), 632 (bl, tr), 639 (tr), 643 (bc), 655 (bl, br), 659 (tr), 670 (bc), 731 (br), 732 (cl), 733 (tc), 736 (tc), 737 (all), 738 (bc), 782 (c), 785 (tr), 786 (bl), 787 (tl, tr), 793 (tr, cl, cr), 795 (cr), 799 (bl, br, tr, cl, bl), 800 (all), 808 (cl, bl), 809 (tr, bl), 812 (cr, cl, br), 813 (cr), 821 (tl), 825 (all), 828 (bl, br), 829 (cl), 832 (bl), 833 (all), 838 (all), 839 (tr, br), 844 (bc), 845 (all), 847 (all), 850 (bl), 851 (all), 872 (tr), 876 (bl), 877 (b)

**Photos by Sergio Purtell:** xix (tl), xx (tl), 9 (t), 12 (tr), 29 (b), 46 (tl), 61 (br), 265 (bl), 278 (bl), 282 (bl), 283 (bl, br), 327 (tr), 330 (tl), 337 (bl), 379 (tr, cr, br), 403 (tr), 419 (l, cl, cr, r, bl, bc, br), 422 (l), 432 (bc), 515 (bc), 518 (tr, cl, c, cr, bl, bc, br), 519 (tc, tr, cl, c, cr, bl, bc, br), 601 (tl, tc, tr, tr), 694 (bl, br, bc), 711 (bl, c, bc, br), 727 (br), 786 (bc, br), 787 (tc)

# Periodic Table of the Elements

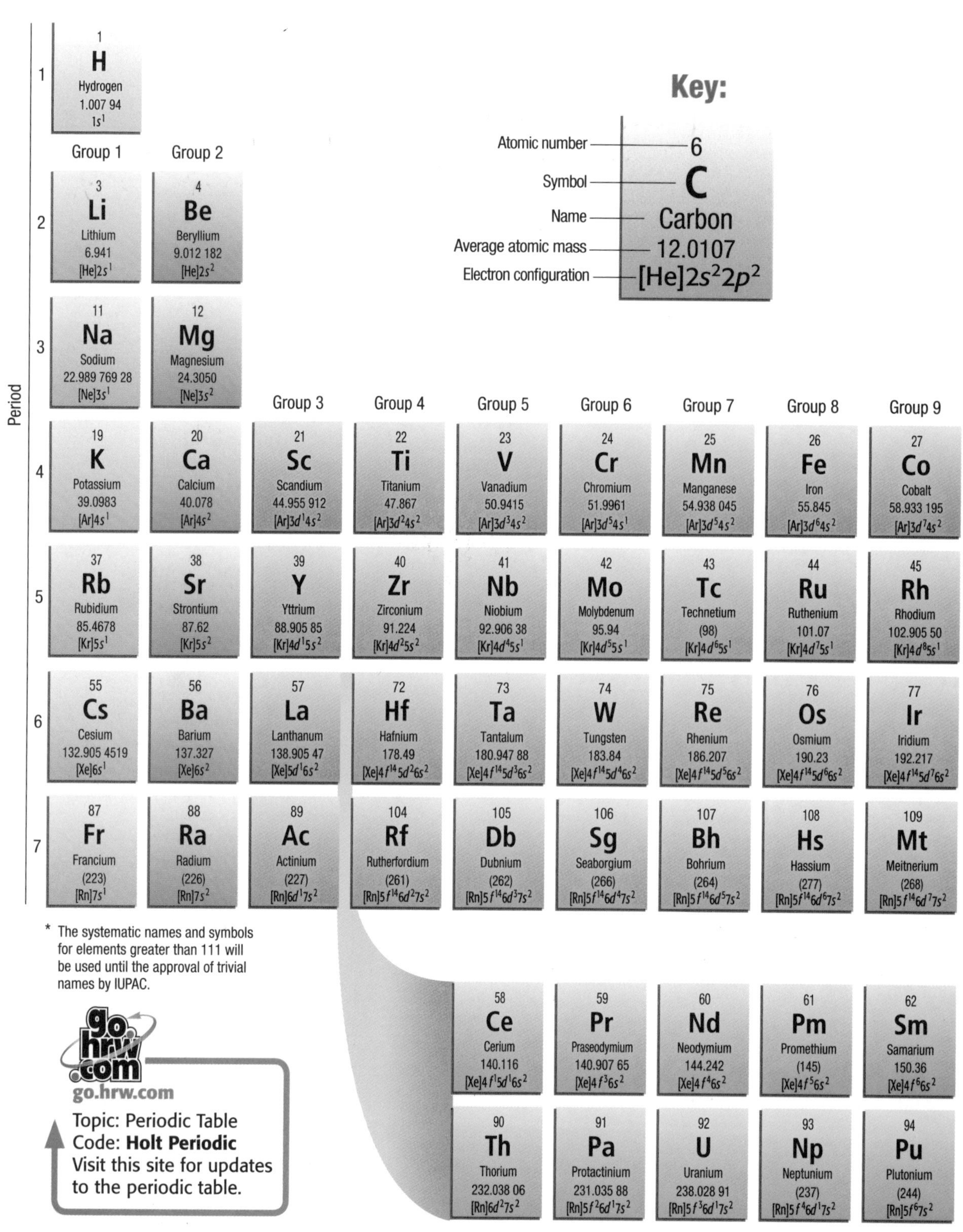